International Acade

Victor Aladjev, Michael Shishakov

Software Etudes in the Mathematica

CreateSpace – 2017

Software Etudes in the Mathematica. Victor Aladjev, Michael Shishakov.– CreateSpace, An Amazon.com Company, 614 p., 2017, ISBN-13: 978-1979037273, ISBN-10: 1979037272.

Systems of computer mathematics find more and more broad use in a number of natural, economical and social fields. One of leaders among means of this class undoubtedly is the *Mathematica* system. The book focuses on an important aspect – procedural and functional programming supported by the *Mathematica*. This aspect is of particular importance not only for appendices but also above all it is quite important in the creation of the user means which extend the most frequently used standard means of the *Mathematica* system and/or eliminate its shortcomings, or complement with the new interesting facilities.

The present book contains over *1140* software etudes not only which are illustrating effective methods of programming in *Mathematica* system and many subtleties and undocumented opportunities of its software, but also being of undoubted interest as the means expanding and supplementing the system means. In a certain historical context etudes have appeared as a result of development of the number of rather large projects in the *Mathematica* system connected with the solution of mathematical problems, computer researches of the classical cellular automata, modeling, etc. In the course of programming of these projects the certain software fragments presenting mass character have been formed later on in the kind of the separate procedures and functions that have made the basis of the package attached to the present book. Many etudes presented here contain a rather useful and effective methods of programming in *Mathematica* system. The presented *etudes* are small by the size of program code and can be in case of need rather easily analysed and, perhaps, are modified for *specific* conditions of application. It must be kept in mind that along with the software having both the applied, and the system character together with illustrating of rather useful methods of programming; at that, the present book represents a rather convenient organization of the user software that supported by a large number of the means for its serving.

Software represented in the book contains a number of useful and effective receptions of the procedural and functional programming in the *Mathematica* system that extend the system software and allow sometimes much more efficiently and easily to program the software for various purposes, above all, wearing system character. Among them there are means which are of interest from the point of view of including of their or their analogs in standard tools of the *Mathematica* system, at the same time they use approaches, useful in programming of applications. The above software rather essentially dilates the *Mathematica* functionality and can be useful enough for programming of many problems above all of *system* character. At the same time, it must be kept in mind that the classification of the represented means by their appointment in a certain measure has a rather *conditional* character because these tools can be crossed substantially among themselves by the functionality. The freeware package *MathToolBox* containing the above means is attached to the present book.

The book is oriented on a wide enough circle of the users of computer mathematics systems, researchers, teachers and students of universities for courses of computer science, physics, mathematics, and a lot of other natural disciplines. This book will be of interest also to the specialists of industry and technology which use the computer mathematics systems in own professional activity. At last, the book is a rather useful handbook with fruitful methods on the procedural and functional programming in the *Mathematica* system.

Contents

Preface	**5**
Chapter 1. Additional tools in interactive mode of the *Mathematica*	**10**
Chapter 2. Additional tools of processing of expressions in the *Mathematica* software	**25**
Chapter 3. Additional tools of processing of symbols and strings in the *Mathematica*	**63**
3.1. Operations on strings	63
3.2. Expressions containing in strings	76
3.3. Replacements and extractions in strings	79
3.4. Operating of substrings in strings	81
3.5. Tools of string processing that are rather useful for certain applications	98
Chapter 4. Additional tools of processing of sequences and lists in the *Mathematica*	**104**
4.1. Additional tools for computer research of cellular automata	176
Chapter 5. The additional tools expanding the standard *Mathematica* functions, or its software as a whole	**200**
5.1. The control branching structures and loop structures in the *Mathematica*	221
5.2. The loop control structures of the *Mathematica* system	223
Chapter 6. Problems of procedural programming in the *Mathematica*	**226**
6.1. Definition of procedures in the *Mathematica* software	226
6.2. Definition of the user functions and pure functions in software of the *Mathematica*	245
6.3. Tools for testing of procedures and functions in the *Mathematica* system	254
6.4. Headings of the user procedures and functions in the *Mathematica* system	276
6.5. Formal arguments of procedures and functions; the tools of their processing in the *Mathematica* software	298
6.6. Local variables of modules and blocks; the means of manipulation by them in the *Mathematica* software	325
6.7. Global variables of modules and blocks; the tools of manipulation by them in the *Mathematica* software	350
6.8. Attributes, options and values by default for the arguments of the user blocks, functions and modules; additional tools of their processing in the *Mathematica* system	365
6.9. Some additional facilities for operating with blocks, functions and modules in the *Mathematica* software	377
Chapter 7. Software for input-output in the *Mathematica* system	**430**
7.1. Tools of the *Mathematica* system for working with internal files	430
7.2. Tools of the *Mathematica* system for working with external files	440
7.3. Tools of the *Mathematica* system for processing of attributes of directories and files	451
7.4. Additional tools for processing of datafiles and directories	457
7.5. Certain special tools for processing of datafiles and directories	474
Chapter 8. The manipulations organization with the user packages in the *Mathematica*	**483**
8.1. Concept of the context, and its use in the software of the *Mathematica*	484
8.1.1. Interconnection of contexts and packages in the software of the *Mathematica*	495
8.2. Definition of the user packages, and their usage in the *Mathematica*	498
8.3. Additional tools for manipulating with the user packages in the *Mathematica*	522

8.4. The organization of the user software in the *Mathematica* system	595
8.5. A *MathToolBox* package for the *Mathematica* system	606
References	609
About the Authors	613
The sponsors of the book	614

Mathematica 2, 5 ÷ 11.2 – trademarks of Wolfram Research Inc.
Maple 4 ÷ 11 – trademarks of MapleSoft Inc.

© *Victor Aladjev, Michael Shishakov. All rights reserved.*

Printed by CreateSpace, An Amazon.com Company

November 7, 2017

<u>*For contacts*</u>: *aladjev@europe.com, aladjev@yandex.ru, aladjev@mail.ru*

© No part of this book may be reproduced, stored in a retrieval system, or transcribed, in any form or by any means electronic, mechanical, recording, photocopying, or otherwise. Software described in this book is furnished under the license agreement and may be used or copied only in accordance with the agreement. The source codes of software represented in the book are protected by Copyrights and at use of any of them the reference to the book and the appropriate software is required. Use of the enclosed software is subject to license agreement and software can be used only in noncommercial purposes with reference to the present book.

Preface

Systems of computer mathematics (SCM) find more and more wide application in a number of natural, economical and social sciences such as: *informatics, chemistry, mathematics, physics, technologies, education, economics, sociology, etc.* Such systems as **Mathematica, Maple, Axiom, Reduce, MuPAD, Derive, Magma, Maxima, Sage, MathPiper** and others are more and more demanded for learning of mathematically oriented disciplines, in scientific researches and technologies. The *SCM* are main means for teachers, scientists, researchers, and engineers. The researches on the basis of technology *SCM*, as a rule, well combine algebraic methods with advanced computing methods. In this sense the *SCM* – a *interdisciplinary* area between informatics and mathematics in which researches are concentrated on the development of algorithms for algebraical *(symbolical)* and numerical calculations and data processing, and on creation of programming languages along with program environment for realization of this kind of algorithms and tasks of different purpose which are based on them.

So, the given book represents a certain set of the selected system problems whose purpose not only to expand or make more effective the *Mathematica* system, but also to give certain help to those users of *Mathematica* who would like to move from the user level to a level of the *programmer* or to those who when using *Mathematica* already faced some its restrictions and want to improve its software. At that, the skilled *Mathematica* programmers probably will also be able to find for themselves in the present book a rather useful information of the applied character, and for thinking.

Therefore, illumination only of certain questions essence without their detailed discussion, certain nuances and consideration of adjacent questions which are interesting enough and important per se often takes place. Moreover, the system tools, presented in the book can be used as rather useful tools at developing own applications in the *Mathematica* software. In our opinion, an analysis of the source codes of the means, presented in the book which use both effective, and nonstandard methods of programming along with quite certain practical interest will allow to master the *Mathematica* system more deeply. For convenience of their use in the given quality the reader has possibility of free loading of **MathToolBox** package for *Mathematica* system of versions $8 \div 11$ which contains these tools [48]. According to the experience of the package users, the presented tools are of interest not only as independent means, but also contain a number of the methods rather useful in practical programming in the *Mathematica* system.

The means considered throughout the present book completely answer to the main goal of the offered book which can be characterized by the following two main directions, namely:

(1) representation of a number of useful enough tools of system character that expand and supplement standard tools of the *Mathematica* system;
(2) illustration on their example of receptions and methods, enough useful in *procedural* and *functional* programming, along with a number of rather essential features of these *paradigms* of programming in the conditions of the *Mathematica* software.

Here is quite appropriate to note a quite natural mechanism of formation of own software tools of the user working in some program environment. In course of programming of one or other tools, or the whole project a certain situation is quite real when is rather expedient to program some additional means that are absent among standard means, either they are more effective, or they are more convenient than standard tools. In many important cases the applicability of these tools can have mass enough character, allowing to form program toolkit of an quite wide range of applicability. At the same time, it should be noted that for bigger convenience, the represented tools are systematized, however their systematization to some extent has a rather conditional character *(according to their basic purpose)* because the majority of the represented tools have multipurpose character. Furthermore, in some cases tools which significantly use each other are in common represented.

Exactly in many respects thanks to the *described* mechanism we have created quite famous library ***UserLib*** for the ***Maple*** along with package ***MathToolBox*** for the ***Mathematica*** which contain more than *850* and *1140* means respectively [47,48]. All above means are supplied with *Freeware* license and have open program code. Such approach to *programming* of many projects both in the ***Mathematica***, and in ***Maple*** also substantially promoted emergence of a number of system means from above-mentioned library and package, when development of software for simplification of its realization revealed expediency of definition of the new accompanying tools of system character that are rather frequently used both in applied and in system programming. So, openness of ***MathToolBox*** package code allows both to modify the tools containing in it, and to program on their basis own tools, or to use their *components* in various appendices. In our opinion, tasks and means of their realization in ***Mathematica*** which are represented in the above package can be rather useful at deeper mastering of the system and in a number of cases will allow to simplify rather significantly programming of appendices in it, first of all, the system problems. At that, the methodological considerations presented in our previous books [29-33,50] fully remain in force relative to the present book.

Means of ***MathToolBox*** have different complexity of organization and the used algorithms. In certain cases, they use effective enough and nonstandard receptions of programming in ***Mathematica***. These means can be used as individually *(for the decision of various problems or for creation on their basis of new means)*, and in structure of ***MathToolBox*** package extending standard means of ***Mathematica***, eliminating a number of its defects and mistakes, raising its *compatibility* relatively to its releases and raising effectiveness of programming of various problems in ***Mathematica***. Means presented in the book are supplied with descriptions and explanations, contain the source codes and the more typical examples of their application. At that, each description is provided by necessary considerations, concerning peculiarities of program execution in ***Mathematica***. Many of the represented tools can be quite useful in practical programming in the ***Mathematica*** system.

The analysis of these source codes can quite initiate useful enough reasons on programming of these or those objects in the ***Mathematica***. At the same time it must be kept in mind, that on the certain represented means of analogous appointment there can be different results, illustrating various algorithms and methods of programming. Similar method pursues the goals of both the training, and comparison of the different approaches.

And it is valid, experience of holding master classes on the ***Mathematica*** system with wide use of the analysis of the initial codes of the means provided in the book and in the attached ***MathToolBox*** package [48], with all evidence confirmed effectiveness of such approach in a rather effective mastering of the built-in ***Math***-language and the ***Mathematica*** system as a whole. A lot of receptions used in the presented means increase the level of functional and procedural programming along with extension of the ***Mathematica*** software as a whole. At the same time it must be kept in mind, that for certain reasons some source codes weren't exposed to complete optimization that can serve as a rather useful exercise for the reader.

That book considers certain principal questions of procedure–functional programming in *Mathematica*, not only for decision of various applied problems, but, above all, for creation of the software expanding frequently used facilities of the system and/or eliminating their defects or expanding the system with new facilities. The software represented in this book contains a series of useful and effective receptions of programming in *Mathematica* system, and extends its software which enables more simply and effectively to programme in the *Mathematica* system the problems of various purpose.

The represented monograph, is mostly for people who want the more deep understanding in the *Mathematica* programming, and particularly those users who would like to make a transition from the user to the programmer, or perhaps those who already have a certain limited experience in *Mathematica* programming but want to improve own possibilities in the system. While the expert *Mathematica* programmers will also probably find an useful enough information for yourself.

At that, it should be noted that the source codes of means given in this book contain calls of non–standard tools that didn't find reflection in the present book in a number of cases, but are presented in our package [48]. Among the presented receptions it should be noted those receptions that, being nonstandard, have been practically tested, in a lot of cases simplifying essentially the programming. Therefore, their detailed analysis requires acquaintance with source codes of these means, at least, at the level of usage on them. Meantime, the principal algorithms of many means of the presented book is rather well looked through and without acquaintance with similar tools, while real use of these tools perhaps only after the loading of this package into the current session.

Along with the illustrative purposes the means represented in this monograph quite can be used and as enough useful means extending *Mathematica* that rather significantly facilitate programming of a wide range of the problems first of all having the system character. The represented means are some kind of program etudes which along with independent interest allow to clear more deeply important nuances of programming in the *Mathematica*. At last, in our opinion, the detailed analysis of the given source codes can be very effective remedy on the path of deeper mastering of programming in *Mathematica*. Experience of holding of the master classes of various levels on *Mathematica* and *Maple* with all evidence confirms expediency of joint use of both the standard tools of the systems of computer mathematics, and the user tools created during of programming of the various appendices [47,48,50].

Tools represented in the book increase the range and efficiency of use of the *Mathematica*, above all, on the *Windows* platform owing to the innovations in three basic directions: *(1) the elimination of a number of basic defects and shortcomings, (2) extending of capabilities of a number of standard means,* and *(3) replenishment of the system by new means which increase capabilities of its program environment, including the means that improve the level of compatibility of versions 8 – 11.* At last, with organization of the user software and programming of large-scale systems in the *Mathematica* along with our standpoint on a question *"Mathematica or Maple?"* the interested reader can familiarize in [29-33,50]. In the given book the certain considerations on organization of the user software are presented. For instance, we propose an *organization of the user packages which is a rather convenient at various processings (for example, editing, programming of various means analyzing means of such or similar organization, etc.)*. At the same time, many means represented in the book are oriented to the given organization, above all. The attached *MathToolBox* package can be a bright example of such organization [48].

Note that *Math*-language isn't the programming system like the majority of languages of a package type because its scope is limited to the *Mathematica.* However acquaintance with it and its peculiarities rather essentially facilitates mastering of the *Mathematica* itself, other programming languages and popular programming paradigms. It is promoted also by the fact, that on a certain number of the principal moments of comparative analysis the systems *Mathematica* and *Maple* seem as undoubted leaders of *SCM.*

At last, a lot of means represented in the above books is intended for extension of standard means of the systems *Mathematica* and *Maple* along with elimination of their shortcomings and mistakes. These means not only more accurately accent distinctions of both systems, but also their problems of common character. And in this relation they allow to look from various points of view on these or other both advantages, and shortcomings of two systems. In the present book we present a lotr of means of similar type concerning the *Mathematica* system. At that, it should be noted, that a mass optimization of procedures have not been performed, procedures in many cases have been written, as they say on *'sheet'*; on the other hand, numerous procedures have been optimized using both the standard tools and newly created means of system character. In this context here there is a magnificent experimental field for increasing of professionalism of the user at operating with *Mathematica* software. On the examples of various means of a rather mass character the receptions, methods and technique which are rather useful in practical programming in the *Mathematica* system, are illustrated. At the same time, along with quite simple means, the means which use rather complex algorithms demanding quite good possession of paradigm of the language of the *Mathematica* and other tools of our package are represented in the book [48]. Furthermore, on a number of examples which appeared as the result of programming and debugging of certain means, have been revealed both the advantages, and the shortcomings of system of *Mathematica*. The most essential of them are presented in the book on concrete examples.

Inclusion of source codes of the procedures and functions presented in this book with their short characteristic directly in the book text allows to operate with them without computer, considering a habit of considerable number of the users of the senior generation to operate with program listings before exit to the computer what in a series of cases promoted better programming in due time at programming in batch mode. In our opinion, skill to operate with program listings is a rather important component of the programmer culture, allowing better to feel the used program environment. In a certain measure it is similar to possession of the musician by the sheet music. In our opinion that is based on conducting a number of courses on the system *Mathematics* in a number of universities, the analysis of source codes of the presented software will allow the user to master the programming paradigm of the *Mathematics* system much better.

Indeed, because of not exactly convenient formatting of the presented means owing to the book format there can be certain difficulties which it is possible to a certain extent to avoid, using `MathToolBox.txt` file which is in archive attached to the present book [48]. Whereas the questions of *linguistic* character arise due to the fact that *English* is not our native tongue. Meanwhile, judging by the reviews of the readers of our previous book and the users of our package from different countries, these problems do not prevent familiarization with this book and the package attached to it.

Moreover, many listings of the presented tools have a rather small size, allowing to analyze them outside of *Mathematica* in the assumption that the reader is sufficiently familiar with its software. At mass existence of personal computers of various type the mentioned visual analysis of the program listings was replaced with the mode of interactive programming, however it is not not the same, and in the first case the process of programming seems to us more better and efficient. Meanwhile, even means with small source code are often useful enough at programming of various applications, in particular, of system character. Whereas others demand for the understanding of serious enough elaboration, including *acquaintance* with our package *MathToolBox* [48,50].

Naturally, the readability of source codes leaves much to be desired because of the booksize format, font and its size, etc., and also because of not absolutely successful structuredness, supported by *Mathematica* itself – in this context the procedures structuredness, supported by *Maple* is presented to us as significantly more preferable. Meantime, this moment should not cause any complications for fairly experienced programmers. In addition, existence of different algorithms for a number of the presented tools, equivalent or almost, is caused by desire to illustrate various methods and aspects of programming useful to use of the built-in *Mathematica*-language in programming of various appendices in *Mathematica*. Namely a certain redundancy of the represented means is caused, first of all, by desire to represent the receptions, methods and approaches useful in practical programming in *Mathematica*.

As a rule, than the problem is more complex, the more time is required for mastering of the tools necessary for its decision. In this context the software *(blocks, procedures, functions, etc.)* which is presented in this book contain a number of rather useful and effective methods of programming in the *Mathematica* environment and extends its program environment, they give opportunity more simply and effectively to program various problems. These means in the process of use of the *MathToolBox* package are updated, taking into account both the new means, and the optimization of already existing means. In many problems of different purpose the package *MathToolBox* showed itself as a rather effective toolkit. The package on the freeware conditions is attached to the present book [48]. This package can be freely uploaded from the website *https://yadi.sk/d/oC5lXLWa3PVEhi*.

The present book is oriented on a wide enough circle of the users of *Computer Mathematics Systems (CMS)*, researchers, mathematicians, physicists, teachers and students of universities for courses of computer science, mathematics, physics, etc. The book will be of interest also to the specialists of industry and technology, economics, medicine, etc., that use the *CMS* in own professional activity.

The authors express deep gratitude and appreciation to Misters **Michael Josten**, **Uwe Teubel** and **Dmitry Vassiliev** – the representatives of firms *REAG Renewable Energy AG* and *Purwatt AG (Switzerland)* – for essential assistance rendered by preparation of the present book.

Chapter 1. Additional tools in interactive mode of the Mathematica system

Further we will distinguish two main operating modes with *Mathematica* – *interactive* and *program*. Under the first mode step-by-step performance with a *Mathematica* document, i.e. from an input **In[n]** up to output **Out[n]** will be understood whereas under the program mode the operating within a *block* or a *module* is understood. In this chapter some additional tools rather useful at work with *Mathematica* in interactive mode are considered.

In a whole series of cases of operating with large documents there is expediency of deleting from the current session of earlier used **Out**-paragraphs with the results unnecessary in the future. This operation is provided by simple **ClearOut** procedure, whose call **ClearOut[x]** returns *nothing* and at the same time deletes **Out**-paragraphs with numbers determined by a whole positive number or their list x. The following fragment represents source code of the **ClearOut** procedure with a typical example of its application. This procedure in some cases also provides allocation of additional memory in work field of system which in case of large documents is quite significant.

In[2520]:= **ClearOut[x_ /; PosIntQ[x] || PosIntListQ[x]] :=**
Module[{a = Flatten[{x}], k = 1}, Unprotect[Out];
For[k, k <= Length[a], k++, Out[a[[k]]] =.]; Protect[Out];]

In[2521]:= **{Out[1508], Out[1510], Out[1511], Out[1515]}**
Out[2521]= {42, 78, 2014, 480}
In[2522]:= **ClearOut[{1508, 1510, 1511, 1515}]**
In[2523]:= **{Out[1508], Out[1510], Out[1511], Out[1515]}**
Out[2523]= {%1508, %1510, %1511, %1515}

In addition, call of used function **PosIntQ[x]** or **PosIntListQ[x]** returns *True* if x – a positive number or a list positive numbers accordingly; otherwise, *False* is returned. These functions are located in our *MathToolBox* package [48]; in addition, many means represented below also use means of this package.

On the other hand, in certain cases of work in the interactive mode a need of replacement of **Out**-paragraphs onto other contents arises that simple **ReplaceOut** procedure implements, whose call **ReplaceOut[x, y]** returns nothing, at the same time carrying out replacement of contents of the existing **Out**-paragraphs which are determined by a whole positive or their list x, by the new expressions determined by y argument. The call assumes parity of factual arguments of x and y; otherwise, the call **ReplaceOut[x, y]** is returned unevaluated. The next fragment represents source code of **ReplaceOut** procedure with typical examples of its use.

In[2025]:= **AgnAvzVsv = 80**
Out[2025]= 80

In[2026]:= **ReplaceOut[x_ /; PosIntQ[x] || PosIntListQ[x], y__] :=**
Module[{a = Flatten[{x}], b = Flatten[{y}], k = 1},
If[b != {}, If[Length[a] != Length[b], Defer[ReplaceOut[x, y]], Unprotect[Out];
For[k, k <= Length[a], k++, Out[a[[k]]] = b[[k]]]; Protect[Out]];, ClearOut[x]]]

In[2027]:= **ReplaceOut[2825, 590]**
In[2028]:= **Out[2825]**

Out[2028]= 480

In[2029]:= **ReplaceOut[2825]**
In[2030]:= **Out[2825]**
Out[2030]= %2825

Moreover, the call **ReplaceOut[*x*]** deletes contents of **Out**-paragraphs that are defined by *x* argument, generalizing the previous **ClearOut** procedure.

Definition of variables in Mathematica. Like the majority of programming languages in the *Mathematica* system for expressions the names *(identifiers)* are used, giving possibility in the future to address to such named expressions on their names. So, on the operator "=" the *immediate* assignment to one or several names of the demanded *expression* is made whereas on the operator "*x*:=" – the *postponed* assignment. Distinction of both types of assignment is supposed well known to the reader. For definition of assignment type that has been applied to a name a simple enough **DefOp** procedure can be used whose call **DefOp[*x*]** returns the type in the string format of assignment applied to the *x* name encoded also in string format, namely: *(1) "Undefined"* – a *x* name isn't defined, *(2) $Failed* – a *x* name determines an object different from a simple variable, *(3) "="* – the immediate assignment has been applied to a *x* name, *(4) ":="* – the postponed assignment has been applied to a *x* name. The next fragment represents source code of the procedure with examples of its application.

In[2040]:= **DefOp[x_ /; StringQ[x] && SymbolQ[x] || SymbolQ[ToExpression[x]], y___]:=**
Module[{a = PureDefinition[x], b = {y}, c, d},
If[a === $Failed, "Undefined", If[SuffPref[a, x <> "[", 1], $Failed,
c[h_] := StringReplace[a, x <> " " <> d <> " " -> "", 1];
If[SuffPref[a, x <> " = ", 1], d = "=", d = ":="]; If[b != {} && ! HowAct[y], y = c[d]]; d]]]

In[2041]:= **v = 78; g = 66; s := 46; Kr = 20; Art := 27; Res := a + b + c; J[x_]:= x;**
In[2042]:= **Map[DefOp, {"v", "g", "s", "Kr", "Art", "Res", "Avz", "J"}]**
Out[2042]= {"=", "=", ":=", "=", ":=", ":=", "Undefined", $Failed}
In[2043]:= **Clear[y]; {DefOp["Art", y], y}**
Out[2043]= {":=", "27"}
In[2044]:= **Clear[y]; {DefOp["Res", y], y}**
Out[2044]= {":=", "a + b + c + d"}

While call **DefOp[*x, y*]** through optional second *y* argument – *an undefined variable* – returns an expression appropriated to a *x* name. The value which has been assigned to a *x* variable remains associated with it until its removal on "*x* = .", or on the functions **Clear**, **ClearAll**, **Remove**, or its redefinition.

For evaluation of assignments the *Math*-language has **Definition** function the call of which **Definition[*x*]** returns all definitions ascribed to a *x* name along with our **DefOpt** procedure *(see fragment above)* that is considered in the present book below. Along with the procedure also other means of return of definitions are considered.

In a number of cases arises a necessity of cleaning of variables of the current session from the values received as a result of dynamic generation. For this purpose it is possible to use the mechanism consisting in accumulation in a list of values of variables which should be removed from the current session subsequently, or be cleared from values and attributes.

For this purpose can be used a function whose call **ClearValues**[*w*] returns the empty list, at the same time deleting all variables having values from the *w* list from the current session; whereas the call **ClearValues**[*w*, *y*] with the second optional *y* argument – *any expression* – returns the empty list, however such variables are only cleared of values and attributes without removal from the current session. The following fragment represents source code of the **ClearValues** function along with typical examples of its application.

In[2070]:= **ClearValues[x_ /; ListQ[x], y___] := Select[Map[If[{y} == {}, Remove, ClearAll], Select[Names["`*"], MemberQ[x, ToExpression[#]] &]], # != "Null" &]**

In[2071]:= **{a = 42, b = 90, c := 75, d = 590, h5 := 69, Kr = 20, Art = x + Sin[y]}**
Out[2071]= {42, 90, Null, 590, Null, 20, x + Sin[y]}
In[2072]:= **ClearValues[{42, 90, 75, 590, 69, 20, x + Sin[y]}]**
Out[2072]= {}
In[2073]:= **Names["`*"]**
Out[2073]= {}
In[2122]:= **{x1, y1, z1, t1, h1, g1, w1, s1} = {45, 78, 27, 20, 20, 20, 20, 20};**
In[2123]:= **Names["`*"]**
Out[2123]= {"g1", "h1", "s1", "t1", "w1", "x1", "y1", "z1"}

In[2124]:= **ClearContextVars[x_ /; MemberQ[Select[Contexts[], StringCount[#, "`"] == 1 &], x], y___] := Map[If[Context[#] === x, ClearAttributes[#, Protected]; If[{y} != {}, ClearAll, Remove][#]; #, Nothing] &, Names["`*"]]**

In[2125]:= **ClearContextVars["Global`"]**
Out[2125]= {"g1", "h1", "s1", "t1", "w1", "x1", "y1", "z1"}
In[2126]:= **Map[Definition1, {x1, y1, z1, t1, h1, g1, w1, s1}]**
Out[2126]= {Null, Null, Null, Null, Null, Null, Null, Null}

In[2210]:= **VarsValues[x_List] := Select[Names["`*"], MemberQ[x, ToExpression[#]] &]**
In[2211]:= **{a = 42, b = 90, c := 75, d = 590, h5 := 69, Kr = 20, Art = x + Sin[y]};**
In[2212]:= **VarsValues[{42, 90, 75, 590, 69, 20, x + Sin[y]}]**
Out[2212]= {"a", "Art", "b", "c", "d", "h5", "Kr"}

Unlike the **ClearValues** function, the function call **ClearContextVars**[*x*] clears all values, definitions, attributes, messages, and defaults associated with symbols having a *x* context while the function call **ClearContextVars**[*x*, *y*] removes the above symbols completely, so that their names are no longer recognized in the current session where *y* – an expression. In addition, in both cases the call returns the list of the cleared/removed symbols. If the used context *x* not belong to the list of main contexts of the current session the call is returned unevaluated. In particular, the **ClearContextVars** function can be useful for clearing of the current session from the unwanted symbols with the given context.

In the second part of the fragment the **VarsValues** function is represented, whose the call **VarsValues**[*x*] returns the list of variables in string format which have values from a *x* list. Both functions present a certain interest during the work in interactive mode of the current session. The recommendations about use of these functions can be found in books [33,50].

In some cases on the basis of a certain value is required to determine names to which in the current session this value was ascribed. The problem is solved by the procedure whose call **Nvalue**[*x*] returns the list of names in string format with a preset value *x*. At that, procedure gives only those global variables whose values have been received in the current session in *In*-paragraphs. In the absence of such names the procedure call returns the empty list, i.e. {}. The next fragment presents source code and an example of use of the **Nvalue** procedure.

In[2725]:= Nvalue[x_] := Module[{a = {}, b = Names["`*"], k = 1},
For[k, k <= Length[b], k++, If[ToExpression[b[[k]]] == x, AppendTo[a, b[[k]]], Next[]]];
Select[a, ! SuffPref[#, "Global`", 1] &]

In[2726]:= {Ag, Av, Art, Kr, V, $Ar, Vs, $Kr, G} = {74, 69, 20, 27, 78, 590, Null, 2016, a*b};
Map[Nvalue, {74, 69, 20, 27, 78, 590, Null, 2016, a*b}]
Out[2726]= {{"Ag"}, {"Av"}, {"Art"}, {"Kr"}, {"V"}, {"$Ar"}, {"Vs"}, {"$Kr"}, {"G"}}

The **Nvalue1** procedure is an extension of *functionality* of the above **Nvalue** procedure. The call **Nvalue1**[*x*] returns the list of names of variables in string format to which in the current session a *x* value has been ascribed. In the next fragment source code of the procedure with examples of its application are represented.

In[4334]:= Nvalue1[x_] := Module[{a = {}, b = Select[Names["*"], StringFreeQ[#, "$"] &], c, k = 1}, While[k <= Length[b], c = ToExpression["Attributes[" <> ToString1[b[[k]]] <> "]"];
If[! MemberQ[c, Protected], AppendTo[a, b[[k]]], Null]; k++];
Select[a, ToExpression[#] === x &]]

In[4335]:= {x, y, z, t, h, g, w, s} = {45, 78, 27, 20, 20, 20, 20, 20}; Nvalue1[20]
Out[4335]= {"g", "h", "s", "t", "w"}

Meanwhile, the **Nvalue1** has not quite satisfactory time characteristics as its algorithm is based on the analysis of all active user and system objects.

For definition of the values ascribed to variables, the procedure **WhatValue** is a quite useful whose call **WhatValue**[*x*] returns value ascribed to a variable *x*; on an undefined variable *x* the list of format {"Undefined", *x*} is returned whereas on a system variable the list of format {"System", *x*}, and on a local *x* variable the list of format {"Local", *x*}, is returned. A fragment below represents source code of the **WhatValue** along with examples of its use.

In[2844]:= WhatValue[x_] := If[SystemQ[x], {"System", x},
If[! SameQ[Definition2[ToString[x]][[1]], ToString[x]], {"Local", x}, {"Undefined", x}]]

In[2845]:= Ag[x_]:= Module[{}, x^2]; Sv[x_]:= Block[{a}, a+x]; F[x_, y_]:= x*y
In[2846]:= Map[WhatValue, {500 + 90*# &, hg, Sin, Ag, Sv, 78, a*b, F, Gs}]
Out[2846]= {{"Undefined", 500 + 90 #1 &}, {"Undefined", hg}, {"System", Sin}, {"Local", Ag}, {"Local", Sv}, {"Undefined", 78}, {"Undefined", a*b}, {"Local", F}, {"Undefined", Gs}}
In[2847]:= M = Module[{avz}, avz]; WhatValue[M]
Out[2847]= {"Local", avz$21552}

The function call **NullQ**[*x*] returns *True* if *x* symbol is no an expression, and *False* otherwise, i.e. its value is *Null* which is not displayed in ordinary output. The next fragment represents source code of the function with examples of its application.

In[3545]:= NullQ[x_] := Quiet[SameQ[ToString[Definition[x]], "Null"]]

In[3546]:= **Map[NullQ, {m, a, Pi, 74, a + b, a/b, G}]**
Out[3546]= {True, True, False, False, False, False, True}

In particular, the above **NullQ** function is a rather useful tool to testing of admissibility of optional arguments through which the return of additional results of the procedures call is provided, for example:

In[3002]:= **Sv[x_, y_ /; NullQ[y], z___] := Module[{a = 74, b = 69, c = 49}, y = Plus[a, b, c];**
If[{z} != {} && NullQ[z], z = Times[a, b, c], 6]; (a + b + c)*x]

In[3003]:= **Clear[m, n]; Sv[2017, m, n]**
Out[3003]= 387264
In[3004]:= **{m, n}**
Out[3004]= {192, 250194}
In[3005]:= **m = 74; Sv[2017, m, n21]**
Out[3005]= Sv[2017, 74, n21]

The above fragment is rather transparent and doesn't demand any special explanations.

The call **Clear[x1, ..., xn]** of the standard function clears symbols {x1, ..., xn}, excepting the symbols with *Protected*-attribute. As a useful generalization of functions **Clear** and **ClearAll** the procedure **Clear1** can be considered whose call **Clear1[h,"x1", ..., "xn"]** returns *Null*, i.e. *nothing*, clearing at condition *h=1* the symbols {x1,x2,...,xn} with saving of all their attributes and options whereas at *h=2*, clearing symbols {x1, x2, ..., xn} as from expressions ascribed to them, and from all attributes and options. The next fragment represents source code of the **Clear1** procedure along with typical examples of its application.

In[2958]:= **Clear1[x_ /; MemberQ[{1, 2}, x], y___] := Module[{a = {y}, b, c, d, k = 1},**
If[y === {}, Null, For[k, k <= Length[a], k++, b = a[[k]];
d = Quiet[ToExpression["Attributes[" <> ToString1[b] <> "]"]];
ToExpression["Quiet[ClearAttributes[" <> ToString1[b] <> ", " <>
ToString[d] <> "]" <> "; Clear" <> If[x == 1, "", "All"] <> "[" <> ToString1[b] <> "]]"]];
If[x == 2, Null, Quiet[Check[ToExpression["SetAttributes[" <> ToString1[b] <> ", " <>
ToString[d] <> "]"], $Failed]]]]]

In[2959]:= **S[x_] := x^2; SetAttributes[S, {Listable, Protected}]; Clear["S"];**
Clear::wrsym: Symbol S is Protected.>>
In[2960]:= **Clear1[1, S]**
In[2961]:= **Definition[S]**
Out[2961]= Attributes[S] = {Listable, Protected}
In[2962]:= **Clear1[2, S]**
In[2963]:= **Definition[S]**
Out[2963]= Null

As a rather useful means the **UnDef** procedure serves, whose call **UnDef[x]** returns *True* if a *x* symbol isn't defined, and *False* otherwise. While call **UnDef[x, y]** with the second optional argument – *an indefined variable* – returns **Head1[x]** value through *y*, where **Head1** is a rather useful generalization of standard function **Head** considered below. At that, in a number of cases of procedural programming the **UnDef** appears as a quite useful means also. The next fragment represents source code of **UnDef** with examples of its application.

In[2490]:= **UnDef[x_, y__]** := Module[{a = {y}, b = Head2[x]},
If[a != {} && ! HowAct[y], y = b]; If[b === Symbol, True, False]]

In[2491]:= x = 78; y = {a, b}; z = a + b; Map[UnDef, {t, h, x, y, z, 590}]
Out[2491]= {True, True, False, False, False, False}

In[2492]:= A[x_ /; UnDef[x]] := Block[{a}, a = 590; a]; y := 2016; {A[y], A[78]}
Out[2492]= {A[2016], A[78]}

In[2493]:= L = {a, b, c, d, h, g, p, v, w}; Select[L, UnDef[#] &]
Out[2493]= {a, b, c, d, h, g, p, v, w}

In[2494]:= M[x_] := x; {UnDef[M, t6], t6}
Out[2494]= {False, "Function"}

Right there it is appropriate to note that on examples of **UnDef1, UnDef2** and **UnDef3** – the **UnDef** procedure modifications – basic distinction between procedures of types *"Module"* and *"Block"* is illustrated [28-33]. Therefore, the type of procedure should be chosen rather circumspectly, giving a certain priority to the procedures of *Module*-type. In addition, as the enclosed procedures the procedures of *Module*-type are used, as a rule.

In a number of cases exists a necessity of definition of a context of an arbitrary symbol. This problem is solved by a simple enough procedure, whose call **Affiliate[x]** returns the context for an arbitrary symbol *x* given in the string format whereas *"Undefined"* is returned on a symbol, completely undefinite for the current session. At that, under *"completely undefinite"* is understood as a concrete expression, and a symbol for the first time used in the current session. The fragment below represents source code of the given procedure and examples of its usage, including examples explaining the essence of the concept *"completely undefinite"*.

In[4280]:= **Affiliate[x_ /; StringQ[x]]** := Module[{a = Quiet[Context[x]]},
If[ToString[a] === "Context[" <> x <> "]", "Undefined", If[MemberQ[Contexts[], a] &&
ToString[Quiet[DefFunc[x]]] == "Null" || Attributes[x] == {Temporary}, "Undefined", a]]]

In[4281]:= G = 69; Map[Affiliate, {"ProcQ", "Sin", "G", "Z", "Map13", "Mapp"}]
Out[4281]= {"AladjevProcedures`", "System`", "Global`", "Undefined",
"AladjevProcedures`", "AladjevProcedures`"}

In[4282]:= {V, G = 74, 69}; Map[Affiliate, {"V", "G", "90", "Sin[20]", "Q", "Map"}]
Out[4282]= {"Undefined", "Global`", "Undefined", "Undefined", "Undefined", "System`"}

The call **WhatObj[x]** of a quite simple procedure returns value depending on location of a *x* symbol activated in the current session: *"System"* – a system function; *"CS"* – symbol whose definition has been determined in the current session; *"Undefined"* – an undefinite symbol; *"Context'"* – a context defining a package uploaded into the current session and containing definition of a *x* symbol; if *x* has a type other than *Symbol*, the procedure call is returned as unevaluated. The following fragment represents source code of **WhatObj** procedure along with typical examples of its application.

In[2139]:= **WhatObj[x_ /; SymbolQ[x]]** := Module[{a = Quiet[Context[x]], t},
If[a === "System`", "System", If[a === "Global`", If[MemberQ[{$Failed, "Undefined"},
PureDefinition[x]], "Undefined", "CS"], a]]]

In[2140]:= w[x_] := Block[{}, x]; Map[WhatObj, {Sin, a/b, ProcQ, t78, h6, w}]
Out[2140]= {"System", WhatObj[a/b], "AladjevProcedures`", "Undefined", "Undefined", "CS"}

For testing of symbols to which expressions are ascribed, two simple functions **HowAct** and **SymbolQ** are defined. The first of them correctly tests the fact of definiteness of a variable in the current session, however on local variables of procedures the call of **HowAct** returns *True* irrespective of existence for them of values. On the other hand, on the undefinite local variables of blocks the **HowAct** returns *False*. The call **SymbolQ**[*x*] of simple though rather useful function returns *True* if *x* is a symbol, and *False* otherwise. This function is used in a number of tools presented in the book. Whereas the procedure call **UndefinedQ**[*x*] returns *True* if *x* is a definite symbol, and *False* otherwise. In addition, unlike the **HowAct** function the **UndefinedQ** procedure returns *True* only on condition of empty definition for a tested symbol irrespective of existence for it of options and attributes. The given distinction is a rather essential, in particular, in a case of programming of procedures at which as formal arguments undefinite variables through which the additional results of procedures calls are returned are used. In this case it is necessary to use the format "*w_ /; ! HowAct[w]*" in the procedures headings. As shows experience of programming in *Mathematica*, in many cases the procedure **HowAct** is more suitable than standard function **ValueQ**, including testing of the local variables in procedures. The last example in the following fragment illustrates the differences between means **ValueQ** and **HowAct**. At that, the call **ValueQ**[*x*] returns *False* only if *x* would not change if it were to be entered as language input. At that, the function call **DefinedActSymbols**[] returns the list of the symbols names different of temporary and *undefined* symbols in the current session. While the function call **SymbolCS**[] without actual arguments returns the sorted list of symbols in the string format that were evaluated in the **Input** paragraphs of *nb*-documents of the current session. The fragment below represents source codes of the above five means with the most typical examples of their application.

In[3942]:= HowAct[x_] := If[Quiet[Check[ToString[Definition[x]], True]] === "Null", False, If[ProtectedQ[x], True, If[Quiet[ToString[Definition[x]]] === "Attributes[" <> ToString[x] <> "] = {Temporary}", False, True]]]

In[3943]:= SymbolQ[x_] := ! SameQ[Quiet[Check[ToExpression["Attributes[" <> ToString[x] <> "]"], $Failed]], $Failed]

In[3944]:= UndefinedQ[x_] := If[SymbolQ[x], If[MemberQ[{$Failed, "Undefined"}, PureDefinition[x]], True, False], False]

In[3945]:= DefinedActSymbols[] := Select[Names["`*"], ! (TemporaryQ[#] || UndefinedQ[#]) &]

In[3946]:= DefinedActSymbols[]
Out[3946]= {"Agn", "Avz", "B", "DefinedActSymbols", "M", "Mb", "P", "Z"}
In[3947]:= Map[HowAct, {590, IAN, "RANS", Cos, Args, TestArgsTypes}]
Out[3947]= {True, False, True, True, True, True}
In[3948]:= Map[SymbolQ, {90, IAN, "RANS", Cos, Args, Label, HowAct}]
Out[3948]= {False, True, True, True, True, True, True, True}
In[3949]:= G[x_] := x; SetAttributes[G, Protected]; ClearAll[V]; S = 49;
In[3950]:= Map18[{HowAct, UndefinedQ}, {G, V, 49, a + b, S}]
Out[3950]= {{True, False, True, True, True}, {False, True, False, False, False}}
In[3951]:= Gs[x_, y_ /; ! HowAct[y]] := {y = Head[x], x^3}[[2]]; {Gs[74, h], h}
Out[3951]= {405 224, Integer}
In[3952]:= v := 74; g = 69; Map18[{ValueQ, HowAct}, {v, g, HowAct, ProcQ}]

Out[3952]= {{False, False, False, False}, {True, True, True, True}}

In[3953]:= **SymbolsCS[] := Sort[Select[Names["Global`*"], ! MemberQ[{"Attributes[" <> ToString[#] <> "] = {Temporary}", "Null"}, ToString1[Definition[#]]] &]]**

In[3954]:= **SymbolsCS[]**
Out[3954]= {"agn", "avz", "h", "Lst", "Lst1", "SymbolsCS", "TGR", "vsv", "xg"}

In certain cases the **SymbolQ1** function, being of a modification of function **SymbolQ** can be useful, whose call **SymbolQ1[x]** returns *True* if *x* is a single symbol, and *False* otherwise [33]. In [33] certain features of usage of **HowAct** for testing of definiteness of local variables of procedures can be found.

On the other hand, the procedure below allows to obtain temporary variables of the current session with contexts, corresponding to them. The procedure call **VariablesCS[j]** returns the simple or nested list, whose sublists as the first element contain context, the second element is word *"Temp"*, whereas others elements define temporary varibles in the string format of the current session, excluding system tools and tools contained in the user packages loaded into the current session and defined by an *j* tuple of contexts accociated with them. Whereas the procedure call **VariablesCS[]** returns the result of the above format on condition that all tools along with temporary variables of the user packages uploaded into the current session are not excluded. The fragment below represents source code of the **VariablesCS** procedure with an example of its application.

In[4582]:= **VariablesCS[x___ /; If[{x} == {}, True, And1[Map[ContextQ[#] &, {x}]]]] := Module[{a, b}, a = Complement[Names["*"], Names["System`*"], Flatten[Map[CNames[#] &, {x}]]];
b = Map[{Context[#], If[TemporaryQ[#], "Temp", Nothing], #} &, DeleteDuplicates[a]];
ReduceLists[Map[DeleteDuplicates, Map[Flatten, Gather[b, #1[[1]] == #2[[1]] &]]]]**

In[4583]:= **VariablesCS["AladjevProcedures`", "Global`"]**
Out[4583]= {{"AladjevProcedures`", "Temp", "a", "a$", "b", "b$", "c", "c$", "d", "d$", "f", "f$", "g", "g$", "n", "n$", "Op$", "p", "p$", "s", "s$", "t", "t$", "x", "x$", "y", "y$", "z", "z$"}, {"Global`", "Temp", "F", "G", "Global", "h", "h$", "j", "k", "k$", "m", "mp", "mp$", "m$", "pf", "Sf", "t1", "t1$", "t2", "t2$", "u", "u$", "v", "v$"}}

The next tool is a natural consequence of the previous procedure; its call **TempPackage[x]** returns the list of temporary variables in the string format of the current session which are conditioned by the user package loaded into the current session and defined by a *x* context associated with it. The next fragment represents source code of the **TempPackage** function with an example of its application.

In[4593]:= **TempPackage[x_ /; ContextQ[x]] := Sort[Select[Complement[Names["*"], Names["System`*"], CNames[x]], Context[#] === x &]]**

In[4594]:= **TempPackage["AladjevProcedures`"]**
Out[4594]= {"a", "a$", "b", "b$", "c", "c$", "d", "d$", "f", "f$", "g", "g$", "n", "n$", "Op$", "p", "p$", "s", "s$", "t", "t$", "x", "x$", "y", "y$", "z", "z$"}

So, the above tools in many cases of procedural programming are applicable enough widely *(see also our books on the **Mathematica** system in collection* [50]).

In a number of cases exists a necessity of removal from the current session of a certain active object having the corresponding value with possibility of its subsequent restoration in the current or other session. This problem is solved by the function whose call **ActRemObj[*x*, *y*]** depending on a value {*"Act"*, *"Rem"*} of the 2nd actual argument *y* deletes an object given by its *x* name in the string format from the current session or activates it in the current or other session respectively. The fragment below represents source code of **ActRemObj** procedure along with typical examples of its application.

In[3647]:= **ActRemObj[x_/; StringQ[x], y_/; MemberQ[{"Act", "Rem"}, y]] :=
Module[{a = $HomeDirectory <> "\\" <> x <> ".$ArKr$", b, c = ToString[Definition4[x]]},
If[c === "$Failed", $Failed, If[HowAct[x] && y == "Rem", b = OpenWrite[a];
WriteString[b, c]; Close[b]; ClearAllAttributes[x]; Remove[x]; "Remove",
If[! HowAct[x] && y == "Act", If[FileExistsQ[a], b = OpenRead[a]; Read[b]; Close[b];
DeleteFile[a]; "Activate", Return[Defer[ActRemObj[x, y]]]]]]]]**

In[3648]:= **F := {74, 69, 49, 20, 27}; SetAttributes[F, Protected]; Definition[F]**
Out[3648]= Attributes[F] = {Protected}
F := {74, 69, 49, 20, 27}
In[3649]:= **ActRemObj["F", "Rem"]**
Out[3649]= "Remove"
In[3650]= **Definition[F]**
Out[3650]= Null
In[3651]:= **ActRemObj["F", "Act"]**
Out[3651]= "Activate"
In[3652]= **Definition[F]**
Out[3652]= Attributes[F] = {Protected}
F := {74, 69, 49, 20, 27}
In[3653]:= **A[x_] := Module[{a = 590}, x + a]; A[x_, y_] := Module[{a = 90}, x + y + a]**
In[3654]:= **{A[100], A[100, 200]}**
Out[3654]= {690, 390}
In[3655]:= **ActRemObj["A", "Rem"]; Definition[A]**
Out[3655]= Null
In[3656]:= **ActRemObj["A", "Act"]; {A[100], A[100, 200]}**
Out[3656]= {690, 390}

Successful removing of an object from the current session returns *"Remove"*, whereas its restoration in the current session returns *"Activate"*. If a datafile containing definition of a removed *x* object, wasn't found in system catalog *$HomeDirectory*, the call of **ActRemObj** procedure is returned *unevaluated*; on an inadmissible *x* argument the call **ActRemObj[*x*, *y*]** returns *$Failed*.

It should be noted that **ClearSymbolsCS** procedure which is based on the previous function **SymbolsCS** allows to *clean* all symbols whose values have been appropriated to them in the current session. In addition, the call **ClearSymbolsCS[]** clears only values and definitions for the symbols while the call **ClearSymbolsCS[*x*]** where *x* is an arbitrary expression clears all values, definitions, attributes, messages, defaults that are associated with these symbols. The successful procedure call returns *Null*, i.e., nothing:

In[4342]:= ClearSymbolsCS[x___] := Module[{a = SymbolsCS[], b},
If[{x} == {}, b = Map[{#, Attributes[#]} &, a]; Map[Unprotect, a]; Map[Clear, a];
Map[SetAttributes1[#[[1]], #[[2]]] &, b], Map[ClearAll, Map[Unprotect, a]]];]

In[4343]:= {avz, agn, vsv} = {75, 70, 50}
Out[4343]= {75, 70, 50}
In[4344]:= SetAttributes[avz, Protected]
In[4345]:= ClearSymbolsCS[]
In[4346]:= {Attributes[avz], avz}
Out[4346]= {{Protected}, avz}

In[4364]:= ClearSymbols[x_ /; ListQ[x], y___] := Module[{a = Select[x, StringQ[#] &], b},
If[{y} == {}, b = Map[{#, Attributes[#]} &, x]; Map[Unprotect, x]; Map[Clear, x];
Map[SetAttributes1[#[[1]], #[[2]]] &, b], Map[ClearAll, Map[Unprotect, x]]];]

In[4365]:= {avz, agn, vsv} = {75, 70, 50}
Out[4365]= {75, 70, 50}
In[4366]:= SetAttributes[avz, Protected]
In[4367]:= ClearSymbols[{"avz", "agn", "vsv"}]
In[4368]:= {Attributes[avz], avz}
Out[4368]= {{Protected}, avz}

The **ClearSymbols** procedure which is a modification of the **ClearSymbolsCS** procedure finishes the previous fragment. The procedure call **ClearSymbols[x]** clears only values and definitions for the symbols in string format from a *x* list whereas the call **ClearSymbols[x, y]** where *y* is an arbitrary expression clears all values, definitions, attributes, messages, and defaults associated with these symbols. Analogously to the **ClearSymbolsCS** procedure, the **ClearSymbols** procedure successfully programmatically processes the situation connected with existence of symbols with the *Protected* attribute. The successful procedure call returns *Null*, i.e., nothing, as the previous fragment illustrated.

System *Maple* has a rather useful *restart* command which causes the *Maple* kernel to clear its internal memory so that system *Maple* acts almost as if just started. Whereas the system *Mathematica* has no similar means in the interactive mode. The next procedure to a certain extent compensates for this deficiency. The call **Restart[]** returns nothing, deleting from the *current session* all objects defined in it. Moreover, from the given list are excluded the objects whose definitions are in the downloaded packages. While the call **Restart[x]** with optional *x* argument – a context defining the user package which has been uploaded into the current session – also returns nothing, additionally deleting from current session all objects whose definitions are contained in the mentioned user package. The procedure is easily extended to the case when the list of contexts is used as the argument *x*. The fragment below presents source code of the **Restart** procedure along with examples of its application.

In[3007]:= Restart[x___] := Module[{},
Map[{Quiet[ClearAttributes[#, Protected]], Quiet[Remove[#]]} &, If[{x} != {} &&
MemberQ[Select[Contexts[], StringCount[#, "`"] == 1 &], x], {Write["590", 90],
Close["590"], Names[x <> "*"]}[[-1]], Names["`*"]]];
If[Quiet[Check[Read["590"], 500]] == 90, DeleteFile[Close["590"]];

```
Unprotect[$Packages, Contexts]; {$Packages, $ContextPath} = Map[Complement[#, {x}] &,
{$Packages, $ContextPath}];
Contexts[] = Select[Contexts[], Quiet[Check[StringTake[#, {1, StringLength[x]}], "Null"]]
!= x &]; Protect[$Packages, Contexts], Null];]
In[3008]:= F := {74, 69, 49, 20, 27}; SetAttributes[F, Protected]; Sv = 49; a := 6;
A[x_] := Module[{a = 590}, x + a]; A[x_, y_] := Module[{a = 90}, x*y*a];
In[3009]:= Restart[]
In[3010]:= Map[Definition1, {F, Sv, A}]
Out[3010]= {"Null", "Null", "Null"}
In[3011]:= Restart["AladjevProcedures`"]
In[3012]:= Names["AladjevProcedures`" <> "*"]
Out[3012]= {}
```

Moreover, the system objects are not affected by the **Restart** means. In a number of cases the function seems a rather useful, allowing to substantially restore an initial state of the current session and to save internal memory of system too. So, the procedure call **Restart[*x*]** deletes from the current session all objects with a *x* context, to some extent allowing to *restore* a state of the current session.

Tools of work with sequential structures. Sequences of expressions *(simply sequences)* in the environment of many languages are formed on the basis of the *comma* operator "," and form a certain base for definition of many types of data *(inquiries of procedures, lists, sets, indexes, etc.)*. At that, in *Mathematica* system the given structure as an independent one is absent, and instead of it the list structure protrudes; some programming languages adhere to the same concept. In this context a number of simple enough tools has been created that ensure operating with the object **Seq[*x*]** defining a sequence of elements *x*. So, the call **SeqToList[*x*]** provides converting of *Seq*-object *x* into the list, the procedure call **ListToSeq[*x*]** provides converting of a *x* list into *Seq*-object, the procedure call **SeqIns[*x*, *y*, *z*]** returns the result of inserting in *Seq*-object *x* of an arbitrary *y* element *(list, Seq-object, expression, etc.)* according to the given *z* position *(z <= 0 – before x, z >= Length[x] – after x, differently – after z – position in x)*, the procedure call **SeqToString[*a*, *b*,...]** returns the list of arguments in string format, while the call **SeqUnion[*x*, *y*,...]** returns result of *merge* of an arbitrary number of sequences. Tools for manipulating with *Seq*-objects can be rather widely expanded, providing the user with rather useful program tools. In a certain relation these tools allow to solve the problem of compatibility with other means, for example, with *Maple* system [28-33] *(see also our books on Mathematica and Maple in the collection* [50]).

Meanwhile, the *Mathematica* system provides the function **Sequence[*a*, ...]** which defines a sequence of arguments which are automatically transferred to a block, function or module. In this context the call **SequenceQ[*s*]** provides testing of the objects that are created on the basis of the **Sequence** function returning *True* if a *s*-object is defined by this function, and *False* otherwise; moreover, the name of *s*-object is coded in string format [33]. On the basis of standard **Sequence** function it is possible to create quite simple tools ensuring working with sequential structures similarly to the *Maple* system; these functions with the *considered* ones in [28-33] are rather useful in work with objects of type *"sequence"*, whose structure isn't supported by *Mathematica* and for work with which system has no standard means.

The call **Sequence[*x1, x2, ..., xn*]** of the standard function determines a sequence of factual arguments *xj (j = 1..n)*, transferred to a function. Meanwhile, with objects of type *"sequence"* *Mathematica* system can work mediately, in particular, on the basis of the list structures. In this regard for expansion of standard **Sequence** function onto list structures the **Sequences** procedure is defined, whose call **Sequences[*x*]** provides insert in a function of arguments *x* given by a sequence or a list; as a simplified variant of **Sequences** the **Sq** function serves. So, the given reception in a number of cases allows to simplify processing of formal arguments of modules, blocks and functions. The next fragment represents source codes of **Sq** function along with the **Sequences** procedure, including their typical applications.

In[3495]:= **Sequences[x__] := Module[{a = Flatten[{x}], b, c},**
b = "Sequence[" <> ToString[a] <> "]"; a = Flatten[StringPosition[b, {"{", "}"}]];
ToExpression[StringReplace[b, {StringTake[b, {a[[1]], a[[1]]}] -> "",
StringTake[b, {a[[-1]], a[[-1]]}] -> ""}]]]

In[3496]:= **{F[Sequence[{x, y, z}]], F[Sequences[{x, y, z}]], F[Sequences[x, y, z]]}**
Out[3496]= {F[{x, y, z}], F[x, y, z], F[x, y, z]}
In[3497]:= **G @@ {a, b, c, Sequences[{x, y, z}], c, d}**
Out[3497]= G[a, b, c, x, y, z, c, d]

In[3499]:= **Sq[x_ /; ListQ[x]] :=**
ToExpression["Sequence[" <> StringTake[ToString1[x], {2, -2}] <> "]"]

In[3501]:= **Plus[Sq[{74, 69, 59, 49, 27, 20}]]**
Out[3501]= 298
In[3502]:= **G[a, b, c, Sequences[x, y, z, h, g, s, t]]**
Out[3502]= G[a, b, c, x, y, z, h, g, s, t]

By understanding a tuple of the elements parted by a comma as a sequence, the next simple function identifies such objects. The function call **SequencesQ[*x*]** returns *True* if *x* defines a sequence, and *False* otherwise. The fragment below presents the source code of the function **SequencesQ** with examples of its application.

In[4109]:= **SequencesQ[x__] := Module[{a}, a[y_] := y; UnevaluatedQ[a, x]]**

In[4110]:= **SequencesQ[{1, 2, 3, a, {b, c}}]**
Out[4110]= False
In[4111]:= **SequencesQ[1, 2, 3, a, {b, c}]**
Out[4111]= True
In[4112]:= **SequencesQ[75]**
Out[4112]= False

The function can be a rather useful means in certain cases of sequences processing. So, it can be useful in the functions extending the logical functions **And, Nand, Nor, Or, Xnor, Xor**, in particular, to case of a list as actual argument. The calls **And1[*x*], Nand1[*x*], Nor1[*x*], Or1[*x*], Xnor1[*x*]** and **Xor1[*x*]** are equivalent to the calls **And[*x*], Nand[*x*], Nor[*x*], Or[*x*], Xnor[*x*]** and **Xor[*x*]** respectively with the difference, that a list or a sequence can be as actual *x* argument. Meanwhile, for extension of the above logical functions onto lists as argument it is possible to use the following definitions, namely:

In[4180]:= **And1[x__] := If[DeleteDuplicates[Map[BooleanQ, Flatten[{x}]]] == {True},**

And @@ Flatten[{x}], If[SequencesQ[x], {x}, x]]

In[4181]:= **And1[{True, True, True}]**
Out[4181]= True
In[4182]:= **And1[True, False, True]**
Out[4182]= False

In[4183]:= **If[And @@ Map[BooleanQ, Flatten[{x}]], And @@ Flatten[{x}], If[SequencesQ[x], {x}, x]]**

In[4184]:= **Nand1[x__] := If[And @@ Map[BooleanQ, Flatten[{x}]], Nand @@ Flatten[{x}], If[SequencesQ[x], {x}, x]]**

In[4185]:= **Nor1[x__] := If[And @@ Map[BooleanQ, Flatten[{x}]], Nor @@ Flatten[{x}], If[SequencesQ[x], {x}, x]]**

In[4186]:= **Or1[x__] := If[And @@ Map[BooleanQ, Flatten[{x}]], Or @@ Flatten[{x}], If[SequencesQ[x], {x}, x]]**

In[4187]:= **Xnor1[x__] := If[And @@ Map[BooleanQ, Flatten[{x}]]}, Xnor @@ Flatten[{x}], If[SequencesQ[x], {x}, x]]**

In[4188]:= **Xor1[x__] := If[And @@ Map[BooleanQ, Flatten[{x}]]}, Xor @@ Flatten[{x}], If[SequencesQ[x], {x}, x]]**

In a lot of cases the possibility of use of the list as the factual argument of the above logical functions simplifies programming, reduces the program code and does it more transparent that, first of all, is convenient in headings of blocks, functions and modules.

At work with sequential structures a rather useful is a procedure, providing converting of strings of a special format into lists, and vice versa. The call **ListStrList[x]** on a list $x=\{a,b,...\}$ returns s string of format "*ahbh...*", while x=**ListStrList[s]** where h=**FromCharacterCode[2]**. In case of absence in s string of h symbol the call **ListStrList[s]** returns the s string. The next fragment represents source code of the procedure along with examples its application.

In[3624]:= **ListStrList[x_ /; StringQ[x] || ListQ[x]] := Module[{a = FromCharacterCode[2]}, If[StringQ[x] && ! StringFreeQ[x, a], Map[ToExpression, StringSplit[x, a]], If[ListQ[x], StringTake[StringJoin[Map14[StringJoin, Map[ToString1, x], a]], {1, −2}], x]]]**
In[3625]:= **L = ListStrList[{Avz, 74, Agn, 69, Art, 27, Kr, 20, Vsv, 49}]**
Out[3625]= "Avz□74□Agn□69□Art□27□Kr□20□Vsv□49"
In[3626]:= **ListStrList[ListStrList[{Avz, 74, Agn, 69, Art, 27, Kr, 20, Vsv, 49}]]**
Out[3626]= {Avz, 74, Agn, 69, Art, 27, Kr, 20, Vsv, 49}

The following procedure serves as a good addition to standard functions of *Mathematica* which are intended for rearranging and restructuring of lists. The call **ListRearrange[x, y]** returns the rearranging result of a x list, using a y list of *ListList* type for change of order of its elements. Elements of the y list are two-element lists of the format $\{n, m\}$ where n – the current position of an element of the x list and m – its new position in the returned list.

Unlike **ListRearrange** procedure, the call **ListListRearrange[x, y]** returns the rearranging result of all sublists of x list of *ListList* type, using the y list of *ListList* type for change of the order of their elements. While elements of y list are 2-element lists of format $\{n, m\}$ where n – the current position of element of sublist of x list, and m – its new position in the returned sublist. At last, the **ListListRearrange1** procedure unlike the previous procedure provides the rearranging between elements belonging to different sublists of a list of the *ListList* type. More precisely, the procedure call **ListListRearrange1[x, y]** returns the rearranging result of *x* list, using *y* list of the *ListList* type for change of order of its elements belonging to various sublists. Elements of the *y* list are 4-element lists of the format {*n1, j2, n2, j2*} where *n1* – the *n1-th* sublist of the *x* list and *j1* – the position of its element, whereas *n2* – the *n2-th* sublist of the *x* list and *j2* – the position of its element; the procedure carries out mutual exchange by these elements of the sublists, returning the result of such rearranging. The above means are rather useful in programming of number of lists processing problems, extending the means of the *Mathematica* system to the nested lists rearranging. The fragment below represents source codes of the above means **ListRearrange, ListListRearrange** and **ListListRearrange1** along with typical examples of their application.

In[3515]:= ListRearrange[x_ /; ListQ[x], y_ /; ListListQ[y] && Length[y[[1]]] == 2] :=
Module[{a = Range[1, Length[x]], b, c = {}, d}, d = Flatten[Map[{#, Reverse[#]} &, y], 1];
b = ReplaceAll[a, Map[Rule[#[[1]], #[[2]]] &, y]];
Do[AppendTo[c, {x[[k]], b[[k]]}], {k, 1, a[[-1]]}];
c = Sort[c, #1[[2]] < #2[[2]] &]; Map[#[[1]] &, c]]

In[3816]:= ListListRearrange[x_ /; ListListQ[x], y_ /; ListListQ[y] && Length[y[[1]]] == 2] :=
Map[ListRearrange[#, y] &, x]

In[3817]:= ListListRearrange[{{1, 2, 3, 4}, {5, 6, 7, 8}, {9, a, j, c}}, {{2, 3}, {4, 1}}]
Out[3817]= {{4, 1, 3, 2}, {8, 5, 7, 6}, {c, 9, j, a}}

In[3818]:= ListRearrange[{1, 2, 3, 4, 5, 6, 7, 8, 9}, {{3, 1}, {4, 2}, {6, 9}, {10, 4}}]
Out[3818]= {3, 4, 1, 2, 5, 9, 7, 8, 6}

In[3897]:= ListListRearrange1[x_ /; ListListQ[x], y_ /; ListListQ[y] && Length[y[[1]]] == 4]:=
Module[{a = x, b}, Do[b = a[[y[[k]][[1]]]][[y[[k]][[2]]]];
a = ReplacePart[a, y[[k]][[1 ;; 2]] -> a[[y[[k]][[3]]]][[y[[k]][[4]]]]];
a = ReplacePart[a, y[[k]][[3 ;; 4]] -> b], {k, 1, Length[y]}]; a]

In[3898]:= L := {{1, 2, 3, 4}, {5, 6, 7, 8}, {x, y, z, g}, {m, n, p, z}}
In[3899]:= ListListRearrange1[L, {{2, 3, 4, 1}, {4, 3, 1, 4}}]
Out[3899]= {{1, 2, 3, p}, {5, 6, m, 8}, {x, y, z, g}, {7, n, 4, z}}

In[4484]:= ListListRearrange2[x_ /; ListListQ[x], y_ /; ListListQ[y] && Length[y[[1]]] == 4]:=
Module[{a = Length[x[[1]]], b}, b = Map[{a*(#[[1]] - 1) + #[[2]], a*(#[[3]] - 1) + #[[4]]} &, y];
Partition[ListRearrange[Flatten[x], b], a]]

In[4485]:= ListListRearrange2[L, {{2, 3, 4, 1}, {4, 3, 1, 4}, {3, 4, 2, 1}}]
Out[4485]= {{1, 2, 3, p}, {4, g, 5, 6}, {8, x, y, z}, {m, 7, n, z}}

In[4491]:= MaxLevelList[x_ /; ListQ[x]] := Module[{b = 0, a = ReplaceAll[x, {} -> {75}]},
Do[If[Level[a, {j}] == {}, Return[b], b++], {j, 1, Infinity}]]

In[4492]:= MaxLevelList[{a, b, {{a, b}, {{m, n, {p, {{{{}}}}}}}, c, {}, m, n, p}]
Out[4492]= 8

In conclusion of the previous fragment, the **ListListRearrange2** procedure that is a certain *modification* of the **ListListRearrange1** procedure and based both on reception of converting of the list of the *ListList* type into the simple list, and on the subsequent application to it of the **ListRearrange** procedure with the subsequent converting of the result into the list of the *ListList* type is represented.

In a like manner to the above **ListListRearrange1** procedure, the call **ListListRearrange2[*x*, *y*]** returns the rearranging result of *x* list, using a *y* list of *ListList* type for change of order of its elements belonging to various sublists. Elements of the *y* list are four-element lists of the format {*n1, j2, n2, j2*} where *n1* – the *n1-th* sublist of the *x* list and *j1* – position of its element, whereas *n2* – the *n2-th* sublist of the *x* list and *j2* – the position of its element; the procedure carries out mutual exchange by these elements of the sublists, returning the result of such rearranging. Meanwhile, the results of use of both procedures on the same tuples of actual arguments aren't identical as a whole, which very visually illustrate examples of application of both procedures. It allows to say that the **ListListRearrange1** and **ListListRearrange2** in general carry out different rearrangings of lists of *ListList* type that are oriented on various problems of lists processing of the *ListList* type. Distinction of the results of execution of the above procedures is caused by distinction of the used algorithms of rearranging of lists of the *ListList* type. The given fragment is ended by the procedure whose call **MaxLevelList[*x*]** returns the maximum nesting level of a *x* list; a simple and empty lists have the *nesting* level *1*. The receptions used at programming of the above procedures can be a rather useful in the practical programming in the *Mathematica* system.

Our versatile experience of the *Mathematica* system use shows undoubted usefulness of the tools represented in the present chapter both in program mode, and in interactive mode of working with the *Mathematica* system. It should be noted that many of these tools are used enough widely by other means of our package and in other numerous applications.

Chapter 2. Additional tools of processing of arbitrary expressions in the *Mathematica* software

A number of useful tools of processing of the expressions supplementing standard tools of *Mathematica* system is presented in the present chapter. Analogously to the most software systems the *Mathematica* understands everything with what it manipulates as "*expression*" *(graphics, lists, formulas, strings, modules, functions, numbers of various type, etc.)*. And although all these expressions at first sight rather significantly differ, *Mathematica* represents them in so-called full format. And only the postponed assignment ":=" has no full format. For the purpose of definition of the heading *(the type defining it)* of an expression the standard **Head** function is used, whose call **Head[***expr***]** returns the heading of an *expr* expression:

In[6]:= **G := S; Z[x_] := Block[{}, x]; F[x_] := x; M[x_] := x; M[x_, y_] := x + y;**
Map[Head, {ProcQ, Sin, 6, a+b, # &, G, Z, Function[{x}, x], x*y, x^y, F, M}]
Out[6]= {Symbol, Symbol, Integer, Plus, Function, Symbol, Symbol, Function, Times, Power, Symbol, Symbol}

For more exact definition of headings we created an useful modification of standard **Head** function in the form of the **Head1** procedure expanding its opportunities, in particular, that concerns testing of blocks, system functions, the user functions, modules, etc. Thus, the call **Head1[***x***]** returns the heading of *x* expression in the context {*Block, Function, Module, System, Symbol, Head[x], PureFunction*}. At that, on the objects of the same name that have one name with several definitions the procedure call returns $*Failed*. The fragment below represents source code of the **Head1** procedure with examples of its application comparatively with the **Head** function as it is illustrated by certain examples of the following fragment on which the functional distinctions of both tools are rather evident.

In[2160]:= **Head1[x_] := Module[{a = PureDefinition[x]},**
If[ListQ[a], $Failed, If[a === "System", System,
If[BlockQ[x], Block, If[ModuleQ2[x], Module,
If[PureFuncQ[x], PureFunction,
If[Quiet[Check[FunctionQ[x], False]], Function, Head[x]]]]]]]]

In[2161]:= **G := S; Z[x_] := Block[{}, x]; F[x_] := x; M[x_] := x; M[x_, y_] := x + y;**
Map[Head, {ProcQ, Sin, 6, a + b, # &, G, Z, Function[{x}, x], x*y, x^y, F, M}]
Out[2161]= {Symbol, Symbol, Integer, Plus, Function, Symbol, Symbol, Function, Times, Power, Symbol, Symbol}
In[2162]:= **Map[Head1, {ProcQ, Sin, 6, a + b, # &, G, Z, Function[{x}, x], x*y, x^y, F, M}]**
Out[2162]= {Module, System, Integer, Plus, PureFunction, Symbol, Block, PureFunction, Times, Power, Function, $Failed}

So, the **Head1** procedure has a quite certain meaning for more exact *(relatively to the system standard)* classification of expressions according to their headings. On many expressions the calls of **Head1** procedure and **Head** function are identical, whereas on a number their calls significantly differ. Below, 2 useful modifications of the **Head1**, namely: **Head2** and **Head3** will be represented. The concept of an expression is the important unifying principle in the system having identical internal structure which allows to confine a rather small amount of the basic operations. Meanwhile, despite identical basic structure of expressions, the system *Mathematica* provides a set of various functions for work both with an expression, and its separate components.

Tools of testing of correctness of expressions. The *Mathematica* has a number of the means providing testing of correctness of syntax of expressions among which only 2 functions are available to the user, namely:

SyntaxQ["*x*"] – *returns True, if x – a syntactic correct expression; otherwise False is returned;*
SyntaxLength["*x*"] – *returns the p number of symbols, since the beginning of a "x" string which determines syntactic correct expression* **StringTake["*x*", {1, *p*}];** *in a case p >* **StringLength["*x*"]** *the system declares that whole "x" string is correct, demanding continuation.*

In our opinion, it isn't very conveniently in case of software processing of the expressions. Therefore extension in the form of **SyntaxLength1** procedure is represented below with its source code and examples of its application.

In[2032]:= SyntaxLength1[x_ /; StringQ[x], y___] :=
Module[{a = "", b = 1, d, h = {}, c = StringLength[x]},
While[b <= c, d = SyntaxQ[a = a <> StringTake[x, {b, b}]];
If[d, AppendTo[h, StringTrim2[a, {"+", "−", " "}, 3]]]; b++];
h = DeleteDuplicates[h]; If[{y} != {} && ! HowAct[{y}[[1]]], {y} = {h}];
If[h == {}, 0, StringLength[h[[−1]]]]]]

In[2437]:= {SyntaxLength1["d[a[1]] + b[2]", g], g}
Out[2437]= {14, {"d", "d[a[1]]", "d[a[1]] + b", "d[a[1]] + b[2]"}}

The call **SyntaxLength1[*x*]** returns the *maximum* number *p* of position in a string *x* such that **ToExpression[StringTake[*x*, {1, *p*}]]** – a syntactically correct expression, otherwise *0* is will be returned; whereas the call **SyntaxLength1[*x*, *y*]** through the second optional *y* argument – *an undefinite variable* – additionally returns the list of substrings of a string *x* representing correct expressions.

Unlike the **SyntaxLength1** procedure, the procedure call **SyntaxLength2[*w*]** gathers correct subexpressions extracted from a string *w* into lists of the expressions identical on the length. The function call **ExtrVarsOfStr1[*w*]** returns the sorted list of all possible symbols in string format which were successfully extracted from a *w* string; if symbols are absent, the empty list is returned. Unlike the above **ExtrVarsOfStr** procedure this function provides the more exhaustive extraction of all possible symbols from the strings. Whereas, the procedure call **FactualVarsStr[*w*]** returns the list of all factual variables extracted from a *w* string; source codes of the above means are represented below.

In[4548]:= SyntaxLength2[x_ /; StringQ[x]] :=
Module[{j = AllSubStrings[x]}, j = Select[j, SyntaxQ[#] &];
j = Mapp[StringTrim, j, ("+" | "−" | " ")...];
j = DeleteDuplicates[Select[j, ! SameQ[#, ""] && ! NumericQ[Quiet[ToExpression[#]]] &]];
Map[Sort, Gather[j, StringLength[#1] == StringLength[#2] &]]]

In[4549]:= SyntaxLength2["a[[1]] + b[2]"]
Out[4549]= {{"a", "b"}, {"b[2]"}, {"a[[1]]"}, {"a[[1]] + b"}, {"a[[1]] + b[2]"}}

In[4552]:= ExtrVarsOfStr1[x_ /; StringQ[x]] :=
Sort[DeleteDuplicates[Select[Mapp[StringTrim, AllSubStrings[x], ("+" | "–" | " ") ...],
SymbolQ[#] &]]]

In[4553]:= V = 74; ExtrVarsOfStr1["74*V + 69*G"]
Out[4553]= {"G", "V"}

In[4560]:= Map[ExtrVarsOfStr1, {"74*v", "Sqrt[74*v + 69g]", "G[Art + 27]"}]
Out[4560]= {{"v"}, {"g", "q", "qr", "qrt", "r", "rt", "S", "Sq", "Sqr", "Sqrt", "t", "v"}, {"A", "Ar", "Art", "G", "r", "rt", "t"}}

In[4562]:= FactualVarsStr[t_ /; StringQ[t]] :=
Module[{b = "", c = {}, p, k, j = 1, d = t <> "[", a = StringLength[t] + 1},
While[j <= a, For[k = j, k <= a, k++, If[SymbolQ[p = StringTake[d, {k, k}]], b = b <> t,
If[b != "", AppendTo[c, b], 6]; b = ""]; j = k + 1]]; c]

In[4563]:= Map[FactualVarsStr, {"7*v[", "Sqrt[74*v + 69g]", "Sin[x] + Cos[y]"}]
Out[4563]= {{"v"}, {"Sqrt", "v", "g"}, {"Sin", "x", "Cos", "y"}}

In[5569]:= FactualVarsStr1[x_ /; StringQ[x]] :=
Module[{b = "", c = {}, h, t, k, a = StringLength[x] + 1, d = x <> "[", j = 1},
While[j <= a, For[k=j, k <= a, k++, If[SymbolQ[t=StringTake[d, {k, k}]] || t == "`", b=b <> t,
If[! MemberQ[{"", "`"}, b], AppendTo[c, {b, If[MemberQ[CNames["AladjevProcedures`"],
b], "AladjevProcedures`", h = If[ContextQ[b], "contexts",
Quiet[ToExpression["Context[" <> b <> "]"]]];
If[h == "AladjevProcedures`", $Context, h]]}], 6]; b = ""]; j = k + 1]];
c = Map[DeleteDuplicates, Map[Flatten, Gather[c, #1[[2]] == #2[[2]] &]]];
c = Map[Sort[#, ContextQ[#1] &] &, c];
c = Map[If[MemberQ[#, "contexts"] && ! MemberQ[#, "Global`"], Flatten[{"contexts",
ReplaceAll[#, "contexts" -> Nothing]}], #] &, c];
c = Map[Flatten[{#[[1]], Sort[#[[2 ;; -1]]]}] &, c];
Map[If[#[[1]] != "Global`" && MemberQ[#, "contexts"], Flatten[{"contexts",
ReplaceAll[#, "contexts" -> Nothing]}], #] &, c]]

In[5570]:= FactualVarsStr1[PureDefinition[FactualVarsStr1]]
Out[5570]= {{"AladjevProcedures`", "CNames", "ContextQ", "FactualVarsStr", "SymbolQ"},
{"Global`", "a", "b", "c", "contexts", "d", "h", "j", "k", "t", "x"}, {"System`", "AppendTo",
"Context", "DeleteDuplicates", "Flatten", "For", "Gather", "If", "MemberQ", "Module",
"Nothing", "Quiet", "Sort", "StringJoin", "StringLength", "StringQ", "StringTake",
"ToExpression", "While", "$Context"}, {"contexts", "AladjevProcedures`", "Global`"}}

The last fragment is ended by the procedure whose the call **FactualVarsStr1[*x*]** on the whole returns the nested list whose sublists have contexts as the first element whereas the others define the symbols extracted from a *x* string which have these contexts. If string *x* contains contexts then *"contexts"* element precedes their sorted tuple in sublist. The **FactualVarsStr1** procedure is an useful modification of the **FactualVarsStr** procedure. The above software is a rather useful in practical programming in the *Mathematica* system, and its source codes contain a number of useful programming techniques.

The following procedure allows to extract from an expression the elements composing it. The procedure call **SymbolsOfString**[*x*] returns the list of symbols that enter an expression represented by a *x* string. While the call **SymbolsOfString**[*x*, *1*] returns the list of symbols different from numbers which enter an expression represented by a *x* string. At last, the call **SymbolsOfString**[*x*, *a*] where *a* – an expression different from *1*, returns the the list of the symbols different from numbers and system symbols that enter an expression represented by a *x* string. The next fragment represents source code of the **SymbolsOfString** procedure with examples of its application.

In[3210]:= SymbolsOfString[x_ /; StringQ[x], y___] :=
Module[{a = Flatten[Map[Range[Sequences[#]] &, {{32, 35}, {37, 47}, {58, 64}, {91, 91}, {93, 96}, {123, 126}}]], b},
b = DeleteDuplicates[StringSplit[StringReplace[x, GenRules[Map[FromCharacterCode, a], " "]]]];
If[{y} == {}, b, If[y === 1, Select[b, ! MemberQ3[Range[48, 57], ToCharacterCode[#]] &], Select[Select[b, ! Quiet[SystemQ[#]] &], NameQ[#] &]]]]

In[3211]:= SymbolsOfString["(74*A1 – S^8*G^6 + Sin[b$ – a]/(c – d)) + S + z + StringLength[\"Agn\"]"]
Out[3211]= {"74", "A1", "S", "8", "G", "6", "Sin", "b$", "a", "c", "d", "z", "StringLength", "Agn"}

In[3212]:= SymbolsOfString["(74*A1 – S^8*G^6 + Sin[b$ – a]/(c – d)) + S + z + StringLength[\"Agn\"]", 1]
Out[3212]= {"A1", "S", "G", "Sin", "b$", "a", "c", "d", "z", "StringLength", "Agn"}

In[3213]:= SymbolsOfString["(74*A1 – S^8*G^6 + Sin[b$ – a]/(c – d)) + S + + StringLength[\"Agn\"]", 90]
Out[3213]= {"b$", "a", "c", "d"}

In[3320]:= ExpressionQ[x_ /; StringQ[x]] := Module[{f = "$ArtKr$.mx", a, b, c},
If[SyntaxQ[x], b = SymbolsOfString[x, 90];
If[b != {}, ToExpression["DumpSave[\"$ArtKr$.mx\"" <> "," <> ToString1[b] <> "]"], Null];
c = Quiet[Check[ToExpression[x], a]];
Quiet[{Get[f], DeleteFile[f]}]; If[SameQ[c, a], False, True], False]]

In[3321]:= {z, a, c, d} = {500, 90, 74, 42};
In[3322]:= SyntaxQ["z=(c+d)*a/0"]
Out[3322]= True
In[3323]:= ExpressionQ["z=(c+d)*a/0"]
Out[3323]= False
In[3324]:= {z, a, c, d}
Out[3324]= {500, 90, 74, 42}
In[3325]:= {a, b, c, z} = {74, 90, 500, 2016}
Out[3325]= {74, 90, 500, 2016}
In[3326]:= ExpressionQ["z=a*c/(b+d)"]
Out[3326]= True
In[3327]:= SyntaxQ["z=a*c/(b+d)"]
Out[3327]= True
In[3328]:= {a, b, c, z}

Out[3328]= {74, 90, 500, 2016}
In[3329]:= {SyntaxQ["2 = 3"], ExpressionQ["2 = 3"]}
Out[3329]= {True, False}

The call **SyntaxQ[x]** of standard *Mathematica* function returns *True* if *x* string corresponds to syntactically correct input for a single expression, and returns *False* otherwise. At that, the function tests only syntax of expression, ignoring its semantics at its evaluation. While the **ExpressionQ** procedure along with the syntax provides testing of an expression regarding semantic correctness. Whereas, the call **ExpressionQ[x]** returns *True* if *x* string corresponds to syntactically and semantically correct single expression, and returns *False* otherwise. The previous fragment represents source code of the **ExpressionQ** procedure with examples of its use in comparison with the standard **SyntaxQ** function.

Means of processing of expressions at the level of their components. Means of this group provide quite effective differentiated processing of expressions. The combined symbolical architecture of the *Mathematica* gives a possibility of direct generalization of the element-oriented list operations onto arbitrary expressions, supporting operations both on separate terms, and on sets of terms at the given levels in trees of the expressions. Without going into details into all tools supporting work with components of expressions, we will give only the main from them that have been complemented by our means. Whereas with more detailed description of standard means of this group, including admissible formats of coding, it is possible to get acquainted or in the *Help*, or in the corresponding literature on *Mathematica* system, for example, in works [50-52,60,66,71].

The call **Variables[p]** of standard function returns the list of all independent variables of a *p* polynomial, while its application to an arbitrary expression has some limitations. Meantime for receiving all independent variables of an expression *x* it is quite possible to use an quite simple function whose call **UnDefVars[x]** returns the list of all independent variables of a *x* expression. Unlike the **UnDefVars** the call **UnDefVars1[x]** returns the list of all *independent* variables in string format of a *x* expression. Source codes of both functions with examples of their application are given below in the comparative context with the **Variables** function. In some cases the mentioned functions have certain preferences relative to standard **Variables** function.

In[2024]:= **UnDefVars[x_] := Select[OP[x], Quiet[ToString[Definition[#]]] == "Null" &]**

In[2025]:= **UnDefVars[(x^2 − y^2)/(Sin[x] + Cos[y]) + a*Log[x + y + z − G[h, t]]]**
Out[2025]= {a, G, h, t, x, y, z}
In[2026]:= **Variables[(x^2 − y^2)/(Sin[x] + Cos[y]) + a*Log[x + y + z − G[h, t]]]**
Out[2026]= {a, x, y, Cos[y], Log[x + y + z − G[h, t]], Sin[x]}

In[2027]:= **UnDefVars1[x_] := Select[ExtrVarsOfStr[ToString[x], 2], ! SystemQ[#] &]**

In[2028]:= **Map[UnDefVars1, {a + b, a*Sin[x]*Cos[y], {a, b}, a*F[h, g, s] + H}]**
Out[2028]= {{"a", "b"}, {"a", "x", "y"}, {"a", "b"}, {"a", "F", "g", "h", "H", "s"}}

The call **Replace[x, r {, j}]** of standard function returns result of application of a *r* rule of the form $a \to b$ or list of such rules for transformation of *x* expression as a whole; application of the *3rd* optional *j* argument defines application of *r* rules to parts of *j* level of a *x* expression. Meanwhile, the standard **Replace** function has a number of restrictions some from which a procedure considerably obviates, whose call **Replace1[x, r]** returns the result of application of *r* rules to all or selective independent variables of *x* expression. In case of detection by the procedure **Replace1** of empty rules the appropriate message is printed with the indication of the list of those *r* rules which were empty, i.e. whose left parts aren't entered into the list of independent variables of *x* expression. Fragment below presents source code of **Replace1** with examples of its use; in addition, comparison with result of application of the **Replace** function on the same expression is given.

In[2052]:= Replace1[x_, y_ /; ListQ[y] && DeleteDuplicates[Map[Head, y]] == {Rule} || Head[y] == Rule] :=
Module[{a = x//FullForm//ToString, b = UnDefVars[x], c, p, l, h = {}, r, k = 1,
d = ToStringRule[DeleteDuplicates[Flatten[{y}]]]},
p = Map14[RhsLhs, d, "Lhs"]; c = Select[p, ! MemberQ[Map[ToString, b], #] &];
If[c != {}, Print["Rules " <> ToString[Flatten[Select[d, MemberQ[c, RhsLhs[#, "Lhs"]] &]]] <> " are vacuous"]];
While[k <= Length[d], l = RhsLhs[d[[k]], "Lhs"];
r = RhsLhs[d[[k]], "Rhs"]; h = Append[h, {"[" <> l -> "[" <> r, " " <> l -> " " <> r, l <> "]" -> r <> "]"}]; k++];
Simplify[ToExpression[StringReplace[a, Flatten[h]]]]]

In[2053]:= X = (x^2 - y^2)/(Sin[x] + Cos[y]) + a*Log[x + y];
Replace[X, {x -> a + b, a -> 90, y -> Cos[a], z -> Log[t]}]
Out[2053]= a*Log[x + y] + (x^2 - y^2)/(Cos[y] + Sin[x])
In[2054]:= **Replace1**[X, {x -> a + b, a -> 90, y -> Cos[a], z -> Log[t], t -> c+d}]
"Rules {z -> (Log[t]), t -> (c + d)} are vacuous"
Out[2054]= 90*Log[a + b + Cos[a]] + ((a + b)^2 - Cos[a]^2)/(Cos[Cos[a]] + Sin[a + b])
In[2055]:= **Replace1**[X, {x -> a + b, a -> 90, y -> Cos[a]}]
Out[2055]= 90*Log[a + b + Cos[a]] + ((a + b)^2 - Cos[a]^2)/(Cos[Cos[a]] + Sin[a + b])

Due to quite admissible impossibility of performance of replacements of subexpressions of expression at the required its levels, there are questions both of belonging of subexpressions of expression to its levels, and testing of belonging of subexpression to the given expression level. The following two procedures in a certain extent solve these problems. The procedure call **SubExprOnLevels**[*x*] returns the nested list whose two-element sublists contain levels numbers as the first elements, and lists of subexpressions on the these levels as the second elements of a *x* expression. Whereas the procedure call **ExprOnLevelQ**[*x, y, z*] returns *True* if *y* subexpression belongs to the *z*-th level of *x* expression, and *False* otherwise. In addition, in a case of *False* return the procedure call **ExprOnLevelQ**[*x, y, z, t*] through the optional *t* argument – an indefinite symbol – additionally returns the list of the levels numbers of the *x* expression that contain the *y* as a subexpression. The following fragment represents source codes of the both procedures with examples of their application.

In[2327]:= SubExprOnLevels[x_] := Module[{a, b, c = {}},
Do[If[Set[a, DeleteDuplicates[Level[x, {j}]]] === Set[b, DeleteDuplicates[Level[x, {j+1}]]], Return[c], AppendTo[c, {j, a}]], {j, Infinity}]]
In[2328]:= **SubExprOnLevels**[(x^2 + y^2)/(Log[x] + a*x^2/b^2)]
Out[2328]= {{1, {x^2 + y^2, 1/((a*x^2)/b^2 + Log[x])}}, {2, {x^2, y^2, (a*x^2)/b^2 + Log[x], -1}}, {3, {x, 2, y, (a*x^2)/b^2, Log[x]}}, {4, {a, 1/b^2, x^2, x}}, {5, {b, -2, x, 2}}}

In[2329]:= ExprOnLevelQ[x_, y_, z_Integer, t___] :=
Module[{a = SubExprOnLevels[x], b = {}, c = {}},
If[! MemberQ[Map[#[[1]] &, a], z], False, If[MemberQ[a[[z]][[2]], y], True,
If[{t} != {} && NullQ[t], Do[If[MemberQ[a[[j]][[2]], y], AppendTo[b, a[[j]][[1]]], 6],
{j, Length[a]}]; t = b; False, 6]]]]

In[2330]:= ExprOnLevelQ[(x^2 + y^2)/(Log[x] + a*x^2/b^2), Log[x], 4, s1]
Out[2330]= False
In[2331]:= s1
Out[2331]= {3}
In[2332]:= ExprOnLevelQ[(x^2 + y^2)/(Log[x] + a*x^2/b^2), x^2, 1, s2]
Out[2332]= False
In[2333]:= s2
Out[2333]= {2, 4}

In certain cases at conversions of the expressions by means of substitutions the necessity of converting into the string format of the left and right parts of rules "a → b" arises. The given problem is solved by a rather simple **ToStringRule** procedure, whose call **ToStringRule**[*x*] returns the rule or the list of rules *x*, whose left and right parts have string format; at that, its right part is taken in parentheses. This procedure is used by the above-presented **Replace1** procedure. The procedure **ToStringRule1** is similar to **ToStringRule**, but the right parts of the result is not taken into parentheses. The following fragment presents source code of the **ToStringRule** with examples of its application.

In[2723]:= ToStringRule[x_ /; ListQ[x] && DeleteDuplicates[Map[Head, x]] == {Rule} ||
Head[x] == Rule] := Module[{a = Flatten[{x}], b = {}, c, k = 1},
While[k <= Length[a], c = a[[k]]; b = Append[b, ToString[RhsLhs[c, "Lhs"]] ->
"(" <> ToString[RhsLhs[c, "Rhs"]] <> ")"]; k++]; If[ListQ[x], b, b[[1]]]]

In[2724]:= {ToStringRule[a -> b], ToStringRule[{a -> b, c -> d, m -> n}]}
Out[2724]= {"a" -> "(b)", {"a" -> "(b)", "c" -> "(d)", "m" -> "(n)"}}

The call **Level**[*x*, *n*] of standard function returns list of all subexpressions of a *x* expression at levels from 1 to *n*. As a rather useful generalization of function is procedure whose call **Levels**[*x*, *h*] returns the list of all subexpressions for a *x* expression at all its possible levels while through the second *h* argument – an independent variable – the maximum number of levels of *x* expression is returned. Generally speaking, the following defining relation takes place **Levels**[*x*, *h*] ≡ **Level**[*x*, *Infinity*], however in case of **Levels** the procedure additionally returns *maximum* level of a *x* expression. While the procedure call **ExprOnLevels**[*x*] returns the enclosed list, whose elements are the lists of subexpressions of a *x* expression which are located on each of its levels from the first to the last. The fragment below represents source codes of both procedures with examples of their application in a comparative context with the **Level** function with the second *Infinity* argument.

In[2868]:= Levels[x_, h_ /; ToString[Definition[h]] == "Null"] := Module[{a = {}, b, k = 1},
While[k < Infinity, b = Level[x, k]; If[a == b, Break[], a = b]; k++]; h = k - 1; a]
In[2869]:= {Levels[(x^2 - y^2)/(Sin[x] + Cos[y]) + a*Log[x + y + z - G[h, t]], g], g}

Out[2869]= {{a, x, y, z, -1, h, 7, G[h, 7], -G[h, 7], x + y + z - G[h, 7], Log[x + y + z - G[h, 7]], a*Log[x + y + z - G[h, 7]], x, 2, x^2, -1, y, 2, y^2, -y^2, x^2 - y^2, y, Cos[y], x, Sin[x], Cos[y] + Sin[x], -1, 1/(Cos[y] + Sin[x]), (x^2 - y^2)/(Cos[y] + Sin[x])}, 6}

In[2870]:= **Level[(x^2 - y^2)/(Sin[x] + Cos[y]) + a*Log[x + y + z - G[h, t]], Infinity]**

Out[2870]= {a, x, y, z, -1, h, 7, G[h, 7], -G[h, 7], x + y + z - G[h, 7], Log[x + y + z - G[h, 7]], a*Log[x + y + z - G[h, 7]], x, 2, x^2, -1, y, 2, y^2, -y^2, x^2 - y^2, y, Cos[y], x, Sin[x], Cos[y] + Sin[x], -1, 1/(Cos[y] + Sin[x]), (x^2 - y^2)/(Cos[y] + Sin[x])}

In[2878]:= **ExprOnLevels[x_] := Module[{a = {}, k = 1},**
While[k <= Depth[x], a = Append[a, MinusList[Level[x, k], Level[x, k-1]]]; k++]; a[[1 ;; -2]]]

In[2879]:= **X = (x^2 - y^2)/(Sin[x] + Cos[y]) + a*Log[x + y + z - G[h, t]];**

In[2880]:= **ExprOnLevels[X]**

Out[2880]= {{a*Log[x + y + z - G[h, t]], (x^2 - y^2)/(Cos[y] + Sin[x])}, {a, Log[x + y + z - G[h, t]], x^2 - y^2, 1/(Cos[y] + Sin[x])}, {x + y + z - G[h, t], x^2, -y^2, Cos[y] + Sin[x], -1}, {x, y, z, x, 2, -1, y^2, Cos[y], Sin[x], -1}, {G[h, t], y, 2, y, x, -1}, {h, t}}

Relative to the above **Levels** procedure, the standard **Depth** function defines on the same expression the maximum number of levels more on *1*, namely:

In[3790]:= **Clear[t]; {Levels[a + b + c^2, t], t, Depth[a + b + c^2]}**
Out[3790]= {{a, b, c, 2, c^2}, 2, 3}

The standard **FreeQ** function provides testing of entries into an arbitrary expression of the subexpressions while a simple **FreeQ1** procedure significantly expands the **FreeQ** function, providing broader testing of entries into an expression of subexpressions. The call **FreeQ1[x, y]** returns *True* if *x* expression doesn't contain *y* subexpressions, otherwise *False* is returned. The **FreeQ2** function expands the **FreeQ** function additionally onto the list as its the second argument. In addition, the call **FreeQ2[x, p]** returns *True* if an expression *x* doesn't contain *p* subexpression or subexpressions from *p* list, otherwise *False* is returned. The next fragment represents source codes of means **FreeQ1** and **FreeQ1** with examples of their applications in a comparative context with the **FreeQ** function.

In[2202]:= **FreeQ1[x_, y_] := Module[{h}, Quiet[FreeQ[Subs[x, y, h = Unique["ArtKr"]], h]]]**

In[2203]:= **{FreeQ1[a/Sqrt[x], Sqrt[x]], FreeQ[a/Sqrt[x], Sqrt[x]]}**
Out[2203]= {False, True}

In[2204]:= **{FreeQ1[{Sqrt[x], 20, 27}, Sqrt[x]], FreeQ[{Sqrt[x], 20, 27}, Sqrt[x]]}**
Out[2204]= {False, False}

In[2250]:= **FreeQ2[x_, p_] := If[ListQ[p], If[AllTrue[Map10[FreeQ, x, p], TrueQ], True, False], FreeQ[x, p]]**

In[2251]:= **L = {a, b, c, d, f, g, h}; {FreeQ[L, {a, d, h}], FreeQ2[L, {a, d, h}]}**
Out[2251]= {True, False}

In[2252]:= **{FreeQ[Cos[x]*Ln[x], {Sin, Ln}], FreeQ2[Cos[x]*Ln[x], {Sin, Ln}]}**
Out[2252]= {True, False}

At last, the procedure call **FreeQ3[x, y, z]** returns *True* if an expression *x* doesn't contain an *y* subexpression or subexpressions from a *y* list, otherwise *False* is returned. Furthermore, the procedure call with the **3rd** optional *z* argument – an undefinite symbol – through it returns the 2-element list or list of the *ListList* type whose first element defines an expression from *y* which composes the *x* expression whereas the second element determines the number of its occurences in *x*. The **FreeQ3** procedure is the most general means of this type. The fragment below represents source code of the **FreeQ3** procedure with examples of its application.

In[4089]:= FreeQ3[x_, y_, z__] :=
Module[{a = ToStringRational[x], b = If[ListQ[y], y, {y}], c},
b = Map[ToStringRational, b]; If[{z} != {} && NullQ[z],
z = ReduceLevelsList[Map[{ToExpression[#], StringCount[a, #]} &, b], 1], 1];
StringFreeQ[a, b]]

In[4090]:= FreeQ3[1/(1 + 1/x^2 + 1/x^3) + 1/(1 + 1/(a + b + 1/x^3)^2) + 1/(1 + 1/x^3), {x^3, x^2}, g47]
Out[4090]= False
In[4091]:= g47
Out[4091]= {{x^3, 3}, {x^2, 1}}
In[4092]:= FreeQ3[a + 1/(1/x^3 + (a + b)^3/x^2), {x^3, x^2}, g70]
Out[4092]= False
In[4093]:= g70
Out[4093]= {{x^3, 1}, {x^2, 1}}
In[4094]:= Clear[g70]; FreeQ3[a + 1/(1/x^3 + (a + b)^3/x^2), {x^3, x^2, x^4}, g70]
Out[4094]= False
In[4095]:= g70
Out[4095]= {{x^3, 1}, {x^2, 1}, {x^4, 0}}

Using the **FullForm** function providing representation of expressions in the full form can be received an useful procedure solving the replacement problem in expressions of the given subexpressions. The call **Replace3[x, y, z]** returns the result of replacement in an arbitrary *x* expression of all entries of *y* subexpressions into it onto the *z* expressions; as arguments {*y*, *z*} separate expressions or their lists can be used. At that, in case of arguments {*y*, *z*} in the form of the list, for them the common length determined by the relation **Min[Map[Length, {y, z}]]** is chosen, allowing to avoid the possible especial and erroneous situations, but with the printing of the appropriate diagnostic information as illustrates an example below. The next fragment represents source code of the procedure with typical examples of its use.

In[2062]:= Replace3[x_, y_, z_] := Module[{a = Flatten[{y}], b = Flatten[{z}], c, t = x, k = 1},
c = Min[Map[Length, {a, b}]];
If[c < Length[a], Print["Subexpressions " <> ToString1[a[[c + 1 ;; -1]]] <> " were not replaced"]]; For[k, k <= c, k++, t = Subs[t, a[[k]], b[[k]]]]; t]
In[2063]:= Replace3[x^2 + Sqrt[1/a^2 + 1/a - Sin[1/a]], 1/a, Cos[h]]
Out[2063]= x^2 + Sqrt[Cos[h] + Cos[h]^2 - Sin[Cos[h]]]
In[2064]:= Replace3[1/(1 + 1/a) + Cos[1/a + Sin[1/a]]*(c + 1/a)^2, 1/a, F[h] + d]
Out[2064]= 1/(1 + d + F[h]) + Cos[d + F[h] + Sin[d + F[h]]]*(c + d + F[h])^2
In[2065]:= Replace3[x^2 + Sqrt[1/a^2 + 1/a - Sin[1/a]], {1/a, 1/b, 1/c}, Cos[h]]
"Subexpressions {b^(-1), c^(-1)} were not replaced"
Out[2065]= x^2 + Sqrt[Cos[h] + Cos[h]^2 - Sin[Cos[h]]]

In the certain cases exists necessity to execute the exchange of values of variables with the corresponding exchange of all them attributes. So, variables *x* and *y* having values 74 and 69 should receive the values *42* and *47* accordingly with the appropriate exchange of all their attributes. The **VarExch** procedure solves this problem, returning *Null*, i.e. nothing. The list of two names of variables in string format which exchange by values and attributes or the nested list of *ListList* type acts as the actual argument; anyway all elements of pairs have to be definite, otherwise the call returns *Null* with print of the appropriate diagnostic message.

On the other hand, the procedure call **Rename[*x, y*]** in regular mode returns *Null*, providing replacement of *x* name of some defined object on *y* name with preservation of all attributes of this object. At that, the *x* name is removed from the current session by means of **Remove** function. But if *y* argument defines a name of a defined object or an undefined name with attributes, the call is returned unevaluated. If the first *x* argument is illegal for renaming, the procedure call returns *Null*; in addition, the **Rename** procedure successfully processes also objects of the same name of type *"Block", "Function"* or *"Module"*. The **Rename1** procedure is a useful modification of the above procedure, being based on the procedure **Definition2**. The call **Rename1[*x, y*]** is similar to the call **Rename[*x, y*]** whereas the call **Rename1[*x, y, z*]** with the third optional *z* argument – *an arbitrary expression* – performs the same functions as the call **Rename1[*x, y*]** without change of an initial *x* object.

The **VarExch1** procedure is a version of the above **VarExch** procedure and is based on use of the **Rename** procedure and global variables; it admits the same type of actual argument, but unlike the 2nd procedure the call **VarExch1[*L*]** in case of detection of undefinite elements of a *L* list or its sublists is returned unevaluated without print of any diagnostic message. In the fragment below, source codes of procedures **Rename, Rename1, VarExch** and **VarExch1** along with examples of their use are presented.

In[2545]:= VarExch[L_List /; Length[L] == 2 || ListListQ[L] && Length[L[[1]]] == 2] :=
Module[{Kr, k = 1}, Kr[p_ /; ListQ[p]] := Module[{a = Map[Attributes, p], b, c, m, n},
ToExpression[{"ClearAttributes[" <> StrStr[p[[1]]] <> "," <> ToString[a[[1]]] <> "]",
"ClearAttributes[" <> StrStr[p[[2]]] <> "," <> ToString[a[[2]]] <> "]"}];
{b, c} = ToExpression[{"ToString[Definition[" <> StrStr[p[[1]]] <> "]]",
"ToString[Definition[" <> StrStr[p[[2]]] <> "]]"}];
If[MemberQ[{b, c}, "Null"], Print[VarExch::"Both arguments should be defined but uncertainty had been detected: ", p]; Return[], Null];
{m, n} = Map4[StringPosition, Map[StrStr, {b, c}], {" := ", " = "}];
{n, m} = {StringTake[b, {1, m[[1]][[1]] – 1}] <> StringTake[c, {n[[1]][[1]], –1}],
StringTake[c, {1, n[[1]][[1]] – 1}] <> StringTake[b, {m[[1]][[1]], –1}]}; ToExpression[{n, m}];
Map[ToExpression, {"SetAttributes[" <> StrStr[p[[1]]] <> "," <> ToString[a[[2]]] <> "]",
"SetAttributes[" <> StrStr[p[[2]]] <> "," <> ToString[a[[1]]] <> "]"}]];
If[! ListListQ[L], Kr[L], For[k, k <= Length[L], k++, Kr[L[[k]]]]];]

In[2546]:= Agn = 69; Avz := 74; Art := 27; Kr = 20; SetAttributes["Agn", Protected];
SetAttributes["Art", {Protected, Listable}]
In[2547]:= Map[Attributes, {"Agn", "Avz", "x", "y", "Art", "Kr"}]
Out[2547]= {{Protected}, {}, {}, {}, {Listable, Protected}, {}}
In[2548]:= VarExch[{{"Avz", "Agn"}, {"x", "y"}, {"Art", "Kr"}}]
VarExch::Both arguments should be defined but uncertainty had been detected: {x, y}

In[2549]:= {Avz, Agn, Art, Kr}
Out[2549]= {69, 74, 20, 27}
In[2550]:= Map[Attributes, {"Agn", "Avz", "Art", "Kr"}]
Out[2550]= {{}, {Protected}, {}, {Listable, Protected}}
In[2551]:= Rename[x_String /; HowAct[x], y_ /; ! HowAct[y]] :=
Module[{a, c, d, b = Flatten[{PureDefinition[x]}]},
If[! SameQ[b, {$Failed}], a = Attributes[x]; c = ClearAllAttributes[x]; d = StringLength[x];
c = Map[ToString[y] <> StringTake[#, {d + 1, -1}] &, b];
Map[ToExpression, c]; Clear[x]; SetAttributes[y, a]]]
In[2552]:= fm = "Art_Kr"; SetAttributes[fm, {Protected, Listable}]; {fm, Attributes[fm]}
Out[2552]= {"Art_Kr", {Listable, Protected}}
In[2553]:= Rename["fm", Tampere]
In[2554]:= {Tampere, Attributes[Tampere], fm}
Out[2554]= {"Art_Kr", {Listable, Protected}, fm}
In[2557]:= VarExch1[L_List /; Length[L] == 2 || ListListQ[L] && Length[L[[1]]] == 2] :=
Module[{Art, k = 1, d},
Art[p_ /; ListQ[p]] := Module[{a = Quiet[Check[Map[Attributes, p], $Aborted]], b, c, m, n},
If[a == $Aborted, Return[Defer[VarExch1[L]]], Null];
If[HowAct[Art], b = Art; Clear[Art]; m = 1, Null];
If[HowAct[Kr], c = Kr; Clear[Kr]; n = 1, Null];
ToExpression[{"ClearAttributes[" <> StrStr[p[[1]]] <> "," <> ToString[a[[1]]] <> "]",
"ClearAttributes[" <> StrStr[p[[2]]] <> ", " <> ToString[a[[2]]] <> "]"}];
ToExpression[{"Rename[" <> StrStr[p[[1]]] <> "," <> "Art" <> "]", "Rename[" <>
StrStr[p[[2]]] <> "," <> "Kr" <> "]"}];
ToExpression["Clear[" <> StrStr[p[[1]]] <> "," <> StrStr[p[[2]]] <> "]"];
ToExpression[{"Rename[" <> StrStr["Kr"] <> "," <> p[[1]] <> "]", "Rename[" <>
StrStr["Art"] <> "," <> p[[2]] <> "]"}];
Map[ToExpression, {"SetAttributes[" <> StrStr[p[[1]]] <> "," <> ToString[a[[2]]] <> "]",
"SetAttributes[" <> StrStr[p[[2]]] <> "," <> ToString[a[[1]]] <> "]"}];
If[m == 1, Art = b, Null]; If[n == 1, Kr = c, Null];];
If[! ListListQ[L], Art[L], For[k, k <= Length[L], k++, Art[L[[k]]]]]]
In[2558]:= Agn = 69; Avz := 74; Art := 27; Kr = 20; SetAttributes["Agn", Protected];
SetAttributes["Art", {Protected, Listable}];
In[2559]:= Map[Attributes, {"Agn", "Avz", "Art", "Kr"}]
Out[2559]= {{Protected}, {}, {Listable, Protected}, {}}
In[2560]:= {Art, Kr} = {90, 500}; VarExch1[{{"Agn", "Avz"}, {"x", "y"}, {"Art", "Kr"}}]
In[2561]:= {{Agn, Avz, Art, Kr}, Map[Attributes, {"Agn", "Avz", "Art", "Kr"}]}
Out[2561]= {{500, 90, 20, 27}, {{}, {Protected}, {}, {Listable, Protected}}}
In[2562]:= {x, y, Art, Kr}
Out[2562]= {x, y, Art, Kr}
In[2572]:= Rename1[x_String /; HowAct[x], y_ /; ! HowAct[y], z___] :=

Module[{a = Attributes[x], b = Definition2[x][[1 ;; -2]], c = ToString[y]},
b = Map[StringReplacePart[#, c, {1, StringLength[x]}] &, b]; ToExpression[b];
ToExpression["SetAttributes[" <> c <> ", " <> ToString[a] <> "]"];
If[{z} == {}, ToExpression["ClearAttributes[" <> x <> ", " <> ToString[a] <> "]";
Remove[" <> x <> "]"], Null]]

In[2574]:= x := 500; y = 500; SetAttributes[x, {Listable, Protected}]
In[2575]:= **Rename1["x", Trg42]**
In[2576]:= **{x, Trg42, Attributes["Trg42"]}**
Out[2576]= {x, 500, {Listable, Protected}}
In[2577]:= **Rename1["y", Trg47, 90]**
In[2578]:= **{y, Trg47, Attributes["Trg47"]}**
Out[2578]= {500, 500, {}}

Use in procedures of global variables, in a lot of cases will allow to simplify programming, sometimes significantly. This mechanism sufficient in detail is considered in [33]. Meantime, the mechanism of global variables in *Mathematica* isn't universal, quite correctly working in case of evaluation of definitions of procedures containing global variables in the current session in the *Input*-paragraph; whereas in general case it isn't supported when the loading in the current session of the procedures containing global variables, in particular, from *nb*-files with the subsequent activation of their contents.

For the purpose of exclusion of similar situation the procedure has been offered, whose call **NbCallProc[x]** reactivates a block, a function or a module *x* in the current session, whose definition was in a *nb*-file loaded into the current session, with return of *Null*, i.e. nothing. The call **NbCallProc[x]** reactivates in the current session all definitions of blocks, functions, modules with the same name *x* and with various headings. All these definitions have to be loaded previously from some *nb*-file into the current session and activated by the function *"Evaluate Notebook"* of the *GUI*. The fragment below represents source code of procedure **NbCallProc** with example of its use for the above **VarExch1** procedure that uses the global variables.

In[2415]:= NbCallProc[x_ /; BlockFuncModQ[x]] :=
Module[{a = SubsDel[StringReplace[ToString1[DefFunc[x]], "\n \n" -> ";"],
"`" <> ToString[x] <> "`", {"[", ","}, -1]}, Clear[x]; ToExpression[a]]

In[2416]:= **NbCallProc[VarExch1]**

The performed verification convincingly demonstrates, that the **VarExch1** containing the global variables and uploaded from the *nb*-file with subsequent its activation *(by "Evaluate Notebook")*, is carried out absolutely correctly and with correct functioning of mechanism of global variables restoring the values after an exit from the **VarExch1** procedure. **NbCallProc** has a number of rather interesting appendices, first of all, if necessary of use of procedures activated in the *Input*-paragraph of the current session.

In certain cases before updating of definitions of objects *(procedure, function, variable, etc.)* it is necessary to check existence for them of the *Protected* attribute that a rather simple function provides; the call **ProtectedQ[x]** returns *True* if *x* object has the *Protected* attribute, and *False* otherwise. A correct expression can act as argument; source code of the **ProtectedQ** function with examples are represented below.

In[2430]:= **ProtectedQ[x_] := If[MemberQ[Attributes1[x], Protected], True, False]**

In[2431]:= **g = 90; Protect[g]; Map[ProtectedQ, {Sin, Protect, AVZ, HowAct, 590, Map, "g"}]**
Out[2431]= {True, True, False, False, False, True, True}

The list structure is one of basic in *Mathematica* in even bigger degree, than at *Maple*. And *Maple*, and in even bigger degree of the *Mathematica* have a quite developed set of means of processing of the list structures. One of such important enough tools is the converting of expressions into lists; for *Maple* such tools has form *convert(Expr, list)* while *Mathematica* of similar means has no, and procedure **ToList** can be in this quality. The call **ToList[***Expr***]** returns the result of converting of an expression *Expr* into the list. At that, in case of a *Expr* string the *Expr* is converted into the symbol–by–symbol list, in case of *Expr* list the list *Expr* is returned while in other cases the converting is based on the standard **Map** function. The following fragment represents source code of the **ToList** with examples of its application.

In[2370]:= **ToList[ex_] := Module[{a, b, c = {}, d, k = 1, n},**
If[StringQ[ex], Characters[ex], If[ListQ[ex], ex, a = ToString[InputForm[Map[b, ex]]];
d = StringSplit[a, ToString[b] <> "["]; For[k, k <= Length[d], k++, n = d[[k]];
c = Append[c, StringTake[n, {1, Flatten[StringPosition[n, "]"]][[-1]] - 1}]]];
ToExpression[c]]]]

In[2371]:= **ToList[(a*Sin[x] + g[b])/(c + d) + (d + c)/(Cos[y] + h)]**
Out[2371]= {(c + d)/(h + Cos[y]), (g[b] + a*Sin[x])/(c + d)}

In[2372]:= **ToList["qwertyuiopasdfgh"]**
Out[2372]= {"q", "w", "e", "r", "t", "y", "u", "i", "o", "p", "a", "s", "d", "f", "g", "h"}

In[2373]:= **ToList[{a, b, c, d, e, f, g, h, a, v, z, a, g, n, A, r, t, K, r}]**
Out[2373]= {a, b, c, d, e, f, g, h, a, v, z, a, g, n, A, r, t, K, r}

The *Maple* has 2 useful means of manipulation with expressions of the type {*range, equation, inequality, relation*}, whose calls *lhs(Exp)* and *rhs(Exp)* return the *left* and the *right* parts of an *Exp* expression respectively. More precisely, the call *lhs(Exp), rhs(Exp)* returns a value *op(1, Exp), op(2, Exp)* respectively. Whereas *Mathematica* has no similar useful means. The given deficiency is compensated by the **RhsLhs** procedure, whose source code with examples of application are given below. The call **RhsLhs[***x, y***]** depending on a value {"*Rhs*", "*Lhs*"} of the second *y* argument returns right or left part of *x* expressions respectively relatively to operator **Head[***x***]**, while the call **RhsLhs[***x, y, t***]** in addition through an undefined *t* variable returns the operator **Head[***x***]** concerning whom splitting of the *x* expression onto left and right parts was made. The **RhsLhs** procedure can be a rather easily modified in the light of expansion of the analyzed operators **Head[***x***]**. The **RhsLhs1** procedure is a certain functional equivalent to the previous procedure [48,50].

In[2700]:= **RhsLhs[x__] := Module[{a = Head[{x}[[1]]], b = ToString[InputForm[{x}[[1]]]],**
d, h = {x}, c = {{Greater, ">"}, {Or, "||"}, {GreaterEqual, ">="}, {Span, ";;"}, {And, "&&"},
{LessEqual, "<="}, {Unequal, "!="}, {Rule, "->"}, {Less, "<"}, {Plus, {"+", "-"}}, {Power, "^"},
{Equal, "=="}, {NonCommutativeMultiply, ""}, {Times, {"*", "/"}}}},**
If[Length[h] < 2 || ! MemberQ[{"Lhs", "Rhs"}, h[[2]]], Return[Defer[RhsLhs[x]]], Null];

If[! MemberQ[Select[Flatten[c], ! StringQ[#] &], a] || a == Symbol,
Return[Defer[RhsLhs[x]]], Null];
d = StringPosition[b, Flatten[Select[c, #[[1]] == a &], 1][[2]]];
a = Flatten[Select[c, #[[1]] == a &]];
If[Length[h] >= 3 && ! HowAct[h[[3]]], ToExpression[ToString[h[[3]]] <> "=" <>
ToString1[a]], Null];
ToExpression[If[h[[2]] == "Lhs", StringTrim[StringTake[b, {1, d[[1]][[1]] - 1}]],
StringTrim[StringTake[b, {d[[1]][[2]] + 1, -1}]]]]]

In[2701]:= Mapp[RhsLhs, {a^b, a*b, a -> b, a <= b, a||b, a && b}, "Rhs"]
Out[2701]= {b, b, b, b, b, b}
In[2702]:= {{RhsLhs[90 ;; 500, "Rhs", s], s}, {RhsLhs[a && b, "Lhs", s1], s1}}
Out[2702]= {{500, {Span, ";;"}}, {a, {And, "&&"}}}

Maple has tools of testing of expressions for the following types, namely:

{`!`, `*`, `+`, `.`, `::`, `<`, `<=`, `<>`, `=`, `@`, `@@`, `^`, `||`, `and`, `or`, `xor`, `implies`, `not`}

In *Mathematica* the means of a such quite wide range are absent and in this connexion the procedure, whose call **TwoHandQ[x]** returns *True* if a x expression has one of the following types, namely:

{"+", ">=", "<=", "&&", "||", "-", "^", "**", "<", "==", "!=", ">", "->"}

and *False* otherwise, is presented below; moreover, if the call **TwoHandQ[x, y]** returns *True*, through the 2nd optional y argument – an undefinite variable – the type of a x expression is returned. The following fragment represents source code of the **TwoHandQ** procedure with examples of its application.

In[2937]:= TwoHandQ[x__] := Module[{a = ToString[InputForm[{x}[[1]]]],
b = {"+", ">=", "<=", "&&", "||", "-", "^", "**", "<", "==", "!=", ">", "->"}, c, d = {x}},
c = StringPosition[a, b];
If[StringFreeQ[a, "->"] && StringFreeQ[a, ">="] && Length[c] > 2 || Length[c] == 0, False,
If[Length[d] > 1 && ! HowAct[d[[2]]] && ! ProtectedQ[d[[2]]],
ToExpression[ToString[d[[2]]] <> "=" <> ToString[Head[{x}[[1]]]]],
Return[Defer[TwoHandQ[x]]]]; True]]

In[2938]:= {TwoHandQ[a3 <= w, h], h}
Out[2938]= {True, LessEqual}
In[2939]:= {TwoHandQ[a -> b, t], t}
Out[2939]= {True, Rule}
In[2940]:= {TwoHandQ[a != b, p], p}
Out[2940]= {True, Unequal}
In[2941]:= Clear[z]; {TwoHandQ[a < b && c, z], z}
Out[2941]= {True, And}
In[2942]:= Clear[p]; {TwoHandQ[a || b + c, p], p}
Out[2942]= {True, Or}

In *Maple* the type of indexed expressions is defined while in *Mathematica* similar tools are absent. For elimination of this drawback we presented a number of procedures eliminating this defect. Among them it is possible to note such procedures as **ArrayInd, Ind, IndexedQ, Index, IndexQ** and **Indices** [30-33,48]. In particular, the call **IndexQ[x]** returns *True*, if x – an indexed expression, and *False* otherwise; at that, the x argument is given in the string format where under the *indexed* is understood an expression whose the reduced form completed by the index bracket "]]". At that, the call **Indices[x]** returns the index component of an indexed expression x given in string format, otherwise the call is returned unevaluated. In the same place rather in details the questions of processing of the indexed expressions are considered. In some cases these tools simplify programming. In particular, on the basis of the previous procedures **ToList** and **Ind** the **OP** procedure is programmed whose call **OP[x]** returns the list of atomic elements composing a x expression. The following fragment represents source code of the **OP** along with typical examples of its application.

In[2620]:= OP[exp_] := Module[{a = ToString[InputForm[expr]], b = {}, c, d, k, h},
If[StringTake[a, {-1, -1}] == "]", a = Flatten[Ind[expr]],
a = DeleteDuplicates[Quiet[ToList[expr]]]]; Label[ArtKr]; d = Length[a];
For[k = 1, k <= Length[a], k++, h = a[[k]]; c = Quiet[ToList[h]];
If[MemberQ[DeleteDuplicates[c], $Failed], AppendTo[b, Ind[h]], AppendTo[b, c]]];
a = DeleteDuplicates[Flatten[b]]; If[d == Length[a], Sort[a], b = {}; Goto[ArtKr]]]

In[2621]:= OP[Sqrt[(a + b)/(c + d)] + Sin[x]*Cos[y]]
Out[2621]= {-1, 1/2, a, b, c, Cos, d, Sin, x, y}
In[2622]:= OP[(Log[(a + b)/(c + d)] + Sin[x]*Cos[y])/(G[h, g, t] - w^2)]
Out[2622]= {-1, 2, a, b, c, Cos, d, g, G, h, Log, Sin, t, w, x, y}
In[2623]:= Map[OP, {{Sin[x]}, G[h, g, t], A[m, p]/G[t, q]}]
Out[2623]= {{Sin, x}, {g, G, h, t}, {-1, A, G, m, p, q, t}}

In *Mathematica* there is no direct equivalent of *op* function of *Maple*, but it can be defined within axiomatics of the systems by the next procedure which in a number of cases is rather convenient at programming of appendices:

In[2672]:= Op[x_] := Module[{a, b},
a = {}; If[ListQ[x], a = x, Do[a = Insert[a, Part[x][[b]], -1], {b, Length[x]}]]; a]

In[2673]:= Op[Sin[x] + Cos[x]]
Out[2673]= {Cos[x], Sin[x]}
In[2674]:= Op[{1, 2, 3, 4, 5, 6, 7, 8, 9}]
Out[2674]= {1, 2, 3, 4, 5, 6, 7, 8, 9}
In[2675]:= Op[Sqrt[a + b] + Sin[x] - c/d]
Out[2675]= {Sqrt[a + b], -(c/d), Sin[x]}
In[2676]:= Op[(x + y*Cos[x])/(y + x*Sin[y])]
Out[2676]= {x + y*Cos[x], 1/(y + x*Sin[y])}
In[2677]:= Map[Op, {Sin[x], Cos[a + b], 1/(a + b)}]
Out[2677]= {{x}, {a + b}, {a + b, -1}}

It is simple to be convinced that the received results of calls of **Op** procedure are *identical* to similar calls of *op* function in *Maple*, taking into account that *Mathematica* doesn't support structure of type "*sequence*" which is replaced with the list. The **Op** procedure is an useful enough means in the programming.

In a number of appendices the undoubted interest presents a certain analog of the *Maple*-procedure *whattype(x)* that returns the type of a *x* expression which is one of basic *Maple*-types. The procedure of the same name acts as a similar analog in *Mathematica* whose call **WhatType[*x*]** returns type of a *x* object of one of basic types {"Module", "DynamicModule", "Block", "Real", "Complex", "Integer", "Rational", "Times", "Rule", "Power", "Alternatives", "And", "List", "Plus", "Condition", "StringJoin", "UndirectedEdge", ...}. The next fragment represents source code of the procedure with examples of its application for identification of the types of various objects.

In[2869]:= WhatType[x_ /; StringQ[x]] := Module[{b = t, d, c = $Packages,
a = Quiet[Head[ToExpression[x]]]},
If[a === Symbol, Clear[t]; d = Context[x]; If[d == "Global`", d = Quiet[ProcFuncBlQ[x, t]];
If[d === True, Return[{t, t = b}[[1]]], Return[{"Undefined", t = b}[[1]]]],
If[d == "System`", Return[{d, t = b}[[1]]], Null]], Return[{ToString[a], t = b}[[1]]]];
If[Quiet[ProcFuncBlQ[x, t]], If[MemberQ[{"Module", "DynamicModule", "Block"}, t],
Return[{t, t = b}[[1]]], t = b; ToString[Quiet[Head[ToExpression[x]]]]], t = b; "Undefined"]]

In[2870]:= t = 590; x = 90; y := 42.47; z = a + b; J[x_] := x;
Map[WhatType, {"Kr", "t", "x", "y", "z", "ProcQ", "Sin", "F[r]", "WhatType", "J"}]
Out[2870]= {"Undefined", "Integer", "Integer", "Real", "Plus", "Module", "System`", "F", "Module", "Function"}
In[2871]:= Map[WhatType, {"a^b", "a**b", "13 + 75*I", "{42, 47}", "a&&b"}]
Out[2871]= {"Power", "NonCommutativeMultiply", "Complex", "List", "And"}
In[2872]:= Map[WhatType, {"a_/; b", "a <> b", "a <-> b", "a | b"}]
Out[2872]= {"Condition", "StringJoin", "UndirectedEdge", "Alternatives"}

However, it should be noted that the **WhatType** procedure does not support exhaustive testing of types, meantime on its basis it is simple to expand the class of the tested types.

The functions **Replace** and **ReplaceAll** of *Mathematica* have very essential restrictions in relation to replacement of subexpressions relatively already of very simple expressions as it will illustrated below. The reason of it can be explained by the following *circumstance*, using the procedure useful enough also as independent tool. The call **ExpOnLevels[*x*, *y*, *z*]** returns the list of a *x* expression levels on which an *y* subexpression is located. While the procedure call with the 3rd optional *z* argument – *an undefinite symbol* – through it additionally returns the nested list of the *ListList* type of all subexpressions of the *x* expression on all its levels. In addition, the first element of each sublist of such *ListList* defines a level of the *x* expression whereas the second element defines the list of subexpressions located on this level. If the *y* subexpression is absent on the levels identified by **Level** function, the procedure call returns the corresponding diagnostic message. The following fragment presents source code of the **ExpOnLevels** procedure with examples of its application.

In[4036]:= ExpOnLevels[x_, y_, z___] := Module[{a = {}, b},
Do[AppendTo[a, {j, Set[b, Level[x, {j}]]}]; If[b == {}, Break[], Continue[]], {j, 1, Infinity}];
a = a[[1 ;; -2]]; If[{z} != {} && NullQ[z], z = a, 75];
b = Map[If[MemberQ[#[[2]], y], #[[1]], Nothing] &, a];
If[b == {}, "Subexpression " <> ToString1[y] <> " can't be identified", b]]

In[4037]:= ExpOnLevels[a + b[t]^3 + 1/x^(b[t]/(a + b[4])) + b[t], b[t]]
Out[4037]= {1, 2, 3}
In[4038]:= ExpOnLevels[a + b^3 + 1/x^(3/(a + 2)) + b[t] + 1/x^2, x^2]
Out[4038]= "Subexpression x^2 can't be identified"
In[4039]:= ExpOnLevels[a + b^3 + 1/x^(3/(a + 2)) + b[t] + a/x^2, x^2, g47]
Out[4039]= "Subexpression x^2 can't be identified"
In[4040]:= g47
Out[4040]= {{1, {a, b^3, a/x^2, x^(-(3/(2 + a))), b[t]}}, {2, {b, 3, a, 1/x^2, x, -(3/(2 + a)), t}}, {3, {x, -2, -3, 1/(2 + a)}}, {4, {2 + a, -1}}, {5, {2, a}}}

So, the **ExpOnLevels** procedure can determine admissible replacements carring out by the means of the standard functions **Replace** and **ReplaceAll**, as they are based on the **Level** function which evaluates the list of all subexpressions of an expression on the given levels.

The call of the standard **Replace** function on unused rules does not return any diagnostical information, at the same time, if all rules were not used, then the function call is returned unevaluated. In turn, the procedure below which is based on the previous **ExpOnLevels** procedure gives full diagnostics concerning the unused rules. The call **ReplaceInExpr**[x, y, z] is analogous to the call **Replace**[x, y, *All*] where y is a rule or their list whereas through the third optional z argument – *an undefined symbol* – additionally is returned the message identifying the list of the unused rules. If unused rules are absent then the z symbol remains undefined. The following fragment represents source code of the **ReplaceInExpr** procedure with examples of its application.

In[4030]:= ReplaceInExpr[x_, y_ /; RuleQ[y] || ListRulesQ[y], z___] :=
Module[{a = x, b = If[RuleQ[y], {y}, y], c = {}},
Do[If[SuffPref[ToString[ExpOnLevels[a, b[[j]][[1]]]], "Sub", 1],
AppendTo[c, j], a = Replace[a, b[[j]], All]], {j, 1, Length[b]}];
If[{z} != {} && NullQ[z], z = "Rules " <> ToString[c] <> " were not used", 75]; a]
In[4031]:= ReplaceInExpr[(a + b[t]) + 1/x^(3/(b[t] + 2)) + b[t] + a/x^2,
{x^2 -> mp, b[t] -> gsv, x^3 -> tag, a -> 75}, gs]
Out[4031]= 75 + 2*gsv + 75/x^2 + x^(-(3/(2 + gsv)))
In[4032]:= gs
Out[4032]= "Rules {1, 3} were not used"

The **ReplaceInExpr** procedure can be rather simply generalized to other admissible formats of the **Replace** call. This problem is left to the reader as a rather useful exercise.

The following procedure is an interesting not equivalent version of the previous procedure **ReplaceInExpr**. At the same time, the procedure algorithm significantly uses the **ToBoxes** function the generating the boxes corresponding to the printed form of an expression in the **StandardForm**. The procedure call **ReplaceInExpr1**[x, y, z] is analogous to the procedure call **ReplaceInExpr**[x, y, z] but not its result where y is a rule or their list while through the third optional z argument – *an undefined symbol* – additionally is returned the message that identifies a list of the unused rules. If unused rules are absent, then the z symbol remains undefined. The fragment below represents source code of the **ReplaceInExpr1** procedure with typical examples of its application. Of the presented examples one can clearly see the difference between both procedures.

In[4014]:= ReplaceInExpr1[x_, r_ /; RuleQ[r] || ListRulesQ[r], y___] :=
Module[{a = ToString1 @@ {ToBoxes @@ {x}}, b, c = If[RuleQ[r], {r}, r], d, h = {}},
Do[b = ToString1 @@ {ToBoxes @@ {c[[j]][[1]]}};
d = ToString1 @@ {ToBoxes @@ {c[[j]][[2]]}};
If[StringFreeQ[a, b], AppendTo[h, j], a = StringReplace[a, b -> d]], {j, 1, Length[c]}];
a = ToExpression[a]; If[{y} != {} && NullQ[y], y = h, 70];
ReleaseHold[MakeExpression[a, StandardForm]]]

In[4015]:= ReplaceInExpr1[x^2 + 1/x^2 + Sin[t], x^2 -> m^3]
Out[4015]= 1/m^3 + m^3 + Sin[t]
In[4016]:= ReplaceInExpr1[x^2 + 1/x^2 + Sin[t], {x^2 -> m^3, t -> Cos[w]}]
Out[4016]= 1/m^3 + m^3 + Sin[Cos[w]]
In[4017]:= ReplaceInExpr1[(a + b^3) + 1/x^(3/(a + 2)) + b[t] + 1/x^2, {b[t] -> Sin[h], x^(3/(a + 2)) -> avz, x^2 -> np}, gsv]
Out[4017]= a + b^3 + 1/np + x^(-(3/(2 + a))) + Sin[h]
In[4018]:= gsv
Out[4018]= "Rules {3} were not used"
In[4019]:= ReplaceInExpr1[(a + b[t]) + 1/x^(3/(b[t] + 2)) + b[t] + a/x^2, {x^2 -> mp, b[t] -> gsv, x^3 -> tag, a -> 75}, gs]
Out[4019]= 75 + 2*gsv + 75/mp + x^(-(3/(2 + gsv)))
In[4020]:= gs
Out[4020]= "Rules {2} were not used"
In[4021]:= ReplaceInExpr[(a + b[t]) + 1/x^(3/(b[t] + 2)) + b[t] + a/x^2, {x^2 -> mp, b[t] -> gsv, x^3 -> tag, a -> 75}, gs1]
Out[4021]= 75 + 2*gsv + 75/x^2 + x^(-(3/(2 + gsv)))
In[4022]:= gs1
Out[4022]= "Rules {1, 3} were not used"

Using like a case of the previous procedure the **ToBoxes** procedure which creates the boxes corresponding to the printed form of expressions in the **StandardForm**, we can allocate the subexpressions composing an expression. The procedure call **SubExpressions**[*x*] returns the list of subexpressions composing an expression *x*, in a case of impossibility the empty list is returned, i.e. {}. The fragment below presents source code of the **SubExpressions** procedure with typical examples of its application.

In[4486]:= SubExpressions[x_] := Module[{a = ToString1[ToBoxes[x]], b, c = {}, d, h, t},
b = Select[ExtrVarsOfStr[a, 2], SystemQ[#] || UserQ[#] &];
Do[h = b[[j]]; d = StringPosition[a, h];
Do[t = "["; Do[If[StringCount[t, "["] == StringCount[t, "]"],
AppendTo[c, h <> t]; Break[], t = t <> StringTake[a, {d[[p]][[2]] + k + 1}]], {k, 1, Infinity}],
{p, 1, Length[d]}], {j, 1, Length[b]}];
c = Map[Quiet[Check[ToExpression[#], Nothing]] &, c];
Map[ReleaseHold[MakeExpression[#, StandardForm]] &, c]]

In[4487]:= SubExpressions[a*b + 1/x^(3/(b[t] + 2)) + Sin[t] + d/x^2]
Out[4487]= {d/x^2, 3/(2 + b[t]), a*b + d/x^2 + x^(-(3/(2 + b[t]))) + Sin[t], a*b, -(3/(2 + b[t])), 2 + b[t], b[t], Sin[t], x^2, x^(-(3/(2 + b[t])))}

In[4488]:= SubExpressions[(a + Sin[x] + b*Log[y])/(c/Levels[t] - d^(m + n))]
Out[4488]= {(a + b*Log[y] + Sin[x])/(-d^(m + n) + c/Levels[t]), c/Levels[t], a + b*Log[y] + Sin[x], b*Log[y], Log[y], Sin[x], -d^(m + n) + c/Levels[t], -d^(m + n), m + n, Levels[t], d^(m + n)}

Unlike the above **SubExpressions** procedure, the **SubExpressions1** procedure is based on the **FullForm** function. The call **SubExpressions1[*x*]** returns the list of subexpressions that compose an *x* expression, whereas in case of impossibility the empty list is returned, i.e. {}. The fragment below represents source code of the **SubExpressions1** procedure along with typical examples of its application.

In[4535]:= SubExpressions1[x_] := Module[{a = ToString[FullForm[x]], b, c = {}, d, h, t},
b = Select[ExtrVarsOfStr[a, 2], SystemQ[#] || UserQ[#] &];
Do[h = b[[j]]; d = StringPosition[a, h];
Do[t = "["; Do[If[StringCount[t, "["] == StringCount[t, "]"], AppendTo[c, h <> t]; Break[],
t = t <> StringTake[a, {d[[p]][[2]] + k + 1}]],
{k, 1, Infinity}], {p, 1, Length[d]}], {j, 1, Length[b]}]; Map[ToExpression[#] &, c]]

In[4536]:= SubExpressions1[a*b + 1/x^(3/(b[t] + 2)) + Sin[t] + d/x^2]
Out[4536]= {a*b + d/x^2 + x^(-(3/(2 + b[t]))) + Sin[t], 2 + b[t], 1/x^2, x^(-(3/(2 + b[t]))), 1/(2 + b[t]), Sin[t], a*b, d/x^2, -(3/(2 + b[t]))}
In[4537]:= SubExpressions1[Sin[a]^Cos[b]]
Out[4537]= {Cos[b], Sin[a]^Cos[b], Sin[a]}
In[4538]:= SubExpressions1[(Sin[a] + Log[c])^Cos[b]]
Out[4538]= {Cos[b], Log[c], Log[c] + Sin[a], (Log[c] + Sin[a])^Cos[b], Sin[a]}

Both procedures **SubExpressions** and **SubExpressions1** clarify the restrictions inherent to the **ReplaceInExpr** procedure for replacement of subexpressions in expressions.

Whereas the procedure call **SubExpressions2[*x*]** returns the sorted list of all subexpressions composing an expression *x*. In this context the procedure call is equivalent to the call of the standard **Level** function to within an order of elements of the returned list. The following fragment represents source code of the **SubExpressions2** procedure with typical examples of its application, including a comparative aspect.

In[4667]:= SubExpressions2[x_] := Module[{a = {x}, b = {}, c = {x}, f},
f[m_, n_] := Module[{p = m},
Do[AppendTo[p, Quiet[Check[Part[n, j], Break[]]]], {j, 1, Infinity}]; p];
Do[b = Join[b, Flatten[Map[f[b, #] &, c]]]; c = b; a = Join[a, b];
If[b == {}, Break[], b = {}], {j, 1, Infinity}]; Sort[DeleteDuplicates[a]]]
In[4668]:= SubExpressions2[a*b + 1/x^(3/(b[t] + 2)) + Sin[t] + d/x^2]
Out[4668]= {-3, -2, -1, 2, a, b, a*b, d, t, 1/x^2, d/x^2, x, x^(-(3/(2 + b[t]))), b[t],
-(3/(2 + b[t])), 1/(2 + b[t]), 2 + b[t], Sin[t], a*b + d/x^2 + x^(-(3/(2 + b[t]))) + Sin[t]}
In[4669]:= Sort[DeleteDuplicates[Level[a*b + 1/x^(3/(b[t] + 2)) + Sin[t] + d/x^2, All]]]
Out[4669]= {-3, -2, -1, 2, a, b, a*b, d, t, 1/x^2, d/x^2, x, x^(-(3/(2 + b[t]))), b[t],
-(3/(2 + b[t])), 1/(2 + b[t]), 2 + b[t], Sin[t], a*b + d/x^2 + x^(-(3/(2 + b[t]))) + Sin[t]}

Thus, both the system **Level** function, and **SubExpressions÷SubExpressions2** procedures allow to outline possibilities of the *Mathematica* system concerning the replacements of the subexpressions in expressions.

As an alternative for the above tools can be offered the **Subs** procedure that is functionally equivalent to the above standard **ReplaceAll** function, but which is relieved of a number of its shortcomings. The procedure call **Subs[x, y, z]** returns the result of substitutions in a x expression of entries of y subexpressions onto z expressions. In addition, if x – an arbitrary correct expression, then as the second and third arguments defining substitutions of format $y \rightarrow z$, an unary substitution or their list coded in form $y \equiv \{y1, y2, ..., yn\}$ and $z \equiv \{z1, z2, ..., zn\}$ appear, determining the list of substitutions $\{y1 \rightarrow z1, y2 \rightarrow z2, ..., yn \rightarrow zn\}$ which are carried out consistently in the order defined at the **Subs** procedure call. The next fragment represents and source code of the **Subs** procedure, and a number of bright examples of its usage on those expressions and with those types of substitutions where the **Subs** procedure surpasses the standard **ReplaceAll** function of *Mathematica*. These examples rather clearly illustrate advantages of the **Subs** procedure before the similar system tools.

```
In[2968]:= Subs[x_, y_, z_] := Module[{d, k = 2, subs}, subs[m_, n_, p_] :=
Module[{a, b, c, h, t}, If[! HowAct[n], m /. n -> p,
{a, b, c, h} = First[{Map[ToString, Map[InputForm, {m, n, p, 1/n}]]}];
t = Simplify[ToExpression[StringReplace[StringReplace[a, b -> "(" <> c <> ")"],
h -> "1/" <> "(" <> c <> ")"]]]; If[t === m, m /. n -> p, t]]];
! ListQ[y] && ! ListQ[z], subs[x, y, z], If[ListQ[y] && ListQ[z] &&
Length[y] == Length[z], d = subs[x, y[[1]], z[[1]]];
For[k, k <= Length[y], k++, d = subs[d, y[[k]], z[[k]]]]; d, Defer[Subs[x, y, z]]]]]]
In[2969]:= (c + x^2)/x^2 /. x^2 -> a
Out[2969]= (a + c)/x^2
In[2970]:= Subs[(c + x^2)/x^2, x^2, a]
Out[2970]= (a + c)/a
In[2971]:= (c + b^2)/x^2 /. x^2 -> Sqrt[z]
Out[2971]= (b^2 + c)/x^2
In[2972]:= Subs[(c + b^2)/x^2, x^2, Sqrt[z]]
Out[2972]= (b^2 + c)/Sqrt[z]
In[2973]:= (a + x^2)/(b + a/x^2) /. x^2 -> Sqrt[a + b]
Out[2973]= (a + Sqrt[a + b])/(b + a/x^2)
In[2974]:= Subs[(a + x^2)/(b + a/x^2), x^2, Sqrt[a + b]]
Out[2974]= (a + Sqrt[a + b])/(b + a/Sqrt[a + b])
In[2975]:= (a + x^2)/(b + 1/x^2) /. x^2 -> Sqrt[a + b]
Out[2975]= (a + Sqrt[a + b])/(b + 1/x^2)
In[2976]:= Subs[(a + x^2)/(b + 1/x^2), x^2, Sqrt[a + b]]
Out[2976]= (a + Sqrt[a + b])/(b + 1/Sqrt[a + b])
In[2977]:= Replace[1/x^2 + 1/y^3, {{x^2 -> a + b}, {y^3 -> c + d}}]
Out[2977]= {1/x^2 + 1/y^3, 1/x^2 + 1/y^3}
In[2978]:= Subs[1/x^2 + 1/y^3, {x^2, y^3}, {a + b, c + d}]
Out[2978]= 1/(a + b) + 1/(c + d)
```

In[2979]:= **Replace[Sqrt[Sin[1/x^2] + Cos[1/y^3]], {{x^2 -> a*b}, {y^3 -> c*d}}]**
Out[2979]= {Sqrt[Cos[1/y^3] + Sin[1/x^2]], Sqrt[Cos[1/y^3] + Sin[1/x^2]]}
In[2980]:= **Subs[Sqrt[Sin[1/x^2] + Cos[1/y^3]], {x^2, y^3}, {a*b, c*d}]**
Out[2980]= Sqrt[Cos[1/(c*d)] + Sin[1/(a*b)]]
In[2981]:= **With[{x = a + c, y = b}, Module[{}, x^2 + y]]**
Out[2981]= b + (a + c)^2
In[2982]:= **With[{x^2 = a + c, y = b}, Module[{}, x^2 + y]]**
With::lvset: Local variable specification {x^2 = a + c, y = b} contains...
Out[2982]= With[{x^2 = a + c, y = b}, Module[{}, x^2 + y]]
In[2983]:= **Subs[Module[{}, x^2 + y], {x, y}, {a + c, b}]**
Out[2983]= b + (a + c)^2
In[2984]:= **Subs[Module[{}, x^2 + y], {x^2, y}, {a + c, b}]**
Out[2984]= a + b + c
In[2985]:= **Replace[(a + x^2/y^3)/(b + y^3/x^2), {{y^3 -> m}, {x^2 -> n}}]**
Out[2985]= {(a + x^2/y^3)/(b + y^3/x^2), (a + x^2/y^3)/(b + y^3/x^2)}
In[2986]:= **Subs[(a + x^2/y^3)/(b + y^3/x^2), {y^3, x^2}, {m, n}]**
Out[2986]= n*(a*m + n)/(m*(m + b*n))
In[2987]:= **Df[x_, y_] := Module[{a}, If[! HowAct[y], D[x, y], Simplify[Subs[D[Subs[x, y, a], a], a, y]]]]**
In[2988]:= **Df[(a + x^2)/(b + a/x^2), x^2]**
Out[2988]= (a^2 + 2*a*x^2 + b*x^4)/(a + b*x^2)^2
In[2989]:= **Df[(x + Sqrt[y])/(y + 2*Sqrt[y])^2, Sqrt[y]]**
Out[2989]= (-4*x - 2*Sqrt[y] + y)/((2 + Sqrt[y])^3*y^(3/2))
In[2990]:= **D[(x + Sqrt[y])/(y + 2*Sqrt[y])^2, Sqrt[y]]**
General::ivar: √y is not a valid variable.>>
Out[2990]= ∂√y ((x + Sqrt[y])/(y + 2 Sqrt[y])^2)
In[2991]:= **Df[(x + Sqrt[a + Sqrt[x]])/(d + 2*Sqrt[x])^2, Sqrt[x]]**
Out[2991]= ((d + 2*Sqrt[x])/Sqrt[a + Sqrt[x]] - 8*(Sqrt[a + Sqrt[x]] + x))/2*(d + 2*Sqrt[x])^3)
In[2992]:= **Df[(x + Sqrt[x + b])/(d + 2*Sqrt[x + b])^2, Sqrt[x + b]]**
Out[2992]= (d - 2*(2*x + Sqrt[b + x]))/(d + 2*Sqrt[b + x])^3
In[2993]:= **ReplaceAll1[x_, y_, z_]:= Module[{a, b, c}, If[! HowAct[y], x /. y -> z, c = If[MemberQ[{Plus, Times, Power}, Head[z]], "(" <> ToString[InputForm[z]] <> ")", ToString[z]]; {a, b} = Map[ToString, Map[InputForm, {x, y}]]; If[StringLength[b] == 1, ReplaceAll[x, y -> z], ToExpression[StringReplace[a, b -> c]]]]]**
In[2994]:= **{ReplaceAll[c/x^2 + x^2, x^2 -> t], ReplaceAll[(1 + c/x^2)/(b + x^2), x^2 -> t]}**
Out[2994]= {t + c/x^2, (1 + c/x^2)/(b + t)}
In[2995]:= **{ReplaceAll1[c/x^2+x^2, x^2, a+b], ReplaceAll1[(1+c/x^2)/(b+x^2), x^2, c+d]}**
Out[2995]= {a + b + c/(a + b), (1 + c/(c + d))/(b + c + d)}
In[2996]:= **Df1[x_, y_] := Module[{a, b, c = "$$Art27$$Kr20$$"}, If[! HowAct[y], D[x, y], {a, b} = Map[ToString, Map[InputForm, {x, y}]]; Simplify[ToExpression[StringReplace[ToString[InputForm[D[ToExpression[StringReplace[a, b -> c]], ToExpression[c]]]], c -> b]]]]]**

In[2997]:= Df2[x_, y_] := Module[{a},
If[! HowAct[y], D[x, y], Simplify[ReplaceAll1[D[ReplaceAll1[x, y, a], a], a, y]]]]

In[2998]:= Df1[(x + Sqrt[a + Sqrt[x]])/(d + 2*Sqrt[x])^2, Sqrt[x]]
Out[2998]= ((d + 2*Sqrt[x])/Sqrt[a + Sqrt[x]] - 8*(Sqrt[a + Sqrt[x]] + x))/2*(d + 2*Sqrt[x])^3)

In[2999]:= Df2[(x + Sqrt[a + Sqrt[x]])/(d + 2*Sqrt[x])^2, Sqrt[x]]
Out[2999]= ((d + 2*Sqrt[x])/Sqrt[a + Sqrt[x]] - 8*(Sqrt[a + Sqrt[x]] + x))/2*(d + 2*Sqrt[x])^3)

In[3000]:= Df2[(a/x^2 + 1/x^2)/(c/x^2 + 1/x^2), 1/x^2]
Out[3000]= -(((a - c)*x^2)/(1 + c)^2)

In[3001]:= Df1[(a/x^2 + 1/x^2)/(c/x^2 + 1/x^2), 1/x^2]
Out[3001]= -(((a - c)*x^2)/(1 + c)^2)

In[3002]:= Df[(a/x^2 + 1/x^2)/(c/x^2 + 1/x^2), 1/x^2]
Out[3002]= -((2*(a - c)*x^6)/(1 + c*x^4)^2)

In[3003]:= Df2[(a + b)/(Sin[x] + Cos[x]), Sin[x] + Cos[x]]
Out[3003]= -((a + b)/(Cos[x] + Sin[x])^2)

In[3004]:= Df2[Cos[x]/(Sin[x] + Cos[x]), Cos[x]]
Out[3004]= Sin[x]/(Cos[x] + Sin[x])^2

A simple example of the previous fragment illustrates application of the **Subs** procedure in realization of the **Df** procedure whose call **Df[x, y]** provides differentiation of a *x* expression on an arbitrary its *y* subexpression, and rather significantly extends the standard **D** function; examples illustrate some opportunities of **Df** procedure. At the end of the above fragment the **ReplaceAll1** procedure functionally equivalent to the standard **ReplaceAll** function is presented, which relieves a number of shortages of the second. So, then on the basis of the procedures **ReplaceAll1** and **StringReplace** some variants of the **Df** procedure, namely the **Df1** and **Df2** which use a number of useful methods of programming are presented. At the same time, they in some cases are more useful than the **Df** procedure what rather visually illustrate the examples given above. At that, the **Df**, **Df1** and **Df2** rather significantly extend the standard function **D**. The fragment represents source codes of the above procedures and some examples of their use where they surpass the standard functions **D**, **ReplaceAll**, **Rule** and **With** of the *Mathematica* system.

At last, **Substitution** is an integrated procedure of the above tools **Subs, Subs1** and **Subs2**. The procedure call **Substitution[x, y, z]** returns the result of substitutions into an arbitrary *x* expression of a *z* expression instead of occurrences in it of all *y* subexpressions. In addition, if as *x* expression any correct expression admitted by *Math*–language is used whereas as a single substitution or their set coded as $y \equiv \{y1, y2,..., yn\}$ and $z \equiv \{z1, z2,..., zn\}$ are allowable as the second and third arguments determining substitutions of the format $y \rightarrow z$, defining a set of substitutions $\{y1 \rightarrow z1, y2 \rightarrow z2,..., yn \rightarrow zn\}$ carried out consistently. The procedure **Substitution** allows rather essentially to extend possibilities of expressions processing. The following fragment represents source code of the **Substitution** procedure along with typical examples of its application, well illustrating its advantages over the standard means.

In[2873]:= Substitution[x_, y_, z_] := Module[{d, k = 2, subs, subs1}, subs[m_, n_, p_] :=
Module[{a, b, c, h, t}, If[! HowAct[n], m /. n -> p,
{a, b, c, h} = First[{Map[ToString, Map[InputForm, {m, n, p, 1/n}]]}];
t = Simplify[ToExpression[StringReplace[StringReplace[a, b -> "(" <> c <> ")"],

h -> "1/" <> "(" <> c <> ")"]]]; If[t === m, m /. n -> p, t]]];
subs1[m_, n_, p_] := ToExpression[StringReplace[ToString[FullForm[m]],
ToString[FullForm[n]] -> ToString[FullForm[p]]]];
If[! ListQ[y] && ! ListQ[z], If[Numerator[y] == 1 && ! SameQ[Denominator[y], 1],
subs1[x, y, z], subs[x, y, z]],
If[ListQ[y] && ListQ[z] && Length[y] == Length[z],
If[Numerator[y[[1]]] == 1 && ! SameQ[Denominator[y[[1]]], 1], d = subs1[x, y[[1]], z[[1]]],
d = subs[x, y[[1]], z[[1]]]];
For[k, k <= Length[y], k++, If[Numerator[y[[k]]] == 1 && ! SameQ[Denominator[y[[k]]], 1],
d = subs1[d, y[[k]], z[[k]]], d = subs[d, y[[k]], z[[k]]]]]; d, Defer[Substitution[x, y, z]]]]]
In[2874]:= Replace[1/x^2 + 1/y^3, {{x^2 -> a + b}, {y^3 -> c + d}}]
Out[2874]= {1/x^2 + 1/y^3, 1/x^2 + 1/y^3}
In[2875]:= Substitution[1/x^2 + 1/y^3, {x^2, y^3}, {a + b, c + d}]
Out[2875]= 1/(a + b) + 1/(c + d)
In[2876]:= Substitution[1/x^2 + 1/y^3, {1/x^2, 1/y^3}, {a + b, c + d}]
Out[2876]= a + b + c + d
In[2877]:= Replace[1/x^2*1/y^3, {{1/x^2 -> a + b}, {1/y^3 -> c + d}}]
Out[2877]= {1/(x^2*y^3), 1/(x^2*y^3)}
In[2878]:= Substitution[1/x^2*1/y^3, {x^2, y^3}, {a + b, c + d}]
Out[2878]= 1/((a + b)*(c + d))
In[2979]:= D[(a/x^2 + 1/x^2)/(c/x^2 + 1/x^2), 1/x^2]
General::ivar: 1/x^2 is not a valid variable.>>
Out[2979]= ∂_{1/x^2} (1/x^2 + a/x^2)/(1/x^2 + c/x^2)
In[2980]:= Simplify[Substitution[D[Substitution[(a/x^2+1/x^2)/(c/x^2+1/x^2), 1/x^2, t], t],
t, 1/x^2]]
Out[2980]= 0
In[2981]:= D[(a/x^2 + 1/x^2)/(c/x^2 + x^2), 1/x^2, x^2]
General::ivar: 1/x^2 is not a valid variable.>>
Out[2981]= ∂1/x^2, x^2 (1/x^2 + a/x^2)/(1/x^2 + c/x^2)
In[2982]:= Simplify[Substitution[D[Substitution[(a/x^2 + 1/x^2)/(c/x^2 + x^2), {1/x^2, x^2},
{t, t1}], t, t1], {t, t1}, {1/x^2, x^2}]]
Out[2982]= ((1 + a)*x^4*(c - x^4))/(c + x^4)^3
In[2883]:= Substitution[Integrate[Substitution[(a/x^2+1/x^2)/(c/x^2+1/x^2), 1/x^2, t], t],
t, 1/x^2]
Out[2883]= (1 + a)/((1 + c)*x^2)
In[2984]:= Integrate[(a/x^2 + 1/x^2)/(c/x^2 + x^2), 1/x^2, x^2]
Integrate::ilim: Invalid integration variable or limit(s) in 1/x^2.>>
Out[2984]= Integrate[(a/x^2 + 1/x^2)/(c/x^2 + x^2), 1/x^2, x^2]
In[2885]:= Simplify[Substitution[Integrate[Substitution[(a/x^2 + 1/x^2)/(c/x^2 + x^2),
{1/x^2, x^2}, {t, t1}], t, t1], {t, t1}, {1/x^2, x^2}]]
Out[2885]= ((1 + a)*(-c*(c - 2*x^4) + 2*(c^2 - x^8)*Log[(c + x^4)/x^2]))/(4*c^2*x^4)
In[2886]:= Integrate[(b + Sin[x]*Cos[x] + a/b)^3, Sin[x], b, a/b]
Integrate::ilim: Invalid integration variable or limit(s) in a/b.>>
Out[2886]= Integrate[(b + Sin[x]*Cos[x] + a/b)^3, Sin[x], b, a/b]

In[2887]:= **Simplify[Substitution[Integrate[Substitution[(b + Sin[x]*Cos[x] + a/b)^3, {Sin[x], b, a/b}, {t1, t2, t3}], t1, t2, t3], {t1, t2, t3}, {Sin[x], b, a/b}]]**
Out[2887]= -((a*Sin[x]*(64*a^3 - 8*b^4 - 192*a*b^4 - 32*b^6 - 16*a*b^2* Log[b] - 384*a^2*b^2*Log[b] + 8*b^2*Cos[4*x]*(b^2 + 2*a*Log[b]) - b*(-96*a^2 + 3*b^2 + 192*a*b^2 + 32*b^4)*Sin[2*x] + b^3*Sin[6*x]))/(128*b^3))

It should be noted that the **Substitution** procedure rather significantly extends the standard tools intended for ensuring replacements of subexpressions in expressions as the following examples rather visually illustrate.

In[3023]:= **ReplaceAll[Defer[(a + b/Sqrt[a + b])/x], Sqrt[a + b] -> m]**
Out[3023]= (a + b/Sqrt[a + b])/x
In[3024]:= **ReplaceAll[(a + b/Sqrt[a + b])/x, Sqrt[a + b] -> m]**
Out[3024]= (a + b/Sqrt[a + b])/x
In[3025]:= **Substitution[(a + b/Sqrt[a + b])/x, Sqrt[a + b], m]**
Out[3025]= (a + b/m)/x
In[3026]:= **ReplaceAll[Defer[(a + b/Sqrt[a + b])/x], 1/Sqrt[a + b] -> m]**
Out[3026]= (a + b/Sqrt[a + b])/x
In[3027]:= **Substitution[(a + b/Sqrt[a + b])/x, 1/Sqrt[a + b], m]**
Out[3027]= (a + b*m)/x
In[3035]:= **ReplaceAll[HoldAll[(a + b/Sqrt[a + b])/x], 1/Sqrt[a + b] -> m]**
Out[3035]= HoldAll[(a + b*m)/x]
In[3042]:= **Substitution1[x_, y_, z_] := Module[{y1, z1, d, k = 2, subst}, subst[m_, n_, p_] := ToExpression[StringTake[StringReplace[ToString1[ReplaceAll[HoldAll[m], n -> p]], "HoldAll[" -> ""], {1, -2}]]; {y1, z1} = Map[Flatten, {{y}, {z}}];
If[ListQ[y1] && ListQ[z1] && Length[y1] == Length[z1], d = subst[x, y1[[1]], z1[[1]]];
For[k, k <= Length[y1], k++, d = subst[d, y1[[k]], z1[[k]]]]; d, Defer[Substitution1[x, y, z]]]]**
In[3043]:= **Substitution1[(a + b/Sqrt[a + b])/x, 1/Sqrt[a + b], m]**
Out[3043]= (a + b*m)/x
In[3044]:= **Substitution1[(a + b/Sqrt[a + b])/(x/Sqrt[a + b]), 1/Sqrt[a + b], m]**
Out[3044]= (Sqrt[a + b]*(a + b*m))/x

The **Substitution1** procedure whose an initial code with examples are given in the previous fragment can be considered as an analog of the **Substitution** procedure. The syntax of the procedure call **Substitution1[x, y, z]** is identical to the procedure call **Substitution[x, y, z]**, returning the result of substitutions into arbitrary *x* expression of *z* subexpression(s) instead of all occurences of *y* subexpression(s).

The following quite simple **Substitution2** function is the simplified version of the previous **Substitution** procedure, its call **Substitution2[x, y, z]** returns the result of substitutions into a *x* expression of a *z* subexpression instead of all occurences of a *y* subexpression. Function significantly uses *FullForm* of expressions and supports a rather wide range of *substitutions*. In context of expressions analysis the procedure whose call **HeadsInExpression[x]** returns the **Heads** list of all subexpressions composing a *x* expression is of a certain interest. While the procedure call **HeadsInExpression[x, y]** through the optional *y* argument – *an undefinite symbol* – additionally returns the list of all subexpressions composing an expression *x*. The procedure can be a rather useful tool at expressions parsing. The next fragment represents source codes of the above two means with typical examples of their applications.

In[3767]:= **Substitution2[x_, y_, z_] := ToExpression[StringReplace[ToString[FullForm[x]], ToString[FullForm[y]] -> ToString[FullForm[z]]]]**

In[3768]:= **Substitution2[Sin[x^2]*Cos[1/b^3], 1/b^3, x^2]**
Out[3768]= Cos[x^2]*Sin[x^2]

In[3850]:= **HeadsInExpression[x_, y___] := Module[{b, c, a = ToString[FullForm[x]]}, If[MemberQ[{ToString[x], ToString1[x]}, a], Head[x], b = ExtrExpr[a, 1, StringLength[a]];**
c = DeleteDuplicates[Flatten[Map[ExtrVarsOfStr[#, 1] &, b]]];
If[{y} != {} && NullQ[y], y = ToExpression[Select[b, Quiet[Check[SystemQ[StringTake[#, {1, DeleteDuplicates[Flatten[StringPosition[#, "["]]][[1]] - 1}]], Nothing]] &]], 75];
Sort[Select[c, SystemQ[#] &]]]]

In[3851]:= **HeadsInExpression[(a + b/Sqrt[a + b])/x, g70]**
Out[3851]= {"Plus", "Power", "Rational", "Times"}
In[3852]:= **g70**
Out[3852]= {(a + b/Sqrt[a + b])/x, a + b/Sqrt[a + b], b/Sqrt[a + b], 1/Sqrt[a + b], a + b, -(1/2), 1/x}

Receiving of similar expansion as well for the standard **Integrate** function which has rather essential restrictions on use of arbitrary expressions as integration variables is presented an quite natural to us. Two variants of such expansion in the form of the simple procedures **Int** and **Int1** which are based on the previous **Subs** procedure have been proposed for the given purpose, whose source codes and examples of application are represented below.

In[2841]:= **Int[x_, y_] := Module[{a},**
If[! HowAct[y], Integrate[x, y], Simplify[Subs[Integrate[Subs[x, y, a], a], a, y]]]]

In[2842]:= **Int1[x_, y_] := Module[{a}, If[! HowAct[y], Integrate[x, y], Simplify[ReplaceAll1[Integrate[ReplaceAll1[x, y, a], a], a, y]]]]**

In[2843]:= {Int[Sin[a + 1/x^2] + c/x^2, 1/x^2], Int1[Sin[a + 1/x^2] + c/x^2, 1/x^2]}
Out[2843]= {-Cos[a + 1/x^2] + c*Log[1/x^2], c/x^4 - Cos[a + 1/x^2]}
In[2844]:= {Int[Sin[n/x^2] + m/x^2, x^2], Int1[Sin[n/x^2] + m/x^2, x^2]}
Out[2844]= {-n*CosIntegral[n/x^2] + m*Log[x^2] + x^2*Sin[n/x^2], -n*CosIntegral[n/x^2] + m*Log[x^2] + x^2*Sin[n/x^2]}
In[2845]:= **Int1[(a*x^2 + b/x^2)/(c*x^2 + d/x^2), x^2]**
Out[2845]= (a*x^2)/c + ((b*c - a*d)*ArcTan[(Sqrt[c]*x^2)/Sqrt[d]])/(c^(3/2)*Sqrt[d])
In[2846]:= **Integrate[(a*x^2 + b/x^2)/(c*x^2 + d/x^2), x^2]**
Integrate::ilim: Invalid integration variable or limit(s) in x^2.>>
Out[2846]= Integrate[(b/x^2 + a*x^2)/(d/x^2 + c*x^2), x^2]

Meanwhile, a simple enough **Subs1** function can be considered as a certain extension and complement of the previous **Subs** procedure. The call **Subs1[x, {y, z}]** returns the result of replacement of all occurrences of a *y* subexpression of an expression *x* onto a *z* expression; at that, the function call qua of the second argument allows both the simple 2-element list, and the list of the *ListList* type. The function call **Subs1Q[x, y]** returns *True* if a call **Subs1[x,** *y*] is allowable, and *False* otherwise. The next fragment represents source codes of functions **Subs1** and **Subs1Q** with examples of their application.

In[2700]:= **Subs1[x_, y_ /; ListQ[y] && Length[y] == 2 || ListListQ[y]] :=**
ToExpression[StringReplace[ToString[FullForm[x]], Map[ToString[FullForm[#[[1]]]] ->
ToString[FullForm[#[[2]]]] &, If[ListListQ[y], y, {y}]]]]

In[2703]:= **Subs1[(a/b + d)/(c/b + h/b), {{1/b, t^2}, {d, 590}}]**
Out[2703]= (590 + a*t^2)/(c*t^2 + h*t^2)

In[2718]:= **Subs1Q[x_, y_] := SameQ[x, Subs1[Subs1[x, y],**
If[ListListQ[y], Map[Reverse, y], Reverse[y]]]]

In[2719]:= **Subs1Q[(a/b + d)/(c/b + h/b), {{1/b, t^2}, {d, 90}}]**
Out[2719]= True

In[2732]:= **Integrate2[x_, y__] := Module[{a, b, d, c = Map[Unique["gs"] &,**
Range[1, Length[{y}]]]}, a = Riffle[{y}, c]; a = If[Length[{y}] == 1, a, Partition[a, 2]];
d = Integrate[Subs1[x, a], Sequences[c]];
{Simplify[Subs1[d, If[ListListQ[a], Map[Reverse, a], Reverse[a]]]], Map[Remove, c]}[[1]]]

In[2733]:= **Integrate2[(a/b + d)/(c/b + h/b), 1/b, d]**
Out[2733]= (d*((2*a)/b + d*Log[1/b]))/(2*(c + h))

In[2734]:= **Integrate2[x^2*y, x, y]**
Out[2734]= (x^3*y^2)/6

In[2735]:= **Integrate2[1/b, 1/b]**
Out[2735]= 1/(2*b^2)

In[2736]:= **Integrate2[(a/b + d)/(c/b + h/t), 1/b, 1/t]**
Out[2736]= -((c*t*(-2*a*b*h + a*c*t + 4*b*c*d*t) + 2*(b*h + c*t)*
(a*b*h - a*c*t - 2*b*c*d*t)*Log[c/b + h/t])/(4*b^2*c^2*h*t^2))

In[2737]:= **Integrate2[Sqrt[a + Sqrt[c + d]*b], Sqrt[c + d]]**
Out[2737]= (2*(a + b*Sqrt[c + d])^(3/2))/(3*b)

In[2738]:= **Integrate2[(a/b + d^2)/(c/b + h/b), 1/b, d^2]**
Out[2738]= (2*a*d^2 + b*d^4*Log[1/b])/(2*b*c + 2*b*h)

In[2739]:= **Integrate2[(a*x^2 + b/x^2)/(c*x^2 + d/x^2), x^2, d/x^2]**
Out[2739]= (-c*x^4*(4*b*c - 2*a*d + a*c*x^4) + 2*(d + c*x^4)*
(2*b*c - a*d + a*c*x^4)*Log[(d + c*x^4)/x^2])/(4*c^2*x^4)

In[2743]:= **Diff1[x_, y__] := Module[{a, b, d, c=Map[Unique["s"] &, Range[1, Length[{y}]]]},**
a = Riffle[{y}, c]; a = If[Length[{y}] == 1, a, Partition[a, 2]];
d = D[Subs1[x, a], Sequences[c]];
{Simplify[Subs1[d, If[ListListQ[a], Map[Reverse, a], Reverse[a]]]], Map[Remove, c]}[[1]]]

In[2744]:= **Diff1[(a*x^2 + b/x^2)/(c*x^2 + d/x^2), x^2, d/x^2]**
Out[2744]= (x^4*(2*b*c - a*d + a*c*x^4))/(d + c*x^4)^3

In[2745]:= **Diff1[c + a/b, c + a/b]**
Out[2745]= 1

In[2746]:= **Diff1[(c + a/b)*Sin[b + 1/x^2], a/b, 1/x^2]**
Out[2746]= Cos[b + 1/x^2]

In[2747]:= **Diff1[(c + a/b)*Sin[d/c + 1/x^2], 1/c, a/b, 1/x^2]**

Out[2747]= -d*Sin[d/c + 1/x^2]

On the basis of the previous **Subs1** function an useful enough procedure has been realized, whose call **Integrate2**[*x, y*] provides integrating of an expression *x* on the subexpressions determined by an *y* sequence. At that, the procedure with the returned result by means of **Simplify** function performs a sequence of algebraic and other transformations and returns the simplest form it finds. The previous fragment represents source code of the **Integrate2** procedure along with typical examples of its use. While the procedure call **Diff1**[*x, y*] which is also realized on the basis of the **Subs1** returns the differentiation result of an arbitrary *x* expression on the generalized {*y, z, ...*} variables which can be an arbitrary expressions. The result is returned in the *simplified* form on the basis of the **Simplify** function. The previous fragment represents source code of the **Diff1** procedure with examples of its application.

The following procedure allows to eliminate the restrictions inherent in means of the above so-called *Subs*-group. The procedure call **SubsInExpr**[*x, r*] returns the result of substitution in an expression *x* given in the form **Hold**[*x*] of the rigth parts of a rule or their list *r* instead of occurences of the left parts corresponding them. In addition, all the left an the rigth parts of *r* rules should be encoded in the *Hold*-form, otherwise the procedure call returns $Failed with printing of the appropriate message. The following fragment represents source code of the **SubsInExpr** procedure with examples of its application.

In[4016]:= SubsInExpr[x_ /; Head[x] == Hold, r_ /; RuleQ[r] || ListRulesQ[r]] :=
Module[{a, b, c, f},
c = Map[Head[(#)[[1]]] === Hold && Head[(#)[[2]]] === Hold &, Set[b, Flatten[{r}]]];
If[! And @@ c, Print["Incorrect tuple of factual arguments"]; $Failed,
f[t_] := StringTake[ToString1[t], {6, -2}]; a = f[x];
c = Map[Rule[f[#[[1]]], "(" <> f[#[[2]]] <> ")"] &, b];
ToExpression[StringReplaceVars[a, c]]]]

In[4017]:= SubsInExpr[Hold[1/(a + 1/x^2)], Hold[x^2] -> Hold[Sin[t]]]
Out[4017]= 1/(a + Csc[t])
In[4018]:= SubsInExpr[Hold[(a + b^3)/(c + d^(-2))], Hold[d^-2] -> Hold[Sin[t]]]
Out[4018]= (a + b^3)/(c + Sin[t])
In[4019]:= SubsInExpr[Hold[1/x^2], Hold[1/x^2] -> Hold[Sin[t]]]
Out[4019]= Sin[t]
In[4020]:= SubsInExpr[Hold[1/x^2], Hold[1/x^2] -> Sin[t]]
"Incorrect tuple of factual arguments"
Out[4020]= $Failed
In[4021]:= SubsInExpr[Hold[1/(a + 1/x^2)], Hold[1/x^2] -> Hold[Sin[t]]]
Out[4021]= 1/(a + Sin[t])
In[4022]:= SubsInExpr[Hold[1/x^2], Hold[x^2] -> Hold[Sin[t]]]
Out[4022]= Csc[t]

The function call **SubsInExpr1**[*x, r*] analogously to the above **SubsInExpr** procedure also returns the result of substitution in an expression *x* given in the string format of the rigth parts of a rule or their list *r* instead of occurences of the left parts corresponding them. At that, in contrast to the the **SubsInExpr** procedure all the left an the rigth parts of the *r* rules should be also coded in the string format like its first argument, otherwise the function call is returned unevaluated. The following fragment presents source code of the **SubsInExpr1** function with examples of its application.

In[4032]:= **SubsInExpr1[x_ /; StringQ[x], r_ /; (RuleQ[r] || ListRulesQ[r]) && (And @@ Map[StringQ[(#)[[1]]] && StringQ[(#)[[2]]] &, Flatten[{r}]])] := ToExpression[StringReplaceVars[x, r]]**

In[4033]:= **SubsInExpr1["1/(a + 1/x^2)", {"x^2" -> "Sin[t]", "a" -> "agn"}]**
Out[4033]= 1/(agn + Csc[t])
In[4034]:= **SubsInExpr1["(a + b^3)/(c + d^(-2))", "d^(-2)" -> "Sin[t]"]**
Out[4034]= (a + b^3)/(c + Sin[t])
In[4035]:= **SubsInExpr1["1/x^2", "1/x^2" -> "Sin[t]"]**
Out[4035]= Sin[t]
In[4036]:= **SubsInExpr1["1/x^2", "x^2" -> "Sin[t]"]**
Out[4036]= Csc[t]

The represented variants of realization of the means **Df, Df1, Df2, Diff1, Diff2, Int, Int1, Integrate2, ReplaceAll1, Subs, Subs1, SubsInExpr** and **SubsInExpr1** illustrate different receptions enough useful in a number of problems of programming in the *Mathematica* system and, first of all, in problems of the system character. Moreover, the above means essentially extend the appropriate system means.

The previous means, expanding similar standard means, at the same time have the certain restrictions. The following means eliminate the defects inherent in the above and standard means, being the most universal in this class for today. As a basis of the following means is the **ToStringRational** procedure. The call **ToStringRational[x]** returns a x expression in the string format that is very convenient for expressions processing, including the replacements of subexpressions, integrating and differentiation on the subexpressions other than simple symbols. Whereas the procedure call **SubsExpr[x, y]** returns the result of substitutions in a x expression of right parts instead of occurences in x expression of left parts defined by a rule or their list y. At last, the next two procedures **Integrate3** and **Differentiation** provide the integrating and differentiation on variables as which can be subexpressions different from simple symbols. The call **Differentiation[x, y, z, ...]** returns result of differentiation of a x expression on subexpressions which can be difer from simple symbols defined by the {y, z, ...} tuple of arguments starting from the second. Whereas the procedure call **Integrate3[x, y, z, ...]** returns the result of integraiting of a x expression on subexpressions that can be difer from simple symbols defined by the {y, z, ...} tuple of arguments starting from the second. It should be noted, the **Integrate3** and **Differentiation** procedures return the result processed by means of standard **Simplify** function which performs a sequence of algebraic and other transformations returning the simplest form it finds. The fragment below represents source code of the above four procedures with examples of their application.

In[4172]:= **ToStringRational[x_] :=**
Module[{a = "(" <> StringReplace[ToString1[x] <> ")", " " -> ""], b, c = {}, h, p, t = "", n},
b = Map[#[[1]] - 1 &, StringPosition[a, "^(-"]];
Do[h = ""; p = SyntaxQ[StringTake[a, {b[[j]]}]];
If[p, Do[h = StringTake[a, {j}];
If[! SyntaxQ[h], AppendTo[c, j + 1]; Break[], 75], {j, b[[j]], 1, -1}],

Do[h = StringTake[a, {j}]; t = h <> t;
If[SyntaxQ[t], AppendTo[c, j]; Break[], 75], {j, b[[j]], 1, -1}]], {j, 1, Length[b]}];
h = StringInsert[a, "1/", c]; h = StringTake[StringReplace[h, "^(-" -> "^("], {2, -2}];
h = StringReplace[h, "1/" -> ToString[n] <> "/"];
h = ToString1[ToExpression[h]]; h = StringReplace[h, ToString[n] -> "1"]]
In[4173]:= ToStringRational[1/x^2 + 1/(1 + 1/(a + b)^2) + 1/x^3]
Out[4173]= "1/(1 + 1/(a + b)^2) + 1/x^3 + 1/x^2"
In[4174]:= ToStringRational[a*b/x^3 + 1/x^(3/(b[t] + 2)) + Sin[a + 1/x^3] +
1/(x^2 + m) - 1/x^3]
Out[4174]= "(a*b)/x^3 - 1/x^3 + 1/x^(3/(2 + b[t])) + 1/(m + x^2) + Sin[a + 1/x^3]"
In[4175]:= ToStringRational[1/(1 + 1/x^2 + 1/x^3) + 1/(1 + 1/(a + b + 1/x^3)^2) +
F[1/(1 + 1/x^3)]]
Out[4175]= "1/(1 + 1/(a + b + 1/x^3)^2) + 1/(1 + 1/x^3 + 1/x^2) + F[1/(1 + 1/x^3)]"
In[4176]:= SubsExpr[x_, y_ /; RuleQ[y] || ListRulesQ[y]] :=
Module[{a = If[RuleQ[y], {y}, y], b = ToStringRational[x], c},
c = Map[Rule[#[[1]], #[[2]]] &, Map[Map[ToStringRational, {#[[1]], #[[2]]}] &, a]];
ToExpression[StringReplace[b, c]]]
In[4177]:= SubsExpr[a*b/x^3 + 1/x^(3/(b[t] + 2)) + 1/f[a + 1/x^3]^2 +
1/(x^2 + m) - 1/x^3, {x^2 -> av, x^3 -> gs}]
Out[4177]= -(1/gs) + (a*b)/gs + 1/(av + m) + x^(-(3/(2 + b[t]))) + 1/f[a + 1/gs]^2
In[4178]:= SubsExpr[1/(1 + 1/x^2 + 1/x^3) + 1/(1 + 1/(a + b + 1/x^3)^2) + 1/(1 + 1/x^3),
{x^2 -> m, x^3 -> n}]
Out[4178]= 1/(1 + 1/(a + b + 1/n)^2) + 1/(1 + 1/n) + 1/(1 + 1/m + 1/n)
In[4179]:= Replace[1/(1 + 1/x^2 + 1/x^3) + 1/(1 + 1/(a + b + 1/x^3)^2) + 1/(1 + 1/x^3),
{x^2 -> m, x^3 -> n}, All]
Out[4179]= 1/(1 + 1/(a + b + 1/x^3)^2) + 1/(1 + 1/x^3) + 1/(1 + 1/x^3 + 1/x^2)
In[4180]:= Differentiation[x_, y__] := Module[{a = {y}, b = x, c},
c = Map[Unique["g"] &, Range[1, Length[a]]];
Do[b = SubsExpr[b, a[[j]] -> c[[j]]], {j, 1, Length[a]}]; b = D[b, Sequences[c]];
Simplify[SubsExpr[b, Map[c[[#]] -> a[[#]] &, Range[1, Length[a]]]]]]
In[4181]:= Differentiation[a*b/x^3 + 1/x^(3/(b[t] + 2)) + Sin[a + 1/x^3] +
1/(x^2 + m) - 1/x^3, x^3]
Out[4181]= -((-1 + a*b + Cos[a + 1/x^3])/x^6)
In[4182]:= Differentiation[a*b/x^3 + 1/x^(3/(b[t] + x^2)) + Sin[a + 1/x^3] +
1/(x^2 + m) - 1/x^3, b[t], x^2]
Out[4182]= -((3*x^(-(3/(x^2 + b[t])))*(2*x^2 + 2*b[t] - 3*Log[x])*Log[x])/(x^2 + b[t])^4)
In[4183]:= Differentiation[1/(1 + 1/x^2 + 1/x^3) + 1/(1 + 1/(a + b + 1/x^3)^2) +
1/(1 + 1/x^3), 1/x^3, x^2]
Out[4183]= -((2*x^5)/(1 + x + x^3)^3)
In[4184]:= Integrate3[x_, y__] := Module[{a = {y}, b = x, c},
c = Map[Unique["g"] &, Range[1, Length[a]]];
Do[b = SubsExpr[b, a[[j]] -> c[[j]]], {j, 1, Length[a]}]; b = Integrate[b, Sequences[c]];

Simplify[SubsExpr[b, Map[c[[#]] -> a[[#]] &, Range[1, Length[a]]]]]

In[4185]:= **Integrate3[1/x^2 + 1/(x^2 + x^3), x^2, x^3]**
Out[4185]= x^2*(-1 + x*Log[x^2] + (1 + x)*Log[x^2*(1 + x)])

In[4186]:= **Integrate3[1/x^2 + 1/(x^2 + x^3), 1/x^2, x^3]**
Out[4186]= (x + 2*Log[x^2*(1 + x)])/(2*x^2)

In[4187]:= **Integrate3[1/(1 + 1/x^2 + 1/x^3) + 1/(1 + 1/(a + b + 1/x^3)^2) + 1/(1 + 1/x^3), 1/x^3, x^2]**
Out[4187]= 1/x - x^2*ArcTan[a + b + 1/x^3] + x^2*Log[1 + 1/x^3] + Log[1 + 1/x + x^2]/(1 + 1/x^3) + x^2*Log[1 + 1/x + x^2]

Unlike **ToString1** procedure the **ToStringRational** procedure provides convenient enough representation of rational expressions in string format, allowing to process the expressions more effectively by means of strings processing tools. The **ToStringRational** and **SubsExpr** procedures, generalizing means of the same orientation, meanwhile, does not belittle them illustrating different useful enough methods of the programming with their advantages and shortcomings.

The fragment below represents the means having both independent value, and a number of useful enough appendices in programming. So, two useful functions used in the subsequent procedures of the fragment preface this fragment. The call **ListRulesQ[*x*]** returns *True* if *x* is a list of rules of the form *a -> b*, and *False* otherwise. While the **Map17** function generalizes the standard **Map** function onto case of a list of rules as its second actual argument. The call **Map17[*f*, {{*a -> b, c -> d, ...*}]** where *f* – the symbol returns the result of format {*f*[*a*] -> *f*[*b*], *f*[*c*] -> *f*[*d*], ...} without demanding any additional explanations in view of its transparency. As a whole, so–called *Map* group consists of 25 our means: **Mapp, Map1 ÷ Map24** [48,50].

Whereas the procedure call **Diff[*x, y, z, ...*]** returns result of differentiation of an expression *x* on the generalized variables {*x,y,z,...*} that are arbitrary expressions. The result is returned in the simplified view on the basis of the **Simplify** function. The procedure call **Integral1[*x, y, z, ...*]** returns the result of integrating of an expression x on the generalized variables {*x, y, z, ...*} which are arbitrary expressions. The result is returned in the simplified view on basis of standard **Simplify** function. The next fragment represents the source codes of the above tools **ListRulesQ, Map17, Diff** and **Integral1** along with typical examples of their use.

In[3321]:= **ListRulesQ[x_ /; ListQ[x]] := AllTrue[Map[RuleQ[#] &, Flatten[x]], TrueQ]**

In[3322]:= **ListRulesQ[{a -> b, c -> d, t -> g, w -> v, h}]**
Out[3322]= False

In[3323]:= **ListRulesQ[{a -> b, c -> d, t -> g, w -> v, h -> 90}]**
Out[3323]= True

In[3324]:= **Map17[x_, y_ /; RuleQ[y] || ListRulesQ[y]] :=
If[RuleQ[y], Map[x, y], Map[Map[x, #] &, y]]**

In[3325]:= **Map17[F, a -> b]**
Out[3325]= F[a] -> F[b]

In[3326]:= **Map17[F, {a -> b, c -> d, t -> g, w -> v, h -> 90}]**
Out[3326]= {F[a] -> F[b], F[c] -> F[d], F[t] -> F[g], F[w] -> F[v], F[h] -> F[90]}

In[3432]:= **Diff[x_, y__] :=**

Module[{c = {}, d = {}, b = Length[{y}], t = {}, k = 1, h = x, n = g,
a = Map[ToString, Map[InputForm, {y}]]},
Clear[g]; While[k <= b, AppendTo[c, Unique[g]]; AppendTo[d, ToString[c[[k]]]];
AppendTo[t, a[[k]] -> d[[k]]];
h = ToExpression[StringReplace[ToString[h // InputForm], t[[k]]]]; h = D[h, c[[k]]];
h = ReplaceAll[h, Map[ToExpression, Part[t[[k]], 2] -> Part[t[[k]], 1]]]; k++];
g = n; Map[Clear, c]; Simplify[h]]

In[3433]:= **Diff[Sin[x^2]*Cos[1/b^3], 1/b^3, x^2]**
Out[3433]= -Cos[x^2]*Sin[1/b^3]
In[3434]:= **Diff[(a + b)/(c + d), a + b, c + d]**
Out[3434]= -(1/(c + d)^2)
In[3435]:= **Diff[(a + b) + m/(c + d), a + b, 1/(c + d)]**
Out[3435]= 0
In[3436]:= **Diff[1/Sqrt[a + b]*(a + b) + Tan[Sqrt[a + b] + c], Sqrt[a + b], a + b]**
Out[3436]= (Sec[Sqrt[a + b] + c]^2*Tan[Sqrt[a + b] + c])/Sqrt[a + b]

In[2257]:= **Integral1[x_, y__] :=**
Module[{d = {}, t = {}, k = 1, h = x, n = g, a = Map[ToString, Map[InputForm, {y}]],
c = {}, b = Length[{y}]},
Clear[g]; While[k <= b, AppendTo[c, Unique[g]]; AppendTo[d, ToString[c[[k]]]];
AppendTo[t, a[[k]] -> d[[k]]];
h = ToExpression[StringReplace[ToString[h // InputForm], t[[k]]]]; h = Integrate[h, c[[k]]];
h = ReplaceAll[h, Map[ToExpression, Part[t[[k]], 2] -> Part[t[[k]], 1]]]; k++];
g = n; Map[Clear, c]; Simplify[h]]

In[2258]:= **g = 90; Integral1[Sin[x^2] + Cos[1/b^3], 1/b^3, x^2]**
Out[2258]= -(Cos[x^2]/b^3) + x^2*Sin[1/b^3]
In[2259]:= **Integral1[Sin[x] + Cos[x], x]**
Out[2259]= -Cos[x] + Sin[x]
In[2260]:= **Integral1[(Sin[x] + Cos[y])*z, x, y, z]**
Out[2260]= (-(1/2))*z^2*(y*Cos[x] - x*Sin[y])
In[2261]:= **Integral1[(a + b)/(c + d), a + b, c + d]**
Out[2261]= (1/2)*(a + b)^2*Log[c + d]
In[2262]:= **Integral1[(a + b) + m/(c + d), a + b, 1/(c + d)]**
Out[2262]= ((a + b)*(a*(c + d) + b*(c + d) + 2*m))/(2*(c + d)^2)
In[2263]:= **Integral1[(a + b)/(c + d), a + b, c + d, c + d]**
Out[2263]= 1/2*(a + b)^2*(c + d)*(-1 + Log[c + d])

Thus, the procedures **Diff** and **Integral1** have the certain limitations that at usage demand corresponding wariness; some idea of such restrictions is illustrated by the next very simple example, namely:

In[3322]:= **Diff[(a + b*m)/(c + d*n), a + b, c + d]**
Out[3322]= -(m/((c + d)^2*n))
In[3323]:= **Integral1[(a + b*m)/(c + d*n), a + b, c + d]**
Out[3323]= ((a + b)^2*m*Log[c + d])/(2*n)

With the view of elimination of these shortcomings 2 modifications of the functions **Replace** and **ReplaceAll** in the form of the procedures **Replace4** and **ReplaceAll2** have been created respectively. These procedures expand standard means and allow to code the previous two procedures **Integral1** and **Diff** with wider range of correct appendices in the context of use of the generalized variables of differentiation and integration. The call **Replace4**[x, a –> b] returns the result of application to an expression x of a substitution a –> b, when as its left part an arbitrary expression is allowed. At absence in the x expression of occurrences of the subexpression a the initial x expression is returned. Unlike previous, the call **ReplaceAll2**[x, r] returns the result of application to a x expression of a r rule or consecutive application of rules from the r list; as the left parts of rules any expressions are allowed.

At last, the procedure call **ReplaceAll3**[x, y, z], where x – an expression, y – a rule or their list and z – undefined symbol, is analogous to the function call **ReplaceAll**[x, y] by allowing to obtain through z argument the two-element list where the first element defines the list of rules from y that are inapplicable to the x expression, while the second element defines the list of subexpressions which are unsuitable for replacing in the x expression. The following fragment represents source code of the **ReplaceAll3** procedure along with examples of its application. In the next fragment source codes of the procedures **ReplaceAll2**, **ReplaceAll3** and **Replace4** along with typical examples of their application are represented.

In[2445]:= **Replace4[x_, r_ /; RuleQ[r]] := Module[{a, b, c, h},**
{a, b} = {ToString[x // InputForm], Map[ToString, Map[InputForm, r]]};
c = StringPosition[a, Part[b, 1]];
If[c == {}, x, If[Head[Part[r, 1]] == Plus, h = Map[If[(#[[1]] == 1 || MemberQ[{" ", "(", "[", "{"},
StringTake[a, {#[[1]] - 1, #[[1]] - 1}]]) && (#[[2]] === StringLength[a] || MemberQ[{" ", ")",
"]", "}", ","}, StringTake[a, {#[[2]] + 1, #[[2]] + 1}]]), #] &, c],
h = Map[If[(#[[1]] === 1 || ! Quiet[SymbolQ[StringTake[a, {#[[1]] - 1, #[[1]] - 1}]]]) &&
(#[[2]] === StringLength[a] || ! Quiet[SymbolQ[StringTake[a, {#[[2]] + 1, #[[2]] + 1}]]]), #]
&, c]]; h = Select[h, ! SameQ[#, Null] &];
ToExpression[StringReplacePart[a, "(" <> Part[b, 2] <> ")", h]]]]

In[2446]:= **Replace4[(c + d*x)/(c + d + x), c + d –> a + b]**
Out[2446]= (c + d*x)/(a + b + x)
In[2447]:= **Replace[Sqrt[a + b*x^2*d + c], x^2 –> a + b]**
Out[2447]= Sqrt[a + c + b*d*x^2]
In[2448]:= **Replace4[Sqrt[a + b*x^2 *d + c], x^2 –> a + b]**
Out[2448]= Sqrt[a + c + b*(a + b)*d]
In[2458]:= **ReplaceAll2[x_, r_ /; RuleQ[r] || ListRulesQ[r]] := Module[{a = x, k = 1},**
If[RuleQ[r], Replace4[x, r], While[k <= Length[r], a = Replace4[a, r[[k]]]; k++]; a]]
In[2459]:= **ReplaceAll[Sqrt[a + b*x^2*d + c], {x^2 –> a + b, a + c –> avz}]**
Out[2459]= Sqrt[avz + b*d*x^2]
In[2460]:= **ReplaceAll2[Sqrt[a + b*x^2 *d + c], {x^2 –> a + b, a + c –> avz}]**
Out[2460]= Sqrt[avz + b*(a + b)*d]
In[2461]:= **ReplaceAll2[x*y*z, {x –> 42, y –> 90, z –> 500}]**
Out[2461]= 1890000
In[2462]:= **ReplaceAll2[Sin[a + b*x^2*d + c*x^2], x^2 –> a + b]**

Out[2462]= Sin[a + (a + b)*c + b*(a + b)*d]

In[2472]:= ReplaceAll3[x_, y_ /; RuleQ[y] || ListQ[y] && And1[Map[RuleQ, y]], z___] :=
Module[{a = x, b, c = {}, r = Flatten[{y}]},
Do[Set[b, ReplaceAll[a, r[[j]]]]; If[a === b, AppendTo[c, r[[j]]], 6]; a = b, {j, 1, Length[r]}];
If[{z} != {} && NullQ[z], z = {c, Map[#[[1]] &, c]}, 6]; a]

In[2473]:= ReplaceAll3[Sin[x]*(a + x^2), Sin -> Cos]
Out[2473]= (a + x^2)*Cos[x]
In[2474]:= ReplaceAll3[Sin[x]*(a + x^2), {Sin -> Cos, y -> m}, gs]
Out[2474]= (a + x^2)*Cos[x]
In[2475]:= gs
Out[2475]= {{y -> m}, {y}}
In[2476]:= ReplaceAll3[(x^2 + y^2)/(Log[x] + a*x^2/b^2), {b^2 -> c^d, Log[x] -> Sin[t], a*x^2 -> (m + n)}, sv]
Out[2476]= (x^2 + y^2)/((m + n)/b^2 + Sin[t])
In[2477]:= sv
Out[2477]= {{b^2 -> c^d}, {b^2}}

In[2488]:= Difff[x_, y__] := Module[{a = x, a1, a2, a3, b = Length[{y}], c = {}, d, k = 1, n = g},
Clear[g]; While[k <= b, d = {y}[[k]]; AppendTo[c, Unique[g]]; a1 = Replace4[a, d -> c[[k]]];
a2 = D[a1, c[[k]]]; a3 = Replace4[a2, c[[k]] -> d]; a = a3; k++]; g = n; Simplify[a3]]

In[2489]:= Difff[(a + b)/(c + d + x), a + b, c + d]
Out[2489]= -(1/(c + d + x)^2)
In[2490]:= Difff[(a + b*m)/(c + d*n), a + b, c + d]
Out[2490]= 0

In[2588]:= Integral2[x_, y__] := Module[{a=x, a1, a2, a3, b = Length[{y}], c = {}, d, k=1, n=g},
Clear[g]; While[k <= b, d = {y}[[k]]; AppendTo[c, Unique[g]];
a1 = Replace4[a, d -> c[[k]]]; a2 = Integrate[a1, c[[k]]];
a3 = Replace4[a2, c[[k]] -> d]; a = a3; k++]; g = n; Simplify[a3]]

In[2589]:= Integral2[(a + b*m)/(c + d*n), a + b, c + d]
Out[2589]= ((a + b)*(c + d)*(a + b*m))/(c + d*n)
In[2590]:= Integral2[Sqrt[a + c + b*(a + b)*d], a + c, a + b]
Out[2590]= (2/3)*(a + b)*(a + c + a*b*d + b^2*d)^(3/2)
In[2591]:= Integral2[Sqrt[a + c + h*g + b*d], c + h, b*d]
Out[2591]= (2/3)*(c + h)*(a + c + b*d + g*h)^(3/2)
In[2592]:= Integral2[(a + c + h*g + b*d)/(c + h), c + h, b*d]
Out[2592]= (1/2)*b*d*(2*a + 2*c + b*d + 2*g*h)*Log[c + h]
In[2593]:= Integral2[(c + h*m)/(c + h), c + h*m]
Out[2593]= (c + h*m)^2/(2*(c + h))

On the basis of the **Replace4** procedure the procedures **Diff** and **Integral1** can be expanded the procedures **Diff** and **Integral1**. The call **Difff**[*x, y, z,...*] returns result of *differentiation* of an arbitrary expression *x* on the generalized variables {*y, z, h, t,...*} that are any expressions. The result is returned in the simplified form on the basis of the standard **Simplify** function. Whereas the call **Integral2**[*x, y, z,...*] returns result of integration of an expression *x* on the generalized variables {y, z, h, ...} that are arbitrary expressions. The result is returned in the simplified form on the basis of the **Simplify**. In the following fragment the source codes of the above means with examples of application are represented. The means given above are rather useful in many cases of manipulations with algebraic expressions which are based on a set of rules, including their symbolical differentiation and integration on the generalized variables that are arbitrary algebraic expressions.

At last, the **Replace5** function basing on the standard **InputString** function provides wide enough opportunities on replacement of subexpressions in expressions in interactive mode. The function call **Replace5[*x*]** creates window through which an expression is introduced, after reading of expression to it a rule or their list *x* is applied, returning the result of such replacements. In addition, the function call tests the *x* rules for the real correctness of the expressions that make up rules; in case of erroneous rules the call is returned unevaluated. Furthermore, both parts of the rules are coded in the string format. In addition, for testing concerning the real correctness the **ExpressionQ** procedure is used that rather essentially generalizes standard **SyntaxQ** function. While the function call in case of existing of errors in the introduced expression returns $*Failed* with printing of the appropriate message. The fragment below represents the source code of the **Replace5** function with examples of its application. So, the first example represents the result of subexpressions replacements in the expression a*b/x^3 + 1/x^(3/(b[t] + 2)) + Sin[t] + 1/x^2.

In[4070]:= **Replace5[x_ /; (RuleQ[x] && StringQ[x[[1]]] && StringQ[x[[2]]] &&
ExpressionQ[x[[1]]] && ExpressionQ[x[[2]]]) || ListRulesQ[x] &&
(And @@ Map[StringQ[#[[1]]] && StringQ[#[[2]]] && ExpressionQ[#[[1]]] &&
ExpressionQ[#[[2]]] &, x])] :=**
Quiet[Check[ToExpression[StringReplace[StringReplace[InputString[], " " -> ""],
Map[Rule @@ Map[StringReplace[#, " " -> ""] &, {#[[1]], #[[2]]}] &, Flatten[{x}]]]],
Print["Incorrect expression"]; $Failed, ToExpression::sntxi]]

In[4071]:= **Replace5[{"x^2" -> "mnp", "x^3" -> "agn", "3/(b[t]+2)" -> "vsg"}]**
Out[4071]= (a*b)/agn + 1/mnp + x^-vsg + Sin[t]
In[4072]:= **Replace[a*b/x^3 + 1/x^(3/(b[t] + 2)) + Sin[t] + 1/x^2, {x^2 -> mnp, x^3 -> agn, 3/(b[t] + 2) -> vsg}, All]**
Out[4072]= (a*b)/x^3 + 1/x^2 + x^(-(3/(2 + b[t]))) + Sin[t]
In[4073]:= **Replace5[{"x^2" -> "np", "x^3" -> "agn", "3/(b[t]+2)" -> "vsg", "a" -> "xyz/0"}]**
Out[4073]= Replace5[{"x^2" -> "np", "x^3" -> "agn", "3/(b[t]+2)" -> "vsg", "a" -> "xyz/0"}]
In[4074]:= **Replace5[{"x^2" -> "mnp", "x^3" -> "agn", "3/(b[t]+2)" -> "vsg"}]**
"Incorrect expression"
Out[4074]= $Failed

At last, the following procedure is intended for replacement of elements of a list which are located on the given nesting levels and meet certain conditions. The call **Replace6[*x, y, z, h*]** returns the result of replacement of elements of a *x* list that are located on the nesting levels determined by nonempty integer list *y* and that meet conditions defined by a *z* list of pure functions onto expressions defined by a nonempty *h* list. In addition, between lists *y*, *z* and *h* one–to–one correspondence in the context of equality of their lengths is supposed. At that, in case of different lengths of lists the general for them **Min[Map[Length, {*y, z, h*}]]** length is chosen. In case of the erroneous or special situations caused by an incorrect tuple of factual arguments, the procedure call returns an initial list or *$Failed*, or is returned *unevaluated*. The next fragment presents source code of the **Replace6** procedure with examples of its use.

In[4182]:= Replace6[x_ /; ListQ[x], y_ /; PosIntListQ[y] && y != {}, z_ /; ListQ[z] && And1[Map[PureFuncQ, z]], h_ /; ListQ[h] && h != {}] :=
Module[{a = ElemsOnLevelList[x], b, c = {}, d, Res = x, p, g},
b = Select[y, MemberQ[Map[#[[1]] &, a], #] &];
If[b == {}, $Failed,
Do[AppendTo[c, Select[a[[j]][[2]], z[[j]]]], {j, 1, Length[z]}];
p = Min[Map[Length, {c, h, z}]]; {c, g, d} = {c[[1 ;; p]], h[[1 ;; p]], z[[1 ;; p]]};
Do[Res = Replace[Res, GenRules[c[[j]], g[[j]]], b[[j]]], {j, 1, p}]; Res]]
In[4183]:= Replace6[{1, 2, 3, 4, 7, {5, 6, 12, {8, 9, 10, 11, 17, 18}}}, {1, 2, 3}, {OddQ[#] &, EvenQ[#] &, PrimeQ[#] &}, {avz, agn, vsv}]
Out[4183]= {1, 2, avz, 4, avz, {5, agn, agn, {8, 9, 10, vsv, vsv, 18}}}
In[4184]:= Replace6[{1, 2, 3, 4, 7, {5, 6, 12, {8, 9, 10, 11, 17, 18}}}, {1, 3}, {OddQ[#] &, EvenQ[#] &}, {avz, agn, vsv}]
Out[4184]= {1, 2, avz, 4, avz, {5, agn, agn, {8, 9, 10, 11, 17, 18}}}

The **SEQ** procedure serves as some analog of the built-in *seq* function of the same name of *Maple*, generating sequences of values. The call **SEQ**[*x*, *y*, *z*] returns the list of values *x*[*y*], where *y* changes within *z* = *m* ;; *n*, or within *z* = *m* ;; *n* ;; *p* with *p* step; at that, values {*m*, *n*, *p*} can accept only positive numerical values; at *m* <= *n p* is considered positive, otherwise negative. Of examples of the next fragment the principle of formation of the list of values depending on the format of the third argument is well visually looked through. In case of zero or negative value of the 3rd argument a call **SEQ**[*x*, *y*, *z*] is returned unevaluated. The next fragment represents source code of the **SEQ** procedure along with typical examples of its application.

In[2334]:= SEQ[x_, y_ /; SymbolQ[y], z_ /; Head[z] == Span] :=
Module[{a = ToString[z], b = {}, c, d = ToString[y], p},
c = ToExpression[StringSplit[a, " ;; "]];
If[DeleteDuplicates[Map[NumberQ, c]] != {True} ||
DeleteDuplicates[Map[Positive, c]] != {True}, Return[Defer[Seq[x, y, z]]],
If[Length[c] > 2 && c[[3]] == 0, Return[Defer[Seq[x, y, z]]], If[c[[1]] <= c[[2]], p = 1, p = 2]]];
For[y = c[[1]], If[p == 1, y <= c[[2]], y >= c[[2]] - If[p == 1 && Length[c] == 2 ||
p == 2 && Length[c] == 2, 0, c[[3]] - 1]],
If[Length[c] == 2, If[p == 1, y++, y--], If[p == 1, y += c[[3]], y -= c[[3]]]], b = Append[b, x]];
{ToExpression["Clear[" <> d <> "]"], b}[[2]]]
In[2335]:= SEQ[F[k], k, 18 ;; 26]
Out[2335]= {F[18], F[19], F[20], F[21], F[22], F[23], F[24], F[25], F[26]}
In[2336]:= SEQ[F[t], t, 1 ;; 75 ;; 8]
Out[2336]= {F[1], F[9], F[17], F[25], F[33], F[41], F[49], F[57], F[65], F[73]}
In[2337]:= SEQ[F[t], t, 100 ;; 95]
Out[2337]= {F[100], F[99], F[98], F[97], F[96], F[95]}

In[2338]:= SEQ[F[t], t, 42.74 ;; 80 ;; 6.47]
Out[2338]= {F[42.74], F[49.21], F[55.68], F[62.15], F[68.62], F[75.09]}
In[2339]:= SEQ[F[k], k, 42 ;; 74 ;; –6]
Out[2339]= SEQ[F[k], k, 42 ;; 74 ;; –6]

The call **ExprsInStrQ[x, y]** of an useful procedure returns *True* if a string *x* contains correct expressions, and *False* otherwise. While thru the second optional *y* argument – *an undefinite variable* – a list of expressions which are in *x* is returned. The following fragment represents source code of the **ExprsInStrQ** procedure along with typical examples of its application.

In[2360]:= ExprsInStrQ[x_ /; StringQ[x], y___] :=
Module[{a = {}, c = 1, d, j, b = StringLength[x], k = 1},
For[k = c, k <= b, k++, For[j = k, j <= b, j++, d = StringTake[x, {k, j}];
If[! SymbolQ[d] && SyntaxQ[d], AppendTo[a, d]]]; c++];
a = Select[Map[StringTrim, Map[StringTrim2[#, {"–", "+", " "}, 3] &, a]], ExpressionQ[#] &];
If[a == {}, False, If[{y} != {} && ! HowAct[{y}[[1]]], y = DeleteDuplicates[a]]; True]]
In[2361]:= ExprsInStrQ["a (c + d) – b^2 = Sin[x] h*/+"]
Out[2361]= True
In[2362]:= {ExprsInStrQ["a (c + d) – b^2 = Sin[x] h*/+", t], t}
Out[2362]= {True, {"a*(c + d)", "a*(c + d) – b", "a*(c + d) – b^2", "(c + d)", "(c + d) – b", "(c + d) – b^2", "c + d", "b^2", "2", "Sin[x]", "Sin[x]*h", "in[x]", "in[x]*h", "n[x]", "n[x]*h"}}
In[2363]:= {ExprsInStrQ["n*(a+c)/c   ", h1], h1}
Out[2363]= {True, {"n*(a + c)", "n*(a + c)/c", "(a + c)", "(a + c)/c", "a + c", "c"}}

The procedure below is of a certain interest whose call **FuncToExpr[f, x]** returns the result of applying of a symbol, a block, a function *(including pure functions)* or a module *f* *(except the f symbol all remaining admissible objects shall have arity 1)* to each variable *(excluding the system symbols)* of a *x* expression. While the procedure call **FuncToExpr[f, x, y]** with the 3rd optional *y* argument – *a list of symbols* – returns the result of applying of a symbol, a block, a function *(including pure function)* or a module *f* *(except f symbol all remaining admissible objects shall have arity 1)* to each variable *(excluding the system symbols and symbols from y list)* of a *x* expression. The next fragment represents source code of the **FuncToExpr** procedure along with typical examples of its application.

In[4635]:= FuncToExpr[f_ /; SymbolQ[f] || BlockFuncModQ[f] || PureFuncQ[f], x_,
y___List] := Module[{a = ToString1[x], b, c}, b = ExtrVarsOfStr[a, 2];
b = Select[b, If[{y} == {}, ! SystemQ[#] &, (! SystemQ[#] &&
! MemberQ[Map[ToString, y], #]) &]];
c = Map[# -> ToString[(f)] <> "@@{" <> # <> "}" &, b];
ReplaceAll[x, Map[ToExpressionRule, c]]]

In[4636]:= FuncToExpr[G, (e^2 + m^g)/(x*Sin[x] + Cos[y])]
Out[4636]= (G[e]^2 + G[m]^G[g])/(Cos[G[y]] + G[x]*Sin[G[x]])
In[4637]:= FuncToExpr[If[SymbolQ[#], h, #] &, (e^2 + m^g)/(x*Sin[x] + Cos[y])]
Out[4637]= (h^2 + h^h)/(Cos[h] + h*Sin[h])
In[4638]:= FuncToExpr[G, {a, b, c, d, 75*Sin[y]}]
Out[4638]= {G[a], G[b], G[c], G[d], 75*Sin[G[y]]}

In[4639]:= **FuncToExpr[f, Sin[m + n]/(x*G[x, y] + S[y, t])]**
Out[4639]= Sin[f[m] + f[n]]/(f[x]*f[G][f[x], f[y]] + f[S][f[y], f[t]])
In[4640]:= **FuncToExpr[f, Sin[m + n]/(x*G[x, y] + S[y, t]), {G, S}]**
Out[4640]= Sin[f[m] + f[n]]/(f[x]*G[f[x], f[y]] + S[f[y], f[t]])

In a whole series of problems of manipulation with expressions, including differentiation & integration on the generalized variables, the question of definition of structure of expression through subexpressions entering in it including any variables is topical enough. The given problem is solved by the **ExprComp** procedure, whose the call **ExprComp[*x*]** returns the set of all subexpressions composing *x* expression, whereas the call **ExprComp[*x*, *z*]**, where the second optional *z* argument – *an undefined variable* – through *z* in addition returns the nested list of subexpressions of an arbitrary expression *x* on levels, since the first level. A fragment below represents source code of the **ExprComp** procedure with examples of its application. The source code contains tools from [48,50] such as **HowAct**, **StringTrim1** and **SymbolQ**.

In[3329]:= **ExprComp[x_, z___] := Module[{a = {x}, b, h = {}, F, q, t = 1},**
F[y_ /; ListQ[y]] := Module[{c = {}, d, p, k, j = 1},
For[j = 1, j <= Length[y], j++, k = 1;
While[k < Infinity, p = y[[j]]; a = Quiet[Check[Part[p, k], $Failed]];
If[a === $Failed, Break[], If[! SameQ[a, {}], AppendTo[c, a]]]; k++]]; c];
q = F[a]; While[q != {}, AppendTo[h, q]; q = Flatten[Map[F[{#}] &, q]]];
If[{z} != {} && ! HowAct[z], z = Map[Select[#, ! NumberQ[#] &] &, h]];
Sort[Select[DeleteDuplicates[Flatten[h], Abs[#1] === Abs[#2] &], ! NumberQ[#] &]]]
In[3330]:= **ExprComp[(1/b + Cos[a + Sqrt[c + d]])/(Tan[1/b] - 1/c^2)]**
Out[3330]= {a, 1/b, b, -(1/c^2), c, d, Sqrt[c + d], c + d, a + Sqrt[c + d], Cos[a + Sqrt[c + d]], 1/b + Cos[a + Sqrt[c + d]], Tan[1/b], 1/(-(1/c^2) + Tan[1/b]), -(1/c^2) + Tan[1/b]}
In[3331]:= **ExprComp[(1/b + Cos[a + Sqrt[c + d]])/(Tan[1/b] - 1/c^2), g]**
Out[3331]= {a, 1/b, b, -(1/c^2), c, d, Sqrt[c + d], c + d, a + Sqrt[c + d], Cos[a + Sqrt[c + d]], 1/b + Cos[a + Sqrt[c + d]], Tan[1/b], 1/(-(1/c^2) + Tan[1/b]), -(1/c^2) + Tan[1/b]}
In[3332]:= **g**
Out[3332]= {{1/b + Cos[a + Sqrt[c + d]], 1/(-(1/c^2) + Tan[1/b])},
{1/b, Cos[a + Sqrt[c + d]], -(1/c^2) + Tan[1/b]}, {b, a + Sqrt[c + d], -(1/c^2), Tan[1/b]},
{a, Sqrt[c + d], 1/c^2, 1/b}, {c + d, c, b}, {c, d}}

An arbitrary expression can be formed by means of arithmetic operators of types: **Plus** ('+', '–'), **Times** ('*', /), **Power** ('^'), **Indexed** *(indexes)* or **Function** *(function)*. At that, expression *a – b* has type "+" with operands {*a*, -*b*}; while expression *a/b* – the type "*" with operands {*a*, *b*^(-1)}; an expression *a*^*b* has type "^" with operands {*a*, *b*}; expression *a*[*b*] has "*Function*" type whereas the expression *a*[[*b*]] has the "*Indexed*" type. In this sense it is possible to use a certain indicator **Cost** for estimation of the *complexity* of calculation of arbitrary expressions. The **Cost** is determined as a polynomial from variables which are names of the above three operators, *Indexed* and *Function* with non–negative integer coefficients. The **Cost** procedure provides calculation of *indicator*; its source code with examples of use presents the fragment below. At creation of source code of the **Cost** the **Sequences** procedure has been used. The procedure call **Sequences[*x*]** generalizes the standard **Sequence** function, allowing a list {*a*, *b*, *c*, ...} as an actual *x* argument with returning of the call **Sequence1[*a*, *b*, *c*, ...]**. The source code of the **Sequences** procedure precedes to the source code of the **Cost** procedure in the fragment below.

In[2452]:= Sequences[x__] := Module[{a = Flatten[{x}], b},
b = "Sequence[" <> ToString1[a] <> "]"; a = Flatten[StringPosition[b, {"{", "}"}]];
ToExpression[StringReplace[b, {StringTake[b, {a[[1]], a[[1]]}] -> "",
StringTake[b, {a[[-1]], a[[-1]]}] -> ""}]]]

In[2453]:= F[a, b, Sequences[{x, y, x}], c, d]
Out[2453]= F[a, b, x, y, x, c, d]

In[2455]:= Cost[x_] := Module[{f = {Plus, Times, Power, Indexed, Function},
a = ToString[InputForm[x]], b = {{"+", "-"}, {"*", "/"}, "^"}, c, d = {}, h, k = 1, j, t},
If[StringFreeQ[a, Flatten[{b, "["}]], 0, c = Map[StringCount[a, #] &, b];
While[k <= 3, h = c[[k]]; If[h != 0, AppendTo[d, {f[[k]], h}]]; k++];
If[Set[b, StringCount[a, "[["]] > 0, AppendTo[d, {f[[4]], b}]];
t = StringPosition[a, "["]; If[t != {}, t = Map[#[[1]] &, t]];
t = Select[Map[If[StringTake[a, {# - 1, # - 1}] != "[" &&
StringTake[a, {# + 1, # + 1}] != "[", #] &, t], ! SameQ[#, Null] &]];
If[t != {}, AppendTo[d, {f[[5]], Length[t]}]];
b = StringPosition[a, "(-"]; {t, b, h} = {0, Map[#[[1]] &, b], StringLength[a]};
For[k = 1, k <= Length[b], k++, c = "";
For[j = b[[k]], j <= h, j++, c = c <> StringTake[a, {j, j}];
If[StringCount[c, "{"] === StringCount[c, "}"], If[ExpressionQ[c], Continue[],
If[NumberQ[Interpreter["Number", Positive][c]], t = t + 1]]; Break[]]]];
d = If[t != 0 && d[[1]][[1]] === Plus, d[[1]][[2]] = d[[1]][[2]] - t; d, d];
Plus[Sequences[Map[#[[2]]*#[[1]] &, d]]]]]

In[2456]:= Cost[z^(h*n - 2) + t^3]
Out[2456]= 3*Plus + 2*Power + Times

In[2457]:= Cost[(z^(h*n - 2) + t^3)/(x*y + c)]
Out[2457]= 4*Plus + 2*Power + 3*Times

In[2458]:= Map[Cost, {42.47, 90*d + p^g, AvzAgnVsv}]
Out[2458]= {0, Plus + Power + Times, 0}

In[2459]:= Cost[(z^(h*n[90] - 2) + t^3)/(x*y + c[590])]
Out[2459]= 2*Function + 4*Plus + 2*Power + 3*Times

In[2460]:= Cost[(a + Sin[-a + v] + x[b[[-90 ;; 590]]]) // Quiet]
Out[2460]= 2*Function + Indexed + 4*Plus

The procedure call **Cost**[*x*] returns the indicator *Cost* of the above format for an arbitrary algebraic *x* expression; at absence for *x* of operators is returned zero. At that, the procedure is a rather simply disaggregated relative to the calculation of number of **Plus** operators. A number of tools of the chapter are rather useful and are located in *MathToolBox* package.

Chapter 3. Additional tools of processing of symbols and string structures in *Mathematica*

Without taking into account the fact that *Mathematica* has rather large set of tools for work with string structures, necessity of tools which are absent in the system arises. Some of such tools are represented in the given chapter; among them are available both simple, and more difficult which appeared in the course of programming of problems of different purpose as additional functions and procedures simplifying or facilitating the programming.

Examples of the present chapter illustrate formalization of procedures in the *Mathematica* which reflects its basic elements and principles, allowing by taking into account the material to directly start creation, at the beginning, of simple procedures of different purpose which are based on processing of string structures. Here only the procedures of so-called `system` character intended for processing of the string structures are considered which, however, represent also the most direct applied interest for the programming of various appendices. Moreover, procedures and functions that have quite foreseeable volume of source code that allows to carry out their rather simple analysis are presented here. Their analysis can serve as a rather useful exercise for the reader both who is beginning programming, and already having rather serious experience in this direction. Later we will understand under **"system"** tools the actually system tools, and our tools oriented on mass application. At that, it should be noted that string structures are of special interest not only as basic structures with which the system and the user operate, but also as a base, in particular, of dynamic generation of the objects in the *Mathematica*, including *procedures* and *functions*. The mechanism of such dynamic generation is quite simple and rather in details is considered in [28-33], whereas examples of its application can be found in examples of source codes of tools of the present book. Below we will present a number of useful enough means for strings processing in the *Mathematica* system.

3.1. Operations on strings

The *Mathematica* language (*Math-language*) provides a variety of functions for *manipulating* strings. Most of these functions are based on a viewing strings as a sequence of characters, and many of the functions are analogous to ones for manipulating lists. The section presents a number of the means providing usefulenough operations on strings that supplement and expand the standard system means.

So, the call **SuffPref[S, s, n]** provides testing of a *S* string regarding to begin *(n=1)*, to finish *(n=2)* by a substring or substrings from the *s* list, or *(n=3)* be limited from both ends by the substrings from *s*. At establishment of this fact the **SuffPref** returns *True*, otherwise *False* is returned. Whereas the call **StrStr[x]** of a simple function provides return of an expression *x* different from a string, in string format, and a double string otherwise. In a number of cases the **StrStr** function is an useful enough in work with strings, in particular, with the standard **StringReplace** function. The following fragment represents source codes of the above tools along with examples of their application.

In[2510]:= StrStr[x_] := If[StringQ[x], "\"" <> x <> "\"", ToString[x]]

In[2511]:= Map[StrStr, {"RANS", a + b, IAN, {74, 69, 49}, F[x, y]}]
Out[2511]= {"\"RANS\"", "a + b", "IAN", "{74, 69, 49}", "F[x, y]"}

In[2512]:= SuffPref[S_ /; StringQ[S], s_ /; StringQ[s] || ListQ[s] &&
AllTrue[Map[StringQ, s], TrueQ], n_ /; MemberQ[{1, 2, 3}, n]] :=
Module[{a, b, c, k = 1}, If[StringFreeQ[S, s], False, b = StringLength[S];
c = Flatten[StringPosition[S, s]];
If[n == 3 && c[[1]] == 1 && c[[-1]] == b, True, If[n == 1 && c[[1]] == 1, True,
If[n == 2 && c[[-1]] == b, True, False]]]]]

In[2513]:= SuffPref["IAN_RANS_RAC_REA_90_500", "90_500", 2]
Out[2513]= True

In[2514]:= SuffPref["IAN_RANS_RAC_REA", {"IAN_RANS", "IAN_"}, 1]
Out[2514]= True

If the above function **StrStr** is intended, first of all, for creation of double strings, then the following simple procedure converts *double* strings and strings of higher nesting level to the usual strings. The procedure call **ReduceString[*x*]** returns the result to converting of a string *x* to the usual classical string.

In[2585]:= ReduceString[x_ /; StringQ[x]] := Module[{a = x},
Do[If[SuffPref[a, "\""", 3], a = StringTake[a, {2, -2}], Return[a]], {j, 1, Infinity}]]

In[2586]:= ReduceString["\"\"\"\"\"{a + b, \"g\", s}\"\"\"\"\""]
Out[2586]= "{a + b, \"g\", s}"

It should be noted that the **SuffPrefList** procedure [48,50] is a useful enough version of the above **SuffPref** procedure concerning the lists. At *n=1*, the procedure call **SuffPrefList[*x, y, n*]** returns the maximal subset common for the lists *x* and *y* with their beginning, whereas at *n=2*, the procedure call **SuffPrefList[*x, y, n*]** returns the the maximal subset common for the lists *x* and *y* with their end, otherwise the call returns two-element sublist whose elements define the above limiting sublists of the lists *x* and *y* with the both ends; moreover, if the call **SuffPrefList[*x, y, n, z*]** uses the optional *z* argument – *an arbitrary function from one argument*, then each element of lists *x* and *y* is previously processed by a *z* function. The next fragment represents source code of the **SuffPrefList** procedure along with an example of its use.

In[3831]:= SuffPrefList[x_ /; ListQ[x], y_ /; ListQ[y], t_ /; MemberQ[{1, 2, 3}, t], z___] :=
Module[{a = Sort[Map[Length, {x, y}]], b = x, c = y, d = {{}, {}}, j},
If[{z} != {} && FunctionQ[z] || SystemQ[z],
{b, c} = {Map[z, b], Map[z, c]}, 6]; Goto[t]; Label[3]; Label[1];
Do[If[b[[j]] === c[[j]], AppendTo[d[[1]], b[[j]]], Break[]], {j, 1, a[[1]]}];
If[t == 1, Goto[Exit], 6]; Label[2];
Do[If[b[[j]] === c[[j]], AppendTo[d[[2]], b[[j]]], Break[]], {j, -1, -a[[1]], -1}];
d[[2]] = Reverse[d[[2]]]; Label[Exit];
If[t == 1, d[[1]], If[t == 2, d[[2]], {d[[1]], d[[2]]}]]]

In[3832]:= SuffPrefList[{x, y, x, y, a, b, c, x, y, x, y}, {x, y, x, y}, 3]
Out[3832]= {{x, y, x, y}, {x, y, x, y}}

The **SuffPrefList1** procedure is an useful addition to the previous procedure. At *n = 1*, the call **SuffPrefList1[*x, y, n*]** returns the maximal sublist *(composed by a multiple concatenation of an y list)* in beginning of a *x* list, whereas at *n = 2*, the call **SuffPrefList1[*x, y, n*]** returns the maximal sublist *(composed by a multiple concatenation of a y list)* in its end, otherwise at $n = 3$ the procedure call returns the two-element sublist whose elements define the above limiting sublists of the x list on the both its ends. The fragment below represents source code of the **SuffPrefList1** procedure and typical examples of its application.

In[3845]:= **SuffPrefList1[x_ /; ListQ[x], y_ /; ListQ[y], t_ /; MemberQ[{1, 2, 3}, t]] :=**
Module[{b}, If[Length[y] > Length[x], $Failed,
b[m_, n_] := Module[{a = Partition[m, Length[n]], c = {}},
Do[If[a[[j]] === n, AppendTo[c, a[[j]]], Break[]], {j, 1, Length[a]}]; Flatten[c]];
If[t == 1, b[x, y], If[t == 2, Reverse[b[Reverse[x], Reverse[y]]],
{b[x, y], Reverse[b[Reverse[x], Reverse[y]]]}]]]]

In[3846]:= **SuffPrefList1[{x, y, x, y, x, y, x, y, a, b, c, x, y, x, y}, {x, y}, 1]**
Out[3846]= {x, y, x, y, x, y, x, y}
In[3847]:= **SuffPrefList1[{x, y, x, y, x, y, x, y, a, b, c, x, y, x, y}, {x, y}, 2]**
Out[3847]= {x, y, x, y}
In[3848]:= **SuffPrefList1[{x, y, x, y, x, y, x, y, a, b, c, x, y, x, y}, {x, y}, 3]**
Out[3848]= {{x, y, x, y, x, y, x, y}, {x, y, x, y}}
In[3849]:= **SuffPrefList1[{x, y, x, y, x, y, x, y, x, y, x, y}, {x, y}, 2]**
Out[3849]= {x, y, x, y, x, y, x, y, x, y, x, y}
In[3850]:= **SuffPrefList1[{x, y, x, y, x, y, x, y, x, y, x, y}, {v, g}, 3]**
Out[3850]= {{}, {}}

As a rather convenient addition to the previous means of strings processing is the testing **StringEndsQ1** procedure which in a certain sense complements the standard **StringEndsQ** function. The procedure call **StringEndsQ1[S, s]** returns the two-element list of format $\{a, b\}$ where $a, b \in \{True, False\}$ which defines the existence in a S string of a substring s as its prefix *(a)* and/or suffix *(b)*. At the same time, if the strings list is used as epy s argument, then the procedure call returns the list of *ListList* type, whose elements – two-element sublists of the above kind. These sublists are in one-to-one correspondence to elements of a s list. The next fragment presents source code of the **StringEndsQ1** procedure with typical examples of its application.

In[4335]:= **StringEndsQ1[S_ /; StringQ[S], s_ /; StringQ[s] || ListQ[s] &&**
AllTrue[Map[StringQ, s], TrueQ]] := Module[{a, b = StringLength[S]},
ReduceLevelsList[Map[{Set[a, StringPosition[S, #]], Quiet[{TrueQ[a[[1]][[1]] == 1],
TrueQ[a[[-1]][[2]] == b]}]}[[2]] &, Flatten[{s}]]][[1]]]

In[4336]:= **StringEndsQ1["dd1dd1ddaabcddd1d1dd1dd1dd1dd1dd1", "dd1"]**
Out[4336]= {True, True}
In[4337]:= **StringEndsQ1["ddd1dd1ddaabcddd1d1dd1dd1dd1dd1dd1", {"dd1", "dd"}]**
Out[4337]= {{False, True}, {True, False}}

The procedure **StringTrim1** is an useful extension of standard function **StringTrim**. The call **StringTrim1[x, y, z]** returns the result of truncation of a string x by a substring y on the left, and by a substring z on the right. In case $y \equiv z \equiv$ "" the call **StringTrim1[x, "", ""]** is equivalent to the call **StringTrim[x]**. The following fragment represents source code of the **StringTrim1** procedure with typical examples of its application.

In[4013]:= StringTrim1[x_ /; StringQ[x], y_ /; StringQ[y], z_ /; StringQ[z]] :=
If[y == z == "", StringTrim[a], ToExpression[ToString[StringTrim[x, (y | z) ...] // FullForm]]]

In[4014]:= **StringTrim1["((123456789))", "(", ")"]**
Out[4014]= "123456789"

In[4015]:= **StringTrim1["((123456789}}}", "(", "}"]**
Out[4015]= "123456789"

The procedure below is a certain extension of the previous procedure. The procedure call **StringTrim2[x, y, z]** returns the result of truncation of a *x* string by *y* symbols on the left *(z = 1)*, on the right *(z = 2)* or both ends *(z = 3)*. In case *x = ""* the call returns the empty string; at that, a single character or a list of them can act as an *y* argument.

In[3847]:= **StringTrim2[x_ /; StringQ[x], y_ /; StringQ[y] ||**
AllTrue[Map[StringQ, Flatten[{y}]], TrueQ], z_ /; MemberQ[{1, 2, 3}, z]] :=
Module[{a = x, b = Flatten[{y}], m = 0, n = 0},
Do[If[z == 1, If[SuffPref[a, b, 1], a = StringDrop[a, 1]; m = 1, m = 0],
If[z == 2, If[SuffPref[a, b, 2], a = StringDrop[a, -1]; n = 1, n = 0],
If[SuffPref[a, b, 1], a = StringDrop[a, 1]; m = 1, m = 0];
If[SuffPref[a, b, 2], a = StringDrop[a, -1]; n = 1, n = 0]]];
If[m + n == 0, Return[a], Null], Infinity]]

In[3848]:= **StringTrim2["+--+--+abcdfgh+--+--", {"+", "-"}, 1]**
Out[3848]= "abcdfgh+--+--"

In[3849]:= **StringTrim2["abcgdfret+--+--", {"+", "-", " "}, 2]**
Out[3849]= "abcgdfret"

In[3850]:= **StringTrim2["+--+--abcbcgdfret----------", {"+", "-", " "}, 3]**
Out[3850]= "abcbcgdfret"

Whereas the following procedure is an useful enough extension of the standard **StringTrim** procedure. The procedure call **StringTrim3[S, s, s1, s2, n, m]** returns the result of truncation of a *S* string by *s* symbols on the left *(n=1)*, on the right *(n=2)* or both ends *(n=3)* a for case of *s1 = ""* and *s2 = ""*, at condition that truncating is done onto *m* depth. While in a case of the *s1* and *s2* arguments different from empty string instead of truncatings the corresponding insertings of strings *s1 (at the left)* and *s2 (on the right)* are done. Thus, the arguments *s1* and *s2* – two string arguments for processing of the ends of the initial *S* string at the left and on the right accordingly are defined. In addition, in a case of *S = ""* or *s = ""* the procedure call returns the initial *S* string; at that, a single character or their string can act as the *s* argument. The following fragment presents source code of the **StringTrim3** procedure with the typical examples of its application.

In[4304]:= **StringTrim3[S_String, s_String, s1_String, s2_String, n_Integer,**
m_ /; MemberQ[{1, 2, 3}, m]] := Module[{a = S, b, c = "", p = 1, t = 1, h},
If[S == "" || s == "", S, Do[b = StringPosition[a, s];
If[b == {}, Break[], a = StringReplacePart[a, "",
If[m == 1, {If[b[[1]][[1]] == 1, p++; b[[1]], Nothing]},
If[m == 2, {If[b[[-1]][[2]] == StringLength[a], t++; b[[-1]], Nothing]},
{If[b[[1]][[1]] == 1, p++; b[[1]], Nothing],

If[b[[-1]][[2]] == StringLength[a], t++; b[[-1]], Nothing]}]]]];
If[a == c, Break[], 6]; c = a, {j, 1, n}]; h = {p, t} - {1, 1};
If[m == 1, StringRepeat[s1, h[[1]]] <> c,
If[m == 2, c <> StringRepeat[s2, h[[2]]], StringRepeat[s1, h[[1]]] <> c <>
StringRepeat[s2, h[[2]]]]]]]

In[4305]:= StringTrim3["dd1dd1ddaabcddd1d1dd1dd1dd1dd1dd1", "dd1", "AVZ", "AGN", 3, 1]
Out[4305]= "AVZAVZddaabcddd1d1dd1dd1dd1dd1dd1"
In[4306]:= StringTrim3["dd1dd1ddaabcddd1d1dd1dd1dd1dd1dd1", "dd1", "", "", 3, 1]
Out[4306]= "ddaabcddd1d1dd1dd1dd1dd1dd1"
In[4307]:= StringTrim3["dd1dd1ddaabcddd1d1dd1dd1dd1dd1dd1", "dd1", "AVZ", "AGN", 3, 2]
Out[4307]= "dd1dd1ddaabcddd1d1dd1dd1AGNAGNAGN"
In[4308]:= StringTrim3["dd1dd1ddaabcddd1d1dd1dd1dd1dd1dd1", "dd1", "AVZ", "AGN", 3, 3]
Out[4308]= "AVZAVZddaabcddd1d1dd1dd1AGNAGNAGN"

Thus, by varying of values of the actual arguments {*s, s1, s2, n, m*}, it is possible to carry out processing of the ends of arbitrary strings in a rather wide scope.

The call **SequenceCases**[*x, y*] of the standard function returns the list of all sublists in a *x* list which match a sequence pattern *y*. Moreover, the default option setting *Overlaps –> False* is assumed, therefore the **SequenceCases** call returns only sublists which do not overlap. In addition to this function the following procedure is presented as a rather useful means. The procedure call **SequenceCases1**[*x, y*] as a whole returns the nested list whose two–element sublists have the following format {*n, h*} where *h* – the sublist of a *x* list which is formed by a maximally admissible continuous concatenation of an *y* list, and *n* – an initial position in the list *x* of such sublist. At that, the procedure call **SequenceCases1**[x, y, z] with the 3rd optional *z* argument – *an undefinite symbol* – through *z* returns the nested list whose the first element defines the sublists maximal in length in format {*m, n, p*}, where *m* – the length of a sublist and *n, p* – its first and end position accordingly, whereas the second element determines the sublists minimal in length of the above format with the obvious modification. In the speccial situations the procedure call returns $Failed or *empty* list. The following fragment represents the source code of the **SequenceCases1** procedure with typical examples of its application.

In[4280]:= SequenceCases1[x_ /; ListQ[x], y_ /; ListQ[y], z___] :=
Module[{a = SequencePosition[x, y], b = 6, c, t},
If[Length[y] > Length[x], $Failed,
While[! SameQ[a, b], a = Gather[a, #1[[2]] == #2[[1]] - 1 &];
a = Map[Extract[#, {{1}, {-1}}] &, Map[Flatten, a]];
b = Gather[a, #1[[2]] == #2[[1]] - 1 &]; b = Map[Extract[#, {{1}, {-1}}] &, Map[Flatten, b]]];
b = Map[{#[[1]], Part[x, #[[1]] ;; #[[-1]]]} &, b];
If[{z} == {}, b, c = Map[{#[[1]], Length[#[[2]]]} &, b]; c = Map8[Max, Min, Map[#[[2]] &, c]];
z = {Map[If[Set[t, Length[#[[2]]]] == c[[1]], {c[[1]], #[[1]], #[[1]] + t - 1}, Nothing] &, b],
Map[If[Set[t, Length[#[[2]]]] == c[[2]], {c[[2]], #[[1]], #[[1]] + t - 1}, Nothing] &, b]};

z = Map[If[Length[#] == 1, #[[1]], #] &, z]; b]]]

In[4281]:= SequenceCases1[{a, x, y, x, y, x, y, x, y, x, y, x, y, x, y, a, m, n, x, y, b, c, x, y, x, y, h, x, y}, {x, y}]

Out[4281]= {{2, {x, y, x, y, x, y, x, y, x, y, x, y, x, y}}, {19, {x, y}}, {23, {x, y, x, y}}, {28, {x, y}}}

In[4282]:= SequenceCases1[{a, x, y, x, y, x, y, x, y, x, y, x, y, x, y, a, m, n, x, y, b, c, x, y, x, y, h, x, y}, {x, y}, g70]

Out[4282]= {{2, {x, y, x, y, x, y, x, y, x, y, x, y, x, y}}, {19, {x, y}}, {23, {x, y, x, y}}, {28, {x, y}}}

In[4283]:= g70

Out[4283]= {{14, 2, 15}, {{2, 19, 20}, {2, 28, 29}}}

In[4284]:= SequenceCases1[{x, y, x, y, x, y, x, y, x, y, x, y, x, y, x, y, x, y, x, y, x, y}, {x, y}]

Out[4284]= {{1, {x, y, x, y, x, y, x, y, x, y, x, y, x, y, x, y, x, y, x, y, x, y}}}

The call **Spos[x, y, p, d]** calculates number of position of the first entrance of a *y* symbol into a *x* string to the *left (d = 0)* or to the *right (d = 1)* from the given *p* position. If an *y* substring doesn't enter into a *x* string in the specified direction concerning *p* position, the call of the **Spos** returns zero. Otherwise, the call **Spos[x, y, p, dir]** returns number of a position of the first entrance of *y* into a *x* string to the left *(dir = 0)* or to the right *(dir = 1)* from the given *p* position; in addition, number of position is counted from the beginning of the *x* string. The **Spos** processes the main erroneous situations, returning on them *False*. The fragment below represents source code of the **Spos** with examples of its application. A number of means of the *MathToolBox* package use this procedure [48,50].

In[6820]:= Spos[x_ /; StringQ[x], y_ /; StringQ[y], p_Integer, dir_Integer] :=
Module[{a, b, c}, If[StringFreeQ[x, y], Return[0], If[StringLength[y] > 1 || dir != 0 &&
dir != 1, Return[False], b = StringLength[x]]];
If[p < 1 || p > b, False,
If[p == 1 && dir == 0, c = 0,
If[p == b && dir == 1, c = 0,
If[dir == 0, For[a = p, a >= 1, a -= 1, If[StringTake[x, {a}] == y, Return[a], c]],
For[a = p, a <= b, a += 1, If[StringTake[x, {a}] == y, Return[a], c]]]]]];
If[a == 0 || a == b + 1, 0, a]]

In[6821]:= Q := "AV99RAN790IN1947"; {Spos[Q, "A", 10, 0], Spos[Q, "4", 3, 1],
Spos[Q, "0", 1, 1], Spos[Q, "Z", 19, 0], Spos[Q, "W", 19, 0], Spos[Q, "P", 1, 1]}

Out[6821]= {6, 15, 10, 0, 0, 0}

In a number of cases the possibilities of the standard functions **Replace** and **StringReplace** are insufficient. In this connection the procedure, whose call **StringReplace2[S, s, E]** returns the result of replacement of all entries into a *S* string of its substrings *s* onto an *E* expression has been created; in addition, the replaced substrings *s* shouldn't be limited by letters. If the *S* string doesn't contain occurrences of *s*, the procedure call returns the initial *S* string while on the empty *S* string the empty string is returned. In a sense the procedure **StringReplace2** combines possibilities of the above system functions. The fragment below represents source code of the **StringReplace2** procedure along with typical examples of its application.

In[4268]:= StringReplace2[S_ /; StringQ[S], s_ /; StringQ[s], Exp_] :=
Module[{b, c, d, k = 1, a = Join[CharacterRange["A", "Z"], CharacterRange["a", "z"]]},

b = Quiet[Select[StringPosition[S, s], ! MemberQ[a, StringTake[S, {#[[1]] - 1, #[[1]] - 1}]]
&& ! MemberQ[a, StringTake[S, {#[[2]] + 1, #[[2]] + 1}]] &]];
StringReplacePart[S, ToString[Exp], b]]

In[4269]:= StringReplace2["Length[\"abSin[x]\"] + Sin[x] + ab - Sin[x]*6", "Sin[x]", "a^b"]
Out[4269]= "Length[\"abSin[x]\"] + a^b + ab - a^b*6"

In[4270]:= StringReplace2["Length[\"abSin[x]\"] + Cos[x] + ab - Cos[x]*6", "abSin[x]", "a^b"]
Out[4270]= "Length[\"a^b\"] + Cos[x] + ab - Cos[x]*6"

In addition to the standard **StringReplace** function and the **StringReplace2** procedure in a number of cases the procedure **StringReplace1** is provided as an useful. The procedure call **StringReplace1[S, L, P]** returns result of substitution in a *S* string of substrings from the *P* list instead of its substrings determined by positions of the nested *L* list of the *ListList* type. The function call **StringReplace2[S, s, Exp]** returns result of repl acement of all occurrences in a *S* string of its substrings *s* onto an *Exp* expression; in addition, the replaced substrings *s* should not be limited by letters. If string *S* doesn`t contain occurrences of *s*, the function call returns the initial string *S* whereas on empty string *S* the empty string is returned, i.e. "".

The procedure call **StringReplace3[W, x, x1, y, y1, z, z1,...]** returns the result of substitution into *W* string of {*x1, y1, z1, ...*} substrings instead of all occurrences of {*x, y, z, ...*} substrings accordingly; in the absence of such occurrences the call returns initial *W* string. This means appears as a very useful tool of processing of string constructions that contain expressions, expanding possibilities of the standard means. At last, the procedure call **StringReplace4[x, y, z]**, where *x* – a string, *y* – a rule or their list and *z* – undefined symbol, is analogous to the function call **StringReplace[x, y]** by allowing to obtain through *z* argument the two-element list where the first element defines the list of rules from *y* that are inapplicable to a *x* string, whereas the second element defines the list of substrings which are unsuitable for replacing. The fragment represents source codes of the **StringReplace1** ÷ **StringReplace4** procedures along with examples of their application.

In[2331]:= StringReplace1[S_ /; StringQ[S], L_ /; ListListQ[L] && Length[L[[1]]] == 2 &&
MatrixQ[L, IntegerQ] && Sort[Map[Min, L]][[1]] >= 1, P_ /; ListQ[P]] :=
Module[{a = {}, b, k = 1},
If[Sort[Map[Max, L]][[-1]] <= StringLength[S] && Length[P] == Length[L], Null,
Return[Defer[StringReplace1[S, L, P]]]];
For[k, k <= Length[L], k++, b = L[[k]];
a = Append[a, StringTake[S, {b[[1]], b[[2]]}] -> ToString[P[[k]]]]]; StringReplace[S, a]]

In[2332]:= StringReplace1["avz123456789agn", {{4, 7}, {8, 10}, {11, 12}}, {" RANS ", Tampere, Sqrt[(a + b)*(c + d)]}]
Out[2332]= "avz RANS TampereSqrt[(a + b)*(c + d)]agn"

In[2333]:= StringReplace2[S_ /; StringQ[S], s_ /; StringQ[s], Exp_] :=
Module[{b, c, d, a = Join[CharacterRange["A", "Z"], CharacterRange["a", "z"]], k = 1},
b = Quiet[Select[StringPosition[S, s], ! MemberQ[a, StringTake[S, {#[[1]] - 1, #[[1]] - 1}]]
&& ! MemberQ[a, StringTake[S, {#[[2]] + 1, #[[2]] + 1}]] &]];
StringReplacePart[S, ToString[Exp], b]]

In[2335]:= StringReplace3[S_ /; StringQ[S], x__] :=
Module[{b = S, c, j = 1, a = Map[ToString, {x}]}, c = Length[a];
If[OddQ[c], S, While[j <= c/2, b = StringReplace2[b, a[[2*j - 1]], a[[2*j]]]; j++]; b]]

In[2336]:= StringReplace3["Module[{a$ = 78, b$ = 90, c$ = 74}, xb$; a$*b$*6;
(a$ + b$ + c$)*(x + y); aa$]", "a$", "a", "b$", "b", "c$", "c"]
Out[2336]= "Module[{a = 78, b = 90, c = 74}, xb$; a*b*6; (a + b + c)*(x + y); aa$]"

In[2348]:= StringReplace4[x_String, y_ /; RuleQ[y] || ListQ[y] && And1[Map[RuleQ, y]],
z___] := Module[{a = x, b, c = {}, r = Flatten[{y}], t}, t = Length[r];
Do[Set[b, StringReplace[a, r[[j]]]]; If[a === b, AppendTo[c, r[[j]]], 6]; a = b, {j, 1, t}];
If[{z} != {} && NullQ[z], z = {c, Map[#[[1]] &, c]}, 6]; a]

In[2349]:= StringReplace["aaanbvfdxvcfgaaa", {"aa" -> "XX", "dy" -> "YY", "bv" -> "66"}]
Out[4350]= "XXan66fdxvcfgXXa"

In[4351]:= StringReplace4["aaanbvfdxvcfgaaa", {"aa" -> "XX", "dy" -> "YY", "bv" -> "66"}, s]
Out[4351]= "XXan66fdxvcfgXXa"

In[4352]:= s
Out[4352]= {{"dy" -> "YY"}, {"dy"}}

Additionally to the standard **StringReplace** function and the above four our procedures **StringReplace1** ÷ **StringReplace4**, the following procedure represents undoubted interest. The procedure call **StringReplaceVars[S, r]** returns the result of replacement in a S string of all occurrences of the left sides of a rule or their list r onto the right sides corresponding to them. In a case of absence of the above left sides entering in the S string the procedure call returns initial S string. Distinctive feature of this procedure is the fact, that it considers the left sides of r rules as separately located expressions in the S string, i.e. framed by the special characters. The procedure is of interest at strings processing. The next fragment represents source code of the **StringReplaceVars** procedure with examples of its application.

In[4047]:= StringReplaceVars[S_ /; StringQ[S], r_ /; RuleQ[r] || ListRulesQ[r]] :=
Module[{a = "(" <> S <> ")",
L = Characters["`!@#%^&*(){}:\"\\\/| <>?~-=+[];:'., 1234567890_"],
R = Characters["`!@#%^&*(){}:\"\\\/| <>?~-=+[];:'., _"], b, c, g = If[RuleQ[r], {r}, r]},
Do[b = StringPosition[a, g[[j]][[1]]];
c = Select[b, MemberQ[L, StringTake[a, {#[[1]] - 1}]] &&
MemberQ[R, StringTake[a, {#[[2]] + 1}]] &];
a = StringReplacePart[a, g[[j]][[2]], c], {j, 1, Length[g]}]; StringTake[a, {2, -2}]]

In[4048]:= StringReplace["Sqrt[t*p] + t^2", "t" -> "(a + b)"]
Out[4048]= "Sqr(a + b)[(a + b)*p] + (a + b)^2"

In[4049]:= StringReplaceVars["Sqrt[t*p] + t^2", "t" -> "(a + b)"]
Out[4049]= "Sqrt[(a + b)*p] + (a + b)^2"

In[4050]:= StringReplaceVars["(12345 123 678 123 90)", {"123" -> "abcd", "678" -> "mn"}]
Out[4050]= "12345 abcd mn abcd 90"

In[4051]:= StringReplaceVars["(12345 123 678 123 90)", "321" -> "abcd"]
Out[4051]= "12345 123 678 123 90"

In[4052]:= StringReplaceVars["(12345 123 678 123 90)", "xyz" -> "abcd"]

Out[4052]= "12345 123 678 123 90"

The following procedure is a version of the above procedure useful in the certain cases. The procedure call **StringReplaceVars1**[*S, x, y, r*] returns the result of replacement in a *S* string of all occurrences of the left sides of a rule or their list *r* onto the right sides corresponding to them. In case of absence of the above left sides entering in the *S* string the procedure call returns an initial *S* string. Distinctive feature of this procedure with respect to the procedure **StringReplaceVars** is the fact that it considers the left sides of r rules as separately located expressions in the *S* string, i.e. they are framed on the left by characters from a *x* string and are framed on the right by characters from a *y* string. This procedure is of interest at strings processing, in particular at processing of definitions in string format of blocks and modules. The fragment below represents source code of the **StringReplaceVars1** procedure with an example of its application.

In[4063]:= **StringReplaceVars1**[S_ /; StringQ[S], x_ /; StringQ[x], y_ /; StringQ[y],
r_ /; RuleQ[r] || ListRulesQ[r]] :=
Module[{a = "(" <> S <> ")", L=Characters[x], R=Characters[y], b, c, g = If[RuleQ[r], {r}, r]},
Do[b = StringPosition[a, g[[j]][[1]]];
c = Select[b, MemberQ[L, StringTake[a, {#[[1]] – 1}]] &&
MemberQ[R, StringTake[a, {#[[2]] + 1}]] &];
a = StringReplacePart[a, g[[j]][[2]], c], {j, 1, Length[g]}]; StringTake[a, {2, –2}]]

In[4064]:= **StringReplaceVars1**["{a = \"ayb\", b = Sin[x], c = {\"a\", 70},
d = {\"a\", \"b\"}}", "{(1234567890", " })", {"a" -> "m", "b" -> "n"}]
Out[4064]= "{m = \"ayb\", n = Sin[x], c = {\"a\", 70}, d = {\"a\", \"b\"}}"

For operating with strings the **SubsDel** procedure represents a quite certain interest whose call **SubsDel**[*S, x, y, p*] returns result of removal from a string *S* of all substrings which are limited on the right *(at the left)* by a *x* substring and at the left *(on the right)* by the first met symbol in string format from the *y* list; moreover, search of *y* symbol is done to the left *(p = –1)* or to the right *(p = 1)*. In addition, the deleted substrings will contain a *x* substring since one end and the first symbol met from *y* since other end. Moreover, if in the course of *search* the symbols from the *y* list weren't found until end of the *S* string, the rest of initial *S* string is removed. The fragment represents source code of the **SubsDel** procedure with examples of its application. Procedure is used by a number of tools from *MathToolBox* package [48].

In[2321]:= **SubsDel**[S_ /; StringQ[S], x_ /; StringQ[x], y_ /; ListQ[y] &&
AllTrue[Map[StringQ, y], TrueQ] && Plus[Sequences[Map[StringLength, y]]] ==
Length[y], p_ /; MemberQ[{-1, 1}, p]] := Module[{b, c = x, d, h = StringLength[S], k},
If[StringFreeQ[S, x], Return[S], b = StringPosition[S, x][[1]]];
For[k = If[p == 1, b[[2]] + 1, b[[1]] – 1], If[p == 1, k <= h, k >= 1],
If[p == 1, k++, k--], d = StringTake[S, {k, k}];
If[MemberQ[y, d] || If[p == 1, k == 1, k == h], Break[], If[p == 1, c = c <> d, c = d <> c];
Continue[]]]; StringReplace[S, c -> ""]]

In[2322]:= **SubsDel**["12345avz6789", "avz", {"8"}, 1]
Out[2322]= "1234589"
In[2323]:= **SubsDel**["12345avz6789", "avz", {"8", 9}, 1]

Out[2323]= SubsDel["12345avz6789", "avz", {"8", 9}, 1]
In[2324]:= **SubsDel["123456789avz6789", "avz", {"5"}, 1]**
Out[2324]= "123456789"

While the procedure call **SubDelStr[x, L]** provides removal from a string *x* of all substrings which are limited by numbers of the positions given by the *L* list of the *ListList* type from 2-element sublists. On incorrect tuples of the actual arguments the procedure call is returned unevaluated. The following fragment presents source code of the procedure with examples of its application.

In[2826]:= **SubDelStr[x_ /; StringQ[x], t_ /; ListListQ[t]] := Module[{k = 1, a = {}},
If[! t == Select[t, ListQ[#] && Length[#] == 2 &] || t[[-1]][[2]] > StringLength[x] || t[[1]][[1]] < 1, Return[Defer[SubDelStr[x, t]]],
For[k, k <= Length[t], k++, AppendTo[a, StringTake[x, t[[k]]] -> ""]]; StringReplace[x, a]]]**

In[2827]:= **SubDelStr["123456789abcdfdh", {{3, 5}, {7, 8}, {10, 12}}]**
Out[2827]= "1269dfdh"
In[2828]:= **SubDelStr["123456789abcdfdh", {{3, 5}, {7, 8}, {10, 12}, {40, 42}}]**
Out[2828]= SubDelStr["123456789abcdfdh", {{3, 5}, {7, 8}, {10, 12}, {40, 42}}]

For receiving of substrings of a string that are given by their positions of end and beginning, *Mathematica* possesses the **StringTake** function having six formats. However, in a number of cases is more convenient a receiving the sublines limited not by positions, but the list of substrings. For this purpose 2 functionally identical procedures **StringTake1 ÷ StringTake3** serve [48]. The call **StringTake{1|2|3}[x, y]** returns the list of substrings of a *x* string which are limited by their *y* substrings; as the second argument can be an expression or their tuple. In addition, for **StringTake2** the strings should not be included in the second argument. The fragment below represents source code of the **StringTake3** procedure with typical examples of its application.

In[2751]:= **StringTake3[x_ /; StringQ[x], y__] :=
Module[{a = FromCharacterCode[2], b = Map[ToString, Flatten[{y}]]},
StringSplit[StringReplace[x, GenRules[b, a]], a]]**

In[2752]:= **StringTake3["ransianavzagnvsvartkr", {"ian", "agn", "art"}]**
Out[2752]= {"rans", "avz", "vsv", "kr"}
In[2753]:= **StringTake3["ransianavzagn590vsvartkr", {ian, 590, art, 90}]**
Out[2753]= {"rans", "avzagn", "vsv", "kr"}
In[2754]:= **StringTake3["ransianavzagnvsvartkr", {ran, ian, agn, art, kr}]**
Out[2754]= {"s", "avz", "vsv"}

For work with strings the following procedure is rather useful, whose call **InsertN[S, L, n]** returns result of inserting into a *S* string after its positions from a *n* list of substrings from a *L* list; in case *n* = {< *1* | ≥ **StringLength[S]**} a substring is located before *S* string or in its end respectively. It is supposed that the actual arguments *L* and *n* may contain various number of elements, in this case the excess *n* elements are ignored. At that, processing of a string *S* is carried out concerning the list of positions for *m* insertions defined according to the relation *m* = **DeleteDuplicates[Sort[n]]**. The procedure call with inadmissible arguments is returned unevaluated. The following fragment represents source code of the **InsertN** procedure with examples of its application.

In[2583]:= InsertN[S_String, L_ /; ListQ[L], n_ /; ListQ[n] && Length[n] ==
Length[Select[n, IntegerQ[#] &]]] :=
Module[{a = Map[ToString, L], d = Characters[S], p, b, k = 1, c = FromCharacterCode[2],
m = DeleteDuplicates[Sort[n]]}, b = Map[c <> ToString[#] &, Range[1, Length[d]]];
b = Riffle[d, b]; p = Min[Length[a], Length[m]];
While[k <= p, If[m[[k]] < 1, PrependTo[b, a[[k]]], If[m[[k]] > Length[d],
AppendTo[b, a[[k]]], b = ReplaceAll[b, c <> ToString[m[[k]]] -> a[[k]]]]]; k++];
StringJoin[Select[b, ! SuffPref[#, c, 1] &]]]

In[2584]:= InsertN["123456789Rans_Ian", {Ag, Vs, Art, Kr}, {6, 9, 3, 0, 3, 17}]
Out[2584]= "Ag123Vs456Art789KrRans_Ian"
In[2585]:= InsertN["123456789", {a, b, c, d, e, f, g, h, n, m}, {4, 2, 3, 0, 17, 9, 18}]
Out[2585]= "a12b3c4d56789efg"

Contrary to the previous procedure the procedure **DelSubStr[S, L]** provides removal from a S string of substrings, whose positions are given by the L list; the L list has nesting 0 or 1, for example, {{3, 4}, {7}, {9}} or {1, 3, 5, 7, 9}, whereas the function call **AddDelPosString[x, y, h, z]** returns the result of truncation of a x string to the substring x[[1 ;; y]] if z – an arbitrary expression and x[[y ;; –1]] if {z} == {}, with replacing of the deleted substring by a h string. In case of an incorrect value y the call returns the initial x string or is returned *unevaluated* [48]. Both these means are rather useful in a number of problems of strings processing of various structure and appointment.

Earlier it was already noted that certain functional facilities of the *Mathematica* need to be reworked both for purpose of expansion of scope of application, and elimination of certain shortcomings. It to the full extent concerns such a rather important function as **ToString[x]** which returns the result of converting of an arbitrary expression x in the string format. This standard procedure incorrectly converts expressions into string format, that contain string subexpressions if to code them in the standard way. By this reason we defined procedure **ToString1[x]** returning result of correct converting of an arbitrary expression x in the string format. The next fragment presents source codes of the **ToString1** procedure and **ToString1** function with examples of its use. In a number of appendices this means is popular enough.

In[2720]:= ToString1[x_] := Module[{a = "$Art27Kr20$.txt", b = "", c, k = 1},
Write[a, x]; Close[a]; For[k, k < Infinity, k++, c = Read[a, String];
If[SameQ[c, EndOfFile], Return[DeleteFile[Close[a]]; b], b = b <> StrDelEnds[c, " ", 1]]]]

In[2721]:= Kr[x_] := Module[{a = "ArtKr", b = " = "}, a <> b <> ToString[x]]
In[2722]:= ToString[Definition[Kr]]
Out[2722]= "Kr[x_] := Module[{a = ArtKr, b = = }, a <> b <> ToString[x]]"
In[2723]:= ToExpression[%]
ToExpression::sntx: Invalid syntax in or before "Kr[x_] := Module[{a = ...".
Out[2723]= $Failed
In[2724]:= ToString1[Definition[Kr]]
Out[2724]= "Kr[x_] := Module[{a = \"Art_Kr\", b = \" = \"}, StringJoin[a, b, ToString[x]]]"
In[2725]:= ToString1[x_] := {Write["$ArtKr", x], Close["$ArtKr"], Read["$ArtKr", String],
DeleteFile[Close["$ArtKr"]]}[[-2]]

In[2748]:= ToString2[x_] := Module[{a}, If[ListQ[x], SetAttributes[ToString1, Listable];

a = ToString1[x]; ClearAttributes[ToString1, Listable]; a, ToString1[x]]]

In[2749]:= ToString2[a + b/74 – Sin[590.90]]
Out[2749]= "–0.27691409532495276 + a + b/74"

In[2750]:= ToString2[{{74, 69}, {47, {a, b, {x, y}, c}, 52}, {27, 20}}]
Out[2750]= {{"74", "69"}, {"47", {"a", "b", {"x", "y"}, "c"}, "52"}, {"26", "19"}}

In[2771]:= ToString3[x_] := StringReplace[ToString1[x], "\"" -> ""]

In[2772]:= ToString3[#1^2 + #2^4 &]
Out[2772]= "#1^2 + #2^4 & "

In[2775]:= ToString4[x_] := If[! SymbolQ[x], "(" <> ToString1[x] <> ")", ToString1[x]]

In[2776]= ToString4[a + b + c + d]
Out[2776]= "(a + b + c + d)"

In[2885]:= ToString5[x_] := Module[{a, b, c, d}, b = ToString[a]; a := x;
c = PureDefinition[b];
d = Flatten[StringPosition[c, " := ", 1]][[-1]]; StringTake[c, {d + 1, -1}]]

In[2886]:= ToString5[{a, b, "c", "d + h"}]
Out[2886]= "{a, b, \"c\", \"d + h\"}"

In[2887]:= ToString1[{a, b, "c", "d + h"}]
Out[2887]= "{a, b, \"c\", \"d + h\"}"

Immediate application of the **ToString1** procedure allows to simplify rather significantly the programming of a number of problems. In addition, examples of the previous fragment visually illustrate application of both means on the concrete example which emphases the advantages of our procedure. While **ToString2** procedure expands the previous procedure onto lists of any level of nesting. So, the call **ToString2**[*x*] on an argument *x*, different from list, is equivalent to the call **ToString1**[*x*], while on *x* list is equivalent to the procedure call **ToString1**[*x*] which is endowed with the *Listable* attribute. The function call **ToString3**[*x*] serves for converting of a *x* expression into the string *InputForm* format. The function has a number of useful enough appendices. Whereas, the call **ToString4**[*x*] is analogous to the call **ToString1**[*x*] if *x* – any symbol, otherwise \"(\" <> **ToString1**[*x*] <> \")\" will be returned. At last, the **ToString5** procedure is a functional analog of the **ToString1** procedure whose source code is based on a different algorithm that does not use the file access. The previous fragment represents source codes of the above five tools with typical examples of their use.

The fragment below represents an useful enough procedure, whose call **SubStr**[*S, p, a, b, r*] returns the substring of a *S* string which is limited at the left by the first symbol other than symbol *a* or other than symbols from the list *a*, and on the right is limited by symbol other than *b* or other than symbols from *b* list. Meantime, thru *r* argument in case of an erroneous situation the corresponding message diagnosing the arisen error situation is returned. The integer *p* argument must be in interval *1 ..* **StringLength**[*S*]. The fragment below represents source code and examples of application of this procedure.

In[2379]:= SubStr[S_ /; StringQ[S], p_ /; IntegerQ[p], a_ /; CharacterQ[a] || ListQ[a] &&
AllTrue[Map[CharacterQ, a], TrueQ], b_ /; CharacterQ[b] || ListQ[b] &&
DeleteDuplicates[Map[CharacterQ, b]] == {True}, r_ /; ! HowAct[r]] :=
Module[{c = Quiet[StringTake[S, {p, p}]], k, t},

If[p >= 1 && p <= StringLength[S], For[k = p + 1, k <= StringLength[S], k++,
t = StringTake[S, {k, k}];
If[If[CharacterQ[b], t != b, ! MemberQ[b, t]], c = c <> t; Continue[], Break[]]];
For[k = p - 1, k >= 1, k--, t = StringTake[S, {k, k}];
If[If[CharacterQ[a], t != a, ! MemberQ[a, t]], c = t <> c; Continue[], Break[]]]; c,
r = "Argument p should be in range 1.." <> ToString[StringLength[S]] <>
" but received " <> ToString[p]; $Failed]]

In[2380]:= SubStr["12345abcd480e80fg6789sewrt", 14, "3", "r", Error]
Out[2380]= "45abcd480e80fg6789sew"
In[2382]:= SubStr["12345abcdefg6789sewrt", 25, "0", "x", Error]
Out[2382]= $Failed
In[2383]:= Error
Out[2383]= "Argument *p* should be in range 1..21 but received 25"
In[2384]:= SubStr["12345ab3c480def80gr6789sewrt", 7, "3", "r", Err]
Out[2384]= "45ab3c480def80g"

Whereas the next fragment represents a rather useful procedure, whose call **StrPartition**[*x*, *W*] returns the list of substrings of a *x* string that are limited by the first symbol of a *x* string and *W* symbol in string format or by their list. In case of impossibility of the above partition of the *x* string the empty list is returned. The fragment below represents source code of the **StrPartition** procedure along with typical examples of its application.

In[2870]:= StrPartition[x_ /; StringQ[x], y_ /; StringQ[y] && StringLength[y] == 1] :=
Module[{a = DeleteDuplicates[Flatten[StringPosition[x, y]]], b = {}},
Flatten[AppendTo[b, Map[StringTake[x, {1, #}] &, a]]]]
In[2871]:= StrPartition["C:\\Users\\Aladjev\\Documents", "\\"]
Out[2871]= {"C:\\", "C:\\Users\\", "C:\\Users\\Aladjev\\"}
In[2872]:= StrPartition["aaaaaaaa", "a"]
Out[2872]= {"a", "aa", "aaa", "aaaa", "aaaaa", "aaaaaa", "aaaaaaa", "aaaaaaaa"}

Thus, the **StrPartition** procedure is used by some means of the package [48,50] and is useful at processing of contexts, directories and full paths to datafiles.

In addition to standard function **StringRiffle**, the call **StringRiffle1**[*x*, *y*, *n*] returns a string which is created from a *x* string by inserting into it a *y* string after every *n*-th character in *x*. If optional *n* argument is omitted then *n* = 2 is supposed. If *n* = {0|1} then inserting of an *y* is done after every character of *x* including insertion of the *y* as suffix and prefix of the *x*. If a *n* is different from an integer or a negative number, then the function call returns $*Failed*. The function **StringRiffle1** uses the **Riffle2** function which extends the standard **Riffle** function onto the case of {0|1} as a value of the optional *n* argument in the call **Riffle**[*x*, *y*, *n*] as the following fragment rather visually illustrates. The next fragment represents source codes of the above two means along with typical examples of their application.

In[6128]:= StringRiffle1[x_ /; StringQ[x], y_ /; StringQ[y], j___] :=
If[{j} != {} && (! IntegerQ[j] || Negative[j]), $Failed, StringJoin[Riffle2[Characters[x], y, j]]]
In[6129]:= StringRiffle1["abcdertfgtyjuk", "xyz"]
Out[6129]= "axyzbxyzcxyzdxyzexyzrxyztxyzfxyzgxyztxyzyxyzjxyzuxyzk"

In[6130]:= **StringRiffle1["abcdertfgtpj", "xyz", 0]**
Out[6130]= "xyzaxyzbxyzcxyzdxyzexyzrxyztxyzfxyzgxyztxyzpxyzjxyz"
In[6131]:= **StringRiffle1["abcdertfgtpj", "xyz", 1]**
Out[6131]= "xyzaxyzbxyzcxyzdxyzexyzrxyztxyzfxyzgxyztxyzpxyzjxyz"
In[6132]:= **Riffle2[x_ /; ListQ[x], y_, z___] :=**
If[Length[{x, y, z}] == 2, Riffle[x, y], If[Length[{z}] == 1 && MemberQ[{0, 1}, {z}[[1]]],
Insert[x, y, Map[List, Range[1, Length[x] + 1]]], Riffle[x, y, z]]]
In[6133]:= **Riffle[{a, b, c, d, h, k, f}, m, 0]**
··· Riffle::rspec: The third argument 0 should be a positive...
Out[6133]= Riffle[{a, b, c, d, h, k, f}, m, 0]
In[6134]:= **Riffle[{a, b, c, d, h, k, f}, m, 1]**
··· Riffle::inclen: The start and end positions and the spacing...
Out[6134]= Riffle[{a, b, c, d, h, k, f}, m, 1]
In[6135]:= **Riffle2[{a, b, c, d, h, k, f}, m, 0]**
Out[6135]= {m, a, m, b, m, c, m, d, m, h, m, k, m, f, m}
In[6136]:= **Riffle2[{a, b, c, d, h, k, f}, m, 1]**
Out[6136]= {m, a, m, b, m, c, m, d, m, h, m, k, m, f, m}

3.2. Expressions containing in strings

In a number of cases of processing of expressions the problem of excretion of one or other type of expressions from strings is quite topical. In this relation an quite certain interest the **ExprOfStr** procedure represents whose source code with examples of its usage represents the following fragment. The call **ExprOfStr[*w*, *n*, *m*, *L*]** returns result of extraction from a *w* string limited by its *n–th* position and the end, of the first correct expression on condition that search is done *on the left (m = –1) / on the right (m = 1)* from the given position; at that, a symbol, next or previous behind the found expression must belong to the *L* list. The call is returned in string format; in the absence of a correct expression $*Failed* is returned, whereas the procedure call on inadmissible arguments is returned unevaluated.

In[2675]:= **ExprOfStr[x_ /; StringQ[x], n_ /; IntegerQ[n] && n > 0, p_ /; MemberQ[{-1, 1}, p],**
L_ /; ListQ[L]] := Module[{a = "", b, k},
If[n >= StringLength[x], Return[Defer[ExprOfStr[x, n, p, L]]], Null];
For[k = n, If[p == -1, k >= 1, k <= StringLength[x]], If[p == -1, k--, k++],
If[p == -1, a = StringTake[x, {k, k}] <> a, a = a <> StringTake[x, {k, k}]];
If[! SyntaxQ[a], Null, If[If[p == -1, k == 1, k == StringLength[x]] ||
MemberQ[L, Quiet[StringTake[x, If[p == -1, {k - 1, k - 1}, {k + 1, k + 1}]]]], Return[a],
Null]]]; $Failed]
In[2676]:= **P[x_, y_] := Module[{a, P1}, P1[z_, h_] := Module[{n}, z^2 + h^2]; x*y + P1[x, y]]**
In[2677]:= **x = ToString1[Definition[P]]; {ExprOfStr[x, 44, 1, {" ", ";", ","}],**
ExprOfStr[x, 39, -1, {" ", ";", ","}]}
Out[2677]= {"Module[{n}, z^2 + h^2]", "P1[z_, h_]"}
In[2679]:= **ExprOfStr[x, 10, 1, {" ", ";", ","}]**
Out[2679]= $Failed
In[2680]:= **ExprOfStr["12345678;F[(a+b)/(c+d)]; AV_2016", 10, 1, {"^", ";"}]**

Out[2680]= "F[(a + b)/(c + d)]"

The **ExprOfStr1** represents an useful enough modification of the previous procedure; its call **ExprOfStr1[x, n, p]** returns a substring of a *x* string, that is minimum on length and in that a boundary element is a symbol in *n–th* position of a *x* string, containing a correct expression. At that, search of such substring is done from *n–th* position to the right and until the end of the *x* string *(p = 1)*, and from the left from *n–th* position of string to the beginning of a string *(p = –1)*. In case of absence of such substring the call returns *$Failed* whereas on inadmissible arguments the procedure call is returned unevaluated [48,50].

In[3748]:= x = "123{a+b}, F[c+d+Sin[a+b]]"; ExprOfStr1[x, 25, –1]
Out[3748]= "F[c+d+Sin[a+b]]"
In[3749]:= x = "123{a+b}, [c+d]"; ExprOfStr1[x, 15, –1]
Out[3749]= $Failed
In[3750]:= x = "123{a+b}, [c+d]"; ExprOfStr1[x, 17, –1]
Out[3750]= $Failed

In a certain relation to the **ExprOfStr** procedure also the **ExtrExpr** procedure adjoins, whose the call **ExtrExpr[S, n, m]** returns omnifarious correct expressions in string format which are contained in the substring of a *S* string limited by positions with numbers *n* and *m*. In a case of absence of correct expressions the empty list is returned. The following fragment presents source code of the **ExprOfStr** procedure with typical examples of its application.

In[3801]:= ExtrExpr[S_ /; StringQ[S], n_ /; IntegerQ[N], n_ /; IntegerQ[M]] :=
Module[{a = StringLength[S], b, c, h = {}, k, j},
If[! (1 <= m <= a && n <= m), {}, b = StringTake[S, {n, m}];
Do[Do[c = Quiet[StringTake[b, {j, m – n – k + 1}]];
If[ExpressionQ[c], AppendTo[h, c]; Break[], Null], {k, 0, m – n + 1}], {j, 1, m – n}];
DeleteDuplicates[Select[Map[StringTrim2[#, {"+", "–", " ", "_"}, 3] &, h],
! MemberQ[{"", " "}, #] &]]]]
In[3802]:= ExtrExpr["z=(Sin[x+y] + Log[x])+G[x,y];", 1, 13]
Out[3802]= {"z", "Sin[x+y]", "in[x+y]", "n[x+y]", "x+y", "y"}
In[3803]:= ExtrExpr["z=(Sin[x+y]+Log[x])-F[x,y]; GS[x_, y_] := x*y; ", 4, 39]
Out[3803]= {"Sin[x+y]+Log[x]", "in[x+y]+Log[x]", "n[x+y]+Log[x]", "x+y", "y", "Log[x]", "og[x]", "g[x]", "x", "F[x,y]; GS[x_, y_]", "GS[x_, y_]", "S[x_, y_]"}

As essential help the **ExtrExpr** procedure uses the **StringTrim2** procedure which is a rather useful extension of standard function **StringTrim** and procedure **StringTrim1**. The above means are useful in a series of appendices, in particular, **ExtrExpr** procedure is connected, first of all, with extraction of expressions from the strings while the **StringTrim2** procedure has quite definite value at solving of different problems connected with strings processing.

Substantially using procedures **CorrSubStrings**, **ExtrVarsOfStr**, **RevRules**, **SubsInString**, **StringReplaceVars** and **ToStringRational**, it is possible to offer one more tool of extraction from an expression of all formally correct subexpressions which are contained in it. The call **SubExprsOfExpr[x]** returns the sorted list of every possible formally correct subexpressions of a *x* expression. Meantime, if *x* expression contains no undefinite symbols, the procedure call returns the evaluated initial expression *x*. The fragment below represents source code of the procedure with examples of its application.

In[4156]:= **SubExprsOfExpr[x_] :=**
Module[{b, c, c1, d = {}, p = 6000, h, f, a = StringReplace[ToStringRational[x], " " -> ""]},
b = StringLength[a]; c = ExtrVarsOfStr[a, 1];
If[c == {}, x, f = Select[c, ! StringFreeQ[a, # <> "["] && StringFreeQ[a, # <> "[["] &];
c1 = Map[# -> FromCharacterCode[p++] &, c]; h = StringReplaceVars[a, c1];
Do[AppendTo[d, CorrSubStrings[h, j]], {j, 1, b}];
d = Map[StringTrim[#, ("+" | "-") ...] &, Flatten[d]];
d = Map[StringReplaceVars[#, RevRules[c1]] &, d];
Do[Set[d, Map[If[MemberQ[{0, 2}, SubsInString[#, f[[j]], "["]], #, Nothing] &, d]],
{j, 1, Length[f]}];
Sort[DeleteDuplicates[ToExpression[d]]]]]

In[4157]:= **SubExprsOfExpr[(a + bc)*Log[z]]**
Out[4157]= {a, bc, a + bc, z, Log[z], (a + bc)*Log[z]}

In[4158]:= **SubExprsOfExpr[(a + b/x^2)/Sin[x*y] + 1/z^3 + Log[y]]**
Out[4158]= {1, 2, 3, a, b, a + b, a + b/x^2, 3 + a + b/x^2, a + b/x, b/x^2, b/x, x, x^2, y, x*y, a + b/x^2 + 1/z^3, 1/z^3, 1/z, z, z^3, a + b/x^2 + z^3, Csc[x*y], (a + b/x^2)*Csc[x*y], 3 + (a + b/x^2)*Csc[x*y], 1/z^3 + (a + b/x^2)*Csc[x*y], z^3 + (a + b/x^2)*Csc[x*y], Log[y], Csc[x*y] + Log[y], (a + b/x^2)*Csc[x*y] + Log[y], 3 + (a + b/x^2)*Csc[x*y] + Log[y], 1/z^3 + (a + b/x^2)*Csc[x*y] + Log[y], z^3 + (a + b/x^2)*Csc[x*y] + Log[y]}

In[4159]:= **SubExprsOfExpr[(a + bc)/(c + dg)]**
Out[4159]= {a, bc, a + bc, c, dg, (a + bc)/(c + dg), c + dg}

In[4160]:= **SubExprOfExpr[75*Sin[42.47] + 70]**
Out[4160]= –4.87171

In[4161]:= **SubExprsOfExpr[(a + Sin[x])/(b + Log[y])]**
Out[4161]= {a, b, x, y, Log[y], b + Log[y], Sin[x], a + Sin[x], (a + Sin[x])/(b + Log[y])}

In[4162]:= **SubExprsOfExpr[(aaa + bcd + bbb)*Log[xyz]]**
Out[4162]= {aaa, bbb, aaa + bbb, bcd, bbb + bcd, aaa + bbb + bcd, xyz, Log[xyz], (aaa + bbb + bcd)*Log[xyz]}

The call **ExtrSubString[x, n, p, f]** returns substring of a *x* string that is limited by a *n* position on the right *(on the left)*, and on the left *(on the right)* by a symbol previous before a *t* symbol, for which *f[t] = False*. At that, search in *x* string is done from right to left at *p = –1*, and from left to right at *p = 1; f* – a pure function. This procedure, representing a certain independent interest, is used by the means of the *MathToolBox* package [48].

In[3382]:= **ExtrSubString[x_ /; StringQ[x], n_ /; IntegerQ[n] && n > 0,**
p_ /; MemberQ[{1, -1}, p], f_ /; PureFuncQ[f]] :=
Module[{a = "", b}, Do[If[Quiet[f[Set[b, StringTake[x, {j}]]]],
If[p == -1, a = b <> a, a = a <> b], Return[a]], {j, If[p == 1, n, n],
If[p == 1, StringLength[x], 1], If[p == 1, 1, -1]}]]

In[3383]:= **Map[ExtrSubString["\.1a$defaultOpts \.0b\.10ReplyTo \.0b", # – 2, –1, LetterQ[#] || DigitQ[#] &] &, {15, 25}]**

Out[3383]= {"defaultOpts", "ReplyTo"}

The string structure is one of the basic structures in *Maple* and *Mathematica*, for ensuring work for which both systems have a number of the effective enough means. However, if *Maple* along with a rather small set of the built-in means has an expanded set of tools from the **StringTools** module and a number of means from our library [47], *Mathematica* in this regard has less representative set of means. Meanwhile, the set of its standard means allows to program rather simply the lacking *Maple*-analogs and other means of strings processing. Our means of the given orientation are represented in [48,50].

Unlike the **StringFreeQ** function, the procedure call **StringDependQ[*x*, *y*]** returns *True*, if a *x* string contains entries of a *y* substring or all substrings given by *y* list, and *False* otherwise. Whereas the call **StringDependQ[*x*, *y*, *z*]** in the presence of the third optional argument – *an undefinite variable* – through it in addition returns list of substrings which don't have entries into a *x* string. The next fragment represents source code of the procedure **StringDependQ** along with typical examples of its application.

In[2611]:= StringDependQ[x_ /; StringQ[x], y_ /; StringQ[y] || ListStrQ[y], z___] :=
Module[{a = Map[StringFreeQ[x, #] &, Flatten[{y}]], b = {}, c = Length[y], k = 1},
If[DeleteDuplicates[a] == {False}, True, If[{z} != {} && ! HowAct[z], z = Select[Flatten[y], StringFreeQ[x, #] &]]; False]]

In[2612]:= {StringDependQ["abcd", {"a", "d", "g", "s", "h", "t", "w"}, t], t}
Out[2612]= {False, {"g", "s", "h", "t", "w"}}
In[2613]:= {StringDependQ["abgschtdw", {"a", "d", "g", "s", "h", "t", "w"}, j], j}
Out[2613]= {True, j}

3.3. Replacements and extractions in strings

In a number of problems of strings processing, there is a need of replacement not simply of substrings but substrings limited by the given substrings. The procedure solves one of such tasks, its call **StringReplaceS[*S*, *s1*, *s2*]** returns the result of substitution into *S* string instead of entries into it of substrings *s1* limited by "*x*" strings on the left and on the right from the specified lists *L* and *R* respectively, by *s2* substrings (**StringLength["*x*"] = 1**); at absence of such entries the procedure call returns *S*. The following fragment represents source code of the **StringReplaceS** procedure with an example of its application.

In[2691]:= StringReplaceS[S_ /; StringQ[S], s1_ /; StringQ[s1], s2_String] :=
Module[{a = StringLength[S], b = StringPosition[S, s1], c = {}, k = 1, p,
L = Characters["`!@#%^&*(){}:\"\\\/|<>?~-=+[];:'., 1234567890"],
R = Characters["`!@#%^&*(){}:\"\\\/|<>?~=+[];:'., "]},
If[b == {}, S, While[k <= Length[b], p = b[[k]];
If[Quiet[(p[[1]] == 1 && p[[2]] == a) ||
(p[[1]] == 1 && MemberQ[R, StringTake[S, {p[[2]] + 1, p[[2]] + 1}]]) ||
(MemberQ[L, StringTake[S, {p[[1]] - 1, p[[1]] - 1}]] &&
MemberQ[R, StringTake[S, {p[[2]] + 1, p[[2]] + 1}]]) || (p[[2]] == a &&
MemberQ[L, StringTake[S, {p[[1]] - 1, p[[1]] - 1}]])], c = Append[c, p]]; k++];
StringReplacePart[S, s2, c]]]

In[2692]:= **StringReplaceS["abc& c + bd6abc – abc78*abc", "abc", "xyz"]**
Out[2692]= "xyz& c + bd6xyz – abc78*xyz"

The procedure, in particular, is a rather useful means at processing of definitions of blocks and modules in respect of operating with their formal arguments and local variables [50].

In a number of cases at strings processing it is necessary to extract from them the substrings limited by the symbol {"}, i.e. *"strings in strings"*. This problem is solved by the procedure, whose call **StrFromStr[*x*]** returns the list of such substrings that are in a string *x*; otherwise, the call **StrFromStr[*x*]** returns the empty list, i.e. {}. The following fragment presents source code of the procedure along with typical examples of its application.

In[3050]:= **StrFromStr[x_ /; StringQ[x]] := Module[{a = "\"", b, c = {}, k = 1},**
b = DeleteDuplicates[Flatten[StringPosition[x, a]]];
For[k, k <= Length[b] – 1, k++, c = Append[c, ToExpression[StringTake[x, {b[[k]], b[[k + 1]]}]]]]; k = k + 1]; c]

In[3051]:= **StrFromStr["12345\"678abc\"xyz\"50090\"mnph"]**
Out[3051]= {"678abc", "50090"}
In[3052]:= **StrFromStr["123456789"]**
Out[3052]= {}

To the above procedure an useful **UniformString** function adjoins. The strings can contain the substrings bounded by "\"" in particular the *cdf*/*nb*-files in string format. To make such strings by uniform, the simple function **UniformString** is used. The call **UniformString[*x*]** returns a *x* string in the uniform format, whereas the call **UniformString[*x*, *y*]** where *y* is an arbitrary expression returns the list of substrings of the *x* string which are bounded by "\"". The following fragment represents source code of the **UniformString** function with typical examples of its application.

In[5420]:= **UniformString[x_ /; StringQ[x], y___] :=**
If[{y} == {}, StringReplace[x, "\"" -> ""], Map[StringReplace[#, "\"" -> ""] &,
StringCases[x, Shortest["\"" ~~ __ ~~ "\""]]]]

In[5421]:= **UniformString["{\"ClearValues\", \"::\", \"usage\"}"]**
Out[5421]= "{ClearValues, ::, usage}"
In[5422]:= **UniformString["{\"ClearValues\", \"::\", \"usage\"}", 74]**
Out[5422]= {"ClearValues", "::", "usage"}
In[5423]:= **UniformString["{ClearValues, ::, usage}"]**
Out[5423]= "{ClearValues, ::, usage}"
In[5424]:= **UniformString["{ClearValues, ::, usage}", 74]**
Out[5424]= {}

The function is a rather useful tool at processing of the string representation of *cdf*/*nb*-files which is based on their internal formats [50].

Unlike standard **StringSplit** function, the call **StringSplit1[*x*, *y*]** performs semantic splitting of a *x* string by symbol *y* onto elements of the returned list. In this case semantics is reduced to the point that in the returned list only those substrings of the *x* string which contain the correct expressions are placed; in case of lack of such substrings the procedure call returns the empty list. The **StringSplit1** procedure appears as an quite useful tools, in particular, at programming of means of processing of the headings of blocks, functions and modules. The comparative analysis of means **StringSplit** and **StringSplit1** speaks well for that. The next fragment represents source code of the procedure **StringSplit1** along with typical examples of its application.

In[2950]:= **StringSplit1**[x_ /; StringQ[x], y_ /; StringQ[y] || StringLength[y] == 1] :=
Module[{a = StringSplit[x, y], b, c = {}, d, p, k = 1, j = 1}, d = Length[a];
Label[G];
For[k = j, k <= d, k++, p = a[[k]];
If[! SameQ[Quiet[ToExpression[p]], $Failed], AppendTo[c, p], b = a[[k]];
For[j = k, j <= d − 1, j++, b = b <> y <> a[[j + 1]]];
If[! SameQ[Quiet[ToExpression[b]], $Failed], AppendTo[c, b];
Goto[G], Null]]]]; Map[StringTrim, c]]

In[2951]:= **StringSplit**["x_String, y_Integer, z_ /; MemberQ[{1, 2, 3, 4, 5}, z] || IntegerQ[z], h_, s_String, c_ /; StringQ[c] || StringLength[c] == 1", ","]
Out[2951]= {"x_String", " y_Integer", " z_ /; MemberQ[{1"," 2"," 3"," 4"," 5}"," z] || IntegerQ[z]", " h_", " s_String", " s_ /; StringQ[y] || StringLength[y] == 1"}

In[2952]:= **StringSplit1**["x_String, y_Integer, z_ /; MemberQ[{1, 2, 3, 4, 5}, z] || IntegerQ[z], h_, s_String, c_ /; StringQ[c] || StringLength[c] == 1", ","]
Out[2952]= {"x_String", "y_Integer", "z_ /; MemberQ[{1, 2, 3, 4, 5}, z] || IntegerQ[z]", "h_", "s_String", "h_ /; StringQ[y] || StringLength[y] == 1"}

3.4. Operating of substrings in strings

A number of the problems dealing with processing of strings do the **SubsStr** procedure as a rather useful, whose call **SubsStr**[*x, y, h, t*] returns result of replacement in a *x* string of all entries of substrings formed by concatenation *(on the right at t = 1 or at the left at t = 0)* of the *y* substrings with strings from a *h* list, onto strings from the *h* list respectively. In case of the impossibility of carrying out replacement initial *x* string is returned. The **SubsStr** procedure appears as a useful tools, for example, at programming of tools of processing of the body of procedure in string format which contains local variables. Whereas the call **SubsBstr**[*S, x, y*] returns the list of all nonintersecting substrings in a *S* string which are limited by symbols *x* and *y*, otherwise the empty list is returned. The following fragment represents source codes of the procedures **SubsStr** and **SubsBstr** along with typical examples of their applications.

In[2209]:= **SubsStr**[x_ /; StringQ[x], y_ /; StringQ[y], h_ /; ListQ[h], t_ /; MemberQ[{0, 1}, t]]:=
Module[{a = Map[ToString, h], b},
If[StringFreeQ[x, y], Return[x], b=If[t == 1, Map3[StringJoin, y, a], Mapp[StringJoin, a, y]]];
If[StringFreeQ[x, b], Return[x], StringReplace[x, Map9[Rule, b, h]]]]

In[2210]:= **SubsStr**["Module[{a$ = $CallProc, b$, c$}, x + StringLength[y] + b$*c$; b$ − c$; a$]", "$", {",", "]", "[", "}", " ", ";", "*", "^", "−"}, 1]
Out[2210]= "Module[{a = $CallProc, b, c}, x + StringLength[y] + b*c; b − c; a]"

In[2438]:= **SubsBstr**[S_ /; StringQ[S], x_ /; CharacterQ[x], y_ /; CharacterQ[y]] :=
Module[{a = {}, c, h, n, m, s = S, p, t},
c[s_, p_, t_] := DeleteDuplicates[Map10[StringFreeQ, s, {p, t}]] == {False};

```
While[c[s, x, y], n = StringPosition[s, x, 1][[1]][[1]];
s = StringTake[s, {n, -1}]; m = StringPosition[s, y, 1];
If[m == {}, Return[], m = m[[1]][[1]]]; AppendTo[a, h = StringTake[s, {1, m}]];
s = StringReplace[s, h -> ""]; Continue[]]; a]
In[2439]:= SubsBstr["1234523335562675243655", "2", "5"]
Out[2439]= {"2345", "23335", "2675", "24365"}
In[2440]:= SubsBstr["1234523335562675243655", "9", "5"]
Out[2440]= {}
```

The procedure call **SubsString**[s, {a, b, c, d, ...}] returns the list of substrings of a s string that are limited by {a, b, c, d, ...} substrings whereas the procedure call **SubsString**[s, {a, b, c, d, e, ...}, p] with the third optional p argument – *a pure function in short format* – returns the list of substrings of a s string which are limited by {a, b, c, d, ...} substrings, meeting the condition determined by a pure p function. Whereas the call **SubsString**[s, {a, b, c, d, ...}, p] with the 3rd optional p argument – an arbitrary expression that different from pure function – returns a list of substrings limited by substrings {a, b, c, d, ...}, with removed prefixes and suffixes {a, b, c, d, ...}[[1]] and {a, b, c, d, ...}[[-1]] accordingly. In absence in a s string of at least one of substrings {a, b, c, d, ...} the procedure call returns the empty list. The following fragment represents source code of the procedure with typical examples of its application.

```
In[3215]:= SubsString[s_ /; StringQ[s], y_ /; ListQ[y], pf___] := Module[{b, c, a = "", k = 1},
If[Set[c, Length[y]] < 2, s, b = Map[ToString1, y]];
While[k <= c - 1, a = a <> b[[k]] <> "~~ Shortest[__] ~~ "; k++];
a = a <> b[[-1]]; b = StringCases[s, ToExpression[a]];
If[{pf} != {} && PureFuncQ[pf], Select[b, pf],
If[{pf} != {}, Map[StringTake[#, {StringLength[y[[1]]] + 1, -StringLength[y[[-1]]] - 1}] &, b],
Select[b, StringQ[#] &]]]]]
In[3216]:= SubsString["adfgbffgbavzgagngbArtggbKgrg", {"b","g"}, StringFreeQ[#, "f"] &]
Out[3216]= {"bavzg", "bArtg", "bKg"}
In[3217]:= SubsString["abcxx7xxx42345abcyy7yyy42345", {"ab", "42"}, 590]
Out[3217]= {"cxx7xxx", "cyy7yyy"}
```

It should be noted, that the **SubsString1** procedure is the **SubsString** procedure extension, being of interest in programming of the problems connected with processing of strings too. The procedure call **SubsString1**[s, y, f, t] returns the list of substrings of a s string which are limited by the substrings of a y list; at that, if a testing pure function acts as f argument, the returned list will contain only the substrings satisfying this test. At that, at t = 1 the returned substrings are limited to ultra substrings of the y list, while at t = 0 substrings are returned without the limiting ultra substrings of the y list. At that, in the presence of the 5th optional r argument – *an arbitrary expression* – search of substrings in s string is done from right to left, that as a whole simplifies algorithms of search of the required substrings. The next fragment represents source code of the **SubsString1** procedure along with typical examples of its use.

```
In[2770]:= SubsString1[s_ /; StringQ[s], y_ /; ListQ[y], pf_ /; IntegerQ[pf] ||
PureFuncQ[pf], t_ /; MemberQ[{0, 1}, t], r___] :=
Module[{c, h, a = "", b = Map[ToString1, y], d = s, k = 1},
```

If[Set[c, Length[y]] < 2, s, If[{r} != {}, b = Map[StringReverse, Reverse[b]];
d = StringReverse[s]]]; While[k <= c - 1, a = a <> b[[k]] <> "~~ Shortest[__] ~~ "; k++];
a = a <> b[[-1]]; h = StringCases[d, ToExpression[a]];
If[t == 0, h=Map[StringTake[#, {StringLength[b[[1]]] - 1, -StringLength[b[[-1]]]+1}] &, h]];
If[PureFuncQ[pf], h = Select[h, pf]]; If[{r} != {}, Reverse[Map[StringReverse, h]], h]]

In[2771]:= SubsString1["12345#xyzttmnptttabc::usage=45678", {"#", "::usage=4"}, 0, 0]
Out[2771]= {"xyzttmnptttabc"}
In[2772]:= SubsString1["2#xaybz::usage=5612#xm90nyz::usage=590#AvzAgn::usage=500", {"#", "::usage="}, 0, 0]
Out[2772]= {"xaybz", "xm90nyz", "AvzAgn"}
In[2773]:= SubsString1["12345#xyz::usage=45612345#x90yz::usage=500#Avz::usage=590", {"#", "::usage="}, 0, 1]
Out[2773]= {"#xyz::usage=", "#x90yz::usage=", "#Avz::usage="}
In[2774]:= SubsString1["12345#xyz::usage=45612345#x590yz::usage=500#Avz::usage=590", {"#", "::usage="}, LetterQ[#] &, 0]
Out[2774]= {"xyz", "Avz"}

When processing substrings in strings is often need of check of existence fact of substrings overlaping that entere to the strings. The function call **SubStrOverlapQ[x, y]** returns *True*, if x string contains overlapping substrings y or substrings from x matching the general string expression y, and *False* otherwise. While the call **SubStrOverlapQ[x, y, z]** through optional z argument – an undefinite symbol – additionally returns the list of consecutive quantities of overlapings of the y sublist in the x string. The fragment below represents source code of the function with examples of its application.

In[3493]:= SubStrOverlapQ[x_String, y_, z___] :=
MemberQ[{If[{z} != {} && NullQ[z], z = {}, 6],
Map[If[Length[#] == 1, True, If[! NullQ[z], Quiet[AppendTo[z, Length[#]]], 6]; False] &,
Split[StringPosition[x, y], MemberQ[Range[#1[[1]] + 1, #1[[2]]], #2[[1]]] &]}[[2]], False]

In[3494]:= SubStrOverlapQ["dd1dd1ddaaaabcdd1d1dd1dd1dd1dd1aaaaaadd1", "aa"]
Out[3494]= True
In[3495]:= SubStrOverlapQ["dd1dd1ddaaaabcdd1d1dd1dd1dd1dd1aaaaaadd1", "aa", g]
Out[3495]= True
In[3496]:= g
Out[3496]= {3, 5}
In[3497]:= SubStrOverlapQ["AAABBBBBAABABBBBCCCBAAAAAA", x_ ~~ x_, g70]
Out[3497]= True
In[3498]:= g70
Out[3498]= {2, 4, 3, 2, 5}

The following procedure **SubStrSymbolParity** presents undoubted interest at processing of definitions of the blocks, functions or modules given in the string format. The procedure call **SubStrSymbolParity[x, y, z, d]** with four arguments returns the list of substrings of a string x that are limited by one-character strings y, z ($y \neq z$); in addtion, search of such substrings in the string x is done from left to right *(d = 0)*, and from right to left *(d = 1)*. Whereas the call **SubStrSymbolParity[x, y, z, d, t]** with the fifth optional argument – *a positive number t > 0* –

provides search in substring of *x* that is limited by *t* position and the end of *x* string at *d = 0*, and by the beginning of *x* string and *t* at *d = 1*. In case of receiving of *inadmissible* arguments the call is returned *unevaluated*, while at impossibility of extraction of demanded substrings the procedure call returns $*Failed*. This procedure is an useful tool, in particular, at solution of problems of extraction from definitions of procedures of the list of the local variables, the headings of procedures, etc. The fragment represents source code of **SubStrSymbolParity** procedure with examples of its application.

```
In[2533]:= SubStrSymbolParity[x_ /; StringQ[x], y_ /; CharacterQ[y], z_ /; CharacterQ[z],
d_ /; MemberQ[{0, 1}, d], t___ /; t == {} || PosIntQ[{t}[[1]]]] :=
Module[{a, b = {}, c = {y, z}, k = 1, j, f, m = 1, n = 0, p, h},
If[{t} == {}, f = x, f = StringTake[x, If[d == 0, {t, StringLength[x]}, {1, t}]]];
If[Map10[StringFreeQ, f, c] != {False, False} || y == z, Return[],
a = StringPosition[f, If[d == 0, c[[1]], c[[2]]]]];
For[k, k <= Length[a], k++, j = If[d == 0, a[[k]][[1]] + 1, a[[k]][[2]] - 1];
h = If[d == 0, y, z]; While[m != n, p = Quiet[Check[StringTake[f, {j, j}], Return[$Failed]]];
If[p == y, If[d == 0, m++, n++]];
If[d == 0, h = h <> p, h = p <> h], If[p == z, If[d == 0, n++, m++];
If[d == 0, h = h <> p, h = p <> h], If[d == 0, h = h <> p, h = p <> h]]];
If[d == 0, j++, j--]]; AppendTo[b, h]; m = 1; n = 0; h = ""]; b]

In[2534]:= SubStrSymbolParity["12345{abcdfgh}67{rans}8{ian}9", "{", "}", 0]
Out[1534]= {"{abcdfgh}", "{rans}", "{ian}"}
In[2535]:= SubStrSymbolParity["12345{abcdfg}67{rans}8{ian}9", "{", "}", 0, 7]
Out[2535]= {"{rans}", "{ian}"}
In[2536]:= SubStrSymbolParity["12345{abcdfgh}67{rans}8{ian}9", "{", "}", 1]
Out[2536]= {"{abcdfgh}", "{rans}", "{ian}"}
In[2537]:= SubStrSymbolParity["12345{abfgh}67{rans}8{ian}9", "{", "}", 1, 25]
Out[2537]= {"{abfgh}", "{rans}"}
In[2538]:= SubStrSymbolParity["12345{abch}67{rans}8{ian}9", "{", "}", 1, -80]
Out[2538]= SubStrSymbolParity["12345{abch}67{rans}8{ian}9", "{", "}", 1, -80]
```

Meanwhile, in many cases it is quite possible to use a simpler and reactive version of this procedure, whose call **SubStrSymbolParity1**[*x, y, z*] with 3 factual arguments returns the list of substrings of a *x* string that are limited by one-character strings {*y, z*} (*y ≠ z*); at that, search of such substrings is done from left to right. In the absence of the desired substrings the procedure call returns the empty list, i.e. {}. The next fragment represents source code of the **SubStrSymbolParity1** procedure along with examples of its application.

```
In[2023]:= SubStrSymbolParity1[x_ /; StringQ[x], y_ /; CharacterQ[y], z_ /; CharacterQ[z]]:=
Module[{c = {}, d, k = 1, j, p, a = DeleteDuplicates[Flatten[StringPosition[x, y]]],
b = DeleteDuplicates[Flatten[StringPosition[x, z]]]},
If[a == {} || b == {}, {}, For[k, k <= Length[a], k++, p = StringTake[x, {a[[k]], a[[k]]}];
For[j = a[[k]] + 1, j <= StringLength[x], j++, p = p <> StringTake[x, {j, j}];
If[StringCount[p, y] == StringCount[p, z], AppendTo[c, p]; Break[]]]]; c]]

In[2024]:= SubStrSymbolParity1["Definition2[Function[{x, y}, x*Sin[y]]", "{", "}"]
```

Out[2024]= {"{x, y}"}
In[2025]:= SubStrSymbolParity1["G[x_String, y_, z_/; ListQ[z]] := Block[{}, {x,y,z}]", "[", "]"]
Out[2025]= {"[x_String, y_, z_/; ListQ[z]]", "[z]", "[{}, {x, y, z}]"}

The following simple enough procedure is an useful enough modification of the procedure **SubStrSymbolParity1**; its call **StrSymbParity**[*S, s, x, y*] returns the list, whose elements are substrings of a *S* string which have format *sw* format on condition of parity of the minimum number of entries into a *w* substring of symbols *x, y (x ≠ y)*. In the lack of such substrings or identity of symbols *x, y*, the procedure call returns the empty list. The fragment represents source code of the **StrSymbParity** procedure with examples of its application.

In[2175]:= StrSymbParity[S_ /; StringQ[S], S1_ /; StringQ[S1], x_ /; StringQ[x] &&
StringLength[x] == 1, y_ /; StringQ[y] && StringLength[y] == 1] :=
Module[{b = {}, c = S1, d, k = 1, j, a = StringPosition[S, S1]},
If[x == y || a == {}, {}, For[k, k <= Length[a], k++, For[j = a[[k]][[2]] + 1,
j <= StringLength[S], j++, c = c <> StringTake[S, {j, j}]];
If[StringCount[c, x] != 0 && StringCount[c, y] != 0 && StringCount[c, x] ===
StringCount[c, y], AppendTo[b, c]; c = S1; Break[]]]]; b]

In[2176]:= StrSymbParity["12345[678]9[abcd]", "34", "[", "]"]
Out[2176]= {"345[678]"}
In[2177]:= StrSymbParity["12345[6[78]9", "34", "[", "]"]
Out[2177]= {}
In[2178]:= StrSymbParity["12345[678]9[ab34cd[x]34[a, b]", "34", "[", "]"]
Out[2178]= {"345[678]", "34cd[x]", "34[a, b]"}

Procedures **SubStrSymbolParity, SubStrSymbolParity1 & StrSymbParity** are rather useful tools, for instance, at processing of definitions of modules and blocks given in string format. These procedures are used by a number of means of our *MathToolBox* package [48,50].

The **SubsStrLim** procedure represents an quite certain interest for a number of appendices which rather significantly use procedure of extraction from the strings of substrings of an quite certain format. The next fragment presents source code of the **SubsStrLim** procedure along with typical examples of its application.

In[2542]:= SubsStrLim[x_ /; StringQ[x], y_ /; StringQ[y] && StringLength[y] == 1,
z_ /; StringQ[z] && StringLength[z] == 1] :=
Module[{a, b = x <> FromCharacterCode[6], c = y, d = {}, p, j, k = 1, n, h},
If[! StringFreeQ[b, y] && ! StringFreeQ[b, z], a = StringPosition[b, y];
n = Length[a]; For[k, k <= n, k++, p = a[[k]][[1]]; j = p;
While[h = Quiet[StringTake[b, {j + 1, j + 1}]]; h != z, c = c <> h; j++]; c = c <> z;
If[StringFreeQ[StringTake[c, {2, -2}], {y, z}], AppendTo[d, c]]; c = y]];
Select[d, StringFreeQ[#, FromCharacterCode[6]] &]]

In[2543]:= SubsStrLim["1234363556aaa36", "3", "6"]
Out[2543]= {"36", "3556", "36"}
In[2544]:= SubsStrLim[DefOpt["SubsStrLim"], "{", "}"]
Out[2544]= {"{}", "{j + 1, j + 1}", "{2, -2}", "{y, z}"}
In[2545]:= SubsStrLim["1234363556aaa363", "3", "3"]

Out[2545]= {"343", "363", "3556aaa3", "363"}

The call **SubsStrLim**[*x*, *y*, *z*] returns the list of substrings of a *x* string which are limited by symbols {*y*, *z*} provided that these symbols don't belong to these substrings, excepting their ends. In particular, the **SubsStrLim** procedure is a quite useful means at need of extracting from of definitions of the functions, blocks and modules given in the string format of some components composing them which are limited by certain symbols, at times, significantly simplifying a number of procedures of processing of such definitions. While the procedure call **SubsStrLim1**[*x*, *y*, *z*] that is an useful enough modification of the previous **SubsStrLim** procedure, returns list of substrings of *x* string that are limited by symbols {*y*, *z*} provided that these symbols or don't enter substrings, excepting their ends, or along with their ends have identical number of entries of pairs {*y*, *z*}, for example [48,50]:

In[2215]:= **SubsStrLim1**["art[kr[xyz]sv][rans]90[[500]]", "[", "]"]
Out[2215]= {"[kr[xyz]sv]", "[xyz]", "[rans]", "[[500]]", "[500]"}
In[2216]:= **SubsStrLim1**["G[x_] := Block[{a = 9, b = 5, c = 90}, (a^2 + b^3 + c^4)*x]", "{", "}"]
Out[2216]= {"{a = 9, b = 5, c = 90}"}

The mechanism of string patterns is quite often used for extraction of some structures from text strings. In a certain degree the the given mechanism we can quite consider as a special programming language of text structures and strings. The mechanism of the string patterns provides a rather serious method to make various processing of string structures. At that, acquaintance with special languages of processing of strings in many cases allows to define string patterns by the notation of regular expressions which are defined in the *Mathematica* system on the basis of **RegularExpression** function. The interested reader is sent to [52,61] or to the reference on the system. In this light the **RedSymbStr** procedure is represented as an quite useful means whose call **RedSymbStr**[*x*, *y*, *z*] returns result of replacement of all substrings consisting of an *y* symbol, of a *x* string onto a symbol or a *z* string. In case of lack of occurrences of the *y* in *x*, the procedure call returns the initial *x* string. The next fragment represents source code of the **RedSymbStr** procedure with typical examples of its use.

In[3202]:= **RedSymbStr**[x_ /; StringQ[x], y_ /; SymbolQ1[y], z_ /; StringQ[z]] :=
Module[{a = StringPosition[x, y], b}, If[StringFreeQ[x, y], x, b = Map[#[[1]] &, a]];
b = Sort[DeleteDuplicates[Map[Length, Split[b, #2 − #1 == 1 &]]], Greater];
StringReplace[x, GenRules[Map3[StringMultiple, y, b], z]]]
In[3203]:= **RedSymbStr**["a b c d ef   gh   x y z", " ", " "]
Out[3203]= "a b c d ef gh x y z"
In[3204]:= **RedSymbStr**["a b c d ef   gh   x y z", " ", ""]
Out[3204]= "abcdefghxyz"
In[3205]:= **RedSymbStr**["a b c d ef   gh   x y z", " ", "GGG"]
Out[3205]= "aGGGbGGGcGGGdGGGefGGGghGGGxGGGyGGGz"
In[3206]:= **RedSymbStr**["a b c d ef   gh   x y z", "x", "GGG"]
Out[3206]= "a b c d ef   gh   GGG y z"

Thus, the strings generated by earlier considered **ToString1** procedure can be called as the **StringStrings** *(strings of strings, or the nested strings)* as in case of lists; a simple function can be used for their testing whose call **StringStringQ**[*x*] returns *True* if a *x* expression presents a string of type *StringStrings*, and *False* otherwise. In a certain sense **ToString1** procedure generates the nested strings analogously to the nested lists, and the level of nesting of a *x* string can be determined by the simple procedure whose call **StringLevels[*x*]** returns the nesting level of a *x* string provided that the zero level corresponds to the standard string, i.e. a string of form *"hhhhh ... h"*. The fragment below represents source codes of function **StringStringQ** and procedure **StringLevels** with typical examples of their applications.

In[2237]:= **StringStringQ[x_] := If[! StringQ[x], False, If[SuffPref[x, "\"", 1] && SuffPref[x, "\"", 2], True, False]]**

In[2238]:= **Map[StringStringQ, {"\"vsvartkr\"", "vsv\\art\\kr", a + b, "\"\\\"vsv\\art\\kr\\\"\""}]**
Out[2238]= {True, False, False, True}

In[2703]:= **StringLevels[x_ /; StringQ[x]] := Module[{a = x, n = -1},**
While[StringQ[a], a = ToExpression[a]; n++; Continue[]]; n]

In[2704]:= **Map[StringLevels, {"agn", "\"vsv\"", "\"\\\"art\\\"\"", rans}]**
Out[2704]= {0, 1, 2, StringLevels[rans]}

For the purpose of simplification of programming of a number of procedures proved useful to define the procedure, whose call **SubsPosSymb[*x*, *m*, *y*, *z*]** returns a substring of *x* string which is limited on the right *(at the left)* by *m* position and at the left *(on the right)* by symbol from a *y* list; in addition, search in *x* string is done from left to right *(z = 1)* and from right to left *(z = 0)* starting with a *m* position. At that, the call on inadmissible arguments is returned *unevaluated*. The following fragment represents source code of the **SubsPosSymb** procedure along with typical examples of its application.

In[2942]:= **SubsPosSymb[x_ /; StringQ[x], n_ /; PosIntQ[n], y_ /; ListQ[y] && AllTrue[Map[CharacterQ, y], TrueQ], z_ /; z == 0 || z == 1] :=**
Module[{a = "", k = n, b}, If[n > StringLength[x], Return[Defer[SubsPosSymb[x, n, y, z]]],
While[If[z == 0, k >= 1, k <= StringLength[x]], b = StringTake[x, {k, k}];
If[! MemberQ[y, b], If[z == 0, a = b <> a, a = a <> b], Break[]]; If[z == 0, k--, k++]]; a]]

In[2943]:= **SubsPosSymb["123456789abcdfght", 5, {"g"}, 1]**
Out[2943]= "56789abcdf"

In[2944]:= **SubsPosSymb["123456789abcdfght", 16, {"z"}, 0]**
Out[2944]= "123456789abcdfgh"

A rather simple procedure **ListStrToStr** represents undoubted interest at processing of lists in string format, more precisely, the call **ListStrToStr[*x*]** where argument *x* has format {*"a"*, *"b"*, ...} converts *x* into string of format *"a, b, c, ..."*, if procedure call uses only an arbitrary actual *x* argument; if the procedure call uses an arbitrary expression as the *second* argument, the call returns a string of *"abcde..."* format. The following fragment represents source code of the **ListStrToStr** procedure along with examples of its application.

In[3828]:= **ListStrToStr[x_ /; ListQ[x] && AllTrue[Map[StringQ, x], TrueQ], p___] :=**
Module[{a = ""}, If[{p} == {}, Do[a = a <> x[[k]] <> ", ", {k, Length[x]}];
StringTake[a, {1, -3}], StringJoin[x]]]

In[3829]:= **ListStrToStr[{"a", "b", "c", "d", "h", "t", "k", "Art", "Kr", "Rans"}]**
Out[3829]= "a, b, c, d, h, t, k, Art, Kr, Rans"

In[3830]:= **ListStrToStr[{"a*b", "*", "t[x]", " - ", "(c - d)", "*", "j[y]", " == ", "6"}, 6]**
Out[3830]= "a*b*t[x] - (c - d)*j[y] == 6"

The following procedure is a rather useful means for ensuring of converting of strings of a certain structure into lists of strings. In particular, such tasks arise at processing of formal arguments and local variables. This problem is solved a rather effectively by the **StrToList** procedure, providing converting of strings of "{*xxxxxxx ... x*}" format into the list of strings received from a "*xxxxxx ... x*" string parted by comma symbols ",". In absence in an initial string of both limiting symbols {"{", "}"} the string is converted into list of symbols according to the call **Characters**["*xxxxx ... x*"]. The next fragment presents source code of the **StrToList** procedure with examples of its application.

In[2190]:= **StrToList[x_ /; StringQ[x]] :=**
Module[{a, b = {}, c = {}, d, h, k = 1, j, y = If[StringTake[x, {1, 1}] ==
"{" && StringTake[x, {-1, -1}] == "}", StringTake[x, {2, -2}], x]},
a = DeleteDuplicates[Flatten[StringPosition[y, "="]] + 2]; d = StringLength[y];
If[a == {}, Map[StringTrim, StringSplit[y, ","]], While[k <= Length[a], c = ""; j = a[[k]];
For[j, j <= d, j++, c = c <> StringTake[y, {j, j}];
If[! SameQ[Quiet[ToExpression[c]], $Failed] && (j == d || StringTake[x, {j + 1, j + 1}] ==
","), AppendTo[b, c -> ToString[Unique[ArtKr$]]]; Break[]]]; k++];
h = Map[StringTrim, StringSplit[StringReplace[y, b], ","]];
Map14[StringReplace, h, RevRules[b]]]]

In[2191]:= **StrToList["Kr, a = 90, b = {x, y, z}, c = {n, m, {42, 47, 67}}"]**
Out[2191]= {"Kr", "a = 90", "b = {x, y, z}", "c = {n, m, {42, 47, 67}}"}
In[2192]:= **StrToList["{a, b = 90, c = {m, n}}"]**
Out[2192]= {"a", "b = 90", "c = {m, n}"}
In[2193]:= **Map[StrToList, {"{a, b, c, d}", "a, b, c, d"}]**
Out[2193]= {{"a", "b", "c", "d"}, {"a", "b", "c", "d"}}

In[2194]:= **RevRules[x_ /; RuleQ[x] || ListQ[x] && AllTrue[Map[RuleQ, x], TrueQ]] :=**
Module[{a = Flatten[{x}], b}, b = Map[#[[2]] -> #[[1]] &, a]; If[Length[b] == 1, b[[1]], b]]
In[2195]:= **RevRules[{x -> a, y -> b, z -> c, h -> g, m -> n}]**
Out[2195]= {a -> x, b -> y, c -> z, g -> h, n -> m}

The above procedure is intended for converting of strings of format "{*x...x*}" or "*x...x*" into the list of strings received from strings of the specified format which are parted by symbols "=" and/or comma ",". Fragment examples an quite visually illustrate the basic principle of performance of the procedure along with formats of the returned results. At that, fragment is ended by a quite simple and useful procedure, whose call **RevRules**[*x*] returns the rule or list of rules that are reverse to the rules defined by a *x* argument – a rule of format *a -> b* or their list. We note that the procedure is essentially used by the above **StrToList** procedure.

The next means are useful at work with string structures. The procedure call **StringPat**[*x, y*] returns the string expression formed by strings of a *x* list and objects {"_", "__", "___"}; the call returns *x* if *x* – a string. The procedure call **StringCases1**[*x, y, z*] returns the list of the substrings in a *x* string which match a string expression, created by the call **StringPat**[*x, y*]. While the function call **StringFreeQ1**[*x, y, z*] returns *True* if no substring in *x* string matches a string expression, created by the call **StringPat[x, y]**, and *False* otherwise. In the fragment below, source codes of the above 3 tools with examples of their applications are presented.

In[2583]:= **StringPat[x_ /; StringQ[x] || ListStringQ[x], y_ /; MemberQ[{"_", "__", "___"}, y]]** :=
Module[{a = "", b}, If[StringQ[x], x, b = Map[ToString1, x];
ToExpression[StringJoin[Map[# <> "~~" <> y <> "~~" &, b[[1 ;; -2]]], b[[-1]]]]]]

In[2584]:= **StringPat[{"ab", "df", "k"}, "__"]**
Out[2584]= "ab" ~~ __ ~~ "df" ~~ __ ~~ "k"

In[2585]:= **StringCases1[x_ /; StringQ[x], y_ /; StringQ[y] || ListStringQ[y],
z_ /; MemberQ[{"_", "__", "___"}, z]]** := Module[{b, c = "", d, k = 1},
Sort[Flatten[Map[DeleteDuplicates, If[StringQ[y], {StringCases[x, y]},
{StringCases[x, StringPat[y, z], Overlaps -> All]}]]]]]

In[2587]:= **StringCases1["abcdfghkaactabcfgfhkt", {"ab", "df", "k"}, "___"]**
Out[2587]= {"abcdfghk", "abcdfghkaactabcfgfhk"}

In[2588]:= **StringFreeQ1[x_ /; StringQ[x], y_ /; StringQ[y] || ListStringQ[y],
z_ /; MemberQ[{"_", "__", "___"}, z]]** :=
If[StringQ[y], StringFreeQ[x, y], If[StringCases1[x, y, z] == {}, True, False]]

In[2589]:= **StringFreeQ1["abcfghkaactabcfghkt", {"ab", "df", "k"}, "___"]**
Out[2589]= True

In[2590]:= **StringFreeQ1["abcdfghkaactabcfghkt", {"ab", "df", "k"}, "___"]**
Out[2590]= False

In[3163]:= **StringCases2[x_ /; StringQ[x], y_ /; ListQ[y] && y != {}]** :=
Module[{a, b = "", c = Map[ToString, y]},
Do[b = b <> ToString1[c[[k]]] <> "~~__~~", {k, 1, Length[c]}];
a = ToExpression[StringTake[b, {1, -7}]]; StringCases[x, Shortest[a]]]

In[3164]:= **StringCases2["a1234b7890000c5a b ca1b2c3", {a, b, c}]**
Out[3164]= {"a1234b7890000c", "a b c", "a1b2c"}

Whereas the call **StringCases2[x, y]** returns a list of the disjoint substrings in a *x* string that match the string expression of the format **Shortest[j1~~__~~j2 ~~__~~...~~__~~jk]**, where *y* = {j1, j2, ..., jk} and *y* is different from the empty list, i.e. {}.

The above tools are used by a number of tools of *MathToolBox* package, enough frequently essentially improving the programming algorithms which deal with string expressions. It should be noted, that specifying patterns for strings by using the string expressions which contain ordinary strings mixed with *Math*-language symbolic pattern objects, we can obtain useful and effective enough methods of string processing. As examples the above **StringPat** procedure and a number of other means represented below can serve.

The following procedure is a rather useful means of strings processing in a cases when it is required to identify in a string of occurrence of substrings of kind *"abc...n"* and *"abc...np"* where *p* – a character. The procedure call **SubsInString[x, y, z]** returns *0*, if substrings *y* and *y<>z* where *y* – a string and *z* – a character are absent in a *x* string; *1*, if *x* contains *y* and not contain *y <> z*; *2*, if *x* contains *y <> z* and not contain *y*, and three otherwise, i.e. the *x* string contains *y* and *y* <> *z*. The next fragment presents source code of the procedure along with examples of its application.

In[4110]:= **SubsInString[x_ /; StringQ[x], y_ /; StringQ[y], z_ /; CharacterQ[z]] :=**
Module[{a = FromCharacterCode[4], b}, b = StringReplace[x, y <> z -> a];
If[StringFreeQ[b, {a, y}], 0, If[! StringFreeQ[b, y] && StringFreeQ[b, a], 1,
If[! StringFreeQ[b, a] && StringFreeQ[b, y], 2, 3]]]]

In[4111]:= **SubsInString["b/x^2*Csc[x*y] + Csc", "Csc", "["]**
Out[4111]= 3

In[4112]:= **SubsInString["b/x^2*Csc[x*y] + 5*Csc[x]", "Csc", "["]**
Out[4112]= 2

Whereas the procedure call **CorrSubStrings[*x*, *n*, *y*]** returns the list of substrings of *x* string which contain all formally correct expressions, at the same time, search is done beginning with *n*-th position of the *x* string from left to right if the third optional *y* argument is absent and from right to left if the *y* argument – an arbitrary expression – exists. The next fragment represents source code of the procedure with an example of its application.

In[4197]:= **CorrSubStrings[x_ /; StringQ[x], n_ /; PosIntQ[n], y___] :=**
Module[{a = {}, b = StringLength[x], c = ""},
If[{y} != {}, Do[If[SyntaxQ[Set[c, StringTake[x, {j}]] <> c]], AppendTo[a, c], 6], {j, n, 1, -1}],
Do[If[SyntaxQ[Set[c, c <> StringTake[x, {j}]]], AppendTo[a, c], 6], {j, n, b}]]; a]

In[4198]:= **CorrSubStrings["(a+b/x^2)/(c/x^3+d/y^2)+1/z^3", 29, 2]**
Out[4198]= {"3", "z^3", "1/z^3", "+1/z^3", "(c/x^3+d/y^2)+1/z^3",
"(a+b/x^2)/(c/x^3+d/y^2)+1/z^3"}

In a number of cases there is a necessity of reducing to the given number of the quantity of entries into the string of its adjacent substrings. This problem is solved successfully by the **ReduceAdjacentStr** procedure represented by the following fragment. The procedure call **ReduceAdjacentStr[*x*, *y*, *n*]** returns a string – the result of reducing to the quantity *n* ≥ *0* of occurrences into a *x* string of its adjacent *y* substrings. If a *x* string not contain *y* substrings, then the call returns the initial *x* string. While the call **ReduceAdjacentStr[*x*, *y*, *n*, *h*]**, where *h* – any expression, returns the above result on condition that at search of the *y* substrings in a *x* string the lowercase and uppercase letters are considered as equivalent letters.

In[55]:= **ReduceAdjacentStr[x_ /; StringQ[x], y_ /; StringQ[y], n_ /; IntegerQ[n], z___] :=**
Module[{a = {}, b = {}, c = Append[StringPosition[x <> FromCharacterCode[0], y,
IgnoreCase -> If[{z} != {}, True, False]], {0, 0}], h, k},
If[c == {}, x, Do[If[c[[k]][[2]] + 1 == c[[k + 1]][[1]], b = Union[b, {c[[k]], c[[k + 1]]}],
b = Union[b, {c[[k]]}]; a = Union[a, {b}]; b = {}], {k, 1, Length[c] - 1}];
a = Select[a, Length[#] >= n &];
a = Map[Quiet[Check[{#[[1]], #[[-1]]}, Nothing]] &,
Map[Flatten, Map[#[[-Length[#] + n ;; -1]] &, a]]];
StringReplacePart[x, "", a]]]

In[56]:= **ReduceAdjacentStr["abababcdcdxmnabmnabab", "ab", 3]**
Out[56]= "abababcdcdxmnabmnabab"

In[57]:= **ReduceAdjacentStr["abababcdcdxmnabmnabab", "ab", 1]**
Out[57]= "abcdcdxmnabmnab"
In[58]:= **ReduceAdjacentStr["abababcdcdxmnabmnabababab", "aB", 2]**
Out[58]= "abababcdcdxmnabmnabababab"
In[59]:= **ReduceAdjacentStr["abababcdcdxmnabmnabababab", "aB", 2, 6]**
Out[59]= "ababcdcdxmnabmnabab"
In[60]:= **ReduceAdjacentStr["aba   Baa baa   baab aa aab   aaa", " ", 1]**
Out[60]= "aba Baa baa baab aa aab aaa"

As against the standard **StringReplacePart** the **StringReplacePart1** procedure provides the *replacements* in strings not on the basis of positions of the replaced substrings but according to ordinal numbers of their entries. So, procedure call **StringReplacePart1[*x, y, z, n*]** returns result of *replacement* in *x* string of *y* substrings onto *z* string according to ordinal number(s) of occurrences of *y* substrings into the *x* string which are defined by an integer or an integer list *n*. In case of impossibility of such replacement, for example, the *n* list contains numbers which are different from order numbers of entries of *y* in a *x*, the procedure call returns the initial *x* string. In addition, the procedure ignores *inadmissible* elements of the *n* list, without initiating an erroneous situation. Whereas the function call **GatherStrLetters[*x*]** of a rather simple function returns the result of gathering of the letters of the *x* string into substrings of identical letters. The next fragment represents source codes of both tools along with typical examples of their applications.

In[3006]:= **StringReplacePart1[x_ /; StringQ[x], y_ /; StringQ[y], z_ /; StringQ[z],**
n_ /; IntegerQ[n] || ListQ[n] && AllTrue[Map[IntegerQ[#] &, n], TrueQ]] :=
Module[{a = StringPosition[x, y]},
If[a == {}, x, StringReplacePart[x, z, Map[Quiet[Check[a[[#]], Nothing]] &, Flatten[{n}]]]]]
In[3007]:= **StringReplacePart1["abababcdcdxmnabmnabab", "ab", "NEW47", {1, 4, 6}]**
Out[3007]= "NEW47ababcdcdxmnNEW47mnabNEW47"
In[3008]:= **StringReplacePart1["abababcdcdxabmnabab", "ab", "NEW47", 5]**
Out[3008]= "abababcdcdxabmnNEW47ab"
In[3009]:= **StringReplacePart1["abababcdxnabmnabab", "ab", "NEW", 25]**
Out[3009]= "abababcdxnabmnabab"

In[3010]:= **GatherStrLetters[x_ /; StringQ[x]] := StringJoin[Map[StringJoin,**
Map[FromCharacterCode, Gather[ToCharacterCode[x], #1 == #2 &]]]]

In[3011]:= **GatherStrLetters["abababcdcdxmnabmnabab"]**
Out[3011]= "aaaaaabbbbbbccddxmmnn"
In[3012]:= **GatherStrLetters["ambvfdsaertdsfweqgh1343267548klhgf"]**
Out[3012]= "aambvfffddsseertwqgghh1334426758kl"

The procedure call **CorrectSubString[*x, n*]** returns the result of extracting from a *x* string of the first syntactically correct expression, beginning from the *n*-th position to the right. At absence of such expression or at *n* beyond the range of {**1, StringLength[*x*]**}, or at *x* == \"\" the procedure call returns $*Failed*. The next fragment presents source code of the procedure and typical examples of its application.

In[3202]:= **CorrectSubString[x_ /; StringQ[x], y_ /; IntegerQ[y], z___] :=**
Module[{a = "", b = StringLength[x], k, t = 0},

If[y >= 1 && y <= b || x == "", If[{z} != {}, Do[a = StringTake[x, {k, k}] <> a;
If[SyntaxQ[a], t = 1; Break[]], {k, y, 1, -1}], Do[a = a <> StringTake[x, {k, k}];
If[SyntaxQ[a], t = 1; Break[]], {k, y, b}]]; If[t == 1, a, $Failed], $Failed]]

In[3203]:= CorrectSubString["{a,y,d={x},h,c,h,d,a=6,h=2,c=7,a},{a d}]", 1]
Out[3203]= "{a,y,d={x},h,c,h,d,a=6,h=2,c=7,a}"
In[3204]:= SyntaxQ["{a,y,d={x},h,c,h,d,a=6,h=2,c=7,a,{a d}]"]
Out[3204]= False
In[3205]:= CorrectSubString["", 0]
Out[3205]= $Failed

This procedure allows to extract correct expressions from strings provided that the symbol which is in the *n* position is not correct expression, in particular, symbol "{". Therefore, the **CorrectSubString** procedure is a convenient enough means for extracting of local variables from modules and blocks.

In contrast to **LongestCommonSubsequence** the call **LongestCommonSubsequence1**[*x, y, J*] in mode *IgnoreCase* –> *J*∈{*True, False*} finds the longest contiguous substrings common to the strings *x* and *y*. Whereas the call **LongestCommonSubsequence1**[*x, y, J, t*] additionally through an undefinite *t* variable returns the list of all common contiguous substrings. The procedure essentially uses the procedure whose call **Intersection1**[*x, y, z, ..., J*] returns the list of elements common to all lists of strings in the mode *IgnoreCase* –> *J*∈{*True, False*}. The next fragment presents source codes of both procedures with typical examples of their use.

In[3324]:= LongestCommonSubsequence1[x_ /; StringQ[x], y_ /; StringQ[y],
Ig_ /; MemberQ[{False, True}, Ig], t___] :=
Module[{a = Characters[x], b = Characters[y], c, d, f},
f[z_, h_] := Map[If[StringFreeQ[h, #], Nothing, #] &, Map[StringJoin[#] &,
Subsets[z]][[2 ;; -1]]];
c = Gather[d = Sort[If[Ig == True, Intersection1[f[a, x], f[b, y], Ig],
Intersection[f[a, x], f[b, y]]], StringLength[#1] <= StringLength[#2] &],
StringLength[#1] == StringLength[#2] &];
If[{t} != {} && ! HowAct[t], t = d, Null]; c = If[c == {}, {}, c[[-1]]];
If[c == {}, {}, If[Length[c] == 1, c[[1]], c]]]

In[3325]:= {LongestCommonSubsequence1["AaAaBaCBbBaCaccccC",
"CacCCbbbAaABaBa", False, gs], gs}
Out[3325]= {{"AaA", "aBa", "Cac"}, {"a", "A", "b", "B", "c", "C", "aA", "Aa", "aB", "ac", "Ba", "Ca", "cC", "AaA", "aBa", "Cac"}}

In[3471]:= Intersection1[x__ /; AllTrue[Map[ListQ[#] &, {x}], TrueQ],
Ig_ /; MemberQ[{False, True}, Ig]] := Module[{b = Length[{x}], c = {}, d = {}},
Do[AppendTo[c, Map[StringQ, {x}[[j]]]], {j, 1, b}];
If[DeleteDuplicates[c] != {True}, $Failed,
If[Ig == False, Intersection[x], Do[AppendTo[d, Map[{j, #, ToUpperCase[ToString[#]]} &,
{x}[[j]]]], {j, 1, b}];
c = Map[DeleteDuplicates, Gather[Flatten[Join[d], 1], #1[[3]] == #2[[3]] &]];

```
c = Flatten[Select[c, Length[#] >= b &], 1];
c = If[DeleteDuplicates[Map[#[[1]] &, c]] !=
Range[1, b], {}, DeleteDuplicates[Map[#[[2]] &, c]]]]]]
In[3472]:= Intersection1[{"AB", "XY", "cd", "Mn"}, {"ab", "cD", "MN", "pq", "mN"},
{"90", "mn", "Ag"}, {"500", "mn", "Av"}, True]
Out[3472]= {"Mn", "MN", "mN", "mn"}
```

The **LongestCommonSubsequence2** procedure is a some extension of the above procedure **LongestCommonSubsequence1** in case of a finite number of strings in which the search for longest common continuous substrings is done. The call **LongestCommonSubsequence2**[*x, y, z,..., h, J*] in the mode *IgnoreCase* –> *J*∈{*True, False*} finds the longest contiguous substrings common to the strings *x, y, ..., h*. In addition, the setting {*True* | *False*} for the last *J* argument is equivalent to the option *IgnoreCase* –> {*True* | *False*} which treats lowercase and uppercase letters as equivalent or not at search of substrings. The next fragment represents source code of the procedure with examples of its application.

```
In[3748]:= LongestCommonSubsequence2[x__ /; AllTrue[Flatten[Map[StringQ, {x}]],
TrueQ], Ig_ /; MemberQ[{False, True}, Ig]] :=
Module[{a = {}, b = {x}, c = Length[{x}], d = {}, h}, h = Subsets[b, 2][[c + 2 ;; -1]];
Do[AppendTo[a, LongestCommonSubsequence1[h[[k]][[1]], h[[k]][[2]], Ig]],
{k, 1, Length[h]}]; a = DeleteDuplicates[Flatten[a]];
Do[If[DeleteDuplicates[Flatten[Map[! StringFreeQ[#, a[[k]], IgnoreCase -> Ig] &, b]]] ==
{True}, AppendTo[d, a[[k]]], Null], {k, 1, Length[a]}]; d]
In[3749]:= LongestCommonSubsequence2["ABxCDH", "ABxCDCABCdc", "ABxC",
"xyzABXC", "xyzABxCF", "mnpABxC", False]
Out[3749]= {"AB"}
In[3750]:= LongestCommonSubsequence2["ABxCDH", "ABxCDCABCdc", "ABxC",
"xyzABXC", "xyzABxC", "mnpABxC", True]
Out[3750]= {"ABxC", "ABXC"}
In[3751]:= LongestCommonSubsequence2["ABxCDH", "ABxCDCABCdc", "ABxC",
"xyzABXC", "xyzABxC", "mnpABxC", "Agn", False]
Out[3751]= {"A"}
In[3752]:= LongestCommonSubsequence2["ABxCDH", "ABxCDCABCdc", "ABxC",
"xyzABXC", "xyzABxC", "mnpABxC", "TRG", False]
Out[3752]= {}
```

In addition to the **Intersection1** procedure the **IntersectStrings** procedure can be an useful enough which solves the question of finding of all contiguous intersections of the symbols between strings of the given tuple. The procedure call **IntersectStrings**[*x, y, z, ..., h, J*] in the mode *IgnoreCase* –> *J*∈{*True, False*} finds *all* contiguous substrings common to the strings *x, y, ..., h*. In addition, the setting {*True* | *False*} for the last argument *J* is equivalent to the option *IgnoreCase* –> {*True* | *False*} that treats lowercase and uppercase letters as equivalent or not at search of common substrings. Furthermore, the call **IntersectStrings**[*x, J*] returns the list of all contiguous substrings of symbols in a *x* string. The procedure is of interesting enough for strings processings problems. The next fragment represents source code of the procedure with examples of its application.

In[3692]:= **IntersectStrings[x__ /; AllTrue[Flatten[Map[StringQ, {x}]], TrueQ],
Ig_ /; MemberQ[{False, True}, Ig]] :=
Module[{a = {}, b = If[Length[{x}] == 1, {x, x}, {x}], c, d = {}, h},
If[x == "", {}, c = Length[b]; h = Subsets[b, 2][[c + 2 ;; -1]];
Do[{ClearAll[p], LongestCommonSubsequence1[h[[k]][[1]], h[[k]][[2]], Ig, p],
AppendTo[a, p]}, {k, 1, Length[h]}];
h = DeleteDuplicates[ToExpression["Intersection1[" <> StringTake[ToString1[a], {2, -2}]
<> "," <> ToString[Ig] <> "]"]];
Flatten[Map[Sort, Gather[h, StringLength[#1] == StringLength[#2] &]]]]]**

In[3693]:= **IntersectStrings["ABxCDxyH", "ABxCDCABCdxy", "ABxCxyz", "xyzABXC",
"ABxCyDCABCxydc", True]**
Out[3693]= {"A", "B", "c", "C", "d", "D", "x", "X", "y", "AB", "Bx", "BX", "xC", "XC", "xy",
"ABx", "ABX", "BxC", "BXC", "ABxC", "ABXC"}

In[3694]:= **IntersectStrings["ABxCDxyH", "ABxCDCABCdxy", "ABxCxyz", "xyzABXC",
"ABxCyDCABCxydc", False]**
Out[3694]= {"A", "B", "C", "x", "y", "AB", "xy"}

In[3695]:= **IntersectStrings["ABx6CD", False]**
Out[3695]= {"6", "A", "B", "C", "D", "x", "6C", "AB", "Bx", "CD", "x6", "6CD", "ABx", "Bx6",
"x6C", "ABx6", "Bx6C", "x6CD", "ABx6C", "Bx6CD", "ABx6CD"}

The **SelectContains** procedure is a certain extension of standard functions **Select, Cases** and **StringCases** in the case of a list of strings. The call **SelectContains[*x, y, w, Ig*]** according to the value *False* or *True* of the *w* argument returns the list of elements-strings of a *x* list which contain elements-strings from *y* list or don't contain occurrences from the *y* list respectively. At that, the setting {*True (the default in the case of the omitted argument)* | *False*} for the optional *Ig* argument is equivalent to the option *IgnoreCase -> {True | False}* that considers lowercase and uppercase letters as equivalent or not at search of substrings. In addition, the procedure essentially uses the procedure whose call **Riffle1[*x*]** restructures a list *x* of *ListList* type into the list of *ListList* type as follows:

Riffle1[{{*a1, b1, c1, ...*}, {*a2, b2, c2, ...*}, ...}] → {{*a1, a2, a3, ...*}, {*b1, b2, b3, ...*}, ...}

In[3503]:= **Riffle1[x_ /; ListListQ[x]] :=
Module[{a = {}}, Do[AppendTo[a, Map[#[[k]] &, x]], {k, 1, Length[x[[1]]]}]; a]**

In[3504]:= **Riffle1[{{"a", "b", "c"}, {m, n, p}, {c, d, h}, {r, s, t}, {1, 2, 3}}]**
Out[3504]= {{"a", m, c, r, 1}, {"b", n, d, s, 2}, {"c", p, h, t, 3}}

In[3507]:= **SelectContains[x_ /; ListQ[x] && AllTrue[Map[StringQ, x], TrueQ],
y_ /; ListQ[y] && AllTrue[Map[StringQ, y], TrueQ], w_ /; MemberQ[{False, True}, w],
Ig_: True] := Module[{a = Riffle1[Map[StringFreeQ[x, #, IgnoreCase -> Ig] &, y]], b},
b = Map[ToExpression["And[" <> StringTake[ToString[#], {2, -2}] <> "]"] &, a];
Map[If[#[[2]] === w, #[[1]], Nothing] &, Riffle1[{x, b}]]]**

In[3508]:= **SelectContains[{"az", "bz", "azb", "50090", "abczcd", "bcdez"}, {"abc", "b", "z"},
True]**
Out[3508]= {"50090"}

In[3509]:= **SelectContains[{"az", "bz", "azb", "50090", "abczcd", "bcdez"}, {"abc", "b", "z"}, False]**
Out[3509]= {"az", "bz", "azb", "abczcd", "bcdez"}
In[3510]:= **SelectContains[{"az", "bz", "azb", "50090", "ABCZCD", "bcdez"}, {"abc", "b", "z"}, True, False]**
Out[3510]= {"50090", "ABCZCD"}

The standard **StringFormat** function returns format name of the type used by the function **Import** or **ImportString**. Meantime, the **StringFormat** uses heuristic methods, and may not give correct results, particularly for *shorter* strings. A modification of **StringFormat** provides clarification of result returned by the **StringFormat**. The procedure call **StringFormat1[*j*, *y*]** returns result of the call **StringFormat[*j*]** as the main result while thru optional *y* argument – *an undefinite symbol* – a type of expression contained in the *j* string is returned. If a *y* string contains an incorrect expression, then *y* variable receives $*Failed* value. At that, on the main result different from {*"Text"*, *"Package"*} the optional *y* argument is returned as unevaluated. The fragment below represents source code of the **StringFormat1** procedure along with the most typical examples of its application.

In[3604]:= **StringFormat1[j_ /; StringQ[j], y___] := Module[{a = StringFormat[j], b, c},**
If[MemberQ[{"Package", "Text"}, a],
If[CallQ[j], b = {"Call", StringTake[j, StringPosition[j, "[", 1][[1]][[1]] – 1]},
b = Quiet[ToString[Head2[c = ToExpression[j]]]];
b = If[c === $Failed, $Failed, If[SameQ[c, Null], "String", b]]];
If[{y} == {}, 6, y = b]; a]; a]
In[3605]:= **StringFormat["Sin[x] + b"]**
Out[3605]= "Package"
In[3606]:= **Clear[t]; {StringFormat1["Sin[x] + b", t], t}**
Out[3606]= {"Package", "Plus"}
In[3607]:= **Clear[t]; {StringFormat1["{a, b, c, d, g, h}", t], t}**
Out[3607]= {"Text", "List"}
In[3608]:= **Clear[t]; {StringFormat1["ProcQ[x]", t], t}**
Out[3608]= {"Text", {"Call", "ProcQ"}}
In[3609]:= **Clear[t]; {StringFormat1["69*agn + #*74&", t], t}**
Out[3609]= {"Text", "ShortPureFunction"}
In[3610]:= **Clear[t]; {StringFormat1["1 2 3\n 5 6 7\n 8 9 0\n", t], t}**
Out[3610]= {"Table", t}
In[3611]:= **Clear[t]; {StringFormat1["1,2\n 3,4\n 5,6\n", t], t}**
Out[3611]= {"CSV", t}
In[3612]:= **Clear[t]; {StringFormat1["1\t2\n 3\t4\n 5\t6\n", t], t}**
Out[3612]= {"TSV", t}

The **CountCharacters** procedure calculates quantity of different characters composing an arbitrary string. Thus, the procedure call **CountCharacters[*x*]** returns the nested list whose elements have format {*"s"*, *n*}, where *"s"* – a character and *n* – its multiplicity in a *x* string. At that, in the resultant list the procedure groups together the elements of the above format depending on the type of *"s"* character from the angle {*letters* | *other symbols*}; in addition, all elements of the above form including the grouped elements of the resultant list are sorted in the ascending order of **ToCharacterCode["s"]**. While the call **ToCharacterCode["s", y]** with the second optional *y* argument – *an indefinite symbol* – thru it additionally returns the type of characters tuple composing the *x* string: *"Letters"* – the *x* contains only letters, *"Symbols"* – the *x* contains characters different from letters, and *"Mixture"* if *x* string contains characters of both types. The fragment below presents source code of the **CountCharacters** procedure with examples of its application.

In[3601]:= **CountCharacters[x_ /; StringQ[x], y___] := Module[{a, b},**
a = GatherBy[Map[{#[[1]], Length[#]} &, Sort[Gather[Characters[x], #1 == #2 &],
ToCharacterCode[#1[[1]]][[1]] <= ToCharacterCode[#2[[1]]][[1]] &]], LetterQ[#[[1]]] &];
b = If[Length[a] == 1, a[[1]], a];
If[{y} != {} && ! HowAct[y], y = If[Length[a] == 2, "Mixture",
If[Quiet[Check[LetterQ[b[[1]][[1]]], False]], "Letters", "Symbols"]], 6]; b]

In[3602]:= **CountCharacters["qwasde*rfd!ewsaghb=vfdrtyujb42+47gfdre"]**
Out[3602]= {{{"!", 1}, {"*", 1}, {"+", 1}, {"2", 1}, {"4", 2}, {"7", 1}, {"=", 1}}, {{"a", 2}, {"b", 2}, {"d", 4}, {"e", 3}, {"f", 3}, {"g", 2}, {"h", 1}, {"j", 1}, {"q", 1}, {"r", 3}, {"s", 2}, {"t", 1}, {"u", 1}, {"v", 1}, {"w", 2}, {"y", 1}}}

In[3603]:= **CountCharacters["!634+74+69"]**
Out[3603]= {{"!", 1}, {"+", 2}, {"3", 1}, {"4", 2}, {"6", 2}, {"7", 1}, {"9", 1}}

In[3604]:= **CountCharacters["! 2016 + 74 + 69", g69]; g69**
Out[3604]= "Symbols"

In[3605]:= **Map[CountCharacters, {"", " ", "   ", "   "}]**
Out[3605]= {{}, {{" ", 1}}, {{" ", 5}}, {{" ", 16}}}

The following procedure provides possibility of application of various functions to various substrings of strings. The procedure call **FuncToStringPart[x, y, z]** returns the string that is result of application to its substrings determined by an *y* position or their list the functions defined by *z* argument – a function or their list. While the call **FuncToStringPart[x, y, z, h]** where *h* – an arbitrary expression also returns the string which is result of application to its substrings determined by an *y* argument the functions defined by the *z* argument, provided that in case of a *j* number of the generated substrings which is greater than a *n* number of *y* functions, the initial *y* list is extended to the left on *j–n* of copies of the first function from *y*, otherwise the extension is made to the right on *j–n* of copies of the last function of the *y*. The procedure uses three auxiliary means, having independent interest as well.

The procedure call **AlignList[x, y, h]** returns the list of the format {x, y*}, where y* = y if the lengths of *x* and *y* are equal, y* = y[[1 ;; Length[y] – Length[x]]], if length of a *x* is lesser than length of *y*, otherwise y* is an extension whose type is defined by optional *h* argument: if *h* *(an arbitrary expression)* is encoded then y* is extension of the initial *y* list to the left on *p = Length[x] – Length[y]* copies of the first element of *y*, otherwise the extension of *y* is made to the right on *p* copies of the last element of the *y*. The call **RepeatList[x, y, n, z]** returns the *x* list, expanded to the right *(to the left, if the optional z argument – an arbitrary expression – was encoded)* on *n* copies of *y*. The procedure call **StringPartition1[x, y]** returns list of substrings that are result of partition of a *x* string by the positions determined by an *y* integer or their list, whereas the procedure call **StringPartition2[x, y]** returns the list of substrings that are result of partition of a *x* string by means of a one-symbol *y* string; in addition, the returned substrings should contain syntactically correct expressions. Procedure has a rather certain interest for the problems of strings processing. Fragment below represents the sourse codes of the above five procedures with examples of their application.

In[3643]:= **FuncToStringPart[x_ /; StringQ[x], y_ /; IntegerQ[y] || IntegerListQ[y], z_ /; DeleteDuplicates[Map[FunctionQ, Flatten[{z}]]] == {True}, h___] :=
Module[{a, b, c = {}}, a = StringPartition1[x, y]; b = AlignList[a, Flatten[{z}], h];
Do[AppendTo[c, b[[2]][[j]] @@ {b[[1]][[j]]}], {j, 1, Length[a]}]; StringJoin[c]]**

In[3644]:= **F1[x_] := x <> "74"; F2[x_] := "69" <> x; F3[x_] := ToUpperCase[x];
FuncToStringPart["avz1234567890mnphgtw", {3, 6, 9, 12}, {F1, F2, F3}, 69]**
Out[3644]= "avz741237445674697890MNPHGTW"

In[3645]:= **FuncToStringPart["avz1234567890mnp", {3, 6, 9, 12}, {F1, F2, F3}]**
Out[3645]= "avz74691234567890MNP"

In[3646]:= **AlignList[x_ /; ListQ[x], y_ /; ListQ[y] && y != {}, z___] :=
Module[{c, a = Length[x], b = Length[y]},
If[a == b, {x, y}, If[a < b, {x, y[[1 ;; a]]}, {x, RepeatList[y, If[{z} != {}, y[[1]], y[[-1]]], a - b, z]}]]]**

In[3647]:= **AlignList[{a, b, c, d, f, g, h}, {1, A, 2}, 6]**
Out[3647]= {{a, b, c, d, f, g, h}, {1, 1, 1, 1, 1, A, 2}}

In[3648]:= **AlignList[{a, b, c, d, f, g, h}, {1, A, 2}]**
Out[3648]= {{a, b, c, d, f, g, h}, {1, A, 2, 2, 2, 2, 2}}

In[3650]:= **RepeatList[x_ /; ListQ[x], y_, n_ /; IntegerQ[n], z___] :=
Module[{a = x}, Do[a = If[{z} != {}, Prepend, Append][a, y], {j, 1, n}]; a]**

In[3651]:= **RepeatList[{a, b, c, d, f, g, h}, m, 6]**
Out[3651]= {a, b, c, d, f, g, h, m, m, m, m, m, m}

In[3652]:= **RepeatList[{x, y, z, h, g, h}, m, 6, 74]**
Out[3652]= {m, m, m, m, m, m, x, y, z, h, g, h}

In[3654]:= **StringPartition1[x_ /; StringQ[x], y_ /; IntegerQ[y] || IntegerListQ[y]] :=
Module[{a=DeleteDuplicates[Sort[Flatten[Prepend[Flatten[{y}], {1, StringLength[x]}]]]], b},
b = a; Do[AppendTo[a, b[[j]] + 1], {j, 2, Length[b] - 1}]; a = Partition[Sort[a], 2];
Map[Quiet[Check[StringTake[x, #], Nothing]] &, a]]**

In[3655]:= **StringPartition1["1234567890mnphgtw", {3, 6, 9, 12}]**
Out[3655]= {"123", "456", "789", "0mn", "phgtw"}

In[3656]:= **StringPartition1["1234567890mnphgtw", {3, 6, 9, 12, 69}]**
Out[3656]= {"123", "456", "789", "0mn", "phgtw"}

In[3898]:= **StringPartition2[x_ /; StringQ[x], y_ /; StringQ[y] && StringLength[y] == 1] :=
Module[{a = y <> x <> y, b, c = {}, g, k = 1, j},
b = DeleteDuplicates[Flatten[StringPosition[a, ","]]];
For[k, k <= Length[b], k++, For[j = k + 1, j <= Length[b], j++,
If[SyntaxQ[Set[g, StringTake[a, {b[[k]] + 1, b[[j]] - 1}]]],
AppendTo[c, g]; Break[], Continue[]]]]; k = j; c]**

In[3899]:= **StringPartition2["x_, y_ /; {IntOddQ[t_] :=**

IntegerQ[t] && OddQ[t], IntOddQ[y]}[[-1]]", ","]
Out[3899]= {"x_"," y_ /; {IntOddQ[t_] := IntegerQ[t] && OddQ[t], IntOddQ[y]}[[-1]]"}
In[3900]:= **StringPartition2["123456789,abcdfgh,", ","]**
Out[3900]= {"123456789", "abcdfgh"}

The following procedure provides extraction from string of continuous substrings of length bigger than *1*. The call **ContinuousSubs[*x*]** returns the nested list whose elements have the format {*s*, {*p11*, *p12*}, ..., {*pn1*, *pn2*}} where *s* – a substring and {*pj1*, *pj2*} (*j* = 1..*n*) determine the first and last positions of copies of a continuous *s* substring which compose the *x* string. The procedure uses an auxiliary means – the **SplitIntegerList** whose call **SplitIntegerList[*x*]** returns the result of splitting of a strictly increasing *x* list of the *IntegerList* type into sublists consisting of strictly increasing tuples of integers. The **SplitIntegerList** procedure has other useful applications too. The next fragment represents source codes of both procedures along with typical examples of their applications.

In[3624]:= **SplitIntegerList[x_ /; IntegerListQ[x]] :=**
Module[{b = {}, c = {}, a = Sort[Flatten[x]]}, a = Sort[AppendTo[a, Max[a] + 6]];
Do[If[a[[j + 1]] − a[[j]] == 1, AppendTo[b, a[[j]]], AppendTo[b, a[[j]]];
AppendTo[c, b]; b = {}], {j, 1, Length[a] − 1}]; c]
In[3625]:= **SplitIntegerList[{1, 2, 3, 5, 6, 7, 8, 9, 22, 23, 25, 25, 42, 43, 47, 48}]**
Out[3625]= {{1, 2, 3}, {5, 6, 7, 8, 9}, {22, 23}, {25}, {25}, {42, 43}, {47, 48}}

In[3639]:= **ContinuousSubs[x_ /; StringQ[x]] := Module[{a},**
a = Select[DeleteDuplicates[Map[StringPosition[x, #] &, Characters[x]]], Length[#] > 1 &];
a = Map[DeleteDuplicates, Map[Flatten, a]]; a = Map[SplitIntegerList, a];
a = Select[Flatten[a, 1], Length[#] > 1 &];
a = Map[{StringTake[x, {#[[1]], #[[−1]]}], {#[[1]], #[[−1]]}} &, a];
a = Gather[Sort[a, #[[1]] &], #1[[1]] === #2[[1]] &];
a = Map[If[Length[#] == 1, #[[1]], DeleteDuplicates[Flatten[#, 1]]] &, a]; SortBy[a, First]]
In[3640]:= **ContinuousSubs["abbbssccchggxxx66xxggazzzaaabbbssz99"]**
Out[3640]= {{"66", {16, 17}}, {"99", {35, 36}}, {"aaa", {26, 28}}, {"bbb", {2, 4}, {29, 31}},
{"ccc", {7, 9}}, {"gg", {11, 12}, {20, 21}}, {"ss", {5, 6}, {32, 33}}, {"xx", {18, 19}}, {"xxx", {13, 15}},
{"zzz", {23, 25}}}

3.5. Tools of string processing that are rather useful for certain applications

The means represented in this section they are intended, first of all, for processing of string structures in special applications, however they can be used an quite successfully also in the problems of string processing of more general character.

The following procedure is an useful enough means supplementing the system tools of the strings processing. The procedure call **SubCfEntries[*x*, *n*, *y*]** generally returns the nested list of the *ListList* type, whose elements – two–element sublists whose first elements define the multiplicity while the second elements define the substrings of *n* length of a *x* string which have the specified multiplicity > *1* of their occurrences into *x* string. At that, with the default argument *y* = *False*, overlapping substrings are not treated as separate whereas the setting *y*

= *True*, the **SubCfEntries** counts substrings which overlap as separate. The fragment below represents source code of the **SubCfEntries** procedure along with examples of its use.

In[3942]:= **SubCfEntries[x_ /; StringQ[x], n_ /; IntegerQ[n] && n >= 1, y_ : False] :=**
Module[{a = Characters[x], b = x, c = {}, d = {}},
If[n > StringLength[x], $Failed, Do[c = Join[c, Partition[Characters[b], n, n]];
c = Gather[Map[StringJoin, c], #1 == #2 &];
Map[AppendTo[d, If[Length[#] > 1, #[[1]], Nothing]] &, c];
c = {}; b = StringTake[b, {2, -1}]; If[StringLength[b] < n, Break[], Null], Infinity];
d = DeleteDuplicates[Flatten[d]]; d = Map[{StringCount[x, #, Overlaps -> y], #} &, d];
If[Length[d] > 1 || d == {}, d, d[[1]]]]]
In[3943]:= **SubCfEntries["01111100110010011", 2]**
Out[3943]= {{4, "01"}, {4, "11"}, {3, "00"}, {3, "10"}}
In[3944]:= **SubCfEntries["0111110011000011", 4]**
Out[3944]= {2, "1100"}
In[3945]:= **SubCfEntries["0111100111001001001001111", 3]**
Out[3945]= {{3, "011"}, {4, "010"}, {3, "111"}, {6, "100"}, {6, "001"}}
In[3946]:= **SubCfEntries["0111100111001001001001111", 6]**
Out[3946]= {{2, "010010"}, {2, "100100"}, {2, "001001"}}
In[3947]:= **SubCfEntries["0111100111001001001001111", 6, True]**
Out[3947]= {{3, "010010"}, {4, "100100"}, {4, "001001"}}

The **SubCfEntries** procedure is of interest as an independent tool of strings processing, and as the tool used at computer research of the configurations reproducibility in *1*-dimensional cellular automata [23,50,72]. While the call **SolidSubStrings[x]** of the following procedure returns the nested list whose the first elements of 2-element sublists define solid substrings of a *x* string which consist of identical characters in quantity > *1*, while the second elements define their counts in the *x* string. In case of lack of such solid substrings the procedure call returns the empty list, i.e. {}.

In[4518]:= **SolidSubStrings[x_ /; StringQ[x]] :=**
Module[{a = DeleteDuplicates[Characters[x]], b, c = {}, d = x, n = 1},
b = Map["[" <> # <> "-" <> # <> "]+" &, a];
b = Map[Sort, Map[StringCases[x, RegularExpression[#]] &, b]];
b = Reverse[Sort[DeleteDuplicates[Flatten[Map[Select[#, StringLength[#] > 1 &] &, b]]]]];
Do[AppendTo[c, StringCount[d, b[[j]]]]; d = StringReplace[d, b[[j]] -> ""],
{j, 1, Length[b]}]; Sort[Map[{#, c[[n++]]} &, b], OrderedQ[{#1[[1]], #2[[1]]}] &]]

In[4519]:= **SolidSubStrings["qwertyuioplkjhgfdsazxcvbnm"]**
Out[4519]= {}
In[4520]:= **SolidSubStrings["cccabaaacdaammmdddddddppphaaaaaccaaa"]**
Out[4520]= {{"aa", 1}, {"aaa", 2}, {"aaaaa", 1}, {"cc", 1}, {"ccc", 1}, {"ddddddd", 1}, {"mmm", 1}, {"pp", 1}}

The next procedure below along with interest at strings processing plays a certain interest for problems of computer research of configurations dymamics of classical *1*-dimension *CA* models. The procedure call **AddEndsToString[S, a, b, n, p]** returns the result of adding to a

S string of a *n* copies of *a* substring and a *p* copies of *b* substring at the left and on the right accordingly. Arbitrary expressions can be as arguments *a* and *b*; the addition of the above substrings is made taking into account already existing substrings *a* and *b* on the *S* string ends. The next fragment represents source code of the **AddEndsToString** procedure with typical examples of its application.

In[3434]:= **AddEndsToString[S_ /; StringQ[S], s_, s1_, n_ /; IntegerQ[n],**
m_ /; IntegerQ[m]] := Module[{a = ToString[s], b = ToString[s1], c = S, k},
For[k = 1, k <= StringLength[c], k++,
If[StringTake[c, {k}] != a, c = StringTake[c, {k, −1}]; Break[], Null]];
For[k = StringLength[c], k >= 1, k−−,
If[StringTake[c, {k}] != b, c = StringTake[c, {1, k}]; Break[], Null]];
Do[c = a <> c, {k, 1, n}]; Do[c = c <> b, {k, 1, m}]; c]

In[3435]:= **AddEndsToString["555aaaaaxyz777", 5, 6, 5, 7]**
Out[3435]= "55555aaaaaxyz7776666666"
In[3436]:= **AddEndsToString["2016AvzRansIan590", 74, 69, 5, 0]**
Out[3436]= "74747474742016AvzRansIan590"

The procedure below along with independent interest appears as an useful enough tool in case of computer research of questions of the reproducibility of finite subconfigurations in *1*-dimensional *CA* models. The procedure call **StringEquiQ[*x*, *y*, *n*]** returns *True* if strings *x* and *y* differ no more, than in *n* positions, and *False* otherwise. Moreover, in the presence of the fifth optional *z* argument – *an indefinite symbol* – through it the message *"Strings lengths aren't equal"*, if lengths of strings *x* and *y* are different, or the nested list {{*n1*, {*x1*, *y1*}}, {*n2*, {*x2*, *y2*}}, ..., {*np*, {*xp*, *yp*}}} are returned whose two–element sublists determine respectively numbers of positions *(nj)*, characters of a *x* string *(xj)* and characters of a *y* string *(yj)* which differ in *nj* positions *(j = 1..p)*. It must be kept in mind that the fourth *r* argument defines the string comparison mode – *lowercase and uppercase letters are considered as different (r = True)*, or *lowercase and uppercase letters are considered as equivalent (r = False)*. The following fragment represents the source code of the **StringEquiQ** procedure with typical examples of its use.

In[3486]:= **StringEquiQ[x_ /; StringQ[x], y_ /; StringQ[y], n_ /; IntegerQ[n], r_:True, z___]:=**
Module[{a = StringLength[x], b = StringLength[y], c = {}, d, m, p, x1, y1},
If[{z} != {} && ! HowAct[z], d = 74, Null];
If[r === True, x1 = x; y1 = y, x1 = ToLowerCase[x]; y1 = ToLowerCase[y]];
If[x1 == y1, True, If[a != b, If[d == 74, z = "Strings are not equal in lengths", Null];
False, {m, p} = Map[Characters, {x1, y1}];
Do[If[m[[j]] != p[[j]], AppendTo[c, {j, {StringTake[x, {j}], StringTake[y, {j}]}}], Null], {j, 1, a}];
If[d == 74, z = c, Null]; If[Length[c] > n, False, True]]]]

In[3487]:= **StringEquiQ["Grsu_2016", "Grsu_2017", 2, False, z42]**
Out[3487]= True
In[3488]:= **z42**
Out[3488]= {{9, {"6", "7"}}}
In[3489]:= **StringEquiQ["Grsu_2016", "Grsu_4247", 2, False, z47]**
Out[3489]= False

In[3490]:= z47
Out[3490]= {{6, {"2", "4"}}, {7, {"0", "2"}}, {8, {"1", "4"}}, {9, {"6", "7"}}}
In[3491]:= **StringEquiQ["Grsu_2016", "Grsu_4247590", 2, True, z67]**
Out[3491]= False
In[3492]:= z67
Out[3492]= "Strings are not equal in lengths"

The call **Partition1**[*x, n*] returns list of all various disjoint substrings of *n* length of a *x* string. On condition **StringLength**[*x*] > *n* the procedure call returns $Failed. This procedure along with auxiliary tool for **StringCases3** is of independent interest at processing strings too. The next fragment presents source code of the **Partition1** procedure with an example of its use.

In[3672]:= **Partition1[x_, n_] := Module[{a = StringLength[x]},
If[a < n, $Failed, If[a == n, {x}, DeleteDuplicates[Map[StringTake[x, {#, # + n - 1}] &,
Range[1, a - n + 1]]]]]]**

In[3673]:= **Partition1["abcdgthyjrx", 4]**
Out[3673]= {"abcd", "bcdg", "cdgt", "dgth", "gthy", "thyj", "hyjr", "yjrx"}

The procedure call **StringCases3**[*x, p, n*] returns the nested list of substrings of *p* length of a *x* string that *in pairs (a, b)* on calls **StringEquiQ**[*a, b, n*] return *True*. It must be kept in mind that the procedure call with the fourth argument *r* determines the string comparison mode – *the lowercase and uppercase letters are considered as different (r = True), or lowercase and uppercase letters are considered as equivalent (r = False)* for the calls **StringEquiQ**[*a, b, n, r*]. The fragment below represents source code of the procedure with an example of its application.

In[3674]:= **StringCases3[x_ /; StringQ[x], m_ /; IntegerQ[m], n_ /; IntegerQ[n], R_: True] :=
Module[{a = StringLength[x], b, c = {}, d},
If[a < m, $Failed, If[a == m, x, b = Partition1[x, m]; d = Length[b];
Do[Do[AppendTo[c, If[StringEquiQ[b[[k]], b[[j]], n], {b[[k]], b[[j]]}, Nothing]],
{k, j + 1, d}], {j, 1, d - 1}];
Map[DeleteDuplicates, Map[DeleteDuplicates, Map[Flatten, Gather[DeleteDuplicates[c],
Intersection[#1, #2] != {} &]]]]]]]**

In[3675]:= **StringCases3["abcabmkgfabcdabmpqasecdrt", 4, 2]**
Out[3675]= {{"abmk", "abca", "abcd", "abmp"}, {"gfab", "bcab", "bcda", "cdab"},
{"fabc", "cabm", "dabm"}, {"bmpq", "bmkg"}, {"abmp", "abcd", "secd"}, {"ecdr", "bcda"},
{"cdrt", "cdab"}}

The following 2 tools along with self–dependent interest for problems of strings processing are of interest for problems programming of the computer research of the *1*-dimensional *CA* models too. The function call **OrderedQ1**[*x, y*] returns *True* if characters of *x* string of length > *1* are in the order determined by the 2nd *y* argument; *y*∈{*Greater, GreaterEqual, LessEqual, Less*}, and *False* otherwise. Whereas the call **LongestOrderedSubStrings**[*x, y*] returns list of the longest ordered substrings of a source string *x* of length >= 2 using the ordering function *y*∈{*Greater, GreaterEqual, Less, LessEqual*}. The fragment below represents source codes of both tools with examples of their application.

In[4282]:= **OrderedQ1[x_ /; StringQ[x] && StringLength[x] > 1,
y_ /; MemberQ[{Greater, GreaterEqual, Less, LessEqual}, y]] :=**

```
y @@ Flatten[Map[ToCharacterCode, Characters[x]]]
In[4283]:= OrderedQ1["BAACBCA", Less]
Out[4283]= False
In[4284]:= OrderedQ1["123456789BCDGH", Less]
Out[4284]= True
In[4285]:= OrderedQ1["987765443221", GreaterEqual]
Out[4285]= True

In[4298]:= LongestOrderedSubStrings[x_ /; StringQ[x] && StringLength[x] > 1,
y_ /; MemberQ[{Greater, GreaterEqual, Less, LessEqual}, y]] := Module[{a, b},
a = Select[Map[StringJoin, Flatten[Map[Partition[Characters[x], #, 1] &,
Range[2, StringLength[x]]], 1]], OrderedQ1[#, y] &];
b = Map[StringLength, a]; Select[a, StringLength[#] == Max[b] &]]
In[4299]:= LongestOrderedSubStrings["123456780BAACBCABCDGHKL", LessEqual]
Out[4299]= {"12345678", "ABCDGHKL"}
In[4300]:= LongestOrderedSubStrings["123456780BAACBCABCDGHKL", Greater]
Out[4300]= {"80", "BA", "CB", "CA"}
```

Both the system tools, and our tools of processing of strings represented in the present book form effective tools for processing of objects of the given type. The above tools of processing of string structures similar to means of the *Maple* have been based as on rather widely used standard tools of system *Mathematica*, and on our tools presented in the present book, very clearly demonstrating relative simplicity of programming in the *Math*-language of the tools similar to tools of the *Maple* as its main competitor. At that, existence in the *Mathematica* of a rather developed set of means for operating with string patterns allows to create effective and developed systems of processing of string structures that by many important indicators surpass possibilities of *Maple*. Furthermore, the means of processing of the string structures which have been programmed in the *Math*-language not only are more effective at *temporal* relation, but also *Mathematica* system for their programming has the advanced functional means, including a rather powerful mechanism of string patterns allowing to speak about a pattern type of programming and providing developed tools of processing of strings on the level which not significantly yield to the specialized languages of text processing [50].

The next simple enough means whose calls **StringMultiple1**[*s*, *p*] and **StringMultiple2**[*s*, *p*] return the results of *p*-fold concatenation of a *s* string are certain versions of the procedure **StringMultiple** [48]. While for case of characters concatenation as an useful tool can be used a function whose call **MultipleCharacter**[*x*, *n*] returns the result of *n*-fold concatenation of a *x* character. The next fragment represents source codes of the above means with examples.

```
In[3470]:= StringMultiple1[x_ /; StringQ[x], n_ /; IntegerQ[n]] := Module[{a = ""},
Do[a = a <> x, {k, 1, n}]; a]
In[3470]:= StringMultiple2[x_ /; StringQ[x], n_ /; IntegerQ[n]] :=
StringJoin[Flatten[Tuples[{x}, n]]]
In[3471]:= StringMultiple2["47", 27]
Out[3471]= "474747474747474747474747474747474747474747474747474747"
```

In[3472]:= **MultipleCharacter[x_ /; CharacterQ[x], n_ /; PosIntQ[n]] :=**
StringJoin[Map[x &, Range[1, n]]]
In[3473]:= **MultipleCharacter["$", 12]**
Out[3473]= "$$$$$$$$$$$$"

So, our experience of usage of both systems for programming of means for operating with string structures showed that standard tools of *Maple* by many essential indicators yield to the means of the same type of *Math*-language. For problems of this type *Math*-language appears simpler not only in connection with more developed means, but also a procedural and functional paradigm allowing to use mechanism of the pure functions. So, the present chapter represents a number of the tools expanding the standard facilities of system that are oriented on work with string structures. These and other tools of this type are located in our package [48]. At that, their correct use assumes that this package is loaded into the current session.

Here pertinently to note that the format of source codes of the software that are presented in the present book differs from the standard *Input*-format of the system because of trim size of the book. At that, it shouldn't cause any special difficulties at their perusal even at lack of any comments because the good code is document itself. Anyway the reader can perlustrate source codes at the loaded *MathToolBox* package [48,50]. By the way, and in the standard *Input* format the source codes aren't so readable. Meantime, for the purpose of *simplification* of viewing of the source codes of the tools presented in the present book can use freewarely distributed *CDF Player*, however, in many cases and it is not so useful. In this conexion the *Maple* is significantly more preferable, allowing rather easily to analyse their source codes with purpose of their modifications, and of familiarization with the efficient programming techniques [6-30,50].

It should be kept in mind that the descriptions of the tools represented in the chapters of the book below can be supplemented by auxiliary tools for processing the strings and lists, that, meanwhile, represent quite a specific independent interest.

Chapter 4. Additional tools of processing of sequences and lists in the *Mathematica*

At programming of many appendices the usage not of separate expressions, but their sets formed in the form of lists is expedient. At such organization instead of calculations of the separate expressions there is an opportunity to do the demanded operations as over lists in a whole – *unified objects* – and over their separate elements. Lists of various types represent important and one of the most often used structures in the *Mathematica*. In *Mathematica* system many functions have *Listable* attribute saying that an operator, a block, a function, a module *F* with this attribute are automatically applicable to each element of the list used respectively as their operand or argument. The call **ListableQ[*x*]** of simple function returns *True* if *x* has the *Listable* attribute, and *False* otherwise [48,50]. Meanwhile, a number of the operations having the *Listable* attribute requires compliance on length of the lists operands, otherwise the corresponding erroneous situations are initiated. With the view of removal of this shortcoming the **ListOp** procedure has been offered whose call **ListOp[*x*, *y*, *z*]** returns the list whose elements are results of application of a procedure, a block, or a function *z* to the corresponding elements of lists *x* and *y*; in addition, in a case of various lengths of such lists the procedure is applied to both lists within their common minimum length, without causing any faulty situations. **ListOp** procedure substantially supposes the pure functions as the third argument what considerably allows to expand a class of functions as the third argument. In principle, the *Listable* attribute can be ascribed to any procedure or function of arity 1, providing its correct call on a list as the factual argument, as a rather simple example illustrates:

In[2450]:= {G[{a, b, c, d, h}], SetAttributes[G, Listable], G[{a, b, c, d, h}]}
Out[2450]= {G[{a, b, c, d, h}], Null, {G[a], G[b], G[c], G[d], G[h]}}

At the formal level for a block, a function and a module *F* of arity *1* it is possible to note the following defining relation, namely:

$$Map[F, \{a, b, c, d, ...\}] \equiv \{F[a], F[b], F[c], F[d], ...\}$$

where in the left part the procedure *F* can be both with the *Listable* attribute, and without it while in the right part the existence of *Listable* attribute for a block, a function or a module *F* is supposed. In addition, for blocks, functions and modules without the *Listable* attribute for receiving its effect the **Map** function is used. For ensuring existence of the *Listable* attribute for a block, function or module the simple **ListableC** procedure can be a rather useful tool [48]. The procedure call **ListableC[*h*]** returns the list of attributes of a *h* object, providing the setting of the *Listable* attribute for *h* object (*the user procedure/function or a standard function*). The following fragment represents source code of the **ListableC** procedure with an example of its application.

In[3828]:= ListableC[x_ /; SystemQ[x] || ProcQ[x] || QFunction[ToString[x]]] :=
Module[{a = Attributes[x], b = If[MemberQ[Attributes[x], Protected], "Protected", "Null"]},
If[MemberQ[a, Listable], a, Unprotect[x]; SetAttributes[x, Listable];
If[b == "Protected", Protect[x]]; Attributes[x]]]

In[3829]:= SetAttributes[Locals, Protected]; ListableC[Locals]

Out[3829]= {Listable, Protected}
In[3830]:= **Attributes[Locals]**
Out[3830]= {Listable, Protected}

Use of the *Listable* attribute allows to make processing of the nested lists, without breaking their internal structure. The procedure call **ListProcessing[*w*, *y*]** returns the list of the same internal organization as a *w* list whose elements are processed by means of an *y* function. A fragment below represents source code of the procedure with examples of its application.

In[4446]:= **ListProcessing[x_ /; ListQ[x], y_ /; FunctionQ[y]] := Module[{f, g},**
If[PureFuncQ[y], f = y; SetAttributes[f, Listable]; Map[f[#] &, x],
g = Attributes[y]; ClearAttributes[y, g]; SetAttributes[y, Listable]; f = Map[y[#] &, x];
ClearAttributes[y, Listable]; SetAttributes[y, g]; f]]

In[4447]:= x = {a, 7, d, c, {c, 5, s, {g, h, 8, p, d}, d}, 4, n}; ListProcessing[x, #^3 &]
Out[4447]= {a^3, 343, d^3, c^3, {c^3, 125, s^3, {g^3, h^3, 512, p^3, d^3}, d^3}, 64, n^3}
In[4448]:= gs[x_] := If[SymbolQ[x], x, GS]; ListProcessing[x, gs]
Out[4448]= {a, GS, d, c, {c, GS, s, {g, h, GS, p, d}, d}, GS, n}
In[4449]:= gv[x_] := If[SymbolQ[x], GS, If[PrimeQ[x], S, x]]; Processing[x, gv]
Out[4449]= {GS, S, GS, GS, {GS, S, GS, {GS, GS, 8, GS, GS}, GS}, 4, GS}
In[4450]:= **ListProcessing[{a, 5, 6, c, d, g, h, 6}, gv]**
Out[4450]= {GS, S, 6, GS, GS, GS, GS, 6}

The following procedure is a rather useful tool in problems of the lists processing that have having certain internal structures. The procedure call **ListClusters[*x*]** returns 2-element list or list of *ListList* type which consists of such sublists where the first element of the returned list *(sublists in the ListList list)* defines a position in *x* list whereas the second element defines the length of the cluster beginning with this position and containing identical elements. In a case of lack of clusters in the *x* list the procedure call **ListClusters[*x*]** returns the empty list, i.e. {}. The fragment below represents source code of the procedure with examples of its use.

In[4454]:= **ListClusters[x_ /; ListQ[x]] := Module[{a = {}, b = Join[x, {Null}], n = 1},**
Do[AppendTo[a, If[! SameQ[b[[j]], b[[j + 1]]], {j - n + 1, n}, n = 1}[[1 ;; 2]], n++; Nothing]],
{j, 1, Length[x]}]; ReduceLevelsList[Select[a, #[[2]] > 1 &]][[1]]]

In[4455]:= gs = {a, b, b, b, a, a, c, d, s, s, s, s, s, d, d, d, d, a, f, g};
In[4456]:= **ListClusters[gs]**
Out[4456]= {{2, 3}, {5, 2}, {9, 5}, {14, 4}}
In[4457]:= **ListClusters[{a, a, a, a, a, b, b}]**
Out[4457]= {{1, 5}, {6, 2}}
In[4458]:= **ListClusters[{a, a, a, a, a, a, a, a}]**
Out[4458]= {1, 8}

The procedure call **ClusterSubLists[*x*]** returns, generally, the nested list, whose 3-element lists determine elements of a *x* list, their positions and lengths of the sublists *(clusters)* which contain more than *1* identical element and which begin with this element. At the same time, the grouping of such sublists on base of their first element is made. In case of lack of clusters in the *x* list the procedure call **ClusterSubLists[*x*]** returns the *empty* list, i.e. {}. The following fragment represents source code of the **ClusterSubLists** procedure with examples of its use.

In[4526]:= **ClusterSubLists[x_ /; ListQ[x]] := Module[{a, b = {}, c, d, h = {}, g = {}, n = 1},**

a = Gather[Map[{#, n++} &, x], #1[[1]] == #2[[1]] &]; a = Select[a, Length[#] > 1 &];
Do[AppendTo[b, Map[#[[2]] &, a[[j]]]], {j, 1, Length[a]}]; b = Map[Differences[#] &, b];
Do[Do[If[b[[j]][[k]] == 1, g = Join[g, {a[[j]][[k]], a[[j]][[k + 1]]}], AppendTo[h, g]; g = {}],
{k, 1, Length[b[[j]]]}]; AppendTo[h, g]; g = {}, {j, 1, Length[b]}];
h = Map[If[# == {}, Nothing, DeleteDuplicates[#]] &, DeleteDuplicates[h]];
ReduceLists[Map[ReduceLists, Gather[Map[Join[#[[1]], {Length[#]}] &, h], #1[[1]] === #2[[1]] &]]]]

In[4527]:= ClusterSubLists[{c, c, c, a, b, c, a, a, ag, a, a, h, a + b, d, a + b, a + b, a + b, a + b, a, a, a, a + b, a + b}]

Out[4527]= {{c, 1, 3}, {{a, 7, 2}, {a, 10, 2}, {a, 19, 3}}, {{a + b, 15, 4}, {a + b, 22, 2}}}

In[4528]:= ClusterSubLists[{a, a, a, a, a, a, a, a, a, a, a, a}]
Out[4528]= {a, 1, 12}

In[4529]:= ClusterSubLists[{a, a, a, a, a, b, b, b, a, a, a, a, a}]
Out[4529]= {{a, 1, 5}, {a, 9, 5}, {a, 9, 8}}

In[4530]:= ClusterSubLists[{a, a, a, c, c, a, a, b, b, b, a, a, a, a, a, p, p, p}]
Out[4530]= {{{a, 1, 3}, {a, 6, 2}, {a, 11, 5}}, {c, 4, 2}, {b, 8, 3}, {p, 16, 3}}

The system functions **DeleteDuplicates** and **DeleteDuplicatesBy** serve for deleting of all duplicates from list at existence of the test to pairs of elements to determine whether they should be considered duplicates or without it, in this case two elements *x*, *y* are considered as duplicates if **SameQ**[*x*, *y*] = *True*. Meanwhile, in some cases it is expedient to know what specifically elements of the list have been removed from it as a result of these operations. The next means solve this problem. The procedure call **DeleteDuplicates1**[*x*] is equivalent the call **DeleteDuplicates**[*x*], whereas the call **DeleteDuplicates1**[*x*, *y*] where *y* is optional argument or their sequence *(a boolean function from two arguments and/or an indefinite symbol)* allows: *(1)* to return the result of deleting of all duplicates from a *x* list, where *y* serves for testing to elements pairs to determine whether they should be considered duplicates, *(2)* if *y* or the third optional argument is an undefinite symbol, then the call additionally to return through it the list of elements positions of the *x* list which have been removed from the list. In case of absent in the *x* list of duplicate elements through *y* the empty list is returned. The following fragment represents source code of the **DeleteDuplicates1** procedure with typical examples of its application.

In[4478]:= DeleteDuplicates1[x_ /; ListQ[x], y___] :=
Module[{a = If[{y} == {}, Sequences[{Nothing}], If[Length[{y}] > 0 &&
FunctionQ[ToExpression[ToString1[{y}[[1]]]]], y, Sequences[{Nothing}]]], b, c = {}, n = 0},
b = DeleteDuplicates[x, a];
Do[Do[AppendTo[c, If[n == 0 && SameQ1[x[[j]], b[[k]], a], n = 1; Nothing,
If[n != 0 && SameQ1[x[[j]], b[[k]], a], j, Nothing]]], {j, 1, Length[x]}]; n=0, {k, 1, Length[b]}];
c = DeleteDuplicates[Sort[c]];
If[Length[{y}] == 1 && NullQ[ToString1[{y}[[1]]]], y = c,
If[Length[{y}] == 2 && NullQ[ToExpression[ToString1[{y}[[2]]]]],
ToExpression[ToString1[{y}[[2]]] <> "=" <> ToString[c]], b]]; b]

In[4479]:= gs = {a, b, b, b, a, a, c, d, s, s, s, s, s, d, d, d, d, a, f, g};

In[4480]:= DeleteDuplicates1[gs]
Out[4480]= {a, b, c, d, s, f, g}
In[4481]:= DeleteDuplicates1[gs, art]; art
Out[4481]= {3, 4, 5, 6, 10, 11, 12, 13, 14, 15, 16, 17, 18}

The above procedure uses one of two simple functions generalizing similar system means and simplifying programming of problems which use the testing expressions. The function call **SameQ1**[x, y] is equivalent the call **SameQ**[x, y], whereas the call **SameQ1**[x, y, f] where optional f argument is a boolean function from two arguments returns *True* if the expression x is identical to the y on condition that f test to pairs of elements to determine whether they should be considered equivalent, and yields *False* otherwise. At that, the call **EqualQ**[x, y, f] where the optional f argument is a boolean function from two arguments returns *True* if the expression x is equal to y on condition that f test to pairs of elements to determine whether they should be considered *equal*, and *False* otherwise. The following fragment represents the source codes of the both functions with typical examples of their application.

In[4401]:= SameQ1[x_, y_, f___] := If[{f} != {} && FunctionQ[f], (f) @@ {x, y}, x === y]

In[4402]:= EqualQ[x_, y_, f___] := If[{f} != {} && FunctionQ[f], (f) @@ {x, y}, x == y]

In[4403]:= SameQ1[75, 70, Abs[#1 - #2] <= 5 &]
Out[4403]= True
In[4404]:= EqualQ[75, 70, Abs[#1 - #2] <= 5 &]
Out[4404]= True

While the **DeleteDuplicates2** procedure is the simplified version of the **DeleteDuplicates1** procedure with maintaining its main functionality. The procedure call **DeleteDuplicates2**[x, y] returns the sorted x list on condition of existing of y test to pairs of elements to determine whether they should be considered duplicates. In addition, the call **DeleteDuplicates2**[x, y, z] where z is the optional argument – *an undefinite symbol* – additionally through it returns the list of elements positions of the x list which have been removed from the list. Moreover, the procedure call **DeleteDuplicates2**[x, y] if y argument is *an undefinite symbol* additionally through it returns the list of elements positions of the x list which have been removed from the list irrespectively existence of the third optional z argument. The next fragment presents source code of the **DeleteDuplicates2** procedure with typical examples of its application.

In[4478]:= DeleteDuplicates2[x_ /; ListQ[x], y_, z___] :=
Module[{a, b, c = If[FunctionQ[y], y, #1[[1]] === #2[[1]] &], d, n = 1},
a = Map[{#, n++} &, x]; b = If[SymbolQ[c], DeleteDuplicatesBy, DeleteDuplicates][a, c];
d = Sort[Map[#[[2]] &, Complement[a, b]]];
If[{z} != {} && NullQ[z], z = d, If[NullQ[y], y = d, 6]]; Map[#[[1]] &, b]]

In[4479]:= DeleteDuplicates2[{1, 3, 4, 5, 3, 2, 3, 6, 5, 4, 3, 3, 4}, Abs[#1[[1]] - #2[[1]]] < 2 &, sg]
Out[4479]= {1, 3, 5}
In[4480]:= sg
Out[4480]= {3, 5, 6, 7, 8, 9, 10, 11, 12, 13}
In[4481]:= DeleteDuplicates2[{1, 3, 4, 5, 3, 2, 3, 6, 5, 4, 3, 3, 4}, Art]
Out[4481]= {1, 3, 4, 5, 2, 6}
In[4482]:= Art
Out[4482]= {5, 7, 9, 10, 11, 12, 13}

In[4483]:= DeleteDuplicates2[{1, 3, 4, 5, 3, 2, 3, 6, 5, 4, 3, 3, 4}, Abs[#1[[1]] - #2[[1]]] <= 2 &]
Out[4483]= {1, 4}
In[4484]:= DeleteDuplicates2[{1, 3, 4, 5, 3, 2, 3, 6, 5, 4, 3, 3, 4}, Art1, Kr]
Out[4484]= {1, 3, 4, 5, 2, 6}
In[4485]:= {Art1, Kr}
Out[4485]= {{5, 7, 9, 10, 11, 12, 13}, Kr}

At that, the above **DeleteDuplicates2** procedure illustrates the organization of return of an auxiliary result through an obligatory formal argument.

The method used in the previous procedure can be used for the solution of the question of definition of elements positions of a list received by means of application to it of a function providing a permutation of list elements. The procedure call **ListPosChange[*x*, *y*]** returns the rules list whose elements *pj* –> *bj* determine the elements positions *pj* of an initial *x* list whereas the right parts *bj* determine the new positions of the same elements of the list – of the result of processing of *x* list by means *y*. Whereas the procedure call **ListPosChange[*x*, *y*, *z*]** returns the above-mentioned result but on condition that optional *z* argument defines the additional argument for the *y* argument that can be a block, a module or a function. The returned rules list is sorted according to the left part of rules in ascending order. As a rule, a pure function from two arguments {#1[[1]], #2[[1]]} is used as *z*, determining the F relations between pairs of the modified *x* list elements; i.e. a function *F[#1, #2]* & for the *y* argument is replaced on the function *F[#1[[1]], #2[[1]]]* & for the modified list *(see fragment below)*. The expediency of use of this reception a quite convincingly is proved by the source code of the **ListPosChange** procedure and examples of its application which are given below.

In[4430]:= ListPosChange[x_ /; ListQ[x], y_ /; SystemQ[y] || ProcFuncBlQ[y, Unique["g"]], z___] := Module[{a, b, n = 1},
a = Map[{#, n++} &, x]; b = y[a, If[{z} == {}, OrderedQ[{#1[[1]], #2[[1]]}] &, z]];
Sort[GenRules[Map[#[[2]] &, b], Map[#[[2]] &, a]], #1[[1]] <= #2[[1]] &]]

In[4431]:= ListPosChange[{1, 3, 75, 4, 5, 28, 3, 2, 6, 40, 4, 3, 20, 3}, Sort]
Out[4431]= {1 -> 1, 2 -> 3, 3 -> 14, 4 -> 7, 5 -> 9, 6 -> 12, 7 -> 4, 8 -> 2, 9 -> 10, 10 -> 13, 11 -> 8, 12 -> 5, 13 -> 11, 14 -> 6}
In[4432]:= ListPosChange[{1, 3, 75, 4, 5, 28, 3, 2, 6, 40, 4, 3, 20, 3}, Sort,
! OrderedQ[{#1[[1]], #2[[1]]}] &]
Out[4432]= {1 -> 14, 2 -> 12, 3 -> 1, 4 -> 8, 5 -> 6, 6 -> 3, 7 -> 11, 8 -> 13, 9 -> 5, 10 -> 2, 11 -> 7, 12 -> 10, 13 -> 4, 14 -> 9}

Whereas a modification of the **ListPosChange** procedure given below differs only in the fact that through the third *s* argument – *an undefinite symbol* – is returned the result of the call *y[x, z]*. It is one more example of organization of return of an auxiliary result through an obligatory formal argument.

In[4438]:= ListPosChange1[x_ /; ListQ[x], y_ /; SystemQ[y] || ProcFuncBlQ[y, Unique["g"]], s_ /; SymbolQ[s] && NullQ[s], z___] :=
Module[{a, b, n = 1}, a = Map[{#, n++} &, x];
b = y[a, If[{z} == {}, OrderedQ[{#1[[1]], #2[[1]]}] &, z]];
s = Map[#[[1]] &, b]; Sort[GenRules[Map[#[[2]] &, b], Map[#[[2]] &, a]],

#1[[1]] <= #2[[1]] &]]

In[4439]:= ListPosChange1[{1, 3, 75, 4, 5, 28, 3, 2, 6, 70, 4, 3, 20, 3}, Sort, gs, OrderedQ[{#1[[1]], #2[[1]]}] &]

Out[4439]= {1 -> 1, 2 -> 3, 3 -> 14, 4 -> 7, 5 -> 9, 6 -> 12, 7 -> 4, 8 -> 2, 9 -> 10, 10 -> 13, 11 -> 8, 12 -> 5, 13 -> 11, 14 -> 6}

In[4440]:= gs

Out[4440]= {1, 2, 3, 3, 3, 3, 4, 4, 5, 6, 20, 28, 70, 75}

At the same time it must be kept in mind that source codes of procedures **ListPosChange** and **ListPosChange1** in the light of use of optional *z* argument are programmed so that at its absence by default the function to pairs of elements in list to determine whether they are in order is used similarly to the standard **Sort** function. Therefore, for the *y* argument other than **Sort**, in source codes of both procedures the corresponding default function should be used.

In difference of standard **Partition** function the **PartitionCond** procedure, supplementing its, allows to partition the list into sublists by its elements satisfying some testing function. The procedure call **PartitionCond[*x*, *y*]** returns the nested list consisting of sublists received by partition of a *x* list by its elements satisfying a testing *y* function. At the same time, these elements don't include in sublists. At absence in the *x* list of the separative elements a initial *x* list is returned. At that, at existing the third optional *z* argument – *an arbitrary expression* – the call **PartitionCond[*x*, *y*, *z*]** returns the above nested list on condition that the sequences of elements in its sublists will be limited by the *z* element. In addition, if the call contains 4 arguments and the *4th argument* is *1* or *2* than the call **PartitionCond[*x*, *y*, *z*, *h*={1|2}]** returns the above nested list on condition that elements sequences in its sublists will be limited by the *z* element at the left (*h*=1) or at the right (*h*=2) accordingly, otherwise the procedure call is equivalent the call **PartitionCond[*x*, *y*]**. The fragment below represents the source code of the **PartitionCond** procedure with typical examples of its application.

In[4498]:= PartitionCond[x_ /; ListQ[x], y_ /; Quiet[ProcFuncBlQ[y, Unique["g"]]], z___] :=
Module[{a, b, c, d},
If[Select[x, y] == {}, x, If[{z} != {} && Length[{z}] > 1,
If[{z}[[2]] == 1, c = {z}[[1]]; d = Nothing,
If[{z}[[2]] == 2, c = Nothing; d = {z}[[1]], c = d = Nothing]],
If[Length[{z}] == 1, c = d = {z}[[1]], c = d = Nothing]]; a = {1, Length[x]}; b = {};
Do[AppendTo[a, If[(y) @@ {x[[j]]}, j, Nothing]], {j, 1, Length[x]}];
a = Sort[DeleteDuplicates[a]];
Do[AppendTo[b, x[[a[[j]] ;; a[[j + 1]]]]], {j, 1, Length[a] - 1}];
b = ReplaceAll[Map[Map[If[(y) @@ {#}, Nothing, #] &, #1] &, b], {} -> Nothing];
Map[{a = #, Quiet[AppendTo[PrependTo[a, c], d]]}[[2]] &, b]]

In[4499]:= PartitionCond[{8, a, b, 3, 6, c, 7, d, h, 75, 70, d, s, 8, k, f, a, 9}, IntegerQ[#] &]
Out[4499]= {{a, b}, {c}, {d, h}, {d, s}, {k, f, a}}
In[4500]:= PartitionCond[{8, a, b, 3, 6, c, 7, d, h, 75, 70, d, s, 8, k, f, a, 9}, ! IntegerQ[#] &]
Out[4500]= {{8}, {3, 6}, {7}, {75, 70}, {8}, {9}}
In[4501]:= PartitionCond[{8, a, b, 3, 6, c, 7, d, h, 75, 70, d, s, 8, k, f, a, 9}, ! IntegerQ[#] &, gs, 1]

Out[4501]= {{gs, 8}, {gs, 3, 6}, {gs, 7}, {gs, 75, 70}, {gs, 8}, {gs, 9}}
In[4502]:= **PartitionCond[{8, a, b, 3, 6, c, 7, d, h, 75, 70, d, s, 8, k, f, a, 9}, ! IntegerQ[#] &, gs, 2]**
Out[4502]= {{8, gs}, {3, 6, gs}, {7, gs}, {75, 70, gs}, {8, gs}, {9, gs}}
In[4503]:= **PartitionCond[{8, a, b, 3, 6, c, 7, d, h, 75, 70, d, s, 8, k, f, a, 9}, ! IntegerQ[#] &, gs]**
Out[4503]= {{gs, 8, gs}, {gs, 3, 6, gs}, {gs, 7, gs}, {gs, 75, 70, gs}, {gs, 8, gs}, {gs, 9, gs}}
In[4504]:= **PartitionCond[{8, a, b, 3, 6, c, 7, d, h, 75, 70, d, s, 8, k, f, a, 9}, ! IntegerQ[#] &, gs, 3]**
Out[4504]= {{8}, {3, 6}, {7}, {75, 70}, {8}, {9}}

The following procedure gives a rather useful way of elements transposition of the list. The procedure call **ListRestruct[x, y]** returns the result of mutual exchanges of elements of x list which are determined by the rule or their list y of the kind $aj \to bj$, where aj – positions of elements of the list x and bj – their positions in the returned list, and vice versa. At the same time, the procedure excludes unacceptable rules from y list. The fragment below represents source code of the **ListRestruct** procedure with examples of its application.

In[4458]:= **ListRestruct[x_ /; ListQ[x], y_ /; RuleQ[y] || ListRulesQ[y]] :=**
Module[{b = If[RuleQ[y], {y}, y], c, d},
b = DeleteDuplicates[DeleteDuplicates[b, #1[[1]] === #2[[1]] &], #1[[1]] === #2[[1]] &];
c = Map[#[[1]] -> x[[#[[2]]]] &, b]; d = ReplacePart[x, c];
c = Map[#[[1]] -> x[[#[[2]]]] &, RevRules[b]]; ReplacePart[d, c]]

In[4459]:= **ListRestruct[{1, 3, 75, 4, 5, 28, 3, 2, 6, 40, 4, 3, 20, 3},**
{1 -> 6, 8 -> 12, 1 -> 14, 8 -> 10, 5 -> 10}]
Out[4459]= {28, 3, 75, 4, 40, 1, 3, 3, 6, 5, 4, 2, 20, 3}
In[4460]:= **ListRestruct[{a, b, c, d}, {1 -> 3, 2 -> 4}]**
Out[4460]= {c, d, a, b}

In particular, for exception from the rules list of unacceptable rules a very simple function providing bijection between parts of rules is used, namely:

In[4463]:= **BijectionRules[x_ /; RuleQ[x] || ListRulesQ[x]] := If[RuleQ[x], x,**
DeleteDuplicates[DeleteDuplicates[x, #1[[1]] === #2[[1]] &], #1[[1]] === #2[[1]] &]]
In[4464]:= **BijectionRules[{a -> b, c -> d, c -> m, f -> g, a -> d, m -> n}]**
Out[4464]= {a -> b, c -> d, f -> g, m -> n}

The function call **BijectionRules[x]** returns the rules list – result of exception from a rules list x of unacceptable rules, by providing providing the bijection between parts of rules. At that, in the returned list remains only rules located in the x list as the first ones.

For testing of a number of important types of lists such means as **SimpleListQ**, **ListListQ**, **FullNestListQ**, **NestListQ** and **NestListQ1** serve, whose source codes with examples of use are represented by the following fragment:

In[3856]:= **SimpleListQ[x_] := ListQ[x] && And[Sequences[Map[! ListQ[#] &, x]]]**

In[3857]:= **SimpleListQ[{1, 1, 1, 3, 3, t + p, 3, 4, 4, 5, a, 5, 5, 4, 1, 1, a, 1, (a + b) + c^c}]**
Out[3857]= True
In[3858]:= **SimpleListQ[{1, 1, 1, 3, 3, t + p, 3, {4}, 4, 5, a, 5, 5, 4, 1, 1, a, 1, (a + b) + c^c}]**
Out[3858]= False
In[3859]:= **SimpleListQ[a + b]**
Out[3859]= False

In[3863]:= NestListQ[x_] := ListQ[x] && AllTrue[Map[ListQ, x], TrueQ]

In[3864]:= NestListQ[{a, b, c, {{x, y, z}, {{m, n, {x, y, z}, p}}}, c, d, g}]
Out[3864]= False

In[3865]:= NestListQ[{{a, b, c}, {{x, y, z}, {{m, n, {x, y, z}, p}}}, {c, d, g}}]
Out[3865]= True

In[3866]:= NestListQ1[x_] := ! (ListQ[x] && Length[Select[x, ListQ[#] &]] == 0)

In[3867]:= NestListQ1[{a, b, c, {{x, y, z}, {{m, n, {x, y, z}, p}}}, c, d, g}]
Out[3867]= True

In[3868]:= FullNestListQ[x_ /; ListQ[x]] := Module[{a},
Do[If[! NestListQ[x[[j]]], a = False; Return[], a = True], {j, 1, Length[x]}]; a]

In[3869]:= FullNestListQ[{a, b, c, {{x, y, z}, {{m, n, {x, y, z}, p}}}, c, d, g}]
Out[3869]= False

In[3870]:= FullNestListQ[{{{a, b, c}}, {{x, y, z}, {{m, n, {x, y, z}, p}}}, {{c, d, g}}}]
Out[3870]= True

In[3871]:= ListListQ[x_] := If[ListQ[x] && x != {} && Length[x] >= 1 &&
Length[Select[x, ListQ[#] && Length[#] == Length[x[[1]]] &]] == Length[x], True, False]

In[3872]:= ListListQ[{{a, b, c}, {m, n, p}, {50, 70, 75}}]
Out[3872]= True

The function call **SimpleListQ[*x*]** returns *True* if *x* – a list whose elements are not lists, and *False* otherwise. The function call **NestListQ[*x*]** returns *True*, if *x* – the nested list, and *False* otherwise. In addition, as the nested list is understood list whose all elements are lists. The function call **NestListQ1[*x*]** returns *True*, if *x* – a nested list, and *False* otherwise. At that, as such nested list is understood list for which at least one element is a list. The procedure call **FullNestListQ[*w*]** returns *True* if all elements of a list *w* are the nested sublists, otherwise *False* is returned. At last, the function call **ListListQ[*x*]** returns *True* if *x* defines a list of lists of identical length, and *False* otherwise.

The **Position1** function extends the standard **Position** function onto the factual arguments which are lists, i.e. a function call **Position1[*x*, *y*]** returns the nested list whose elements are 2–element lists whose first elements belongs to a *y* list whereas the second element – list of positions of these elements in a *x* list as a rather visually illustrates the following fragment:

In[4209]:= Position1[x_ /; ListQ[x], y_ /; ListQ[y]] :=
ReduceLevelsList[Map[{#, Flatten[Position[x, #]]} &, y], 1]

In[4210]:= Position1[{1, 2, 3, 4, 5, 3, 5, 2, 1}, {1, 2, 3, 5}]
Out[4210]= {{1, {1, 9}}, {2, {2, 8}}, {3, {3, 6}}, {5, {5, 7}}}

The following a rather simple function allows to ascribe to each element of the simple list the list of positions on which he is located in the list. The function call **Position2[*x*]** returns the nested list of 2–element sublists whose the first elements are elements of a simple list *x* whereas the second elements – list of their positions in the *x* list. The returned list is sorted on the first elements of sublists. The fragment below represents source code of the **Position2** function with an example of its application.

In[4375]:= Position2[x_ /; SimpleListQ[x]] := Map[{#[[1]], Flatten[#[[2]]]} &,

Map[{#, Position[x, #]} &, Sort[DeleteDuplicates[x]]]]]

In[4376]:= **Position2[{a, b, h + d, x, a, y, a, m, f}]**

Out[4376]= {{a, {1, 5, 7}}, {b, {2}}, {f, {9}}, {d + h, {3}}, {m, {8}}, {x, {4}}, {y, {6}}}

In a number of the problems which deal with lists processing, it is very expedient to reduce lists to a view with the minimum pair of the limiting brackets {.....} provided that an object still remains as the object of the *List* type. For example, {{{{{a, {{b}}, c}}}}} to {a, {{b}}, c}. The **ReduceLevelsList** procedure solves the problem; the call **ReduceLevelsList[x]** returns the 2-element list whose first element defines result of reducing of an initial list *x* to the above kind, whereas the second element determines the nesting level of a list *x* as a whole. At the same time, the reduced list has the nesting 1. Whereas the call **ReduceLevelsList[x, y]** with the second optional *y* argument – *an arbitrary expression* – returns the fully reduced list only. The next fragment presents source code of the **ReduceLevelsList** procedure with examples of its application.

In[3880]:= **ReduceLevelsList[x_ /; ListQ[x], y___] := Module[{a = x, b = 0, c},**

Do[a = Quiet[Check[ToExpression[StringTake[Set[c, ToString1[a]], {2, -2}]], $Failed]]; b++;

If[ListQ[a], Continue[], Break[]], {k, 1, Infinity}];

If[{y} != {}, ToExpression[c], {ToExpression[c], b}]]

In[3881]:= **ReduceLevelsList[{{{a, b, {c}, {{d}}, h}}}]**
Out[3881]= {{a, b, {c}, {{d}}, h}, 3}
In[3882]:= **ReduceLevelsList[{{{a, b, c, d, h}}}]**
Out[3882]= {{a, b, c, d, h}, 3}
In[3883]:= **ReduceLevelsList[{{{{{{{}}}}}}}, gs]**
Out[3883]= {}
In[3884]:= **ReduceLevelsList[{{{{{{a, b, {c}, {{d}}, h}}}}}}]**
Out[3884]= {{a, b, {c}, {{d}}, h}, 6}

Unlike the **ReduceLevelsList** procedure the procedure call **ReduceLists[x]** returns the result of reducing of a *x* list to the simple list what its source code with examples of use illustrate.

In[4000]:= **ReduceLists[x_ /; ListQ[x]] := Module[{a = ToString1[x], b},**

Do[b = a; If[! SyntaxQ[Set[a, StringTake[a, {2, -2}]]], Return[ToExpression[b]]],

{j, 1, Infinity}]]

In[4001]:= **ReduceLists[{{{{{{{{{{{"\"a + b\"", c, "a – m", {{{k}}}}}}}}}}}}}}]**
Out[4001]= {"\"a + b\"", c, "a – m", {{{k}}}}
In[4002]:= **ReduceLists[{"\"a + b\"", c, "a – m", {{{k}}}}]**
Out[4002]= {"\"a + b\"", c, "a – m", {{{k}}}}

The *Mathematica* system at manipulation with the list structures has certain shortcomings among which impossibility of direct assignment to elements of a list of expressions is, as the following simple example illustrates:

In[2412]:= **{a, b, c, d, h, g, s, x, y, z}[[10]] = 590**
Set::setps: {a, b, c, d, h, g, s, x, y, z} in the part assignment is not a symbol.>>
Out[2412]= 590
In[2413]:= **z**
Out[2413]= z

In order to *simplify* the implementation of procedures that use similar direct assignments to the list elements, the **ListAssignP** procedure is used, whose call **ListAssignP**[*x, n, y*] returns the updated value of a *x* list which is based on results of assignment of a *y* value or the list of values to *n* elements of the *x* list where *n* – one position or their list. Moreover, if the lists *n* and *y* have different lengths, their common minimum value is chosen. The **ListAssignP** expands functionality of *Mathematica*, doing quite correct assignments to the list elements what the system fully doesn't provide. Fragment represents source code of the **ListAssignP** procedure along with examples of its application.

In[2693]:= **ListAssignP[x_ /; ListQ[x], n_ /; PosIntQ[n] || PosIntListQ[n], y_] :=
Module[{a = DeleteDuplicates[Flatten[{n}]], b = Flatten[{y}], c, k = 1},
If[a[[-1]] > Length[x], Return[Defer[ListAssignP[x, n, y]]], c = Min[Length[a], Length[b]]];
While[k <= c, Quiet[Check[ToExpression[ToString[x[[a[[k]]]]] <> " = " <>
ToString1[If[ListQ[n], b[[k]], y]]], Null]]; k++]; If[NestListQ1[x], x[[-1]], x]]**

In[2694]:= **Clear[x, y, z]; ListAssignP[{x, y, z}, 3, 500]**
Out[2694]= {x, y, 500}
In[2695]:= **Clear[x, y, z]; ListAssignP[{x, y, z}, {2, 3}, {74, 69}]**
Out[2695]= {x, 74, 69}
In[2696]:= **Clear[x, y, z]; ListAssignP[{x, y, z}, 3, {42, 74, 2016}]**
Out[2696]= {42, 74, 2016}

The next procedure is a certain modification of the **ListAssignP**, its call **ListAssign1**[*x, n, y*] returns the updated value of a *x* list which is based on results of assignment of a *y* value or the list of values to *n* elements of the *x* list where *n* – one position or their list. Moreover, if the lists *n* and *y* have different lengths, their common minimum value is chosen. At that, the update of the *x* list is done in situ. The **ListAssign1** procedure also expands functionality of the *Mathematica*, doing quite correct assignments to the list elements what the system fully doesn't provide. The following fragment represents source code of the **ListAssign1** along with examples of its application.

In[2770]:= **ListAssign1[x_ /; ListQ[x], n_ /; PosIntQ[n] || PosIntListQ[n], y_] :=
Module[{a = DeleteDuplicates[Flatten[{n}]], b = Flatten[{y}], c, d, k = 1},
If[a[[-1]] > Length[x], Return[Defer[ListAssignP[x, n, y]]], c = Min[Length[a], Length[b]]];
While[k <= c, d = ReplacePart[x, a[[k]] -> If[ListQ[n], b[[k]], y]]; k++];
Quiet[ToExpression[ToString[x] <> "=" <> ToString1[ReduceLevelsList[d][[1]]]]]]**

In[2771]:= **x := {m, n, p}; ListAssign1[x, 3, 300]**
Out[2771]= {m, n, 300}
In[2772]:= **x**
Out2772]= {m, n, 300}
In[2773]:= **ListAssign1[{m, n, 100}, 2, 200]**
Out[2773]= {m, 200, 300}
In[2774]:= **x**
Out[2774]= {m, 200, 300}

Along with the **ListAssignP** procedure expediently to in addition define a simple function whose call **ListStrQ**[*x*] returns *True* if all elements of a *x* list – expressions in string format, and *False* otherwise. The following fragment represents source code of the **ListStrQ** function with an example of its application.

In[3599]:= **ListStrQ[x_ /; ListQ[x]] :=**
Length[Select[x, StringQ[#] &]] == Length[x] && Length[x] != 0

In[3600]:= **Map[ListStrQ, {{"a", "b", "a", "b"}, {"a", "b", a, "a", b}, {"A", "K"}}]**
Out[3600]= {True, False, True}

The following procedure carries out exchange of elements of a list which are defined by the pairs of positions. The procedure call **SwapInList[x, y]** returns the exchange of elements of a *x* list which are defined by pairs of positions or their list *y*. At the same time, if the *x* list is explicitly encoded at the procedure call, the updated list is returned, if *x* is determined by a symbol *(that defines a list)* in string format then along with returning of the updated list also value of the *x* symbol is updated in situ. The procedure processes the erroneous situation caused by the indication of non-existent positions in the *x* list with returning $*Failed* and the appropriate message. It is recommended to consider a reception used for updating of a list in situ. The procedure is of a certain interest at the operating with lists. The fragment below represents source code of the **SwapInList** procedure with typical examples of its application which rather visually illustrate the told.

In[3884]:= **SwapInList[x_ /; ListQ[x] || StringQ[x] && ListQ[ToExpression[x]],**
y_ /; SimpleListQ[y] || ListListQ[y] && Length[y[[1]]] == 2] :=
Module[{a, b, c = ToExpression[x], d, h = If[SimpleListQ[y], {y}, y]},
d = Complement[DeleteDuplicates[Flatten[y]], Range[1, Length[c]]];
If[d != {}, Print["Positions " <> ToString[d] <> " are absent in list "<>ToString[c]]; $Failed,
Do[a = c[[h[[j]][[1]]]]; b = c[[h[[j]][[2]]]]; c = ReplacePart[c, h[[j]][[1]] -> b];
c = ReplacePart[c, h[[j]][[2]] -> a], {j, 1, Length[h]}];
If[StringQ[x], ToExpression[x <> "=" <> ToString[c]], c]]]

In[3885]:= **SwapInList[{1, 2, 3, 4, 5, 6, 7, 8, 9}, {{1, 3}, {4, 6}, {8, 10}}]**
"Positions {10} are absent in {1, 2, 3, 4, 5, 6, 7, 8, 9}"
Out[3885]= $Failed

In[3886]:= **d = {1, 2, 3, 4, 5, 6}**
Out[3886]= {1, 2, 3, 4, 5, 6}

In[3887]:= **SwapInList["d", {{1, 3}, {4, 6}}]**
Out[3887]= {3, 2, 1, 6, 5, 4}

In[3888]:= **d**
Out[3888]= {3, 2, 1, 6, 5, 4}

In[3889]:= **Clear[a, b, c, d, f, h, k, t, w]; g = {a, b, c, d, f, h, k, t, w}**
Out[3889]= {a, b, c, d, f, h, k, t, w}

In[3890]:= **SwapInList["g", {1, 9}]**
Out[3890]= {w, b, c, d, f, h, k, t, a}

In[3891]:= **g**
Out[3891]= {w, b, c, d, f, h, k, t, a}

In[3892]:= **SwapInList[{1, 2, 3, 4, 5, 6, 7, 8, 9}, {{1, 3}, {4, 6}}]**
Out[3892]= {3, 2, 1, 6, 5, 4, 7, 8, 9}

Software Etudes in the Mathematica

The following procedure is useful enough in procedural programming, the procedure call **ListAssign[x, y]** provides assignment of values of a *x* list to the generated variables of the *y$nnn* format, returning the nested list, whose the first element determines the list of the generated "*y$nnn*" variables in the string format, whereas the second defines the list of the values assigned to them from the *x* list. The **ListAssign** procedure is of interest, first of all, in problems of the dynamical generation of variables with assigning values to them. The fragment below represents source code of the **ListAssign** procedure with an example of its application.

In[2221]:= ListAssign[x_ /; ListQ[x], y_ /; SymbolQ[y]] := Module[{a = {}, b},
Do[a = Append[a, Unique[y]], {k, Length[x]}]; b = Map[ToString, a];
ToExpression[ToString[a] <> "=" <> ToString1[x]]; {b, a}]

In[2222]:= ListAssign[{49, 27, 590, 69, 74}, h]
Out[2222]= {{"h$814", "h$815", "h$816", "h$817", "h$818"}, {49, 27, 590, 69, 74}}

In the *Mathematica* for grouping of expressions along with simple lists also more complex list structures in the form of the nested lists are used, whose elements are lists *(sublists)* too. In this connection the lists of the *ListList* type, whose elements – sublists of identical length are of special interest. For simple lists the system has testing function; whose call **ListQ[x]** returns *True*, if *x* – a list, and *False* otherwise. While for testing of the nested lists we defined the useful enough functions **NestListQ, NestListQ1, NestQL, ListListQ** [33, 48]. These tools are quite often used as a part of the testing components of the headings of procedures and functions both from our *MathToolBox* package, and in the different blocks, functions and modules first of all that are used in different problems of the system character [28-33,48,50].

In addition to the above testing functions some useful functions of the same class which are useful enough in programming of means to processing of the list structures of an arbitrary organization have been created [28,33,48]. Among them can be noted testing means such as **BinaryListQ, IntegerListQ, ListNumericQ, ListSymbolQ, PosIntListQ, ListExprHeadQ** and **PosIntListQ, PosIntQ**. In particular, the call **ListExprHeadQ[w, h]** returns *True* if a *w* list contains only elements meeting the condition **Head[a] = h**, and *False* otherwise. At that, the testing means process all elements of the analyzed list, including all its sublists of any level of nesting. The next fragment represents source code of the **ListExprHeadQ** function along with examples of its application.

In[2576]:= ListExprHeadQ[x_ /; ListQ[x], h_] :=
Length[x] == Length[Select[x, Head[#] === h&]]

In[2577]:= {ListExprHeadQ[{a + b, c – d}, Plus], ListExprHeadQ[{a*b, c/d}, Times],
ListExprHeadQ[{a^b, (c + a)^d}, Power]}
Out[2577]= {True, True, True}

The above means are often used at programming of the problems oriented on processing of the list structures. These and other means of the given type are located in our *MathToolBox* package [48,50]. In addition, their correct use assumes that the package is uploaded into the current session.

A rather useful **SelectPos** function provides the choice from list of elements by their given positions. The function call **SelectPos[x, y, z]** returns the list with elements of a *x* list, whose numbers of positions are different from elements of a *y* list *(at z = 1)* whereas at *z* = 2 the list with elements of the *x* list whose numbers of positions coincide with elements of the integer list *y* is returned. Fragment below represents source code of the function with examples of its application.

In[2696]:= SelectPos[x_ /; ListQ[x], y_ /; ListQ[y] &&
AllTrue[Map[IntegerQ[#] && # > 0 &, y], TrueQ], z_ /; MemberQ[{1, 2}, z]] :=
Select[x, If[If[z == 2, Equal, Unequal][Intersection[Flatten[Position[x, #]], y], {}], False, True] &]

In[2697]:= SelectPos[{a, b, c, d, e, f, g, h, m, n, p}, {1, 3, 5, 7, 9, 11, 13, 15, 17, 19, 21}, 2]
Out[2697]= {a, c, e, g, m, p}
In[2698]:= SelectPos[{a, b, c, d, e, f, g, h, m, n, p}, {1, 3, 5, 7, 9, 11, 13, 15, 17, 19, 21}, 1]
Out[2698]= {b, d, f, h, n}

It must be kept in mind that numbers of positions of the *y* list outside the range of positions of elements of the *x* list are ignored, without initiating an erroneous situation what is quite convenient for ensuring continuous execution of program without situations processing.

In problems of processing of simple *w* lists on which the call **SimpleListQ[*w*]** returns *True*, the procedure below is of a certain interest. The procedure call **ClusterList[*x*]** returns the the nested list of *ListList* type whose 2–element sublists by the first element determine element of a simple nonempty *x* list whereas by the second element determine its sequential number in a cluster of identical elements to which this element belongs. The next fragment presents source code of the **ClusterList** procedure with examples of its application.

In[3873]:= ClusterList[x_ /; x != {} && SimpleListQ[x]] :=
Module[{a = {}, b = {}, c = Join[x, {x[[-1]]}], d = Map[{#, 1} &, DeleteDuplicates[x]], n},
Do[n = d[[Flatten[Position[d, Flatten[Select[d, #[[1]] == c[[j]] &]][[1]]]][[2]]]]++;
Flatten[Select[d, #[[1]] == c[[j]] &]][[2]];
If[c[[j]] === c[[j + 1]], AppendTo[a, {c[[j]], n}],
AppendTo[b, a]; AppendTo[b, {c[[j]], n}]; a = {}], {j, 1, Length[c] – 1}];
AppendTo[b, a]; b = ToString1[Select[b, # != {} &]];
b = If[SuffPref[b, "{{{", 1], b, "{" <> b];
b = ToExpression[StringReplace[b, {"{{" -> "{", "}}" -> "}"}]]]

In[3874]:= ClusterList[{1, 1, 1, 3, 3, 3, 4, 4, 5, 5, 5, 4, 1, 1, 1}]
Out[3874]= {{1, 1}, {1, 2}, {1, 3}, {3, 1}, {3, 2}, {3, 3}, {4, 1}, {4, 2}, {5, 1}, {5, 2}, {5, 3}, {4, 3}, {1, 4}, {1, 5}, {1, 6}}
In[3875]:= ClusterList[{1, 1, 1, 3, 3, t + p, 3, 4, 4, 5, a, 5, 5, 4, 1, 1, a, 1, (a + b) + c^c}]
Out[3875]= {{1, 1}, {1, 2}, {1, 3}, {3, 1}, {3, 2}, {p + t, 1}, {3, 3}, {4, 1}, {4, 2}, {5, 1}, {a, 1}, {5, 2}, {5, 3}, {4, 3}, {1, 4}, {1, 5}, {a, 2}, {1, 6}, {a + b + c^c, 1}}
In[3876]:= ClusterList[{6, 6, 6, 6, 6, 6, 6, 6, 6, 6, 6, 6}]
Out[3876]= {{6, 1}, {6, 2}, {6, 3}, {6, 4}, {6, 5}, {6, 6}, {6, 7}, {6, 8}, {6, 9}, {6, 10}, {6, 11}, {6, 12}}
In[3877]:= ClusterList[{74}]
Out[3877]= {{74, 1}}

For the solution of a number of the problems dealing with the nested lists, in certain cases can arise problems which are not solved by direct standard means, demanding in similar situations of programming of tasks by the tools which are provided by the *Mathematica*. It an quite visually illustrates an example of the problem consisting in definition of number of the elements different from the list, at each level of nesting of a list and simple list *(a nesting level 0)*, and the nested. The problem is solved by the procedure whose call **ElemLevelsN[x]** returns the nested list whose elements are two-element lists whose first element determines the nesting level while the second – number of elements of this level with the type different from the *List*. Procedure **ElemLevelsL** is a rather useful modification of the above procedure [33, 48]. The fragment below represents source codes of the both procedures with examples their application.

In[2733]:= ElemLevelsN[x_ /; ListQ[x]] := Module[{a = x, c = {}, m = 0, n, k = 0},
While[NestListQ1[a], n = Length[Select[a, ! ListQ[#] &]]; AppendTo[c, {k++, n − m}];
m = n; a = Flatten[a, 1]; Continue[]]; Append[c, {k++, Length[a] − m}]]

In[2734]:= L = {a, b, a, {d, c, s}, a, b, {b, c, {x, y, {v, g, z, {90, {500, {}, 74}}, a, k, a}, z}, b}, c, b};
In[2735]:= ElemLevelsN[L]
Out[2735]= {{0, 7}, {1, 6}, {2, 3}, {3, 6}, {4, 1}, {5, 2}, {6, 0}}
In[2736]:= Map[ElemLevelsN, {{}, {a, b, c, d, r, t, y, c, s, f, g, h, 74, 90, 500, s, a, q, w}}]
Out[2736]= {{{0, 0}}, {{0, 19}}}

In[2874]:= ElemLevelsL[x_ /; ListQ[x]] :=
Module[{a = ReplaceAll[x, {} -> Null], c = {}, m = {}, n, k = 0},
While[NestListQ1[a], n = Select[a, ! ListQ[#] &];
AppendTo[c, {k++, Complement[n, m]}]; m = n; a = Flatten[a, 1];
Continue[]]; c = Append[c, {k++, Complement[a, m]}]; ReplaceAll[c, Null -> {}]]

In[2875]:= ElemLevelsL[L]
Out[2875]= {{0, {a, b, c}}, {1, {d, s}}, {2, {x, y, z}}, {3, {g, k, v}}, {4, {90}}, {5, {74, 500}}, {6, {}}}

The following procedure provides return of all possible sublists of the nested list. The call **SubLists[x]** returns a list of all possible sublists of the nested *x* list, taking into account their nesting. At that, if the *x* list is simple, the call **SubLists[x]** returns the empty list, i.e. {}. The fragment below represents source code of the **SubLists** procedure with examples of its use.

In[2339]:= SubLists[x_ /; ListQ[x]] := Module[{a, b, c = {}, k = 1},
If[! NestListQ1[x], {}, a = ToString[x];
b = DeleteDuplicates[Flatten[StringPosition[a, "{"]]];
While[k <= Length[b], AppendTo[c, SubStrSymbolParity1[StringTake[a, {b[[k]], −1}],
"{", "}"][[1]]]; k++]; DeleteDuplicates[ToExpression[c[[2 ;; −1]]]]]]

In[2340]:= L = {a, b, a, {d, c, s}, a, b, {b, c, {x, y, {v, g, z, {90, {500, {}, 74}}, a, k, a}}, b}, c, b};
In[2341]:= SubLists[Flatten[L]]
Out[2341]= {}
In[2342]:= SubLists[L]
Out[2342]= {{d, c, s}, {b, c, {x, y, {v, g, z, {90, {500, {}, 74}}, a, k, a}}, b}, {x, y, {v, g, z, {90, {500, {}, 74}}, a, k, a}}, {v, g, z, {90, {500, {}, 74}}, a, k, a}, {90, {500, {}, 74}}, {500, {}, 74}, {}}
In[2343]:= SubLists[{a, b, {c, d, {g, h, {g, s}}, {n, m}}, {90, 500}}]
Out[2343]= {{c, d, {g, h, {g, s}}, {n, m}}, {g, h, {g, s}}, {g, s}, {n, m}, {90, 500}}

Means of operating with levels of the nested list are of a special interest. In this context the following tools can be rather useful. As one of such means the **MaxLevel** procedure can be considered, whose call **MaxLevel[x]** returns the maximum nesting level of *x* list *(in addition, the nesting level of a simple x list is supposed equal to zero)*. At that, **MaxNestLevel** procedure is a *equivalent* version of the previous procedure. While the call **ListLevels[x]** returns the list of nesting levels of a *x* list; in addition, for a simple list or empty list the procedure call returns zero. The next fragment represents source codes of the above procedures along with typical examples of their applications.

In[2562]:= **MaxLevel[x_ /; ListQ[x]] := Module[{a = x, k = 0},**
While[NestListQ1[a], k++; a = Flatten[a, 1]; Continue[]]; k]
In[2563]:= **Map[MaxLevel, {{a, b}, {a, {b, c, d}}, {{{a, b, c}}}, {a, {{c, {d}, {{h, g}}}}}}]**
Out[2563]= {0, 1, 2, 4}
In[2564]:= **MaxLevel[{a, b, c, d, f, g, h, s, r, t, w, x, y, z}]**
Out[2564]= 0

In[2581]:= **ListLevels[x_ /; ListQ[x]] := Module[{a = x, b, c = {}, k = 1},**
If[! NestListQ1[x], {0}, While[NestListQ1[a], b = Flatten[a, 1];
If[Length[b] >= Length[a], AppendTo[c, k++], AppendTo[c, k]]; a = b; Continue[]]; c]]
In[2582]:= **ListLevels[{a, b, c, d, f, g, h, s, r, t, w, x, y, z}]**
Out[2582]= {0}
In[2583]:= **ListLevels[{a, {{{{{}}}}}, b, c, {d, f, g, {h, s, {z, y, g}, r}, t}, w, {x, {{{a, b, c}}}, y}, z}]**
Out[2583]= {1, 2, 3, 4, 5}

In[586]:= **MaxNestLevel[L_ /; ListQ[L]] := Module[{a = Flatten[L], b = L, c = 0},**
While[! a == b, b = Flatten[b, 1]; c = c + 1]; c]
In[2587]:= **L = {{a, {b, {m, {x, y, {p, q, {g, 2016}}}, n}, x}, c, {{{{{{{{69, 780}}}}}}}}}};**
Map[MaxNestLevel, {L, {a, b, c}}]
Out[2587]= {8, 0}

Moreover, between the above tools the next defining relations take place:

Flatten[x] ≡ Flatten[x, MaxLevel[x]]; MaxLevel[x] ≡ ListLevels[x][[-1]]

The call **ElemMaxLevel[w, y]** returns the maximal nesting level of a *w* list containing an *y* element; in case of lack of the *y* element in the list the $*Failed* is returned with output of the corresponding message. Whereas the procedure call **ElemMaxLevel[w, y, h]** with the third optional *h* argument – an indefinite symbol – through it is returned the list of all elements of the *w* list at this nesting level. Whereas the call **ElemsMaxLevels[w, y]** returns the list of the *ListList* type whose 2–element sublists have elements of *y* list as the first elements, and their maximal nesting levels in a *w* list as the second elements. The **ElemsMaxLevels** procedure processes the main especial situations.

In[3606]:= **ElemMaxLevel[x_ /; ListQ[x], y_, h___] := Module[{a = MaxLevelList[x], b, c = {}},**
If[FreeQ[x, y], Print["List not contain " <> ToString1[y]]; $Failed,
b = Map[{#, Level[x, {#}]} &, Range[1, a]];
Do[AppendTo[c, If[FreeQ[b[[j]][[2]], y], Nothing, j]], {j, 1, a}];
If[{h} != {} &&! HowAct[h], h = Level[x, {c[[-1]]}], Null]; c[[-1]]]]

In[3607]:= L := {a, b, {{a, b}, {{m, n, {p, {{{{}}}}}}}, c, {}, m, n, p, {{{{a + b}, g}}}}
In[3608]:= {ElemMaxLevel[L, g, g69], g69}
Out[3608]= {4, {m, n, {p, {{{}}}}, {a + b}, g}}
In[3609]:= ElemsMaxLevels[x_ /; ListQ[x], y_ /; ListQ[y]] :=
Module[{a = MaxLevelList[x], b, c = {}, d = {}, h}, b = {Map[FreeQ[x, #] &, y], y};
If[Count[b[[1]], True] == Length[y], Print["List not contain " <> ToString1[y]]; $Failed,
If[MemberQ[b[[1]], True], Do[AppendTo[c, If[b[[1]][[j]], b[[2]][[j]], Nothing]],
{j, 1, Length[b[[1]]]}], 6];
If[c == {}, 6, PrintTemporary["List not contain " <> ToString1[c]]; Pause[2]];
h = Map[{#, Level[x, {#}]} &, Range[1, a]]; b = Select[y, ! MemberQ[c, #] &];
Do[Do[AppendTo[d, If[FreeQ[h[[j]][[2]], b[[k]]], Nothing, {b[[k]], j}]],
{k, 1, Length[b]}], {j, 1, a}]; d = Gather[d, #1[[1]] == #2[[1]] &];
d = Map[Sort[#, #1[[2]] >= #2[[2]] &] &, d]; Map[#[[1]] &, d]]]
In[3610]:= ElemsMaxLevels[L, {{}, Avz, {{}}, g, Agn, Vsv, a + b}]
"List not contain {Avz, Agn, Vsv}"
Out[3610]= {{{}, 8}, {{{}}, 7}, {g, 4}, {a + b, 5}}
In[3611]:= ElemsMaxLevels[L, {a, n, m, {a + b}, {{}}}]
Out[3611]= {{a, 6}, {n, 4}, {m, 4}, {{a + b}, 4}, {{{}}, 7}}
In[3505]:= AllElemsMaxLevels[x_ /; ListQ[x]] := Module[{g = ToString1[x], c, Agn},
If[x == {}, {}, Agn[z_ /; ListQ[x], y_] := Module[{a = MaxLevelList[z], d = {}, h},
h = Map[{#, Level[z, {#}]} &, Range[1, a]];
Do[Do[AppendTo[d, If[FreeQ[h[[j]][[2]], y[[k]]], Nothing, {y[[k]], j}]],
{k, 1, Length[y]}], {j, 1, a}]; d = Gather[d, #1[[1]] == #2[[1]] &];
d = Map[Sort[#, #1[[2]] >= #2[[2]] &] &, d]; Map[#[[1]] &, d]];
c = AllSubStrings[g, 0, ExprQ[#] &];
g = DeleteDuplicates[ToExpression[c]]; g = Agn[x, g]; If[Length[g] == 1, g[[1]], g]]]
In[3509]:= AllElemsMaxLevels[L]
Out[3509]= {{a, 6}, {b, 6}, {m, 4}, {n, 4}, {p, 5}, {c, 1}, {g, 4}, {{}, 8}, {{{}}, 7}, {a + b, 5}, {{a, b}, 2},
{{{{}}}, 5}, {{a + b}, 4}, {{p, {{{}}}}, 4}, {{{a + b}, g}, 3}, {{{{a + b}, g}}, 2}, {{{{{a + b}, g}}}, 1},
{{m, n, {p, {{{}}}}}, 3}, {{{m, n, {p, {{{}}}}}}, 2}, {{{a, b}, {m, n, {p, {{{}}}}}}, 1}, {{a, b, {{a, b},
{{m, n, {p, {{{}}}}}}, c, {}, m, n, p, {{{{a + b}, g}}}}, 1}}

Thus, the **AllElemsMaxLevels** procedure of the previous fragment extends the procedure **ElemsMaxLevels** onto all expressions composing the analyzed list. **AllElemsMaxLevels**[x] returns the list of the *ListList* type whose 2-element sublists have all possible elements of a x list as the first elements, and their maximal nesting levels in a x list as the second elements.

The next rather useful procedure of work with lists has structural character, first of all, for the nested lists. Generally speaking, the procedure call **ElemOnLevels**[x] returns the nested list whose elements are sublists whose first elements are levels of a nested list x whereas the others – elements of these levels. For lack of elements on j level the sublist has the form {j}; the call **ElemOnLevels**[x] on a simple x list returns {0, x}, i.e. the simple list has the nesting level *0*. In the fragment below the source code of the **ElemOnLevels** procedure and typical examples of its application are represented.

In[2736]:= **ElemOnLevels[x_ /; ListQ[x]] := Module[{a, b, c, d, p = 0, k, j = 1},**
If[! NestListQ1[x], Flatten[{0, x}], {a, c, d} = {x, {}, {}};
While[NestListQ1[a], b = {p++}; For[k = 1, k <= Length[a], k++, If[! ListQ[a[[k]]],
AppendTo[b, a[[k]]], AppendTo[c, k]]];
AppendTo[d, b]; a = Flatten[Delete[a, Map[List, c]], 1]; {b, c} = {{}, {}}; j++];
AppendTo[d, Flatten[{p++, a}]]]]

In[2737]:= **ElemOnLevels[{a, b, {c, d, {f, h, d}, s, {p, w, {n, m, r, u}, t}}, x, y, z}]**
Out[2737]= {{*0*, a, b, x, y, z}, {*1*, c, d, s}, {2, f, h, d, p, w, t}, {3, n, m, r, u}}
In[2738]:= **ElemOnLevels[{a, b, c, d, f, h, d, s, p, w, n, m, r, u, t, x, y, z}]**
Out[2738]= {*0*, a, b, c, d, f, h, d, s, p, w, n, m, r, u, t, x, y, z}
In[2739]:= **ElemOnLevels[{{{a, b, c, d, f, h, d, s, p, w, n, m, r, u, t, x, y, z}}}]**
Out[2739]= {{*0*}, {*1*}, {2, a, b, c, d, f, h, d, s, p, w, n, m, r, u, t, x, y, z}}
In[2740]:= **Map[ElemOnLevels, {{{{{{}}}}}, {{}}, {{{}}}, {{{{{{}}}}}}}]**
Out[2740]= {{{*0*}, {*1*}, {2}, {3}}, {{*0*}, {*1*}}, {{*0*}, {*1*}, {2}}, {{*0*}, {*1*}, {2}, {3}, {4}, {5}}}

The procedure **ElemsOnLevelList** below in certain cases is more preferable than the above procedure. The procedure call **ElemsOnLevelList[*x*]** returns the nested list whose elements – the nested two–element lists, whose the first elements are nesting levels of a *x* list whereas the second elements – the lists of elements at these nesting levels. If *x* is empty list, then {} is returned. Below, the source code of the procedure with an example are represented.

In[2860]:= **ElemsOnLevelList[x_ /; ListQ[x]] := Module[{a, b, c = {}, d = {}, k = 1, t, f, h, g},**
f = ReplaceAll[x, {{} -> Set[g, FromCharacterCode[3]], 2 -> h}]; b = Flatten[f];
a = LevelsOfList[f]; Do[AppendTo[c, {a[[t = k++]], b[[t]]}], {Length[a]}];
c = Map[Flatten, Gather[c, #1[[1]] == #2[[1]] &]]; k = 1;
Do[AppendTo[d, {c[[t = k++]][[1]], Select[c[[t]], EvenQ[Flatten[Position[c[[t]], #]][[1]] &]}], {Length[c]}];
c = ReplaceAll[d, {Null -> Nothing, h -> 2}];
ReplaceAll[Sort[c, #1[[1]] < #2[[1]] &], g -> Nothing]]

In[2861]:= **ElemsOnLevelList[{a, {{{{{{}}}}}}, b, {c, d, {f, h, d}, s, {p, w, {n, m, r, u}, t}}, x, y, z}]**
Out[2861]= {{1, {a, b, x, y, z}}, {2, {c, d, s}}, {3, {f, h, d, p, w, t}}, {4, {n, m, r, u}}, {5, {}}}

Using the previous procedure, we can define a tool of converting of any list into a canonical form, i.e. in the list of format {*Level1*, {*Level2*, {*Level3*, {*Level4*, ..., *Leveln*} ...}}}; at the same time, all elements of a *Levelj* level are sorted {*j = 1..n*}. The function is provided with means whose call **RestructLevelsList[*x*]** returns a *x* list in the canonical format. The next fragment represents source code of the procedure with examples of its application.

Unlike the previous procedure, the procedure call **ElemsInList[*x*, *y*]** returns the 2–element list whose first element defines an *y* element whereas the second – the list of nesting levels of the *x* list on which the *y* element is located. In case of absence of the *y* element in the *x* list the empty list, i.e. {} will be as the second element of the returned list. If the list acts as the second *y* element, the procedure call returns the nested list whose elements have the above kind. The next fragment represents source code of the procedure with examples of its use.

In[3075]:= ElemsInList[x_ /; ListQ[x], y_] := Module[{a = ElemsOnLevels[x], b = {}},
If[! ListQ[y], {y, Map[If[#[[1]] === y, #[[2]], Nothing] &, a]},
Do[AppendTo[b, {y[[j]], Map[If[#[[1]] == y[[j]], #[[2]], Nothing] &, a]}], {j, 1, Length[y]}]; b]]
In[3076]:= x = {a, b, d, c, {c, d, s, {g, h, t, p, d}, d}, m, n}; ElemsInList[x, d]
Out[3076]= {d, {1, 2, 3, 2}}
In[3077]:= ElemsInList[x, {d, c, y}]
Out[3077]= {{d, {1, 2, 3, 2}}, {c, {1, 2}}, {y, {}}}
In[4380]:= RestructLevelsList[x_ /; ListQ[x]] :=
Module[{a, b = FromCharacterCode[3], g = FromCharacterCode[4], c, d, h = {}},
d = b; a = ElemsOnLevelList[ReplaceAll[x, {} -> {g}]];
c = Map[{AppendTo[h, #[[1]]]; #[[1]], Join[Sort[#[[2]]], {b}]} &, a];
h = Flatten[{1, Differences[h]}];
Do[d = ReplaceAll[d, b -> If[c[[j]][[1]] - j == 1, c[[j]][[2]], Nest[List, c[[j]][[2]], h[[j]] - 1]]],
{j, 1, Length[h]}];
ReplaceAll[d, {b -> Nothing, g -> {}}]]
In[4381]:= L = {s, "a", g, {{{{{}}}}}, m, 75, m, c, m, {f, d, 70, s, h, m, {m + p, {{}}, n, 50, p, a}}, 9};
In[4382]:= ElemsOnLevelList[L]
Out[4382]= {{1, {s, "a", g, m, 75, m, c, m, 9}}, {2, {f, d, 70, s, h, m}}, {3, {m + p, n, 50, p, a}},
{4, {}}, {5, {}}}
In[4383]:= L1 = RestructLevelsList[L]
Out[4383]= {9, 75, "a", c, g, m, m, m, s, {70, d, f, h, m, s, {50, a, n, p, m + p, {{}, {{}}}}}}
In[4384]:= ElemsOnLevelList[L1]
Out[4384]= {{1, {9, 75, "a", c, g, m, m, m, s}}, {2, {70, d, f, h, m, s}}, {3, {50, a, n, p, m + p}},
{4, {}}, {5, {}}}
In[4385]:= L2 = RestructLevelsList[{s, "a", g, m, 75, m, c, {{{{{{{{{art}}}}}}}}}, m, 90, {f, d, 70, s,
h, m, {m + p, n, 50, p, a, {{{gs}, {{{vg}}}}}}}}]
Out[4385]= {75, "a", c, g, m, m, s, {90, m, {70, d, f, h, m, s, {50, a, n, p, m + p, {{{gs, {{vg,
{art}}}}}}}}}}
In[4386]:= ElemsOnLevelList[L2]
Out[4386]= {{1, {75, "a", c, g, m, m, s}}, {2, {90, m}}, {3, {70, d, f, h, m, s}}, {4, {50, a, n, p,
m + p}}, {7, {gs}}, {9, {vg}}, {10, {art}}}
In[4387]:= RestructLevelsList[{p, 6, 7, 3, f, m, d, a, 4, h, w, g, s, 2}]
Out[4387]= {2, 3, 4, 6, 7, a, d, f, g, h, m, p, s, w}

The following procedure has algorithm different from the previous procedure and defines a tool of converting of any list into the above canonical form, i.e. in the list of format {*Level1*, {*Level2*, {*Level3*, {*Level4*, ..., *Leveln*}...}}}; in addition, all elements of *Levelj* level are sorted {*j* = 1..*n*}. The procedure call **CanonListForm**[*x*] returns a *x* list in the canonical format. The next fragment presents source code of the **CanonListForm** procedure with typical examples of its application.

In[4390]:= CanonListForm[x_ /; ListQ[x]] :=
Module[{a = Map[{#[[1]], Sort[#[[2]]]} &, ElemsOnLevelList[x]], b, c, h = {}, p, m, s, f, n = 2,
d = FromCharacterCode[3]},

b = Max[Map[#[[1]] &, a]]; AppendTo[h, c = "{" <> d <> "1,"];
Do[Set[c, "{" <> d <> ToString[n++] <> ","]; AppendTo[h, c], {j, 2, b}];
p = StringJoin[h] <> StringMultiple["}", b];
m = Map[Rule[d <> ToString[#[[1]]], StringTake[ToString1[#[[2]]], {2, -2}]] &, a];
m = Map[If[#[[2]] == "", Rule[#[[1]], "{}"], #] &, m]; s = StringReplace[p, m];
f[t_] := If[! StringFreeQ[ToString[t], d], Nothing, t];
SetAttributes[f, Listable]; Map[f, ToExpression[StringReplace[s, ",}" -> "}"]]]]

In[4391]:= L = {s, "a", g, {{{{{{}}}}}}, m, 75, m, c, m, {f, d, 70, s, h, m, {m + p, {{}}, n, 50, p, a}}, 9};
L1 = {s, "a", g, {{{{{{m}}}}}}, m, 75, m, c, m, {f, d, 70, s, h, m, {m + p, {{p}}, n, 50, p, a}}, 9};
In[4392]:= CanonListForm[L]
Out[4392]= {9, 75, "a", c, g, m, m, m, s, {70, d, f, h, m, s, {50, a, n, p, m + p, {{}, {{}}}}}}
In[4393]:= CanonListForm[L1]
Out[4393]= {9, 75, "a", c, g, m, m, m, s, {70, d, f, h, m, s, {50, a, n, p, m + p, {{p, {m}}}}}}

The **CanonListForm** uses a number of the receptions useful in practical programming of the problems dealt of lists of various type. While the following simple function allows to obtain a representation of a *x* list in a slightly different canonical format: {{*L1*}, {{*L2*}}, {{{*L3*}}}, ..., {{{...{*Ln*}...}}}} where *Lj* present the sorted list elements at appropriate nesting *j* level of the *x* list *(j = 1..n)*, for example:

In[4395]:= CanonListForm1[x_ /; ListQ[x]] :=
Map[Nest[List, #[[2]], #[[1]] - 1] &, Map[{#[[1]], Sort[#[[2]]]} &, ElemsOnLevelList[x]]]
In[4396]:= CanonListForm1[{a, b, {c, d, {g, h, {x, {y, {z}}}}}}]
Out[4396]= {{a, b}, {{c, d}}, {{{g, h}}}, {{{{x}}}}, {{{{{y}}}}}, {{{{{{z}}}}}}}
In[4397]:= Map[LevelsList[#] &, CanonListForm1[{a, b, {c, d, {g, h, {x, {y, {z}}}}}}]]
Out[4397]= {1, 2, 3, 4, 5, 6}

At the same time, the nesting of elements of a list returned by the **CanonListForm1** function can be determined, for example, by **LevelsList** procedure calls as illustrates the last example of the previous fragment.

On the basis of the previous procedure the **NumElemsOnLevels** function useful enough in a number of appendices can be quite easily programmed. The call **NumElemsOnLevels**[*x*] returns the list of *ListList* type whose 2-element sublists define nesting levels and quantity of elements on them respectively. While the function call **NumElemsOnLevel**[*x*, *p*] returns the quantity of elements of a *x* list on its *p* nesting level. In case of absence of the *p* level the function call returns $Failed with printing of the appropriate message. The source codes of both functions with examples of their application are represented below.

In[4002]:= NumElemsOnLevels[x_ /; ListQ[x]] :=
Map[{#[[1]], Length[#[[2]]]} &, ElemsOnLevelList[x]]
In[4003]:= NumElemsOnLevel[x_ /; ListQ[x], y_ /; IntegerQ[y] && y >= 1] :=
If[MemberQ[LevelsOfList[x], y], Length[Select[ElemsOnLevels[x], #1[[2]] == y &]],
Print["Level " <> ToString[y] <> " is absent"]; $Failed]
In[4004]:= NumElemsOnLevel[{t, c, {{{{{{}}}}}}, {74, 69}, {{{a + b, h}}}, {m, n, f}, {{{{74, g}}}}}, 5]
Out[4004]= 3

In[4005]:= **NumElemsOnLevel[{t, c, {{{{{}}}}}, {74, 69}, {{{a + b, h}}}, {m, n, f}, {{{{74, g}}}}}, 9]**
"Level 9 is absent"
Out[4005]= $Failed
In[4006]:= **NumElemsOnLevels[{t, c, {{{{{}}}}}, {74, 69}, {{{a + b, h}}}, {m, n, f}, {{{{74, g}}}}}]**
Out[4006]= {{1, 2}, {2, 5}, {4, 2}, {5, 2}, {6, 0}}

On the basis of the **ElemsOnLevelList** procedure the **ElemsLevelOnCond** function useful in a number of appendices can be easily programmed. The call **ElemsLevelOnCond[x, y]** returns the nested list whose elements – the nested 2–element lists, whose the first elements are nesting levels of a x list while the second elements – the lists of elements at these nesting levels that coincide with an y expression or satisfy to the test defined by a pure y function. In case if the required elements are absent in the list x, the empty list is returned. The source code of the **ElemsLevelOnCond** function with examples of its use are represented below.

In[4225]:= **ElemsLevelOnCond[x_ /; ListQ[x], y_] :=**
ReduceLevelsList[Select[If[PureFuncQ[y], Map[{#[[1]], Select[#[[2]], y]} &,
ElemsOnLevelList[x]], Map[{#[[1]], Select[#[[2]], # == y &]} &, ElemsOnLevelList[x]]],
#[[2]] != {} &]][[1]]

In[4226]:= **ElemsLevelOnCond[{{1, 2, 3}, {4, b, 5}, {6, 2, 7, {8, 7, 8, {5, 6, 7, b}}}}, OddQ[#] &]**
Out[4226]= {{2, {1, 3, 5, 7}}, {3, {7}}, {4, {5, 7}}}
In[4227]:= **ElemsLevelOnCond[{{1, 2, 3}, {4, b, 4, b, 5}, {6, 2, 7, {8, b, 8, {5, b, 6, 7, b}}}}, b]**
Out[4227]= {{2, {b, b}}, {3, {b}}, {4, {b, b}}}

Procedure below is a rather useful extension of the above **ElemsLevelOnCond** function. The call **ElemsLevelOnCond1[x, y]** returns the nested list whose elements - the nested 2-element lists, whose the first elements are nesting levels of a x list whereas the second elements – the 2-element sublists whose the *first* elements determine elements at these nesting levels which coincide with an y expression or belong to their y list, or satisfy to the test defined by a pure y function while the second elements define their serial numbers on these nesting levels. In a case if the required elements are absent in the list x, the empty list is returned. The source code of the **ElemsLevelOnCond1** procedure with examples of its use are presented below.

In[4238]:= **ElemsLevelOnCond1[x_ /; ListQ[x], y_] :=**
Module[{a = ElemsOnLevelList[x], b, c, d = {}}, b = Map[{#[[1]], Select3[#[[2]], y]} &, a];
Do[AppendTo[d, {b[[j]][[1]], Position1[a[[j]][[2]], DeleteDuplicates[b[[j]][[2]]]]}],
{j, 1, Length[a]}]; d]

In[4239]:= **ElemsLevelOnCond1[{{1, 2, 3}, {4, b, 4, b, 5}, {6, 2, 7, {7, b, 8, {5, b, 6, 7, b}}}}, b]**
Out[4239]= {{2, {b, {5, 7}}}, {3, {b, {2}}}, {4, {b, {2, 5}}}}
In[4240]:= **ElemsLevelOnCond1[{{1, 2, 3}, {4, b, 4, b, 5}, {6, 2, 7, {7, b, 8, {5, b, 6, 7, b}}}}, {b, 4}]**
Out[4240]= {{2, {{4, {4, 6}}, {b, {5, 7}}}}, {3, {b, {2}}}, {4, {b, {2, 5}}}}
In[4241]:= **ElemsLevelOnCond1[{{1, 2, 2, 3}, {4, b, 4, 5}, {6, 2, 7, {8, 7, 8, {5, 6, 7, b}}}},**
PrimeQ[#] || SymbolQ[#] &]
Out[4241]= {{2, {{2, {2, 3, 10}}, {3, {4}}, {b, {6}}, {5, {8}}, {7, {11}}}}, {3, {7, {2}}}, {4, {{5, {1}}, {7, {3}}, {b, {4}}}}}

The procedure call **LevelsOfList[x]** returns the list of levels of elements of a list **Flatten[x]** of a source x list. In addition, in case the empty x list, {} is returned; in case of a simple x list the single list of length **Length[Flatten[x]]**, i.e. {1, 1, ..., 1} is returned, i.e. level of all elements of a simple list is equal *1*. On lists of the kind {{{{...{{}}...}}}} the procedure call returns the empty list, i.e. {}. The following fragment represents source code of the procedure with an example of its application.

In[3854]:= LevelsOfList[x_ /; ListQ[x]] :=
Module[{L, L1, t, p, k, h, g, j, s, w = ReplaceAll[x, {} -> {FromCharacterCode[2]}]},
{j, s} = ReduceLevelsList[w]; j = Prepend[j, 1];
Delete[If[j == {}, {}, If[! NestListQ1[j], Map[#^0 &, Range[1, Length[j]]],
If[FullNestListQ[j], Map[#^0 &, Range[1, Length[Flatten[j]]]],
{p, h, L, L1, g} = {1, FromCharacterCode[1], j, {}, {}}; ClearAll[t];
Do[For[k = 1, k <= Length[L], k++,
If[! ListQ[L[[k]]] && ! SuffPref[ToString[L[[k]]], h, 1],
AppendTo[g, 0]; AppendTo[L1, h <> ToString[p]],
If[! ListQ[L[[k]]] && ! SuffPref[ToString[L[[k]]], h, 1],
AppendTo[g, 0]; AppendTo[L1, L[[k]]], AppendTo[g, 1]; AppendTo[L1, L[[k]]]]]];
If[! MemberQ[g, 1], L1, L = Flatten[L1, 1]; L1 = {}; g = {}; p++], {Levels[j, t]; t}];
ToExpression[Map[StringDrop[#, 1] &, L]]]]] + s - 1, 1]]
In[3855]:= LevelsOfList[{a, m, n, {{b}, {c}, {{m, {{{g}}}, n, {{{{{gs}}}}}}}}, d}]
Out[3855]= {1, 1, 1, 3, 3, 4, 7, 4, 9, 1}
In[3856]:= LevelsOfList[{{{{{1, 2, 3, a}, 7}}}}]
Out[3856]= {5, 5, 5, 5, 4}
In[3857]:= LevelsOfList[{1, {a}, 3, 5}]
Out[3857]= {1, 2, 1, 1}
In[3858]:= LevelsOfList[{{{{}}}}]
Out[3858]= {4}
In[3859]:= LevelsOfList[{{{{{a, b}, {c, d}}}}}]
Out[3859]= {5, 5, 5, 5}
In[3860]:= LevelsOfList[{{{{{}, {{}}}}}, {}}]
Out[3860]= {5, 6, 2}
In[3853]:= ElemsOnLevels[x_ /; ListQ[x]] := Module[{a, b, c, f = ReplaceAll[x, {} -> Null]},
a = Flatten[f]; b = LevelsOfList[f]; c = Map[{a[[#]], b[[#]]} &, Range[1, Length[a]]];
ReplaceAll[c, Null -> {}]]
In[3854]:= ElemsOnLevels[{a, b, c, {{x, y, z}, {{m, n, p}}}, c, d}]
Out[3854]= {{a, 1}, {b, 1}, {c, 1}, {x, 3}, {y, 3}, {z, 3}, {m, 4}, {n, 4}, {p, 4}, {c, 1}, {d, 1}}
In[3855]:= ElemsOnLevels[Flatten[{a, b, c, {{x, y, z}, {{m, n, p}}}, c, d}]]
Out[3855]= {{a, 1}, {b, 1}, {c, 1}, {x, 1}, {y, 1}, {z, 1}, {m, 1}, {n, 1}, {p, 1}, {c, 1}, {d, 1}}
In[3897]:= ElemsOnLevels1[x_ /; ListQ[x]] :=
Module[{a, b, c = ReplaceAll[x, {} -> {Null}], n = 1},
a = LevelsOfList[c]; SetAttributes[b, Listable];
b[t_] := {t, a[[n++]]}; c = Map[b, c]; ReplaceAll[c, Null -> {}]]
In[3898]:= ElemsOnLevels1[{b, t, c, {{3, 2, 1, {g, s, a}, k, 0}, 2, 3, 1}, 1, 2, {m, n, f}}]
Out[3898]= {{b, 1}, {t, 1}, {c, 1}, {{{3, 3}, {2, 3}, {1, 3}, {{g, 4}, {s, 4}, {a, 4}}, {k, 3}, {0, 3}}, {2, 2},

{3, 2}, {1, 2}}, {1, 1}, {2, 1}, {{m, 2}, {n, 2}, {f, 2}}}
In[3899]:= ElemsOnLevels1[{}]
Out[3899]= {{{}, 1}}
In[3900]:= ElemsOnLevels1[{{{a, {{}, {}}}}}]
Out[3900]= {{{{a, 3}, {{{{}, 5}}, {{{}, 5}}}}}}
In[3901]:= ElemsOnLevels1[{{a, b, {{{d}}}}, c}]
Out[3901]= {{{a, 2}, {b, 2}, {{{{d, 5}}}}}, {c, 1}}
In[3902]:= ElemsOnLevels1[{{}, {{}}, {{{}}}, {{{{}}}}}]
Out[3902]= {{{{}, 2}}, {{{{}, 3}}}, {{{{{}, 4}}}}, {{{{{{}, 5}}}}}}
In[3925]:= ElemsOnLevels2[x_ /; ListQ[x]] :=
Module[{a, b = ReplaceAll[x, {} -> {Null}], c, d, p},
a = ElemsOnLevels[b]; d = DeleteDuplicates[LevelsOfList[b]];
Do[p = 1; Do[If[(a[[k]][[2]] == d[[j]]) && (Length[a[[k]]] == 2),
c = AppendTo[a[[k]], p++]; ListAssignP[a, c, k], Null], {k, 1, Length[a]}], {j, 1, Length[d]}];
ReplaceAll[a, Null -> {}]]
In[3926]:= ElemsOnLevels2[{b, t, c, {{3, 2, 1, {g, s, a}, k, 0}, 2, 3, 1}, 1, 2, {m, n, f}}]
Out[3926]= {{b, 1, 1}, {t, 1, 2}, {c, 1, 3}, {3, 3, 1}, {2, 3, 2}, {1, 3, 3}, {g, 4, 1}, {s, 4, 2}, {a, 4, 3}, {10, 3, 4}, {0, 3, 5}, {2, 2, 1}, {3, 2, 2}, {1, 2, 3}, {1, 1, 4}, {2, 1, 5}, {m, 2, 4}, {n, 2, 5}, {f, 2, 6}}
In[3927]:= ElemsOnLevels2[{{a, b, {{{d}}}}, c}]
Out[3927]= {{a, 2, 1}, {b, 2, 2}, {d, 5, 1}, {c, 1, 1}}
In[3928]:= ElemsOnLevels2[{{{{a, b, {}, {{{d, {}}, {}}}}, c}}}]
Out[3928]= {{a, 4, 1}, {b, 4, 2}, {{}, 5, 1}, {d, 7, 1}, {{}, 8, 1}, {{}, 7, 2}, {c, 3, 1}}
In[3929]:= ElemsOnLevels3[x_ /; ListQ[x]] :=
Map[{#[[1]], Position2[#[[2]]]} &, ElemsOnLevelList[x]]
In[3930]:= ElemsOnLevels3[{{1, 2, 3}, {4, b, 4, b, 5}, {6, 2, 7, {7, b, 8, {5, b, 6, 7, d + c}}}}]
Out[3930]= {{2, {{1, {1}}, {2, {2, 10}}, {3, {3}}, {4, {4, 6}}, {5, {8}}, {6, {9}}, {7, {11}}, {b, {5, 7}}}}, {3, {{7, {1}}, {8, {3}}, {b, {2}}}}, {4, {{5, {1}}, {6, {3}}, {7, {4}}, {b, {2}}, {c + d, {5}}}}}

ElemsOnLevels3 function replenishes the previous fragment. The call **ElemsOnLevels**[*x*] returns the list of *ListList* type; the first element of its two-elements sublists determines an element of a *x* list without regard to its nesting level, while the 2nd element determines the nesting level of this element. The **ElemsOnLevels** algorithm uses the above **LevelsOfList** procedure. In addition, unlike the **ElemsOnLevels** procedure the call **ElemsOnLevels1**[*x*] returns the list structurally identical to an initial *x* list to whose elements the nested levels on that they are located are ascribed, i.e. elements of the returned list have the kind {*elems, levl*} where *elems* – an element and *levl* – its nesting level. The **ElemsOnLevels1** algorithm essentially uses the procedures **LevelsOfList** and **MapListAll**. Unlike the **ElemsOnLevels** procedure the procedure call **ElemsOnLevels2**[*x*] returns the list of the *ListList* type; the *first* element of its 3-elements sublists defines an element of a *x* list without regard to its nesting level, the second element determines the nesting level of this element and the third element defines sequential number of element on its nesting level. The **ElemsOnLevels2** algorithm essentially uses the **ElemsOnLevels** and **LevelsOfList** procedures. At that, the function call **ElemsOnLevels3**[*x*] returns the nested list whose elements – the nested two-element lists, whose the first elements are nesting levels of a *x* list whereas the second elements – the two-element sublists whose the first elements define elements at these nesting levels whereas the second elements define the lists of their serial numbers on these nesting levels. The source codes of the above tools and examples of their application complete the previous fragment. These means are of interest, first of all, to the problems dealing with the nested lists.

The result of the **ElemsOnLevels2** procedure call can be given in the kind more convenient for many applications which use processing of the nested lists, namely. The procedure call **DispElemsInList[x]** returns the list whose 3-element sublists define a x list elements as the first element of these sublists whereas the second their element defines the list *(or nested list)* of nesting levels of the elements and the their sequential numbers on these nesting levels. Naturally, the **DispElemsInList** algorithm essentially uses the **ElemsOnLevels2** procedure. The fragment below represents source code of the **DispElemsInList** procedure and typical examples of its application.

In[4285]:= DispElemsInList[x_ /; ListQ[x]] := Module[{a = ElemsOnLevels2[x], b},
b = Map[{#[[1]][[1]], Map[#1[[2 ;; -1]] &, #]} &, Gather[a, #1[[1]] === #2[[1]] &]];
b = Map[If[Length[#[[2]]] == 1, {#[[1]], #[[2]][[1]]}, #] &, b];
Sort[b, ToCharacterCode[ToString1[#1[[1]]]][[1]] <=
ToCharacterCode[ToString1[#2[[1]]]][[1]] &]]

In[4286]:= g = {a, b, 2, m, c, m, {f, d, 5, s, h, m, {m + p, n, 7, p, a}}}; DispElemsInList[g]
Out[4286]= {{2, {1, 3}}, {5, {2, 3}}, {7, {3, 3}}, {a, {{1, 1}, {3, 5}}}, {b, {1, 2}}, {c, {1, 5}}, {d, {2, 2}},
{f, {2, 1}}, {h, {2, 5}}, {m, {{1, 4}, {1, 6}, {2, 6}}}, {m + p, {3, 1}}, {n, {3, 2}}, {p, {3, 4}}, {s, {2, 4}}}

In[4287]:= Clear[g]; DispElemsInList[{a, 1, 2, h, 3, 4, 5, g, 6, 7, v, 8, 9}]
Out[4287]= {{1, {1, 2}}, {2, {1, 3}}, {3, {1, 5}}, {4, {1, 6}}, {5, {1, 7}}, {6, {1, 9}}, {7, {1, 10}},
{8, {1, 12}}, {9, {1, 13}}, {a, {1, 1}}, {g, {1, 8}}, {h, {1, 4}}, {v, {1, 11}}}

Using the **ElemsOnLevels2** procedure, it is possible to program the procedure allowing to process by the given symbol the list elements which are defined by their arrangements on nesting levels and their location at the nested levels. The call **SymbToElemList[x, {m, n}, s]** returns the result of application of a symbol s to an element of a x list which is located on a nesting level m, and be n-th one at this nesting level. The nested list {{$m1, n1$}, ..., {mp, np}} can be as the second argument of the **SymbToElemList**, allowing to execute processing by the s symbol the elements of the x list, whose locations are defined by pairs {mj, nj} {$j = 1..p$} of the above format. At that, the structure of an initial x list is preserved. The next fragment represents source code of the **SymbToElemList** procedure and typical examples of its use.

In[4386]:= SymbToElemList[x_ /; ListQ[x], y_ /; NonNegativeIntListQ[y] && Length[y] ==
2 || ListListQ[y] && And1[Map[Length[#] == 2 && NonNegativeIntListQ[#] &, y]],
G_Symbol] :=
Module[{a, b, c, d, h, g = If[ListListQ[y], y, {y}], f, n = 1, u},
SetAttributes[d, Listable]; f = ReplaceAll[x, {} -> Set[u, {FromCharacterCode[6]}]];
h = Flatten[f]; a = ElemsOnLevels2[f]; d[t_] := "g" <> ToString[n++]; c = Map[d[#] &, f];
h = GenRules[Map["g" <> ToString[#] &, Range[1, Length[h]]], h];
SetAttributes[b, Listable]; a = ElemsOnLevels2[c];
Do[b[t_] := If[MemberQ[a, {t, g[[j]][[1]], g[[j]][[2]]}], G[t], t];
Set[c, Map[b[#] &, c]], {j, 1, Length[g]}];

ReplaceAll[ReplaceAll[c, h], {G[u[[1]]] -> G[], u -> {}}]]

In[4387]:= Lst = {s, "a", g, {{{{{{}}}}}}, b, 75, m, c, m, {f, d, 70, s, h, m, {m + p, {{}}, n, 50, p, a}}};

In[4388]:= SymbToElemList[Lst, {{4, 1}, {6, 1}, {3, 1}, {1, 1}, {5, 1}, {1, 6}, {2, 3}}, S]

Out[4388]= {S[s], "a", g, {{{{{S[]}}}}}, b, 75, S[m], c, m, {f, d, S[70], s, h, m, {S[m + p], {{S[]}}, n, 50, p, a}}}

In[4389]:= SymbToElemList[{{}, {{{}}, {{{}}}}}, {{2, 1}, {4, 1}, {5, 1}}, S]

Out[4389]= {{S[]}, {{{S[]}}, {{{S[]}}}}}

In[4390]:= SymbToElemList[{{{S[m + n]}}}, {{{a, S[18]}}, {{{S[28]}}}}}, {{3, 1}, {4, 1}, {5, 1}}, G]

Out[4390]= {{{G[S[m + n]]}}, {{{G[a], S[18]}}, {{{G[S[28]]}}}}}

Unlike the previous procedure, the **SymbToLevelsList** procedure provides processing by a symbol of all elements of a list which are located at the given nesting levels. The procedure call **SymbToLevelsList** [*x, y, G*] returns the result of application of *G* symbol to all elements of *x* list which are located on *y* nesting levels of the list; at the same time, the separate whole positive number or their list *y* can be as the second argument of the procedure. Whereas the call **SymbToLevelsList**[*x, y, G, t*] with the fourth optional argument *t* – *an undefinite variable* – through it additionally returns the list of nonexisting nesting levels of the *x* list from the *y* list. The fragment below represents source code of the **SymbToLevelsList** procedure with typical examples of its application.

In[4459]:= SymbToLevelsList[x_ /; ListQ[x], y_, G_Symbol, z___] :=
Module[{a, b, c, d, h, f, k = 0, g = If[ListQ[y], y, {y}], n = 1, p = {}, u},
SetAttributes[d, Listable]; f = ReplaceAll[x, {} -> Set[u, {FromCharacterCode[6]}]];
h = Flatten[f]; a = ElemsOnLevels[f]; d[t_] := "g" <> ToString[n++]; c = Map[d[#] &, f];
h = GenRules[Map["g" <> ToString[#] &, Range[1, Length[h]]], h];
SetAttributes[b, Listable]; a = ElemsOnLevels[c];
Do[b[t_] := If[MemberQ[a, {t, y[[j]]}], k++; G[t], t];
Set[c, Map[b[#] &, c]]; AppendTo[p, k]; k = 0, {j, 1, Length[g]}];
c = ReplaceAll[ReplaceAll[c, h], {G[u[[1]]] -> G[], u -> {}}];
If[{z} != {} && NullQ[z], z = Sort[Map[If[#[[2]] === 0, #[[1]], Nothing] &,
Partition[Riffle[g, p], 2]]]]; 6]; c]

In[4460]:= Lst = {s, "a", g, {{{{{{}}}}}}, b, 75, m, c, m, {f, d, 70, s, h, m, {m+p, {{}}, n, 50, p, a}}, 6};

In[4461]:= Clear[t]; SymbToLevelsList[Lst, {1, 28, 2, 5, 6, 12, 15}, S, t]

Out[4461]= {S[s], S["a"], S[g], {{{{{S[]}}}}}, S[b], S[75], S[m], S[c], S[m], {S[f], S[d], S[70], S[s], S[h], S[m], {m + p, {{S[]}}, n, 50, p, a}}, S[6]}

In[4462]:= t

Out[4462]= {12, 15, 28}

In[4463]:= SymbToLevelsList[RandomInteger[{1, 20}, 10], {0, 1, 28, 2, 5, 6, 12, 15}, S, p]

Out[4463]= {S[10], S[16], S[3], S[18], S[4], S[3], S[10], S[15], S[9], S[16]}

In[4464]:= p

Out[4464]= {0, 2, 5, 6, 12, 15, 28}

Using the **ElemsOnLevels2** procedure, it is possible to program the procedure allowing to expand a list by means of inserting into the given positions (nestings levels and sequential numbers on them) of a certain list. The procedure call **ExpandLevelsList**[*x, y, z*] returns the result of inserting of a *z* list to a nesting level *m* relative to *n*–th position at this nesting level;

in addition, the second *y* argument in common case is the nested list {{*m, n*}, *p*}, ..., {*mt, nt*}, *pt*}}, allowing to execute inderting to positions, whose locations are defined by pairs {*mj, nj*} {*j = 1..t*} *(nestings levels and sequential numbers on them)*, while *pt*∈{*1, -1, 0*}, defining insertion at the right, at the left and at situ relative to the given position. The argument *y* has the kind {{*m, n*}, *p*} or the kind of the above nested list {{*m1, n1*}, *p1*}, ..., {*mt, nt*}, *pt*}}. Thus, the call of **ExpandLevelsList** gives the chance of the differentiated inserting of lists, including empty and nested, in an initial *x* list of an arbitrary nesting. At that, the structure of the initial *x* list is preserved. The next fragment represents source code of the **ExpandLevelsList** procedure with typical examples of its application.

In[4485]:= **ExpandLevelsList[x_ /; ListQ[x], y_, z_ /; ListQ[z]] :=**
Module[{a, b, c, d, h, g = If[Length[Flatten[y]] == 3, {y}, y], f, n = 1, u, p = ToString[z]},
SetAttributes[d, Listable]; f = ReplaceAll[x, {} -> Set[u, {FromCharacterCode[2]}]];
h = Flatten[f]; a = ElemsOnLevels2[f]; d[t_] := "g" <> ToString[n++]; c = Map[d[#] &, f];
h = GenRules[Map["g" <> ToString[#] &, Range[1, Length[h]]], h];
SetAttributes[b, Listable]; a = ElemsOnLevels2[c];
Do[b[t_] := If[MemberQ[a, {t, g[[j]][[1]][[1]], g[[j]][[1]][[2]]}],
If[g[[j]][[2]] == -1, p <> "," <> t, If[g[[j]][[2]] == 1, t <> "," <> p, p, 6]], t];
Set[c, Map[b[#] &, c]], {j, 1, Length[g]}]; c = ToExpression[ToString[c]];
ReplaceAll[ReplaceAll[c, Map[ToExpression[#[[1]]] -> #[[2]] &, h]], u[[1]] -> {}]]

In[4486]:= **ExpandLevelsList[{a, d, {b, h, {c, d}}}, {{{1, 1}, 1}, {{2, 1}, 0}, {{3, 1}, -1}}, {{x, y, z}}]**
Out[4486]= {a, {{x, y, z}}, d, {{{x, y, z}}, h, {{{x, y, z}}, c, d}}}
In[4487]:= **ExpandLevelsList[{a, d, {b, h, {c, d}}}, {{{1, 1}, 1}, {{2, 1}, 0}, {{3, 1}, -1}}, {{}}]**
Out[4487]= {a, {{}}, d, {{{}}, h, {{{}}, c, d}}}
In[4488]:= **ExpandLevelsList[{}, {{1, 1}, 0}, MultiEmptyList[3]]**
Out[4488]= {{{{}}}}

Unlike the **ElemsOnLevels2** procedure the procedure call **ElemOfLevels[x, y]** returns the 3-element list whose the first element defines an *y* element, the second element defines the list of nesting level of this element and the third element determines, generally, the nested list of sequential numbers of the *y* element on its nesting levels. In addition, the **ElemOfLevels** algorithm essentially uses the **ElemsOnLevels2**. In case of absense of the *y* element in the *x* list the procedure call returns $*Failed*. The following fragment represents source code of the **ElemOfLevels** procedure and typical examples of its use. The procedure is of interest, first of all, for the problems dealing with the nested lists.

In[4613]:= **ElemOfLevels[x_ /; ListQ[x], y_] := Module[{a = ElemsOnLevels[x], b, c, d},**
b = Select[a, SameQ[#[[1]], y] &]; If[b == {}, $Failed,
b = Map[Flatten, Gather[b, #1[[2]] == #2[[2]] &]];
b = Map[#[[2]] &, b]; c = Map[Length, b]; d = Select[a, MemberQ[b, #[[2]]] &];
d = Map[Flatten, Gather[d, #1[[2]] == #2[[2]] &]];
d = Map[Delete1[#, EvenQ[#] &] &, d]; d = Map[SequencePosition[#, {y}] &, d];
d = Map[DeleteDuplicates, Map[Flatten, d]];
Map[If[ListQ[#] && Length[#] == 1, Flatten[#], #] &, {y, b, d}]]]

In[4614]:= **ElemOfLevels[{a, b, c, m, c, m, {f, d, m, s, h, m, {m, n, m, p, a}}}, m]**

Out[4614]= {m, {1, 2, 3}, {{4, 6}, {3, 6}, {1, 3}}}
In[4615]:= ElemOfLevels[{a, b, c, m, c, m, {f, d, x, s, h, {m, n, m, p, a}}}, x]
Out[4615]= {x, {2}, {3}}

In particular, using the previous procedure the following useful testing procedure can be programmed, namely. The procedure call **DispElemInListQ**[*x, y, n, m*] returns *True* if an *y* element is *m*–th on *n* nesting level of a nonempty *x* list, and *False* otherwise. The following fragment represents source code of the **DispElemInListQ** procedure and typical examples of its application.

In[4633]:= **DispElemInListQ**[x_ /; ListQ[x] && x != {}, y_, n_ /; PosIntQ[n],
m_ /; PosIntQ[m]] := Module[{a = ElemOfLevels[x, y], b = {}, c, d},
Do[AppendTo[b, Flatten[{a[[2]][[j]], a[[3]][[j]]}]], {j, 1, Length[a[[2]]]}];
a = If[NestListQ[a[[3]]], a, Join[a[[1 ;; 2]], {{a[[3]]}}]]; c = Length[a[[2]]];
d = Map[{a[[2]][[#]], a[[3]][[#]]} &, Range[1, c]];
Or1[Map[If[d[[#]][[1]] === n && MemberQ[d[[#]][[2]], m], True, False] &, Range[1, c]]]]

In[4634]:= **DispElemInListQ**[{a, b, 2, m, c, m, {f, d, 5, s, h, m, {m, n, 7, p, a}}}, m, 4, 3]
Out[4634]= False
In[4635]:= **DispElemInListQ**[{a, b, 2, m, c, m, {f, d, 5, s, h, m, {m, n, 7, p, a}}}, m, 1, 6]
Out[4635]= True
In[4636]:= **DispElemInListQ**[{a, b, 2, m, c, m, {f, d, 5, s, h, m, {m, n, 7, p, a}}}, 7, 3, 3]
Out[4636]= True

In addition to the above means of processing of the nested lists the following function is an useful enough tool. The function call **ElemOnLevelListQ**[*x, y, n*] returns *True*, if *y* element belongs to *n*–th nesting level of a *x* list, and *False* otherwise.

In[4683]:= **ElemOnLevelListQ**[x_ /; ListQ[x], y_, n_ /; PosIntQ[n]] :=
MemberQ[Map[If[{#[[1]], #[[2]]} === {y, n}, True, False] &, ElemsOnLevels[w]], True]

In[4684]:= t = {a, b, c, m, c, m, {f, d, m, s, h, m, {m, n, m, p, a}}}; **ElemOnLevelListQ**[t, m, 3]
Out[4684]= True
In[4685]:= **ElemOnLevelListQ**[t, m, 5]
Out[4685]= False

When processing of sublists in the lists is often need of check of the existence fact of sublists overlaping that entere to the lists. The procedure call **SubListOverlapQ**[*x, y, z*] returns *True*, if *x* list on nesting level *z* contains overlapping sublists *y*, and *False* otherwise. While the call **SubStrOverlapQ**[*x, y, z, n*] thru optional n argument – an undefinite symbol – additionally returns the list of consecutive quantities of overlapings of the *y* sublist on the *z* nesting level of the *x* list. In case of the nesting level *z* nonexisting for the *x* list, the procedure call returns *$Failed* with printing of the appropriate message. The next fragment represents source code of the procedure with examples of its application.

In[4330]:= **SubListOverlapQ**[x_List, y_List, z_Integer, n___] :=
Module[{a = ElemsOnLevels[x], b = {}, c = FromCharacterCode[5], d, f},
If[MemberQ[Set[d, DeleteDuplicates[LevelsOfList[x]]], z],
f[t_, h_, d___] := SubStrOverlapQ[ToString1[t], StringTake[ToString1[h], {2, -2}], d];
Do[b = Join[b, Quiet[Check[If[a[[j]][[2]] != z, {a[[j]]}, If[{a[[j]][[1]], a[[j]][[2]]} ===

{a[[j + 1]][[1]], a[[j + 1]][[2]]}, {a[[j]]}, {a[[j]], c}]], {a[[j]], c}]]], {j, 1, Length[a]}]
b = Map[If[# === c, c, If[#[[2]] == z, #[[1]], Nothing]] &, b];
If[{n} != {} && NullQ[n], f[b, y, n], f[b, y]], Print["Nesting level " <> ToString[z] <> " should be from the " <> ToString[Sort[d]] <> " list"]; $Failed]]

In[4331]:= L = {m, "j", m, m, m, m, {{{{{m, m, m, m}}}}}, m, 75, m, m, m, c, m, {f, d, 70, s, h, m, {m, m, {{p}}, n, 50, p, a}}, m, m, m};
In[4332]:= **SubListOverlapQ[L, {m, m}, 1]**
Out[4332]= True
In[4333]:= **SubListOverlapQ[L, {m, m}, 1, gs]**
Out[4333]= True
In[4334]:= **gs**
Out[4334]= {3, 2, 2}
In[4335]:= **SubListOverlapQ[L, {m, m}, 8, p]**
"Nesting level 8 should be from the {1, 2, 3, 5, 6} list"
Out[4335]= $Failed

The previous procedure uses some useful programming techniques. In particular, it uses processing of the special situations inherent in cyclic constructions the essence of which is illustrated by the following simple and visual example:

In[4422]:= a = {1, 2, 3, 4, 5}; Do[Print[Quiet[Check[{a[[j]], a[[j + 1]]}, {a[[j]]}]]], {j, 1, 5}]
{1, 2}
{2, 3}
{3, 4}
{4, 5}
{5}

In some problems of programming that use the list structures arises a quite urgent need of replacement of values of a list which are located at the given nesting levels. The standard functions of the *Mathematica* system don't give such opportunity. In this connection the procedure has been created whose call **ReplaceLevelList**[*x*, *n*, *y*, *z*] returns the result of the replacement of *y* element of a *x* list which is located at a nesting level *n* onto a *z* value. Lists which have identical length also can act as arguments *y*, *n* and *z*. At violation of the given condition the procedure call returns $*Failed*. In case of lack of the *fourth* optional *z* argument the call **ReplaceLevelList**[*x*, *n*, *y*] returns result of removal of *y* elements which are located on a nesting level *n* of the *x* list. The fragment below represent source code of the procedure with some examples of its application.

In[2866]:= **ReplaceLevelList[x_ /; ListQ[x], n_ /; IntegerQ[n] && n > 0 || IntegerListQ[n], y_, z___] :=**
Module[{a, c = Flatten[x], d, b = SetAttributes[ToString4, Listable],
h = FromCharacterCode[2], k, p = {}, g = FromCharacterCode[3],
u = FromCharacterCode[4], m, n1 = Flatten[{n}], y1 = Flatten[{y}], z1},
If[{z} != {}, z1 = Flatten[{z}], z1 = y1];
If[Length[DeleteDuplicates[Map[Length, {n1, y1, z1}]]] != 1, $Failed, a = ToString4[x];
SetAttributes[StringJoin, Listable];

b = ToExpression[ToString4[StringJoin[u, a, g <> h]]];
b = ToString[b]; m = StringPosition[b, h]; d = LevelsOfList[x];
b = StringReplacePart[ToString[b], Map[ToString, d], m];
For[k = 1, k <= Length[n1], k++, AppendTo[p, u <> Map[ToString4, y1][[k]] <> g <>
Map[ToString, n1][[k]] -> If[{z} == {}, "", Map[ToString, z1][[k]]]]];
b = StringReplace[b, p]; d = Map[g <> # &, Map[ToString, d]];
Map[ClearAttributes[#, Listable] &, {StringJoin, ToString4}];
ToExpression[StringReplace[b, Flatten[{u -> "", ", }" -> "}", "{," -> "{", ",," -> ",", " ," -> "",
" , " -> "", GenRules[d, ""]}]]]]]

In[2867]:= L := {a, m, n, {{b + d}, {c}, {{m, {{{g}}}, n, {{{{{{gsv, vgs}}}}}}}}, d}
In[2868]:= L1 := {a, m, n, {{b}, {c}, {{m, {{{g}}}, n, {{{{{{Ggsv, vgs}}}}}}}}, d}
In[2870]:= ReplaceLevelList[L, 9, gsv, Art]
Out[2870]= {a, m, n, {{b + d}, {c}, {{m, {{{g}}}, n, {{{{{Art, vgs}}}}}}}}, d}
In[2871]:= ReplaceLevelList[L1, 9, gsv, Art]
Out[2871]= {a, m, n, {{b}, {c}, {{m, {{{g}}}, n, {{{{{Ggsv, vgs}}}}}}}}, d}
In[2872]:= ReplaceLevelList[L, {3, 9}, {b + d, gsv}, {Art, Kr}]
Out[2872]= {a, m, n, {{Art}, {c}, {{m, {{{g}}}, n, {{{{{Kr, vgs}}}}}}}}, d}
In[2883]:= FullNestListQ[x_ /; ListQ[x]] := Module[{a},
Do[If[! NestListQ[x[[j]]], a = False; Return[]], a = True, {j, 1, Length[x]}]; a]
In[2884]:= FullNestListQ[L]
Out[2884]= False
In[2885]:= Map[FullNestListQ, {{{{a, b}}, {{c, d}}, {{m, n}, {p, c}}}, {{{{{a, b}}}}}}]
Out[2885]= {True, True}

The simple enough procedure **FullNestListQ** completes the above fragment; the procedure call **FullNestListQ**[*x*] returns *True* if all elements of a *x* list are the nested sublists, and *False* otherwise. This procedure can be rather useful at lists processing.

In[2968]:= MapNestList[x_ /; ListQ[x], f_ /; SymbolQ[f], y___] :=
Module[{a = ToString1[x], b, c, d, h = FromCharacterCode[3]},
b = StringPosition[a, "{"]; d = StringReplacePart[a, ToString[f] <> "[" <> h, b];
b = StringPosition[d, "}"];
ToExpression[StringReplace[StringReplacePart[d, If[{y} != {}, "}, " <>
StringTake[ToString1[{y}], {2, -2}] <> "]", "}]"], b], h -> "{"]]]
In[2969]:= L := {6, 3, 8, {11, 8, 26, {{{}, 5, 7, 9}}, {{3, 0, {5, 3, 7, 2}, 2}}}}, 19}
In[2970]:= MapNestList[L, Sort, #1 > #2 &]
Out[2970]= {8, 6, 3, {26, 11, 8, {{{}, 9, 7, 5}}, {{3, 0, {7, 5, 3, 2}, 2}}}}, 19}

Whereas the procedure call **MapNestList**[*x*, *f*, *y*] of the previous fragment returns the result of application to all nesting levels of *x* list of a *f* function with transfer to it of the arguments determined by the optional *y* argument.

The procedure call **LevelsList**[*x*] returns the nesting level of a list *x* of the kind {{{{{{.....}}}}}}, so-called lists of strict nesting. For example, **LevelsList**[{{{{{{a, b, c}, {{x, y, z}}, m, n}}}}}] = 5 and **LevelsList**[{{a, b, c}, {{x, y}}, m, n}] = 1. The procedure is useful enough at processing of certain types of the nested lists. The next fragment represents source code of the **LevelsList** procedure with an example of its application.

In[3961]:= **LevelsList[x_ /; ListQ[x]] := Module[{a = ToString1[x], b = 1},**
Do[a = Quiet[Check[StringTake[a, {2, -2}], "$Failed"]];
If[! SyntaxQ[a] | | ! ListQ[ToExpression[a]] | | a === Null, Break[], b++], {k, 1, Infinity}]; b]
In[3962]:= **Map[LevelsList, {{{{{{{{a, b}}}}}}}, {c, "d", {{{x, y}}}}}]**
Out[3962]= {6, 1}
In[3963]:= **Map[LevelsList, {{{{{{{{{}}}}}}}}, {{{{-c, "d", {{{}}}}}}}}]**
Out[3963]= {6, 4}

Whereas the procedure call **ReduceLevelsList[x][[1]]** returns the list formed from a x list by reducing of its nesting level to *1*, for example:

In[3964]:= **ReduceLevelsList[{{{{{{{{9 + a*b - c, {{{x, {{{y}}}}}}}}}}}}}}][[1]]**

Out[3964]= {9 + a*b - c, {{{x, {{{y}}}}}}}

The call **MapAt[f, e, n]** of the standard **MapAt** function applies *f* to the element at position *n* in the *e* expression; whereas other its formats allow to apply *f* to the elements at the given positions in an *e* expression. At the same time, the following procedure allows to apply *f* to the elements located on the given nesting levels with the given sequential numbers on the these nesting levels in a list. The procedure call **MapAtLevelsList[f, x, y]** returns the result of applying of *f* to the elements of a *x* list that are located on the given nesting levels $L1$, ... , Lk with the given sequential numbers $p1$, ..., pk on these nesting levels; at that, the second argument is a *y* *ListList*-list of the format {{$L1$, $p1$}, ..., {Lk, pk}}, as examples below a rather visually illustrate. Whereas the procedure call **MapAtLevelsList[f, x, y, z]** with *3rd* optional *z* argument – an undefined symbol – through it additionally returns the *ListList* list whose elements are three–elements sublists for which the *1st* elements define elements of the list **Flatten[x]**, the *2nd* elements define their positions in the **Flatten[x]** list, and the *3rd* elements define their nesting levels in the *x* list. On a *x* list of the kind {{{{...{{{...}}}...}}}} the procedure call returns {{{{...{{{f[]}}}...}}}}. Whereas the call **MapAtLevelsList[f, x, y, z]** additionally thru the optional *z* argument returns the list of kind {{{}, 1, MaxLevel[x]}}. This procedure is of certain interest in the problems of the lists processing. The next fragment represents source code of the procedure along with typical examples of its application.

In[3904]:= **MapAtLevelsList[f_ /; SymbolQ[f], x_ /; ListQ[x], y_ /; ListListQ[y], z___] :=**
Module[{a, b, c = FromCharacterCode[2], d, g, p, n = 1, s},
s = ReplaceAll[x, {} -> {c}]; a = LevelsOfList[s]; d = ClusterList[a];
b = Map[c <> # &, Map[ToString, y]];
f[t_] := {"(" <> If[t === Null, "f[]", ToString1[t]] <> ")" <> c <> ToString[d[[n++]]]}[[1]];
d = MapListAll[f, s]; Clear[f];
g[t_] := If[MemberQ[b, StringTake[t, {Set[p, Flatten[StringPosition[t, c]][[-1]]], -1}]],
ToString[f] <> "[" <> StringTake[t, {1, p - 1}] <> "]", StringTake[t, {1, p - 1}]];
SetAttributes[g, Listable]; If[{z} != {} && NullQ[z],
z = ReplaceAll[Map[{Flatten[s][[#]], #, a[[#]]} &, Range[1, Length[a]]], "\.02" -> {}], 75];
n = ToExpression[Map[g, d]]; n = ReplaceAll[n, "\.02" -> Null];
ReplaceAll[n, {f[Null] -> f[], {Null} -> {}}]]

In[3905]:= **MapAtLevelsList[f, {a, b, c, {{x, y, z}, {{m, n*t, p}}}, c, d}, {{1,1}, {1,5}, {3,3}, {4,2}}]**
Out[3905]= {f[a], b, c, {{x, y, f[z]}, {{m, f[n*t], p}}}, c, f[d]}
In[3906]:= **MapAtLevelsList[f, {{{{{a, b, c}, {x, y, z}}}}}, {{5, 1}, {5, 5}, {5, 3}}]**
Out[3906]= {{{{{f[a], b, f[c]}, {x, f[y], z}}}}}
In[3907]:= **MapAtLevelsList[f, {{{{{a, b, c}, {x, y, z}}}}}, {{5, 1}, {5, 5}, {5, 3}}, g70]**
Out[3907]= {{{{{f[a], b, f[c]}, {x, f[y], z}}}}}
In[3908]:= **g70**
Out[3908]= {{a, 1, 5}, {b, 2, 5}, {c, 3, 5}, {x, 4, 5}, {y, 5, 5}, {z, 6, 5}}
In[3909]:= **MapAtLevelsList[f, {a*b, b, c, {{x, y, z}, {{m, n + t + y*z, p}}}, c, d}, {{1, 1}, {1, 5}, {3, 3}, {4, 2}}, v75]**
Out[3909]= {f[a*b], b, c, {{x, y, f[z]}, {{m, f[n + t + y*z], p}}}, c, f[d]}
In[3910]:= **v75**
Out[3910]= {{a*b, 1, 1}, {b, 2, 1}, {c, 3, 1}, {x, 4, 3}, {y, 5, 3}, {z, 6, 3}, {m, 7, 4}, {n + t + y*z, 8, 4}, {p, 9, 4}, {c, 10, 1}, {d, 11, 1}}
In[3911]:= **MapAtLevelsList[f, {{{{{a, b, c}, {x + y, y, z}}}}}, {{5, 4}}]**
Out[3911]= {{{{{a, b, c}, {f[x + y], y, z}}}}}
In[3912]:= **MapAtLevelsList[G, {{{{{{{}}}, 74, 69, {}}}}}, {{5, 1}, {7, 1}, {4, 2}}]**
Out[3912]= {{{{{{{G[]}}}, 74, G[69], {G[]}}}}}
In[3913]:= **MapAtLevelsList[F, {}, {{1, 1}}]**
Out[3913]= {F[]}
In[3914]:= **MapAtLevelsList[F, {{{{{{{{{{}}}}}}}}}}, {{10, 1}}]**
Out[3914]= {{{{{{{{{F[]}}}}}}}}}
In[3915]:= **MapAtLevelsList[F, {{{{{{{{{{}}}}}}}}}}, {{10, 1}}, s50]**
Out[3915]= {{{{{{{{{F[]}}}}}}}}}
In[3916]:= **s50**
Out[3916]= {{{}, 1, 10}}

Now, using the above two procedures **LevelsOfList** and **MapAtLevelsList** we can easily reprogram the procedures **MapListAll** and **MapListAll1** as the **MapListAll2** function. The call **MapListAll2[f, j]** returns the result of applying of *f* to all elements of an *j* list. On an *j* list of the kind {{{....{{{.....}}}....}}} the procedure call returns {{{.....{{{f[]}}}.....}}}. The procedure call **MapListAll2[x, y, z]** returns the result of application of a *y* symbol to all elements of a *x* list; at the same time, on empty sublists **y[]** is returned, whereas in case of coding of the 3rd optional *z* argument – *any expression* – on empty sublists **y[{}]** is returned. The next fragment represents source code of the **MapListAll2** function along with examples of its application.

In[3914]:= **MapListAll2[f_ /; SymbolQ[f], x_ /; ListQ[x], z___] := MapListAll3[x, f, z]**

In[3915]:= **MapListAll2[F, {a, b, "c", {{x, y + h, z}, {{"m", n*t, p}}}, c, "d"}]**
Out[3915]= {F[a], F[b], F["c"], {{F[x], F[h + y], F[z]}, {{F["m"], F[n*t], F[p]}}}, F[c], F["d"]}
In[3916]:= **MapListAll2[F, {{{{{{a, b, c, x, y + z, c/d}}}}}}]**
Out[3916]= {{{{{{F[a], F[b], F[c], F[x], F[y + z], F[c/d]}}}}}}
In[3917]:= **MapListAll2[F, {a, b, c, x, y + z, c/d}]**
Out[3917]= {F[a], F[b], F[c], F[x], F[y + z], F[c/d]}
In[3918]:= **MapListAll2[F, {{{{{{{}}}}}}}]**
Out[3918]= {{{{{{F[]}}}}}}

Use of *Listable* attribute to a symbol defining a block, function or a module allows to apply the symbol to all elements of the simple or nested list. Meanwhile, application of the symbol to elements – the simple or nested empty lists – leaves them without change, that generally speaking, is not absolutely correctly. Therefore the procedure below eliminates this defect, allowing to process the empty sublists too. The procedure call **MapListAll3[x, y, z]** returns the result of application of a *y* symbol to all elements of a *x* list; at the same time, on empty sublists is returned **y[]**, whereas in case of encoding of the third optional *z* argument – any expression – on *empty* sublists is returned **y[{}]**. The procedure is useful enough in problems dealing with the nested lists. The next fragment represents source code of the **MapListAll3** procedure with examples of its application.

In[3955]:= **MapListAll3[x_ /; ListQ[x], y_ /; SymbolQ[y], z___] :=**
Module[{a = ReplaceAll[x, {} -> {Null}], b = Attributes[y], c},
ClearAttributes[y, b]; SetAttributes[y, Listable]; c = Map[y, a];
ClearAttributes[y, Listable]; SetAttributes[y, b];
ReplaceAll[c, {y[Null]} -> If[{z} != {}, y[{}], y[]]]]

In[3956]:= SetAttributes[G, Listable]; Map[G, P]
Out[3956]= {G[a], G[b + c], {{{{G["gs"], {}}}}}, {{{{}}}}, {G[j + k], G[d^c]}, G[m], {}}
In[3957]:= P = {a, b + c, {{{{"gs", {}}}}}, {{{{}}}}, {k + j, d^c}, m, {}};
In[3958]:= **MapListAll3[P, H]**
Out[3958]= {H[a], H[b + c], {{{{H["gs"], H[]}}}}, {{{H[]}}}, {H[j + k], H[d^c]}, H[m], H[]}
In[3959]:= **MapListAll3[P, H, g]**
Out[3959]= {H[a], H[b + c], {{{{H["gs"], H[{}]}}}}, {{{H[{}]}}}, {H[j + k], H[d^c]}, H[m], H[{}]}

The **MapListAll3** procedure is equivalent to the above **MapListAll2** function.

The following simple enough procedure also uses *Listable* attribute to the symbol defining a block, a function or a module allowing to apply the symbol to all elements of the simple or the *nested* list under the condition that the *empty* lists remain without change. The procedure call **MapAtAllList[f, x]** returns the result of application of a symbol or a pure function *f* of a short format to all elements of the *x* list leaving the empty sublists unchanged. Procedure is useful enough in the problems dealing with the nested lists. The fragment below represents source code of the **MapAtAllList** procedure with examples of its application.

In[4462]:= **MapAtAllList[f_ /; SymbolQ[f] || ShortPureFuncQ[f], x_ /; ListQ[x]] :=**
Module[{a},
SetAttributes[a, Listable]; If[SymbolQ[f], a[t_] := f[t], a[t_] := (f) @@ {t}]; (a) @@ {x}]

In[4463]:= **MapAtAllList[gs, {{{a}, bc, {x, y, z}, {{m, {a, b, c}, n}}}, h}]**
Out[4463]= {{{gs[a]}, gs[bc], {gs[x], gs[y], gs[z]}, {{gs[m], {gs[a], gs[b], gs[c]}, gs[n]}}}, gs[h]}
In[4464]:= **MapAtAllList[gs, {a, {}, c, {m, {{{}}}, n, {{{}},{{{}}}}}}]**
Out[4464]= {gs[a], {}, gs[c], {gs[m], {{{}}}, gs[n], {{{}}, {{{}}}}}
In[4465]:= **MapAtAllList[IntegerQ[#] &, {{{a}, 75, {x, 21, z}, {{m, {a, 70, c}, n}}}, 28}]**
Out[4465]= {{{False}, True, {False, True, False}, {{False, {False, True, False}, False}}}, True}

Unlike the **MapAtLevelsList** the procedure below allows to apply a set of functions to the specified elements of a list depending on a nesting level at which they are located. The call **MapAtLevelsList1[x, y, z]** returns the result of applying of a function from a *z* list to the elements of the x list which are located on the given nesting levels $L_1, ..., L_k$ with the given sequential numbers $p_1, ..., p_k$ on these nesting levels; in addition, the 2nd argument is a y list of the format $\{\{L_1, p_1\}, ..., \{L_k, p_k\}\}$. Whereas the third argument is a z list of the format $\{\{F_1, L_1\}, ..., \{F_p, L_p\}\}$ where a sublist $\{F_j, L_j\}$ defines applying of a F_j function on a nesting level L_j. In case if in the list z there are different functions at the same level, then only the first of them is used. This procedure is of a certain interest in problems of the lists processing. The following fragment represents source code of the procedure along with typical examples of its application which very visually illustrate the above told.

```
In[3997]:= MapAtLevelsList1[x_ /; ListQ[x], y_ /; ListListQ[y], z_ /; ListListQ[z]] :=
Module[{a, b, c = FromCharacterCode[2], d, g, f, p, n = 1, s, u, v},
s = ReplaceAll[x, {} -> {c}]; a = LevelsOfList[s];
If[MemberQ3[a, Set[v, Map[#[[2]] &, z]]], d = ClusterList[a];
b = Map[c <> # &, Map[ToString, y]];
f[t_] := {"(" <> If[t === Null, "[]", ToString1[t]] <> ")" <> c <> ToString[d[[n++]]]}[[1]];
d = MapListAll[f, s]; Clear[f];
g[t_] := If[MemberQ[b, Set[u, StringTake[t, {Set[p, Flatten[StringPosition[t, c]][[-1]]],
-1}]]], ToString[Select[z, #[[2]] == ToExpression[StringTake[u, {2, -1}]][[1]] &][[1]][[1]]] <>
"[" <> StringTake[t, {1, p - 1}] <> "]", StringTake[t, {1, p - 1}]]];
SetAttributes[g, Listable]; n = ToExpression[Map[g, d]];
n = ReplaceAll[n, "\.02" -> Null]; u = Map[#[Null] -> #[] &, Map[#[[1]] &, z]];
ReplaceAll[n, AppendTo[u, {Null} -> {}]], Print["Third argument contains the nonexistent
nesting levels " <> ToString[Complement[v, a]] <> "; nesting levels should be from a list
" <> ToString[DeleteDuplicates[a]]]; $Failed]]
In[3998]:= MapAtLevelsList1[{{{{{a, b, {{}}, {}, c}, {x + y, y, z}}}}}, {{5, 2}, {7, 1}, {5, 5}}, {{G, 7},
{F, 9}}]
"Third argument contains the nonexistent nesting levels {9}; nesting levels should be from a
list {5, 7, 6}"
Out[3998]= $Failed
In[4000]:= MapAtLevelsList1[{{{{{a, b, {{}}, {}, c}, {x + y, y, z}}}}}, {{5, 2}, {5, 3}, {7, 1}, {5, 5}},
{{G, 7}, {F, 5}}]
Out[4000]= {{{{{a, F[b], {{G[]}}, {}, F[c]}, {x + y, F[y], z}}}}}
In[4001]:= MapAtLevelsList1[{{}, {}, {{}}, {{{}}}}, {{2, 1}, {2, 2}, {3, 1}, {4, 1}}, {{G, 2}, {H, 2},
{H, 3}, {W, 4}}]
Out[4001]= {{G[]}, {G[]}, {{H[]}}, {{{W[]}}}}
In[4002]:= MapAtLevelsList1[{{}, {}, {{}}, {{{}}}, {}}, {{2, 1}, {2, 2}, {2, 3}, {3, 1}, {4, 1}}, {{G, 2},
{H, 2}, {H, 3}, {W, 4}}]
Out[4002]= {{G[]}, {G[]}, {{H[]}}, {{{W[]}}}, {G[]}}
In[4003]:= MapAtLevelsList1[a, Map[{1, #} &, a], {{W, 3}, {S, 2}}]
"Third argument contains the nonexistent nesting levels {2, 3}; nesting levels should be from
a list {1}"
Out[4003]= $Failed
In[4004]:= a = Range[1, 10]; MapAtLevelsList1[a, Map[{1, #} &, a], {{W, 1}, {S, 1}}]
Out[4004]= {W[1], W[2], W[3], W[4], W[5], W[6], W[7], W[8], W[9], W[10]}
```

The next procedure gives possibility to apply a function to all elements of the given nesting levels of a list. The call **SymbolToLevelsList[x, m, Sf]** returns the list which is structurally similar to a list *x* and to its elements at the nesting levels *m* (list or separate integer) function *Sf* is applied. In a case of absence of real nesting levels in *m* (i.e. nonexisting levels in the *x* list) the call returns *$Failed* with printing of the appropriate message. The next fragment submits the source code of the procedure with typical examples of its application.

In[4235]:= **SymbolToLevelsList[x_ /; ListQ[x], m_ /; IntegerQ[m] || PosIntListQ[m], Sf_Symbol] :=**
Module[{a, b = ReplaceAll[x, {} -> {Null}], c, d, f, g, h = {}, mp, n = 1, p, s, v, u,
z = Flatten[{m}], t1 = FromCharacterCode[6]},
a = LevelsOfList[b]; d = DeleteDuplicates[a];
If[! MemberQ3[d, z], Print["Levels " <> ToString[m] <> " are absent in the list; " <>
"nesting levels must belong to " <> ToString[Range[1, Max[d]]]]; $Failed,
f[t_] := "{" <> ToString1[t] <> "}" <> "_" <> ToString1[a[[n++]]];
SetAttributes[f, Listable]; c = Map[f, b]; SetAttributes[StringSplit, Listable];
c = Map[StringSplit[#, "__"] &, c];
mp[t1_, t2_] := Map[t1, t2]; SetAttributes[mp, Listable]; c = mp[f, c];
g[t_] := If[MemberQ[z, ToExpression[StringTake[t, {Set[p,
Flatten[StringPosition[t, "_"]][[1]]] + 1, -1}]]],
ToString[Sf] <> "@@" <> StringTake[t, {1, p - 1}] <> t1, StringTake[t, {1, p - 1}]];
SetAttributes[g, Listable]; c = ToString1[Map[g, c]];
c = StringReplace[c, {"{\"{" -> "", "\"}" -> "", "{\"" -> "", "}\"}" -> "", t1 -> "", ToString[Sf] <>
"@@{Null}" -> "", "Null" -> ""}]; ToExpression[c]]]

In[4236]:= **SymbolToLevelsList[{a, d, g, h, d, s, {h, j, d, s, {z, y, x, {k, l, v, c, x}}}}, {4, 6, 5}, F]**
"Levels {5, 6} are absent in the list; nesting level must belong to {1, 2, 3, 4}"
Out[4236]= $Failed
In[4237]:= **SymbolToLevelsList[{a, d, g, {}, h, d, s, {h, j, k, d + j, s, {z, y, x, {k, l, v, c, x}}}}, {2, 4}, F]**
Out[4237]= {a, d, g, {}, h, d, s, {F[h], F[j], F[k], F[d + j], F[s], {z, y, x, {F[k], F[l], F[v], F[c], F[x]}}}}
In[4238]:= **SymbolToLevelsList[{a, d, g, {}, h, d, s, {h, j, k, d + j, s, {z, y, x, {k, l, v, c, x}}}}, 1, G]**
Out[4238]= {G[a], G[d], G[g], {}, G[h], G[d], G[s], {h, j, k, d + j, s, {z, y, x, {k, l, v, c, x}}}}
In[4239]:= **SymbolToLevelsList[{a, d, g, {}, h, d, s, {h, j, k, d + j, s, {z, y, x, {k, l, v, {{{}}}, c, x}}}}, 4, G]**
Out[4239]= {a, d, g, {}, h, d, s, {h, j, k, d + j, s, {z, y, x, {G[k], G[l], G[v], {{{}}}, G[c], G[x]}}}}

The **SymbolToLevelsList** procedure allows some modifications, useful in applications. In the fragment it is necessary to pay attention to an artificial reception (*in a number of cases a rather useful*) which had been used for temporary assignment to the standard **Map** function of the *Listable* attribute. The following fragment a quite visually illustrates application of the *Listable* atribute when processing elements of a list with maintaining its structure.

The call **SymbolToLists[x, F]** returns x list when to all its elements had been applied symbol F, whereas the procedure call **SymbolToLists[x, F, pf]** returns x list when to its elements on which pure *pf* function takes value *True*, had been applied F symbol, leaving other elements unchanged. The next fragment represents source code of the procedure with rather evident and typical examples of its application.

In[4334]:= SymbolToLists[x_ /; ListQ[x], F_Symbol, pf___] := Module[{a},
a[t_] := If[{pf} != {} && PureFuncQ[pf], If[pf @@ {t}, F[t], t], F[t]];
SetAttributes[a, Listable]; Map[a, x]]

In[4335]:= SymbolToLists[{a, b, 2, m, c, m, {f, d, 5, s, h, m, {m, n, 7, p, a}}}, G]
Out[4335]= {G[a], G[b], G[2], G[m], G[c], G[m], {G[f], G[d], G[5], G[s], G[h], G[m], {G[m], G[n], G[7], G[p], G[a]}}}

In[4336]:= SymbolToLists[{a, b, 2, m, c, m, {f,d,5,s,h,m, {m, n, 7, p, m}}}, G, SameQ[#, m] &]
Out[4336]= {a, b, 2, G[m], c, G[m], {f, d, 5, s, h, G[m], {G[m], n, 7, p, G[m]}}}

The fragment illustrates some opportunities of the *Listable* attribute even more evidently.

The standard **ReplaceList** function attempts to transform an expression by applying a rule or list of rules in all possible ways, and returns a list of the results obtained. The procedure below is a rather useful modification of the **ReplaceList** function. The call **ReplaceList1[x, y, z, p]** returns the list which is the result of replacement in x list of elements whose positions are determined by a y list at a nesting level p onto appropriate expressions that are defined by a z list. In addition, if a certain element should be deleted then in the z list the key word *"Nothing"* is coded in the appropriate position. The procedure processes the main espesial situations. The next fragment presents source code of the procedure and examples of its use.

In[3539]:= ReplaceList1[x_ /; ListQ[x], y_ /; IntegerListQ[y], z_ /; ListQ[z],
p_ /; IntegerQ[p]] := Module[{a = MaxLevelList[x], b, c = {}},
If[Length[y] != Length[z], Print["The 2nd and 3rd arguments have different lengths"];
$Failed, If[p > a, Print["The given nesting level is more than maximal"]; $Failed,
b = Level[x, {p}];
Do[AppendTo[c, If[y[[j]] <= Length[b], b[[y[[j]]]] -> If[z[[j]] === "Nothing", Nothing, z[[j]]], Nothing]], {j, 1, Length[y]}]; If[c == {}, x, Replace[x, c, {p}]]]]]

In[3540]:= L := {a, b, {{a, b}, {{m, n, {p, {{{}}}}}}, c, {}, m, n, p, {{{{a + b}, g}}}}
In[3541]:= ReplaceList1[L, {1, 2, 5}, {Avz, Agn, Vsv}, 4]
Out[3541]= {a, b, {{a, b}, {{Avz, Agn, {p, {{{}}}}}}, c, {}, m, n, p, {{{{a + b}, Vsv}}}}
In[3542]:= ReplaceList1[L, {1, 2, 4, 6, 7}, {Avz, Agn, Vsv, Art, Kr}, 10]
"The given nesting level is more than maximal"
Out[3542]= $Failed
In[3543]:= ReplaceList1[L, {1, 2, 3}, {"Nothing", Nothing, "Nothing"}, 5]
"The 2nd and 3rd arguments have different lengths"
Out[3543]= $Failed
In[3544]:= ReplaceList1[L, {1, 2, 3}, {"Nothing", "Nothing", "Nothing"}, 5]
Out[3544]= {a, b, {{a, b}, {{m, n, {}}}}, c, {}, m, n, p, {{{{}, g}}}}
In[3545]:= ReplaceList1[L, {1, 2}, {{Avz, Agn}, {74, 69}}, 2]
Out[3545]= {a, b, {{Avz, Agn}, {74, 69}}, c, {}, m, n, p, {{{{a + b}, g}}}}

The next procedure is based on our procedures **ReplaceList1** and **Sequences** and attempts to transform a list by including of expressions in the tuples of its elements that are located on the given nesting level. The **InsertToList** procedure is a rather useful modification of the standard **Insert** function. So, the procedure call **InsertToList[*x, y, z, h, p*]** returns the list that is result of inserting into *x* list on a nesting level *p* of expressions from a *z* list; the positions for inserting are defined by the appropriate *y* list which defines the positions of elements of the *x* list on the *p*-th nesting level. In addition, between lists *y* and *z* should be one–to–one correspondence.

Moreover, a *h* integer or their list defines the inserting mode for expressions from a *z* list: *1* – the inserting after an element and *0* – the inserting before an element on the nesting level *p*. The **InsertToList** procedure processes the main erroneous situations. The next fragment represents source code of the **InsertToList** procedure along with typical examples of its use.

```
In[7075]:= InsertToList[x_ /; ListQ[x], y_ /; IntegerListQ[y], z_ /; ListQ[z],
h_ /; MemberQ[{0, 1}, h] || BinaryListQ[h], p_ /; IntegerQ[p]] :=
Module[{a = MaxLevelList[x], b, c = {}, d = Flatten[{h}]},
If[Length[y] != Length[z], Print["The 2nd and 3rd arguments have different lengths"];
$Failed, If[p > a, Print["The given nesting level is more than maximal"]; $Failed,
b = Level[x, {p}];
Do[AppendTo[c, If[y[[j]] <= Length[b], b[[y[[j]]]] -> Sequences[If[Quiet[Check[d[[j]], 1]]
== 0, {z[[j]], b[[y[[j]]]]}, {b[[y[[j]]]], z[[j]]}]], Nothing]], {j, 1, Length[y]}];
If[c == {}, x, Replace[x, c, {p}]]]]]

In[7076]:= L := {a, b, {{a, b}, {{m, n, {p, {{{}}}}}}}, c, {}, m, n, p, {{{{a + b}, g}}}}
In[7077]:= InsertToList[L, {1, 3, 5}, {Avz, Agn, Vsv}, {0, 1, 0}, 4]
Out[7077]= {a, b, {{a, b}, {{Avz, m, n, p, Agn}}}, c, {}, m, n, p, {{{{a + b}, Vsv, g}}}}
In[7078]:= InsertToList[L, {2, 3}, {Avz, {Agn, Vsv}}, {0, 1}, 5]
Out[7078]= {a, b, {{a, b}, {{m, n, {p, Avz}}}}, c, {}, m, n, p, {{{{a + b, Agn, Vsv}, g}}}}
In[7079]:= InsertToList[L, {1, 3, 5}, {Avz, Agn, Vsv}, 0, 4]
Out[7079]= {a, b, {{a, b}, {{Avz, m, n, p, Agn}}}, c, {}, m, n, p, {{{{a + b}, g, Vsv}}}}
```

The next procedure represents a certain generalization of the standard **Insert** function for a case of simple lists as well as the simplified version of the previous procedure **InsertToList** without taking into account the nesting levels of the processed lists. The call **Insert1[*x, y, p*]** returns the list which is the result of inserting into a *x* list of an *y* expression or their list; in addition, the positions for inserting are defined by a *p* integer or their list. If the call uses an optional *w* argument – an arbitrary expression – the insertions are done before the given positions, in the opposite case the insertions are done after the given positions. The **Insert1** procedure ignores all *inadmissible* positions for insertions, printing the appropriate message about it; if there are no valid positions for the insertions the procedure call returns original *x* list. The next fragment represents source code of the procedure with examples of its use.

```
In[4550]:= Insert1[x_ /; ListQ[x], y_, p_ /; IntegerQ[p] || IntegerListQ[p], t___] :=
Module[{a, b = Flatten[{y}], c = Flatten[{p}]},
a = Select[c, ! MemberQ[Range[1, Length[x]], #] &];
If[a != {}, Print["Positions " <> ToString[a] <> " are invalid"], 6];
```

ReplacePart[x, Flatten[Map[{# -> If[{t} == {}, Sequences[x[[#]], b], Sequences[b, x[[#]]]]} &, Select[c, MemberQ[Range[1, Length[x]], #] &]]]]]

In[4551]:= L := {a, b, c, d, f, h, g, m, n, p}
In[4553]:= Insert1[L, {x, y, z}, 4, 74]
Out[4553]= {a, b, c, x, y, z, d, f, h, g, m, n, p}
In[4554]:= Insert1[L, {x, y, z}, {2, 4, 8}]
Out[4554]= {a, b, x, y, z, c, d, x, y, z, f, h, g, m, x, y, z, n, p}
In[4555]:= Insert1[L, {x, y, z}, {2, 4, 6}, 69]
Out[4555]= {a, x, y, z, b, c, x, y, z, d, f, x, y, z, h, g, m, n, p}
Out[4556]= {a, b, x, y, z, c, d, x, y, z, f, h, g}
In[4557]:= Insert1[L, {x, y, z}, {2, 4, 20, 30}, 69]
"Positions {20, 30} are invalid"
Out[4557]= {a, x, y, z, b, c, x, y, z, d, f, h, g, m, n, p}
In[4558]:= Insert1[L, {}, {2, 4, 6}, 69]
Out[4558]= {a, b, c, d, f, h, g, m, n, p}

In[5524]:= Insert2[x_ /; ListQ[x], y_, p_ /; IntegerQ[p] || IntegerListQ[p], t___] :=
ReplacePart[x, Flatten[Map[If[! MemberQ[Range[1, Length[x]], #], Print["Position " <> ToString[#] <> " is invalid"]; Nothing, {# -> If[{t} == {}, Sequences[x[[#]], Flatten[{y}]], Sequences[Flatten[{y}], x[[#]]]]}] &, Flatten[{p}]]]]

In[5525]:= Insert2[L, {x, y, z}, {2, 4, 47, 47}, 69]
"Position 42 is invalid"
"Position 47 is invalid"
Out[5525]= {a, x, y, z, b, c, x, y, z, d, f, h, g, m, n, p}
In[5526]:= Insert2[L, {x, y, z}, {2, 4, 42}]
"Position 42 is invalid"
Out[5526]= {a, b, x, y, z, c, d, x, y, z, f, h, g, m, n, p}
In[5527]:= Insert2[L, {}, {2, 4, 6}, 69]
Out[5527]= {a, b, c, d, f, h, g, m, n, p}
In[3530]:= Insert2[L, {x, y, z, h, Av, Ag, Vs}, 74, 74]
"Position 74 is invalid"
Out[3530]= {a, b, c, d, f, h, g, m, n, p}

A functional version of the **Insert1** procedure completes the above fragment. The function call **Insert2[x, y, p]** returns the list that is the result of inserting in *x* list of an *y* expression or their list; the positions for inserting of the expressions are determined by a *p* integer or their list. If the call **Insert2[x, y, p, h]** uses the optional *h* argument – an arbitrary expression then insertions are done before the given positions, otherwise insertions are done after the given positions. In addition, the **Insert2** function ignores all inadmissible positions for insertions, printing the appropriate messages about them; if there are no valid positions for whatever insertions then the function call returns initial *x* list. Note that both the **Insert1** procedure, and the **Insert2** function use our **Sequences** function, allowing insertings in the lists of both separate expressions, and their sequences.

The built-in *Mathematica* language normally assumes that all variables are global. It means that every time using some name like *y*, *Mathematica* normally assumes that the referring to the same object is done. However, in a number of cases is not desirable that all variables be global. In this case the *Math*-language allows to use the blocks and modules in that it is possible to define variables as *local* with scope only in such objects. In the previous fragment 2 analogs **Insert1** and **Insert2** with use and without of local variables respectively have been defined for what algorithm of the problem has been programmed in the form of function.

Meanwhile, in certain cases using the expressions lists in which the evaluations are done in series, it is possible to use so-called *"indirect"* local variables. The fragment represents an analog of the above means **Insert1** and **Insert2** which had been programmed in the form of the **Insert3** list. So, for definition of variables as indirect local variables their definitions are saved in a file *"avz" (Save2)*, whereupon the algorithm uses them as local variables and the result is kept in other *"sagn" file (Write)*, then restoration of initial values of local variables *(Get)*, the reading in the current session of the received result *(Read)* and with followed by removal of all *temporary* files are done. The next source code of the **Insert3** list very visually illustrates the above mechanism.

In[4513]:= **Insert3[x_ /; ListQ[x], y_, p_ /; IntegerQ[p] || IntegerListQ[p], t___] :=**
{Save2["avz", {"a", "b", "c"}],
a = Select[Flatten[{p}], ! MemberQ[Range[1, Length[x]], #] &], b = Flatten[{y}],
c = Flatten[{p}], If[a != {}, Print["Positions " <> ToString[a] <> " are invalid"], 6],
Write["sagn", ReplacePart[x, Flatten[Map[{# -> If[{t} == {}, Sequences[x[[#]], b],
Sequences[b, x[[#]]]]} &, Select[c, MemberQ[Range[1, Length[x]], #] &]]]]], Close["sagn"],
Clear["a", "b", "c"], Get["avz"], DeleteFile["avz"], Read["sagn"],
DeleteFile[Close["sagn"]]}[[-2]]

In[4514]:= **{a, b, c} = {42, 47, 67}; L := {q, t, v, w, g, h, z, m, n, p}**
In[4515]:= **Insert3[L, {x, y, z}, {2, 4, 42, 20, 30}]**
"Positions {42, 20, 30} are invalid"
Out[4515]= {q, t, x, y, z, v, w, x, y, z, g, h, z, m, n, p}
In[4516]:= **{a, b, c}**
Out[4516]= {42, 47, 67}

In[4546]:= **Uv[x_ /; StringQ[x], n_ /; IntegerQ[n] && Positive[n], y___] := Module[{a},**
If[FileExistsQ[x], a = Quiet[Check[{Read[x][[n]], Close[x]},
Print["Part " <> ToString[n] <> " does not exist."]; Return[$Failed]]];
If[{y} == {}, Symbol[a[[1]]], ToExpression[a[[1]] <> "=" <> ToString1[y]]],
Write[x, Map[ToString, Map[Unique, Characters[StringRepeat["j", n]]]]]; Close[x]]]

In[4547]:= **Uv["j", 6]; {Read["j"], Close["j"]}[[1]]**
Out[4547]= {"j85", "j86", "j87", "j88", "j89", "j90"}
In[4548]:= **{Uv["j", 3], Uv["j", 3, 74], Uv["j", 5, {m, n, p}], Uv["j", 3]*Uv["j", 5]}**
Out[3548]= {j87, 74, {m, n, p}, {74*m, 74*n, 74*p}}

In[4551]:= **Insert4[x_ /; ListQ[x], y_, p_ /; IntegerQ[p] || IntegerListQ[p], f_ /; StringQ[f],**
t___] :=
{Uv[f, 3], Uv[f, 1, Select[Flatten[{p}], ! MemberQ[Range[1, Length[x]], #] &]],
Uv[f, 2, Flatten[{y}]], Uv[f, 3, Flatten[{p}]], If[! SameQ[Uv[f, 1], {}], Print["Positions " <>
ToString1[Uv[f, 1]] <> " are invalid"], 6],
ReplacePart[x, Flatten[Map[{# -> If[{t} == {}, Sequences[x[[#]], Uv[f, 2]],

Software Etudes in the Mathematica

Sequences[Uv[f, 2], x[[#]]]]} &, Select[Uv[f, 3],
MemberQ[Range[1, Length[x]], #] &]]]], {Map[Remove, Read[f]], DeleteFile[Close[f]]}}[[-2]]
In[4552]:= **Insert4[L, {x, y, z}, {2, 4, 8}, "Avz", 69]**
Out[4552]= {q, x, y, z, t, v, x, y, z, w, g, h, z, x, y, z, m, n, p}

The function **Insert3** can be simplified using the **Uv** procedure based on **Unique** function and providing work with unique variables in the program mode in the current session. If a string *f* not defines file then the call **Uv[*f*, *n*]** creates a *f* file containing the list with *n* unique variables in the string format; if a *f* string determines a file then the call **Uv[*f*, *n*]** returns the current value of the *n-th* variable of *f* file while the call **Uv[*f*, *n*, *y*]** returns a *y* value assigned to the *n-th* variable of *f* file. List-function **Insert4** illustrates a version of the **Insert3** with use of the **Uv** procedure. Heading of **Insert4** differs from heading of **Insert3** only by the fourth *f* argument defining a file which is used by **Uv** procedure. The previous fragment represents source codes of both tools, whereas the **Uv** is a rather useful means in problems that use the unique variables.

The fragment below represents one more useful enough mechanism which is also based on the **Unique** function for working with unique variables of the current session. In addition, this fragment begins with the simple testing function whose call **NumericListQ[*x*]** returns *True* if all elements of a list *x* have *Numeric* type, otherwise *False* is returned. The function is useful tool at programming of problems dealing with numeric lists. Meantime, the **PrevUv** procedure is directly designed to handle the unique variables of the current session. So, the procedure call **PrevUv[*x*, *n*]** returns the *n*-th unique variable since the end in the sequence of the unique variables which were earlier generated in the current session from *x* string. At that, the used algorithm is based on the fact that the call **Unique[*x*]** enumerates the created symbols sequentially, since *1* for each new call. Whereas the procedure call **PrevUv[*x*, *n*, *y*]** with optional *y* argument – *an arbitrary expression* – returns a *y* value of *n–th* unique variable that has been assigned it.

The function below is one more useful addition of standard **Unique** function. The function call **ToNewSymbol[*x*, *y*, *z*]** in string format returns name of variable, unique for the current session that is based on symbol-string *x* with assignment to the new symbol of *y* expression whereas the third *z* argument defines assignment mode *(Set, SetDelayed)*. Hereinafter with this variable it is possible to operate without fear of crossing with other variables of current session. The following fragment presents source codes of the **ToNewSymbol** function with examples of its application.

In[4530]:= **ToNewSymbol[x_ /; StringQ[x], y_, z_ /; MemberQ[{Set, SetDelayed}, z]]** :=
{Put[Unique[x], "ag"], ToString[Get["ag"]], ToExpression[ToString[z] <> "[" <>
ToString1[Get["ag"]] <> "," <> ToString1[y] <> "]"]; DeleteFile["ag"]}[[2]]

In[4531]:= **ToNewSymbol["b", x*y*z, SetDelayed]**
Out[4531]= "b47"
In[4532]:= **Definition[b47]**
Out[4532]= b47 := x*y*z
In[4533]:= **ToNewSymbol["b", x*y*z, Set]**
Out[4533]= "b48"
In[4534]:= **Definition[b48]**

Out[4534]= b48 = x*y*z

The function **Insert5** completes the following fragment, illustrating a version of the function **Insert4** with use of the **PrevUv** procedure. The source code of **Insert5** function very visually illustrates the above mechanism. In addition, heading of the **Insert5** function fully complies with heading of the **Insert3** function, and its calls on the same tuples of factual arguments return the same results. The next fragment represents source codes of the above means with examples of their application.

In[4738]:= **NumericListQ[x_] := If[! ListQ[x], False, If[AllTrue[Map[NumericQ, x], TrueQ], True, False]]**

In[4739]:= **Map[NumericListQ, {{1, 2, Pi, Sqrt[2]}, {1, m, a, 5, Pi}}]**
Out[4739]= {True, False}

In[4742]:= **PrevUv[x_ /; StringQ[x], n_ /; IntegerQ[n], y___] :=**
Module[{a = ToString[Unique[x]], b, c},
b = StringJoin[TakeWhile[Characters[a], SymbolQ[#] &]];
ToExpression[c = b <> ToString[FromDigits[StringReplace[a, b -> ""]] - n]];
If[{y} != {}, Quiet[Check[ToExpression[c <> "=" <> ToString1[y]], Return["Number " <> ToString[n] <> " is inadmissible"]]], 6]; Symbol[c]]

In[4743]:= **Map[{Unique["a"], #}[[1]] &, Range[1, 10]]**
Out[4743]= {a814, a815, a816, a817, a818, a819, a820, a821, a822, a823}
In[4744]:= **Map[PrevUv["a", #] &, Range[1, 10]]**
Out[4744]= {a823, a823, a823, a823, a823, a823, a823, a823, a823, a823}
In[4745]:= **PrevUv["a", 823, Sqrt[(a + b)/(c + d)]]**
Out[4745]= Sqrt[(a + b)/(c + d)]
In[4746]:= **PrevUv["$a", 95, Sqrt[(a + b)/(c + d)]]**
Out[4746]= "Number 95 is inadmissible"

In[4755]:= **Insert5[x_ /; ListQ[x], y_, p_ /; IntegerQ[p] || IntegerListQ[p], t___] :=**
{ToExpression[ToString[Unique["$a"]] <> "=" <> ToString1[Select[Flatten[{p}],
! MemberQ[Range[1, Length[x]], #] &]]],
ToExpression[ToString[Unique["$b"]] <> "=" <> ToString[Flatten[{y}]]],
ToExpression[ToString[Unique["$c"]] <> "=" <> ToString[Flatten[{p}]]],
If[! SameQ[PrevUv["$a", 3], {}], $6947 = 5; $7442 = 3;
Print["Positions " <> ToString1[PrevUv["$a", 4]] <> " are invalid"], $6947 = 4; $7442 = 2],
Quiet[ReplacePart[x, Flatten[Map[{# -> If[{t} == {}, Sequences[x[[#]]],
PrevUv["$b", $6947++]],
Sequences[PrevUv["$b", $6947++], x[[#]]]} &, Select[PrevUv["$c", $7442],
MemberQ[Range[1, Length[x]], #] &]]]]]}[[-1]]

In[4756]:= **L := {q, t, v, w, g, h, z, m, n, p}**
In[4757]:= **Insert5[L, {x, y, z}, {2, 4, 42, 20, 30}, 69]**
"Positions {42, 20, 30} are invalid"
Out[4757]= {q, x, y, z, t, v, x, y, z, w, g, h, z, m, n, p}
In[4758]:= **Insert5[L, {x, y, z}, {2, 4, 42, 20, 30}]**
"Positions {42, 20, 30} are invalid"

Out[4758]= {q, t, x, y, z, v, w, x, y, z, g, h, z, m, n, p}
In[4759]:= **Insert5[L, {x, y, z}, {2, 4, 8}, 69]**
Out[4759]= {q, x, y, z, t, v, x, y, z, w, g, h, z, x, y, z, m, n, p}
In[4760]:= **Insert5[{}, {x, y, z}, {2, 4, 8}, 69]**
"Positions {2, 4, 8} are invalid"
Out[4760]= {}

In addition to the standard functions of so-called *Replace*-group a rather simple procedure **ReplaceListCond** provides conditional replacement of elements of a list. The procedure call **ReplaceListCond[x, f, y]** returns result of replacement of the elements of a *x* list which meet a condition defined by the testing Boolean *f* function onto an *y* expression. At that, lists can be used as *f* and *y*; more precisely, *j* objects for which **FunctionQ[j]** = *True* or **SysFuncQ[j]** = *True* are admitted as a *f* argument. While the procedure call **PositionsListCond[x, f]** returns list of positions of elements of *x* list which meet a condition defined by the testing Boolean *f* function or their list. The fragment below represents sources codes of the procedures along with typical examples of their application.

In[3374]:= **ReplaceListCond[x_ /; ListQ[x], f_ /; SymbolQ[f] || ListQ[f] && AllTrue[Map[SysFuncQ[#] || FunctionQ[#] &, f], TrueQ], y__] := Module[{a, b, func},
func[x1_ /; ListQ[x1], f1_, y1_] := Map[If[! UnevaluatedQ[f1, #] && f1[#] || f1[#], Replace[#, # -> y1], #] &, x1];
If[! ListQ[f], func[x, f, y], {a, b} = {x, Flatten[{y}]};
Quiet[Do[a = func[a, f[[k]], If[Length[b] == 1, b[[1]], b[[k]]]], {k, 1, If[Length[b] == 1, Length[f], Min[{Length[f], Length[b]}]]}]]**

In[3375]:= **hgs[t_] := 69 === t; ReplaceListCond[{a, b, 42, 69, 47, m, n, 2016, agn, 69, 23}, {EvenQ, PrimeQ, hgs}, {"gs", "vg", 590}]**
Out[3375]= {a, b, "gs", 590, "vg", m, n, "gs", agn, 590, "vg"}
In[3376]:= **ReplaceListCond[{a, b, 42, 69, 47, m, n, 2016, agn, 69, 23}, {EvenQ, PrimeQ, # === 69 &}, {"gs", "vg", 590}]**
Out[3376]= {a, b, "gs", 590, "vg", m, n, "gs", agn, 590, "vg"}

In[3394]:= **PositionsListCond[x_ /; ListQ[x], f_ /; SymbolQ[f] || ListQ[f] && AllTrue[Map[SysFuncQ[#] || FunctionQ[#] &, f], TrueQ]] :=
Module[{a, b = {}}, Do[If[MemberQ[Map[#[x[[k]]] &, Flatten[{f}]], True], AppendTo[b, k], Null], {k, 1, Length[x]}]; b]**

In[3395]:= **PositionsListCond[{avz, 42, {}, 74, 47, agn, 74, {}, 23}, {EvenQ, PrimeQ}]**
Out[3395]= {2, 4, 5, 7, 9}

In addition to the above **ReplaceListCond** procedure can be *succesfully* used a rather simple procedure **ReplaceCond** that provides *replacement* of all subelements of a certain expression that meet a condition. The procedure call **ReplaceCond[x, f, y]** returns result of replacement of all subelements of an *x* expression which meet a condition defined by the testing Boolean *f* function onto expression *y*.

While the call **ReplaceCond[x, f, y, z]** provided that the optional *z* argument is a nonempty expression and *y* argument is a symbol returns result of replacement of all *w* subelements of an *x* expression composing *x* that meet a condition defined by testing Boolean *f* function onto *y[w]* expressions. In addition, the *replacement* acts on all subexpressions of *x* expression that are on all its levels. The fragment below represents sources codes of the **ReplaceCond** procedure with typical examples of its application.

In[4388]:= **ReplaceCond[x_, f_/; FunctionQ[f], y_, z___] :=**
Module[{a = Level[x, {0, Infinity}], b},
b = Map[If[TrueQ[f @@ {#}], # -> If[SymbolQ[y] && {z} != {}, y[#], y], Nothing] &, a];
ReplaceAll[x, b]]

In[4389]:= **ReplaceCond[a + x/b^2 + c*y, IntegerQ[#] &, G]**
Out[4389]= a + b^G*x + c*y

In[4390]:= **ReplaceCond[a + x/b^2 + c*y, Head[#] == Power &, G]**
Out[4390]= a + G*x + c*y

In[4391]:= **ReplaceCond[{a, x/b^2, c*y}, Head[#] == Power &, G, t]**
Out[4391]= {a, x*G[1/b^2], c*y}

In[4392]:= **ReplaceCond[{a, x/b^2, c*y}, IntegerQ[#] &, G, t]**
Out[4392]= {a, b^G[-2]*x, c*y}

The procedure below is a rather useful version of the system **Position** function concerning lists. The procedure call **PositionList[x, y]** returns the nested list whose 2-element sublists by the first element define the nesting level of a *x* list whereas by the second element define the list of positions at this level of the elements coinciding with an *y* expression or satisfying to the test defined by a pure *y* function. In this case, all nesting levels of a list *x* are analyzed. Whereas the procedure call **PositionList[x, y, z]** with the optional *z* argument – *a nesting level or their list* – returns the above result relatively to the *z* nesting levels. It should be noted that the procedure as an auxiliary tool uses a procedure, whose call **PosList[x, y]** returns the list of elements positions of *x* list that coincide with an *y* expression or satisfy to the test defined by a pure *y* function. The fragment below represents source codes of both procedures along with typical examples of their application.

In[4248]:= **PositionList[x_ /; ListQ[x], y_, z___] :=**
Module[{a = ElemsOnLevelList[x], b, c, d}, d = Map[#[[1]] &, a];
c = If[{z} != {}, Select[Flatten[{z}], MemberQ[d, #] &], d];
ReduceLevelsList[Map[If[MemberQ[c, #[[1]]], {#[[1]], If[PureFuncQ[y], PosList[#[[2]], y],
Flatten[Position[#[[2]], y]]]}, Nothing] &, a]][[1]]]

In[4249]:= **Position[{{a, b, b}, {b, b, a}, {a, b, {b, b, {a, b}}}}, b]**
Out[4249]= {{1, 2}, {1, 3}, {2, 1}, {2, 2}, {3, 2}, {3, 3, 1}, {3, 3, 2}, {3, 3, 3, 2}}

In[4250]:= **PositionList[{{a, b, b}, {b, b, a}, {a, b, {b, b, {a, b}}}}, b]**
Out[4250]= {{2, {2, 3, 4, 5, 8}}, {3, {1, 2}}, {4, {2}}}

In[4251]:= **PositionList[{{1, 2, 3}, {4, 4, 5}, {6, 7, {8, 8, {5, 6, 7, b}}}}, EvenQ[#] &]**
Out[4251]= {{2, {2, 4, 5, 7}}, {3, {1, 2}}, {4, {2}}}

In[4252]:= **PositionList[{{a, b, b}, {b, b, a}, {a, b, {b, b}}}, b, 3]**
Out[4252]= {3, {1, 2}}

In[4253]:= **PositionList[{{1, 2, 3}, {4, 4, 5}, {6, 7, {8, 8, {5, 6, 7, b}}}}, EvenQ[#] &, 2]**
Out[4253]= {2, {2, 4, 5, 7}}

In[4254]:= **PositionList[{{1, 2, 3}, {4, 4, 5}, {6, 7, {8, 8, {5, 6, 7, b}}}}, EvenQ[#] &, {3, 4}]**
Out[4254]= {{3, {1, 2}}, {4, {2}}}

In[4263]:= **PosList[x_ /; ListQ[x], y_] := Module[{n = 1},**

Software Etudes in the Mathematica

If[PureFuncQ[y], Map[#[[2]] &, Select[Map[{#, n++} &, x], y @@ {#[[1]]} &]],
Flatten[Position[x, y]]]]

In[4264]:= PosList[{1, 7, 2, 3, 7, 4, 5, 6, 7, 8, 7, 9}, 7]
Out[4264]= {2, 5, 9, 11}
In[4265]:= PosList[{1, 7, 2, 3, 7, 4, 5, 6, 7, 8, 7, 9}, OddQ[#] || PrimeQ[#] &]
Out[4265]= {1, 2, 3, 4, 5, 7, 9, 11, 12}

The next function allows to extract from a list its elements, that meet the condition defined by the pure function. The function call **ElemsListOnCond[x, y]** generally returns the nested list whose 2-element sublists by the first element define the elements of a *x* list which satisfy to the test determined by a pure function *y* whereas by the second element define simple or nested 2-element sublists whose the first elements define nesting levels at which are located these elements whereas second elements determine their sequential numbers at these levels respectively. At that, in pure *y* function of the short format as an argument it is necessary to use #[[1]] instead of #. In the lack of the required elements in a *x* list the function call returns the empty list, i.e. {}. The fragment below represents source code of the **ElemsListOnCond** function with typical examples of its application.

In[4055]:= ElemsListOnCond[x_ /; ListQ[x], y_ /; PureFuncQ[y]] :=
ReduceLevelsList[Map[{#[[1]], ReduceLevelsList[#[[2]], 74]} &,
Map[{#[[1]][[1]], Map[#[[2 ;; 3]] &, #]} &,
Gather[Select[ElemsOnLevels2[x], y], #1[[1]] == #2[[1]] &]]], 69]

In[4057]:= L := {6, 3, 8, {11, 8, 26, {{{}, 5, 7, 9}}, {{{3, 0, {5, 3, 7, 2}, 2}}}}, 19}
In[4058]:= ElemsListOnCond[L, PrimeQ[#[[1]]] &]
Out[4058]= {{3, {{1, 2}, {5, 2}, {6, 2}}}, {11, {2, 1}}, {5, {{4, 1}, {6, 1}}}, {7, {{4, 2}, {6, 3}}}, {2, {{6, 4}, {5, 4}}}, {19, {1, 4}}}
In[4059]:= ElemsListOnCond[{t, c, {{{{}}}}, {74, 69}, {{{a + b, h}}}, {m, n, f}, {{{{74, g}}}}},
SymbolQ[#[[1]]] &]
Out[4059]= {{t, {1, 1}}, {c, {1, 2}}, {{}, {5, 1}}, {h, {4, 2}}, {m, {2, 3}}, {n, {2, 4}}, {f, {2, 5}}, {g, {5, 3}}}
In[4060]:= ElemsListOnCond[{{{}, {}}, {{{}}, {{{{}}}}}}, #[[1]] == {} &]
Out[4060]= {{}, {{3, 1}, {3, 2}, {4, 1}, {6, 1}}}
In[4061]:= gs := Function[x, If[PrimeQ[x[[1]]], True, False]]
In[4062]:= ElemsListOnCond[L, gs]
Out[4062]= {{3, {{1, 2}, {5, 2}, {6, 2}}}, {11, {2, 1}}, {5, {{4, 1}, {6, 1}}}, {7, {{4, 2}, {6, 3}}}, {2, {{6, 4}, {5, 4}}}, {19, {1, 4}}}

For assignment of the same value to the variables can be used very simple construction *x1* = *x2* = ... = *a1*, while for assignment to variables of different values can be used a construction {*x1*, *x2*, *x3*, ...} = {*a1*, *a2*, *a3*, ...} provided that lengths of both lists are identical, otherwise an erroneous situation arises. In order to eliminate this shortcoming the following procedure call **ListsAssign[x, y]** can be used, returning result of assignment of values of *y* list to *x* list.

In[2766]:= ListsAssign[x_ /; ListQ[x], y_ /; ListQ[y]] :=
Module[{b, c, d = {}, a = Min[Map[Length, {x, y}]], k = 1},
If[a == 0, Return[x], Off[Set::setraw]; Off[Set::write]; Off[Set::wrsym]];
While[k <= a, {b, c} = {x[[k]], y[[k]]}; AppendTo[d, b = c]; k++];
x = {Sequences[d[[1 ;; a]]], Sequences[x[[a + 1 ;; -1]]]};

On[Set::setraw]; On[Set::write]; On[Set::wrsym]; x]

In[2767]:= L = {x, 90, a + b, Sin, t, s}; P = {a, b, c, w, 74}; ListsAssign[L, P]

Out[2767]= {a, 90, a + b, Sin, 74, s}

In[2768]:= {x, y, z, h, g, w, t} = {a, b, c}

Set::shape: Lists {x, y, z, h, g, w, t} and {a, b, c} are not the same shape.>>

Out[2768]= {a, b, c}

In[2769]:= ListsAssign[{x, y, z, h, g, w, t}, {a, b, c}]; {x, y, z}

Out[2769]= {a, b, c}

In[2770]:= ListAppValue[x_List, y_] := Quiet[x = PadLeft[{}, Length[x], y]]

In[2771]:= x = 90; ListAppValue[{x1, y, z, h, g, w, t}, 74]; {x1, y, z, h, g, w, t, x}

Out[2771]= {74, 74, 74, 74, 74, 74, 74, 90}

At that, the call **ListsAssign[x, y]** returns the list x updated by assignments; in addition, the procedure processes the erroneous and especial situations caused by the assignments $x = y$. Whereas the function call **ListAppValue[x, y]** provides assignment of the same y value to all elements of a x list. The previous fragment presents source codes of the above tools with examples of their applications.

The next simple enough procedure is intended for grouping of elements of a list according to their multiplicities. The call **GroupIdentMult[x]** returns the nested list of the format:

$$\{\{\{n_1\}, \{x_1, x_2, ..., x_a\}\}, \{\{n_2\}, \{y_1, y_2, ..., y_b\}\}, ..., \{\{n_k\}, \{z_1, z_2, ..., z_c\}\}\}$$

where $\{x_i, y_j, ..., z_p\}$ – elements of a x list and $\{n_1, n_2, ..., n_k\}$ – multiplicities corresponding to them $\{i = 1..a, j = 1..b, ..., p = 1..c\}$. The following fragment represents source code of the procedure along with examples of its application.

In[2997]:= GroupIdentMult[x_ /; ListQ[x]] := Module[{a = Gather[x], b},
b = Map[{DeleteDuplicates[#][[1]], Length[#]} &, a];
b = Map[DeleteDuplicates[#] &, Map[Flatten, Gather[b, SameQ[#1[[2]], #2[[2]]] &]]];
b = Map[{{#[[1]]}, Sort[#[[2 ;; -1]]]} &, Map[Reverse, Map[If[Length[#] > 2,
Delete[Append[#, #[[2]]], 2], #] &, b]]];
b = Sort[b, #1[[1]][[1]] > #2[[1]][[1]] &]; If[Length[b] == 1, Flatten[b, 1], b]]

In[2998]:= L = {a, c, b, a, a, c, g, d, a, d, c, a, c, c, h, h, h, h, h};

In[2999]:= GroupIdentMult[L]

Out[2999]= {{{5}, {a, c, h}}, {{2}, {d}}, {{1}, {b, g}}}

In[3000]:= GroupIdentMult[{a, a, a, a, a, a, a, a, a, a, a, a, a, a, a, a, a, a, a}]

Out[3000]= {{19}, {a}}

In[3001]:= GroupIdentMult[RandomInteger[42, 74]]

Out[3001]= {{{7}, {34}}, {{5}, {37}}, {{4}, {11, 36}}, {{3}, {0, 9, 38}}, {{2}, {3, 6, 13, 14, 20, 22, 23, 24, 26, 27, 28, 29, 31, 33, 40, 41}}, {{1}, {7, 8, 10, 12, 15, 16, 18, 19, 25, 32, 35, 39, 42}}}

In[3161]:= Sum[%[[k]][[1]]*Length[%[[k]][[2]]], {k, 1, Length[%]}][[1]]

Out[3161]= 74

At that, elements of the returned nested list are sorted in decreasing order of multiplicities of groups of elements of the initial x list.

At processing of list structures the problem of grouping of elements of the nested lists of the *ListList* type on the basis of *n–th* elements of their sublists represents a quite certain interest. This problem is solved by the following procedure, whose call **ListListGroup[x, n]** returns the nested list – result of grouping of a *ListList* list *x* according to *n–th* element of its sublists. The next fragment represents source code of the procedure along with examples of its use.

In[2369]:= ListListGroup[x_ /; ListListQ[x], n_ /; IntegerQ[n] && n > 0] :=
Module[{a = {}, b = {}, k = 1},
If[Length[x[[1]]] < n, Return[Defer[ListListGroup[x, n]]],
For[k, k <= Length[x], k++, AppendTo[b, x[[k]][[n]]]];
b = DeleteDuplicates[Flatten[b]]]];
For[k=1, k <= Length[b], k++, AppendTo[a, Select[x, #[[n]] == b[[k]] &]]]; a]

In[2370]:= **ListListGroup[{{90, 2}, {500, 6}, {20, 2}, {27, 2}, {74, 6}}, 2]**
Out[2370]= {{{90, 2}, {20, 2}, {26, 2}}, {{500, 6}, {74, 6}}}
In[2371]:= **ListListGroup[{{90, 2}, {500, 6}, {20, 2}, {27, 2}, {74, 67}}, 6]**
Out[2371]= ListListGroup[{{90, 2}, {500, 6}, {20, 2}, {27, 2}, {74, 67}}, 6]

Whereas, on inadmissible factual arguments the procedure call is returned unevaluated. For example, the procedure is quite often used at processing of long enough lists containing the repeating elements.

The following procedure expands the standard **MemberQ** function onto the nested lists, its call **MemberQ[x, y]** returns *True* if an *y* expression belongs to any nesting level of *x* list, and *False* otherwise. While the call with the third optional *z* argument – an undefinite variable – in addition through *z* returns the list of the *ListList* type, the first element of each its sublist defines a level of the *x* list, whereas the second determines quantity of *y* elements on this level provided that the main output is *True*, otherwise *z* remains undefinite. The fragment below represents source code of the procedure along with the most typical examples of its application.

In[2532]:= MemberQL[x_ /; ListQ[x], y_, z___] := Module[{b, a = ElemOnLevels[x]},
If[! NestListQ[a], a = {a}, Null];
b = Map[If[Length[#] == 1, Null, {#[[1]], Count[#[[2 ;; -1]], y]}] &, a];
b = Select[b, ! SameQ[#, Null] && #[[2]] != 0 &];
If[b == {}, False, If[{z} != {} && ! HowAct[z], z = b, Null]; True]]

In[2533]:= **MemberQL[{a, b, {c, d, {f, h, d}, s, {p, w, {n, m, r, u}, t}}, x, y, z}, d]**
Out[2533]= True
In[2534]:= **MemberQL[{a, b, {c, d, {f, h, d}, s, {p, w, {n, m, r, u}, t}}, x, y, z}, d, z]**
Out[2534]= True
In[2535]:= z
Out[2535]= {{1, 1}, {2, 1}}
In[2536]:= **MemberQL[{a, b}, d, z]**
Out[2536]= False

The procedure call **ListToString[x, y]** returns result of converting into an unified string of all elements of a *x* list, disregarding its nesting, that are parted by an *y* string; whereas a *x* string is converted into the list of the substrings of a *x* string parted by an *y* string. The next fragment represents source code of the **ListToString** procedure with typical examples of its application.

In[2813]:= **ListToString[x_ /; ListQ[x] || StringQ[x], y_ /; StringQ[y]]** :=
Module[{a, b = {}, c, d, k = 1},
If[ListQ[x], a = Flatten[x]; For[k, k < Length[a], k++, c = a[[k]];
AppendTo[b, ToString1[c] <> y]];
a = StringJoin[Append[b, ToString1[a[[-1]]]]], a = FromCharacterCode[14];
d = a <> StringReplace[x, y -> a] <> a;
c = Sort[DeleteDuplicates[Flatten[StringPosition[d, a]]]];
For[k = 1, k < Length[c], k++, AppendTo[b, StringTake[d, {c[[k]] + 1, c[[k + 1]] - 1}]]];
ToExpression[b]]]

In[2814]:= **ListToString[{a + b, {"Agn", 69}, Kr, 20, Art, 27, "RANS", {{{Avz || 74}}}}, "&"]**
Out[2814]= "a + b&\"Agn\"&69&Kr&20&Art&27&\"RANS\"&Avz||74"
In[2815]:= **ListToString["a + b&\"Agn\"&69&Kr&20&Art&27& Avz || 74", "&"]**
Out[2815]= {a + b, "Agn", 69, Kr, 20, Art, 27, Avz || 74}

In a number of cases exists need to carry out the assignments to those expressions, whose number isn't known in advance and which is defined in the course of some calculations, for example, of cyclic character to the variables. This problem is solved by a simple procedure **ParVar**. The call **ParVar[x, y]** provides assignment of elements of y list to a list of variables generated on the basis of a x symbol with return of list of these variables in the *string format*. The procedure is widely used in problems dealing with generating of in advance unknown number of expressions. The fragment below represents source code of the **ParVar** procedure with an example of its application.

In[2610]:= **ParVar[x_ /; SymbolQ[x], y_ /; ListQ[y]]** := Module[{a = {}, b, k = 1},
For[k, k <= Length[y], k++, AppendTo[a, Unique[x]]]; b = ToString[a];
{b, ToExpression[b <> "=" <> ToString1[y]]}[[1]]]

In[2611]:= **W = ParVar[GS, {74, 69, 49, 27, 20}]**
Out[2611]= "{GS$17436, GS$17437, GS$17438, GS$17439, GS$17440}"
In[2612]:= **ToExpression[W]**
Out[2612]= {74, 69, 49, 27, 20}

In certain problems dealing with lists exists necessity of calculation of difference between two lists x and y which is determined as a list, whose elements are included into a x list, but don't belong to a y list. For solution of the problem the following procedure is used. The call **MinusLists[x, y, 1]** returns result of subtraction of y list from x list that consists in deletion in the x list of *all* occurrences of elements from the y list. Whereas the call **MinusLists[x, y, 2]** returns result of subtraction of an y list from a x list which consists in parity removing from the x list of entries of elements from the y list, i.e. the number of the elements deleted from x list strictly correspond to their number in the y list. The next fragment presents source code of the **MinusLists** procedure along with typical examples of its application.

In[2980]:= **MinusLists[x_ /; ListQ[x], y_ /; ListQ[y], z_ /; MemberQ[{1, 2}, z]]** :=
Module[{a, b, c, k = 1, n}, If[z == 1, Select[x, ! MemberQ[y, #] &], a = Intersection[x, y];
b = Map[Flatten, Map[Flatten[Position[x, #] &], a]]; c = Map[Count[y, #] &, a];

Software Etudes in the Mathematica

n = Length[b]; For[k, k <= n, k++, b[[k]] = b[[k]][[1 ;; c[[k]]]]];
c = Map[GenRules[#, Null] &, b]; Select[ReplacePart[x, Flatten[c]], ! SameQ[#, Null] &]]]

In[2981]:= MinusLists[{a, b, c, a, d, a, b, b, a, e, c, c}, {a, n, b, b, b, a, d, c}, 2]
Out[2981]= {a, a, e, c, c}
In[2982]:= MinusLists[{a, b, c, a, d, a, b, b, a, e, c, c}, {a, n, b, b, b, a, d, c}, 1]
Out[2982]= {e}

To the procedure two tools **MinusList** and **MinusList1** directly adjoin which are of interest as auxiliary tools at realisation of a number of our procedures [33,48], and also independent interest at processing of lists.

At programming of certain procedures of access to files has been detected the expediency of creation of a procedure useful also in other appendices. Thus, in this context the procedure **PosSubList** has been created, whose call **PosSubList**[x, y] returns a nested list of initial and final elements for entry into a simple x list of the tuple of elements set by an y list. The next fragment represents the source code of the **PosSubList** procedure and typical examples of its application.

In[2260]:= PosSubList[x_ /; ListQ[x], y_ /; ListQ[y]] :=
Module[{d, a = ToString1[x], b = ToString1[y], c = FromCharacterCode[16]},
d = StringTake[b, {2, -2}];
If[! StringFreeQ[a, d], b = StringReplace[a, d -> c <> "," <>
StringTake[ToString1[y[[2 ;; -1]]], {2, -2}]];
Map[{#, # + Length[y] - 1} &, Flatten[Position[ToExpression[b], ToExpression[c]]], {}]]

In[2261]:= PosSubList[{a, a, b, a, a, a, b, a, x, a, b, a, y, z, a, b, a}, {a, b, a}]
Out[2261]= {{2, 4}, {6, 8}, {10, 12}, {15, 17}}
In[2262]:= PosSubList[{a, a, b, a, a, a, b, a, x, y, z, a, b, a}, {a, x, a, b, c}]
Out[2262]= {}

The similar approach once again visually illustrates incentive motives and prerequisites for programming of the user means expanding the *Mathematica* software. Many of tools of our *MathToolBox* package appeared exactly in this way [28-33,48,50].

The procedures **Gather1** and **Gather2** a little extend the standard function **Gather1**, being an useful in a number of applications. The call **Gather1**[L, n] returns the nested list formed on the basis of the L list of the *ListList* type by means of grouping of sublists of the L by its n-th element. Whereas call **Gather2**[L] returns either the simple list, or the list of the *ListList* type which determines only multiple elements of the L list with their multiplicities. At absence of multiple elements in L the procedure call returns the empty list, i.e. {} [48,50]. The fragment below represents source codes of both tools with examples of their application.

In[3832]:= Gather1[L_ /; ListListQ[L], n_ /; IntegerQ[n]] := Module[{a = {}, b = {}, c, k},
If[! (1 <= n && n <= Length[L[[1]]]), Return[Defer[Gather1[L, n]]],
Do[a = Append[a, L[[k]][[n]]], {k, 1, Length[L]}]; a = Map[List, DeleteDuplicates[a]];
For[k = 1, k <= Length[a], k++, a[[k]] = Select[L, #[[n]] == a[[k]][[1]] &]]; a]

In[3833]:= Gather2[x_ /; ListQ[x]] :=
Module[{a = Select[Gather[Flatten[x]], Length[#] > 1 &], b = {}},

```
If[a == {}, {}, Do[AppendTo[b, {a[[k]][[1]], Length[a[[k]]]}], {k, Length[a]}];
ReduceLists[b]]]
In[3834]:= L = {{42, V, 1}, {47, G, 2}, {64, S, 1}, {69, V, 2}, {64, G, 3}, {44, S, 2}}; Gather1[L, 3]
Out[3834]= {{{42, V, 1}, {64, S, 1}}, {{47, G, 2}, {69, V, 2}, {44, S, 2}}, {{64, G, 3}}}
In[3835]:= Gather2[{"a", 500, "a", 90, "y", 500, "d", "h", "c", "d", 90, 500, 90}]
Out[3835]= {{"a", 2}, {500, 3}, {90, 3}, {"d", 2}}
```

The following group of means serves for ensuring sorting of lists of various type. Among them can be noted such as **SortNL, SortNL1, SortLpos, SortLS, SortNestList**. For example, the procedure call **SortNL1[*x*, *p*, *b*]** returns the result of sorting of a *x* list of the *ListList* type according to the elements in a *p* position of its sublists on the basis of their unique decimal codes, and *b* = {*Greater* | *Less*}. Whereas the call **SortNestList[*x*, *p*, *y*]** returns result of sorting of a nested numeric or symbolical list *x* by *p*-th element of its sublists according to sorting functions *Less, Greater* for numerical lists, and *SymbolGreater, SymbolLess* for symbolical lists. In both cases the nested list with the nesting level *1* as actual *x* argument is supposed, otherwise an initial *x* list is returned. In addition, in case of symbolical lists the comparison of elements is done on the basis of their character codes. The following fragment represents source code of the procedure with examples of its application.

```
In[2738]:= SortNestList[x_ /; NestListQ[x], p_ /; PosIntQ[p], y_] :=
Module[{a = DeleteDuplicates[Map[Length, x]], b},
b = If[AllTrue[Map[ListNumericQ, x], TrueQ]] && MemberQ[{Greater, Less}, y], y,
If[AllTrue[Map[ListSymbolQ, x], TrueQ]] && MemberQ[{SymbolGreater, SymbolLess},
y], y], Return[Defer[SortNestList[x, p, y]]]];
If[Min[a] <= p <= Max[a], Sort[x, b[#1[[p]], #2[[p]]] &], Defer[SortNestList[x, p, y]]]]
In[2739]:= SortNestList[{{42, 47, 69}, {74, 69, 49}, {27, 20}}, 2, Greater]
Out[2739]= {{74, 69, 49}, {42, 47, 69}, {27, 20}}
In[2740]:= SortNestList[{{"a", Av, b}, {x4, Ag70, y3}, {V75, G70}, {R, Ia}}, 2, SymbolGreater]
Out[2740]= {{x4, Ag70, y3}, {V75, G70}, {"a", Av, b}, {R, Ia}}
```

At that, at programming of the **SortNestList** procedure for the purpose of expansion of its applicability both onto numerical, and symbolical nested lists it was expedient to determine three new functions, namely **SymbolGreater** and **SymbolLess** as analogs of the operations **Greater** and **Less** *respectively*, and the function whose call **ListSymbolQ[*x*]** returning *True*, if all elements of *x* list, including its sublists of an arbitrary nesting level have the *Symbol* type, otherwise the function call **ListSymbolQ[*x*]** returns *False* [2,28-33,48,50]. The next fragment represents source code of the **ListSymbolQ** function with an example of its application.

```
In[3821]:= ListSymbolQ[x_ /; ListQ[x]] := AllTrue[SymbolQ /@ Flatten[x], TrueQ]
In[3822]:= Map[ListSymbolQ, {{a, b, c, d}, {v, 74, g, 69, x, y, z}}]
Out[3822]= {True, False}
```

The next modification of the standard **Sort** function in certain situations is a rather useful means of lists processing. So, as a similar problem it is possible to note the sorting problem of the list whose elements are re-structured by means of gathering into sublists each set of elements in a list which give the same value when the pure function is applied to them. So, the procedure call **Sort1[*x*, *y*]** returns the list whose first elements are elements of *x* list that give the same value when the pure *y* function is applied to them, after which the remaining sorted elements of the list *x* follow. Whereas the procedure call **Sort1**[*x, y, z*] with the third optional *z* argument – an arbitrary expression – returns the result that differs from previous only in that the elements of *x* list which give the same value when pure *y* function is applied to them end the returned list. The next fragment presents source code of the procedure with typical examples of its application.

In[4238]:= **Sort1[x_ /; ListQ[x], y_ /; PureFuncQ[y], z___] := Module[{a, b, c},**
If[Select[x, y] == {}, x, a = Sort[x, y]; c = If[{z} != {}, -1, 1];
a = If[c == -1, Reverse[a], a]; a = GatherBy[a, a[[c]]];
ReduceLists[If[c == 1, b = 2 ;; -1; Join[a[[1]], Sort[Flatten[a[[b]]]]],
Join[Sort[Flatten[a[[1 ;; -2]]]], a[[-1]]]]]]]

In[4239]:= **Sort1[{m, n, h, a, d, c, s, x, a, m, p}, SameQ[#, a] &]**
Out[4239]= {a, a, c, d, h, m, m, n, p, s, x}
In[4240]:= **Sort1[{m, n, h, a, d, c, s, x, a, m, p}, SameQ[#, a] &, 6]**
Out[4240]= {c, d, h, m, m, n, p, s, x, a, a}
In[4241]:= **Sort1[{m, n, h, a, d, c, s, x, a, m, p}, SameQ[#, abc] &, 6]**
Out[4241]= {m, n, h, a, d, c, s, x, a, m, p}
In[4242]:= **Sort1[{a, x, z, t}, SameQ[#, a] &, 6]**
Out[4242]= {t, x, z, a}
In[4243]:= **Sort1[{"ReduceLevelsList", "AladjevProcedures`", "HeadPF", "BlockFuncModQ"}, ContextQ[#] &]**
Out[4243]= {"AladjevProcedures`", "BlockFuncModQ", "HeadPF", "ReduceLevelsList"}
In[4248]:= **Sort1[x_ /; ListQ[x], y_ /; PureFuncQ[y], z___] := Module[{a = Select[x, y], b, c, d},**
If[a == {}, x, {c, d} = Map[Length, {a, x}]; b = If[{z} != {}, Reverse[Sort[x, y]], Sort[x, y]];
If[{z} != {}, Join[Sort[b[[1 ;; d - c]]], Sort[b[[d - c + 1 ;; -1]]]],
Join[Sort[b[[1 ;; c]]], Sort[b[[c + 1 ;; -1]]]]]]]

In[4249]:= **Sort1[{m, n, h, a, d, c, s, x, a, m, p}, SameQ[#, a] &, 6]**
Out[4249]= {c, d, h, m, m, n, p, s, x, a, a}
In[4250]:= **Sort1[{m, n, h, a, d, c, s, x, a, m, p}, SameQ[#, a] &]**
Out[4250]= {a, a, c, d, h, m, m, n, p, s, x}
In[4251]:= **Sort1[{a, x, z, t}, SameQ[#, a] &, 6]**
Out[4251]= {t, x, z, a}
In[4252]:= **Sort1[{m, n, h, a, d, c, s, x, a, m, p}, SameQ[#, abc] &, 6]**
Out[4252]= {m, n, h, a, d, c, s, x, a, m, p}
In[4349]:= **Sort2[x_ /; ListQ[x], y_, z___] :=**
Module[{a = Select[x, MemberQ[Flatten[{y}], #] &], b, c, d},
If[a == {}, x, {c, d} = Map[Length, {a, x}];
b = If[{z} != {}, Reverse[Sort[x, MemberQ[Flatten[{y}], #] &]],
Sort[x, MemberQ[Flatten[{y}], #] &]];
If[{z} != {}, Join[{Sort[b[[1 ;; d - c]]]}, {Sort[b[[d - c + 1 ;; -1]]]}], Join[{Sort[b[[1 ;; c]]]}, {Sort[b[[c + 1 ;; -1]]]}]]]]

In[4350]:= **Sort2[{m, n, h, a, d, c, s, x, a, m, p}, {m, c, a}]**
Out[4350]= {{a, a, c, m, m}, {d, h, n, p, s, x}}

In[4351]:= **Sort2[{m, n, h, a, d, c, s, x, a, m, p}, {m, c, a}, 70]**
Out[4351]= {{d, h, n, p, s, x}, {a, a, c, m, m}}
In[4352]:= **Sort2[{m, n, h, a, d, c, s, x, a, m, p}, d, 70]**
Out[4352]= {{a, a, c, h, m, m, n, p, s, x}, {d}}

In addition, the **Sort1** procedure has one more transparent and effective analog represented above. In particular, the **Sort1** procedure is convenient in that case when in the sorted list as the *first* element is its element defining the type of other sorted list elements. At last, a rather useful version of **Sort1** procedure ends the preveous fragment. The call **Sort2[x, y]** where *y* is an expression or their list returns the nested list whose the first element defines the sorted list of *y* element(s), while the second element defines the sorted list of remaining elements of the *x* list. Meanwhile, the procedure call **Sort2[x, y, z]** with the third optional *z* argument – an arbitrary expression – returns the result that differs from previous only in that the sorted list of *y* element(s) ends the returned list. In toto, procedures **Sort1** and **Sort2** can be enough simply combined in the uniform procedure what remains to the reader as an useful enough practical exercise.

Unlike the previous procedures of sorting, the procedure call **Sort3[x, y]** makes sorting of a *x* list on the basis of sorting of its elements defined by their *y* positions. While the procedure call **Sort3[x, y, z]** with optional *z* argument – *a pure function* – additionally sorts *x* list using the ordering function *z*. In case of existence of inadmissible positions in *y* list the procedure call makes sorting on admissible positions whereas on inadmissible positions the call prints the corresponding message. The next fragment presents source code of the **Sort3** procedure with typical examples of its application.

In[4174]:= **Sort3[x_ /; ListQ[x], y_ /; ListQ[y], z___] := Module[{a, b, c = Range[1, Length[x]]},**
a = Select[y, MemberQ[c, #] &];
b = If[y == a, y, Select[y, MemberQ[c, #] &]]; a = Complement[y, b];
If[a == {}, 75, Print["Positions " <> ToString[a] <> " are incorrect"]];
ReplacePart[x, GenRules[b, Sort[Map[x[[#]] &, b], z]]]]
In[4175]:= **Sort3[{q, w, e, r, t, y, u, i, o, p, a, s, d, f, g, h, j, k, l, z, x, c, v, b, n, m},**
{1, 5, 47, 8, 15, 22, 25, 42}]
"Positions {42, 47} are incorrect"
Out[4175]= {c, w, e, r, g, y, u, i, o, p, a, s, d, f, n, h, j, k, l, z, x, q, v, b, t, m}
In[4176]:= **Sort3[{q, w, e, r, t, y, u, i, o, p, a, s, d, f, g, h, j, k, l, z, x, c, v, b, n, m},**
{2, 5, 47, 8, 15, 22, 25, 42}, #1 < #2 &]
"Positions {42, 47} are incorrect"
Out[4176]= {q, w, e, r, t, y, u, i, o, p, a, s, d, f, g, h, j, k, l, z, x, c, v, b, n, m}
In[4177]:= **Sort3[{q, w, e, r, t, y, u, i, o, p, a, s, d, f, g, h, j, k, l, z, x, c, v, b, n, m}, {1, 5, 8, 15, 22, 25}]**
Out[4177]= {c, w, e, r, g, y, u, i, o, p, a, s, d, f, n, h, j, k, l, z, x, q, v, b, t, m}

The function call **SortCount[x]** sorts a list *x* both on quantities of elements located in it, and elements oneself; by default in increasing order, whereas the call **SortCount[x, y]** where *y* is an arbitrary expression, sorts the *x* list in decreasing order of quantities of its elements, and elements oneself. The next fragment represents source code of the **SortCount** function with typical examples of its application.

In[4226]:= SortCount[x_ /; ListQ[x], y___] := Flatten[Map[Map[#1[[1]] &, #] &,
Sort[Map[Sort[#, If[{y} == {}, OrderedQ[{#1, #2}] &, ! OrderedQ[{#1, #2}] &]] &,
Gather[Map[{#, Count[x, #]} &, x], #1[[2]] == #2[[2]] &]], If[{y} == {}, #1[[1]][[2]] <=
#2[[1]][[2]], #1[[1]][[2]] >= #2[[1]][[2]] &]]]

In[4227]:= SortCount[{a, b, c, b, m, a, b, c, d, d, m, b, d, a}]
Out[4227]= {c, c, m, m, a, a, a, d, d, d, b, b, b, b}
In[4228]:= SortCount[{a, b, c, b, m, a, b, c, d, d, m, b, d, a}, 70]
Out[4228]= {b, b, b, b, d, d, d, a, a, a, m, m, c, c}

The function call **SortGather[x, y, z]** does the gathering of *x* list according to *y* pure function with subsequent sorting of the all elements of the obtained list **Gather[y, z]** according to a *z* pure function.

In[4247]:= SortGather[x_ /; ListQ[x], y_ /; PureFuncQ[y], z_ /; PureFuncQ[z]] :=
Map[Sort[#, z] &, Gather[x, y]]
In[4248]:= SortGather[{1, 2, 12, 3, 4, 5, 3, 6, 7, 9, 10, 4, 5}, Abs[#1 - #2] <= 2 &, #1 < #2 &]
Out[4248]= {{1, 2, 3, 3}, {10, 12}, {4, 4, 5, 5, 6}, {7, 9}}

Sorting of the nested list at the nesting levels composing it is of an quite certain interest. In this regard the following procedure can be a rather useful tool. The call **SortOnLevel[x, m]** returns the sorting result of a *x* list at its nesting level *m*. If the nesting level *m* is absent then the procedure call returns $Failed with printing of the appropriate message. It must be kept in mind that by default the sorting is made in the symbolical format, i.e. all elements of the sorted *x* list are presented in the string format. While the call **SortOnLevel[x, m, Sf]** returns the sorting result of the *x* list at its nesting level *m* depending on the sorting pure *Sf* function that is the optional argument. In addition, the cross-cutting sorting at the set nesting level is made. The next fragment represents source code of the **SortOnLevel** procedure with typical examples of its application.

In[4003]:= SortOnLevel[x_ /; ListQ[x], m_ /; IntegerQ[m], Sf___] :=
Module[{a, b = ReplaceAll[x, {} -> {Null}], c, d, f, g, h = {}, n = 1, p, v},
a = LevelsOfList[b]; d = DeleteDuplicates[a];
If[! MemberQ[d, m], Print["Level " <> ToString[m] <> " is absent in the list; " <> "nesting level must belong to " <> ToString[Range[1, Max[d]]]]; $Failed,
f[t_] := "(" <> ToString1[t] <> ")" <> "_" <> ToString1[a[[n++]]];
SetAttributes[f, Listable]; c = Map[f, b];
g[t_] := If[SuffPref[t, "_" <> ToString[m], 2], AppendTo[h, t], Null];
SetAttributes[g, Listable]; Map[g, c];
p = Sort[Map[StringTake[#, {1, Flatten[StringPosition[#, "_"]][[-1]] - 1}] &, h], Sf]; n = 1;
v[t_] := If[ToExpression[StringTake[t, {Flatten[StringPosition[t, "_"]][[-1]] + 1, -1}]] == m,
p[[n++]], StringTake[t, {1, Flatten[StringPosition[t, "_"]][[-1]] - 1}]];
SetAttributes[v, Listable]; c = ToExpression[Map[v, c]]; ReplaceAll[c, Null -> Nothing]]]

In[4004]:= SortOnLevel[{b, t, "c", {{3, 2, 1, {g, s + t, a}, k, 0}, 2, 3, 1}, 1, 2, {m, n, f}}, 1]
Out[4004]= {1, 2, b, {{3, 2, 1, {g, s + t, a}, k, 0}, 2, 3, 1}, "c", t, {m, n, f}}
In[4005]:= SortOnLevel[{b, t, "c", {{3, 2, 1, {g, s + t, a, {}}, k, 0}, 2, 3, 1}, 1, 2, {m, n, f}}, 4]
Out[4005]= {b, t, "c", {{3, 2, 1, {a, g, s + t, {}}, k, 0}, 2, 3, 1}, 1, 2, {m, n, f}}

In[4006]:= **SortOnLevel[{b, t, "c", {{3, 2, 1, {g, s + t, a, {}}, k, 0}, 2, 3, 1}, 1, 2, {m, n, f}}, 6]**
"Level 6 is absent in the list; nesting level must belong to {1, 2, 3, 4, 5}"
Out[4006]= $Failed
In[4007]:= **SortOnLevel[Range[1, 20], 1]**
Out[4007]= {1, 10, 11, 12, 13, 14, 15, 16, 17, 18, 19, 2, 20, 3, 4, 5, 6, 7, 8, 9}
In[4008]:= **SortOnLevel[Range[1, 20], 1, ToExpression[#1] < ToExpression[#2] &]**
Out[4008]= {1, 2, 3, 4, 5, 6, 7, 8, 9, 10, 11, 12, 13, 14, 15, 16, 17, 18, 19, 20}
In[4009]:= **SortOnLevel[{b, t, "c", {{3, 2, 1, {g, a, s || t, a, {}, a}, k, 0}, 2, 3, 1}, 1, 2, {m, n, f}}, 4]**
Out[4009]= {b, t, "c", {{3, 2, 1, {a, a, a, g, {}, s || t}, k, 0}, 2, 3, 1}, 1, 2, {m, n, f}}
In[4010]:= **SortOnLevel[{{5}, {3}, {g}, {75}, {2}, {v}, {7}, {50}, {a}, {4}, {9}, {s}, {70}}, 2]**
Out[4010]= {{2}, {3}, {4}, {5}, {50}, {7}, {70}, {75}, {9}, {a}, {g}, {s}, {v}}
In[4011]:= **SortOnLevel[{{5}, {3}, {g}, {75}, {2}, {v}, {7}, {50}, {a}, {4}, {9}, {s}, {70}}, 2, ToCharacterCode[#1][[1]] > ToCharacterCode[#2][[1]] &]**
Out[4011]= {{70}, {s}, {9}, {4}, {a}, {50}, {7}, {v}, {2}, {75}, {g}, {3}, {5}}
In[4012]:= **SortOnLevel[{{m}, {n}, {g}, {d}, {a}, {b}, {s}, {h, k}, {u, t, s}, {w, z}}, 2]**
Out[4012]= {{a}, {b}, {d}, {g}, {h}, {k}, {m}, {n, s}, {s, t, u}, {w, z}}

The represented examples rather visually illustrate the sorting principle of the procedure.

The following procedure is a rather natural generalization of the previous procedure. The call **SortOnLevels[x, m, Sf]** where the optional *Sf* argument defines a sorting pure function analogously to the previous procedure returns the sorting result of *x* list at its nesting levels *m*. Furthermore, as an argument *m* can be used a single level, the levels list or `All` word which determines all nesting levels of the *x* list which are subject to sorting. If all *m* levels are absent then the call returns $*Failed* with printing of appropriate message, otherwise the call prints the message concerning only levels absent in the *x* list. It must be kept in mind, that by default the sorting is made in symbolical format, i.e. all elements of the sorted *x* list before sorting by means of the standard **Sort** function are represented in the string format. Whereasthe procedure call **SortOnLevels[x, m, S]** returns the sorting result of a *x* list at its nesting levels *m* depending on a sorting pure *S* function that is the optional argument. The next fragment represents source code of the **SortOnLevels** procedure with typical examples of its application.

In[4003]:= **SortOnLevels[x_ /; ListQ[x], m_ /; IntegerQ[m] || IntegerListQ[m] || m === All, Sf___] := Module[{a, b, c = ReplaceAll[x, {} -> {Null}], d, h, t, g, s},**
a = LevelsOfList[c]; d = Sort[DeleteDuplicates[a]];
If[m === All || SameQ[d, Set[h, Sort[DeleteDuplicates[Flatten[{m}]]]]], t = d,
If[Set[g, Intersection[h, d]] == {}, Print["Levels " <> ToString[h] <> " are absent in the list; " <> "nesting levels must belong to " <> ToString[Range[1, Max[d]]]];
Return[$Failed], t = g; s = Select[h, ! MemberQ[d, #] &];
If[s == {}, Null, Print["Levels " <> ToString[s] <> " are absent in the list; " <> "nesting levels must belong to " <> ToString[Range[1, Max[d]]]]]]];
Map[Set[c, SortOnLevel[c, #, Sf]] &, t]; ReplaceAll[c, Null -> Nothing]]

In[4063]:= **SortOnLevels[{b, t, "c", {{3, 2, 1, {g, s + t, a}, k, 0}, 2, 3, 1}, 1, 2, {m, n, f}}, {2, 3, 6, 7, 8}]**
"Levels {6, 7, 8} are absent in the list; nesting levels must belong to {1, 2, 3, 4}"
Out[4063]= {b, t, "c", {{0, 1, 2, {g, s + t, a}, 3, k}, 1, 2, 3}, 1, 2, {f, m, n}}

In[4064]:= **SortOnLevels[{b, t, "c", {{3, 2, 1, {g, s + t, a}, k, 0}, 2, 3, 1}, 1, 2, {m, n, f}}, 1]**
Out[4064]= {1, 2, b, {{3, 2, 1, {g, s + t, a}, k, 0}, 2, 3, 1}, "c", t, {m, n, f}}
In[4065]:= **SortOnLevels[{b, t, "c", {{3, 2, 1, {g, s + t, a}, k, 0}, 2, 3, 1}, 1, 2, {m, n, f}}, {7, 5, 0, 4}]**
"Levels {0, 5, 7} are absent in the list; nesting levels must belong to {1, 2, 3, 4}"
Out[4065]= {b, t, "c", {{3, 2, 1, {a, g, s + t}, k, 0}, 2, 3, 1}, 1, 2, {m, n, f}}
In[4066]:= **SortOnLevels[{b, t, "c", {{3, 2, 1, {g, s + t, a}, k, 0}, 2, 3, 1}, 1, 2, {m, n, f}}, {7, 5, 0}]**
"Levels {0, 5, 7} are absent in the list; nesting levels must belong to {1, 2, 3, 4}"
Out[4066]= $Failed
In[4067]:= **SortOnLevels[{b, t, "c", {{3, 2, 1, {g, s + t, a}, k, 0}, 2, 3, 1}, 1, 2, {m, n, f}}, All]**
Out[4067]= {1, 2, b, {{0, 1, 2, {a, g, s + t}, 3, k}, 1, 2, 3}, "c", t, {f, m, n}}
In[4068]:= **SortOnLevels[{{b, c, d}, {1, {4, 3, 2}, {}, {{}}, h, g, f, d, s, {{{9, 8, 6}, {{}}}}}, All]**
Out[4068]= {{1, b, c}, {d, {2, 3, 4}, {}, {{}}, d, f, g, h, s, {{{6, 8, 9}, {{}}}}}}

The possibility of exchange by elements of the nested lists which are at the different nesting levels is of quite certain interest. The problem is successfully solved by the **SwapOnLevels** procedure. The procedure call **SwapOnLevels[x, y]** returns result of exchange of elements of a *x* list, being at the nesting levels and with their sequential numbers at these levels that are defined by the nested list *y* of the format {{{s1, p1}, {s2, p2}}, ..., {{sk1, pk1}, {sk2, pk2}}} where a pair {{sj1, pj1}, {sj2, pj2}} defines replacement of an element which is at the nesting level *sj1* with a sequential number *pj1* at this level by an element that is at the nesting level *sj2* with sequential number *pj2* at this level, and vice versa. In case of impossibility of such exchange because of lack of a nesting level *sj* or/and a sequential number *pj* the procedure call prints the appropriate message. At the same time, in case of absence in the *y* list of the acceptable pairs for exchange the procedure call returns *$Failed* with printing of the above messages. The next fragment represents source code of the **SortOnLevels** procedure along with typical examples of its application.

In[7835]:= **SwapOnLevels[x_ /; ListQ[x], y_ /; ListListQ[y]] :=**
Module[{a = ElemsOnLevels2[x], b, c, d, f, g, h, p, n, s, z, u=0, w=ReplaceAll[x, {} -> Null]},
g[t_] := "(" <> ToString1[t] <> ")"; SetAttributes[g, Listable]; f[t_] := h[[n++]];
SetAttributes[f, Listable]; s[t_] := ToExpression[t][[1]]; SetAttributes[s, Listable];
Do[z = y[[j]]; n = 1; If[MemberQ5[a, #[[2 ;; 3]] == z[[1]] &] &&
MemberQ5[a, #[[2 ;; 3]] == z[[2]] &],
b = Select[a, #[[2 ;; 3]] == z[[1]] &][[1]]; c = Select[a, #[[2 ;; 3]] == z[[2]] &][[1]];
a = ReplaceAll[a, b -> d]; a = ReplaceAll[a, c -> h];
a = ReplaceAll[a, d -> c]; a = ReplaceAll[a, h -> b];
p = Map[g, w]; h = Map[ToString1, a]; h = Map[s, Map[f, p]], u++;
Print["Pairs " <> ToString[z] <> " are incorrect for elements swap"]], {j, 1, Length[y]}];
If[u == Length[y], $Failed, ReplaceAll[h, Null -> Nothing]]]
In[7836]:= **SwapOnLevels[{b, t, c, {{3, 2, 1, {g, s, a}, k, 0}, 2, 3, 1}, 1, 2, {m, n, f}}, {{{1, 5}, {4, 3}}, {{1, 1}, {3, 3}}}]**
Out[7836]= {1, t, c, {{3, 2, b, {g, s, 2}, k, 0}, 2, 3, 1}, 1, a, {m, n, f}}
In[7837]:= **SwapOnLevels[{b, t, c, {{3, 2, 1, {g, s, a}, k, 0}, 2, 3, 1}, 1, 2, {m, n, f}}, {{{1, 5}, {4, 3}}, {{5, 1}, {2, 3}}, {{1, 1}, {4, 2}}}]**
"Pairs {{5, 1}, {2, 3}} are incorrect for elements swap"

In[7837]= {s, t, c, {{3, 2, 1, {g, b, 2}, k, 0}, 2, 3, 1}, 1, a, {m, n, f}}
In[7838]:= **SwapOnLevels[{b, t, c, {{3, 2, 1, {g, s, a}, k, 0}, 2, 3, 1}, 1, 2, {m, n, f}}, {{{7, 1}, {2, 3}}, {{8, 1}, {3, 3}}}]**
"Pairs {{{7, 1}, {2, 3}}, {{8, 1}, {3, 3}}} are incorrect for the elements swap"
Out[7838]= $Failed
In[7839]:= **SwapOnLevels[{b, t, c, {}, {{3, 2, 1, {g, s, a}, k, 0}, 2, 3, 1}, 1, 2, {{{{}}}, {m, n, f}}, {{{2, 1}, {4, 1}}, {{5, 1}, {1, 1}}}]**
Out[7839]= {{}, t, c, g, {{3, 2, 1, {{}, s, a}, k, 0}, 2, 3, 1}, 1, 2, {{{b}}}, {m, n, f}}
In[7840]:= **SwapOnLevels[{t, c, {{{a + b, h}}}, {m, n, f}, {{{{c/d, g}}}}}, {{{4, 1}, {5, 1}}, {{2, 3}, {5, 2}}}]**
Out[7840]= {t, c, {{{c/d, h}}}, {m, n, g}, {{{{a + b, f}}}}}

The call **Replace[e, r, lev]** of the standard function applies rules *r* to parts of *e* list specified by the nesting levels *lev*. In addition, all rules are applied to all identical *e* elements of the *lev*. An useful enough addition to the **Replace** function is the procedure, whose procedure call **ReplaceOnLevels[x, y]** returns the result of replacement of elements of a *x* list, being at the nesting levels and with their *sequential* numbers at these levels which are defined by the nested list *y* of the format {{$s1, p1, e1$}, {$s2, p2, e2$}, ..., {sk, pk, ek}}, where sublist {sj, pj, ej} ($j = 1..k$) defines replacement of an element that is located at nesting level *sj* with sequential number *pj* at this level by an *ej* element. If such substitution is not possible because of lack of a nesting level *sj* or/and a sequential number *pj* the procedure call prints the appropriate message. At the same time, in case of absence in the *y* list of the acceptable values {sj, pj, ej} for replacement the call returns $*Failed* with printing of the appropriate messages. The next fragment represents source code of the **ReplaceOnLevels** procedure with typical examples of its application.

In[3963]:= **Replace[{{a, b, c, a, p, a}}, a -> x, 2]**
Out[3963]= {{x, b, c, x, p, x}}
In[3964]:= **ReplaceOnLevels[{{a, b, c, a, p, a}}, {{2, 1, a + b}, {2, 6, m^n}}]**
Out[3964]= {{a + b, b, c, a, p, m^n}}

In[3970]:= **ReplaceOnLevels[x_ /; ListQ[x], y_ /; ListQ[y]] :=
Module[{a, b, d = {}, f, g, h, p, n, s, z, u = 0, w = ReplaceAll[x, {} -> Null],
r = If[ListListQ[y], y, {y}]},
a = ElemsOnLevels2[w]; b = Map[#[[2 ;; 3]] &, a];
g[t_] := "(" <> ToString1[t] <> ")"; SetAttributes[g, Listable];
f[t_] := h[[n++]]; SetAttributes[f, Listable];
s[t_] := ToExpression[t][[1]]; SetAttributes[s, Listable];
Do[z = r[[j]]; n = 1; If[MemberQ[b, z[[1 ;; 2]]],
Do[If[a[[k]][[2 ;; 3]] == z[[1 ;; 2]],
AppendTo[d, PrependTo[a[[k]][[2 ;; 3]], z[[3]]]],
AppendTo[d, a[[k]]]], {k, 1, Length[a]}]; a = d; d = {};
p = Map[g, w]; h = Map[ToString1, a]; h = Map[s, Map[f, p]], u++;
Print["Data " <> ToString[z] <> " for replacement are incorrect"]], {j, 1, Length[r]}];
If[u == Length[r], $Failed, ReplaceAll[h, Null -> Nothing]]]**

In[3971]:= ReplaceOnLevels[{t, c, {{{a + b, h}}}, {m, n, f}, {{{{c/d, g}}}}}, {{4, 1, m + n}, {5, 1, Sin[x]}}]

Out[3971]= {t, c, {{{m + n, h}}}, {m, n, f}, {{{{Sin[x], g}}}}}

In[3972]:= ReplaceOnLevels[{t, c, {{{a + b, h}}}, {m, n, f}, {{{{c/d, g}}}}}, {{4, 1, m + n}, {8, 3, avz}, {5, 1, Sin[x]}}]

"Data {8, 3, avz} for replacement are incorrect"

Out[3972]= {t, c, {{{m + n, h}}}, {m, n, f}, {{{{Sin[x], g}}}}}

In[3973]:= ReplaceOnLevels[{t, c, {{{a + b, h}}}, {m, n, f}, {{{{c/d, g}}}}}, {{9, 1, m + n}, {8, 3, avz}, {7, 1, Sin[x]}}]

"Data {9, 1, m + n} for replacement are incorrect"
"Data {8, 3, avz} for replacement are incorrect"
"Data {7, 1, Sin[x]} for replacement are incorrect"

Out[3973]= $Failed

In[3974]:= ReplaceOnLevels[{t, c, {{{}}}, {m, n, f}, {{{{}}}}}, {{4, 1, m + n}, {3, 1, Sin[x]}}]

Out[3974]= {t, c, {{Sin[x]}}, {m, n, f}, {{{m + n}}}}

In turn, the **ReplaceOnLevels1** procedure works similar to the previous **ReplaceOnLevels** procedure with a rather important difference. The call **ReplaceOnLevels1**[x, y] returns the result of replacement of elements of a x list, being at the nesting levels and satisfying given conditions which are determined by the nested list y of the format {{$s1$, $c1$, $e1$}, {$s2$, $c2$, $e2$}, ..., {sk, ck, ek}}, where sublist {sj, cj, ej} ($j = 1..k$) determines replacement of an element that is located at nesting level sj and satisfies given condition cj by an ej element. If substitution is not possible because of absence of a nesting level sj or/and falsity of testing condition cj the procedure call prints the appropriate message. At the same time, in a case of absence in y list of any acceptable values {sj, cj, ej} for replacement the call returns $*Failed* with print of the appropriate messages. The next fragment presents source code of the **ReplaceOnLevels1** procedure along with typical examples of its application.

In[3990]:= ReplaceOnLevels1[x_ /; ListQ[x], y_ /; ListQ[y]] :=
Module[{a, b, d = {}, f, g, h, p, n, s, z, u = 0, w = ReplaceAll[x, {} -> Null]},
r = If[ListListQ[y], y, {y}]};
a = ElemsOnLevels2[w]; b = Map[#[[2]] &, a];
g[t_] := "(" <> ToString1[t] <> ")"; SetAttributes[g, Listable];
f[t_] := h[[n++]]; SetAttributes[f, Listable];
s[t_] := ToExpression[t][[1]]; SetAttributes[s, Listable];
Do[z = r[[j]]; n = 1; If[! MemberQ[b, z[[1]]] && ! FunctionQ[z[[2]]], u++;
Print["Level and function are incorrect in argument " <> ToString1[z]]],
If[! MemberQ[b, z[[1]]], u++;
Print["Level " <> ToString[z[[1]]] <> " is incorrect in argument " <> ToString1[z]]],
If[! FunctionQ[z[[2]]], u++;
Print["Condition " <> ToString[z[[2]]] <> " is incorrect in argument " <> ToString1[z]]],
Do[If[a[[k]][[2]] == z[[1]] && z[[2]][a[[k]][[1]]],
AppendTo[d, PrependTo[a[[k]][[2 ;; 3]], z[[3]]]],
AppendTo[d, a[[k]]]], {k, 1, Length[a]}]; a = d; d = {}; p = Map[g, w];
h = Map[ToString1, a]; h = Map[s, Map[f, p]]]], {j, 1, Length[r]}];

If[u == Length[r], $Failed, ReplaceAll[h, Null -> Nothing]]]

In[3991]:= f[t_] := SameQ[Head[t], Plus]; h[t_] := EvenQ[t]
In[3992]:= **ReplaceOnLevels1[{t, c, {{{a + b, h}}}, {m, n, f}, {{{{74, g}}}}}, {{4, f, Log[x]}, {5, h, Tan[x]}}]**
Out[3992]= {t, c, {{{Log[x], h}}}, {m, n, f}, {{{{Tan[x], g}}}}}
In[3993]:= **ReplaceOnLevels1[{t, c, {{{a + b, h}}}, {m, n, f}, {{{{69, g}}}}}, {{4, f, Log[x]}, {5, h, Tan[x]}}]**
Out[3993]= {t, c, {{{Log[x], h}}}, {m, n, f}, {{{{69, g}}}}}
In[3994]:= **ReplaceOnLevels1[{t, c, {{{a + b, h}}}, {m, n, f}, {{{{69, g}}}}}, {{4, S, Log[x]}, {9, G, Tan[x]}, {9, f, m^2}}]**
"Condition S is incorrect in argument {4, S, Log[x]}"
"Level and function are incorrect in argument {9, G, Tan[x]}"
"Level 9 is incorrect in argument {9, f, m^2}"
Out[3994]= $Failed
In[3995]:= **ReplaceOnLevels1[{t, c, {{{a + b, h}}}, {m, n, f}, {{{{74, g}}}}}, {{4, f, Log[x]}, {5, h, Tan[x]}, {9, G, m^2}}]**
"Level and function are incorrect in argument {9, G, m^2}"
Out[3995]= {t, c, {{{Log[x], h}}}, {m, n, f}, {{{{Tan[x], g}}}}}

An useful enough addition to the **ReplaceOnLevels** function is the next procedure, whose call **ExchangeListsElems**[*x*, *y*, *z*] returns the result of exchange by elements of a *x* list and a *y* list that are located at the nesting levels and with their sequential numbers at these levels. The *z* factual argument is defined by the nested list of the format {{{*s11*, *p11*}, {*s21*, *p21*}}, ..., {{*sk1*, *pk1*}, {*sk2*, *pk2*}}} where the pair {{*sj1*, *pj1*}, {*sj2*, *pj2*}} defines the levels and sequential numbers of elements of the 1st and the 2nd list accordingly. If a pair is not possible because of lack of a nesting level {*sj1*/*sj2*} or/and sequential number {*pj1*/*pj2*} the procedure call prints the appropriate message. At the same time, in case of absence in the *z* list of any acceptable pair {{*sj1*, *pj1*}, {*sj2*, *pj2*}} for exchange, then the procedure call returns $*Failed* with printing of the appropriate messages. The fragment presents source code of the **ExchangeListsElems** procedure along with typical examples of its application.

In[4966]:= **ExchangeListsElems[x_ /; ListQ[x], y_ /; ListQ[y], z_ /; ListListQ[z]] :=
Module[{a, a1, a3, a4, b, b1, c = {}, d, h, q, f = ReplaceAll[x, {} -> Null],
g = ReplaceAll[y, {} -> Null], r = If[MaxLevelList[z] == 2, {z}, z], u = 0},
a = ElemsOnLevels2[f]; b = Map[#[[2 ;; 3]] &, a];
a1 = ElemsOnLevels2[g]; b1 = Map[#[[2 ;; 3]] &, a1];
Do[q = r[[j]]; Map[If[MemberQ[b, q[[1]]] && MemberQ[b1, q[[2]]], AppendTo[c, q],
u++; Print["Pairs " <> ToString[q] <> " are incorrect"]]], {j, 1, Length[r]}];
If[u == Length[r], $Failed, Do[q = c[[j]]; a3 = Select[a, #[[2 ;; 3]] == q[[1]] &][[1]][[1]];
a4 = Select[a1, #[[2 ;; 3]] == q[[2]] &][[1]][[1]]; f = ReplaceOnLevels[f, Flatten[{q[[1]], a4}]];
g = ReplaceOnLevels[g, Flatten[{q[[2]], a3}]], {j, 1, Length[c]}];
Map[ReplaceAll[#, Null -> Nothing] &, {f, g}]]]**

In[4967]:= x = {a, b + c, {{1, 2, 3}}, {k + j, d^c}, m, n + g}; y = {a, b*c, m, {{1, 2, 3}, {k, c, h}}, {r + t, t^c}, m, z*g};
In[4957]:= **ExchangeListsElems[x, y, {{{3, 2}, {2, 2}}, {{5, 2}, {4, 2}}}]**

"Pairs {{5, 2}, {4, 2}} are incorrect"
Out[4957]= {{a, b + c, {{1, t^c, 3}}, {1 + k, d^c}, m, g + n}, {a, b*c, m, {{1, 2, 3}, {k, c, h}}, {r + t, 2}, m, g*z}}
In[4968]:= ExchangeListsElems[x, y, {{{7, 1}, {2, 2}}, {{5, 2}, {4, 2}}}]
"Pairs {{7, 1}, {2, 2}} are incorrect"
"Pairs {{5, 2}, {4, 2}} are incorrect"
Out[4968]= $Failed
In[4969]:= ExchangeListsElems[x, y, {{{3, 2}, {2, 2}}, {{1, 2}, {1, 5}}}]
Out[4969]= {{a, g*z, {{1, t^c, 3}}, {1 + k, d^c}, m, g + n}, {a, b*c, m, {{1, 2, 3}, {k, c, h}}, {r + t, 2}, m, b + c}}
In[4970]:= x = {a, b + c, {{{{"gs", {}}}}}, {{1, 2, 3}}, {k + j, d^c}, m, n + g};
y = {a, b*c, m, {{{1, 2, 3}, {k, c, h}}}, {r + t, t^c}, m, z*g};
In[4971]:= ExchangeListsElems[x, y, {{7, 2}, {2, 2}}]
"Pairs {{7, 2}, {2, 2}} are incorrect"
Out[4971]= $Failed
In[4972]:= ExchangeListsElems[x, y, {{{3, 2}, {2, 2}}, {{5, 1}, {4, 6}}}]
Out[4972]= {{a, b + c, {{{{h, {}}}}, {{1, t^c, 3}}, {1 + k, d^c}, m, g + n}, {a, b*c, m, {{1, 2, 3}, {k, c, "gs"}}, {r + t, 2}, m, g*z}}

The methods used by algorithms of the above procedures **LevelsOfList, ElemsOnLevels** ÷ **ElemsOnLevels2, SortOnLevel, SwapOnLevels, ReplaceOnLevels, ReplaceOnLevels1** and **ExchangeListsElems** that are of independent interest are of certain interest to the problems dealing with the nested lists too.

Unlike the standard **Insert** function the following procedure is a rather convenient means for inserting of expressions to the given place of any nesting level of the list. The procedure call **InsertInLevels**[*x, y, z*] returns the result of inserting in a *x* list of *expj* expressions which are defined by the second *y* argument of the format {{*lev1, ps1, expr1*}, ..., {*levk, psk, expk*}} where *levj* defines the nesting level of *x, psj* defines the sequential number of this element on the level and *expj* defines an expression that is inserted before *(z = 1)* or after *(z = 2)* this element *(j = 1..k)*. On inadmissible pairs {*levj, psj*} the procedure call prints the appropriate messages. Whereas, in a case of lack in the *y* list of any acceptable {*levj, psj*} for inserting the procedure call returns $*Failed* with print of the appropriate messages. At the same time, the fourth optional *g* argument – an uncertain symbol – allows to insert in the list the required sublists, increasing nesting level of *x* list in general. In this case, the expression *expj* is coded in the form g[*a, b, c, d, ...*] which admits different useful compositions as the examples of the fragment below along with source code of the procedure very visually illustrate.

In[3998]:= InsertInLevels[x_ /; ListQ[x], y_ /; ListQ[y], z_ /; MemberQ[{1, 2}, z], g___] :=
Module[{a, b, c, d, h, f = ReplaceAll[x, {} -> Null], p, u = 0, r = If[ListListQ[y], y, {y}]},
a = ElemsOnLevels2[f]; b = Map[#[[2 ;; 3]] &, a];
d[t_] := If[StringQ[t] && SuffPref[t, "Sequences[", 1], ToExpression[t], t];
SetAttributes[d, Listable];
Do[p = r[[j]]; If[Set[h, Select[a, #[[2 ;; 3]] == p[[1 ;; 2]] &]] == {}, u++;
Print["Level and/or position " <> ToString[p[[1 ;; 2]]] <> " are incorrect"],
c = If[z == 2, "Sequences[" <> ToString[{h[[1]][[1]], p[[3]]}] <> "]",

"Sequences[" <> ToString[{p[[3]], h[[1]][[1]]}] <> "]"];
f = Map[d, ReplaceOnLevels[f, {Flatten[{p[[1 ;; 2]], c}]}]]], {j, 1, Length[r]}];
If[u == Length[r], $Failed, ReplaceAll[f, {If[{g} != {} && NullQ[g], g -> List, Nothing],
Null -> Nothing}]]]

In[3999]:= InsertInLevels[{t, c, {{{a + b, h}}}, {m, n, f}, {{{{74, g}}}}, 74, 69}, {{4, 1, avz}, {5, 2, agn}}, 1]
Out[3999]= {t, c, {{{avz, a + b, h}}}, {m, n, f}, {{{{74, agn, g}}}}, 74, 69}
In[4000]:= InsertInLevels[{t, c, {{{a + b, h}}}, {m, n, f}, {{{{74, g}}}}, 74, 69}, {{4, 1, avz}, {5, 2, agn}}, 2]
Out[4000]= {t, c, {{{a + b, avz, h}}}, {m, n, f}, {{{{74, g, agn}}}}, 74, 69}
In[4001]:= InsertInLevels[{t, c, {{{a + b, h}}}, {m, n, f}, {{{{74, g}}}}, 74, 69}, {{7, 1, avz}, {9, 2, agn}}, 2]
"Level and/or position {7, 1} are incorrect"
"Level and/or position {9, 2} are incorrect"
Out[4001]= $Failed
In[4002]:= InsertInLevels[{t, c, {{{a + b, h}}}, {m, n, f}, {{{{74, g}}}}, 74, 69}, {{7, 1, avz}, {5, 2, agn}}, 2]
"Level and/or position {7, 1} are incorrect"
Out[4002]= {t, c, {{{a + b, h}}}, {m, n, f}, {{{{74, g, agn}}}}, 74, 69}
In[4003]:= InsertInLevels[{t, c, {{{a + b, h}}}, {m, n, f}, {{{{74, g}}}}, 74, 69}, {{4, 1, F[{avz, 1, 2, 3}]}, {5, 2, F[{agn, art, kr}]}}, 2, F]
Out[4003]= {t, c, {{{a + b, {avz, 1, 2, 3}, h}}}, {m, n, f}, {{{{74, g, {agn, art, kr}}}}}, 74, 69}
In[4004]:= InsertInLevels[{t, c, {{{a + b, h}}}, {m, n, f}, {{{{75, g}}}}, 75, 70}, {{4, 1, G[{avz, 1, G[{m, n, p}], 2, 3}]}, {5, 2, G[{agn, art, kr}]}}, 1, G]
Out[4004]= {t, c, {{{{avz, 1, {m, n, p}, 2, 3}, a + b, h}}}, {m, n, f}, {{{{75, {agn, art, kr}, g}}}}, 75, 70}
In[4005]:= InsertInLevels[{1, 2, 3, 4, 5, 6, 7, 8, 9}, {{1, 3, F[{avz, a, b, c}]}, {1, 7, F[{agn, art, kr}]}}, 2, F]
Out[4005]= {1, 2, 3, {avz, a, b, c}, 4, 5, 7, {agn, art, kr}, 7, 8, 9}
In[4006]:= InsertInLevels[{1, 2, 3, 4, 5, 6, 7, 8, 9}, {{1, 3, F[{avz, a, F[m, n], b, c}]}, {1, 7, F[{agn, art, kr}]}}, 2, F]
Out[4006]= {1, 2, 3, {avz, a, {m, n}, b, c}, 4, 5, 7, {agn, art, kr}, 7, 8, 9}
In[4007]:= InsertInLevels[{1, 2, 3, 4, 5, 6, 7, 8, 9}, {{1, 3, {a, b, c}}, {1, 7, {{agn, art, kr}}}}, 2, F]
Out[4007]= {1, 2, 3, a, b, c, 7, agn, art, kr, 5, 6, 7, 8, 9}
In[4008]:= InsertInLevels[{1, 2, 3, 4, 5, 6, 7, 8, 9}, {{1, 3, F[F[{{{x, a, F[{{m, n}}], b, c}}}]]}}, 2, F]
Out[4008]= {1, 2, 3, {{x, a, {m, n}, b, c}}, 4, 5, 6, 7, 8, 9}
In[4009]:= InsertInLevels[{1, 2, 3, 4, 5, 6, 7, 8, 9}, {{1, 5, F[F[F[F[{a, b, c}]]]]}}, 1, F]
Out[4009]= {1, 2, 3, 4, {{{{a, b, c}}}}, 5, 6, 7, 8, 9}

Unlike the standard **Delete** function the following procedure is a rather convenient means for deleting of expressions on the given place of any nesting level of the list. The procedure call **DeleteAtLevels[x, y]** returns result of deleting in a *x* list of its elements that are defined by the second *y* argument of the format {{*lev1*, *ps1*}, ..., {*levk*, *psk*}} where *levj* determines the nesting level of *x* and *psj* defines the sequential number of this element on the level (*j* = 1..*k*). On inadmissible pairs {*levj*, *psj*} the procedure call prints the corresponding messages. Whereas in case of absence in the *y* list of any acceptable {*levj*, *psj*} pair for the deleting the procedure call returns $Failed with printing of the appropriate messages. The next fragment represents source code of the **DeleteAtLevels** procedure with examples of its application.

In[3972]:= DeleteAtLevels[x_ /; ListQ[x], y_ /; ListQ[y]] :=
Module[{a, b, c = 0, d, h, f = ReplaceAll[x, {} -> Null], r = If[ListListQ[y], y, {y}]},
a = ElemsOnLevels2[f]; b = Map[#[[2 ;; 3]] &, a];
d[t_] := If[t === "Nothing", ToExpression[t], t]; SetAttributes[d, Listable];
Do[h = r[[j]]; If[Select[b, # == h &] == {}, c++;
Print["Level and/or position " <> ToString[h] <> " are incorrect"],
f = ReplaceOnLevels[f, {Flatten[{h, "Nothing"}]}]]], {j, 1, Length[r]}];
f = Map[d, f]; If[c == Length[r], $Failed, ReplaceAll[f, Null -> Nothing]]]

In[3973]:= DeleteAtLevels[{1, 2, 3, 4, 5, 6, 7, 8, 9, 10}, {{1, 5}, {1, 8}, {1, 3}}]
Out[3973]= {1, 2, 4, 6, 7, 9, 10}

In[3974]:= DeleteAtLevels[{1, 2, 3, 4, 5, 6, 7, 8, 9, 10}, {{1, 25}, {1, 12}, {1, 20}}]
"Level and/or position {1, 25} are incorrect"
"Level and/or position {1, 12} are incorrect"
"Level and/or position {1, 20} are incorrect"
Out[3974]= $Failed

In[3975]:= DeleteAtLevels[{1, 2, 3, 4, 5, 6, 7, 8, 9, 10}, {{1, 5}, {1, 12}, {1, 8}, {1, 20}}]
"Level and/or position {1, 12} are incorrect"
"Level and/or position {1, 20} are incorrect"
Out[3975]= {1, 2, 3, 4, 6, 7, 9, 10}

In[3976]:= DeleteAtLevels[{t, c, {{{a*b, h}}}, {m, n, f}, {{{{74, g}}}}, 74, 69}, {{4, 1}, {4, 2}, {5, 2}}]
Out[3976]= {t, c, {{{}}}, {m, n, f}, {{{{74}}}}, 74, 69}

The **PartialSums** procedure of the same name with the *Maple* procedure, similarly returns the list of the partial sums of elements of the list *x* with one difference that at coding of the *x* symbol in the string format the procedure call **PartialSums[x]** updates an initial *x* list *in situ*. The next fragment represents source code of the **PartialSums** procedure along with typical examples of its application.

In[2317]:= PartialSums[L_ /; ListQ[L] || StringQ[L] && ListQ[ToExpression[L]]] :=
Module[{a = {}, b = ToExpression[L], k = 1, j},
For[k, k <= Length[b], k++, AppendTo[a, Sum[b[[j]], {j, k}]]];
If[StringQ[L], ToExpression[L <> " = " <> ToString[a]], a]]

In[2318]:= PartialSums[{1, 2, 3, 4, 5, 6, 7, 8, 9, 10, 11, 12, 13, 14, 15, 16, 17, 18}]
Out[2318]= {1, 3, 6, 10, 15, 21, 28, 36, 45, 55, 66, 78, 91, 105, 120, 136, 153, 171}

In[2319]:= GS = {1, 2, 3, 4, 5, 6, 7, 8, 9, 10, 11, 12, 13, 14, 15, 16, 17}; PartialSums["GS"]; GS
Out[2319]= {1, 3, 6, 10, 15, 21, 28, 36, 45, 55, 66, 78, 91, 105, 120, 136, 153}

In[2320]:= SV = {a, b, c, d, e, f}; PartialSums["SV"]; SV
Out[2320]= {a, a + b, a + b + c, a + b + c + d, a + b + c + d + e, a + b + c + d + e + f}

In a number of cases exists a need of generation of the list of variables in the format *Vk* (*k* = 1..*n*), where *V* – a name and *n* – a positive integer. The standard functions **CharacterRange** and **Range** of *Mathematica* don't solve the given problem therefore for these purposes it is rather successfully possible to use the procedures **Range1, Range2, Range3, Range3**, whose source codes along with typical examples of their use can be found in [32,48,50]. So, the call **Range1[*j1, jp*]** returns the list of variables in shape *{j1, j2, ..., jp}*; at that, the *actual* arguments are coded in *$xxx_yyyN* format *(N = {0..p | 1..p})* whereas the call **Range2[*j, p*]** returns the list of variables in standard format, providing *arbitrariness* in choice of identifier of an *j* variable, namely: *{j1, j2, j3, ..., jp}*; from other party, the call **Range3[*j, p*]** returns the list in the format *{j1_, j2_, ..., jp_}* where *j* – an identifier and *p* – an integer. The procedure **Range4** combines standard functions **Range & CharacterRange** with an extension of possibilities of the *second* function. At last, the function call **Range5[*x*]** returns the list which is formed on the basis of a *x* tuple consisting from simple elements and spans. More detailed description of the above tools of *Range* type with their source codes can be found in [28-33,48]. Whereas some typical examples of their application with source codes are given below:

In[3100]:= **Range2[x_, y_ /; IntegerQ[y] && y >= 1]** := Module[{a = {}, b = Range[1, y], k = 1}, For[k, k <= Length[b], k++, a = Append[a, If[ToString[x] === "#1", "#", ToString[x]] <> ToString[b[[k]]]]]; ToExpression[a]]

In[3101]:= **Range3[x_, y_ /; IntegerQ[y] /; y >= 1]** := Module[{a = {}, k = 1, b = Range[1, y]}, For[k, k <= Length[b], k++, AppendTo[a, ToString[x] <> ToString[b[[k]]] <> "_"]]; ToExpression[a]]

In[3102]:= **Range4[x_, y__]** :=
Module[{a = Select[Flatten[{x, If[{y} != {}, {y}, Null]}], # != "Null" &], b},
If[AllTrue[Map[NumberQ, a], TrueQ], Range[Sequences[a]],
b = Map[FromCharacterCode, Range[32, 4096]];
If[Length[{x, y}] == 2 && MemberQ3[b, {x, y}], CharacterRange[x, y],
If[Length[{x, y}] == 1 && StringQ[x], Select[b, ToCharacterCode[#][[1]] <= ToCharacterCode[x][[1]] &], $Failed]]]]

In[3103]:= **Range5[x__]** :=
Flatten[Map[If[Head[#] === Span, Range[Part[#, 1], Part[#, 2]], #] &, Flatten[{x}]]]

In[3104]:= **Range1[$Kr_Art1, $Kr_Art6]**
Out[3104]= {$Kr_Art1, $Kr_Art2, $Kr_Art3, $Kr_Art4, $Kr_Art5, $Kr_Art6}
In[3105]:= **Range2[Kr, 12]**
Out[3105]= {Kr1, Kr2, Kr3, Kr4, Kr5, Kr6, Kr7, Kr8, Kr9, Kr10, Kr11, Kr12}
In[3106]:= **Range2[#, 10]**
Out[3106]= {#1, #2, #3, #4, #5, #6, #7, #8, #9, #10}
In[3107]:= **Range3[h, 12]**
Out[3107]= {h1_, h2_, h3_, h4_, h5_, h6_, h7_, h8_, h9_, h10_, h11_, h12}
In[3108]:= **Range4[42, 74, 2]**
Out[3108]= {42, 44, 46, 48, 50, 52, 54, 56, 58, 60, 62, 64, 66, 68, 70, 72, 74}
In[3109]:= **Range5[74, 34 ;; 38, 40 ;; 48, 90]**
Out[3109]= {74, 34, 35, 36, 37, 38, 40, 41, 42, 43, 44, 45, 46, 47, 48, 90}

In[3118]:= **CodeEncode[x__]** :=
Module[{a = ToString[x], b = Map[{#, Prime[#]} &, Range5[2 ;; 126]], c = "", d},
d = ToCharacterCode[a];
Do[c = c <> FromCharacterCode[Select[b, #[[If[Max[d] <= 126, 1, 2]]] == d[[k]] &][[1]]

[[If[Max[d] <= 126, 2, 1]]]], {k, 1, Length[d]}]; c]

In[3119]:= CodeEncode["C:/MathToolBox/MathToolBox.mx"]

Out[3119]= "ïďÓǽɪ?dzʉǽîqǽȳ8Óǽɪ?dzʉǽîqǽȳ8Çďʒ"

In[3120]:= CodeEncode[CodeEncode["C:/MathtoolBox/MathtoolBox.mx"]]

Out[3120]= "C:/MathToolBox/MathToolBox.mx"

The above tools of so–called *Range* group are rather useful at processing of the lists. So, the coder–decoder **CodeEncode**, operating on the principle of switch, uses 2 functions **Range5** and **Prime**. The procedure call **CodeEncode[x]** returns the coded *x* string of Latin printable *ASCII*–symbols, and vice versa.

The **CodeEncode1** tool is a rather useful extension of the previous **CodeEncode** procedure in the event of datafiles of *ASCII* format. The procedure call **CodeEncode1[x]** is equivalent to a call **CodeEncode[x]** if *x* is the string consisting of *ASCII* symbols. While the procedure call **CodeEncode1[j]** in case of *j* argument defining a file consisting from the *ASCII* symbols, returns nothing, updating in situ the initial uncoded *j* file onto the encoded *j* file. At last, the procedure call **CodeEncode1[j]** in case of *j* argument defining a coded file consisting of the *ASCII* symbols, returns contents of the decoded *j* file, at the same time updating in situ an encoded *j* file onto the decoded *j* file. The following fragment represents source code of the procedure **CodeEncode1** with typical examples of its application.

In[3147]:= CodeEncode1[x_ /; FileExistsQ[x] || StringQ[x]] := Module[{a},
If[FileExistsQ[x], a = ReadString[x, "\n" | "\n\n" | "\r\n"];
If[Quiet[Check[StringCases[a, "Attributes[a$" ~~ Shortest[X__] ~~ "] = {Temporary}"][[1]],
$Failed]] === $Failed, a = CodeEncode[ReadString[x]]; DeleteFile[x];
Save[x, a], a = Get[x]; a = CodeEncode[a];
a = If[SuffPref[a, "\"", 1] && SuffPref[a, "\r\n", 2], ToExpression[StringTake[a, {1, -3}]], a];
WriteString[x, a]; Close[x]; CodeEncode[CodeEncode[a]]], CodeEncode[x]]]

In[3148]:= CodeEncode1["Asdfcxsertybnhgf jkhgty=+\"xcvbnAgnVsv"]

Out[3148]= "Ĺωʒõîʒω8ʁʕìəφȳõ ?qφȳʁʕěɀ ʒîꟼìəĹȳə2ωɫ"

In[3149]:= CodeEncode1["Ĺωʒõîʒω8ʁʕìəφȳõ ?qφȳʁʕěɀ ʒîꟼìəĹȳə2ωɫ"]

Out[3149]= "Asdfcxsertybnhgf jkhgty=+\"xcvbnAgnVsv"

In[3150]:= CodeEncode1["C:\\Temp\\Cinema_2016.txt"]

In[3151]:= CodeEncode1["C:\\Temp\\Cinema_2016.txt"]

Out[3151]= "http://computersysstems.webs.com
http://cellularautomata.webs.com
http://aladjev-maple-book.narod.ru/Index.htm
http://bbian.webs.com/Files/Mathematica_Maple.pdf
http://viperson.ru/wind.php?ID=535085
http://reocities.com/ResearchTriangle/station/7432/index.htm
http://www.famous-scientists.ru/2763"

The next group of facilities serves for expansion of the standard **MemberQ** function, and its tools are quite useful in work with list structures. So, the **MemberQ1** procedure in a certain degree expands the standard **MemberQ** function onto the nested lists while the **MemberQ2** procedure expands the same function, taking into account number of entries of expression into a list [48]. The procedure call **MemberQ1[L, x, y]** returns *True* if *x* is an element of any nesting level of list *L* *(provided that a simple list has nesting level 0)*; otherwise *False* is returned. In case of return of *True* through, the third *y* argument the call returns list of levels of the *L* list that contain occurrences of *x*. While the procedure call **MemberQ2[*L*, *x*, *y*]** returns *True* if *x* – an element of a *L* list; otherwise *False* is returned. In addition, at return of *True*, via the 3rd argument *y* the number of entries of *x* into the *L* list is returned. The call **MemberQ3[*x*, *y*]** returns *True* if all elements of an *y* list belong to a *x* list excluding the nesting, and *False* otherwise. While the call **MemberQ3[*x*, *y*, *t*]** with the 3rd optional argument – *an expression* – returns *True*, if the *y* list – a sublist of the *x* list at arbitrary nesting level, and *False* otherwise.

The call **MemberQ4[*x*, *y*]** returns *True* if at least *1* element of a *y* list or an *y* element belongs to a *x* list, and *False* otherwise. If there the 3rd optional *z* argument, *True* is returned only in a case of number of *occurrences* of the *y* elements not smaller than *z*. The call **MemberQ5[*x*, *y*]** returns *True* if at least one element of *x* list satisfies to pure *y* function, and *False* otherwise. In addition to the above tools the following 2 simple means present an quite certain interest. The procedure call **MemberT[*L*, *x*]** returns total number of occurrences of an expression *x* into the *L* list, whereas the call **MemberLN[*L*, *x*]** returns the list of *ListList* type whose each sublist determines number of a nesting level of the *L* list by its first element, and number of *occurrences* of *x* expression into this nesting level by its *second* element. Facilities **MemberQ1**, **MemberQ2**, **MemberQ3** and **MemberQ4** along with the means **MemberT** and **MemberLN** are useful in the lists processing. In principle, these means allow interesting modifications significantly broadening the sphere of their application. Source codes of the above means of so–called *Member*–group along with examples of their application can be found in [48,50].

The procedure below serves for expansion of the standard **Intersection** function, and it is an quite useful in work with list structures. The procedure call **Intersection2[*x*, *y*, *z*, ...]** returns the list of *ListList* type whose 2–element sublists contain elements common for the lists {*x*, *y*, *z*, ...} as the first elements, while the 2nd elements – their minimal multiplicities accordingly. In case of the only list as an argument the procedure call returns list of *ListList* type whose 2–element sublists define list elements as the first elements whereas the second elements – their multiplicities. On the basis of the **Intersection2** and **ElemsOnLevelList** procedures the next procedure can be programmed which allows to receive intersection of the elements of nesting levels of a list. The procedure call **ElemsLevelsIntersect[*x*]** returns the nested list whose two–element sublists has the format {{*n*, *m*}, {{*e1*, *p1*}, {*e2*, *p2*}, ...}} where {*n*, *m*} – the nesting levels of a *x* list (*n* ÷ *m*) and {*ej*, *pj*} determines common *ej* element for the nesting levels {*n*, *m*} whereas *pj* is its common minimal multiplicity for both nesting levels. In case of the only list as an argument *x* the procedure call returns the empty list. The next fragment represents source codes of the procedures **Intersection2** and **ElemsOnLevelList** along with examples of their application.

In[4357]:= Intersection2[x__List] := Module[{a = Intersection[x], b = {}},
Do[AppendTo[b, DeleteDuplicates[Flatten[Map[{a[[j]], Count[#, a[[j]]]} &, {x}]]]],
{j, 1, Length[a]}]; b]

In[4358]:= Intersection2[{a + b, a, b, a + b}, {a, a + b, d, b, a + b}, {a + b, b, a, d, a + b}]
Out[4358]= {{a, 1}, {b, 1}, {a + b, 2}}

In[4364]:= ElemsLevelsIntersect[x_ /; ListQ[x]] := Module[{a = ElemsOnLevelList[x], b,
c = {}, d, h = {}}, d = Length[a];

```
Do[Do[If[k == j, Null, If[Set[b, Intersection2[a[[k]][[2]], a[[j]][[2]]]] != {},
AppendTo[c, {{a[[k]][[1]], a[[j]][[1]]}, b}], Null]], {j, k, d}], {k, 1, d}];
Do[AppendTo[h, {c[[j]][[1]], Map[{#[[1]], Min[#[[2 ;; -1]]]} &, c[[j]][[2]]]}], {j, 1, Length[c]}]; h]
In[4365]:= ElemsLevelsIntersect[{a, c, b, b, c, {b, b, b, c, {c, c, b, b}}}]
Out[4365]= {{{1, 2}, {{b, 2}, {c, 1}}}, {{1, 3}, {{b, 2}, {c, 2}}}, {{2, 3}, {{b, 2}, {c, 1}}}}
```

The procedure call **ToCanonicList[w]** converts a *w* list of *ListList* type, whose sublists have format {a, hj} and/or {{a1, ..., ap}, hj}, into the equivalent nested classical list where *a, ak* are elements of list *(k = 1..p)* and *hj* – the nesting levels on which they have to be in the *resultant* list. The nested list with *any* combination of sublists of the above formats is allowed as the *w* argument. The fragment below represents source code of the **ToClassicList** procedure with an example of its use which well illustrates the procedure essence.

```
In[4496]:= ToCanonicList[x_ /; ListQ[x] && ListListQ[x] && Length[x[[1]]] == 2] :=
Module[{a, b, c, d, y, v, h, f, m, g = FromCharacterCode[6]},
v[t_] := Join[Map[{{#, t[[2]]}} &, t[[1]]]]; h[t_] := If[ListQ[t[[1]]], Map[{#, t[[2]]} &, t[[1]]], t];
f[t_] := Module[{n = 1}, Map[If[OddQ[n++], #, Nothing] &, t]];
y = Partition[Flatten[Join[Map[If[ListQ[#[[1]]], v[#], {#}] &, x]]], 2];
a = Sort[y, #1[[2]] <= #2[[2]] &];
a = Map[{#[[1]][[-1]], Flatten[#]} &, Gather[a, #1[[2]] == #2[[2]] &]];
a = Map[{#[[1]], Sort[f[#[[2]]]]} &, a]; m = Length[a]; d = Map[#[[1]] &, a];
d = Flatten[{d[[1]], Differences[d]}];
a = Map[{#[[1]], b = #[[2]]; AppendTo[b, g]} &, a]; c = MultiList[a[[1]][[2]], d[[1]] - 1];
Do[c = Quiet[ReplaceAll[c, g -> MultiList[a[[j]][[2]], d[[j]] - 1]]], {j, 2, m}];
ReplaceAll[c, g -> Nothing]]
In[4497]:= ToCanonicList[{{a + b, 2}, {b, 2}, {{z, m, n}, 12}, {c, 4}, {d, 4}, {{n, y, w, z}, 5},
{b, 2}, {m*x, 5}, {n, 5}, {t, 7}, {g, 7}, {x, 12}, {y, 12}}]
Out[4497]= {{b, b, a + b, {{c, d, {n, n, w, m*x, y, z, {{g, t, {{{{{m, n, x, y, z}}}}}}}}}}}}
In[4498]:= ToCanonicList[{{a, 1}, {b, 2}, {c, 3}, {d, 4}, {g, 5}}]
Out[4498]= {a, {b, {c, {d, {g}}}}}
```

Due to the canonical representation of lists, the procedure is of a certain interest whose call **ExchangeLevels[x, n, m]** returns a *x* list in the canonical format on condition of exchange of its nesting levels *n* and *m*. In addition, if the nesting level *m* is absent then it is created. The fragment below represents source code of the **ExchangeLevels** procedure with examples of its application.

```
In[4594]:= ExchangeLevels[x_ /; ListQ[x], n_ /; IntegerQ[n], m_ /; IntegerQ[m]] :=
Module[{a = ElemsOnLevels[x], b = {}},
Map[AppendTo[b, If[#[[2]] == n, ReplacePart[#, 2 -> m],
If[#[[2]] == m, ReplacePart[#, 2 -> n], #]]] &, a]; ToCanonicList[b]]
In[4595]:= ExchangeLevels[{a, b, {c, d, {g, h, t}, d}, m}, 1, 3]
Out[4595]= {g, h, t, {c, d, d, {a, b, m}}}
In[4596]:= ExchangeLevels[{a, b, {c, d, {g, h, t}, d}, m}, 5, 6]
Out[4596]= {a, b, m, {c, d, d, {g, h, t}}}
```

In[4597]:= **ExchangeLevels[{a, b, {c, d, {g, h, t}, d}, m}, 1, 6]**
Out[4597]= {{c, d, d, {g, h, t, {{{a, b, m}}}}}}
In[4598]:= **ExchangeLevels[{a, b, {c, d, {g, h, t}, d}, m}, 3, 5]**
Out[4598]= {a, b, m, {c, d, d, {{{g, h, t}}}}}

In connection with the previous procedure quite naturally there is a problem of exchange of the nesting levels of two various lists which is solved by the following procedure. The call **ListsExchLevels[x, y, n]** returns the nested list whose the first element defines the canonical form of a *x* list with preliminary replacement of its nesting level *n* onto level *n* of *y* list while the second element defines the canonical form of the *y* list with preliminary replacement of its nesting level *n* onto level *n* of the *x* list. In addition, only one integer or their list can be as the *third n* argument of the procedure. The following fragment represents source code of the **ListsExchLevels** procedure with examples of its application.

In[4672]:= **ListsExchLevels[x_ /; ListQ[x], y_ /; ListQ[y], n_ /; PosIntQ[n] || PosIntListQ[n]] :=**
Module[{a = Map[ElemsOnLevels, {x, y}], b, c, d, m = Flatten[{n}]},
Do[b = Mapp[Select, {a[[1]], a[[2]]}, #[[2]] == m[[j]] &];
d = Map9[Complement, {a[[1]], a[[2]]}, {b[[1]], b[[2]]}];
d = Map9[Join, {d[[1]], d[[2]]}, {b[[2]], b[[1]]}];
a = {d[[1]], d[[2]]}, {j, 1, Length[m]}]; Map[ToCanonicList, d]]

In[4673]:= x = {a, b, {c, d, {g, h, t}, d}, m}; y = {h, r, {d, s, {k, a, w, t}}};
In[4674]:= **ListsExchLevels[x, y, 3]**
Out[4674]= {{a, b, m, {c, d, {a, k, t, w}}}, {h, r, {d, s, {g, h, t}}}}
In[4675]:= **ListsExchLevels[x, y, {1, 3}]**
Out[4675]= {{h, r, {c, d, {a, k, t, w}}}, {a, b, m, {d, s, {g, h, t}}}}
In[4676]:= **ListsExchLevels[x, y, {3, 6}]**
Out[4676]= {{a, b, m, {c, d, {a, k, t, w}}}, {h, r, {d, s, {g, h, t}}}}

Using the method on which the last procedures are based, it is simple to program the means focused on typical manipulations with the nested lists. The procedure call **AddDelLevels[x, n]** returns the canonical format of a *x* list which preliminary has been complemented by the nesting levels defined by the *n* list whose elements have format {*a, hj*} and/or {{*a1, ..., ap*}, *hj*}, where *a, ak* – elements of the list *(k=1..p)* and *hj* – the nesting levels on which they have to be in the resultant list. While the procedure call **AddDelLevels[x, n, y]** where the optional *y* argument is an arbitrary expression returns the canonical format of the *x* list from which have preliminary been deleted, namely: *(1)* all nesting levels, if the *n* argument determines an positive integer or their list, *(2)* only elements that yield *False* on testing by pure function *n*, at last *(3)* only elements that are defined by the list whose elements have the above format {*a, hj*} and/or {{*a1, ..., ap*}, *hj*}. The fragment below represents source code of the procedure **AddDelLevels** with examples of its application.

In[4775]:= **AddDelLevels[x_ /; ListQ[x], n_, y___] := Module[{a = ElemsOnLevels[x], b},**
If[{y} == {} && ListListQ[n], ToCanonicList[Join[a, n]],
If[{y} != {} && PureFuncQ[n], ToCanonicList[Select[a, n]],
If[{y} != {} && (PosIntQ[n] || PosIntListQ[n]),
ToCanonicList[Select[a, ! MemberQ[Flatten[{n}], #[[2]]] &]],

If[{y} !== {} && NestListQ[n], b[t_] := If[Length[t] == 2 &&
ListQ[t[[1]]], Map[{#, t[[2]]} &, t[[1]]], t];
ToCanonicList[Select[a, ! MemberQ[Map[b, n], #] &]], $Failed]]]]

In[4776]:= x1 = {a, b, c, {c, d, s, {g, h, t, p}, d}, m, n};
In[4777]:= AddDelLevels[x1, 3, 8]
Out[4777]= {a, b, c, m, n, {c, d, d, s}}
In[4778]:= AddDelLevels[x1, {1, 3}, 8]
Out[4778]= {{c, d, d, s}}
In[4779]:= AddDelLevels[x1, {{x, 3}, {y, 3}, {m, 1}, {{1, 2, 3}, 1}}]
Out[4779]= {1, 2, 3, a, b, c, m, m, n, {c, d, d, s, {g, h, p, t, x, y}}}
In[4780]:= AddDelLevels[x1, 6]
Out[4780]= $Failed
In[4781]:= AddDelLevels[{a, 1, b, c, {c, 2, b, {4, 5, a, 6}}}, SymbolQ[#[[1]]] &, 75]
Out[4781]= {a, b, c, {b, c, {a}}}

On the basis of the method used in the last procedures it is possible to implement different manipulations with the nested lists with their subsequent converting in lists of the canonical format.

The system considers a list as the object allowing multiple *occurrences* into it of elements and keeping the order of elements that has been given at its definition. For determination of the *multiplicity* of elements entering the list is possible to use the function **MultEntryList** whose call **MultEntryList[x]** returns the list of *ListList* type; the 1st element of its sublists defines an element of a x list, whereas the second element defines its multiplicity in the x list regardless of its nesting. The source code of the **MultEntryList** function with examples of its use can be found in [33,48,50], for example:

In[2720]:= MultEntryList[{"a", b, "a", c, h, 74, g, {"a", b, c, g, 74}, g, h, {74, g, h, 74}}]
Out[2720]= {{"a", 3}, {b, 2}, {c, 2}, {h, 3}, {74, 4}, {g, 4}}

Unlike two standard functions **Split** and **SplitBy** the procedure call **Split1[x, y]** splits a x list into sublists consisting of its elements which are located between occurrences of an element or elements of y list. If y don't belong to the x list, the initial x list is returned. The following fragment represents source code of the **Split1** procedure with typical examples of its use.

In[2746]:= Split1[x_ /; ListQ[x], y_] := Module[{a, b, c = {}, d, h, k = 1},
If[MemberQ3[x, y] || MemberQ[x, y], a = If[ListQ[y], Sort[Flatten[Map[Position[x, #] &, y]]], Flatten[Position[x, y]]];
h = a; If[a[[1]] != 1, PrependTo[a, 1]];
If[a[[-1]] != Length[x], AppendTo[a, Length[x]]]; d = Length[a];
While[k <= d - 1, AppendTo[c, x[[a[[k]] ;; If[k == d - 1, a[[k + 1]], a[[k + 1]] - 1]]]]; k++];
If[h[[-1]] == Length[x], AppendTo[c, {x[[-1]]}]]; c, x]]

In[2747]:= Split1[{a, a, a, b, a, b, c, d, a, b, a, b, c, d, a, b, d}, a]
Out[2747]= {{a}, {a}, {a, b}, {a, b, c, d}, {a, b}, {a, b, c, d}, {a, b, d}}
In[2748]:= Split1[{a, b, a, b, c, d, a, b, a, b, c, d, a, b, d}, {a, c, d}]
Out[2748]= {{a, b}, {a, b}, {c}, {d}, {a, b}, {a, b}, {c}, {d}, {a, b, d}, {d}}
In[2749]:= Split1[{a, b, a, b, c, d, a, b, a, b, c, d, a, b, d}, {x, y, z}]

Out[2749]= {a, b, a, b, c, d, a, b, a, b, c, d, a, b, d}

If during the operating in the *interactive* mode diagnostic messages have quite certain sense, in the software mode *(continuous)* of the execution, for example, of procedures the messages concerning the especial situations don't have any sense, complicating software processing of such situations. In this context it is more natural to identify a special situation by return of a conveniently processed expression, for example, $Failed. The next procedure can serve as an example. The successful call **ElemsList[x, y]** returns the elements of a x list depending on list of their positions given by an y list. The y list format in the general case has the view $\{n1, ..., nt, \{m1 ;...; mp\}\}$, returning elements of a x list according to standard relation $x[[n1]]$ ... $[[nt]]$ $[[m1; ...; mp]]$. In addition, the y argument allows the following encoding formats $\{n1, ..., nt\}$, $\{m1;...;mp\}\}$, {}; whose results of application are given in the next fragment with source code of the **ElemsList** procedure.

In[3378]:= **ElemsList[x_ /; ListQ[x], y_ /; ListQ[y]] :=**
Module[{c = "", k = 1, a = Select[y, ! ListQ[#] &], b = Select[y, ListQ[#] &]},
If[a == {} && b == {}, x, If[a == {}, Quiet[Check[ToExpression[ToString[x] <> "[[" <> StringTake[ToString[b], {3, -3}] <> "]]"], $Failed]], If[b == {}, c = ToString[x];
While[k <= Length[a], c = c <> "[[" <> ToString[a[[k]]] <> "]]"; k++];
Quiet[Check[ToExpression[c], $Failed]], c = ToString[x];
While[k <= Length[a], c = c <> "[[" <> ToString[a[[k]]] <> "]]"; k++];
Quiet[Check[ToExpression[c <> "[[" <> StringTake[ToString[b], {3, -3}] <> "]]"],
$Failed]]]]]]

In[3379]:= L = {{avz, agn, vsv, art, kr}, {d, e, f, g, h, {20, 27, 49, 53, 69, 74}}, {g, h, j}};
In[3380]:= **ElemsList[{}, {}]**
Out[3380]= {}
In[3381]:= **ElemsList[L, {}]**
Out[3381]= {{avz, agn, vsv, art, kr}, {d, e, f, g, h, {20, 27, 49, 53, 69, 74}}, {g, h, j}}
In[3382]:= **ElemsList[L, {{1 ;; 3}}]**
Out[3382]= {{avz, agn, vsv, art, kr}, {d, e, f, g, h, {20, 27, 49, 53, 69, 74}}, {g, h, j}}
In[3383]:= **ElemsList[L, {2, 6, {3 ;; –1}}]**
Out[3383]= {49, 53, 69, 74}
In[3384]:= **ElemsList[L, {2, 6, 5}]**
Out[3384]= 69
In[3385]:= **ElemsList[L, {2, 90.500, 5}]**
Out[3385]= $Failed
In[3386]:= **L[[2]][[6]][[3 ;; 0]]**
Part::take: Cannot take positions 3 through 0 in {19, 26, 49, 53, 69, 74}...>>
Out[3386]= {20, 27, 49, 53, 69, 74}[[3 ;; 0]]
In[3387]:= **ElemsList[L, {2, 6, {3 ;; 0}}]**
Out[3387]= $Failed

The two procedures below expand the system means oriented on work with list structures, giving a certain possibility to simplify programming *(in certain cases rather significantly)* of a number of problems that use the lists.

Software Etudes in the Mathematica

The fragment below represents source codes of the procedures with examples of their use. The call **ReduceList**[*l*, *x*, *z*, *t*] returns the result of reducing of elements of a *l* list which are defined by a separate *x* element or their list to a multiplicity defined by a separate *z* element or their list. If elements of *x* don't belong to the *l* list the procedure call returns the initial *l* list. At that, if **Length**[*z*] < **Length**[*x*] a *z* list is padded on the right by *1* to the list length *x*. In addition, the *fourth t* argument defines direction of reducing in the list *l* (*on the left at* **t** = *1*, *and on the right at* **t** = *2*).

While the call **SplitList**[*l*, *x*] returns result of *splitting* of a *l* list onto sublists by an element or elements *x*; at that, *x* dividers are removed from the result. If *x* elements don't belong to the *l* list, the procedure call returns the initial *l* list. In a number of cases both procedures are rather claimed. A number of means from *MathToolBox* package a rather essentially use the mentioned procedures **ReduceList** and **SplitList** [48,50]. These means arose in the result of programming of other our certain means.

```
In[2520]:= ReduceList[L_ /; ListQ[L], x_, z_, t_ /; MemberQ[{1, 2}, t]] :=
Module[{a = Map[Flatten, Map[Position[L, #] &, Flatten[{x}]]], b = {}, m = Flatten[{x}],
n = Flatten[{z}], k = 1},
n = If[Length[m] > Length[n], PadRight[n, Length[m], 1], n];
For[k, k <= Length[a], k++, If[Length[a[[k]]] >= n[[k]], AppendTo[b, a[[k]]], Null]];
For[k = 1, k <= Length[a], k++, a[[k]] = If[t == 1, a[[k]][[1 ;; Length[a[[k]]] - n[[k]]]],
a[[k]][[-Length[a[[k]]] + n[[k]] ;; -1]]]];
Select[ReplacePart[L, GenRules[Flatten[a], Null]], ! SameQ[#, Null] &]]

In[2521]:= ReduceList[{f, d, .d, d, d, d, f, f, f, f, f, d}, {d, f}, 3, 2]
Out[2521]= {f, d, d, d}
In[2522]:= ReduceList[{f, d, d, d, d, d, f, f, f, f, f, d}, {d, f}, 3, 1]
Out[2522]= {d, d, f, d}
In[2523]:= ReduceList[{a, f, b, c, f, d, f, d, f, f, f, g}, {d, f}, {1, 2}, 1]
Out[2523]= {a, b, c, d, f, f, g}
In[2524]:= ReduceList[{f, f, a, b, c, d, d, f, f, f, g, f}, {d, f}, {1, 2}, 2]
Out[2524]= {f, f, a, b, c, d, g}
In[2525]:= L = {a, a, a, b, b, b, b, c, c, c, c, c, d, d, d, d, d, d, e, e, e, e, e, e, e};
In[2526]:= ReduceList[L, DeleteDuplicates[L], {1, 2, 3, 4, 5}, 1]
Out[2526]= {a, b, b, c, c, c, d, d, d, d, e, e, e, e, e}

In[3340]:= SplitList[L_ /; ListQ[L], x_] :=
Module[{a = Flatten[{x}], c, d, h, b = ToString[Unique["$a"]]},
c = Map[ToString[#] <> b &, a]; d = StringJoin[Map[ToString[#] <> b &, L]];
h = Select[StringSplit[d, c], # != "" &]; h = Map[StringReplace[#, b -> ","] &, h];
h = ToExpression[Map["{" <> StringTake[#, {1, -2}] <> "}" &, h]];
Remove[b]; If[Length[h] == 1, h[[1]], h]]

In[3341]:= SplitList[{f, f, a, b, c, d, p, p, d, p, d, f, f, f, g, f}, {d, f}]
Out[3341]= {{a, b, c}, {p, p}, {p}, {g}}
In[3342]:= SplitList[{f, f, a, b, c, d, p, d, f, f, f, g, f}, {h, f}]
Out[3342]= {{a, b, c, d, p, d}, {g}}
```

The call {**MinimalBy**[{*x1, x2, ..., xp*}, *f*] | **MaximalBy**[{*x1, x2, ..., xp*}, *f*]} of standard function {**MinimalBy**| **MaximalBy**} returns the list of *xk* values for which a value *f*[*xk*] is {*minimal* | *maximal*}. The **MinMaxBy** procedure being a modification of the above functions serves as a rather useful means for processing of the numeric lists. The procedure call **MinMaxBy**[*x, f*] returns the list of the form {{*min*, {*x`kj*,...}, {*max*, {*x``np*,...}}} where *min* and *max* are *minimal* and *maximal* values of *f*[*xk*], and {*x`kj*} and {*x``np*} are lists of the *x* elements appropriate to them. The call **MinMaxBy**[*x, f, y*] with optional *y* argument different from *0* returns the list of the above form for all elements of *x* list, while the call **MinMaxBy**[*x, f, d*] with optional *d* argument which differs from zero returns the above results provided that **Abs**[*f*[*xk*] - *f*[*xp*]] <= *d* is a test to pairs of values to determine, if they should be considered identical. The call **RandomNumericRange**[*x, y, j*] returns a list of *j* random numbers in the interval [*x, y*]; it is used as a certain subsidiary tool due to the illustration of the **MinMaxBy** use. However, the **RandomNumericRange** procedure represents the certain independent interest too. The next fragment represents both the source codes of the procedures **RandomNumericRange** and **MinMaxBy** along with the typical examples of their application.

In[3779]:= **RandomNumericRange**[x_ /; NumericQ[x], y_ /; NumericQ[y],
n_ /; IntegerQ[n]] :=
Module[{a, b}, a = If[IntegerQ[x] && IntegerQ[y], b = 6; RandomInteger; RandomReal];
Map[a[If[b === 6, {x, y}, Map[N, {x, y}]]] &, Range[1, n]]]

In[3780]:= **RandomNumericRange**[42.6, 47, 7]
Out[3780]= {46.2084, 42.6476, 44.7955, 45.7908, 43.97, 46.0904, 43.6753}

In[3781]:= **MinMaxBy**[x_ /; ListQ[x], f_Symbol, y_: 0, d_: 0] := Module[{a},
a = Map[Flatten, Gather[Sort[Map[{#, N[f[#]]} &, x], Abs[#1[[2]] - #2[[2]]] <= d &],
Abs[#1[[2]] - #2[[2]]] <= d &]];
a = Map[{#[[-1]], ReplacePart[#, Map[#1 -> Nothing &, Range[2, Length[#], 2]]]} &, a];
a = Sort[a, #1[[1]] <= #2[[1]] &]; a = If[y === 0, {a[[1]], a[[-1]]}, a];
If[Length[a] == 1, a[[1]], a]]

In[3782]:= F[x_] := x; MinMaxBy[RandomNumericRange[42, 47, 10], F, 0, 2]
Out[3782]= {{42., {42, 42, 43, 42}}, {47., {46, 45, 47, 46, 45, 47}}}

At operating with numerical lists there is a grouping problem of their elements on condition of their hit in the set intervals. The following procedure solves one of similar problems. The call **GroupSort**[*x, y*] returns the nested list whose elements contain tuples of elements of the initial numerical *x* list which hit in the set intervals defined by an *y* list of the *ListList* type of the format {{*a1, a2*}, {*b1, b2*}, ...}. At the same time, hit of a *t* element in an interval {*n1, n2*} is defined by the condition *n1* <= *t* < *n2*. While the procedure call **GroupSort**[*x, y, z*] with the third optional *z* argument – *an indefinite symbol* – additionally thru it returns the nested list of the above format with that difference that as elements the grouped and reduced elements of *x* list with their multiplicities are returned. For simplification of the procedure algorithm the simple procedure that is an useful version of the standard **IntervalMemberQ** function has been determined whose call **IntervalMemberQ1**[{*a, b*}, *t*] returns *True*, if *a* <= *t* < *b*, and *False* otherwise. The following fragment represents source codes of both procedures along with examples of their application.

In[4175]:= **IntervalMemberQ1**[t_ /; ListNumericQ[t] && Length[t] == 2, z_] :=

Module[{a = Sort[Map[N, t]]}, If[a[[1]] <= z && z < a[[2]], True, False]]

In[4176]:= **IntervalMemberQ[Interval[{2, 5}], 5]**
Out[4176]= True
In[4177]:= **IntervalMemberQ1[{2, 5}, 5]**
Out[4177]= False
In[4178]:= **GroupSort[x_ /; ListNumericQ[x], y_ /; ListListQ[y] && ListNumericQ[y], z___] := Module[{a = Sort[Map[Sort, y]], b, c = {}, d, p = Length[a]},**
b = Map[{} &, Range[1, p]];
Do[Map[If[IntervalMemberQ1[a[[j]], #], AppendTo[b[[j]], #], 6] &, x], {j, 1, p}];
b = Map[Sort, b]; d = Length[b];
If[{z} != {} && NullQ[z], Do[AppendTo[c, Map[{#, Count[b[[j]], #]} &, b[[j]]]], {j, 1, d}];
z = Map[DeleteDuplicates, c], 6]; b]
In[4179]:= **GroupSort[RandomInteger[{10, 40}, 30], {{10, 20}, {20, 30}, {30, 40}}]**
Out[4179]= {{11, 12, 13, 14, 15, 17, 17, 17, 17, 17, 18, 18, 18, 19}, {20, 22, 24, 24, 26, 26, 26, 27, 28}, {30, 32, 34, 35, 36, 37, 39}}
In[4180]:= **GroupSort[RandomInteger[{10, 40}, 30], {{10, 20}, {20, 30}, {30, 40}}, h]; h**
Out[4180]= {{{11, 2}, {12, 1}, {13, 1}, {14, 1}, {15, 4}, {17, 1}, {18, 3}}, {{20, 3}, {21, 2}, {23, 1}, {24, 1}, {25, 2}, {26, 2}, {28, 1}}, {{33, 1}, {35, 1}, {38, 1}, {39, 1}}}

The following function provides sorting of elements of the list on the basis of multiplicity of occurrences of its elements. The function call **SortMultiple[x, y]** returns the result of sorting of the *x* list on the basis of multiplicities of its elements according to the ordering *y* function {*Greater,LessEqual,LessThan*}; in case of absence of *y* function by default the sorting according to increase of *multiplicities* of elements is done, i.e. *y=Less*. In turn, the sublists with identical multiplicities of the returned list are sorted according to increase of their elements. The next fragment represents source code of the **SortMultiple** function with examples of its use.

In[4210]:= **SortMultiple[x_ /; ListQ[x], y___] := Flatten[Map[Drop1[#, EvenQ[#] &] &, Map[Flatten, Sort[Gather[Map[{#, Count[x, #]} &, Sort[x]], #1[[2]] == #2[[2]] &], If[{y} != {} && MemberQ[{Greater, LessEqual, LessThan}, y], y[#1[[1]][[2]], #2[[1]][[2]]] &, #1[[1]][[2]] < #2[[1]][[2]] &]]]]**
In[4211]:= **SortMultiple[{5, 3, 5, 2, 2, 6, 7, 5, 4, 3, 7, 7, 8, 5, 1, 5, 4}, Greater]**
Out[4211]= {5, 5, 5, 5, 5, 7, 7, 7, 2, 2, 3, 3, 4, 4, 1, 6, 8}
In[4212]:= **SortMultiple[{5, 3, 5, 2, 2, 6, 7, 5, 4, 3, 7, 7, 8, 5, 1, 5, 4}]**
Out[4212]= {1, 6, 8, 2, 2, 3, 3, 4, 4, 7, 7, 7, 5, 5, 5, 5, 5}
In[4213]:= **SortMultiple[{a, b, a, c, a, b, d, e, c, c, f, a}, Greater]**
Out[4213]= {a, a, a, a, c, c, c, b, b, d, e, f}
In[4214]:= **SortMultiple[{a, b, a, c, a, b, d, e, c, c, f, a}]**
Out[4214]= {d, e, f, b, b, c, c, c, a, a, a, a}

The previous function uses the **Drop1** function which is an useful enough version of system **Drop** function. The function call **Drop1[x, y]** returns the result of dropping of elements of *x* list that are defined by their *y* positions – the list of positions or the list of positions selected on the basis of a pure function. The following fragment represents source code of the **Drop1** function with examples of its application.

In[4220]:= **Drop1[x_ /; ListQ[x], y_ /; PosIntListQ[y] || PureFuncQ[y]]** :=
If[ListQ[y], Delete[x, Map[List, Complement[y, Complement[y, Range[1, Length[x]]]]]],
Delete[x, Map[List, Select[Range[1, Length[x]], y]]]]

In[4221]:= **Drop1[{a, b, c, d, e, f, h, m, n, p, t}, {1, 3, 5, 7, 9}]**
Out[4221]= {b, d, f, m, p, t}

In[4222]:= **Drop1[{a, b, c, d, e, f, h, m, n, p, t}, {1, 3, 5, 7, 9, 20, 28}]**
Out[4222]= {b, d, f, m, p, t}

In[4223]:= **Drop1[{a, b, c, d, e, f, h, m, n, p, t}, EvenQ[#] &]**
Out[4223]= {a, c, e, h, n, t}

The next function is the natural consequence of the previous function, being a rather useful version of the standard **Delete** function. The function call **Delete1[x, y]** returns the result of deleting of elements of a *x* list which are defined by their *y* positions – the list of positions or the list of positions selected on the basis of a pure function. The fragment below represents source code of the **Delete1** function with examples of its application.

In[4166]:= **Delete1[x_ /; ListQ[x], y_ /; PosIntListQ[y] || PureFuncQ[y]]** :=
If[ListQ[y], Delete[x, Map[List, Complement[y, Complement[y, Range[1, Length[x]]]]]],
Delete[x, Map[List, Select[Range[1, Length[x]], y]]]]

In[4167]:= **Delete1[{a, b, c, d, w, e, r, t, y, u, p, x, v, y, z}, {3, 8, 9, 12, 42}]**
Out[4167]= {a, b, d, w, e, r, u, p, v, y, z}

In[4168]:= **Delete1[{a, b, c, d, w, e, r, t, y, u, p, x, v, y, z}, OddQ[#] &]**
Out[4168]= {b, d, e, t, u, x, y}

In the context of the previous two tools a version of the standard **ReplacePart** function is of a certain interest. The call **ReplacePart1[x, y, z]** returns the result of replacing of elements of *x* list which are determined by their *y* positions – the list of positions or the list of positions selected on the basis of a pure function onto the new elements defined by a *z* list. Between lists *y* and *z* one-to-one correspondence within the framework of the first **Min[{Length[y], Length[z]}]** elements is established. The following fragment represents source code of the **ReplacePart1** function with examples of its application. Additionally, the fragment below represents the function **ReplacePart1** programmed as the module.

In[4180]:= **ReplacePart1[x_ /; ListQ[x], y_ /; PosIntListQ[y] || PureFuncQ[y],
z_ /; ListQ[z]]**:=
If[ListQ[y], ReplacePart[x, Map[Rule[y[[#]], z[[#]]] &, Range[1, Min[Map[Length,
{y, z}]]]]], ReplacePart[x, Map[Rule[Select[Range[1, Length[x]], y][[#]], z[[#]]] &,
Range[1, Min[Map[Length, {Select[Range[1, Length[x]], y], z}]]]]]]

In[4181]:= **ReplacePart1[x_ /; ListQ[x], y_ /; PosIntListQ[y] || PureFuncQ[y],
z_ /; ListQ[z]] := Module[{a = Length[x]},
If[ListQ[y], ReplacePart[x, Map[Rule[y[[#]], z[[#]]] &, Range[1, Min[Length[y],
Length[z]]]]],
ReplacePart[x, Map[Rule[Select[Range[1, a], y][[#]], z[[#]]] &, Range[1, Min[Map[Length,
{Select[Range[1, a], y], z}]]]]]]]**

In[4182]:= **ReplacePart1[{a, b, c, d, e, f, g, h}, {2, 5, 8}, {xxx, yyy, zzz, ggg}]**
Out[4182]= {a, xxx, c, d, yyy, f, g, zzz}

In[4183]:= ReplacePart1[{a, b, c, d, e, f, g, h}, OddQ[#] &, {xxx, yyy, zzz, ggg}]
Out[4183]= {xxx, b, yyy, d, zzz, f, ggg, h}

At last, the call **CountsList[w]** of simple and useful function returns the list of *ListList* type; the first element of its two–element sublists define an element of *w* list whereas the second element define its multiplicity. In addition, the call **CountsList[w, y]**, if the second optional *y* argument – *an arbitrary expression* – exists, returns the result of reducing of **CountsList[w]** to the simple list as that the source code with examples of its application illustrate.

In[4539]:= CountsList[w_ /; ListQ[w], y___] :=
If[{y} != {}, ReduceLists, And][Map[{#, Count[w, #]} &, DeleteDuplicates[w]]]

In[4540]:= x = {a, b, c, a, a, {a, b}, c, c, {a, b}}; CountsList[x]
Out[4540]= {{a, 3}, {b, 1}, {c, 3}, {{a, b}, 2}}

In[4541]:= CountsList[{a, a, a, a, a, a, a, a, a, a}, 75]
Out[4541]= {a, 10}

In[4542]:= CountsList[{a, a, a, a, a, a, a, a, a, a}]
Out[4542]= {{a, 10}}

In addition, it is recommended to pay attention to an useful reception used at programming of the function.

Of certain problems of the functional processing of lists the following procedure arises. The procedure call **FuncOnLists[w, y]** returns the result of aplllying of a module, a function or a block *w* to each element of list obtained by means of *riffling (analogously to the **Riffle** function but relative to indefinite number of lists)* of the nonempty lists of an *y* tuple. In addition, if *w* is different from a module, a function or a block the call **FuncOnLists[w, y]** returns the result of riffling of the nonempty lists of an *y* tuple, to some extent expanding the standard **Riffle** function. The following fragment presents source code of the **FuncOnLists** procedure with examples of its application.

In[4637]:= FuncOnLists[w_, y__ /; And1[Map[ListQ[#] && # != {} &, {y}]]] :=
Module[{a, b = Min[Map[Length[#] &, {y}]]}, a = Map[Part[{y}, All, #] &, Range[1, b]];
If[BlockFuncModQ[w], b = Arity[w]; Map[w @@ Quiet[Check[#[[1 ;; b]], #]] &, a], a]]

In[4638]:= G[x_, y_, z_, t_] := x + y + z + t; Gs[x_, y_] := x + y
In[4639]:= FuncOnLists[G, {a, b, c, d}, {m, n, p, g, h}, {d, k, w, s, f, s}, {x, y, z, u}]
Out[4639]= {a + d + m + x, b + k + n + y, c + p + w + z, d + g + s + u}
In[4640]:= FuncOnLists[S, {a, b, c, d}, {m, n, p, g, h}, {d, k, w, s, f, s}, {x, y, z, u}]
Out[4640]= {{a, m, d, x}, {b, n, k, y}, {c, p, w, z}, {d, g, s, u}}
In[4641]:= FuncOnLists[G, {a, b, c, d}]
Out[4641]= {G[a], G[b], G[c], G[d]}
In[4642]:= FuncOnLists[S, {a, b, c, d}]
Out[4642]= {{a}, {b}, {c}, {d}}
In[4643]:= FuncOnLists[Gs, {a, b, c, d}]
Out[4643]= {Gs[a], Gs[b], Gs[c], Gs[d]}

A rather simple procedure provides increase in the external nesting level of the list on the given number. The procedure call **ExpListLevel[x, n]** returns the initial list *x* with extension of its external level on a value *n*. If an integer number *n* <= 0, then the procedure call returns the initial *x* list. The next fragment presents source code of the **ExpListLevel** procedure with an example of its application.

In[4685]:= **ExpListLevel[x_ /; ListQ[x], n_ /; IntegerQ[n]] :=**
Module[{a = x, t = 1}, While[t <= n, a = List[a]; t++]; a]

In[4686]:= **ExpListLevel[{a, b, {{c}}, d}, 5]**
Out[4686]= {{{{{{{a, b, {{c}}, d}}}}}}}
In[4687]:= **ExpListLevel[{}, 8]**
Out[4687]= {{{{{{{{{}}}}}}}}}
In[4688]:= **ExpListLevel[{a, b, {{c}}, d}, 0]**
Out[4688]= {a, b, {{c}}, d}

The next procedure is intended for selection of elements of the nested lists whose elements – sublists with arbitrary *external* nesting levels. The procedure call **SelectNestList[x, y]** returns the nested list of the same structure as an initial *x* list on condition of saving in it of values meeting a testing pure function *y*. The next fragment presents source code of the procedure with an example of its application.

In[4770]:= **SelectNestList[x_ /; NestListQ[x], y_ /; PureFuncQ[y]] :=**
Module[{a = Map[ReduceLevelsList[#] &, x], b, c, n = 1}, c = Map[#[[1]] &, a];
a = Map[#[[2]] &, a]; b = Map[Select[Select[#, # == # &], y] &, c];
Map[ExpListLevel[#, a[[n++]] – 1] &, b]]

In[4771]:= gs = {{{1, 2, 6, 3}}, {{4, 5, 6}}, {4, 7, 9}, {{{8}}}, {{7, 8, 9}}, {{11, 75}}};
In[4772]:= **SelectNestList[gs, PrimeQ[#] &]**
Out[4772]= {{{2, 3}}, {{5}}, {7}, {{{}}}, {{7}}, {{11}}}
In[4773]:= y = {{{1, 2, 3}}, {{{4, 5, 6, m, n}}}, {{{{7, 8, 9, a + b}}}}, {{{11, m*n}}}};
In[4774]:= **SelectNestList[y, If[# === #, Nothing, True] &]**
Out[4774]= {{{}}, {{{}}}, {{{{}}}}, {{{}}}}

In particular, the last example of the previous fragment illustrates a possibility of obtaining empty structure of an initial list on the basis of the **SelectNestList** procedure. The procedure has also other useful appendices in list processing problems.

At last, the following simple procedure is a some kind of generalization of the **Map** function to lists of arbitrary structure. The procedure call **MapList[f, x]** returns the result of applying of a symbol, a block, a function, a module or a pure function *f (except f symbol all remaining admissible objects shall have arity 1)* to each element of a *x* list with maintaining its structure. It is supposed that sublists of the list *x* have the unary nesting levels, otherwise the procedure call is returned unevaluated. The next fragment presents source code of the procedure with examples of its application.

In[4603]:= **MapList[f_ /; SymbolQ[f] || BlockFuncModQ[f] || PureFuncQ[f], x_ /; ListQ[x] &&**
And1[Map[Length[DeleteDuplicates[LevelsOfList[#]]] == 1 &, x]]] :=
Module[{g}, SetAttributes[g, Listable]; g[t_] := (f) @@ {t}; Map[g, x]]

In[4604]:= F[g_] := g^3; **MapList[F, {{a, b, c}, {{m, n}}, {}, {{{h, p}}}}]**
Out[4604]= {{a^3, b^3, c^3}, {{m^3, n^3}}, {}, {{{h^3, p^3}}}}
In[4605]:= s[g_] := If[IntegerQ[g], g^3, Nothing]; **MapList[s, {{a, 2, c}, {{m, 3}}, {}, {{{4, 5}}}}]**
Out[4605]= {{8}, {{27}}, {}, {{{64, 125}}}}

In[4606]:= F[g_] := If[IntegerQ[g], g^3, Nothing]; MapList[F, {a, 2, c, m, 3, 4, 5}]
Out[4606]= {8, 27, 64, 125}
In[4607]:= MapList[G, {{a, 2, c}, {{m, 3}}, {}, {{{4, 5}}}}]
Out[4607]= {{G[a], G[2], G[c]}, {{G[m], G[3]}}, {}, {{{G[4], G[5]}}}}
In[4608]:= MapList[If[IntegerQ[#], Nothing, #] &, {{a, 2, c}, {{m, 3}}, {}, {{{4, b, 5, c}}}}]
Out[4608]= {{a, c}, {{m}}, {}, {{{b, c}}}}

The following function is a rather useful version of the **MapList** procedure. The function call **MapList1**[*f, x*] returns the result of applying of a symbol, a block, a function or a module *f* (*except f symbol all remaining admissible objects shall have arity 1*) to each element of *x* list with full maintaining its structure. It must be kept in mind that unlike the **MapList** procedure the function does not admit a pure function as the *first* actual argument because of impossibility of direct ascribing to it of attributes, in particular, of the *Listable* attribute. The next fragment represents source code of the **MapList1** function with examples of its application.

In[4670]:= MapList1[f_ /; SymbolQ[f] || BlockFuncModQ[f], x_ List] :=
If[MemberQ[Attributes[f], Listable], (f) @@ {x}, {SetAttributes[f, Listable], (f) @@ {x},
ClearAttributes[f, Listable]}[[If[MemberQ[Attributes[f], Listable], 1 ;; -1, 2]]]

In[4672]:= SetAttributes[G, Listable]; Map[Attributes, {S, G}]
Out[4672]= {{}, {Listable}}
In[4673]:= MapList1[S, {a, {b}, {{c, d}}, {{{1, 2, 3}}}}]
Out[4673]= {S[a], {S[b]}, {{S[c], S[d]}}, {{{S[1], S[2], S[3]}}}}
In[4674]:= MapList1[G, {a, {b}, {{c, d}}, {{{1, 2, 3}}}}]
Out[4674]= {G[a], {G[b]}, {{G[c], G[d]}}, {{{G[1], G[2], G[3]}}}}
In[4675]:= Map[Attributes, {S, G}]
Out[4675]= {{}, {Listable}}
In[4676]:= MapList1[Head, {a, {b, a + b, {g^{t + h}}}, {{c, 5, d}}, {{{1, m/n, 3}}}}]
Out[4676]= {Symbol, {Symbol, Plus, {{Power}}}, {{Symbol, Integer, Symbol}},
{{{Integer, Times, Integer}}}}
In[4677]:= MapList1[SymbolQ, {a, {b, a + b, {g^{t + h}}}, {{c, 5, d}}, {{{1, m/n, 3}}}}]
Out[4677]= {True, {True, False, {{False}}}, {{True, False, True}}, {{{False, False, False}}}}
In[4593]:= T[t_] := If[SymbolQ[t], Nothing, G @@ {t}]; MapList1[T, {a, {b, a + b, {g^{t + h}}},
{{c, 5, d}}, {{{1, m/n, 3}}}}]
Out[4593]= {{G[a + b], {{G[g^(h + t)]}}}, {{G[5]}}, {{{G[1], G[m/n], G[3]}}}}

At last, the call **MapList2**[*f, x*] of simple function, that unlike **MapList1** is based on function **Map**, returns the result of applying of a symbol, a block, a function (*including pure function*), a module *f* (*except a f symbol all remaining admissible objects shall have arity 1*) to each element with head different from *Symbol* of a *x* list with full maintaining its structure. The following fragment represents source code of the **MapList2** function with examples of its application.

In[4604]:= MapList2[f_ /; SymbolQ[f] || BlockFuncModQ[f] || PureFuncQ[f], x_List] :=
{SetAttributes[Map, Listable], Map[f, x], ClearAttributes[Map, Listable]}[[2]]

In[4605]:= MapList2[G, {ab, b*c, c, d + h, e^2 + m^g}]
Out[4605]= {ab, G[b]*G[c], c, G[d] + G[h], G[e^2] + G[m^g]}
In[4606]:= Map[G, {ab, b*c, c, d + h, e^2 + m^g}]
Out[4606]= {G[ab], G[b c], G[c], G[d + h], G[e^2 + m^g]}

In[4607]:= **MapList2[If[! SameQ[Head[#], Symbol], #^3, s[#]] &, {a, b*c, c, d+h, e^2+m^g}]**
Out[4607]= {a, s[b]*s[c], c, s[d] + s[h], e^6 + m^(3*g)}

In addition, the **MapList2** function admits a lot of interesting enough modifications. So, the next examples illustrate certain differences between **Map**, **MapList**, **Maplist1** and **Maplist2**.

In[4579]:= **Map[G, {ab, b*c, {a, b}, c, d + h, {{{c, d}}}, e^2 + m^g}]**
Out[4579]= {G[ab], G[b*c], G[{a, b}], G[c], G[d + h], G[{{{c, d}}}], G[e^2 + m^g]}
In[4580]:= **MapList[G, {ab, b*c, {a, b}, c, d + h, {{{c, d}}}, e^2 + m^g}]**
Out[4580]= {G[ab], G[b*c], {G[a], G[b]}, G[c], G[d + h], {{{G[c], G[d]}}}, G[e^2 + m^g]}
In[4581]:= **MapList1[G, {ab, b*c, {a, b}, c, d + h, {{{c, d}}}, e^2 + m^g}]**
Out[4581]= {G[ab], G[b*c], {G[a], G[b]}, G[c], G[d + h], {{{G[c], G[d]}}}, G[e^2 + m^g]}
In[4582]:= **MapList2[G, {ab, b*c, {a, b}, c, d + h, {{{c, d}}}, e^2 + m^g}]**
Out[4582]= {ab, G[b]*G[c], {a, b}, c, G[d] + G[h], {{{c, d}}}, G[e^2] + G[m^g]}

A number of the additional means expanding the *Mathematica*, in particular, for effective programming of problems of manipulation with the list structures of various organization is presented in the given present chapter. These and other our tools of the given orientation are presented a quite in details in [28-33,48,50]. In general, the *Mathematica* provides the mass of useful and effective means of processing, except already the mentioned, of the list structures and objects that are based on structures of the given type. Being additional tools for work with lists – *basic structures* in the *Mathematica* – these means are rather useful in a number of applications of various purpose. Meanwhile, other means that can be used quite successfully at processing lists of various format are also represented in the book. A number of means were already considered, while others will be considered below along with means that are directly not associated with lists, but quite accepted for work with separate formats of the lists. Many means presented here and below, arose in the process of programming a variety of applications as tools wearing a rather mass character. Some of them use *techniques* which are rather useful in the practical programming in the *Mathematica*. In particular, the above relates to a computer study of the *Cellular Automata (CA; Homogeneous Structures; HS)*.

4.1. Additional tools for computer research of cellular automata

In spite of such extremely simple concept of the classical cellular automata *(CA)*, they have, generally speaking, a complex enough dynamics. In very many cases theoretical research of their dynamics collides with essential enough difficulties. Therefore, computer simulation of these structures that in the empirical way allows to research their dynamics is a powerful enough tool. For this reason this question is quite natural for considering within the present chapter, considering the fact that *cellular automata* at the formal level present the dynamical systems of highly parallel substitutions. The detailed enough discussion of the problem of computer simulation of the cellular automata *(CA)* can be found in our publications [50,72].

At present, the problem of computer modeling of the **CA** is solved at 2 levels: *(1)* software modelling dynamics on computing systems of traditional architecture, and *(2)* simulation on the hardware architecture that as much as possible corresponds to **CA** concept; so–called **CA**–oriented architecture of computing systems. Thus, computer simulation of **CA** models plays a rather essential part at theoretical researches of their dynamics, in the same time it is even more important at practical realizations of **CA** models of various processes. At present time, a whole series of rather interesting systems of software and hardware for giving help to researchers of different types of *CA* models has been developed; their characteristics can be found in [50,72]. In our works many programs in various program systems for different computer platforms had been represented. In particular, tools of the *Mathematica* system support algebraic substitutions rules that allow to easily model the local transition functions of the classical *1*-dimension *CA*. In this context many interesting programs for simulation of *CA* models in the *Mathematica* system can be found, for example, in references to the books [2,50,72]. On the basis of computer modelling a whole series of rather interesting theoretical results on the theory of classical *CA* models and their use in the fields such as mathematics, computer sciences, developmental biology, etc. had been received.

By way of illustration a number of the procedures providing the computer research of some aspects of dynamics of the classical *1-CA* in *Mathematica* is presented below. In particular, the procedure call **CFsequences**[*Co, A, f, n*] prints the sequence of configurations generated by a *1-CA* with alphabet of internal states $A = \{0, 1, 2, 3, ..., p\}$ ($p = 1..9$) and local transition function *f* from a finite *Co* configuration given in the string format for *n* steps of the given automaton.

In[3345]:= CFsequences[C_ /; StringQ[C] && C != "", A_ /; ListQ[A] &&
MemberQ[Map[Range[0, #] &, Range[9]], A], Ltf_ /; ListQ[Ltf] &&
AllTrue[Map[RuleQ[#] &, Ltf], TrueQ] || FunctionQ[Ltf], n_ /; IntegerQ[n] && n >= 0]:=
Module[{a = StringTrim2[C, "0", 3], b, c, t = {}, t1 = {}, t2 = {}, t3 = {}, f, p = n},
If[! MemberQ3[Map[ToString, A], Characters[C]], Print["Initial configuration <"<> C <>
"> is incorrect"]; $Failed, If[FunctionQ[Ltf], b = Arity[Ltf], Map[{{AppendTo[t,
StringQ[#[[1]]]], AppendTo[t1, StringLength[#[[1]]]]}, {AppendTo[t2, StringQ[#[[2]]]],
AppendTo[t3, StringLength[#[[2]]]]}} &, Ltf]; b = Map[DeleteDuplicates[#] &, {t, t1, t2, t3}];
If[! (MemberQ3[{True}, {b[[1]], b[[3]]}] && Map[Length, {b[[2]], b[[4]]}] == {1, 1} &&
Length[t1] == Length[A]^(b = b[[2]][[1]])), Print["Local transition function is incorrect"];
Return[$Failed], f=Map[ToExpression[Characters[#[[1]]]] -> ToExpression[#[[2]]] &, Ltf]]];
c = StringMultiple2["0", b]; Print[a]; While[p > 0, p--; a = c <> a <> c;
a = Partition[ToExpression[Characters[a]], b, 1];
a = If[FunctionQ[Ltf], Map[Ltf @@ # &, a], ReplaceAll[a, f]];
a = StringJoin[Map[ToString, a]]; Print[StringTrim2[a, "0", 3]]];]]

In[3346]:= CFsequences["100111100001", {0, 1}, {"00" -> "0", "01" -> "1", "10" -> "1",
"11" -> "0"}, 10]
"100111100001"
"1101000100011"
"10111001100101"
"111001010101111"
"1001011111110001"
"11011100000010011"
"101100100000110101"
"1110101100001011111"
"10011110100011100001"
"110100011100100100011"
"1011100100101101100101"
In[3347]:= Ltf1[x_, y_, z_] := Mod[x + y + z, 5]

In[3348]:= CFsequences["4012013121020302401400024", Range[0, 4], Ltf1, 10]
"4012013121020302401400024"
"4403334014332030110004 2114"
"4332140200303003422104124104"
"4203120122331333243030022 20044"
"4110413330232224344 2133241424334"
"4012003241002213411021234242040024"
"4403323042012401331233014403 11442114"
"43321330211332104221131404324014024104"
"4203112103402313013040030324410001120044"
"4110404434221012444424433104040 10124324334"
"40120433114303232022000102404340123244440024"
In[3349]:= CFsequences["0001201121020032010020", {0, 1, 2}, Ltf1, 10]
"Initial configuration <0001201121020032010020> is incorrect"
Out[3349]= $Failed
In[3350]:= CFsequences["100111100001", {0, 1}, {"00" -> "0", "10" -> "1"}, 10]
"Local transition function is incorrect"
Out[3350]= $Failed

At the same time, a function of the kind $F[x, y, z, ..., t] := x*$, and the list of substitutions of the kind "$xyz ... t$" -> "$x*$" $\{x, x*, y, z, ..., t\} \in A$ can act as the 3rd *F* argument. The procedure processes basic mistakes arisen at encoding an initial *Co* configuration, an *A* alphabet and/or a local transition function *F*, returning $*Failed* with output of strings with the corresponding messages. The fragment above presents source code of the **CFsequences** procedure with the typical examples of its application.

The following procedure is a rather useful modification of the **CFsequences** procedure. The procedure call **CFsequences1[*Co*, *A*, *f*, *n*]** prints the sequence of configurations generated by a *1–CA* with alphabet of states $A = \{0, 1, ..., p\}$ ($p = 1..9$), local transition function *f* from a *Co* finite configuration given in numeric or string format for *n* steps of the model.

The procedure *arguments* are analogous to the case of the **CFsequences** procedure with that difference if a *Co* configuration is encoded in the string format, the procedure call returns the sequence of configurations if *Co* configuration is encoded in the numberic format, the procedure call returns numerical sequence that is equivalent to sequence of configurations presented numerically on the base *10*. The following fragment represents source code of the **CFsequences1** procedure with typical examples of its application.

In[3650]:= CFsequences1[Co_ /; StringQ[Co] && Co != "" || IntegerQ[Co] && Co != 0,
A_ /; ListQ[A] && MemberQ[Map[Range[0, #] &, Range[9]], A], f_ /; ListQ[f] &&
AllTrue[Map[RuleQ[#] &, f], TrueQ] || FunctionQ[f], n_ /; IntegerQ[n] && n >= 0] :=
Module[{a = StringTrim2[ToString[Co], "0", 3], b, c, d, t1 = {}, t2 = {}, t3 = {}, t4 = {}, tf, p = n},
If[! MemberQ3[Map[ToString, A], Characters[a]] ||
! MemberQ3[A, IntegerDigits[ToExpression[Co]]], Print["Initial configuration <" <>
ToString[Co] <> "> is incorrect"];
$Failed, If[FunctionQ[f], b = Arity[f], Map[{{AppendTo[t1, StringQ[#[[1]]]],
AppendTo[t2, StringLength[#[[1]]]]}, {AppendTo[t3, StringQ[#[[2]]]],

AppendTo[t4, StringLength[#[[2]]]]} &, f]; b = Map[DeleteDuplicates[#] &, {t1, t2, t3, t4}];
If[! (MemberQ3[{True}, {b[[1]], b[[3]]}] && Map[Length, {b[[2]], b[[4]]}] == {1, 1} &&
Length[t2] == Length[A]^(b = b[[2]][[1]])), Print["Local transition function is incorrect"];
Return[$Failed], tf = Map[ToExpression[Characters[#[[1]]]] -> ToExpression[#[[2]]] &, f]]];
c = StringMultiple2["0", b]; Print[Co];
If[IntegerQ[Co], d[a_] := Print[FromDigits[StringTrim2[a, "0", 3], 2]],
d[a_] := Print[StringTrim2[a, "0", 3]]]; While[p > 0, p--; a = c <> a <> c;
a = Partition[ToExpression[Characters[a]], b, 1];
a = If[FunctionQ[f], Map[f @@ # &, a], ReplaceAll[a, tf]];
a = StringJoin[Map[ToString, a]]; d[a]];]]

In[3651]:= CFsequences1["11", {0, 1}, {"000" -> "0", "001" -> "1", "010" -> "1", "011" -> "0",
"100" -> "1", "101" -> "0", "110" -> "0", "111" -> "1"}, 5]
"11"
1001
111111
10111101
1100110011
100110011001

In[3652]:= CFsequences1[11, {0, 1}, {"000" -> "0", "001" -> "1", "010" -> "1", "011" -> "0",
"100" -> "1", "101" -> "0", "110" -> "0", "111" -> "1"}, 5]
11
9
63
189
819
2457

Note, modification of a block, function or module operatively *(for the required time)* can be performed by means of the **CallTemp** procedure. This procedure is intended for temporal modification of a block, function or module activated in the current session. The procedure call **CallTemp[*f*]** returns nothing, uploading into the current session the "*f.m*" datafile with definition of a *f* object *(function, block, module)* which earlier had been saved in the directory *"Directory[]"*; in case of absence of this file $*Failed* returns with output of the corresponding message. Whereas the procedure call **CallTemp[*f, r*]** also returns nothing, activating in the current session a modification of a *f* object by means of the replacement of the occurrence into its definition of a *X* construction onto an *Y* construction where both components are represented in the string format by the argument *r* = {*X, Y*}. At the same time, the previous definition the *f* object is saved in the "*f.m*" datafile located in the above directory. After that, all calls of the *f* object will belong to its new definition. At that, the old object definition *f* is recovered in the current session by means of the procedure call **CallTemp[*f*]**. The fragment below represents source code of the procedure with examples of its application concerning the above **CFsequences** procedure.

In[3942]:= CallTemp[f_ /; BlockFuncModQ[f], r_: {}] := Module[{a = ToString[f] <> ".m", b},
If[r === {}, Clear[f]; Get[a]; DeleteFile[a], DumpSave[a, f];

ToExpression[StringReplace[PureDefinition[f], Rule[r[[1]], r[[2]]]]]]]

In[3943]:= CFsequences["11", {0, 1}, {"000" -> "0", "001" -> "1", "010" -> "0", "011" -> "1", "100" -> "1", "101" -> "0", "110" -> "0", "111" -> "1"}, 5]
"11"
"1101"
"110001"
"11010101"
"1100000001"
"110100000101"

In[3944]:= CallTemp[CFsequences, {"Print[StringTrim2[a, \"0\", 3]]", "Print[FromDigits[ToExpression[Characters[StringTrim2[a, \"0\", 3]]], 2]]"}]   (1)

In[3945]:= CFsequences["11", {0, 1}, {"000" -> "0", "001" -> "1", "010" -> "0", "011" -> "1", "100" -> "1", "101" -> "0", "110" -> "0", "111" -> "1"}, 5]
"11"
13
49
213
769
3333

In[3946]:= CallTemp[CFsequences]

In[3947]:= CFsequences["11", {0, 1}, {"000" -> "0", "001" -> "1", "010" -> "0", "011" -> "1", "100" -> "1", "101" -> "0", "110" -> "0", "111" -> "1"}, 5]
"11"
"1101"
"110001"
"11010101"
"1100000001"
"110100000101"

In[3948]:= CallTemp[CFsequences, {"Print[StringTrim2[a, \"0\", 3]]", "t = FromDigits[ToExpression[Characters[StringTrim2[a, \"0\", 3]]], 2]; If[PrimeQ[t], Print[{n - p, t}], Null]"}]   (2)

In[3949]:= CFsequences["11", {0, 1}, {"000" -> "0", "001" -> "1", "010" -> "0", "011" -> "1", "100" -> "1", "101" -> "0", "110" -> "0", "111" -> "1"}, 2016]
"11"
{1, 13}
{4, 769}
{850, 1726111023767246351758350972380580814767846 0117009}

It is supposed that the possibility of modification of a *w* object is already provided at a stage of its designing and programming by means of including in its definition of certain unique replaceable constructions. In particular, two examples of use of the **CallTemp** procedure in the above fragment concerning the **CFsequence** procedure allow to research sequences of the integral and prime numbers *(examples 1 and 2 respectively; number of a CA step and a prime number)* that are generated by *1*-dimensional binary *CA* models.

Indeed, the technology represented above on the basis of modifications of the **CFsequence** procedure allows to obtain a number of rather interesting properties of *numeric* sequences, generated by *1*-dimensional binary *CA* models. So, the computer analysis by means of the above software allows to formulate rather interesting assumptions, namely: *1*-*dimensional binary CA model with the local transition function* **Ltf[x_, y_, w_] := Mod[$x + y + w$, 2]** *from a configuration Co = "111...111"* (**StringLength[Co] = 2k; k = 1, 2, 3, ...**) *generates the numerical sequence which not contains prime numbers*; *whereas from a configuration different from a Co the above binary CA model generates the numerical sequence that contains only finite number of prime numbers; more precisely, since some step that depends on initial Co configuration, such binary CA model doesn't generate prime numbers. Additionally, the 1-dimensional binary CA with the local transition function* **Ltf[x_, y_] := Mod[$x + y$, 2]** *from configurations of the form Co = "100...001"* (**StringLength[Co] >= 14**) *generates numerical sequences that not contain prime numbers. While the 1-dimensional binary CA model with local transition function* **Ltf[0, 0, 0] = 0, Ltf[0, 0, 1] = 1**, *and* **Ltf[x_, y_, w_] := Mod[$x + y + w + 1$, 2]** *otherwise, generates the infinite sequence of prime numbers from the initial Co = "11" configuration*. In the same time, there are also a number of other results interesting enough in this direction [2,23,31-33,72,73] *(see also our books on the CA problematics in the collection* [50]).

So, the procedure call **CFPrimeDensity[Co, A, f, n]** prints the sequence of two-element lists whose the first element defines the number of step of *1-CA*, the second element defines the density of primes on this interval; the arguments of this procedure fully complies with the formal arguments of the **CFsequences** procedure. Fragment below represents source code of the **CFPrimeDensity** procedure with an example of its use for exploration of *primes* density, generated by means of a *1-CA*.

```
In[4433]:= CFPrimeDensity[Co_ /; StringQ[Co] && Co != "" || IntegerQ[Co] && Co != 0,
A_ /; ListQ[A] && MemberQ[Map[Range[0, #] &, Range[9]], A], f_ /; ListQ[f] &&
AllTrue[Map[RuleQ[#] &, f], TrueQ] || FunctionQ[f], n_ /; IntegerQ[n] && n >= 0] :=
Module[{a = StringTrim2[ToString[Co], "0", 3], b, d, d1 = 0, c,
t1 = {}, t2 = {}, t3 = {}, t4 = {}, tf, p = n},
If[! MemberQ3[Map[ToString, A], Characters[a]] || ! MemberQ3[A,
IntegerDigits[ToExpression[Co]]], Print["Initial configuration <" <> ToString[Co] <> ">"
is incorrect"]; $Failed, If[FunctionQ[f], b = Arity[f], Map[{{AppendTo[t1, StringQ[#[[1]]]],
AppendTo[t2, StringLength[#[[1]]]]}, {AppendTo[t3, StringQ[#[[2]]]],
AppendTo[t4, StringLength[#[[2]]]]}} &, f]; b = Map[DeleteDuplicates[#] &, {t1, t2, t3, t4}];
If[! (MemberQ3[{True}, {b[[1]], b[[3]]}] && Map[Length, {b[[2]], b[[4]]}] == {1, 1} &&
Length[t2] == Length[A]^(b = b[[2]][[1]])), Print["Local transition function is incorrect"];
Return[$Failed], tf = Map[ToExpression[Characters[#[[1]]]] -> ToExpression[#[[2]]] &, f]]];
c = StringMultiple2["0", b]; Print[Co]; While[p > 0, p--; a = c <> a <> c;
a = Partition[ToExpression[Characters[a]], b, 1];
a = If[FunctionQ[f], Map[f @@ # &, a], ReplaceAll[a, tf]];
a = StringJoin[Map[ToString, a]]; d = FromDigits[StringTrim2[a, "0", 3], Length[A]];
If[PrimeQ[d], d1++; Print[{n - p, N[d1/(n - p)]}], Null]];]]

In[4434]:= CFPrimeDensity[11, {0, 1}, {"000" -> "0", "001" -> "1", "010" -> "0", "011" -> "1",
"100" -> "0", "101" -> "1", "110" -> "1", "111" -> "0"}, 1000]
11
```

....
{306, 0.163399}

....
{518, 0.1139}

....
{995, 0.0934673}

The procedure below is of interest in the context of computer research of *1*-dimensional *CA* models along with special applications when processing the rules. The call **SubsRules[*x*, *y*, *n*]** returns the strings list that are formed by merge of substrings of *xj* of a *x* list where *xj* = **StringTake[*xj*, {–*n*, –1}]**, with the right parts of the *yk* rules of a *y* list for which the relations **StringTake[*xj*, {–*n*, –1}] == StringTake[*yk*, {1, *n*}]** take place. In addition, it is supposed that strings of the *x* list have identical length > *1*, and the left parts of rules of the *y* list also have identical length > *1* too. The next fragment presents source code of the **SubsRules** procedure along with an example of its application.

In[3334]:= SubsRules[x_ /; ListQ[x] && AllTrue[Map[StringQ[#] &, x], TrueQ],
y_ /; ListQ[y] && AllTrue[Map[RuleQ[#] &, y], TrueQ], n_ /; IntegerQ[n]] :=
Module[{a, b = {}, c = {}}, a = x;
Do[Do[If[StringTake[a[[k]], {–n, –1}] === StringTake[y[[j]][[1]], {1, n}],
AppendTo[b, a[[k]] <> y[[j]][[2]]], Null], {k, 1, Length[x]}, {j, 1, Length[y]}];
Do[AppendTo[c, StringLength[b[[k]]]], {k, 1, Length[b]}];
Select[b, StringLength[#] == Max[c] &]]

In[3335]:= x = {"abc", "cdf", "pkz", "hkz", "abc", "mnp"}; y = {"bcf" -> "p1", "bcg" -> "p2", "dff" -> "p3", "kzf" -> "p4"}; SubsRules[x, y, 2]

Out[3335]= {"abcp1", "abcp1", "abcp2", "abcp2", "cdfp3", "pkzp4", "hkzp4"}

A rather simple function along with independent interest represents a certain interest for software elaboration for a computer research of the classical *CA* models. The function call **CollectRules[*r*]** returns the nested list whose elements have format {*p1*, {*x1*,..., *xn*}},..., {*pk*, {*y1*, ..., *yg*}} where *pj* – the right parts of rules of a *r* list, and {*xj*, ...,*yt*} – the left parts which correspond to them {*j* = *1..n*, *t* = *1..g*}, collecting rules of the *r* list by the principle of equality of their right parts. Whereas the call **CollectRules[*r*, *w*]** where *w* – an arbitrary expression – returns the nested list whose elements have format {*p1*, {*x1*,...,*xn*}}, ..., {*pk*, {*y1*,...,*yg*}} where *pj* – the left parts of rules of *r* list, and {*xj*,...,*yt*} – the right parts that correspond to them {*j* = *1..n*, *t* = *1..g*}, collecting all rules of the *r* list by the principle of the equality of their left parts. The next fragment represents source code of the procedure with typical examples of its use.

In[3486]:= CollectRules[r_ /; ListQ[r] && AllTrue[Map[RuleQ[#] &, r], TrueQ], g_ : "r"] :=
Map[If[g == "r", {#[[1]][[2]], Map[#1[[1]] &, #]}, {#[[1]][[1]], Map[#1[[2]] &, #]}] &,
Gather[r, If[g == "r", #1[[2]] == #2[[2]] &, #1[[1]] == #2[[1]] &]]]

In[3487]:= r = {a -> x, b -> y, c -> x, h -> y, g -> y, s -> x}; CollectRules[r]
Out[3487]= {{x, {a, c, s}}, {y, {b, h, g}}}

In[3488]:= j = {a -> x, b -> x, a -> z, b -> v, b -> p, a -> g}; CollectRules[j, 6]
Out[3488]= {{a, {x, z, g}}, {b, {x, v, p}}}

The procedure call **ListToRules[*x*, *y*___]** returns the rules list generated from a *x* list, and vice versa if optional second *y* argument – an arbitrary expression – is specified. Along with

Software Etudes in the Mathematica

certain interest in case of list processing the given function appears as a rather useful means when programming of software for the computer research of the *CA* models. The following fragment represents source code of the **ListToRules** function with examples of its use.

In[3627]:= **ListToRules[x_ /; ListQ[x], y___] := Module[{a = {}},**
If[{y} == {}, Do[AppendTo[a, x[[k]] -> x[[k + 1]]], {k, 1, Length[x] - 1}],
a = Flatten[Map[{#[[1]], #[[2]]} &, x]]]; a]
In[3628]:= y1 = {a, b, c, d}; x1 = {a1 -> x, b1 -> y, c1 -> z, d1 -> h};
In[3629]:= **ListToRules[y1]**
Out[3629]= {a -> b, b -> c, c -> d}
In[3630]:= **ListToRules[x1, m]**
Out[3630]= {a1, x, b1, y, c1, z, d1, h}

The procedure call **RulesOrFunction[***f, x, g***]** returns nothing; in addition, if local transition function *x* of a *1-CA* with a *g* alphabet of internal states is given in the format of the list of parallel substitutions of the format *x1 ... xn -> x'1*, then *f* will define a function of type *f[x1, x2, x3, ..., xn] = x'1*, if *x* argument defines a function of the above format, then a *f* symbol will determine the list of parallel substitutions *(xj, x'1 ∈ g; n - the arity of a x function)*, and *f* - an *indefinite* symbol. The optional *g* argument has value {0, 1} by default, defining the alphabet of internal states of a *1-CA*. The following fragment represents source code of the procedure along with typical examples of its application.

In[3725]:= **RulesOrFunction[F_ /; SymbolQ[F], x_ /; ListQ[x] &&**
AllTrue[Map[RuleQ[#] &, x], TrueQ] || FunctionQ[x], A_: {0, 1}] :=
Module[{a, b}, If[ListQ[x], b = Map[F @@ (Characters[#[[1]]]) &, x];
Do[ToExpression[ToString1[b[[k]]] <> ":= " <> ToString1[x[[k]][[2]]]], {k, 1, Length[x]}],
a = Tuples[A, Arity[x]]; F = {};
Do[AppendTo[F, StringJoin[Map[ToString, a[[k]]]] -> ToString[x @@ a[[k]]]],
{k, 1, Length[a]}]]]
In[3726]:= R = {"00" -> "0", "01" -> "1", "10" -> "1", "11" -> "0"};
In[3727]:= **RulesOrFunction[G, R]**
In[3728]:= {G["0", "0"], G["0", "1"], G["1", "0"], G["1", "1"]}
Out[3728]= {"0", "1", "1", "0"}
In[3729]:= Clear[G]; G[x_, y_] := Mod[x + y, 2]; **RulesOrFunction[F, G]; Definition[F]**
Out[3729]= F = {"00" -> "0", "01" -> "1", "10" -> "1", "11" -> "0"}

The next procedure can be useful for computer research of *1-dimensional CA* models too. The procedure call **CfLtfCf1[***S, Ltf***]** returns the result of the simulation of generation in a single step of a configuration from an initial *S* configuration by means of the local transition function *(Ltf)* of a *1-dimensional CA* model. At the same time, local transition function can be given both by the list of parallel substitutions, and the function of the standard format. In addition, if *Ltf* is given in the format of standard function of one argument *(Ltf[x])*, the call demands the encoding of the third optional *k* argument - the length of left parts of parallel substitutions. The fragment below represents source code of the **CfLtfCf1** procedure with typical examples of its application.

In[3776]:= CfLtfCf1[S_ /; StringQ[S], Ltf_ /; ListQ[Ltf] && ListTrueQ[Ltf, RuleQ] || FunctionQ[Ltf], k_: 2] := Module[{n = If[FunctionQ[Ltf] && {k} != {} && IntegerQ[k] && k >= 2, k, StringLength[Ltf[[1]][[1]]]], a},
a = AddEndsToString[S, "0", "0", n, n]; a = Map[StringJoin, Partition[Characters[a], n, 1]];
StringJoin[If[FunctionQ[Ltf], Map[Ltf, a], ReplaceAll[a, Ltf]]]]

In[3777]:= ListTrueQ[x_, f_] := If[! ListQ[x] || ! SymbolQ[f], False, AllTrue[Map[f, x], TrueQ]]

In[3778]:= Ltf = {"00" -> "0", "01" -> "1", "10" -> "1", "11" -> "0"};
S = "11000101010110001110011";

In[3779]:= CfLtfCf1[S, Ltf]
Out[3779]= "010100111111110100100101010"

In[3780]:= Ltf[j_String] := ToString[Mod[ToExpression[StringTake[j, {1}]] + ToExpression[StringTake[j, {2}]], 2]]; CfLtfCf1[S, Ltf, 2]
Out[3780]= "010100111111110100100101010"

The procedure call **ToFunction[G, x]** returns nothing, providing conversion of the parallel substitutions given by a *x* list of rules into the function given by a *G* symbol. The following fragment represents source code of the **ToFunction** procedure with an example of its use.

In[3947]:= ToFunction[G_Symbol, x_ /; ListQ[x] && DeleteDuplicates[Map[RuleQ[#] &, x]] == {True}] := Module[{b},
b = Map[G @@ (Characters[#[[1]]]) &, x];
Do[ToExpression[ToString1[b[[k]]] <> ":= " <> ToString1[x[[k]][[2]]]], {k, 1, Length[x]}]]

In[3948]:= X = {"abc" -> "x", "bvc" -> "y", "kjh" -> "z", "agn" -> "p"}
Out[3948]= {"abc" -> "x", "bvc" -> "y", "kjh" -> "z", "agn" -> "p"}

In[3949]:= ToFunction[G, X]
In[3950]:= {G["a", "b", "c"], G["b", "v", "c"], G["k", "j", "h"], G["a", "g", "n"]}
Out[3950]= {"x", "y", "z", "p"}

Along with classical rules of parallel substitutions determining the local transition functions of *1*-dimensional *CA* models, of the format *x1x2x3 ... xn → x'1* use of the generalized local transition functions determined by parallel substitutions of the format *x1x2 ... xn → y1y2 ... ym (xj, x'1, yk∈A = {0, 1, ..., a-1}; j = 1..n; k = 1..m)* is of a certain interest; in addition, tuples <x1x2 ... xn>, <y1y2 ... ym> can have arbitrary length >= 1. The following function provides implementation of one step of a *1*-dimensional *CA* model with generalized local transition function. The call **GeneralizedLtf[r, S]** returns the result of simulation of generation in the single step of a configuration from an initial *S* configuration by means of a generalized local transition function *(r)* of *1*-dimensional *CA* model. Whereas the call **GeneralizedLtf[r, S, t]** returns the result of simulation of generation in single step of a configuration from an initial *S* configuration by means of the *generalized* local transition function *(r)* of *1*-dimensional *CA* model on condition that an initial configuration is parted on blocks with a *t* offset *(by default t = 1)*. The following fragment represents source code of the **GeneralizedLtf** procedure with the typical examples of its application.

In[3822]:= GeneralizedLtf[r_ /; ListQ[r] && AllTrue[Map[RuleQ[#] &, r], TrueQ], c_ /; StringQ[c], t_: 1] := StringJoin[ReplaceAll[Map[StringJoin,

Flatten[Map[Partition[Characters[c], #, If[{t} != {} && IntegerQ[t] && t >= 1 &&
t <= #, t, 1]] &, DeleteDuplicates[Map[StringLength[#[[1]]] &, r]]], 1]], r]]

In[3823]:= r = {"a" -> "ab", "ac" -> "abc", "bd" -> "ab", "d" -> "ab", "aa" -> "acb",
"cc" -> "dabc", "ad" -> "ab"}; S = "abcddabcdabbccd";

In[3824]:= GeneralizedLtf[r, S]

Out[3824]= "abbcabababbcababbbccababbccddddaabbccddaabbbbcdabccd"

In[3825]:= r = {"00" -> "0", "01" -> "1", "10" -> "1", "11" -> "0"}; S = "1110100100011111";

In[3826]:= GeneralizedLtf[r, S]

Out[3826]= "001110110010000"

In[3827]:= r = {"00" -> "0", "01" -> "1", "10" -> "1", "11" -> "0"}; S = "1110100100011111";

In[3828]:= GeneralizedLtf[r, c, 2]

Out[3828]= "01110100"

We will represent some more procedures of processing of the *CA* models which have been programmed in the *Mathematica* system. So, the procedure call **Predecessors[L, Co, n]** on the basis of a *L* list that determines the local transition function of a *1*-dimensional classical cellular automaton, of a *n* size of its neighbourhood template and initial *Co* configuration – *a finite block of states of elementary automata* – returns the list of *configurations-predecessors* for the block *Co* configuration. At that, parallel substitutions *x1x2x3 ... xn -> x*1* that define the local transition function of the classical *1-CA* in the *L* list are represented by strings of the format *"x1x2x3...xnx*1"*. The procedure can identify existence for an arbitrary classical *1-CA* model of the nonconstructability of *NCF*-type, printing the appropriate message. While the procedures **PredecessorsL** and **PredecessorsR** protrude as certain extensions of the above procedure [48,50,72].

The procedure call **SelfReprod[c, n, p, m]**, programmed in *Mathematica* system returns the number of iterations of a linear global transition function with neighbourhood index $X = \{0, 1, 2, ..., n - 1\}$ and alphabet $A = \{0, 1, 2, ..., p - 1\}$ *(p – an arbitrary integer)* that was required to generate *m* copies of an initial *c* configuration. In application, in case of a rather long run of procedure, it can be interrupted, by monitoring through the list {d, t} the reality of obtaining the required number of copies of *c* configuration, where *d* – number of the iterations and *t* – the quantity of initial *c* configuration. While **SelfReprod1** and **SubConf** procedures acts as certain extensions of the above procedure. The procedures HSD and HS serve for study of configurations dynamics of the classical *1-CA* and *1-CA* with delays accordingly [48,50,72].

The next procedure serve for study of self-reproducibility of the classical *1-CA* models too. The *first* 3 arguments {*Co, A, f*} of the procedure are fully equivalent to the above procedure **CFsequenses**, while *n* argument defines the demanded number of copies of a configuration *Co* in configurations that are generated by *CA* model, and *m* argument defines an interval of the generating when the inquiry on continuation or termination of operating of procedure is done *(key "Enter"* – *continuation, No – termination)*. The call **SelfReproduction[Co, A, f, n, m]** returns the 2-element list whose first element defines the number of the *CA* step on which the demanded number of *Co* copies has been obtained, while the second element defines the really obtained number of *Co* copies. The procedure call in response to *"No"* returns *nothing*, terminating the procedure. The following fragment represents source code of the procedure **SelfReproduction** with an example of its application.

In[4727]:= SelfReproduction[Co_ /; StringQ[Co] && Co != "" || IntegerQ[Co] && Co != 0,
A_ /; ListQ[A] && MemberQ[Map[Range[0, #] &, Range[9]], A], f_ /; ListQ[f] &&
AllTrue[Map[RuleQ[#] &, f], TrueQ] || FunctionQ[f], n_ /; IntegerQ[n] && n > 1, m_ /;
IntegerQ[m]] :=
Module[{a = StringTrim2[ToString[Co], "0", 3], b, d, d1, c, t1 = {}, t2 = {}, t3 = {}, t4 = {}, tf, p = 0},
If[! MemberQ3[Map[ToString, A], Characters[a]] ||
! MemberQ3[A, IntegerDigits[ToExpression[Co]]], Print["Initial configuration <" <>
ToString[Co] <> "> is incorrect"]; $Failed, If[FunctionQ[f], b = Arity[f],
Map[{{AppendTo[t1, StringQ[#[[1]]]], AppendTo[t2, StringLength[#[[1]]]]},
{AppendTo[t3, StringQ[#[[2]]]], AppendTo[t4, StringLength[#[[2]]]]}} &, f];
b = Map[DeleteDuplicates[#] &, {t1, t2, t3, t4}];
If[! (MemberQ3[{True}, {b[[1]], b[[3]]}] && Map[Length, {b[[2]], b[[4]]}] == {1, 1} &&
Length[t2] == Length[A]^(b = b[[2]][[1]])), Print["Local transition function is incorrect"];
Return[$Failed], tf = Map[ToExpression[Characters[#[[1]]]] -> ToExpression[#[[2]]] &, f]]];
c = StringMultiple2["0", b]; While[p < Infinity, p++; a = c <> a <> c;
a = Partition[ToExpression[Characters[a]], b, 1];
a = If[FunctionQ[f], Map[f @@ # &, a], ReplaceAll[a, tf]];
a = StringJoin[Map[ToString, a]]; d = StringTrim2[a, "0", 3];
If[Set[d, StringCount[d, Co]] >= n, Print[{p, d}]; Break[],
If[Mod[p, m] == 0, d1 = Input["Continue?"]; If[d1 === No, Break[], Null], Null]]];]]

In[4728]:= G[x_, y_, z_, t_] := Mod[x + y + z + t, 2];
SelfReproduction["11010010001", {0, 1}, G, 75, 500]
{1360, 256}

In some cases at computer research of a *1–CA* it is preferable to define their local transition functions not functionally in the form *Ltf[x_, y_, z_, t_ ...] := x**, but in the form of the list of parallel substitutions of format *"xyz ... t" –> "x*"*. This problem is solved by a rather simple function, whose call **FunctionToRules[x, A]** returns list of parallel substitutions of the above format on the basis of a *x* function and alphabet *A = {0, 1, 2, ..., n} (n = 1..9)*.

In[3334]:= Ltf[x_, y_, z_] := Mod[x + y + z, 2]

In[3335]:= FunctionToRules[x_ /; SymbolQ[x], A_ /; ListQ[A] &&
MemberQ[Map[Range[0, #] &, Range[9]], A]] :=
Map[StringJoin[Map[ToString, #]] -> ToString[x @@ #] &, Tuples[A, Arity[x]]]

In[3336]:= FunctionToRules[Ltf, {0, 1}]
Out[3336]= {"000" -> "0", "001" -> "1", "010" -> "1", "011" -> "0", "100" -> "1", "101" -> "0", "110" -> "0", "111" -> "1"}

The procedure call **RevBlockConfig[C, Ltf]** returns *True* if the list of block configurations which are predecessors of a *C* configuration of a finite block, relative to a local transition function *Ltf* given by the list of rules *(the parallel substitutions)* is other than the empty list, and *False* otherwise. Whereas the procedure call **RevBlockConfig[C, Ltf, h]** with optional third *h* argument – *an indefinite symbol* – through it returns the list of all predecessors of the *C* configuration of finite block. The next fragment represents source code of the procedure **RevBlockConfig** with the most typical examples of its application.

In[4448]:= RevBlockConfig[C_ /; StringQ[C], Ltf_ /; ListQ[Ltf] &&
AllTrue[Map[RuleQ[#] &, Ltf], TrueQ], h___] :=
Module[{a = CollectRules[Ltf], b = Characters[C], c = {}, d,
p, n = StringLength[Ltf[[1]][[1]]] - 1, g},
d = Flatten[Map[ListToRules, a], 2]; c = Flatten[AppendTo[c, Replace[b[[1]], d]]];
Do[c = RepSubStrings1[c, If[Set[g, Replace[b[[k]], d]] === b[[k]], g = 75; Break[], g], n],
{k, 2, Length[b]}];
If[g === 75, Return[False], Null]; If[{h} != {} && ! HowAct[h], h = c, Null];
If[Max[Map[StringLength, c]] == StringLength[C] + n, True, False]]

In[4449]:= RevBlockConfig["0110111101010", {"00" -> "0", "01" -> "1", "10" -> "1", "11" -> "0"}]
Out[4449]= True

In[4450]:= {RevBlockConfig["0110111101010", {"00" -> "0", "01" -> "1", "10" -> "1",
"11" -> "0"}, v74], v74}
Out[4450]= {True, {"00100101001100", "11011010110011"}}

In[4451]:= {RevBlockConfig["0110111101010", {"00" -> "0", "01" -> "0", "10" -> "0",
"11" -> "0"}, g69], g69}
Out[4451]= {False, g69}

In[4452]:= {RevBlockConfig["01101111010100", {"000" -> "0", "001" -> "1", "010" -> "1",
"011" -> "0", "100" -> "1", "101" -> "0", "110" -> "0", "111" -> "1"}, g69], g69}
Out[4452]= {True, {"0001010010101011", "0111100100011101", "1010001001110000",
"1100111111000110"}}

The following procedure unlike the **CFsequences** procedure is also a rather useful means in case of computer exploration of questions of *reproducibility* of finite subconfigurations in *1-dimensional CA* models. The following fragment presents source code of the procedure and examples of its application.

In[4783]:= **SubCFgenerate[Co_ /; StringQ[Co] && Co != "", A_ /; ListQ[A] &&
MemberQ[Map[Range[0, #] &, Range[9]], A], Ltf_ /; ListQ[Ltf] &&
AllTrue[Map[RuleQ[#] &, Ltf], TrueQ] || FunctionQ[Ltf], n_ /; ListQ[n] &&
AllTrue[Map[IntegerQ[#] &, n], TrueQ], m_: 1, v_: 1] :=**
Module[{a = StringTrim2[Co, "0", 3], b, c, t1 = {}, t2 = {}, t3 = {}, t4 = {}, tf, p = Max[n],
h = StringLength[Co], g = 0},
If[! MemberQ3[Map[ToString, A], Characters[Co]], Print["Initial configuration <" <>
Co <> "> is incorrect"]; $Failed, If[FunctionQ[Ltf], b = Arity[Ltf], Map[{{AppendTo[t1,
StringQ[#[[1]]]], AppendTo[t2, StringLength[#[[1]]]]}, {AppendTo[t3, StringQ[#[[2]]]],
AppendTo[t4, StringLength[#[[2]]]]}} &, Ltf];
b = Map[DeleteDuplicates[#] &, {t1, t2, t3, t4}];
If[! (MemberQ3[{True}, {b[[1]], b[[3]]}] && Map[Length, {b[[2]], b[[4]]}] == {1, 1} &&
Length[t2] == Length[A]^(b = b[[2]][[1]])), Print["Local transition function is incorrect"];
Return[$Failed], tf = Map[ToExpression[Characters[#[[1]]]] -> ToExpression[#[[2]]] &,
Ltf]]]; c = StringMultiple2["0", b]; Print[a]; While[p > 0, p--; g++; a = c <> a <> c;
a = Partition[ToExpression[Characters[a]], b, 1];
a = If[FunctionQ[Ltf], Map[Ltf @@ # &, a], ReplaceAll[a, tf]];
a = StringTrim2[StringJoin[Map[ToString, a]], "0", 3];

If[MemberQ[n, g], If[m == 1, Print[{g, StringCount[a, Co]}], Print[{g, Length[Select[Partition1[a, h], StringEquiQ[Co, #, v, False] &]]}]], Continue[]]]]]
In[4784]:= SubCFgenerate["101", {0, 1}, {"000" -> "0", "001" -> "1", "010" -> "1", "011" -> "0", "100" -> "1", "101" -> "0", "110" -> "0", "111" -> "1"}, Range[1, 6]]
101
{1, 1}
{2, 0}
{3, 0}
{4, 3}
{5, 3}
{6, 2}
In[4785]:= SubCFgenerate["101", {0, 1}, {"000" -> "0", "001" -> "1", "010" -> "1", "011" -> "0", "100" -> "1", "101" -> "0", "110" -> "0", "111" -> "1"}, Range[69, 74], 2, 2]
101
{69, 6}
{70, 4}
{71, 7}
{72, 4}
{73, 6}
{74, 4}

The first three formal arguments of the procedure call **SubCFgenerate[Co, A, Ltf, n, m, w]** are fully analogous to the corresponding arguments of the above **CFsequences** procedure. The fourth *n* argument determines the integer list that represents numbers of *CA* steps for which the information should be printed. Whereas the *fifth* optional *m* argument determines the search mode of substrings, that are equivalent to a *Co* initial string, in the strings which are generated by *1*-dimensional *CA* model with local transition function *Ltf*, namely: *m = 1* *(by default)* – substrings shall be strictly equivalent to the *Co* configuration; in opposite case the substrings are relied equivalent if they differ not more than in *w* appropriate positions *(by default w = 1)*. Depending on the tuple of actual arguments, the call **SubCFgenerate[Co, A, Ltf, n, m, w]** prints two–element lists whose the first element defines the step number of generation of the *CA* model whereas the second element defines the number of substrings, equivalent to the initial *Co* string, on this step; in addition, the equivalence of the strings is defined by parameters *m* and *w* in the context stated above.

An one–dimensional classical *CA* models with alphabet *A = {0, 1, 2, ..., a–1}* of the internal states of elementary automaton along with size *m* of neighbourhood template, whose local transition functions are determined as follows

$$Ltf[x1\_, x2\_, x3\_, ..., xm\_] := Mod[xj1 + xj2 + xj3 + ... + xjp, g] \qquad (g70)$$

$(\forall jk)\ (\forall jp)\ (jk \neq jp);\ 1 \leq jk < jp \leq m;\ k, p \in \{1, 2, ..., m\};\ g$ – a prime number

do not possess the nonconstructability of the *NCF* type, posessing all finite configurations as self-reproducing in the *Moore* sense [72]. Obviously, that the number of such *CA* models is at least $2^{\wedge}n - n - 1$. The next modification of the **SubCFgenerate** procedure allows both to research the constructability of finite configurations in the above classical *CA* models, and visually illustrate such process of self–reproducibility. The next fragment represents source code of the **CfReprod** procedure with typical examples of its application.

In[3805]:= CfReprod[Co_ /; StringQ[Co] && Co != "", A_ /; ListQ[A] &&
MemberQ[Map[Range[0, #] &, Range[9]], A], f_ /; ListQ[f] && AllTrue[Map[RuleQ[#] &,
f], TrueQ] || FunctionQ[f], n_ /; IntegerQ[n]] :=
Module[{a = StringTrim2[Co, "0", 3], b, c, t1 = {}, t2 = {}, t3 = {}, t4 = {}, tf, p,
h = StringLength[Co], g = 0},
If[! MemberQ3[Map[ToString, A], Characters[Co]], Print["Initial configuration <" <>
Co <> "> is incorrect"]; $Failed, If[FunctionQ[f], b = Arity[f], Map[{{AppendTo[t1,
StringQ[#[[1]]]], AppendTo[t2, StringLength[#[[1]]]]}, {AppendTo[t3, StringQ[#[[2]]]],
AppendTo[t4, StringLength[#[[2]]]]}} &, f];
b = Map[DeleteDuplicates[#] &, {t1, t2, t3, t4}];
If[! (MemberQ3[{True}, {b[[1]], b[[3]]}] && Map[Length, {b[[2]], b[[4]]}] == {1, 1} &&
Length[t2] == Length[A]^(b = b[[2]][[1]])), Print["Local transition function is incorrect"];
Return[$Failed], tf = Map[ToExpression[Characters[#[[1]]]] -> ToExpression[#[[2]]] &,
f]]]; c = StringMultiple2["0", b];
Do[g++; a = c <> a <> c; a = Partition[ToExpression[Characters[a]], b, 1];
a = If[FunctionQ[f], Map[f @@ # &, a], ReplaceAll[a, tf]];
a = StringTrim2[StringJoin[Map[ToString, a]], "0", 3];
p = StringCount[a, Co]; If[p >= n, Break[], Continue[]], {k, 1, Infinity}]]; {Co, g, p}]
In[3806]:= Ltf[x_, y_] := Mod[x + y, 2]
In[3807]:= CfReprod["100101", {0, 1}, Ltf, 20]
Out[3807]= {"100101", 248, 32}
In[3808]:= Ltf1[x_, y_, z_] := Mod[x + y + z, 2]
In[3809]:= CfReprod["100101", {0, 1}, Ltf1, 20]
Out[3809]= {"100101", 120, 21}
In[3810]:= Ltf2[x_, y_, z_] := Mod[x + z, 2]
In[3811]:= CfReprod["100101", {0, 1}, Ltf2, 20]
Out[3811]= {"100101", 124, 32}
In[3812]:= Ltf3[x_, y_, z_, t_] := Mod[x + z + t, 2]
In[3813]:= CfReprod["100101", {0, 1}, Ltf3, 6]
Out[3813]= {"100101", 104, 21}
In[3814]:= Ltf4[x_, y_, z_, t_, h_, d_, g_] := Mod[x + z + d + g, 2]
In[3815]:= CfReprod["100101", {0, 1}, Ltf4, 20]
Out[3815]= {"100101", 56, 26}
In[3816]:= Ltf5[x_, y_, z_, t_, h_, d_, g_, k_, s_] := Mod[x + z + d + g + s, 2]
In[3817]:= CfReprod["100101", {0, 1}, Ltf5, 74]
Out[3817]= {"100101", 184, 93}
In[3818]:= CfReprod["1010010001", {0, 1}, Ltf5, 74]
Out[3818]= {"1010010001", 368, 93}
In[3819]:= Ltf6[x_, y_, z_, t_, h_, d_, g_, k_, s_] := Mod[x + z + d + k + s, 2]
In[3820]:= CfReprod["1111001011011110011011", {0, 1}, Ltf6, 74]
Out[3820]= {"1111001011011110011011", 608, 79}
In[3821]:= Ltf7[x_, y_, z_, t_, h_, d_, g_, k_, s_] := Mod[x + z + d + k + s, 3]
In[3822]:= CfReprod["1121001021011220012012", {0, 1, 2}, Ltf7, 74]
Out[3822]= {"1121001021011220012012", 837, 82}

In[3823]:= **Ltf8[x_, y_, z_, t_, h_, d_, g_, k_, s_] := Mod[x + z + d + k + s, 7]**
In[3824]:= **CfReprod["132100402106522004206", {0, 1, 2, 3, 4, 5, 6}, Ltf8, 27]**
Out[3824]= {"132100402106522004206", 931, 28}

The first 3 formal arguments of the procedure call **CfReprod[Co, A, f, n]** are fully similar to the corresponding arguments of the above **CFsequences** procedure. The fourth *n* argument determines the number of substrings *Co* which are generated by means of a *CA* model with local transition function *f* determined in *A* alphabet. The call **CfReprod[Co, A, f, n]** returns three-element list whose the first element determines an initial *Co* configuration, the second element determines the steps number of generation of a *CA* model during which of *Co* has been generated a configuration containing at least *n* disjoint copies of subconfiguration *Co*, whereas the third element defines factual number of substrings, contained in the obtained final configuration.

For the purpose of computer simulation of dynamics of the *1*-dimensional *CA* whose local transition functions which in particular are described by relations *(g70)* and which change from a step to a step of generation of *1-CA* within the maximum neighbourhood template the following tools seem rather useful. At the same time, the first two of them have an quite definite interest for the processing of lists too, whereas the third means may be useful when dealing with functions. The procedure call **Range6[x, p]** returns the list {$x1\_, x2\_, x3\_,...,xp\_$} whereas the procedure call **Range6[x, p, t]** returns the list {$x1\_\_, x2\_\_, x3\_\_, ..., xp\_\_$}, where *x* is a name, *p* is an positive integer and *t* – an arbitrary expression. Whereas the procedure call **Permutat[x, n]** returns the list of the sorted tuples of *n* length of different elements of a *x* list *(the tuples contain no identical elements)*, whereas the call **Permutat[x, n, p]** returns the *p-th* element of the above tuples list. Moreover, an unsuccessful call of both procedures returns $Failed. The **GenLtf** function is intended for generation of functions whose quantity of the essential arguments no more than quantity of the formal arguments; thereby, the generated functions may have the *fictive* arguments. The function call **GenLtf[f, g, j, n, p]** generates the definition of a function $f[j1, j2, ..., jn] = g[c]$ where *c* is a tuple of length $p <= n$ of elements from the set {$j1, j2, j3, ..., jn$} that are different, returning the evaluation result of $g[c]$ on the factual arguments {*f, g, x, n, m*}; moreover, the *c* tuple is chosen by a random manner. At the same time the function call **GenLtf[f, g, j, n, p, z]** with optional *z* argument - *an integer* - uses *z-th* tuple from list of all tuples formed on the basis of elements from the set {$j1, j2, j3,..., jn$} with indexes **Permutat[Range[1, n], p, z]** as the *c* tuple. So, for **Permutat[Range[1, 6], 4, 3]** = {1, 2, 3, 6} we have c = {$j1, j2, j3, j6$}. In addition, the unsuccessful call of the **GenLtf** function returns $Failed. The following fragment represents source codes of the above 3 means with typical examples of their application.

In[3730]:= **Range6[x_, y_ /; IntegerQ[y] /; y >= 1, z___] := Module[{a = {}, b = Range[1, y]},**
Do[AppendTo[a, ToString[x] <> ToString[b[[k]]] <> If[{z} != {}, "__", "_"]];
If[{z} != {}, Return[ToExpression[a]]], {k, 1, Length[b]}]; ToExpression[a]]
In[3731]:= **Range6[x, 8, h]**
Out[3731]= {x1__}
In[3732]:= **Range6[h, 10]**
Out[3732]= {h1_, h2_, h3_, h4_, h5_, h6_, h7_, h8_, h9_, h10_}
In[3747]:= **Permutat[x_ /; ListQ[x], n_ /; IntegerQ[n], p___] := Module[{a,**

a = DeleteDuplicates[Map[Sort, Permutations[x, {n}]]];
Quiet[Check[a = If[{p} == {}, a, a[[p]]]; If[{p} == {} && Length[a] == 1, a[[1]], a], $Failed]]]
In[3785]:= GenLtf[f_ /; SymbolQ[f], g_ /; SymbolQ[g], j_ /; SymbolQ[x], n_ /; IntegerQ[n], m_ /; IntegerQ[m], z___] := f[Sequences[Range6[j, n]]] = g @@ If[{z} == {}, DeleteDuplicates[RandomChoice[Range2[j, n], m]], ToExpression[Map[ToString[j] <> ToString[#] &, Permutat[Range[1, n], m, z]]]]

In[3786]:= **Clear[F, G]; GenLtf[F, G, y, 7, 4]**
Out[3786]= G[y1, y7, y4]
In[3787]:= **Definition[F]**
Out[3787]= F[y1_, y2_, y3_, y4_, y5_, y6_, y7_] = G[y1, y7, y4]
In[3788]:= **F[a, b, c, d, f, g, s]**
Out[3788]= G[f, s, c]
In[3789]:= **Clear[F, G]; GenLtf[F, Plus, y, 6, 4, 3]**
Out[3789]= y1 + y2 + y3 + y6
In[3790]:= **Definition[F]**
Out[3790]= F[y1_, y2_, y3_, y4_, y5_, y6_] = y1 + y2 + y3 + y6
In[3791]:= **GenLtf[F, Plus, y, 6, 4, 7]**
In[3792]:= **F[a, b, c, d, g, h]**
Out[3792]= a + b + c + h

At last, on condition of existence of the functions, blocks and modules with fictive formal arguments there is a need of determination for them of the actual, but not formal arity. The **FactualArityC** procedure solves the problem. For case of *unique* definition of a function with heading, a block or module, the procedure **FactualArityC** is used whose the procedure call **FactualArityC[y]** returns the factual arity of an object of the above type *(block, function with heading, module)*. At the same time the call **FactualArityC[y, w]** additionally through second optional *w* argument – an undefinite symbol – returns the list of fictive arguments of an *y* object. The **FactualArityC** procedure extends the facilities of procedures **FactualArity** and **FactualArityM** [48] on the case of multiple definitions of a function with heading, block or module. The procedure call **FactualArityC[y]** returns the list *(generally speaking, the nested list)* of the arities of the objects that compose an initial *y* object, whereas the procedure call **FactualArityC[y, v]** additionally through 2nd optional *v* argument – an undefinite symbol – returns the nested list of fictive arguments of the objects composing the *y* object. The next fragment represents source code of the **FactualArityC** procedure with typical examples of its application.

In[3877]:= FactualArityC[y_ /; BlockFuncModQ[y], v___] := Module[{Gs, d, g = {}, s = {}, u = Unique["Avz"], m}, Gs[x_, t___] := Module[{a = Args[x, 0], b = HeadPF[x], c},
c = StringReplace[PureDefinition[x], b -> "", 1];
c = ExtrVarsOfStr[c, 2]; c = Select[a, MemberQ[c, #] &];
If[{t} != {} && ! HowAct[t], t = Complement[a, c]; Length[c], Length[c]]];
d = Flatten[{PureDefinition[y]}];
Do[ToExpression[StringReplace[d[[j]], ToString[y] <> "[" -> ToString[u]<> "[", 1]];
If[{v} != {} && ! HowAct[v], Clear[m]; AppendTo[g, Gs[u, m]];
AppendTo[s, m], AppendTo[g, Gs[u]]; AppendTo[s, {}]]; Clear[u, m], {j, 1, Length[d]}];

If[{v} != {} && ! HowAct[v], If[Length[s] == 1, v = s[[1]], v = s]; Remove[u];
If[Length[g] == 1, g[[1]], g], If[Length[g] == 1, g[[1]], g]]]

In[3878]:= F[x_, y_, z_] := x + z; F[x_, y_, z_, t_] := Module[{a, b, c}, x + z*t];
F[y1_, y2_, y3_, y4_, y5_, y6_, y7_] := G[y2, y4, y7]; F[x_, y_List, z_] := x*z
In[3879]:= FactualArityC[F, g70]
Out[3879]= {2, 2, 3, 3}
In[3880]:= g70
Out[3880]= {{"y"}, {"y"}, {"y"}, {"y1", "y3", "y5", "y6"}}

In view of features of the contexts mechanism supported by the *Mathematica* software in certain cases there can be especial situations at loading into the current session of the nested procedures [50]. Therefore it is recommended to upload them, for example, by means of the call **ReloadPackage["... \\MathToolBox.m"]** [48].

In general, and the local variables not always successfully solve problems of use them as the temporary names of the objects generated in the body of procedures. Let's illustrate that moment on a rather simple example using an useful enough approach, effective, above all, when processing the blocks, functions with headings, and modules which have multiple definitions under the same name (*so-called objects under the same name* [50]). The following fragment represents two versions of the procedure, whose call **ArityC[*x*]** has to return the list of arities of a function with heading, block or a *x* module. At the same time, definition of the *x* object can be both single, and multiple. An quite natural method was the basis for such algorithm: into a definition provided in the string format, of the next component composing an initial *x* object of the same name, its common *x* name is replaced onto a local *c* variable and its evaluation by means of the standard **ToExpression** function is executed, obtaining the activated *c* object as a result for which the determined arity is added to the *b* list. The procedure call returns the formed *b* list. Meantime, the obtained result is not as expected. Therefore the second version of the **ArityC** the procedure **ArityC1** uses the same algorithm, but as a temporary name is used a global variable, unique for the current session. The next fragment represents source codes of both procedures with examples of their application.

In[3756]:= **ArityC[x_ /; BlockFuncModQ[x]] :=**
Module[{b = {}, c, a = Flatten[{PureDefinition[x]}]}, Do[Clear[c];
ToExpression[StringReplace[a[[k]], ToString[x] <> "[" -> "c[", 1]];
AppendTo[b, Arity[c]]; ClearAll[c], {k, 1, Length[a]}]; b]

In[3757]:= **ArityC1[x_ /; BlockFuncModQ[x]] :=**
Module[{b = {}, j = Unique["x"], a = Flatten[{PureDefinition[x]}]},
Do[ToExpression[StringReplace[a[[i]], ToString[x] <> "[" -> ToString[j] <> "[", 1]];
AppendTo[b, Arity[j]]; Clear[j], {i, 1, Length[a]}]; b]

In[3758]:= F[x_] := x; F[x_, y_] := Block[{}, x*y]; F[x_, y_, z_] := x*y*z
In[3759]:= **ArityC[F]**
Out[3759]= {Arity[c$8089], Arity[c$8089], Arity[c$8089]}
In[3760]:= **ArityC1[F]**
Out[3760]= {1, 2, 3}

This moment should be meant at procedures programming of similar kind.

In problems of computer research of dynamic properties of a *1-dimensional CA* when the configurations generated by them are represented in format of strings, the **AllSubStrings** procedure is of a certain interest. The procedure call **AllSubStrings[x]** or **AllSubStrings[x, 0]** returns the list of all possible substrings contained in a *x* string, including substrings that overlap. While the call **AllSubStrings[x, j]** where *j* – an arbitrary expression different from zero, returns the list of all possible substrings contained in a *x* string, which includes only substrings that do not *overlap*. At last, the use of the *3rd* optional *z* argument – *a filter function* – allows to exclude from the list of the previously received strings the substrings which not satisfy the filter function. The fragment below represents the source code of the procedure **AllSubStrings** along with the typical examples of its application.

In[3552]:= **AllSubStrings[x_ /; StringQ[x], y_: 0, z___] := Module[{a = Characters[x]},**
Select[Map[StringJoin[#] &, Catenate[Map[Partition[a, #, If[y === 0, 1, #]] &,
Range[Length[a]]]]], If[{z} == {}, # === # &, z]]]

In[3553]:= **Map[AllSubStrings, {"", "a", "ab"}]**
Out[3553]= {{}, {"a"}, {"a", "b", "ab"}}

In[3554]:= **AllSubStrings["avzagnvsv"]**
Out[3554]= {"a", "v", "z", "a", "g", "n", "v", "s", "v", "av", "vz", "za", "ag", "gn", "nv", "vs", "sv", "avz", "vza", "zag", "agn", "gnv", "nvs", "vsv", "avza", "vzag", "zagn", "agnv", "gnvs", "nvsv", "avzag", "vzagn", "zagnv", "agnvs", "gnvsv", "avzagn", "vzagnv", "zagnvs", "agnvsv", "avzagnv", "vzagnvs", "zagnvsv", "avzagnvs", "vzagnvsv", "avzagnvsv"}

In[3555]:= **AllSubStrings["avzagnvsv", 6]**
Out[3555]= {"a", "v", "z", "a", "g", "n", "v", "s", "v", "av", "za", "gn", "vs", "avz", "agn", "vsv", "avza", "gnvs", "avzag", "avzagn", "avzagnv", "avzagnvs", "avzagnvsv"}

In[3556]:= **AllSubStrings["avzagnvsv", 0, StringFreeQ[#, "z"] &]**
Out[3556]= {"a", "v", "a", "g", "n", "v", "s", "v", "av", "ag", "gn", "nv", "vs", "sv", "agn", "gnv", "nvs", "vsv", "agnv", "gnvs", "nvsv", "agnvs", "gnvsv", "agnvsv"}

Among research problems of the dynamics of sequences of configurations, generated by the *CA*, the research of diversity of subconfigurations composing the generated configurations plays a rather essential part. In the same time, this problem in theoretical plan is a complex enough, therefore the computer research is used enough widely. Thus, the procedure below allows to research the diversity for the *1-dimensional CA*. The call **SubCFdiversity[Co, A, f, n]** prints the sequence of *3-element* lists whose the first element defines the number of step of *1-dimensional CA* model, the *2nd* element defines the quantity of various *subconfigurations (including substrings that overlap)* that are contained in a configuration generated by means of the *CA* with *A* alphabet and local transition function *f* from initial *Co* configuration on this step while the *3rd* element defines the quantity of various non–overlaping *subconfigurations*.

At last, the *4th n* argument determines quantity of steps of the *CA* model on which research of the specified phenomenon is made. In addition, the first argument admits both the string, and numeric format, *A = {0, 1, ..., p} (p = 1..9)* while a list of rules, or function can be as third argument. The following fragment represents source code of the **SubCFdiversity** procedure along with examples of its application.

In[3474]:= **SubCFdiversity[Co_ /; StringQ[Co] && Co != "" || IntegerQ[Co] && Co != 0,**
A_ /; ListQ[A] && MemberQ[Map[Range[0, #] &, Range[9]], A], f_ /; ListQ[f] &&
AllTrue[Map[RuleQ[#] &, f], TrueQ] || FunctionQ[f], n_ /; IntegerQ[n] && n >= 0] :=

```
Module[{a = StringTrim2[ToString[Co], "0", 3], b, d, d1, d2, c, t1 = {}, t2 = {}, t3 = {},
t4 = {}, tf, p = n},
If[! MemberQ3[Map[ToString, A], Characters[a]] ||
! MemberQ3[A, IntegerDigits[ToExpression[Co]]], Print["Initial configuration <" <>
ToString[Co] <> "> is incorrect"]; $Failed, If[FunctionQ[f], b = Arity[f],
Map[{{AppendTo[t1, StringQ[#[[1]]]], AppendTo[t2, StringLength[#[[1]]]]},
{AppendTo[t3, StringQ[#[[2]]]], AppendTo[t4, StringLength[#[[2]]]]}} &, f];
b = Map[DeleteDuplicates[#] &, {t1, t2, t3, t4}];
If[! (MemberQ3[{True}, {b[[1]], b[[3]]}] && Map[Length, {b[[2]], b[[4]]}] == {1, 1} &&
Length[t2] == Length[A]^(b = b[[2]][[1]])), Print["Local transition function is incorrect"];
Return[$Failed], tf = Map[ToExpression[Characters[#[[1]]]] -> ToExpression[#[[2]]] &, f]]];
c = StringMultiple2["0", b]; Print[Co]; While[p > 0, p--; a = c <> a <> c;
a = Partition[ToExpression[Characters[a]], b, 1];
a = If[FunctionQ[f], Map[f @@ # &, a], ReplaceAll[a, tf]];
a = StringJoin[Map[ToString, a]]; d = StringTrim2[a, "0", 3];
d1 = Length[DeleteDuplicates[Map[StringJoin, Flatten[Map[Partition[Characters[d], #, 1]
&, Range[2, StringLength[d]]], 1]]]];
d2 = Length[DeleteDuplicates[Map[StringJoin, Flatten[Map[Partition[Characters[d], #, #]
&, Range[2, StringLength[d]]], 1]]]]; Print[{n - p, d1, d2}];]]
In[3475]:= SubCFdiversity[11, {0, 1}, {"000" -> "0", "001" -> "1", "010" -> "1", "011" -> "0",
"100" -> "1", "101" -> "0", "110" -> "0", "111" -> "1"}, 5]
11
{1, 6, 4}
{2, 5, 5}
{3, 22, 11}
{4, 30, 13}
{5, 38, 17}
```

In the light of research of attainability of subconfigurations in the chains of configurations generated by the *CA* models the following procedure is a rather useful. The procedure call **CFattainability**[*x*, *y*, *A*, *f*, *n*] prints the two-element list whose first element determines the number of step of *1-CA* with alphabet *A* and local transition function *f*, the second element defines the number of *y* subconfigurations containing in a configuration generated by the *CA* model from a *x* configuration, and *n* argument defines the interval of generating, when the inquiry on continuation or termination of the procedure operating is done *(key "Enter" – continuation, "No" – termination)*. The call in response to *"No"* returns nothing, terminating the procedure, whereas in response to *"other"* a new configuration is requested as a sought *y* configuration. At that, value in the answer is coded in string format. The fragment below represents source code of the **CFattainability** procedure with examples of its application.

```
In[3678]:= CFattainability[x_ /; StringQ[x] && x != "" || IntegerQ[x] && x != 0,
y_ /; StringQ[y] && y != "" || IntegerQ[y], A_ /; ListQ[A] &&
MemberQ[Map[Range[0, #] &, Range[9]], A], f_ /; ListQ[f] &&
AllTrue[Map[RuleQ[#] &, f], TrueQ] || FunctionQ[f], n_ /; IntegerQ[n] && n > 1] :=
Module[{a, b, d, d1, c, tf, p = 0, h = ToString[y]},
```

```
If[FunctionQ[f], b = Arity[f], b = StringLength[f[[1]][[1]]]];
tf = Map[ToExpression[Characters[#[[1]]]] -> ToExpression[#[[2]]] &, f]];
c = StringMultiple2["0", b]; Label[New]; a = StringTrim2[ToString[x], "0", 3];
While[p < Infinity, p++; a = c <> a <> c; a = Partition[ToExpression[Characters[a]], b, 1];
a = If[FunctionQ[f], Map[f @@ # &, a], ReplaceAll[a, tf]];
a = StringJoin[Map[ToString, a]]; d = StringTrim2[a, "0", 3];
If[Set[d, StringCount[d, h]] >= 1, Print[{p, d}]; Break[],
If[Mod[p, n] == 0, Print[p]; d1 = Input["Continue?"];
If[SameQ[d1, Null], Continue[], If[d1 === "No", Break[], If[d1 === "other", d1 = Input["A
new configuration in string format"]; p = 0; h = d1; Goto[New], Break[]]], Null]]];]

In[3679]:= f[x_, y_] := Mod[x + y, 2]; CFattainability[1, 11000011, {0, 1}, f, 100]
{11, 1}
In[3680]:= g[x_, y_, z_] := Mod[x + y + z, 2]; CFattainability[1101, 1100011, {0, 1}, g, 30]
30
Continue? - "Enter"
60
Continue? - "Enter"
90
Continue? - "other"
"A new confiduration in string format"
"1101110100001101000011011101000000000000000000000000000000001101110100001101
000011011101"
30
Continue? - "Enter"
60
Continue? - "Enter"
{76, 1}
```

For convenience of a tracking of quantity of the steps generated by means of the **CA** model the numbers of steps, multiple to value of the *n* argument are printed. This information is then used for decision-making concerning the further choice of a way of operating with the **CFattainability** procedure.

The following procedure along with interest in the context of development of means of the computer research of *1*-dimensional **CA** models is of a quite certain interest for processing problems, first of all, of lists, expanding the standard software of the *Mathematica* system.

The call **Select[p, f]** of the standard function returns all *xj* elements of a *p* list for which the calls *f[xj]* are *True*. The **Select1** procedure extends the above function. If the *p* list is simple then the procedure call **Select1[p, f]** returns the list of *ListList* type, the first *xj* elements of its 2-element sublists define the elements of the *p* list for which the calls *f[xj]* are *True*, whereas the second elements determine their positions in the *p* list. If the *p* list is the nested list then the procedure call **Select1[p, f]** returns the nested list, the first elements of its two-element sublists define the nesting levels *gk* of the *xj* elements of a *p* list for which the calls *f[xj]* are *True*, whereas the second element defines 2-element lists of the *ListList* type, their the first elements define the *xj* elements of the *p* list on *gk* nesting levels for which the calls *f[xj]* are

True, whereas the *second* elements determine their positions in the *p* list on *gk* nesting levels. In addition, elements of the simple list are at the first nesting level. The following fragment represents source code of the **Select1** procedure with examples of its application.

In[3993]:= **Select1[p_, f_ /; FunctionQ[f]] := Module[{a, b = {}, d = {}, c = If[ListQ[p], ElemOnLevels[p], ToExpression[SymbolsOfString[ToString1[p]]]]},**
If[c == {}, {}, c = If[NestListQ[c], c, {c}];
Do[a = 0; Map[{a++, If[f @@ {#}, AppendTo[b, {#, a}], 6]} &, c[[j]][[2 ;; -1]]];
If[b != {}, AppendTo[d, {c[[j]][[1]] + 1, b}], 6]; b = {}, {j, 1, Length[c]}];
d = Map[Flatten[#, 1] &, d]; d = If[Length[d] == 1, d[[1]][[2 ;; -1]], d];
If[ListQ[p], d, Map[#[[1]] &, d]]]]

In[3994]:= **Select1[{1, 2, b, 4, 5, 74, 6, 69, 7, 8, b}, OddQ[#] || SymbolQ[#] &]**
Out[3994]= {{1, 1}, {b, 3}, {5, 5}, {69, 8}, {7, 9}, {b, 11}}

In[3995]:= **Select1[{1, 2, b, 4, 5, 74, {a, b, {m, p, {{x, y, z}}, d}, c}, 6, 69, 7, 8, b}, OddQ[#] || SymbolQ[#] &]**
Out[3995]= {{1, {1, 1}, {b, 3}, {5, 5}, {69, 8}, {7, 9}, {b, 11}}, {2, {a, 1}, {b, 2}, {c, 3}}, {3, {m, 1}, {p, 2}, {d, 3}}, {5, {x, 1}, {y, 2}, {z, 3}}}

In[3996]:= **Select1[(74*v + 69 + g)/(49*s + 20) + G[x + 69]*S[y + 49] - Sqrt[z], OddQ[#] || SymbolQ[#] &]**
Out[3996]= {g, v, 49, s, Sqrt, z, G, x, S, y}

The following procedure is direct extension of the previous procedure on case of a list as the second argument. If the *p* list is simple then the procedure call **Select2[*p*, *f*]** returns the list of *ListList* type, the first *xj* elements of its two-element sublists determine the elements of the *p* list for which the calls *f*[*xj*] are *True* or which belong to a list *f*, whereas the second elements determine their positions in the *p* list. If the *p* list is the nested list then the call **Select2[*p*, *f*]** returns the nested list, the first elements of its two-element sublists define the nesting levels *gk* of the *xj* elements of the *p* list for which the calls *f*[*xj*] are *True*, or which belong to a list *f*, whereas the second elements defines 2-element lists of the *ListList* type, their first elements define *xj* elements of the *p* list on *gk* nesting levels for which the calls *f*[*xj*] are *True* or which belong to a list *f*, while the second elements define their positions in the *p* list on *gk* nesting levels. In addition, elements of the simple *p* list are at the first nesting level. The fragment below represents source code of the **Select2** procedure with examples of its application.

In[4202]:= **Select2[p_, f_ /; FunctionQ[f] || ListQ[f]] :=**
Module[{a, b = {}, c = If[ListQ[p], ElemOnLevels[p], ToExpression[SymbolsOfString[ToString1[p]]]], d = {}},
If[c == {}, {}, c = If[NestListQ[c], c, {c}];
Do[a = 0; Map[{a++, If[If[ListQ[f], MemberQ[f, #], f @@ {#}], AppendTo[b, {#, a}], 6]} &, c[[j]][[2 ;; -1]]];
If[b != {}, AppendTo[d, {c[[j]][[1]] + 1, b}], 6]; b = {}, {j, 1, Length[c]}];
d = Map[Flatten[#, 1] &, d]; d = If[Length[d] == 1, d[[1]][[2 ;; -1]], d];
If[ListQ[p], d, Map[#[[1]] &, d]]]]

In[4203]:= **Select2[{5, {5, b, 6, 7, {6, 7, a}}}, OddQ[#] &]**
Out[4203]= {{1, {5, 1}}, {2, {5, 1}, {7, 4}}, {3, {7, 2}}}

In[4204]:= **Select2[{5, {5, b, 6, 7, {6, 7, a}}}, {5, 7}]**
Out[4204]= {{1, {5, 1}}, {2, {5, 1}}, {7, 4}}, {3, {7, 2}}}
In[4205]:= **Select2[{5, {5, b, 6, 7}}, {42, 75}]**
Out[4205]= {}
In[4206]:= **Select2[{5, 5, b, 6, 7, 6, 7, a}, {5, 7}]**
Out[4206]= {{5, 1}, {5, 2}, {7, 5}, {7, 7}}

If in the both procedures call the first p argument defines an expression different from the list, then the list of elements composing the string **ToString1**[p] and satisfying the f selection filter is returned without regard to their nesting levels. This procedure essentially uses tools **SymbolsOfString, NestListQ, ToString1** and **ElemOnLevels** [48,50].

In a number of cases the following simple function is very convenient means of processing of the simple lists. The function call **Select3**[x, y] returns the list of elements of a simple x list which satisfy pure function y, belong to an y list or coincide with an y expression. The next fragment represents source code of the **Select3** procedure with examples of its application.

In[4445]:= **Select3[x_ /; SimpleListQ[x], y_] :=**
Select[x, If[PureFuncQ[y], y @@ {#} &, If[! ListQ[y], y === # &, MemberQ[y, #] &]]]
In[4446]:= **Select3[{f, d, 75, s, m, h, 50, a + b, m, 70}, {a + b, m}]**
Out[4446]= {m, a + b, m}
In[4447]:= **Select3[{f, d, 75, s, m, h, 50, a + b, m, 70}, m]**
Out[4447]= {m, m}
In[4448]:= **Select3[{f, d, 75, s, m, h, 50, a + b, m, 70}, SymbolQ[#] &]**
Out[4448]= {f, d, s, m, h, m}

One more useful modification of the standard **Select** function is the **Select4** function whose call returns the list elements of a w list which satisfy a testing function g *(a block, a function, a pure function or a module of one argument)* or whose positions are defined by the list of *positive integers* g. At the same time, the positions that are absent in the g list are ignored or the call is returned unevaluated. The fragment below represents source code of the **Select4** function with typical examples of its application.

In[4452]:= **Select4[x_ /; ListQ[x], g_ /; Quiet[ProcFuncBlQ[g, Unique["s"]]] ||**
PosIntListQ[g]] := If[PureFuncQ[g], Select[x, g], If[BlockFuncModQ[g], Map[g, x],
Map[If[Intersection[g, Flatten[Position[x, #]]] != {}, #, Nothing] &, x]]]
In[4453]:= **Select4[{a, b, 3, 6, m, 7, 8, d, 70, m, a + b, 75}, SymbolQ[#] &]**
Out[4453]= {a, b, m, d, m}
In[4454]:= **Select4[{a, b, 3, 6, m, 7, 8, d, 70, m, a + b, 75}, {1, 4, 7, 9, 12}]**
Out[4454]= {a, 6, 8, 70, 75}
In[4455]:= **h[j_] := If[IntegerQ[j], j^3, Nothing]; Select4[{a, b, 3, 6, m, 7, 8, d, 70, m, a/b, 75}, j]**
Out[4455]= {27, 216, 343, 512, 343000, 421875}

The tools represented here and in [50,72] and intended for computer research of dynamical properties of the *1-*dimensional *CA* models, are of interest not only especially for specifical applications of the given type but many of them can be successfully used as auxiliary tools at programming in the *Mathematica* system of other problems of the computer research of the *1-*dimensional *CA* models.

The tools presented here and in [50,72,73] and intended for computer research of dynamical properties of the *1*-dimensional *CA* models, are of interest not only especially for specifical applications of the given type but many of them can be successfully used as auxiliary tools at programming in the *Mathematica* system of other problems of the computer research of the *1*-dimensional *CA* models. The complex of procedures and functions developed by us which are focused both on the computer research of *CA* models, and on expansion of the *Mathematica* software are located in the *MathToolBox* package which contains more than *1140* tools with freeware license. This package can be freely downloaded from web-site [48]. This package is represented in the form of the archive included five files of formats {*cdf, m, mx, nb, txt*} which, excepting *mx*-format, can be used on all known computing platforms.

Meanwhile, the procedures presented in the chapter are intended for the computer research *CA* of models focused on *1*-dimensional models. Experience of use of similar means for case of 2-dimensional *CA* models has revealed expediency of use for these purposes of the *Maple* system, but not the *Mathematica* system. The main reason for it consists that performance of the nested cyclic structures in the *Maple* is essential more fast than in the *Mathematica*. At that, for these purposes it is the most expedient to use the parallel systems of information processing focused on *CA*-like computing architectures [50,72,73].

At last, we will make one essential enough remark concerning of place of the *CA* problems in scientific structure. By a certain contraposition to the standpoint on the *CA*-problematics that is declared by the *S. Wolfram* our vision of this question is being presented as follows. Our experience of researches in the *CA*-problematics both on theoretical, and applied level speaks entirely another:

(1) CA-models represent one of special classes of infinite abstract automata with the specific internal organization which provides high-parallel level of the information processing and calculations; these models form a specific class of discrete dynamic systems that function in especially parallel way on base of a principle of local short-range interaction;

(2) CA-models can serve as an quite satisfactory model of high-parallel calculations just as the *Turing* machines (*Markov normal algorithms, Post machines, productions systems,* etc.) serve as formal models of sequential calculations; from this standpoint *CA*-models it is possible to consider and as algebraical systems of processing of finite or/and infinite words, defined in finite alphabets, on basis of a finite set of rules of parallel substitutions; in particular, any *CA*-model can be interpreted as a some system of parallel programming where the rules of parallel substitutions act as a parallel language of the lowest level;

(3) principle of *local interaction* of elementary automata composing a *CA*-model that in result defines their global dynamics allows to use the *CA* and as a fine environment of modelling of a rather broad range of processes, phenomena and objects; in addition, this phenomenon as the reversibility permitted by the *CA* does their by interesting enough means for physical modelling, and for creation of very perspective computing structures that are based on the nanotechnologies;

(4) at last, the *CA*-models represent an interesting enough independent mathematic object whose essence consists in high-parallel processing of words in finite or infinite alphabets.

At that, it is possible to associate the *CA*-oriented approach with certain model analogue of the differential equations in partial derivatives describing those or another processes with that the difference, that if the differential equations describe a process at the average, then in a *CA*-model defined in appropriate way, a certain researched process is really embedded and dynamics of the *CA*-model enough evidently represents the qualitative behaviour of a researched process. Thus, it is necessary to define for elementary automata of the model the necessary properties and rules of their local interaction by appropriate way. Thus, the *CA*-approach can be used and for research of the processes described by complex differential equations which have not of analytical solution, and for processes, that it is not possible to describe by such equations. Furthermore, the *CA* models represent a perspective modelling environment for research of those phenomena, objects, processes, phenomena for that there are no known classical means or they are difficult enough.

As we already noted, as against many other modern fields of science, theoretical component of *CA* problems is no so appreciably crossed with its second applied component, therefore, it is possible to consider *CA* problems as two independent enough directions: *(1)* research of the *CA* as mathematical objects and *(2)* use of the *CA* for simulating; in addition, the second direction is characterized also by the wider spectrum. At that, the level of development of the second direction is appreciably being defined by possibilities of the modern computing systems since *CA*-models, as a rule, are being designed on base of the immense number of elementary automata and, as a rule, with complex enough rules of local interaction among themselves. The indubitable interest to them amplifies also a possibility of realization of the high-parallel computing *CA*-models on the basis of modern successes of microelectronics and prospects of the information processing at molecular level *(methods of nanotechnology)*; while the itself *CA*-concept provides creation of both conceptual and practical models of spatially-distributed dynamic systems of which namely various physical systems are the most interesting and perspective. Namely, from this standpoint the *CA*-models of various type represent a special interest, above all, from the applied standpoint at research of a lot of processes, phenomena, objects in different fields and, first of all, in physics, computer science and development biology. As a whole if classical *CA*-models represent first of all formal mathematical systems researched in the appropriate context, then their numerous generalizations present *perspective* modelling environment of various processes and objects.

Chapter 5. The additional tools expanding the standard *Mathematica* functions, or its software as a whole

The string and list structures – some of the most important in the *Mathematica* system, they both are considered in the previous two chapters in the context of means, additional to the system means, without regard to a large number of the standard functions of processing of structures of this type. Naturally, here it isn't possible to consider all range of the system functions of this type, sending the interested reader to the help information on the system *Mathematica* or to the corresponding numerous publications. It is possible to find many of these editions on the website *http://www.wolfram.com/books*. Having presented the means expanding the standard *Mathematica* software in the context of processing of *string* and *list* structures in the present chapter we will represent the means expanding the *Mathematica* system that are oriented on processing of other types of objects. First of all, we will present a number of tools of bit–by–bit processing of arbitrary symbols.

The **Bits** procedure an quite significantly uses function **BinaryListQ**, providing a number of the useful functions during of work with symbols. On the tuple of factual arguments <*x*, *p*>, where *x* – a *1*-symbol string *(character)* and *p* – an integer in the range *0 .. 8*, the call **Bits[*x*, *p*]** returns binary representation of the *x* in the format of the list, if *p = 0*, and *p–th* bit of such representation of a *x* symbol otherwise. Whereas on a tuple of the actual arguments <*x*, *p*>, where *x* – the nonempty binary list of length no more than *8* and *p = 0*, the procedure call returns a symbol corresponding to the given binary *x* list; in other cases the call **Bits[*x*, *p*]** is returned as the unevaluated. The fragment below represents source code of the procedure **Bits** along with examples of its application.

In[2819]:= Bits[x_, P_ /; IntegerQ[P]] := Module[{a, k},
If[StringQ[x] && StringLength[x] == 1, If[1 <= P <= 8,
PadLeft[IntegerDigits[ToCharacterCode[x][[1]], 2], 8][[P]],
If[P == 0, PadLeft[IntegerDigits[ToCharacterCode[x][[1]], 2], 8], Defer[Bits[x, P]]]],
If[BinaryListQ[x] && 1 <= Length[Flatten[x]] <= 8, a = Length[x];
FromCharacterCode[Sum[x[[k]]*2^(a - k), {k, 1, a}]], Defer[Bits[x, P]]]]]

In[2820]:= Map9[Bits, {"A", "A", {1, 0, 0, 0, 0, 0, 1}, "A", {1, 1, 1, 1, 0, 1}}, {0, 2, 0, 9, 0}]
Out[2820]= {{0, 1, 0, 0, 0, 0, 0, 1}, 1, "A", Bits["A", 9], "="}

If the previous **Bits** procedure provides rather *simple* processing of symbols, the following 2 procedures **BitSet1** and **BitGet1** provide the expanded bit–by–bit information processing like our *Maple* procedures. In the *Maple* we created a number of procedures *(Bit, Bit1, xNB, xbyte1, xbyte)* which provide bit–by–bit information processing [47]; the *Mathematica* has similar means too, in particular, the call **BitSet[*n*, *k*]** returns the result of setting of *1* into the *k-th* position of binary representation of a *n* integer. The following fragment represents the procedure, whose call **BitSet1[*n*, *p*]** returns the result of setting into positions of the binary representation of a *n* integer that are determined by the first elements of sublists of a nested *p* list, {*0* | *1*} – values; in addition, in case of non–nested *p* list the value replacement only in a single position of *n* integer is made. Both procedure **BitSet1** and **BitGet1** are included in the *MathToolBox* package [48,50].

In[2338]:= BitSet1[n_ /; IntegerQ[n] && n >= 0, p_ /; ListQ[p]] :=

Module[{b = 1, c, d, h = If[ListListQ[p], p, {p}], a =
ToExpression[Characters[IntegerString[n, 2]]]},
If[ListListQ[h] && Length[Select[h, Length[#] == 2 && IntegerQ[#[[1]]] &&
IntegerQ[#[[2]]] && MemberQ[{0, 1}, #[[2]]] &]] == Length[h], Null,
Return[Defer[BitSet1[n, p]]]];
For[b, b <= Length[h], b++, {c, d} = {h[[b]][[1]], h[[b]][[2]]};
If[c <= Length[a], a[[c]] = d, Null]];
Sum[a[[k]]*2^(Length[a] – k), {k, Length[a]}]]

In[2339]:= {BitSet1[480, {{3, 1}, {6, 0}, {9, 1}}], BitSet1[80, {4, 0}], BitSet1[80, {7, 1}]}
Out[2339]= {481, 80, 81}
In[2340]:= BitSet1[480, {{3, 1}, {6, 0}, {9, 2}}]
Out[2340]= BitSet1[480, {{3, 1}, {6, 0}, {9, 2}}]

In[89]:= BitGet1[x___, n_ /; IntegerQ[n] && n >= 0, p_ /; IntegerQ[p] && p > 0 || ListQ[p]]:=
Module[{b = 1, c = {}, d, h = If[ListQ[p], p, {p}],
a = ToExpression[Characters[IntegerString[n, 2]]]},
For[b, b <= Length[a], b++, c = Append[c, If[MemberQ[h, b], a[[b]], Null]]];
If[! HowAct[x], x = Length[a], Null]; Select[c, ToString[#] != "Null" &]]

In[90]:= {BitGet1[h, 80, {1, 5, 7}], h, BitGet1[47, {1, 5, 7}], BitGet1[p, 480, {1, 3, 5}], p}
Out[90]= {{1, 0, 0}, 7, {1, 1}, {1, 1, 0}, 9}

Examples of application of the procedures **BitSet1** and **BitGet1** very visually illustrate the told. It should be noted that the **BitSet1** procedure functionally expands both the standard function **BitSet**, and **BitClear** of the *Mathematica* system, whereas the procedure **BitGet1** functionally extands the standard functions **BitGet** and **BitLength** of the system. The call **BitGet1[n, p]** returns the list of bits in the positions of binary representation of an integer *n* that are defined by a *p* list; in addition, in case of a *p* integer the bit in a *p* position of binary representation of *n* integer is returned. While the procedure call **BitGet1[x, n, p]** through a *x* symbol in addition returns number of bits in the binary representation of an integer *n*. The examples of the previous fragment very visually illustrate the aforesaid without the need of any additional explanations.

In the *Mathematica* the *transformation rules* are generally determined by the **Rule** function, whose the call **Rule[a, b]** returns the transformation rule in the format *a –> b*. These rules are used in transformations of expressions by the following functions *ReplaceAll, Replace, ReplaceRepeated, ReplacePart, StringReplaceList, StringCases, StringReplace* which use either one rule, or their list as simple list, and a list of *ListList* type. For dynamic generation of such rules the **GenRules** procedure can be a rather useful, whose the call **GenRules[x, y]** depending on a type of its arguments returns single rule or list of rules; the procedure call **GenRules[x, y, z]** with the third optional *z* argument – *any expression* – returns the list with single transformation rule or the nested list of the *ListList* type. Depending on the encoding format, the procedure call returns result in the following format, namely:

(1) GenRules[{x, y, z, ...}, a] $\Rightarrow$ {x –> a, y –> a, z –> a, ...}
(2) GenRules[{x, y, z, ...}, a, h] $\Rightarrow$ {{x –> a}, {y –> a}, {z –> a}, ...}
(3) GenRules[{x, y, z, ...}, {a, b, c, ...}] $\Rightarrow$ {x –> a, y –> b, z –> c, ...}

(4) **GenRules[{x, y, z, ... }, {a, b, c, ... }, h]** ⇒ {{x –> a}, {y –> b}, {z –> c}, ... }
(5) **GenRules[x, {a, b, c, ... }]** ⇒ {x –> a}
(6) **GenRules[x, {a, b, c, ... }, h]** ⇒ {x –> a}
(7) **GenRules[x, a]** ⇒ {x –> a}
(8) **GenRules[x, a, h]** ⇒ {x –> a}

The **GenRules** procedure is useful, in particular, when in some procedure it is necessary to dynamically generate the transformation rules depending on conditions. The next fragment represents source code of the **GenRules** procedure with most typical examples of its use on all above-mentioned cases of coding of its call.

In[4040]:= GenRules[x_, y_, z___] := Module[{a, b = Flatten[{x}]},
c = Flatten[If[ListQ /@ {x, y} == {True, False}, PadLeft[{}, Length[x], y], {y}]]};
a = Min[Length /@ {b, c}]; b = Map9[Rule, b[[1 ;; a]], c[[1 ;; a]]];
If[{z} == {}, b, b = List /@ b; If[Length[b] == 1, Flatten[b], b]]]

In[4041]:= {GenRules[{x, y, z}, {a, b, c}], GenRules[x, {a, b, c}], GenRules[{x, y}, {a, b, c}], GenRules[x, a], GenRules[{x, y}, a]}
Out[4041]= {{x –> a, y –> b, z –> c}, {x –> a}, {x –> a, y –> b}, {x –> a}, {x –> a, y –> a}}
In[4042]:= {GenRules[{x, y, z}, {a, b, c}, 74], GenRules[x, {a, b, c}, 42], GenRules[x, a, 6], GenRules[{x, y}, {a, b, c}, 47], GenRules[{x, y}, a, 69]}
Out[4042]= {{{x –> a}, {y –> b}, {z –> c}}, {x –> a}, {{x –> a}, {y –> b}}, {x –> a}, {{x –> a}, {y –> a}}}

In[4043]:= GenRules1[x_, y_, z___] := Module[{a, b},
b = If[ListQ[x] && ! ListQ[y], a = Map[Rule[#, y] &, x], If[ListQ[x] &&
ListQ[y], a = Rule @@ {x, y}, {x –> Flatten[{y}][[1]]}]];
b = If[{z} != {}, SplitBy[b, Head[#] & == Rule], b];
If[NestListQ[b] && Length[b] == 1, b[[1]], b]]

In[4044]:= {GenRules1[{x, y, z}, {a, b, c}], GenRules1[x, {a, b, c}], GenRules1[{x, y}, {a, b, c}], GenRules1[x, a], GenRules1[{x, y}, a]}
Out[4044]= {{x, y, z} –> {a, b, c}, {x –> a}, {x, y} –> {a, b, c}, {x –> a}, {x –> a, y –> a}}
In[4045]:= {GenRules[{x, y, z}, {a, b, c}], GenRules[x, {a, b, c}], GenRules[{x, y, z}, {a, b, c}], GenRules[x, a], GenRules[{x, y}, a]}
Out[4045]= {{x –> a, y –> b, z –> c}, {x –> a}, {x –> a, y –> b, z –> c}, {x –> a}, {x –> a, y –> a}}
In[4046]:= {GenRules[{x, y, z}, {a, b, c}, 74], GenRules[x, {a, b, c}, 42], GenRules[x, a, 6], GenRules[{x, y}, a, 69]}
Out[4046]= {{{x –> a}, {y –> b}, {z –> c}}, {x –> a}, {x –> a}, {{x –> a}, {y –> a}}}

In[2457]:= GenRules2[x_ /; ListQ[x], y_] := If[ListQ[y], Map[Rule[x[[#]], y[[#]]] &,
Range[1, Min[Length[x], Length[y]]]], Map[Rule[x[[#]], y] &, Range[1, Length[x]]]]

In[2458]:= {GenRules2[{x, y, z}, {a, b, c}], GenRules2[{x, y, z}, h], GenRules2[{x, y, z}, {a, b}], GenRules2[{x, y, z}, {a, b, c, d}]}
Out[2458]= {{x –> a, y –> b, z –> c}, {x –> h, y –> h, z –> h}, {x –> a, y –> b}, {x –> a, y –> b, z –> c}}

The **GenRules** procedure of the same name which is functionally equivalent to the initial procedure is given as an useful enough modification provided that lists *x* and *y* as two first arguments have identical length. The simple **GenRules2** function which depending on type of the 2nd argument generates the list of transformation rules of the above formats *(1)* and *(3)* respectively finishes the fragment as illustrate very transparent examples. In certain cases these tools allows quite significantly to reduce source code of the procedures. Some means of the *MathToolBox* package essentially use these tools [48,50].

Along with the considered transformation rules of the form *a -> b* the system allows to use also of the *delayed* rules *(RuleDelayed)* of the form *a :> b* or *a :→ b* which are realized only at the time of their usage. In the rest they are similar to the already considered transformation rules. For generation of list of transformation *rules* of similar type can be used the **GenRules** procedure represented above for which the **Rule** function is replaced by the **RuleDelayed** function, or can be used its **GenRules3** modification adapted to application of one or other function by the corresponding encoding of the third argument at the call **GenRules3[*x, y, h, z*]**, where *x, y, z* – arguments completely similar to the arguments of the same name of the procedure **GenRules** whereas the third *h* argument determines the mode of generation of the list of the usual or delayed rules on the basis of the received value "rd" *(delayed rule)* or "r" *(simple rule)*. The fragment below represents a source code of the **GenRules3** procedure along with the most typical examples of its application.

In[2623]:= GenRules3[x_, y_, h_ /; h == "r" || h == "rd", z___] := Module[{a, b = Flatten[{x}]},
c = Flatten[If[Map[ListQ, {x, y}] == {True, False}, PadLeft[{}, Length[x], y], {y}]]},
a = Min[Map[Length, {b, c}]]; b = Map9[If[h == "r", Rule, RuleDelayed], b[[1 ;; a]], c[[1 ;; a]]];
If[{z} == {}, b, b = Map[List, b]; If[Length[b] == 1, Flatten[b], b]]]

In[2624]:= GenRules3[{x, y, z}, {a, b, c}, "r", 590]
Out[2624]= {{x -> a}, {y -> b}, {z -> c}}
In[2625]:= GenRules3[{x, y, z}, {a, b, c}, "rd", 90]
Out[2625]= {{x :→ a}, {y :→ b}, {z :→ c}}
In[2626]:= GenRules3[{x, y, z}, a, "r"]
Out[2626]= {x -> a, y -> a, z -> a}
In[2627]:= GenRules3[{x, y, z}, a, "rd"]
Out[2627]= {x :→ a, y :→ a, z :→ a}
In[2628]:= GenRules3[{x, y}, {a, b, c, d}, "rd", 590]
Out[2628]= {{x :→ a}, {y :→ b}}
In[2629]:= GenRules3[x, a, "rd", 90]
Out[2629]= {x :→ a}

Considering the importance of the *map* function, since the *Maple 10*, the option `inplace`, admissible only at usage of this function with rectangular *rtable*-objects at renewing these objects in situ was defined. While for objects of other type this mechanism isn't supported as certain examples from [25-27] illustrate. For the purpose of disposal of this shortcoming we offered a quite simple **MapInSitu** procedure [27,47]. Along with it the similar tools and for *Mathematica* in the form of 2 functions **MapInSitu** and **MapInSitu1** together with the **MapInSitu2** procedure have been offered. The following fragment represents source codes of the above tools with typical examples of their application.

In[2650]:= MapInSitu[x_, y_ /; StringQ[y]] :=
ToExpression[y <> "=" <> ToString[Map[x, ToExpression[y]]]]

In[2651]:= y = {a, b, c}; h = {{4.2, 7.4}, {4.7, 6.9}}; {MapInSitu[G, "y"], MapInSitu[Sin, "h"]}
Out[2651]= {{G[a], G[b], G[c]}, {{-0.871576, 0.898708}, {-0.999923, 0.57844}}}

In[2652]:= {y, h}
Out[2652]= {{G[a], G[b], G[c]}, {{-0.871576, 0.898708}, {-0.999923, 0.57844}}}
In[2653]:= {H, G} = {{8.48, 47.69, 20.27}, {7.8, 47.69, 20.27}}
Out[2653]= {{8.48, 47.69, 20.27}, {7.8, 47.69, 20.27}}

In[2654]:= MapInSitu1[x_, y_] :=
ToExpression[ToString[Args[MapInSitu, 90]] <> "=" <> ToString[Map[x, y]]]

In[2655]:= y = {{80.42, 25.57}, {80.45, 80.89}}; MapInSitu1[Sin, y]
Out[2655]= {{-0.95252, 0.423458}, {-0.942959, -0.711344}}
In[2656]:= y
Out[2656]= {-0.942959, -0.711344}

In[2657]:= MapInSitu2[x_, y_] := Module[{a = Map[x, y], b = ToString[y], h, d = {}, k = 1,
c = Select[Names["`*"], StringFreeQ[#, "$"] &]},
For[k, k <= Length[c], k++, h = c[[k]];
If[ToString[ToExpression[h]] === b, d = Append[d, h], Null]];
For[k = 1, k <= Length[d], k++, h = d[[k]]; ToExpression[h <> " = " <> ToString[a]]]; a]

In[2658]:= MapInSitu2[Sin, {7.4, 47.69, 20.27}]
Out[2658]= {0.898708, -0.536353, 0.988718}
In[2659]:= {H, G}
Out[2659]= {{8.48, 47.69, 20.27}, {7.8, 47.69, 20.27}}

With the mechanisms used by the *Maple*-procedure **MapInSitu** and other *Math*-functions **MapInSitu** of the same name and **MapInSitu1** can familiarize in [25-33,47,48,50]. The tool **MapInSitu** for both systems are characterized by the prerequisite, the second argument at their call points out on an identifier in the string format to which a certain value has been ascribed earlier and that is updated in situ after its processing by the {*map*|**Map**} function.

The call **MapInSitu1**[*x*, *y*] provides assignment to all identifiers to which in current session the values coinciding with value of the second *y* argument have been ascribed, of the result of the call of **Map**, updating their values in situ. Anyway, the calls of these tools return the **Map**[*x*, *y*] as a result. The previous fragment presents source codes of all these procedures along with typical examples of their application.

The standard **Part** function is a quite useful at analysis and processing of the expressions in addition to the **Head** function, allowing six formats of encoding [60]. Between the functions **Head**, **Level** and **Part** some useful relations take place that can be used for problems of the testing of expressions, in particular, **Part**[*Ex*, *0*] ≡ **Head**[*Ex*], **Level**[*Ex*, *1*][[1]] ≡ **Part**[*Ex*, *1*], **Level**[*Ex*, *Infinity*] ≡ **Level**[*Ex*, *-1*], where *Ex* – an arbitrary expression, etc. The given means can be used quite successfully for testing and processing of expressions. Thus, the following fragment represents source code of the procedure, whose the call **Decomp**[*x*] returns the list of all unique atomic components of an expression *x*, including the names of the procedures, variables, functions, operations along with constants. This procedure significantly uses the above functions **Level** and **Head**; application of the functions **Head**, **Level**, **Part** in a number of functions and procedures of the package [48] proved their effectiviness.

In[2417]:= Decomp[x_] := Module[{c = DeleteDuplicates[Flatten[Level[x, Infinity]],
Abs[#1] === Abs[#2] &], b = {}, k},

Software Etudes in the Mathematica

```
Label[ArtKr];
For[k = 1, k <= Length[c], k++, b = Append[b, If[AtomQ[c[[k]]], c[[k]], {Level[c[[k]], -1],
Head[c[[k]]]}]]];
b = DeleteDuplicates[Flatten[b], Abs[#1] === Abs[#2] &];
If[c == b, Return[b], c = b; b = {}; Goto[ArtKr]]]
In[2418]:= Decomp[{6*Cos[x] - n*Sin[y]/(Log[h] - b), ProcQ[c, d]}]
Out[2418]= {6, x, Cos, Times, -1, n, b, h, Log, Plus, Power, y, Sin, c, d, ProcQ}
```

The following procedure makes grouping of the expressions that are given by *L* argument according to their types defined by the **Head2** procedure; in addition, a separate expression or their list is coded as the *L* argument. The procedure call **GroupNames[L]** returns simple list or nested list, whose elements are lists, whose first element – an object type according to the **Head2** procedure, whereas the others – expressions of this type. So, the fragment below represents source code of the **GroupNames** procedure with examples of its application.

```
In[2486]:= GroupNames[L_] :=
Module[{a = If[ListQ[L], L, {L}], c, d, p, t, b = {{"Null", "Null"}}, k = 1},
For[k, k <= Length[a], k++, c = a[[k]]; d = Head2[c]; t = Flatten[Select[b, #[[1]] === d &]];
If[t == {} && (d === Symbol && Attributes[c] === {Temporary}),
AppendTo[b, {Temporary, c}],
If[t == {}, AppendTo[b, {d, c}], p = Flatten[Position[b, t]][[1]]; AppendTo[b[[p]], c]]]];
b = b[[2 ;; -1]]; b = Gather[b, #1[[1]] == #2[[1]] &];
b = Map[DeleteDuplicates[Flatten[#]] &, b]; If[Length[b] == 1, Flatten[b], b]]
In[2487]:= GroupNames[{Sin, Cos, ProcQ, Locals2, 80, Map1, StrStr, 69/74, Avz, Nvalue1,
a + b, Avz, 74, Agn, If, Vsv}]
Out[2487]= {{System, Sin, Cos, If}, {Module, ProcQ, Locals2, Nvalue1}, {Integer, 80, 74},
{Function, Map1, StrStr}, {Rational, 69/74}, {Symbol, Avz}, {Plus, a + b},
{Temporary, Avz, Agn, Vsv}}
In[2489]:= L = GroupNames[Names["*"]]
Out[2489]= {{Function, "AcNb", ..., "$ProcName"},
{String, "ActionMenu", ..., "GroebnerBasis"},
{Module, "ActiveProcess", ..., "WhichN"},
{Temporary, "Avz", ..., "$Vsv"},
{System, "\[FormalA]", ..., "CallPacket"}}
In[2490]:= Map[Length, L] - 1
Out[2490]= {356, 32, 920, 75, 6928}
```

Particularly, from the above examples of the **GroupNames** use follows, that names of the current session belong to five groups: *Function, String, Module, Temporary* and *System*, the number of elements in which is *356, 32, 920, 75* and *6928* respectively. It should be noted, for receiving this result a rather considerable time expenditure is needed, because of the need of testing of a rather large number of means in the current session.

In addition to the **GroupNames** procedure a certain interest can represent a rather simple procedure, whose call **LocObj[x]** returns the three-element list whose first element defines an object *x*, the second element determines its type in the context *{"Module", "SFunction"* *(system function)*, **"Expression"**, **"Function"**}, whereas the third element – its location in the context {**"Global`"** – the current session, **"System`"** – the kernel or the *Mathematica* library, **"Context"** – a system or user package which has been uploaded into the current session and which contains definition of the *x* object}. The following fragment represents source code of the **GroupNames** procedure and the most typical examples of its application.

In[2244]:= LocObj[x_] := Module[{a = Head1[x], b},

b[y_] := Context[y]; If[a === Module, {x, "Module", b[x]},

If[a === Function, {x, "Function", b[x]}, If[SystemQ[x], {x, "SFunction", b[x]},

{x, "Expression", "Global`"}]]]]

In[2245]:= Map[LocObj, {PureDefinition, ProcQ, StrStr, Sin, a + b, 500}]
Out[2245]= {{PureDefinition, "Module", "AladjevProcedures`"},
{ProcQ, "Module", "AladjevProcedures`"}, {StrStr, "Function", "AladjevProcedures`"},
{Sin, "SFunction", "System`"}, {a + b, "Expression", "Global`"}, {500, "Expression", "Global`"}}

While the call **Names1[]** returns the nested 4-element list whose *1st* element defines the list of names of procedures, the *2nd* element – the list of names of functions, the third element – the list of names whose definitions have been evaluated in the current session whereas the fourth element defines the list of other names associated with the current session. The next fragment represents source code of the **Names1** procedure with an application example.

In[2545]:= Names1[x___ /; {x} == {}] :=
Module[{c = 1, d, h, b = {{}, {}, {}, {}}, a = Select[Names["`*"], StringTake[#, {1, 1}] != "$" &]},
While[c <= Length[a], d = a[[c]]; If[ProcQ[d], AppendTo[b[[1]], d],
If[Quiet[Check[QFunction[d], False]], AppendTo[b[[2]], d],
h = ToString[Quiet[DefFunc[d]]];
If[! SameQ[h, "Null"] && h == "Attributes[" <> d <> "] = {Temporary}", AppendTo[b[[3]], d]],
AppendTo[b[[4]], d]]]; c++]; b]

In[2546]:= Names1[]
Out[2546]= {{"Bt", "Mas", "Names1", "W"}, {"F", "G"}, {"Art27$", "Kr20"}, {}}

The **Names1** procedure is a rather useful tools in a number of appendices, in particular, in certain questions of procedural programming, in certain relations expanding the standard **Names** function of the *Mathematica* system. Though, during work in the current session, the **Names1** call demands the increasing time expenditure, assuming its circumspect use.

On the other hand, the procedure call **CurrentNames[]** without arguments returns a nested list, whose elements define sublists of names in string format of tools of the current session which by the first element are identified by their context other than the context **"System'"**. Whereas the procedure call **CurrentNames[x]**, where *x* – an undefinite symbol – through *x* returns the nested list of the above format whose first element of sublists is a context while the others define symbols with this context that have no *definitions*, i.e. so-called *concomitant* symbols of different types. The next fragment represents source code of the **CurrentNames** procedure with an example of its application.

In[3893]:= CurrentNames[x__] :=
Module[{b, c, d = {}, a = Complement[Names["*"], Names["System`*"]]},
b = Map[{Context[#], #} &, a]; c = Gather[b, #1[[1]] == #2[[1]] &];

c = Map[DeleteDuplicates[Flatten[#]] &, c];
If[{x} != {} && ! HowAct[x], Map[Do[AppendTo[d, {#[[1]], If[MemberQ[{$Failed, "Undefined"}, PureDefinition[#[[k]]]], #[[k]], Nothing]}], {k, 2, Length[#]}] &, c];
x = Map[DeleteDuplicates[Flatten[#]] &, Gather[d, #1[[1]] == #2[[1]] &]], Null]; c]

In[3894]:= CurrentNames[g47]
Out[3894]= {{"AladjevProcedures`", "a", "A", "a1", "a1$", "AcNb", "ActBFM", ... },
{"Global`", "ActionFunction", "AladjevProcedures", ... },
{"PacletManager`", "CreatePaclet", "PackPaclet", ... },
{"Parallel`Debug`", "LapPerformance", "MathLink", ... },
{"Parallel`Debug`Perfmon`", "masterAbs", ..., "subIDs"}}

In[3895]:= g47
Out[3895]= {{"AladjevProcedures`", "a", "A", "a1", "a1$", "a$", "A$", "b", ... },
{"Global`", "ActionFunction", "AladjevProcedures", ... },
{"PacletManager`", "PacletManager", "PacletSite"},
{"Parallel`Debug`", "MathLink", "Perfmon", "Queueing", "SendReceive", "SharedMemory", "TraceHandler", "Tracers", "$SystemDebug"}, {"Parallel`Debug`Perfmon`"}}

The procedure call **RemoveNames[]** without arguments provides removal from the current *Mathematica* session of the names, whose types are other than procedures and functions, and whose definitions have been evaluated in the current session; moreover, the names are removed so that aren't recognized by the *Mathematica* system any more. The procedure call **RemoveNames[]** along with removal of the above names from the current session returns the nested 2-element list whose first element defines the list of names of procedures, while the second element – the list of names of functions whose definitions have been evaluated in the current session. The following fragment represents source code of the **RemoveNames** procedure with typical examples of its application.

In[2565]:= RemoveNames[x___] := Module[{a = Select[Names["`*"],
ToString[Definition[#]] != "Null" &], b},
ToExpression["Remove[" <> StringTake[ToString[MinusList[a, Select[a, ProcQ[#] ||
! SameQ[ToString[Quiet[DefFunc[#]]], "Null"] ||
Quiet[Check[QFunction[#], False]] &]]], {2, -2}] <> "]"];
b = Select[a, ProcQ[#] &]; {b, MinusList[a, b]}]

In[2566]:= {Length[Names["`*"]], RemoveNames[], Names["`*"]}
Out[2566]= {80, {{"Ar", "Kr", "Rans"}, {"Ian"}}, {"Ar", "Kr", "Rans", "Ian"}}
In[2567]:= RemoveNames[]
Out[2567]= {{"Art", "Kr", "Rans"}, {"Ian"}}
In[2568]:= RemoveNames[]
Out[2568]= {{"M", "M1", "M2"}, {"F", "F42", "F47", "$LoadContexts"}}

The **RemoveNames** procedure is a rather useful means in some appendices connected with cleaning of the working *Mathematica* field from definitions of the non-used symbols. The given procedure confirmed a certain efficiency in management of random access memory.

The **Remove** function plays an important enough part in work with symbols and contexts. So, the **Remove** function can be used to get rid of symbols that are not needed, and which may shadow the symbols in contexts later on a context path. The call **Remove[*x*, *y*, *z*, *f*, ...]**

removes {*x*, *y*, *z*, *f*, ...} symbols completely, so that their names are no longer recognized in the current session. In addition, the **Remove** does not affect the symbols with the *Protected* attribute. It is impossible to address itself to a removed symbol without its recreating. If an expression contains a symbol which was removed, the removed symbol will be printed as *Removed["n"]*, where its *n* name is given in string format. The procedure call **RemovedQ[*x*]** returns *True*, if *x* symbol was removed of the current session, and *False* otherwise. The next fragment represents source code of the **RemovedQ** procedure along with typical examples of its application.

In[3308]:= RemovedQ[x_] := Module[{a = DeleteDuplicates[(StringTake[#, {1, Flatten[StringPosition[#, "`"]][[1]]}] &) /@ Contexts[]], b},
If[MemberQ4[Flatten[(NamesContext[#] &) /@ a], ToString[x]], False, True]]

In[3309]:= {Attributes["\[FormalH]"], Unprotect["\[FormalH]"], Remove["\[FormalH]"], RemovedQ["\[FormalH]"]}
Out[3309]= {{Protected}, {"\[FormalH]"}, Null, True}
In[3310]:= avz := 74; {RemovedQ["avz"], Remove[avz], RemovedQ["avz"]}
Out[3310]= {False, Null, True}

In[3320]:= MultipleContexts[x_] := Module[{a = DeleteDuplicates[Map[StringTake[#, {1, Flatten[StringPosition[#, "`"]][[1]]}] &, Contexts[]]], b},
b = Map[{#, NamesContext[#]} &, a];
Map[If[MemberQ4[#[[2]], {ToString[x], #[[1]] <> ToString[x]}], #[[1]], Nothing] &, b]]

In[3321]:= ProcQ[x_, y_, z_] := x*y*z
In[3322]:= MultipleContexts[ProcQ]
Out[3322]= {"AladjevProcedures`", "Global`"}

The mechanism of contexts of the *Mathematica* system allows the existence in the current session of symbols of the same name with different contexts. The call **MultipleContexts[*x*]** returns the list of contexts attributed to a *x* symbol. The above fragment represents source code of the **MultipleContexts** procedure with an example of its application.

Using our procedures and functions such as **DefFunc3, HeadPF, ToString1, SymbolQ** and **PrefixQ**, it is possible to obtain the more developed means of testing of program objects of the *Mathematica* system; the **ObjType** procedure acts as a similar tool. The procedure call **ObjType[*x*]** returns the type of a *x* object in the context {*DynamicModule, Function, Block or Module*}, in other cases the type of an expression assigned in the current session to *x* symbol by assignment operators {:=, =} is returned. The following fragment represents source code of the **ObjType** procedure along with typical application examples.

In[2220]:= ObjType[x_] := Module[{a, b, c, d = {}, h},
If[ToString1[HeadPF[x]] === "HeadPF[" <> ToString1[x] <> "]" || SymbolQ[HeadPF[x]], Return[Head[x]], b = Flatten[{Definition1[x]}]; c = Length[b]];
Do[AppendTo[d, h = StringSplit[b[[k]], " := "]; {h[[1]], If[PrefixQ["Module[{", h[[2]]], Module, If[PrefixQ["Block[{", h[[2]]], Block, If[PrefixQ["Function[", h[[2]]], Function, If[PrefixQ["DynamicModule[{", h[[2]]], DynamicModule, {Function, Head[ToExpression[h[[2]]]]}]]]]}]; Flatten[d, 1]]

In[2221]:= Sv[x_, y_] := x + y; G[x_] := Block[{}, x^2]; V[x_] := If[EvenQ[x], x, 2*x];
V[x_, y_] := Block[{a = If[PrimeQ[x], NextPrime[y]]}, a*(x + y)]
In[2222]:= Map[ObjType, {ObjType, 590, a + b, ProcQ}]
Out[2222]= {{"ObjType[x_]", Module}, Integer, Plus, {"ProcQ[x_]", Module}}
In[2223]:= Map[ObjType, {Sv, G, V}]
Out[2223]= {{"Sv[x_, y_]", {Function, Plus}}, {"G[x_]", Block}, {"V[x_]", {Function, Times}, "V[x_, y_]", Block}}
In[2224]:= ObjType[DefFunc3]
Out[2224]= {"DefFunc3[x_ /; BlockFuncModQ[x]]", Module}
In[2225]:= F := Function[{x, y}, x + y]; {F[90, 500], ObjType[F]}
Out[2225]= {590, Function}
In[2226]:= F1 := #1*#2 &; {F1[90, 500], ObjType[F1]}
Out[2226]= {45000, Function}
In[2227]:= Map[ObjType, {Head1, StrStr}]
Out[2227]= {{"Head1[x_]", Module}, {"StrStr[x_]", {Function, String}}}
In[2228]:= Agn := "4247&689886"; Avz = 2016; Map[ObjType, {Agn, Avz}]
Out[2228]= {String, Integer}

Here is quite appropriate to make one explanation: the **ObjType** procedure attributed to the *Function* type not only especially functional objects, but also definitions of the format such as **Name[x_, y_, z_, ...] := *Expression*;** in this case the call returns the list of the next format, namely: {"**Name[x_, y_, z_, ...]**", {*Function*, *Head*[*Expression*]}}. Because of the aforesaid the **ObjType** procedure is represented to us as a rather useful means at testing of the objects of various type in the current session in problems of procedural programming.

In a number of cases exists an urgent need of determination of the program objects along with their types activated directly in the current session. This problem is solved by means of the **TypeActObj** procedure whose call **TypeActObj[]** returns the nested list, whose sublists in the string format by the first element contain types of active objects of the current session, whereas other elements of the sublist are names corresponding to this type; in addition, the types recognized by the *Mathematica*, or types of expressions defined by us, in particular, {*Procedure, Function*} can protrude as a type. In a certain sense the **TypeActObj** procedure supplements the **ObjType** procedure. The following fragment represents the source code of the **TypeActObj** procedure with examples of its application.

In[2787]:= TypeActObj[] := Module[{a = Names["`*"], b = {}, c, d, h, p, k = 1},
Quiet[For[k, k <= Length[a], k++, h = a[[k]]; c = ToExpression[h];
p = StringJoin["0", ToString[Head[c]]];
If[! StringFreeQ[h, "$"] || (p === Symbol && "Definition"[c] === Null), Continue[],
b = Append[b, {h, If[ProcQ[c], "0Procedure",
If[Head1[c] === Function, "0Function", p]]}]]]];
a = Quiet[Gather1[Select[b, ! #1[[2]] === Symbol &], 2]];
a = ToExpression[StringReplace[ToString1[DeleteDuplicates /@ Sort /@ Flatten /@ a],
"AladjevProcedures`TypeActObj`" -> ""]];
Append[{}, Do[a[[k]][[1]] = StringTake[a[[k]][[1]], {2, -1}], {k, Length[a]}]]; a]
In[2788]:= TypeActObj[]

Out[2788]= {{"Symbol", "A", "B", "g", "H3", "m", "n", "PacletFind", "System", "Procedure"}, {"Procedure", "As", "Kr"}, {"Function", "G", "V"}, {"List", "xyz"}}

In[2826]:= **TypeActObj[]**

Out[2826]= {{"String", "Agn"}, {"Symbol", "atr", "F2", "F47", "M", "Sv", "V"}, {"Integer", "Avz"}, {"Function", "F", "F1"}, {"Procedure", "G", "M2", "M3", "M4", "M5", "RemoveNames"}}

In the context of use of the standard functions **Nest** and **Map** for definition of the new pure functions on the basis of the available ones, it is possible to offer the procedure as an useful generalization of the standard **Map** function, whose call **Mapp[F, E, x]** returns the result of application of a function or procedure *F* to an *E* expression with transfer to it of the factual arguments determined by a tuple of *x* expressions which can be and empty. In a case of the empty *x* tuple the identity **Map[F, E]** ≡ **Mapp[F, E]** takes place. As formal arguments of the standard function **Map[f, g]** act the *f* name of a procedure or function whereas as the second argument – an arbitrary *g* expression, to whose operands of the 1st level the *f* is applied. The following fragment represents source code of the **Mapp** procedure with typical examples of its application.

In[2634]:= **Mapp[f_ /; ProcQ[f] || SysFuncQ[f] || SymbolQ[f], Ex_, x___] :=
Module[{a = Level[Ex, 1], b = {x}, c = {}, h, g = Head[Ex], k = 1},
If[b == {}, Map[f, Ex], h = Length[a];
For[k, k <= h, k++, AppendTo[c, ToString[f] <> "[" <> ToString1[a[[k]]] <> ", " <>
ListStrToStr[Map[ToString1, {x}]] <> "]"]]; g @@ Map[ToExpression, c]]]**

In[2635]:= **Mapp[F, {a, b, c}, x, y, z]**
Out[2635]= {F[a, x, y, z], F[b, x, y, z], F[c, x, y, z]}

In[2636]:= **Mapp[F, a + b + c, x, y, z]**
Out[2636]= F[a, x, y, z] + F[b, x, y, z] + F[c, x, y, z]

In[2637]:= **Mapp[F, (m + n)/(g + h) + Sin[x], a, b, c]**
Out[2637]= F[(m + n)/(g + h), a, b, c] + F[Sin[x], a, b, c]

In[2638]:= **Mapp[StringPosition, {"11123", "33234"}, {"2", "3", "23"}]**
Out[2638]= {{{4, 4}, {4, 5}, {5, 5}}, {{1, 1}, {2, 2}, {3, 3}, {3, 4}, {4, 4}}}

In[2639]:= **Mapp[StringReplace, {"123525", "2595"}, {"2" -> "V", "5" -> "G"}]**
Out[2639]= {"1V3GVG", "VG9G"}

In[2640]:= **Map[F, {{a, b}, {c, d, e}}]**
Out[2640]= {F[{a, b}], F[{c, d, e}]}

In[2641]:= **Mapp[F, {{a, b}, {c, d, e}}, x, y, z]**
Out[2641]= {F[{a, b}, x, y, z], F[{c, d, e}, x, y, z]}

In[2642]:= **Mapp[ProcQ, {Sin, ProcQ, Mapp, PureDefinition, SysFuncQ}]**
Out[2642]= {False, True, True, True, False}

In[2653]:= **Mapp1[f_ /; SymbolQ[f], L_ /; ListQ[L]] := Module[{b, a = Attributes[f]},
SetAttributes[f, Listable]; b = Map[f, L]; ClearAllAttributes[f]; SetAttributes[f, a]; b]**

In[2654]:= **Map[F, {{a, b, c}, {x, y, {c, d, {h, k, t}}}}]**
Out[2654]= {F[{a, b, c}], F[{x, y, {c, d, {h, k, t}}}]}

In[2655]:= **Mapp[F, {{a, b, c}, {x, y, {c, d, {h, k, t}}}}]**
Out[2655]= {F[{a, b, c}], F[{x, y, {c, d, {h, k, t}}}]}

In[2656]:= **Mapp1[F, {{a, b, c}, {x, y, {c, d, {h, k, t}}}}]**

Out[2656]= {{F[a], F[b], F[c]}, {F[x], F[y], {F[c], F[d], {F[h], F[k], F[t]}}}}

We will note that realization of algorithm of the **Mapp** procedure is based on the following relation, namely:

Map[*F*, *Expr*] ≡ Head[*Expr*][Sequences[Map[*F*, Level[*Expr*, 1]]]]

Whose rightness follows from definition of system functions **Head, Map, Level,** and also of the **Sequences** procedure considered in the present book. A simple example rather visually illustrates the aforesaid:

In[4942]:= Map[F, (m + n)/(g + h) + Sin[x]] == Head[(m + n)/(g + h) + Sin[x]][Sequences[Map[F, Level[(m + n)/(g + h) + Sin[x], 1]]]]
Out[4942]= True

The given relation can be used and at realization of cyclic structures for the solution of the problems of other directionality, including programming on the basis of use of mechanism of the pure functions. Whereas the **Mapp** procedure in the certain cases rather significantly simplifies programming of various tasks. The *Listable* attribute for a *f* function defines that the *f* function will be automatically applied to elements of the list that acts as its argument. Such approach can be used rather successfully in a number of cases of programming of the blocks, functions and modules.

Thus, in this context a rather simple **Mapp1** procedure is of interest, whose call **Mapp1[*x*, *y*]** unlike the call **Map[*x*, *y*]** of standard function returns result of applying of a block, function or a *x* module to all elements of *y* list, regardless of their location on list levels. The previous fragment presents source code of the **Mapp1** procedure with comparative examples relative to the system **Map** function.

Meanwhile, for a number of functions and expressions the *Listable* attribute does not work, and in this case the system provides two special functions **Map** and **Thread** that in a certain relation can quite be referred to the structural tools that provide application of functions to parts of expressions. In this conexion we created a group of enough simple and at the same time useful procedures and functions, so-called *Map*-means that rather significantly expand the system **Map** function. Two means of this group – the procedures **Mapp** and **Mapp1** that have a number of appendices in means of the *MathToolBox* package [48] have already been presented above, we will present also other means of this *Map*-group. The fragment below represents source codes of means of this group with typical examples of their applications which on the formal level rather visually illustrate results of calls of these means on correct factual arguments. Similar representation allows to significantly minimize descriptions of tools when on the basis of formal results of calls it is quite simple to understand an essence of each means of the above *Map*-group.

In[2625]:= Map1[x_ /; ListQ[x] && AllTrue[Map[SymbolQ[#] &, x], TrueQ], y_List] := Map[Symbol[ToString[#]][Sequences[y]] &, x]

In[2626]:= Map1[{F, G, H, V}, {x, y, z, h, p, t}]
Out[2626]= {F[x, y, z, h, p, t], G[x, y, z, h, p, t], H[x, y, z, h, p, t], V[x, y, z, h, p, t]}

In[2627]:= Map2[F_ /; SymbolQ[F], c_ /; ListQ[c], d_ /; ListQ[d]] := Map[Symbol[ToString[F]][#, Sequences[d]] &, c]

In[2628]:= Map2[F, {a, b, c, d, e, g}, {x, y, z, p, q, h}]

Out[2628]= {F[a, x, y, z, p, q, h], F[b, x, y, z, p, q, h], F[c, x, y, z, p, q, h], F[d, x, y, z, p, q, h], F[e, x, y, z, p, q, h], F[g, x, y, z, p, q, h]}

In[2629]:= Map3[f_ /; SymbolQ[f], g_, j_ /; ListQ[j]] := Map[Symbol[ToString[f]][g, #] &, j]

In[2630]:= Map3[F, H, {x, y, z, h, p, h, m, n}]
Out[2630]= {F[H, x], F[H, y], F[H, z], F[H, h], F[H, p], F[H, h], F[H, m], F[H, n]}

In[2631]:= Map4[f_ /; SymbolQ[f], j_ /; ListQ[j], x_] := Map[Symbol[ToString[f]][#, x] &, j]

In[2632]:= Map4[F, {a, b, c, d, h, g, m, n}, x]
Out[2632]= {F[a, x], F[b, x], F[c, x], F[d, x], F[h, x], F[g, x], F[m, x], F[n, x]}

In[2633]:= Map5[F_, L_ /; NestListQ[L]] := Map[F[Sequences[#]] &, L]

In[2634]:= Map5[S, {{x1, y1, z1, t1}, {x2, y2, z2}, {x3, y3}, {x4, y4, z4, t4, m, n}}]
Out[2634]= {S[x1, y1, z1, t1], S[x2, y2, z2], S[x3, y3], S[x4, y4, z4, t4, m, n]}

In[2635]:= F[x_, y_, z_, h_] := a[x]*b[y]*d[z]*g[z] − c[x, y, z]

In[2636]:= Map5[F, {{x1, y1, z1, t1}, {x2, y2, z2}, {x3, y3}, {x4, y4, z4, t4, m, n}}]
Out[2636]= {−c[x1,y1,z1] + a[x1]*b[y1]*d[z1]*g[z1], F[x2,y2,z2], F[x3,y3], F[x4,y4,z4,t4,m,n]}

In[2637]:= Map6[F_ /; PureFuncQ[F], L_ /; ListListQ[L]] :=
Module[{a, h, p, b = Length[L], c = Length[L[[1]]], d = {}, k = 1},
h = StringTake[ToString[F], {1, −4}];
For[k, k <= b, k++, a = {}; AppendTo[d, StringReplace[h, Flatten[{For[p = 1, p <= c, p++,
AppendTo[a, "#" <> ToString[p] -> ToString[L[[k]][[p]]]], a}][[2 ;; −1]]]]]; ToExpression[d]]

In[2638]:= Map6[a[#1]*b[#2]*d[#3]*g[#4] − c[#1, #2, #3] &, {{x1, y1, z1, t1}, {x2, y2, z2, t2}, {x3, y3, z3, t3}, {x4, y4, z4, t4}}]
Out[2638]= {−c[x1, y1, z1] + a[x1]*b[y1]*d[z1]*g[t1], −c[x2, y2, z2] + a[x2]*b[y2]*d[z2]*g[t2], −c[x3, y3, z3] + a[x3]*b[y3]*d[z3]*g[t3] − c[x4, y4, z4] + a[x4]*b[y4]*d[z4]*g[t4]}

In[2639]:= Map7[x__ /; AllTrue[Map[SymbolQ, {x}], TrueQ], y_ /; ListQ[y]] :=
Map[FunCompose[Reverse[Map[Symbol, Map[ToString, {x}]]], #] &, y]

In[2640]:= Map7[F, G, H, {a, b, c, d, h}]
Out[2640]= {F[G[H[a]]], F[G[H[b]]], F[G[H[c]]], F[G[H[d]]], H[G[F[h]]]}

In[2641]:= Map7[Sin, Sqrt, N, {20, 27, 48, 68, 73, 590}]
Out[2641]= {−0.971278, −0.885251, 0.601213, 0.924059, 0.771232, −0.746526}

In[2642]:= Map8[x__ /; AllTrue[Map[SymbolQ, {x}], TrueQ], y_ /; ListQ[y]] :=
Map[Symbol[ToString[#]][Sequences[y]] &, {x}]

In[2643]:= Map8[x, y, z, h, g, {a, b, c, d}]
Out[2643]= {x[a, b, c, d], y[a, b, c, d], z[a, b, c, d], h[a, b, c, d], g[a, b, c, d]}

In[2644]:= Map9[F_ /; SymbolQ[F], x_ /; ListQ[x], y_ /; ListQ[y]] :=
If[Length[x] == Length[y], Map13[F, {x, y}], Defer[Map9[F, x, y]]]

In[2645]:= Map9[F, {a, b, c, d, g, p}, {x, y, z, h, s, w}]
Out[2645]= {F[a, x], F[b, y], F[c, z], F[d, h], F[g, s], F[p, w]}

In[2646]:= Map9[Rule, {"74a", "69g", "48s", "90b"}, {"a", "b", "c", "d"}]
Out[2646]= {"74a" −> "a", "69g" −> "b", "48s" −> "c", "90b" −> "d"}

In[2647]:= Map9[Rule, {a, b, c, d, m, p}, {x, y, z, t, n, q}]

Out[2647]= {a -> x, b -> y, c -> z, d -> t, m -> n, p -> q}
In[2648]:= **Map9[Plus, {a, b, c, d, g, p, u}, {x, y, z, h, s, w, t}]**
Out[2648]= {a + x, b + y, c + z, d + h, g + s, p + w, t + u}
In[2649]:= **Map10[F_ /; SymbolQ[F], x_, L_ /; ListQ[L], y___] :=**
Map[Symbol[ToString[F]][x, #, Sequences[{y}]] &, L]
In[2650]:= **Map10[F, x, {a, "b", c, d}, y, "z", h]**
Out[2650]= {F[x, a, y, "z", h], F[x, "b", y, "z", h], F[x, c, y, "z", h], F[x, d, y, "z", h]}
In[2651]:= **Map10[F, "x", {a, "b", c, d, f, g}]**
Out[2651]= {F["x", a], F["x", "b"], F["x", c], F["x", d], F["x", f], F["x", g]}
In[2652]:= **Map10[SuffPref, "C:/89b8fc17cbdce3/mxdwdrv.dll", {".nb", ".m", ".dll", ".cdf"}, 2]**
Out[2652]= {False, False, True, False}
In[2653]:= **Map11[x_ /; SymbolQ[x], y_ /; ListQ[y], z_] :=**
(If[ListQ[#1], (x[#1, z] &) /@ #1, x[#1, z]] &) /@ y
In[2654]:= **Map11[G, {x, y, z, m, n, g}, t]**
Out[2654]= {G[x, t], G[y, t], G[z, t], G[m, t], G[n, t], G[g, t]}
In[2655]:= **Map12[F_ /; SymbolQ[F], x_ /; NestListQ1[x]] :=**
Module[{c, a = ToString1[x], b = ToString[F] <> "@"},
c = StringReplace[a, {"{" -> "{" <> b, ", " -> "," <> b}];
c = StringReplace[c, b <> "{" -> "{"]; ToExpression[c]]
In[2656]:= **Map12[F, {{a, b, c}, {x, y, z}, h, {m, {{"p"}}, n, p, {{{x, "y"}}}}}]**
Out[2656]= {{F[a], F[b], F[c]}, {F[x], F[y], F[z]}, F[h], {F[m], {{F["p"]}}, F[n], F[p], {{{F[x], F["y"]}}}}}
In[2657]:= **Map12[ToString1, {{a, b, c}, {x, y, z}, "h", {m, {"x"}, n, p}}]**
Out[2657]= {{"a", "b", "c"}, {"x", "y", "z"}, "\"h\"", {"m", {"\"x\""}, "n", "p"}}
In[2658]:= **Map13[x_ /; SymbolQ[x], y_ /; ListListQ[y]] :=**
Module[{k, j, a = Length[y], b = Length[y[[1]]], c = {}, d = {}},
For[k = 1, k <= b, k++, For[j = 1, j <= a, j++,
AppendTo[c, y[[j]][[k]]]]; AppendTo[d, Apply[x, c]]; c = {}]; d]
In[2659]:= **Map13[F, {{a, b, c, s}, {x, y, z, g}, {m, n, p, w}}]**
Out[2659]= {F[a, x, m], F[b, y, n], F[c, z, p], F[s, g, w]}
In[2660]:= **Map13[ProcQ, {{ProcQ}}]**
Out[2660]= {True}
In[2661]:= **Map13[Plus, {{a, b, c, g, t}, {x, y, z, g, t}, {m, n, p, h, g}}]**
Out[2661]= {a + m + x, b + n + y, c + p + z, 2 g + h, g + 2 t}
In[2662]:= **G[x_, y_] := x + y; Map13[G, {{a, b, c}, {x, y, z}, {m, n, p}}]**
Out[2662]= {G[a, x, m], G[b, y, n], G[c, z, p]}
In[2663]:= **Map13[G, {{a, b, c, g, h}, {x, y, z, t, v}}]**
Out[2663]= {a + x, b + y, c + z, g + t, h + v}
In[2664]:= **Map14[x_ /; SymbolQ[x], y_ /; ListQ[y], z_, t___] :=**
Module[{a = Map[x[#, z] &, y]}, If[{t} == {}, a, Map[ToString, a]]]
In[2665]:= **Clear[G]; Map14[G, {a, b, c, d, f, g, h}, Kr]**
Out[2665]= {G[a, Kr], G[b, Kr], G[c, Kr], G[d, Kr], G[f, Kr], G[g, Kr], G[h, Kr]}

In[2666]:= **Map14[G, {a, b, c, d, f, g}, Kr, 500]**
Out[2666]= {"G[a, Kr]", "G[b, Kr]", "G[c, Kr]", "G[d, Kr]", "G[f, Kr]", "G[g, Kr]"}

In[2668]:= **Map15[x__ /; AllTrue[Map[SymbolQ, {x}], TrueQ], y_] := Map[#[y] &, {x}]**

In[2669]:= **Map15[F, G, H, P, Q, X, Y, (a + b)]**
Out[2669]= {F[a + b], G[a + b], H[a + b], P[a + b], Q[a + b], X[a + b], Y[a + b]}

In[2670]:= **Map16[f_ /; SymbolQ[f], l_ /; ListQ[l], x__] :=**
Quiet[(f[#1, FromCharacterCode[6]] &) /@ l /. FromCharacterCode[6] -> Sequence[x]]

In[2671]:= **Map16[F, {x, y, z, t}, h, m, p]**
Out[2671]= {F[x, h, m, p], F[y, h, m, p], F[z, h, m, p], F[t, h, m, p]}

In[2672]:= **Map17[x_, y_ /; RuleQ[y] || ListRulesQ[y]] :=**
If[RuleQ[y], Map[x, y], Map[Map[x, #] &, y]]

In[2673]:= **Map17[F, {a -> b, c -> d, t -> g, w -> v, h -> 90}]**
Out[2673]= {F[a] -> F[b], F[c] -> F[d], F[t] -> F[g], F[w] -> F[v], F[h] -> F[90]}

In[2674]:= **Map18[x_ /; ListQ[x] && AllTrue[Map[SymbolQ, x], TrueQ], y_ /; ListQ[y]] :=**
Map[Map[#, y] &, x]

In[2675]:= **Map18[{x, y, z}, {a, b, c}]**
Out[2675]= {{x[a], x[b], x[c]}, {y[a], y[b], y[c]}, {z[a], z[b], z[c]}}

In[2676]:= **Map19[x_ /; ListQ[x], y_ /; ListQ[y]] := Module[{a = {}, k = 1},**
If[Length[x] == Length[y] && AllTrue[Map[SymbolQ[#] &, x], TrueQ],
Do[AppendTo[a, Flatten[{x[[k]], y[[k]]}]], {k, Length[x]}];
Map[#[[1]] @@ #[[2 ;; -1]] &, a], $Failed]]

In[2677]:= **Map19[{x, y, z, h, g}, {a, b, c, d, e}]**
Out[2677]= {x[a], y[b], z[c], h[d], g[e]}

In[3891]:= **Map20[x_ /; ListQ[x], y_ /; NestListQ[y]] :=**
If[Length[x] != Length[y], $Failed, Map[#[[1]] @@ #[[2]] &, Partition[Riffle[x, y], 2]]]

In[3892]:= **Map20[{F, G, H}, {{a, b}, {c, d}, {m, n}}]**
Out[3892]= {F[a, b], G[c, d], H[m, n]}

In[3893]:= **Map21[x_ /; SymbolQ[x], y__] := F @@ {y}**

In[3894]:= **Map21[F]**
Out[3894]= F[]

In[3895]:= **Map21[F, a, b, c, d, f, g, h]**
Out[3895]= F[a, b, c, d, f, g, h]

In[3896]:= **Map21[x_ /; SymbolQ[x], y__] := F[Sequences[{y}]]**

In[3897]:= **Map21[F, a, b, c, d, f, g, h]**
Out[3897]= F[a, b, c, d, f, g, h]
In[3898]:= **Map21[F]**
Out[3898]= F[]

In[3899]:= **Map22[x_ /; ListQ[x], y__] := Map[# @@ {y} &, x]**

In[3900]:= **Map22[{X, Y, Z}, a, b, c]**

Out[3900]= {X[a, b, c], Y[a, b, c], Z[a, b, c]}

The **Map21** definition is represented in two functionally equivalent versions.

The previous fragment represents the source codes of means of the above *Map*–group with examples of their application, from which the structure of the results returned by them is an quite visually visible:

Map1[{F, G, H, ...}, {x, y, ...}], Map2[F, {a, b, ...}, {x, y, ...}], Map3[F, H, {x, y, ...}]

return respectively lists of the following format, namely:

{F[x, y, ...], G[x, y ,...], H[x, y, ...], ...}; {F[a, x, y, ...], F[b, x, y, ...], F[c, x, y, ...], ...};
{F[H, x], F[H, y], F[H, z], F[H, h], ..., F[H, g], F[H, m], F[H, n], ...}.

The call **Map4[x, y, z]** returns the result in the format {x[a1, z], x[a2, z], x[a3, z], ...}, where y = {a1, a2, a3, a4,...}. Whereas two procedures **Map5** and **Map6** expand action of the system function **Map** onto cases of classical and pure functions with any number of arguments. The call **Map7[F, G, ..., V, {a, b, ..., v}]** where F, G, ..., V – symbols and {a, b, c, ..., v} – the list of arbitrary expressions, returns result of the following format, namely:

{F[G[... V[a]]]] ...], F[G[... V[b]]]] ...], F[G[... V[c]]]] ...], ..., F[G[... V[v]]]] ...]}

without demanding any additional explanations in view of transparency.

Quite certain interest is represented by quite simple **Map8** function, whose call **Map8[F, G, H, ..., V, {a, b, c, ..., v}]**, where to F, G, ..., V – the symbols whereas {a, b, c, ..., v} – the list of arbitrary expressions, returns result of the following format:

{F[a, b, c, ..., v], G[a, b, c, ..., v], H[a, b, c, ..., v], ..., V[a, b, c, ..., v]}

without demanding any additional explanations in view of transparency; in addition, the **Map8** function is a rather useful means, in particular, at organization of comparisons of the results of the calls of functionally similar blocks, functions or modules on identical tuples of the actual arguments. Whereas the call **Map9[x, {a, b, c, ..., v}, {a1, b1, c1, ..., v1}]** where x – a symbol, {a, b, c, ..., v} and {a1, b1, c1, ..., v1} are lists of arbitrary expressions of identical length, returns result of the following format, namely:

{x[a, a1], x[b, b1], x[c, c1], x[d, d1], ..., x[v, v1]}

The call **Map10[F, x, {a, b, c, ..., v}, c1, c2, ..., cn]**, where F – a symbol, x and {a, b, c, ..., v} – an expression and lists of expressions respectively, c1, c2, ..., cn – the optional arguments, returns result of the following format, namely:

{F[x, a, c1, c2, ...], F[x, b, c1, c2, ...], F[x, c, c1, c2, ...], ..., F[x, v, c1, c2, ...]}

The **Map12** procedure generalizes the standard **Map** function onto a case of the nested list as its second actual argument. The call **Map12[F, {{a, b, c, ..., v}, {a1, b1, c1, ..., v1}, ..., p, ..., {ap, bp, h, cp, ..., vp}}]** where F – a symbol, and the second argument – the nested list of the arbitrary expressions, returns result of the following format, namely:

{**Map**[F, {a, b, c,...,v}], **Map**[F, {a1, b1, c1,...,v1}], ..., F[p], ..., **Map**[F, {ap, bp, h, cp,...,vp}]}

Whereas the **Map13** procedure generalizes the standard **Map** function onto case of a list of *ListList* type as its second factual argument. The procedure call **Map13[F, {{a, b, c, ..., v}, {a1, b1, c1, ..., v1}, ..., {ap, bp, cp, ..., vp}}]**, where F – a symbol, and the second argument – the list of *ListList* type of expressions, returns result of the following format, namely:

$$\{F[a, a1, a2, ..., ap], F[b, b1, b2, ..., bp], F[c, c1, c2, ..., cp], ..., F[v, v1, v2, ..., vp]\}$$

In case of an undefinite symbol *x* the concept of arity is ignored; meanwhile, if the factual *x* argument defines a procedure or function of the user, at that, the call of **Map13** is returned unevaluated if *x arity* is other than length of sublists of *y*. The call **Map14**[*F*, {*a, b, c, ..., v*}, *y*] where *F* – a symbol, the second argument is a list of arbitrary expressions and *y* – arbitrary expression, returns result of the following format, namely:

$$\{F[a, y], F[b, y], F[c, y], F[d, y], ..., F[v, y]\}$$

At that, an use at the call **Map14**[*F*, {*a, b, c, ..., v*}, *y, t*] of the optional 4th factual argument – an arbitrary expression – returns result of the following format, namely:

$$\{"F[a, y]", "F[b, y]", "F[c, y]", "F[d, y]", ..., "F[v, y]"\}$$

The call **Map15**[*x1, x2, x3, ..., xp, t*], where *xj* – the symbols, and *t* – an arbitrary admissible expression, returns result of the following format, namely:

$$\{x1[t], x2[t], x3[t], x4[t], x5[t], ..., xp[t]\}$$

The call **Map16**[*F*, {*a, b, ..., v*}, *c1, c2, ..., cn*], where *F* – a symbol whereas {*a, b, c, ..., v*} – a list of arbitrary expressions, and *c1, c2, ..., cn* – optional arguments accordingly – returns the list of the following format, namely:

$$\{F[a, c1, c2, ...], F[b, c1, c2, ...], F[c, c1, c2, ...], ..., F[v, c1, c2, ...]\}$$

The call **Map17**[*F*, {*a -> b, c -> d, ...*}], where *F* – a symbol whereas {*a -> b, c -> d, ...*} – a list of rules returns the list of the following format, namely:

$$\{F[a] \to F[b], F[c] \to F[d], ...\}$$

without demanding any additional explanations in view of its transparency.

The call **Map18**[*x, y*], where *x* – a list {*x1, x2, ..., xn*} of symbols and *y* – a list {*y1, y2, ..., yp*} of arbitrary expressions, returns the nested list of the following format, namely:

$$\{\{x1[y1], x1[y2], ..., x1[yp]\}, \{x2[y1], x2[y2], ..., x2[yp]\}, ..., \{xn[y1], xn[y2], ..., xn[yp]\}\}$$

The result returned by the call **Map18** is transparent enough and of any special explanations doesn't demand.

The call **Map19**[*x, y*], where *x* – a list {*x1, x2, ..., xj, ..., xp*} of symbols and *y* – a list {*y1, y2, ..., yj, ..., yp*} of the arbitrary expressions returns the nested list of the following format: {*x1[y1], x2[y2], ..., xj[yj], ..., xp[yp]*} (*j* = 1..*p*). If *yj* = {*a, b, c, ...*} then *xj*[*a, b, c, ...*]. The result returned by the call **Map19** is transparent enough and of any special explanations doesn't demand.

The call **Map20**[*x, y*], where *x* – the list {*x1, x2, ..., xj, ..., xp*} of symbols and *y* – the nested list {{*y1*}, {*y2*}, ..., {*yj,..., yjn*}, ..., {*yp*}} of *NestList* type of arbitrary expressions, returns the nested list of the following format, namely:

$$\{x1[y1], x2[y2], ..., xj[yj, ..., yjn], ..., xp[yp]\} \ (j = 1..p).$$

If *yj* = {*a*, {*b*}, *c, ...*} then *xj*[*a*, {*b*}, *c, ...*]. The result returned by the call **Map20** is transparent enough and of special explanations doesn't demand.

The function call **Map21**[*F, y*], where *F* – a symbol and *y* – a list {*y1, y2, ..., yp*} returns *F*[*y1, y2, ..., yp*] (*j* = 1..*p*). If the *y* argument is absent the *F*[] is returned. Whereas the function call **Map22**[*F, a, b, c, ...*], where *F* – a list of {*y1, y2, ..., yp*} symbols, returns a list {*y1*[*a, b, c, ...*], *y2*[*a, b, c, ...*], ..., *yp*[*a, b, c, ...*]} (*j* = 1..*p*). The function call **Map23**[*F, y*], where *F* – a symbol and *y* – a list {*y1, y2, ..., yp*} returns {*F[y1], F[y2], ..., F[yp]*} where lists can be as *yj* (*j = 1..p*). If the *x* argument is the empty list then {} is returned. A rather simple **Map24**[*F, y*] function is natural generalization of the **Map23**[*F, y*] function on a case when the separate symbol or their list is used as its first *F* argument. In addition, an unsuccessful call returns *$Failed*.

In[4576]:= Map23[F_ /; SymbolQ[F], y_ /; ListQ[y]] :=
Map[F @@ Flatten[{y[[#]]}] &, Range[1, Length[y]]]

In[4578]:= Map23[g, {{a, b, c, p, d}, gs, {m, n, p, c, d}, m}]
Out[4578]= {g[a, b, c, p, d], g[gs], g[m, n, p, c, d], g[m]}

In[4579]:= Map24[F_, y_ /; ListQ[y]] := If[SymbolQ[F], Map23[F, y],
If[ListQ[F] && And1[Map[SymbolQ, F]], Map[Map23[#, y] &, F], $Failed]]

In[4580]:= Map24[{g, s, h}, {{a, b, c, p, d}, gs, {m, n, p, c, d}, m}]
Out[4580]= {{g[a, b, c, p, d], g[gs], g[m, n, p, c, d], g[m]}, {s[a, b, c, p, d], s[gs], s[m, n, p, c, d], s[m]}, {h[a, b, c, p, d], h[gs], h[m, n, p, c, d], h[m]}}

An useful enough modification of standard **Map** function is the **MapEx** function whose call returns the list of application of a symbol *f* to those elements of *w* list which satisfy a testing function *g* (*block, function, pure function, or module from one argument*) or whose positions are defined by the list of positive integers *g*. At the same time, the positions which are absent in the *g* list are ignored or the procedure call is returned unevaluated. The following fragment represents source code of the **MapEx** function with typical examples of its application.

In[4432]:= MapEx[f_Symbol, g_ /; Quiet[ProcFuncBlQ[g, Unique["s"]]] || PosIntListQ[g],
w_ /; ListQ[w]] := Map[f[#] &, If[FunctionQ[g], If[PureFuncQ[g], Select[w, g], Map[g, w]],
Map[If[Intersection[g, Flatten[Position[w, #]]] != {}, #, Nothing] &, w]]]

In[4433]:= MapEx[f, IntegerQ[#] &, {a, b, 3, 6, m, 7, 8, d, 70, m, a + b, 75}]
Out[4433]= {f[3], f[6], f[7], f[8], f[70], f[75]}

In[4434]:= MapEx[f, {2, 4, 6, 8, 9, 10, 12, 100}, {a, b, 3, 6, m, 7, 8, d, 70, m, a + b, 75}]
Out[4434]= {f[b], f[6], f[m], f[7], f[d], f[70], f[m], f[75]}

In[4435]:= MapEx[f, {0, 1, 2, 4, 6, 15}, {a, b, 3, 6, m, 7, 8, d}]
Out[4435]= MapEx[f, {0, 1, 2, 4, 6, 15}, {a, b, 3, 6, m, 7, 8, d}]

In[4436]:= h[t_] := If[SymbolQ[t], t^3, Nothing]; MapEx[f, h, {a, b, 3, 6, m, 8, d, 7, m, a/b, 5}]
Out[4436]= {f[a^3], f[b^3], f[m^3], f[d^3], f[m^3]}

The function call **MapAll**[*f, exp*] applies *f* symbol to all subexpressions of an *exp* expression which are on all its levels. Whereas the procedure call **MapToExpr**[*f, y*] returns the result of application of a symbol or their list *f* only to all symbols of *y* expression. Furthermore, from the list *f* are excluded symbols entering into the *y* expression. For example, if *f* = {*G, S*} then applying of *f* to a *x* symbol gives *G[S[x]]*. In case of absence of acceptable *f* symbols the call returns the initial *y* expression. The procedure call **MapToExpr**[*f, y, z*] with the 3rd optional *z* argument – a symbol or their list – allows exclude the *z* symbols from applying to them *f* symbols. In certain cases the procedure is a rather useful means at expressions processing. Meanwhile, it should be noted, the procedure significantly uses the procedure whose call **CorrPosStr**[*x, y, z, h*] returns the minimal *t* position of a *z* character in a *x* string forming the substring on <*y, t*> positions that contains identical number of occurrences of the boundary characters. In addition, if *z = 0* then search is done from left to right, otherwise from right to left. The following fragment represents source codes of both procedures along with typical examples visually illustrating their application.

In[4078]:= CorrPosStr[x_ /; StringQ[x], y_ /; PosIntQ[y], z_ /; StringQ[z] &&
StringLength[z] == 1, h_ /; MemberQ[{0, 1}, h]] :=
Module[{a = "", b = y, c}, c = StringTake[x, {b}];
Do[If[h == 0, a = a <> StringTake[x, {b++}], a = StringTake[x, {b--}] <> a];
If[StringCount[a, c] == StringCount[a, z], Break[], 6], {j, y, StringLength[x]}]; b - 1]

In[4079]:= CorrPosStr["1234avz[x+y*z]5678", 8, "]", 0]
Out[4079]= 14

In[4080]:= CorrPosStr["1234avz[x+y*z]5678", 14, "[", 1]
Out[4080]= 8

In[4099]:= MapToExpr[f_ /; SymbolQ[f] || ListQ[f] &&
And @@ Map[SymbolQ, f], y_, z___] :=
Module[{a = "(" <> StringReplace[ToStringRational[y], " " -> ""] <> ")", b, c, d, h, g, m, n, s},
b = ExtrVarsOfStr[a, 1]; If[b == {}, y, If[{z} == {}, b, If[SymbolQ[z] ||
ListQ[z] && And @@ Map[SymbolQ, z],
b = Complement[b, Map[ToString, Flatten[{z}]]], b]];
s = Complement[Map[ToString, Flatten[{f}]], b];
If[s == {}, y, {m, n} = {"", ""}; Map[{m = m <> # <> "[", n = n <> "]"} &, s];
Do[{h, g} = {{}, {}}; c = StringPosition[a, b[[j]]];
d = Map[If[! SyntaxQ[StringTake[a, {#[[1]] - 1}]] &&
! SyntaxQ[StringTake[a, {#[[2]] + 1}]], #, Nothing] &, c];
Do[AppendTo[h, If[! StringTake[a, {d[[k]][[2]] + 1}] == "[", d[[k]],
{d[[k]][[1]], CorrPosStr[a, d[[k]][[2]] + 1, "]", 0]}]], {k, 1, Length[d]}];
Do[AppendTo[g, m <> StringTake[a, h[[p]]] <> n], {p, 1, Length[h]}];
a = StringReplacePart[a, g, h], {j, 1, Length[b]}]; ToExpression[a]]]]

In[4100]:= MapToExpr[F, (1 + 1/x^(n + b*x^2 + g[a])^Sin[x]^2)^x^2]
Out[4100]= (1 + F[x]^-(F[n] + F[b]*F[x]^2 + F[g[F[a]]])^F[Sin[F[x]]]^2)^F[x]^2

In[4101]:= MapToExpr[F, (a + 1/x^(n + G[b*x^2] + S[a])^Sin[x]^2)^(a + b)]
Out[4101]= (F[a] + F[x]^-(F[n] + F[G[F[b]*F[x]^2]] + F[S[F[a]]])^F[Sin[F[x]]]^2)^(F[a] + F[b])

In[4102]:= MapToExpr[{S, G, V}, (a + 1/x^(n + G[b*x^2] + S[a])^Sin[x]^2)^(a + b)]
Out[4102]= (V[a]+V[x]^-(V[n]+V[G[V[b]*V[x]^2]]+V[S[V[a]]])^V[Sin[V[x]]]^2)^(V[a]+V[b])

In[4103]:= MapToExpr[{G, S}, {a, Sin[b], c/d, f*g, h, p + t, r, s^g}]
Out[4103]= {G[S[a]], G[S[Sin[G[S[b]]]]], G[S[c]]/G[S[d]], G[S[f]]*G[S[g]], G[S[h]], G[S[p]] + G[S[t]], G[S[r]], G[S[s]]^G[S[g]]}

In[4104]:= MapToExpr[{S, G, V}, {500, 90}]
Out[4104]= {500, 90}

In[4105]:= MapToExpr[{S, G}, (a + 1/x^(n + G[b*x^2] + S[a])^Sin[x]^2)^(a + b)]
Out[4105]= (a + x^-(n + G[b*x^2] + S[a])^Sin[x]^2)^(a + b)

In[4106]:= MapToExpr[F, (a + 1/x^2)/(b + 1/y^2), {a, b}]
Out[4106]= (a + 1/F[x]^2)/(b + 1/F[y]^2)

In[4107]:= MapToExpr[F, (a + 1/x^2)/(c/x^3 + 1/y^2), {a, c}]

Out[4107]= (a + 1/F[x]^2)/(c/F[x]^3 + 1/F[y]^2)

The means, represented above, form so-called *Map*-group that rather significantly expands functionality of the standard **Map** function. From the presented information the formats of the returned results of calls of the above means are transparent enough, without the need of demanding any additional explanations. Tools of the *Map*-group in a number of cases allow to simplify programming of procedures and functions, significantly extending the standard **Map** function. The *MathToolBox* package also use these means [48,50].

The following procedure **MapListAll** substantially adjoins the above *Map*-group. The call **MapAt[***f*, *express*, *n***]** of the standard **MapAt** function provides applying *f* to the elements of an *express* at its positions *n*. While the procedure call **MapListAll[***f*, *j***]** returns the result of applying *f* to all elements of a *j* list. In addition, a simple analog of the above procedure that is based on mechanism of temporary change of attributes for a factual *f* argument in the call **MapListAll1[***f*, *j***]** solves the problem analogously to **MapListAll** procedure. The procedure call **MapListAll1[***f*, *j***]** returns the result of applying *f* symbol to all elements of a *j* list. On an *j* list of the kind {{...{{{{...}}}}...}} both procedures returns {{...{{{f[]}}}...}}. The next fragment represents the source code of the procedures **MapListAll** and **MapListAll1** with examples of their application.

In[3903]:= **MapListAll[f_ /; SymbolQ[f], x_ /; ListQ[x]]** :=
Module[{a, b, c = SetAttributes[ToString1, Listable], d, g = ReplaceAll[x, {} -> Null]},
a = DeleteDuplicates[Flatten[g]]; b = Map[ToString[f] <> "[" <> ToString1[#] <> "]" &, a];
d = GenRules[Map[ToString1, a], b]; d = ToExpression[ReplaceAll[ToString1[g], d]];
ClearAttributes[ToString1, Listable]; ReplaceAll[d, Null -> Sequences[{Nothing}]]]

In[3904]:= **MapListAll[F, {a, b, "c", {{x, y + h, z}, {{"m", n*t, p}}}, c, "d"}]**
Out[3904]= {F[a], F[b], F["c"], {{F[x], F[h + y], F[z]}, {{F["m"], F[n*t], F[p]}}}, F[c], F["d"]}
In[3905]:= **MapListAll[F, {a, b, "c", x, y + h, z, "m", n*t, p, c, "d"}]**
Out[3905]= {F[a], F[b], F["c"], F[x], F[h + y], F[z], F["m"], F[n*t], F[p], F[c], F["d"]}
In[3906]:= **MapListAll[G, {{{{{{}}}}}}]**
Out[3906]= {{{{{G[]}}}}}
In[3907]:= **MapListAll[F, {a, b, "c", {}, {{x, y + h, z}, {{"m", n*t, p, {{{{}}}}}}, c, "d", {{}}}]**
Out[3907]= {F[a], F[b], F["c"], F[], {{F[x], F[h + y], F[z]}, {{F["m"], F[n*t], F[p], {{{F[]}}}}}}, F[c], F["d"], {F[]}}

In[3964]:= **MapListAll1[f_ /; SymbolQ[f], x_ /; ListQ[x]]** := Module[{a = Attributes[f], b, c},
ClearAttributes[f, a]; SetAttributes[f, Listable]; c = ReplaceAll[x, {} -> Null];
b = {Map[f, c], ClearAttributes[f, Listable], SetAttributes[f, a]}[[1]];
ReplaceAll[b, Null -> Sequences[{Nothing}]]]

In[3965]:= **MapListAll1[F, {a, b, "c", {{x, y + h, z}, {{"m", n*t, p}}}, c, "d"}]**
Out[3965]= {F[a], F[b], F["c"], {{F[x], F[h + y], F[z]}, {{F["m"], F[n*t], F[p]}}}, F[c], F["d"]}
In[3966]:= **MapListAll1[G, {{{{{{}}}}}}]**
Out[3966]= {{{{{G[]}}}}}

It is rather expedient to programmatically process all especial and erroneous situations that arise in the course of calculation for which the *Mathematica* has quite enough means in the *Input* mode, while at procedural processing of such situations the question is a slightly more complex. For this reason the **Try** function that presents a certain analog of the *try*-sentence of the *Maple* whose mechanism is effective enough in the *Input* mode and at the procedural processing of especial and erroneous situations, when such situations without any serious reason don't lead to a procedure completion without return the corresponding diagnostical messages has been offered. The next fragment presents the source code of the **Try** function along with examples of its typical application.

In[2458]:= **G::norational = "actual argument `1` is not rational"**
Out[2458]= "actual argument `1` is not rational"
In[2459]:= **G[x_] := If[Head[x] === Rational, Numerator[x]^9 + Denominator[x]^9, Message[G::norational, x]; Defer[G[x]]]**
In[2460]:= **G[42.74]**
G::norational: actual argument 42.74` is not rational
Out[2460]= G[42.74]

In[2461]:= **Try[x_ /; StringQ[x], y_] := Quiet[Check[ToExpression[x], {y, $MessageList}]]**
In[2462]:= **Try["G[42/74]", "Res"]**
Out[2462]= 130756019841658
In[2463]:= **Try["G[42.74]", "Res"]**
Out[2463]= {"Res", {G::norational}}
In[2464]:= **Try["1/0", "Error"]**
Out[2464]= {"Error", {Power::infy}}
In[2465]:= **Ag[x_Integer, y_Integer] := Module[{a = Try[ToString[x] <> "/" <> ToString[y], "Error"]}, If[ListQ[a], If[a[[1]] === "Error", {x, y, a[[2]]}], x/y]]**
In[2466]:= **Ag[90, 500]**
Out[2466]= 9/50
In[2467]:= **Ag[590, 0]**
Out[2467]= {590, 0, {Power::infy}}

Above all, for illustration of operating of the **Try** function the message with *"G::norational"* name that is used by simple function **G[x]** in case of its call on a *x* argument different from a rational number is used. Such call outputs this message with returning of an *unevaluated* call *(in addition, only simplifications of a x expression can be done)*. The **Try** function is similar to the *try*-clause of the *Maple* system, providing processing of the *x* depending on the messages initiated by evaluation of *x*. Furthermore, it is necessary to note that all messages initiated by such evaluation of the *x* expression, should be activated in the current session. The call of the **Try** function has the following format, namely:

Try["*x-expression*", *y*}}]

where the first *x* argument determines a *x* expression in string format whereas the second argument defines the message associated with a possible special or erroneous situation at calculation of a *x* expression. In case evaluation of a *x* expression is correct, the result of its evaluation *(for example, the procedure call)* is returned, otherwise the nested list of the format {*y*, {*Mess*}} is returned where *Mess* defines the system message generated as a result of the processing of a erroneous or special situation by the system. The function **Try** proved itself as a rather convenient tool for processing of a number of especial and erroneous situations at programming of various applied and system problems. For the rather experienced users

Software Etudes in the Mathematica

of the *Mathematica* system the codes of the illustrative examples and tools of this section are quite transparent and of any special additional explanations don't demand.

5.1. The control branching structures and loop structures in the *Mathematica*

Rather difficult algorithms of calculations and/or control algorithms *(first of all)* can not use especially consequent schemes, including various constructions changing consequent order of an algorithm execution depending on these or those conditions, namely: *conditional* and *unconditional* transitions, loops, branchings *(the structures of such type in a number of cases are called as control structures)*. In particular, for the organization of the control structures of the branching type the *Math*-language of the *Mathematica* has rather effective means provided with the **If** function having three formats of encoding [28-33,50,60]. In a number of cases the simple **Iff** procedure from number of arguments from *1* to *n* that generalizes the standard **If** function is quite useful means; it is very convenient at number of arguments, starting with *1*, what is rather convenient in those cases when calls of the **Iff** function are generated in a certain procedure automatically, simplifying processing of *erroneous* and *especial* situations arising by a call of such procedure on number of arguments from range *2..4*. The following fragment represents source code of the **Iff** procedure with an example. In addition, it must be kept in mind that all actual arguments of *y*, since the second, are coded in string format in order to avoid their premature calculation at the call **Iff**[*x*, ...] when the factual arguments are being calculated/simplified.

In[2745]:= Iff[x_, y__ /; StringQ[y]] := Module[{a = {x, y}, b}, b = Length[a];
If[b == 1 || b >= 5, Defer[Iff[x, y]], If[b == 2, If[x, ToExpression[y]],
If[b == 3, If[x, ToExpression[y], ToExpression[a[[3]]]],
If[b == 4, If[x, ToExpression[a[[2]]], ToExpression[a[[3]]], ToExpression[a[[4]]]], Null]]]]]

In[2746]:= a = {}; For[k = 1, k <= 74, k++, Iff[PrimeQ[k], "AppendTo[a, k]"]]; a
Out[2746]= {2, 3, 5, 7, 11, 13, 17, 19, 23, 29, 31, 37, 41, 43, 47, 53, 59, 61, 67, 71, 73}

Thus, the **If** function represents the most typical instrument for ensuring of the branching algorithms. In this context it should be noted that *If* means of the *Maple* and *Mathematica* are considerably equivalent, however readability of difficult enough branching algorithms realized by the *if* offers of the *Maple* system is being perceived slightly more clearly. So, the *Maple* system allows the conditional *if* offer of the following format, namely:

if lc1 then v1 elif lc2 then v2 elif lc3 then v3 elif lc4 then v4 ... else vk end if

where *j–th lcj* – a logical condition and *vj* – an arbitrary expression, whose sense is a rather transparent and considered, for example, in books [25-27,50]. This offer is very convenient at programming of a number of conditional structures. For definition of a similar structure in the *Mathematica* system, the **IFk** procedure whose source code with examples of its use represents the following fragment can be used, namely:

In[2340]:= IFk[x__] := Module[{a = {x}, b, c = "", d = "If[", e = "]", h = {}, k = 1}, b = Length[a];
If[For[k, k <= b - 1, k++, AppendTo[h, b >= 2 && ListQ[a[[k]]] && Length[a[[k]]] == 2]];
DeleteDuplicates[h] != {True}, Return[Defer[Ifk[x]]], k = 1];
For[k, k<=b-1, k++, c=c <> d <> ToString[a[[k]][[1]]] <> "," <> ToString[a[[k]][[2]]] <> ","];
c = c <> ToString[a[[b]]] <> StringMultiple[e, b - 1]; ToExpression[c]]

221

In[2341]:= IFk[{a, b}, {c, d}, {g, s}, {m, n}, {q, p}, h]
Out[2341]= If[a, b, If[c, d, If[g, s, If[m, n, If[q, p, h]]]]]
In[2342]:= IFk[{False, b}, {False, d}, {False, s}, {True, G}, {False, p}, h]
Out[2342]= G
In[2343]:= IFk[{False, b}, {False, d}, {False, s}, {False, n}, {g, p}, h]
Out[2343]= If[g, p, h]

In[2060]:= IFk1[x__] := Module[{a = {x}, b, c = "", d = "If[", e = "]", h = {}, k = 1},
b = Length[a];
If[For[k, k <= b - 1, k++, AppendTo[h, b >= 2 && ListQ[a[[k]]] && Length[a[[k]]] == 2]];
DeleteDuplicates[h] != {True}, Return[Defer[IFk1[x]]], {h, k} = {{}, 1}];
If[For[k, k <= b - 1, k++, AppendTo[h, a[[k]][[1]]]];
Select[h, ! MemberQ[{True, False}, #] &] != {}, Return[Defer[IFk1[x]]], k = 1];
For[k = 1, k <= b - 1, k++, c = c <> d <> ToString[a[[k]][[1]]] <> "," <>
ToString[a[[k]][[2]]] <> ","];
c = c <> ToString[a[[b]]] <> StringMultiple[e, b - 1]; ToExpression[c]]

In[2061]:= IFk1[{False, b}, {False, d}, {False, s}, {False, n}, {g, p}, h]
Out[2061]= IFk1[{False, b}, {False, d}, {False, s}, {False, n}, {g, p}, h]
In[2062]:= IFk1[{False, b}, {False, d}, {False, s}, {True, G}, {False, p}, h]
Out[2062]= G
In[2063]:= IFk1[{a, b}, {c, d}, {g, s}, {m, n}, {q, p}, h]
Out[2063]= IFk1[{a, b}, {c, d}, {g, s}, {m, n}, {q, p}, h]
In[2065]:= IFk1[{True, b}]
Out[2065]= IFk1[{True, b}]
In[2066]:= IFk1[{False, b}, Agn]
Out[2066]= Agn

The call of the **IFk** procedure uses any number of the actual arguments more than one; the arguments use the two-element lists of the format {lcj, vj}, except the last. Whereas the last actual argument is a correct expression; at that, a testing of lcj on Boolean type isn't done. The call of the **IFk** procedure on a tuple of the correct factual arguments returns the result equivalent to execution of the corresponding *Maple if* offer [25-27,50].

At that, the **IFk1** procedure is an useful extension of the previous procedure which unlike **IFk** allows only Boolean expressions as the factual arguments lcj, otherwise returning the unevaluated call. In the rest, the procedures **IFk** and **IFk1** are functionally identical. Thus, similarly to the *if* offer of the *Maple* system the procedures **IFk** and **IFk1** are quite useful at programming of the branching algorithms of the different types. With that said, the above procedures **IFk** and **IFk1** are provided with a quite developed mechanism of testing of the factual arguments transferred at the procedure call whose algorithm is easily seen from the source code. Now, using the described approach fairly easy to program in *Math*-language an arbitrary construction of the *Maple*-language describing the branching algorithms [28-33,50]. To a certain degree it is possible to refer to *If* constructions also the **Which** function of the following format

Which[*lc1*, *w1*, *lc2*, *w2*, *lc3*, *w3*, ..., *lck*, *wk*]

which returns result of evaluation of the *first wj* expression for which Boolean expression *lcj* (*j = 1..k*) accepts *True* value, for example:

In[2735]:= G[x_] := Which[–Infinity <= x < 90, Sin[x], 90 <= x < 500, Cos[x], 500 <= x <= Infinity, x^2]
In[2736]:= {G[69], G[90.500], G[500], G[2016], G[–27.20]}
Out[2736]= {Sin[69], –0.821826, 250000, 4064256, –0.879273}

This example illustrates the definition of a piecewise–defined function through the **Which** function. If some of the evaluated conditions *lcj* doesn't return {*True* | *False*} the function call is returned unevaluated while in case of *False* for all *lcj* conditions (*j = 1..k*) the function call returns *Null*, i.e. nothing. At dynamical generation of a *Which* object the simple procedure **WhichN** can be a rather useful which allows any even number of arguments similar to the **Which** function, otherwise returning result unevaluated. In the rest, the **WhichN** is similar to the **Which** function; the next fragment represents source code of the **WhichN** procedure along with typical examples of its application.

In[4731]:= WhichN[x__] := Module[{a = {x}, c = "Which[", d, k = 1}, d = Length[a];
If[OddQ[d], Defer[WhichN[x]], ToExpression[For[k, k <= d, k++, c = c <>
ToString[a[[k]]] <> ","]; StringTake[c, {1, –2}] <> "]"]]]

In[4732]:= WhichN[a, b, c, d, f, g, h, r]
Out[4732]= Which[a, b, c, d, f, g, h, r]
In[4733]:= f = 90; WhichN[False, b, f == 90, SV, g, h, r, t]
Out[4733]= SV

The above procedures **IFk, IFk1, Which** represent a quite certain interest at programming a number of applications of various purpose, first of all, of the system character *(similar means are considered in our collection* [50]).

5.2. The loop control structures of the *Mathematica* system

So, one of the main loop structures of the system is based on the function **For** which has the following general format of coding, namely:

For[w, <lc>, b, <Body of a loop construction>]

Since the given *w*, the body of a construction which contains offers of the *Math*-language, with loop increment of a loop variable on a *b* magnitude so long as a logical condition *(lc)* doesn't accept *True* is cyclically calculated. Simple example of application of this function is represented below, namely:

In[2942]:= For[k = 1; h = 1, k < 10000, k = k + 1, h = h^2 + 90*h + k; If[k < 5, Continue[], Print[h]; Break[]]]
63183009994842320223844638948475 80

For continuation of a **For** loop and exit from it the control words **Continue** and **Break** serve respectively as it very visually illustrates a simple example above. While other quite widely used tools in the *Mathematica* system for organization of loop calculations is **Do** function that has five formats of encoding whose descriptions with examples can be found in books [28-33,50,60]. Meantime, unlike the *Maple* system the *Mathematica* system has no analog of very useful loop constructions of types *(1.b)* and *(1.d)* [27] which allow to execute the loop calculations at subexpressions of a certain expression that provides possibility on their basis to program quite interesting constructions as illustrate rather simple fragments [25-27]. In this context we will represent the procedure whose call **DO[*x*, *y*, *j*]** returns the list of results of loop calculation of a *x* expression on a cycle *j* variable that accepts values from the **Op[*y*]** list. The construction in a certain relation is analog of the loop construction *for_in* for *Maple* system [25-27,47,50].

In[2274]:= DO[x_, y_, k_] := Module[{a = x, b = Op[y], c, d = 1, R = {}}, c := Length[b] + 1;
While[d < c, R = Insert[R, a /. k -> b[[d]], -1]; a := x; d++]; R]
In[2275]:= DO[k^2 + Log[k], f[g[a, b], h[c, d, e, j, k, l]], k]
Out[2275]= {g[a, b]^2 + Log[g[a, b]], h[c, d, e, j, k, l]^2 + Log[h[c, d, e, j, k, l]]}

In our books [28-33] the reciprocal functional equivalence of both systems is quite visually illustrated when the most important computing constructions of the *Mathematica* system with this or that efficiency are simulated by the *Maple* constructions and vice versa. Truly, in principle, it is a quite expected result because the built-in languages of both systems are universal and in this regard with one or the other efficiency they can program an arbitrary algorithm. But in the time relation it is not so and at using of the loop structures of a large enough nesting level the *Maple* can have essential enough advantages before *Mathematica*. For confirmation we will give a simple example of a loop construction programmed both in the *Maple*, and the *Mathematica* system.

The results speak for themselves – if in the *Maple 11* the execution of a certain construction requires **7.8 s**, the *Mathematica 11* for execution of the same construction requires already **49.7 s**, i.e. approximately **6.4** times more *(estimations have been obtained on **Dell OptiPlex 3020**, i5-4570 3.2 GHz with 64-bit Windows 7 Professional 6.1.7601 Service Pack 1 Build 7601)*. At that, with growth of the nesting depth and range of a loop variable at implementation of the loop constructions this difference rather significantly grows.

> t := time(): for k1 to 10 do for k2 to 10 do for k3 to 10 do for k4 to 10 do for k5 to 10 do for k6 to 10 do for k7 to 10 do for k8 to 10 do 80 end do end do end do end do end do end do end do end do: time() – t;   # *(Maple 11)*
7.800
In[2693]:= n = 10; t = TimeUsed[]; For[k1 = 1, k1 <= n, k1++, For[k2 = 1, k2 <= n, k2++,
For[k3 = 1, k3 <= n, k3++, For[k4 = 1, k4 <= n, k4++, For[k5 = 1, k5 <= n, k5++,
For[k6 = 1, k6 <= n, k6++, For[k7=1, k7 <= n, k7++, For[k8 = 1, k8 <= n, k8++, 90]]]]]]]];
TimeUsed[] – t
Out[2693]= 49.671

Naturally, the received estimations are determined by the main resources of the computer however on identical resources this basic relation retains. From the given example follows that the *Maple* uses more effective algorithms in the time relation for realization of the loop constructions of a large nesting depth and a range of loop variable, than it takes place for its main competitor – the *Mathematica* system even of its latest version *11.2.0*. A lot of rather interesting comparisons relative to estimations of time characteristics of performance of the mass tools of processing and calculations is represented in our books [25-27,30,50]. Of these comparisons follows, that according to time characteristics the *Maple* system in some cases is more preferable than the *Mathematica* system what in each concrete case supposes the appropriate comparative analysis. Naturally, the above time estimations in a certain degree depend on the current state of the computing platform and available main resources of the computer, however the comparative time trend remains stable.

Among special types of loop control structures in the *Mathematica* system it is possible to note a series of interesting enough ones, some of them have various level of analogy with similar tools of the *Maple* system [28-33,50]. However in general, tools of the *Mathematica* system are more preferable at generation of the nested expressions and, first of all, of pure functions which play especially essential part in problems of functional programming in the *Mathematica* system. At comparative consideration of the control structures of branching and loop which are supported by both systems, two main groups have been distinguished, namely: *basic* and *additional* resources of providing the specified control structures. So, the *if* offer of the *Maple* system and the **If** function of the *Mathematica* system represent the most typical tools of ensuring of the branching algorithms. At operating with both tools a point of view has been formed, the tools are being represented as substantially equivalent, however these tools defined by the *if* offers of the *Maple* for rather complex branching algorithms are being slightly more simply perceived in the sence of their readability. So, in other respects it is rather difficult to give preference to any of these control means and in these respects both leading systems can quite be considered as equivalent. An interesting enough comparative analysis of the systems *Mathematica* and *Maple*, which is based on the practical application of both systems in a variety of appendices can be found in works [28-30,49,50]. In addition, note that the above comparative analysis was based on the *Maple 11* and *Mathematica 11*.

Chapter 6. Problems of procedural programming in the *Mathematica*

Procedural programming is one of basic paradigms of the *Mathematica* which in an quite essential degree differs from the similar paradigm of the well-known traditional procedural programming languages. The given circumstance is the cornerstone of a number of system problems relating to a question of procedural programming in the *Mathematica*. Above all, similar problems arise in the field of distinctions in *realization* of the above paradigms in the *Mathematica* and in the environment of traditional procedural languages. Along with that, unlike a number of traditional and built-in languages the built-in *Math*–language has no a number of useful enough means for operating with procedural objects. Some such tools are represented in our books [28-33] and *MathToolBox* package [48]. A number of the problems connected with such tools is considered in the present chapter, previously having discussed the concept of `procedure` in the *Mathematica* system as bases of its procedural paradigm. In addition, tools of analysis of this section concern only the user procedures and functions because definitions of all system functions *(unlike, say, from the Maple system)* from the user are hidden, i.e. are inaccessible for processing by the standard tools of the *Mathematica*.

6.1. Definition of procedures in the *Mathematica* software

Procedures in the *Mathematica* system formally present functional objects of the following two simple formats, namely:

$$M[x\_/; Test_x, y\_/; Test_y, ...] \{:= | =\} \text{Module}[\{locals\}, \text{Procedure Body}]$$

$$B[x\_/; Test_x, y\_/; Test_y, ...] \{:= | =\} \text{Block}[\{locals\}, \text{Block Body}]$$

i.e., the procedures of both types represent the functions from two arguments – the *body* of a procedure *(Body)* and *local variables (locals)*. Local variables – the list of names, perhaps, with the initial values which are attributed to them. These variables have the local character concerning procedure, i.e. their values aren't crossed with values of the symbols of the same name outside of the procedure. All other variables in the procedure have global character, sharing field of variables of the *Mathematica* current session. In addition, in the definition of procedures it is possible to distinguish six following component, namely:

– *procedure name* (M *in the first procedure definition)*;
– *procedure heading* (M[x_/; Test$_x$, y_/; Test$_y$, ...] *in the both procedures definitions)*;
– *procedural brackets* (**Module**[...] *or* **Block**[...]);
– *local variables* (*list of local variables {locals}; can be empty list)*;
– *procedure body; can be empty*;
– *testing Test$_x$ function (the function call Test[x] returns True or False depend on permissibility of the factual x argument; can absent)*.

It is necessary to highlight that in the *Mathematica* system as correct objects *{Function, Block, Module}* only those objects are considered that contain the patterns of the formal arguments located in a certain order, namely:

1. The coherent group of formal arguments with patterns "_" has to be located at the very beginning of the tuple of formal arguments in headings of the above objects

2. Formal arguments with patterns "__" or "___" can to close the tuple of formal arguments; at that, couples of adjacent arguments with patterns consisting from {"__", "___"} are inadmissible because of possible violation of correctness (in sense of planned algorithm of calculations) of calls of the above objects as the following fragment illustrates:

In[4220]:= A[x_, y__, z___] := x*y^2*z^3
In[4222]:= {A[x, y, z], A[x, y, h, z], A[x, y, h, x, a, b]}
Out[4222]= {x*y^2*z^3, h^z^3*x*y^2, h^x^a^b^3*x*y^2}
In[4223]:= G[x_, y__, z___] := x + y + z
In[4224]:= {G[x, y, z], G[x, y, m, n, z], G[x, y, z, h]}
Out[4224]= {x + y + z, m + n + x + y + z, h + x + y + z}

Other rather simple examples illustrate told. Thus, the real correctness of the tuple of formal arguments can be quite coordinated to their arrangement in the tuple in context of patterns {"_", "__", "___"}. At the same time, for all templates for formal arguments the testing $Test_x$ function of a rather complex kind can be used as the following evident fragment illustrates:

In[4566]:= Sg[x_/; StringQ[x], y__/; If[Length[{y}] == 1, IntegerQ[y], MemberQ3[{Integer, List, String}, Map[Head, {y}]]]] := {x, y}

In[4567]:= Sg["agn", 70]
Out[4567]= {"agn", 70}
In[4568]:= Sg["agn", 70, 75, "sv", {a, b}]
Out[4568]= {"agn", 70, 75, "sv", {a, b}}

In[4569]:= Sg1[x_/; StringQ[x], y___/; If[{y} == {}, True, If[Length[{y}] == 1, IntegerQ[y], MemberQ3[{List, String, Integer}, Map[Head, {y}]]]]] := {x, y}

In[4570]:= Sg1["agn", 70, 75, "sv", {a, b}]
Out[4570]= {"agn", 70, 75, "sv", {a, b}}
In[4571]:= Sg1["agn"]
Out[4571]= {"agn"}
In[4572]:= Sg1["agn", 70, 75, "sv", {a, b}, a + b]
Out[4572]= Sg1["agn", 70, 75, "sv", {a, b}, a + b]

The problem for testing of correctness of the tuple of formal arguments in the user modules, blocks or functions can be solved by the procedure whose procedure call **CorrTupleArgs[x]** returns *True* if the tuple of formal arguments of a block, a function or a module *x* is correct in the sense stated above, and *False* otherwise. The following fragment presents source code of the procedure with examples of its application.

In[4307]:= f[x_, y__, z___] := x + y + z; f1[x_, y__, y__, z___] := x + y + y + z;
In[4308]:= CorrTupleArgs[x_/; BlockFuncModQ[x]] := Module[{a = ArgsU[x], b},
a = If[NestListQ[a], a, {a}];
b = DeleteDuplicates[Map[If[StringCount[#[[2]], "_"] == 1, 1,
If[StringCount[#[[2]], "_"] == 2, 2, If[StringCount[#[[2]], "_"] == 3, 3]]] &, a]];
If[OrderedQ[b] && ! (MemberQ3[b, {2, 2}] && MemberQ3[b, {2, 3}]), True, False]]

In[4309]:= CorrTupleArgs[Attrib]
Out[4309]= True
In[4310]:= Map[CorrTupleArgs, {f, f1}]

Out[4310]= {False, False}

On the other hand, the problem of preliminary determination of correctness of the factual arguments passing to a block, a function or a module is of a rather interesting. If a tool has no mechanisms of testing of the factual arguments passing to it at a call, then the call on the incorrect factual arguments, as a rule, is returned unevaluated. The following rather simple procedure is one of variants of solution of the problem. The procedure call **TestActArgs[*x*, *y*]** returns the empty list if the tuple of actual arguments meets the tuple of testing functions of the corresponding formal arguments, otherwise the procedure call returns the integer list of numbers of the formal arguments to which inadmissible actual arguments are supposed to be passed. The following fragment presents source code of the procedure with examples of its application.

In[4548]:= **TestActArgs[x_ /; BlockFuncModQ[x], y_ /; ListQ[y]] :=**
Module[{a = Args[x], b, c = {}, n = 1}, b = Map[ToString1, a];
b = Map[Map[StringTrim, StringSplit[#, "/;"]] &, b];
Do[If[Length[b[[j]]] == 1, AppendTo[c, True],
AppendTo[c, ToExpression[StringReplaceVars[b[[j]][[2]],
StringTrim[b[[j]][[1]], {"_", "__", "___"}] -> ToString1[y[[j]]]]]], {j, 1, Length[b]}];
If[And1[c], {}, Map[If[#, n++; Nothing, n++] &, c]]]

In[4549]:= **Gs[x_ /; StringQ[x], y_, z_ /; ListQ[z]] := {x, y, z}**
In[4550]:= **TestActArgs[Gs, {"75", 70, {a, b}}]**
Out[4550]= {}
In[4551]:= **TestActArgs[Gs, {75, 70, a + b}]**
Out[4551]= {1, 3}
In[4552]:= **Sg[x_ /; StringQ[x], y__ /; If[Length[{y}] == 1, IntegerQ[y], MemberQ3[{Integer, List, String}, Map[Head, {y}]]]] := {x, y}**
In[4553]:= **TestActArgs[Sg, {agn, "70", 75, "sv", {a, b}, a + b}]**
Out[4553]= {1, 2}

At that, use of this procedure assumes that testing for correctness of the factual arguments for formal arguments with patterns {"__", "___"} is carried out only for the first elements of tuples of the factual arguments passing to formal arguments with the appropriate patterns. Further development of the procedure is left to the interested reader as an useful exercise.

In addition, it should be noted the following important circumstance. If in the traditional programming languages the identification of an arbitrary procedure or a function is made according to its *name*, in case of the *Math*-language identification is made according to its *heading*. This circumstance is caused by that the definition of a procedure or a function in the *Math*-language is made by the manner different from traditional [4,33]. Simultaneous existence of the procedures or functions of the same name with different headings in such situation is admissible as it illustrates the following fragment, namely:

In[2434]:= **M[x_, y_] := Module[{}, x + y]; M[x_] := Module[{}, x^2];**
M[y_] := Module[{}, y^3]; M[x__] := Module[{}, {x}]
In[2435]:= **Definition[M]**
Out[2435]= M[x_, y_] := Module[{}, x + y]
M[y_] := Module[{}, y^3]

M[x__] := Module[{}, {x}]
In[2436]:= {M[500, 90], M[90], M[42, 47, 67, 27, 20]}
Out[2436]= {590, 729000, {42, 47, 67, 27, 20}}
In[2437]:= G[x_Integer] := Module[{}, x]; G[x_] := Module[{}, x^2]; G[500]
Out[2437]= 500

At the call of procedure or function of the same name from the list is chosen the one, whose formal arguments of the heading correspond to the factual arguments of the call, otherwise the call is returned *unevaluated*, except for simplifications of factual arguments according to the standard system agreements. Moreover, at compliance of formal arguments of heading with the factual ones the component of x procedure or function is caused, whose definition is above in the list returned at the **Definition[*x*]** call; in particular, whose definition has been calculated in the *Mathematica* current session by the first.

Right there, it should be noted one a rather essential moment. Definition of the testing $Test_x$ function can be directly included in the procedure heading, becoming active in the current session by the first procedure call. A mechanism of such approach very visually illustrates the following fragment, namely:

In[3850]:= P[x_, y_ /; {IntOddQ[t_] := IntegerQ[t] && OddQ[t], IntOddQ[y]}[[-1]]] := x*y
In[3851]:= P[42, 47]
Out[3851]= 1974
In[3852]:= P[42, 590]
Out[3852]= P[42, 590]
In[3853]:= **Definition[IntOddQ]**
Out[3853]= IntOddQ[t_] := IntegerQ[t] && OddQ[t]

Analogous mechanism can be used also with local variables as the following simple enough fragment visually illustrates:

In[4210]:= Vsv[x_, y_] := Module[{a = {IntOddQ[t_] := IntegerQ[t] && OddQ[t], If[IntOddQ[y], x*y, x + y]}[[-1]], b, c}, a]
In[4211]:= Vsv[74, 69]
Out[4211]= 5106
In[4212]:= Vsv[75, 70]
Out[4212]= 145
In[4213]:= **Definition[IntOddQ1]**
Out[4213]= IntOddQ[t_] := IntegerQ[t] && OddQ[t]

This mechanism works when determining the headings and local variables of the functions, blocks and modules. Meanwhile, it must be kept in mind that the represented mechanism with good reason can be carried to so-called non-standard methods of programming which are admissible, correct and are a collateral consequence of the built-in *Math*-language. At the same time, taking into account this circumstance to programming of processing means of elements of the procedures and functions (*headings, arguments, local variables, etc.*) certain additional demands are made. This mechanism can be considered especially facultative, i.e. absolutely optional to programming of procedures and functions. At the same time it must be kept in mind that definitions of the tools coded in formal arguments and local variables become active in the all domain of the current session that isn't always acceptable. The vast majority of the means represented in the present book don't use this mechanism. However certain our means, presented in this book, cover this mechanism, presenting certain ways of its processing.

In general, the return of results of call of objects of the type {*Block, Module*} can be organized through *(1)* the last offer of an object, *(2)* through the **Return**-offer and through *(3)* a formal argument, for example:

In[4227]:= **A1[x_] := Module[{a = 75, b = 70, c}, c = a + b; c*x];**
A2[x_] := Module[{a = 75, b = 70, c}, c = a + b; Return[x + 10]; c*x];
In[4228]:= **{A1[2017], A2[2017]}**
Out[4228]= {292465, 2027}
In[4229]:= **A3[x_, y_] := Module[{a = 75, b = 70, c}, c = a + b; y = {a, b}; c*x];**
In[4230]:= **{A3[2017, h], h}**
Out[4230]= {292465, {75, 70}}

In particular, the third case can be used for returning of additional results of a call, values of local variables, etc. In the present book a number of fragments of such approach is visually illustrated. In addition, formal argument in *heading* of an object through which it is planned to return a result has to be of the form {$g\_, g\_\_, g\_\_\_$}, i.e. without a testing *Test$_x$* function.

Further is being quite often mentioned about return of result of a function or a procedure by unevaluated, it concerns both the standard system tools, and the user tools. In any case, the call of a procedure or a function on an inadmissible tuple of actual arguments is returned by unevaluated, except for standard simplifications of the actual arguments. In this connection the **UnevaluatedQ** procedure providing testing of a certain procedure or function regarding of the return of its call unevaluated on a concrete tuple of the factual arguments has been programmed. The procedure call **UnevaluatedQ[*F, x*]** returns *True* if the call *F[x]* is returned unevaluated, and *False* otherwise; on an erroneous call *F[x]* "ErrorInNumArgs" is returned. The fragment below represents source code of the **UnevaluatedQ** procedure with examples of its application. This procedure represents a certain interest for program processing of the results of calls of procedures and functions.

In[3246]:= **UnevaluatedQ[F_ /; SymbolQ[F], x___] :=**
Module[{a = Quiet[Check[F[x], "error", F::argx]]},
If[a === "error", "ErrorInArgs", If[ToString1[a] === ToString[F] <> "[" <>
If[{x} == {}, "", ListStrToStr[Map[ToString1, {x}]] <> "]", True, False]]]
In[3247]:= **{UnevaluatedQ[F, x, y, z], UnevaluatedQ[Sin, x, y, z]}**
Out[3247]= {True, "ErrorInArgs"}
In[3248]:= **{UnevaluatedQ[Sin, 50090], UnevaluatedQ[Sin, 500.90], UnevaluatedQ[Sin]}**
Out[3248]= {True, False, "ErrorInArgs"}
In[3673]:= **UnevaluatedQ1[F_, x___] := If[! SymbolQ[F], True,**
ToString1[F[x]] === ToString[F] <> "[" <> StringTake[ToString1[{x}], {2, -2}] <> "]"]
In[3674]:= **G[x_, y_, z_Integer] := x*y*z**
In[3675]:= **UnevaluatedQ1[G, 74, 69, 49]**
Out[3675]= False
In[3676]:= **UnevaluatedQ1[G, 74, 69, "S"]**

Out[3676]= True

The **UnevaluatedQ1** function completes the previous fragment being a functional analog of the **UnevaluatedQ** procedure. The function call **UnevaluatedQ1[F, x]** returns *True* if the call *F[x]* is returned unevaluated, and *False* otherwise.

Meanwhile, the standard **Definition** function in the case of the procedures/functions of the same name in a number of cases is of little use for solution of problems which are connected with processing of definitions of such objects. Above all, it concerns the procedures whose definitions are located in the user packages loaded into the current *Mathematica* session as illustrates a simple example of receiving definition of the **SystemQ** procedure [48,50]:

In[3247]:= **Definition["SystemQ"]**
Out[3247]= SystemQ[AladjevProcedures`SystemQ`S_] := If[Off["Definition"::"ssle"];
! ToString["Definition"[AladjevProcedures`SystemQ`S]] === Null &&
MemberQ[Names["System`*"], ToString[AladjevProcedures`SystemQ`S]],
On["Definition"::"ssle"]; True, On["Definition"::"ssle"]; False]

The call **Definition[x]** of the standard function in a number of cases returns the definition of some *x* object with the context corresponding to it what at a rather large definitions becomes badly foreseeable and less acceptable for the subsequent program processing as evidently illustrates the previous example. Moreover, the name of an object or its string format also can act as an actual argument. For elimination of this shortcoming we defined a number of tools allowing to obtain definitions of procedures or functions in thea certain optimized format. As such means it is possible to note the following: **DefOptimum, Definition1, Definition2, Definition3, Definition4, DefFunc, DefFunc1, DefFunc2, DefFunc3, DefOpt**. These means along with some others are represented in books [28-33] and included in the *MathToolBox* package [48]. The following fragment represents source codes of the most used of them with examples of their application.

In[2470]:= **Definition2[x_ /; SameQ[SymbolQ[x], HowAct[x]]] :=**
Module[{a, b = Attributes[x], c},
If[SystemQ[x], Return[{"System", Attributes[x]}], Off[Part::partw]];
ClearAttributes[x, b]; Quiet[a = ToString[InputForm[Definition[x]]];
Mapp[SetAttributes, {Rule, StringJoin}, Listable];
c = StringReplace[a, Flatten[{Rule[StringJoin[Contexts1[], ToString[x] <> "`"], ""]}]];
c = StringSplit[c, "\n \n"]; Mapp[ClearAttributes, {Rule, StringJoin}, Listable];
SetAttributes[x, b]; a = AppendTo[c, b];
If[SameQ[a[[1]], "Null"] && a[[2]] == {}, On[Part::partw]; {"Undefined", Attributes[x]},
If[SameQ[a[[1]], "Null"] && a[[2]] != {} && ! SystemQ[x], On[Part::partw]; {"Undefined",
Attributes[x]}, If[SameQ[a[[1]], "Null"] && a[[2]] != {} && a[[2]] != {}, On[Part::partw];
{"System", Attributes[x]}, On[Part::partw]; a]]]]]

In[2471]:= **Definition2[SystemQ]**
Out[2471]= {"SystemQ[S_] := If[Off[MessageName[Definition, \"ssle\"]];
! ToString[Definition[S]] === Null && MemberQ[Names[\"System`*\"], ToString[S]],
On[MessageName[Definition, \"ssle\"]]; True, On[MessageName[Definition, \"ssle\"]];
False]", {}}

In[2472]:= **Definition2[Tan]**
Out[2472]= {"System", {Listable, NumericFunction, Protected}}
In[2473]:= **Definition2[(a + b)/(c + d)]**
Out[2473]= Definition2[(a + b)/(c + d)]

In[2502]:= **Definition3[x_ /; SymbolQ[x], y_ /; ! HowAct[y]] :=**
Module[{a = Attributes[x], b = Definition2[x]},
If[b[[1]] == "System", y = x; {"System", a}, b = Definition2[x][[1 ;; -2]];
ClearAttributes[x, a]; If[BlockFuncModQ[x, y], ToExpression[b];
SetAttributes[x, a]; Definition[x], SetAttributes[x, a]; Definition[x]]]]

In[2503]:= **Definition3[SystemQ, y]**
Out[2503]= SystemQ[S_] := If[Off["Definition"::"ssle"];
! ToString["Definition"[S]] === Null && MemberQ[Names["System`*"], ToString[S]],
On["Definition"::"ssle"]; True, On["Definition"::"ssle"]; False]
In[2504]:= **y**
Out[2504]= "Function"
In[2505]:= **Definition3[Sin, z]**
Out[2505]= {"System", {Listable, NumericFunction, Protected}}
In[2506]:= **z**
Out[2506]= Sin

In[2598]:= **Definition4[x_ /; StringQ[x]] := Module[{a},**
a = Quiet[Check[Select[StringSplit[ToString[InputForm[Quiet[Definition[x]]]], "\n"],
 # != " " && # != x &], $Failed]];
If[a === $Failed, $Failed, If[SuffPref[a[[1]], "Attributes[", 1], a = AppendTo[a[[2 ;; -1]],
a[[1]]]]]; If[Length[a] != 1, a, a[[1]]]]

In[2599]:= **W = 90; G := 500; Map[Definition4, {"W", "G", "74", "a + b", "If"}]**
Out[2599]= {"W = 90", "G := 500", $Failed, $Failed, "Attributes[If] = {HoldRest, Protected}"}
In[2600]:= **A[x_] := Module[{a = 90}, x + a]; A[x_, y_] := Module[{a = 6}, x + y + a];**
A[x_, y_List] := Block[{}, {x, y}]; A[x_Integer] := Module[{a = 500}, x + a]; A := {a, b, c, d, h};
SetAttributes[A, {Flat, Listable, Protected}];
In[2601]:= **Definition4["A"]**
Out[2601]= {"A := {a, b, c, d, h}", "A[x_Integer] := Module[{a = 500}, x + a]",
"A[x_] := Module[{a = 90}, x + a]", "A[x_, y_List] := Block[{}, {x, y}]",
"A[x_, y_] := Module[{a = 6}, x + y + a]", "Attributes[A] = {Flat, Listable, Protected}"}

A number of functional means of the *Math*-language as the actual arguments assume only objects of the types {*Symbol, String, HoldPattern[Symbol]*} what in certain cases is an quite inconvenient at programming of problems of different purpose. In particular, the standard **Definition** function refers to these tools too [28–33,50]. For the purpose of expansion of the **Definition** function onto types, different from the mentioned ones, **Definition1** procedure can be used, whose call **Definition1[x]** returns definition of *x* object in string format, *"Null"* if *x* isn't determined, otherwise *$Failed* is returned.

So, a fragment in [33] represents the procedure code with typical examples of its application from which certain advantages of the **Definition1** concerning the **Definition** function are quite visually visible. The **Definition1** procedure has been programmed with usage of our

ToString1 procedure [28,33] which unlike the standard **ToString** function provides correct converting of expressions in string format. The **Definition1** procedure processes the main especial and erroneous situations. Meanwhile, the **Definition1** procedure does not rid the returned definitions from contexts and is correct only for the objects with unique names. In addition, in case of the multiple contexts the **Definition1** procedure call returns definitions with a context which answers the last user package uploaded into the current *Mathematica* session. On system functions, the **Definition1** procedure call returns *"Null"*.

As an expansion of the **Definition1** procedure, the **Definition2** procedure presented by the previous fragment can serve. This procedure uses our means **Contexts1**, **HowAct**, **Mapp**, **SymbolQ** and **SystemQ** considered in the present book and in [28–33,48,50]. These means are rather simple and are used in our means enough widely [48].

Unlike the previous procedure **Definition1**, the **Definition2** procedure rids the returned definitions from contexts, and is correct for the program objects with unique names. The **Definition2** call on system functions returns the nested list, whose first element – *"System"*, whereas the second element – the list of attributes ascribed to a factual argument. While on the user function or procedure x the call **Definition2**[x] also returns the nested list, whose first element – the optimized definition of x *(in the sense of absence of contexts in it)*, whereas the second element – the list of attributes ascribed to x; in their absence the empty list acts as the second element of the returned list. In case of *False* value on a test ascribed to a formal x argument, the procedure call **Definition2**[x] will be returned unevaluated. Analogously to the previous procedure, the procedure **Definition2** processes the main both the erroneous, and especial situations. In addition, both procedures **Definition1** and **Definition2** return definitions of objects in the string format.

The call **Definition3**[w, y] returns the optimum definition of a procedure or a function w, whereas through the second y argument– an undefined variable – the type of w in a context {*"Procedure"*, *"Function"*, *"Procedure&Function"*} is returned if w is a procedure or a function, on system functions the procedure call returns the list {*"Function"*, {*Attributes*}}, while thru the second y argument the first argument is returned; at inadmissibility of the first actual w argument the procedure call is returned unevaluated, i.e. **Definition3**[w].

The call **Definition4**[w] in a convenient format returns the definition of a w object, whose name is encoded in the string format, namely: *(1)* on a system function w its attributes are returned, *(2)* on the user block, function, module the procedure call returns the definition of a w object in the string format with the attributes, options and/or values by default for the formal arguments ascribed to it *(if such are available)*, *(3)* the call returns the definition of a w object in the string format for assignments by operators {":=", "="} whereas *(4)* in other cases the procedure call returns *$Failed*. The procedure has a number of interesting appendices at programming of various system applications.

The following **DefOpt** procedure presents a quite certain interest that in a number of cases is more acceptable than the **Definition** function along with procedures **DefFunc**, **DefFunc1**, **DefFunc2** and **DefFunc3** considered in [28-33] that are intended for obtaining definitions of procedures and functions in the convenient format acceptable for processing. The fragment below represents source code of the **DefOpt** procedure with examples of its application.

In[2342]:= **DefOpt[x_/; StringQ[x]] := Module[{a = If[SymbolQ[x], If[SystemQ[x],**

b = "Null", ToString1[Definition[x]], "Null"]], b, c},
If[! SameQ[a, "Null"], b = Quiet[Context[x]]];
If[! Quiet[ContextQ[b]], "Null", c=StringReplace[a, b <> x <> "`" -> ""]; ToExpression[c]; c]]

In[2343]:= **DefOpt["SystemQ"]**
Out[2343]= SystemQ[S_] := If[Off[MessageName[Definition, \"ssle\"]];
! ToString[Definition[S]] === Null && MemberQ[Names[\"System`*\"], ToString[S]],
On[MessageName[Definition, \"ssle\"]]; True, On[MessageName[Definition, \"ssle\"]];
False]

In[2344]:= **DefFunc[$TypeProc]**
Out[2344]= Attributes[$Failed] = {HoldAll, Protected}

In[2345]:= **DefOpt["$TypeProc"]**
Out[2345]= "$TypeProc := CheckAbort[If[$Art27$Kr20$ = Select[{Stack[Module],
Stack[Block], Stack[DynamicModule]}, #1 != {} &]; If[$Art27$Kr20$ == {},
Clear[$Art27$Kr20$]; Abort[], $Art27$Kr20$ = ToString[$Art27$Kr20$[[1]][[1]]]];
SuffPref[$Art27$Kr20$, \"Block[{\", 1], Clear[$Art27$Kr20$]; \"Block\",
If[SuffPref[$Art27$Kr20$, \"Module[{\", 1] && ! StringFreeQ[$Art27$Kr20$,
\"DynamicModule\"], Clear[$Art27$Kr20$]; \"DynamicModule\", Clear[$Art27$Kr20$];
\"Module\"]], $Failed]"

In[2346]:= **Map[DefOpt, {"If", "Sin", "Goto", "a + b", "90", 590}]**
Out[2346]= {Null, Null, Null, Null, Null, DefOpt[590]}

On the other hand, our certain procedures are unsuitable in case of necessity of receiving definitions of a number of procedural variables, for instance, **$TypeProc** as illustrate some examples in [33]. And only the procedure call **DefOpt[*x*]** returns definition of an arbitrary *x* object in the optimum format irrespective of type of the user *x* object. In addition, the call **DefOpt[*x*]** not only returns an *optimum* form of definition of a *x* object in the string format, but also evaluates it in the current session what in a number of cases is useful enough; at the procedure call the name of the *x* object is encoded in the string format; while on the system functions and other string expressions the procedure call **DefOpt[*x*]** returns "*Null*". At the same time it must be kept in mind that the **DefOpt** procedure is inapplicable to procedures or functions of the same name, i.e. having several definitions with different headings. The previous fragment represents source code of the **DefOpt** with examples of its application.

The **OptDefinition** procedure is a rather interesting modification of the previous **DefOpt** procedure; its source code with examples of usage represents the following fragment. The call **OptDefinition[*x*]** returns the definition of a procedure or a function *x* optimized in the above sense i.e. without context associated with the user package containing the definition of a procedure or a function *x*.

In[3298]:= **OptDefinition[x_ /; Quiet[ProcQ[x] || FunctionQ[x]]] :=**
Module[{c = $Packages, a, b, d, h = Definition2[x]}, {a, b} = {h[[1 ;; -2]], h[[-1]]};
ClearAllAttributes[x]; d = Map[StringJoin[#, ToString[x] <> "`"] &, c];
ToExpression[Map[StringReplace[#, GenRules[d, ""]] &, a]];
SetAttributes[x, b]; Definition[x]]

In[3299]:= **SetAttributes[ToString1, {Listable, Protected}]; Definition[ToString1]**
Out[3299]= Attributes[ToString1] = {Listable, Protected}

ToString1[AladjevProcedures`ToString1`x_] :=
Module[{AladjevProcedures`ToString1`a = "$$Art27$Kr20$$.txt",
AladjevProcedures`ToString1`b = "", AladjevProcedures`ToString1`c,
AladjevProcedures`ToString1`k = 1}, Write[AladjevProcedures`ToString1`a,
AladjevProcedures`ToString1`x]; Close[AladjevProcedures`ToString1`a];
For[AladjevProcedures`ToString1`k, AladjevProcedures`ToString1`k < \[Infinity],
AladjevProcedures`ToString1`k++, AladjevProcedures`ToString1`c =
Read[AladjevProcedures`ToString1`a, String]; If[AladjevProcedures`ToString1`c ===
EndOfFile, Return[DeleteFile[Close[AladjevProcedures`ToString1`a]];
AladjevProcedures`ToString1`b], AladjevProcedures`ToString1`b =
AladjevProcedures`ToString1`b <> StrDelEnds[AladjevProcedures`ToString1`c, " ", 1]]]]

In[3300]:= **OptDefinition[ToString1]**

Out[3300]= Attributes[ToString1] = {Listable, Protected}
ToString1[x_] := Module[{a = "$$Art27$Kr20$$.txt", b = "", c, k = 1}, Write[a, x]; Close[a];
For[k, k < ∞, k++, c = Read[a, String]; If[c === EndOfFile, Return[DeleteFile[Close[a]]; b],
b = b <> StrDelEnds[c, " ", 1]]]]

It is necessary to pay attention to use of the **GenRules** procedure providing generation of the list of transformation rules for providing of replacements in the string definition of a *x* object. In a number of cases such approach is a rather effective at strings processing.

The **DefOptimum** procedure realized in a different manner is a full analog of the previous procedure, whose call **DefOptimum[x]** returns the definition of a function or a procedure *x* optimized in the respect that it doesn't contain a context of the user package which contains definition of the procedure or function *x*. The following fragment represents source code of the **DefOptimum** procedure with a typical example of its application.

In[2245]:= **SetAttributes[OptDefinition, {Listable, Protected}]; Definition[OptDefinition]**
Out[2245]= Attributes[OptDefinition] = {Listable, Protected}
OptDefinition[x_ /; ProcQ[x] || FunctionQ[x]] := Module[{a = Definition2[x][[1 ;; -2]],
b = Definition2[x][[-1]], AladjevProcedures`OptDefinition`c = $Packages,
AladjevProcedures`OptDefinition`d, AladjevProcedures`OptDefinition`h},
ClearAllAttributes[ToString1]; AladjevProcedures`OptDefinition`d =(#1 <> (ToString[x] <>
"`") &) /@ AladjevProcedures`OptDefinition`c; ToExpression[(StringReplace[#1,
GenRules[AladjevProcedures`OptDefinition`d, ""]] &) /@ a]; SetAttributes[x, b];
"Definition"[x]]

In[2246]:= **DefOptimum[x_ /; Quiet[ProcQ[x] || FunctionQ[x]]] :=**
Module[{a = "", b = ToString[x], c, d = Context[x], f = Attributes[x], k = 1},
ClearAttributes[x, f]; Save[b, x]; For[k = 1, k < Infinity, k++, c = Read[b, String];
If[c === " ", Break[], a = a <> StringReplace[c, StringJoin[d, b, "`"] -> ""]]];
DeleteFile[Close[b]]; Clear[x]; ToExpression[a]; SetAttributes[x, f]; Definition[x]]

In[2247]:= **DefOptimum[OptDefinition]**
Out[2247]= Attributes[OptDefinition] = {Listable, Protected}
OptDefinition[x_ /; Quiet[ProcQ[x] || FunctionQ[x]]] := Module[{c = $Packages, a, b, d,
h = Definition2[x]}, {a, b} = {h[[1 ;; -2]], h[[-1]]}; ClearAllAttributes[x];

d = (#1 <> (ToString[x] <> "`") &) /@ c; ToExpression[(StringReplace[#1, GenRules[d, ""]] &) /@ a]; SetAttributes[x, b]; "Definition"[x]]

In[2500]:= **DefOpt1[x_] := Module[{a = ToString[x], b, c},**
If[! SymbolQ[a], $Failed, If[SystemQ[x], x, If[ProcQ[a] || FunctionQ[a], b = Attributes[x];
ClearAttributes[x, b];
c = StringReplace[ToString1[Definition[x]], Context[a] <> a <> "`" -> ""];
SetAttributes[x, b]; c, $Failed]]]]

In[2501]:= **DefOpt1[StrStr]**
Out[2501]= "StrStr[x_] := If[StringQ[x], \"<>x<>\", ToString[x]]"
In[2502]:= **Map[DefOpt1, {a + b, 74, Sin}]**
Out[2502]= {$Failed, $Failed, Sin}

Thus, the algorithm of the above **DefOptimum** procedure is based on saving of the current definition of a block, function, module x in *ASCII* format file by means of the **Save** function with the subsequent *string-by-string* reading of the file in common string with preliminary deleting of occurrences of a package context in which definition of the x object is located. Whereupon such common string is processed by **ToExpression** function with return of the optimized definition of the x object.

Meanwhile, the last **DefOpt1** procedure of the previous fragment is seemed as an effective enough for receiving of definition of the user procedure or function in optimized format in the above sense, i.e. without context. The procedure call **DefOpt1[x]** on a system function x returns its name, on the user function or procedure returns its optimized code in the string format whereas on other values of a x argument $*Failed* is returned. The previous fragment represents source code of the procedure **DefOpt1** along with examples of its application.

At last, the following two simple functions resolve the question of receiving the optimized code of the definition of a block, function or module too. The functions calls **OptimalDef[x]** and **OptimalDef1[x]** return the definition of a block, function or module x in the optimized format, i.e without context associated with the user package containing the x. The definition becomes active in the current session. The next fragment represents source codes of the both functions with typical examples of their application.

In[4109]:= **OptimalDef[x_ /; BlockFuncModQ[x]] :=**
{ToExpression[StringReplace[ToString1[Definition[x]], {"Global`" <> ToString[x] <>
"`" -> "", Context[x] <> ToString[x] <> "`" -> ""}]], Definition[x]}[[-1]]

In[4110]:= **Definition[FactualVarsStr]**
Out[4110]= FactualVarsStr[x_ /; StringQ[x]] := Module[{a = StringLength[x] + 1, b = "",
c = {}, d = x <> "[", t, Global`FactualVarsStr`k, Global`FactualVarsStr`j = 1},
While[Global`FactualVarsStr`j <= a, For[Global`FactualVarsStr`k = Global`FactualVarsStr`j,
Global`FactualVarsStr`k <= a, Global`FactualVarsStr`k++,
If[SymbolQ[t = StringTake[d, {Global`FactualVarsStr`k, Global`FactualVarsStr`k}]],
b = b <> t, If[b != "", AppendTo[c, b], 6]; b = ""];
Global`FactualVarsStr`j = Global`FactualVarsStr`k + 1]]; c]

In[4111]:= **OptimalDef[FactualVarsStr]**
Out[4111]= FactualVarsStr[x_ /; StringQ[x]] := Module[{a = StringLength[x] + 1, b = "",

c = {}, d = x <> "[", t, k, j = 1}, While[j <= a, For[k = j, k <= a, k++, If[SymbolQ[t = StringTake[d, {k, k}]], b = b <> t, If[b != "", AppendTo[c, b], 6]; b = ""]; j = k + 1]]; c]

In[4112]:= **OptimalDef1[x_ /; BlockFuncModQ[x]] := {ToExpression[PureDefinition[x]], Definition[x]}[[-1]]**

In[4113]:= **OptimalDef1[OptDef]**
Out[4113]= OptDef[x_ /; SymbolQ[x], y___] := Quiet[ToExpression[StringReplace[ToString1["Definition"[x]], {Context[x] <> ToString[x] <> "`" -> If[{y} != {} && ContextQ[y], y, ""], Context[x] -> If[{y} != {} && ContextQ[y], y, ""]}]]]

At last, the function call **DefMeans[x]** returns definition of a *x* symbol in the above *optimum* format, i.e. without contexts entering in it expressions of format {Context[*x*] <> ToString[*x*] <> "`", "Global`" <> ToString[*x*] <> "`"}.

In[4356]:= **DefMeans[x_Symbol] :=**
{ToExpression[StringReplace[ToString1[Definition[x]], GenRules[Map[# <> ToString[x] <> "`" &, {Context[x], "Global`"}], ""]]], Definition[x]}[[2]]

In[4357]:= **Definition[PureFuncQ]**
Out[4357]= PureFuncQ[Global`PureFuncQ`F_] := Quiet[(StringTake[ToString1[Global`PureFuncQ`F], {-3, -1}] == " & " && ! StringFreeQ[ToString[Global`PureFuncQ`F], "#"]) || SuffPref[ToString["InputForm"[Global`PureFuncQ`F]], "Function[", 1]]

In[4358]:= **DefMeans[PureFuncQ]**
Out[4358]= PureFuncQ[F_] := Quiet[(StringTake[ToString1[F], {-3, -1}] == " & " && ! StringFreeQ[ToString[F], "#"]) || SuffPref[ToString["InputForm"[F]], "Function[", 1]]

In addition to the above means, the procedure is of interest, whose call **OptDefPackage[x]** returns the two-element list whose the first element – the list with names of tools of the user package with *x* context, uploaded into the current session whose definitions received by the **Definition** function are optimized in the above sense whereas the second element – the list with names of tools with a *x* context whose definitions aren't optimized in the above sense. In turn, the procedure call **OptDefPackage[x, y]** with the second optional *y* argument – an arbitrary expression – returns the above 2-element list, in addition converting the means of the second sublist into tools with the *optimized* format in the current session. In addition, the procedure call on an inactive *x* context returns $Failed. The next fragment represents source code of the **OptDefPackage** procedure with typical examples of its application.

In[3767]:= **OptDefPackage[x_ /; ContextQ[x], j___] := Module[{a = {{}, {}}, b},**
If[MemberQ[$Packages, x], Map[If[StringFreeQ[ToString[Definition[#]], x <> # <> "`"],
AppendTo[a[[1]], #], AppendTo[a[[2]], #]] &, CNames[x]];
If[{j} != {}, Map[{ClearAttributes[#, b = Attributes[#]], ToExpression[PureDefinition[#]],
SetAttributes[#, b]} &, a[[2]]], 6]; a, $Failed]]

In[3768]:= **Map[Length, OptDefPackage["AladjevProcedures`"]]**
Out[3768]= {1057, 66}
In[3769]:= **OptDefPackage["AladjevProcedures`", 590];**
In[3770]:= **Map[Length, OptDefPackage["AladjevProcedures`"]]**
Out[3770]= {1123, 0}

```
In[3887]:= SymbolsFromMx[x_ /; FileExistsQ[x] && FileExtension[x] == "mx", y___] :=
Module[{a = ReadFullFile[x], c, h, p = {{}, {}}, t, b = Map[FromCharacterCode, Range[0, 31]],
d = ContextFromMx[x]},
If[d === $Failed, {}, h = StringCases[a, Shortest[d ~~ __ ~~ "`"]];
h = Sort[DeleteDuplicates[Select[Map[StringTake[#, {StringLength[d] + 1, -2}] &, h],
SymbolQ[#] &]]]; c = StringSplit[a, "\.0b"];
c = Map[StringTrim[StringReplace[#, GenRules[b, ""]]] &, c];
c = Select[c, StringFreeQ[#, " "] && PrintableASCIIQ[#] &]; c = Select[c, SymbolQ[#] &];
c = Select[c, {b = StringTake[#, {1, 1}], LetterQ[b] && UpperCaseQ[b]}[[2]] &];
Map[If[SystemQ[#], AppendTo[p[[2]], #], AppendTo[p[[1]], #]] &, c];
a = {h, t = Sort[Select[p[[1]], StringFreeQ[#, "`"] &]], Sort[p[[2]]]};
If[{y} != {} && ! HowAct[y], If[MemberQ[$Packages, d],
y = {h, MinusList[Sort[DeleteDuplicates[Select[t, Context[#] == d &&
! TemporaryQ[#] &]]], h]}, Get[x];
y = {h, MinusList[Sort[DeleteDuplicates[Select[t, Context[#] == d &&
! TemporaryQ[#] &]]], h]}; RemovePackage[d]], Null]; a]]
In[3888]:= Map[Length, SymbolsFromMx["c:/AVZ/MathToolBox.mx", g70]]
Out[3888]= {68, 1142, 378}
In[3889]:= Map[Length, g70]
Out[3889]= {68, 941}
```

The previous fragment contains an useful enough **SymbolsFromMx** procedure that allows to check a *mx*-file with the user package for entering of symbols in it without uploading of the file into the current session. The procedure call **SymbolsFromMx**[*x*] returns the three-element list whose first element – the list with names of tools of the user package, contained in a *mx*-file *x*, whose definitions received by system **Definition** function are not optimized in the above sense, while the second element represents the list with names of tools with the context ascribed to the *x* datafile; at last, the third element represents the list with names of system means used by the user package located in the *x* datafile. In turn, the procedure call **SymbolsFromMx**[*x, y*] with second optional *y* argument – *an indefinite symbol* – additionally returns the 2-element list whose the first element – the list with names of means of the user package, located in a *mx*-file *x*, whose definitions received by means of system **Definition** function are not optimized in the above sense, whereas the second element is the list with names of tools of the user package *x*, whose definitions obtained by means of the standard **Definition** function are optimized in the above sense. The previous fragment presents the source code of the procedure with examples of its application.

Meanwhile, the oprtimization problem of the source code of a block, a function or a module loaded into the current session is considered in broader aspect. The matter is that the source code of such means may contain expressions of a type $a <> b <> $ "`" where *a* – a context from the system list *$Packages* and *b* – a name of this means. Therefore the following procedure is of quite certain interest. The procedure call **OptimizedQ**[*x*] returns *True* if source text of a block, a function or a module *x* does not contain expressions of the type $a <>$ "*x*`" in the call **Definition**[*x*] where *a* – a context from the list *$Packages*, and *False* otherwise. While the call **OptimizedQ**[*x, y*] where the second optional *y* argument – *an undefinite symbol* – through it additionally returns the list of contexts from the list *$Packages* only if *False* is returned thru the main result, otherwise *y* remains undefinite. The next fragment represents source code of the **OptimizedQ** procedure with typical examples of its application.

In[4514]:= **OptimizedQ[x_ /; BlockFuncModQ[x], y___] :=**
Module[{a = ToString1[Definition[x]], b, c = ToString[x]},
b = Select[$Packages, ! StringFreeQ[a, # <> c <> "`"] &];
If[b == {}, True, If[{y} != {} && SymbolQ[y] && NullQ[y], y = b;
ToExpression[StringReplace[a, Map[(# <> c <> "`" -> "") &, b]]]]; False]]

In[4515]:= **OptimizedQ[Locals]**
Out[4515]= False
In[4516]:= **OptimizedQ[Locals, gs]**
Out[4516]= False
In[4517]:= **gs**
Out[4517]= {"Global`"}
In[4518]:= **OptimizedQ[Locals]**
Out[4518]= True

On the basis of the previous procedure it is possible to program a rather simply procedure regarding the analysis of existence in the user package uploaded into the current session of means *x* whose definitions obtained by the means of the call **Definition[x]** aren't *completely optimized*, i.e. contain constructions of the kind *j* <> "*x*`" where *j* – a context from the system list *$Packages*. The procedure call **DefAnalysis[x]** returns the list of *ListList* type whose 2-element sublists as the first elements defines *w* context *(one or more)* while the last elements define quantity of means *j* *(blocks, functions, modules)* of the user package with *x* context that is uploaded into the current session, whose definitions **Definition[j]** contains constructions of the kind *w* <> "*j*`" where *w* – a context from the system list *$Packages*. At that, the first element of the returned list has kind {*"Total"*, *n*} where *n* defines the total of means of the analyzed package that have type {*Block, Function, Module*}. At the same time it must be kept in mind that the procedure call translate all definitions of blocks, functions and modules of a package *x* to *fully optimized* format in the current session. At last, the call **DefAnalysis[x, y]** with the optional *y* argument – an indefinite symbol – thru it additionally returns the nested list of names of tools whose definitions have nonoptimized format; its sublists contains tools names of the package *x* with a context preceeding them. The following fragment represents source code of the **DefAnalysis** procedure along with examples of its application.

In[4523]:= **DefAnalysis[x_ /; MemberQ[$Packages, x], y___] :=**
Module[{a = CNames[x], b, c = {}, d, p = t, g = 0, h},
Do[ClearAll[t]; If[! BlockFuncModQ[Set[d, a[[j]]]], 6, g++;
Quiet[OptimizedQ[d, t]]; If[NullQ[t], 6, AppendTo[c, {t, d}]]], {j, 1, Length[a]}]; t = p;
If[{y} != {} && NullQ[y], y = Gather[c, #1[[1]] === #2[[1]] &];
y = Map[DeleteDuplicates, Map[Flatten, y]], 6];
h = CountsList[Flatten[Map[#[[1]] &, c]]]; PrependTo[h, {"Total", g}]]

In[4524]:= **DefAnalysis["AladjevProcedures`", gs]**
Out[4524]= {{"Total", 1102}, {"Global`", 536}, {"AladjevProcedures`", 66}}

In[4525]:= **gs**
Out[4525]= {{"Global`", "ActBFMuserQ", "ActCsProcFunc", ..., "VarExch", "VarExch1"}, {"AladjevProcedures`", "AllElemsMaxLevels", "BitGet1", ..., "TypeActObj", "WhichN"}}
In[4526]:= **Map[Length, %]**
Out[4526]= {537, 67}

Thus, from the represented example follows that **48.73%** of definitions of blocks, functions and modules of the package with context *"AladjevProcedures'"* are not *completely optimized* in the above sense. At the same time it must be kept in mind that this indicator is *dependable* on the version of the *Mathematica* and the user package, uploading in the current session.

The following fragment contains the useful **OptimizedDefPackage** procedure that allows to check the user package located in a *mx*-file x for existing in it of means whose definitions in case of uploading of the datafile in the current session are optimized in the above sense. The procedure call **OptimizedDefPackage[x]** returns the 2-element list whose the first element – the list with names of means of the user package, located in a *mx*-file x whose definitions are optimized in the above sense, while the second element represents the list with names of tools that are not optimized. At the same time, the procedure call converts all means of the x package whose definitions will be optimized in the current session. This procedure can be applied both to the unloaded, and the uploaded *mx*-file. At that, if the *mx*-file is unloaded, then this datafile remains unloaded.

In[4275]:= **OptimizedDefPackage[x_ /; FileExistsQ[x] && FileExtension[x] == "mx"] :=**
Module[{a = ContextFromFile[x], b, c = {{}, {}}},
If[a === $Failed, $Failed, If[MemberQ[$Packages, a], b = 75, Get[x]];
Map[If[StringFreeQ[ToString[Definition[#]], a <> # <> "`"], AppendTo[c[[1]], #],
{AppendTo[c[[2]], #], Map[ToExpression, Flatten[{PureDefinition[#]}]]}] &, CNames[a]];
If[b === 75, Null, RemovePackage[a]]; c]]

In[4276]:= **OptimizedDefPackage["C:\\MathtoolBox\\MathtoolBox.mx"]**
Out[4276]= {{"AcNb", "ActBFM", "Affiliate", "ArityBFM", "ArrayInd", "AssignL", "Attributes1", "AttributesH", "AttributesQ", "Avg", "BlockQ", "BlockQ1", "BootDrive1", "CallListable", ..., "$TestArgsTypes", "$UserContexts", "$Version1", "$Version2"}, {"ActUcontexts", "AddMxFile", "Adrive", "Adrive1", ..., "VarsInBlockMod", "VolDir", "WhatObj", "WhatType", "WhichN", "XOR1", "$Line1", "$ProcName", "$TypeProc"}}
In[4277]:= **Map[Length, %]**
Out[4277]= {1057, 66}
In[4278]:= **Map[Length, OptimizedDefPackage["C:/agn/MathToolBox.mx"]]**
Out[4278]= {1123, 0}

Whereas the procedure call **OptimizedMfile[x, y]** ensures the saving of means definitions with x context that are optimized in the above sense in a *m*-file y, with returning y. In turn, the call **OptimizedMfile[x, y, z]** additionally through the third z argument – an indefinite symbol – returns the three-element list whose the 1st element determines list of tools whose definitions are optimized, the 2nd element determines list of tools whose definitions are not optimized, and the 3rd element determines the list of temporary symbols which have been generated at upload of the user package with a x context into the current session. The next fragment represents source code of the **OptimizedMfile** procedure along with the typical examples of its application.

In[3337]:= **OptimizedMfile[x_ /; ContextQ[x], y_ /; FileExtension[y] == "m", z___] :=**
Module[{a = Save[y, x], b = CNames[x], c, c1, d, d1, g, p, t, m = {}, n = {}},
c = ReadString[y]; t = Map[x <> # <> "`" &, b]; c1 = StringReplace[c, GenRules[t, ""]];
d = DeleteDuplicates[StringCases[c1, "Attributes[" ~~ X_ ~~ "$] = {Temporary}"]];
If[{z} != {} && ! HowAct[z], Map[{g = StringReplace[#, {x -> "", "`" -> ""}],
If[StringFreeQ[c, #], AppendTo[m, g], AppendTo[n, g]]} &, t];
d1 = Sort[Flatten[Map[StringTake[p = StringCases[#, "[" ~~ __ ~~ "]"], {2, -2}] &, d]]];
z = {m, n, d1}, Null];
c = StringReplace[c1, GenRules[d, ""]]; WriteString[y, c]; Close[y]]

In[3338]:= **OptimizedMfile["AladjevProcedures`", "MathToolBox.m", g70]**
Out[3338]= "MathToolBox.m"
In[3339]:= **g70**
Out[3339]= {{"AcNb", "ActBFM", "Affiliate", "ArityBFM", "ArrayInd", ...}, {"ActBFMuserQ", "ActCsProcFunc", "ActivateMeansFromCdfNb", ...}, {"a$", "A$", "b$", "c$", "d$", "e$", "f$", "F$", "g$", "G$", "h$", "H$", ..., "v$", "w$", "x$", "y$", "z$", "Z$"}}
In[3340]:= **Map[Length, %]**
Out[3340]= {1071, 52, 19}

At last, the function call **OptDefPack[x]** returns the empty list, i.e. {}, providing reload of all symbols whose definitions are in the user package with a *x* context activated in the current session, doing possible to receive their definitions in the optimized format, i.e without the *x* context. The fragment presents source codes of the function and its analog with an example.

In[3942]:= **OptDefPack[x_ /; ContextQ[x]] :=**
ReplaceAll[Map[Quiet[OptimalDef[#]]; &, CNames[x]], Null -> Nothing]

In[3943]:= **OptDefPack[x_ /; ContextQ[x]] :=**
ReplaceAll[Map[Quiet[OptimalDef1[#]]; &, CNames[x]], Null -> Nothing]

In[3944]:= **OptDefPack["AladjevProcedures`"]**
Out[3944]= {}

For a number of applications, including applications of the system character, the standard **Definition** function seems as important enough tools whose call **Definition**[*x*] returns the definition of a *x* object with attributes ascribed to it; in the absence of a definition the *Null*, i.e. nothing, or the ascribed attributes to an undefined *x* symbol is returned, namely:

Attributes[*x*] = *The list of attributes ascribed to a symbol x*

As very visually illustrate the following simple examples, namely:

In[2839]:= **SetAttributes[h, Listable]; Definition[h]**
Out[2839]= Attributes[h] = {Listable}
In[2840]:= **Definition[Sin]**
Out[2840]= Attributes[Sin] = {Listable, NumericFunction, Protected}

Meanwhile, on the other hand, a lot of problems of processing of objects are based, strictly speaking, on their definitions in their pure form. Therefore the allotment of definition of an arbitrary *x* object in pure form can be provided, in particular, by means of two mechanisms whose essence is explained by the examples in [28-33,50] by means of the means **Def1** and **Def**; the following example gives definition of the **Def1** function, namely:

In[2526]:= **Def1[x_ /; StringQ[x]] := If[! SymbolQ[x] || SystemQ[x], $Failed, ReduceLists[Definition2[x][[1 ;; -2]]]]**

In[2527]:= **B[x_] := x; B[x_, y_] := Module[{a, b, c}, x + y];
B[x_ /; IntegerQ[x]] := Block[{a, b, c, d}, x]**

In[2528]:= **SetAttributes[B, {Protected}]; Attributes[B]**

Out[2528]= {Protected}

In[2529]:= **Def1["B"]**

Out[2529]= {"B[x_ /; IntegerQ[x]] := Block[{a, b, c}, x]", "B[x_] := x", "B[x_, y_] := Module[{a, b, c, d}, x + y]"}

In[2530]:= **Definition[B]**

Out[2530]= Attributes[B] = {Protected}
B[x_ /; IntegerQ[x]] := Block[{}, x]}
B[x_] := x
B[x_, y_] := Module[{}, x + y]

In event of a *x* object of the same name the function call **Def1[*x*]** returns the list of optimized definitions of the *x* object in string format without the attributes ascribed to it. If *x* defines an unique name, the call returns the optimized definition of the *x* object in the string format without the attributes ascribed to it. The name of a *x* object is given in string format; at that, on unacceptable values of *x* argument $*Failed* is returned.

An extension of the standard **Attributes** function is presented by the simple function whose call **Attributes1[*x*, *y*, *z*, *t*,...]** unlike standard function on objects *x*, *y*, *z*, *t*,..., that differ from admissible ones, returns the empty list, i.e. {}, without output of any erroneous messages what in a number of cases more preferably from standpoint of processing of the erroneous situations. While on admissible objects *x*, *y*, *z*, ... the call **Attributes1[*x*, *y*, *z*, ...]** returns the list of the attributes ascribed to objects *x*, *y*, *z*, ... The next fragment represents source code of the **Attributes1** function along with typical examples of its application.

In[2796]:= **Attributes1[x__] := ReduceLists[Map[Quiet[Check[Attributes[#], {}]] &, {x}]]**

In[2797]:= **L := {42, 49, 68, 27, 20}; SetAttributes[L, {Flat, Protected, Listable}]**

In[2798]:= **Attributes1[L[[5]], Sin, ProcQ]**

Out[2798]= {{}, {Listable, NumericFunction, Protected}, {}}

In[2799]:= **Attributes1[74, a + b, Attributes1, While, If]**

Out[2799]= {{}, {}, {}, {HoldAll, Protected}, {HoldRest, Protected}}

The **Attributes1** function is a rather useful means in a number of appendices. The means of processing of the attributes specifical to the procedures/functions in the form of procedures **AttributesH** and **DefAttributesH** are presented below.

As it was noted above, the strict differentiation of the blocks, functions and modules in the *Mathematica* is carried out not by means of their names as it is accepted in the majority of known programming languages and systems, but by means of their headings. For that in a number of cases of the advanced procedural programming, an important enough problem of the organization of mechanisms of the differentiated processing of these objects on the basis of their headings arises. A number of such means is represented in the present book, here we will determine two means ensuring work with attributes of objects on the basis of their headings. The following fragment represents source codes of 2 tools **DefAttributesH** and **AttributesH** along with typical examples of their applications.

The call **DefAttributesH**[*x, y, z, p, h, g, ...*] returns *Null*, i.e. nothing, assigning {*y* = *"Set"*} or deleting {*y* = *"Clear"*} the attributes determined by the arguments for an object with heading *x*. While in attempt of assigning or deleting of an attribute nonexistent in the current version of the system, the procedure call returns the list whose the first element is *$Failed*, whereas the second element – the list of the expressions different from the current attributes. At that, the call **AttributesH**[*x*] returns the list of attributes ascribed to an object with *x* heading. An useful function whose call **ClearAllAttributes**[*x, y, z, ...*] returns *Null*, i.e. nothing, canceling all attributes ascribed to the symbols *x, y, z, ...* completes the given fragment.

In[2880]:= **DefAttributesH**[x_ /; HeadingQ[x], y_ /; MemberQ[{"Set", "Clear"}, y], z___] :=
Module[{a}, If[AttributesQ[{z}, a = Unique[g]], ToExpression[y <> "Attributes[" <>
HeadName[x] <> ", " <> ToString[{z}] <> "]"], {$Failed, a}]]

In[2881]:= M[x__] := Module[{}, {x}]; M[x__, y_] := Module[{}, {x}]; M[x__, y_, z_] := x*y*z
In[2882]:= **DefAttributesH**["M[x___, y_, z_]", "Set", Flat, Protected, Listable]
In[2883]:= **Attributes[M]**
Out[2883]= {Flat, Listable, Protected}
In[2884]:= **DefAttributesH**["M[x___, y_, z_]", "Set", AvzAgn]
Out[2884]= {$Failed, {AvzAgn}}

In[2930]:=**AttributesH**[x_ /; HeadingQ[x]] := Attributes1[Symbol[HeadName[x]]]

In[2972]:= **AttributesH**["M[x___, y_, z_]"]
Out[2972]= {Flat, Listable, Protected}

In[2973]:= **ClearAllAttributes**[x__] :=
Map[Quiet[ClearAttributes[#, Attributes[#]];] &, {x}][[1]]

In[2974]:= SetAttributes[G, {Flat, Protected}]; SetAttributes[V, {Protected}]
In[2975]:= Map[Attributes, {G, V}]
Out[2975]= {{Flat, Protected}, {Protected}}
In[2976]:= **ClearAllAttributes**[G, V]; Attributes[G]
Out[2976]= {}

The represented means equally with **Attributes1** and **SetAttributes1** [33,48] of work with attributes which are most actual for objects of the type {*Function, Block, Module*}, in some cases are rather useful. At that, these means can be used quite effectively at programming and other means of different purpose, first of all, of tools of the system character.

The mechanism of the *Mathematica* attributes is quite effective means both for protection of objects against modifications, and for management of a mode of processing of arguments at calls of the blocks, functions or modules. By means of assignment to a procedure or function of the *Listable* attribute can be specified that procedure or function has to be automatically applied to all actual arguments as for the list elements. In the following fragment the simple procedure is represented, whose call **CallListable**[*x, y*] returns the list **Map**[*x*, **Flatten**[{*y*}]], where *x* – a block, function, module from one formal argument, and *y* – the list or sequence of the actual arguments which can be and empty. The fragment represents source code and the most typical examples of application of the **CallListable** procedure.

In[2977]:= **ToString[{a, b, c + d, 74, x*y, (m + n)*Sin[p − t]}]**
Out[2977]= "{a, b, c + d, 74, x*y, (m + n)*Sin[p − t]}"

In[2978]:= **CallListable[x_ /; SystemQ[x] || BlockFuncModQ[x], y___] :=**
Module[{a = Attributes[x]},
If[MemberQ[a, Listable], x[Flatten[{y}]], SetAttributes[x, Listable];
{x[Flatten[{y}]], ClearAttributes[x, Listable]}[[1]]]]

In[2979]:= **CallListable[ToString, {a, b, c + d, 90, x*y, (m + n)*Sin[p − t]}]**
Out[2979]= {"a", "b", "c + d", "90", "x*y", "(m + n)*Sin[p − t]"}
In[2980]:= **CallListable[ToString, a, b, c + d, 500, x*y, (m + n)*Sin[p − t]]**
Out[2980]= {"a", "b", "c + d", "500", "x*y", "(m + n)*Sin[p − t]"}
In[2981]:= **CallListable[ToString]**
Out[2981]= {}

The approach used by the **CallListable** procedure is an quite effective and can be used in a number of the appendices programmed in the *Mathematica* system.

In conclusion of this section some useful means for receiving the optimized definitions of procedures/functions are in addition represented. So, the call **DefFunc[x]** provides return of the optimized definition of a *x* object whose definition is located in the user package or *nb*-document and that has been loaded into the current session. At that, the *x* name should define an object without any attributes and options; otherwise a erroneous situation arises. The fragment below represents source code of the **DefFunc** procedure with examples of its application.

In[2461]:= **DefFunc[x_ /; SymbolQ[x] || StringQ[x]] :=**
Module[{a = GenRules[Map14[StringJoin, {"Global`", Context[x]}, ToString[x] <> "`"], ""],
b = StringSplit[ToString[InputForm[Definition[x]]], "\n \n"]},
ToExpression[Map[StringReplace[#, a] &, b]]; Definition[x]]

In[2462]:= **Definition[ListListQ]**
Out[2462]= ListListQ[AladjevProcedures`ListListQ`L_] := If[AladjevProcedures`ListListQ`L != {} && ListQ[AladjevProcedures`ListListQ`L] && Length[Select[AladjevProcedures`ListListQ`L, ListQ[#1] && Length[#1] == Length[AladjevProcedures`ListListQ`L[[1]]] &]] == Length[AladjevProcedures`ListListQ`L], True, False]

In[2463]:= **DefFunc[ListListQ]**
Out[2463]= ListListQ[L_] := If[L != {} && ListQ[L] && Length[Select[L, ListQ[#1] && Length[#1] == Length[L[[1]]] &]] == Length[L], True, False]

Naturally, the standard **Definition** function also is suitable for receiving of definition of an object activated in the current session, however in case of a *m*-file or a *nb*-document exists a rather essential distinction as is well illustrated by the return of definition of the **ListListQ** function from the *MathToolBox* package [48] by means of both the **Definition** function, and our **DefFunc** procedure. Thus, in the second case the obtained definition is essentially more readably, above all, for large source codes of procedures and functions. With the procedures

DefFunc1, DefFunc2 and **DefFunc3** which are quite useful versions of the above **DefFunc** procedure, the interested reader can familiarize oneself in [28-33]; the means are presented and in our package [48,50]. These means also are functionally adjoined by the **ToDefOptPF** procedure and the **OptRes** function [28,48,50]. Meanwhile, the **ToDefOptPF** procedure is inefficient for case when the user packages with identical contexts have been loaded into the current session. Note, we for the similar purposes widely use the above **Definition2** means.

Withal, having provided loading of the user package, for instance, *UserPackage* by the call **LoadMyPackage["... \\UserPackage.mx", Context]**, all definitions containing in it will be in the optimized format, i.e. they will not contain the context associated with the *UserPackage* package. At that, processing of tools of a package loaded thus will be significantly simpler. The **LoadMyPackage** procedure is considered in appropriate section. In the presented book below, the means of manipulation with the main components of the definitions of the user procedures and functions are considered.

6.2. Definition of the user functions and pure functions in software of the *Mathematica* system

First of all, we will notice that so-called *functional programming* isn't any discovery of the *Mathematica* system, and goes back to a number of software which appeared long before the above system. In this regard we quite pertinently have focused slightly more in details the attention on the concept of functional programming in the historical context [30-33,50]. While here we only will note certain moments characterizing specifics of the paradigm of functional programming. We will note only that the foundation of *functional* programming has been laid approximately at the same time, as *imperative* programming that is the most widespread now, i.e. in the *30th* years of the last century. *A. Church (USA)* – the author of λ-calculus and one of founders of the concept of *Homogeneous structures (Cellular Automata)* in connection with his works in the field of infinite abstract automata and mathematical logic along with *H. Curry (England)* and *M. Schönfinkel (Germany)* which have developed the mathematical theory of combinators, with good reason can be considered as the principal founders of mathematical foundation of functional programming. In additiom, functional programming languages, especially purely functional ones such as the *Hope* and *Rex*, have largely been used in academical circles rather than in commercial software development. Whereas prominent functional programming languages such as *Lisp* have been used in the industrial and commercial applications. Today, functional programming paradigm is also supported in some domain-specific programming languages for example by the *Mathem-*language of the *Mathematica* system. From rather large number of languages of functional programming it is possible to note the following languages that exerted a great influence on progress in this field, namely: *Lisp, Scheme, ISWIM,* family *ML, Miranda, Haskell,* etc. [33]. By and large, if the imperative languages are based on operations of assignment and cycle, the functional languages on recursions. The most important advantages of the functional languages are considered in our books in detail [50,71], namely:

– *programs on functional languagess as a rule are much shorter and simpler than their analogs on the imperative languages;*
– *almost all modern functional languages are strictly typified ensuring the safety of programs; at that the strict typification allows to generate more effective code;*

– *in a functional language the functions can be transferred as an argument to other functions or are returned as result of their call;*
– *in the pure functional languages (which aren't allowing by–effects for the functions) there is no an operator of assigning, the objects of such language can't be modified and deleted, it is only possible to create new objects by decomposition and synthesis of the existing. In the pure functional languages all functions are free from by–effects.*

Meanwhile, functional languages can imitate the certain useful imperative properties. Not all functional languages are pure forasmuch in a lot of cases the admissibility of by–effects allows to essentially simplify programming. However today the most developed functional languages are as a rule pure. With many interesting enough questions concerning a subject of functional programming, the reader can familiarize oneself, for example, in [51]. Whereas with an quite interesting critical remarks on functional languages and possible ways of their elimination it is possible to familiarize oneself in [28-33,50,71].

A series of concepts and paradigms are specific for *functional* programming and are absent in *imperative* programming. Meanwhile, many programming languages, as a rule, are based on several paradigms of programming, thus imperative programming languages can quite use and concepts of functional programming. In particular, as an important enough concept are so–called the ***pure functions***, whose results of performance depends only on their actual arguments. Such functions possess certain useful properties a part of which it is possible to use for optimization of a program code and parallelization of calculations. The questions of realization of certain properties of pure functions in the imperative *Maple*-language have been considered in [28-33]. In principle, there are no special difficulties for programming in the functional style in languages that aren't the functional. The *Math*-language professing the mixed paradigm of functional and procedural programming supports also the *functional* programming, whereas the *Maple*-language professing the concept of especially procedural programming at the same time allows the certain elements of the functional programming.

Meanwhile, first of all, the few words about the system functions, i.e. the functions *belonging* properly to the *Mathematica* language and its software. Generally speaking, to call these system means by functions is not entirely correct since realization of many of them is based on the procedural organization, however we stopped on such terminology inherent actually to the system.

So, the *Mathematica* system has a very large number of the built–in functions, at the same time it provides rather simple enough mechanisms for the user functions definition. In the simplest case a certain *F* function with several formal arguments *x, y, z, ...* has the following very simple format, namely:

F[*x_, y_, z_,...*] {:= | =} *an expression dependent on variables x, y, z,... as a rule*

So, $F[x\_] := x^3 + 90$ defines the function $F(x) = x^3 + 90$ in standard mathematical notation; the call of such function on a concrete factual argument is defined as *F[x]*, in particular:

In[2442]:= F[x_] := x^3 + 90; F[590]
Out[2442]= 205379090

For receiving of definition of an arbitrary function *(and not only functions, but also an arbitrary definition on the basis of operator of postponed ":=" or immediate "=" assignments)*, excepting the built–in functions, serve the built–in **Definition** function along with our tools considered in the previous section, allowing to receive the optimized definitions in the above sense of as procedures and functions. We will consider briefly elements of functional programming in the *Mathematica* system in whose basis the concept of the *pure function* lays. Thus, the *pure functions* – one of the basic concepts of functional programming which is a component of all programming system in the *Mathematica* in general. Further, the questions relating to this component will be considered in more detail, here we will define only basic concepts. In the *Mathematica* the pure functions are defined as follows. A pure function in the environment of the *Mathematica* has the following three formats of encoding, namely:

Function[x, Function body] – *a pure function with one formal argument x;*
Function[{x1, x2, ..., xp}, Function body] – *a pure function with formal arguments x1, x2, ..., xp;*
(Function body) & – *a pure function with formal arguments #, #1, #2, ..., #n.*

At that, at using of the third format that is often called as short form of pure function for its identification the *ampersand (&)* serves whose absence causes either erroneous situations or incorrect results at impossibility to identify the demanded pure function. Note, the reader familiar with the formal logic or the *Lisp* programming language can simply identify pure functions with *unnamed* functions or λ–expressions. Moreover, the pure functions are rather close to mathematical concept of the operators. In addition, in defition of the *pure* function so–called substitutes (#) of variables are used, namely:

– *the first variable of a pure function;*
#n – *n–th variable of a pure function;*
– *sequence of all variables of a pure function;*
##n – *sequence of variables of a pure function starting with n–th variable.*

At application of the *pure* functions, unlike traditional functions and procedures, there is no need to designate their names, allowing to code their definitions directly in points of their call that is caused by that the results of the calls of pure functions depend only on values of the actual arguments received by them. Selection from a *x* list of elements meeting certain conditions and elementwise application of a function to elements of a *x* list can be carried out by constructions of the format **Select[x, Test[#] &]** and **Map[F[#] &, x]** respectively as illustrate the following simple examples, namely:

In[2341]:= **Select[{a, 72, 75, 42, g, 67, Art, Kr, 2016, s, 47, 500}, IntegerQ[#] &]**
Out[2341]= {72, 75, 42, 67, 2016, 47, 500}
In[2342]:= **Map[(#^2 + #) &, {1, 2, 3, 4, 5, 6, 7, 8, 9, 10, 11, 12}]**
Out[2342]= {2, 6, 12, 20, 30, 42, 56, 72, 90, 110, 132, 156}

At use of the *short* form of a pure function it is necessary to be careful at its coding because the ampersand has quite low priority. For example, the expression *#1 + #2 – #3 + #2*#4 &* without parentheses is correct while, generally speaking, they are obligatory, in particular, at use of a pure function as the right part of a transformation rule as illustrate very simple examples:

In[2392]:= {a /. a –> #1 + #2 + #3 &, a /. a –> (#1 + #2 + #3 &)}
Out[2392]= {a /. a –> #1 + #2 + #3 &, #1 + #2 + #3 &}
In[2393]:= {Replace[a, a –> #1*#2*#3 &], a /. a –> (#1*#2*#3 &)}

Replace::reps: {a -> #1*#2*#3&} is neither a list of replacement rules nor a valid dispatch table, and so cannot be used for replacing.>>
Out[2393]= {Replace[a, a -> #1*#2*#3 &], #1*#2*#3 &}

The universal format of the call of a pure *y* function is defined as *y* @@ {*args*}, for example,

In[4202]:= **OddQ[#] || PrimeQ[#] & @@ {75}**
Out[4202]= True
In[4203]:= **Select[{5, 7, 11, 3, 9, 6, 2, 4, 9}, OddQ[#1] & || PrimeQ[#1] &]**
Out[4203]= {5, 7, 11, 3, 2}

In combination with a number of functions, in particular, **Map, Select** and some others the using of pure functions is rather convenient, therefore the question of converting from the traditional functions into the pure functions seems an quite topical; for its decision various approaches, including creation of the program converters can be used. Thus, we used pure functions a rather widely at programming of a number of problems of various types of the applied, and the system character [28-33,48,50].

The next procedure provides converting of a function defined by the format g[*x*_, *y*_, ...] := W(*x, y, z, ...*) into a pure function of any admissible format, namely: the call **FuncToPure[*x*]** returns the pure function that is an analog of a *x* function of the third format, while the call **FuncToPure[*x, p*]** where *p* – an arbitrary expression, returns a pure function of the two first formats. The following fragment represents source code of the **FuncToPure** procedure with typical examples of its application.

In[2822]:= **FuncToPure[x_ /; QFunction[ToString[x]], y___] :=**
Module[{d, t, a = HeadPF[x], b = Map[ToString, Args[x]],
c = Definition2[x][[1]], k = 1, h, g = {}, p},
d = Map[First, Mapp[StringSplit, b, "_"]]; p = StringTrim[c, a <> " := "];
h = "Hold[" <> p <> "]"; {t, h} = {Length[b], ToExpression[h]};
While[k <= t, AppendTo[g, d[[k]] <> " -> #" <> ToString[k]]; k++];
h = ToString1[ReplaceAll[h, ToExpression[g]]]; g = StringTake[h, {6, -2}];
ToExpression[If[{y} != {}, "Function[" <> If[Length[b] == 1,
StringTake[ToString[d], {2, -2}], ToString[d]] <> ", " <> p <> "]", g <> " &"]]]

In[2823]:= **G[x_Integer, y_Integer, z_Real] := z*(x + y) + Sin[x*y*z]; FuncToPure[G]**
Out[2823]= #3*(#1 + #2) + Sin[#1*#2*#3] &
In[2824]:= **G[x_Integer, y_Integer, z_Real] := z*(x + y) + Sin[x*y*z]; FuncToPure[G, 90]**
Out[2824]= Function[{x, y, z}, z*(x + y) + Sin[x*y*z]]
In[2825]:= **V[x_ /; IntegerQ[x]] := If[PrimeQ[x], True, False]; Select[{47, 74, 27, 20, 500, 13, 7, 41, 561, 2, 123, 322, 27, 20}, FuncToPure[V]]**
Out[2825]= {47, 13, 7, 41, 2}
In[2826]:= **{S[x_] := x^2 + 27*x + 20; FuncToPure[S, 47], FuncToPure[S][90]}**
Out[2826]= {Function[x, x^2 + 27*x + 20], 10550}

However, at use of the **FuncToPure** procedure for converting of some traditional function into the pure function it must be kept in mind a number of the essential enough moments. First of all, the resultant pure function won't have attributes, options and initial values of arguments along with logic tests for admissibility of the factual arguments. Secondly, any converting automatically doesn't do the resultant function as a pure function if an original traditional function such wasn't, i.e. result of the procedure call should depend only on the obtained actual arguments. A number of useful tools of operating with pure functions will be considered in the present book slightly below.

Unlike the previous **FuncToPure** procedure, the procedure below allows to keep the main testing conditions for arguments of the converted functions of the general kind

$$F[x\_/; Test[x], y\_H, z\_, h\_\_H1, t\_\_, ...] := \Re[x, y, z, h, t, ...]$$

by converting an initial F function in a pure function of short format, i.e. the procedure call **FuncToPureFunction[F]** returns the pure function in the kind

If[*Test*[#1] && HQ[#2] && True && H1Q[#4] && True && ..., $\Re$[#1, #2, #3, #4, #5, ...],
*IncorrectArgs[Sequential numbers of incorrect factual arguments]***] &**

where {*heads H and H1*} can absent. Moreover, for formal arguments of type {*h__H1, t__*} the resultant pure function considers only their first factual value.

At the same time, only one of the {*Complex, Integer, List, Rational, Real, String, Symbol*} list is allowed as the head H for an y expression. In case of inadmissibility of at least one factual argument and/or its testing *(for example, incorrect head H or H1)* the call of the pure function returns the formal call of the kind **IncorrectArgs**[*n1, n2, ..., np*] where {*n1, n2, ..., np*} determine sequential numbers of incorrect factual arguments. The following fragment represents source code of the procedure with typical examples of its application that quite clearly illustrate the results returned by the **FuncToPureFunction** procedure.

In[3988]:= **FuncToPureFunction[x_ /; FunctionQ[x]] :=**
Module[{a, b = ProcBody[x], c = 1, d, g, h, p, s = Map[ToString, {Complex, Integer, List, Rational, Real, String, Symbol}]}, a = ArgsBFM1[x];
g = Map[{Set[d, "#" <> ToString[c++]]; d, StringReplaceVars[#[[2]], #[[1]] -> d]} &, a];
h = Map[If[! StringFreeQ[#[[2]], #[[1]]], #[[2]], If[#[[2]] == "Arbitrary", "True",
If[MemberQ[s, #[[2]]], #[[2]] <> "Q[" <> #[[1]] <> "]", "False"]]] &, g];
p = Map["(" <> # <> ")" &, h]; p = Riffle[p, "&&"];
a = Map[#[[1]] &, a]; c = Map[#[[1]] &, g]; a = StringReplaceVars[b, GenRules[a, c]];
ToExpression["If[" <> p <> "," <> a <> "," <> "IncorrectArgs@@Flatten[Position[" <>
ToString[h] <> ", False]]" <> "]&"]]

In[3989]:= f[x_ /; IntegerQ[x], y_ /; y == 69, z_List, t_, p__, h___] := x*y*h + Length[z]*t
In[3990]:= **FuncToPureFunction[f]**
Out[3990]= If[IntegerQ[#1] && #2 == 69 && ListQ[#3] && True && True && True,
#1*#2*#6 + Length[#3]*#4, IncorrectArgs @@ Flatten[Position[{IntegerQ[#1], #2 == 69, ListQ[#3], True, True, True}, False]]] &
In[3991]:= %[74, 69, {a, b, c}, 22, 27, 50, 6]
Out[3991]= 255366
In[3992]:= %%[74.5, 69, {a, b, c}, 22, 27, 50, 6]
Out[3992]= IncorrectArgs[1]
In[3993]:= G[x_, y_ /; IntegerQ[y], z_ /; z == 74, t__Real, h___Rational] :=
(x^2 + y^2)/ (z^2*t^2 + h)
In[3994]:= **FuncToPureFunction[G]**

Out[3994]= If[True && IntegerQ[#2] && #3 == 74 && RealQ[#4] && RationalQ[#5], (#1^2 + #2^2)/(#3^2*#4^2 + #5), IncorrectArgs @@ Flatten[Position[{True, IntegerQ[#2], #3 == 74, RealQ[#4], RationalQ[#5]}, False]]] &

In[3995]:= %[69, 50, 74, 90.500, 7/6]
Out[3995]= 0.000161896
In[3996]:= %%[69, 50, 74, 590, 7/6]
Out[3996]= IncorrectArgs[4]
In[3997]:= G1[x_, y_ /; IntegerQ[y], z_ /; z == {75, 70, 50, 28, 21} || ListListQ[z], t__Real, h___Rational] := (x^2 + Length[z]^2)/(y^2*t^2 + h)
In[3998]:= H = FuncToPureFunction[G1]
Out[3998]= If[True && IntegerQ[#2] && (#3 == {75, 70, 50, 28, 21} || ListListQ[#3]) && RealQ[#4] && RationalQ[#5], (#1^2 + Length[#3]^2)/(#2^2*#4^2 + #5), IncorrectArgs @@ Flatten[Position[{True, IntegerQ[#2], #3 == {75, 70, 50, 28, 21} || ListListQ[#3], RealQ[#4], RationalQ[#5]}, False]]] &
In[3999]:= H[500, 90, {{500, 90}, {42, 47}}, 70.75, 8/3]
Out[3999]= 0.00616608
In[4000]:= H[500, 500.90, {{500, 90}, {42, 47}}, 69, 75]
Out[4000]= IncorrectArgs[2, 4, 5]

Using the approach applied when programming the **FuncToPureFunction** procedure to the reader it is recommended to extend area of applicability of the procedure to functions with other types of the testing conditions ascribed to arguments of the convertible functions as an useful enough exercise. So, the approach used above allows simply to convert the algebraic expressions in pure functions of the short format. The call **AlgToPureFunction[x, y]** returns the result of converting of an algebraical x expression in the pure function of short format. Whereas the procedure call with the second optional y argument – an indefinite symbol – through it returns generally speaking the *ListList* list whose 2-elements establish one-to-one correspondence between indefinite symbols included in the x expression and the slots that correspond to them. The next fragment represent source code of the procedure with typical examples of its application.

In[4026]:= **AlgToPureFunction[x_, y___]** :=
Module[{a = "(" <> ToString1[x] <> ")&", b, c = {}, n = 1},
b = ExtrVarsOfStr[a, 2]; b = Select[b, ! SystemQ[#] && PureDefinition[#] === $Failed &];
Do[AppendTo[c, b[[j]] -> "#" <> ToString[n++]], {j, 1, Length[b]}];
If[{y} != {} && NullQ[y], y = ReduceLevelsList[ToExpression[Map[{#[[1]], #[[2]]} &, c]], 75], 70]; ToExpression[StringReplaceVars[a, c]]]

In[4027]:= **AlgToPureFunction[(a*x + 5*y^2)/(m*c - n*Sin[d]) - x*Sqrt[y]]**
Out[4027]= -(#6*Sqrt[#7]) + (#1*#6 + 5*#7^2)/(#2*#4 - #5*Sin[#3]) &
In[4028]:= **AlgToPureFunction[(a*x + 5*y^2)/(m*c - n*Sin[d]) - x*Sqrt[y], gsv]**
Out[4028]= -(#6*Sqrt[#7]) + (#1*#6 + 5*#7^2)/(#2*#4 - #5*Sin[#3]) &
In[4029]:= **gsv**
Out[4029]= {{a, #1}, {c, #2}, {d, #3}, {m, #4}, {n, #5}, {x, #6}, {y, #7}}
In[4030]:= **{AlgToPureFunction[x^3 + 75*x^2 + 70*x + 50, gs], gs}**
Out[4030]= {50 + 70*#1 + 75*#1^2 + #1^3 &, {x, #1}}

On the other hand, the procedure call **PureFuncToShort**[*x*] returns the result of converting of a pure function *x* to its short format.

In[4110]:= **PureFuncToShort**[x_ /; PureFuncQ[x]] := Module[{a, b, c, d},
If[ShortPureFuncQ[x], x, a = ArgsPureFunc[x]; d = a; b = Map[ToExpression, a];
Map[ClearAll, a]; a = Map[ToExpression, a]; c = Quiet[GenRules[a, Range2[#, Length[a]]]];
{ToExpression[ToString1[ReplaceAll[x[[2]], c]] <> "&"],
ToExpression[ToString[d] <> "=" <> ToString1[b]]}[[1]]]]

In[4111]:= **PureFuncToShort**[Function[{x, y, z, h}, (x + y)*z^h]]
Out[4111]= (#1 + #2)*#3^#4 &

In[4112]:= **PureFuncToShort**[(#1 + #2)*#3^#4 &]
Out[4112]= (#1 + #2)*#3^#4 &

On the other hand, the following procedure in a certain measure is inverse to the previous procedure, its call **PureToFunc**[*x*, *y*], where *x* – the definition of a pure function, and *y* – an unevaluated symbol – returns *Null*, i.e. nothing, providing converting of the definition of a pure *x* function into the evaluated definition of equivalent function with a *y* name. At that, on inadmissible actual arguments the procedure call is returned unevaluated. The fragment below represents source code of the procedure with an example of its application.

In[2525]:= **PureToFunc**[x_ /; PureFuncQ[x], y_ /; ! HowAct[y]] :=
Module[{a = Sort[Select[ExprComp[x], Head[#] === Slot &]], b = {}, c = {}, k},
Do[AppendTo[c, Unique["x"]], {k, 1, Length[a]}];
Do[AppendTo[b, a[[k]] –> c[[k]]], {k, 1, Length[a]}];
ToExpression[StringTake[ToString[y @@ Map[ToExpression, Map[# <> "_" &,
Map[ToString, c]]]] <> ":=" <> ToString1[ReplaceAll[x, b]], {1, -2}]]]

In[2526]:= **PureToFunc**[#4*(#1 + #2)/(#3 – #4) + #1*#4 &, Gs]
In[2527]:= **Definition**[Gs]
Out[2527]= Gs[x6_, x7_, x8_, x9_] := (x9*(x6 + x7))/(x8 – x9) + x6*x9

For converting of a clean function of the short format the following function can be useful, whose call **ShortPureToFunc**[*x*, *g*, *y*] returns nothing, converting a pure function *x* into the classical function *g* with arguments whose names begin with *y*. The next fragment presents source code of the **ShortPureToFunc** procedure with examples of its application.

In[2536]:= **ShortPureToFunc**[x_ /; ShortPureFuncQ[x], g_ /; SymbolQ[g],
y_ /; SymbolQ[y]] := Module[{a = ArgsPureFunc[x], b}, b = Range3[y, Length[a]];
ToExpression[ToString[g[Sequences[b]]] <> ":=" <> StringReplace[ToString1[x],
{"#" –> ToString[y], "&" –> ""}]]]

In[2537]:= **ShortPureToFunc**[(#1^2 + #2^3)*#5^4/(#3 – #4) &, g, x]
In[2538]:= **Definition**[g]
Out[2538]= g[x1_, x2_, x3_, x4_, x5_] := ((x1^2 + x2^3)*x5^4)/(x3 – x4)

The following procedure has the generalizing character whose call **PureFuncToFunction**[*x*, *y*] returns nothing, providing the converting of a pure function *x* or a pure function *x* of the short format in a classical *y* function. The following fragment represents source code of the **PureFuncToFunction** procedure with examples of its application.

In[4536]:= **PureFuncToFunction[x_ /; PureFuncQ[x], y_ /; ! HowAct[y]] :=**
Module[{a = ArgsPureFunc[x], b, c},
If[ShortPureFuncQ[x], b = Map[StringReplace[#, "#" -> "x"] &, a];
c = StringReplace[ToString1[x], GenRules[a, b]];
b = Map[ToExpression, Sort[Map[# <> "_" &, b]]];
ToExpression[ToString1[y[Sequences[b]]] <> ":=" <> StringTake[c, {1, -3}]],
a = Map[# <> "_" &, a]; ToExpression[ToString1[y[Sequences[Map[ToExpression, a]]]] <> ":=" <> ToString1[x[[2]]]]]]

In[4537]:= **PureFuncToFunction[Function[{x, y, z, h}, (x + y)*z^h], gs1]**
In[4538]:= **Definition[gs1]**
Out[4538]= gs1[x_, y_, z_, h_] := (x + y)*z^h
In[4539]:= **PureFuncToFunction[(#1 + #2)*#3^#4 &, gs2]**
In[4540]:= **Definition[gs2]**
Out[4540]= gs2[x1_, x2_, x3_, x4_] := (x1 + x2)*x3^x4

Unlike **FuncToPure**, the call **ModToPureFunc[x]** provides the converting of a module or a block x into pure function under following conditions: *(1)* the module or block x can't have local variables or all local variables should have initial values; *(2)* a module or block x can't have active *global* variables, i.e. variables for which in an arbitrary x object assignments are done; *(3)* formal arguments of the returned function don't save tests for their admissibility; *(4)* the returned function inherits attributes and options of the x object. The fragment below represents source code of the procedure with examples of its application.

In[2428]:= **ModToPureFunc[x_ /; QBlockMod[x]] :=**
Module[{a, c, d, p, j, t, Atr = Attributes[x], O = Options[x], n = "$$$" <> ToString[x], b = Flatten[{PureDefinition[x]}][[1]], k = 1, q = {}},
ToExpression["$$$" <> b]; c = LocalsGlobals1[Symbol[n]]; a = Args[Symbol[n], 90];
d = StringReplace[PureDefinition[n], HeadPF[n] <> " := " -> "", 1];
ToExpression["ClearAll[" <> n <> "]"]; If[c[[3]] != {}, Return[{$Failed, "Globals", c[[3]]}]];
c = Map[{#, ToString[Unique[#]]} &, Join[a, c[[1]]]];
While[k <= Length[c], p = c[[k]]; d = StringReplaceS[d, p[[1]], p[[2]]]; k++];
d = ToString[ToExpression[d]]; t = Map[ToString, UnDefVars[ToExpression[d]]];
t = Map[StringTake[#, {1, If[StringFreeQ[#, "$"], -1,
Flatten[StringPosition[#, "$"]][[1]] - 1]}] &, t]; k = 1;
While[k <= Length[t], j = 1; While[j <= Length[c], If[t[[k]] == c[[j]][[2]],
AppendTo[q, c[[j]][[1]]]]; j++]; k++]; k = 1;
While[k <= Length[c], p = c[[k]]; d = StringReplaceS[d, p[[2]], p[[1]]]; k++];
If[p = MinusList[q, a]; p != {}, {$Failed, "Locals", p}, ToExpression["ClearAll[" <> n <> "]"];
n = "$$$" <> ToString[x];
ToExpression[n <> " := Function[" <> ToString[a] <> ", " <> d <> "]"];
If[Atr != {}, ToExpression["SetAttributes[" <> n <> "," <> ToString[Atr] <> "]"]];
If[O != {}, ToExpression["SetOptions[" <> n <> "," <> ToString[O] <> "]"]]; n]]

In[2429]:= **B[x_, y_] := Block[{a, b = 90, c, d}, (a + b + c)*(x + y + d)];**

B1[x_, y_] := Block[{a = 500, b = 90, c = 74}, (a + b + c)*(x + y)];
SetAttributes[B1, {Protected, Listable}];
B2[x_, y_] := Block[{a = 500, b = 90}, h = (a + b)*(x + y); t = 42];
B3[x_, y_] := Block[{a = 500, b, c}, h = (a + b + c)*(x + y); g = 69];
B4[x_, y_] := Block[{a = 500, b = 90}, h = (a + b)*(x + y); t = z];
B5[x_, y_] := Module[{a = 500, b, c, d = 90}, (a + b)*(c + d)]
In[2430]:= **ModToPureFunc[B]**
Out[2430]= {$Failed, "Locals", {"a", "c", "d"}}
In[2431]:= **ModToPureFunc[B1]**
Out[2431]= "$$$B1"
In[2432]:= **Definition["$$$B1"]**
Out[2432]= Attributes[$$$B1] = {Listable, Protected}
$$$B1 := Function[{x, y}, 664*(x + y)]
In[2433]:= **ModToPureFunc[B2]**
Out[2433]= {$Failed, "Globals", {"h", "t"}}
In[2434]:= **ModToPureFunc[B3]**
Out[2434]= {$Failed, "Globals", {"h", "g"}}
In[2435]:= **ModToPureFunc[B4]**
Out[2435]= {$Failed, "Globals", {"h", "t"}}
In[2436]:= **ModToPureFunc[B5]**
Out[2436]= {$Failed, "Locals", {"b", "c"}}
In[2437]:= A[m_, n_, p_ /; IntegerQ[p], h_ /; PrimeQ[h]] := Module[{a=42.74}, h*(m+n+p)/a]
In[2438]:= **ModToPureFunc[A]**
Out[2438]= "$$$A"
In[2439]:= **Definition["$$$A"]**
Out[2439]= $$$A := Function[{m, n, p, h}, 0.0233973*h*(m + n + p)]
In[2440]:= M[x_, y_ /; StringQ[y]] := Module[{a, b = 90, c = 6, d}, a*x/b*y + d]
In[2441]:= **SetAttributes[M, Protected]; ModToPureFunc[M]**
Out[2441]= {$Failed, "Locals", {"a", "d"}}
In[2442]:= **G[x_] := Module[{a = 90, b = 500}, a + b]; ModToPureFunc[G]; Definition[$$$G]**
Out[2442]= $$$G := Function[{x}, 590]

A successful call **ModToPureFunc[*x*]** returns the name of the resultant pure function in the form **ToString[Unique[*x*]]**, otherwise the procedure call returns the nested list of the format {*$Failed*, {"*Locals*" | "*Globals*"}, {*list of variables in string format*}} whose the first element *$Failed* determines inadmissibility of converting, 2nd element – the type of the variables that were as a reason of it whereas the third element – a list of variables of this type in the string format. At that, the name of a block or a module should be as the factual *x* argument, otherwise the procedure call is returned unevaluated. Along with standard means the procedure in very essential degree uses our procedures **HeadPF, Args, LocalsGlobals1, ClearAllMinusList, PureDefinition, StringReplaceS, QBlockMod** and **UnDefVars** which are considered in the present book and in [28-33,50], that allowed to considerably simplify programming of this procedure. These means and at programming some other appendices are useful enough, it must be kept in mind that the mechanism of the *pure* functions composes a certain kind of core of the paradigm of functional programming in the *Mathematica* system.

6.3. Tools for testing of procedures and functions in the *Mathematica*

Having defined procedures of two types *(Module and Block)* and functions, including *pure* functions, at the same time we have no standard means for identification of objects of the given types. In this regard we created a series of means that allow to identify objects of the specified types. In the present section non-standard means for testing of procedural and functional objects are considered. In addition, it should be noted that the *Mathematica* – a rather closed system in contradistinction, for example, to its main competitor – the *Maple* system in which perusal of source codes of its software which are located both in the main and in the auxiliary libraries is admissible. Whereas the *Mathematica* system has no similar opportunity. In this connection the software represented below concerns only to the user functions and procedures uploaded into the current session from a package *(m– or mx–file)*, or a document *(nb–file; also may contain a package)* and activated in it.

It is known that for providing of the modularity of the software the procedures are rather widely used that in the conditions of the *Mathematica* system by the modular and block constructions is provided. Both a module *(Module)*, and a block *(Block)* provide the closed domain of variables that is supported via the mechanism of local variables. The procedures on the basis of both modular, and block structure provide, in general, a rather satisfactory mechanism of the modularity. Above we attributed the modular and block objects to the procedure type, but here not everything so unambiguously and this is why. In procedural programming a procedure represents some kind of so–called *"black box"* whose contents is hidden from the external software with which it interacts only through arguments and the global variables *(if they are used by the procedure body)*. While domain of definition of the local variables is limited by the procedure body only, without crossing with variables of the same name outside of the procedure. Meanwhile, between procedures of the modular and block types exists a rather essential distinction which is based on mechanism of *local* variables that are used by both types of procedures. In brief the essence of such distinction consists in the following.

Traditional programming languages at work with variables use mechanism *"lexical scope"*, that is similar to the modular mechanism in *Mathematica*, while the modular mechanism is similar to *"dynamic scope"* that is used, for example, in the symbolic languages like *Lisp*. So, if *lexical scope* considers the *local* variables connected with module, dynamic scope considers the *local* variables connected only with a concrete segment of history of a block execution. In books [28-33] the question of preference of procedures on the basis of the *modular* structure, than on the basis of block structure is considered in details. Meanwhile, the *block* procedures are often convenient in a case of organization of different interactive calculations. Generally, supposing existence of procedures of the above two types *(module and block)* in the system *Mathematica*, for ensuring *reliability* it is recommended to use the procedures of the *Module* type. Distinctions of procedures on both basics can be illustrated with the following typical examples, namely:

In[2254]:= B[x_] := Block[{a, b, c, d}, x*(a + b + c + d)]
In[2255]:= {a, b, c, d} = {42, 47, 67, 6}
Out[2255]= {42, 47, 67, 6}
In[2256]:= {B[100], a, b, c, d}
Out[2256]= {16200, 42, 47, 67, 6}

In[2257]:= B[x_] := Block[{a = 90, b = 500, c, d}, x*(a + b + c + d)]
In[2258]:= {B[100], a, b, c, d}
Out[2258]= {66300, 42, 47, 67, 6}
In[2259]:= M[x_] := Module[{a = 90, b = 500, c, d}, x*(a + b + c + d)]
In[2260]:= {M[100], a, b, c, d}
Out[2260]= {100*(590 + c$502 + d$502), a, b, c, d}
In[2261]:= {a, b, c, d} = {42, 47, 20, 27};
In[2262]:= B2[x_] := Block[{a, b, c, d}, {a, b, c, d} = {74, 68, 90, 500}; Plus[a, b, c, d]]
In[2263]:= {B2[100], {a, b, c, d}}
Out[2263]= {732, {42, 47, 20, 27}}

From the represented fragment follows, if local variables of a modular object aren't crossed with domain of values of the variables of the same name which are external in relation to it, the absolutely other picture takes place in a case with the local variables of a block object, namely: if initial values or values are ascribed to all local variables of such object in its body, they save effect in the object body; those variables of an object to which such values weren't ascribed accept values of the variables of the same name which are the external in relation to the block object. So, at fulfillment of the listed conditions the modular and block objects relative to the local variables *(and in general as procedural objects)* can quite be considered as equivalent. Naturally, the told remains in force also for block objects with empty lists of the local variables. The specified reasons were used as a basis of the algorithm programmed by the **RealProcQ** procedure represented by the following fragment.

In[2347]:= RealProcQ[x_] := Module[{a, b = " = ", c, d, k = 1, p},
If[! ProcQ[x], False, If[Set[a, Locals1[x]] == {} || ModuleQ[x], True, c = PureDefinition[x];
d = Map[#[[1]] - 1 &, StringPosition[c, b]]; p = Map[ExprOfStr[c, #, -1, {" ", "{", "["}] &, d];
p = DeleteDuplicates[Flatten[Map[StrToList, p]]]; If[p == a, True, False]]]]

In[2348]:= B1[x_] := Block[{a = 90, b = 50, c = 75, d = 42}, x*(a + b + c + d)]; RealProcQ[B1]
Out[2348]= True
In[2349]:= M2[x_] := Block[{a = 90, b = 50, c, d}, {c, d} = {42, 47}; x*a*b*c*d]; RealProcQ[M2]
Out[2349]= True
In[2350]:= M3[x_] := Block[{a = 90, b = 49, c, h}, h = 75; x*h]; RealProcQ[M3]
Out[2350]= False

Experience of use of the **RealProcQ** procedure confirmed its efficiency at testing objects of the type *"Block"* which are considered as real procedures. At that, we will understand an object of the type {*Module, Block*} as a *real* procedure which in the *Mathematica* software is functionally equivalent to a *Module*, i.e. is certain procedure in its classical understanding. The procedure call **RealProcQ**[*x*] returns *True* if the *x* symbol defines a *Module* or a *Block* which is equivalent to a *Module*, and *False* otherwise. At that, it is supposed that a certain block is equivalent to the module if it has no the local variables or all its local variables have initial values or some local variables have initial values, whereas others obtain values by by means of the operator "=" in the block body. The procedure along with the standard means uses as well procedures **ExprOfStr, ProcQ, Locals1, ModuleQ, PureDefinition, StrToList** which are considered in the present book and in [33]. Note, from all our means solving the testing problem of arbitrary procedural objects, the **RealProcQ** procedure with the greatest possible reliability identifies the given procedure in its classical understanding; so, the real procedure can be of the type {*Module, Block*}.

In the context of providing of an object of the type {*Module, Block*} to be the real procedure recognized by the testing **RealProcQ** procedure, the **ToRealProc** procedure is of a certain interest, whose call **ToRealProc[*x*, *y*]** returns nothing, converting a module or a block *x* into the object of the same type and of the same name with the *empty* list of local variables which are placed in the object body at once behind the *empty* list of the local variables. At the same time, all local variables of the *x* object are replaced with the symbols, unique in the current session, which are generated by means of the **Unique** function. The procedure call with the second optional *y* argument – *an undefinite symbol* – additionally through it returns the list of the format {{"*loc1*", "*$n1*"}, ..., {"*locp*", "*$np*"}} where *locj* and *$nj* are a local variable of the initial *x* object and a variable replacing it accordingly *(j = 1..p)*. In addition, along with some specified purpose, the returned procedure provides a possibility of more effective *debugging* in the *interactive* mode of the procedure, allowing to do dynamic control of change of values of its local variables in the procedure run on concrete factual arguments. The next fragment represents source code of the **ToRealProc** procedure with examples of its application.

In[4011]:= **ToRealProc[x_, y___] := Module[{a, b, c, d, h},**
If[! BlockModQ[x], $Failed, a = HeadPFU[x]; b = ToString[Locals[x]]; c = Locals1[x];
d = Unprotect[x]; c = Map[{#, ToString[Unique["$"]]} &, c];
h = "{}, " <> StringReplaceVars1[b, "{ 1234567890", " }", Map[Rule @@ # &, c]] <> ";";
d = StringReplace[PureDefinition[x], a -> "", 1]; d = StringReplace[d, b -> "7570", 1];
d = StringReplaceVars[d, Map[Rule @@ # &, c]]; d = StringReplace[d, "7570," -> h];
If[{y} != {} && NullQ[y], y = ReduceLevelsList[c, 6], 50]; ToExpression[a <> d]]]

In[4012]:= **H[x_] := Module[{a = "xyz", b = Sin[x], c = {70, 50}, d = {"a", "b"}},**
x*Length[d]*c + StringLength[a <> "abcdefghptrkwqxyz"] - b*Length[d]]

In[4013]:= **ToRealProc[H, g70]**

In[4014]:= **g70**
Out[4014]= {{"a", "$19"}, {"b", "$20"}, {"c", "$21"}, {"d", "$22"}}

In[4015]:= {H[70.75], $22}
Out[4015]= {{9923., 7093.}, {"a", "b"}}

In[4016]:= **Definition[H]**
Out[4016]= H[x_] := Module[{}, {$19 = "xyz", $20 = Sin[x], $21 = {70, 50}, $22 = {"a", "b"}};
x*Length[$22]*$21 + StringLength[$19 <> "abcdefghptrkwqxyz"] - $20*Length[$22]]

In some cases in addition to the above means of testing of the *Math*–objects a rather useful and quite simple procedure can be used whose call **BlockQ[*x*]** returns *True* if the *x* symbol defines a block object, and *False* otherwise. The following fragment represents source code of the **BlockQ** procedure along with the most typical examples of its application.

In[2377]:= **BlockQ[x_] :=**
Module[{b, a = If[SymbolQ[x], Flatten[{PureDefinition[x]}][[1]], $Failed]},
If[MemberQ[{$Failed, "System"}, a], False, b = Mapp[StringJoin, {" := ", " = "}, "Block[{"];
If[SuffPref[a, Map3[StringJoin, HeadPF[x], b], 1], True, False]]]

In[2378]:= Sv[x_] := Module[{}, y := 74; z:=69; {y, z}]; Agn[x_] := Block[{a=90}, a*x];
Kr[x_] := Block[{y = a, h = b}, (y^2 + h^2)*x]; Art[x_] := Module[{a = 74}, x*a]

In[2379]:= Map[BlockQ, {Sv, Kr, Agn, Art, a + b, 590}]

Out[2379]= {False, True, True, False, False, False}

In[2380]:= BlockQ1[x_] := If[SymbolQ[x] && TestBFM[x] === "Block", True, False]

In[2381]:= Map[BlockQ1, {Sv, Kr, Agn, Art, 590}]

Out[2381]= {False, True, True, False, False}

In[2382]:= ModuleQ1[x_] := If[SymbolQ[x] && TestBFM[x] === "Module", True, False]

In[2383]:= Map[ModuleQ1, {Sv, Kr, Agn, Art, 590}]

Out[2383]= {True, False, False, True, False}

In[2384]:= ModuleQ2[x_] :=
Module[{b, a = If[SymbolQ[x], Flatten[{PureDefinition[x]}][[1]], $Failed]},
If[MemberQ[{$Failed, "System"}, a], False, b=Map14[StringJoin, {" := ", " = "}, "Module[{"];
If[SuffPref[a, Map3[StringJoin, HeadPF[x], b], 1], True, False]]]

In[2385]:= Map[ModuleQ2, {Sv, Kr, Agn, Art, 590}]

Out[2385]= {True, False, False, True, False}

The above fragment is completed by an example with the simple **BlockQ1** function which is *functionally* equivalent to the previous **BlockQ** procedure and which is based on procedure **TestBFM**; at that, this fragment represents also not less simple **ModuleQ1** function, whose call **ModuleQ1**[*x*] returns *True* if *x* symbol defines a modular structure, and *False* otherwise. The result of the procedure call **ModuleQ2**[*x*] is analogous to the call **ModuleQ1**[*x*].

We will note, the previous tools of testing of objects of the type {*Module, Block, Function*} support only single objects, but not objects of the same name, i.e. for each such object in the current session of the *Mathematica* the only definition should be activated. Therefore the tools of testing of objects in independence from number of the definitions standing behind them are of special interest. This problem is solved by means of the next **FuncBlockModQ** procedure, whose result of a call **FuncBlockModQ**[*x, y*] returns *True*, if *x* – a symbol defines an object of type {*Function, Module, Block*}; at that, in the presence for the *x* symbol of several definitions the *True* is returned only if all its definitions generate an object of the same type. While through the second *y* argument – *an undefinite variable* – an object type in the context of {*"Function", "Block", "Module"*} is returned. If a *x* symbol determines an object of the same name whose definitions are associated with subobjects of the different types, the procedure call **FuncBlockModQ**[*x, y*] returns *False* whereas through the second argument *y* *"Multiple"* is returned. The fragment below represents source code of the **FuncBlockModQ** procedure along with the most typical examples of its application.

In[2654]:= FuncBlockModQ[x_ /; SymbolQ[x], y_ /; ! HowAct[y]] :=
Module[{b, c, m, n, a = PureDefinition[x]},
If[MemberQ[{"System", $Failed}, a], False, a = Flatten[{a}]; b = Flatten[{HeadPF[x]}];
c = Join[Mapp[StringJoin, b, " := "], Mapp[StringJoin, b, " = "]]; c = GenRules[c, ""];
c = StringReplace[a, c]; {m, n} = Map[Length, {Select[c, SuffPref[#,"Block[{", 1] &],
Select[c, SuffPref[#, "Module[{", 1] &]}];

If[Length[a] == m, y = "Block"; True, If[Length[a] == n, y = "Module"; True, If[m + n == 0, y = "Function"; True, y = "Multiple"; False]]]]]

In[2655]:= Sv[x_] := Module[{}, y := 74; z := 69; {y, z}];
Agn[x_] := Block[{a = 90}, a*x]; B[x_] := Block[{a, b, c, d}, x*(a + b + c + d)];
B[x_, y_] := Block[{}, x + y]; M[x_] := Module[{a, b, c, d}, x*(a + b + c + d)];
M[x_, y_] := Module[{}, x + y]; V[x_] := Module[{a, b, c, d}, x*(a + b + c + d)];
V[x_, y_] := Block[{}, x + y]; F[x_, y_] := x + y; F[x_, y_, z_] := x + y + z
In[2656]:= {FuncBlockModQ[Sv, y], y}
Out[2656]= {True, "Module"}
In[2657]:= {FuncBlockModQ[B, y1], y1}
Out[2657]= {True, "Block"}
In[2658]:= {FuncBlockModQ[M, y2], y2}
Out[2658]= {True, "Module"}
In[2659]:= {FuncBlockModQ[V, y3], y3}
Out[2659]= {False, "Multiple"}
In[2660]:= {FuncBlockModQ[While, y4], y4}
Out[2660]= {False, y4}
In[2661]:= {FuncBlockModQ[F, y4], y4}
Out[2661]= {True, "Function"}

This procedure along with standard means uses also our means **GenRules, PureDefinition, HeadPF, HowAct, Mapp, SuffPref** and **SymbolQ** which are considered in this book and in [32,33]. Below, other means of testing of the objects of type {*"Function", "Block", "Module"*} will be represented too, though already the above means allow to considerably solve this a rather important problem.

Insofar as procedures of both types (*Module, Block*) along with the user functions are basic objects of procedural programming in the *Mathematica*, then a very important problem of creation of means for testing of belonging of an object to the type {*Module, Block, Function*} exists. The next fragment represents the **TestBFM** procedure which is successfully solving this a rather important problem.

In[2620]:= TestBFM[x_] := Module[{a = Flatten[{PureDefinition[x]}], b, d, h, p, k, j, t = {}},
If[MemberQ[{$Failed, "System"}, a[[1]]], Return[$Failed], b = Flatten[{HeadPF[x]}];
For[k = 1, k <= Length[a], k++, d = a[[k]]; p = Map[b[[k]] <> # &, {" := ", " = "}];
h = StringReplace[d, {p[[1]] -> "", p[[2]] -> ""}, 1];
If[SuffPref[h, "Module[{", 1], t = AppendTo[t, "Module"], If[SuffPref[h, "Block[{", 1],
t = AppendTo[t, "Block"], If[SuffPref[h, "DynamicModule[{", 1],
t = AppendTo[t, "DynamicModule"], t = AppendTo[t, "Function"]]]]]]; ReduceLists[t]]
In[2621]:= M[x_] := x; M[x_, y_] := Module[{}, x + y]; M[x_, y_, z_] := Block[{}, x + y + z]
In[2622]:= PureDefinition[M]
Out[2622]= {"M[x_] := x", "M[x_, y_] := Module[{}, x+y]", "M[x_, y_, z_] := Block[{}, x + y + z]"}
In[2623]:= TestBFM[M]
Out[2623]= {"Function", "Module", "Block"}
In[2624]:= Map[TestBFM, {a + b, AVZ, Sin, SuffPref, For, 2016}]
Out[2624]= {$Failed, $Failed, $Failed, "Module", $Failed, $Failed}

The procedure call **TestBFM[x]** returns the type of a functional, modular or block object *x* in the format *"Function", "Module", "DynamicModule", "Block"*, whereas on a *x* argument of other types the procedure call returns $Failed. At that, if a *x* argument determines an object of the same name, the procedure call **TestBFM[x]** returns the list of types of the subobjects composing it, having bijection with the list of definitions that is returned by the procedure call **PureDefinition[x]**.

At that, the following procedure can appear as an useful enough tool of testing of objects, its call **ProcFuncBlQ[x, y]** returns *True* if *x* is a procedure, function or block; otherwise *False* is returned. At that, at return of *True*, thru *y* argument – an indefinite variable – a *x*–object type is returned {"Block", "Module", "DynamicModule", "Function", "PureFunction"}, otherwise the 2nd argument remains indefinite. The next fragment represents source code of the procedure along with the most typical examples of its application.

```
In[3178]:= ProcFuncBlQ[x_, y_ /; ! HowAct[y]] :=
Module[{a = ToString[HeadPF[x]], b = ToString[y] <> " = ", c = PureDefinition[x]},
If[ListQ[c], False, If[SuffPref[a, "HeadPF[", 1],
If[SuffPref[a, " & ]", 2], y = "PureFunction"; True, False],
If[HeadingQ[a], If[SuffPref[c, a <> " := Module[{", 1], y = "Module"; True,
If[SuffPref[c, a <> " := Block[{", 1], y = "Block"; True,
If[SuffPref[c, a <> " := DynamicModule[{", 1],
y = "DynamicModule"; True, y = "Function"; True]]], False]]]]

In[3179]:= Dm[] := DynamicModule[{x}, {Slider[Dynamic[x]], Dynamic[x]}]
In[3180]:= DPOb[] := Module[{a = 90, b = 69, c = 20, d = 27}, Plus[a, b, c, d]]
In[3181]:= B[x_] := Block[{a}, a = x]; G := Function[500 + 90*# &];
In[3182]:= Clear[g, g1, g2, g3, g4, g5]; {ProcFuncBlQ[Dm, g], ProcFuncBlQ[DPOb, g1],
ProcFuncBlQ[B, g2], ProcFuncBlQ[G, g3], ProcFuncBlQ[500 + 90*# &, g4],
ProcFuncBlQ[590, g5]}
Out[3182]= {True, True, True, True, True, False}
In[3183]:= {g, g1, g2, g3, g4, g5}
Out[3183]= {"DynamicModule", "Module", "Block", "PureFunction", "PureFunction", g5}
In[3184]:= ClearAll[t]; F[x_] := 500 + 90*x; {ProcFuncBlQ[F, t], t}
Out[3184]= {True, "Function"}
```

It should be noted that this procedure is correctly executed only on objects of the above type provided that they have single definitions, otherwise returning *False*. The procedure along with the standard tools uses also our means **HeadingQ, HeadPF, HowAct, PureDefinition** and **SuffPref** that are considered in the present book and in our previous books [32,33,50].

The following procedure can appear as a rather useful extension for the testing of objects, its call **ProcFuncBlQ1[x, y]** returns *True* if *x* is a procedure, function or block, otherwise *False* is returned. At that, at return of *True*, thru *y* argument – an undefinite variable – a *x* object type is returned {"Block", "Module", "DynamicModule", "Function", "PureFunction"}, otherwise the second argument remains *indefinite*. It should be noted that the above procedure is correctly executed both on single objects, and on the objects of the same name, otherwise is returned *False*. The next fragment represents source code of the **ProcFuncBlQ1** procedure along with the most typical examples of its application.

In[3117]:= ProcFuncBlQ1[x_, y_ /; ! HowAct[y]] :=
Module[{b = {}, d = {}, k, a = Flatten[{HeadPF[x]}], c = Flatten[{PureDefinition[x]}]},
Do[If[SuffPref[ToString[x], " & ", 2], AppendTo[b, "PureFunction"]; AppendTo[d, True],
If[c[[k]] === $Failed, AppendTo[b, $Failed]; AppendTo[d, False],
If[SuffPref[c[[k]], a[[k]] <> " := Module[{", 1], AppendTo[b, "Module"];
AppendTo[d, True],
If[SuffPref[c[[k]], a[[k]] <> " := Block[{", 1], AppendTo[b, "Block"]; AppendTo[d, True],
If[SuffPref[c[[k]], a[[k]] <> " := DynamicModule[{", 1], AppendTo[b, "DynamicModule"];
AppendTo[d, True], AppendTo[b, "Function"]; AppendTo[d, True]]]]]], {k, 1, Length[c]}];
{b, d} = Map[If[Length[#] == 1, #[[1]], #] &, {b, d}]; y = b; d]

In[3118]:= Clear[g, g1, g2, g3, g4, g5, g6]; {ProcFuncBlQ1[Dm, g], ProcFuncBlQ1[DPOb, g1],
ProcFuncBlQ1[B, g2], ProcFuncBlQ1[G, g3], ProcFuncBlQ1[500 + 90*# &, g4],
ProcFuncBlQ1[590, g5], ProcFuncBlQ1[ProcQ, g6]}
Out[3118]= {True, True, True, {True, True, True}, True, False, True}

In[3119]:= {g, g1, g2, g3, g4, g5, g6}
Out[3119]= {"DynamicModule", "Module", "Block", {"Block", "Block", "Function"},
"PureFunction", $Failed, "Module"}

In[3120]:= Clear[G]; G[x_, y_] := x + y; {ProcFuncBlQ1[G, h27], h27}
Out[3120]= {True, "Function"}

As it was already noted above, in general case between procedures of types *"Module"* and *"Block"* exist principal enough distinctions which don't allow a priori to consider the block structure as the full procedure. Such distinctions are based on various used mechanisms of local variables as that was visually illustrated with examples slightly above. It is possible to give more complex examples of similar distinctions [50]. Therefore the type of a procedure should be chosen rather circumspectly, giving preference to the procedures of the *"Module"* type. Therefore, the **BlockToModule** procedure can be usefull enough whose procedure call **BlockToModule[*x*]** returns *Null*, providing converting of procedure of the *"Block"* type into procedure of the *"Module"* type. The next fragment represents source code of the procedure **BlockToModule** along with typical examples of its application.

In[2468]:= BlockToModule[x_Symbol] :=
Module[{b, c, d, h = {}, k = 1, n, m, a = Definition2[x]},
If[ListQ[a] && a[[1]] == "System" || UnevaluatedQ[Definition2, x], $Failed, b = a[[-1]]];
ClearAllAttributes[x]; c = a[[1 ;; -2]]; d = Flatten[{HeadPF[x]}];
For[k, k <= Length[d], k++, {n, m} = {c[[k]], d[[k]]};
If[SuffPref[n, {m <> " := Block[{", m <> " = Block[{"}, 1],
AppendTo[h, StringReplace[n, "Block[{" -> "Module[{", 1]], AppendTo[h, n]]];
Map[ToExpression, h]; SetAttributes[x, b]]]

In[2469]:= V[x_] := Module[{a, b}, x*(a + b)]; V[x_, y_] := Block[{}, x + y]; V[x__] := {x}
In[2470]:= Options[V] = {agn -> 69, asv -> 49}; SetAttributes[V, {Protected, Listable}]
In[2471]:= Definition2[V]
Out[2471]= {"V[x_] := Module[{a, b}, x*(a + b)]", "V[x_, y_] := Block[{}, x + y]",
"V[x__] := {x}", "Options[V] = {agn -> 69, asv -> 49}", {Listable, Protected}}

In[2472]:= **BlockToModule[V]**
In[2473]:= **Definition2[V]**
Out[2473]= {"V[x_] := Module[{a, b}, x*(a + b)]", "V[x_, y_] := Module[{}, x + y]",
"V[x__] := {x}", "Options[V] = {agn -> 69, asv -> 49}", {Listable, Protected}}
In[2474]:= **G[x_] := Block[{}, x^2]; G[x_, y_] = Block[{}, x*y]; G[x__] := Block[{}, {x}]**
In[2475]:= **Options[G] = {ian -> 90, rans -> 590}; SetAttributes[G, {Protected, Listable}]**
In[2476]:= **Definition2[G]**
Out[2476]= {"G[x_] := Block[{}, x^2]", "G[x_, y_] = x*y", "G[x__] := Block[{}, {x}]",
"Options[G] = {ian -> 90, rans -> 590}", {Listable, Protected}}
In[2477]:= **BlockToModule[G]; Definition2[G]**
Out[2477]= {"G[x_] := Module[{}, x^2]", "G[x_, y_] = x*y", "G[x__] := Module[{}, {x}]",
"Options[G] = {ian -> 90, rans -> 590}", {Listable, Protected}}

The call **BlockToModule[*x*]** returns *Null*, i.e. nothing, simultaneously with converting of a *x* procedure of the block type into the procedure of the modular type of the same name with preservation of all attributes and options of a source procedure of the block type. Moreover several definitions of modules, blocks or functions also can be associated with a *x* object, but the procedure call **BlockToModule[*x*]** provides converting only of the block components of a *x* object in modular structures. The above examples quite visually illustrate the aforesaid. The following procedure generalizes the **BlockToModule** procedure.

As it was already noted above, the procedural type is recommended to be chosen a rather circumspectly, giving preference to the procedural objects of the *"Module"* type. Hence, the **BlockFuncToModule** procedure can be usefull enough, its the call **BlockFuncToModule[*x*]** returns nothing simultaneously with converting of a *x* procedure of block type or function into the procedure of modular type of the same name with preservation of all its attributes and options of an initial *x* object of the type {*Block, Function, Module*}. Moreover, several definitions of *modules*, *blocks* or/and *functions* also can be associated with *x* object, however the procedure call **BlockFuncToModule[*x*]** provides converting only of above components of the *x* object into the *modular* structures. The following fragment represents source code of the **BlockFuncToModule** procedure along with typical examples of its application. At that, the examples below quite visually illustrate the aforesaid.

In[3715]:= **BlockFuncToModule[x_ /; SymbolQ[x]] :=
Module[{b, c, d, h = {}, k = 1, n, m, a = Definition2[x]},
If[ListQ[a] && a[[1]] == "System" || UnevaluatedQ[Definition2, x], $Failed, b = a[[-1]]];
ClearAllAttributes[x]; c = a[[1 ;; -2]]; d = Flatten[{HeadPF[x]}];
For[k, k <= Length[d], k++, {n, m} = {c[[k]], d[[k]]};
If[SuffPref[n, {m <> " := Block[{", m <> " = Block[{"}, 1],
AppendTo[h, StringReplace[n, "Block[{" -> "Module[{", 1]],
If[SuffPref[n, {m <> " := Module[{", m <> " = Module[{"}, 1], AppendTo[h, n],
AppendTo[h, m <> " := " <> "Module[{}, " <> StringReplace[n, {m <> " = " -> "",
m <> " := " -> ""}, 1] <> "]"]]]]; Map[ToExpression, h]; SetAttributes[x, b]]]**

In[3716]:= **V6[x_] := Module[{a, b}, x*(a + b)]; V6[x_, y_] := Block[{}, x + y];
V6[x_, y__] := x^2 + StringLength[y]**
In[3717]:= **BlockFuncToModule[6]**

In[3718]:= **Definition[6]**
Out[3718]= V6[x_] := Module[{a, b}, x*(a + b)]
V6[x_, y_] := Module[{}, x + y]
V6[x_, y__] := Module[{}, x^2 + StringLength[y]]

Due to the mechanism of the global variables used by blocks and modules it is necessary to make certain explanations. In this context it is possible to distinguish two types of the global variables – *passive* and *active* ones. Passive global variables are characterized by that, they are only used by an object, without changing their values outside of the object. Whereas the assignment of values by means of operators {":=", "="} for active global variables is done in object body, changing their values and outside of the object. In view of the above the active global variables are of interest at processing of blocks, modules, and procedures in general. A number of our means processing the objects of this type whose definitions contain active global variables consider the specified circumstance, doing processing of objects of the type {"*Module*", "*Block*"} so that not to change values of the active global variables used by them outside of their scope. In this relation the procedures **BlockModQ**, **BlockFuncModQ** and **BlockQ**, **ModuleQ** represented below are indicative enough.

The call **BlockFuncModQ[x]** returns *True*, if *x* – a symbol defining a typical *(with a heading)* function, a block or a module, and *False* otherwise. While the call **BlockFuncModQ[x, y]** on condition of the main return of *True* through the second optional *y* argument – *an undefinite variable* – returns type of a *x* object in the context of {"*Block*", "*Function*", "*Module*"}. On the other hand, the call **BlockModQ[x]** returns *True*, if *x* – a symbol defining a block or module, and *False* otherwise. Whereas the call **BlockModQ[x, y]** on condition of the main return of *True* through optional *y* argument – *an undefinite variable* – returns type of the *x* object in the context {"*Block*", "*Module*"}. The following fragment submits source codes of the procedures **BlockModQ** and **BlockFuncModQ** along with typical examples of their applications.

In[2612]:= **BlockFuncModQ[x_, y___] :=**
Module[{b, c, a = Flatten[{PureDefinition[x]}][[1]]},
If[MemberQ[{$Failed, "System"}, a], False, b = StringSplit[a, {" := ", " = "}, 2];
If[StringFreeQ[b[[1]], "["], False, c = If[SuffPref[b[[2]], "Module[{", 1], "Module",
If[SuffPref[b[[2]], "Block[{", 1], "Block", "Function"]]];
If[{y} != {} && ! HowAct[y], y = c]; True]]]
In[2613]:= M[x_, y_] := Module[{a = 90, b = 590}, x*y*a*b]; F[x_] := x; B[_] := Block[{}, x]
In[2614]:= {BlockFuncModQ[M, y], y}
Out[2614]= {True, "Module"}
In[2615]:= {BlockFuncModQ[F, y1], y1}
Out[2615]= {True, "Function"}
In[2616]:= {BlockFuncModQ[B, y2], y2}
Out[2616]= {True, "Block"}
In[2639]:= **BlockModQ[x_, y___] :=**
Module[{s = FromCharacterCode[6], a = Flatten[{PureDefinition[x]}][[1]], b, c},
If[MemberQ[{$Failed, "System"}, a], False, b = StringReplace[a, {" := " -> s, " = " -> s}, 1];
b = StringTake[b, {Flatten[StringPosition[b, s]][[1]] + 1, -1}];

```
c = If[SuffPref[b, "Module[{", 1], "Module", If[SuffPref[b, "Block[{", 1], "Block"]];
If[{y} != {} && ! HowAct[y], y = c]; If[c === Null, False, True]]]
```

In[2640]:= Clear[y3, y4, y5]; {BlockModQ[M, y3], y3}
Out[2640]= {True, "Module"}
In[2641]:= {BlockModQ[F, y4], y4}
Out[2641]= {False, Null}
In[2642]:= {BlockModQ[B, y5], y5}
Out[2642]= {True, "Block"}

From the aforesaid follows, at programming of the tools that manipulate with objects of the type {"Block", "Module"} and which use *global* variables, it is necessary to consider *possibility*, what in the course of the calls of these means for their global variables the assignments are done what can conflict with values of variables of the same name which have been received in the current session earlier. Naturally, general speaking, it isn't so essential for the reason that by the call of such objects, the *global* variables used by them and so will receive values if is being not envisaged the contrary. In order to avoid possible *misunderstanding* a procedure has to provide saving of values of global variables which have been received by them up to the procedure call with restoration them at exit from the procedure. Simple enough example illustrates mechanism of saving of values of an *y* variable of the current session that is used as a global variable of the simple *Kr* procedure, namely:

In[2495]:= Kr[x_] := Module[{a = 90, b = y}, y = 590; {a + y + x, y = b}[[1]]]
In[2496]:= y = 42; {Kr[450], y}
Out[2496]= {1130, 42}

Functions of the *Mathematica* system have a number of interesting means for support of a work with dynamic objects. We recall that dynamical module **DynamicModule[{x, y, z, ...}, W]** represents an object that supports the same local status for variables *x, y, z, ...* during of evaluation of all dynamic objects of a *W* body. The variables specified in **DynamicModule** by default have values throughout all current session. In addition, the dynamical object can act not only directly as an expression, but also, in particular, as a coordinate in the graphical primitive, as an object of the type *"slider"*, as a setting for an option. Meanwhile, unlike the standard module the dynamic module directly doesn't allow to receive its definition by the standard **Definition** function, only our procedures **Definition2** and **PureDefinition** allow to solve this problem as it illustrates the following fragment, namely:

In[2760]:= Dm[x_, y_ /; PrimeQ[y]] := DynamicModule[{a = 90, b = 590}, a + b*(x + y)]; Definition[Dm]
Out[2760]= Dm[x_, y_ /; PrimeQ[y]] := a$$ + b$$*(x + y)
In[2761]:= Definition2[Dm]
Out[2761]= {"Dm[x_, y_ /; PrimeQ[y]] := DynamicModule[{a = 90, b = 590}, a + b*(x + y)]", {}}
In[2762]:= PureDefinition[Dm]
Out[2762]= "Dm[x_, y_ /; PrimeQ[y]] := DynamicModule[{a = 90, b = 590}, a + b*(x + y)]"
In[2799]:= ModuleQ[x_, y___ /; y == Null || SymbolQ[y] && ! HowAct[y]] :=
Module[{a = PureDefinition[x], b},
If[ListQ[a] || a == "System" || a === $Failed, False, b = HeadPF[x];
If[SuffPref[a, b <> " := " <> "Module[{", 1],

If[{y} != {}, y = "Module"]; True, If[SuffPref[a, b <> " := " <> "DynamicModule[{", 1],
If[{y} != {}, y = "DynamicModule"]; True, False]]]]
In[2800]:= {ModuleQ[Dm, t3], t3}
Out[2800]= {True, "DynamicModule"}
In[2801]:= V[x_] := Module[{a, b}, x*(a + b)]; {ModuleQ[V, t5], t5}
Out[2801]= {True, "Module"}
In[2802]:= V[x_, y_] := Block[{}, x + y]; V[x__] := {x}; {ModuleQ[V, t7], t7}
Out[2802]= {False, t7}
In[2803]:= {ModuleQ[Sin, t8], t8}
Out[2803]= {False, t8}
In[2804]:= {ModuleQ[590, t9], t9}
Out[2804]= {False, t9}

The useful enough **ModuleQ** procedure completes this fragment whose call **ModuleQ[x]** returns *True* if a *x* object, given by a symbol, is a module, and *False* otherwise; whereas the call **ModuleQ[x, y]** with the second optional *y* argument – *an indefinite variable* – through *y* returns module type *x* in the context {*"Module"*, *"DynamicModule"*}. At that, the procedure call on a tuple of incorrect actual arguments is returned unevaluated. In other cases the call **ModuleQ[x, y]** returns *False*. The procedure along with standard tools uses also our means **HeadPF, HowAct, PureDefinition, SymbolQ, SuffPref** which are considered in this book and in [32,33,50]. Meanwhile, several essential enough moments concerning the **ModuleQ** procedure should be noted. First of all, the **ModuleQ** procedure is oriented onto a modular object *x* which has single definition, returning *False* on the objects of the same name. At that, the procedure algorithm assumes that the definition of the modular *x* object is based on the operator of postponed assignment ":=" but not on the operator "=" of immediate assignment because in the latter case the *x* object will be recognized both by the **Definition** function and our testing means as a function. In our opinion, the **ModuleQ** procedure is an useful enough tool at programming of various type of problems.

For testing of objects onto procedural type we proposed a number of means among which it is possible to note such as **ProcQ, ProcQ1, ProcQ2**. The call **ProcQ[x]** provides testing of a *x* object be as the procedural object {*"Module"*, *"Block"*}, returning accordingly *True* or *False*; whereas the **ProcQ1** procedure is a useful enough modification of the **ProcQ** procedure, its call **ProcQ1[x, t]** returns *True*, if *x* – an object of the type *Block*, *Module* or *DynamicModule*, and *"Others"* or *False* otherwise; at that, the type of *x* object is returned through the factual *t* argument – an *indefinite variable*. The source codes of the above procedures, their description along with the most typical examples of their application are presented in our books [30-33] and in our *MathToolBox* package [48]. A number of receptions used at their creation can be useful enough in the practical programming. The **ProcQ** procedure is an quite fast, processes attributes and options, however has certain restrictions, first of all, in a case of objects of the same name [33]. The fragment below represents source codes of both procedures along with typical examples of their applications.

In[2492]:= ProcQ[x_] := Module[{a, atr = Quiet[Attributes[x]], b, c, d, h},
If[! SymbolQ[x], False, If[SystemQ[x], False, If[UnevaluatedQ[Definition2, x], False,
If[ListQ[atr] && atr != {}, ClearAllAttributes[x]];

```
a = StringReplace[ToString[InputForm[Definition[x]]],
Context[x] <> ToString[x] <> "`" -> ""];
Quiet[b = StringTake[a, {1, First[First[StringPosition[a, {" := Block[{", " :=Block[{"}] - 1]]}];
c = StringTake[a, {1, First[First[StringPosition[a, {" := Module[{"," :=Module[{"}] - 1]]}];
d = StringTake[a, {1, First[First[StringPosition[a,
{" := DynamicModule[{", " :=DynamicModule[{"}] - 1]]}]];
If[b === ToString[HeadPF[x]], SetAttributes[x, atr]; True,
If[c === ToString[HeadPF[x]], SetAttributes[x, atr]; True,
If[d === ToString[HeadPF[x]], SetAttributes[x, atr]; True,
SetAttributes[x, atr]; False]]]]]]
```

In[2493]:= Map[ProcQ, {Sin, a + b, ProcQ1, ProcQ, 74, UnevaluatedQ}]
Out[2493]= {False, False, True, True, False, True}

In[2620]:= ProcQ1[x_, y___ /; y === Null || SymbolQ[y] && ! HowAct[y]] :=
Module[{a = Quiet[Check[Flatten[{PureDefinition[x]}], $Failed]],
b = StringLength[ToString[x]], c, g = ToString[Unique["agn"]], h = {},
p = $$$74, k = 1, t = {}, v = {}},
If[SubsetQ[{$Failed, "System"}, a], False, For[k, k <= Length[a], k++, Clear[$$$74];
ToExpression[g <> StringTake[a[[k]], {b + 1, -1}]]; AppendTo[v, g];
AppendTo[h, c = ProcQ[g]]; BlockFuncModQ[g, $$$74];
AppendTo[t, If[c && $$$74 == "Function", "DynamicModule", $$$74]];
g = ToString[Unique["agn"]]]; $$$74 = p;
Map[Remove[#] &, Flatten[{g, v}]]; If[{y} != {}, y = {h, t}, Null];
If[AllTrue[h, TrueQ], True, False]]]

In[2621]:= V[x_] := Module[{a, b}, x*(a + b)]; V[x_, y_] := Block[{}, x + y]; V[x__] := {x};
{ProcQ1[V, y7], y7}
Out[2621]= {False, {{True, True, False}, {"Module", "Block", "Function"}}}

In[2622]:= G[x_] := Module[{a = 74}, a*x^2]; G[x_, y_] := Module[{}, x*y];
G[x__] := Module[{a = 90, b = 590}, Length[{x}] + a*b]; {ProcQ1[G, u], u}
Out[2622]= {True, {{True, True, True}, {"Module", "Module", "Module"}}}

In[2686]:= ProcBMQ[x_ /; BlockModQ[x], y___] := Module[{a, b, c = " = ", d, p},
If[! SingleDefQ[x], "Object <" <> ToString[x] <> "> has multiple definitions",
If[ModuleQ[x], True, {a, b} = {PureDefinition[x], Locals1[x]};
d = Map[#[[1]] - 1 &, StringPosition[a, c]]; p = Map[ExprOfStr[a, #, -1, {" ", "{", "["}] &, d];
p = DeleteDuplicates[Flatten[Map[StrToList, p]]];
If[{y} != {}, y = MinusList[b, p], Null]; If[p == b, True, False]]]]

In[2687]:= P[x_] := Block[{a = 90, b = 590, c, d, h, g}, h = (a + b)*x; h^2]; {ProcBMQ[P, q], q}
Out[2687]= {False, {"c", "d", "g"}}

In[2688]:= T[x_] := Block[{a = 590, b = 90, c, d, h, g}, {c, d, h, g} = {1, 2, 3, 4}];
{ProcBMQ[T, v], v}
Out[2688]= {True, {}}

In[2689]:= G[x_] := Block[{a, b}, x]; G[x_, y_] := Block[{a, b}, x + y]; ProcBMQ[G]

Out[2689]= "Object <G> has multiple definitions"

In[2690]:= **SingleDefQ[x_] := If[Length[Flatten[{PureDefinition[x]}]] == 1 || SameQ["System", PureDefinition[x]], True, False]**

In[2691]:= **G[x_] := Block[{}, x]; G[x_, y_] := Block[{a}, x*y]; SingleDefQ[G]**
Out[2691]= False

In[2692]:= **a[x_] := x; a[x_, y_] := x/y; Map[SingleDefQ, {74, c/b, If, ProcQ, a}]**
Out[2692]= {True, True, True, True, False}

In this context we created the **ProcQ1** procedure that generalizes the **ProcQ** procedure, first of all, in case of the objects of the same name. The previous fragment represents the source code of the **ProcQ1** procedure with examples of its most typical application. At that, the call **ProcQ1[x]** returns *True* if the symbol *x* defines a procedural object of the type {*Block, Module, DynamicModule*} with unique definition, with an object consisting of their any combinations with different headings *(the objects of the same name)*. Moreover, in case of a separate object or *x* object of the same name *True* is returned only when all its *components* is procedural objects in the sense stated above, i.e. they have type {*Block, DynamicModule, Module*}. Meanwhile, the procedure call **ProcQ1[x, y]** with the second optional *y* argument – *an indefinite variable* – thru it returns simple or the nested list of the following format, namely:

$$\{\{a1, a2, a3, a4, ..., ap\}, \{b1, b2, b3, b4, ..., bp\}\}$$

where $aj \in \{True, False\}$ while $bj \in \{$"Block", "DynamicModule", "Function", "Module"$\}$; at that, between elements of the above sublists exists one-to-one correspondence while pairs {*aj, bj*} (*j = 1..p*) correspond to subobjects of the *x* object according to their order as a result of the function call **Definition[x]**.

The **ProcQ1** procedure is rather widely used and is an useful enough in many appendices, it differs from the previous **ProcQ** procedure in the following context: *(1)* an quite successfully processes the objects of the same name, *(2)* defines procedurality in case of the objects of the same name, whose subobjects are blocks and functions. The procedure along with standard tools significantly uses as well our tools such as **HowAct, PureDefinition, SymbolQ, ProcQ, BlockFuncModQ** which are considered in the present book and in [28-33,50].

The previous fragment presents the **ProcBMQ** procedure whose call **ProcBMQ[x]** with one argument returns *True*, if a block or a module *x* – a *real* procedure in the above context, and *False* otherwise; the procedure call **ProcBMQ[x, y]** with the second optional *y* argument – *an undefinite variable* – returns through it the list of local variables of the *x* block in string format which have no initial values or for which in a body of the *x* block the assignments of values weren't made. We will note, that the **ProcBMQ** procedure is oriented only on one–defined objects whose definitions are unique while the message "*Object <x> has multiple definitions*" is returned on *x* objects of the same name. The procedure along with standard means uses also our means **ExprOfStr, BlockModQ, ModuleQ, PureDefinition, Locals1, SingleDefQ, MinusList, StrToList** which are considered in this book and in books [30-33]. In particular, the procedure essentially uses rather simple and useful function, whose call **SingleDefQ[x]** returns *True* if the actual *x* argument determines the name of procedure, block or a function having single definition; in other cases the function call returns *False*. The above fragment represents the source code of the **SingleDefQ** function with the most typical examples of its application.

In addition to our means for testing of *procedural* objects, we will note the simple procedure, whose call **UprocQ[*x*]** returns *False* if a *x* object isn't a procedure or is an object of the same name, and the 2-element list otherwise; in this case its *first* element is *True* while the *second* – the type {"*DynamicModule*" | "*Block*" | "*Module*"} of the *x* object. While on the functions the 2-element list of the format {*False*, "*Function*"} is returned. On inadmissible *factual* argument *x* the procedure call is returned unevaluated. The fragment below represents source code of the **UprocQ** procedure along with typical examples of its application.

In[2515]:= **UprocQ[x_ /; SymbolQ[x]] := Module[{a = Unique["agn"], b},**
If[SingleDefQ[x], b = ProcQ1[x, a]; {b, a[[2]][[1]]}, False]]

In[2516]:= **a[x_] := x^3; Dm[] := DynamicModule[{x}, {Slider[Dynamic[x]], Dynamic[x]}];**
P[x_] := Block[{a = 90, b = 590, h}, h = a*b*x; h^2]
In[2517]:= **Map[UprocQ, {ProcQ, P, Dm, 74, a, m + n}]**
Out[2517]= {{True, "Module"}, {True, "Block"}, {True, "DynamicModule"}, UprocQ[74], {False, "Function"}, UprocQ[m + n]}

Having considered the main means of testing of procedural objects which are absent among standard means of the *Mathematica* system it is reasonable to consider the means similar to them for testing of the functional objects where under functional means we will understand objects whose definitions have the following format, namely:

$$F[x\_ /; Test_x, y\_ /; Test_y, z\_ /; Test_z, ...] := W(x, y, z, ...)$$

or pure functions of one of the following formats, namely:

Function[*Body*] or short form ***Body*** **&** *(formal arguments # {#1}, #2, #3, etc.)*
Function[*x*, *Body*] – *a pure function with single formal argument x*
Function[{*x1*, *x2*, ...}, *Body*] – *a pure function with formal arguments {x1, x2, ...}*

We will give some simple examples onto these types of functions, namely:

In[2325]:= **y := Function[{x, y}, x + y]; y1 = Function[{x, y}, x + y]; z := #1 + #2 &;**
z1 = #1 + #2 &; F[x_, y_] := x + y
In[2326]:= **{y[90, 590], y1[90, 590], z[90, 590], z1[90, 590], F[90, 590]}**
Out[2326]= {680, 680, 680, 680, 680}

On objects of the above functional type the calls of the procedures **ProcQ1** and **ProcQ** return *False*, therefore for testing of functional type and other means considered below are offered. However, first of all, we will consider means testing the system functions, i.e. functions of the *Math*-language along with its environment. By and large, these system tools are called by *functions* not entirely correctly, because implementation of many of them is based on the *procedural* organization, meanwhile, we stopped on the given terminology, inherent actually to the system. And in this regard it is possible to present tools for testing of *system* functions besides that, the testing of objects regarding to be standard functions of the *Mathematica* in a number of important enough problems arises need. In this regard a rather simple function **SysFuncQ** solves the given problem; its call **SysFuncQ[*x*]** returns *True* if certain *x* object is a standard function of *Mathematica* system, and *False* otherwise; whereas simple **SysFuncQ1** function is a functionally equivalent modification of the previous **SysFuncQ** procedure. The following fragment represents source codes of the above tools with examples of their use.

In[2419]:= SysFuncQ[x_] := If[UnevaluatedQ[Definition2, x], False,
If[SameQ[Definition2[x][[1]], "System"], True, False]]

In[2420]:= Map[SysFuncQ, {Sin, Tan, While, If, Do, ProcQ, 6, Length, a/b}]
Out[2420]= {True, True, True, True, True, False, False, True, False}

In[3037]:= SysFuncQ1[x_] := MemberQ[Names["System`*"], ToString[x]]

In[3038]:= Map[SysFuncQ1, {Sin, Tan, While, If, Do, ProcQ, 6, Length, a/b}]
Out[3038]= {True, True, True, True, True, False, False, True, False}

We will consider the means of testing of the user functional objects, the first of which is the procedure **QFunction** that is the most general means for testing of *x* objects of the functional type, whose call **QFunction**[*x*] returns *True* on traditional *x* function and objects, generated by the function **Compile**, and *False* otherwise. At that, a construction of the format F[*x_, y_, ...*] {:= | =} F(*x, y, ...*) is understood as the traditional function. The next fragment represents source code of the **QFunction** procedure with examples of its application. In addition, this procedure along with the standard tools uses and our means such as **HeadPF, Definition2, SymbolQ, Map3, SuffPref, ToString1** and **ToString3** which are considered in the book and in our works [28-33,50].

In[2393]:= QFunction[x_] := Module[{a = Quiet[Definition2[x][[1]]],
b = ToString3[HeadPF[x]]}, If[! SingleDefQ[x], False, If[SuffPref[ToString1[a],
{"CompiledFunction[","Function["}, 1] || SuffPref[ToString1[a], " & ", 2], True,
If[SameQ[a, x], False, If[SuffPref[b, "HeadPF[", 1], False,
b = Map3[StringJoin, b, {" := ", " = "}];
If[MemberQ[{SuffPref[StringReplace[a, b -> ""], "Module[", 1],
SuffPref[StringReplace[a, b -> ""], "Block[", 1]}, True], False, True]]]]]]

In[2394]:= V := Compile[{{x, _Real}, {y, _Real}}, x/y]; Kr := (#1^2 + #2^4) &;
Art := Function[{x, y}, x*Sin[y]]; GS[x_ /; IntegerQ[x], y_ /; IntegerQ[y]] := Sin[7] + Cos[4];
Sv[x_ /; IntegerQ[x], y_ /; IntegerQ[y]] := x^2 + y^2;
S := Compile[{{x, _Integer}, {y, _Real}}, (x + y)^3];
In[2395]:= Map[QFunction, {V, S, Art, Kr, Pi, 42.74, GS, Sv}]
Out[2395]= {True, True, True, True, False, False, True, True}
In[2396]:= G[x_Integer, y_Real, z_Real] := x*y^2 + z
In[2397]:= Map[QFunction, {#1*#2*#3 &, Function[{x, y, z}, x*y*z], G, ProcQ}]
Out[2397]= {True, True, True, False}

In[2642]:= QFunction1[x_ /; StringQ[x]] :=
Module[{a, b, p, d = {}, h = {}, k, c = ToString[Unique["agn"]]},
If[UnevaluatedQ[Definition2, x], False, If[SysFuncQ[x], False,
a = Definition2[x][[If[Options[x] == {}, 1 ;; -2, 1 ;; -3]]];
For[k = 1, k <= Length[a], k++, p = c <> ToString[k];
AppendTo[h, p <> x]; ToExpression[p <> a[[k]]];
AppendTo[d, Qfunction[Symbol[p <> x]]]]; Map[Remove, Flatten[{c, h}]];
If[AllTrue[d, TrueQ], True, False]]]]

In[2643]:= F[x_] := x^2; F[x_, y_] = x + y; F := Compile[{{x, _Real}, {y, _Real}}, (x + y)^2];
F = Compile[{{x, _Real}, {y, _Real}}, (x + y)^2];

In[2644]:= Map[QFunction1, {"Sin", "F", "Art", "V", "Kr", "GS", "Sv", "S"}]
Out[2644]= {False, True, True, True, True, True, True, True}
In[2645]:= ClearAllAttributes["G"]; G[x_] := x; SetAttributes[G, Protected];
{QFunction[G], QFunction1["G"]}
Out[2645]= {True, True}
In[2646]:= {Map[QFunction, {Art, Kr}], Map[QFunction1, {"Art", "Kr"}]}
Out[2646]= {{True, True}, {True, True}}
In[2647]:= Sv[x_] := x; Sv[x_, y_] := x + y; {QFunction[Sv], QFunction1["Sv"]}
Out[2647]= {False, True}

However, the **QFunction** procedure, successfully testing the functional objects which are determined both by the traditional functions with headings and generated by the standard **Compile** function along with pure functions; at that, this procedure doesn't process also the functional objects of the same name as a visually illustrate the last example of the previous fragment. Whereas the **QFunction1** procedure solves the given problem, whose source code is presented in the second part of the previous fragment. The procedure call **QFunction1[*x*]** returns *True* on a traditional function or object *x*, which has been generated by the **Compile** function, and *False* otherwise; moreover, on *x* object of the same name *True* is returned only if all its components are traditional functions and/or are generated by the **Compile** function. At that, the call **QFunction1[*x*]** assumes coding of a factual *x* argument in the string format. Both procedures enough effectively process options and attributes of the tested objects. In addition, both the **QFunction1** procedure, and the **QFunction** procedure can't correctly test, generally, pure functions as quite visually illustrate examples of the previous fragment.

Along with the above types of functions, the *Mathematica* uses also the **Compile** function intended for compilation of the functions which calculate numerical expressions at certain assumptions. The **Compile** function has the following four formats of coding, each of which is oriented on a separate type of compilation, namely:

Compile[{*x1, x2,...*}, *G*] – *compiles a function for calculation of an expression G in the assumption that all values of arguments xj {j = 1, 2, ...} have numerical character;*

Compile[{{*x1, t1*}, {*x2, t2*}, {*x3, t3*}, ...}, *G*] – *compiles a function for calculation of a G expression in the assumption that all values of xj arguments have accordingly type tj {j = 1, 2, 3,...};*

Compile[{{*x1, p1, w1*}, {*x2, p2, w2*},...}, *J*] – *compiles a function for calculation of a J expression in the assumption that values of xj arguments are wj ranks of array of objects, each of that corresponds to a pj type {j = 1, 2, 3,...};*

Compile[*s, W,* {{*p1, pw1*}, {{*p2, pw2*}, ...}] – *compiles a function for calculation of a W expression in the assumption that its s subexpressions which correspond to the pk templates have the pwj types accordingly {k = 1, 2, 3, ...}.*

The **Compile** function processes both procedural and functional objects, matrix operations, numerical functions, functions of work with lists, etc. **Compile** function generates a special object **CompiledFunction**. The function call **Compile[..., Evaluate[*expr*]]** is used to specify that *expr* should be evaluated symbolically before compilation.

For testing of functions of this type a simple enough **CompileFuncQ** function is presented, whose call **CompileFuncQ[*x*]** returns *True* if a *x* represents the **Compile** function, and *False* otherwise. The following fragment represents source code of the **CompileFuncQ** function with the most typical examples of its application.

In[2367]:= V := Compile[{{x, _Real}, {y, _Real}}, x*y^2]; Kr := (#1*#2^4) &;
Art := Function[{x, y}, x*Sin[y]]; H[x_] := Block[{}, x]; H[x_, y_] := x + y;
SetAttributes["H", Protected]; P[x__] := Plus[Sequences[{x}]];
GS[x_ /; IntegerQ[x], y_ /; IntegerQ[y]] := Sin[78] + Cos[42];
Sv[x_ /; IntegerQ[x], y_ /; IntegerQ[y]] := x^2 + y^2;
Sv = Compile[{{x, _Integer}, {y, _Real}}, (x + y)^6]; S := Compile[{{x, _Integer}, {y, _Real}},
(x + y)^3]; G = Compile[{{x, _Integer}, {y, _Real}}, (x + y)]; P[x_] := Module[{}, x]
In[2368]:= CompileFuncQ[x_] := If[SuffPref[ToString[InputForm[Definition2[x]]],
"Definition2[CompiledFunction[{", 1], True, False]

In[2369]:= Map[CompileFuncQ, {Sv, S, G, V, P, Art, Kr, H, GS, ProcQ}]
Out[2369]= {True, True, True, True, False, False, False, False, False, False}
In[2370]:= Map[CompileFuncQ, {590, avz, a + b, Sin, While, 42.74}]
Out[2370]= {False, False, False, False, False, False}

The **CompileFuncQ** procedure expands possibilities of testing of functional objects in the *Mathematica* system, by representing a quite certain interest, first of all, for the problems of the system programming.

The **PureFuncQ** function represented below is oriented for testing of the pure functions, its call **PureFuncQ[*f*]** returns *True* if *f* defines a *pure function*, and *False* otherwise. The fragment represents source code of the **PureFuncQ** function along with examples of its typical use.

In[2385]:= PureFuncQ[f_] := Quiet[StringTake[ToString[f], {-3, -1}] == " & " &&
! StringFreeQ[ToString[f], "#"] || SuffPref[ToString[InputForm[f]], "Function[", 1]]

In[2386]:= Map[PureFuncQ, {#1 + #2 &, Function[{x, y, z}, x + y], G, ProcQ}]
Out[2386]= {True, True, False, False}
In[2387]:= Map[PureFuncQ, {Sin, F, Art, V, Kr, GS, Sv, S}]
Out[2387]= {False, False, True, False, True, False, False, False}
In[2388]:= Z := Function[{x, y, z}, x + y + z]; SetAttributes[Z, Protected]
In[2389]:= {PureFuncQ[Z], Attributes[Z]}
Out[2389]= {True, {Protected}}

In[2390]:= FunctionQ[x_] := If[StringQ[x], PureFuncQ[ToExpression[x]] || QFunction1[x],
PureFuncQ[x] || QFunction[x]]

In[2391]:= Map[FunctionQ, {"G", "ProcQ", "Function[{x, y, z}, x + y*z]", "#1 + #2*#3 &"}]
Out[2391]= {True, False, True, True}
In[2392]:= Map[FunctionQ, {"V", "S", "Art", "Kr", "Pi", "42.74", "GS", "Sv", "F"}]
Out[2392]= {True, True, True, True, False, False, True, True, True}
In[2393]:= Map[QFunction, {V, S, Art, Kr, Pi, 42.74, GS, Sv, F}]
Out[2393]= {True, True, True, True, False, False, True, True, True}

The simple enough **FunctionQ** function completes the previous fragment; the function call **FunctionQ[*x*]** returns *True* if a *x* object is the function of any of types {*traditional*, *pure*}, and *False* otherwise. In addition, the *x* name of an object can be coded both in symbolical, and in string formats; in the 2nd case correct testing of object *x* is supported, permitting multiplicity of its definitions, i.e. the *x* object can be of the same name in the above sense. It must be kept in mind that the testing tools that are represented above refers to the testing tools of the user functions, and aren't intended for standard functions of the *Mathematica* system, returning on them, as a rule, *False*. Thereby a number of means for the differentiated identification of the user functions, traditional functions, and pure functions has been defined, in particular, procedures and functions **FunctionQ, QFunction, QFunction1, PureFuncQ** respectively. These tools provide strict differentiation of such basic element of functional and procedural programming, as the *function*. These and tools similar to them are useful enough in applied and system programming in the *Mathematica* system.

Meanwhile, here it is necessary to make one a rather essential remark once again. As it was already noted, unlike the majority of the known languages the *Math*-language identifies procedures and functions not on their names, but on the headings, allowing not only the procedures of the same name with the different headings, but also their combinations with functions. Thus the question of testing of objects in context of the type {*Procedure, Function*} isn't so unambiguous. The testing tools presented above {**ProcQ, QFunction1, FunctionQ, PureFuncQ**, *etc.*} allow as a argument a *x* object or only with one heading or the first object returned by the system call **Definition**[*x*] as it was illustrated above. At that, for on objects of the same name the calls of a series of means, considered above return *True* only in a case when the definitions composing them are associated with subobjects of the same type.

In this connection it is very expedient to define some testing procedure which determines belonging of an object *x* to the group {**Block, CompiledFunction, Function, PureFunction, Module, ShortPureFunction**}. As *one* of similar approaches it is possible to suppose the next procedure, whose call **ProcFuncTypeQ**[*x*] returns the list of format {*True*, {*t1, t2, ..., tp*}} if a simple *x* object or subobjects of a *x* object of the same name whose *x* name is encoded in the string format have the *tj* types from the set {*CompiledFunction, PureFunction, Block, Module, Function, ShortPureFunction*}, otherwise the list of format {*False, x, "Expression"*} or {*False, x, "System"*} is returned. In case of a *x* object of the same name a sublist of types {*t1, t2, ..., tp*} (*j* = 1..*p*) of subobjects composing *x* is returned; while "*System*" and "*Expression*" defines a system function *x* and a *x* expression respectively. Thus, the **ProcFuncTypeQ** procedure can be applied as a group test for belonging of a *x* object to the above types. The next fragment represents source code of the **ProcFuncTypeQ** procedure with the most typical examples of its application.

In[2528]:= ProcFuncTypeQ[x_ /; StringQ[x]] := Module[{a, b, d = {}, k = 1, p},
If[ShortPureFuncQ[x], {True, "ShortPureFunction"},
a = Definition2[x][[If[Options[x] == {}, 1 ;; -2, 1 ;; -3]]];
If[SuffPref[x, "Function[{", 1], {True, "PureFunction"},
If[a === Definition2[], {False, x, "Expression"}, If[SysFuncQ[x], {False, x, "System"},
For[k, k <= Length[a], k++, b = Map[StringSplit[#, {" := ", " = "}] &, a]; p = b[[k]][[2]];
If[SuffPref[p, {"Compile[{", "CompiledFunction[{"}, 1],
AppendTo[d, "CompiledFunction"], If[SuffPref[p, "Block[{", 1], AppendTo[d, "Block"],
If[SuffPref[p, "Module[", 1], AppendTo[d, "Module"],
If[SuffPref[p, "Function[{", 1], AppendTo[d, "PureFunction"],
If[ShortPureFuncQ[p], AppendTo[d, "ShortPureFunction"],
If[PureFuncQ[ToExpression[x]], AppendTo[d, "PureFunction"],
AppendTo[d, "Function"]]]]]]]]; {True, d}]]]]
In[2529]:= V := Compile[{{x, _Real}, {y, _Real}}, (x^3 + y)^2];

```
Sv[x_] := Module[{}, x]; Art := Function[{x, y}, x*Sin[y]];
GS[x_ /; IntegerQ[x], y_ /; IntegerQ[y]] := Sin[x] + y;
Sv[x_ /; IntegerQ[x], y_ /; IntegerQ[y]] := x^2 + y^2;
Sv = Compile[{{x, _Integer}, {y, _Real}}, (x + 6*y)^6];
S := Compile[{{x, _Integer}, {y, _Real}}, (x + y)^3]; Kr := (#1*#2^4) &;
G = Compile[{{x, _Integer}, {y, _Real}}, (x + y)]; H[x_] := Block[{a}, x];
H[x_, y_] := x + y; SetAttributes["H", Protected]
In[2530]:= ProcFuncTypeQ["Sv"]
Out[2530]= {True, {"CompiledFunction", "Module", "Function"}}
In[2531]:= ProcFuncTypeQ["H"]
Out[2531]= {True, {"Block", "Function"}}
In[2532]:= ProcFuncTypeQ["G"]
Out[2532]= {True, {"CompiledFunction"}}
In[2533]:= A[x_, y_] := x + y; A[x_] := x; ProcFuncTypeQ["A"]
Out[2533]= {True, {"Function", "Function"}}
In[2534]:= ProcFuncTypeQ["Art"]
Out[2534]= {True, {"PureFunction"}}
In[2535]:= ProcFuncTypeQ["Function[{x, y}, x+y]"]
Out[2535]= {True, "PureFunction"}
In[2536]:= ProcFuncTypeQ["Kr"]
Out[2536]= {True, {"ShortPureFunction"}}
In[2537]:= ProcFuncTypeQ["a+g+s*#&"]
Out[2537]= {True, "ShortPureFunction"}
In[2538]:= ProcFuncTypeQ["GS"]
Out[2538]= {True, {"Function"}}
In[2539]:= ProcFuncTypeQ["S"]
Out[2539]= {True, {"CompiledFunction"}}

In[2543]:= ShortPureFuncQ[x_] := PureFuncQ[ToExpression[If[StringQ[x], x,
ToString1[x]]]] && StringTake[StringTrim[ToString[If[StringQ[x], ToExpression[x],
ToString1[x]]]], {-1, -1}] == "&"

In[2544]:= Map[ShortPureFuncQ, {"a+g+s*#&", Kr, "Kr", a + g + s*# &}]
Out[2544]= {True, True, True, True}
In[2545]:= ProcFuncTypeQ["2016"]
Out[2545]= {False, "2016", "Expression"}
In[2546]:= ProcFuncTypeQ["While"]
Out[2546]= {False, "While", "System"}
```

Along with the **ProcFuncTypeQ** procedure the above fragment presents a simple and rather useful function, whose call **ShortPureFuncQ[*x*]** returns *True* if *x* determines a pure function in the short format, and *False* otherwise. In particular, this function is used by the procedure **ProcFuncTypeQ** too. In some appendices of both the applied, and system character which are connected with processing of procedures and functions the **ProcFuncTypeQ** procedure is a rather effective testing group tools.

The procedure call **ShortPureToFunction[*F, w, g*]** returns definition of a classical *F* function with heading and formal arguments with the main name *w*, at the same time converting a pure *g* function of short format into the function *F*, equivalent to the *g*. The fragment below represents source code of the procedure with typical examples of its application.

In[4588]:= ShortPureToFunction[F_ /; SymbolQ[F], w_ /; SymbolQ[w], g_ /; ShortPureFuncQ[g]]:=
Module[{a = ArgsPureFunc[g], b, c, n = 1}, b = Range3[w, Length[a]];
c = Range2[w, Length[a]]; c = Map[Rule[#, c[[n++]]] &, a];
c = ReplaceAll[ToExpression[StringReplace[ToString1[g], "&" -> ""]],
Map[Rule[ToExpression[#[[1]]], #[[2]]] &, c]];
Quiet[ToExpression[ToString1[F @@ b] <> ":=" <> ToString1[c]]]; Definition[F]]

In[4589]:= ShortPureToFunction[G, x, (a*#1 + #2*Sin[#1])/(c*#3 - #4*Cos[#3]) &]
Out[4589]= G[x1_, x2_, x3_, x4_] := (a*x1 + x2*Sin[x1])/(c*x3 - x4*Cos[x3])
In[4590]:= G[Pi/2, 1, 0, 1]
Out[4590]= -1 - (a*π)/2
In[4591]:= S=ToExpression[ToString1[Plus[Sequences[Map[#^3 &, Range2[#, 6]]]]] <> "&"];
In[4592]:= ShortPureToFunction[gs, t, S]
Out[4592]= gs[t1_, t2_, t3_, t4_, t5_, t6_] := t1^3 + t2^3 + t3^3 + t4^3 + t5^3 + t6^3

While the procedure call **ClassicFuncToPure[*x*]** returns result of converting of a *x* function of classical format with heading into pure function of short format. At the same time, if the heading of the *x* function contains tests for admissibility of formal arguments, then function call returns $Failed. The function call returns *x* if *x* defines the pure function *(including a pure function of short format)*; in addition, in case of *x* argument of other types the function call is returned unevaluated. The following fragment presents source code of the procedure with typical examples of its application.

In[4661]:= ClassicFuncToPure[x_ /; FunctionQ[x]] := Module[{a, b, c},
If[PureFuncQ[x], x, ClearAll[c]; a = ArgsBFM2[x, c]; a = Map[StringTrim[#, "_"] &, a];
a = If[Complement[Map[#[[2]] &, c], {"Arbitrary"}] != {}, $Failed,
b = Map[ToString, Range2["#", Length[a]]]; b = Map[ToExpressionRule, GenRules[a, b]];
ToExpression[ToString1[ReplaceAll[ToExpression[ProcBody[x]], b]] <> "&"]]]]
In[4662]:= H1[x_ /; IntegerQ[x], y_, z_Integer, t_, h_] := (a*x + Cos[b*y])*z/h^t;
In[4663]:= ClassicFuncToPure[H1]
Out[4663]= $Failed
In[4664]:= H[x_, y_, z_, t_, h_] := (a*x + Cos[b*y])*z/h^t;
In[4665]:= ClassicFuncToPure[H]
Out[4665]= ((Cos[b*#2] + a*#1)*#3)/#5^#4 &
In[4666]:= ClassicFuncToPure[Function[{x, y, z}, (x + y)*z]]
Out[4666]= Function[{x, y, z}, (x + y)*z]

For identification of functional objects *(traditional and pure functions)* in the *Mathematica* system exist quite limited means which are based only on the calls of the system functions **Part[*x*, 0]** and **Head[*x*]** that return the headings of a *x* expression; at that, on pure functions the *Function* is returned, whereas on the traditional functions the *Symbol* is returned as a simple enough fragment enough visually illustrates, namely:

In[2905]:= G[x_Integer, y_Real, z_Real] := x*y^2 + z

In[2906]:= **Map[Head, {#1*#2*#3 &, Function[{x, y, z}, x + y*z], G, ProcQ}]**
Out[2906]= {Function, Function, Symbol, Symbol}
In[2907]:= **Mapp[Part, {#1*#2*#3 &, Function[{x, y, z}, x*y*z], G, ProcQ}, 0]**
Out[2907]= {Function, Function, Symbol, Symbol}
In[2908]:= **Map[PureFuncQ, {#1*#2 &, Function[{x, y, z}, x*y*z], G, ProcQ}]**
Out[2908]= {True, True, False, False}
In[2909]:= **Map[QFunction, {#1*#2 &, Function[{x, y, z}, x/y*z], G, ProcQ}]**
Out[2909]= {True, True, True, False}
In[2910]:= **Map[FunctionQ, {#1*#2 &, Function[{x, y, z}, x*y*z], G, ProcQ}]**
Out[2910]= {True, True, True, False}
In[2911]:= **{m, n} = {#1 + #2*#3 &, Function[{x, y}, x*y]}; Map[Head, {m, n}]**
Out[2911]= {Function, Function}
In[2912]:= **{Mapp[Part, {m, n}, 0], Map[QFunction, {m, n}]}**
Out[2912]= {{Function, Function}, {True, True}}
In[2913]:= **{Map[FunctionQ, {m, n}], Map[PureFuncQ, {m, n}]}**
Out[2913]= {{True, True}, {True, True}}

In this context the **Head2** procedure seems as an useful enough tools that is a modification of the **Head1** procedure and that is based on the previous **ProcFuncTypeQ** procedure and the standard **Head** function. The procedure call **Head2[x]** returns the heading or the type of a certain x object, given in the string format. In principle, the *type* of an object may fully be considered as a *heading* in its broad understanding. The **Head2** procedure serves to such problem generalizing the standard **Head** function and returning the heading of an arbitraty x expression in the context of {*Block, CompiledFunction, Function, Module, PureFunction, ShortPureFunction, Symbol, System,* **Head[x]**}. The examples of application of both means on the same list of the tested objects that in a number of cases confirm a preference of the **Head2** procedure are given as a comparison. The following fragment presents source code of the **Head2** procedure and the most typical examples of its use. While the **Head3** function presented here expands the system function **Head** along with our procedures **Head1, Head2** upon condition, that the tested x expression is considered apart from the sign; distinction is visually illustrated by results of the call of these means on the identical actual arguments. In general, the function call **Head3[x]** is similar to the procedure call **Head1[x]**.

In[2651]:= **Head2[x_] := Module[{b, a = Quiet[Check[ProcFuncTypeQ[ToString[x]], {Head[x]}]]},**
If[SameQ[a[[-1]], "System"], "System", If[SameQ[a[[-1]], "Expression"], Head[x],
If[ListQ[a], b = a[[-1]]]]; If[Length[b] == 1, b[[1]], b]]]]

In[2652]:= **Map[Head2, {"#1 + #2*#3&", "Function[{x, y, z}, x + y*z]", "G", "ProcQ", "a + b", "{x, y, z}", "\"ransian\"", Avz, While}]**
Out[2652]= {"ShortPureFunction", "PureFunction", {"CompiledFunction", "Function"}, "Module", String, String, String, Symbol, "System"}
In[2653]:= **Map[Head2, {"V", "Art", "G", "ProcQ", "GS", "Sv", "S", "H", "Ag ", 59, 42.47, Kr}]**
Out[2653]= {"CompiledFunction", "PureFunction", {"CompiledFunction", "Function"}, "Module", "Function", {"CompiledFunction", "Module", "Function"}, "CompiledFunction", {"Block", "Function"}, String, Integer, Real, "ShortPureFunction"}
In[2654]:= **Map[Head, {V, Art, G, ProcQ, GS, Sv, S, H, Agn, 590, 42.47, Kr}]**

Out[2654]= {CompiledFunction, Function, CompiledFunction, Symbol, Symbol, CompiledFunction, CompiledFunction, Symbol, Symbol, Integer, Real, Function}

In[2655]:= Head3[x_] := If[Part[x, 1] === -1, Head1[-1*x], Head1[x]]]

In[2656]:= {Head[Sin[-a + b]], Head2[Sin[-a + b]], Head3[Sin[-a + b]]}
Out[2656]= {Times, Times, Sin}

At last, quite natural interest represents the question of existence of the user procedures and functions activated in the current session. Solution of the question can be received by means of the procedure whose call **ActBFMuserQ[]** returns *True* if such objects exist in the current session, and *False* otherwise; meanwhile, the call **ActBFMuserQ[x]** thru optional *x* argument – an undefinite variable – returns the 2-element nested list whose the first element contains name of the user object in the string format while the second defines list of its types in string format respectively. The fragment below represents source code of the **ActBFMuserQ** with examples of its application.

In[2570]:= ActBFMuserQ[x___ /; If[{x} == {}, True, If[Length[{x}] == 1 && ! HowAct[x], True, False]]] := Module[{b = {}, c = 1, d, h, a = Select[Names["`*"],
! UnevaluatedQ[Definition2, #] &]},
For[c, c <= Length[a], c++, h = Quiet[ProcFuncTypeQ[a[[c]]]];
If[h[[1]], AppendTo[b, {a[[c]], h[[-1]]}], Null]];
If[b == {}, False, If[{x} != {}, x = ReduceLists[b]]; True]]

In[2571]:= V := Compile[{{x, _Real}, {y, _Real}}, (x^3 + y)^2];
Art := Function[{x, y}, x*Sin[y]]; Kr := (#1^2 + #2^4) &;
GS[x_ /; IntegerQ[x], y_ /; IntegerQ[y]] := Sin[90] + Cos[42];
G = Compile[{{x, _Integer}, {y, _Real}}, x*y]; P[x_, y_] := Module[{}, x*y]
H[x_] := Block[{}, x]; H[x_, y_] := x + y; SetAttributes["H", Protected]
P[x_] := Module[{}, x]; P[y_] := Module[{}, y];
P[x__] := Plus[Sequences[{x}]]; P[x___] := Plus[Sequences[{x}]];
P[y_ /; PrimeQ[y]] := Module[{a = "Agn"}, y]; T42[x_, y_, z_] := x*y*z
P[x_ /; StringQ[x]] := Module[{}, x]; P[x_ /; ListQ[x]] := Module[{}, x];
R[x_] := Module[{a = 590}, x*a]; GSV := (#1^2 + #2^4 + #3^6) &

In[2572]:= ActBFMuserQ[]
Out[2572]= True

In[2573]:= {ActBFMuserQ[t75], t75}
Out[2573]= {True, {{"Art", {"PureFunction"}}, {"G", {"CompiledFunction"}}, {"GS", {"Function"}}, {"H", {"Block", "Function"}}, {"P1", {"Function"}}, {"W", {"Function"}}, {"R", {"Module"}}, {"Kr", "ShortPureFunction"}, {"V", {"CompiledFunction"}}, {"P", {"Module", "Module", "Module", "Module", "Module", "Function", "Function"}, {"T42", {"Function"}}, {"GSV", "ShortPureFunction"}}}}

In addition, the given procedure along with the standard tools uses and our means such as **Definition2, HowAct, ProcFuncTypeQ, UnevaluatedQ** that are considered in the present book and in books [28-33,50]. The procedure is represented as a rather useful means, first of all, in the system programming. A number of some means of our *MathToolBox* package [48] use this procedure.

6.4. Headings of the user procedures and functions in the *Mathematica*

In many contexts, it is not necessary to know the exact value of an arbitrary expression; it suffices to know that the given expression belongs to a certain broad class, or a group, of expressions which share some common properties. These classes or groups are known as *types*. If *T* represents a type, then an expression is of *T* type if it belongs to the class that *T* presents. For example, an expression is said to be of the type *Integer* if it belongs to definite class of expressions denoted by the name *Integer*, that is the set of integers. Many functions and procedures use types to direct the flow of control in algorithms or to decide whether an expression is a valid input. For example, the behavior of a function or procedure, generally, depends on the types of its actual arguments. At that, the result of a number of operations is determined by type of their arguments. The *type* – the fundamental concept of the theory of programming, defining an admissible set of values or operations that can be applied to such values and, perhaps, a way of realization of values storage and performance of operations.

Any objects with which the programs operate, belong to certain types. The concept of data type in programming languages of high level appeared as an absolutely natural reflection of that fact that the data and expressions which are processed by a program can have various sets of admissible values, be stored in *RAM* of the computer in different ways, they can be processed by different commands of the processor. In addition, the type of any object can be determined in two ways, namely: by a set of all values belonging to this type, or by a certain predicate function defining object belonging to this type. Advantages from use of types of objects are reduced to three highlights: *(1)* protection against errors of assignment, incorrect operations along with inadmissible factual arguments passed to a procedure or function; *(2)* the standardization provided by agreements on the types supported by the majority of the programming systems, *(3)* documenting of software in many respects becomes simpler with use of the standard typification of objects and data used in them. In the modern languages of programming are used several systems of typification a brief characteristic of which can be found in [33,50] while more in detail it is possible to familiarize with them in a number of the books on modern programming systems. Considering the importance of typification of language objects, this aspect is considered by us also and concerning *Mathematica* in books [28-33]. In particular, in our book [30] rather in details from point of view of development of the mechanism of typification both the *Mathematica*, and the *Maple* systems are considered as computer mathematics systems which are the most developed and popular for today.

Unlike *209* types, for example, of the *Maple 11* which are tested by the *type* procedure *(apart from considerable enough set of the user types connected to the Maple by means of our library* [47])*, the *Mathematica 9* has only *60* testing *Q*–functions whose names have the form *NameQ*, for example, the call **SyntaxQ[x]** returns *True* if the contents of *x* string is correct *Mathematica* expression, and *False* otherwise. To some extent to this function the **ToExpression** function adjoins which evaluates all expressions which are in the argument of the string format with returning *Null*. By results of their performance these functions can be considered as testing means of correctness of the expressions which are in a string. In addition, if in the first case we receive value {*True, False*}, in the 2nd case the *correctness* can be associated with returning *Null*. In this connection the **ToExpression** function to a certain extent is similar to the `parse` procedure of the *Maple* system [10,14-16,27]. If necessary, the user can create own functions with names of the form *NameQ* that will significantly expand the range of similar standard system means.

In addition to the standard **ToExpression** function in some cases its simple modification is an quite certain interest, namely. Like the standard **ToExpression** function the function call **ToExpression1[*x*]** returns the expression obtained by interpreting strings or boxes as *Math* language input on condition that double substrings contained in an initial string expression *x* are previously converted to the usual strings. The fragment below represents source code of the **ToExpression1** function along with examples of its application.

In[4482]:= ToExpression1[x_ /; StringQ[x]] := ToExpression[StringReplace[x, "\"" -> ""]]

In[4483]:= ToExpression["{a, \"b\", c, d, \"g\", m, \"a + b\"}"]
Out[4483]= {a, "b", c, d, "g", m, "a + b"}
In[4484]:= ToExpression1["{a, \"b\", c, d, \"g\", m, \"a + b\"}"]
Out[4484]= {a, b, c, d, g, m, a + b}
In[4485]:= ToExpression1[StrStr["{a, b, c, d}"]]
Out[4485]= {a, b, c, d}

Below, this question largely is detailed on specific examples of such means.

Coding of definitions of types directly in the headings of procedures/functions takes place only for the *Mathematica* system, allowing in the point of call of a procedure or a function without its execution and without appeal to external tools to execute testing on the subject of admissibility of factual arguments received by the procedure or function. Such approach increases efficiency of execution of procedure or function, doing it by the more mobile. This approach is especially convenient in the case where the type posesses the highly specialized character or its definition is described by small and a rather clear program code. Indeed, in a number of cases the inclusion of definitions of the testing means directly into headings is very conveniently. So, this approach is used rather widely in means from the *MathToolBox* package [48]. In general, this approach allows to typify quite in details in many important applied data; its essence rather visually illustrates the following simple fragment, namely:

In[2524]:= ArtKr[x_ /; {T[z_] := If[z <= 90 && z >= 8, True, False], T[x]}[[2]],
y_ /; StringQ[y] && ! SuffPref[y, {"avz", "agn", "vsv"}, 1]] :=
Module[{a = 74, b = 69}, y <> " = " <> ToString[x + a + b]]
In[2525]:= {T[6], Map7[ArtKr, Sequences, {{74, "h"}, {42, "j"}, {50, "avagvs"}}], T[6]}
Out[2525]= {T[6], {"h = 217", "j = 185", "avagvs = 193"}, False}
In[2526]:= Definition[T]
Out[2526]= T[z_] := If[z <= 90 && z >= 8, True, False]

The example of the simple *ArtKr* procedure of the modular type an quite visually illustrates opportunities on the organization of the typified testing of factual arguments of procedure when definition of a *T* type is given directly in heading of the procedure and is activated at once after the 1st call of *ArtKr* procedure. One more interesting enough example of this kind has been represented above. One more interesting enough example of the similar kind has been represented above. Many of means of the *MathToolBox* package use similar approach in own organization [48] *(see books and software in our collection [50])*. On the assumption of the general definition of a procedure, in particular, of modular type

$$M[x\_/; Test_x, y\_/; Test_y, ...] := \text{Module}[\{Locals\}, Procedure\ body]$$

and of that fact that concrete definition of the procedure is identified not by its *name*, but its *heading* we will consider a set of useful enough tools that provide the various manipulations with the headings of procedures and functions and play an important part in the procedural programming and, first of all, programming of problems of the system character.

Having defined such object rather useful in many appendices as the *heading* of a procedure or function in the form "*Name*[*List of formal arguments with the testing tools ascribed to them*]", quite naturally arises the question of the creation of means for a testing of objects regarding their relation to the `Heading` type. It is possible to represent the **HeadingQ** procedure as a such means whose source code with examples of its usage is represented by the following fragment. So, the procedure call **HeadingQ**[*x*] returns *True* if a *x* object, given in the string format, can be considered as a syntactically correct heading; otherwise *False* is returned; in case of an inadmissible *x* argument the procedure call **HeadingQ**[*x*] is returned *unevaluated*. The **HeadingQ** procedure is a rather essentially used in a series of means from the package *MathToolBox* [48,50].

```
In[3385]:= HeadingQ[x_ /; StringQ[x]] := Module[{a, b, c, k = 1, m = True, n = True},
If[StringTake[x, {-1, -1}] == "]" && StringCount[x, {"[", "]"}] == 2 &&
! StringFreeQ[StringReplace[x, " " -> ""], "[]"], Return[m],
If[! Quiet[StringFreeQ[RedSymbStr[x, "_", "_"], "[_]"]], Return[! m]]];
Quiet[Check[ToExpression[x], Return[False]]];
If[DeleteDuplicates[Map3[StringFreeQ, x, {"[", "]"}]] === {False},
c = StringPosition[x, "["][[1]][[2]];
If[c == 1, Return[False], a = StringTake[x, {c, -1}]], Return[False]];
b = StringPosition[a, "["][[1]][[1]]; c = StringPosition[a, "]"][[-1]][[1]];
a = "{" <> StringTake[a, {b + 1, c - 1}] <> "}"; a = Map[ToString, ToExpression[a]];
If[DeleteDuplicates[Mapp[StringFreeQ, a, "_"]] == {False}, Return[True]];
If[{c, a} == {2, {}}, Return[True], If[a == {} || StringTake[a[[1]], {1, 1}] == "_", Return[False],
For[k, k <= Length[a], k++, b = a[[k]];
If[StringReplace[b, "_" -> ""] != "" && StringTake[b, {-1, -1}] == "_" ||
! StringFreeQ[b, "_"] || ! StringFreeQ[b, "_:"] || ! StringFreeQ[b, "_."],
m = True, n = False]]]; m && n]]

In[3386]:= {HeadingQ["D[x_, y_ /; ListQ[y], z_: 75, h_]"], HeadingQ["D[x_, y_, z_: 75, h_]"],
HeadingQ["D[x_, y_ /; ListQ[y], z_: 75, _]"]}
Out[3386]= {True, True, True}
In[3387]= {HeadingQ["D[x_, y_ /; ListQ[y], z_: 7, h]"], HeadingQ["[x_, y_ /; ListQ[y], z: 7]"]}
Out[3387]= {False, False}
In[3388]:= {HeadingQ["g[]"], HeadingQ["t[x__]"], HeadingQ["p[x__]"], HeadingQ["h[_]"]}
Out[3388]= {True, True, True, False}
In[3389]:= {HeadingQ["D[_, x_]"], HeadingQ["Z[x_]"], HeadingQ["Q[x___]"]}
Out[3389]= {True, True, True}
In[3390]:= {HeadingQ["D[x_, y_ /; ListQ[y], z_: 7, h]"], HeadingQ["V[x_, y_ /; ListQ[y], z_.]"]}
Out[3390]= {False, True}
```

At that, the procedure along with standard tools uses and our means such as **RedSymbStr**, **Map3** and **Mapp** which are considered in the present book and in [28-33]. The procedure is presented as rather useful means, above all, in system programming, for example, at testing of objects types in definitions of the procedures and functions similarly to the means **Head1** and **Head2** that are considered in the present book too.

The following **HeadingQ1** procedure represents an useful enough expansion of the above **HeadingQ** procedure concerning its opportunity of testing of the headings relative to their correctness. The procedure call **HeadingQ1[x]** returns *True*, if the factual *x* argument, given in the string format, can be considered as a syntactically correct heading; otherwise *False* is returned. The following fragment represents source code of the **HeadingQ1** procedure with examples of its application.

In[2512]:= HeadingQ1[x_ /; StringQ[x]] :=
Module[{h = ToString[Unique["j"]], b, c = {}, d, k,
a = Quiet[StringTake[x, {Flatten[StringPosition[x, "[", 1]][[1]] + 1, -2}]]},
If[StringFreeQ[x, "["], False, b = StringSplit1[a, ","];
For[k = 1, k <= Length[b], k++, d = b[[k]];
AppendTo[c, If[StringFreeQ[d, "_"], False, If[MemberQ[ToString /@ {Complex, Integer, List, Rational, Real, String, Symbol},
StringTake[d, {Flatten[StringPosition[d, "_"]][[-1]] + 1, -1}]], True,
HeadingQ[h <> "[" <> d <> "]"]]]]]; If[AllTrue[c, TrueQ], True, False]]]

In[2513]:= Map[HeadingQ1, {"H[s_String, x_ /; StringQ[x], y_]", "T[x_, y_ /; ListQ[y], z_List]", "V[x_, y_ /; ListQ[y] && Length[L] == 90]", "E[x__, y_/; ListQ[y], z___]"}]
Out[2513]= {True, True, True, True}
In[2514]:= {Map[HeadingQ, {"H[s_Integer]", "G[n_Integer,L_List]", "G[n___Integer]"}],
Map[HeadingQ1, {"H[s_Integer]", "G[n_Integer, L_List]", "G[n___Integer]"}]}
Out[2514]= {{True, True, True}, {True, True, True}}

In addition to the system tools the **HeadingQ1** procedure uses procedure **StringSplit1** that represents an useful generalization of the system function **StringSplit**. It should be noted that regardless of the correct testing of an quite wide type of headings, meantime, the above **HeadingQ** procedure along with the **HeadingQ1** procedure is not comprehensive because of a number of features of syntactical control of the *Math*-language. The following example very visually illustrates that; from it follows, that the system testing tools perceive incorrect headings as correct expressions.

In[2567]:= ToExpression["W[x__/;_StringQ[x]]"]
Out[2567]= W[x__ /; _StringQ[x]]
In[2568]:= SyntaxQ["W[x__/;_StringQ[x]]"]
Out[2568]= True

At the same time two these procedures are rather useful in many cases.

Meanwhile, on the basis of **ArgsTypes** procedure designed for testing of formal arguments of a function or a procedure which has been activated in the current session perhaps further expansion of the testing opportunities of the **HeadingQ1,** allowing in some cases to expand types of the correctly tested headings of procedures/functions. At that, here it is possible to tell only about extension of opportunities at certain cases but not about extension as a whole. The following fragment represents source code of the **HeadingQ2** procedure along with the most typical examples of its application.

In[2942]:= **HeadingQ2[x_ /; StringQ[x]] := Module[{a, b, c, d = ToString[Unique["agn"]]}, {a, b} = Map[DeleteDuplicates, Map[Flatten, Map3[StringPosition, x, {"[", "]"}]]]; If[StringLength[x] == b[[-1]] && SymbolQ[c = StringTake[x, {1, a[[1]] - 1}]], Quiet[Check[ToExpression[StringReplace[x, c <> "[" -> d <> "[", 1] <> " := 72"], False]]; c = Map[SyntaxQ, ArgsTypes[d]]; ToExpression["Remove[" <> d <> "]"]; If[AllTrue[c, TrueQ], True, False], False]]**

In[2943]:= **Map8[HeadingQ1, HeadingQ2, {"V[x__/_String]"}]**
Out[2943]= {True, False}
In[2944]:= **Map8[HeadingQ1, HeadingQ2, {"V[x_/; StringQ[x]]"}]**
Out[2944]= {True, True}
In[2945]:= **Map[HeadingQ2, {"F[x_/; StringQ[x]]", "F[x/; StringQ[x]]", "F[x; StringQ[x]]", "F[x_/_ StringQ[x]]", "F[x_//; StringQ[x]]", "F[x_; y_; z_]"}]**
Out[2945]= {True, True, True, False, False, True}
In[2946]:= **Map[HeadingQ1, {"F[x_/; StringQ[x]]", "F[x/; StringQ[x]]", "F[x; StringQ[x]]", "F[x_/_ StringQ[x]]", "F[x_//; StringQ[x]]", "F[x_; y_; z_]"}]**
Out[2946]= {True, False, False, True, False, True}
In[2947]:= **Map[HeadingQ, {"F[x_/; StringQ[x]]", "F[x/; StringQ[x]]", "F[x; StringQ[x]]", "F[x_/_ StringQ[x]]", "F[x_//; StringQ[x]]", "F[x_; y_; z_]"}]**
Out[2947]= {True, False, False, True, False, True}
In[2948]:= **Map[#["F[x_/_ StringQ[x]]"] &, {HeadingQ, HeadingQ1}]**
Out[2948]= {True, True}
In[2949]:= **Map[#["F[x_/_ StringQ[x]]"] &, {HeadingQ2, HeadingQ3}]**
Out[2949]= {False, False}
In[2950]:= **Map[#["F[x_/_StringQ[x]]"] &, {HeadingQ, HeadingQ1}]**
Out[2950]= {True, True}
In[2951]:= **Map[#["F[x_/_StringQ[x]]"] &, {HeadingQ2, HeadingQ3}]**
Out[2951]= {False, False}

Analogously to the procedures **HeadingQ, HeadingQ1**, the procedure call **HeadingQ2[x]** returns *True* if actual *x* argument, set in string format, can be considered as a syntactically correct heading; otherwise *False* is returned. At that, the examples represented in the above fragment of applications of the procedures **HeadingQ, HeadingQ1** and **HeadingQ2** an quite visually illustrate distinctions between their functionality. At that, the group of these means includes also the **HeadingQ3** procedure which in the functional relation is equivalent to the **HeadingQ2** procedure; its call **HeadingQ3[x]** returns *True* if an actual *x* argument, set in the string format can be considered as a syntactically correct heading; otherwise the call returns *False*. At the same time, between pairs of the procedures {**HeadingQ[x], HeadingQ1[x]**} and {**HeadingQ2[x], HeadingQ3[x]**} principal distinctions exist.

In particular, on the headings {**F[x_/_StringQ[x]], F[x_ / _StringQ[x]**} the first pair returns *True* while the second pair returns *False* as a quite visually illustrates the above fragment. It is also necessary to note that the *1st* pair of testing functions is more high-speed what is very essential at their use in real programming. Meanwhile, considering similar and some other unlikely encoding formats of the headings of the functions and procedures, the presented 4 procedures **HeadingQ[x], HeadingQ1[x], HeadingQ2[x], HeadingQ3[x]** can be considered as rather useful testing tools in modular programming. At that, from experience of their use and their timecharacteristics it became clear that it is quite enough to be limited oneself only by procedures **HeadingQ[x]** and **HeadingQ1[x]** that cover a rather wide range of erroneous coding of headings. Furthermore, taking into account the mechanism of expressions parse for their correctness that the *Mathematica* system uses, creation of comprehensive means of testing of the headings is a rather difficult. Naturally, it is possible to use the non-standard receptions for receiving the testing means for the headings having a rather wide set of the deviations from the standard, but such outlay often do not pay off by the received benefits.

In particular, the possibilities of the **HeadingQ ÷ HeadingQ3** procedures are overlapped by opportunities of the procedure whose call **TestHeadingQ[x]** returns *True*, if a x represents the heading in string format of a block, module, function, and *False* otherwise. Whereas the procedure call **TestHeadingQ[x, y]** with the 2nd optional y argument – *an indefinite variable* – through it additionally returns information specifying the reasons of the incorrectness of a x *heading*. Meantime, on x objects of the same name *(multiple objects)* the procedure call returns *$Failed*; the extension of the procedure onto case of the multiple objects does not cause much difficulty. The fragment below represents source code of the **TestHeadingQ** procedure with the comparative examples of its application concerning the **HeadingQ ÷ HeadingQ3** means which say in favor of its preference for practical programming in the *Mathematica* system.

```
In[3212]:= TestHeadingQ[x_ /; StringQ[x], y___] :=
Module[{a, b, d = {}, h, c = Map[ToString, {Arbitrary, Complex, Integer, List, Rational,
Real, String, Symbol}], g = {}, f},
If[QmultiplePF[x], $Failed, f[t_] := If[{y} != {} && ! HowAct[y], y = t, Null];
b = Quiet[Check[Args[a, 90], $Failed]];
If[b === $Failed, f[h]; Remove[a]; False, b = Quiet[Check[ArgsTypes[a], $Failed]];
If[b === $Failed, f[h]; Remove[a]; False, b = If[! ListListQ[b], {b}, b];
Map[If[MemberQ[c, #[[2]]] || #[[2]] == "." || SuffPref[#[[2]], ":", 1] ||
StringMatchQ[#[[2]], X__ ~~ ":" ~~ Y__] || MemberQ[{True, False},
Quiet[Check[ToExpression[#[[2]]], $Failed]]], AppendTo[d, True], AppendTo[g, #]] &, b];
If[g == {}, f[{}]; True, f[g]; False]]]]]]
In[3213]:= {TestHeadingQ["Agn[a_,aa_.,t_/;mn,p_:0,y_List,z_ppp,u_v:W,
h___,g_/;SymbolQ[g]]", g69], g69}
Out[3213]= {False, {{"t", "mn"}, {"z", "ppp"}}}
In[3214]:= {HeadingQ["D[x_, y_/; ListQ[y], z_:5, h]"], HeadingQ["[x_, y_/; ListQ[y], z:5]"]}
Out[3214]= {False, False}
In[3215]:= {TestHeadingQ["D[x_, y_/;ListQ[y], j_:1, h]"], HeadingQ["[x_, y_/;ListQ[y], j:1]"]}
Out[3215]= {False, False}
In[3216]:= {HeadingQ["g[]"], HeadingQ["p[x__]"], HeadingQ["h[_]"]}
Out[3216]= {True, True, False}
In[3217]:= Map[TestHeadingQ, {"g[]", "p[x__]", "h[_]"}]
Out[3217]= {False, True, False}
In[3218]:= {HeadingQ["D[_, x_]"], HeadingQ["Q[x___]"]}
```

Out[3218]= {True, True}
In[3219]:= {TestHeadingQ["D[_, x_]"], TestHeadingQ["Q[x___]"]}
Out[3219]= {False, True}
In[3220]:= {HeadingQ["D[x_, y_/; ListQ[y], z_:5, h]"], HeadingQ["V[x_, y_/;ListQ[y], z_.]"]}
Out[3220]= {False, True}
In[3221]:= Map[HeadingQ1, {"H[s_String,x_/;StringQ[x],y_]", "T[x_,y_/;ListQ[y],z_List]", "V[x_, y_/; ListQ[y]&&Length[L] == 90]", "E[x__, y_/; ListQ[y], z___]"}]
Out[3221]= {True, True, True, True}
In[3222]:= Map[TestHeadingQ, {"H[s_String,x_/;StringQ[x],y_]", "T[x_,j_/;ListQ[j],z_List]", "V[x_, y_/; ListQ[y]&&Length[L] == 90]", "E[x__, y_/; ListQ[y], z___]"}]
Out[3222]= {True, True, True, True}
In[3223]:= {Map[TestHeadingQ, {"H[s_Integer]", "G[n_Integer,j_List]", "G[n___Integer]"}], Map[TestHeadingQ, {"H[s_Integer]", "G[n_Integer,L_List]", "G[n___Integer]"}]}
Out[3223]= {{True, True, True}, {True, True, True}}
In[3224]:= Map8[HeadingQ1, HeadingQ2, {"V[x__/_String]"}]
Out[3224]= {True, False}
In[3225]:= TestHeadingQ["V[x__/_String]"]
Out[3225]= False
In[3226]:= Map[HeadingQ2, {"F[x_/; StringQ[x]]", "F[x/; StringQ[x]]", "F[x; StringQ[x]]", "F[x_/_ StringQ[x]]", "F[x_//; StringQ[x]]", "F[x_; y_; z_]"}]
Out[3226]= {True, True, True, False, False, True}
In[3227]:= Map[TestHeadingQ, {"F[x_/; StringQ[x]]", "F[x/; StringQ[x]]", "F[x; StringQ[x]]", "F[x_/_ StringQ[x]]", "F[x_//; StringQ[x]]", "F[x_; y_; z_]"}]
Out[3227]= {True, False, False, False, False, False}
In[3228]:= Map[HeadingQ1, {"F[x_/; StringQ[x]]", "F[x/; StringQ[x]]", "F[x; StringQ[x]]", "F[x_/_ StringQ[x]]", "F[x_//; StringQ[x]]", "F[x_; y_; z_]"}]
Out[3228]= {True, False, False, True, False, True}
In[3229]:= Map[TestHeadingQ, {"F[x_/; StringQ[x]]", "F[x/; StringQ[x]]", "F[x; StringQ[x]]", "F[x_/_ StringQ[x]]", "F[x_//; StringQ[x]]", "F[x_; y_; z_]"}]
Out[3229]= {True, False, False, False, False, False}
In[3230]:= Map[#["F[x_/_StringQ[x]]"] &, {HeadingQ, HeadingQ1}]
Out[3230]= {True, True}
In[3231]:= TestHeadingQ["F[x_/_StringQ[x]]"]
Out[3231]= False
In[3232]:= Map[TestHeadingQ, {"G[x_y,/;z_]", "G[x___abc]", "G[x_ y_ z_]"}]
Out[3232]= {False, False, False}
In[3233]:= Map[HeadingQ, {"G[x_y,/;z_]", "G[x___abc]", "G[x_ y_ z_]"}]
Out[3233]= {False, True, True}
In[3234]:= Map[TestHeadingQ, {"d[x_;]", "d[x_:ab]", "d[x_:ab]", "d[x_a:b]", "d[x_;a]", "d[x_:ab]", "d[x:ab]", "d[a_b]", "d[x_/;mnp]", "d[x_;y_;b_]"}]
Out[3234]= {False, True, True, True, False, True, False, False, False, False}

In[3273]:= HeadName1[x_ /; StringQ[x]] := Module[{a},
If[! ExpressionQ[ToString[Unique["gs"]] <> x <> ":=74"], $Failed,
If[SuffPref[x, "]", 2] && ! SuffPref[x, "[", 1] &&

SymbolQ[a = StringTake[x, {1, Flatten[StringPosition[x, "["]][[1]] – 1}]], a, $Failed]]]

In[3274]:= HeadName1["Avz[x_, y_/; ListQ[y], z_:75, h_]"]

Out[3274]= "Avz"

In[3275]:= ExpressionQ["Avz[x_, y_/; ListQ[y], z_:75, h:]"]

Out[3275]= False

So, of the detailed analysis follows, that the **TestHeadingQ** procedure on the opportunities surpasses the above testing means of the same purpose. The previous fragment represents also the **HeadName1** procedure used by the **TestHeadingQ** procedure; the procedure call **HeadName1**[*x*] returns the name heading of a correct *x* heading, and *False* otherwise. This procedure has independent meaning too.

In the light of real correctness of the tuple of formal arguments which has been determined in section *6.1* and is caused by mutual accommodations of formal arguments in the context of the patterns {"_", "__", "___"} we can significantly generalize the above group **HeadingQ** ÷ **HeadingQ3** of the procedures intended for testing of correctness of headings of the user blocks, functions and modules, additionally using the above **CorrTupleArgs** procedure. For this purpose the **HeadingsUQ** procedure can be used. The procedure call **HeadingsUQ**[*x*] returns *True* if all components composing a *x* object in the context of the **Definition**[*x*] have correct headings, and *False* otherwise. While the call **HeadingsUQ**[*x*, *y*] in addition through the second optional argument – *an undefined y variable* – returns the list whose elements are or *True* if the heading of the appropriate component of a *x* object is correct, or the list whose first element determines incorrect heading of a component of the *x* object, while the second element defines of the component number with this heading concerning **Defition**[*x*]. The fragment below represents source code of the **HeadingsUQ** procedure with some examples of its application.

In[4280]:= HeadingsUQ[x_/; BlockFuncModQ[x], y___] :=
Module[{a = Flatten[{PureDefinition[x]}], b, c = {}, d = 0, gsv},
b = Map[ToString[Unique[gsv]] &, Range[1, Length[a]]];
gsv = Flatten[{Map[ToString1, HeadPF[x]]}]; Do[d++; If[d > Length[a], Break[],
ToExpression[StringReplace[a[[d]], ToString[x] <> "[" -> b[[d]] <> "[", 1]]];
AppendTo[c, If[CorrTupleArgs[b[[d]]] && HeadingQ1[HeadPF[b[[d]]]], True,
{gsv[[d]], d}]], Infinity]; Quiet[Remove["gsv"]];
If[{y} != {} && NullQ[y], y = ReduceLevelsList[c, 1], y = ReduceLevelsList[c, 1]];
And1[Map[TrueQ, c]]]

In[4281]:= Clear[s]; HeadingsUQ[ProcQ, s]

Out[4281]= True

In[4282]:= s

Out[4282]= {True}

In[4283]:= h[x_, y_] := x*y; h[x_Integer] := x^2; Clear[s]; HeadingsUQ[h, s]

Out[4283]= True

In[4284]:= s

Out[4284]= {True, True}

In[4285]:= gs[x_] := x^2; gs[x_, y__, z___] := x*y*z; gs[x_, y_, z___] := x*y*z;
gs[x_, y__, y__, z___] := x*y*z; gs[x_Integer] := x^3; gs[x_, y_, z_, t_] := x*y*z*t;

In[4286]:= **Clear[s]; HeadingsUQ[gs, s]**
Out[4286]= False
In[4287]:= **s**
Out[4287]= {True, True, True, True, {"gs[x_, y__, y__, z___]", 5}, {"gs[x_, y__, z___]", 6}}
In[4288]:= **Definition[gs]**
Out[4288]= gs[x_Integer] := x^3
gs[x_] := x^2
gs[x_, y_, z_, t_] := x*y*z*t
gs[x_, y_, z___] := x*y*z
gs[x_, y__, y__, z___] := x*y*z
gs[x_, y__, z___] := x*y*z

The **HeadingsUQ** procedure rather exhaustively tests the correctness of the headings of the blocks, functions and modules.

The following procedure serves as an useful enough means at manipulating with functions and procedures, its call **HeadPF[*x*]** returns heading in string format of a block, a module or a function with a *x* name activated in the current session, i.e. of the function in its traditional understanding with heading. Whereas on other values of the *x* argument the call is returned unevaluated. Meanwhile, the problem of definition of headings is actual also in a case of the objects of the above type of the same name which have more than one heading. In this case the procedure call **HeadPF[*w*]** returns the list of headings in string format of the subobjects composing a *w* object as a whole. The following fragment represents the source code of the **HeadPF** procedure along with the most typical examples of its application.

In[2942]:= **HeadPF[x_ /; BlockFuncModQ[x]] :=**
Module[{b, c = ToString[x], a = Select[Flatten[{PureDefinition[x]}],
! SuffPref[#, "Default[", 1] &]},
b = Map[StringTake[#, {1, Flatten[StringPosition[#, {" := ", " = "}]][[1]] – 1}] &, a];
If[Length[b] == 1, b[[1]], b]]

In[2943]:= **G[x_, y_] := x*Sin[y] + y*Cos[x]; s[] := 90*x; g := 590**
In[2944]:= **Map[HeadPF, {G, s, Sin, 2017, g}]**
Out[2944]= {"G[x_, y_]", "s[]", HeadPF[Sin], HeadPF[2017], HeadPF[590]}
In[2945]:= **Map[HeadPF, {If, Tan, Log, True, G, "Infinity", For, Do, ProcQ}]**
Out[2945]= {HeadPF[If], HeadPF[Tan], HeadPF[Log], HeadPF[True], "G[x_, y_]", HeadPF["Infinity"], HeadPF[For], HeadPF[Do], "ProcQ[x_]"}
In[2946]:= **M[x_ /; x == "avzagn"] := Module[{a}, a*x]; M[x_, y_, z_] := x*y*z;**
M[x_ /; IntegerQ[x], y_String] := Module[{a, b, c}, x]; M[x_String] := x;
M[x_, y_] := Module[{a, b, c}, "abc"; x + y]
In[2947]:= **HeadPF[M]**
Out[2947]= {"M[x_ /; x == \"avzagn\"]", "M[x_, y_, z_]", "M[x_ /; IntegerQ[x], y_String]", "M[x_String]", "M[x_, y_]"}

So, the call **HeadPF[*x*]** returns the heading in string format of an object with a *x* name of the type {*Block, Function, Module*} which has been activated in the current session. At that, for a *x* object which has several various headings, the procedure call **HeadPF[*x*]** returns the list of the headings whose order fully meets the order of the definitions returned by the function call **Definition[x]**. In this regard the testing of a *x* object regarding to be of the same name is enough actually; the **QmultiplePF** procedure solves the problem whose source code along with typical examples of its application the following fragment represents.

In[2780]:= **QmultiplePF[x_, y___] := Module[{a = Flatten[{PureDefinition[x]}]},**
If[MemberQ[{{"System"}, {$Failed}}, a] || Length[a] == 1, False,
If[{y} != {} && ! HowAct[y], y = If[Length[a] == 1, a[[1]], a]]; True]]

In[2781]:= M[x_ /; x == "avzagn"] := Module[{a, b, c}, x]; M[x_String] := x;
M[x_, y_, z_] := x*y*z; M[x_List, y_] := Block[{a}, Length[x] + y];
M[x_ /; IntegerQ[x], y_String] := Module[{a, b, c}, x];
M[x_, y_] := Module[{a, b, c}, "abc"; x + y];
In[2782]:= **QmultiplePF[M]**
Out[2782]= True
In[2783]:= **{QmultiplePF[M, s49], s49}**
Out[2783]= {True, {"M[x_ /; x == \"avzagn\"] := Module[{a, b, c}, x]", "M[x_String] := x",
"M[x_, y_, z_] := x*y*z", "M[x_List, y_] := Block[{a, b, c}, \"abc\"; Length[x] + y]",
"M[x_ /; IntegerQ[x], y_String] := Module[{a, b, c}, x]",
"M[x_, y_] := Module[{a, b, c}, \"abc\"; x + y]"}}
In[2784]:= **Map[QmultiplePF, {M, 590, Avz, Sin, If, a + b}]**
Out[2784]= {True, False, False, False, False, False}

The procedure call **QmultiplePF[x]** returns *True*, if *x* – an object of the same name *(Function, Block, Module)*, and *False* otherwise. Whereas the procedure call **QmultiplePF[x, y]** with the second optional *y* argument – *an undefinite variable* – thru *y* returns the list of definitions of all subobjects with a *x* name. The **QmultiplePF** procedure realization significantly uses the earlier considered **PureDefinition** procedure, and also our **HowAct** function. In a number of cases the **QmultiplePF** procedure despite the relative simplicity is a convenient enough means at testing of objects of the specified types.

Here, it is necessary to make one essential remark concerning the means dealing with the *headings* of procedures and functions. The matter is that as it was shown earlier, the testing means ascribed to the formal arguments, as a rule, consist of the earlier determined testing functions or the reserved keywords defining the type, for example, *Integer*. While as a side effect the built–in *Math*-language allows to use the constructions containing definitions of the testing means, directly in the headings of procedures and functions. Certain interesting examples of that have been presented above. Meanwhile, despite of such opportunity, the programmed means are oriented, as a rule, on use for testing of admissibility of the factual arguments or the predefined means, or including the testing algorithms in the body of the procedures and functions. For this reason, the **HeadPF** procedure presented above in such cases can return incorrect results. While the **HeadPFU** procedure covers also such peculiar cases. The procedure call **HeadPFU[x]** correctly returns the heading in the string format of a block, a module or a function with a *x* name activated in the current session regardless of a way of definition of testing of factual arguments. The fragment below represents the source code of the **HeadPFU** procedure with examples of its application.

In[3845]:= **P[x_, y_ /; {IntOddQ[t_] := IntegerQ[t] && OddQ[t], IntOddQ[y]}[[-1]]] := x*y**
In[3846]:= **HeadPF[P]**

Out[3846]= "P[x_, y_ /; {IntOddQ[t_]"

In[3847]:= HeadPFU[x_/; BlockFuncModQ[x]] :=
Module[{a = Flatten[{PureDefinition[x]}], b = {}, c, g},
Do[c = Map[#[[1]] - 1 &, StringPosition[a[[j]], " := "]];
Do[If[SyntaxQ[Set[g, StringTake[a[[j]], {1, c[[k]]}]]], AppendTo[b, g]; Break[], Null],
{k, 1, Length[c]}], {j, 1, Length[a]}]; If[Length[b] == 1, b[[1]], b]]

In[3848]:= HeadPFU[P]
Out[3848]= "P[x_, y_ /; {IntOddQ[t_] := IntegerQ[t] && OddQ[t], IntOddQ[y]}[[-1]]]"

In[3849]:= HeadPFU[Args]
Out[3849]= "Args[P_, z___]"

At testing of objects often arises necessity of allotment among them of the system functions; this problem is solved by a simple function, whose the call **SystemQ**[x] returns *True* if object x is a system function, i.e. is determined by built-in language of the *Mathematica*, and *False* otherwise. The function very simply is defined *directly* on the basis of the standard functions **Definition, Names** and **ToString**. Whereas the function call **UserQ**[x] returns *True*, if the x object is the user object (*Block, Function, Module*) activated in the current session, and *False* otherwise. The following fragment represents source code of the both functions with typical examples of their application. In a lot of appendices these functions present an quite certain interest and, first of all, giving an opportunity enough effectively to categorize software.

In[2975]:= SystemQ[S_] := If[Off[Definition::ssle]; ! ToString[Definition[S]] === Null && MemberQ[Names["System`*"], ToString[S]], On[Definition::ssle]; True, On[Definition::ssle]; False]

In[2976]:= Map[SystemQ, {90, G, Sin, Do, While, False, ProcQ, a/b^2, M}]
Out[2976]= {False, False, True, True, True, True, False, False, False}

In[4025]:= UserQ[x_] := BlockFuncModQ[x] && ! SystemQ[x]

In[4026]:= Map[UserQ, {Sin, ProcQ, SubsInExpr, StringReplaceVars, Hold, Length}]
Out[4026]= {False, True, True, True, False, False}

Above all, the **SystemQ** function is often used in the *headings* of procedures and functions, testing the actual arguments for admissibility. Thus, in addition to the **SystemQ** function it makes sense to represent an useful enough function whose call **LangHoldFuncQ**[x] returns *True* if x – a basic function of *Math*-language, and *False* otherwise. At that, under the *basic* function is understood a system function with one of the attributes ascribed to it, namely: **HoldFirst, HoldAll** or **HoldRest**. The function is represented as a quite useful means in the case of necessity of more accurate differentiation of software. The next fragment represents source code of the **LangHoldFunc** function along with examples of its typical application.

In[2299]:= LangHoldFuncQ[x_] := If[SystemQ[x] && Intersection[Quiet[Check[Attributes[x], False]], {HoldAll, HoldFirst, HoldRest}] != {}, True, False]

In[2300]:= Map[LangHoldFuncQ, {If,Goto,Do,Sin,Rule,Break,While,Switch,Which,For}]
Out[2300]= {True, False, True, False, False, False, True, True, True, True}

For a number of problems of the system character the **LangHoldFuncQ** function allows to differentiate the set of all system functions of the built-in *Math*-language according to the specified feature.

Right there pertinently to note some more means linked with the **HeadPF** procedure. So, the **Headings** procedure – an useful enough expansion of the **HeadPF** procedure in the case of blocks, functions and modules of the same name but with the different headings. Generally, the call **Headings[x]** returns the nested list whose elements are the sublists which determine respectively headings of subobjects composing a *x* object; the first elements of such sublists defines the types of subobjects, whereas others define the headings corresponding to them. The fragment below represents source code of the **Headings** procedure along with the most typical examples of its application.

In[2385]:= Headings[x_ /; BlockFuncModQ[x]] :=
Module[{n, d, h, p, t, k = 1, c = {{"Block"}, {"Function"}, {"Module"}},
a = Flatten[{PureDefinition[x]}]},
While[k <= Length[a], d = a[[k]]; n = ToString[Unique["agn"]];
ToExpression[n <> d]; ClearAll[p]; h = HeadPF[t = n <> ToString[x]];
d = StringTake[h, {StringLength[n] + 1, -1}]; BlockFuncModQ[t, p];
If[p == "Block", AppendTo[c[[1]], d], If[p == "Function", AppendTo[c[[2]], d],
AppendTo[c[[3]], d]]];
ToExpression["Remove[" <> t <> "," <> n <> "]"]; k++];
c = Select[c, Length[#] > 1 &]; If[Length[c] == 1, c[[1]], c]]

In[2386]:= M[x_ /; SameQ[x, "avz"], y_] := Module[{a, b, c}, y];
M[x_, y_, z_] := x + y + z; L1[x_, y_] := Block[{a, b, c}, x + y];
M[x_ /; x == "avz"] := Module[{a, b, c}, x]; L[x_] := x;
M[x_ /; IntegerQ[x], y_String] := Module[{a, b, c}, x];
M[x_, y_] := Module[{a, b, c}, "agn"; x + y]; M[x_String] := x;
M[x_ /; ListQ[x], y_] := Block[{a, b, c}, "agn"; Length[x] + y]

In[2387]:= Headings[M]
Out[2387]= {{"Block", "M[x_ /; ListQ[x], y_]"}, {"Function", "M[x_, y_, z_]", "M[x_String]"}, {"Module", "M[x_ /; x === \"avz\", y_]", "M[x_ /; x == \"avz\"]", "M[x_ /; IntegerQ[x], y_String]", "M[x_, y_]"}}

In[2388]:= V1[x_] = x; Map[Headings, {L, L1, 590, Sin, agn, V1}]
Out[2388]= {{"Function", "L[x_]"}, {"Block", "L1[x_, y_]"}, Headings[590], Headings[Sin], Headings[agn], {"Function", "V1[x_]"}}

In[2389]:= G[x_] := x; Headings[G]
Out[2389]= {"Function", "G[x_]"}

In[2390]:= h = 590; P[x_] := Module[{a = 90, b = 590}, h = (a + b)*x; h^2]; {Headings[P], h}
Out[2390]= {{"Module", "P[x_]"}, 590}

On *x* arguments different from block, function or module, the procedure call **Headings[x]** is returned unevaluated. The tool is of interest, first of all, from the *programmer* standpoint. In a number of the appendices which use the procedural programming, the **Headings** is useful enough. At that, the given procedure along with standard tools uses and our means such as **BlockFuncModQ**, **PureDefinition** and **HeadPF** that are considered in the present book and in [28-33,50]. At that, examples of the previous fragment very visually illustrate structure of the results returned by the given procedure.

In a number of the appendices which widely use procedural programming, a rather useful is the **HeadingsPF** procedure that is an expansion of the previous procedure. Generally, the procedure call **HeadingsPF[]** returns the nested list, whose elements are sublists, defining respectively the headings of functions, blocks and modules, whose definitions have been evaluated in the current session; the first element of each such sublist determines an object type in the context of {*"Block", "Module", "Function"*} while the others define the headings corresponding to it. The procedure call returns simple list if any of sublists does not contain headings; in addition, if in the current session the evaluations of definitions of objects of the specified 3 types weren't made, the procedure call returns empty list. At that, the procedure call with any arguments is returned unevaluated. The following fragment represents source code of the **HeadingsPF** procedure along with examples of its typical application.

In[2913]:= **HeadingsPF[x___ /; SameQ[x, {}]] :=**
Module[{a = {}, d = {}, k = 1, b, c = {{"Block"}, {"Function"}, {"Module"}}, t},
Map[If[Quiet[Check[BlockFuncModQ[#], False]], AppendTo[a, #], Null] &, Names["`*"]];
b = Map[Headings[#] &, a]; While[k <= Length[b], t = b[[k]];
If[NestListQ[t], d = Join[d, t], AppendTo[d, t]]; k++];
Map[If[#[[1]] == "Block", c[[1]] = Join[c[[1]], #[[2 ;; -1]]],
If[#[[1]] == "Function", c[[2]] = Join[c[[2]], #[[2 ;; -1]]],
c[[3]] = Join[c[[3]], #[[2 ;; -1]]]]] &, d]; c = Select[c, Length[#] > 1&];
If[Length[c] == 1, c[[1]], c]]
In[2915]:= **M[x_ /; SameQ[x, "avz"], y_] := Module[{a, b, c}, y]; L1[x_] := x;**
M[x_, y_, z_] := x + y + z; L[x_, y_] := x + y; M[x_ /; x == "avz"] := Module[{a, b, c}, x];
M[x_ /; IntegerQ[x], y_String] := Module[{a, b, c}, x];
M[x_, y_] := Module[{a, b, c}, "agn"; x + y]; M[x_String] := x;
M[x_ /; ListQ[x], y_] := Block[{a, b, c}, "agn"; Length[x] + y];
F[x_ /; SameQ[x, "avz"], y_] := {x, y}; F[x_ /; x == "avz"] := x
In[2916]:= **HeadingsPF[]**
Out[2916]= {{"Block", "M[x_ /; ListQ[x], y_]"}, {"Function", "F[x_ /; x === \"avz\", y_]",
"F[x_ /; x == \"avz\"]", "L[x_, y_]", "L1[x_]", "M[x_, y_, z_]", "M[x_String]"},
{"Module", "M[x_ /; x === \"avz\", y_]", "M[x_, y_]", "M[x_ /; x == \"avz\"]",
"M[x_ /; IntegerQ[x], y_String]"}}
In[2917]:= **Restart[]**
In[2918]:= **HeadingsPF[]**
Out[2918]= {}
In[2919]:= **V[x_, y_] := x*y; F[x_String] := x <>"avz"; G[x_] := x^2; L[y_] := y**
In[2920]:= **HeadingsPF[]**
Out[2920]= {"Function", "F[x_String]", "G[x_]", "L[y_]", "V[x_, y_]"}

In addition, the given procedure along with the standard means uses and our tools such as **BlockFuncModQ, Headings** and **NestListQ** that are considered in the present book and in [28-33]. The examples of the previous fragment enough visually illustrate structure of the results returned by the procedure. However, it must be kept in mind, that performance of the procedure directly depends on a state of the current session when the **HeadingsPF** has been called and how many definitions of the user tools of the type {*Function, Module, Block*} were evaluated in the *Mathematica* current session.

In certain problems of processing of the headings at times arises the question of evaluation of the name of a heading whose decision a simple enough function gives; the function call **HeadName[x]** returns the name of *x* heading in string format but provided that the heading is distinguished by procedure **HeadingQ** or **HeadingQ1** as a syntactically correct heading, i.e. the call **HeadingQ[x]** or **HeadingQ1[x]** returns *True*; otherwise, the call **HeadName[x]** will be returned unevaluated. The next fragment represents source code of the **HeadName** function along with typical examples of its application.

In[2645]:= **HeadName[x_ /; HeadingQ[x] || HeadingQ1[x]] :=**
StringTake[x, {1, StringPosition[x, "[", 1][[1]][[1]] - 1}]

In[2646]:= **Map[HeadName, {"V[x_/; StringQ[x]]", "G[x_String]", "S[x_/; IntegerQ[x]]",**
"Kr[x_/; StringQ[x], y__]", "Art[]"}]
Out[2646]= {"V", "G", "S", "Kr", "Art"}

In[2647]:= **Map[HeadName, {"V[j_; StringQ[j]]", "S[j/; IntegerQ[j]]"}]**
Out[2647]= {HeadName["V[j_; StringQ[j]]"], HeadName["S[j/; IntegerQ[j]]"]}

In some cases of procedural programming, for example, in a case of necessity of insertion of calls of procedures/functions on the basis of their headings in structures of the string type, the **HeadToCall** procedure is represented as a quite useful tool, whose call **HeadToCall[w]** in string format returns the call of a procedure or a function on the basis of its heading on `pure` formal arguments (i.e. without the testing for an admissibility ascribed to them), where *w* – admissible heading of a procedure or a function. The following fragment represents source code of the **HeadToCall** procedure along with examples of its application.

In[2511]:= **HeadToCall[j_ /; HeadingQ[j]] := Module[{a = HeadName[j], b},**
b = "{" <> StringTake[StringReplace[j, a <> "[" -> "", 1], {1, -2}] <> "}";
b = Select[StrToList[b], ! StringFreeQ[#, "_"] &];
b = Map[StringTake[#, {1, Flatten[StringPosition[#, "_"]][[1]] - 1}] &, b];
a <> "[" <> StringTake[ToString[b], {2, -2}] <> "]"]

In[2512]:= **HeadToCall["G[x_, y_/; StringQ[y], z_/; MemberQ[{0, 1, 2}, z], t_Symbol, h_/;**
IntegerQ[h], z__, p___]"]
Out[2512]= "G[x, y, z, t, h, z, p]"

In[2513]:= **HeadToCall["V[x_List, y_/; PrimeQ[y] && y < 590, z_/; ! HowAct[z],**
t_Integer, z__, p___]"]
Out[2513]= "V[x, y, z, t, z, p]"

At that, it must be kept in mind that the procedure call returns also optional arguments of the studied heading.

In the light of possibility of existence in the current *Mathematica* session of the procedures and functions of the same name with different headings the problem of removal from the session of an object with the concrete heading represents a certain interest; this problem is solved by the procedure **RemProcOnHead**, whose source code along with examples of its application are represented below.

In[2437]:= **RemProcOnHead[x_ /; HeadingQ[x] || HeadingQ1[x] || ListQ[x] &&**
AllTrue[Map[HeadingQ[#] &, x], TrueQ]] :=
Module[{b, c, d, p, a = HeadName[If[ListQ[x], x[[1]], x]]},
If[! MemberQ[Names["`*"] || ! HowAct[a], a], $Failed, b = Definition2[a];
c = b[[1 ;; -2]]; d = b[[-1]];
ToExpression["ClearAttributes[" <> a <> "," <> ToString[d] <> "]"];
y = Map[StandHead, Flatten[{x}]]; p = Select[c, ! SuffPref[#, x, 1] &];
ToExpression["Clear[" <> a <> "]"]; If[p == {}, "Done", ToExpression[p];
ToExpression["SetAttributes[" <> a <> "," <> ToString[d] <> "]"]; "Done"]]]

In[2438]:= **M[x_ /; SameQ[x, "avz"], y_] := Module[{a, b, c}, y]; L1[x_] := x;**
M[x_, y_, z_] := x + y + z; L[x_, y_] := x + y;
M[x_ /; x == "avz"] := Module[{a, b, c}, x];
M[x_ /; IntegerQ[x], y_String] := Module[{a, b, c}, x];
M[x_, y_] := Module[{a, b, c}, "agn"; x + y]; M[x_String] := x;
M[x_ /; ListQ[x], y_] := Block[{a, b, c}, "agn"; Length[x] + y];
F[x_ /; SameQ[x, "avz"], y_] := {x, y}; F[x_ /; x == "avz"] := x

In[2439]:= **Definition[M]**
Out[2439]= M[x_ /; x === "avz", y_] := Module[{a, b, c}, y]
M[x_, y_, z_] := x + y + z
M[x_ /; x == "avz"] := Module[{a, b, c}, x]
M[x_ /; IntegerQ[x], y_String] := Module[{a, b, c}, x]
M[x_ /; ListQ[x], y_] := Block[{a, b, c}, "agn"; Length[x] + y]
M[x_, y_] := Module[{a, b, c}, "agn"; x + y]
M[x_String] := x

In[2440]:= **RemProcOnHead[{"M[x_,y_,z_]", "M[x_ /;ListQ[x],y_]"}]**
Out[2440]= "Done"

In[2441]:= **Definition[M]**
Out[2441]= M[x_ /; x === "avz", y_] := Module[{a, b, c}, y]
M[x_ /; x == "avz"] := Module[{a, b, c}, x]
M[x_ /; IntegerQ[x], y_String] := Module[{a, b, c}, x]
M[x_, y_] := Module[{a, b, c}, "agn"; x + y]
M[x_String] := x

In[2530]:= **G[x_, y_ /; IntegerQ[y]] := x + y**
In[2531]:= **RemProcOnHead["G[x_,y_/;IntegerQ[y]]"]**
Out[2531]= "Done"
In[2532]:= **Definition[G]**
Out[2532]= Null
In[2533]:= **Definition[F]**
F[x_ /; x === "avz", y_] := {x, y}
F[x_ /; x == "avz"] := x
In[2534]:= **RemProcOnHead["F[x_ /;x==\"avz\"]"]**
Out[2534]= "Done"
In[2535]:= **Definition[F]**
Out[2535]= F[x_ /; x === "avz", y_] := {x, y}

In[2541]:= V[x_] := Module[{}, x^6]; V[x_Integer] := x^2; Definition[V]
Out[2541]= V[x_Integer] := x^2
V[x_] := Module[{}, x^6]
In[2542]:= {RemProcOnHead["V[x_Integer]"], RemProcOnHead["V[x_]"]}
Out[2542]= {"Done", "Done"}
In[2543]:= Definition[V]
Out[2543]= Null
In[2544]:= Map[RemProcOnHead, {"L[x_, y_]", "L1[x_]"}]
Out[2544]= {"Done", "Done"}
In[2545]:= {Definition[L1], Definition[L]}
Out[2545]= {Null, Null}

In[2508]:= StandHead[x_ /; HeadingQ[x] || HeadingQ1[x]] :=
Module[{a = HeadName[x], b}, b = StringReplace[x, a <> "[" -> "", 1];
b = ToString1[ToExpression["{" <> StringTake[b, {1, -2}] <> "}"]];
a <> "[" <> StringTake[b, {2, -2}] <> "]"]

In[2509]:= StandHead["V[x_,y_Integer,z_/;StringQ[z]]"]
Out[2509]= "V[x_, y_Integer, z_ /; StringQ[z]]"
In[2510]:= StandHead["F[x_/;x===\"avz\",y_]"]
Out[2510]= "F[x_ /; x === \"avz\", y_]"

The successful call of the procedure **RemProcOnHead**[*x*] returns *"Done"*, having removed from the current session a procedure or a function or their list with heading or accordingly with list of the *x* headings that are given in the string format; in addition, on an inadmissible factual *x* argument the call returns $*Failed*, or is returned unevaluated. At the same time, the remaining subobjects with the name of a *x* object that have been processed by the procedure **RemProcOnHead** save and options, and attributes, except in case when *x* object is removed completely. At that, it is necessary to do two remarks, namely: *(1)* the tools of this fragment that are used as examples have only formally correct code, no more, and *(2)* heading in the procedure call **RemProcOnHead**[*x*] is encoded according to the format **ToString1**[*x*].

The previous fragment contains source code of the **RemProcOnHead** with examples of its usage along with control of the obtained results. It must be kept in mind that realization of algorithms of a number of the procedures which significantly use the headings requires the coding of headings in the format corresponding to the system agreements at evaluation of definitions of a procedure, function or block. For automation of representation of a heading in the standard format the **StandHead** procedure can be a rather useful whose source code along with examples of its use completes the previous fragment. So, the call **StandHead**[*h*] returns a *h* heading of block, procedure or function in the format which corresponds to the system agreements at evaluation of its definition.

So, if in the *Maple* system as identifier of a procedure or a function is its name, then in the *Mathematica* system an object heading performs this function, i.e. the construction of the kind "*Name*[*List of formal arguments*]" that it is necessary to consider at programming of the tools for processing of specified objects. Therefore, the **Names** function needs to be applied in the combination with the **Definition** function because the first returns only the names of procedures and functions and tells nothing about existence in the current session of the user procedures and/or functions of the same name with different headings as nice illustrates the following simple fragment, namely:

In[2620]:= G[x_] := Module[{a = 590}, x^2 + a];
G[x_ /; PrimeQ[x]] := Module[{a = 590}, x + a];
V[x_ /; ListQ[x]] := Module[{}, Length[x]]; V[x_] := Module[{}, x^2]
In[2621]:= Select[Names["`*"], ProcQ1[#] &]
Out[2621]= {"G", "V"}
In[2622]:= Definition[G]
Out[2622]= G[x_ /; PrimeQ[x]] := Module[{a = 590}, x + a]
G[x_] := Module[{a = 590}, x^2 + a]
In[2623]:= Definition[V]
Out[2623]= V[x_ /; ListQ[x]] := Module[{}, Length[x]]
V[x_] := Module[{}, x^2]

In[2624]:= MdP[x___] :=
Module[{b = {}, c, d, a = Select[Names["`*"], BlockFuncModQ[#] &]},
d = Flatten[Map[ToString, {x}]];
a = If[a == {}, {}, If[d == {}, a, If[MemberQ4[a, d], Intersection[a, d], {}]]];
If[a == {}, $Failed,
c = Map[AppendTo[b, {#, Length[Flatten[{PureDefinition[#]}]]}] &, a][[-1]];
If[Length[c] > 1, c, c[[1]]]]]

In[2625]:= MdP[]
Out[2625]= {{"G", 2}, {"V", 2}}
In[2626]:= MdP[G, V, H]
Out[2626]= {{"G", 2}, {"V", 2}}
In[2627]:= Clear[G, V]; MdP[]
Out[2627]= $Failed
In[2628]:= MdP[G1, V1, H]
Out[2628]= $Failed
In[3502]:= MdP[]
Out[3502]= {{"F", 2}, {"G", 2}, {"L", 1}, {"L1", 1}, {"M", 7}, {"V", 2}}

The previous fragment determines the procedure, whose call **MdP[x]** returns a simple two-element list, in which the *first* element – an object name in the string format and the second element – number of headings with such name *(if x defines procedure, function, block activated in the current session; in the absence of similar object $Failed is returned)*; the nested list whose 2-element sublists have the structure described above *(if a x object defines the list of the modules, functions or blocks activated in the current session)*, the nested list of the previous format *(if x is empty, defining the list of all functions, blocks or modules activated in the current session)*.

In the absence of the functions, modules and blocks activated in the current session the call **MdP** returns *$Failed*. At that, the procedure along with standard means uses and our means such as **BlockFuncModQ, PureDefinition, MemberQ4** which are considered in the present book and in books [28-33]. The examples of the previous fragment rather visually illustrate structure of the results returned by the **MdP** procedure.

As it was already noted, the current session may contain several different definitions of the procedure, function, block with the same name that differ only at the level of their headings. The procedure call **Definition2[*x*]** in an optimum format returns the list of all definitions in string format of a block, procedure or function with a *x* name, accompanying it with options and the list of attributes that are ascribed to *x* symbol. According to the system agreements the procedures, functions or blocks of the same name have the same ascribed options and attributes as illustrates the following fragment:

In[3389]:= G[x_, y_] := x^2*y^2
In[3390]:= Options[G] = {Art -> 27, Kr -> 20};
In[3391]:= SetOptions[G, Art -> 27, Kr -> 20]
Out[3391]= {Art -> 27, Kr -> 20}
In[3392]:= Definition2[G]
Out[3392]= {"G[x_, y_] := x^2*y^2", "Options[G] := {Art -> 27, Kr -> 20}", {}}
In[3393]:= G[x_] := x^2; G[x_, y_, z_] := x + y + z; SetAttributes[G, Protected]
In[3394]:= Definition2[G]
Out[3394]= {"G[x_, y_] := x^2*y^2", "G[x_] := x^2", "G[x_, y_, z_] := x + y + z",
"Options[G] := {Art -> 27, Kr -> 20}", {Protected}}

In[3395]:= DefOnHead[x_ /; HeadingQ[x]] := Module[{a, b, c, d,
h = Quiet[Check[RedSymbStr[StringReplace[StandHead[x], "," -> ", ", " ", " "], x]]},
a = HeadName[h]; b = Definition2[ToExpression[a]];
c = Select[b, SuffPref[#, Map3[StringJoin, h, {" := ", " = "}], 1] &];
d = Select[b, SuffPref[#, Quiet[Map3[StringJoin, "Options[" <> a <> "]", {" = ", " := "}]], 1] &];
If[MemberQ[b, "Undefined"], $Failed,
If[d == {}, AppendTo[c, b[[-1]]], Join[c, {d[[1]], b[[-1]]}]]]]

In[3396]:= DefOnHead["G[x_,y_,z_]"]
Out[3396]= {"G[x_, y_, z_] := x + y + z", "Options[G] := {Art -> 27, Kr -> 20}", {Protected}}
In[3397]:= DefOnHead["G[x_,y_]"]
Out[3397]= {"G[x_, y_] := x^2*y^2", "Options[G] := {Art -> 27, Kr -> 20}", {Protected}}
In[3398]:= DefOnHead["G[x_]"]
Out[3398]= {"G[x_] := x^2", "Options[G] := {Art -> 24, Kr -> 17}", {Protected}}

For receiving of definition of the procedure, function or block *x* with the given heading *(the main identifier)* a number of means one of which is represented by the previous fragment is created; more precisely the **DefOnHead** procedure whose call **DefOnHead[*j*]** returns the list whose the first element – definition in the string format of a procedure, function or block with the given *j* heading *(or list of definitions for the subobjects of the same name)* whereas other elements are options *(if they exist)* and list of attributes ascribed to the procedure, function or block *w*. At that, the following defining relation **HeadName[*j*]** = *w* takes place. As a whole, it is recommended to use a certain unique name for each definition, for providing of such possibility the system functions **Clear** and **ClearAll** can be used at modifications of means if their headings change.

Thus, at the call of a procedure, function or block from the list of definitions of its subobjects namely a definition with the heading corresponding to the actual arguments, i.e. which are admissible for the formal arguments with the ascribed tests for an admissibility is chozen.

Moreover, a heading of the format **G[x_, y_, ...]** has the minimum priority among headings of other formats irrespective of the evaluation order in the current session of the definitions of procedures, functions or blocks of the same name as visually illustrates the next a rather simple fragment, namely:

In[2863]:= **G[x_, y_] := StringJoin[x, y] <> "RansIan"**
In[2864]:= **G[x_Integer, y_Integer] := x + y**
In[2865]:= **G[x_String, y_Integer] := y*StringLength[x]; Definition2[G]**
Out[2865]= {"G[x_Integer, y_Integer] := x + y", "G[x_String, y_Integer] := y*StringLength[x]", "G[x_, y_] := StringJoin[StringJoin[x, y], \"RansIan\"]", {}}
In[2866]:= **{G[90, 500], G["AvzAgnVsvArtKr", 590]}**
Out[2866]= {590, 8260}
In[2867]:= **G["AvzAgnVsvArtKr", "Tallinn"]**
Out[2867]= "AvzAgnVsvArtKrTallinnRansIan"
In[2868]:= **G[x_, y__] := If[{y} == {}, x^2, {y} = {x}; x^2]; G[590]**
Out[2868]= 348100
In[2869]:= **G["90", "500"]**
Out[2869]= "90500RansIan"
In[2870]:= **ClearAll[G]**
In[2871]:= **G[x_] := x^2; G[x_, y_ /; ! HowAct[y] === Null] := {y = x, x^2}[[2]]**
In[2872]:= **Definition2[G]**
Out[2872]= {"G[x_] := x^2", "G[x_, y_ /; ! HowAct[y] === Null] := {y = x, x^2}[[2]]", {}}

Above, it was already noted that in the most cases is expedient to use only one definition of a procedure, a function or a block, that at times quite significantly simplifies its processing. Meanwhile, in certain cases is quite convenient the use of a number of functions, blocks or procedures of the same name, for example, for the purpose of simplification of their *program* realization. So, realization of the *G* function from undefinite number of formal arguments of the second part of the previous fragment can serve as an example. The definition of two *G* functions covering all cases of the *G* function in some cases allows to simplify its realization. In this example such *simplification* isn't so obvious since it only illustrates reception while in case of rather complex procedures that in the body have to execute processing of undefinite quantity of the received actual arguments such approach can be very effective.

As it was noted above, in generally, the user procedure, function and block can has both the ascribed attributes, and options. In addition, some of earlier considered means were based, mainly on the call of our **Definition2[x]** procedure returning the list whose the last element contains the list of attributes ascribed to a *x* symbol while the sublist **Definition2[x][[1 ;; –2]]** contains definitions of the procedure, function or block together with options if those exist. The next **PureDefinition** procedure solves the problem of receiving of pure definitions of a procedure, a function or a block without options and the ascribed attributes.

In[2826]:= **G[x_] := x; G[x_, y_ /; ! HowAct[y] === Null] := {y = x, x^2}[[2]]**
In[2827]:= **Options[G] = {Art -> 27, Kr -> 20}; SetOptions[G, Art -> 27, Kr -> 20]**
Out[2827]= {Art -> 27, Kr -> 20}
In[2828]:= **SetAttributes[G, {Listable, Protected}]; Definition2[G]**
Out[2828]= {"G[x_] := x", "G[x_, y_ /; !HowAct[y] === Null] := {y = x, x}[[2]]", "Options[G] := {Art -> 27, Kr -> 20}", {Listable, Protected}}

In[2834]:= PureDefinition[x_, t___] := Module[{b, c, d, h = ToString[x] <> " " /: Default[",
a = If[UnevaluatedQ[Definition2, x], $Failed, Quiet[Check[Definition2[x], $Failed]]]},
If[a === $Failed, Return[$Failed]]; b = a[[1 ;; -2]];
c = If[SuffPref[b[[-1]]], Map3[StringJoin, "Options[" <> ToString[x] <> "]", {" = ", " := "}], 1],
b[[1 ;; -2]], b]; If[{t} != {} && ! HowAct[t], d = MinusList[a, c];
t = Join[If[Length[d] > 1, d, Flatten[d]], Select[a, SuffPref[#, h, 1] &]]];
c = Select[c, ! SuffPref[#, h, 1] &];
c = Map[StringReplace[#, Context[x] <> ToString[x] <> "`" -> ""] &, c];
If[Length[c] == 1, c[[1]], c]]

In[2835]:= {PureDefinition[G, g70], g70}
Out[2835]= {{"G[x_] := x", "G[x_, y_ /; !HowAct[y] === Null] := {y = x, x}[[2]]"},
{"Options[G] := {Art -> 27, Kr -> 20}", {Listable, Protected}}}

The procedure call **PureDefinition[x]** returns definition in the string format or their list of a block, function or module *x* without options, ascribed attributes and values by default for formal arguments while the call **PureDefinition[x, t]** with the second optional *t* argument – *an undefinite variable* – thru it returns the list of the options, attributes and values by default attributed to a *x* symbol. In the case of inadmissible *x* argument the procedure call returns $Failed, including also a call on **Compile** functions. The previous fragment presents source code of the **PureDefinition** procedure with examples of its application. The **PureDefinition** procedure is an useful enough means in various processing of objects whose definitions are returned in the *optimized* format, i.e. without occurrences **Context[x] <> ToString[x] <> "`"**.

On the basis of the above **PureDefinition** procedure, an useful enough procedure can be programmed, whose call **DefSymbol[x]** where *x* – a symbol in the string format, generally returns the nested list whose elements have next formats {{"=" | ":="}, *Type*, *Body*} and/or {*Optimized definition*, *Type*}. The first element corresponds to a simple symbol, that defines assignment type, type of its value, and value in the string format accordingly, whereas the second element defines the optimized definition and type in string format accordingly for an object that composes many–valued definition of the *x* symbol different from the simple. The *"Block"*, *"Function"*, *"Module"*, *"others"* may be as a type of definition of such object; at that, *"Others"* can be finished by the subsequent development of the procedure. On a *x* argument different from a symbol the procedure call is returned unevaluated. The source code of the **DefSymbol** procedure with an example of its application is given below.

In[4247]:= DefSymbol[x_ /; StringQ[x] && SymbolQ[x]] :=
Module[{a, b, d = {}, p, g, h, z = {}},
If[SystemQ[x], "System", a = ToString[Unique[x]]; b = Flatten[{PureDefinition[x]}];
Do[If[PrefixQ[p = x <> Set[h, " = "], b[[j]]], AppendTo[d, {StringTrim[h],
{Head[g = ToExpression[StringReplace[b[[j]], p -> "", 1]]], g}}],
If[PrefixQ[p = x <> Set[h, " := "], b[[j]]], AppendTo[d, {StringTrim[h],
{Head[g = ToExpression[StringReplace[b[[j]], p -> "", 1]]], g}}], a = ToString[Unique[x]];
AppendTo[z, a]; ToExpression[StringReplace[b[[j]], x <> "[" -> a <> "[", 1]];
AppendTo[d, {b[[j]], If[FunctionQ[a], "Function", If[BlockQ[a], "Block", If[ModuleQ[a],
"Module", "Other"]]]}]]], {j, 1, Length[b]}];

Map[Remove, z]; d = Map[Flatten, d]; If[Length[d] == 1, d[[1]], d]]]

In[4248]:= G[x_] := x; G[x_, y_] := Module[{}, x^2]; G[x_String] := Block[{}, x <> "74"];
G = x + # &;

In[4249]:= DefSymbol["G"]

Out[4249]= {{"=", Function, x + #1 &}, {"G[x_String] := Block[{}, StringJoin[x, \"74\"]]", "Block"}, {"G[x_] := x", "Function"}, {"G[x_, y_] := Module[{}, x^2]", "Module"}}

The concept of the *Mathematica* allows existence of a few blocks, functions or procedures, of the same name that are identified by their headings but not names. Operating with these objects is supported by a number of the means represented in the present book, and in the *MathToolBox* package [48,50]. In this connection the **ExtrProcFunc** procedure represents a certain interest, whose call **ExtrProcFunc[*h*]** returns an unique name of the generated block, function or procedure which in the list of definitions has a *h* heading; otherwise, $Failed is returned. The **ExtrProcFunc** procedure is characteristic in that, leaves all *definitions* of *symbol* **HeadName[*h*]** without changes. At that, the returned object saves all options and attributes ascribed to the symbol **HeadName[*h*]**. The following fragment represents source code of the **ExtrProcFunc** procedure along with typical examples of its application.

In[2860]:= ExtrProcFunc[x_ /; HeadingQ[x]] :=
Module[{a = StandHead[x], c, d, b = HeadName[x], g, p},
If[! HowAct[b], $Failed, c = Definition2[ToExpression[b]];
If[c[[1]] === "Undefined", $Failed, d = Select[c, SuffPref[#, a <> " := ", 1] &];
c = ToString[Unique[b]]; If[d != {}, ToExpression[c <> d[[1]]]]; g = AttrOpts[b];
p = c <> b; Options[p] = g[[1]]; SetOptions[p, g[[1]]];
ToExpression["SetAttributes[" <> p <> "," <> ToString[g[[2]]] <> "]"];
Clear[c]; p, Clear[c]; $Failed]]]]

In[2861]:= H[x_] := x^2; H[x_, y_] := x + y; H[x_, y_, z_] := x + y + x; H[x_Integer] := x;
H[x_, y_Integer] := x + y; H[x_String] := x <> "Agn"; Options[H] = {Art -> 27, Kr -> 20};
SetOptions[H, {Art -> 27, Kr -> 20}]; SetAttributes[H, {Listable, Protected}]

In[2862]:= Definition2[H]
Out[2862]= {"H[x_Integer] := x", "H[x_String] := StringJoin[x, \"Agn\"]", "H[x_] := x^2", "H[x_, y_Integer] := x + y", "H[x_, y_] := x + y", "H[x_, y_, z_] := x + y + x", "Options[H] = {Art -> 27, Kr -> 20}", {Listable, Protected}}

In[2863]:= ExtrProcFunc["H[x_,y_,z_]"]
Out[2863]= "H81H"

In[2864]:= Definition["H81H"]
Out[2864]= Attributes[H81H] = {Listable, Protected}
H81H[x_, y_, z_] := x + y + x
Options[H81H] = {Art -> 27, Kr -> 20}

In[2865]:= ExtrProcFunc["H[x_,y_,z_String]"]
Out[2865]= $Failed

In[2866]:= ExtrProcFunc["H[x_String]"]
Out[2866]= "H11H"

In[2867]:= Definition["H11H"]
Out[2867]= Attributes[H11H] = {Listable, Protected}

H11H[x_String] := x <> "Agn"
Options[H11H] = {Art -> 27, Kr -> 20}
In[2868]:= **H11H["AvzAgnVsvArtKr"]**
Out[2868]= "AvzAgnVsvArtKrAgn"
In[2869]:= **H9H[42, 2016, 74]**
Out[2869]= 2100

In[3543]:= **AttrOpts[x_ /; BlockFuncModQ[x]] := Module[{b, c, d, a = Definition2[x]},**
b = a[[-1]]; c = Select[a, SuffPref[#, "Options[" <> ToString[x] <> "]", 1] &];
If[c == {}, d = c, d = StringSplit[c[[1]], " := "][[2]]]; {ToExpression[d], b}]
In[3544]:= **AttrOpts[H]**
Out[3544]= {{Art -> 27, Kr -> 20}, {Listable, Protected}}
In[3545]:= **Sv[x_, y_, z_] := x^2 + y^2 + z^2; AttrOpts[Sv]**
Out[3545]= {{}, {}}

At that, the procedure along with standard means uses and our means such as **HeadingQ**, **Definition2**, **HeadName**, **StandHand**, **SuffPref** and **AttrOpts** which are considered in the present book and in [28-33]. Moreover, the last **AttrOpts** procedure completes the previous fragment. The procedure call **AttrOpts[w]** returns the two-element nested list whose first element determines options whereas the second element determines the list of the attributes ascribed to a *w* symbol of type {*Block, Funcion, Module*}. On a *w* symbol without options and attributes ascribed to it, the procedure call **AttrOpts[w]** returns {{}, {}}. The examples of the previous fragment rather visually illustrate structures of the results which are returned by both the procedure **ExtrProcFunc**, and the **AttrOpts** procedure.

In addition, in definition of the **ExtrProcFunc** procedure one artificial reception essential in the practical programming has been used. So, direct application of our and standard means {**Attributes, ClearAllAttributes, SetAttributes**} for processing of attributes in the body of a procedure in certain cases doesn't give of the desired result hence it is necessary to use the special constructions the organization of which is a rather transparent and doesn't demand any special explanations. The reception presented in source code of **ExtrProcFunc** procedure from the previous fragment is used in some other means that are represented in the present book and in our *MathToolBox* package [48]. The **RemProcOnHead** procedure, considered above, also significantly uses the given reception.

The call **ActBFM[]** of the next rather simple function returns the list of names in the string format of the user blocks, functions and modules, whose definitions have been activated in the current session. The following fragment represents source code of the **ActBFM** function along with an example of its application.

In[2824]:= **ActBFM[] := Select[Sort[Names["Global`*"]], ! TemporaryQ[#] && BlockFuncModQ[#] &]**

In[2825]:= **ActBFM[]**
Out[2825]= {"Agn", "Avz", "B", "F", "G", "H", "H11H", "M", "Name", "Sv"}

The above **ActBFM** function has a number of interesting appendices at programming of the various problems above all of the system character. For example, **ActBFM** function plays a rather essential part at searching of the user objects, whose definitions have been evaluated in the current *Mathematica* session.

6.5. Formal arguments of procedures and functions; the tools of their processing in the *Mathematica* software

Having considered in the previous two sections the means of manipulation with definitions of blocks, functions or modules, and also their headings, we pass to consideration of means whose scope of interests includes a number of a rather important problems connected with manipulation by the formal arguments which compose headings of definitions of the user procedures and functions. In addition, these components are extremely important and their total absence in headings does not allow system in general to consider objects with similar headings as procedures or functions. In the previous section the means of processing of the headings of procedures, blocks or functions have been considered; of them the **HeadingQ1** procedure in the best way tests an arbitrary string as a heading what visually illustrates the following simple example:

In[2546]:= Map[HeadingQ1, {"G[]", "G[ ]", "G[   ]"}]
Out[2546]= {False, False, False}
In[2547]:= G[] := x; {FunctionQ[G], Clear[G]}[[1]]
Out[2547]= True
In[2548]:= G[x_ /; SameQ[{x}, {}]] := x; FunctionQ[G]
Out[2548]= True
In[2549]:= HeadingQ["G[x_ /; SameQ[{x}, {}]]"]
Out[2549]= True
In[2550]:= G[x___] := {x}; G[]
Out[2550]= {}
In[2551]:= {HeadingQ["G[x___]"], HeadingQ1["G[x___]"]}
Out[2551]= {True, True}

Of the represented example follows, that strings of the type "G[ ]" can't be considered as syntactic correct headings, and definitions on their basis can't be considered as procedures or functions. Meanwhile, in case of necessity to define procedures or functions whose calls make sense on the empty list of actual arguments, it is possible to code their headings as it is stated above; in this case our tools identify them properly. Further consideration of tools of manipulation with formal arguments of procedures, blocks and functions assumes short introduction into templates concept; in more detail this question is considered in usage on the system and, in particular, in the books [29-33].

Templates (patterns) are used in the *Mathematica* system for representation of the classes of expressions. Very simple example of a template is an expression *h[x_]* which represents a class of expressions of the type *h[any expression]*. As the prerequisite of introduction of the concept *"Template"* into the *Mathematica* the fact served, what many enough operations support work not only with separate expressions but also with templates representing the whole classes of expressions. So, in particular, it is possible to use the templates in rules of transformation for the indicating of that how properly to transform classes of expressions. The templates can be used for calculation of positions of all expressions in some class along with a number of other applications of the sufficiently developed templates mechanism.

The basic identifier that determines, practically, all templates in the *Mathematica* is the "_" symbol *(symbol of underlining)* that is being ascribed to some symbol on the right. In this case the *Mathematica* considers such symbol as any admissible expression used as its value. The call **Head**[*x*] of the earlier mentioned function on *x* pattern returns **Pattern** whereas the call **PatternQ**[*x*] of very simple function returns *True* if *x* – a template, and *False* otherwise:

In[2570]:= **PatternQ[x_] := If[Head[x] === Pattern, True, False]**
In[2571]:= **Map18[{PatternQ, Head}, {agn_, _, _a _, x_, _^_, avz__, __}]**
Out[2571]= {{True, False, False, True, False, True, False}, {Pattern, Blank, Times, Pattern, Power, Pattern, BlankSequence}}

In[2572]:= **Map18[x_ /; ListQ[x] && AllTrue[Map[SymbolQ[#] &, x], TrueQ], y_ /; ListQ[y]] := Map[Map[#, y] &, x]**
In[2573]:= **Map18[{X, Y, Z}, {a, b, c}]**
Out[2573]= {{X[a], X[b], X[c]}, {Y[a], Y[b], Y[c]}, {Z[a], Z[b], Z[c]}}

Along with the **PatternQ** function and comparative examples for it and the standard **Head** function the previous fragment represents the simple and useful **Map18** function in many appendices in addition to the represented means of the *Map*-group. The call **Map18**[*x, y*], where *x* – list {*x1, x2,...,xn*} of symbols and *y* – list {*y1, y2,...,yp*} of expressions, returns the nested list of the following format, namely:

{{*x1*[*y1*], *x1*[*y2*], ..., *x1*[*yp*]}, {*x2*[*y1*], *x2*[*y2*], ..., *x2*[*yp*]}, ..., {*xn*[*y1*], *xn*[*y2*], ..., *xn*[*yp*]}}

Result returned by the function call **Map18**[*x, y*] is transparent enough and doesn't demand of any special explanations. In principle, it is possible to place "_" symbol in any place of an expression, defining thus the pattern corresponding to some group of expressions received by replacement of this symbol by an arbitrary expression. Several simple enough examples of patterns are given below, namely:

h[*x_*] – *the heading of a block, a function or a procedure **h** with one formal x argument where x – an arbitrary expression;*

h[*x_, y_*] – *the heading of a block, function or procedure **h** with two formal arguments x, y where x, y – arbitrary expressions;*

h[*x_, x_*] – *the heading of a block, function or procedure **h** with two identical x arguments where x – an arbitrary expression;*

*x^n_* – *determines an arbitrary x expression in an arbitrary n degree;*
*x_^n_* – *determines an arbitrary x expression in an arbitrary n degree;*
*x_ + y_ + z_* – *determines the sum of three arbitrary expressions x, y and z;*
{*x_, y_, z_*} – *determines the list of three arbitrary expressions x, y and z;*
*90*x_^y_ + 500*x_*y_ + z_* – *determines an expression with five patterns.*

The *basic* patterns in the *Mathematica* system are the following three patterns, namely:

_ or **Blank[]** *(in the full form)* – *the pattern defining an arbitrary expression;*
_*t* or **Blank[*t*]** *(in the full form)* – *the pattern defining an arbitrary expression with a t heading;*
__ *(two symbols "_")* or **BlankSequence[]** *(in the full form)* – *the pattern determining an arbitrary expression or sequence of arbitrary expressions;*
__*w* or **BlankSequence[*w*]** *(in the full form)* – *the pattern determining an arbitrary expression or a sequence of arbitrary expressions with a w heading each;*
___ *(3 symbols "_")* or **BlankNullSequence[]** *(in the full form)* – *the pattern which defines absence of expressions, or sequence of arbitrary expressions;*

___t or **BlankNullSequence[t]** *(in the full form)* – *the pattern which defines absence of expressions or sequence of arbitrary expressions with t heading each.*

At that, in the full form the expressions that contains patterns of the types {"___", "__", "_"} are represented in the formats illustrated by the next example:

In[2500]:= **Map[FullForm, {x_, x__, x___}]**
Out[2500]= {Pattern[x,Blank[]],Pattern[x,BlankSequence[]],Pattern[x,BlankNullSequence[]]}

A rather simple **ExprPatternQ** function provides testing of an expression *regarding* existence in it of patterns of types {"_", "__", "___"}, whose the call **ExprPatternQ[x]** returns *True* if a *x* expression contains at least one of the patterns {"_", "__", "___"}, otherwise *False* is returned. The following fragment represents source code of the **ExprPatternQ** function with typical examples of its application.

In[2502]:= **ExprPatternQ[x_] := ! StringFreeQ[ToString[FullForm[x]], {"BlankSequence[]", "BlankNullSequence[]", "Blank[]"}]**

In[2503]:= **Map[ExprPatternQ, {a*Sin[x], 6*x_^y_ + a*x_*y_, x_^y_, x__, z___}]**
Out[2503]= {False, True, True, True, True}

The user has possibility to create patterns for expressions with an arbitrary structure but the most widespread way of use of templates is a block, function or procedure definition when formal arguments are specified in its heading. In addition, the coding of formal arguments without the above patterns doesn't allow to consider these objects as the *blocks*, *functions* and *procedures* as illustrates a simple enough example:

In[2589]:= **G[x, y] := x^2 + y^2; G1[x_, y_] := x^2 + y^2**
In[2590]:= **{G[90, 500], G1[90, 500]}**
Out[2590]= {G[90, 500], 258100}

Once again it is necessary to emphasize, that patterns in the *Math*-language represent the classes of expressions with the given structure when one pattern corresponds to a certain expression and if the structure of pattern coincides with structure of an expression, i.e. by a filling of the patterns it is possible to receive an arbitrary expression. Moreover, even two expressions, mathematically equivalent, can not be represented by the same template if they do not have the same structure. For example, the expression $(a + b)^2$ is equivalent to the expression $a^2 + 2*a*b + b^2$ however these expressions are not equivalent at the level of patterns representing them, for the reason, that both have various full form as illustrates a simple enough example:

In[2507]:= **FullForm[(a + b)^2]**
Out[2507]//FullForm =
Power[Plus[a, b], 2]
In[2508]:= **FullForm[a^2 + 2*a*b + b^2]**
Out[2508]//FullForm =
Plus[Power[a, 2], Times[2, a, b], Power[b, 2]]

The fact that patterns define structure of expressions, is very important for the solution of the problem of determination of the transformation rules of changing of structure of the expressions without change of their mathematical equivalence. The system has not other general criterion that would allow to define equivalence of two expressions. For realization of algorithm of the comparison of expressions the system uses reduction them upto the full form determined by the **FullForm** function. In the reference on the *Mathematica* a number of important mechanisms of creation of the patterns for a quite wide class of expressions is discussed while in other manuals the receptions used by the *Mathematica* for the purpose of expansion and restriction of the classes of expressions represented by patterns are being considered. For determination of the expressions that coincide with the given pattern it is possible to apply the **Cases** function allowing five coding formats; thus, the call **Cases[g, w]** according to the first format returns the elements-expressions of a *g* list that are structurally correspond to a *w* pattern as very visually illustrates the following simple example:

In[2610]:= Cases[{a + b*c^5, 5 + 6*y^7, a + b*p^m, a + b*m^(-p)}, a + b*x_^n_]
Out[2610]= {a + b*c^5, a + b*p^m, a + b*m^-p}

Meanwhile, for testing of 2 arbitrary expressions for equivalence a simple function, whose call **EquivalenceQ[x, y]** returns *True*, if expressions *x* and *y* are equivalent, and in opposite case *False* can be used, as a rather visually illustrates the following simple fragment:

In[4215]:= EquivalenceQ[x_, y_] := SameQ @@ Map[FullForm, Map[Simplify, {x, y}]]
In[4216]:= EquivalenceQ[a + b*c^(c + d^c), b*c^(d^c + c) + a]
Out[4216]= True

Meanwhile, without being distracted by details, we only will note that *Mathematica* system has a number of the functions providing the functioning with expressions at the level of the patterns representing them as in general, and at the level of the subexpressions composing them; at that, the reader can familiarize with these tools, in particular, in [50,51,60,65,68,71].

Meanwhile, along with the system functions there is a number of the means expanding or supplementing the possibilities of the first ones. For example, the following procedure is an extension of the above **Cases** function in case of the pure function of short format from two variables is used as the 2nd argument. The procedure call **Cases1[L, w]** returns the nested list whose 2-element sublists contain the two-element list of elements of a *L* list, whose values are connected by the relation defined by a pure *w* function of short format from 2 variables as the second argument, while the first element defines its multiplicity; in case of absence in the *L* list of elements which of pairwise satisfy the *w* relation the empty list is returned. The procedure **Cases2** is a rather useful modification of **Cases1** procedure. The procedure call **Cases2[h, f]** returns the nested list whose *n*-element sublists contain the elements of a *h* list, whose values are connected by the relation defined by a pure *f* function from *n* arguments; in case of absence in the *h* list of elements that satisfy the *h* relation the *empty* list is returned. These procedures represent a certain interest for problems of lists processing. The fragment below represents source codes of the procedures with examples of their application.

In[3742]:= Cases1[L_ /; ListQ[L], w_ /; ShortPureFuncQ[y]] :=
Module[{a = Args[w], b = {}, c = ToString1[L], d, p = Length[L], h},
d = Partition[Riffle[a, {c <> "[[k]]", c <> "[[j]]"}], 2]; d = Map[Rule[#[[1]], #[[2]]] &, d];
h = Quiet[ToExpression[StringReplace[StringReplace[ToString[InputForm[w]],
" &" -> ""], d]]];
Do[Do[AppendTo[b, If[TrueQ[h], {L[[j]], L[[k]]}, Nothing]], {k, j + 1, p}], {j, 1, p - 1}];
Map[{Length[#], #[[1]]} &, Gather[b]]]
In[3743]:= Cases1[{1, 2, 4, 6, 16, 8, 7, 9, 64, 36}, #1 == #2^2 &]

Out[3743]= {{1, {2, 4}}, {1, {4, 16}}, {1, {6, 36}}, {1, {8, 64}}}

In[2]:= Cases2[j_ /; ListQ[j], f_ /; PureFuncQ[f]] :=
Module[{b = {}, a = Select[DeleteDuplicates[Subsets[Join[j, Reverse[j]],
{Length[ArgsPureFunc[f]]}]], ! SameQ[#[[1]], #[[2]]] &]},
a = Gather[a, PermutationQ[#1, #2] &];
Map[If[f @@ #, AppendTo[b, #], Nothing] &, Map[#[[1]] &, a]]; b]

In[3]:= Cases2[{1, 2, 4, 6, 16, 8, 7, 9, 64, 36}, Function[{x, y}, TrueQ[x^2 == y]]]
Out[3]= {{2, 4}, {4, 16}, {6, 36}, {8, 64}}

In[4]:= f := Function[{x, y, z}, PrimeQ[x + y + z]]; Cases2[{1, 5, 6, 4, 8, 9, 5, 3}, f]
Out[4]= {{1, 5, 5}, {1, 6, 4}, {1, 4, 8}, {1, 9, 3}, {5, 6, 8}, {5, 4, 8}, {5, 9, 5}, {5, 9, 3}, {5, 5, 3}, {6, 4, 9}, {6, 4, 3}, {6, 8, 9}, {6, 8, 5}, {6, 8, 3}, {4, 8, 5}, {9, 5, 3}}

In[5]:= g := Function[{x, y, z, t}, PrimeQ[x + y + z*t]]; Cases2[{1, 5, 6, 4, 8, 9, 5, 3, 6, 3, 7}, g]
Out[5]= {{1, 5, 5, 7}, {1, 6, 4, 9}, {1, 6, 4, 3}, {1, 6, 4, 6}, {1, 6, 4, 3}, {1, 6, 8, 9}, {1, 6, 8, 5}, {1, 6, 8, 3}, {1, 6, 8, 3}, {1, 6, 9, 6}, {1, 6, 5, 6}, {1, 4, 8, 3}, {1, 4, 8, 6}, ..., {8, 3, 6, 3}, {8, 3, 6, 7}, {9, 5, 3, 3}, {5, 3, 3, 7}}

In[6]:= Cases2[{1, 2, 4, 6, 16, 8, 7, 9, 64, 36}, Function[{x, y}, EvenQ[x + y]]]
Out[6]= {{1, 7}, {1, 9}, {2, 4}, {2, 6}, {2, 16}, {2, 8}, {2, 64}, {2, 36}, {4, 6}, {4, 16}, {4, 8}, {4, 64}, {4, 36}, {6, 16}, {6, 8}, {6, 64}, {6, 36}, {16, 8}, {16, 64}, {16, 36}, {8, 64}, {8, 36}, {7, 9}, {64, 36}}

In[3753]:= SymbolsOfString1[x_ /; StringQ[x], y___] :=
Module[{a = Flatten[Map[Range[Sequences[#]] &, {{32, 34}, {37, 47}, {58, 64}, {91, 91}, {93, 96}, {123, 126}}]], b},
b = DeleteDuplicates[StringSplit[StringReplace[x, GenRules[Map[FromCharacterCode, a], " "]]]];
If[{y} == {}, b, If[y === 1, Select[b, ! MemberQ3[Range[48, 57], ToCharacterCode[#]] &],
Select[Select[b, ! Quiet[SystemQ[#]] &], NameQ[#] &]]]]

In[3467]:= SymbolsOfString1["EvenQ[#1 + #2 + #3 + #4]&"]
Out[3467]= {"EvenQ", "#1", "#2", "#3", "#4"}

In[3754]:= ArgsPureFunc[x_ /; PureFuncQ[x]] := If[StringFreeQ[ToString[x], "#"], Args[x],
Select[SymbolsOfString1[ToString[x], 1], SuffPref[#1, "#", 1] &]]

In[3755]:= Map[ArgsPureFunc, {EvenQ[#1 + #3] &, #1*#2*#3 &,
Function[{x, y}, EvenQ[x + y]]}]
Out[3755]= {{"#1", "#3"}, {"#1", "#2", "#3"}, {"x", "y"}}

In[3756]:= ArityPureFunc[x_ /; PureFuncQ[x]] := Length[ArgsPureFunc[x]]

In[3757]:= ArityPureFunc[(a*#1 + b*#2)/(c*#3 - d*#4) &]
Out[3757]= 4

In[3794]:= ContainsStrong[x_ /; ListQ[x], y_ /; ListQ[y]] :=
MemberQ[Partition[x, Length[y], 1], y]

In[3795]:= Map9[ContainsStrong, {{a, b, c, a, d}, {b, a}}, {{a, b, c}, {a, b, c}}]
Out[3795]= {True, False}

In[3797]:= PermutationQ[x_, y_] := If[ListQ[x] && ListQ[y] && Length[x] == Length[y],
MemberQ[Permutations[x], y], False]

In[3798]:= **PermutationQ[{a, b, c, d, g, h}, {h, b, c, a, g, d}]**
Out[3798]= True

The method which has been used in the **Cases1** procedure for formation of the *h* variable that is used as a logical condition in a double **Do** cycle for search of pairs of elements of the *L* list which satisfy to the relation defined by a pure function of the short format from two variables is of a certain interest in a number of applications. While in the **Cases2** definition for the purpose of increase of its universality a rather useful modification of the procedure **SymbolsOfString** had been used. The procedure call **SymbolsOfString1[*x*]** returns the list of the symbols that enter an expression presented by a *x* string. Whereas the procedure call **SymbolsOfString1[*x*, 1]** returns the list of symbols different from numbers which enter an expression represented by a *x* string. In addition, the procedure call **SymbolsOfString1[*x*, *a*]** where *a* – an expression different from 1, returns the the list of the symbols different from numbers and system symbols which enter an expression represented by a *x* string. On the basis of the **Args** and **SymbolsOfString1** procedures the function allowing to evaluate the formal arguments of pure functions including the generalized pure functions in the short format has been programmed. Thus, the function call **ArgsPureFunc[*w*]** returns the list of the formal arguments in the string format of a pure *w* function; in addition, the generalized pure functions in the short format are allowed. Whereas the call **ArityPureFunc[*w*]** of the function based on the **ArgsPureFunc** function returns the arity of a pure *w* function.

In addition to the standard four functions **ContainsExactly**, **ContainsNone**, **ContainsAll**, **ContainsAny**, the function call **ContainsStrong[*x*, *y*]** returns *True* if *x* list contains the same elements, and in the same order as an *y* list, and *False* otherwise. Whereas the function call **PermutationQ[*x*, *w*]** returns *True* if a *w* list is a permutation of the elements of a *x* list, and *False* otherwise, i.e. the both lists are equivalent up to a permutation.

As it was noted, it is possible to apply the **Cases** function for definition of the expressions coinciding with a given pattern, however not all problems of expressions comparison with patterns are solved by the standard tools. For solution of the problem in broader aspect the **EquExprPatt** procedure can be rather useful whose call **EquExprPatt[*x*, *p*]** returns *True* if a *x* expression corresponds to the given *p* pattern, and *False* otherwise. The following fragment represents source code of the **EquExprPatt** procedure with examples of its application.

In[3395]:= EquExprPatt[x_, y_ /; ExprPatternQ[y]] := Module[{c, d = {}, j, t, v = {}, k = 1, p,
g = {}, s = {}, a = Map[FullForm, Map[Expand, {x, y}]],
b = Mapp[MinusList, Map[OP, Map[Expand, {x, y}]], {FullForm}],
z = SetAttributes[ToString, Listable], w},
{b, c} = ToString[{b, a}]; p = StringPosition[c[[2]], {"Pattern[", "Blank[]]"}];
While[k = 2*k − 1; k <= Length[p], AppendTo[d, StringTake[c[[2]],
{p[[k]][[1]], p[[k + 1]][[2]]}]]; k++]; {t, k} = {ToExpression[d], 1};
While[k <= Length[t], AppendTo[v, StringJoin[ToString[Op[t[[k]]]]]]; k++];
v = ToString[v]; v = Map13[Rule, {d, v}]; v = StringReplace[c[[2]], v];
b = Quiet[Mapp[Select, b, ! SystemQ[#] || BlockFuncModQ[ToString[#]] &]];
{b, k, j} = {ToString[b], 1, 1};
While[k <= Length[b[[1]]], z = b[[1]][[k]]; AppendTo[g, {"[" <> z <> "," −> "[w", " " <>
z <> "," −> " w", "[" <> z <> "]" −> "[w]", " " <> z <> "]" −> " w]"}]; k++];

While[j <= Length[b[[2]]], z = b[[2]][[j]]; AppendTo[s, {"[" <> z <> "," -> "[w", " " <> z <> "," -> " w", "[" <> z <> "]" -> "[w]", " " <> z <> "]" -> " w]"}]; j++];
ClearAttributes[ToString, Listable];
z = Map9[StringReplace, {c[[1]], v}, Map[Flatten, {g, s}]];
SameQ[z[[1]], StringReplace[z[[2]], Join[GenRules[Flatten[Map[# <> "," &, Map[ToString, t]]], "w"], GenRules[Flatten[Map[# <> "]" &, Map[ToString, t]]], "w]"], GenRules[Flatten[Map[# <> ")" &, Map[ToString, t]]], "w)"]]]]]

In[3396]:= **EquExprPatt[a*Sin[x] – 5*b*c^5, a*Sin[x] – 5*b*x_^n_]**
Out[3396]= True
In[3397]:= **EquExprPatt[a*Sin[x] – 5*b*c^5, 90*Sin[x] – 500*b*x_^n_]**
Out[3397]= True
In[3398]:= **EquExprPatt[a^2 + 2*a*b + b^2, (x_ + y_)^2]**
Out[3398]= True
In[3399]:= **Mapp[EquExprPatt, {a + b*c^5, 5 + 6*y^7, a + b*p^m, a + b*m^p}, a + b*x_^n_]**
Out[3399]= {True, True, True, True}
In[3400]:= **Mapp[Cases, {{a + b*c^5}, {5 + 6*y^7}, {a + b*p^m}, {a + b*m^p}}, a + b*x_^n_]**
Out[3400]= {{a + b*c^5}, {}, {a + b*p^m}, {a + b*m^p}}
In[3401]:= **EquExprPatt1[a^2 + 2*a*b + b^2, (a + b)^2]**
Out[3401]= True

At that, the definition of the **EquExprPatt** along with standard means uses and our means such as **ExprPatternQ, Map9, Map13, Mapp, MinusList, ProcQ, QFunction, SystemQ, Op, OP** which are considered in the present book and in books [28-33]. The last examples of the fragment illustrate as well the more ample *possibilities* of **EquExprPatt** procedure concerning the standard **Cases** function. As the algorithm of this procedure is based on presentation of expressions and patterns in the full form *(FullForm)*, in principle, as the second argument of the **EquExprPatt** procedure it is possible to apply any expression, having coded the second argument as a *y_* in definition of the **EquExprPatt**, having modified it in the **EquExprPatt1** procedure different from the **EquExprPatt** only by this condition. In this case it is possible to test 2 any expressions regarding their structural equivalence what represents an important question in a number of problems of the expressions analysis. Attention should be paid to realization of this procedure which uses a quite useful reception of the temporary endowing the system **ToString** function the *Listable* attribute. In [50] questions of manipulations with patterns are considered in detail.

Determination of types of expression in patterns. For this purpose it is quite possible to use headings of *w* expressions *(they are defined by function call* **Head[w]**), which define their main essence. So, the patterns *_h* and *x_h* will represent expressions with *h heading;* the following headings from which are the most often used, namely:

x_h – a x expression with h heading:
x_Integer – a x expression with heading **Integer** *(integer)*
x_Real – a x expression with heading **Real** *(real number)*
x_Complex – a x expression with heading **Complex** *(complex number)*
x_List – a x expression with heading **List** *(list)*
x_String – a x expression with heading **String** *(string)*

Software Etudes in the Mathematica

x_Symbol – *a x expression with heading **Symbol** (symbol)*
x_Plus – *a x expression with heading **Plus** (addition, subtraction)*
x_Times – *a x expression with heading **Times** (product, division)*
x_Power – *a x expression with heading **Power** (power)*

In principle, any admissible *heading* can act as some heading and the part of a pattern. We will give examples of such patterns, namely:

In[2415]:= G[x_Plus] := x^2; S[x_Power] := x^2; {G[9], G[a + b], S[5], S[a^b], G[c – d], 5^(-1)}
Out[2415]= {G[9], (a + b)^2, S[5], a^(2*b), (c – d)^2, 1/5}

Meanwhile, in certain cases of standardly defined headings isn't enough for assignment of patterns, quite naturally bringing up the question of addition to their list of the headings determined by the user. Since for evaluation of a heading, standard **Head** function is used, therefore naturally to modify this function regarding testing by it of the wider class of the headings. For this purpose the **RepStandFunc** procedure has been determined, whose the call **RepStandFunc**[*x*, *y*, *z*] returns the call of a *y* means of the same name with standard *y* function, and whose definition is determined in the string format by the *x* argument, on the *z* argument of its factual arguments. At the same time, call of the **RepStandFunc** procedure is once-only in the sense, that after the call the initial state of standard *y* function remains without change. The next fragment represents source code of the **RepStandFunc** procedure and some examples of its application, and of testing of aftereffect of result of its call; along with that, in other part of the fragment the means illustrating the aforesaid are represented.

In[3380]:= **RepStandFunc[x_ /; StringQ[x], y_ /; SymbolQ[y], z__] :=**
Module[{a = Unique[y], b}, ToExpression[StringReplace[x, ToString[y] <> "[" –>
ToString[a] <> "[", 1]]; b = a[z]; Remove[a]; b]

In[3381]:= x = "Sin[x__] := Plus[Sequences[Map[#^2 &, {x}]]]";
RepStandFunc[x, Sin, 74, 69, 590, 2016]
Out[3381]= 4422593
In[3382]:= x = "Sin[x_] := x^5"; **RepStandFunc[x, Sin, 69]**
Out[3382]= 1564031349
In[3383]:= **Definition[Sin]**
Out[3383]= Attributes[Sin] = {Listable, NumericFunction, Protected}
In[3384]:= **Sin[74.50090]**
Out[3384]= –0.78166

In[3390]:= **Headd := "Head[x_] := Module[{b = {ListListQ, ProcQ, SystemQ, NestListQ,**
QFunction}, c = {ListList, Procedure, System, NestList, Function},
h = SetAttributes[SetAttributes, Listable], d = 90, k = 1}, SetAttributes1[c, Protected];
Quiet[For[k = 1, k <= Length[b], k++, If[b[[k]][x], d = c[[k]]; Break[]]]];
ClearAttributes[SetAttributes, Listable]; If[d === 90, x[[0]], d]]"

In[3391]:= **RepStandFunc[Headd, Head, {{a}, {b, c}, {d}}]**
Out[3391]= NestList
In[3392]:= **Definition[Head]**
Out[3392]= Attributes[Head] = {Protected}
In[3393]:= **Head[{{a}, {b, c}, {d}}]**
Out[3393]= List

In[3394]:= G[h_NestList] := Length[h]
In[3395]:= G[{{a}, {b}, {c}, {d, t}, {f}, {g}, {v}}]
Out[3395]= G[{{a}, {b}, {c}, {d, t}, {f}, {g}, {v}}]
In[3396]:= G[h_List] := Length[h]
In[3397]:= G[{{a}, {b}, {c}, {d, t}, {f}, {g}, {v}}]
Out[3397]= 7
In[3398]:= ClearAllAttributes[Head]; Clear[Head]; ToExpression[Headd]
In[3399]:= G[h_List] := Length[h]
In[3400]:= G[{{a}, {b}, {c}, {d, t}, {f}, {g}, {v}}]
Out[3400]= 7

In[3795]:= SetAttributes1[x_, y_] :=
ToExpression["SetAttributes[SetAttributes, Listable];
SetAttributes[" <> ToString[x] <> ", " <> ToString[y] <> "];
ClearAttributes[SetAttributes, Listable]"]

In[3796]:= t = {x, y, z}; SetAttributes1[t, Listable];
Map[Attributes, Flatten[{t, SetAttributes}]]
Out[3796]= {{Listable}, {Listable}, {Listable}, {HoldFirst, Protected}}

In the previous fragment the string structure **Headd** has been presented which represents definition of the **Head** procedure of the same name with the standard **Head** function with expansion of functionality of the last. As an example the call **RepStandFunc[Headd, Head, {{{a}, {b, c}, {d}}}]** is presented whose result is a modification of the **Head** *(Headd)* function whose once-only application to a list of *NestList*-type returns the heading *NestList* on such list, whereas the **Head** function on this list returns the heading *List*. Modifications of **Head** procedure in string structure **Headd** are an quite simple *(by an appropriate extension of the lists represented by the local variables b and c)*, in principle, allowing to expand the list of headings arbitrarily widely. However, these headings are not distinguished by the *Mathematica* as components of "*x_h*" patterns as the fragment example with the **G** function very visually illustrates. Moreover, this result takes place both at using of the **RepStandFunc** procedure, and at the *prolonged* replacement *(for the duration of the Mathematica current session)* of the standard **Head** function by its modification which is located in string structure **Headd**. As a result of similar procedure the *Mathematica* restart is required for recovery of the original version of the **Head** function if before, it wasn't kept in a datafile of *mx*-format from which it could be uploaded into the current session as that the **RepStandFunc** procedure does. In addition, it is supposed that a block, procedure or function replacing a standard *x* function shouldn't contain calls of the initial *x* function; otherwise emergence of the erroneous or/and special situations up to the *looping* is quite real, demanding the restart of the *Mathematica*.

The **SetAttributes1** function completes the previous fragment; the call **SetAttributes1[w, y]** expands the standard **SetAttributes** function onto the form of representation of the first *w* argument, for which the indexed variables, lists, etc. can be used, in particular, providing the ascribing of an *y* attributes to elements of a *w* list. Meanwhile, the above mechanism of once-only use of the substitutes of the same name of standard functions in certain cases is a rather effective method, Meantime, prolongation of such substitutes in the current session can cause conflict situations with its functions that significantly use originals of the replaced tools. So, the given mechanism should be used a rather circumspectly.

The question of processing of the formal arguments with good reason can be considered as the first problem relating to the calculations of the tuples of formal arguments of the user functions, modules, blocks which have been activated in the current session directly or on the basis of download of the packages containing their definitions. In the previous works [30-33,48] certain tools for the solution of this problem have been offered in the form of the procedures **Args, Args0, Args1, Args2,** below we will represent similar means in narrower assortment and with the improved functional characteristics. First of all, as a rather useful tool, we will represent the **Args** procedure whose call **Args**[x] returns the list of the formal arguments of the user module, block or function x. The following fragment represents the sourse code of the **Args** procedure with the most typical examples of its application.

```
In[2322]:= V := Compile[{{x, _Real}, {y, _Real}}, (x^3 + y)^2];
Kr := (#1^2 + #2^4 - 590*#3) &; H[x_] := Block[{}, x];
Art := Function[{x, y}, x*Sin[y]]; P[y_] := Module[{}, y];
P[x__] := Plus[Sequences[{x}]]; H[x_, y_] := x + y;
GS[x_ /; IntegerQ[x], y_ /; IntegerQ[y]] := Sin[74] + Cos[42];
Sv[x_ /; IntegerQ[x], y_ /; IntegerQ[y]] := x^2 + y^2;
Sv = Compile[{{x, _Integer}, {y, _Real}}, (x + y)^6];
S := Compile[{{x, _Integer}, {y, _Real}}, (x + y)^3];
G = Compile[{{x, _Integer}, {y, _Real}}, (x + y)];
T := Compile[{{x, _Real}}, (x + y)]; SetAttributes[H, Protected];

In[2323]:= Args[P_, z___] := Module[{a, b, c, d = {}, k = 1, Vt},
If[CompileFuncQ[P] || BlockFuncModQ[P],
Vt[y_ /; ListQ[y]] := Module[{p = 1, q = {}, t},
While[p <= Length[y], q = Append[q, t = ToString[y[[p]]];
StringTake[t, {1, StringPosition[t, "_"][[1]][[1]] - 1}]]; p++]; q];
If[CompileFuncQ[P], a = StringSplit[ToString[InputForm[Definition2[P]]], "\n \n"][[1]];
b = Quiet[SubStrSymbolParity1[a, "{", "}"]];
b = Select[b, ! StringFreeQ[#, "_"] ||  ! StringFreeQ[a, " Function[" <> #] &];
b = Mapp[StringSplit, b, ", "]; b = Mapp[StringReplace, b, {"{" -> "", "}" -> ""}];
b = Mapp[Select, b, StringFreeQ[#, "Blank$"] &]; c = b[[2]];
For[k, k <= Length[c], k++, d = Append[d, c[[k]] <> b[[1]][[k]]]]; d = ToExpression[d];
If[{z} == {}, d, Flatten[Map[Vt, {d}]]], If[BlockFuncModQ[P], a = Flatten[{HeadPF[P]}];
For[k, k <= Length[a], k++, d = Append[d, If[{z} != {}, Vt[ToExpression["{" <>
StringTake[a[[k]], {StringLength[ToString[P]] + 2, -2}] <> "}"]], ToExpression["{" <>
StringTake[a[[k]], {StringLength[ToString[P]] + 2, -2}] <> "}"]]]];
If[Length[d] == 1, d[[1]], d],
a = StringTake[StringReplace[ToString[InputForm[Definition2[P]]],
"Definition2[" -> "", 1], {1, -2}];
If[SuffPref[a, "Function[{", 1], b = SubStrSymbolParity1[a, "{", "}"];
b = Select[b, ! StringFreeQ[a, "Function[" <> #] &][[1]];
a = StringSplit[StringTake[b, {2, -2}], ", "], a = StringReplace[a, "#" -> "$$$$$"];
a = Map[ToString, UnDefVars[ToExpression[a]]]];
```

Map[ToString, ToExpression[Mapp[StringReplace, a, "$$$$$" -> "#"]]]]], $Failed]]

In[2324]:= **Map[Args, {V, S, Sv, T}]**
Out[2324]= {{x_Real, y_Real}, {x_Integer, y_Real}, {x_Integer, y_Real}, {x_Real}}

In[2325]:= **Mapp[Args, {V, S, Sv, T}, gs]**
Out[2325]= {{"x", "y"}, {"x", "y"}, {"x", "y"}, {"x"}}

In[2326]:= **Map[Args, {H, P, GS}]**
Out[2326]= {{{x_}, {x_, y_}}, {{y_}, {x__}}, {x_ /; IntegerQ[x], y_ /; IntegerQ[y]}}

In[2327]:= **Mapp[Args, {H, P, GS}, gsv]**
Out[2327]= {{{"x"}, {"x", "y"}}, {{"y"}, {"x"}}, {"x", "y"}}

In[2328]:= **Map[Args, {Art, Kr}]**
Out[2328]= {{"x", "y"}, {"#1", "#2", "#3"}}

In[2329]:= **Mapp[Args, {Art, Kr}, gsv]**
Out[2329]= {{"x", "y"}, {"#1", "#2", "#3"}}

In[2330]:= **Map[Args, {avz, 50090, a + b}]**
Out[2330]= {$Failed, $Failed, $Failed}

In[2556]:= **Args1[x_ /; BlockFuncModQ[x]] :=**
Module[{b = 1, c = {}, h = {}, d, p, t, a = Flatten[{PureDefinition[x]}]},
For[b, b <= Length[a], b++, t = ToString[Unique["agn"]];
p = t <> ToString[x]; ToExpression[t <> a[[b]]]; d = Unique["avz"];
AppendTo[h, {ToString[d], p, t}]; AppendTo[c, {Args[p], BlockFuncModQ[p, d]; d}];
d = ToUpperCase[d]]; Map[Remove, Flatten[h]]; If[Length[c] == 1, c[[1]], c]]

In[2557]:= **Args1[H]**
Out[2557]= {{{x_}, "Block"}, {{x_, y_}, "Function"}}

In[2558]:= **Args1[GS]**
Out[2558]= {{x_ /; IntegerQ[x], y_ /; IntegerQ[y]}, "Function"}

In[2559]:= **Args1[P]**
Out[2559]= {{{y_}, "Module"}, {{x__}, "Function"}}

At that, the format of the result returned by the call **Args**[*x*] is defined by type of a *x* object, namely:

– the list of formal arguments with the types ascribed to them is returned on the **Compile** function;

– the list of the formal arguments with the tests for an admissibility of the factual arguments ascribed to them or without them is returned on {*module, block, typical function*}; in addition, the **Args** procedure processes the situation *"objects of the same name with the various headings"*, returning the nested list of the formal arguments concerning all subobjects composing the *x* object in the order that is determined by the call **Definition2**[*x*];

– the list of slots {#1, ..., #*n*} in the string format of formal arguments is returned on a pure function in the short format whereas for standard pure function the list of formal arguments in the string format is returned.

Moreover, the procedure call **Args**[*Wg, h*] with the 2nd optional *h* argument – *any admissible expression or any their sequence* – returns the result similar to the call with the first argument, with that difference that all formal arguments are coded in string format, however without types ascribed to arguments and tests for admissibility. On an inadmissible actual argument the call **Args**[*x*] returns *$Failed*. Told very visually is looked through in the examples which are represented in the previous fragment.

At that, the definition of the **Args** along with standard means uses and our means such as **BlockFuncModQ, CompileFuncQ, Definition2, SuffPref, SubStrSymbolParity1, Mapp, HeadPF** and **UnDefVars** which are considered in the present book and in [28-33,50]. This procedure is used quite widely, first of all, in the problems of system programming in the *Mathematica*, significantly expanding the above procedures **Args, Args0, Args1, Args2**. In the same context we will note that a number of means presented in [32,50] are absent in the present book because of replacement their by more high-speed and functionally developed tools; like this, the **ArgsProc** procedure whose functions are overlapped by **Args** procedure.

The **Args1** procedure completes the previous fragment, whose call **Args1**[*x*] returns simple or the nested list, whose elements are 2-element lists, whose first element represents the list of formal arguments with the types and tests, ascribed to them while the second – an object type in the context {"*Module*", "*Block*", "*Function*"}. As an argument *x* the objects on which **BlockFuncModQ**[*x*] returns *True* are allowed. On unacceptable *x* argument the procedure call **Args1**[*x*] is returned unevaluated.

The **ArgsBFM** procedure is a rather useful means in addition to the procedures **Args1** and **Args**; it is intended for evaluation of formal arguments of a block, a function or a module. The fragment below represents source code of the procedure **ArgsBFM** along with typical examples of its application.

```
In[2396]:= ArgsBFM[x_ /; BlockFuncModQ[x], y___] :=
Module[{b, c = {}, p, a = Flatten[{HeadPF[x]}], d = {}, n = ToString[x] <> "[", k = 1},
b = Map[ToExpression["{" <> StringTake[#, {StringLength[n] + 1, -2}] <> "}"] &, a];
c = Map[Map[ToString, #] &, b];
While[k <= Length[c], p = c[[k]];
AppendTo[d, Map[StringTake[#, {1, Flatten[StringPosition[#, "_"]][[1]] - 1}] &, p]]; k++];
If[{y} != {} && ! HowAct[y], y = ReduceLevelsList[c, 69]]; ReduceLevelsList[d, 74]]

In[2397]:= G[x_ /; IntegerQ[x], y_ /; IntegerQ[y]] := x + y; G[x_, y__] := x + y;
G[x_, y_ /; IntegerQ[y], z_] := x + y + z; G[x_Integer, y__] := x + y;
G[x_ /; x == {42, 47, 67}, y_ /; IntegerQ[y]] := Length[x] + y; G[x_ /; IntegerQ[x]] := x
In[2398]:= ArgsBFM[G]
Out[2398]= {{"x", "y"}, {"x", "y", "z"}, {"x", "y"}, {"x", "y"}, {"x", "y"}, {"x"}}
In[2399]:= ArgsBFM[G, gsw]
Out[2399]= {{"x", "y"}, {"x", "y", "z"}, {"x", "y"}, {"x", "y"}, {"x", "y"}, {"x"}}
In[2400]:= gsw
Out[2400]= {{"x_ /; IntegerQ[x]", "y_ /; IntegerQ[y]"}, {"x_", "y_ /; IntegerQ[y]", "z_"},
{"x_Integer", "y__"}, {"x_ /; x == {42, 47, 67}", "y_ /; IntegerQ[y]"}, {"x_", "y__"},
{"x_ /; IntegerQ[x]"}}
```

The procedure call **ArgsBFM**[*x*] returns the list of formal arguments in the string format of a block, a function or a module *x* whereas the call **ArgsBFM**[*x, y*] with the second optional *y* argument – *an undefinite variable* – in addition returns thru it the list of formal arguments of the block, function or module *x* with the tests for admissibility in the string format that are ascribed to them.

The following procedure is a rather useful modification of the previous procedure. The call **ArgsBFM1[x]** generally returns the list of the *ListList* type whose two-element sublists in the string format determine the name of the formal argument *(1st element)* and its admissibility test *(2nd element)* of a block, function or module *x*. Lack of the test is coded as *"Arbitrary"*; at the same time, under lack of test is understood not only its actual lack, but also the optional and default patterns ascribed to the formal argument. The procedure successfully processes the objects of the same name too, i.e. objects with several headings. The following fragment represents source code of the **ArgsBFM1** procedure with typical examples of its application.

In[3333]:= **ArgsBFM1[x_ /; BlockFuncModQ[x]] :=**
Module[{b, c, d, g = {}, t, a = ToString2[Args[x]]},
a = If[QmultiplePF[x], a, {a}]; Do[{b, c, d} = {{}, {}, {}}; t = a[[j]];
Do[AppendTo[b, If[ListQ[t[[k]]],
Map[StringSplit[#, {"/;", "__", "___", "_", ":", "_:", "_."}] &, t[[k]]],
StringSplit[t[[k]], {"/;", "__", "___", "_", ":", "_:", "_."}]]], {k, 1, Length[t]}];
Do[AppendTo[c, If[NestListQ[b[[k]]], Map[Map[If[#1 == " " || #1 == "", Nothing,
StringTrim[#1]] &, #] &, b[[k]]], Map[If[# == " " || #1 == "", Nothing,
StringTrim[#]] &, b[[k]]]]], {k, 1, Length[b]}];
Do[AppendTo[d, If[NestListQ[c[[k]]],
Map[If[Length[#1] == 1, {#1[[1]], "Arbitrary"}, #1] &, c[[k]]],
If[Length[c[[k]]] == 1, {c[[k]][[1]], "Arbitrary"}, c[[k]]]]], {k, 1, Length[c]}];
d = If[Length[d] == 1, d[[1]], d]; AppendTo[g, d], {j, 1, Length[a]}];
If[Length[g] == 1, g[[1]], g]]

In[3334]:= **ArgsBFM1[Attribs]**
Out[3334]= {{"x", "FileExistsQ[x] || DirectoryQ[x]"}, {"y", "Arbitrary"}}
In[3335]:= **G[x_, y_List, z_: 74, h___] := Module[{}, Body]; G[x_, y_List, z_: 74,**
{x1_, x2_List, x3_: 90}, h___] := Module[{}, Body]
In[3336]:= **ArgsBFM1[G]**
Out[3336]= {{{"x", "Arbitrary"}, {"y", "List"}, {"z", "74"}, {{"x1", "Arbitrary"}, {"x2", "List"},
{"x3", "90"}}, {"h", "Arbitrary"}}, {{"x", "Arbitrary"}, {"y", "List"}, {"z", "74"}, {"h", "Arbitrary"}}}

The next procedure is a certain addition to previous procedures **ArgsBFM** and **ArgsBFM1**. The procedure call **ArgsBFM2[x]** in the string format returns the list of formal arguments of the user block, function or module *x* with the admissibility *tests* attributed to them. Whereas procedure call **ArgsBFM2[x, y]** with the second optional *y* argument – *an undefinite symbol* – additionally returns the list whose, in general, 2-element sublists define as the first element a formal argument in string format, whereas the second element – its admissibility test. In addition, sublists of the list returned through the second argument *y* by the second element along with the admissibility tests may contain a certain specifying information concerning the corresponding arguments, namely: *"Arbitrary"*, *"Default"* and *"Optional = value at its absence"*. The **ArgsBFM2** procedure can be rather easily extented to the objects processing of the same name, i.e. the objects with several headings. The following fragment represents source code of the procedure with examples of its application.

In[4195]:= **ArgsBFM2[x_ /; BlockFuncModQ[x], y___] :=**

Module[{a = StringTake[HeadPF[x], {StringLength[ToString[x]] + 2, -1}], b = "", c = {}, d, k = 1, j = 1, p}, d = StringLength[a];
For[j, j <= d, j++, For[k = j, k <= d, k++,
If[SyntaxQ[Set[b, b <> StringTake[a, {k}]]] && MemberQ[{",", "]"}, StringTake[a, {k + 1}]],
AppendTo[c, b]; b = ""; Break[]]]; j = k + 2];
k = Map[StringSplit[StringReplace[#, {"___" -> "_", "__" -> "_"}], "_"] &, c];
If[{y} != {} && NullQ[y],
p = ReduceLevelsList[Map[If[Length[#] == 1, {#[[1]], "Arbitrary"},
{#[[1]], Do[If[SyntaxQ[Set[d, StringTake[#[[2]], {j, StringLength[#[[2]]]}]]],
Return[StringTrim[d]]], {j, 1, StringLength[#[[2]]]}]}, {j, 1, StringLength[#[[2]]]}] &, k]][[1]];
y = {}; Do[AppendTo[y, If[! StringFreeQ[c[[j]], "_:"], {p[[j]][[1]], "Optional = " <> p[[j]][[2]]},
If[! StringFreeQ[c[[j]], "_."], {p[[j]][[1]], "Default"}, p[[j]]]]], {j, 1, Length[c]}]]; c]

In[4196]:= **Kr[x_: 21, z_., t_ /; IntegerQ[t], p__, y___ /; IntegerListQ[{x}]] := {x, y, z, t, p}**
In[4197]:= **ArgsBFM2[Kr, Sv]**
Out[4197]= {"x_:21", "z_.", "t_ /; IntegerQ[t]", "p__", "y___ /; IntegerListQ[{x}]"}
In[4198]:= **Sv**
Out[4198]= {{"x", "Optional = 21"}, {"z", "Default"}, {"t", "IntegerQ[t]"}, {"p", "Arbitrary"}, {"y", "IntegerListQ[{x}]"}}
In[4199]:= **G[] := x; {ArgsBFM2[G, svg], svg}**
Out[4199]= {{}, {}}
In[4200]:= **ArgsBFM2[CFattainability, vgs]**
Out[4200]= {"x_ /; (StringQ[x] && x != \"\") || (IntegerQ[x] && x != 0)",
"y_ /; (StringQ[y] && y != \"\") || IntegerQ[y]", "A_ /; ListQ[A] &&
MemberQ[(Range[0, #1] &) /@ Range[9], A]", "f_ /; (ListQ[f] &&
AllTrue[(RuleQ[#1] &) /@ f, TrueQ]) || FunctionQ[f]", "n_ /; IntegerQ[n] && n > 1"}
In[4201]:= **vgs**
Out[4201]= {{"x", "(StringQ[x] && x != \"\") || (IntegerQ[x] && x != 0)"},
{"y", "(StringQ[y] && y != \"\") || IntegerQ[y]"}, {"A", "ListQ[A] &&
MemberQ[(Range[0, #1] &) /@ Range[9], A]"}, {"f", "(ListQ[f] &&
AllTrue[(RuleQ[#1] &) /@ f, TrueQ]) || FunctionQ[f]"}, {"n", "IntegerQ[n] && n > 1"}}
In[4202]:= **SG[x_String, y_List, z_Integer] := {x, y, z}; ArgsBFM2[SG, vg]**
Out[4202]= {"x_String", "y_List", "z_Integer"}
In[4203]:= **vg**
Out[4203]= {{"x", "String"}, {"y", "List"}, {"z", "Integer"}}

Here it is necessary to make one essential remark concerning the means that deal with the arguments of procedures and functions. The matter is that as it was shown earlier, testing means ascribed to the formal arguments, as a rule, consist of the earlier determined testing functions or the reserved key words defining the type, for example, *Integer*. While as a side effect the builtin *Math*-language allows to use the constructions that contain the definitions of the testing means, directly in headings of the procedures and functions. Some interesting examples of that have been represented above. Meanwhile, despite of such possibility, the programmed means are oriented, as a rule, on use for testing of admissibility of the factual arguments or the predefined means, or including the testing algorithms in the body of the procedures and functions. For this reason, the **Args** procedure and similar to it in such cases can return incorrect results. Whereas the **ArgsU** procedure covers also such peculiar cases. The procedure call **ArgsU**[*x*] regardless of way of definition of testing of factual arguments in the general case returns the nested list whose elements are 3-element sublists of strings; the *first* element of such sublists is the name of formal argument, the *second* element defines template ascribed to this formal argument, and the third element defines a testing function, a construction including definition of the testing function, a key word, or an optional value, otherwise the third element is the empty string, i.e. "". The next fragment represents source code of the **ArgsU** procedure with examples of its application.

In[3892]:= ArtKr[x_, h_ /; IntegerQ[h], y_ /; {IntOddQ[t_ /; IntegerQ[t]] :=
Module[{}, IntegerQ[t] && OddQ[t]], IntOddQ[y]}[[-1]], p_: 74, t_.] := x*y*h*p*t
In[3893]:= Args[ArtKr]
ToExpression::sntx: Invalid syntax in or before "{x_, h_ /; IntegerQ[h],
y_ /; {IntOddQ[t_ /; IntegerQ[t]]}".
Out[3893]= $Failed

In[3894]:= ArgsU[x_ /; BlockFuncModQ[x]] := Module[{a = HeadPFU[x], b, c, d = {}, g},
a = StringTake[a, {StringLength[ToString[x]] + 2, -2}]; c = StringPartition2[a, ","];
b[t_] := {StringTake[t, {1, Set[g, Flatten[StringPosition[t, "_"]][[1]]] - 1}],
StringTake[t, {g, -1}]}; c = Quiet[Map[StringTrim@b@# &, c]];
c = Quiet[Map[{#[[1]], StringReplace[#[[2]], " /; " -> "", 1]} &, c]];
Map[If[SuffPref[#[[2]], "___", 1], AppendTo[d, {#[[1]], "___", StringTrim2[#[[2]], "_", 1]}],
If[SuffPref[#[[2]], "__", 1], AppendTo[d, {#[[1]], "__", StringTrim2[#[[2]], "_", 1]}],
If[SuffPref[#[[2]], "_:", 1], AppendTo[d, {#[[1]], "_:", StringReplace[#[[2]], "_:" -> "", 1]}],
If[SuffPref[#[[2]], "_.", 1], AppendTo[d, {#[[1]], "_.", StringReplace[#[[2]], "_." -> "", 1]}],
If[SuffPref[#[[2]], "_", 1], AppendTo[d, {#[[1]], "_", StringTrim2[#[[2]], "_", 1]}]]]]]] &, c];
If[Length[d]==1, d[[1]], d]]

In[3895]:= ArgsU[ArtKr]
Out[3895]= {{"x", "_", ""}, {"h", "_", "IntegerQ[h]"}, {"y", "_", "{IntOddQ[t_ /; IntegerQ[t]] :=
Module[{}, IntegerQ[t] && OddQ[t]], IntOddQ[y]}[[-1]]"}, {"p", "_:", "74"}, {"t", "_.", ""}}
In[3896]:= GS1[x_, y_List, z_: 74, x1_, x2_List, x3_: 590, h___] := Module[{}, Body]
In[3897]:= ArgsU[GS1]
Out[3897]= {{"x", "_", ""}, {"y", "_", "List"}, {"z", "_:", "74"}, {"x1", "_", ""}, {"x2", "_", "List"},
{"x3", "_:", "590"}, {"h", "___", ""}}

The next **ArgsTypes** procedure serves for testing of the formal arguments of block, function or module activated in the current session. So, the call **ArgsTypes**[*x*] returns the nested list, whose two-element sublists in the string format define *names* of formal arguments and their admissible types *(in the broader sense the tests for their admissibility with initial values by default)* respectively. In lack of a type an argument it is defined as *"Arbitrary"* that is characteristic for arguments of *pure functions* and *arguments* without the tests and/or initial values ascribed to them, and also which have format patterns {"__", "___"}. The fragment below represents source code of the **ArgsTypes** procedure along with typical examples of its application.

In[2775]:= V := Compile[{{x, _Real}, {y, _Real}}, (x^3 + y)^2];

Software Etudes in the Mathematica

```
Kr := (#1^2 + #2^4 - 590*#3) &; H[x_] := Block[{}, x];
Art := Function[{x, y}, x*Sin[y]]; H[x_, y_] := x + y;
P[x__] := Plus[Sequences[{x}]]; GS[x__] := x;
P[x_ /; StringQ[x], y_] := StringLength[x];
GS[x_ /; IntegerQ[x], y_ /; IntegerQ[y]] := Sin[74] + Cos[42];
Sv[x_ /; IntegerQ[x], y_ /; IntegerQ[y]] := x^2 + y^2;
Sv = Compile[{{x, _Integer}, {y, _Real}}, (x + y)^6];
S := Compile[{{x, _Integer}, {y, _Real}}, (x + y)^3];
G = Compile[{{x, _Integer}, {y, _Real}}, (x + y)];
P[y_] := Module[{}, y]; P[x__] := Plus[Sequences[{x}]];
T := Compile[{{x, _Real}}, (x + y)]; GS[x_, y_String] := {x, y}

In[2776]:= ArgsTypes[x_ /; CompileFuncQ[x] || BlockFuncModQ[x] || PureFuncQ[x]] :=
Module[{a = Args[x], c = {}, d = {}, k = 1},
If[CompileFuncQ[x], a = Mapp[StringSplit, Map[ToString, a], "_"];
If[Length[a] == 1, a[[1]], a], If[PureFuncQ[x], a = Map[{#, "Arbitrary"} &, a];
If[Length[a] == 1, a[[1]], a], SetAttributes[ToString, Listable]; a = Map[ToString, a];
ClearAttributes[ToString, Listable]; a = If[NestListQ[a], a, {a}]];
For[k, k <= Length[a], k++, c = Append[c, Mapp[StringSplit,
Mapp[StringSplit, a[[k]], "_/; "], {"___", "__", "_"}]]];
For[k = 1, k <= Length[c], k++, d = Append[d, Map[Flatten, c[[k]]]]]; c = {};
For[k = 1, k <= Length[d], k++, c = Append[c, Map[If[Length[#] == 1, {#[[1]], "Arbitrary"},
{#[[1]], StringReplace[#[[2]], "\\" -> ""]}] &, d[[k]]]]];
c = Map[If[Length[#] == 1, #[[1]], #] &, c]; If[Length[c] == 1, c[[1]], c]]]]

In[2777]:= Map[ArgsTypes, {GS, Args}]
Out[2777]= {{{{"x", "IntegerQ[x]"}, {"y", "IntegerQ[y]"}}, {{"x", "Arbitrary"}, {"y", "String"}},
{"x", "Arbitrary"}}, {{"P", "Arbitrary"}, {"z", "Arbitrary"}}}
In[2778]:= ArgsTypes[P]
Out[2778]= {{{"x", "StringQ[x]"}, {"y", "Arbitrary"}}, {"y", "Arbitrary"}, {"x", "Arbitrary"}}
In[2779]:= Map[ArgsTypes, {Art, Kr}]
Out[2779]= {{{"x", "Arbitrary"}, {"y", "Arbitrary"}}, {{"#1", "Arbitrary"}, {"#2", "Arbitrary"},
{"#3", "Arbitrary"}}}
In[2780]:= Map[ArgsTypes, {V, Sv, S, G, T}]
Out[2780]= {{{"x", "Real"}, {"y", "Real"}}, {{"x", "Integer"}, {"y", "Real"}},
{{"x", "Integer"}, {"y", "Real"}}, {{"x", "Integer"}, {"y", "Real"}}, {"x", "Real"}}
```

Moreover, the **ArgsTypes** procedure successfully processes the above situation *"objects of the same name with various headings"*, returning the nested two-element lists of formal arguments concerning the subobjects composing a *x* object, in the order determined by the **Definition** function. And in this case 2-element lists have the format, presented above while for objects with empty list of formal arguments the empty list is returned, i.e. {}. Unlike **ArgsTypes** of the same name [29,30] this procedure processes blocks, modules or functions, including *pure* functions and **Compile** functions. At that, the call **ArgsTypes[*x*]** onto an illegal *x* argument is returned unevaluated.

Multiple patterns of formats `x__` and `x___` allow to determine any number of admissible factual arguments of a block, function or module; at that, if the first pattern defines not less than one argument, the second pattern allows absence of the actual arguments. The above-mentioned patterns formats of formal arguments allow to define the objects of the specified type, allowing any number of the factual arguments at their calls. This circumstance is the basis for programming of the tools which define arity of the user block, function or module, i.e. number of the factual arguments allowed at the object calls of a specified type which doesn't cause special *(unevaluated calls)* or the erroneous situations caused by discrepancy between number of the received factual arguments and of admissible at determining of an object. The question of calculation of arity of the user block, function or module is a rather important in many appendices and, first of all, of system character, but *Mathematica* has no tools for its solution therefore certain procedures for the solution of the question have been created such as **Arity, Arity1, Arity2, ArityM, ArityPF** that solve this problem with one or another degree of generality [30-32]. The next fragment represents source code of the **Arity** procedure which generalizes all above-mentioned means solving the arity problem along with examples of its most typical application.

```
In[2565]:= V := Compile[{{x, _Real}, {y, _Real}}, (x^3 + y)^2];
Kr := (#1^2 + #2^4 - 590*#3) &; H[x_, y_] := x + y;
Art := Function[{x, y}, x*Sin[y]]; H[x_] := Block[{}, x];
P[x__] := Plus[Sequences[{x}]]; SetAttributes[H, Protected];
GS[x_/; IntegerQ[x], y_/; IntegerQ[y]] := Sin[590] + Cos[42];
Sv[x_/; IntegerQ[x], y_/; IntegerQ[y]] := x^2 + y^2;
Sv = Compile[{{x, _Integer}, {y, _Real}}, (x + y)^6];
S := Compile[{{x, _Integer}, {y, _Real}}, (x + y)^3];
G = Compile[{{x, _Integer}, {y, _Real}}, (x + y)];
P[y_] := Module[{}, y]; T := Compile[{{x, _Real}}, (x + y)];
Vs[x_/; SameQ[{x}, {}]] := {x}; W[x_] := x; W[x_, y_] := x + y;
W[x_, y_, z_, t_] := Module[{}, x*y*z*t]; W[x_, y_Integer] := x + y

In[2566]:= Arity[P_/; SystemQ[P] || CompileFuncQ[P] || PureFuncQ[P] ||
BlockFuncModQ[P]] := Module[{a}, If[SystemQ[P], "System", a = Args[P];
Mapp[SetAttributes, {ToString, StringFreeQ}, Listable]; a = Map[ToString, a];
a = Map[If[DeleteDuplicates[StringFreeQ[#, "__"]] === {True}, Length[#], "Undefined"] &,
If[NestListQ[a], a, {a}]];
Mapp[ClearAttributes, {ToString, StringFreeQ}, Listable]; If[Length[a] == 1, a[[1]], a]]]

In[2567]:= Map[Arity, {V, S, Sv, T}]
Out[2567]= {2, 2, 2, 1}
In[2568]:= Map[Arity, {H, P, GS}]
Out[2568]= {{2, 1}, {1, "Undefined"}, 2}
In[2569]:= Map[Arity, {Art, Kr, ProcQ, Sin, For}]
Out[2569]= {2, 3, 1, "System", "System"}
In[2570]:= Map[Arity, {avz, 590, a + b}]
Out[2570]= {Arity[avz], Arity[590], Arity[a + b]}
In[2571]:= Arity[W]
Out[2571]= {1, 2, 2, 4}
```

In[2666]:= **Arity1[P_ /; SystemQ[P] || CompileFuncQ[P] || PureFuncQ[P] ||
BlockFuncModQ[P]] := Module[{a},
If[SystemQ[P], "System", a = Args[P]; a = Mapp1[ToString, a];
a = Map[If[DeleteDuplicates[StringFreeQ[#, "_"]] === {True}, Length[#], "Undefined"] &,
If[NestListQ[a], a, {a}]]; If[Length[a] == 1, a[[1]], a]]]**

In[2667]:= **Map[Arity1, {V, S, Sv, T}]**
Out[2667]= {2, 2, 2, 1}
In[2668]:= **Map[Arity1, {H, P, GS}]**
Out[2668]= {{2, 1}, {1, "Undefined"}, 2}
In[2669]:= **Map[Arity1, {Art, Kr, ProcQ, Sin, For}]**
Out[2669]= {2, 3, 1, "System", "System"}
In[2670]:= **Arity1[W]**
Out[2670]= {1, 2, 2, 4}
In[2671]:= **Map[Arity1, {avz, 590, a + b}]**
Out[2671]= {Arity1[avz], Arity1[590], Arity1[a + b]}

On blocks, functions or modules with an undefinite number of arguments the call **Arity**[*x*] returns *"Undefined"*, on the system functions the call **Arity**[*x*] returns *"System"* while on the objects having the *fixed* number of actual arguments their number is returned, in other cases the call is returned unevaluated. We will note that the **Arity** procedure processes the special situation *"objects of the same name with various headings"*, returning list of arities of subobjects composing a *x* object. At that, between this list and the list of definitions of subobjects which is returned on the call **Definition**[*x*] there is one-to-one correspondence. The definition of the **Arity** procedure along with standard tools uses and our tools such as **Args, PureFuncQ, BlockFuncModQ, CompileFuncQ, Mapp, SystemQ, NestListQ** which are considered in the present book and in [28-33]. At that, at programming of **Arity** in the light of simplification of its algorithm is expedient for the period of its call to ascribe to system functions **ToString, StringFreeQ** the *Listable* attribute, allowing to considerably reduce source code of the **Arity** procedure. Finally, **Arity1** procedure – *a rather effective equivalent analog of* **Arity** *procedure* – completes the previous fragment.

The **ArityBFM** procedure defining arity of objects of the type {*module, classical function, block*} serves as quite useful addition to the procedures **Arity** and **Arity1**. The following fragment represents source code of the **ArityBFM** and the most typical examples of its application.

In[2474]:= **ArityBFM[x_ /; BlockFuncModQ[x]] := Module[{b, a = Flatten[{HeadPF[x]}]},
b = Map[If[! StringFreeQ[#, {"_", "___"}], "Undefined", Length[ToExpression["{" <>
StringTake[StringReplace[#, ToString[x] <> "[" -> ""], 1], {1, -2}] <> "}"]]] &, a];
If[Length[b] == 1, b[[1]], b]]**

In[2475]:= **G[x_ /; IntegerQ[x], y_ /; IntegerQ[y]] := x + y;
G[x_Integer, y__] := x*y; G[x_, y_ /; IntegerQ[y], z_] := x + y + z;
G[x_, y__] := x + y; G[x_ /; IntegerQ[x]] := x;
G[x_ /; x == {42, 47, 67}, y_ /; IntegerQ[y]] := Length[x] + y**
In[2476]:= **ArityBFM[G]**
Out[2476]= {2, "Undefined", 3, 2, "Undefined", 1}
In[2477]:= **S[x_, y_] := x*y; V[x__] := {x}; Map[ArityBFM, {S, V}]**

Out[2477]= {2, "Undefined"}
In[2478]:= V[a_, b_, c_, d_, h_] := N[h*(3*a*b + (c - b)*d + (d - a)*c)/3000]
In[2479]:= {V[27, 20, 49, 74, 69], ArityBFM[V]}
Out[2479]= {139.587, "Undefined"}

The procedure call **ArityBFM**[*x*] returns the *arity (number of arguments)* of a *x* object of type {*block, function, module*}; at that, a function of classical type is understood as a *x* function, i.e. some function with *heading*. In the presence in heading of formal arguments with patterns {"__", "___"} arity is determined as undefinite *("Undefined")* because arity is understood as a real number of the factual arguments, admissible at a call of a *x* object which in this case can be undefinite. On the *x* objects of type, different from the specified, the procedure call is returned unevaluated.

At last, the procedure below provides more detailed information on the arity of a function, a block or a module. The procedure call **ArityBFM1**[*x*] returns the *arity (number of the formal arguments)* of a block, function or module *x* in the format of four-element list whose the *first*, the *second* and the *third* elements define quantity of formal arguments with the patterns "_", "__" and "___" accordingly. Whereas the *fourth* element defines common quantity of formal arguments which can be different from the quantity of factual arguments. In addition, the *x* heading should has classical type as the next fragment illustrates, i.e. it should not include non-standard, but acceptable methods of headings definition. The unsuccessful procedure call returns $Failed.

In[3385]:= Av[x_, y_, z_] := x*y*z; Av[x_, y__: 69, z___] := Block[{}, {x, y, z}]
In[3386]:= Av[x_Integer, y_ /; PrimeQ[y], z__] := Module[{}, x + y + z]
In[3387]:= ArityBFM1[x_Symbol] := Module[{a, b, c, d = {}}, Map[ClearAll, {a, c}];
If[DeleteDuplicates[Flatten[{ProcFuncBlQ1[x, c]}]] != {True}, $Failed,
Quiet[Check[ArgsBFM[x, a], Return[$Failed]]];
Do[b = {0, 0, 0}; Map[If[! StringFreeQ[#, "___"], b[[3]]++,
If[! StringFreeQ[#, "__"], b[[2]]++, b[[1]]++]] &, a[[k]]];
AppendTo[d, AppendTo[b, Plus[0, Sequences[b]]]];
b = {0, 0, 0}, {k, 1, Length[a]}]; If[Length[d] == 1, d[[1]], d]]]

In[3388]:= ArityBFM1[Av]
Out[3388]= {{3, 0, 0, 3}, {2, 1, 0, 3}, {1, 1, 1, 3}}
In[3389]:= Sd[x_ /; {a[b_] = b^2 + 90; If[x >= a[5], True, False]}[[1]]] :=
Module[{a = 27, b = 20}, x*(a + b)]
In[3390]:= {Sd[2016], Definition[a]}
Out[3390]= {94752, a[b_] = 90 + b^2}
In[3391]:= Sd1[x_ /; {a[b_] = b^2 + 90, If[x >= a[5], True, False], ClearAll[a]}[[2]]] :=
Module[{a = 27, b = 20}, x*(a + b)]
In[3392]:= {Sd1[2016], Definition[a]}
Out[3392]= {94752, Null}
In[3393]:= TestHeadingQ["Sd1[x_ /; {a[b_] = b^2 + 90, If[x >= a[5], True, False], ClearAll[a]}[[2]]]"]
Out[3393]= False

Software Etudes in the Mathematica

The procedure below serves for definition of arity of system functions. The procedure call **AritySystemFunction[*x*]** generally returns the two-element list whose first element defines number of formal arguments, whereas the second element – quantity of admissible factual arguments. Whereas the procedure call **AritySystemFunction[*x*, *y*]** with the second optional *y* argument – an undefinite variable – through it returns the generalized template of formal arguments. The infinity symbol says about arbitrary number of factual arguments. Thus, the **AritySystemFunction** procedure uses the **SysFunctionQ** procedure as an auxiliary means, whose call **SysFunctionQ[*x*]** returns *True,* if *x* determines the function of the *Mathematica* language, and *False* otherwise; its source code and examples of its use are represented at the beginning of the fragment below.

```
In[3450]:= SysFunctionQ[x_] := Module[{a},
If[! SymbolQ[x], False, If[! SystemQ[x], False, a = SyntaxInformation[x];
If[a == {}, False, If[Select[a[[1]][[2]], ! SameQ[#, OptionsPattern[]] &] == {}, False, True]]]]]

In[3451]:= Map[SysFunctionQ, {Goto, Sin, Trace, Catch, For, Module, If,
SyntaxInformation, Return, Plot}]
Out[3451]= {True, True, True, True, True, True, True, True, True, True}

In[3452]:= Map[SysFunctionQ, {ProcQ, $Packages, Continue, Break, End, True, Listable,
Abort, $ExportFormats, Next}]
Out[3452]= {False, False, False, False, False, False, False, False, False, False}

In[3550]:= AritySystemFunction[x_, y___] := Module[{a, b, c, d, g, p},
If[! SysFunctionQ[x], $Failed, a = SyntaxInformation[x];
If[a == {}, $Failed, c = {0, 0, 0, 0}; b = Map[ToString, a[[1]][[2]]];
b = Map[If[SuffPref[#, "{", 1], "_",
If[SuffPref[#, {"Optional", "OptionsPattern"}, 1], "_.", #]] &, b];
If[{y} != {} && ! HowAct[y], y = Map[ToExpression[ToString[Unique["x"]] <> #] &, b], 6];
Map[If[# == "_", c[[1]]++, If[# == "_.", c[[2]]++, If[# == "__", c[[3]]++, c[[4]]++]]] &, b];
{p, c, d, g} = c; d = DeleteDuplicates[{p + d, If[d != 0 || g != 0, Infinity, p + c]}];
If[d != {0, Infinity}, d, Quiet[x[Null]]]; If[Set[p, Messages[x]] == {}, d,
p = Select[Map[ToString, Map[Part[#, 2] &, p]], ! StringFreeQ[#, " expected"] &];
p = Map[StringTake[#, {Flatten[StringPosition[#, ";"]][[1]] + 1, -2}] &, p];
p = ToExpression[Flatten[StringCases[p, DigitCharacter..]]];
If[p == {}, {1}, If[Length[p] > 1, {Min[p], Max[p]}, p]]]]]]]

In[3551]:= {AritySystemFunction[Catch, g47], g47}
Out[3551]= {{1, 3}, {x80_, x81_., x82_.}}
In[3552]:= {AritySystemFunction[ContinuousTask, k], k}
Out[3552]= {{1, 3}, {x27_, x28_., x29_.}}
In[3553]:= {AritySystemFunction[StringJoin, v42], v42}
Out[3553]= {{1, ∞}, {x85_, x86_., x87___}}
```

The **AritySystemFunction1** procedure is similar to the previous **AritySystemFunction** tool, but is based on other basis; the call **AritySystemFunction1[*x*]** generally returns a 2-element list whose *1st* and *2nd* element determine *minimal* and *maximal* number of admissible factual arguments accordingly. In case of their coincidence *1*-element list is returned. Whereas the procedure call **AritySystemFunction1**[*x, y*] with the 2*nd* optional *y* argument – an indefinite symbol – thru it returns the generalized template of formal arguments. At that, the infinity symbol (∞) says about an arbitrary number of factual arguments. An *unsuccessful* procedure call returns $*False*. The next fragment represents source code of the **AritySystemFunction1** procedure with typical examples of its application.

In[3670]:= **AritySystemFunction1**[x_ /; SystemQ[x], y___] :=
Module[{b, c, a = FindFile1["FunctionInformation.m", $InstallationDirectory], d = "",
k, p, g = {0, 0, 0, 0}},
a = StringReplace[StringReplace[ReadString[a], {"\n" -> "", "\r" -> ""}], "   " -> " "];
If[StringFreeQ[a, c = ToString1[p = ToString[x]]], $Failed,
c = Flatten[StringPosition[a, "{" <> c]][[1]];
For[k = c, k < Infinity, k++, d = d <> StringTake[a, {k, k}];
If[SyntaxQ[d], Break[]]]; d = ToExpression[d][[2]];
If[{y} != {} && ! HowAct[y], y = d, Null]; d = Map[ToString, d];
d = Flatten[Map[If[SuffPref[#, {"Optional", "OptionsPattern"}], 1], "_.",
If[SuffPref[#, "{", 1], "_", #]] &, d]]; Map[If[# == "_", g[[1]]++, If[# == "_.", g[[2]]++,
If[# == "__", g[[3]]++, g[[4]]++]]] &, d]; {p, c, d, g} = g;
d = Flatten[DeleteDuplicates[{p + d, If[d != 0 || g != 0, Infinity, p + c]}]]]]

In[3671]:= Clear[t]; {AritySystemFunction1[AmbiguityList, t], t}
Out[3671]= {{1, 3}, {{__}, _., Optional[{__}]}}
In[3672]:= Clear[t]; {AritySystemFunction1[AiryAiZero, t], t}
Out[3672]= {{1, 2}, {_, _.}}
In[3674]:= Clear[t]; {AritySystemFunction1[FailureDistribution, t], t}
Out[3674]= {{2}, {_, {{_, _}, {_, _}, ___}}}
In[3675]:= Clear[t]; {AritySystemFunction1[RevolutionPlot3D, t], t}
Out[3675]= {{2, ∞}, {_, {_, _, _}, ___, OptionsPattern[]}}

In certain cases the processing of messages generated by the calls of blocks, functions and modules in the program mode, for example, in a module body is required. The problem is solved by the procedure whose call **MessagesOut**[*x*] returns the message generated by a *G* block, a function or a module call given in the format *x* = "*G*[*z*]". Whereas the procedure call **MessagesOut**[*x, y*] with the 2*nd* optional *y* argument – an undefinite symbol – thru it returns the messages in the format {*MessageName, "Message"*}. In the absence of any messages the empty list, i.e. {}, is returned. An unsuccessful procedure call returns $*Failed*. The fragment below represents source code of the **MessagesOut** procedure with illustrative examples of its application.

In[3390]:= **MessagesOut**[x_ /; StringQ[x], y___] := Module[{a, b},
If[! (SyntaxQ[x] && CallQ[x]), $Failed, a = HeadName1[x];
If[BlockFuncModQ[a] || SysFunctionQ[Symbol[a]], ToExpression["Messages[" <>
a <> "] = {}"]; Quiet[ToExpression[x]];
b = ToExpression["Messages[" <> a <> "]"]; ToExpression["Messages[" <> a <> "] = {}"];
If[{y} != {} && ! HowAct[y], y = Select[Map[{Part[#[[1]], 1], Part[#, 2]} &, b],
! SameQ[#[[1]], $Off[]] &]; y = If[Length[y] == 1, y[[1]], y], Null]; b, $Failed]]]

In[3391]:= **MessagesOut["Integrate[a]"]**
Out[3391]= {HoldPattern[Integrate::argmu] :> "`1` called with 1 argument; ... are expected.", HoldPattern[Integrate::gener] :> $Off[]}
In[3392]:= **Clear[g70]; MessagesOut["Plot[a]", g70]**
Out[3392]= {HoldPattern[Plot::argr] :> "`1` called with 1 argument; ...", HoldPattern[Plot::argrx] :> "`1` called with `2` arguments; ...
In[3393]:= **g70**
Out[3393]= {{Plot::argr, "`1` called with 1 argument; ... are expected."}, {Plot::argrx, "`1` called with `2` arguments; ... are expected."}}
In[3394]:= **MessagesOut["ProcQ[]"]**
Out[3394]= {HoldPattern[ProcQ::usage] :> "The call ProcQ[x] returns the True if x is a procedure and the False otherwise."}
In[3395]:= **Mnpq[x_ /; StringQ[x]] := Module[{a, b, c}, MessagesOut[x]]**
In[3396]:= **Mnpq["Plot[]"]**
Out[3396]= {HoldPattern[Plot::argrx] :> "`1` called with `2` arguments; ...", HoldPattern[Plot::invmapf] :> $Off[]}

Similarly to the *Maple* system, the *Mathematica* system doesn't give any possibility to test inadmissibility of all actual arguments in a block, function or module in a point of its call, interrupting its call already on the first inadmissible actual argument. Meanwhile, in view of importance of determination of all inadmissible factual arguments only for one pass, the **TestArgsTypes** procedure solving this important enough problem and represented in our book [30] and the *MathToolBox* package [48] has been created. In addition, the emergence of the new tools and updating of our existing functional tools allows to update also and the these tools, represented by the procedure of the same name. The next fragment represents source code of the **TestArgsTypes** procedure with one its useful enough **TestArgsTypes1** modification and examples of their application.

In[2760]:= **TestArgsTypes[P_ /; ModuleQ[P] || BlockQ[P] || QFunction[P], y_] :=**
Module[{c, d = {}, h, k = 1, a = Map[ToString, Args[P]], b = ToString[InputForm[y]]},
ClearAll["$TestArgsTypes"];
If[! SuffPref[b, ToString[P] <> "[", 1], Return[y], c = Map[ToString1, ToExpression["{" <> StringTake[b, {StringLength[ToString[P]] + 2, -2}] <> "}"]]];
If[Length[a] != Length[c], $TestArgsTypes = "Quantities of formal and factual arguments are different"; $Failed, For[k, k <= Length[a], k++, d = Append[d, ToExpression["{" <> c[[k]] <> "}" <> " /. " <> a[[k]] <> " -> True"]]]; d = Map[If[ListQ[#], #[[1]], #] &, d];
h = Flatten[Map3[Position, d, Cases[d, Except[True]]]];
h = Map[{#, If[ListQ[d[[#]]], Flatten[d[[#]], 1], d[[#]]]} &, h];
$TestArgsTypes = If[Length[h] == 1, h[[1]], h]; $Failed]]

In[2761]:= **P[x_, y_String, z_ /; If[z === 90, True, False]] := {x, y, z}**
In[2762]:= **TestArgsTypes[P, P[agn, "ArtKr", 90]]**
Out[2762]= {agn, "ArtKr", 90}
In[2763]:= **TestArgsTypes[P, P[x, y, z]]**
Out[2763]= $Failed
In[2764]:= **$TestArgsTypes**

```
Out[2764]= {{2, y}, {3, z}}
In[2765]:= {TestArgsTypes[P, P[x, "y", {590}]], $TestArgsTypes}
Out[2765]= {$Failed, {3, {590}}}
In[2766]:= TestArgsTypes[P, P[x, a + b, {590}]]
Out[2766]= $Failed
In[2767]:= $TestArgsTypes
Out[2767]= {{2, a + b}, {3, {590}}}
In[2768]:= VS[x_, n_/; IntegerQ[n], y_, z_/; StringQ[z], j_/; ListQ[j] && MemberQ[{{0},
 {1}, {0, 1}}, Sort[DeleteDuplicates[Flatten[j]]]]] := Block[{}, j[[StringLength[y <> z] + n]]]
In[2769]:= VS[6, -4, "A", "vz", {0, {1, 0, 1}, {1, 0, 0, 0, 1, 1, 1, 0, 0, 1}}]
Out[2769]= {1, 0, 0, 0, 1, 1, 1, 0, 0, 1}
In[2770]:= TestArgsTypes[VS, VS[9, 7.4, A, "v", {0, {1, 0, 1}, {1, 0, 1, 1, 0, 1}}]]
Out[2770]= $Failed
In[2771]:= $TestArgsTypes
Out[2771]= {2, 7.4}
In[2772]:= TestArgsTypes[VS, VS[9, 7.4, A, vz, {0, {1, 0, 1}, {2, 0, 0, 0, 7, 2}}]]
Out[2772]= $Failed
In[2773]:= $TestArgsTypes
Out[2773]= {{2, 7.4}, {4, vz}, {5, {0, True, 2, 0, 0, 0, 7, 2}}}
In[2774]:= TestArgsTypes[VS, VS[9, 0, "A", "v", {0, {1, 0, 0, 1}, {1, 0, 1, 0, 1}}]]
Out[2774]= {1, 0, 0, 1}
In[2862]:= TestArgsTypes1[P_/; ModuleQ[P] || BlockQ[P] || QFunction[P], y_] :=
Module[{c, d = {}, h, k = 1, n, p, w, w1, a = Quiet[ArgsTypes[P]],
g = Map[ToString1, Args[P]], b = ToString[InputForm[y]]},
a = Map[{#[[1]], StringReplace[#[[2]], "\\\\" -> ""]} &, a];
ClearAll["$TestArgsTypes", "$$Art$Kr$$"];
If[! SuffPref[b, ToString[P] <> "[", 1], Return[y], c = Map[ToString1, ToExpression["{" <>
StringTake[b, {StringLength[ToString[P]] + 2, -2}] <> "}"]]];
If[Length[a] != Length[c], Return[$TestArgsTypes = "Quantities of formal and factual
arguments are different"; $Failed],
w = Map[StringTake[#, {1, StringPosition[#, "_"][[1]][[1]] - 1}] &, g];
w1 = Map[ToString, Unique[w]];
While[k <= Length[w], ToExpression[w1[[k]] <> " = " <> w[[k]]]; k++];
Map[ClearAll, w]; For[k = 1, k <= Length[a], k++, p = a[[k]];
If[p[[2]] === "Arbitrary", d = Append[d, True], If[StringFreeQ[g[[k]], " /; "],
If[ToExpression["Head[" <> c[[k]] <> "] === " <> p[[2]]], d = Append[d, True],
d = Append[d, False]], $$Art$Kr$$ = ToExpression[p[[1]]];
n = ToExpression[{p[[1]] <> " = " <> c[[k]], p[[2]]}];
ToExpression[p[[1]] <> " = " <> "$$Art$Kr$$"];
If[n[[-1]], d = Append[d, True], d = Append[d, False]]]]];
h = DeleteDuplicates[Flatten[Map3[Position, d, Cases[d, Except[True]]]]];
h = Map[{#, If[ListQ[c[[#]]], Flatten[c[[#]], 1], c[[#]]]} &, h];
$TestArgsTypes = If[Length[h] == 1, h[[1]], h]; k = 1;
```

While[k <= Length[w], ToExpression[w[[k]] <> " = " <> w1[[k]]]; k++];
ClearAll["$$Art$Kr$$"]; $Failed]

In[2863]:= TestArgsTypes1[P, P[x, a + b, {590}]]
Out[2863]= $Failed
In[2864]:= $TestArgsTypes
Out[2864]= {{2, "a + b"}, {3, "{590}"}}
In[2865]:= TestArgsTypes1[P, P[agn, "ArtKr", 90]]
Out[2865]= {agn, "ArtKr", 90}
In[2866]:= TestArgsTypes1[P, P[x, y, z, h]]
Out[2866]= $Failed
In[2867]:= $TestArgsTypes
Out[2867]= "Quantities of formal and factual arguments are different"
In[2868]:= TestArgsTypes1[P, P[x, y, z]]
Out[2868]= $Failed
In[2869]:= $TestArgsTypes
Out[2869]= {{2, "y"}, {3, "z"}}
In[2870]:= TestArgsTypes1[VS, VS[9, 7.4, A, vz, {0, {1, 0, 1}, {2, 0, 1, 5, 6, 2}}]]
Out[2870]= $Failed
In[2871]:= $TestArgsTypes
Out[2871]= {{2, "7.4"}, {4, "vz"}, {5, "{0, {1, 0, 1}, {2, 0, 1, 5, 6, 2}}"}}

In[2920]:= TestArgsTypes2[x_ /; ModuleQ[x] || BlockQ[x] || QFunction[x], y__] :=
Module[{a = Quiet[ArgsTypes[x]], b = Map[ToString1, {y}], c = {y}, d = {}, k = 1, p},
If[Length[c] != Length[a], "Quantities of formal and factual arguments are different",
For[k, k <= Length[c], k++, p = a[[k]];
AppendTo[d, If[p[[2]] === "Arbitrary", True, If[SymbolQ[p[[2]]], ToString[Head[c[[k]]]]
=== p[[2]], ToExpression[StringReplace[p[[2]], {"[" <> p[[1]] <> "]" -> "[" <> b[[k]] <> "]",
" " <> p[[1]] <> " " -> " " <> b[[k]] <> " ", " " <> p[[1]] <> "]" -> " " <> b[[k]] <> "]"}]]]]]];
If[MemberQ[d, False], Partition[Riffle[{y}, d], 2], {True, x[y]}]]]

In[2921]:= TestArgsTypes2[VS, 90, 590]
Out[2921]= "Quantities of formal and factual arguments are different"
In[2922]:= F[x_, y_String, z_Integer, t_ /; ListQ[t]] := Module[{}, x*z +
StringLength[y]*Length[t]]
In[2923]:= TestArgsTypes2[F, 90, 590, 74, a + b]
Out[2923]= {{90, True}, {590, False}, {74, True}, {a + b, False}}
In[2924]:= TestArgsTypes2[F, 90, "Agn", 590, {r, a, n, s}]
Out[2924]= {True, 53112}
In[2925]:= TestArgsTypes2[P, x, y, z]
Out[2925]= {{x, True}, {y, False}, {z, False}}

In[2932]:= TrueCallQ[x_ /; BlockFuncModQ[x], y__] :=
Quiet[Check[If[UnevaluatedQ[x, y], False, x[y]; True], False]]
In[2933]:= TrueCallQ[VS, 9, 7.4, A, vz, {0, {1, 0, 1}, {2, 0, 1, 5, 6, 2}}]
Out[2933]= False
In[2934]:= TrueCallQ[P, x, y, z, h]

Out[2934]= False
In[2935]:= **TrueCallQ[VS, 9, 7.4, A, "vz", {0, {1, 0, 1}, {1, 0, 0, 0, 1, 1, 1, 0, 0, 1}}]**
Out[2935]= False
In[2936]:= **TrueCallQ[P, agn, "ArtKr", 90]**
Out[2936]= True

Call of the above procedure **TestArgsTypes[x, x[.....]]** processes the procedure *x* call in way which returns the result of a procedure call *x*[.....] in case of absence of inadmissible factual arguments and equal number of the factual and formal arguments in the point of procedure call *x*; otherwise $Failed is returned. In addition, through the *global* variable **$TestArgsTypes** the nested list is returned, whose two-element sublists define the set of inadmissible factual arguments, namely: the first element of a sublist defines number of an inadmissible factual argument whereas the second element – its value. At discrepancy of number of the formal arguments to number of factual arguments thru **$TestArgsTypes** the appropriate diagnostic message is returned, namely: *"Quantities of formal and factual arguments are different"*.

Meanwhile, for simplification of the testing algorithm realized by the above procedure it is supposed that formal arguments of a certain procedure *x* are typified by the pattern "_" or by the construction *"Argument_ /; Test"*. Moreover, it is supposed that the unevaluated call *x* is caused by discrepancy of types of the factual arguments to the formal arguments or by discrepancy of their quantities only. Thus, the question of testing of the actual arguments is considered at the level of the heading of a block, a function or a module only for case when their number is fixed. If a procedure or a function allows the optional arguments, then their typifying assumes correct use of any expressions as the factual values, i.e. the type of format "*x_*" is supposed. In this regard at necessity, their testing should be made in the body of the procedure or function as it is illustrated by useful examples in [32]. At difficult algorithms of check of the received factual arguments onto admissibility it is recommended to program them in the body of blocks or modules what is more appropriate as a whole.

Meantime, as an expansion of the **TestArgsTypes** procedure the possibility of testing of the factual arguments onto admissibility on condition of existence in the headings of the formal arguments of types {"*x__*", "*x___*"} can be considered. Receptions, used in **TestArgsTypes1** procedure that is one useful modification of the above **TestArgsTypes** procedure is a rather perspective prerequisite for further expansion of the functionality of these tools. A result of call **TestArgsTypes1[x, x[...]]** is similar to the call **TestArgsTypes[x, x[...]]** with the difference that values of inadmissible actual arguments are given in string format. In addition, without reference to smaller reactivity of the 2nd procedure, the algorithm used at its programming is rather interesting for the number of usages, above all, of system character; its analysis can be a rather useful to the interested reader who wishes to learn *Math*-language more deeply. This remark concerns some other means of the present book.

Meanwhile, it must be kept in mind that use by the above procedures **TestArgsTypes** and **TestArgsTypes1** of the global variable **$TestArgsTypes** through which information on the inadmissible actual arguments received by a tested block, procedure at its calls is returned, should be defined in the user's package that contains definitions of these procedures, i.e. to be predetermined, otherwise diagnostic information isn't returned through it. It can be done, for example, by means of inclusion in the *MathToolBox* package of the following block:

Begin["`$TestArgsTypes`"]

$TestArgsTypes = 50090
End[]

with obligatory providing a reference *(usage)* for this variable, for example, of the kind:

$TestArgsTypes::usage = "The global variable **$TestArgsType** defined by the procedures **TestArgsTypes** and **TestArgsTypes1**."

That remark should be considered at programming of procedures which use the global $-variables for additional return of results, i.e. such variables should be initiated, for example, in a package containing the definitions of means with their usage.

In some cases the **TestArgsTypes2** procedure which is a rather useful modification of the previous procedures **TestArgsTypes** and **TestArgsTypes1** is a rather useful means; the call **TestArgsTypes2[*P, w*]**, where *P* – a block, a function with the heading, or a module and *w* – a nonempty sequence of the factual arguments passed to the *P*, returns the list of the format {*True, P[w]*} if all factual *w* arguments are admissible; the procedure call returns the nested list whose elements are two-element sublists whose first element defines a factual argument whereas the second element determines its admissibility {*True, False*}; in addition, in case of discrepancy of quantities of the formal and factual arguments the next message is returned: *"Quantities of formal and factual arguments are different"*. The above fragment contains source code of the **TestArgsTypes2** procedure with examples of its application.

At last, in contrast to the above procedures **TestArgsTypes** – **TestArgsTypes2** that provide the differentiated testing of the factual arguments received by the tested object for their admissibility, the simple function **TrueCallQ** provides testing of correctness of the call of an object of the type {*Block, Function, Module*} as a whole; the function call **TrueCallQ[*x, args*]** returns *True* if the call *x[args]* is correct, and *False* otherwise. In addition, the lack of the fact of the unevaluated call, and lack of the especial and erroneous situations distinguished by the *Mathematica* is understood as a correctness of the call. The source code of the function with typical examples of its application completes the previous fragment. It is necessary to note the interesting possibilities of further development of the procedures **TestArgsTypes** – **TestArgsTypes2** in a number of rather important directions, for instance, in case of variable number of the factual arguments, which we leave to the interested reader.

To the tools **TestArgsTypes** – **TestArgsTypes2** and **TrueCallQ** function in a certain degree the **TestArgsCall** procedure adjoins whose call allows to allocate definitions of a function, a block or a module on which the call with the given factual arguments is quite correct. The following fragment represents source code of the **TestArgsCall** procedure with the typical examples of its application.

In[2889]:= TestArgsCall[x_ /; BlockFuncModQ[x], y___] := Module[{d, p, h = {}, k = 1,
a = Flatten[{PureDefinition[x]}], b = Flatten[{HeadPF[x]}], c = "$$$", n = ToString[x]},
While[k <= Length[b], d = c <> n; ToExpression[c <> b[[k]] <> ":=90"];
p = Symbol[d][y]; ToExpression["Remove[" <> d <> "]"];
If[p === 90, AppendTo[h, a[[k]]]]; k++]; If[Length[h] == 1, h[[1]], h]]

In[2890]:= G[x_ /; IntegerQ[x], y_ /; IntegerQ[y]] := x + y;
G[x_Integer, y__] := x + y; G[x_, y__] := x+y;
G[x_, y_ /; IntegerQ[y], z_] := x+y+z; G[x_ /; IntegerQ[x]] := x;

G[x_ /; x == {42, 47, 67}, y_ /; IntegerQ[y]] := Length[x] + y;
In[2891]:= TestArgsCall[G, 19.42, 590]
Out[2891]= "G[x_, y__] := x + y"
In[2892]:= V[x_ /; IntegerQ[x], y_ /; IntegerQ[y]] := x + y; TestArgsCall[V, 19.42, 590]
Out[2892]= {}
In[2893]:= TestArgsCall[Avz, 19.42, 590]
Out[2893]= TestArgsCall[Avz, 19.42, 590]

The procedure call **TestArgsCall[*x, y*]** returns a definition or the definitions list of a block, a function or a module *x* on which the call with the tuple of factual *y* arguments is correct, i.e. their types correspond to admissible types of formal arguments. Otherwise, the procedure call returns the empty list, i.e. {}; on an inadmissible *x* argument, different from a function, a block or a module, the call is returned unevaluated.

While the procedure call **TestFactArgs[*x, y*]** returns the list from *True* and *False* that defines who of the actual arguments determined by a *y* sequence will be admissible in the call *x*[*y*], where *x* – an object name with the heading *(block, function, module)*. The procedure assumes equal number of the formal and actual arguments determined by an *y* sequence, along with existence for an object *x* of the fixed number of arguments; otherwise, the call **TestFactArgs** returns $*Failed*. The fragment below represents source code of the **TestFactArgs** procedure along with typical examples of its application.

In[2535]:= **TestFactArgs[x_ /; ProcQ[x] || QFunction[x], y__] :=**
Module[{b, c = {}, d, p = {y}, k = 1, a = Flatten[{HeadPF[x]}][[1]]},
b = StrToList["{" <> StringTake[a, {StringLength[ToString[x]] + 2, -2}] <> "}"];
b = Map[StringSplit[#, "_"] &, b];
If[Length[b] == Length[p] && StringFreeQ[a, "__"], While[k <= Length[b], d = b[[k]];
If[Length[d] == 1, AppendTo[c, True],
If[Length[d] == 2 && SymbolQ[d[[2]]], AppendTo[c, Head[p[[k]]] === Symbol[d[[2]]]],
If[SuffPref[d[[2]], " /; ", 1], AppendTo[c, ToExpression[StringReplace3[StringTake[d[[2]], {5, -1}], d[[1]], ToString[p[[k]]]]]]]]]; k++]; c, $Failed]]

In[2536]:= **VGS[x_, y_Integer, z_ /; ListQ[z]] := Flatten[{x, y, z}]**
In[2537]:= **TestFactArgs[VGS, avz, 74, {g, s, a, k}]**
Out[2537]= {True, True, True}
In[2538]:= **TestFactArgs[VGS, 42, ag, a + b]**
Out[2538]= {True, False, False}
In[2539]:= **TestFactArgs[VGS, 90, ag, a + b, 590]**
Out[2539]= $Failed

The **TestFactArgs** procedure is a *generalization* of the **CheckArgs** procedure of **Maple** system in case of definition of *admissibility* of the factual arguments for blocks, functions or modules. The presented means of testing of the factual arguments at calls of procedures can be useful enough at the organization of robust program systems of a rather large size. So, these means allow rather effectively beforehand to test the correctness of the procedures calls on those or other tuples of factual arguments.

6.6. Local variables of modules and blocks; the means of manipulation by them in the *Mathematica* software

Having considered in the previous two sections the means of manipulation with definitions of the blocks, functions, modules along with their headings, we move on to consideration of means whose circle of interests includes the problems, linked with manipulation with the following major component of definitions of blocks and modules – the *local variables*. So, this component determines the first leading variable in a block or a module definition, as a function from two variables – the list of local variables, and its body. The *local* variables take place only for the procedural objects *(Module and Block)* of the *Math*-language whereas for functions such concept is absent. The local variables have only the module body as an area of their action, without crossing with the variables of the same name outside of its domain. Meanwhile, namely between objects of types of *{Block and Module}* there is a very essential distinction which is based on mechanisms of local variables which are used by both types of objects and which are considered in [30-33,50] enough in detail.

The *Block* is a *scoping* construct that localizes symbols by separating the values they assume inside the block from values they might assume outside its. The *Block* implements dynamic scoping of variables, meaning the name of the local symbol stays the same. When the local symbol has a value, this value is used; otherwise, the value in the enclosing function is used. The *Block* localizes values only but does not substitute them. In contrast, the *Module* does the lexical scoping, meaning a new, unique copy of the variable is created in each invocation which is used nowhere else in any enclosing function or subsequent call to the *Module*. The *Block* is typically faster than *Module*, so use of *Block* may result in faster evaluation when functions with *scoped variables* are called many times. In view of the importance of the given component for which the *Mathematica* has no means of manipulation it is very desirable to have similar means. Meanwhile, previously has the meaning to consider this component of blocks and modules in more detail *(concerning the **Maple** system this question is considered in the collection* [50]).

First of all, as for admissibility of the local variables for traditional functions. The statement about their inadmissibility isn't absolutely right, namely. The local variables shouldn't have crossing with the variables of the same name, outside of the object body in which they are defined. Using this postulate, on the basis of an artificial reception it is possible to solve also this problem. Basic principle of this reception is presented on a simple example.

In[2617]:= **PrevNextVar[x_ /; SymbolQ[x], t_ /; IntegerQ[t], y___]** :=
Module[{a = ToString[x], b, c = {}, d, k, n}, b = Characters[a]; n = Length[b];
For[k = n, k >= 1, k--, If[IntegerQ[ToExpression[b[[k]]]], AppendTo[c, b[[k]]],
d = StringJoin[b[[1 ;; k]]]; Break[]]];
k = ToExpression[c = StringJoin[Reverse[c]]];
If[SameQ[k, Null] || {y} == {} && k - t <= 0, x, If[c == "", x,
ToExpression[d <> ToString[k + If[{y} != {}, t, -t]]]]]]

In[2618]:= **PrevNextVar[avz1942, 2, 5]**
Out[2618]= avz1944
In[2619]:= **PrevNextVar[avz1942, 2]**
Out[2619]= avz1940

In[2620]:= **PrevNextVar[ab590xyz, 5]**
Out[2620]= ab590xyz
In[2621]:= **G[x_, y_] := {ListAssignP[{Unique["a"]}, 1, 75], ListAssignP[{Unique["b"]}, 1, 70], PrevNextVar[Unique["a"], 2]*x + PrevNextVar[Unique["b"], 2]*y}[[-1]]**
In[2622]:= **G[90, 590]**
Out[2622]= 48050

Above all, we will need the **PrevNextVar** procedure for a special processing of the symbols of the format *<symbol><integer>* which end with an integer. The call **PrevNextVar[x, t]** on a *x* symbol of the mentioned format *<symbol><integer>* returns the symbol of format *<symbol><integer - t>* while the call **PrevNextVar[x, t, h]**, where *h* - an arbitrary expression returns a symbol of the format *<symbol><integer + t>*. At condition `integer - t <= 0` or in case of the *x* format, different from the mentioned, the source symbol *x* is returned. Previous fragment represents source code of the procedure with examples of its use. This procedure represents as independent interest, and is essentially used for solution of the problem of local variables in case of definition of the user traditional functions.

For solution of the problem of use of local variables for functions along with the previous **PrevNextVar** procedure our **ListAssignP** procedure providing assignment of a value to a list element with the set number, and system **Unique** function generating the symbols new for the current session every time at its call are used. The general format of definition of a function with local variables can be represented as follows.

F[x_, y_, ...] := {ListAssignP[{Unique["a1"]}, 1, b1], ListAssignP[{Unique["a2"]}, 1, b2],
=========
ListAssignP[{Unique["at"]}, 1, bt],
BODY[x, y, ..., PrevNextVar[Unique["a1"], j], ...,
PrevNextVar[Unique["at"], j]}[[-1]]; j = kt (k = 1..n)

According to the above format, a function is defined in the format of the list, whose the first *t* elements define the local variables with initial values ascribed to them whereas the body of this function is a certain function from formal arguments and local variables whose each encoding has the following view **PrevNextVar[Unique["ap"], j]**, *j = kt (k = 1..n)*, where *n* – number of usage of a local *"ap"* variable in the function body. In addition, the last element of such list determines result of the call of a function given in similar format as very visually illustrates example of the *G* function of the previous fragment. Thus, the described artificial reception allows to use local variables in functions, however their opportunities are rather limited. In addition, each call of function of this kind generates the mass of variables which aren't crossed with the previous variables of the current session, however they can enough significantly litter the area of variables of the current session; in this the reader can a rather simply make sure by the means of the call **Names["`*"]**. Therefore, the artificial possibility of use of the local variables by functions, and the expedience of this is not entirely the same. Meanwhile, the represented reception can be a rather useful at programming of the certain problems, first of all, of system character.

Blocks and modules in the *Mathematica* function as follows. At each call of a module for its local variables the new symbols which define their names, unique in the current session are generated. Each local variable of a module is identified by a symbol of the kind *Name$num* where *Name* – the name of a local variable determined in the module, and *num* – its current number in the current session. At that, the number is defined by *$ModuleNumber* variable as it illustrates the following a rather simple fragment, namely:

In[2572]:= G[x_, y_, z_] := Module[{a, b, c}, h = a*x+b*y+c*z;
{h, a, b, Symbol["a" <> "$" <> ToString[$ModuleNumber – 1]]}]
In[2573]:= {$ModuleNumber, G[72, 67, 47], $ModuleNumber}
Out[2573]= {72757, {72*a$72757 + 67*b$72757 + 47*c$72757, a$72757, b$72757, a$72757}, 72758}
In[2574]:= {$ModuleNumber, G[72, 67, 47], $ModuleNumber}
Out[2574]= {72761, {72*a$72761 + 67*b$72761 + 47*c$72761, a$72761, b$72761, a$72761}, 72762}
In[2575]:= G[x_, y_, z_] := Block[{a, b, c}, h = a*x + b*y + c*z;
{h, a, b, Symbol["a" <> "$" <> ToString[$ModuleNumber – 1]]}]
In[2576]:= {$ModuleNumber, G[72, 67, 47], $ModuleNumber}
Out[2576]= {72768, {72*a + 67*b + 47*c, a, b, a$72767}, 72768}
In[2577]:= n = 1; While[n <= 3, Print[$ModuleNumber]; n++]
72771
72771
72771
In[2578]:= {$ModuleNumber, $ModuleNumber}
Out[2578]= {72774, 72774}

Of the given example the principle of assignment of current numbers to the local variables quite accurately is traced at each new reference to a module containing them. Also from the fragment follows that increase of the current numbers for local variable blocks at their calls isn't done in view of different mechanisms of processing of modules and blocks. At that, on condition of knowledge of the current numbering for local variables of a module there is an opportunity to dynamically obtain their values outside of a module after each its call as this illustrates the following a rather simple and very evident fragment, namely:

In[2555]:= S[x_, y_] := Module[{a = $ModuleNumber – 1, b = $ModuleNumber – 1,
c = $ModuleNumber – 1}, h := a*x + b*y + c; {h, Symbol["a$" <>
ToString[$ModuleNumber – 1]], Symbol["b$" <> ToString[$ModuleNumber – 1]],
Symbol["c$" <> ToString[$ModuleNumber – 1]], a b, c}]
In[2556]:= S[77, 67]
Out[2556]= {10552955, 72779, 72779, 72779, 5296782841, 72779}
In[2557]:= g := {a$72780, b$72780, c$72780}
In[2558]:= S[72, 67]
Out[2558]= {10195780, 72827, 72827, 72827, 5303771929, 72827}
In[2559]:= d := {g, {a$72828, b$72828, c$72828}}
In[2560]:= S[72, 67]
Out[2561]= {10197460, 72839, 72839, 72839, 5305519921, 72839}
In[2562]:= {d, {a$72840, b$72840, c$72840}}
Out[2562]= {{{72779, 72779, 72779}, {72827, 72827, 72827}}, {72839, 72839, 72839}}

Thus, the user has opportunity to work with the local variables and outside of module that contains them, i.e. as a matter of fact at the level of global variables what in certain cases can be used quite effectively at programming of different problems and, above all, of problems of the system character.

In[2587]:= **Kr[x_, y_] := Module[{a, b}, h := a*x + b*y; {{a, b, h}, h}]**
In[2588]:= **Kr[20, 27]**
Out[2588]= {{a$3243, b$3243, 20*a$3243 + 27*b$3243}, 20*a$3243 + 27*b$3243}
In[2589]:= **%[[1]][[1]]^2 + Take[%[[1]], {2, 2}]^2**
Out[2589]= {a$3243^2 + b$3243^2}
In[2590]:= **Kr[x_, y_] := Module[{a, b}, a = 96; b = 89; h := a*x + b*y;**
Print[{"a$" <> ToString[$ModuleNumber − 1], "b$" <> ToString[$ModuleNumber − 1]}];
{Symbol["a$" <> ToString[$ModuleNumber − 1]],
Symbol["b$" <> ToString[$ModuleNumber − 1]]}]
In[2591]:= **Kr[20, 27]**
{a$72857, b$72857}
Out[2591]= {96, 89}
In[2592]:= **%[[1]]^2 + %[[−1]]^2**
Out[2592]= 17137

The previous a rather simple fragment rather visually illustrates the aforesaid. As a rule, the user shouldn't operate with values of the local variables outside of module; meanwhile, in case of operating with module in the dialogue mode or at using for monitoring of module performance of function, in particular, **Trace** these local variables will be visualized. At that, this opportunity can be used for non-standard evaluations, but effect from it is completely defined by experience and skills of the user, his knowledge of the system. In the *Maple* the similar explicit mechanism of operating with local variables outside of procedures is absent though the similar mechanism can be realized by some special receptions, in particular, on the basis of so-called method of *"disk transits"* [22]. However, such approach does variables of procedure as *really local* variables with scope limited by the procedure. In this case local variables are inaccessible outside of the procedure, what in certain respects it is possible to consider as some prerequisite for the definition of a *"black box"* and quite natural transition to the paradigm of the modular organization in programming.

In certain cases it is necessary to generate object names that are *unique* to the current session. For this purpose, the afore-mentioned system **Unique** function is designed which generates the names without the attributes ascribed to them. In addition, for ensuring of uniqueness of the generated symbols each call of the system **Unique** function provides an increment for a value of the system predefined variable *$ModuleNumber*. The mechanism of functioning of the **Unique** is similar to the mechanism of generating of names for the local variables of a module. The simple example illustrates one of approaches to software realization of **Unique** by means of **Un** procedure, whose source code with examples are given below, while useful procedure **Unique2** completes the fragment; the call **Unique2[x, y]** returns the 2-element list whose the first element defines the unique name for a *x* symbol in the string format whereas the second element defines an *y* value ascribed to the obtained unique symbol based on *x*.

In[2555]:= **Un[x___] := Module[{a}, If[{x} == {}, Symbol["$" <> ToString[$ModuleNumber]],**
a[y_] := If[StringQ[y], Symbol[y <> ToString[$ModuleNumber]], If[Head[y] == Symbol,

Symbol[ToString[y] <> "$" <> ToString[$ModuleNumber]], y]];
If[ListQ[x], Map[a, Flatten[x]], a[x]]]]

In[2556]:= {Un[], Un[S], Un["G"], Un[{x, y, z}], Un[V]}
Out[2556]= {$72867, S$72868, G72869, {x$72870, y$72870, z$72870}, V$72871}

In[2570]:= Unique1[x_, y___] := Module[{a = Unique[y], b}, b = ToString[a];
ToExpression[ToString[a] <> "=" <> ToString1[x]]; b]

In[2571]:= {Unique1[90, agn], Unique1[500]}
Out[2571]= {"agn$72883", "$25"}
In[2572]:= ToExpression[{"agn$72883", "$25"}]
Out[2572]= {90, 500}

In[2622]:= Unique2[x_ /; SymbolQ[x], y_] := Module[{a}, a = Unique[ToString[x]];
{ToString[a], ToExpression[ToString[a] <> "=" <> ToString1[y]]}]

In[2623]:= Unique2[gs, (a + b)/(c + d)]
Out[2623]= {"gs20", (a + b)/(c + d)}
In[2624]:= gs20
Out[2624]= (a + b)/(c + d)

By the standard call ?*Name* it is possible to obtain information concerning all symbols with the given **Name** which have been generated in modules or by means of the **Unique** function as it illustrates the following very simple fragment, namely:

In[2699]:= n = 1; Clear[x, y, z]; While[n < 5, Unique[{x, y, z}]; n++]
In[2700]:= ?x*
▼Global`
x10   x13 x16   x4   x7   x$72870
▼AladjevProcedures`
x   x$ x$72898   x$72899   x$72900   x$72901

Therefore, the names generated by the module behave in the same way, as other names concerning calculations. However, these names have the temporary character that defines, that they have to be completely removed from the system in the absence of need for them. Thus, the majority of the names generated in modules will be removed after performance of these modules. Only names returned by the modules explicitly remain. Moreover, outside of modules their local variables remain *undefinite* even if in modules they received the initial values. Meanwhile, it must be kept in mind that use of names of the form *name$nnn* is the agreement of the *Mathematica* for the local variables generated by modules.

So, in order to avoid any conflict situations with names of the specified format the user isn't recommended to use names of such format in own programs. It must be kept in mind, that the variables generated by modules are *unique* only during the current *Mathematica* session. The mechanism of use of *local* variables at the call of a module is considered rather in details in [30,50]. The *local* variables of the modules allow assignment to them of initial values in the form of *any* expressions, including expressions, whose values quite can depend on the *actual* arguments received at a module call or from external variables, for example:

In[2943]:= G[x_, y_] := Module[{a = If[PrimeQ[x], NextPrime[y], If[PrimeQ[y], NextPrime[x], z]]}, a*(x + y)]

In[2944]:= z = 90; {G[7, 590], G[27, 20], G[74, 69]}
Out[2944]= {354021, 4230, 12870}

The *Mathematica* system allows use of definitions of modules and functions in the domain of local variables of the procedures, providing their correct application in body of the same procedures. Moreover, after calls of procedures such definitions remain active in the current session. The following fragment rather visually illustrates told.

In[4234]:= **Ag[x_, y_Symbol] := Module[{a = {If[x <= 70, y[t_] := t^2, If[x < 75, y[t_] := t^3, y[t_] := Module[{}, t^4]]]}}, {x, y[x]}]**

In[4235]:= **Ag[50, h]**
Out[4235]= {50, 2500}
In[4236]:= **Definition[h]**
Out[4236]= h[t_] := t^2
In[4237]:= **Ag[74, h]**
Out[4237]= {74, 405224}
In[4238]:= **Definition[h]**
Out[4238]= h[t_] := t^3
In[4239]:= **Ag[90, h]**
Out[4239]= {90, 65610000}
In[4240]:= **Definition[h]**
Out[4240]= h[t_] := Module[{}, t^4]

In certain cases the above reception can be a rather useful.

In addition, at the level of local variables not exists of any opportunity immediate *(without execution of offers of procedure body)* of exit from procedure, for example, in case of calculation of the initial expressions ascribed to the local variables as that illustrates a simple fragment, the exception is the use of the call **Abort[]** which initiates return by the procedure $Aborted:

In[2487]:= G[x_, y_] := Module[{a = If[PrimeQ[x], NextPrime[y], Return[x]]}, a*(x + y)]
In[2488]:= G[90, 590]
Out[2488]= 61200
In[2489]:= G[x_, y_] := Module[{a = If[PrimeQ[x], NextPrime[y], Defer[G[x]]]}, a*(x + y)]
In[2490]:= G[90, 590]
Out[2490]= 680*G[90]
In[2491]:= G[x_, y_] := Module[{a = If[PrimeQ[x], NextPrime[y], Abort[]]}, a*(x + y)]
In[2492]:= G[90, 590]
Out[2492]= $Aborted

The concept of the *modules* in the context of the mechanism of local variables quite closely is adjoined the objects of *block* type, whose organization has the following kind, namely:

Block[{a, b, c, ...}, Body] – *Body is evaluated, using the local values for {a, b, c, ...} variables;*

Block[{a = a0, b = b0, c = c0, ...}, Body] – *Body at initial values for {a, b, c, ...} variables localized in a block is evaluated.*

In modular structure the local variables are such by definition while in block structure the variables, defined as local, operates only within the block. At that, if to them in block aren't ascribed values, they accept values of the variables of the same name that are external with respect to a block, while in case of assignment of values by it in the block, values of *variables* of the same name *outside* of the block remain without change. Therefore, by the *circumstance* the mechanisms of local variables of modules and blocks enough significantly differ.

For this reason, speaking about procedures of types {"*Module*", "*Block*"}, we have to analyze block objects regarding character of their local variables, namely: lack of the local variables or existence for each local variable of an initial value says that this object can be considered as the procedure that receives at a call an information only from the factual arguments. On such principle our tests considered here and in our books [30-32,50] for check of a block to be as an actual procedure are built. Thus, the general rule for a block structure is defined by the principle – the variables located outside of a block, until the block and after the block, save values, acting in relation to the block as *global* variables while in the block the variables of the same name can arbitrarily change the values according to the demanded algorithm.

As it was noted above, the local variable *b* in a structure **Module[{b}, Body]** correlates with an unique symbol which is modified every time when the given module is used; the given symbol differs from the global name *b*. While the variable *b* in a structure **Block[{b}, Body]** is global variable outside of the block, it in the course of performance of the block can accept any values but by exit from the block restores a value that it had on entrance to the block. If in a case of a *Module*–construction the local variables in such procedure body are especially temporary, in a *Block*–construction they aren't considered as such. Without going into detail, we only will note that for providing of the robustness of procedures it is recommended to program them, generally, on the basis of **Module**-constructions, or on the basis of the *Block*-constructions for which there are no local variables or all local variables have initial values.

Meanwhile, it should be noted, within of modular structure a mechanism of localization of the global variables can be quite realized similarly to mechanism used in a block structure; two variants have been offered in [28,32]. Moreover, also other variants of realization of the mechanism of localization of global variables which are used by blocks, and on the basis of other approaches one of which is considered in [28,30,50] are possible. In this regard quite appropriate to note, that there is an quite simple and universal mechanism of work with the global variables in the body of procedures keeping their values at the time of an entrance to procedure and of an exit from it. Formally its essence can be presented visually on the basis of the following rather simple scheme:

$$h = x; G[x\_, y\_, ...] := Module[\{b = h, ...\}, Body<h, ..., \{h = b, Res\}[[-1]]>]$$

Suppose, outside of the body of a *G* procedure the *global h* variable, used in the procedure as a *local* variable, received a *x* value. The local *b* variable of the *G* procedure receives *x* as an initial value, keeping it upto each potential exit from the procedure. In the future, the algorithm realized by the procedure body can use the *h* variable arbitrarily, and only each possible exit from the *G* procedure together with returning of a result (*Res*) has to provide assignment to the *h* variable of its initial *x* value upto exit from the procedure. So, a rather simple example visually illustrates the described mechanism of use of global variables in a procedure body at the local level, namely:

In[2517]:= h = 90; P[x_] := Module[{a = h, R}, h = 6; R = h*x; {h = a, R}[[-1]]]
In[2518]:= {P[590], h}
Out[2518]= {3540, 90}

Thereby, the block constructions allow to determine effectively *"environment"* in which it is temporarily possible to change values of global variables; the global variables are used by a block body as local variables, and only on exit from the block they restore own values upto entrance to the block. In the general understanding, block structures serve as certain *"fields"* of the current session in which the values changes of the variables located outside of these domain without change of their values outside of such domain is admissible, i.e. some kind of localization of global variables of the current session in certain fields of computing space in general is provided. This possibility was used a rather effectively in a number of means composing our *MathToolBox* package [48,50]. In addition, the block structure is implicitly used in realization of a number of the *Mathematica* functions, e.g. **Do, Product, Table, Sum,** etc., mainly, of iterative type for localization of variables of indexing as that a rather visually illustrates a very simple example, namely:

In[2520]:= n := 90; {{Sum[n^2, {n, 20}], n}, {Product[n, {n, 27}], n}}
Out[2520]= {{2870, 90}, {10888869450418352160768000000, 90}}

As a rule, the system considers any variable, determined by the user in the current session if the opposite isn't specified as a global variable. However, in the certain cases is required to localize a global variable for some period, that the block structure quite successfully allows to make. At the same time it should be noted once again, the variables localized in a block only then are the local variables if in the block the values are ascribed to them; otherwise their values in the block will *coincide* with values of the variables of the same name that are external relative to the block. Therefore, if for a localized variable in a block an initial value wasn't defined, the real localization for such variable isn't made. Thus, in the certain cases it makes sense to create the procedural objects on the basis of both the modular, and the block organization. Therefore, in a general sense under procedural objects in the *Mathematica* it is quite possible to consider the objects, created as on the basis of the modular, and the block organizations on condition of fulfillment by the block organization of the above conditions – absence for it of the local variables or existence for each local variable of an initial value. We will represent some means of manipulation with local variables of modules and blocks that play essential enough part in various problems of procedural programming.

First of all, it is very desirable to have the means for definition of the *local* variables of blocks and modules which are absent among standard means of the *Mathematica* system. As such tool, it is possible to consider the **Locals** procedure whose source code with examples of its application the following fragment represents. The procedure is intended for evaluation of the local variables of the user blocks and modules.

In[2538]:= M[x_, y_] := Module[{a = 90, b = 500}, (x + y)*(a + b)];
M[x_] := x; M[x_ /; IntegerQ[x]] := Block[{}, x^2];
M[x_Integer, y_ /; ListQ[y]] := Block[{a, b = 90}, x^2];
P[x__] := Module[{a = h, R}, h = 90; R = h*x; {h = a, R}[[-1]]]
In[2539]:= Locals[x_ /; ProcQ1[x], R___] := Module[{c, d = {}, p, t, q, Sg, Sv,
a = Flatten[{PureDefinition[x]}], b = Flatten[{HeadPF[x]}], k = 1},
Sg[y_String] := Module[{h = 1, v = {}, j, s = "", z = StringLength[y] – 1}, Label[avz];
For[j = h, j <= z, j++, s = s <> StringTake[y, {j, j}];
If[! SameQ[Quiet[ToExpression[s]], $Failed] && StringTake[y, {j + 1, j + 1}] == ",",

AppendTo[v, s]; h = j + 3; s = ""; Goto[avz]]]; AppendTo[v, s <> StringTake[y, {-1, -1}]]];
Map[If[Quiet[StringTake[#, {1, 2}]] === ", ", StringTake[#, {3, -1}], #] &, v]];
c = Flatten[Map[Map3[StringJoin, #, {" := ", " = "}] &, b]];
c = Map[StringReplace[#, Map[Rule[#, ""] &, c]] &, a];
For[k, k <= Length[a], k++, p = c[[k]];
If[SuffPref[p, "Module[{", 1], t = 8, If[SuffPref[p, "Block[{", 1], t = 7, t = 0;
AppendTo[d, "Function"]]];
If[t != 0, AppendTo[d, SubStrSymbolParity1[StringTake[p, {t, -1}], "{", "}"][[1]]]];
Continue[]];
d = Map[StringReplace[#, {"{" -> "{$$90$$", ", " -> ", $$90$$", "= " -> "= $$90$$"}] &, d];
d = Map[If[MemberQ[{"Function", "{}"}, #], #, Sg[StringTake[#, {2, -2}]]] &, d];
d = Map[If[FreeQ[Quiet[ToExpression[#]], $Failed], #, StringJoin1[#]] &, d];
d = Map[If[# === {""}, "{}", #] &, Mapp[StringReplace, d, {"$$90$$" -> "", "\\" -> ""}]];
Map[ClearAll, Names["`$$90$$*"]];
If[{R} != {} && ! HowAct[R], Sv[y_List] := Map[Flatten, Map[{q = StringPosition[#, " = "],
If[q == {}, {#, "No"},
{StringTake[#, {1, q[[1]][[1]] - 1}], StringTake[#, {q[[1]][[2]] + 1, -1}]}}][[2 ;; -1]] &, y]];
R = {}; Do[AppendTo[R, If[ListQ[d[[k]]], Sv[d[[k]]], d[[k]]]], {k, 1, Length[d]}];
R = If[ListQ[HeadPF[x]], R, R[[1]]], Null];
d = If[Length[d] == 1, Flatten[d], d], If[d == {"{}"}, {}, d]]]

In[2540]:= **Locals[M]**
Out[2540]= {{"a", "b = 90"}, {"a = 90", "b = 500"}, "{}", "Function"}
In[2541]:= **Locals[P]**
Out[2541]= {"a = h", "R"}
In[2542]:= **Map[Locals, {ModuleQ, Definition2, Locals}]**
Out[2542]= {{"a = PureDefinition[x]", "b"}, {"a", "b = Attributes[x]", "c"}, {"c", "d = {}", "p", "t", "a = Flatten[{PureDefinition[x]}]", "b = Flatten[{HeadPF[x]}]", "k = 1", "Sg", "Sv"}}
In[2543]:= **G[x_, y_] := Module[{a = If[PrimeQ[x], NextPrime[y], If[PrimeQ[y], NextPrime[x], z]]}, a*(x + y)]; Locals[G]**
Out[2543]= {"a = If[PrimeQ[x], NextPrime[y], If[PrimeQ[y], NextPrime[x], z]]"}
In[2544]:= **Locals[P, g70]**
Out[2544]= {"a = h", "R"}
In[2545]:= **g70**
Out[2545]= {{"a", "h"}, {"R", "No"}}
In[2546]:= **Locals[M, v75]**
Out[2546]= {{"a", "b = 90"}, {"a = 90", "b = 500"}, "{}", "Function"}
In[2547]:= **v75**
Out[2547]= {{{"a", "No"}, {"b", "90"}}, {{"a", "90"}, {"b", "500"}}, "{}", "Function"}
In[2548]:= **Z[x_] := x; Z[x_, y_] := x + y; Z[x_, y_, z_] := x + y + z; Locals[Z, t9]**
Out[2548]= {"Function", "Function", "Function"}
In[2549]:= **t9**
Out[2549]= {"Function", "Function", "Function"}
In[2550]:= **Locals[G, s50]**

Out[2550]= {"a = If[PrimeQ[x], NextPrime[y], If[PrimeQ[y], NextPrime[x], z]]"}
In[2551]:= s50
Out[2551]= {"a", "If[PrimeQ[x], NextPrime[y], If[PrimeQ[y], NextPrime[x], z]]"}
In[2552]:= B[x_] := Module[{a}, x]; {Locals[B, t42], t42}
Out[2552]= {{"a"}, {"a", "No"}}
In[2553]:= V[x_] := Module[{a, b, c, d}, x]; Locals[V, t55]
Out[2553]= {"a", "b", "c", "d"}
In[2554]:= t55
Out[2554]= {{"a", "No"}, {"b", "No"}, {"c", "No"}, {"d", "No"}}
In[3156]:= A[m_] := Block[{a = 42.74, b = {m, n = 590}, q, t}, Body]; {Locals[A, s49], s49}
Out[3156]= {{{"a = 42.74", "b = {m, n = 590}", "q", "t"}}, {{{"a", "42.74"}, {"b", "{m, n = 590}"}, {"q", "No"}, {"t", "No"}}}}

The represented **Locals** procedure on functionality covers both the procedure of the same name, and the **Locals1** procedure that are considered in [30-32]. The call **Locals**[*x*] returns the list whose elements in the string format represent local variables of a block or a module *x* together with their initial values. Whereas the call **Locals**[*x, y*] with the second optional *y* argument – an undefinite variable – provides in addition return through *y* or of the simple two-element list, or the list of the *ListList* type with 2–element sublists whose first elements determine names of local variables of a block or module *x* in the string format, whereas the second element – the initial values, ascribed to them in the string format; absence of initial values is defined by the *"No"* symbol. If a *x* object has no *local* variables, the procedure call **Locals**[*x, y*] returns empty list, i.e. {}, the same result is returned thru the second optional *y* argument. Moreover, on typical function the call of the procedure returns *"Function"*. The **Locals** procedure is rather widely used in problems connected with various manipulation with the local variables.

In[2352]:= **StringJoin1**[x_ /; ListQ[x] && AllTrue[Map[StringQ, x], TrueQ]] :=
Module[{a = x, b = Length[x], c = "", k = 1},
While[k <= b - 1, c = c <> a[[k]] <> ", "; k++]; c <> a[[-1]]]

In[2353]:= **StringJoin1**[{"Avz", "Agn", "Vsv", "Art", "Kr"}]
Out[2353]= "Avz, Agn, Vsv, Art, Kr"
In[2354]:= **StringJoin1**[{"Avz", 590, x + y, "Art", Sin}]
Out[2354]= StringJoin1[{"Avz", 590, x + y, "Art", Sin}]

The definition of the **Locals** procedure along with standard means uses and our means such as **BlockFuncModQ**, **PureDefinition**, **SuffPref**, **HowAct**, **HeadPF**, **Mapp**, **Map3**, **NestListQ**, **SubStrSymbolParity1** considered in the present book and in [28-33]. At that, for realization of this procedure along with the above tools the expediency became clear to define a simple **StringJoin1** procedure for the purpose of special processing of strings lists which is a rather useful modification of the standard **StringJoin** function. The procedure call **StringJoin1**[*x*] returns result of consecutive concatenation of string elements of a *x* list which are separated by commas as very visually illustrates a example of the previous fragment with source code of this procedure. The **StringJoin1** procedure belongs to group of the means operating with string structures, however it is considered exactly here in the context of **Locals** procedure; note, the **StringJoin1** procedure has a rather wide range of appendices.

Meanwhile, in certain cases it is required to define only the list of names of local variables irrespectively from the initial values ascribed to them. The **Locals1** procedure replacing two former procedures **Locals1** and **Locals2** [28,30] can be used for this purpose. The procedure call **Locals1[x]** returns the list of names in the string format of local variables of a block or a module *x*; in a case of absence of local variables for a *x* object the procedure call returns the empty list, i.e. {}. Furthermore, in a case of an object of the same name *x* which contains the subobjects of the same name with different headings the nested list is returned, elements of which are bijective with *x* subobjects, according to their order at call of the **PureDefinition** procedure on the *x* object. The following fragment represents source code of the procedure **Locals1** along with the most typical examples of its application.

In[2587]:= Locals1[x_ /; BlockFuncModQ[x]] := Module[{a, b = {}, c, k = 1, kr},
kr[y_List] := Module[{d = {}, v = Flatten[y], j = 1}, While[j <= Length[v]/2,
AppendTo[d, v[[2*j - 1]]]; j++]; d]; ClearAll[a]; Locals[x, a];
If[NestListQ1[a], For[k, k <= Length[a], k++, c = a[[k]]];
AppendTo[b, If[MemberQ[{"{}", "Function"}, c], c, kr[c]]]];
If[StringQ[PureDefinition[x]], Flatten[b], b], kr[a]]]

In[2588]:= **Locals1[P]**
Out[2588]= {"a", "R"}
In[2589]:= **Locals1[G]**
Out[2589]= {"a"}
In[2590]:= **Locals1[M]**
Out[2590]= {{"a", "b"}, {"a", "b"}, "{}", "Function"}

For examples of this fragment the means, given in the fragment above, have been used. At that, right there we will note that the **Locals1** procedure represents one of the most effective tools in the problems of processing of local variables of blocks and modules.

As one more useful means of this kind it is possible to note also the **Locals2** procedure that should be preceded by the procedure, in many cases useful and intended for testing of the objects of the same name which have several definitions of various type. The procedure call **QBlockMod[x]** returns *True* if definitions of a *x* object have type {*Module, Block*}, and *False* otherwise. This procedure assumes that in the presence among definitions of *x* of definitions of other type, such object in general can't be considered by the object of type {*Module, Block*}. It allows to allocate from the objects of the same name the objects of the type {*Module, Block*}. The fragment represents source code of the **QBlockMod** procedure with examples of its use.

In[2585]:= M[x_, y_] := Module[{a = 90, b = 590}, (x + y)*(a + b)]; M[x_] := x;
A[m_, n_] := Module[{a = 42.74, b = {m, n=90}}, h*(m + n + p)/(a + b)];
A[m_] := Block[{a = 42.74, b = {m, n = 90}, q, t}, h*(m + n + p)/(a +b)]

In[2586]:= QBlockMod[x_] := Module[{a = Flatten[{PureDefinition[x]}], b, c = True, k = 1},
If[MemberQ[{"System", $Failed}, a[[1]]], False, b = Flatten[{HeadPF[x]}];
While[k <= Length[a], If[! SuffPref[StringReplace[a[[k]], b[[k]] <> " := " -> ""], 1],
{"Module[{", "Block[{"}, 1], c = False; Break[]]; k++]; c]]

In[2587]:= A[x_] := Block[{}, x^3]; QBlockMod[M]
Out[2587]= False

In[2588]:= Map[QBlockMod, {ProcQ, A, ToString1, StrStr, 590, Sin}]
Out[2588]= {True, True, True, False, False, False}

In the context of the previous **QBlockMod** procedure the following **Locals2** procedure on x objects of the type {*Module, Block*} returns the nested list of their local variables in the string format without initial values assigned to them if the x object contains several definitions, in the opposite case the simple list is returned. The next fragment presents the procedure code along with examples of its use; these examples are tooken from the previous fragment.

In[2710]:= Locals2[x_ /; QBlockMod[x]] := Module[{c = {}, d, p, h, q, k = 1, g = {},
a = Flatten[{PureDefinition[x]}], b = Flatten[{HeadPF[x]}], Sv},
While[k <= Length[a], AppendTo[c, d = StringReplace[a[[k]], Mapp[Rule,
Map[b[[k]] <> " := " <> # &, {"Module[", "Block["}], ""], 1];
Quiet[SubStrSymbolParity[d, "{", "}", 1][[-1]]]]; k++];
Sv[y_List] := Map[Flatten, Map[{q = StringPosition[#, " = "],
If[q == {}, #, {StringTake[#, {1, q[[1]][[1]] - 1}],
StringTake[#, {q[[1]][[2]] + 1, -1}]}]}[[2 ;; -1]] &, y]]; Locals[x]; c = If[NestListQ1[c], c, {c}];
Do[AppendTo[g, Map[#[[1]] &, If[ListQ[c[[k]]], Quiet[Check[Sv[c[[k]]], c[[k]]]], c[[k]]]]],
{k, 1, Length[c]}];
g = If[Length[b] > 1, g, If[g == {{}}, {}, If[Length[g[[1]]] > 1, g[[1]], g[[1]][[1]]]]];
If[StringQ[g], {g}, g]]

In[2711]:= Locals2[A]
Out[2711]= {{"a", "b", "q", "t"}, {"a", "b"}, "{}"}

The procedure **Locals3** essentially uses the procedure **StringToList**, and its call **Locals3**[x] returns the list whose elements in string format represent the local variables of a block or a module x or lists of such variables together with their initial values. Whereas, on the typical functions the procedure call returns *"Function"*. The following fragment represents source codes of both tools with examples of their application.

In[3126]:= StringToList[x_ /; StringQ[x]] := Module[{a, b, c = {}, d = {}, k, j, t = "", t1, n = 1},
b = DeleteDuplicates[Flatten[StringPosition[x, ","]]];
PrependTo[b, 0]; AppendTo[b, StringLength[x] + 1];
Do[AppendTo[c, StringTake[x, {b[[k]] + 1, b[[k + 1]] - 1}]], {k, 1, Length[b] - 1}];
a = Length[c]; Do[For[j = n, j <= a, j++, t = t <> c[[j]] <> ","; t1 = StringTrim[t, {",", " "}];
If[SyntaxQ[t1], AppendTo[d, t1]; t = ""; n = j + 1; Break[]]], {k, 1, a}]; d]

In[3127]:= StringToList["m = 90, b = {m,n=90}, h, c={x,y,z}, a=590, z={1,2,3}"]
Out[3127]= {"m=90", "b={m,n=90}", "h", "c={x,y,z}", "a=590", "z={1,2,3}"}

In[3197]:= Locals3[x_ /; BlockFuncModQ[x]] := Module[{c = {}, d, h, q, g = {}, S,
a = Flatten[{PureDefinition[x]}], b = Flatten[{HeadPF[x]}]},
Do[d = StringReplace[a[[k]], {b[[k]] <> " := " -> "", b[[k]] <> " = " -> ""}, 1];
h = If[SuffPref[d, {"Module[", "Block["}, 1], StringTrim[d, {"Module[", "Block["}],
"Function"];
AppendTo[c, If[h == "Function", "Function", CorrectSubString[h, 1]]], {k, 1, Length[a]}];
c = Map[If[MemberQ[{"Function", "{}"}, #], #, StringToList[StringTake[#, {2, -2}]]] &, c];

```
S[y_] := Map[{q = StringPosition[#, " = "], If[q == {}, #, {StringTake[#, {1, q[[1]][[1]] - 1}],
StringTake[#, {q[[1]][[2]] + 1, -1}]}]}[[2 ;; -1]] &, y];
Do[AppendTo[g, If[MemberQ[{"Function", "{}"}, c[[k]]], c[[k]], Map[#[[1]] &, S[c[[k]]]]]],
{k, 1, Length[c]}]; Flatten[g, LevelsList[g] - 1]]
```
In[3198]:= **Locals3[M]**
Out[3198]= {{"a", {"b", "90"}}, {{"a", "90"}, {"b", "590"}}, "{}", "Function"}

The procedure below is a rather useful and instructive version of the previous procedure, using certain useful receptions. The procedure call **Locals4[*x*]** returns the list whose sublists in the string format represent the local variables of a block or a module *x* together with their initial values, if they exist. In case of *emply* tuple of local variables the procedure call returns the empty list. However, the procedure is intended for *unique* objects of type {*Block, Module*}, i.e. the objects having single definitions. Meantime, the procedure can be simply adapted to objects of the same name, i.e. objects having *multiple* headings. The next fragment represents source code of the procedure with evamples of its use.

```
In[4125]:= Locals4[x_ /; BlockModQ[x]] :=
Module[{a = StringReplace[PureDefinition[x], HeadPF[x] <> " := " <>
TestBFM[x] <> "[" -> ""], b = "", c = {}, k, j, d},
Do[If[SyntaxQ[Set[b, b <> StringTake[a, {j}]]], Break[]], {j, StringLength[a]}];
{a, b} = {b, ""}; d = StringLength[a];
For[j = 2, j <= d, j++, For[k = j, k <= d, k++,
If[SyntaxQ[Set[b, b <> StringTake[a, {k}]]] && MemberQ[{",", "}"}, StringTake[a, {k + 1}]],
AppendTo[c, b]; b = ""; Break[]]]; j = k + 2];
Map[StringTrim[#] &, Map[StringSplit[#, "=", 2] &, c]]]
In[4126]:= G[x_, y_, z_] := Module[{a = 75, b = 70, c = If[x > 56, x^2, x^3]}, a*x + b*y + c*z]
In[4127]:= G[75, 70, 50]
Out[4127]= 291775
In[4128]:= Locals4[G]
Out[4128]= {{"a", "75"}, {"b", "70"}, {"c", "If[x > 56, x^2, x^3]"}}
```

The procedure call **StringToList[*x*]** returns the list of syntactically correct substrings of a *x* string which are parted by the comma. This procedure is useful enough at programming of problems, connected, in particular, with processing of the headings and local variables.

In a number of cases there is a necessity of dynamical extension of the list of local variables for a block or a module that is activated in the current session, without change of the object code on the *storage* medium. The **ExpLocals** procedure presented by the following fragment solves the problem. So, the procedure call **ExpLocals[*x, y*]** returns the list of local variables in the string format with the initial values ascribed to them on which local variables of a *x* object are expanded. At that, generally speaking this list can be less than a *y* list given at the procedure call *(or at all empty)* because the variables which are available in the *x* object as the formal arguments or local variables are excluded from it.

```
In[2757]:= ExpLocals[P_ /; ModuleQ[P] || BlockQ[P], L_ /; ListQ[L] &&
AllTrue[Map[StringQ, L], TrueQ]] :=
Module[{a = Flatten[{PureDefinition[P]}][[1]], b = Locals1[P], c = Args[P, 90], d, p, p1, h,
```

```
Op = Options[P], Atr = Attributes[P], t}, Quiet[d = Map[If[StringFreeQ[#, {" = ", "="}], #,
StringSplit[#, {" = ", "="}][[1]]] &, L]; p = Locals[P]; h = MinusList1[d, Flatten[{b, c}]];
If[h == {}, Return[{}]]; ClearAll[t]; BlockModQ[P, t];
h = Flatten[Map[Position[d, #] &, h]]; d = Join[p, c = Map[L[[#]] &, h]];
ToExpression["ClearAllAttributes[" <> ToString[P] <> "]"]; ClearAll[P];
ToExpression[StringReplace[a, t <> "[" <> ToString[p] -> t <> "[" <> ToString[d], 1]]];
If[Op != {}, SetOptions[P, Op]]; SetAttributes[P, Atr]; c]
```

In[2758]:= **Avz[x_] := Module[{a = 90, b, c}, a + x^2]; SetAttributes[Avz, Protected];**
Agn[x_] := Module[{}, {x}]; Z[x_ /; IntegerQ[x]] := Module[{a, b, c, d}, {a, b, c, d}[[x]]]

In[2759]:= **ExpLocals[Agn, {"x", "a = c + d", "b", "Art = 27", "Sv", "Kr = 20"}]**
Out[2760]= {"a = c + d", "b", "Art = 27", "Sv", "Kr = 20"}

In[2761]:= **Definition[Agn]**
Out[2761]= Agn[x_] := Module[{a = c + d, b, Art = 27, Sv, Kr = 20}, {x}]

In[2762]:= **ExpLocals[Avz, {"x", "a = c+d", "b", "Art = 27", "Sv", "Kr = 20"}]**
Out[2762]= {"Art = 27", "Sv", "Kr = 20"}

In[2763]:= **Definition[Avz]**
Out[2763]= Attributes[Avz] = {Protected}
Avz[x_] := Module[{a = 90, b, c, Art = 27, Sv, Kr = 20}, a + x^2]

In[2764]:= **ExpLocals[Avz, {"x", "a = c+d", "b", "Art = 27", "Sv", "Kr = 20"}]**
Out[2764]= {}

In[2765]:= **ExpLocals[Z, {"m = 90", "n = 590", "p = 74"}]**
Out[2765]= {"m = 90", "n = 500", "p = 74"}

In[2766]:= **Definition[Z]**
Out[2766]= Z[x_ /; IntegerQ[x]] := Module[{a, b, c, d, m = 90, n = 590, p = 74}, {a, b, c, d}[[x]]]

The above fragment contains source code of the **ExpLocals** procedure with examples of its application to simple enough procedures **Agn, Avz, Z** for the purpose of extension of their list of local variables the part of which has initial values; at that, in the second procedure the list of local variables is the empty while for the first procedure there is a nonempty crossing of the joint list of formal arguments and local variables with the list of variables on which it is necessary to expand the list of local variables of the procedure. In addition, if the joint list coincides with *y* list, the procedure call returns empty list, i.e. {}, without changing an initial *x* object in the current session. It must be kept in mind, that elements of the *y* list need to be encoded in string format in order to avoid assignment of values to them of variables of the same name of the current session and/or calculations according to the initial values ascribed to them. The result of a modification of an initial *x* object preserves options and attributes of the initial *x* object.

It is well known that activation in the current session of a module or a block in the domain of names of variables of the *Mathematica* system adds all their local variables as illustrates a simple example, namely:

In[2582]:= **Mb[x_] := Block[{Art = 27, Kr = 20, Sv = 49}, x]; Mb[590];**
In[2583]:= **B[x_] := Block[{Art1 = 27, Kr1 = 20, Sv1 = 49}, x]; B[590];**
In[2584]:= **Names["`*"]**
Out[2584]= {"Art", "Art1", "B", "Kr", "Kr1", "Mb", "Sv", "Sv1"}

Therefore, economical use of the local variables is a quite important problem. Meanwhile, in the course of programming of blocks/modules quite really emersion of the so-called *excess local variables*. The **RedundantLocals** procedure that is based on the **ProcBMQ** procedure, in a certain degree solves this problem. The following fragment represents source code of the **RedundantLocals** procedure with examples of its application.

In[2571]:= RedundantLocals[x_ /; BlockFuncModQ[x]] :=
Module[{a, b, c, p, g, k = 1, j, v, t = {}, z = ""},
{a, b} = {PureDefinition[x], Locals1[x]};
If[StringQ[a], If[b == {}, True, p = Map[#[[1]] &, StringPosition[a, {"} = ", "} := "}]]];
p = Select[p, ! MemberQ[{"{\"}", " \"}"}, StringTake[a, {# - 2, #}]] &];
c = Map[Map3[StringJoin, #, {" := ", " = "}] &, b];
g = Select[b, StringFreeQ[a, Map3[StringJoin, #, {" := ", " = "}]] &];
While[k <= Length[p], v = p[[k]];
For[j = v, j >= 1, j--, z = StringTake[a, {j, j}] <> z;
If[! SameQ[Quiet[ToExpression[z]], $Failed], AppendTo[t, z]]]; z = ""; k++];
t = MinusList[g, Flatten[Map[StrToList, t]]];
If[t == {}, t, p = Select[Map[" " <> # <> "[" &, t], ! StringFreeQ[a, #] &]; g = {};
For[k = 1, k <= Length[p], k++, v = StringPosition[a, p[[k]]];
v = Map[#[[2]] &, v]; z = StringTake[p[[k]], {2, -2}]; c = 1;
For[j = c, j <= Length[v], j++, For[b = v[[j]], b <= StringLength[a], b++, z = z <>
StringTake[a, {b, b}]; If[! SameQ[Quiet[ToExpression[z]], $Failed], AppendTo[g, z];
c = j + 1; z = StringTake[p[[k]], {2, -2}]; Break[]]]]];
MinusList[t, Map[HeadName[#] &, Select[g, HeadingQ1[#] &]]]]]],
"Object <" <> ToString[x] <> "> has multiple definitions"]]

In[2572]:= Map[RedundantLocals, {ProcQ, Locals1, RedundantLocals}]
Out[2572]= {{"h"}, {"a"}, {}}
In[2573]:= Vsv[x_, y_] := Module[{a, b, c = 90, d, h}, b = 590; d[z_] := z^2 + z + 590;
h[t_] := Module[{}, t]; d[c + b] + x + y + h[x*y]]
In[2574]:= RedundantLocals[Vsv]
Out[2574]= {"a"}
In[2575]:= Map[RedundantLocals, {ProcQ, Globals, RedundantLocals, Locals, Locals1}]
Out[2575]= {{"h"}, {}, {}, {}, {"a"}}
In[3384]:= RedundantLocalsM[x_ /; BlockFuncModQ[x]] :=
Module[{d, b = {}, k = 1, c = ToString[Unique["g"]], a = Flatten[{PureDefinition[x]}]},
While[k <= Length[a], d = c <> ToString[x]; ToExpression[c <> a[[k]]];
AppendTo[b, If[QFunction[d], "Function", RedundantLocals[d]]];
ToExpression["ClearAll" <> d <> "]"]; k++]; Remove[c]; If[Length[b] == 1, b[[1]], b]]
In[3385]:= Vsv[x_, y_] := Module[{a, b, c = 90, d, h}, b = 590; d[z_] := z*x + 590;
h[t_] := Module[{}, t]; d[c + b] + x + y + h[x*y]]; Vsv[x_, y_, z_] := Module[{a, b, c = 90, d, h},
a = 6; d[p_] := z + p + 590; h[t_] := Module[{}, t]; d[c + b] + x + y + h[x*y*z]]; Vsv[x_] := x
In[3386]:= RedundantLocalsM[Vsv]

339

Out[3386]= {{"a"}, {"b"}, "Function"}

The procedure call **RedundantLocals[x]** returns the list of local variables in string format of a block or a module *x* which the procedure considers excess variables in the context, what both the initial values, and values in body of the *x* object weren't ascribed to them, or these variables aren't names of the internal functions or modules, blocks defined in body of the *x* object. At that, the local variables used as an argument at the call of one or the other function in body of a *x* object *(in particular, it takes place for* **Locals1** *procedure that uses the call* **Locals[x, a]** *in which through the 2nd optional a argument – an undefinite variable – the return of additional result is provided)* also can get in such list. We will note, that this procedure like the previous **ProcBMQ** procedure is oriented on the single objects, whose definitions are unique whereas on the objects of the same name the call prints message *"Object <x> has multiple definitions"*. Meantime, unlike the previous **ProcBMQ** procedure, the **RedundantLocals** procedure quite successfully processes also the objects containing in their bodies the definitions of the typical functions *(with headings)*, modules and blocks. But the considering of this moment as a certain shortcoming of **ProcBMQ** procedure isn't quite competent, discussion of that can be found in our books [32,33,50].

The **RedundantLocalsM** procedure completes the previous fragment, the given procedure expands the **RedundantLocals** procedure on the objects of the same name. The procedure call **RedundantLocalsM[x]** on a single object {*Block, Module*} is similar to the procedure call **RedundantLocals[x]** whereas on a traditional function *"Function"* is returned; on a *x* object of the same name {*Block, Traditional function, Module*} the list of results of application of the **RedundantLocals** to all subobjects of the *x* object is returned. Meanwhile, results of calls of the above procedures **RedundantLocals** and **RedundantLocalsM** suggest certain additional analysis of a *x* object concerning the excess local variables, i.e. procedures can be considered as rather effective means for the preliminary analysis of the blocks or modules regarding an exception of the *excess* local variables. As shows our experience, in the most important cases the results of application of procedures **RedundantLocalsM** and **RedundantLocals** can be considered as ultimate without demanding any additional researches of the analyzed object.

In addition, in the *Mathematica* the evaluation of definitions of modules and blocks which contain the *duplicated local variables* is made quite correctly without initiation of any especial or erroneous situations that arise only at the time of a call of a block and a module, initiating erroneous situation with the system message *Block::dup* and *Module::dup* respectively, with returning of the unevaluated call of a block or a module. Meantime, the given mechanism of identification of a duplicated local *h* variable isn't clear because in the list of local variables in definition of the *Proc* procedure *at first* the variables *a* and *d* are located as rather visually illustrates the following quite simple fragment. For definition of the fact of *duplication* of the local variables in definitions of objects like block or module that are activated in the current *Mathematica*, the procedure has been created, whose call **DuplicateLocalsQ[x]** returns *True* in case of existence in definition of *x* procedure of the *duplication* of *local* variables, otherwise *False* is returned. In addition, in case of returning *True* through the 2nd optional *y* argument – *an indefinite symbol* – simple list or list of the *ListList* type is returned whose elements define names of the duplicated local variables with multiplicities of their entries into the list of the local variables. The next fragment presents source code of the **DuplicateLocalsQ** procedure along with examples of its use.

In[2560]:= Proc[x__] := Module[{a, y, d = {x}, h, c, h, d, a = 6, h = 2, c = 7, a}, a*d]
In[2561]:= Proc[90, 590]
Module::dup: Duplicate local variable h found in local variable specification
{a, y, d = {90, 590}, h, c, h, d, a = 6, h = 2, c = 7, a}...>>
Out[2561]= Module[{a, y, d = {90, 590}, h, c, h, d, a = 6, h = 2, c = 7, a}, a*d]
In[2562]:= Blok[x__] := Block[{a, y, d = {x}, h, c, h, d, a = 6, h = 2, c = 7, a}, a*d]
In[2563]:= Blok[90, 590]
Block::dup: Duplicate local variable h found in local variable specification
{a, y, d = {90, 590}, h, c, h, d, a = 6, h = 2, c = 7, a}...>>
Out[2563]= Block[{a, y, d = {90, 590}, h, c, h, d, a = 6, h = 2, c = 7, a}, a*d]
In[2564]:= DuplicateLocalsQ[P_ /; BlockModQ[P], y___] :=
Module[{a, b = Locals1[P]}, If[b == {}, False, b = If[NestListQ[b], b[[1]], b];
a = Select[Gather2[b], #[[2]] > 1 &];
If[a == {}, False, If[{y} != {} && ! HowAct[y], y = a]; True]]]
In[2565]:= {DuplicateLocalsQ[Proc, y69], y69}
Out[2565]= {True, {{"a", 3}, {"d", 2}, {"h", 3}}}
In[2566]:= B[x_, y_] := Module[{a = 74}, a*x*y]; {DuplicateLocalsQ[B, t], t}
Out[2566]= {False, t}
In[3590]:= Proc[x_] := Module[{a, y, d = {x}, h, c, h, d, a = 6, h = 2, c = 7, a}, a*d];
Proc1[x_] := Module[{}, {x}]; Proc2[x_] := Module[{a, a = 590}, a*x];
Blok42[x_] := Block[{a, y, d = {x}, h, c, h, d, a = 6, h = 2, c = 7, a}, a*d];
In[3591]:= DuplicateLocals[x_ /; BlockModQ[x]] := Module[{a = Locals1[x]},
a = Select[Map[{#, Count[a, #]} &, DeleteDuplicates[a]], #[[2]] > 1 &];
a = Sort[a, ToCharacterCode[#1[[1]]][[1]] < ToCharacterCode[#2[[1]]][[1]] &];
If[Length[a] > 1 || a == {}, a, a[[1]]]]
In[3592]:= DuplicateLocals[Proc]
Out[3592]= {{"a", 3}, {"c", 2}, {"d", 2}, {"h", 3}}
In[3593]:= DuplicateLocals[Proc1]
Out[3593]= {}
In[3594]:= DuplicateLocals[Proc2]
Out[3594]= {"a", 2}
In[3595]:= DuplicateLocals[Blok42]
Out[3595]= {{"a", 3}, {"c", 2}, {"d", 2}, {"h", 3}}

So, the **DuplicateLocals** procedure completes the antecedent fragment, the procedure call **DuplicateLocals**[*x*] returns the simple or the nested list the first element of a list or sublists of which defines a name in string format of a multiple local variable of a block or module *x* while the second defines its multiplicity. In the absence of *multiple* local variables the empty list, i.e. {} is returned. In this regard, a certain interest the procedure represents whose call **DelDuplLocals**[*x*] returns the *name* of a module or block *x*, reducing its *local* variables of the same name to *1* with activation of the updated definition *x* in the current session. While the call **DelDuplLocals**[*x*, *y*] with the second optional *y* argument – an indefinite symbol – thru *y* returns the list of excess local variables. In addition, first of all only simple local variables *(without initial values)* are reduced. This procedure a rather well supplements the previous

DuplicateLocals procedure. The next fragment presents source code of the **DelDuplLocals** procedure along with examples of its typical application.

In[2657]:= Ag[x_, y_] := Module[{a, b, b = 90, c, b = 74, c = 590, c, d}, (a*b + c*d)*(x + y)];
Av[x_] := Block[{a = 90, a = 590}, a*x];
In[2658]:= As[x_] := Module[{a, b, c, a, c}, x]
In[2659]:= SetAttributes[Ag, {Protected, Listable}]; Art[x_] := Module[{}, x]
In[2660]:= DelDuplLocals[x_ /; BlockModQ[x], y___] :=
Module[{b = {}, d, c = {}, a = Locals[x], p},
If[a == {}, x, d = Attributes[x]; ClearAttributes[x, d];
Map[If[StringFreeQ[#, "="], AppendTo[b, #], AppendTo[c, #]] &, a];
b = DeleteDuplicates[b];
c = DeleteDuplicates[Map[StringSplit[#, " = ", 2] &, c], #1[[1]] == #2[[1]] &];
p = Map[#[[1]] &, c]; b = Select[b, ! MemberQ[p, #] &];
c = Map[StringJoin[#[[1]], " = ", #[[2]]] &, c];
b = StringRiffle[Join[b, c], ", "]; p = PureDefinition[x];
ToExpression[StringReplace[p, StringRiffle[a, ", "] -> b, 1]]; SetAttributes[x, d];
If[{y} != {} && ! HowAct[y], y = MinusList[a, StrToList[b]], Null]; x]]

In[2661]:= DelDuplLocals[Ag]
Out[2661]= Ag
In[2662]:= Definition[Ag]
Out[2662]= Attributes[Ag] = {Listable, Protected}
Ag[x_, y_] := Module[{a, d, b = 90, c = 590}, (a*b + c*d)*(x + y)]
In[2663]:= DelDuplLocals[Av]
Out[2663]= Av
In[2664]:= Definition[Av]
Out[2664]= Av[x_] := Block[{a = 90}, a*x]
In[2665]:= DelDuplLocals[As]
Out[2665]= As
In[2666]:= Definition[As]
Out[2666]= As[x_] := Module[{a, b, c}, x]
In[3667]:= Ag[x_, y_] := Module[{a, b, b = 90, c, b = 74, c = 590, c, d}, (a*b + c*d)*(x + y)];
DelDuplLocals[Ag, w];
In[3668]:= w
Out[3668]= {"b", "c", "b = 74", "c"}

Procedure provides processing of the objects having single definitions, however it is easily generalized to the objects of the same name. The fragment below represents the procedure expanding the previous procedure on a case of the blocks and modules of the same name. The call **DelDuplLocalsM[x, y]** is completely analogous to the call **DelDuplLocals[x, y]**.

In[4717]:= Ag[x_, y_] := Module[{a, b, b = 90, c, b = 74, c = 590, c, d}, (a*b + c*d)*(x + y)];
Ag[x_] := Block[{a, b, b = 90, c, c = 590}, a*b*c*x]
In[4718]:= Ag[x_, y_, z_] := Module[{a = 74, a, b, b = 90, c = 590, c}, a*x + b*y + c*z];
SetAttributes[Ag, {Protected, Listable}]
In[4719]:= Definition[Ag]

Out[4719]= Attributes[Ag] = {Listable, Protected}
Ag[x_, y_] := Module[{a, b, b = 90, c, b = 74, c = 590, c, d}, (a*b + c*d) *(x + y)]
Ag[x_] := Block[{a, b, b = 90, c, c = 590}, a*b*c*x]
Ag[x_, y_, z_] := Module[{a = 74, a, b = 90, c = 590, c}, a*x + b*y + c*z]

In[4720]:= DelDuplLocalsM[x_ /; BlockModQ[x], y___] :=
Module[{b, d, p, a = Flatten[{PureDefinition[x]}], h = ToString[x], c = {}, z = {}},
If[Length[a] == 1, DelDuplLocals[x, y],
If[{y} != {} && ! HowAct[y] || {y} === {}, b = Attributes[x];
ClearAttributes[x, b], Return[Defer[DelDuplLocalsM[x, y]]]];
Map[{AppendTo[c, d = ToString[Unique["vgs"]]],
ToExpression[StringReplace[#, h <> "[" -> d <> "[", 1]]} &, a];
p = Map[PureDefinition[#] &, Map[{DelDuplLocals[#, y], Quiet[AppendTo[z, y]],
Clear[y]}[[1]] &, c]];
ToExpression[Map[StringReplace[#, GenRules[Map[# <> "[" &, c], h <> "["], 1] &, p]];
SetAttributes[x, b]; Map[Remove[#] &, c]; If[{y} != {}, y = z, Null]; x]]

In[4721]:= DelDuplLocalsM[Ag, w74]
Out[4721]= Ag
In[4722]:= Definition[Ag]
Out[4722]= Attributes[Ag] = {Listable, Protected}
Ag[x_, y_] := Module[{a, d, b = 90, c = 590}, (a*b + c*d)*(x + y)]
Ag[x_] := Block[{a, b = 90, c = 590}, a*b*c*x]
Ag[x_, y_, z_] := Module[{a = 74, b = 90, c = 590}, a*x + b*y + c*z]
In[4723]:= w74
Out[4723]= {{"b", "c", "b = 74", "c"}, {"b", "c"}, {"a", "b", "c"}}

While the procedure call **OptimalLocals[x]** returns the name of a module or a block *x* with optimization in the current session of its local variables in the context of eliminating their duplication and redundancy.

In[3633]:= **OptimalLocals[x_ /; BlockModQ[x]] :=**
Module[{at, b, c, d, p, t, a = DelDuplLocals[x], h, k, j, f},
a = Locals[x]; b = RedundantLocals[x];
If[a == {} || b == {}, x, t = a; c = PureDefinition[x]; h = HeadPF[x];
at = Attributes[x]; ClearAttributes[x, at];
f[z_ /; StringQ[z]] := If[StringFreeQ[z, "="], z,
StringTrim[StringTake[z, {1, Flatten[StringPosition[z, "="]][[1]] -1}]]];
d = StringReplace[c, h <> " := " -> ""]; d = StringTake[d, {If[ModuleQ[x], 8, 7], -1}];
p = SubStrSymbolParity1[d, "{", "}"][[1]];
For[k = 1, k <= Length[b], k++, For[j = 1, j <= Length[t], j++,
If[f[t[[j]]] == b[[k]], t = Delete[t, j]]]];
ToExpression[StringReplace[c, p -> ToString[t], 1]]; SetAttributes[x, at]; x]]

In[3634]:= **Vsv2[x_, y_] := Module[{a, b, c = 590, d, c, v, h, a, t, p, b, q}, Procedure body];
SetAttributes[Vsv2, Protected]**

In[3635]:= OptimalLocals[Vsv2]; Definition[Vsv2]
Out[3635]= Attributes[Vsv2] = {Protected}
Vsv2[x_, y_] := Module[{c = 590}, Procedure body]

In[3643]:= ReplaceLocals[x_ /; BlockQ[x] || FunctionQ[x] || ModuleQ[x],
y_ /; AllTrue[Map[StringQ, Flatten[{y}]], TrueQ]] :=
Module[{a = Locals[x], b = Flatten[{y}], c = PureDefinition[x], d, p, h = HeadPF[x], k, j, f},
f[z_ /; StringQ[z]] := If[StringFreeQ[z, "="], z,
StringTrim[StringTake[z, {1, Flatten[StringPosition[z, "="]][[1]] - 1}]]];
d = StringReplace[c, h <> " := " -> ""]; d = StringTake[d, {If[ModuleQ[x], 8, 7], -1}];
p = SubStrSymbolParity1[d, "{", "}"][[1]];
For[k = 1, k <= Length[a], k++, For[j = 1, j <= Length[b], j++,
If[f[a[[k]]] == f[b[[j]]], a[[k]] = b[[j]]]]];
ToExpression[StringReplace[c, p -> ToString[a]]]]

In[3644]:= J[x_, y_] := Module[{a, b, c = 90, d, h}, b = 590; PB]
In[3645]:= ReplaceLocals[J, {"a=74", "h=69", "b=2017"}]; Definition[J]
Out[3645]= J[x_, y_] := Module[{a = 74, b = 2017, c = 90, d, h = 69}, b = 590; PB]

The **ReplaceLocals** procedure completing the previous fragment provides the dynamical replacement of local variables of a block or module *x* for a period of the current session. The procedure call **ReplaceLocals[x, y]** returns *Null*, i.e. nothing, providing replacement of local variables of block or module *x* by the new local variables of the same name, including their initial values which are defined by the second *y* argument – a separate string of the format *"name"* or *"name = initial value"*, or their list. Only those local variables of the *x* object are subjected to replacement whose *names* are in the *y*. The source codes of both procedures and examples of their application are represented in the fragment above.

The procedure **OptimalLocalsM** is an extension of the above **OptimalLocals** procedure onto case of objects (*Blocks, Functions, Modules*) of the same name. The call **OptimalLocalsM[*x*]** returns the definition of *x* object, providing optimization of its local variables in the current *Mathematica* session in the context of eliminating duplication and redundancy of variables. At that, **OptimalLocalsM** procedure succesfully processes single objects too. The fragment below represents source code of the procedure with an example of its use.

In[3897]:= Vsv[x_, y_] := Module[{a, b, c = 90, d, c, v, h, a, t, p, b, q}, Body];
Vsv[x_, y_, z_] := Block[{a, b, c = 90, d, c, v, h, a, t, p, b, q, g, v}, Body];
Vsv[x_, y_, z_, n_] := Block[{a, b, c = 90, d, c, v, h, a, t, p, b, q, g, v}, Body];
Vsv[x_] := x^2 + x + 590; SetAttributes[Vsv, {Listable, Protected}]

In[3898]:= OptimalLocalsM[x_ /; BlockFuncModQ[x]] :=
Module[{d = {}, a = PureDefinition[x], atr = Attributes[x], b = ClearAllAttributes[x],
c = FromCharacterCode[6], p = 1, t = {}, h = ToString[x]},
If[StringQ[a], OptimalLocals[h]; SetAttributes[x, atr]; Definition[x],
b = Map[{AppendTo[d, h <> c <> ToString[p++]],
ToExpression[StringReplace[#, h <> "[" -> h <> c <> ToString[p - 1] <> "[", 1]]} &, a];
b = Select[DeleteDuplicates[Flatten[b]], ! SameQ[#, Null] &];

Map[If[BlockQ[#] || ModuleQ[#], OptimalLocals[#], Null] &, b];
Map[ToExpression, Map[StringReplace[PureDefinition[#], GenRules[# <>
"[", h <> "["], 1] &, b]]; Map[ClearAll, b]; SetAttributes[x, atr]; Definition[x]]]

In[3899]:= OptimalLocalsM[Vsv]

Out[3899]= Attributes[Vsv] = {Listable, Protected}

Vsv[x_, y_] := Module[{c = 90}, Body]
Vsv[x_, y_, z_] := Block[{c = 90}, Body]
Vsv[x_, y_, z_, n_] := Block[{c = 90}, Body]
Vsv[x_] := x^2 + x + 590

In[3900]:= Agn[x_, y_, z_] := Block[{a, b, c = 90, d, c, v, h, a, t, p, b, q, g, v}, Body];
SetAttributes[Agn, {Listable, Protected}]; OptimalLocalsM[Agn]

Out[3900]= Attributes[Agn] = {Listable, Protected}

Agn[x_, y_, z_] := Block[{c = 90}, Body]

The procedure **OptimalLocalsN** is an extension of the above **OptimalLocals** procedure onto case of the nested objects *(blocks and modules)*. The call **OptimalLocalsN**[*x*] returns definition of block or module *x*, providing optimization in the current session of its local variables and of local variables of all subobjects *(blocks, modules)* composing it in the context of eliminating duplication and redundancy of local variables. In addition, the **OptimalLocalsN** procedure succesfully processes simple blocks or modules *(i.e. objects that are non–nested)* too. The next fragment represents source code of the procedure along with typical examples of its use.

In[3575]:= OptimalLocalsN[x_ /; BlockModQ[x]] :=
Module[{b, c, d, h, t, a = SubsProcs[x], k = 1},
If[a === {}, OptimalLocals[x]; Definition[x], b = Attributes[x];
ClearAllAttributes[x]; OptimalLocals[x];
c = PureDefinition[x]; d = Flatten[SubsProcs[x]];
t = Map[StringTake[#, {1, Flatten[StringPosition[#, "["]][[1]] – 1}] &, d];
h = Select[t, ! MemberQ[{"Undefined", $Failed}, PureDefinition[#]] &];
If[h != {}, ToExpression["Save[\"$ArtKr$.m\"," <> ToString[h] <> "]"];
Map[ClearAllAttributes, h]; Map[Clear, h], Null];
For[k, k <= Length[d], k++, ToExpression[d[[k]]]; OptimalLocals[t[[k]]];
c = StringReplace[c, d[[k]] –> PureDefinition[t[[k]]], 1];
ToExpression["Clear[" <> t[[k]] <> "]"]]; ToExpression[c];
Quiet[Check[Get["$ArtKr$.m"], Null]]; Quiet[Check[DeleteFile["$ArtKr$.m"], Null]];
SetAttributes[x, b]; Definition[x]]]

In[3576]:= B[x_, y_] := Module[{a, b, a, Z1, Z, b, Z, Z1, c, d}, a = 6;
Z[t_] := Module[{c, d, d, m, n, p, a, b, c, h}, d = 74; H[p_] := Module[{Q, s, w},
Q[k_] := Block[{m, n, v, u1, u2}, t^2]; p]; t^2*d*H[t]];
Z1[m_] := Module[{g = 90, l, k, j}, g*m]; (Z[x*y] + Z1[x*y])/Z1[x + y]];
SetAttributes[B, {Listable, Protected}]

In[3577]:= B[590, 90]

Module::dup: Duplicate local variable a$ found in local variable specification {a$, b$, a$, Z1$, Z$, b$, Z$, Z1$, c$, d$}}... >>

345

Out[3577]= Module[{a$, b$, a$, Z1$, Z$, b$, Z$, Z1$, c$, d$}, a$ = 6; Z$[t_] := Module[{c, d, d, m, n, p, a, b, c, h}, d = 74; H[p_] := Module[{Q, s, w}, Q[k_] := Block[{m, n, v, u1, u2}, t^2]; p]; t^2*d*H[t]]; Z1$[m_] := Module[{g = 90, l, k, j}, g*m];
(Z$[590*90] + Z1$[590*90])/Z1$[590 + 90]]

In[3578]:= **OptimalLocalsN[B]**
Out[3578]= Attributes[B] = {Listable, Protected}
B[x_, y_] := Module[{a, Z1, Z}, a = 6; Z[t_] := Module[{d}, d = 74;
H[p_] := Module[{Q}, Q[k_] := Block[{}, t^2]; p]; t^2*d*H[t]];
Z1[m_] := Module[{g = 90}, g*m]; (Z[x*y] + Z1[x*y])/Z1[x + y]]

In[3579]:= **N[B[590, 90]]**
Out[3579]= 1.81036*10^11

In[3580]:= **Definition[Z]**
Out[3580]= Attributes[Z] = {Listable, Protected}
Z[x_, y_, z_] := x + y + z

In[3581]:= Art[x_] := Module[{a, b, c, a, b = 74, c}, c = 590; *Procedure Body*];
SetAttributes[Art, {Listable, Protected}]

In[3582]:= **OptimalLocalsN[Art]**
Out[3582]= Attributes[Art] = {Listable, Protected}
Art[x_] := Module[{c, b = 74}, c = 590; *Procedure Body*]

The **ReplaceSubProcs** procedure is intended for replacement in an arbitrary procedure of its subprocedures of type {*Block, Module*}. The procedure call **ReplaceSubProcs[x, y]** returns the result of replacement in a *x* procedure of type {*Block, Module*} of subprocedures which is defined by the *2nd y* argument that has the format {*a1, b1*} or {{*a1, b1*}, ..., {*ap, bp*}}, defining replacements of the *aj* subprocedures of the *x* procedure onto the *bj* procedures of the type {*Block, Module*}; if *bj* = "" (*empty string*) then the appropriate *aj* subprocedure is deleted (*j* = *1..n*). The optimization of local variables of the main *x* procedure and all its subprocedures is carried out. The next fragment represents source code of the procedure **ReplaceSubProcs** with typical examples of its application.

In[4642]:= **ReplaceSubProcs[x_ /; BlockModQ[x], y_ /; ListQ[y] && Length[y] == 2 || ListListQ[y] && Length[y[[1]]] == 2, z___] :=
Module[{a = Flatten[SubsProcs[x]], b, c, h, g, f, k},
If[a == {}, OptimalLocals[x]; Definition[x], b = Attributes[x];
ClearAllAttributes[x]; f = PureDefinition[x]; c = SubProcs[x];
Map[ClearAll[#] &, c[[2]]]; h = Map[HeadName[#] &, c[[1]]][[2 ;; -1]];
c = Select[If[ListListQ[y], y, {y}], BlockModQ[#[[1]]] && BlockFuncModQ[#[[2]]] &&
MemberQ[h, ToString[#[[1]]]] || #[[2]] == "" &];
c = ToStringRule1[Map[#[[1]] -> #[[2]] &, c]]; c = If[RuleQ[c], {c}, c];
g = {}; For[k = 1, k <= Length[c], k++, AppendTo[g, Select[a, SuffPref[#, Part[c[[k]], 1] <>
"[", 1] &][[1]] -> If[Part[c[[k]], 2] == "", "", PureDefinition[Part[c[[k]], 2]]]]];
ToExpression[StringReplace[StringReplace[f, g], {" , " -> "", " ; " -> ""}]];
If[{z} != {}, Map[ClearAllAttributes, h]; Map[ClearAll, h], Null];
OptimalLocalsN[x]; SetAttributes[x, b]; Definition[x]]]**

In[4643]:= Z1[m_] := Module[{a, b, c, a, b, c, t, w, d, s, o}, m^2 + m + 590];

Q[z_] := Module[{m, n, p, g, h}, z^2]
In[4644]:= B[x_, y_] := Module[{a, b, a, Z1, Z, b, Z, Z1, c, d}, a = 6; Z[t_] := Module[{c, d, d, m, n, p, a, b, c, h}, d=75; H[p_] := Module[{Q, s, w}, Q[k_] := Block[{m, n, v, u1, u2}, t^2]; p]; t^2*d*H[t]]; Z1[m_] := Module[{g = 90, l, k, j}, g*m]; (Z[x*y] + Z1[x*y])/Z1[x + y]];
SetAttributes[B, {Listable, Protected}]
In[4645]:= **ReplaceSubProcs[B, {Q, Q}, 590]**
Out[4645]= Attributes[B] = {Listable, Protected}
B[x_, y_] := Module[{a, Z1, Z, d}, a = 6; Z[t_] := Module[{d}, d = 75;
H[p_] := Module[{Q}, Q[z_] := Module[{}, z^2]; p]; t^2*d*H[t]];
Z1[m_] := Module[{g = 90}, g*m]; (Z[x*y] + Z1[x*y])/Z1[x + y]]
In[4646]:= **N[B[590, 90]]**
Out[4646]= 1.81036*10^11
In[4647]:= **ReplaceSubProcs[B, {{Q, Q}, {Z1, Z1}}]**
Out[4647]= Attributes[B] = {Listable, Protected}
B[x_, y_] := Module[{a, Z1, Z, d}, a = 6; Z[t_] := Module[{d}, d = 75;
H[p_] := Module[{Q}, Q[z_] := Module[{}, z^2]; p]; t^2*d*H[t]];
Z1[m_] := Module[{}, m^2 + m + 590]; (Z[x*y] + Z1[x*y])/Z1[x + y]]
In[4648]:= **N[B[590, 90]]**
Out[4648]= 2.3895*10^10
In[4649]:= **ReplaceSubProcs[B, {{H, ""}, {Z1, Z1}}]**
Out[4649]= Attributes[B] = {Listable, Protected}
B[x_, y_] := Module[{a, Z1, Z, d}, a = 6; Z[t_] := Module[{d}, d = 74; t^2*d*H[t]];
Z1[m_] := Module[{}, m^2 + m + 590]; (Z[x*y] + Z1[x*y])/Z1[x + y]]

Whereas the procedure call **ProcUniToMod[x]** returns definition of a block or a module x which can be the object of the same name, with replacement of all blocks by modules along with optimization of the local variables of all subobjects composing the x object.

In[2909]:= B[x_, y_] := Block[{a, b, a, Z1, Z, b, Z, Z1, c, d}, a = 6; Z[t_] := Module[{c, d, d, m, n, p, a, b, c, h}, d = 74; H[p_] := Block[{Q, s, w}, Q[k_] := Block[{m, n, v, u1, u2}, t^2]; p]; t^2*d*H[t]]; Z1[m_] := Module[{g = 90, l, k, j}, g*m]; (Z[x*y] + Z1[x*y])/Z1[x + y]];
In[2910]:= B[x_, y_, z_] := Block[{a, b, a, Z1, Z, b, Z, Z1, c, d}, a = 6; Z[t_] := Module[{c, d, d, m, n, p, a, b, c, h}, d = 74; H[p_] := Block[{Q, s, w}, Q[k_] := Block[{m, n, v, u1, u2}, t^2]; p]; t^2*d*H[t]]; Z1[m_] := Module[{g = 90, l, k, j}, g*m]; (Z[x*y] + Z1[x*y])/Z1[x + y]^z];
SetAttributes[B, {Listable, Protected}]
In[2911]:= **B[590, 90, 6]**
Block::dup: Duplicate local variable a found in local variable... >>
Out[2911]= Block[{a, b, a, Z1, Z, b, Z, Z1, c, d}, a=6;... (Z[590*90]+Z1[590*90])/Z1[590+90]^6]

In[2912]:= ProcUniToMod[j_ /; BlockModQ[j]] :=
Module[{b = Attributes[j], a = Flatten[{PureDefinition[j]}], c = ClearAllAttributes[j]},
Clear[j]; c = {}; Map[{ToExpression[#], OptimalLocalsN[j],
AppendTo[c, PureDefinition[j]], Clear[j]} &, a];
Map[ToExpression[StringReplace[#, " := Block[{" -> " := Module[{"]] &, c];
SetAttributes[j, b]; Definition[j]]

In[2913]:= **ProcUniToMod[B]**

Out[2913]= Attributes[B] = {Listable, Protected}
B[x_, y_] := Module[{a, Z1, Z, d}, a = 6; Z[t_] := Module[{d}, d = 74;
H[p_] := Module[{Q}, Q[k_] := Module[{}, t^2]; p]; t^2*d*H[t]];
Z1[m__] := Module[{g = 90}, g*m]; (Z[x*y] + Z1[x*y])/Z1[x + y]]
B[x_, y_, z_] := Module[{a, Z1, Z, d}, a = 6; Z[t_] := Module[{d}, d = 74;
H[p_] := Module[{Q}, Q[k_] := Module[{}, t^2]; p]; t^2*d*H[t]];
Z1[m__] := Module[{g = 90}, g*m]; (Z[x*y] + Z1[x*y])/Z1[x + y]^z]

Along with that it should be noted that the above procedures such as **ReplaceSubProcs**, **OptimalLocals**, **OptimalLocalsN**, **OptimalLocalsM** and **ProcUniToMod** allow a series of interesting enough modifications and extensions.

At last, the **VarsInBlockMod** procedure provides the structural analysis of all variables that entere in a block or a module. Procedure call **VarsInBlockMod[x]** returns the 4-element list, whose first element defines the list of formal arguments, the second element defines the list of local variables, the *third* element defines the list of global variables and the *fourth* element defines the list of the variables other than system variables and names. The fragment below represents source code of the procedure with an example of its application.

In[2859]:= **VarsInBlockMod[x_/; BlockQ[x] || ModuleQ[x]]** :=
Module[{a = Locals1[x], b = Globals[x], c, d},
c = ExtrVarsOfStr[StringReplace[PureDefinition[x], HeadPF[x] <> " := " -> ""], 1], 1];
c = Select[c, ! Quiet[Check[SystemQ[#], True]] &];
{d = Args[x, 90], a, b, MinusList[c, Flatten[{a, b, d}]]}]

In[2860]:= **VarsInBlockMod[ProcQ]**
Out[2860]= {{"x"}, {"a", "atr", "b", "c", "d", "h"}, {}, {"SymbolQ", "SystemQ", "UnevaluatedQ", "Definition2", "ClearAllAttributes", "HeadPF"}}

As noted above, the *Mathematica* at evaluation of definitions of objects of the type {*Block, Function, Module*} does not identify situations of the duplication of formal arguments, local variables and their intersections as a fragment below clearly illustrates. But these situations are tested by means of the procedure whose call **TestArgsLocals[x]** returns *False* if a block, a function or a module *x* has a duplication of formal arguments, local variables and/or their intersections, and *True* otherwise. Whereas the procedure call **TestArgsLocals[x, y]** through the 2nd optional *y* argument – an undefinite symbol – in case of the main return *False* returns the 2-element list whose elements-sublists are in 1-to-1 correspondence. The first element determines the definitions, composing a *x* object, for which the above situations take place, while the second element defines the list of sublists of the format {*t1, t2, t3*}; (*tj*∈{*True, False*}; *j* = 1÷3); its *tj* elements determine the duplication of formal arguments, duplication of local variables, and/or their intersections {*False/True*} accordingly. In addition, this procedure essentially uses the procedure **RestListList** which represents independent interest. The call **RestListList[x]** returns the result of restructuring of a list {{$x1, x2, ..., xn$}, {$y1, y2, ..., yn$}, ..., {$z1, z2, ..., zn$}} of the *ListList* type into the list of the same type of the kind {{$x1, y1, ..., z1$}, {$x2, y2, ..., z2$}, ...}. The following fragment represents source codes of the both tools along with the most typical examples of their application.

In[3478]:= **G[x_] := Module[{a = 90, b = 69, a = 590}, *Body*]; G[74]**
Module::dup: Duplicate local variable a$ found in local variable... >>

Out[3478]= Module[{a$ = 90, b$ = 69, a$ = 590}, *Body*]

In[3479]:= **G1[x_, y_, x_] := Module[{a = 90, b = 590}, Body]; G1[74, 69, 49]**

Out[3479]= G1[74, 69, 49]

In[3480]:= **G2[x_, y_] := Module[{a = 90, y = 590}, Body]; G2[74, 69]**

Module::lvset: Local variable specification {a$ = 90, 69 = 590} contains... >>

Out[3480]= Module[{a$ = 90, 69 = 590}, *Body*]

In[3482]:= **RestListList[x_ /; ListListQ[x]] :=**
Module[{a, b = Length[x[[1]]], c = Length[x], d = {}},
Do[a = {}; Do[AppendTo[a, x[[j]][[k]]], {j, 1, c}]; AppendTo[d, a], {k, 1, b}]; d]

In[3483]:= **RestListList[{{a, b, c}, {x, y, z}}]**

Out[3483]= {{a, x}, {b, y}, {c, z}}

In[3288]:= **Map[RestListList, {{{}, {}, {}}, {{a}, {b}, {c}}}]**

Out[3288]= {{}, {{a, b, c}}}

In[3484]:= **RestListList[{{a, b, c}, {x, y, z}, {m, n, p}, {p, g, h}}]**

Out[3484]= {{a, x, m, p}, {b, y, n, g}, {c, z, p, h}}

In[3485]:= **TestArgsLocals[x_ /; BlockFuncModQ[x], y__] :=**
Module[{a = ArgsBFM[x, 90], b, a1, b1, c1 = {}, d1 = {}, c, g, n, f,
p = Flatten[{PureDefinition[x]}]},
b = If[Length[p] > 1, Locals1[x], {Locals1[x]}]; g = Length[p];
b = Map[If[# === "Function", {}, #] &, b];
a1 = Map[Length[#] == Length[DeleteDuplicates[#]] &, a];
b1 = Map[Length[#] == Length[DeleteDuplicates[#]] &, b];
Do[AppendTo[c1, Intersection[a[[k]], b[[k]]] == {}], {k, 1, g}];
c = If[MemberQ[Flatten[Set[n, {a1, b1, c1}]], False], False, True];
d1 = RestListList[n]; f[z_] := MemberQ[z, False];
If[{y} != {} && ! HowAct[y] && ! c, y = p[[PositionsListCond[d1, f]]], Null]; c]

In[3486]:= **{TestArgsLocals[G1, s49], s49}**

Out[3486]= {False, {{"G1[x_, y_, x_] := Module[{a=90, b=590, x}, Body]"}, {False, True, False}}}

In[3487]:= **G2[x_, y_, y_List] := Module[{a = 90, y = 69, a}, a*x*y];**
G2[x_, y_, z_] := Module[{a = 90, y = 69, b}, a*x*y]; G2[x_, y_, x_] := x*y
G2[x_List, y_Integer] := y*Length[x]; G2[x_Integer, x_String] := x^2

In[3488]:= **G2[74, 69]**

Out[3488]= G2[74, 69]

In[3489]:= **{TestArgsLocals[G2, s50], s50}**

Out[3489]= {False, {{"G2[x_, y_, y_List] := Module[{a=90, y=69, a}, a*x*y]",
"G2[x_, y_, x_] := x*y", "G2[x_, y_, z_] := Module[{a=90, y=69, b}, a*x*y]",
"G2[x_Integer, x_String] := x^2"}, {{False, False, False}, {False, True, True},
{True, True, False}, {False, True, True}}}}

The procedure **RestListList1** is a rather useful analog of the **RestListList** procedure.

The above means play rather essential part at debugging functions, modules and blocks of a rather large size, allowing on the first stages to detect the fact of *duplicating* of local variables

349

and formal arguments of the same name, and provide their reducing to one. At that, along with it, the facts of intersection of lists of local variables and formal arguments are tested.

6.7. Global variables of modules and blocks; the tools of manipulation by them in the *Mathematica* software

Concerning the *Maple*, the *Mathematica* functions have the more *limited* opportunities both relative to the mechanism of global variables, and on returning of results of performance. If in case of a *Maple* procedure an arbitrary variable has been declared in *global*-section of the description, or which didn't receive values in the body of the procedure on the operator of assignment ":=", or on the system *assign* procedure *(upto version Maple 11)* is considered as a global variable, then in a *Mathematica* procedure all those variables which are manifestly not defined as local variables are considered as the global variables. The following example rather visually illustrates the aforesaid, namely:

In[2678]:= Sv[x_] := Module[{}, y := 74; z = 69; {y, z}]
In[2679]:= {y, z} = {42, 47}; {Sv[2016], y, z}
Out[2679]= {{74, 69}, 74, 69}

Therefore, any redefinition in a *Mathematica* procedure *(module or block)* of a *global variable* automatically redefines the variable of the same name outside of the procedure, what will demand significantly bigger attentiveness for the purpose of prevention of possible special and undesirable situations than in a similar situation with the *Maple* procedures. Thus, the level of providing the robustness of software in the *Mathematica* system at operating with the procedures is presented to us a little lower of the mentioned level of the *Maple* system. It should be noted that *Mathematica* allows definition of global variables of the procedures by means of a quite simple reception of modification of the testing mechanism of the actual arguments at the time of the procedure call as it quite visually illustrates the following very simple fragment, namely:

In[2543]:= Art[x_ /; If[! IntegerQ[x], h = 90; True, h = 590; True], y_] :=
Module[{a = 2016}, x + y + h + a]
In[2544]:= {Art[90, 590], Art[20.27, 590]}
Out[2544]= {3286, 2716.27}
In[2545]:= Kr[x_, y_] := Module[{a = If[IntegerQ[x], 90, 590]}, x + y + a]
In[2546]:= {Kr[20.27, 590], Kr[90, 590]}
Out[2546]= {1200.27, 770}
In[2547]:= Sv[x_, y_] := Module[{a = If[IntegerQ[x] && PrimeQ[y], 90, 590]}, x + y + a]
In[2548]:= {Sv[90, 590], Kr[20, 590]}
Out[2548]= {1270, 700}
In[2549]:= H[x_: 90, y_, z_] := Module[{}, x + y + z]
In[2550]:= {H[200, 270, 590], H[220, 270], H[590]}
Out[2550]= {1060, 580, H[590]}

In a number of cases this mechanism is a rather useful whereas for the *Maple* the similar modification of the mechanism of testing of types of the factual arguments at the time of a procedures call is inadmissible. Naturally, the similar mechanism is allowed and for *Maple* when an algorithm determined in the form of a test *(Boolean function)* of arguments is coded not in the heading of a procedure, however it is defined by separate type with its activation in the current session. In this case standard format *x::test* is used for testing of a *x* argument. By natural manner we can determine also the initial values of *local* variables in a point of the procedure call depending on received values of its *actual* arguments as illustrate 2 examples of the previous fragment. At that, if the *Maple* system doesn't allow assignment of values by default to intermediate arguments of a procedure, *Mathematica* system allows, that a rather significantly expands possibilities of programming of procedures; so, the last example of the previous fragment represents a certain illustration to the told.

Meanwhile, it must be kept in mind that at use of the mechanism of return through global variables the increased attentiveness is required in order to any conflict situations with the *global variables* of the same name outside of procedures does not arise. Since the procedures as a rule will be repeatedly used in various sessions, the return through global variables is inexpedient. However, to some extent this problem is solvable at use, in particular, of the special names whose probability of emergence in the current session is extremely small, for example, on the basis of the **Unique** function. In a case of creation of certain procedures of our *MathToolBox* package [48] the similar approach for return of the results through global variables was used. In certain cases this approach is an quite effective.

Analogously to the case of the local variables the question of determination of existence in a procedure of global variables represents undoubted interest; in the first case the problem is solved by the procedures **Locals** and **Locals1** considered above, in the second – by means of two procedures **Globals** and **Globals1**. As a natural addition to the **Locals1** procedure, the procedure whose the call **Globals[*x*]** returns the list of global variables in string format of a *x* procedure acts. The next fragment represents source code of the **Globals** procedure along with the most typical examples of its application.

```
In[2522]:= Globals[P_ /; ProcBMQ[P]] := Module[{c, d = {}, p, g = {}, k = 1,
b = ToString1[DefFunc[P]], a = Sort[Locals1[P]]},
If[P === ExprOfStr, Return[{}], c = StringPosition[b, {" := ", " = "}][[2 ;; -1]]];
For[k, k <= Length[c], k++, p = c[[k]];
AppendTo[d, ExprOfStr[b, p[[1]], -1, {" ", ",", "\"", "!", "{"}]]];
For[k = 1, k <= Length[d], k++, p = d[[k]];
If[p != "$Failed" && p != " ", AppendTo[g, If[StringFreeQ[p, {"{", "}"}], p,
StringSplit[StringReplace[p, {"{" -> "", "}" -> ""}], ","]], Null]];
g = Flatten[g]; d = {}; For[k = 1, k <= Length[g], k++, p = g[[k]];
AppendTo[d, If[StringFreeQ[p, {"[", "]"}], p, StringTake[p, {1, Flatten[StringPosition[p,
"["]][[1]] - 1}]]]]; g = d;
d = {}; For[k = 1, k <= Length[g], k++, p = g[[k]];
AppendTo[d, StringReplace[p, {"," -> "", " " -> ""}]]];
d = Sort[Map[StringTrim, DeleteDuplicates[Flatten[d]]]];
Select[d, ! MemberQ[If[ListListQ[a], a[[1]], a], #] &]]
In[2523]:= Sv[x_, y_] := Module[{a, b = 90, c = 500}, a = (x^2 + y^2)/(b + c); {z, h} = {a, b};
t = z + h; t];
GS[x_] := Module[{a, b = 90, c = 42}, Kr[y_] := Module[{}, y^2 + Sin[y]]; a = x^2;
{z, h, p} = {a, b, 20}; t = z + h*Kr[20] - Cos[x + Kr[90]]; t];
```

Ar[x_] := Module[{a, b = 90, c = 42, Kr, z}, Kr[y_] := Module[{}, y^2 + Sin[y]]; a = x^2;
{z, h, p} = {a, b, 20}; t = z + h*Kr[20] − Cos[x + Kr[90]]; t]
In[2524]:= Map[Globals, {Locals1, Locals, Globals, ProcQ, ExprOfStr, GS, DefFunc, Sv, Ar}]
Out[2524]= {{"d", "j", "v"}, {"h", "R", "s", "v", "z"}, {}, {}, {}, {"h", "Kr", "p", "t", "z"}, {},
{"h", "t", "z"}, {"h", "p", "t"}}

The definition of the **Globals** procedure along with the standard means uses and our means such as **ProcBMQ, DefFunc, ExprOfStr, Locals1, ToString1, ListListQ** that are considered in this book and in [28-33]. It should be noted that the procedure call **Globals[P]** returns the objects names of a procedure body to which assignments by operators {":=", "="} are made and that differ from local variables of the main *P* procedure; they are understood as global variables. Therefore, the situation when a local variable of a subprocedure in a *P* procedure can be defined by the procedure call **Globals[P]** as a global variable as it visually illustrates an example of application of the **Globals** procedure to our procedures **Locals** and **Locals1** containing the nested subprocedures *Sg* and *Kr* respectively is a quite possible. In it case an additional research is required, or the **Globals** can be extended and to it case, interesting as a rather useful exercise. For the solution of this problem, in particular, it is possible to use the procedures **Locals1** and **Globals** in conjunction with the **MinusList** procedure [48,50].

One of simple enough variants of the generalization of the **Globals** (*based on the Globals*) on case of the *nested* procedures can be presented by a quite simple procedure **Globals1**, whose call **Globals1[x]** returns the list of global variables in string format of a *x* procedure; at that, an actual *x* argument can be as a procedure that isn't containing in the body of *subprocedures* of various level of nesting, and procedure containing such subprocedures. Also some others interesting and useful in practical programming the approaches for the solution of the given problem are possible. The fragment below presents source code of the **Globals1** procedure along with examples of its application.

In[3116]:= Globals1[P_ /; ProcQ[P]] := Module[{a = SubProcs[P], b, c, d = {}},
{b, c} = Map[Flatten, {Map[Locals1, a[[2]]], Map[Globals, a[[2]]]}];
MinusList[DeleteDuplicates[c], b]]

In[3117]:= Map[Globals1, {Locals1, Locals,Locals3, ProcQ,ExprOfStr, GS, DefFunc, Sv, Ar}]
Out[3117]= {{}, {"R"}, {}, {}, {}, {"h", Kr", "p", "t", "z"}, {}, {"h", "t", "z"}, {"h", "p", "t"}}
In[3118]:= P[x_, y_] := Module[{a, b, P1, P2}, P1[z_, h_] := Module[{m, n}, T = z^2 + h^2; T];
P2[z_] := Module[{P3}, P3[h_] := Module[{}, Q = h^4; Q]; P3[z]];
V = x*P2[x] + P1[x, y] + P2[y]; V]; P1[x_] := Module[{}, {c, d} = {90, 590}; c*d + x];
Map[Globals1, {P, P1}]
Out[3118]= {{"Q", "T", "V"}, {"c", "d"}}
In[3119]:= Sv[x_, y_] := Module[{a, b = 90, c = 590}, a = (x^2 + y^2)/(b + c);
{z, h} = {a, b}; t = z + h; gs = t^2]; Globals1[Sv]
Out[3119]= {"gs", "h", "t", "z"}

In[3120]:= LocalsGlobals[x_ /; ProcQ[x]] := {Locals[x], Globals1[x]}

In[3121]:= LocalsGlobals[Sv]
Out[3121]= {{"a", "b = 90", "c = 590"}, {"gs", "h", "t", "z"}}

Thus, the first example is represented for comparison of results of calls of the procedures **Globals** and **Globals1** on the same tuple of arguments; so, if in the first case as the global variables the subprocedures were defined, in the second such variables as global don't act any more. The function call **LocalsGlobals[*x*]** returns the nested list, whose the 1st element – the list of local variables with initial values if such variables exist in string format while the second element determines the list of global variables of a *x* procedure *(block or module)*. The **ExtrNames** procedure is represented as a quite useful tools at working with procedures, its source code with examples of application is represented by the following fragment:

In[2720]:= ExtrNames[x_ /; ProcQ[x]] :=
Module[{a = BlockToModule[x], b, c, d, f, p = {}, g, k = 1},
{f, a} = {ToString[Locals[x]], Locals1[x]}; {b, c} = {HeadPF[x], PureDefinition[x]};
g = StringReplace[c, {b <> " := Module[" -> "", ToString[f] <> ", " -> ""}];
d = Map[If[ListQ[#], #[[1]], #] &, StringPosition[g, {" := ", " = "}]];
For[k, k <= Length[d], k++, AppendTo[p, ExtrName[g, d[[k]], -1]]];
p = Select[p, # != "" &]; {a, Complement[a, p], Complement[p, a]}]

In[2721]:= GS[x_] := Block[{a = 90, b, c}, b = 590; c = 6; x = a + b + c; x]
In[2722]:= ExtrNames[GS]
Out[2722]= {{"a", "b", "c"}, {"a"}, {"x"}}
In[2723]:= ExtrNames[ProcQ]
Out[2723]= {{"a", "atr", "b", "c", "d", "h"}, {"atr", "h"}, {}}
In[2724]:= ExtrNames[ExtrNames]
Out[2724]= {{"a", "f", "b", "c", "d", "p", "g", "k"}, {"a", "b", "c", "f", "k"}, {}}

In[2727]:= Globals2[x_ /; ProcQ[x] || ModuleQ[x] || BlockQ[x]] := ExtrNames[x][[3]]
In[2728]:= GS[h_] := Module[{a = 90, b, c}, b = 590; c = 6; x = a + b + c; x + h]
In[2729]:= VG[h_] := Block[{a = 90, b, c}, b = 590; c = 6; x = a + b + c; y = h^2]
In[2730]:= Map[Globals2, {GS, VG, ProcQ, Tuples1, TestArgsTypes, LoadFile}]
Out[2730]= {{"x"}, {"x", "y"}, {}, {"Res"}, {"$TestArgsTypes"}, {"$Load$Files$"}}

The procedure call **ExtrNames[*x*]** returns the nested 3–element list, whose the first element defines the list of all local variables of a *x* procedure in the string format, the second element determines the list of local variables of the *x* procedure in the string format to which in the procedure body *x* are ascribed the values, whereas the third element determines the list of global variables to which in the procedure body *x* are ascribed the values by the operators {":=", "="}. A rather simple **Globals2** function completes the fragment, the given function is based on the previous procedure and in a certain measure expands the possibilities of the considered procedures **Globals** and **Globals1** on procedures of any type; the function call **Globals2[*x*]** returns the list of names in string format of global variables of a *x* procedure.

Nevertheless, the previous tools which are correctly testing existence at a module, a block of the global variables defined by assignments by the operators {":=", "="}, are not effective in cases when definitions of the tested modules/blocks use assignments of type {*a, b, ...*} {= | :=} {*a1, b1, c1, ...*} or *a*[[*k*]] {= | :=} *b*, simply ignoring them. The given defect is eliminated by the **LocalsGlobals1** procedure, whose call **LocalsGlobals1[*x*]** returns the nested 3–element list whose the first sublist contains names in the string format of the local variables, the second sublist contains local variables with initial values in the string format, and the third sublist – global variables in the string format of a block, or a module *x*. On the *x* argument of the type different from a block or a module, the procedure call is returned *unevaluated*. The fragment represents source code of the **LocalsGlobals1** procedure with typical examples of its use.

In[2483]:= LocalsGlobals1[x_ /; QBlockMod[x]] :=
Module[{c = "", d, j, h = {}, k = 1, p, G, L, a = Flatten[{PureDefinition[x]}][[1]],
b = Flatten[{HeadPF[x]}][[1]]},
b = StringReplace[a, {b <> " := Module[" -> "", b <> " := Block[" -> ""}, 1];
While[k <= StringLength[b], d = StringTake[b, {k, k}]; c = c <> d;
If[StringCount[c, "{"] == StringCount[c, "}"], Break[]]; k++];
b = StringReplace[b, c <> "," -> "", 1];
L = If[c == "{}", {}, StrToList[StringTake[c, {2, -2}]]];
d = StringPosition[b, {" := ", " = "}]; d = (#1[[1]] - 1 &) /@ d;
For[k = 1, k <= Length[d], k++, c = d[[k]]; p = "";
For[j = c, j >= 1, j--, p = StringTake[b, {j, j}] <> p;
If[! Quiet[ToExpression[p]] === $Failed && StringTake[b, {j - 1, j - 1}] == " ",
AppendTo[h, p]; Break[]]]];
G = Flatten[(If[StringFreeQ[#1, "{"], #1, StrToList[StringTake[#1, {2, -2}]]] &) /@
(StringTake[#1, {1, Quiet[Check[Flatten[StringPosition[#1, "["]][[1]], 0]] - 1}] &) /@ h];
b = (If[StringFreeQ[#1, " = "], #1, StringTake[#1, {1, Flatten[StringPosition[#1,
" = "]][[1]] - 1}]] &) /@ L;
d = DeleteDuplicates[Flatten[(StringSplit[#1, ", "] &) /@ MinusList[G, b]]];
d = Select[d, ! Quiet[SystemQ[#1]] && ! MemberQ[Flatten[{"\\", "#", "\"", "", "+", "-",
ToString /@ Range[0, 9]}], StringTake[#1, {1, 1}]] &];
{Select[b, ! MemberQ[ToString /@ Range[0, 9], StringTake[#1, {1, 1}]] &], L,
MinusList[d, b]}]

In[2484]:= M[x_, y_] := Module[{a = 90, b = 590, c = {v, r}}, h = x*y*a*b; m = 72; t := (a + b);
g[[6]] = 74; t[z_] := a; {g, p} = {69, 74}; {k, j} := {42, 74}; x + y];
{h, m, t, g, p, k, j} = {1, 2, 3, 4, 5, 6, 7}; {LocalsGlobals1[M], {h, m, t, g, p, k, j}}
Out[2484]= {{{"a", "b", "c"}, {"a = 90", "b = 590", "c = {v, r}"}, {"h", "m", "t", "g", "p", "k", "j"}},
{1, 2, 3, 4, 5, 6, 7}}
In[2485]:= Sv[x_, y_] := Module[{a, b = 90, c = {n, m}}, a = (x^2 + y^2)/(b + c); {z, h} = {a, b};
t = z + h; gs = t^2]; LocalsGlobals1[Sv]
Out[2485]= {{"a", "b", "c"}, {"a", "b = 90", "c = {n, m}"}, {"z", "h", "t", "gs"}}
In[2486]:= Vt[x_, y_] := Module[{a, b = 90, c = {n, m, {42, 74}}}, a = (x^2 + y^2)/(b + c);
{z, h} = {a, b}; t = z + h; gs = t^2]; LocalsGlobals1[Vt]
Out[2486]= {{"a", "b", "c"}, {"a", "b = 90", "c = {n, m, {42, 74}}"}, {"z", "h", "t", "gs"}}

In[2495]:= LocalsGlobalsM[x_ /; QBlockMod[x]] :=
Module[{b = "$$90$", c, d = {}, k = 1, a = Flatten[{PureDefinition[x]}]},
While[k <= Length[a], c = b <> ToString[x]; ToExpression[b <> a[[k]]];
AppendTo[d, LocalsGlobals1[c]]; ToExpression["Clear[" <> c <> "]"]; k++];
If[Length[d] == 1, d[[1]], d]]
In[2496]:= M[x_, y_] := Module[{a = 90, b = 590, c}, h = x*y*a*b; m = 74; t := (a + b);

g[[6]] = 75; t[z_] := a; {g, p} = {69, 74}; x + y];
M[x_] := Block[{a, b}, y = x]; M[x__] := Block[{a, b}, {y, z} := {a, b}];
P1[x_] := Module[{a, b = {90, 590}}, {c, d} = {p, q}; {a, b, h, g} = {42, 49, 74, 69}; c*d + x]
In[2497]:= LocalsGlobalsM[M]
Out[2497]= {{{"a", "b", "c"}, {"a = 90", "b = 590", "c"}, {"h", "m", "t", "g", "p"}},
{{"a", "b"}, {"a", "b"}, {"y"}}, {{"a", "b"}, {"a", "b"}, {"y", "z"}}}
In[2498]:= LocalsGlobalsM[P1]
Out[2498]= {{"a", "b"}, {"a", "b = {90, 590}"}, {"c", "d", "h", "g"}}

Meanwhile, the **LocalsGlobals1** procedure correctly operates only with blocks or modules having unique definitions, i.e. with the objects other than objects of the same name. While the **LocalsGlobalsM** procedure expands the **LocalsGlobals1** procedure onto a case of the blocks or modules of the same name; the procedure call **LocalsGlobalsM**[*x*] returns the list of the nested *three*-element lists of the format similar to the format of results of return on the calls **LocalsGlobals1**[*x*] whose elements are *biunique* with subobjects of *x*, according to their order at application to the *x* object of the **PureDefinition** procedure. On *x* arguments of type different from {*block, module*}, the procedure call **LocalsGlobalsM**[*x*] is returned *unevaluated*. The source code of the **LocalsGlobalsM** procedure with examples of its usage complete the previous fragment. Meanwhile, it must be kept in mind that the returned list of the global variables doesn't contain multiple names though the identical names and can belong to the objects of various type as a visually illustrates *1st* example to the **LocalsGlobals1** procedure in the previous fragment in which the "*t*" symbol acts as a global variable twice. Indeed, the simple example below very visually illustrates the aforesaid, namely:

In[2538]:= t[z_] := z; t := (a + b + c); Definition[t]
Out[2538]= t := (a + b + c)
t[z_] := z

Therefore carrying out the additional analysis regarding definition of the types of the global variables used by the tested block or module in event of need is required. Definition of the **LocalsGlobals1** procedure along with standard tools uses and our means such as **HeadPF**, **QBlockMod**, **PureDefinition**, **MinusList**, **StrToList**, **SystemQ** considered in this book and in [28-33]. The procedure has a number of application at programming of various problems, first of all, of the system character.

Additionally to the above procedure, the procedure call **ArgsLocalsGlobals**[*x*], in general, returns the 3-element list whose the first element defines the formal arguments, the second element defines the local variables and the third element defines the global variables of a *x* object; at that, in case of a *x* object with the same name the elements of the returned list are the nested sublists whose elements are biunique with subobjects of a *x*, according to their order at application of the **PureDefinition** procedure to the *x* object. Whereas the procedure call **ArgsLocalsGlobals**[*x, y*] where the second optional *y* argument – *an indefinite symbol* – through it returns the 3-element list whose the first list defines the system tools, the second element determines the tools of **BlockFuncModQ** type, and the third element defines other global symbols; at that, in case of a *x* object with the same name the elements of the returned list are the nested sublists whose elements are biunique with subobjects of a *x*, according to their order at use of the **PureDefinition** procedure to the *x* object. On factual *x* argument of the type different from block, function or module, the procedure calls **ArgsLocalsGlobals**[*x*] and **ArgsLocalsGlobals**[*x, y*] are returned as the unevaluated ones. The following fragment represents source code of the **ArgsLocalsGlobals** procedure with examples of its use.

In[3784]:= G[x_ /; IntegerQ[x]] := Module[{a=75, b=70}, x*m*(a+b); ProcQ[x]]; G[x_, y_] := Block[{}, (x + Cos[y])/n]; S[x_] := x^2 + h; F[x_ /; StringQ[x]] := Module[{a = 49}, x*a]

In[3784]:= ArgsLocalsGlobals[x_ /; BlockFuncModQ[x], y__] :=
Module[{a = Flatten[{PureDefinition[x]}, 1], b = Flatten[{Args[x, 6]}, 1],
c = Flatten[{Locals1[x]}, 1], d = {}, h, h1, g = {}, g1 = {}, s = {}, s1 = {}, p = {}, p1 = {}},
h = Map[Complement[ExtrVarsOfStr[#, 2], {ToString[x]}] &, a];
h1 = Map[Select[#, #1 != ToString[x] && ! SystemQ[#1] &] &, h];
Do[AppendTo[d, Complement[h1[[j]], Join[Flatten[{b[[j]]}]],
Quiet[Flatten[{c[[j]]}]]]]], {j, 1, Length[a]}];
If[{y} != {} && ! HowAct[y], Do[Map[If[SystemQ[#], AppendTo[g, #],
If[BlockFuncModQ[#], AppendTo[s, #], AppendTo[p, #]]] &, h[[j]]];
AppendTo[g1, DeleteDuplicates[Sort[g]]]; g = {};
AppendTo[s1, DeleteDuplicates[Sort[s]]]; s = {};
AppendTo[p1, Complement[DeleteDuplicates[Sort[p]],
Join[Quiet[Flatten[{b[[j]]}]], Quiet[Flatten[{c[[j]]}]]]]]; p = {}, {j, 1, Length[h]}];
y = {g1, s1, p1}; y = Map[If[Length[#] == 1, #[[1]], #] &, y], 75];
{b, c, If[Length[d] == 1, Quiet[d[[1]]], d]}]

In[3785]:= ArgsLocalsGlobals[G, g70]
Out[3785]= {{{"x"}, {"x", "y"}}, {{"a", "b"}, "{}"}, {{"m", "ProcQ"}, {"n"}}}
In[3786]:= g70
Out[3786]= {{{"IntegerQ", "Module"}, {"Block", "Cos"}}, {{"ProcQ"}, {}}, {{"m"}, {"n"}}}
In[3787]:= ArgsLocalsGlobals[F, v75]
Out[3787]= {{"x"}, {"a"}, {}}
In[3788]:= v75
Out[3788]= {{"Module", "StringQ"}, {}, {}}
In[3789]:= ArgsLocalsGlobals[S, s50]
Out[3789]= {{"x"}, {}, {"h"}}
In[3790]:= s50
Out[3790]= {{}, {}, {"h"}}

The next procedure is a rather useful version of the previous **ArgsLocalsGlobals** procedure. The procedure call **ArgsLocalsGlobals1**[*x*] returns the 3–element list whose the *first* element defines the list containing the formal arguments in string format of a block or module *x*, the *second* element determines the list containing the local variables in the string format of the *x*, while the *third* element defines the nested list containing other sorted symbols in the string format of *x* which are grouped accordingly to their contexts; at that, the contexts are located as the first elements in groups corresponding to these symbols. However, the procedure is intended for unique objects of type {*Block, Module*}, i.e. the objects having single definitions. Meantime, the procedure can be simply adapted to objects of the same name, i.e. the objects having multiple headings. The following fragment represents source code of the procedure with examples of its application.

In[4212]:= ArgsLocalsGlobals1[x_ /; BlockModQ[x]] :=
Module[{a = ExtrVarsOfStr[PureDefinition[x], 2], b = Sort[Map[#[[1]] &, Locals4[x]]], c, d},
d[t_] := Sort1[t, ContextQ[#] &]; ClearAll[c]; ArgsBFM2[x, c];
c = Map[#[[1]] &, If[Length[c] == 1, {c}, c]];
{c, b, ReduceLevelsList[Map[d, Map[DeleteDuplicates[Flatten[#]] &, Gather[Map[{#, Context[#]} &, Complement[a, Join[c, b, {ToString[x]}]]], #1[[2]] == #2[[2]] &]]]][[1]]]}]

In[4213]:= ArgsLocalsGlobals1[ArgsBFM2]
Out[4213]= {{"x", "y"}, {"a", "b", "c", "d", "j", "k", "p"}, {{"System`", "AppendTo", "Break", "Default", "Do", "For", "If", "Length", "MemberQ", "Module", "Optional", "Return", "StringFreeQ", "StringJoin", "StringLength", "StringReplace", "StringSplit", "StringTake", "StringTrim", "SyntaxQ", "ToString"}, {"Global`", "Arbitrary"}, {"AladjevProcedures`", "BlockFuncModQ", "HeadPF", "NullQ", "ReduceLevelsList"}}}

In[4214]:= G[x_, y_, z_] := Module[{a = 75, b = 70, c}, (a + Sin[b] + c)*x*y*z*j/u]

In[4215]:= ArgsLocalsGlobals1[G]
Out[4215]= {{"x", "y", "z"}, {"a", "b", "c"}, {{"System`", "Module", "Sin"}, {"Global`", "j", "u"}}}

In[4216]:= ArgsLocalsGlobals1[ArgsLocalsGlobals1]
Out[4216]= {{"x"}, {"a", "b", "c", "d"}, {{"AladjevProcedures`", "ArgsBFM2", "BlockModQ", "ContextQ", "ExtrVarsOfStr", "Locals4", "PureDefinition", "ReduceLevelsList", "Sort1", "t"}, {"System`", "ClearAll", "Complement", "Context", "DeleteDuplicates", "Flatten", "Gather", "If", "Join", "Length", "Module", "Sort", "ToString"}}}

The **ArgsLocalsGlobals1** procedure can be a rather easily extented to the objects processing of the same name, i.e. *Blocks* and *Modules* with several headings. It should be noted, that the **ExtrVarsOfStr** procedure used by the two previous procedures allows to make a rather interesting *structural* analysis of source codes of definitions of the user blocks, functions and modules. At that, this tool is also useful for the structural analysis of arbitrary expressions.

The procedure call **GlobalsInFunction[x]** returns the list of global symbols and/or constants (*excepting system symbols*) which are in definition of a *x* function (*including pure functions of short format*). If *x* function has no global symbols and/or constants, the function call returns the empty list, i.e. {}. The fragment below represents source code of the **GlobalsInFunction** procedure with evamples of its application.

In[4652]:= GlobalsInFunction[x_ /; FunctionQ[x] || ShortPureFuncQ[x]] := Module[{a, b},
If[ShortPureFuncQ[x], b = Complement[ExtrVarsOfStr[ToString1[x], 2], ArgsPureFunc[x]],
a = If[UnevaluatedQ[ArgsBFM, x], Args[x], ArgsBFM[x]]; b = PureDefinition[x];
b = If[b === $Failed, ToString1[x], b]; b = ExtrVarsOfStr[b, 2];
b = Complement[b, a, {"Function", ToString[x]}]]; Select[b, ! SystemQ[#] &]]

In[4653]:= GlobalsInFunction[Function[{x, y, z}, Sin[(x + y)*z]]]
Out[4653]= {}

In[4654]:= H[x_, y_, z_] := (a*x + Cos[b*y])*z/m^d; GlobalsInFunction[H]
Out[4654]= {"a", "b", "d", "m"}

In[4655]:= GlobalsInFunction[(a*#1 + #2*Sin[d*#1])/(c*#3 − #4*Cos[b*#3]) &]
Out[4655]= {"a", "b", "c", "d"}

Above we determined so-called *active* global variables as global variables to which in the objects of type {*Block, Module*} the assignments are done, whereas we understand the global variables different from arguments as the *passive* global variables, whose values are only used in objects of the specified type. In this regard tools which allow to evaluate the passive global variables for the user blocks and modules are being represented as a very interesting. One of similar means – the **BlockFuncModVars** procedure which solves even more general problem. The fragment below represents source code of the procedure **BlockFuncModVars** along with the most typical examples of its application.

In[2337]:= BlockFuncModVars[x_ /; BlockFuncModQ[x]] :=
Module[{d, t, c = Args[x, 90], a = If[QFunction[x], {}, LocalsGlobals1[x]], s = {"System"},
u = {"Users"}, b = Flatten[{PureDefinition[x]}][[1]], h = {}, d = ExtrVarsOfStr[b, 2];
If[a == {}, t = Map[If[Quiet[SystemQ[#]], AppendTo[s, #],
If[BlockFuncModQ[#], AppendTo[u, #], AppendTo[h, #]]] &, d];
{s, u = Select[u, # != ToString[x] &], c, MinusList[d, Join[s, u, c, {ToString[x]}]]},
Map[If[Quiet[SystemQ[#]], AppendTo[s, #],
If[BlockFuncModQ[#], AppendTo[u, #], AppendTo[h, #]]] &, d];
{Select[s, ! MemberQ[{"$Failed", "True", "False"}, #] &], Select[u, # != ToString[x] &&
! MemberQ[a[[1]], #] &], c, a[[1]], a[[3]], Select[h, ! MemberQ[Join[a[[1]], a[[3]],
c, {"System", "Users"}], #] &]}]]

In[2338]:= A[m_, n_, p_ /; IntegerQ[p], h_ /; PrimeQ[h]] := Module[{a = 74},
h*(m + n + p)/a + StringLength[ToString1[z]]/(Cos[c] + Sin[d])]
In[2339]:= BlockFuncModVars[A]
Out[2339]= {{"System", "Cos", "IntegerQ", "Module", "PrimeQ", "Sin", "StringLength"},
{"Users", "ToString1"}, {"m", "n", "p", "h"}, {"a"}, {}, {"c", "d", "z"}}
In[2340]:= BlockFuncModVars[StringReplaceS]
Out[2340]= {{"System", "Append", "Characters", "If", "Length", "MemberQ", "Module",
"Quiet", "StringLength", "StringPosition", "StringQ", "StringReplacePart", "StringTake",
"While"}, {"Users"}, {"S", "s1", "s2"}, {"a", "b", "c", "k", "p", "L", "R"}, {}, {}}
In[2341]:= BlockFuncModVars[BlockFuncModVars]
Out[2341]= {{"System", "AppendTo", "Flatten", "If", "Join", "MemberQ", "Module", "Quiet",
"Select", "ToString"}, {"Users", "Args", "BlockFuncModQ", "ExtrVarsOfStr",
"LocalsGlobals1", "MinusList", "PureDefinition", "QFunction", "SystemQ"}, {"x"},
{"d", "t", "c", "a", "s", "u", "b", "h"}, {}, {}}
In[2342]:= BlockFuncModVars[LocalsGlobals1]
Out[2342]= {{"System", "Append", "Block", "Break", "Check", "DeleteDuplicates", "Flatten",
"For", "If", "Length", "MemberQ", "Module", "Quiet", "Range", "Select", "StringCount",
"StringFreeQ", "StringJoin", "StringLength", "StringPosition", "StringReplace", "StringSplit",
"StringTake", "ToExpression", "ToString", "While"}, {"Users", "HeadPF", "MinusList",
"PureDefinition", "QBlockMod", "StrToList", "SystemQ"}, {"x"}, {"c", "d", "j", "h", "k", "p",
"G", "L", "a", "b"}, {}, {}}
In[2343]:= BlockFuncModVars[StrStr]
Out[2343]= {{"System", "If", "StringJoin", "StringQ", "ToString"}, {"Users"}, {"x"}, {}}

The procedure call **BlockFuncModVars**[*x*] returns the nested 6-element list, whose the first element – the list of the *system* functions used by a block or module *x*, whose first element is *"System"* while other names are system functions in string format; the second element – the list of the user tools used by the block or module *x*, whose the first element is *"Users"* while the others define names of tools in string format; the third element defines the list of formal arguments in the string format of the block or module *x*; the fourth element – the list of local variables in the string format of the block or module *x*; the fifth element – the list of active global variables in string format of the block or module *x*; at last, the sixth element defines the list of *passive* global variables in the string format of the block or module *x*. While on the user *x* function the procedure call **BlockFuncModVars**[*x*] returns the nested 4-element list, whose the first element – the list of the *system* functions used by a *x* function, whose the first element is *"System"* while other names are system functions in the string format; the second element – the list of the user tools used by the *x* function, whose the first element is *"Users"* whereas the others determine names of tools in string format; the third element defines the list of formal arguments in the string format of the *x* function; the fourth element – the list of global variables in the string format of the *x* function. The procedure provides the structural analysis of the user blocks, functions or modules in the following contexts, namely: *(1)* the used system functions, *(2)* the user tools, active in the current session, *(3)* formal arguments, *(4)* the local variables, *(5)* the active global variables, and *(6)* the passive local variables. The means has a number of interesting enough appendices, first of all, of the system character.

The following procedure belongs to group of the means processing the strings, however, it is presented exactly here as it is very closely connected with the previous procedure; along with other means it is the cornerstone of algorithm of the **BlockFuncModVars** procedure. The following fragment represents source code of the **BlockFuncModVars** procedure with the most typical examples of its application.

In[2478]:= ExtrVarsOfStr[S_ /; StringQ[S], t_ /; MemberQ[{1, 2}, t], x__] :=
Module[{k, j, d = {}, p, a, q = Map[ToString, Range[0, 9]], h = 1, c = "",
L = Characters["`!@#%^&*(){}:\"\\\/|<>?~-=+[];:'., 1234567890_"],
R = Characters["`!@#%^&*(){}:\"\\\/|<>?~-=+[];:'., _"], s = "," <> S <> ","},
a = StringLength[s]; Label[G]; For[k = h, k <= a, k++, p = StringTake[S, {k, k}];
If[! MemberQ[L, p], c = c <> p; j = k + 1; While[j <= a, p = StringTake[S, {j, j}];
If[! MemberQ[R, p], c = c <> p, AppendTo[d, c]; h = j; c = ""; Goto[G]]; j++]]];
AppendTo[d, c]; d = Select[d, ! MemberQ[q, #] &];
d = Select[Map[StringReplace[#, {"+" -> "", "-" -> "", "_" -> ","}] &, d], # != "" &];
d = Flatten[Select[d, ! StringFreeQ[S, #] &]]; d = Flatten[Map[StringSplit[#, ", "] &, d]];
If[t == 1, Flatten, Sort][If[{x} != {}, Flatten, DeleteDuplicates][Select[d, ! MemberQ[{"\\",
"#", ""}, StringTake[#, {1, 1}]] &]]]]

In[2479]:= A[m_, n_, p_ /; IntegerQ[p], h_ /; PrimeQ[h]] := Module[{a=42.74}, h*(m+n+p)/a]
In[2480]:= ExtrVarsOfStr[Flatten[{PureDefinition[A]}][[1]], 2]
Out[2480]= {"a", "A", "h", "IntegerQ", "m", "Module", "n", "p", "PrimeQ"}
In[2481]:= G[x_, y_ /; IntegerQ[y]] := Module[{a, b = Sin[c+590*d], h}, z = x+y; V[m] + Z[n]]
In[2482]:= ExtrVarsOfStr[PureDefinition[G], 1, 90]

Out[2482]= {"G", "x", "y", "IntegerQ", "y", "Module", "a", "b", "Sin", "c", "d", "h", "z", "x", "y", "V", "m", "Z", "n"}

In[2483]:= V[x_, y_ /; PrimeQ[y]] := Block[{a, b = 83/590, c = m*n}, If[x > t + w, x*y, S[x, y]]]

In[2484]:= ExtrVarsOfStr[PureDefinition[V], 2]

Out[2484]= {"a", "b", "Block", "c", "If", "m", "n", "PrimeQ", "S", "t", "V", "w", "x", "y"}

In[2485]:= F[x_] := a*x + Sin[b*x] + StringLength[ToString1[x + 590*c]];
BlockFuncModVars[F]

Out[2485]= {{"System", "Sin", "StringLength"}, {"Users", "ToString1"}, {"x"}, {"a", "b", "c"}}

In[2486]:= ExtrVarsOfStr["G[x_] := Module[{Vg, H74},
Vg[y_] := Module[{}, y^3]]", 1]

Out[2486]= {"G", "x", "Module", "Vg", "H74", "y"}

In[2487]:= ExtrVarsOfStr["(a + b)/(c + d) + 74*Sin[c]*Cos[d + 590*h]", 2]

Out[2487]= {"a", "b", "c", "Cos", "d", "h", "Sin"}

In[2488]:= ExtrVarsOfStr["(a + b)/(c + 590*d) + Sin[c]*Cos[d + h]", 2, 90]

Out[2488]= {"a", "b", "c", "c", "Cos", "d", "d", "h", "Sin"}

The procedure call **ExtrVarsOfStr[*S*, *t*]** at *t* = 2 returns the sorted and at *t* = 1 unsorted list of variables in the string format which managed to extract from a *S* string; at the absence of the similar variables the empty list, i.e. {} is returned. The procedure call **ExtrVarsOfStr[*S*, *t*, *x*]** with the 3rd optional *x* argument – an arbitrary expression – returns the list of the variables included in the *S* string without reduction of their multiplicity to *1*. Along with the standard mechanism of local variables the *Mathematica* system allows use the mechanism of global variables of the current session in the body of procedures as the local variables. Experience of use of the procedure confirms its high reliability in the extraction of variables; the given procedure is an quite simply adjusted onto the especial situations arising in the course of its work. For correct use of the **ExtrVarsOfStr** procedure it is supposed that an expression *Exp*, determined in a *S* string is in the *InputForm*-format, i.e. *S* = **ToString[InputForm[*Exp*]]**. The procedure is effectively used at manipulations with definitions of the user functions, blocks and procedures. So, in the previous **BlockFuncModVars** procedure it is used significantly. The **ExtrVarsOfStr** procedure is used in the **ContentsBFM** procedure represented below.

The next **VarsInExpr2** procedure represents an useful enough version of the **ExtrVarsOfStr** procedure. The procedure call **ExtrVarsOfStr2[*S*, *t*]** returns the sorted list of variables in the string format that managed to extract from a *S* string; at the absence of the similar variables the empty list, i.e. {} is returned. Whereas the procedure call **ExtrVarsOfStr2[*S*, *t*, *x*]** with the 3rd optional *x* argument – *the list of strings of the length 1* – returns the list of the variables of *S* on condition that at the above extracting, the elements from the *x* list are not ignored. The following fragment represents source code of the **ExtrVarsOfStr2** procedure with a typical example of its application.

In[4576]:= ExtrVarsOfStr2[S_ /; StringQ[S], x___ /; If[{x} == {}, True, ListQ[x]]] :=
Module[{k, j, d = {}, p, a, q = Map[ToString, Range[0, 9]], h = 1, c = "",
L = Characters["`!@#%^&*(){}:\"\\V|<>?~-=+[];:'., 1234567890_"],
R = Characters["`!@#%^&*(){}:\"\\V|<>?~-=+[];:'., _"], s = "," <> S <> ","},
a = StringLength[s]; If[{x} == {}, 6, {L, R} = Map[Select[#, ! MemberQ[x, #] &] &, {L, R}]];
Label[Gs];

```
For[k = h, k <= a, k++, p = StringTake[s, {k, k}]; If[! MemberQ[L, p], c = c <> p; j = k + 1;
While[j <= a, p = StringTake[s, {j, j}];
If[! MemberQ[R, p], c = c <> p, AppendTo[d, c]; h = j; c = ""; Goto[Gs]]; j++]]];
AppendTo[d, c]; d = Select[d, ! MemberQ[q, #] &];
d = Select[Map[StringReplace[#, {"+" -> "", "-" -> "", "_" -> ","}] &, d], # != "" &];
d = Flatten[Select[d, ! StringFreeQ[s, #] &]];
Sort[DeleteDuplicates[Flatten[Map[StringSplit[#, ", "] &, d]]]]]
In[4577]:= ExtrVarsOfStr2["(a*#1 + b*#2)/(c*#3 - d*#4) + m*#1*#4", {"#"}]
Out[4577]= {"#1", "#2", "#3", "#4", "a", "b", "c", "d", "m"}
In[4578]:= ExtrVarsOfStr2["(a*#1 + b*#2)/(c*#3 - d*#4) + m*#1*#4"]
Out[4578]= {"a", "b", "c", "d", "m"}
```

The next **VarsInExpr** procedure represents a rather useful version of the **ExtrVarsOfStr** and **ExtrVarsOfStr1** procedures. The call **VarsInExpr**[x] returns the sorted list of variables in the string format, which managed to extract from a x expression; in a case of absence of similar variables the empty list is returned. At that, it is supposed that a x expression can be coded in the string format, i.e. **ToString[InputForm[x]]**. The following fragment represents source code of the **VarsInExpr** procedure with the typical examples of its application.

```
In[4170]:= VarsInExpr[x_] := Module[{a = StringReplace[ToStringRational[x], " " -> ""],
b = Join[Range5[33 ;; 35, 37 ;; 47], Range[58, 64], Range[91, 96], Range[123, 126]]},
Sort[DeleteDuplicates[Select[StringSplit[a, Map[FromCharacterCode[#] &, b]],
SymbolQ[#] && # != "" &]]]]
In[4171]:= VarsInExpr[Log[x] + (a + b/x^2)*Csc[x*y] + Tan[y]]
Out[4171]= {"a", "b", "Csc", "Log", "Tan", "x", "y"}
In[4172]:= VarsInExpr[(a + bc)/(c + dg)]
Out[4172]= {"a", "bc", "c", "dg"}
In[4173]:= VarsInExpr[(a + b/x^2)/Sin[x*y] + 1/z^3 + Log[y]]
Out[4173]= {"a", "b", "Csc", "Log", "x", "y", "z"}
In[4174]:= VarsInExpr["(a + b)/(c + 590*d$) + Sin[c]*Cos[d + h]"]
Out[4174]= {"a", "b", "c", "Cos", "d", "d$", "h", "Sin"}
```

In general, the both procedures **ExtrVarsOfStr** and **VarsInExpr** can be also useful enough for structural analysis of algebraic expressions.

The procedure call **ContentsBFM**[x] returns the six-element list whose:

- the first element defines the type of a x object {*"Block"*, *"Function"*, *"Module"*},
- the second element defines the list of its formal arguments,
- the third element defines the list of local variables of the x object,
- the fourth element defines the list of names of the system functions used by the x object,
- the fifth element defines the list of names of the user means used by the x object,
- the sixth element defines the list of the global variables used by the x object.

All components composing the returned list are represented in the string format. The next fragment represents source code of the **ContentsBFM** procedure with examples of its use.

```
In[4035]:= ContentsBFM[x_ /; BlockFuncModQ[x]] :=
```

Module[{a = PureDefinition[x], b = ArgsBFM[x], c = Locals1[x], d, h = {}, g = {}, s = {}},
a = ExtrVarsOfStr[a, 2]; d = Complement[a, b, c, {ToString[x], "Block", "Module"}];
Quiet[Map[If[SystemQ[#], AppendTo[g, #], If[UserQ[#], AppendTo[s, #],
AppendTo[h, #]]] &, d]];
{If[BlockQ[x], "Block", If[ModuleQ[x], "Module", "Function"]], b, c, g, s, h}]

In[4036]:= F[x_] := a*x + Sin[b*x] + StringLength[ToString1[x + 590*c]]
In[4037]:= ContentsBFM[F]
Out[4037]= {"Function", {"x"}, {}, {"Sin", "StringLength"}, {"ToString1"}, {"a", "b", "c"}}
In[4038]:= ContentsBFM[StringReplaceVars]
Out[4038]= {"Module", {"S", "r"}, {"a", "L", "R", "b", "c", "g"}, {"Characters", "Do", "If", "Length", "MemberQ", "Select", "StringJoin", "StringPosition", "StringQ", "StringReplacePart", "StringTake"}, {"ListRulesQ", "RuleQ"}, {"j"}}

As a rather useful *addition* to the previous procedure the **ContextsInExpr** procedure appears whose source code with examples of its use the fragment below represents. The procedure call **ContextsInExpr["x"]** as a whole returns the nested list whose elements have the format {"Ch'", "h"} where h – a symbol entering a x expression, presented in the string format, and "Ch'" – its context in the current session. Whereas the procedure call **ContextsInExpr["x", y]** with 2nd optional y argument – an arbitrary expression – as subject of the analysis considers the definition of a x symbol which can be both single, and multiple, i.e. to define an object of the same name. At that, on an uncertain w symbol the procedure call **ContextsInExpr["w"]** returns the empty list, whereas the call **ContextsInExpr["w", expr]** where *expr* – an arbitrary expression – returns the list {"System'", "$Failed"}. The grouping of symbols entering the definition of the x object is made according to their contexts on all object as a whole.

In[3775]:= ContextsInExpr[x_ /; ListQ[x] && And @@ Map[StringQ, x] || StringQ[x], y___]:=
Module[{a = If[{y} != {}, PureDefinition[x], x], b, vgs},
vgs[z_, t___] := Map[Sort[#, ContextQ[#1] &] &, Map[DeleteDuplicates, Map[Flatten,
Gather[Sort[DeleteDuplicates[Map[Quiet[Check[{#, Context[#]}, Nothing]] &,
ExtrVarsOfStr[If[{t} != {}, PureDefinition[z], ToString[z]], 2]]]], #1[[2]] === #2[[2]] &]]]];
b = Map[Join[{#[[1]]}, Sort[#[[2 ;; -1]]]] &, b];
b = If[StringQ[x], vgs[a], Map[vgs[#] &, a]]; If[Length[b] == 1, b[[1]], b]]

In[3776]:= kdp[x_] := Module[{a, b, c}, x]; kdp[y_, z_] := (y + z)*h75;
kdp[y_, z_, t_] := Block[{m, n}, (m*y + z + n*t)*g70]; kdp[x_Integer] := G*x
In[3777]:= ContextsInExpr["kdp"]
Out[3777]= {"Global`", "kdp"}
In[3778]:= ContextsInExpr["kdp", 75]
Out[3778]= {{"AladjevProcedures`", "a", "b", "c", "t", "x", "y", "z"},
{"System`", "Block", "Integer", "Module"}, {"Global`", "G", "g69", "h74", "kdp", "m", "n"}}

A quite useful reception of ensuring use of the global variables which isn't changing values of the variables of the same name outside of a procedure body was already given above. In addition to earlier described reception, we will present the procedure which automates this process of converting at the time of *performance* of an arbitrary procedure of global variables to the local variables of this procedure. The similar problem arises, for example, in the case when it is required to execute a procedure having global variables without changing their values outside of the procedure and without change of source code of the procedure in the current session. In other words, it is required to execute the procedure call with division of domains of definition of global variables of the current session of *global* and *system* variables of the same name of the procedure. While in other points of procedure call such restrictions aren't imposed.

The **GlobalToLocal** procedure solves the problem, whose call **GlobalToLocal[x]** provides converting of definition of a x procedure into definition of the $\$\$\$x$ procedure in which all global variables of the initial x procedure are included into the tuple of local variables; the procedure call returns a procedure name activated in the current session that has no global variables. Whereas the call **GlobalToLocal[x, y]** with the second optional y argument – an undefinite variable – in addition through it returns the nested list whose first element is the sublist of local variables and the 2nd element is sublist of global variables of a x procedure. The procedure in a number of cases solves the problem of protection of variables, external relative to a x procedure. The fragment below represents source code of the **GlobalToLocal** procedure with the most typical examples of its application.

In[2526]:= GlobalToLocal[x_ /; QBlockMod[x], y___] := Module[{b, c, a=LocalsGlobals1[x]},
If[Intersection[a[[1]], a[[3]]] == a[[3]] || a[[3]] == {}, x, b=Join[a[[2]], MinusList[a[[3]], a[[1]]]];
c = "$$$" <> StringReplace[PureDefinition[x], ToString[a[[2]]] -> ToString[b], 1];
If[{y} != {} && ! HowAct[y], y = {a[[1]], a[[3]]}]; ToExpression[c];
Symbol["$$$" <> ToString[x]]]]

In[2527]:= GS[x_] := Module[{a, b = 590, c = {m, n}}, Kr[y_] := Module[{}, y^2 + Sin[y]];
a = x^2; {z, h, p} = {a, b, 5}; t = z + h*Kr[6] − Cos[x + Kr[9]]; t]

In[2528]:= GlobalToLocal[GS]
Out[2528]= $$$GS

In[2529]:= Definition[$$$GS]
Out[2529]= $$$GS[x_] := Module[{a, b = 590, c = {m, n}, Kr, z, h, p, t}, Kr[y_] := Module[{}, y^2 + Sin[y]]; a = x^2; {z, h, p} = {a, b, 5}; t = z + h*Kr[6] − Cos[x + Kr[9]]; t]

In[2530]:= {GlobalToLocal[GS, g69], g69}
Out[2530]= {$$$GS, {{"a", "b", "c"}, {"Kr", "z", "h", "p", "t"}}}

In[2531]:= LocalsGlobals1[$$$GS]
Out[2531]= {{"a", "b", "c", "Kr", "z", "h", "p", "t"}, {"a", "b = 590", "c = {m, n}", "Kr", "z", "h","p", "t"}, {}}

The algorithm used by the **GlobalToLocal** procedure is a rather simple and consists in the following. In a case of absence for a x procedure of global variables the x name is returned; otherwise, on the basis of definition of the x procedure, the definition of the procedure with $\$\$\$x$ name which differs from the initial procedure only in that that the global variables of the x procedure are included into a tuple of local variables of the $\$\$\$x$ procedure is formed. Whereat the definition is activated in the current session with return of $\$\$\$x$ name, allowing to carry out the $\$\$\$x$ procedure in the current session without change of values of the global variables of the current session.

At the same time, the converting problem of a block or a module x into an object of the same type in which the global variables are included in a tuple of local variables of the returned x

object of the same name with both the same attributes and options is of certain interest. The **GlobalToLocalM** procedure solves this problem; the next fragment represents source code of the procedure **GlobalToLocalM** along with typical examples of its application.

In[2651]:= GlobalToLocalM[x_/; QBlockMod[x]] := Module[{d, h = "$$$", k = 1, n, p = {},
b = Attributes[x], c = Options[x], a = Flatten[{PureDefinition[x]}]},
While[k <= Length[a], d = a[[k]]; n = h <> ToString[x];
ToExpression[h <> d]; GlobalToLocal[Symbol[n]];
AppendTo[p, PureDefinition["$$$" <> n]];
ToExpression["ClearAll[" <> n <> "]"]; k++]; ClearAllAttributes[x]; ClearAll[x];
ToExpression[Map[StringReplace[#,"$$$$$$" -> "", 1] &, p]];
SetAttributes[x, b]; If[c != {}, SetOptions[x, c]];]

In[2652]:= A[x_] := Block[{}, g = x; {m, n} = {90, 74}]; A[x_, y_] := Module[{}, h = x + y;
z = h*x]; SetAttributes[A, {Listable, Protected}]; GlobalToLocalM[A]
In[2653]:= Definition[A]
Out[2653]= Attributes[A] = {Listable, Protected}
A[x_] := Block[{g, m, n}, g = x; {m, n} = {90, 74}]
A[x_, y_] := Module[{h, z}, h = x + y; z = h*x]
In[2654]:= GS[x_] := Module[{a, b = 590, c = {m, n}}, Kr[y_] := Module[{}, y^2 + Sin[y]];
a = x^2; {z, h, p} = {a, b, 20}; t = z + h*Kr[20] – Cos[x + Kr[90]]; t];
GS[x_, y_] := Block[{a, b = {90, 590}, c}, z = x + y; d = Art]; SetAttributes[GS, {Protected}];
GlobalToLocalM[GS]
In[2655]:= Definition[GS]
Out[2655]= Attributes[GS] = {Protected}
GS[x_] := Module[{a, b = 590, c = {m, n}, Kr, z, h, p, t}, Kr[y_] := Module[{}, y^2 + Sin[y]];
a = x^2; {z, h, p} = {a, b, 20}; t = z + h*Kr[20] – Cos[x + Kr[90]]; t]
GS[x_, y_] := Block[{a, b = {90, 590}, c, z, d}, z = x + y; d = Art]
In[2656]:= GSV[x_] := Module[{a, b = 590, c = {m, n}}, Kr[y_] := Module[{}, y^2 + Sin[y]];
a = x^2; {z, h, p} = {a, b, 20}; t = z + h*Kr[20] + Cos[x + Kr[590]]; w = t^2];
GSV[x_, y_] := Block[{a, b = {90, 50}, c}, z = x + y; d = Art; t = Length[b]*z];
SetAttributes[GSV, {Protected}]; GlobalToLocalM[GSV]
In[2657]:= Definition[GSV]
Out[2657]= GSV[x_] := Module[{a, b = 590, c = {m, n}, Kr, z, h, p, t, w}, Kr[y_] := Module[{},
y^2 + Sin[y]]; a = x^2; {z, h, p} = {a, b, 20}; t = z + h Kr[20] + Cos[x + Kr[590]]; w = t^2]
GSV[x_, y_] := Block[{a, b = {90, 50}, c, z, d, t}, z = x + y; d = Art; t = Length[b]*z]

The procedure call **GlobalToLocalM[x]** returns *Null*, i.e. nothing, herewith converting block or module *x* into *x* object of the same type and with the same attributes and options in that the global variables *(if they were)* of the initial object receive the local status. In the case of the objects of the same *x* name the call provides the correct converting of all components of the object defined by different definitions. The fragment examples enough visually clarify the sense of similar converting.

It must be kept in mind, our *MathToolBox* package [48] contains a number of other tools for the analysis of the procedures regarding existence in them of local and global variables, and also for manipulation with *arguments*, *local* and *global* variables of objects of the types {*Block*,

Function, Module}. Means for operating with local and global variables that are represented here and in [48] are quite useful in procedural programming in the *Mathematica* system.

Meantime, it must be kept in mind that a series of means of the *MathToolBox* package can depend on a version of the *Mathematica,* despite the a rather high level of prolongation of the built-in *Math*-language. Therefore in certain cases a certain tuning of separate means of the package on the current version of the system can be demanded, what in principle for the rather experienced user shouldn't cause special difficulties. In addition, similar tuning can be demanded even in case of passing from one operation platform to another, for example, from *Windows XP Professional* to *Windows 7 Professional.*

6.8. Attributes, options and values by default for the arguments of the user blocks, functions and modules; additional tools of their processing in the *Mathematica* system

The *Mathematica* system provides the possibility of assignment to variable, in particular, to names of the blocks, functions or modules of the certain special attributes determining their different properties. So, the *Listable* attribute for a *S* function determines, that the *S* function will be automatically applied to all elements of list which acts as its argument. The current tenth version of the *Mathematica* system has *19* attributes of various purpose, the operating with them is supported by *three* functions: **Attributes, ClearAttributes, SetAttributes** whose formats are discussed, for example, in [33,50]. These 3 functions provide such operations as: *(1) return of list of attributes ascribed to a x object; (2) deletion of all or separate attributes ascribed to a x object; (3) redefinition of the list of the attributes ascribed to a x object*. At that, in a number of cases of these means it isn't enough or they are not so effective. Therefore, a number of tools in this direction that expand the above standard *Mathematica* functions have been offered.

Above all, since eventually new *Mathematica* versions quite can both change the standard set of attributes and to expand it, the problem of testing of an arbitrary symbol to be qua of an admissible attribute is an quite natural. The **AttributesQ** procedure solves the problem whose call **AttributesQ[***x***]** returns *True*, if a *x* – the list of admissible attributes of the current version of the system, and *False* otherwise. Moreover, the call **AttributesQ[***x, y***]** with the 2nd optional *y* argument – an undefinite variable – returns through it the list of elements of the *x* list which aren't attributes. The fragment below presents source code of the procedure with typical examples of its application.

In[2550]:= **AttributesQ[x_ /; ListQ[x], y__] := Module[{a, b = {}},**
Map[If[Quiet[Check[SetAttributes[a, #], $Failed]] === $Failed, AppendTo[b, #]] &, x];
If[b != {}, If[{y} != {} && ! HowAct[y], y = b]; False, True]]

In[2551]:= **{AttributesQ[{Listable, Agn, Protected, Kr, Art}, h74], h74}**
Out[2551]= {False, {Agn, Kr, Art}}
In[2552]:= **{AttributesQ[{Protected, Listable, HoldAll}, g69], g69}**
Out[2552]= {True, g69}

The given means is an quite useful in a number of system appendices; at that, expanding the testing means of the *Mathematica* system.

Definitions of the user blocks, functions and modules in the **Mathematica** system allow qua of conditions and initial values for formal arguments, and initial values for local variables to use rather complex constructions as the following simple fragment illustrates:

In[4173]:= G[x_Integer, y_ /; {v[t_] := Module[{}, t^2], If[v[y] > 2017, True, False]}[[2]]] :=
Module[{a = {g[z_] := Module[{}, z^3], If[g[x] < 2017, 74, 590]}[[2]]}, Clear[v, g]; x*y + a]

In[4174]:= {a, b} = {590, 90}; {G[42, 74], G[42, 590], G[0, 0]}

Out[4174]= {3698, 25370, G[0, 0]}

In[4175]:= **Map[PureDefinition, {v, g}]**

Out[2565]= {"v[t_] := Module[{}, t^2]", $Failed}

In[4176]:= G[x_Integer, y_ /; {v[t_] := Module[{}, t^2], If[v[a] > 2016, True, False]}[[2]]] :=
Module[{a = {g[z_] := Module[{}, z^3], If[g[b] < 2016, 74, 590]}[[2]]}, x*y + a]

In[4177]:= {a, b} = {590, 74}; {G[42, 74], G[42, 590], G[0, 0]}

Out[4177]= {3698, 25370, 590}

In[4178]:= **Map[PureDefinition, {v, g}]**

Out[4178]= {"v[t_] := Module[{}, t^2]", "g[z_] := Module[{}, z^3]"}

For possibility of use of sequence of offers, including as well definitions of procedures, as a condition for a formal *y* argument and initial value for a local variable *a* the reception that is based on the list has been used in the previous fragment. The offers sequences were defined as elements of lists with value of their last element as *condition* and *initial* value respectively. If in body of the main *G* procedure a cleaning of symbols *v* and *g* from their definitions was not done, the procedures *v* and *g* will be available in the current session, otherwise not. The given question is solved depending on an objective, previous fragment illustrates the told. The above reception can be applied rather effectively also for programming of means of the different purpose what illustrates a number of the procedures represented in [28-33,50].

The mechanisms of typification of formal arguments of the user functions, modules, blocks enough in details are considered in [30,50]. At that, along with mechanism of typification of formal arguments, the **Mathematica** has definition mechanisms for the formal arguments of values *by default*, i.e. values that obtain the corresponding actual arguments at their absence at the calls. But, the system mechanism of setting of values by default assumes definition of such values before evaluation of definitions of blocks, functions and modules on the basis of standard **Default** function whose format supports installation of various values by default serially for separate formal arguments or of the same value for all arguments. The following fragment represents the **Defaults1[*F*, *y*]** procedure that provides the setting of expressions as values by default for the corresponding formal arguments of any subtuple of the tuple of formal arguments of the user function, block or module *F* that is determined by these two-element *y* list *(the first element – the number of position of an argument, the second element is any expression)*. For several values by default the *y* list has *ListList* type whose sublists have the above format. The procedure successfully works with the user block, function or module *F* of the same name, processing only the first subobject from the list of subobjects which are returned at the call **Definition[*F*]**. At that, the procedure call returns $Failed, or is returned unevaluated in especial situations. The next fragment represents source code of the **Defaults** procedure with examples of its use.

In[2640]:= **Defaults[x_ /; BlockFuncModQ[x], y_ /; ListQ[y] && Length[y] == 2 ||
ListListQ[y] && AllTrue[Map[IntegerQ[#[[1]]] &, y], TrueQ]] :=**

```
Module[{a = Flatten[{Definition2[x]}], atr = Attributes[x], q, t, u,
b = Flatten[{HeadPF[x]}][[1]], c = Args[x], d, p, h = {}, k = 1, g = If[ListListQ[y], y, {y}]},
If[Max[Map[#[[1]] &, y]] <= Length[c] && Min[Map[#[[1]] &, y]] >= 1,
c = Map[ToString, If[NestListQ[c], c[[1]], c]]; q = Map[#[[1]] &, y];
d = StringReplace[a[[1]], b -> "", 1];
While[k <= Length[q], p = c[[q[[k]]]]; t = StringSplit[p, "_"];
If[MemberQ[q, q[[k]]]], u = If[Length[t] == 2, t[[2]] = StringReplace[t[[2]], " /; " -> ""];
If[Quiet[ToExpression["{" <> t[[1]] <> "=" <> ToString[y[[k]][[2]]] <> "," <> t[[2]] <>
"}"]][[2]] || Quiet[Head[y[[k]][[2]]] === Symbol[t[[2]]]], True, False], True];
If[u, c[[q[[k]]]] = StringTake[p, {1, Flatten[StringPosition[p, "_"]][[2]]}] <> "."]]; k++];
ClearAllAttributes[x]; ClearAll[x]; k = 1;
While[k <= Length[q], ToExpression["Default[" <> ToString[x] <> ", " <>
ToString[q[[k]]] <> "]" <> " = " <> ToString1[y[[k]][[2]]]]; k++];
ToExpression[ToString[x] <> "[" <> StringTake[ToString[c], {2, -2}] <> "]" <> d];
Map[ToExpression, MinusList[a, {a[[1]]}]]; SetAttributes[x, atr], $Failed]]
```

In[2641]:= G[x_, y_ /; IntegerQ[y]] := x+y; G[x_, y_, z_] := x*y*z; G[x_, y_, z_, h_] := x*y*z*h

In[2642]:= SetAttributes[G, {Listable, Protected, Flat}]

In[2643]:= Defaults[G, {{2, 590}, {1, 74}}]

In[2644]:= Definition[G]

Out[2644]= Attributes[G] = {Flat, Listable, Protected}

G[x_., y_.] := x + y

G[x_, y_, z_] := x*y*z

G[x_, y_, z_, h_] := x*y*z*h

G /: Default[G, 1] = 74

G /: Default[G, 2] = 590

In[2645]:= {G[42, 47], G[74], G[]}

Out[2645]= {89, 664, 664}

In[2646]:= ClearAllAttributes[G]; G[x_, y_ /; IntegerQ[y]] := x + y; G[x_, y_, z_] := x*y*z;
G[x_, y_, z_, h_] := x*y*z*h

In[2647]:= SetAttributes[G, {Listable, Protected, Flat}]

In[2648]:= Defaults[G, {2, 2016}]

In[2649]:= Definition[G]

Out[2649]= Attributes[G] = {Flat, Listable, Protected}

G[x_, y_.] := x + y

G[x_, y_, z_] := x*y*z

G[x_, y_, z_, h_] := x*y*z*h

G /: Default[G, 2] = 2016

In[2650]:= Defaults[G, {1, 1942}]

In[2651]:= Definition[G]

Out[2651]= Attributes[G] = {Flat, Listable, Protected}

G[x_., y_.] := x + y

G[x_, y_, z_] := x*y*z

G[x_, y_, z_, h_] := x*y*z*h

G /: Default[G, 1] = 1942
G /: Default[G, 2] = 2016
In[2652]:= {G[], G[74, 69], G[590]}
Out[2652]= {3958, 143, 2606}

The successful call **Defaults[G, y]** returns *Null*, i.e. nothing, carrying out all *y* settings of the values *by default* for formal arguments of a block, a function or a module *j*. It is necessary to emphasize once again that in a case of a *w* object of the same name the call **Defaults[w, y]** processes only the first subobject from the list of subobjects which is returned on the call **Definition[w]**. And this is a rather essential remark since the assignment mechanism to the formal arguments of *w* of values by default for case of an object of the same name, using the **Default** function, is other than ascribing to the objects of such type, for instance, attributes. In the latter case the attributes are ascribed to all subobjects of an *w* object of the same name while for values by default the mechanism is valid only concerning the first subobject from the list of the subobjects returned on the call **Definition[w]**. The mechanism is realized as by the standard reception with use of the call **Default[j, n]** = *default* with template definition for *n*–th formal argument of the *j* object in the kind "_." and by the call **Defaults[j, {n, default}]** as it rather visually illustrates the following fragment, namely:

In[2673]:= **Clear[V]; Default[V, 2] = 590; V[x_, y_.] := {x, y}; V[x_, y_., z_, h_] := {x, y, z, h}**
In[2674]:= **Definition[V]**
Out[2674]= V[x_, y_.] := {x, y}
V[x_, y_., z_, h_] := {x, y, z, h}
V /: Default[V, 2] = 590
In[2675]:= {V[590], V[42, 47, 67]}
Out[2675]= {{590, 590}, {42, 590, 47, 67}}
In[2676]:= **Clear[V]; Default[V, 2] = 590; V[x_, y_.] := {x, y}; V[x_, y_, z_, h_] := {x, y, z, h}**
In[2677]:= **Definition[V]**
Out[2677]= V[x_, y_.] := {x, y}
V[x_, y_, z_, h_] := {x, y, z, h}
V /: Default[V, 2] = 590
In[2678]:= {V[590], V[42, 47, 67]}
Out[2678]= {{590, 590}, V[42, 47, 67]}
In[2679]:= **Clear[V]; V[x_, y_] := {x, y}; V[x_, y_, z_, h_] := {x, y, z, h}; Defaults[V, {2, 90}]**
In[2680]:= **Definition[V]**
Out[2680]= V[x_, y_.] := {x, y}
V[x_, y_, z_, h_] := {x, y, z, h}
V /: Default[V, 2] = 90
In[2681]:= {V[590], V[42, 47, 67]}
Out[2681]= {{590, 90}, V[42, 47, 67]}

While the **DefaultsM** procedure expands the previous **Defaults** procedure onto case of the objects of the same name of type {*Block, Function, Module*}. The successful procedure call **DefaultsM[g, y]** returns *Null*, i.e. nothing, in addition, carrying out all settings of *y* values by default for formal arguments of a block, function or module *g*. In addition, for a *g* object of the same name that is composed from subobjects of the above types the settings of the *y* values by default for formal arguments of all subobjects of the *g* object are carried out. The next fragment represents source code of the **DefaultsM** procedure with typical examples of its application.

In[2556]:= DefaultsM[x_ /; BlockFuncModQ[x], y_ /; ListQ[y] && Length[y] == 2 || ListListQ[y] && AllTrue[Map[IntegerQ[#[[1]]] &, y], TrueQ]] :=
Module[{ArtKr, atr = Attributes[x], q, k = 1, a = Flatten[{PureDefinition[x]}],
g = If[ListListQ[y], y, {y}]}, ClearAllAttributes[x]; ClearAll[x]; q = Map[#[[1]] &, g];
While[k <= Length[g], ToExpression["Default[" <> ToString[x] <> ", " <>
ToString[g[[k]][[1]]] <> "]" <> " = " <> ToString1[g[[k]][[2]]]]; k++];
ArtKr[s_String, def_List] := Module[{n = Unique[AVZ], b, c, d, t, j = 1, h},
h = ToString[n] <> ToString[x]; ToExpression[ToString[n] <> s];
b = HeadPF[h]; d = StringReplace[PureDefinition[h], b -> ""];
c = Select[Map[ToString, Args[h]], # != "$Failed" &];
While[j <= Length[c], If[MemberQ[q, j], t = c[[j]];
c[[j]] = StringTake[t, {1, Flatten[StringPosition[t, "_"]][[2]]}] <> "."]; j++];
ToExpression[ToString[x] <> "[" <> StringTake[ToString[c], {2, -2}] <> "]" <> d];
ClearAll[h, n]]; k = 1;
While[k <= Length[a], ArtKr[a[[k]], g]; k++]; SetAttributes[x, atr]]
In[2557]:= Clear[G]; G[x_, y_, z_Integer] := x + y + z; G[x_, y_] := x + y; G[x_] := Block[{}, x];
G[x_, y_, z_, h_] := Module[{}, x*y*z*h]; SetAttributes[G, {Flat, Protected, Listable}];
In[2558]:= DefaultsM[G, {{2, 74}, {3, 590}}]
In[2559]:= Definition[G]
Out[2559]= Attributes[G] = {Flat, Listable, Protected}
G[x_] := Block[{}, x]
G[x_, y_.] := x + y
G[x_, y_., z_.] := x + y + z
G[x_, y_., z_., h_] := Module[{}, x*y*z*h]
G /: Default[G, 2] = 74
G /: Default[G, 3] = 590
In[2550]:= {G[69], G[42, 47], G[67, 20, 27]}
Out[2550]= {69, 89, 114}

The **DefaultsM** procedure provides a rather useful expansion of the standard means of this type, supporting as the single objects of the type {*Block, Function, Module*}, and the objects of the same name as evidently illustrate examples of the previous fragment.

It is necessary to focus attention on one rather important point once again. As it was already noted earlier, the procedures can be defined on the basis of constructions of types {*Module, Block*}. However, proceeding from certain considerations, it is generally recommended to give a preference to the constructions of the *Module* type because in a number of cases *(that question has been considered slightly above in [33,50] in details)* the constructions of *Block* type are carried out incorrectly, without output of diagnostic messages. As a certain illustration we will give an example of realization of the **Default1** procedure which concerns the theme of values by default, on the basis of two types of the constructions – on the basis of the types *Module* and *Block*. The procedure call **Default1[*x, y, z*]** returns *Null*, i.e. nothing, providing settings of values by default defined by a *z* list for arguments of a *x* object, whose positions are given by a *y* list of the *PosIntList* type for a block, a function or a module *x*. The fragment below from the *standpoint* of formalization presents almost *identical* realizations of definition of the **Default1** procedure on the basis of constructions of type *Module*, and *Block*. And if the first realization is carried out quite correctly regardless of names of local variables, then the correctness of the second, generally speaking, depends on crossing of a list of names of local variables with a list of values by default for arguments, in particular, of a function as an quite visually illustrates the following fragment in case when the local *a* variable exists in addition and in the list of values by default for a simple *G* function. The following fragment represents source codes along with corresponding typical examples of their applications.

In[3792]:= **Default1[x_Symbol, y_ /; PosIntListQ[y], z_ /; ListQ[z]] :=**
Module[{k=1, a=Min[Map[Length, {y, z}]]}, While[k <= a, Default[x, y[[k]]] = z[[k]]; k++];]

In[3793]:= **ClearAllAttributes["G"]; Clear[G]; Default1[G, {1, 2}, {a, b}];**
G[x_., y_.] := {x, y}; Clear[Default1]; DefaultValues[G]
Out[3793]= {HoldPattern[Default[G, 1]] :> a, HoldPattern[Default[G, 2]] :> b}

In[3794]:= **Default1[x_Symbol, y_ /; PosIntListQ[y], z_ /; ListQ[z]] :=**
Block[{k = 1, a = Min[Map[Length, {y, z}]]}, While[k <= a, Default[x, y[[k]]] = z[[k]]; k++];]

In[3795]:= **ClearAllAttributes["G"]; ClearAll[G]; Default1[G, {1, 2}, {a, b}];**
G[x_., y_.] := {x, y}; DefaultValues[G]
Out[3795]= {HoldPattern[Default[G, 1]] :> 2, HoldPattern[Default[G, 2]] :> b}

In[3796]:= **Default1[x_Symbol, y_ /; PosIntListQ[y], z_ /; ListQ[z]] :=**
Module[{k=1, h=Min[Map[Length, {y, z}]]}, While[k <= h, Default[x, y[[k]]]=z[[k]]; k++];]

In[3797]:= **Default1[G, {1, 2}, {a, b}]; G[x_., y_.] := {x, y}; Clear[Default1]; DefaultValues[G]**
Out[3797]= {HoldPattern[Default[G, 1]] :> a, HoldPattern[Default[G, 2]] :> b}

In[3798]:= **Default1[x_Symbol, y_ /; PosIntListQ[y], z_ /; ListQ[z]] :=**
Block[{k=1, h = Min[Map[Length, {y, z}]]}, While[k <= h, Default[x, y[[k]]] = z[[k]]; k++];]

In[3799]:= **ClearAll[G]; Default1[G, {1, 2}, {a, b}]; G[x_., y_.] := {x, y}; DefaultValues[G]**
Out[3799]= {HoldPattern[Default[G, 1]] :> a, HoldPattern[Default[G, 2]] :> b}

So, the mechanisms of local variables used by procedures on the basis of types *Module* and *Block*, generally, are not identical. Consequently, in general it is necessary to give a certain preference to definition of the procedures on the basis of a **Module** construction, however, taking into account the aforesaid there are many cases when both types of the organization of procedures are equivalent, demanding the preliminary analysis concerning the existence of such equivalence. This question rather in details is considered in [28,33,50]. In general, for definition of the procedures we recommend to use structures on the basis of type *Module* in order to avoid necessity of carrying out a certain additional analysis regarding *procedurality* and *universality* in all cases of appendices.

For definition of values by default for formal arguments of a function, a block or a module it is possible to use both the tools **Defaults, DefaultsM, Default,** and directly in their *headings* on the basis of constructions of the format *"x_:expression"*, or by combining both specified methods. But, the system **DefaultValues** function returns the settings of values by default, executed only by means of the standard **Default** function, for example:

In[2269]:= **Default[G5, 2] = 90; G5[x_, y_: 590, z_: 42] := {x, y, z}; DefaultValues[G5]**
Out[2269]= {HoldPattern[Default[G5, 2]] :> 90}
In[2270]:= **G5[Agn]**
Out[2270]= {Agn, 590, 42}
In[2271]:= **Default[S4, 2] = 90; S4[x_, y_., z_: 42] := {x, y, z}; DefaultValues[S4]**
Out[2271]= {HoldPattern[Default[S4, 2]] :> 90}
In[2272]:= **S4[Avz]**
Out[2272]= {Avz, 90, 42}

At that, if for argument a value by default has been defined and via **Default,** and directly in heading by the construction "_:", then the second way has the maximum priority as it very visually illustrates the previous example with *G5* function. At that, standard **DefaultValues** function possesses serious enough shortcomings. First of all, this function doesn't reflect the values by default defined in a block, a function or a module heading, and only set thru the **Default** function. But generally it is incorrect because for arguments the assignment of the values by default as through the **Default** function, and directly in headings is admissible; in addition, the priority belongs exactly to the second method what often can contradict result of a call of the **DefaultValues** function as it is illustrated with the previous examples.

For riddance of such shortcomings, the **DefaultValues1** procedure has been programmed, whose the call **DefaultValues1**[*x*] returns the list of the format {{*N1*} :> *V1*, ..., {*Np*} :> *Vp*}, where *Nj* and *Vj* (*j = 1..p*) define numbers of positions of formal arguments in the heading of a block/function/module, and values by default ascribed to them respectively, regardless of method of their definition, taking into account the priority (*the setting of values by default in headings of blocks, functions or modules has the highest priority*). The next fragment represents source code of the **DefaultValues1** procedure with typical examples of its use.

In[3079]:= **DefaultValues1[x_ /; BlockFuncModQ[x]] :=
Module[{d = {}, h, k, a = {SetAttributes[String, Listable]},
b = Map[ToString, Args[x]], c = Map[ToString, DefaultValues[x]]},
ClearAttributes[ToString, Listable];
If[b != {}, For[a = 1, a <= Length[b], a++, h = b[[a]];
If[! StringFreeQ[h, "_:"], AppendTo[d, ToExpression["{" <> ToString[a] <> "} :> " <>
StringTake[h, {Flatten[StringPosition[h, "_:"]][[2]] + 1, -1}]]]]]];
If[c != {}, If[c != {}, c = ToExpression[Mapp[StringReplace, Mapp[StringReplace,
c, {"HoldPattern[Default[" <> ToString[x] -> "{", "]]" -> "}"}], {"{, " -> "{", "{}" -> "{2017}"}]]];
h = c[[1]][[1]]; If[Op[h] == {2017}, a = {}; For[k = 1, k <= Length[b], k++,
AppendTo[a, ToExpression[ToString[{k}] <> " :> " <> ToString[c[[1]][[2]]]]]]; c = a];
If[PosIntListQ[h] && Length[h] > 1, a = {}; b = h;
For[k = 1, k <= Length[b], k++, AppendTo[a, ToExpression[ToString[{k}] <> " :> " <>
ToString[c[[1]][[2]]]]]]; c = a]];
If[d == {} && c == {}, Return[{}], c = Sort[Join[d, c], Op[#1][[1]][[1]] <= Op[#2][[1]][[1]] &]];
{k, h} = {1, {}};
While[k <= Length[c] - 1, AppendTo[h, If[Op[c[[k]]][[1]] == Op[c[[k+1]]][[1]], k+1]]; k++];
Select[ReplacePart[c, Mapp[Rule, Select[h, # != "Null" &], Null]], ! SameQ[#, Null] &]]**

In[3080]:= **Default[G] = 590; G[x_, y_., z_: 90] := {x, y, z}; DefaultValues1[G]**
Out[3080]= {{1} :> 590, {2} :> 590, {3} :> 90}
In[3081]:= **Default[S2, 2, 3] = 90; S2[x_, y_., z_] := {x, y, z}; DefaultValues1[S2]**
Out[3081]= {{1} :> 90, {2} :> 90}
In[3082]:= **Default[S3, {1, 2, 3}, {42, 47, 27}]; S3[x_: 590, y_., z_.] := {x, y, z};**
DefaultValues1[S3]
Out[3082]= {{1} :> 590}
In[3083]:= **Default[S4, 2] = 2016; S4[x_: 590, y_: 47, z_: 42] := {x, y, z}; DefaultValues1[S4]**
Out[3083]= {{1} :> 590, {2} :> 47, {3} :> 42}
In[3084]:= **Default[S5, 2] = 90; S5[x_, y_: 590, z_: 42] := {x, y, z}; DefaultValues1[S5]**
Out[3084]= {{2} :> 590, {3} :> 42}
In[3085]:= **Default1[V3, {1, 2, 3, 4}, {a, b, c, d}]; V3[x_., y_., z_., t_.] := {x, y, z, t};**
DefaultValues1[V3]
Out[3085]= {{1} :> a, {2} :> b, {3} :> c, {4} :> d}
In[3086]:= **Default1[V4, {1, 2, 3, 4}, {a, b, c, d}]; V4[x_., y_: 90, z_., t_: 590] := {x, y, z, t};**
DefaultValues1[V4]
Out[3086]= {{1} :> a, {2} :> 90, {3} :> c, {4} :> 590}

Definition of the **DefaultValues1** procedure along with the standard tools uses our means such as **Args, BlockFuncModQ, Mapp, PosIntListQ, Op** that are considered in the present book and in [28-33]. Thus, our procedure **DefaultValues1** rather significantly expands the possibilities of the standard **DefaultValues** function, and quite its replaces at condition of existence of the *MathToolBox* package [48] loaded into the current *Mathematica* session.

The **DefaultValues2** procedure to a certain degree extends the previous procedure, its call **DefaultValues2**[*x*, *y*, *z*], where *y* – the list of the positions of arguments in the heading of *x* and *z* – the list of default values corresponding to them, returns a list of format {{*N1*} –> *V1*, ..., {*Np*} –> *Vp*}, where *Nj* and *Vj* (*j* = 1..*p*) – the numbers of positions of formal arguments in a function or procedure *x* and default values, ascribed to them, accordingly, irrespective of the method of their definition; at that, the priority is taken into account *(the settings of default values in heading of the functions/procedures have the highest priority)*. The procedure call does in the current session the *x* as an active object of the above type with the new default values with saving of options and attributes of the old *x* object. The following fragment represents source code of the **DefaultValues2** procedure with an example of its use.

In[3157]:= **DefaultValues2[x_ /; BlockFuncModQ[x], y_ /; IntegerListQ[y], z_ /; ListQ[z]] :=**
Module[{a = Attributes[x], b = Map[ToString, Args[x]], c = HeadPF[x],
d = PureDefinition[x], p, h = {}, y1, z1, g = {}}, ClearAttributes[x, a];
p = Min[Map[Length, {y, z}]]; y1 = y[[1 ;; p]]; z1 = z[[1 ;; p]];
If[y1 == {}, Null, Do[AppendTo[h, If[! MemberQ[y1, k], b[[k]], If[SuffPref[b[[k]], "_", 2],
AppendTo[g, {k} -> z1[[k]]];
b[[k]] <> ":" <> ToString1[z1[[k]]], If[SuffPref[b[[k]], "_.", 2], AppendTo[g, {k} -> z1[[k]]];
StringTake[b[[k]], {1, -2}] <> ":" <> ToString1[z1[[k]]], b[[k]]]]]], {k, 1, Length[b]}]; Clear[x];
ToExpression[StringReplace[d, c -> ToString[x] <> "[" <>
StringTake[ToString[h], {2, -2}] <> "]", 1]]; SetAttributes[x, a]; g]]
In[3158]:= **S49[x_: 590, y_., z_., t_] := {x, y, z, t}**

In[3159]:= **DefaultValues2[S49, {1, 2, 3, 4}, {a, b, "c", a + b}]**
Out[3159]= {{2} -> b, {3} -> "c", {4} -> a + b}
In[3160]:= **Definition[S49]**
Out[3160]= S3[x_ : 590, y_ : b, z_ : "c", t_ : a + b] := {x, y, z, t}

Considering existence of three admissible mechanisms of assignment of values by default to formal arguments of blocks, functions and modules, the problem of definition of this kind of values for objects of the *specified* type represents a quite certain interest. In this connexion the **DefaultsQ** procedure solves the given problem whose call **DefaultsQ[w]** returns *True* if definitions of the blocks, functions or modules *w* contain values by default for their formal arguments, and *False* otherwise. Whereas the procedure call **DefaultsQ[x, y]** where the 2nd *y* argument – *an undefinite variable* – in addition through *y* returns the list of the used types of values by default {"_.", "_:"}. The fragment below represents source code of the **DefaultsQ** procedure along with the most typical examples of its application.

In[2776]:= **DefaultsQ[x_ /; BlockFuncModQ[x], y___] :=**
Module[{c = {}, d, a = Args[x], b = {"_.", "_:"}, k = 1},
a = Map[ToString, If[NestListQ[a], a[[1]], a]]; While[k <= Length[a], d = a[[k]];
If[! StringFreeQ[d, b[[1]]], AppendTo[c, b[[1]]], If[! StringFreeQ[d, b[[2]]],
AppendTo[c, b[[2]]]]]; k++];
If[c == {}, False, If[{y} != {} && ! HowAct[y], y = DeleteDuplicates[Flatten[c]]]; True]]
In[2777]:= **PureDefinition[G]**
Out[2777]= {"G[x_., y_.] := x + y", "G[x_, y_, z_] := x*y*z", "G[x_, y_, z_, h_] := x*y*z*h"}
In[2778]:= **{DefaultsQ[G, t74], t74}**
Out[2778]= {True, {"_."}}
In[2779]:= **Default[S, 1] = 590; S[x_., y_: 590, z_] := x + y + z; Kr[x_, y_, z_] := Block[{}, x*y*z]**
In[2780]:= **{Map9[DefaultsQ, {S, Kr}, {v1, v2}], {v1, v2}}**
Out[2780]= {{True, False}, {{"_.", "_:"}, v2}}

According to the *Mathematica* agreements, x_:y is an object that represents an expression of the *x* form, that, if omitted, should be replaced by a *y*. Meantime, this mechanism has rather serious restrictions not allowing to use an expression as *y*. For removing of the restrictions it is possible to use, eg, in heading of a block, a function or a module vague number of formal arguments with their subsequent appropriate processing as examples of the next fragment illustrate *(modules m1 ÷ m3)*. So, the **Tally1** procedure uses this reception. The call **Tally1[x]** tallies the elements in a *x* list, returning all distinct elements together with their *multiplicities* whereas the call **Tally1[x, y]** uses *y* test to define pairs of elements of a *x* list that should be considered as equivalent, and returns a list of the first representatives of each equivalence class, together with their multiplicities. Meantime, the calls **Tally1[x, y]** and **Tally1[x, y, z]** with second *(y)* or third *(z)* optional argument accordingly – an indefinite symbol – through it return the results of gathering of elements of the *x* list into sublists of identical elements. The fragment below represents source code of the **Tally1** procedure, illustrating the above-mentioned method.

In[3675]:= **m1[x_, y_: #1 === #2 &] := Module[{}, {x, y}]; {m1[a, b], m1[a]}**
Out[3675]= {m1[a, b], m1[a]}
In[3676]:= **m2[x_, y_] := Module[{}, {x, y}]; {m2[a, b], m2[a, #1 === #2 &]}**

Out[3676]= {{a, b}, {a, #1 === #2 &}}
In[3677]:= m3[x_, y___] := Module[{}, If[{y} == {}, {x, #1 === #2 &}, {x, y}]]
In[3678]:= {m3[a, b], m3[a]}
Out[3678]= {{a, b}, {a, #1 === #2 &}}
In[3680]:= Tally1[x_ /; ListQ[x], y___] := Module[{a = {y}, b},
b = Gather[x, If[{y} == {} || ! HowAct[a[[1]]], #1 === #2 &, a[[1]]]];
If[Length[a] == 1 && ! HowAct[y], y = b, If[Length[a] == 2 && ! HowAct[a[[2]]],
ToExpression[ToString[a[[2]]] <> "=" <> ToString[b]], 6]]; Map[{#[[1]], Length[#]} &, b]]
In[3681]:= Clear[t]; {Tally1[{a, a, b, a, c, b, a}, t], t}
Out[3681]= {{{a, 4}, {b, 2}, {c, 1}}, {{a, a, a, a}, {b, b}, {c}}}
In[3682]:= {Tally1[{{a, j}, {j, x}, S, {j, x}, S}, Head[#1] === Head[#2] &, h], h}
Out[3682]= {{{{a, j}, 3}, {S, 2}}, {{{a, j}, {j, x}, {j, x}}, {S, S}}}

Along with attributes and values by default for the formal arguments of a block, a function or a module, these objects can use mechanism of the *options*. Above all, the mechanism of options is rather widely used by the system means. Thus, for a number of functions in the *Mathematica* system *(eg, the Plot function)*, the options available both for installation, and for redefinition are ascribed. The system supports the general mechanisms for work with such options. The call **Options[G]** returns the list of the current settings in the format {*a -> a1, b -> b1, ...*} for all options of a block, function or module *G* while the call **Options[G, h]** returns the current setting for a *h* option. In turn, the call **SetOptions[G, a -> a2, b -> b2, ...]** provides a reinstalling of values for options {*a, b, c, ...*} of a block, a function or a module *G* which remains active up to the next reinstalling in the current session. Whereas the function call **SystemOptions[]** returns list of the current settings for all preinstalled internal options and suboptions of the system. These settings are determined as the used platform, and in certain cases also by the current session of the *Mathematica*. Thus, for receiving quantity of all system options and their quantities in the context as the groups of options, and separate options, the next procedure **CountOptions** whose source code with the typical examples of its application are given below is used, namely:

In[3252]:= CountOptions[h___] := Module[{a = SystemOptions[], b = {}, d, c = 1, k},
While[c <= Length[a], d = a[[c]]; AppendTo[b, If[ListQ[Part[d, 2]],
{Part[d, 1], Length[Part[d, 2]]}, d]]; c++];
b = Flatten[Gather[b, Head[#1] == Head[#2] &], 1];
If[{h} == {}, b, If[HowAct[h], Defer[CountOptions[h]], d = 0;
Do[If[ListQ[b[[k]]], d = d + b[[k]][[2]], d = d + 1], {k, Length[b]}]; {h} = {d}; b]]
In[3253]:= CountOptions[]
Out[3253]= {{"AlgebraicsOptions", 8}, ..., "ZeroTestNumericalPrecision" -> 80.}
In[3254]:= CountOptions[g70]; g70
Out[3254]= 437

The call **CountOptions[]** returns the nested list whose elements are the lists and separate options. The list as the first element contains a name of group of options, whereas the 2nd element – number of options in this group. Whereas the call **CountOptions[w]** in addition through *w* argument – *an undefinite symbol* – returns total of the preset system options and suboptions. Furthermore, settings for a concrete system *w* option can be redefined by the function call **SetSystemOptions[*w* -> *value*]**, however except for separate cases, it is not desirable in order to avoid the possible conflicts with the system settings. In addition, the *Mathematica* system doesn't support operations of removal of the options, therefore in the following fragment we present the **DeleteOptsAttr** procedure, decisive the given problem.

The procedure call **DeleteOptsAttr[*x*]** returns *Null*, i.e. nothing, canceling for a *x* symbol the options ascribed to it. Whereas the procedure call **DeleteOptsAttr[*w*, *y*]**, returning *Null*, i.e. nothing, cancels both the options, and the attributes that are ascribed to a *w* symbol, where *y* – an expression; so, the default values are stored. The following fragment presents source code of the procedure **DeleteOptsAttr** with the most typical examples of its application.

In[2576]:= G[x_, y_] := x^2 + y^2; Options[G] = {Art -> 27, Kr -> 20}
Out[2576]= {Art -> 27, Kr -> 20}
In[2577]:= SetOptions[G, Art -> 27, Kr -> 20]
Out[2577]= {Art -> 27, Kr -> 20}
In[2578]:= SetAttributes[G, {Protected, Listable, Flat}]
In[2579]:= Definition2[G]
Out[2579]= {"G[x_, y_] := x^2 + y^2", "Options[G] := {Art -> 27, Kr -> 20}", {Flat, Listable, Protected}}

In[2580]:= DeleteOptsAttr[x_ /; BlockFuncModQ[x], y___] :=
Module[{b, a = Definition2[x], c = "Options[" <> ToString[x] <> "]"},
b = a[[-1]]; ClearAllAttributes[x]; ClearAll[x];
ToExpression[Select[a, StringFreeQ[ToString[#], c] &]];
If[{y} == {}, If[b != {}, SetAttributes[x, b]]]]

In[2581]:= DeleteOptsAttr[G]
In[2582]:= Definition2[G]
Out[2582]= {"G[x_, y_] := x^2 + y^2", {Flat, Listable, Protected}}
In[2583]:= Vs[x_, y_] := x^2 + y^2; Options[Vs] = {v -> 74, g -> 69};
In[2584]:= SetOptions[Vs, {v -> 74, g -> 69}]; SetAttributes[Vs, Protected]
In[2585]:= Definition2[Vs]
Out[2585]= {"Vs[x_, y_] := x^2 + y^2", "Options[Vs] := {v -> 74, g -> 69}", {Protected}}
In[2586]:= DeleteOptsAttr[Vs, 590]
In[2587]:= Definition2[Vs]
Out[2587]= {"Vsv[x_, y_] := x + y", {}}

At that, it must be kept in mind that this procedure isn't applicable to the standard system functions, returning on them the unevaluated call as it well illustrates the example below:

In[2618]:= {DeleteOptsAttr[Sin, 590], DeleteOptsAttr[Sin]}
Out[2618]= {DeleteOptsAttr[Sin, 590], DeleteOptsAttr[Sin]}

For certain builtin *Mathematica* functions, in particular **Plot**, are ascribed the options whose values can be redetermined. At that, if at a function call the values for its admissible options aren't determined, then for them values by default are used. The call **Options[*w*, *op*]** allows to obtain values by default for an option *op* of a *w* function, for example:

In[2620]:= **Options[Plot, {PlotLabel, FrameStyle, PlotStyle, PlotRange, ColorOutput}]**

Out[2620]= {PlotLabel -> None, FrameStyle -> {}, PlotStyle -> Automatic, PlotRange -> {Full, Automatic}, ColorOutput -> Automatic}

The mechanism of options that is supported by the *Mathematica* system can be successfully used in development of both the applications of various type, and a separate software. The interested reader can familiarize with the mechanism more in details in the well-developed help-base of the *Mathematica* system, or in the books [31-33,50,52,59,61].

In conclusion of the represent section we in brief will stop on application of transformations rules to the procedures. The mechanism of transformations rules supported by the system remains in force not only for symbols, but also for algebraic expressions. In principle, this mechanism can be adapted onto an arbitrary expression. Moreover, as an essential enough property of this mechanism it is possible to note the circumstance that allows to use and the patterns, and the symbolic constructions, for example:

In[2837]:= **Sin[x^2]^2 + Cos[y + h]^2 /. {x^2 -> x, y + h -> x}**
Out[2837]= Cos[x]^2 + Sin[x]^2
In[2838]:= **Sin[a + b*c]*(Sin[x^2] + Cos[y + h]) /. {Sin[_] -> x, Cos[_] -> y}**
Out[2838]= x*(x + y)

Thus, between purely symbolic transformations rules and rules that include the patterns, in particular, "_" there is one fundamental difference that is considered in details in the books [31-33]. In addition, the more detailed description of mechanisms of patterns programming for transformations rules of an expression can be found in reference on the *Mathematica*.

At the same time the system doesn't dispose the mechanism of use of transformations rules to procedures and for this purpose the next procedure can be offered, whose procedure call **ReplaceProc[x, w]** returns the definition in the string format of the procedure – the result of application to a *x* procedure of rules of *w* transformations *(one rule or their list)*; at that, those rules are excluded from *w* rules, whose left parts coincide with formal arguments of the *x* procedure. The fragment below represents source code of the procedure with examples of its application along with a simple testing function whose call **RuleQ[w]** returns *True*, if *w* – a transformation rule, and *False* otherwise. Thus, in the **ReplaceProc** procedure definition of the given function is used in its heading.

In[2859]:= **RuleQ[x_] := If[MemberQ[{Rule, RuleDelayed}, Head[x]], True, False]**
In[2860]:= **Map[RuleQ, {a -> b, c -> d + h, Sin, a + b, ProcQ, a :> b, c :> d + h}]**
Out[2860]= {True, True, False, False, False, True, True}

In[2861]:= **ReplaceProc[x_ /; ProcQ[x], r_ /; AllTrue[Map[RuleQ, Flatten[{r}]], TrueQ]] :=**
Module[{a = Definition2[x], b = HeadPF[x], c, d = Flatten[{r}]},
c = ToExpression["Hold[" <> StringTrim[a[[1]], b <> " := "] <> "]"];
d = Select[d, ! MemberQ[Args1[x], ToString[Part[#, 1]]] &];
c = ToString1[ReplaceAll[c, d]]; b <> " := " <> StringTake[c, {6, -2}]]

In[2862]:= **ArtKr[x_ /; IntegerQ[x], y_ /; StringQ[y]] :=**
Module[{a = StringLength[y], b = 90, ab = 590}, (a + x)*(b + y) + ab]
In[2863]:= **ReplaceProc[ArtKr, {a -> Art, b -> Kr, y -> 42, x -> 590}]**
Out[2863]= "ArtKr[x_ /; IntegerQ[x], y_ /; StringQ[y]] := Module[{Art = StringLength[42], Kr = 90, ab = 590}, (Art + 590)*(Kr + 42) + ab]"

It makes sense to stop on one moment useful for programming. Supra, a lot of procedures which return additional result through argument – *an undefinite symbol* – were considered. However such mechanism requires or of choice of some undefinite variable in the current session, demanding generally of its cleaning in the absence of necessity for it, or saving of value of a certain variable with subsequent its cleaning in a procedure and restoration of an initial value before any outcome from the procedure. At that, for such purpose the similar mechanism which is based on the **UniqueV** procedure can be used, whose call **UniqueV[*x*, *y*]** returns a name in the string format *"xn"* of an unique variable of the current session to which *y* value was ascribed, where *x* – *a symbol*, *n* – *an integer* and *y* – *an arbitrary expression*. Further the **UniqueV** procedure is used for ensuring of returning of additional result by the simple *A6* procedure through an unique variable. The fragment below is rather transparent and of any special additional explanations doesn't demand.

In[2571]:= **UniqueV[x_ /; SymbolQ[x], y_] := Module[{a = ToString[Unique[ToString[x]]]}, ToExpression[a <> " = " <> ToString1[y]]; a]**

In[2572]:= **UniqueV["agn", 50090]**
Out[2572]= "agn11"
In[2573]:= **agn11**
Out[2573]= 50090
In[2579]:= **A6[x_, y___] := Module[{a = 6, b = 7}, If[{y} == {}, a*x, {a*x, UniqueV["ag", b*x]}]]**
In[2580]:= **{A6[75], A6[42, 6]}**
Out[2580]= {450, {252, "ag12"}}
In[2581]:= **ag12**
Out[2581]= 294

Below, a lot of tools providing higher level of the procedural programming in *Mathematica* system will be represented; which in a certain degree were wafted by similar means of the *Maple* system and by other systems of procedural programming. It should be noted that the values by default for the system attributes and options given in the present section, and in the book as a whole concern the *Mathematica* system of versions *11.0.1.0 – 11.2*. Therefore, in the subsequent *Mathematica* versions there can quite be certain differences.

6.9. Some additional facilities for operating with blocks, functions and modules in the *Mathematica* software

If the previous sections of the head represent main tools of work with an object of the type {*Block, Function, Module*}, the present section represents additional, but quite important tools of work in a number of appendices with objects of this type. Meanwhile, having the basic purpose, these tools can be functionally crossed with tools presented in the previous sections of this head. Note, it should not cause any particular surprise because the similar situation takes place pretty often among means, practically, of any software system. And still the tools of the present section have a little more specific character and aren't so sought after as tools of the previous sections. At the same time, ascribing them to this section in a certain degree has conditional character and is caused by our experience of their use.

First of all, again we will return to the question of syntactical correctness of a module and a block. Examples of two types of syntactic mistakes at definition of the procedures of types {*Module, Block*} are presented below, that aren't distinguished by the system at evaluation of their definitions, and in certain cases even at a call of such procedures. At that, repeated calls of procedures of the *Module* type as very much demonstrate the fragment examples, yield formally correct results. For testing of the procedures of both types regarding their syntactical correctness in the above context the **SyntCorProcQ** procedure has been offered, whose source code with typical examples of its use the following fragment represents:

In[5081]:= **Art[x_, y_] := Module[{a, b},]; Art1[x_, y_] := Module[{a, b}]**
In[5082]:= **Kr[x_, y_] := Block[{a, b},]; {Art[90, 590], Art1[90, 590]}**
Module::argr: Module called with 1 argument; 2 arguments are expected.
Out[5083]= {Null, Module{a, b}]}
In[5084]:= {Art[90, 590], Art1[90, 590]}
Out[5084]= {Null, Module[{a, b}]}
In[5085]:= **SyntaxQ["Kr[x_,y_]:=Block[{a,b},];Kr1[x_,y_]:=Block[{a,b}]"]**
Out[5085]= True
In[5086]:= **ExpressionQ["Kr[x_,y_]:=Block[{a,b},];Kr1[x_,y_]:=Block[{a,b}]"]**
Out[5086]= False

In[5087]:= **SyntCorProcQ[x_ /; BlockModQ[x]] :=**
Module[{d, h, c = Kr, b = PureDefinition[x], a = HeadPF[x]},
ClearAll[Kr]; Kr = ProcFuncTypeQ[ToString[x]][[2]][[1]];
h = Quiet[Check[Locals2[x], Locals1[x]]];
h = If[h === {}, "{}", ToString[h]]; d = a <> " := " <> Kr <> "[" <> h;
d = StringReplace[b, d -> "", 1]; Kr = c; ! MemberQ[{"]", ", Null]"}, d]]

In[5088]:= **Map[SyntCorProcQ, {ProcQ, Kr, Kr1, Art, Art1}]**
Out[5088]= {True, False, False, False, False}
In[5089]:= **KrArt[x_, y_, z_] := Module[{a, b, c}, 590 + x + y + z]**
In[5090]:= **Map[SyntCorProcQ, {Locals, Mapp, BlockToModule, KrArt}]**
Out[5090]= {True, True, True, True}
In[5091]:= **Map[SyntCorProcQ, {Art2, Do, If}]**
Out[5091]= {SyntCorProcQ[Art2], SyntCorProcQ[Do], SyntCorProcQ[If]}

As appears from examples of the above fragment the syntactic incorrectness of definitions of the module and block isn't distinguished by the **SyntaxQ** function, but distinguished by our **ExpressionQ** procedure. So, the procedure call **SyntCorProcQ[x]** returns *True*, if the definition of a block or a module *x* activated in the current session is syntactical correct in the above context, and *False* otherwise. If a *x* – not a block or a module, the call is returned unevaluated. The definition of the above **SyntCorProcQ** procedure along with the standard functions uses our means such as **ProcFuncTypeQ, Locals2, PureDefinition, BlockModQ,** and **HeadPF** considered in the present book and in [48,50].

In a number of applications of system character it is desirable for the user block, function or module to have information regarding use by it of means in context {*system tools, user tools*}. The **SysUserSoft** procedure solves the problem whose call **SysUserSoft[x]** generally returns the nested two–element list, whose first element contains 2-element sublists, whose the first element – the name in the string format of a system function, and the second element – its multiplicity, whereas the second element of the list also contains 2-element sublists, whose first element – the name in the string format of the user means {*Block, Function, Module*}, and the second element – its multiplicity. In the absence for a *x* object tools of the specified types the procedure call **SysUserSoft[x]** returns the empty list, i.e. {}. In addition, if the type of the factual argument *x* is different from *(Block, Function, Module)*, then the call **SysUserSoft[x]** is returned unevaluated. The next fragment represents source code of the procedure along with typical examples of its application.

In[2580]:= **SysUserSoft[x_ /; BlockFuncModQ[x]] := Module[{b, s = {}, u = {}, h = Args[x, 6],**
c, a = Flatten[{PureDefinition[x]}][[1]], d = If[QFunction[x], {}, LocalsGlobals1[x]]},
b = ExtrVarsOfStr[a, 2, 90];
c = Select[b, ! MemberQ[Flatten[{ToString[x], h, "True", "False", "$Failed", Quiet[d[[1]]],
Quiet[d[[3]]]}], #] &];
Map[If[Quiet[SystemQ[#]], AppendTo[s, #], If[BlockFuncModQ[#],
AppendTo[u, #]]] &, c]; c = Map[Gather, {s, u}];
c = {Map[Flatten[#] &, Map[{#, Length[#]} &, c[[1]]]], Map[Flatten[#] &,
Map[{#, Length[#]} &, c[[2]]]]};
c = {Map[DeleteDuplicates[#] &, c[[1]]], Map[DeleteDuplicates[#] &, c[[2]]]};
If[Flatten[c] == {}, {}, c]]

In[2581]:= **A[m_, n_, p_ /; IntegerQ[p], h_ /; PrimeQ[h]] := Module[{a = 74},**
h*(m + n + p)/a + StringLength[ToString1[z]]/(Cos[c] + Sin[d])]
In[2582]:= **SysUserSoft[A]**
Out[2582]= {{{"Cos", 1}, {"IntegerQ", 1}, {"Module", 1}, {"PrimeQ", 1}, {"Sin", 1}, {"StringLength", 1}}, {{"ToString1", 1}}}
In[2583]:= **SysUserSoft[SysUserSoft]**
Out[2583]= {{{"AppendTo", 2}, {"DeleteDuplicates", 2}, {"Flatten", 5}, {"Gather", 1}, {"If", 4}, {"Length", 2}, {"MemberQ", 1}, {"Module", 1}, {"Quiet", 3}, {"Select", 1}, {"ToString", 1}}, {{"Args", 1}, {"BlockFuncModQ", 2}, {"ExtrVarsOfStr", 1}, {"LocalsGlobals1", 1}, {"PureDefinition", 1}, {"QFunction", 1}, {"SystemQ", 1}}}
In[2584]:= **G[x_] := x^2 + 90*x + 590; SysUserSoft[G]**
Out[2584]= {}
In[2585]:= **F[x_] := a*x + Sin[b*x] + StringLength[ToString1[x + c]]; SysUserSoft[F]**
Out[2585]= {{{"Sin", 1}, {"StringLength", 1}}, {{"ToString1", 1}}}
In[2586]:= **SysUserSoft[QFunction]**
Out[2586]= {{{"Block", 1}, {"CompiledFunction", 1}, {"If", 5}, {"MemberQ", 1}, {"Module", 2}, {"Quiet", 1}, {"StringJoin", 1}, {"StringReplace", 2}}, {{"Definition2", 1}, {"HeadPF", 2}, {"Map3", 1}, {"SingleDefQ", 1}, {"SuffPref", 5}, {"ToString1", 2}, {"ToString3", 1}}}

As showed our expirience, the **SysUserSoft** procedure is an useful enough in the structural analysis of the user software of the types *{Block, Function, Module}*.

In some cases the **RenBlockFuncMod** procedure is an useful means of manipulation by the blocks, functions, modules of the same name. The procedure call **RenBlockFuncMod[x, y]** returns a new name of a function, a block or a module *x* in string format determined by the format **Unique[y] <> H**, where *y* – a symbol, whereas *H* – one of symbols *{"B", "F", "M"}* depending on the type of a *x* object or of type of its subobject composing it in case of the *x* object of the same name. At that, the *x* object is removed from the current session whereas the result of such renaming keeps options and attributes of the original *x* object. The next fragment represents source code of the procedure with typical examples of its application.

In[2526]:= Pr[x_, y_String, z_ /; If[z === 90, True, False]] := {x, y, z}; Pr[x_, y_ /; StringQ[y], z_ /; If[z === 90, True, False]] := Module[{}, {x, y, z}];
SetAttributes[Pr, Protected]; Pr1[x_, y_String, z_ /; If[z === 90, True, False]] := {x, y, z};
SetAttributes[Pr1, {Protected, Listable}]

In[2527]:= **RenBlockFuncMod[x_ /; BlockFuncModQ[x], y_Symbol]** :=
Module[{t = {}, h, a = Options[x], b = Attributes[x], n, c = Flatten[{PureDefinition[x]}], k = 1, d = Flatten[{HeadPF[x]}]},
For[k, k <= Length[c], k++, h = StringReplace[c[[k]], StringJoin[d[[k]], " := "] -> ""];
h = If[SuffPref[h, "Module[{", 1], "M", If[SuffPref[h, "Block[{", 1], "B", "F"]];
n = ToString[Unique[y]] <> h; AppendTo[t, n];
ToExpression[StringReplace[c[[k]], ToString[x] <> "[" -> n <> "[", 1]];
If[a != {}, ToExpression["SetOptions[" <> n <> ", " <> ToString[a] <> "]"]];
If[b != {}, ToExpression["SetAttributes[" <> n <> ", " <> ToString[b] <> "]"]]];
ClearAllAttributes[x]; ClearAll[x]; If[Length[t] == 1, t[[1]], t]]

In[2528]:= **RenBlockFuncMod[Pr1, Sv]**
Out[2528]= "Sv$61404F"
In[2529]:= **Definition["Sv$61404F"]**
Out[2529]= Attributes[Sv$61404F] = {Listable, Protected}
Sv$61404F[x_, y_String, z_ /; If[z === 90, True, False]] := {x, y, z}
In[2530]:= **RenBlockFuncMod[Pr, Sv]**
Out[2530]= {"Sv$61997F", "Sv$61999M"}
In[2531]:= **Definition["Sv$61997F"]**
Out[2531]= Attributes[Sv$61997F] = {Protected}
Sv$61997F[x_, y_String, z_ /; If[z === 90, True, False]] := {x, y, z}
In[2532]:= **Definition["Sv$61999M"]**
Out[2532]= Attributes[Sv$61999M] = {Protected}
Sv$61999M[x_, y_String, z_ /; If[z === 90, True, False]] := Module[{}, {x, y, z}]
In[2533]:= **Map[Definition, {Pr, Pr1}]**
Out[2533]= {Null, Null}

In addition, the **RenBlockFuncMod** procedure is most of all convenient in case of necessity of differentiating of a *x* object of the same name onto the single subobjects composing it.

In certain cases at the procedures calls which are in the user package *(files of the types {"cdf", "m", "mx"})* which is uploaded into the current session, their local variables, including local variables of the nested procedures, in the field of the *Mathematica* variables are associated with context ascribed to the given package. This mechanism the more in details here is not considered. It also concerns the symbolical results returned by a procedure of this package through such local variables. In this case the symbolic result accepts the following standard format, namely:

<Context ascribed to a package>`<Procedure name>`Result

For the purpose of *elimination* of such situation and receiving so-called *reduced result (which contains no forms w`m`)* that is significantly better adapted for the subsequent processing, to a result returned by procedure of the user package, can be applied the **ReductRes** function whose call **ReductRes[x, w]** returns the reduced w result returned by a x procedure of the user package that has been loaded into the current session. The fragment below represents both variants of the **Head1** procedure without usage and with usage of such mechanism with an illustration of results of the calls of both procedures. The received results a rather visually illustrate the basic distinction arising from the mechanism of reduction of results on the basis of the represented **ReductRes** function. The following fragment represents source code of the **ReductRes** function with examples of its application.

In[3282]:= **ReductRes[x_ /; SymbolQ[x], y_] := ToExpression[StringReplace[ToString[y], Context[x] <> ToString[x] <> "`" -> ""]]**

In[3283]:= **ReductRes[Head1, AladjevProcedures`Head1`System]**
Out[3283]= System

In[3284]:= **Map[Head, {ProcQ, Sin, 90, a + b, Function[{x, y}, x + y], G[x], J[6], Head1}]**
Out[3284]= {Symbol, Symbol, Integer, Plus, Function, G, J, Symbol}

In[3285]:= **Map[ReductRes[Head1, #] &, Map[Head1, {ProcQ, Sin, 90, a+c, Function[{x, y}, x + y], G[x], J[6], Head1, a/c, a -> b, a^b, a := b}]]**
Out[3285]= {Module, System, Integer, Plus, PureFunction, G, J, Module, Times, Rule, Power, System}

In[3286]:= **Head1[a := b]**
Out[3286]= AladjevProcedures`Head1`System

The following useful **Avg** procedure is internal, i.e. the procedure call **Avg[]** makes a sense only in the body of other procedure, returning a list of nesting {1 | 2} whose elements define the two–element lists whose first elements determine local variables in the string format of a procedure, external in relation to the **Avg** whereas the second – their initial values in string format; at that, lack of the initial value is coded by the symbol *"None"*. In case of more than one local variable the *ListList* list is returned, whose sublists have the above format. At lack of the local variables for external procedure the procedure call **Avg[]** returns the empty list – {}. The call **Avg[]** outside of other procedure doesn't make special sense, returning the list of the above format for two *local* variables {a, b} of the procedure **Avg** as visually illustrates the following fragment.

In[2723]:= **Avg[]:= Module[{b,**
a = ToString[ToExpression[ToString[InputForm[Stack[_][[1]]]]]],
a = If[! SuffPref[a, {"Module[", "Block["}, 1], "Module[{}," <> a <> "]", a];
a = StringReplace[a, "$" -> ""];
a = StringReplace[a, If[SuffPref[a, "Block[", 1], "Block[", "Module["] -> "", 1];
a = SubStrSymbolParity1[a, "{", "}"][[1]];
If[a == "{}", {}, b = StrToList[StringTake[a, {2, -2}]]];
b = Map[StringSplit[#, " = "] &, b]; Map[If[Length[#] == 1, {#[[1]], "None"}, #] &, b]]]

In[2724]:= **Z[m_, n_, p_ /; IntegerQ[p]] := Module[{h, x = 90, y = {a, b}}, m + n + p;**
h = Avg[]; h]
In[2725]:= **Z[74, 90, 590]**

381

Out[2725]= {{"h", "None"}, {"x", "90"}, {"y", "{a, b}"}}
In[2726]:= G[m_, n_, p_ /; IntegerQ[p]] := Module[{a, b = 74, c, d = 590},
d = Avg[]; m + n + p; d]
In[2727]:= G[t, p, 590]
Out[2727]= {{"a", "None"}, {"b", "74"}, {"c", "None"}, {"d", "590"}}
In[2728]:= A[m_, n_, p_ /; IntegerQ[p], h_ /; PrimeQ[h]] :=
Module[{a = 590.90, b, c, t, q, d = 74, z = 47}, b = Avg[]; m + n + p + h; m*n; b]
In[2729]:= A[x, y, 42, 47]
Out[2729]= {{"a", "590.9"}, {"b", "None"}, {"c", "None"}, {"t", "None"}, {"q", "None"},
{"d", "74"}, {"z", "47"}}
In[2730]:= B[m_, n_, p_, h_ /; PrimeQ[h]] :=
Module[{a = 590.90, b, c = {h, p}, t, q, d = 74, z = p*t, s}, b = Avg[]; m + n + p + h; m*n; b]
In[2731]:= B[x, y, 42, 47]
Out[2731]= {{"a", "590.9"}, {"b", "None"}, {"c", "{47, 42}"}, {"t", "None"}, {"q", "None"},
{"d", "74"}, {"z", "42 t"}, {"s", "None"}}
In[2732]:= T[m_, n_, p_, h_ /; PrimeQ[h]] := Module[{}, m*n*p*h; Avg[]]; T[27, 20, 42, 47]
Out[2732]= {}
In[2733]:= Avg[]
Out[2733]= {{"b", "None"}, {"a", "ToString[ToExpression[ToString[Stack[_]][[1]]]]"}}

The previous fragment represents source code of the **Avg** procedure along with examples of its use for receiving in the body of a procedure of the list of its local variables. It should be noted that a number of system means of *MathToolBox* package [48,50] use the above **Avg** procedure.

Here once again quite pertinently to note the important circumstance, that the functions, blocks, modules differ by their headings as it was repeatedly illustrated above. In addition, at the call of an object of this type the first of the complete list of the subobjects of the same name determined by the standard **Definition** function is choosen on which the tuple of the factual arguments is admissible. This circumstance should be considered at programming, and it has been considered by us at programming of many means of *MathToolBox* package [48]. At that, as objects of the same name can be as objects of type {*Block, Function, Module*}, and in combination with the objects of other types, in a number of cases at calculations with such objects, causing especial and erroneous situations. For elimination from the objects of the same name of subobjects of types different from {*Block, Function, Module*} a quite simple procedure serves whose call **ProcCalls**[*w*] returns *Null*, i.e. nothing, deleting from the list of the object of the same *w* name *(w in the string format)* of subobjects of types, different from {*Block, Function, Module*}. The following fragment represents source code of the **ProcCalls** procedure along with the most typical examples of its application.

In[2780]:= A[x_] := Module[{a = 50}, x + a]; A[x_, y_] := Module[{a = 90}, x + y + a];
A[x_, y_List] := Block[{}, {x, y}]; A[x_Integer] := Module[{a = 42}, x + a]; A := {a, b, c, d, h};
SetAttributes[A, {Flat, Listable, Protected}]
In[2781]:= Definition[A]
Out[2781]= Attributes[A] = {Flat, Listable, Protected}
A := {a, b, c, d, h}
A[x_Integer] := Module[{a = 42}, x + a]

A[x_] := Module[{a = 50}, x + a]
A[x_, y_List] := Block[{}, {x, y}]
A[x_, y_] := Module[{a = 90}, x + y + a]

In[2782]:= **ProcCalls[x_ /; StringQ[x]] :=**
Module[{a = Select[StringSplit[ToString[InputForm[Definition[x]]], "\n"], # != " " &&
 # != x &&! SuffPref[#, x <> " := ", 1] &], b = Attributes[x]},
a = If[SuffPref[a[[1]], "Attributes[", 1], a[[2 ;; -1]], a]; ClearAttributes[x, b]; Clear[x];
Map[ToExpression, a]; SetAttributes[x, b]]

In[2783]:= **ProcCalls["A"]**

In[2784]:= **Definition[A]**
Out[2784]= Attributes[A] = {Flat, Listable, Protected}
A[x_Integer] := Module[{a = 42}, x + a]
A[x_] := Module[{a = 50}, x + a]
A[x_, y_List] := Block[{}, {x, y}]
A[x_, y_] := Module[{a = 90}, x + y + a]

In[3280]:= **A[x_] := Module[{a = 590}, x + a];**
A[x_, y_] := Module[{a = 90}, x + y + a]; A[x_, y_List] := Block[{}, {x, y}];
A[x_Integer] := Module[{a = 42}, x + a]; A := {a, b, c, d, h};
SetAttributes[A, {Flat, Listable, Protected}]

In[3281]:= **TestDefBFM[x_ /; StringQ[x], y_ /; StringQ[y]] :=**
Module[{a = ToString[Unique["S"]], b, c}, b = a <> y;
ToExpression[a <> x]; c = BlockFuncModQ[b]; ToExpression["Remove[" <> b <> "]"]; c]

In[3282]:= **TestDefBFM["A[x_] := Module[{a = 590}, x + a]", "A"]**
Out[3282]= True

In[3283]:= **TestDefBFM["A := {1, 2, 3}", "A"]**
Out[3283]= False

In[3284]:= **ProcCalls1[x_ /; StringQ[x]] :=**
Module[{c = Attributes[x], d = {}, a = Flatten[{PureDefinition[x], p}]}, ClearAttributes[x, c];
p = Length[a]; Do[If[TestDefBFM[a[[k]], x], AppendTo[d, a[[k]]], Null], {k, 1, p}];
Clear[x]; ToExpression[d]; SetAttributes[x, c]]

In[3285]:= **ProcCalls1["A"]**

In[3286]:= **Definition[A]**
Out[3286]= Attributes[A] = {Flat, Listable, Protected}
A[x_Integer] := Module[{a = 42}, x + a]
A[x_] := Module[{a = 590}, x + a]
A[x_, y_List] := Block[{}, {x, y}]
A[x_, y_] := Module[{a = 90}, x + y + a]

In[3785]:= **ScanLikeProcs[x_: {}] := Module[{b = {}, c = {}, d, h, k = 1, a = Select[Names["`*"],**
StringFreeQ[#, "$"] && Quiet[Check[BlockFuncModQ[#], False]] &]},
Off[Definition::ssle]; If[a == {}, Return[{}], For[k, k <= Length[a], k++,
d = Definition2[a[[k]]][[1 ;; -2]];

If[Length[d] > 1, AppendTo[b, Map[StringTake[#, {1, Flatten[StringPosition[#, " := "]][[1]] − 1}] &, d]];
AppendTo[c, a[[k]]]]]]]; On[Definition::ssle]; If[! HowAct[x], x = b, Null]; c]

In[3786]:= G[x_] := Module[{a = 590}, x^2 + a];
G[x_ /; PrimeQ[x]] := Module[{a = 90}, x + a]; G[x_, y_] := Module[{}, x + y];
G[x_, y_ /; ListQ[y], z_] := Module[{}, x + Length[y] + z]

In[3787]:= V[x_] := Module[{}, x]; V[x_ /; ListQ[x]] := Module[{}, Length[x]]

In[3788]:= {ScanLikeProcs[], ScanLikeProcs[Sv], Sv}

Out[3788]= {{"A", "G", "V"}, {"A", "G", "V"}, {{"A[x_Integer]", "A[x_, y_List]", "A[x_, y_]", "A[x_]"}, {"G[x_ /; PrimeQ[x]]", "G[x_]", "G[x_, y_]", "G[x_, y_ /; ListQ[y], z_]"}, {"V[x_ /; ListQ[x]]", "V[x_]"}}}

The **ProcCalls1** procedure is a rather interesting analog of the **ProcCalls** procedure. This procedure is based on the **TestDefBFM** procedure, whose call **TestDefBFM[x, w]** returns *True* if a *x* string contains the definition of an object of type {*Block, Function, Module*} with a *w* name, set in the string format, and *False* otherwise. The previous fragment represents source codes of both tools with examples of their typical applications.

In addition to the above *two* procedure for the purpose of definition of blocks, functions and modules of the same name of the current session of the system a quite simple procedure is intended whose call **ScanLikeProcs[]** returns the list of the blocks, functions or modules of the same name that are activated in the current session whereas as a result of the procedure call **ScanLikeProcs[w]** in addition through an undefinite *w* variable the list of headings in string format of objects of the specified type is returned. The previous fragment represents source code of the **ScanLikeProcs** procedure with examples of its use. In certain appendices these tools are rather useful, above all, at elaboration of the system means for manipulations with procedures.

In a number of cases the structural analysis of objects of the type {*Block, Module, Function*} represents the undoubted interest. In conexion with this the next **StructProcFunc** procedure providing a certain structural analysis of objects of this type was created. The next fragment represents the **StructProcFunc** procedure whose call **StructProcFunc[x]** returns a simple or a nested list whose elements depending on the type {*"Block", "Module", "Function"*} of an actual *x* argument have format {*Type, Heading, Locals, Body*} for {*"Block", "Module"*} and {*Type, Heading, Body*} for *"Function"*; furthermore, as a function is understood an object *x* such as **BlockFuncModQ[x]** = *True*. This fragment represents source code of the procedure along with examples of its use off which the format of the result returned by the procedure is highly obvious.

In[3223]:= StructProcFunc[x_ /; BlockFuncModQ[x]] :=
Module[{c, d, h = {}, p, k = 1, t, b = Flatten[{HeadPF[x]}], a = Flatten[{PureDefinition[x]}]},
c = Map9[StringReplace, a, Map[StringJoin[#, " := "] −> "" &, b]];
While[k <= Length[b], d = c[[k]];
If[SuffPref[d, "Module[{", 1], t = "Module", If[SuffPref[d, "Block[{", 1], t = "Block", t = ""]];
If[t != "", AppendTo[h, {t, b[[k]], p = SubStrSymbolParity1[d, "{", "}"][[1]];

StrToList[p], StringReplace[StringTake[d, {1, –2}], t <> "[" <> p <> ", " -> ""]}],
AppendTo[h, {"Function", b[[k]], StringReplace[d, b[[k]] <> " := " -> ""]}]]; k++];
If[Length[h] == 1, h[[1]], h]]

In[3224]:= Agn[x_] := Block[{a = 90, b = 590}, x^2*a*b]; Agn[x_, y_] := x + y

In[3225]:= Agn[x_, y_, z_] := Module[{a = 590}, a*(x + y + z)]

In[3226]:= StructProcFunc[Agn]

Out[3226]= {{"Block", "Agn[x_]", {"a = 90", "b = 590"}, "x^2*a*b"}, {"Function", "Agn[x_, y_]", "x + y"}, {"Module", "Agn[x_, y_, z_]", {"a = 590"}, "a*(x + y + z)"}}

In[3227]:= Avz[x__] := Module[{a = 74, b = Stack[_]}, a + x; b; $InBlockMod]

In[3228]:= StructProcFunc[Avz]

Out[3228]= {"Module", "Avz[x__]", {"a = 74", "b = Stack[_]"}, "a + x; b; $InBlockMod"}

In certain cases, the problem of structural analysis of the nested procedures of the *Module* type arises; the **StrNestedMod** procedure solves the given problem in a certain degree. The procedure call **StrNestedMod[*x*]** returns the nested list of names in the string format of the subprocedures of a *x* module; at that, each name is located at an appropriate level of *nesting*. Meanwhile, the procedure call **StrNestedMod[*x, w*]** with the second optional *w* argument – an indefinite variable – thru *w* returns the list of names in string format of subprocedures of a *x* procedure, in which the first element – a *x* name in string format of the main procedure. If the *x* procedure does not contain subprocedures, the procedure call **StrNestedMod[*x, w*]** returns {\"*x*\"} whereas the second *w* argument retains own value. The following fragment represents source code of the **StrNestedMod** procedure with typical examples of its use.

In[2870]:= StrNestedMod[x_ /; ModuleQ[x], y___] :=
Module[{c, d, g, p, t, a = SubProcs[x][[2]], h = {}, k = 1, n},
If[Length[a] == 1, Map[Remove, a]; {ToString[x]},
c = Map[{d = DeleteDuplicates[Flatten[StringPosition[#, "$"]]],
StringTake[#, {1, d[[-1]] – 1}]}[[-1]] &, Map[ToString, a]]; b = Map[Symbol, c];
For[k, k <= Length[a], k++, AppendTo[h, b[[k]] = {c[[k]], Select[Locals[a[[k]]],
MemberQ[c, #] &]}]];
h = Select[h, #[[2]] != {} &]; Map[Remove, a]; If[{y} != {} && ! HowAct[y], y = c, Null];
For[k = Length[h], k >= 2, k--, If[MemberQ[h[[k – 1]][[2]], h[[k]][[1]]], h[[k – 1]][[2]] =
AppendTo[h[[k – 1]][[2]], h[[k]][[-1]]]]]; h[[1]]]]

In[2871]:= Avz[x_, y_, z_] := Module[{Art, Gal, b = 6}, Art[a_] := Module[{Es}, a^2 + Es[a]];
Gal[b_, c_] := Module[{Kr, Sv}, Kr[d_] := Module[{Vg}, Vg[p_] := Module[{a, Gr},
Gr[m_] := Module[{}, m]; p^1]; Vg[d]*d^3]; Sv[p_] := Module[{}, p^4]; Kr[b]*Sv[c]];
Art[x]*Gal[y, z]];

In[2872]:= {StrNestedMod[Avz, w69], w69}

Out[2872]= {{"Avz", {"Art", "Gal", {"Kr", "Sv", {"Vg", {"Gr"}}}}}, {"Avz", "Art", "Gal", "Kr", "Vg", "Gr", "Sv"}}

The *Mathematica* system allows to use the nested procedures containing other procedures of various nesting in their bodies. At that, similar organization of the nested procedures is supposed as correct when the name of each nested procedure has to be in the list of the local variables of a procedure, that directly its contains. In this case by the call of main procedure the access to all its *subprocedures* is inaccessible, for instance, by means of standard function

Definition. For testing of correctness of the above type of a procedure of the type *Module*, a procedure has been programmed, whose call **NotSubsProcs[x, y]** returns the list of names in string format of subprocedures of a procedure *x* which don't satisfy to the above-specified agreement and whose definitions are available in the current session after the *x* procedure call. While through the 2nd optional *y* argument – an undefinite variable – the list of names in string format of all subprocedures of the *x* procedure without their *nesting* is returned. As an indication of correctness of the nested *x* procedure is the return of the empty list, i.e. {}, by means of the call **NotSubsProcs[x]**. So, the procedure is intended for testing of the nested procedures of the *Module* type with one heading however it can be extended on procedures of the same name.

In[3869]:= NotSubsProcs[x_ /; ModuleQ[x], y___] :=
Module[{a = SubsProcs[x], at = Attributes[x], b, c, d, h, t = {}},
If[a == {}, {}, b = PureDefinition[x]; ClearAttributes[x, at];
c = HeadPF[x]; d = Args[x, 90]; h = ToString[Unique["a"]];
ToExpression[StringReplace[b, c -> h <> "[" <> StringTake[ToString[Map[# <> "_" &, d]],
{2, -2}] <> "]", 1]];
Quiet[Check[ToExpression[h <> "[" <> StringTake[ToString[d], {2, -2}] <> "]"], Null]];
d = Map[StringTake[#, {1, Flatten[StringPosition[#, "[", 1]][[1]] - 1}] &, a];
If[{y} != {} && ! HowAct[y], y = d, Null];
Map[If[UnevaluatedQ[HeadPF, #] || ! StringFreeQ3[HeadPF[#], "$_"],
AppendTo[t, #], Null] &, d]; ToExpression[b]; t = MinusList[d, t];
SetAttributes[x, at]; {t, Quiet[Map[ClearAll, Flatten[{h, d}]]]}[[1]]]]

In[3870]:= B[x_, y_ /; IntegerQ[y]] := Module[{}, Z[t_] := Module[{}, H[p_] := Module[{Q},
Q[k_] := Module[{}, k]; p]; t^2*H[t] + Q[t]]; x*y + Z[x*y]]; {NotSubsProcs[B, t], t}
Out[3870]= {{"Z", "H"}, {"Z", "H", "Q"}}

As block and module are fundamental objects of procedural programming, the concept of the procedure in general is based on their basis. The following procedure provides testing of procedures *(blocks, modules)* regarding their nesting. The procedure call **NestedProcQ[x]** returns *True*, if definition of a block or a module *x* contain definitions of other blocks and/or modules; otherwise, *False* is returned. Whereas the procedure call **NestedProcQ[x, y]** with the second optional *y* argument – *an indefinite symbol* – thru it returns in a whole the nested list whose the first element is from the object names {*"Block"*, *"Module"*} in the string format whereas the second element defines number of occurrences of the corresponding objects. In addition, the first element of the first sublist of the *y* list defines the type of the *x* object, i.e. *"Block"* or *"Module"*. The following fragment represents source code of the **NestedProcQ** procedure with typical examples of its application.

In[4646]:= NestedProcQ[x_ /; BlockModQ[x], y___] :=
Module[{a, b = {" := Block[{", " := Module[{"}, c}, ClearAll[c];
 a = Map[{StringTake[#, {5, -3}], StringCount[PureDefinition[x], #]} &, b];
BlockModQ[x, c]; b = Sort[a, #[[1]] === c &];
If[Plus @@ {b[[1]][[2]], b[[2]][[2]]} >= 2, a = True, a = False];
If[{y} != {} && NullQ[y], y = ReduceLevelsList[Select[b, #[[2]] != 0 &]][[1]]; a, a]]

In[4647]:= Sv[x_, y_] := Module[{a, c, d}, a[z_] := Module[{b}, z^2]; c[z_] := Block[{}, z^3]; d[p_] := Module[{n = 6}, n*p]; a[x + y]*c[x]*d[y]]
In[4648]:= Gs[x_, y_] := Block[{a, c, d}, a[z_] := Module[{b}, z^2]; c[z_] := Block[{}, z^3]; d[p_] := Block[{n = 6}, n*p]; a[x + y]*c[x]*d[y]]
In[4649]:= **NestedProcQ[Sv]**
Out[4649]= True
In[4650]:= **NestedProcQ[Gs]**
Out[4650]= True
In[4651]:= {NestedProcQ[Sv, gs], gs}
Out[4651]= {True, {{"Module", 3}, {"Block", 1}}}
In[4652]:= {NestedProcQ[Gs, vg], vg}
Out[4652]= {True, {{"Block", 3}, {"Module", 1}}}
In[4653]:= **NestedProcQ[ExtrVarsOfStr]**
Out[4653]= False
In[4654]:= {NestedProcQ[ExtrVarsOfStr, st], st}
Out[4654]= {False, {"Module", 1}}

The procedure admits an expansion on a case of the blocks and modules of the same name, being a rather useful exercise for the reader. In addition, the above fragment represent one of possible approaches to testing of blocks and modules, and as a whole of the procedures regarding their nesting.

For the purpose of elimination of ambiguity of modules, functions and blocks of the same name it is recommended to apply standard means to the cleaning of the current session off concrete definitions, using the cancellation of *Protected* attribute for them, if it is necessary. For cleaning of symbols off the ascribed values the *Mathematica* system has three functions **Clear**, **ClearAll** and **Remove** which are considered, for example, in [32]. However, the given functions demand the concrete designation of the symbols which are subject to the cleaning off the ascribed expressions. Whereas the following fragment represents source code of the **ClearCS** procedure with examples of its usage, whose call **ClearCS[*ClearAll*]** returns *Null*, i.e. nothing, clearing all symbols and off the ascribed values received by them in the current session, and off attributes, messages and values by default, associated with such symbols; while the call **ClearCS[*Remove*]** returns *Null*, i.e. nothing, deleting from the field of names of the system all symbols which received values in the current *Mathematica* session.

In[2640]:= ClearCS[x_ /; MemberQ[{ClearAll, Remove}, x]] :=
Module[{a = Join[Names["Global`*"], {"a", "b", "c", "d", "h", "k", "p", "S", "x", "y"}]},
Quiet[Mapp[ClearAttributes, a, Protected]]; Quiet[Map[x, a]];]
In[2641]:= {x, y, t, g, h} = {42, 74, 47, 69, 2016}; ClearCS[Remove]; {x, y, t, g, h}
Out[2641]= {Removed[x], Removed[y], Removed[t], Removed[g], Removed[h]}
In[2642]:= {x, y, t, g, h} = {42, 74, 47, 69, 2016}; ClearCS[ClearAll]; {x, y, t, g, h}
Out[2642]= {x, y, t, g, h}
In[2643]:= G[x_] := Module[{a = 590}, x^2 + a]; V[x_] := Module[{}, x^2];
G[x_ /; PrimeQ[x]] := Module[{a = 590}, x + a]; V[x_ /; ListQ[x]] := Module[{}, Length[x]]
In[2644]:= ClearCS[ClearAll]; Map[Definition, {G, V}]
Out[2644]= {Null, Null}

In certain appendices the **ClearCS** procedure appears as an useful enough means, in many respects providing recovery of initial status of the current session. The procedure is used by some means of *MathToolBox* package [48], carrying out a function of preliminary cleaning of the current session.

In problems of formal processing of functional expressions the **ExpArgs** procedure presents a quite certain interest whose call **ExpArgs[G, {x, y,...}]** provides extension of the list of the formal arguments of a module, function or block *G* onto the list of arguments {*x, y, z, ...*} to the right concerning the tuple of formal arguments of the *G* object with return of *Null* value, i.e. nothing, and with activation in the current session of the updated definition of *G* object. The expansion of tuple of formal arguments is made for *G* object only onto variables from the list {*x, y, ...*} which aren't its formal arguments or local variables; otherwise expansion is not made. List elements {*x, y, z, ...*} onto updating can be symbols in the string format along with names of the formal arguments with tests for admissibility of the corresponding actual arguments ascribed to them. At that, the procedure call **ExpArgs[G, x]** on an inadmissible *G* object, for instance, on a system function or on the empty *x* list is returned unevaluated. The following fragment represents source code of the **ExpArgs** procedure along with some most typical examples of its application.

In[2547]:= A[x_] := Module[{a = 6}, x*a]; A[x_, y_] := Module[{a = 7}, x*y*a];
A[x_, y_List] := Block[{}, {x, y}]; A[x_Integer] := Module[{a = 5}, x*a];
SetAttributes[A, {Flat, Listable, Protected}];
Art[x_, y_ /; PrimeQ[y]] := Module[{a = 2, b = 6}, Length[Join[x, y]]*a*b]

In[2548]:= ExpArgs[f_ /; BlockFuncModQ[f], x_ /; ListQ[x] &&
AllTrue[Map[! StringFreeQ[ToString[#], "_"] || StringQ[#] &, x], TrueQ]] :=
Module[{a, b, c, d, t, h, g = {}, k = 1}, a = Flatten[{Definition4[ToString[f]]}];
b = Args[f, 90]; b = If[NestListQ[b], b[[1]], b]; d = Locals1[f];
d = If[NestListQ[d], d[[1]], d]; c = Flatten[{HeadPF[f]}][[1]]; t = Map[ToString, x];
h = Map[#[[1]] &, Map[StringSplit[#, "_"] &, t]]; b = Join[b, d];
While[k <= Length[h], If[! MemberQ[b, h[[k]]], d = t[[k]];
AppendTo[g, If[StringFreeQ[d, "_"], d <> "_", d]]]; k++];
If[g == {}, Return[], g = ToString[g];
d = StringTake[c, {1, -2}] <> ", " <> StringTake[g, {2, -2}] <> "]"; ClearAllAttributes[f];
ClearAll[f]; a[[1]] = StringReplace[a[[1]], c -> d, 1]; Map[ToExpression, a]];]

In[2549]:= ExpArgs[Art, {"x", "z_", "h", p_ /; String[p], c_String, h_ /; ListQ[h] &&
Length[h] >= 90}]
In[2550]:= Definition[Art]
Out[2550]= Art[x_, y_ /; PrimeQ[y], z_, h_, p_ /; String[p], c_String, h_ /; ListQ[h] &&
Length[h] >= 90] := Module[{a = 2, b = 6}, Length[Join[x, y]]*aVb]
In[2551]:= ExpArgs[Art, {"x", "z_", "h", p_ /; String[p], c_Integer, h_ /; ListQ[h] &&
Length[h] >= 90}]
In[2552]:= Definition[Art]
Out[2552]= Art[x_, y_ /; PrimeQ[y], z_, h_, p_ /; String[p], c_String, h_ /; ListQ[h] &&
Length[h] >= 90] := Module[{a = 2, b = 6}, Length[Join[x, y]]*a*b]
In[2553]:= ExpArgs[A, {"x", "z_", "h", p_ /; String[p], c_Integer, h_ /; ListQ[h] &&

Length[h] >= 90}]
In[2554]:= **Definition[A]**
Out[2554]= Attributes[A] = {Flat, Listable, Protected}
A[x_, y_List, z_, h_, p_ /; String[p], c_Integer, h_ /; ListQ[h] && Length[h] >= 90] := Module[{a = 5}, x*a]
A[x_] := Module[{a = 6}, x*a]
A[x_, y_List] := Block[{}, {x, y}]
A[x_, y_] := Module[{a = 7}, x*y*a]
In[2555]:= **ExpArgs[A, {"x", "z_", "h", p_ /; String[p], c_Integer, h_ /; ListQ[h] && Length[h] >= 90}]**
In[2556]:= **Definition[A]**
Out[2556]= Attributes[A] = {Flat, Listable, Protected}
A[x_Integer, z_, h_, p_ /; String[p], c_Integer, h_ /; ListQ[h] && Length[h] >= 90] := Module[{a = 5}, x*a]
A[x_] := Module[{a = 6}, x*a]
A[x_, y_List] := Block[{}, {x, y}]
A[x_, y_] := Module[{a = 7}, x*y*a]

Definition of the **ExpArgs** procedure along with the standard tools uses a series of our tools such as **Args, BlockModQ, ClearAllAttributes, HeadPF, Definition4, NestListQ, Locals1** which are considered in the present book and in [33]. The **ExpArgs** procedure has a series of rather interesting appendices, above all, applications of the system character. The procedure directly adjoins to next **ExtensionHeading** procedure, using a slightly different approach.

The procedure call **ExtensionHeading[G, y1, ...]** provides expansion of the tuple of formal arguments of a function, a module or a block G by {y1,y2,...} arguments to the right from the tuple, with returning *Null*, i.e. nothing, and activation in the current session of the updated definition of the G object. Expansion of the tuple of formal arguments is made for G object only on variables from the {y1, y2,...} list which aren't its formal arguments; otherwise any expansion isn't made. List {y1, y2,...} for updating can be both symbols in string format, and names of arguments with tests ascribed to it for their admissibility. At that, the procedure significantly uses the procedure, whose call **ReduceArgs[x]** returns nothing, providing the removing of *"excess"* formal arguments of a block, a function or a module x in the current session, leaving only their first entries in the tuple of its formal arguments. This procedure has also independent interest as the *Mathematica* even at the time of the function call with excess formal arguments can't correctly identify this situation. In turn, the given procedure uses a rather useful function whose call **FirstPositionsList[x]** returns the list of positions of only first occurrences of elements in a x list, i.e. ignoring their multiplicities.

Whereas the **ExtHeadPF** is a version of the **ExtensionHeading** procedure; the procedure call **ExtHeadPF[x, y]** provides expansion of tuple of formal arguments of a block, a function or a module x by elements of an y list to the right from the tuple with returning *Null*, i.e. *nothing*, and activation in the current session of the updated definition of the x object. Expansion of a tuple of formal arguments is made for x object only on elements from the y list which aren't checked for admissibility as formal arguments *(duplicating, existence of patterns, etc.)*, ensuring correctness of elements of the y list lies on the user. Furthermore, the **ExtHeadPF** procedure provides the processing of x obiects with the same names in the above sense. At last, the call

MultipleArgsQ[*x*] returns *True* if at least one object composing the definition of a function, a module or a block *x* has multiple occurrences of formal arguments, and *False* otherwise. A fragment below represents source codes of the above means with examples of their use.

In[3376]:= G[x_, y_Integer] := x*y; G[x_, y_, z_] := Module[{a}, a*(x + y + x)]

In[3377]:= ExtensionHeading[x_ /; BlockFuncModQ[x], y__] :=
Module[{a = Flatten[{PureDefinition[x]}], b = Flatten[{HeadPF[x]}],
c = If[StringQ[x], Symbol[x], x], d, atr = Attributes[x]},
ClearAttributes[x, atr]; d = Args[x]; Clear[x]; d = Map[Join[#, {y}] &, d];
d = Map[ToString1, Map[c @@ # &, d]];
Do[ToExpression[StringReplace[a[[k]], b[[k]] -> d[[k]], 1]], {k, 1, Length[a]}];
Map[ToExpression, d]; ReduceArgs[x]; SetAttributes[x, atr]]

In[3378]:= ExtensionHeading[G, x_Integer, b_ /; PrimeQ[b], y_Integer, c__]

In[3379]:= Definition[G]

Out[3379]= G[x_, y_Integer, b_ /; PrimeQ[b], c__] := x*y
G[x_, y_, z_, b_ /; PrimeQ[b], c__] := Module[{a}, a*(x + y + x)]

In[3380]:= ExtHeadPF[x_ /; BlockFuncModQ[x], y_ /; ListQ[y]] :=
Module[{a = Flatten[{HeadPF[x]}][[1]], b},
b = "{" <> StringTake[a, {StringLength[HeadName[a]] + 2, -2}] <> "}";
ToExpression[StringReplace[Flatten[{PureDefinition[x]}][[1]],
a -> HeadName[a] <> "[" <> ToString1[Join[ToExpression[b], y]] <> "]"]]]

In[3381]:= g[x_, y_, z_ /; IntegerQ[z]] := x + y*z

In[3382]:= Definition[g]

Out[3382]= g[x_, y_, z_ /; IntegerQ[z]] := x + y*z

In[3383]:= ExtHeadPF[g, {a_, b_ /; StringQ[b], c_}]

In[3384]:= Definition[g]

Out[3384]= g[x_, y_, z_ /; IntegerQ[z]] := x + y*z
g[{x_, y_, z_ /; IntegerQ[z], a_, b_ /; StringQ[b], c_}] := x + y*z

In[3385]:= ExtHeadPF[g, {m_, n_ /; ListQ[n], p_Symbol}]

In[3386]:= Definition[g]

Out[3386]= g[x_, y_, z_ /; IntegerQ[z]] := x + y*z
g[{x_, y_, z_ /; IntegerQ[z], a_, b_ /; StringQ[b], c_}] := x + y*z
g[{x_, y_, z_ /; IntegerQ[z], m_, n_ /; ListQ[n], p_Symbol}] := x + y*z

In[3387]:= ReduceArgs[x_ /; BlockFuncModQ[x]] := Module[{a, b, d = {}, d1 = {}, d2 = {},
c = Flatten[{PureDefinition[x]}], h = Flatten[{HeadPF[x]}], atr = Attributes[x]},
ClearAll[b]; ClearAttributes[x, atr]; a = ArgsBFM[x, b]; ClearAll[x];
Do[AppendTo[d, Join[a[[k]], b[[k]]]], {k, 1, Length[c]}];
d = Map[{#[[1 ;; Length[#]/2]], #[[Length[#]/2 + 1 ;; -1]]} &, d];
Do[AppendTo[d1, FirstPositionsList[d[[k]][[1]]]], {k, 1, Length[d]}];
Do[AppendTo[d2, Part[d[[k]][[2]], d1[[k]]]], {k, 1, Length[d]}];
d2 = Map[ToString[x] <> "[" <> StringTake[#, {2, -2}] <> "]" &, Map[ToString, d2]];

Do[ToExpression[StringReplace[c[[k]], h[[k]] -> d2[[k]], 1]], {k, 1, Length[c]}];
SetAttributes[x, atr]]

In[3388]:= Agn[x_, y_, x_List] := Module[{a = Stack[]}, x*y; a];
Agn[t_Integer, y_, x_.] := Module[{a = Stack[]}, x*y; a];

In[3389]:= ReduceArgs[Agn]

In[3390]:= Definition[Agn]

Out[3390]= Agn[x_, y_] := Module[{a = Stack[]}, x*y; a]
Agn[t_Integer, y_, x_.] := Module[{a = Stack[]}, x*y; a]

In[3391]:= FirstPositionsList[x_ /; ListQ[x]] :=
DeleteDuplicates[Map[#[[1]][[1]] &, Map[SequencePosition[x, {#}] &, x]]]

In[3392]:= FirstPositionsList[{a, a, b, c, a, c, d, a, c, x, y, x, a, z, y, x, c, d, g}]

Out[3392]= {1, 3, 4, 7, 10, 11, 14, 19}

In[3399]:= MultipleArgsQ[x_ /; BlockFuncModQ[x]] :=
Or @@ Map[Length[#] > Length[DeleteDuplicates[#]] &, ArgsBFM[x]]

In[3400]:= MultipleArgsQ[Agn]

Out[3400]= True

The next fragment represents a rather useful procedural **$ProcType** variable which has been implemented by a simple function on the basis of system **Stack** function and making sense only in the body of a block or a module, returning type {*Block, Module*} in the string format of an object containing it. Outside of objects of the above type the variable accepts the value *"ToString"* which doesn't have especial meaning. The next fragment represents source code of the **$ProcType** variable along with some typical examples of its application. The variable **$ProcType** has a number of rather useful appendices.

In[2562]:= $ProcType := ToString[Stack[][[1]]]

In[2563]:= Agn[x_, y_] := Block[{a = 90, b = 500, c = $ProcType}, a + b + c; {$ProcType, c}]

In[2564]:= Agn[42, 47]

Out[2564]= {"Block", "Block"}

In[2565]:= Clear[Agn]; Agn[x_, y_] := Module[{a = 90, b = 500, c = $ProcType}, a + b + c; {$ProcType, c}]

In[2566]:= Agn[42, 47]

Out[2566]= {"Module", "Module"}

In[2567]:= Clear[Agn]; Agn[x_, y_] := Module[{c = $ProcType, a = 2016, b = 590}, a + b + c; {$ProcType, c}]

In[2568]:= Agn[42, 47]

Out[2568]= {"Module", "Module"}

In[2569]:= $ProcType

Out[2569]= "ToString"

To the previous procedural variable another procedural **$TypeProc** variable directly adjoins which is also used only in body of a block or a module of any type. The variable **$TypeProc** receives value of type in string format of a *G* object that contains it, in the context {*"Block"*, *"DynamicModule"*, *"Module"*}; outside of a block or a module the variable receives *$Failed* value as clearly illustrates the following fragment presenting source code of the procedural **$TypeProc** variable along with examples of its most typical application.

In[2572]:= $TypeProc := CheckAbort[If[$a27k20$ =
Select[{Stack[Module], Stack[Block], Stack[DynamicModule]}, # != {} &];
If[$a27k20$ == {}, Clear[$a27k20$]; Abort[], $a27k20$ = ToString[$a27k20$[[1]][[1]]]];
SuffPref[$a27k20$, "Block[{", 1], Clear[$a27k20$]; "Block", If[SuffPref[$a27k20$,
"Module[{", 1] && ! StringFreeQ[$a27k20$, "DynamicModule"], Clear[$a27k20$];
"DynamicModule", Clear[$a27k20$]; "Module"]], $Failed]

In[2573]:= M[x_] := Module[{a = 90, b = 590, c = $TypeProc}, c]; M[74]
Out[2573]= "Module"
In[2574]:= G[x_] := Module[{a = 6, b = 7, c}, c = a*b*x; c^2; $TypeProc]; G[74]
Out[2574]= "Module"
In[2575]:= B[x_] := Block[{a = 90, b = 590, c = $TypeProc}, c]; B[69]
Out[2575]= "Block"
In[2576]:= DM[x_] := DynamicModule[{a, c = $TypeProc}, x; c]; DM[69]
Out[2576]= "DynamicModule"
In[2577]:= $TypeProc
Out[2577]= $Failed
In[2578]:= F[x_ /; ListQ[x]] := Append[Select[x, OddQ[#] &], $TypeProc]; F[{69, 74, 27, 20}]
Out[2578]= {69, 27, $Failed}

In certain cases of the procedural programming the **$TypeProc** variable with the **$ProcType** variable are useful enough facilities.

At last, to the previous procedural variables the **$CallProc** variable directly adjoins whose call returns contents in string format of the body of a block or a module which contains it at the time of a call. In addition, for a module the body with local variables with "$" symbols ascribed to them while for a block its body in the standard format are returned. The call of this variable outside of a block or a module returns "*StringTake[ToString1[Stack[_]][[1]]], {10, -2}]*". The following fragment represents source code of the procedural **$CallProc** variable along with the typical examples of its application.

In[2584]:= $CallProc := StringTake[ToString1[Stack[_]][[1]]], {10, -2}]

In[2585]:= M[x_, y_ /; StringQ[y]] := Module[{a = $CallProc, b, c}, x*StringLength[y]; a]
In[2586]:= M[6, "vak"]
Out[2586]= "Module[{a$ = $CallProc, b$, c$}, 6*StringLength[\"vak\"]; a$]"
In[2587]:= B[x_, y_ /; PrimeQ[y]] := Block[{a = $CallProc, b}, x + y; a]
In[2588]:= B[590, 29]
Out[2588]= "Block[{a = $CallProc, b}, 590 + 29; a]"
In[2589]:= $CallProc
Out[2589]= "StringTake[ToString1[Stack[_]][[1]]], {10, -2}]"

The procedural **$CallProc** variable provides possibility of processing of the body of a block or a module, containing it, within the confines of the object, presenting a certain interest for a number of applications, first of all, of the system character.

Use of tools of preservation of definitions in the *ASCII* format files allows to program quite effective and useful means of the analysis of the structural organization of the user blocks, functions and modules. The following fragment represents source code of the **CompActPF** procedure with the typical examples of its application, whose call **CompActPF[*x*]** returns a nested two–element list whose the first element determines the list of all blocks, functions or modules which enter in the definition of a block, function or module *x*, including *x* whereas the second element determines the list of headings in string format of these means. At that, the lists include only the user tools whose definitions were activated in the current session of the *Mathematica* system; moreover, for the calls which enter into the *x* object, are added respectively and all their calls onto the full depth of their nesting.

In[5134]:= G[x_] := Module[{}, a*x + b]; G1[x_] := a*x + b + V[x, 2016];
S[y_] := Module[{}, y^2 + 90]; S1[y_] := y^2 + G[y];
V[x_, y_] := Module[{G, S}, G[x] + S[y^2]];
V1[x_, y_] := G1[x] + S1[y^2] + h*Sin[x*y] + v*Cos[x*y]

In[5135]:= CompActPF[x_ /; BlockFuncModQ[x]] := Module[{b = {}, c = "", d, h = "",
a = ToDefOptPF[x], f = ToString[x] <> ".txt"},
Put[FullDefinition[x], f]; Quiet[While[! SameQ[h, EndOfFile], h = Read[f, String];
If[h != " ", c = c <> h;
If[HeadingQ[d = StringTake[c, {1, Flatten[StringPosition[c, " := "]][[1]] – 1}]],
AppendTo[b, d]; c = ""]; Continue[]]]];
DeleteFile[Close[f]]; {Map[HeadName, b], b}]

In[5136]:= CompActPF[V1]
Out[5136]= {{"V1", "G1", "V", "G", "S", "S1"}, {"V1[x_, y_]", "G1[x_]", "V[x_, y_]", "G[x_]", "S[y_]", "S1[y_]"}}

In[5137]:= CompActPF[V]
Out[5137]= {{"V", "G", "S"}, {"V[x_, y_]", "G[x_]", "S[y_]"}}

In[5138]:= CompActPF1[x_ /; BlockFuncModQ[x]] := Module[{d = {}, k = 1, b = Args[x, 90],
a = Flatten[{PureDefinition[x]}][[1]], c = Locals1[x], p},
{b, c} = {If[NestListQ1[b], b[[1]], b], If[NestListQ1[c], c[[1]], c]};
a = Select[ExtrVarsOfStr[a, 2], ! MemberQ[Flatten[{ToString[x],
Join[b, c, {"Block", "Module"}]}], #] &];
While[k <= Length[a], p = a[[k]];
AppendTo[d, If[BlockFuncModQ[p], {p, HeadPF[p]}, If[SystemQ[p], {p, "System"},
{p, "Undefined"}]]]; k++];
a = Map[Flatten, Gather[d, ! StringFreeQ[#1[[2]], "_"] && ! StringFreeQ[#2[[2]], "_"] &]];
b = Map[Flatten, Gather[a, #1[[2]] == "System" && #2[[2]] == "System" &]];
d = Map[Flatten, Gather[b, #1[[2]] == "Undefined" && #2[[2]] == "Undefined" &]];
Map[If[#[[-1]] == "System", Prepend[MinusList[#, {"System"}], "System"],
If[#[[-1]] == "Undefined", Prepend[MinusList[#, {"Undefined"}], "Undefined"], #]] &, d]]

In[5139]:= CompActPF1[V1]
Out[5139]= {{"System", "Cos", "Sin"}, {"G1", "G1[x_]", "S1", "S1[y_]"}, {"Undefined", "h", "v"}}
In[5140]:= CompActPF1[V]

Out[5140]= {}
In[5141]:= Z[x_ /; StringQ[x], z_ /; ! HowAct[z]] :=
Block[{a = Sin[x]}, Cos[a] + StringLength[x]]
In[5142]:= CompActPF1[Z]
Out[5142]= {{"System", "Cos", "Sin", "StringLength", "StringQ"}, {"HowAct", "HowAct[x_]"}}

We will note, that for effective processing of the saved complete definitions of the functions, blocks and modules in definition of **CompActPF** procedure the procedure has been used, whose the call **ToDefOptPF[x]** optimizes definition of the user block, function or module *x* in the current session. The truth, for optimization of definitions there are also other means considered in the present book above. A quite useful modification of **CompActPF** procedure completes the previous fragment whose call **CompActPF1[x]** returns the nested list whose elements represent sublists of the following format:

– sublist with the first *"System"* element defines calls of system functions in definition of a block, a function or a module *x*;

– sublist with the first *"Undefined"* element defines names of objects which aren't included into the list of arguments and local variables of a function, a block or a module *x*;

– sublist of a format different from above-mentioned contains the user pairs {*block, function or module, its heading*}, whose calls are available in definition of a *x* object.

The **CompActPF1** procedure is an useful tool in a number of applications, first of all, of the system character, providing the structural analysis of the user means of the types {*Function, Block, Module*}.

As it is well known [25], the **Maple** system has a number of the procedural variables *(where under procedural variables are understood the variables making sense only in the body of a block or a module and receiving values about components of the object containing them)* which provide, for example, the possibility to receive the list of formal arguments of the block or module in its body at a call. Whereas in the **Mathematica** system similar tools are absent though in many cases represent quite certain interest. Some tools of this kind for the **Mathematica** are given above. It is simple to notice that tools of the **Maple** in this respect are more developed, than similar tools of the **Mathematica**, that in some cases rather *significantly* simplifies procedural programming.

A block or a module provide four main mechanisms of return of results of its call, namely: *(1)* through the *last* offer of the body, *(2)* on the basis of **Return** function, *(3)* through global variables, and *(4)* through formal arguments. The given question was considered enough in detail in our books [25-33,50].

The following fragment on the example of a rather simple *P* procedure visually illustrates a mechanism of return of any number of results through *z* argument – the tuple of undefinite variables. At that, for simplification of assignment of the returned results to elements of a *z* list a simple and at the same time the useful enough **AssignL** function is used.

In[2550]:= P[x_, y_, z___ /; AllTrue[Map[! HowAct[#] &, {z}], TrueQ]] :=
Module[{a = 90, b = 590, c = 74}, If[x*y > 590, AssignL[{z}[[1]], a]; AssignL[{z}[[2]], b];
AssignL[{z}[[3]], c]]; (x + y)*(a + b + c)]
In[2551]:= P[42, 47, m, n, p]
Out[2551]= 67106

In[2552]:= {m, n, p}
Out[2552]= {90, 590, 74}
In[2553]:= **First[{x, y, z}] = 590**
Set::write: Tag First in First[{x, y, z}] is Protected... >>
Out[2553]= 590
In[2554]:= **{x, y, z}**
Out[2554]= {x, y, z}
In[2555]:= **{x, y, z}[[2]] = 590**
Set::setps: {x, y, z} in the part assignment is not a symbol... >>
Out[2555]= 590
In[2556]:= **{x, y, z}**
Out[2556]= {x, y, z}
In[2557]:= **AssignL[x_, y_, z___] := Quiet[If[{z} != {}, x := y, x = y]]**
In[2558]:= **AssignL[{x, y, z}[[2]], 590]**
Out[2558]= 590
In[2559]:= **{x, y, z}**
Out[2559]= {x, 590, z}
In[2560]:= **AssignL[{a1, a2, a3, a4, a5, a6}[[3 ;; 5]], {74, 49, 69}]**
Out[2560]= {74, 49, 69}
In[2561]:= **{a1, a2, a3, a4, a5, a6}**
Out[2561]= {a1, a2, 74, 49, 69, a6}
In[2562]:= **AssignL[{{a, b}, {c, d}}[[1, 2]], 590, Delayed]**
In[2563]:= **{{a, b}, {c, d}}**
Out[2563]= {{a, 590}, {c, d}}
In[2564]:= **AssignL[{{a, b}, {c, d}}[[1, 2]], 590, Delayed]**
Ot[2564]= $Failed

The function call **AssignL[x, y]** provides correct assignment to elements *(to all or only given elements)* of an arbitrary expression or expressions from the *y* list, modeling assignments on the basis of constructions of the format {x, y, z,...}[[n]] = *Expr* and {x, y, z,...}[[n ;; p]] = {Ex_n, Ex_{n+1}, ..., Ex_p} and to them similar which the system doesn't support, whereas the function call **AssignL[x, y, j]** where *j – an arbitrary expression –* provides correct delayed assignments of the above–stated kind, as very visually illustrates the previous fragment. In addition, the function call on inadmissible appointments returns *$Failed*.

As it was already noted earlier and it was used in certain procedures, in the *Mathematica* along with the simple procedures that aren't containing in the body of definitions of other procedures, the application of the so–called *nested* procedures, i.e. of such procedures whose definitions are in body of other procedures is allowed. The nesting level of such procedures is determined by only a size of working field of the system. In this regard rather interesting problem of definition of the list of subprocedures whose definitions are in the body of an arbitrary procedure of the type {*Block, Module*} arises. The **SubProcs** procedure successfully solves the problem whose call **SubProcs[x]** returns the nested two-element list of the *ListList* type whose first element defines the sublist of headings of blocks and modules composing a main procedure *x*, while the second element determines the sublist of the generated names of the blocks and modules composing the main procedure *x*, including procedure *x* itself, and which are activated in the current session of *Mathematica* system. The next fragment represents source code of the **SubProcs** procedure with the most typical examples of its use.

```
In[2525]:= SubProcs[P_ /; BlockModQ[P]] :=
Module[{b, c = {}, d, t, h, k = 1, p = {}, g = {}, a = Flatten[{PureDefinition[P]}][[1]]},
b = StringPosition[a, {"] := Block[{", "] := Module[{"}];
For[k, k <= Length[b], k++, d = b[[k]]; AppendTo[p, ExprOfStr[a, d[[1]], -1, {" ", ",", ";"}]];
AppendTo[c, h = ExprOfStr[a, d[[1]], -1, {" ", ",", ";"}] <> " := " <>
ExprOfStr[a, d[[1]] + 5, 1, {" ", ",", ";"}]; t = Flatten[StringPosition[h, "["]];
h = Quiet[StringReplacePart[h, ToString[Unique[ToExpression[StringTake[h,
{1, t[[1]] - 1}]]]], {1, t[[1]] - 1}]];
AppendTo[g, StringTake[h, {1, Flatten[StringPosition[h, "["]][[1]] - 1}]]; h]];
Map[ToExpression, c]; {p, Map[ToExpression, g]}]

In[2526]:= P[x_, y_] := Module[{a, b, B, P1, P2}, P1[z_, h_] := Module[{m, n}, z + h];
B[h_] := Block[{}, h]; P2[z_] := Module[{P3}, P3[h_] := Module[{}, h]; P3[z]]; x*P2[x] +
P1[x, y] + P2[y]]
In[2527]:= P[90, 590]
Out[2527]= 9370
In[2528]:= SubProcs[P]
Out[2528]= {{"P[x_, y_]", "P1[z_, h_]", "B[h_]", "P2[z_]", "P3[h_]"}, {P$117705, P1$117709,
B$117713, P2$117717, P3$117721}}
In[2529]:= DefFunc[P2$117717]
Out[2529]= P2$117717[z_] := Module[{P3}, P3[h_] := Module[{}, h]; P3[z]]
```

So, between elements of sublists of the returned nested list the one-to-one correspondence takes place. The definition of the **SubProcs** procedure along with the standard means uses a number of our means such as **BlockModQ**, **ExprOfStr**, **PureDefinition** that are considered in the present book and in [28–33,50]. The procedure admits a number of a rather interesting extensions and modifications.

A quite useful **SubProc1** procedure provides testing of a block or a module *x* regarding the existence in its definition of the interior blocks or modules. The procedure call **SubProcs1**[*x*] depending on existence of an object *x* of the same name with various headings or with one heading returns the nested or simple list; in addition, the first elements of the list or sublists define headings of a *x* object whereas the second define number of blocks or modules which enter into definition of the *x* object with the corresponding headings. At that, if the *x* object is not block, function or module, the procedure call **SubProcs1**[*x*] is returned unevaluated. The fragment represents source code of the procedure with the most typical examples of its application. The **SubProcs1** procedure can be quite simply extended onto extraction of all subprocedures of a *x* procedure.

```
In[2532]:= SubProcs1[x_ /; BlockFuncModQ[x]] :=
Module[{b = {}, c, d, k = 1, a = Flatten[{PureDefinition[x]}]},
For[k, k <= Length[a], k++, c = a[[k]];
d = StringPosition[c, {"] := Module[{", "] := Block[{"}];
If[d == {}, Continue[]]; AppendTo[b, {StringTake[c, {1, d[[1]][[1]]}], Length[d] - 1}]];
```

If[Length[b] == 1, Flatten[b], b]]

In[2533]:= G[x_, y_, z_] := x + y + z; G[x_] := Module[{V, H}, V[y_] := Module[{}, y^3];
H[z_] := Module[{}, z^4]; x + V[x] + H[x]]; G[x_, z_] := Module[{V, H, P},
V[t_] := Module[{}, t^3 + t^2 + 590]; H[t_] := Module[{}, t^4];
P[h_] := Module[{a = 590}, a^2 + h^2]; x + V[x] + H[z]*P[x]];
H[t_] := Module[{P}, P[h_] := Module[{a = 90}, a^2 + h^2]; x + P[x]]

In[2534]:= SetAttributes[G, {Protected, Listable}]; {G[2016], G[2016, 74]}
Out[2534]= {16526370375648, 132319646140014}

In[2535]:= SubProcs1[G]
Out[2535]= {{"G[x_]", 2}, {"G[x_, z_]", 3}}

In[2536]:= SubProcs1[H]
Out[2536]= {"H[t_]", 1}

In[2537]:= SubProcs1[590]
Out[2537]= SubProcs1[590]

In[2538]:= P[x_ /; {j[b_] := Module[{}, b^2], If[OddQ[x], True, False]}[[2]]] :=
Module[{a = {c[d_] := Module[{}, d]}}, {j[x], c[x]}]

In[2539]:= P[2017]
Out[2539]= {4068289, 2017}

In[2540]:= Map[Definition1, {j, c}]
Out[2540]= {"j[b_] := Module[{}, b^2]", "c[d_] := Module[{}, d]"}

Very simple example illustrating some admissible mechanisms of definition of heading and local variables of block or module which are useful for procedural programming completes the previous fragment. These mechanisms are used also by a number of tools that compose our *MathToolBox* package [48,50] while the **SubProcs2** procedure presents a quite essential extension of the **SubProcs1** procedure. The following fragment represents source code of the **SubProcs2** procedure along with examples of its typical application.

In[2386]:= G[x_] := Module[{V, H}, Vg[y_] := Module[{}, y^3]; H72[z_] := Module[{}, z^4];
x + Vg[x] + H72[x]]; G[x_, z_] := Module[{Vt, H, P}, Vt[t_] := Module[{}, t^3 + t^2 + 590];
H[t_] := Module[{}, t^4]; P[h_] := Module[{a = 590}, a^2 + h^2]; x + Vt[x] + H[z]*P[x]];
H[t_, z_] := Module[{P}, P[h_] := Module[{a = 90}, a^2 + h*z]; t + P[t]]; F[x_, y] := x + y;
SetAttributes[G, {Protected, Listable}]; {G[2016], G[2016, 74]}
Out[2386]= {16526370375648, 132319646140014}

In[2387]:= SubProcs2[y_, z___] := Module[{n={}, m=1, SB, v=Flatten[{PureDefinition[y]}]},
If[BlockFuncModQ[y], SB[x_String] :=
Module[{b = "Module[", c, d, h, g = "", t, k, p, q, j, s, w, a = Map[#[[1]] &,
StringPosition[x, "Module[{"]]},
If[a == {}, Return[]]; If[Length[a] == 1, Return[$Failed], d = Map[# - 5 &, a]];
c = {StringTake[x, {1, d[[1]]}]};
For[k = Length[a], k > 1, k--, h = b; g = ""; t = "";
For[j = a[[k]] + 7, j < Infinity, j++, h = h <> StringTake[x, {j, j}];
If[SameQ[Quiet[Check[ToExpression[h], "Error"]], "Error"], Continue[],
For[j = d[[k]], j > 1, j--, g = StringTake[x, {j, j}] <> g;
If[SameQ[Quiet[Check[ToExpression[g], "Error"]], "Error"], Continue[], Break[]]];

```
While[j > 1, p = StringTake[x, {j, j}]; If[! SameQ[p, " "], t = p <> t, Break[]]; j--];
p = StringPosition[x, " " <> t <> "["][[1]];
s = Flatten[SubStrSymbolParity1[StringTake[x, {p[[1]], -1}], "[", "]"]];
w = 1; While[w <= Length[s] - 1, q = s[[w]];
If[! StringFreeQ[q, "_"], s = t <> q <> " := Module" <> s[[w + 1]];
Break[]]; w++]; AppendTo[c, s]; Break[]]]]; c];
For[m, m <= Length[v], m++, AppendTo[n, SB[v[[m]]]]];
n = Select[n, ! SameQ[#, Null] &]; If[n == {}, $Failed, n = If[Length[n] == 1, n[[1]], n];
If[{z} != {}, ToExpression[n]]; n], $Failed]]
In[2388]:= SubProcs2[G, 90]
Out[2388]= {{"G[x_]", "H72[z_] := Module[{}, z^4]", "Vg[y_] := Module[{}, y^3]"},
{"G[x_, z_]", "P[h_] := Module[{a = 590}, a^2 + h^2]", "H[t_] := Module[{}, t^4]",
"Vt[t_] := Module[{}, t^3 + t^2 + 590]"}}
In[2389]:= {H72[90], Vg[590], P[27], H[20], Vt[69]}
Out[2389]= {65610000, 205379000, 348829, 160000, 333860}
In[2390]:= SubProcs2[H]
Out[2390]= {{"H[t_, z_]", "P[h_] := Module[{a = 90}, a^2 + h*z]"}, $Failed}
In[2391]:= Map[SubProcs2, {F, 590}]
Out[2391]= {$Failed, $Failed}
```

The procedure call **SubProcs2[*y*]** depending on an unique *y* procedure or of the same name with various headings, returns simple or nested list. For the returned list or sublists the first element is the procedure *y* heading, whereas the others – definitions in the string format of subprocedures of the *Module* type which enter into the *y* definition. In absence for the *y* of subprocedures of the specified type or in the case of type of the *y* argument, different from *Module*, the procedure call **SubProcs2[*y*]** returns *$Failed*. In case of the 2nd optional argument *z* – *an arbitrary expression* – the procedure call **SubProcs3[*y*, *z*]** returns the similar result with simultaneous activation of these subprocedures in the current session.

The **SubProcs3** procedure is a further certain extension of the **SubProcs2** procedure; its call **SubProcs3[*y*]** differs from a call **SubProcs2[*y*]** by the following 2 moments, namely: *(1)* the user block, function or module can act as a factual *y* argument, and *(2)* the returned list as the first element contains heading of the *y* object whereas other elements of the list present definitions of functions, blocks and modules in string format entering into the *y* definition. In case of *y* object of the same name, the returned list will be the nested list, whose sublists have the above–mentioned format. At that, the call **SubProcs3[*y*, *z*]** with the *second* optional *z* argument – *an arbitrary expression* – returns the above list and at the same time activates in the current session all objects of the above type, which enter into the *y*. The fragment below presents source code of the **SubProcs3** procedure along with the typical examples of its use.

```
In[2630]:= G[x_] := Module[{Vg, H74}, Vg[y_] := Module[{}, y^3]; H74[z_] := Module[{},
z^4]; x + Vg[x] + H74[x]]; G[x_, z_] := Module[{Vt, H, P}, Vt[t_] := Module[{}, t^3 + t^2 +
590]; H[t_] := Module[{}, t^4]; P[h_] := Module[{a = 90}, a^2 + Cos[h^2]]; Sin[x] + Vt[x] +
H[z]*P[x]]; H[t_] := Module[{P}, P[h_] := Module[{a = 90}, a^2*h^2]; Cos[t]*P[t]];
F[x_, y_] := Sin[x+y] + Cos[x - y]; V[x_] := Block[{a, b, c}, a[m_] := m^2; b[n_] := n + Sin[n];
c[p_] := Module[{}, p]; a[x]*b[x]*c[x]]; SetAttributes[G, {Protected, Listable}]
```

In[2631]:= SubProcs3[y_, z___] := Module[{u={}, m=1, Sv, v=Flatten[{PureDefinition[y]}]},
If[BlockFuncModQ[y], Sv[S_String] := Module[{a = ExtrVarsOfStr[S, 1], b, c = {}, d, t = 2,
k = 1, cc = {}, n, p, j, h = {StringTake[S, {1, Flatten[StringPosition[S, " := "]][[1]] - 1}]}},
a = Select[a, ! SystemQ[Symbol[#]] && ! MemberQ[{ToString[G]}, #] &];
b = StringPosition[S, Map[" " <> # <> "[" &, a]];
p = Select[a, ! StringFreeQ[S, " " <> # <> "["] &];
b = Flatten[Map[SubStrSymbolParity1[StringTake[S, {#[[1]], -1}], "[", "]"] &, b]];
For[j = 1, j <= Length[p], j++, n = p[[j]]];
For[k = 1, k <= Length[b] - 1, k++, d = b[[k]];
If[! StringFreeQ[d, "_"] && StringTake[b[[k + 1]], {1, 1}] == "[", AppendTo[c, Map[n <> d
<> " := " <> # <> b[[k + 1]] &, {"Block", "Module"}]]]]; c = DeleteDuplicates[Flatten[c]];
For[k = 1, k <= Length[c], k++, d = c[[k]];
If[! StringFreeQ[S, d], AppendTo[h, d], AppendTo[cc, StringTake[d, {1,
Flatten[StringPosition[d, " := "]][[1]] - 1}]]]]; {h, cc} = Map[DeleteDuplicates, {h, cc}];
p = Map[StringTake[#, {1, Flatten[StringPosition[#, "["]][[1]]}] &, h];
cc = Select[Select[cc, ! SuffPref[#, p, 1] &], ! StringFreeQ[S, #] &];
If[cc == {}, h, For[k = 1, k <= Length[cc], k++, p = cc[[k]];
p = StringCases[S, p <> " := " ~~ __ ~~ "; "];
AppendTo[h, StringTake[p, {1, Flatten[StringPosition[p, ";"]][[1]] - 1}]]]; Flatten[h]];
For[m, m <= Length[v], m++, AppendTo[u, Sv[v[[m]]]]];
u = Select[u, ! SameQ[#, Null] &];
u = If[Length[u] == 1, u[[1]], u]; If[{z} != {}, ToExpression[u]]; u, $Failed]]

In[2632]:= **SubProcs3[G]**
Out[2632]= {{"G[x_]", "Vg[y_] := Module[{}, y^3]", "H74[z_] := Module[{}, z^4]"},
{"G[x_, z_]", "Vt[t_] := Module[{}, t^3 + t^2 + 590]", "H[t_] := Module[{}, t^4]",
"P[h_] := Module[{a = 90}, a^2 + Cos[h^2]]"}}
In[2633]:= **SubProcs3[H]**
Out[2633]= {"H[t_]", "P[h_] := Module[{a = 90}, a^2*h^2]"}
In[2634]:= **SubProcs3[F]**
Out[2634]= {"F[x_, y_]"}
In[2635]:= **SubProcs3[V]**
Out[2635]= {"V[x_]", "c[p_] := Module[{}, p]", "a[m_] := m^2", "b[n_] := n + Sin[n]"}
In[2636]:= **SubProcs3[V, 590]**
Out[2636]= {"V[x_]", "c[p_] := Module[{}, p]", "a[m_] := m^2", "b[n_] := n + Sin[n]"}
In[2637]:= {**V[590], a[42], b[47], c[67]**}
Out[2637]= {205379000*(590 + Sin[590]), 1764, 47 + Sin[47], 67}

If a function with heading acts as a *y* object, only its heading is returned; the similar result takes place and in case of *y* object which doesn't contain subobjects of the above type while on the *y* object different from the user block, function or module, the call of the **SubProcs3** procedure returns *$Failed*.

In some cases there is a necessity of definition for a block and a module of the subobjects of the type {*Block, Function, Module*}. The call **SubsProcQ[x, y]** returns *True* if *y* is the global active subobject of a *x* object of the above type, and *False* otherwise. However, as the Math objects of this type differ not by names as that is accepted in the majority of programming systems, but by headings then thru the third optional argument the procedure call returns the nested list whose sublists as first element contain headings with a *x* name, whereas the second element contain the headings of subobjects corresponding to them with *y* name. On the first two arguments {*x*, *y*} of the types, different from given in a procedure heading, the procedure call **SubsProcQ**[*x*, *y*] returns *False*. The next fragment represents the source code of the **SubsProcQ** procedure with examples of its application.

In[2650]:= SubsProcQ[x_, y_, z___] := Module[{a, b, k = 1, j = 1, Res = {}},
If[BlockModQ[x] && BlockFuncModQ[y], {a, b} = Map[Flatten,
{{Definition4[ToString[x]]}, {Definition4[ToString[y]]}}];
For[k, k <= Length[b], k++, For[j, j <= Length[a], j++, If[! StringFreeQ[a[[j]], b[[k]]],
AppendTo[Res, {StringTake[a[[j]], {1, Flatten[StringPosition[a[[j]], " := "]][[1]] - 1}],
StringTake[b[[k]], {1, Flatten[StringPosition[b[[k]], " := "]][[1]] - 1}]}], Continue[]]]];
If[Res != {}, If[{z} != {} && ! HowAct[z], z = If[Length[Res] == 1, Res[[1]], Res]; True],
False], False]]

In[2651]:= V[x_] := Block[{a, b, c}, a[m_] := m^2; b[n_] := n + Sin[n]; c[p_] := Module[{}, p];
a[x]*b[x]*c[x]]; c[p_] := Module[{}, p]; V[x_, y_] := Module[{a, b, c}, a[m_] := m^2; b[n_] :=
n + Sin[n]; c[p_] := Module[{}, p]; a[x]*b[x]*c[x]]; c[p_] := Module[{}, p]; p[x_] := x;
SetAttributes[V, Protected]
In[2652]:= {SubsProcQ[V, c, g69], g69}
Out[2652]= {True, {{"V[x_]", "c[p_]"}, {"V[x_, y_]", "c[p_]"}}}
In[2653]:= SubsProcQ[V, Avz]
Out[2653]= False
In[2654]:= SubsProcQ[Sin, h]
Out[2654]= False
In[2655]:= SubsProcQ[p, c]
Out[2655]= False

In principle, on the basis of the above five means {**SubProcs** ÷ **SubProcs3**, **SubsProcQ**} it is possible to program a number of useful enough means of operating with expressions of the types {*Block*, *Module*}.

In a certain regard the procedural variable **$ProcName** which is used only in the body of a procedure activated in the current session is of interest; the variable returns the list whose first element defines a name whereas the second element – the heading in the string format of procedure containing it. Moreover, for providing of the given possibility in a list of the local variables of a procedure containing **$ProcName** variable it is necessary to encode the expression of the type $$NameProc$$ = *"Procedure_Name"*, otherwise the call as a value of **$ProcName** variable returns *"UndefinedName"*. The next fragment represents source code of the procedural **$ProcName** variable along with typical examples of its application.

In[2530]:= $ProcName := Module[{d = "$$ArtKr$$", a, b, c, t = "", k},
a = ToString1[Stack[_]]; d = Flatten[StringPosition[a, d]][[1]];
b = Flatten[StringPosition[a, "$$NameProc$$"]][[1]];
If[b > d || ToString[b] == "", Return["UndefinedName"], k = b];

```
For[k = b, k <= d, k++, c = StringTake[a, {k, k}];
If[MemberQ[{",", "}"}, c], Break[], t = t <> c; Continue[]]];
{b = ToExpression[ToExpression[StringSplit[t, "="][[2]]]], HeadPF[b]}]
In[2531]:= Avz[x_, y_, z_] := Module[{$$NameProc$$ = "Avz", b}, b=$ProcName; x+y+z; b]
In[2532]:= Agn[x_, y_, z_] := Module[{b, $$NameProc$$ = "Agn"}, x+y+z; b=$ProcName; b]
In[2533]:= Ian[x_, y_, z_] := Module[{b, c, h}, x + y + z; b = $ProcName; b]
In[2534]:= Agn[49, 69, 74]
Out[2534]= {Agn, "Agn[x_, y_]"}
In[2535]:= Avz[49, 69, 74]
Out[2535]= {Avz, "Avz[x_, y_, z_]"}
In[2536]:= Ian[49, 69, 74]
Out[2536]= "UndefinedName"
```

This variable in a certain degree was wafted by the procedural *"procname"* variable of the *Maple* system which plays a quite essential part, first of all, in procedural programming of various problems of the system character.

The **BFMSubsQ** procedure represents a certain interest; the procedure call **BFMSubsQ[x]** returns the list of format {*True, Heading*} if definition of the user block or module *x* contains definitions of blocks, functions or modules, otherwise the list {*False, Heading*} is returned. In case of a *x* object of the same name of the above type the procedure call returns the *nested* list whose sublists have the *specified* format. On a *x* object of the type, different from {*Block, Module*}, the procedure call returns *False*. At that, the procedure call **BFMSubsQ[x, y]** with the second optional *y* argument – *an undefinite variable* – through *y* returns the list of format {*Heading, N*} where *N* defines number of blocks, functions and modules which enter into a subobject with the heading *Heading* of an object of the same *x* name. The fragment below represents source code of the **BFMSubsQ** procedure with the typical examples of its use.

```
In[2545]:= G[x_] := Module[{Vg, H7}, Vg[y_] := Module[{}, y^3]; H7[z_] := Module[{}, z^4];
x + Vg[x] + H7[x]]; G[x_, z_] := Module[{Vt, H, P}, Vt[t_] := Module[{}, t^3 + t^2];
H[t_] := Module[{}, t^4]; P[h_] := Module[{a = 6}, a^2 + Cos[h^2]]; Sin[x] + Vt[x] + H[z]*
P[x]]; H[t_] := Module[{P}, P[h_] := Module[{a = 6}, a^2 + h]]; T[x_] := Block[{a},
a[y_] := y^2; x + a[500]]; T[x_, y_] := Module[{a = 6}, x*y + a* Cos[t] + P[t]];
F[x_, y_] := Sin[x/y] + Cos[x*y]; SetAttributes[G, {Protected, Listable}]]
In[2546]:= BFMSubsQ[x_, y___] := Module[{a, b, c, d = {}, k = 1, p, h, g = {}},
If[! BlockModQ[x], False, {a, b} = Map[Flatten, {{PureDefinition[x]}, {HeadPF[x]}}];
For[k, k <= Length[a], k++, p = a[[k]]; p = StringReplace[p, b[[k]] <> " := " -> "", 1];
c = Select[ExtrVarsOfStr[p, 1], ! SystemQ[#] &];
h = Flatten[Map[StrSymbParity[p, " " <> #, "[", "]"] &, c]];
h = Select[h, SuffPref[#, Map[StringJoin[" " <> # <> "["] &, c], 1] && ! StringFreeQ[#, "_"] &];
AppendTo[g, {b[[k]], Length[h]}]; AppendTo[d, {If[h != {}, True, False], b[[k]]}]];
If[{y} != {} && ! HowAct[y], y = g]; If[Length[d] == 1, d[[1]], d]]]
In[2547]:= BFMSubsQ[H]
Out[2547]= {True, "H[t_]"}
In[2548]:= BFMSubsQ[G]
```

Out[2548]= {{True, "G[x_]"}, {True, "G[x_, z_]"}}
In[2549]:= **BFMSubsQ[T]**
Out[2549]= {{True, "T[x_]"}, {False, "T[x_, y_]"}}
In[2550]:= **Map[BFMSubsQ, {F, 590, Agn, Sin}]**
Out[2550]= {False, False, False, False}
In[2551]:= **BFMSubsQ[G, g70]**
Out[2551]= {{True, "G[x_]"}, {True, "G[x_, z_]"}}
In[2552]:= **g70**
Out[2552]= {{"G[x_]", 2}, {"G[x_, z_]", 3}}

The definition of the **BFMSubsQ** procedure along with the standard tools uses a number of our tools such as **BlockModQ, PureDefinition, HeadPF, HowAct, StrSymbParity, SuffPref, ExtrVarsOfStr** and **SystemQ** that are considered in the present book and in [30,33,50]. This procedure generalizes and extends the above our procedures **SubsProcQ** and **SubProcsQ ÷ SubProcsQ3**; the **BFMSubsQ** procedure is useful enough in a number of appendices which are connected with processing of procedures of type {*Module, Block*} and, first of all, of the system character.

On the basis of our 5 procedures **BlockModQ, HeadPF, Mapp, SubStrSymbolParity1** and **PureDefinition** which are considered in the present book, also the useful enough **ProcBody** procedure has been programmed whose call **ProcBody[x]** returns the body in string format of the user block, module or function *x* with heading. The procedure successfully processes also the objects of the same *x* name, returning the list of bodies of subobjects that compose a *x* object. The fragment below represents source code of the **ProcBody** procedure along with typical examples of its application.

In[2093]:= **ProcBody[x_ /; BlockFuncModQ[x]] :=**
Module[{c, p, d = {}, k = 1, a = Flatten[{PureDefinition[x]}], b = Flatten[{HeadPF[x]}], t},
While[k <= Length[a], p = StringReplace[a[[k]], b[[k]] <> " := " -> ""];
If[SuffPref[p, {"Block[", "Module["}, 1],
p = StringReplace[p, {"Block[" -> "", "Module[" -> ""}, 1];
AppendTo[d, StringReplace[p, SubStrSymbolParity1[p, "{", "}"][[1]] <> ", " -> "", 1]],
AppendTo[d, p]]; k++]; If[Length[d] == 1, d[[1]], d]]
In[2094]:= **Art[x_, y_, z_] := Module[{a = x + y + z, c = {m, n}, b = 90}, a^2 + a + b]**
In[2095]:= **ProcBody[Art]**
Out[2095]= "a^2 + a + b"
In[2096]:= **T[x_] := Block[{a}, a[y_] := y^2; x + a[590]]; T[x_, y_] := Module[{a = 590}, x*y + a]**
In[2097]:= **ProcBody[T]**
Out[2097]= {"a[y_] := y^2; x + a[590]", "x*y + a"}
In[2098]:= **F[x_, y_] := x + y + x*y; F[x_] := Sin[x] + x*Cos[x]; ProcBody[F]**
Out[2098]= {"x + y + x*y", "Sin[x] + x*Cos[x]"}

The **ProcBody** procedure plays a rather essential part in tasks of procedural programming dealing with various manipulations with definitions of classical functions and procedures of the type {*Block, Module*} along with components composing them.

In a number of the tasks caused by a processing of string representation of definitions of the user procedures and blocks the questions of partition of this representation onto two main components – procedure body and its frame with the final procedural "]" bracket a certain interest can represent. In this context and the **PartProc** procedure can be an quite useful. The procedure call **PartProc[x]** returns the two–element list, whose first element in string format represents a procedure frame with the final procedural "]" bracket; the place of the body of a procedure is taken by substring *"Procedure Body"* whereas the second element of the list in string format presents a procedure body *x*. At that, as a procedure frame the construction of the format "**Heading := Module[{***Locals*}, ...]" will be understood. In the case of erroneous situations the procedure call is returned unevaluated or returns *$Failed*. The fragment below represents source code of the **PartProc** procedure along with typical examples of its use.

In[2049]:= **PartProc[P_ /; BlockModQ[P]] := Module[{a = ProcBody[P]},**
{StringReplace[PureDefinition[P], a -> "Procedure Body", 1], a}]

In[2050]:= **Kr[x_, y_, z_] := Module[{a = x + y + z, b = 590}, b*a + a^2 + b]; PartProc[Kr]**
Out[2050]= {"Kr[x_, y_, z_] := Module[{a=x+y+z, b=590}, Procedure Body]", "b*a + a^2 + b"}

In[2054]:= **ReplaceProcBody[x_ /; BlockModQ[x], y_ /; StringQ[y]] :=**
ToExpression[StringReplace[PureDefinition[x], ProcBody[x] -> y]]

In[2055]:= **ReplaceProcBody[Kr, "b*(x + y + z)"]; Definition[Kr]**
Out[2055]= Kr[x_, y_, z_] := Module[{a = x + y + z, b = 590}, b*(x + y + z)]

An quite simple **ReplaceProcBody** function completes the previous fragment; the function call **ReplaceProcBody[x, y]** returns *Null*, providing replacement of the body of a block or a module *x* by a new *y* body which is given in the string format. Furthermore, the updated *x* object is activated in the current *Mathematica* session. Both the **PartProc** procedure, and the **ReplaceProcBody** function are based on the above **ProcBody** procedure. Exactly the given circumstance provides a quite simple algorithm of these means.

Except the means considered in books [28,30-33,50] a number of means for operating with the subprocedures is presented, here we will represent a useful procedure that analyzes the blocks and modules regarding presence in their definitions of subobjects of the type {*Block, Module*}. The procedure call **SubsProcs[x]** returns generally the nested list of definitions in string format of all subobjects of the type {*Block, Module*} whose definitions are in the body of an object *x* of type {*Block, Module*}. In addition, the first sublist determines subobjects of *Module* type, the second sublist defines subobjects of the *Block* type. In the presence of only one sublist the simple list is returned whereas in the presence of the *1*–element simple list its element is returned. At lack of subobjects of the above type the call **SubsProcs[x]** returns the *empty* list, i.e. {} whereas on a *x* object, different from {*Block, Module*}, the call **SubsProcs[x]** is returned unevaluated. The fragment represents source code of the **SubsProcs** procedure and the most typical examples of its application.

In[2580]:= **SubsProcs[x_ /; BlockModQ[x]] := Module[{d, s = {}, g, k = 1, p, h = "", v = 1,**
R = {}, Res = {}, a = PureDefinition[x], j, m = 1, n = 0, b = {" := Module[{", " := Block[{"},
c = ProcBody[x]},
For[v, v <= 2, v++, If[StringFreeQ[c, b[[v]]], Break[], d = StringPosition[c, b[[v]]]];
For[k, k <= Length[d], k++, j = d[[k]][[2]]; While[m != n, p = StringTake[c, {j, j}];
If[p == "[", m++; h = h <> p, If[p == "]", n++; h = h <> p, h = h <> p]]; j++];
AppendTo[Res, h]; m = 1; n = 0; h = ""];

```
Res = Map10[StringJoin, If[v == 1, " := Module[", " := Block["], Res];
g = Res; {Res, m, n, h} = {{}, 1, 0, "]"};
For[k = 1, k <= Length[d], k++, j = d[[k]][[1]] - 2;
While[m != n, p = StringTake[c, {j, j}];
If[p == "]", m++; h = p <> h, If[p == "[", n++; h = p <> h, h = p <> h]]; j--];
AppendTo[Res, h]; s = Append[s, j]; m = 1; n = 0; h = "]"];
Res = Map9[StringJoin, Res, g]; {g, h} = {Res, ""}; Res = {};
For[k = 1, k <= Length[s], k++, For[j = s[[k]], j >= 1, j--, p = StringTake[c, {j, j}];
If[p == " ", Break[], h = p <> h]]; AppendTo[Res, h]; h = ""];
AppendTo[R, Map9[StringJoin, Res, g]]; {Res, m, n, k, h, s} = {{}, 1, 0, 1, "", {}}];
R = If[Length[R] == 2, R, Flatten[R]]; If[Length[R] == 1, R[[1]], R]]
In[2581]:= P[x_, y_] := Module[{Art, Kr, Gs, Vg, a}, Art[c_, d_] := Module[{b}, c + d];
Vg[h_] := Block[{p = 90}, h^3 + p]; Kr[n_] := Module[{}, n^2]; Gs[z_] := Module[{}, x^3];
a = Art[x, y] + Kr[x*y]*Gs[x + y] + Vg[x*y]]
In[2582]:= P[90, 590]
Out[2582]= 2205216981000770
In[2583]:= SubsProcs[P]
Out[2583]= {{"Art[c_, d_] := Module[{b}, c + d]", "Kr[n_] := Module[{}, n^2]",
"Gs[z_] := Module[{}, x^3]"}, {"Vg[h_] := Block[{p = 90}, h^3 + p]"}}
In[2584]:= H[t_] := Module[{P}, P[h_] := Module[{a = 90}, a*h]; Cos[t] + P[t]]
In[2585]:= SubsProcs[H]
Out[2585]= "P[h_] := Module[{a = 90}, a*h]"
```

The **SubsProcs** procedure can be rather simply expanded, in particular, for determination of the nesting levels of subprocedures, and also onto unnamed subprocedures. The **SubsProcs** procedure significantly uses also our tools **BlockModQ**, **Map10**, **Map9**, **PureDefinition** and **ProcBody** considered above.

Moreover, in connection with the problem of nesting of the blocks and modules essential enough distinction between definitions of the nested procedures in the systems *Maple* and *Mathematica* takes place. So, in the *Maple* the definitions of subprocedures allow usage of lists of formal arguments identical with the main procedure containing them, while in the system *Mathematica* similar combination is *inadmissible*, causing in the course of evaluation of definition of the main procedure erroneous situations [30-33,50]. Generally speaking, the given circumstance causes certain inconveniences, demanding a special attentiveness in the process of programming of the nested procedures. In a certain measure the similar situation arises and in the case of crossing of lists of formal arguments of the main procedure and the local variables of its subprocedures while that is quite admissible in the *Maple* [10-22,25-27]. In this context the **SubsProcs** procedure can be applied quite successfully and to procedures containing subprocedures of the type {*Block, Module*}, on condition of nonempty crossing of the list of formal arguments of the main procedure along with the list of local variables of its subprocedures *(see also books on the systems Maple and Mathematica in* the collection [50]).

The following procedure provides return of the list of all blocks, functions and modules of the user packages uploaded into the current session, along with other active objects of the

Software Etudes in the Mathematica

specified types. The next fragment represents source code of the **ProcsAct** procedure along with examples of its applications.

In[3052]:= ProcsAct[] := Module[{a = Names["*"], b = Names["System`*"], c, d = {}, k = 1, j, h, t, g = {{"Module"}, {"Block"}, {"DynamicModule"}, {"Function"}, {"Others"}}},
c = Select[a, ! MemberQ[b, #] &];
c = Select[c, ToString[Definition[#]] != "Null" && ToString[Definition[#]] != "Attributes[" <> ToString[#] <> "] = {Temporary}" && ! MemberQ[{ToString[#] <> " = {Temporary}", ToString[#] <> " = {Temporary}"}, ToString[Definition[#]]] &];
For[k, k <= Length[c], k++, h = c[[k]]; ClearAll[t];
Quiet[ProcQ1[Symbol[h], t]]; t = Quiet[Check[t[[2]][[1]], $Failed]];
If[t === "Module", AppendTo[g[[1]], h], If[t === "Block", AppendTo[g[[2]], h],
If[t === "DynamicModule", AppendTo[g[[3]], h], If[QFunction[h], AppendTo[g[[4]], h],
AppendTo[g[[5]], h]]]]]]; g]

In[3053]:= ProcsAct[]
Out[3053]= {{"**Module**", "ActBFMuserQ", "ActCsProcFunc", "ActRemObj", "ActUcontexts", "AddMxFile", "Adrive",...}, {"**Block**"}, {"**DynamicModule**"},
{"**Function**", "AcNb", "ActBFM", "AssignL", "AttributesH", "BinaryListQ", "BlockQ1", ...},
{"**Others**", "Paclet", "PacletCheckUpdate", "PacletDirectoryAdd", ...}}

In[3054]:= Map[Length[#] – 1 &, %]
Out[3054]= {912, 0, 0, 220, 47}

The procedure call **ProcsAct[]** returns the nested 5-element list whose sublists define as the first element the types of objects in the context {*"Block"*, *"DynamicModule"*, *"Function"*, *"Module"*, *"Others"*} which are activated in the current session whear other elements define names of objects corresponding to the first element of type. Meanwhile, it should be noted the performance of the **ProcsAct** procedure quite significantly depends on quantity of both the user means and system means activated in the current session. Again it should be noted that in the *Mathematica* procedures local variables initially aren't considered as undefinite; but, it is possible to give them the status undefinite in the body of a procedure what visually illustrates the following rather transparent example, namely:

In[2547]:= A[x___] := Module[{a, b, c}, b = {Attributes[a], Definition[a]}; ClearAll[a];
c = {Attributes[a], Definition[a]}; {b, c}]
In[2548]:= A[]
Out[2548]= {{{Temporary}, Null}, {{}, Null}}

Such reception is used and in the **ProcsAct** procedure, providing return of the type of a *h* object through the second *t* argument – an undefinite variable – at the call **ProcQ1[*h*, *t*]**. In general, the **ProcsAct** procedure represents an quite certain interest for certain appendices, above all, in procedural programming of problems of system character.

The next fragment represents a rather useful function **NamesProc**, whose call **NamesProc[]** returns the sorted list of names of the user modules, functions and blocks activated in the current session. In certain cases the **NamesProc** function can appear as a rather useful tool. The following fragment represents source code of the **NamesProc** function with the typical examples of its application.

In[3617]:= NamesProc[] := Select[Sort[Names["`*"]], Quiet[BlockFuncModQ[#]] && ToString[Definition[#]] != "Null" && ToString[Definition[#]] != "Attributes[" <> ToString[#] <> "] = {Temporary}" && ! MemberQ[{ToString[#] <> " = {Temporary}", ToString[#] <> " = {Temporary}"}, ToString[Definition[#]]] &]

In[3618]:= NamesProc[]

Out[3618]= {A, Art, Df, F, G, H, Kr, NamesProc, ProcQ, Spos, Subs, Uprocs}

As one more example we will represent the **Uprocs** procedure which is a quite useful in the practical relation and also illustrates an approach to a certain expansion of standard means. The procedure call **Uprocs[]** returns simple or the nested list. In the first case in the current session the user procedures of any of 2 types {*Block, Module*} have been not activated, while in the second case the list elements returned by the **Uprocs** procedure are 3-element sublists whose first elements define names of the user blocks and modules activated in the current session, the second define their headings in string format, the third elements define the type {*Block | Module*} of procedures {*Block | Module*}. The following fragment represents source code of the **Uprocs** procedure and the most typical example of its application.

In[2448]:= Gs[x_] := Block[{a, b, c}, Evaluate[(a*x + x^b)/c]]
In[2449]:= Sv[x_] := Block[{y = a, h = b}, G[Pi/2, y*x]]
In[2450]:= H[x_] := Module[{y = a, h = b}, G[Pi/2, y*x]]
In[2451]:= P[x_, y_] := Block[{z = a, h = b}, G[Pi/2, (y*x)/z]]
In[2452]:= Bl[y_] := Block[{h = z}, G[Pi/2, y]]
In[2453]:= MM[x_, y_] := Module[{}, x + y]

In[2454]:= Uprocs[] := Module[{a, b, c, d, h, g, k, t1, t2},
a := "_$Art27_Kr20$_.txt"; {c, g} = {{}, {}}; Save[a, "`*"];
b := Map[ToString, Flatten[DeleteDuplicates[ReadList[a, String]]]];
For[k = 1, k <= Length[b], If[StringCount[First[b[[{k}]]], " := Module[{"] != 0 && StringTake[First[b[[{k}]]], {1}] != " " || StringCount[First[b[[{k}]]], " := Block[{"] != 0 && StringTake[First[b[[{k}]]], {1}] != " ", AppendTo[c, First[b[[{k}]]]], Null]; k = k + 1];
For[k = 1, k <= Length[c], d = Quiet[First[c[[{k}]]]];
h = Quiet[Symbol[StringTake[d, First[First[StringPosition[d, "["]]] - 1]]];
t1 = If[StringCount[d, " := Module[{"] != 0, Module, Block];
t2 = Quiet[StringTake[d, Last[First[StringPosition[d, "]"]]]]];
If[BlockModQ[h], AppendTo[g, {h, t2, t1}], Null]; k = k + 1]; DeleteFile[a]; g]

In[2455]:= Uprocs[]
Out[2455]= {{Bl, "Bl[y_]", Block}, {Gs, "Gs[x_]", Block}, {H, "H[x_]", Module}, {MM, "MM[x_, y_]", Module}, {P, "P[x_, y_]", Block}, {Sv, "Sv[x_]", Block}}

The procedure call **ExtrCall[*w*, *y*]** returns *True* if the user block, function, module *y* contains the calls of a block, a function or a module *w*, otherwise *False* is returned. If the call as a *w* argument defines the list of names of the blocks, functions or modules, the sublist of names of the blocks, functions or modules from the *w* whose calls enter into an *y* object is returned. In case if the first optional *w* argument is absent, then the call **ExtrCall[*y*]** returns the list of the system means whose calls enter into definition of the user function, block or module *y*.

The following fragment represents source code of the **ExtrCall** procedure with examples of its application.

In[2547]:= ExtrCall[z___, y_ /; BlockFuncModQ[y]] :=
Module[{b, p, g, x, a = Join[CharacterRange["A", "Z"], CharacterRange["a", "z"]]},
If[{z} == {}, p = PureDefinition[y]; If[ListQ[p], Return[$Failed]]; g = ExtrVarsOfStr[p, 2];
g = Select[g = Map[" " <> # <> "[" &, g], ! StringFreeQ[p, #] &];
g = Select[Map[If[SystemQ[p = StringTake[#, {2, -2}]], p] &, g], ! SameQ[#, Null] &];
If[Length[g] == 1, g[[1]], g], b[x_] := Module[{c = DefFunc3[ToString[y]], d, h, k = 1, t = {}},
h = StringPosition[c, ToString[x] <> "["];
If[h == {}, Return[False], d = Map[First, h]]; For[k, k <= Length[d], k++,
AppendTo[t, If[! MemberQ[a, StringTake[c, {d[[k]] - 1, d[[k]] - 1}]], True, False]]]; t[[1]]];
If[! ListQ[z], b[z], Select[z, b[#] &]]]]

In[2548]:= Map3[ExtrCall, Run, {Attrib, SearchDir, SearchFile, Df, Uprocs}]
Out[2548]= {True, False, True, False, False}
In[2549]:= ExtrCall[{Run, Write, Read, If, Return}, Attrib]
Out[2549]= {Run, Read, If, Return}
In[2550]:= Map[ExtrCall, {BlockFuncModQ, ExtrCall}]
Out[2550]= {{"Flatten", "If", "Module", "StringSplit"}, {"AppendTo", "CharacterRange", "For", "If", "Join", "Length", "Module", "Return", "Select", "StringJoin", "StringPosition", "StringTake"}}

The definition of the **ExtrCall** procedure along with the *standard* tools uses a number of our tools such as **BlockFuncModQ**, **PureDefinition**, **SystemQ**, **DefFunc3**, **ExtrVarsOfStr** which are considered in the present book and in [30,33,50]. The **ExtrCall** procedure has a number of useful appendices, above all, in problems of the system character. Meanwhile, it must be kept in mind that the **ExtrCall** procedure correctly processes only the *unique* objects, but not objects of the same name by returning on them *$Failed*.

In addition to earlier presented **TestArgsTypes** procedure providing the call of a specified block, function and module in such manner that returns result of this procedure call in the absence of inadmissible factual arguments or the list consisting from values {*True, False*} whose order corresponds to an order of the factual arguments at a call of the tested object of the specified type the **TestProcCalls** procedure is of a certain interest. The procedure call **TestProcCalls**[*x*, *y*] returns the nested list whose elements have format {*j*, "*n*", *True* | *False*} where *j* – the ordinal number of a formal argument, "*n*" – a formal argument in the string format, {*True* | *False*} – a value that determines admissibility *(True)* or inadmissibility *(False)* of a factual value determined by a *y* list and received by a formal argument {*j*, *n*} in a point of the call of the *x* object. Moreover, it is supposed that a *x* object defines the fixed number of formal arguments and the lengths of lists defining formal arguments and *y* are identical, otherwise the procedure call returns *$Failed*.

In[5057]:= TestProcCalls[x_ /; BlockFuncModQ[x], y_ /; ListQ[y]] :=
Module[{d, p, a = Args[x], b = {}, r, c = "_ /; ", k = 1, v},
a = Map[ToString1, If[NestListQ[a], a[[1]], a]];
If[Length[a] != Length[y] || MemberQ[Map[! StringFreeQ[#, "__"] &, a], True], $Failed,

```
v = If[NestListQ[v = Args[x, 90]], v[[1]], v]; For[k, k <= Length[a], k++, p = a[[k]];
AppendTo[b, If[StringTake[p, {-1, -1}] == "_", True, If[! StringFreeQ[p, c],
d = StringSplit[p, c]; r = ToExpression[d[[1]]];
{ToExpression[{d[[1]] <> "=" <> ToString1[y[[k]]], d[[2]]}][[2]],
ToExpression[d[[1]] <> "=" <> ToString[r]}][[1]], d = StringSplit[p, "_"];
ToString[Head[y[[k]]]] == d[[2]]]]]]; {k, d} = {1, Partition[Riffle[v, b], 2]};
While[k <= Length[d], PrependTo[d[[k]], k]; k++]; d]]
In[5058]:= TestProcCalls[SuffPref, {"IAN_RANS_RAC_90_74", "90_74", 2}]
Out[5058]= {{1, "S", True}, {2, "s", True}, {3, "n", True}}
In[5059]:= TestProcCalls[SuffPref, {"IAN_RANS_RAC_90_74", 590.90, 7.4}]
Out[5059]= {{1, "S", True}, {2, "s", False}, {3, "n", False}}
In[5060]:= F[x_String, y_/; IntegerQ[y]] := {x, y}; TestProcCalls[F, {6, "avz"}]
Out[5060]= {{1, "x", False}, {2, "y", False}}
```

The previous fragment represents source code of the **TestProcCalls** procedure with certain examples of its application. The procedure call **TestProcCalls**[*x*] successfully processes the unique objects and the objects of the same name; in addition, in the second case the first subobject from the list returned by the call **Definition**[*x*] is processed. At checking of the values on admissibility in the case of a formal argument of the format *"arg_ /; Test(arg)"* is required previously to calculate *arg* and only then to check its logical value *Test*[*arg*]. But this operation in body of the **TestProcCalls** procedure updates *arg* outside of the procedure what, in general, is inadmissible. Therefore, for elimination of this situation a quite simple reception *(that can be easily seen from the presented procedure code)* without redefinition of the global variables of the current session which have the same name with formal arguments of the tested *x* object of the type stated above has been used. The represented approach to the organization of algorithm of the procedure a quite answers the concept of so-called *robust* programming. In addition, the **TestProcCalls** procedure allows a number of modifications useful enough for procedural programming in the *Mathematica* system.

In contrast to the previous procedures the next **ProcActCallsQ** procedure tests existence in the user block, a function and a module *w* the existence of calls of the user means active in the current session which are provided by the usages. The procedure call **ProcActCallsQ**[*w*] returns *True* if definition of a module, a block or a function *w* contains the calls of means of the similar type, otherwise *False* is returned. Moreover, thru the second optional *y* argument – an undefinite variable – the procedure call **ProcActCallsQ**[*x*, *y*] returns the list of the user software whose calls are in the definition of a block, a function or a module *w*.

```
In[5070]:= ProcActCallsQ[x_ /; BlockFuncModQ[x], y___] :=
Module[{a, b, c = {}, d, k = 1, h = "::usage = "}, Save[b = "Art27$Kr20", x];
For[k, k < Infinity, k++, d = Read[b, String];
If[SameQ[d, EndOfFile], Break[], If[! StringFreeQ[d, h], AppendTo[c,
StringSplit[StringTake[d, {1, Flatten[StringPosition[d, h]][[1]] - 1}], " /: "][[1]]]]]];
DeleteFile[Close[b]]; c = Select[c, SymbolQ[#] &];
b = If[MemberQ[c, ToString[x]], Drop[c, 1], c];
If[{y} != {} && ! HowAct[{y}[[1]]], {y} = {b}]; If[b == {}, False, True]]
```

In[5071]:= {ProcActCallsQ[ProcQ, v74], v74}
Out[5071]= {True, {"SymbolQ", "SystemQ", "UnevaluatedQ", "ToString1", "StrDelEnds", "SuffPref", "ListStrToStr", "Definition2", "HowAct", "Mapp", "SysFuncQ", "Sequences", "Contexts1", "ClearAllAttributes", "SubsDel", "HeadPF", "BlockFuncModQ", "PureDefinition", "Map3", "MinusList"}}

In[5072]:= {ProcActCallsQ[ToString1, g69], g69}
Out[5072]= {True, {"StrDelEnds", "SuffPref"}}

In[5073]:= G[x_String, y_ /; ! HowAct[y]] := If[StringLength[x] == 90, y = x, y = x <> "590"];
{ProcActCallsQ[G, Gs1], Gs1}
Out[5073]= {True, {"HowAct", "ProtectedQ", "Attributes1"}}

In[5074]:= {ProcActCallsQ[StrStr, Sv1], Sv1}
Out[5074]= {False, {}}

In[5075]:= {ProcActCallsQ[ProcActCallsQ, Gsv3], Gsv3}
Out[5075]= {True, {"BlockFuncModQ", "PureDefinition", "UnevaluatedQ", "SymbolQ", "ToString1", "StrDelEnds", "SuffPref", "ListStrToStr", "Definition2", "HowAct", "SystemQ", "Mapp", "ProcQ", "ClearAllAttributes", "SubsDel", "Sequences", "HeadPF", "SysFuncQ", "Contexts1", "Map3", "MinusList"}}

In[5076]:= Fs[x_] := If[NestListQ[x], x, ToString1[x]]
In[5077]:= {ProcActCallsQ[Fs, v42], v42}
Out[5077]= {True, {"NestListQ", "ToString1", "StrDelEnds", "SuffPref"}}

The previous fragment gives source code of the **ProcActCallsQ** procedure along with some typical examples of its usage. The procedure is of an interest at the structural analysis of the user blocks, functions or modules; furthermore, the exhaustive analysis belongs only to the user tools active in the current session of the system and provided by the standard usage.

In certain cases the question of definition of all means used by the user block, function or module which are activated in the current session including tools for which the usage are missing represents a certain interest. This problem is solved by the **ProcContent** procedure which provides the analysis of an activated x object of the above type with correct heading, concerning the existence in its definition of the user tools both internal, and external, which are supplied with usages or without them. The procedure call **ProcContent**[x] returns the nested 3-element list whose first element defines the name of a block, function or module x, the second element determines the list of names of all external blocks, functions or modules used by the x object whereas the third element determines the list of names of the internal blocks, functions or modules defined in body of the x object. The next fragment represents source code of the **ProcContent** procedure along with typical examples of its application.

In[5080]:= Kr[x_, y_] := Plus[x, y]; Art[x_] := Module[{a=90, b = 590, c = ToString1[x], d, g}, c = Kr[a, b]; d[y_] := Module[{}, y]; g[z_] := Block[{}, z + 90]; c];
V[x_] := Module[{c = StrStr[x], d, g}, G[a, b]; d[y_] := Module[{}, y]; g[z_] := Block[{}, z]; c]

In[5081]:= ProcContent[x_ /; BlockFuncModQ[x]] := Module[{a, f, b = SubProcs[x][[1]]}, Map[ClearAll, SubProcs[x][[2]]];
f[y_] := Module[{a1 = "$Art2720Kr$", b1 = "", c = {y}, d, h = "", p}, Save[a1, y];
While[! SameQ[b1, EndOfFile], b1 = Read[a1, String];
If[! MemberQ[{" ", "EndOfFile"}, ToString[b1]], h = h <> ToString[b1]; Continue[], d = Flatten[StringPosition[h, " := ", 1]]];

If[d == {}, h = ""; Continue[], p = StringTake[h, {1, d[[1]] - 1}];
If[! SameQ[Quiet[ToExpression[p]], $Failed], AppendTo[c, StringTake[p, {1,
Flatten[StringPosition[p, "[", 1]][[1]] - 1}]];
h = "", Null]]]; a1 = Map[ToExpression, {DeleteFile[Close[a1]], c}[[2]]];
DeleteDuplicates[a1]]; a = f[x]; {x, If[Length[a] > 1, a[[2 ;; -1]], {}],
If[Length[b] > 1, Map[ToExpression, Map[HeadName, b[[2 ;; -1]]]], {}]}]

In[5082]:= ProcContent[V]
Out[5082]= {V, {StrStr}, {d, g}}
In[5083]:= ProcContent[Art]
Out[5083]= {Art, {ToString1, StrDelEnds, SuffPref, Kr}, {d, g}}
In[5084]:= ProcContent[ToString1]
Out[5084]= {ToString1, {StrDelEnds, SuffPref}, {}}
In[5085]:= J[x_] := Module[{a = 5, b = 590, c, d, g, Gt}, c = Gt[a, b]; d[y_] := Module[{}, y];
g[z_] := Block[{a = 6, b = 9}, z/74]; ToString1[x] <> StrStr[x]]
In[5086]:= ProcContent[J]
Out[5086]= {J, {ToString1, StrDelEnds, SuffPref, StrStr}, {d, g}}

At that, the **ProcContent** procedure along with standard functions enough essentially uses our procedures **BlockFuncModQ** and **SubProcs** together with a simple function, whose call **HeadName**[*x*] returns the name of a *x* heading in the string format. The given means were considered in the present book above.

The next procedure provides the analysis of means of a package uploaded into the current session regarding existence in their definitions of calls of the tools supplied with usage. The procedure call **CallsInMean**[*x*] returns the 2-element list, whose the first element is *x* – the symbol defining the tools name of a package whereas the second element – the list of names of the tools that enter in definition of *x* symbol. In turn, the **CallsInMeansPackage** which is based on the previous procedure provides the analysis of all means of the package given by a *x* context and uploaded into the current session, regarding existence in their definitions of calls of the means supplied with references.

The call **CallsInMeansPackage**[*x*] returns the 3-element list, whose the first element defines the list of names of the tools which aren't containing such calls, the second element – the list of names of tools containing such calls, and the 3rd element – list returned by the procedure call **CallsInMean** for the tools having the maximum number of such calls occurrences. The next fragment represents source codes of the above two procedures with examples of their application.

In[5954]:= CallsInMean[x_ /; SymbolQ[x]] := Module[{a = Context[x], b, c},
If[! MemberQ[$Packages[[1 ;; -3]], a], $Failed,
b=StringCases[ToString[FullDefinition[x]], "\n \n" ~~ X__ ~~ " /: " ~~ X__ ~~ "::usage ="];
{ToString[x], Select[Sort[DeleteDuplicates[Map[StringTake[#,
{4, Flatten[StringPosition[#, " /: "]][[1]] - 1}] &, b]]], # != ToString[x] &]}]]
In[5955]:= CallsInMean[DelOfPackage]
Out[5955]= {"DelOfPackage", {"ContextQ", "StrDelEnds", "SuffPref", "SymbolQ",
"ToString1"}}

In[5982]:= CallsInMeansPackage[x_ /; ContextQ[x]] := Module[{a = {{}, {}}, b, c, d = 0},
If[! MemberQ[$Packages[[1 ;; –3]], x], $Failed, Map[{b = Quiet[CallsInMean[#]],
If[b === $Failed, b = Null, If[b[[2]] == {}, AppendTo[a[[1]], #], AppendTo[a[[2]], #]],
If[Set[c, Length[b[[2]]]] > d, d = c, Null]]} &, CNames[x]]; If[a == {{}, {}}, {}, {a, b}]]]

In[5983]:= CallsInMeansPackage["AladjevProcedures`"]
Out[2983]= {{{"AcNb", "Adrive", "AllContexts", "AssignL", "AtomicQ", ... }}}
In[2984]:= Map[Length, {%[[1]][[1]], %[[1]][[2]], %[[2]][[2]]}]
Out[2984]= {217, 906, 0}

The function call **ProcFuncCS[]** returns the nested three-element list whose sublists define names in string format according of the user blocks, modules or functions whose definitions were evaluated in the current session. The fragment represents source code of the function **ProcFuncCS** together with a typical example of its application.

In[2532]:= ProcFuncCS[]:= Quiet[Map3[Select, Names["`*"], {BlockQ[#] &, FunctionQ[#] &, ModuleQ[Symbol[#]] &}]]

In[2533]:= G[x_String, y_ /; ! HowAct[y]] := If[StringLength[x] == 90, y = x, y = x <> "590"];
GS[x_] := Block[{a = 90, b = 590}, x]; F1[x_] := If[NestListQ[x], x, ToString1[x]];
GG[y_] := Module[{a = 90, b = 590, c = 2016, d = {42, 47, 67}}, y]; ProcFuncCS[]
Out[2533]= {{"GS"}, {"F1", "G"}, {"GG"}}

The operator **HeadCompose[a, b, c, d]** that was in the previous releases of the system *(now the operator isn't documented)* returns the composition of the identifiers in the next format:

In[2545]:= HeadCompose[G69, x, y, z]
Out[2545]= G69[x][y][z]

Such format, for example, can be useful in various functional transformations. The operator can be useful enough also at the organization of the user functions, allowing to transfer in quality of the actual values for their formal arguments the headings of functions along with their formal arguments. At the same time, this tool in general doesn't represent an especial interest what induced its bringing outside the system. On the other hand, it is possible to represent a certain analog of this means which has significantly larger applied interest, the **FunCompose** procedure whose call **FunCompose[L, x]** allows to create the nested functions from a *L* list of functions, modules or blocks from an expression given by its 2nd *x* argument. The following a quite simple fragment rather visually illustrates the aforesaid.

In[2551]:= FunCompose[t_ /; ListQ[t], x_] := Module[{a, k = 2}, a = t[[1]]@x;
For[k, k <= Length[t], k++, a = t[[k]]@a]; a]

In[2552]:= FunCompose[{F, G, H, T, W, Q, V, U}, Sin[z]]
Out[2552]= U[V[Q[W[T[H[G[F[Sin[z]]]]]]]]]
In[2553]:= {FunCompose[{Sin, Cos, Log}, 74.42], FunCompose[{Sin, Cos, Tan, Sqrt}, 59.90]}
Out[2553]= {–0.392687, 1.21894}

For organization of transfering of identifiers of functions as the actual values it is possible to use constructions, for example, of the following rather simple formats, namely:

In[2555]:= F[x_] := x^3; SV[z_] := F@z + z^3; VSV[Id_, z_] := Module[{}, Id@(z^2 + 6)];
{VSV[F, h], SV[47]}
Out[2555]= {(6 + h^2)^3, 207646}

along with a number of similar useful enough constructions.

For temporary removal from the current session of the **Mathematica** of the user functions, blocks or modules quite useful **DelRestPF** procedure serves whose source code along with typical examples of application represents the following fragment.

In[2579]:= F[x_] := x^3; SV[z_] := F@z + z^3; VSV[Id_, z_] := Module[{}, Id@(z^2 + 6)];
F[x_, y_] := x + y; SetAttributes[F, {Protected, Listable}]; SetAttributes[SV, Listable]

In[2580]:= DelRestPF[r_ /; MemberQ[{"d", "r"}, r], x__] := Module[{b, c, p, k = 1,
f = "$Art27Kr20$.mx", a = Quiet[Select[{x}, BlockFuncModQ[#] &]]},
If[r == "d", b = Map[Definition2, a]; Save[f, b];
Map[ClearAllAttributes, a]; Map[Remove, a];, c = Get[f]; DeleteFile[f];
For[k, k <= Length[c], k++, p = c[[k]]; ToExpression[p[[1 ;; -2]]];
ToExpression["SetAttributes[" <> StringTake[p[[1]], {1, Flatten[StringPosition[p[[1]],
"["]][[1]] - 1}] <> "," <> ToString[p[[-1]]] <> "]"]]]]

In[2581]:= DelRestPF["d", F, SV, VSV]
In[2582]:= Map[Definition2, {F, SV, VSV}]
Out[2582]= {Definition2[F], Definition2[SV], Definition2[VSV]}
In[2583]:= DelRestPF["r"]
In[2584]:= Map[Definition2, {F, SV, VSV}]
Out[2584]= {{"F[x_] := x^3", "F[x_, y_] := x + y", {Listable, Protected}},
{"SV[z_] := F[z] + z^3", {Listable}}, {"VSV[Id_, z_] := Module[{}, Id[z^2 + 6]]", {}}}

In[2585]:= DelRestPF1[r_ /; MemberQ[{"d", "r"}, r], f_ /; StringQ[f], x__] :=
Module[{a = Quiet[Select[{x}, BlockFuncModQ[#] &]], b, c, p, k = 1},
If[r == "d", b = Map[Definition2, a]; Save[f, b];
Map[ClearAllAttributes, a]; Map[Remove, a];, c = Get[f]; DeleteFile[f];
For[k, k <= Length[c], k++, p = c[[k]]; ToExpression[p[[1 ;; -2]]];
ToExpression["SetAttributes[" <> StringTake[p[[1]], {1, Flatten[StringPosition[p[[1]],
"["]][[1]] - 1}] <> "," <> ToString[p[[-1]]] <> "]"]]]]

In[2586]:= DelRestPF1["d", "C:\\Temp\\Tallinn", F, SV, VSV]
In[2587]:= Map[Definition2, {F, SV, VSV}]
Out[2587]= {Definition2[F], Definition2[SV], Definition2[VSV]}
In[2588]:= DelRestPF1["r", "C:\\Temp\\Tallinn"]
In[2589]:= Map[Definition2, {F, SV, VSV}]
Out[2589]= {{"F[x_] := x^3", "F[x_, y_] := x + y", {Listable, Protected}},
{"SV[z_] := F[z] + z^3", {Listable}}, {"VSV[Id_, z_] := Module[{}, Id[z^2 + 6]]", {}}}

The call **DelRestPF["*d*", *x, y, ...*]** returns *Null*, i.e. nothing, deleting from the current session the user blocks, functions and modules {*x, y,...*} whereas the subsequent call **DelRestPF["*r*"]** returns *Null*, i.e. *nothing*, restoring their availability in the current session or in other session with preservation of the options and attributes ascribed to them. The procedure is a rather useful in a number of applications, first of all, of system character. Moreover, the procedure is oriented onto work only with one list of objects, creating only a fixed file with the saved objects. Meanwhile, a very simple modification of the procedure provides its expansion on any number of lists of the user blocks, functions or modules, allowing temporarily to delete them at any moments from the current session with the subsequent their restoration in the current session or other session of the system. So, the previous fragment is completed by *1* of similar useful modifications that has a number of useful use of the system character.

The procedure call **DelRestPF1["d", *w*, *x*, *y,z,...*]** returns *Null*, i.e. nothing, deleting from the current session the user blocks, functions and modules {*x, y, z, ...*} with saving of them in a *w* file, whereas the subsequent call **DelRestPF1["r", *w*]** returns *Null*, i.e. nothing, restoring their availability in the current session or in other session from the *w* file with preservation of the options and attributes ascribed to them.

The built-in *Math*-language for programming of the branching algorithms along with the "If" offer allows use of unconditional transitions on the basis of the **Goto** function which is encoded in the **Goto[*h*]** form, unconditionally passing control into a point defined by the **Label[*h*]** construction. As a rule, the **Goto** function is used the in procedural constructions, however unlike the built-in *goto*-function of the *Maple* system it can be used also in the input constructions of the *Mathematica*. Moreover, as a **Label** any correct expression is allowed, including also sequence of expressions whose the last expression defines actually label; in addition, the **Label** concerning a module can be both the global variable, and the local variable. Meanwhile, in order to avoid any possible misunderstandings, the **Label** is recommended to be defined as a local variable because the global **Label** calculated outside of a module is always acceptable for the module, however calculated in the module body quite can distort calculations outside of the module. At that, multiplicity of occurrences of identical **Goto** functions into a procedure is a quite naturally and is defined by the realized algorithm while with the corresponding tags **Label** the similar situation, *generally speaking*, is inadmissible; in addition, it is not recognized at evaluation of a procedure definition and even at a stage of its performance, often substantially distorting the planned task algorithm. In this case only point of the module body which is marked by the first such **Label** receives the control. Moreover, it must be kept in mind that lack of a **Label[*a*]** for the corresponding call **Goto[*a*]** in a block or module at a stage of evaluation of its definitions isn't recognized, however only at the time of performance with the real appeal to such **Goto[*a*]**. The rather interesting examples illustrating the told can be found in our books [28-33,50].

In this connection the **GotoLabel** procedure can represent a certain interest the call of which **GotoLabel[*P*]** allows to analyse a procedure *P* on the subject of formal correctness of use of **Goto** functions and the **Label** tags corresponding to them. The procedure call **GotoLabel[*P*]** returns the nested 3-element list whose first element defines the list of all **Goto** functions used by a *P* module, the *second* element defines the list of all tags *(without their multiplicity)*, the third element determines the list, whose sublists determine **Goto** functions with the tags corresponding to them *(at that, as the first elements of these sublists the calls of the* **Goto** *function appear, whereas multiplicities of functions and tags remain)*. The following fragment represents source code of the **GotoLabel** procedure along with typical examples of its application.

In[2540]:= GotoLabel[x_ /; BlockModQ[x]] :=
Module[{b, c = {{}, {}, {}}, d, p, k = 1, j, h, v = {}, t, a = Flatten[{PureDefinition[x]}][[1]]},
b = ExtrVarsOfStr[a, 1]; b = DeleteDuplicates[Select[b, MemberQ[{"Label", "Goto"}, #] &]];
If[b == {}, c, d = StringPosition[a, Map[" " <> # <> "[" &, {"Label", "Goto"}]];
t = StringLength[a]; For[k, k <= Length[d], k++, p = d[[k]]; h = ""; j = p[[2]];

While[j <= t, h = h <> StringTake[a, {j, j}];
If[StringCount[h, "["] == StringCount[h, "]"], AppendTo[v, StringTake[a, {p[[1]] + 1, p[[2]] - 1}] <> h]; Break[]]; j++]];
h = DeleteDuplicates[v]; {Select[h, SuffPref[#, "Goto", 1] &], Select[h, SuffPref[#, "Label", 1] &], Gather[Sort[v], #1 == StringReplace[#2, "Label[" -> "Goto[", 1] &]}]]

In[2541]:= ArtKr[x_ /; IntegerQ[x]] := Module[{prime, agn}, If[PrimeQ[x], Goto[9; prime], If[OddQ[x], Goto[agn], Goto[Sin]]]; Label[9; prime]; Print[x^2]; Goto[Sin]; Print[NextPrime[x]]; Goto[Sin]; Label[9; prime]; Null]

In[2542]:= Kr[x_ /; IntegerQ[x]] := Module[{prime, agn, y}, If[PrimeQ[x], Goto[prime], If[OddQ[x], Goto[agn], Goto[agn]]]; Label[9; prime]; y = x^2; Goto[agn]; Label[agn]; y = NextPrime[x]; Label[agn]; y]

In[2543]:= **GotoLabel[ArtKr]**

Out[2543]= {{"Goto[9; prime]", "Goto[agn]", "Goto[Sin]"}, {"Label[9; prime]"}, {{"Goto[9; prime]", "Label[9; prime]", "Label[9; prime]"}, {"Goto[agn]"}, {"Goto[Sin]", "Goto[Sin]", "Goto[Sin]"}}}

In[2544]:= **GotoLabel[Kr]**

Out[2544]= {{"Goto[prime]", "Goto[agn]"}, {"Label[9; prime]", "Label[agn]"}, {{"Goto[agn]", "Goto[agn]", "Goto[agn]", "Label[agn]", "Label[agn]"}, {"Goto[prime]"}, {"Label[9; prime]"}}}

In[2545]:= **Map[GotoLabel, {GotoLabel, TestArgsTypes, CallsInMean}]**

Out[2545]= {{{}, {}, {}}, {{}, {}, {}}, {{}, {}, {}}}

In[2546]:= **Map[GotoLabel, {SearchDir, StrDelEnds, OP, BootDrive}]**

Out[2546]= {{{}, {}, {}}, {{}, {}, {}}, {{"Goto[ArtKr]"}, {"Label[ArtKr]"}, {{"Goto[ArtKr]", "Label[ArtKr]"}}}, {{"Goto[avz]"}, {"Label[avz]"}, {{"Goto[avz]", "Goto[avz]", "Goto[avz]", "Label[avz]"}}}}

We will note that existence of a nested list with the third sublist containing **Goto**-functions without tags corresponding to them, in the result returned by the means call **GotoLabel[P]** not necessarily speaks about existence of the function calls **Goto[x]** for which not exists any **Label[x]** tag. It can be, for example, in the case of generation of a value depending on some condition.

In[2550]:= **Av[x_ /; IntegerQ[x], y_Integer, p_ /; MemberQ[{1, 2, 3}, p]] := Module[{}, Goto[p]; Label[1]; Return[x + y]; Label[2]; Return[N[x/y]]; Label[3]; Return[x*y]]**

In[2551]:= **Map[Av[590, 90, #] &, {1, 2, 3, 4}]**

Out[2551]= {680, 6.55556, 53100, Av[590, 90, 4]}

In[2552]:= **GotoLabel[Av]**

Out[2552]= {{"Goto[p]"}, {"Label[1]", "Label[2]", "Label[3]"}, {{"Goto[p]"}, {"Label[1]"}, {"Label[2]"}, {"Label[3]"}}}

For example, according to simple example of the previous fragment the call **GotoLabel[Av]** contains {"Goto[p]"} in the third sublist what, at first sight, it would be possible to consider as a certain impropriety of the corresponding call of **Goto** function. However, all the matter is that a value of the actual *p* argument in the call *Av[x,y,p]* and defines a tag, really existing in definition of the procedure, i.e. **Label[p]**. Therefore, the **GotoLabel** procedure only at the formal level analyzes existence of the **Goto** functions, *"incorrect"* from its point of view with *"excess"* tags. Whereas refinement of the results received on the basis of a call **GotoLabel[P]** lies on the user, above all, by the means of analysis of accordance of source code of the *P* to the correctness of the required algorithm.

The structured paradigm of programming doesn't assume application in programs of the *goto* constructions allowing to transfer control from bottom to top. At the same time, in some cases the use of **Goto** function is effective, in particular, at needing of embedding into the *Mathematica* environment of a program which uses unconditional transitions on the basis of the *goto* offer. For example, *Fortran* programs can be adduced as a typical example that are very widespread in the scientific appendices. From our experience follows, that the use of **Goto** function allowed significantly to simplify the embedding into the *Mathematica* system of a number of rather large *Fortran* programs relating to engineering and physical applications which very widely use the *goto* constructions. Right there it should be noted that from our standpoint the **Goto** function of the *Mathematica* system is more preferable, than *goto* function of the *Maple* system in respect of efficiency in the light of application in procedural programming of various appendices, including also appendices of the system character.

As it was already noted, the *Mathematica* allows existence of the objects of the same name with various headings which identify objects, but not their names. The standard **Definition** function along with our procedures **Definition2, PureDefinition,** and others by name of an object allow to receive definitions of all active subobjects in the current session with *identical* names, but with various headings. Therefore there is quite specific problem of removal from the current *Mathematica* session not of all objects with a concrete name, but only subobjects with concrete headings.

The **RemovePF** procedure solves the problem; its call **RemovePF[*x*]** returns *Null*, providing removal from the current session of the objects with *x* headings which are determined by a factual *x* argument *(a heading in string format or their list)*. In case of the incorrect headings defined by means of *x* argument, the procedure call **RemovePF[*x*]** is returned unevaluated. The procedure is an quite useful in procedural programming. The next fragment represents source code of the **RemovePF** procedure with examples of its application for removing of subobjects at the objects of the same name.

In[2620]:= **RemovePF[x_/; HeadingQ1[x] || ListQ[x] &&**
AllTrue[Map[HeadingQ1, x], TrueQ]] :=
Module[{b, c = {}, d, p, k = 1, j, a = Map[StandHead, DeleteDuplicates[Map[HeadName,
Flatten[{x}]]]]}, b = Map[If[UnevaluatedQ[Definition2, #], {"90", {}},
Definition2[#]] &, a]; For[k, k <= Length[a], k++, p = b[[k]];
AppendTo[c, Select[Flatten[{p[[1 ;; -2]], "SetAttributes[" <> a[[k]] <> ", " <>
ToString[p[[-1]]] <> "]"}], ! SuffPref[#, Map[StandHead, x], 1] &]]];
Map[ClearAllAttributes, a]; Map[Remove, a]; Map[ToExpression, c];
a = Definition2[b = HeadName[x]]; If[a[[1]] === "Undefined",
ToExpression["ClearAttributes[" <> b <> "," <> ToString[a[[2]]] <> "]"], Null]]]

In[2621]:= **M[x_/; SameQ[x, "avz"], y_] := Module[{a, b, c}, y];**
F[x_, y_Integer] := x + y; F[x_, y_] := x + y; F[x_, y_, z_] := x*y*z;
M[x_/; x == "avz"] := Module[{a, b, c}, x]; M[x_, y_, z_] := x*y*z;
M[x_/; IntegerQ[x], y_String] := Module[{a, b, c}, x];

M[x_, y_] := Module[{a, b, c}, "agn"; x + y]; M[x_String] := x;
M[x_ /; ListQ[x], y_] := Block[{a, b, c}, "agn"; Length[x] + y];
SetAttributes[M, {Flat, Protected}]; SetAttributes[F, Listable]
In[2622]:= **Definition[M]**
Out[2622]= Attributes[M] = {Flat, Protected}
"M[x_ /; x === \"avz\", y_] := Module[{a, b, c}, y]"
"M[x_ /; x == \"avz\"] := Module[{a, b, c}, x]"
"M[x_, y_, z_] := x*y*z"
"M[x_ /; IntegerQ[x], y_String] := Module[{a, b, c}, x]"
"M[x_ /; ListQ[x], y_] := Block[{a, b, c}, \"agn\"; Length[x] + y]"
"M[x_, y_] := Module[{a, b, c}, \"agn\"; x + y]"
"M[x_String] := x"
In[2623]:= **Definition[F]**
Out[2623]= Attributes[F] = {Listable}
"F[x_, y_Integer] := x + y"
"F[x_, y_] := x + y"
"F[x_, y_, z_] := x*y*z"
In[2624]:= **RemovePF[{"M[x_, y_]", "F[x_, y_, z_]", "M[x_String]", "M[x_, y_, z_]",
"F[x_, y_Integer]", "v[t_]"}]**
In[2625]:= **Definition[M]**
Out[2625]= Attributes[M] = {Flat, Protected}
"M[x_ /; x === \"avz\", y_] := Module[{a, b, c}, y]"
"M[x_ /; x == \"avz\"] := Module[{a, b, c}, x]"
"M[x_ /; IntegerQ[x], y_String] := Module[{a, b, c}, x]"
"M[x_ /; ListQ[x], y_] := Block[{a, b, c}, \"agn\"; Length[x] + y]"
In[2626]:= **Definition[F]**
Out[2626]= Attributes[F] = {Listable}
"F[x_, y_] := x + y"
In[2627]:= **Definition[W]**
Out[2627]= Null

For ensuring of correct uploading of the user block, function or module *x* into the current session on condition of possible need of additional reloading in the current session also of non-standard blocks, functions, modules whose calls are used in *x* object, the **CallsInProc** procedure can be useful enough, whose call **CallsInProc[*x*]** returns the list of all standard functions, external and internal blocks, functions or modules, whose calls are used by the *x* object of the specified type. The fragment below represents source code of the **CallsInProc** procedure along with the typical examples of its application.

In[2660]:= **CallsInProc[P_ /; BlockFuncModQ[P]] :=
Module[{b, c = {}, k = 1, a = ToString[FullDefinition[P]], TN},
TN[S_ /; StringQ[S], L_ /; ListQ[L] && Length[Select[L, IntegerQ[#] &]] == Length[L] &&
L != {}] := Module[{a1 = "", c1, b1 = {}, k1, p = 1},
For[p, p <= Length[L], p++, For[k1 = L[[p]] - 1, k1 != 0, k1--, c1 = StringTake[S, {k1, k1}];
a1 = c1 <> a1; If[c1 === " ", a1 = StringTake[a1, {2, -1}];
If[Quiet[Check[Symbol[a1], False]] === False, a1 = ""; Break[], AppendTo[b1, a1];**

a1 = ""; Break[]]]]]; b1];
b = TN[a, b = DeleteDuplicates[Flatten[StringPosition[a, "["]]]][[2 ;; −1]];
b = Sort[DeleteDuplicates[Select[b, StringFreeQ[#, "`"] &&
! MemberQ[{"Block", ToString[P], "Module"}, #] &&
ToString[Definition[#]] != "Null" &]]]; k = Select[b, SystemQ[#] &];
c = MinusList[b, Flatten[{k, ToString[P]}]]; {k, c, DeleteDuplicates[Map[Context, c]]}]

In[2661]:= CallsInProc[StringDependQ]
Out[2661]= {{"Attributes", "Flatten", "HoldPattern", "If", "Length", "ListQ", "Select", "StringFreeQ", "StringQ"}, {"Attributes1", "HowAct", "ListStrQ", "ProtectedQ"}, {"AladjevProcedures`"}}

In[2662]:= G[x_] := ToString1[x]; CallsInProc[G]
Out[2662]= {{"Close", "DeleteDuplicates", "Flatten", "For", "If", "MemberQ", "Read", "Return", "StringLength", "StringQ", "StringTake", "StringTrim", "While", "Write"}, {"StrDelEnds", "SuffPref", "ToString1"}, {"AladjevProcedures`"}}

The procedure call **CallsInProc[*x*]** returns the nested 3-element list whose the first element defines the list of standard functions, the second element determines the list of external and internal functions, blocks and modules of the user, whose calls uses a *x* object whereas the third element defines the list of contexts which correspond to the user tools and which are used by the *x* object. The **CallsInProc** procedure represents essential interest for analysis of the user means regarding existence of calls in them of both the user means, and the system software.

The following **CallsInFuncBlockMod** procedure serves for calculation of calls of the means entering the definition of a *x* object of the type {*Block, Function, Module*}; at the same time, the object can be both unique, and of the same name. Definition of **CallsInFuncBlockMod** procedure is preceded by a procedure whose call **FuncBlockModQ1[*x*]** returns *True* if the *x* determines an object of the type {*Block, Function, Module*}; otherwise, *False* is returned; at the same time, the *x* object can be both unique, and of the same name. In case of an object of the same name all its components should have of type {*Block, Function, Module*}, otherwise *False* is returned.

The procedure call **CallsInFuncBlockMod[*x*]** returns as a rule the nested list of the format {*x1, x2, ..., xn*} where *xj* sublists define the calls of the means entering in definitions of the components of the type {*Block, Function, Module*} which compose an object *x* of the same name. At the same time, sublists of the returned list are also nested lists whose first element defines the list of names in string format of system tools while the second element defines the nested sublists whose elements define the grouped names of means, different from the system tools, with the contexts attributed to them. While the call **CallsInFuncBlockMod[*x, y*]** with the second optional *y* argument – an undefinite symbol – through it additionally returns as a rule the nested list whose the sorted sublists define the grouped names of the indexed means, different from the system tools, with the contexts attributed to them. In case of impossibility of determination of a context the identifier *"Undefined"* is identified. On the *x* argument different from {*Block, Function, Module*} the call is returned unevaluated. The fragment below represents the source code of the **CallsInFuncBlockMod** procedure along with the most typical examples of its application.

In[3862]:= S[x_] := x*Sin[x]/Cos[x]; S[x_, y_] := Module[{}, N[x*y]];
S[x_ /; IntegerQ[x], y_ /; StringStringQ[y]] := N[Sin[x]]*StringLength[y];
S[x_ /; StringQ[x], y_ /; IntegerQ[y]] := StrStr[x] <> ToString1[y] <> m[x*y];
S[x_, y_List, z_] := Module[{a = {42, 47, 67, 28}}, z*Map[Length, {a[[1 ;; 3]], y[[1 ;; 6]]}]];
m := "agn"; ContextToSymbol1["m", "avz`"]

In[3863]:= FuncBlockModQ1[x_] := Module[{a}, ClearAll[a];
If[UnevaluatedQ[FuncBlockModQ[x, a]] || ! MemberQ[{"Block", "Function", "Module", "Multiple"}, a], False, True]]

In[3864]:= FuncBlockModQ1[S]
Out[3864]= True

In[3865]:= CallsInFuncBlockMod[x_ /; FuncBlockModQ1[x]] :=
Module[{a = Flatten[{PureDefinition[x]}], b = {}, c, d, d1, h, p = {}, f},
c = Map[ExtrVarsOfStr[#, 2] &, a];
f[t_] := If[t === {{}}, {}, If[NestListQ[t] && Length[t] == 1, t[[1]], t]];
c = Map[Complement[#, {ToString[x], "Block", "Module"}] &, c];
If[{y} != {} && ! HowAct[y],
Do[AppendTo[p, d1 = Select[c[[j]], ! StringFreeQ[a[[j]], # <> "[["] &];
d1 = Map[{#, Quiet[Check[Context[#], "Undefined"]]} &, d1];
d1 = Gather[d1, #1[[2]] === #2[[2]] &]; d1 = Mapp[Flatten, d1, 1];
d1 = Map[Join[Sort[Replace[#[[1 ;; -2]], #[[-1]] -> Nothing, All]], {#[[-1]]}] &, d1]],
{j, 1, Length[c]}]; y = Map[f, p], 74];
Do[AppendTo[b, d = Select[c[[j]], StringFreeQ[a[[j]], # <> "[["] &&
! StringFreeQ[a[[j]], # <> "["] &];
h = Select[d, Quiet[SystemQ[#]] &]; d = Complement[d, h];
d = Map[{#, Quiet[Check[Context[#], "Undefined"]]} &, d];
d = Gather[d, #1[[2]] === #2[[2]] &]; d = Mapp[Flatten, d, 1];
d = Map[Join[Sort[Replace[#[[1 ;; -2]], #[[-1]] -> Nothing, All]], {#[[-1]]}] &, d]; {h, f[d]}]],
{j, 1, Length[c]}]; f[b]]

In[3866]:= CallsInFuncBlockMod[S, g70]
Out[3866]= {{{"Cos", "Sin"}, {}}, {{"IntegerQ", "N", "Sin", "StringLength"},
{{"StringStringQ", "AladjevProcedures`"}}, {{"IntegerQ", "StringJoin", "StringQ"},
{{"m", "avz`"}, {"StrStr", "ToString1", "AladjevProcedures`"}}}, {{"N"}, {}}, {{}, {}}}
In[3767]:= g70
Out[3767]= {{}, {}, {}, {}, {"a", "y", "AladjevProcedures`"}}
In[3868]:= CallsInFuncBlockMod[CallsInFuncBlockMod]
Out[3868]= {{"AppendTo", "Complement", "Context", "Do", "Flatten", "Gather", "If", "Join",
"Length", "Replace", "Select", "Sort", "StringFreeQ", "StringJoin", "ToString"},
{"ExtrVarsOfStr", "FuncBlockModQ1", "HowAct", "Mapp", "PureDefinition", "SystemQ",
"AladjevProcedures`"}}

For operating with procedures and functions, whose definitions have been evaluated in the current session, a simple **CsProcsFuncs** function is an useful tool whose call **CsProcsFuncs[]** returns the list of blocks, functions and modules, whose definitions were evaluated in the current session. The fragment represents source code of the function with an example of its application.

In[2719]:= CsProcsFuncs[] := Select[CNames["Global`"], ProcQ[#] || FunctionQ[#] &]

In[2720]:= CsProcsFuncs[]
Out[2720]= {"A", "ArtKr", "Av", "B", "H74", "Kr", "V", "Vg", "W"}

Naturally, the given list does not include the procedures and functions from the packages uploaded into the current session, of both system tools, and user means for the reason that similar tools are associated with contexts of the corresponding packages. Moreover, due to necessity of analysis of a quite large number of means of the current *Mathematica* session the performance of this function can demand noticeable time costs.

The **CsProcsFuncs1** procedure is an useful modification of the previous function whose call **CsProcsFuncs1[]** returns the nested list whose elements define lists whose the first elements determine means similarly to the **CsProcsFuncs** function whereas the second elements – the *multiplicities* of their definitions. The next fragment represents source code of the procedure **CsProcsFuncs1** along with typical examples of its application.

In[2532]:= CsProcsFuncs1[] := Module[{a = CsProcsFuncs[], b, c},
b = Map[Definition2, ToExpression[a]];
c = Quiet[Mapp[Select, b, StringFreeQ[#1, ToString[#1] <> "Options[" <>
ToString[#1] <> "] := "] &]];
Select[Map9[List, a, Map[Length, c]], ! MemberQ[#, "CsProcsFuncs1"] &]]

In[2533]:= CsProcsFuncs1[]
Out[2533]= {{"LocalVars", 1}, {"V", 4}, {"W", 2}, {"Z", 2}, {"Art", 6}, {"Kr", 4}}

Analogously to **CsProcsFuncs** function, the call **CsProcsFuncs1[]** of the previous procedure because of necessity of analysis of a quite large number of means which are activated in the current session can demand enough noticeable time costs.

The next procedure **ActCsProcFunc** is a means rather useful in the practical relation, its call **ActCsProcFunc[]** returns the nested 2–element list whose elements are sublists of variable length. The first element of the first sublist – *"Procedure"* while others define the 2–element lists containing names of procedures with their headings activated in the current session. Whereas the first element of the second sublist – *"Function"* while others determine the 2–element lists containing names of functions with their headings which were activated in the current *Mathematica* session. At that, the procedures can contain in own composition the blocks, and modules. The following fragment represents source code of the **ActCsProcFunc** procedure along with the most typical examples of its application.

In[2742]:= ActCsProcFunc[] :=
Module[{a = Names["Global`*"], h = {}, d, t, k = 1, v, b = {"Procedure"}, c = {"Function"}},
Map[If[TemporaryQ[#] || HeadPF[#] === #, Null,
AppendTo[h, ToString[t = Unique["g"]]]; v = BlockFuncModQ[#, t];
If[v && MemberQ[{"Block", "Module"}, t], AppendTo[b, {#, HeadPF[#]}]],
If[v && t === "Function", AppendTo[c, {#, HeadPF[#]}]]]] &, a]; Map[Remove, h]; {b, c}]

In[2743]:= TemporaryQ[x_] := If[SymbolQ[x], MemberQ[{"Attributes[" <>

ToString[x] <> "] = {Temporary}", "Null"}, ToString[Definition[x]]], False]

In[2744]:= **Map[TemporaryQ, {gs47, gs, a + b}]**
Out[2744]= {True, True, False}
In[2745]:= **g[x_] := Module[{}, x]; s[x_, y_] := Block[{}, x + y]; v[x_] := x; n[x_] := x;
vs[x_, y_] := x + y; gs[x_] := x^2; hg[x__] := Length[{x}]; hh[x_, y_] := x^2 + y^2;
nm[x_, y_] := Module[{}, x*y]; ts[x_Integer]:=Block[{a=74}, x+a]; w[x_]:=x; w[x_, y_]:=x*y;**
In[2746]:= **ActCsProcFunc[]**
Out[2746]= {{"Procedure", {"g", "g[x_]"}, {"nm", "nm[x_, y_]"}, {"s", "s[x_, y_]"},
{"ts", "ts[x_Integer]"}}, {"Function", {"gs", "gs[x_]"}, {"hg", "hg[x__]"}, {"hh", "hh[x_, y_]"},
{"n", "n[x_]"}, {"TemporaryQ", {"TemporaryQ[x_/; SymbolQ[x]]", "TemporaryQ[x_]"}},
{"v", "v[x_]"}, {"vs", "vs[x_, y_]"}, {"w", {"w[x_]", "w[x_, y_]"}}}}
In[2747]:= **A[___] := Module[{a, b = 590}, Map[TemporaryQ, {a, b}]]; A[]**
Out[2747]= {True, False}

This procedure materially uses **TemporaryQ** function, whose call **TemporaryQ[x]** returns *True* if a *x* symbol determines the temporary variable, and *False* otherwise. So, for a local *x* variable without initial value a call **TemporaryQ[x]** returns *True*. The **TemporaryQ** function is useful in many uses, above all of the system character. The previous fragment represents source code of the function with typical examples of its application.

Analogously to the **CsProcsFuncs** and **CsProcsFuncs1**, the procedure call **ActCsProcFunc** because of necessity of analysis of a quite large number of the means which are activated in the current session can demand noticeable enough time costs. Concerning the procedure **ActCsProcFunc** it should be noted that it provides return only of the blocks, functions and modules the definitions of which have been evaluated in the *Input* paragraph mode without allowing to receive objects of this type which were uploaded into the current session in the *Input* paragraph mode, in particular, as a result of loading of the user package by means of the **LoadMyPackage** procedure as illustrate the last examples of the previous fragment. The reason for this is that these objects are associated with context of a package containing them but not with the *"Global`"* context.

As it was noted above, the strict differentiation of objects in the *Mathematica* is carried out not by their names, but by their headings. For this reason in a number of cases of procedural programming the problem of organization of mechanisms of the differentiated processing of such objects on the basis of their headings arises. At that, certain such tools is represented in the present book, here we will define 2 procedures ensuring the differentiated operating with attributes of the objects. Unlike the **Rename** procedure, **RenameH** procedure provides in a certain degree selective renaming of blocks, functions or modules of the same name on the basis of their headings. The successful call **RenameH[x, y]** returns *Null*, renaming object (*block, function, module*) with a *x* heading onto a name *y* with saving of its attributes; at that, the initial object with the *x* heading is removed from the current *Mathematica* session.

In[2563]:= **RenameH[x_ /; HeadingQ1[x], y_ /; ! HowAct[y], z___] :=
Module[{c, a = HeadName[x], d = StandHead[x],
b = ToExpression["Attributes[" <> HeadName[x] <> "]"]},
c = Flatten[{PureDefinition[a]}];
If[c == {$Failed}, $Failed,**

```
If[c == {}, Return[$Failed], ToExpression["ClearAllAttributes[" <> a <> "]"]];
ToExpression[ToString[y] <> DelSuffPref[Select[c, SuffPref[#, d <> " := ", 1] &][[1]], a, 1]];
If[{z} == {}, RemProcOnHead[d]];
If[! SameQ[PureDefinition[a], $Failed], ToExpression["SetAttributes[" <>
ToString[a] <> "," <> ToString[b] <> "]"]];
ToExpression["SetAttributes[" <> ToString[y] <> "," <> ToString[b] <> "]"];]]
In[2564]:= M[x_ /; SameQ[x, "avz"], y_] := Module[{a, b, c}, y];
M[x_, y_] := Module[{a, b, c}, "agn"; x + y]; M[x_String] := x;
M[x_ /; ListQ[x], y_] := Block[{a, b, c}, "agn"; Length[x] + y];
SetAttributes[M, {Flat, Protected}]
In[2565]:= RenameH["M[x_,y_]", V]
In[2566]:= Definition[V]
Out[2566]= Attributes[V] = {Flat, Protected}
V[x_, y_] := Module[{a, b, c}, "agn"; x + y]
In[2567]:= Definition[M]
Out[2567]= Attributes[M] = {Flat, Protected}
M[x_ /; x === "avz", y_] := Module[{a, b, c}, y]
M[x_ /; ListQ[x], y_] := Block[{a, b, c}, "agn"; Length[x] + y]
M[x_String] := x
In[2568]:= RenameH["M[x_String]", S, 590]
In[2569]:= Definition[S]
Out[2569]= Attributes[S] = {Flat, Protected}
S[x_String] := x
In[2570]:= Definition[M]
Out[2570]= Attributes[M] = {Flat, Protected}
M[x_ /; x === "avz", y_] := Module[{a, b, c}, y]
M[x_ /; ListQ[x], y_] := Block[{a, b, c}, "agn"; Length[x] + y]
M[x_String] := x
```

In addition, the procedure call **RenameH[*x*, *y*, *z*]** with the third optional *z* argument – any expression – renames an object with *x* heading onto an *y* name with saving of the attributes; meanwhile, the object with *x* heading remains active in the current session. On inadmissible tuple of factual arguments the call returns $*Failed*, or is returned unevaluated. The previous fragment represents source code of the **RenameH** procedure with the most typical examples of its application.

Unlike the **RenameH** the **RenameH1** procedure also provides the selective renaming of the blocks, functions or modules of the same name on the basis of *unique* symbols. The *successful* call **RenameH1[*x*, *y*]** returns the list of new names of components composing a *x* object with saving of its attributes; in addition, an initial object is removed from the current session. The new names are formed as **Unique[ToString[*x*]]**. At that, the procedure call **RenameH1[*x*, *y*, *z*]** with the 3rd optional *z* argument – an arbitrary expression – selectively renames a *x* object with saving of the attributes; meanwhile, the *x* object remains active in the current session. On an inadmissible tuple of actual arguments the procedure call returns $*Failed* or returned unevaluated. The fragment represents source code of the **RenameH1** procedure along with the most typical examples of its application.

In[3864]:= RenameH1[x_ /; BlockFuncModQ[x], y_ /; SymbolQ[y] && NullQ[y], z___] :=
Module[{a=Attributes[x], b=Flatten[{PureDefinition[x]}], c={}, d=ClearAllAttributes[x]},
Do[d = Unique[ToString[y]]; AppendTo[c, d];
ToExpression[StringReplace[b[[k]], ToString[x] <> "[" -> ToString[d] <> "[", 1]],
{k, 1, Length[b]}]; Map[SetAttributes[#, a] &, c]; If[{z} == {}, c, Remove[x]; c]]

In[3865]:= kdp[x_] := Module[{a = 74}, a*x]; kdp[x_, y_] := Module[{a = 69}, a*x*y];
SetAttributes[kdp, Protected]

In[3866]:= **RenameH1[kdp, Agn, 74]**
Out[3866]= {Agn2021, Agn2022}

In[3867]:= **Definition[Agn2021]**
Out[3867]= Attributes[Agn2021] = {Protected}
Agn2021[x_] := Module[{a = 74}, a*x]

In[3868]:= **Definition[Agn2022]**
Out[3868]= Attributes[Agn2022] = {Protected}
Agn2022[x_, y_] := Module[{a = 69}, a*x*y]

In a number of procedures intended for processing of definitions or calls of other functions or procedures, the problem of identification of the call format, i.e. format of the type *F[args]* where *F* – the name of a procedure or a function, and *args* – the tuple of factual or formal arguments is a rather topical. The following fragment represents source code of the **CallQ** procedure along with typical enough examples of its application.

In[2540]:= CallQ[x_] := Module[{b, c, a=ToString[If[Quiet[Part[x, 1]] == -1, Part[x, 1]*x, x]]},
b = Flatten[StringPosition[a, "["]];
If[b == {}, False, c = b[[1]]; If[SymbolQ[StringTake[a, {1, c - 1}]] &&
StringTake[a, {c + 1, c + 1}] != "[" && StringTake[a, -1] == "]", True, False]]]

In[2541]:= **Clear[A]; CallQ[A[x, y, z]]**
Out[2541]= True

In[2542]:= **Map[CallQ, {Sin[-590], Sin[590.0]}]**
Out[2542]= {True, False}

In[2543]:= FormalArgs[x_] := Module[{a, b = Quiet[Part[x, 1]]},
If[CallQ[x], a = ToString[If[b === -1, Part[x, 1]*x, x]]; ToExpression["{" <>
StringTake[a, {Flatten[StringPosition[a, "["]][[1]] + 1, -2}] <> "}"], $Failed]]

In[2544]:= **Map[FormalArgs, {Agn[x, y, x], Sin[-a+b], Agn[x_ /; StringQ[x], y_Integer, z_]}]**
Out[2544]= {{x, y, x}, {a - b}, {x_ /; StringQ[x], y_Integer, z_}}

In[2545]:= **Map[FormalArgs, {Agn[], a + b, 590, {a, b, c}}]**
Out[2545]= {{}, $Failed, $Failed, $Failed}

The procedure call **CallQ[x]** up to a sign returns *True* if *x* is an expression of format *F[args]* where *F* – the name of a procedure or function and *args* – the tuple of the factual arguments, and *False* otherwise. The above **CallQ** procedure is of interest as a testing tools for checking of actual arguments of objects for their *admissibility*. Whereas the call **FormalArgs[x]** returns the list of formal arguments of a *x* heading irrespectively off definition ascribed to it; on an inadmissible *x* heading *$Failed* is returned. The previous fragment represents source code of the procedure along with an example of its application.

In the *Maple* in problems of procedural programming the procedural *"procname"* variable is rather useful, whose use in the body of a certain procedure allows to receive the heading of procedure in a point of its call. The variable is useful enough at realization of some *special* mechanisms of processing in procedures what was widely used by us for programming of system tools expanding the software of the *Maple* system [10-22,25-27,47]. Similar means in the *Mathematica* system are absent, meanwhile, tools of similar character are rather useful at realization of the procedural paradigm of the system. As one useful means of this type it is quite possible to consider the **$InBlockMod** variable whose call in the body of a block or a module in string format returns source code of an object containing it without a heading in a point of its call. The fragment below adduces source code of the **$InBlockMod** variable along with examples of its typical application.

In[2552]:= **$InBlockMod** := Quiet[Check[StringTake[If[Stack[Block] != {},
ToString[InputForm[Stack[Block][[1]]]], If[Stack[Module] != {},
StringReplace3[ToString[InputForm[Stack[Module][[1]]]],
Sequences[Riffle[Select[StringReplace[StringSplit[StringTake[SubStrSymbolParity1[To
String[InputForm[Stack[Module][[1]]]], "{", "}"][[1]], {2, -2}], " "], "," -> ""],
StringTake[#, -1] == "$" &],
Mapp[StringTake, Select[StringReplace[StringSplit[StringTake[SubStrSymbolParity1[
ToString[nputForm[Stack[Module][[1]]]], "{", "}"][[1]], {2, -2}], " "], "," -> ""],
StringTake[#, -1] == "$" &], {1, -2}]]]]], $Failed], {10, -2}], Null]]

In[2553]:= **Avz[x_]** := Block[{a = 6, b = 50, c = $InBlockMod}, Print[c]; a*b*x]
In[2554]:= **Avz[74]**
"Block[{a = 6, b = 50, c = $InBlockMod}, Print[c]; a*b*74]"
Out[2554]= 22200
In[2555]:= **Agn[x_]** := Module[{a = 6, b = 50, c = $InBlockMod}, Print[c]; a*b*x]
In[2556]:= **Agn[69]**
"Module[{a = 6, b = 50, c = $InBlockMod}, Print[c]; a*b*69]"
Out[2556]= 20700
In[2557]:= **Avs[x_]** := Module[{a=$InBlockMod, b=50, c=590}, Print[a]; b*c*x^2]; Avs[590]
"Block[{a = $InBlockMod, b = 50, c = 590}, Print[a]; b*c*590^2]"
Out[2557]= 10268950000
In[2558]:= **Av[x_]** := Module[{a = $InBlockMod, b = 50, c=590}, Print[a]; b*c*x^2]; Av[590]
"Module[{a = $InBlockMod, b = 50, c = 590}, Print[a]; b*c*590^2]"
Out[2558]= 10268950000
In[2559]:= **$InBlockMod**
In[2560]:= **G[x_, y_]** := {90*x + 590*y, $InBlockMod}; G[74, 69]
Out[2560]= {47370, Null}

At that, for realization of algorithm of the above variable the **StringReplace3** procedure that is an extension of the **StringReplace2** procedure is rather significantly used. At using of the procedural **$InBlockMod** variable it must be kept in mind that it makes sense only in body of a procedure of type {*Block, Module*}, returning *Null*, in other expressions or in an *Input*-paragraph as illustrate examples of application of the **$InBlockMod** variable in the previous fragment. In addition, it must be kept in mind in order to avoid of any misunderstanding the call of the **$InBlockMod** variable is recommended to do at the beginning of procedures, for example, in the field of local variables.

The procedure below is useful for work with blocks, functions and modules. The procedure call **FullUserTools[*x*]** returns the list of names, which enter in definition of the active user block, function or module *x*; in addition, the 1st element of the list is a context of these tools. Whereas in a case of means with various contexts a call returns the nested list of sublists of the above format. In turn, a procedure call **FullUserTools[*x*, *y*]** thru the optional *y* argument – *an undefinite variable* – returns two-element list whose the first element defines list of tools without an usage, and the second element determines the unidentified tools. The following fragment presents source code of the **FullUserTools** procedure with typical examples of its application.

```
In[2718]:= FullUserTools[x_ /; BlockFuncModQ[x], y___] :=
Module[{a, b, c, d, p = {}, n = {}}, Save[Set[a, ToString[x] <> ".txt"], x];
b = ReadString[a]; DeleteFile[a]; c = StringSplit[b, "\r\n \r\n"];
b = Select[c, ! StringFreeQ[#, "::usage = \""] &];
d = MinusList[c, b]; c = Map[StringSplit[#, " /: ", 2][[1]] &, b];
d = Map[StringSplit[#, " := "][[1]] &, d];
Quiet[Map[If[HeadingQ[#], AppendTo[p, HeadName[#]], AppendTo[n, #]] &, d]];
{a, p} = {Join[c, p ], MinusList[c, p]}; b = Map[MinusList[#, {ToString[x]}] &, {a, p}][[1]];
b = DeleteDuplicates[Map[{#, Context[#]} &, b]]; b = Gather[b, #1[[2]] == #2[[2]] &];
b = Map[Sort[DeleteDuplicates[Flatten[#]]] &, b]; d = Map[Sort[#, ContextQ[#1] &] &, b];
d = Map[Flatten[{#[[1]], Sort[#[[2 ;; -1]]]}] &, d]; d = If[Length[d] == 1, d[[1]], d];
If[{y} != {} && ! HowAct[y], y = {p, n}; d, d]]

In[2719]:= FullUserTools[UnevaluatedQ]
Out[2719]= {{"AladjevProcedures`", "ListStrToStr", "StrDelEnds", "SuffPref", "SymbolQ", "ToString1"}}

In[2720]:= F[x_, y_] := Module[{a = 90, b = 590, c}, a*b*x*y; c = ToString1[c]];
Sv[x_, y_] := x*y; G[x_, y_] := Module[{}, {ToString1[x*y], F[x] + Sv[x, y]}]
In[2721]:= FullUserTools[G]
Out[2721]= {{"AladjevProcedures`", "StrDelEnds", "SuffPref", "ToString1"}, {"Global`", "F", "Sv"}}
```

Unlike the **FullUserTools** procedure the **FullToolsCalls** procedure provides the analysis of the user block, function and module regarding existence in its definition of calls of both the user and system tools. The procedure call **FullToolsCalls[*x*]** returns the list of names, whose calls are in definition of the active user block, function and module *x*; in addition, the first element of the list is a context of these tools. Whereas in case of tools with different contexts the procedure call returns the nested list of sublists of the above format. In case of absence in a *x* definition of the user or system calls the procedure call **FullToolsCalls[*x*]** returns the empty list, i.e. {}.

```
In[2920]:= FullToolsCalls[x_ /; BlockFuncModQ[x]] :=
Module[{b, c = {}, d, a = Flatten[{PureDefinition[x]}][[1]], k = 1, g = {}, p, j, n},
b = Gather[Map[#[[1]] &, StringPosition[a, "["]], Abs[#1 - #2] == 1 &];
```

```
b = Flatten[Select[b, Length[#] == 1 &]];
For[k, k <= Length[b], k++, n = ""; For[j = b[[k]] - 1, j >= 0, j--,
If[SymbolQ[p = Quiet[StringTake[a, {j}]]] || IntegerQ[Quiet[ToExpression[p]]],
n = p <> n, AppendTo[c, n]; Break[]]]];
c = MinusList[c, Join[Locals[x], Args[x, 90], {"Block", "Module"}]];
c = Map[{#, Quiet[Context[#]]} &, MinusList[c, {ToString[x]}]];
b = Map[Sort[DeleteDuplicates[Flatten[#]]] &, c];
d = Map[Flatten, Gather[Map[Sort[#, Quiet[ContextQ[#1]] &] &, b], #1[[1]] == #2[[1]] &]];
d = Map[Flatten[{#[[1]], Sort[#[[2 ;; -1]]]}] &, Map[DeleteDuplicates, d]];
d = If[Length[d] == 1, d[[1]], d]; Select[d, ! Quiet[SameQ[#[[1]], Context[""]]] &]]
In[2921]:= AH[x_] := (Sv[x] + GSV[x, 90, 590])*Sin[x] + Z[[a]] + Art[x]/Kr[x]
In[2922]:= FullToolsCalls[AH]
Out[2922]= {{"Tallinn`","Sv"}, {"RansIan`","GSV"}, {"System`", "Sin"}, {"Global`", "Art", "Kr"}}
In[2923]:= FullToolsCalls[UnevaluatedQ]
Out[2923]= {{"AladjevProcedures`", "ListStrToStr", "SymbolQ", "ToString1"},
{"System`", "Check", "If", "Quiet", "StringJoin", "ToString"}}
```

Unlike the previous procedure the **FullToolsCallsM** procedure provides the analysis of the user block, function or module of the same name.

```
In[2954]:= FullToolsCallsM[x_ /; BlockFuncModQ[x]] :=
Module[{b, c = {}, a = Flatten[{PureDefinition[x]}], k = 1, n = ToString[x]},
If[Length[a] == 1, FullToolsCalls[x], For[k, k <= Length[a], k++,
b = ToString[Unique["sv"]];
ToExpression[StringReplace[a[[k]], n <> "[" -> b <> "[", 1]];
AppendTo[c, FullToolsCalls[b]]; Quiet[Remove[b]]];
c = Map[If[NestListQ[#] && Length[#] == 1, #[[1]], #] &, c];
Map[If[! NestListQ[#] && Length[#] == 1, {},
If[! NestListQ[#] && Length[#] > 1, #, Select[#, Length[#] > 1 &]]] &, c]]]
In[2955]:= Ah[x_] := (Sv[x] + GSV[x, 90, 590])*Sin[x] + Z[[a]] + Art[x]/Kr[x];
Ah[x_Integer] := Block[{a = 90}, ToString1[a*Cos[x]]];
Ah[x_String] := Module[{a = "6"}, ToString1[x <> a]]; FullToolsCallsM[Ah]
Out[2956]= {{{"AladjevProcedures`", "ToString1"}, {"System`", "Cos"}},
{{"AladjevProcedures`", "ToString1"}, {"System`", "StringJoin"}},
{{"Global`", "Art", "GSV", "Kr", "Sv"}, {"System`", "Sin"}}}
In[2957]:= G[x_, y_, z_] := Module[{}, x*y*z]; G[x_] := Module[{a = 69}, x/a]
In[2958]:= FullToolsCallsM[G]
Out[2958]= {{}, {}}
In[2959]:= FullToolsCallsM[ToString1]
Out[2959]= {{"System`", "Close", "DeleteFile", "For", "If", "Read", "Return", "StringJoin",
"Write"}, {"AladjevProcedures`", "StrDelEnds"}}
In[2960]:= Avz[x_] := Module[{a = 590}, StrStr[x] <> ToString[a]]
In[2961]:= Map[#[Avz] &, {FullToolsCalls, FullToolsCallsM}]
```

Out[2961]= {{{"System`", "StringJoin", "ToString"}, {"AladjevProcedures`", "StrStr"}}, {{"System`", "StringJoin", "ToString"}, {"AladjevProcedures`", "StrStr"}}}

The procedure call **FullToolsCallsM[*x*]** returns the nested list of results of application of the **FullToolsCalls** procedure to subobjects *(blocks, functions, modules)* which compose an object of the same *x* name. The order of elements in the returned list corresponds to the order of definitions of the subobjects returned by the call **Definition[*x*]**. Whereas, the call **AllCalls[*x*]** returns the nested list of sublists containing the full format of calls entering in definitions of subobjects that compose an object of the same name or a simple *x* object. At that, the order of elements in the returned list corresponds to the order of definitions of the subobjects that are returned by the function call **Definition[*x*]**.

In[2840]:= AllCalls[x_ /; BlockFuncModQ[x]] :=
Module[{a1, ArtKr, k1, b1, c1 = {}, d1, m = ToString[x]},
a1 = Flatten[{PureDefinition[x]}];
ArtKr[y_] := Module[{a = Flatten[{PureDefinition[y]}][[1]], b, c = {}, d, k, g = {}, p, j, n},
b = Gather[Map[#[[1]] &, StringPosition[a, "["]], Abs[#1 - #2] == 1 &];
b = Flatten[Select[b, Length[#] == 1 &]];
For[k = 1, k <= Length[b], k++, n = ""; For[j = b[[k]] - 1, j >= 0, j--,
If[SymbolQ[p = Quiet[StringTake[a, {j}]]] || IntegerQ[Quiet[ToExpression[p]]],
n = p <> n, AppendTo[c, n]; Break[]]]];
For[k = 1, k <= Length[b], k++, For[j = b[[k]], j <= StringLength[a], j++,
SubStrSymbolParity1[StringTake[a, {j, StringLength[a]}], "[", "]"][[1]];
AppendTo[g, SubStrSymbolParity1[StringTake[a, {j, StringLength[a]}], "[", "]"][[1]]];
Break[]]];
n = Select[Map[StringJoin[#] &, Partition[Riffle[c, g], 2]], # != HeadPF[y] &];
If[FunctionQ[y], n, n[[2 ;; -1]]]];
If[Length[a1] == 1, ArtKr[x], For[k1 = 1, k1 <= Length[a1], k1++,
b1 = ToString[Unique["v"]];
ToExpression[StringReplace[a1[[k1]], m <> "[" -> b1 <> "[", 1]];
AppendTo[c1, ArtKr[b1]]; Quiet[Remove[b1]]]; c1]]

In[2841]:= AH[x_] := (Sv[x] + GSV[x, 90, 590])*Sin[x] + Z[[a]] + Art[x]/Kr[x];
AH[x_Integer] := Block[{a = 90}, ToString1[a*Cos[x]]]; AH[x_String] := Module[{a = "590"},
ToString1[x <> a]]; AH1[x_] := (Sv[x] + GSV[x, 90, 590])*Sin[x] + Z[[a]] + Art[x]/Kr[x];
F[x_, y_] := x + y

In[2842]:= **AllCalls[AH]**
Out[2842]= {{"ToString1[a*Cos[x]]", "Cos[x]"}, {"ToString1[StringJoin[x, a]]", "StringJoin[x, a]"}, {"Sv[x]", "GSV[x, 90, 590]", "Sin[x]", "Art[x]", "Kr[x]"}}

In[2843]:= **AllCalls[F]**
Out[2843]= {}

In[2844]:= **AllCalls[AH1]**
Out[2844]= {"Sv[x]", "GSV[x, 90, 590]", "Sin[x]", "Art[x]", "Kr[x]"}

The call **ContextsInModule[*x*]** returns the nested list of the following format, namely:

{{"*Args*", ...}, {"*Locals*", ...}, {"*SubProcs*", ...}, {"*Context1`*", ...}, ..., {"*ContextN`*", ...}}

Software Etudes in the Mathematica

where the first sublist determines formal arguments of block or module x, the second sublist defines its local variables, the third sublist defines names of subprocedures of procedure x whereas other sublists, starting with the fourth, determine variables of the x module with the contexts corresponding to them. All elements of sublists of the returned list have string format. In the fragment below the source code of the procedure along with an example of its application are represented.

In[2880]:= **ContextsInModule[x_ /; BlockQ[x] || ModuleQ[x]] :=**
Module[{a = Select[ExtrVarsOfStr[PureDefinition[x], 1],
! MemberQ[{"Block", "Module"}, #] &], b, c, d, h, Sf},
Sf[y_] := Flatten[{Select[y, ! StringFreeQ[#, "`"] &], Select[y, StringFreeQ[#, "`"] &]}];
ClearAll[h]; NotSubsProcs[x, h];
a = MinusList[a, Flatten[{b = Args[x, 90], c = Locals1[x], h}]];
h = {PrependTo[b, "Args"], PrependTo[c, "Locals"], PrependTo[h, "SubProcs"]};
Flatten[{h, Map[Sf, Map[DeleteDuplicates, Map[Flatten, Gather[Map[{#, Context[#]} &, a],
#1[[2]] == #2[[2]] &]]]]}, 1]]

In[2881]:= **Avz[x_, y_, z_] := Module[{Art, Gal, b}, Art[a_] := Module[{Es}, a^2 + Es[a]];**
Gal[b_, c_] := Module[{Kr, Sv}, Kr[d_]:=Module[{Vg}, Vg[p_] := Module[{a, Gr}, Gr[m_]:=
Module[{}, m]; p^1]; Vg[d]*d^3]; Sv[p_] := Module[{}, p^4]; Kr[b]*Sv[c]]; Art[x]*Gal[y, z]]
In[2882]:= **ContextsInModule[Avz]**
Out[2882]= {{"Args", "x", "y", "z"}, {"Locals", "Art", "Gal", "b"}, {"SubProcs", "Art", "Gal", "Kr", "Vg", "Gr", "Sv"}, {"Global`", "Avz", "Es", "p", "m"}, {"AladjevProcedures`", "a", "c", "d"}}

In some cases it is necessary to determine structure of the means composing the user block, function or module with the contexts attributed to them. The problem is solved by means of the **ContentObj** procedure represented below.

In[2887]:= **ContentObj[x_ /; BlockQ[x] || FunctionQ[x] || ModuleQ[x]] :=**
Module[{a = ToString1[FullDefinition[x]], b}, a = StringCases[a, X__ ~~ "`: " ~~ X__];
If[a=={}, {}, a=Map[StringTake[#, {1, Flatten[StringPosition[#, "`: "]][[1]] – 1}] &, a][[2 ;; –1]];
a = Map[DeleteDuplicates, Map[Flatten, Gather[Map[{Context[#], #} &, a],
#1[[1]] == #2[[1]] &]]];
a = Map[Flatten[{#[[1]], Sort[#[[2 ;; –1]]]}] &, a]; If[Length[a] == 1, a[[1]], a]]]

In[2888]:= **ContentObj[ProcQ]**
Out[2888]= {"AladjevProcedures`", "Attributes1", "BlockFuncModQ", "ClearAllAttributes", "Contexts1", "Definition2", "HeadPF", "HowAct", "ListStrToStr", "Map3", "Mapp", "MinusList", "ProtectedQ", "PureDefinition", "StrDelEnds", "SuffPref", "SymbolQ", "SysFuncQ", "SystemQ", "ToString1", "UnevaluatedQ"}
In[2889]:= **Avz[x_, y_, z_] := Module[{Art, Gal, b}, Art[a_] := Module[{Es}, a^2 + Es[a]];**
Gal[b_, c_] := Module[{Kr, Sv}, Kr[d_] := Module[{Vg}, Vg[p_]:=Module[{a, Gr}, Gr[m_]:=
Module[{}, m]; p^1]; Vg[d]*d^3]; Sv[p_] := Module[{}, p^4]; Kr[b]*Sv[c]]; Art[x]*Gal[y, z]]
In[2890]:= **ContentObj[Avz]**
Out[2890]= {}

The procedure call **ContentObj**[x] returns the list of the format {$Context_j$, j_1, j_2,...}, where j_k – the user means, used by a block, a function or a module x, and $Context_j$ – the context that corresponds to them. In a case of several contexts the nested list is returned whose sublists have the above-mentioned format. The call returns all tools of the user packages on which a *x* object depends. In the absence of such tools the procedure call returns the *empty* list, i.e. {}. The previous fragment represents source code of the **ContentObj** procedure along with the typical examples of its application.

Whereas the call **SymbolsInBlockFuncMod[*f*]** of the procedure analyzes symbolic contents of a block, a function *(including pure function)* or a module by returning the nested list whose the *first* element defines the list of the formal arguments in string format, the *second* element defines the list of local variables in string format *(in case of their absence or in case of f function the empty list is returned)* while the *third* element defines the nested list whose elements have a context as the first element, while remaining elements in string format define symbols of *f* object with this context. The following fragment presents source code of the procedure with typical examples of its application.

In[4581]:= **SymbolsInBlockFuncMod[f_ /; BlockFuncModQ[f] || PureFuncQ[f]] :=**
Module[{a = If[PureFuncQ[f], ToString1[f], PureDefinition[f]], b, c},
a = ExtrVarsOfStr[a, 2]; b = If[PureFuncQ[f], ArgsPureFunc[f], ArgsBFM[f]];
c = If[FunctionQ[f] || PureFuncQ[f], {}, Map[#[[1]] &, Locals4[f]]];
= Map[{Quiet[Check[Context[#], "Global`"]], #} &, Complement[a, b, c, {ToString[f]}]];
a = Gather[a, #1[[1]] === #2[[1]] &]; a = Map[DeleteDuplicates, Map[Flatten, a]];
a = Map[SortBy[#, ! ContextQ[#] &] &, a]; {b, c, a}]

In[4582]:= G[x_, y_] := Sin[x + y + h]; **SymbolsInBlockFuncMod[G]**
Out[4582]= {{"x", "y"}, {}, {{"Global`", "h"}, {"System`", "Sin"}}}
In[4583]:= **SymbolsInBlockFuncMod[ProcQ]**
Out[4583]= {{"x"}, {"a", "atr", "b", "c", "d", "h"}, {{"System`", "Attributes", "Block", "Context", "Definition", "DynamicModule", "False", "First", "If", "InputForm", "ListQ", "Module", "Quiet", "SetAttributes", "StringJoin", "StringPosition", "StringReplace", "StringTake", "ToString", "True"}, {"AladjevProcedures`", "ClearAllAttributes", "Definition2", "HeadPF", "SymbolQ", "SystemQ", "UnevaluatedQ"}}}
In[4584]:= **SymbolsInBlockFuncMod[mp*Args[#1] + nh*Sin[#2] &]**
Out[4584]= {{"#1", "#2"}, {}, {{"Global`", "mp", "nh"}, {"AladjevProcedures`", "Args"}, {"System`", "Sin"}}}
In[4585]:= Gs[x_, y_, z_] := Module[{}, x*y*z]; **SymbolsInBlockFuncMod[Gs]**
Out[4585]= {{"x", "y", "z"}, {}, {{"System`", "Module"}}}
In[4586]:= **SymbolsInBlockFuncMod[SymbolsInBlockFuncMod]**
Out[4586]= {{"f"}, {"a", "b", "c"}, {{"AladjevProcedures`", "ArgsBFM", "ArgsPureFunc", "BlockFuncModQ", "ContextQ", "ExtrVarsOfStr", "FunctionQ", "Locals4", "PureDefinition", "PureFuncQ", "ToString1"}, {"System`", "Complement", "Context", "DeleteDuplicates", "Flatten", "Gather", "If", "Module", "SortBy", "ToString"}}}
In[4587]:= **SymbolsInBlockFuncMod[Locals]**
Out[4587]= {{"x", "R"}, {"c", "d", "p", "q", "t", "a", "b", "k", "Sg", "Sv"}, {{"System`", "AppendTo", "Block", "ClearAll", "Continue", "Do", "Flatten", "For", "FreeQ", "Function", "Goto", "If", "Label", "Length", "List", "ListQ", "MemberQ", "Module", "Names", "Null", "Quiet", "StringJoin", "StringLength", "StringPosition", "StringQ", "StringReplace",

"StringTake", "ToExpression", "$Failed"},
{"Global`", "avz", "h", "j", "No", "v", "$$90$$"},
{"AladjevProcedures`", "BlockFuncModQ", "HeadPF", "HowAct", "Map3", "Mapp",
"PureDefinition", "s", "StringJoin1", "SubStrSymbolParity1", "SuffPref", "y", "z"}}}

On that the presentation of tools, serving for processing of the user objects, is completed; in addition, some tools accompanying them are considered below or were already considered above. Classification of our means has in a certain measure a subjective character which is caused by their basic use or frequency of usage at programming of the tools represented in the given book and in a number of important uses of the applied and the system character. These means are mainly used at programming of the system tools. In addition, a number of the means represented in our package are focused on the solution of identical problems, but they use various algorithms programmed with usage of various approaches. They not only illustrate variety of the useful receptions but also reveal their shortcomings and advantages, useful both in practical and system programming. In our opinion, such approach opens a wide field for awakening of creative activity of the reader in respect of the improvement of his skills at programming in the *Mathematica* system.

Chapter 7. Software for input–output in the *Mathematica* system

The *Mathematica* language being the built-in programming language which first of all is oriented onto symbolical calculations and processing has rather limited facilities for data processing which first of all are located in external memory of the computer. In this regard the language significantly concedes to the traditional programming languages *C++*, *Basic*, *Fortran*, *Cobol*, *PL/1*, *ADA*, *Pascal*, etc. At the same time, being oriented, first of all, onto solution of tasks in symbolic view, the *Mathematica* language provides a set of means for access to datafiles which can quite satisfy a rather wide range of the users of mathematical applications of the *Mathematica* system. In this chapter the tools of access to datafiles are considered a rather superficially owing to the limited volume, extensiveness of this theme and purpose of the present book. The reader who is interested in tools of access to files of the *Mathematica* system quite can appeal to documentation delivered with the system. At the same time, for the purpose of development of methods of access to file system of the computer we programmed a number of rather effective means that are represented in the *MathToolBox* package [48]. Whereas in the present chapter the attention is oriented on the tools expanding standard tools of the *Mathematica* system for ensuring work with files of the computer. Some of them are rather useful to practical application in the software of the *Mathematica* system.

7.1. Tools of the *Mathematica* for work with internal files

Means of *Math*-language provide access of the user to files of several types which can be conditionally divided into two large groups, namely: *internal* and *external* files. During the routine work the system deals with three various types of internal files from which we will note the files having extensions {".nb", ".m", ".mx"}, their structure is distinguished by the standard system tools and which are important enough already on the first stages of work with system. Before further consideration we will note that the concept of *file qualifier* (**FQ**) defining the full path to the required file in file system of the computer or to its *subdirectory*, practically, completely coincides with similar concept for already mentioned *Maple* system excepting that if in the *Maple* for **FQ** the format of type {*symbol*, *string*} is allowed whereas in the *Mathematica* system for **FQ** the string format is admissible only.

So, the call **Directory[]** of the system function returns an active subdirectory of the current session of the system whereas the call **SetDirectory[*x*]** returns a *x* directory, doing it active in the current session; in addition, as an *active (current)* directory is understood the directory whose datafiles are processed by means of means of access if only their names, but not full paths to them are specified. At that, defining at the call **SetDirectory[*x*]** the system variable **$UserDocumentsDirectory** as a factual *x* argument, it is possible to *redefine* the user current subdirectory by default. Meanwhile, the **SetDirectory** allows only real–life subdirectories as argument, causing on nonexistent directories an erroneous situation with returning $*Failed*. On the other hand, a **SetDir** procedure provides possibility to determine also nonexistent subdirectories as the current subdirectories. The call **SetDir[*x*]** on an existing subdirectory *x* does it current while a nonexistent subdirectory is previously created and then it is defined as the current subdirectory. At that, if the actual *x* argument at the call **SetDir[*x*]** is defined by a chain without name of the *IO* device, in particular, "*aa*\\\\.......*bb*", then a chain of the subdirectories **Directory[]** <> "*aa*\\\\.......*bb*" is created which determines a full path to the created current subdirectory. The unsuccessful procedure call returns $*Failed*, for example, at an inactive *IO* device. The next fragment represents source code of the **SetDir** procedure with examples of its application.

In[2531]:= **Directory[]**
Out[2531]= "C:\\\\Users\\\\Aladjev\\\\Documents"
In[2532]:= **SetDirectory["E:\\\\MathToolBox"]**
SetDirectory::cdir: Cannot set current directory to E:\\\\MathToolBox... >>
Out[2532]= $Failed
In[2533]:= **SetDirectory[$UserDocumentsDirectory]**
Out[2533]= "C:\\\\Users\\\\Aladjev\\\\Documents"
In[2534]:= **SetDirectory[]**
Out[2534]= "C:\\\\Users\\\\Aladjev"

In[2535]:= **SetDir[x_ /; StringQ[x]] := Module[{a, b, c},**
If[StringLength[x] == 1 || StringLength[x] >= 2 && StringTake[x, {2, 2}] != ":",
Quiet[SetDirectory[Quiet[CreateDirectory[StringReplace[Directory[] <> "\\\\" <> x,
"\\\\\\\\" -> "\\\\"]]]]], If[Run["Dir " <> StringTake[x, {1, 2}]] != 0, $Failed,
b = FileNameSplit[x]; c = b[[1]]; Do[c = c <> "\\\\" <> b[[k]];
Quiet[CreateDirectory[c]], {k, 2, Length[b]}]; SetDirectory[c]]]]

In[2536]:= **SetDir["C:\\\\Temp\\\\111\\\\222\\\\333\\\\444\\\\555\\\\666\\\\777"]**
Out[2536]= "C:\\\\Temp\\\\111\\\\222\\\\333\\\\444\\\\555\\\\666\\\\777"
In[2537]:= **SetDir["H:\\\\111\\\\222\\\\333\\\\444\\\\555\\\\666\\\\777"]**
Out[2537]= $Failed
In[2538]:= **Directory[]**
Out[2538]= "C:\\\\Temp\\\\111\\\\222\\\\333\\\\444\\\\555\\\\666\\\\777"
In[2539]:= **SetDir["kr\\\\6"]**
Out[2539]= "C:\\\\Temp\\\\111\\\\222\\\\333\\\\444\\\\555\\\\666\\\\777\\\\kr\\\\6"
In[2540]:= **SetDir["E:\\\\MathToolBox"]**
Out[2540]= "E:\\\\MathToolBox"

In[2541]:= **Adrive[] := Module[{a, b, c, d}, {a, b} = {CharacterRange["A", "Z"], {}};**
Do[d = Directory[]; c = a[[k]]; AppendTo[b, If[Quiet[SetDirectory[c <> ":\\\\"]] === $Failed,
Nothing, SetDirectory[d]; c]], {k, 1, Length[a]}]; Sort[b]]

In[2542]:= **Adrive[]**
Out[2542]= {"C", "D", "E", "F", "G"}

Meanwhile, in attempt of definition of a nonexistent directory as the current directory the emergence of a situation is quite real when as a *IO* device has been specified a device which at the moment isn't existing in the system or inaccessible. Therefore rather actually to have means allowing to verify availability of *IO* devices in the system. In this regard the **Adrive** procedure solves this problem, whose call **Adrive[]** returns the list of logical names in string format of *IO* devices, available at the moment. This procedure is an useful enough analog of procedure of the same name for the *Maple*, the last part of the previous fragment represents source code of the **Adrive** procedure with an example of its use [47]. Both procedures of the previous fragment are useful enough at programming in the *Mathematica* of various tools of access to the datafiles.

The following **Adrive1** procedure extends the above **Adrive** procedure and returns the two-element nested list whose first element represents the list with names in string format of all active direct access devices while the second element represents the list with names in string format of all inactive direct access devices of the computer. The fragment below represents source code of the **Adrive1** procedure along with a typical example of its application.

In[3206]:= **Adrive1[]** := Module[{a = CharacterRange["A", "Z"], b = {}, c, h, d = {}},
Do[c = a[[k]]; If[DirQ[c <> ":\\"], AppendTo[b, c], Null], {k, 1, Length[a]}];
Do[h = Directory[]; c = a[[k]]; AppendTo[d, If[Quiet[SetDirectory[c <> ":\\"]] === $Failed,
Nothing, SetDirectory[h]; c]], {k, 1, Length[a]}]; Map[Sort, {d, MinusList[b, d]}]]]

In[3207]:= **Adrive1[]**
Out[3207]= {{"C", "D", "G"}, {"A", "E"}}
In[3208]:= **Adrive1[]**
Out[3208]= {{"C"}, {"D"}}
In[3209]:= **SetDir1**[x_ /; StringQ[x]] :=
Module[{a = Quiet[Check[SetDirectory[x], $Failed]], b, c},
If[! SameQ[a, $Failed], a, b = Adrive[]; c = Map[FreeSpaceVol, b];
c = SortNL1[c, 2, Greater]; SetDir[StringJoin[c[[1]][[1]], StringTake[x, {2, -1}]]]]]
In[3210]:= **SetDir1**["G:\\Galina/Svetla\\ArtKr/Tampere\\Tallinn"]
Out[3210]= "C:\\Galina/Svetla\\ArtKr/Tampere\\Tallinn"

At last, the **SetDir1** procedure represented at the end of the previous fragment extends the **SetDir** onto the case when attempt to create a chain of directories meets an *especial* situation caused by lack of the demanded device on which creation of this chain of subdirectories was planned. In the absence of such device of direct access the procedure call **SetDir1**[*x*] returns the created chain of subdirectories on a device having the greatest possible volume of the available memory among all active devices of the direct access in the current session of the *Mathematica* system.

Files with documents which in one of *11* formats by the chain of command *"File -> {Save As|Save}"* of the *GUI* *(the most used formats "nb", "m")* are saved, the files with the objects saved by the **Save** function *(input format)*, and files with the *Mathematica* packages *(format "m", "mx")* belong to the internal files. These datafiles represent an quite certain interest at the solution of many problems demanding both the standard methods, and the advanced methods of programming. For standard support of operating with them the *Mathematica* system has a number of tools whereas for ensuring expanded work with similar datafiles a set of tools can be created, some of which are considered in the present book and also have been included to our *MathToolBox* package [48,50]. In addition, files of any of the specified formats with the definitions of objects saved in them by the **Save** function as a result of the uploading of these datafiles by the **Get** function into the subsequent sessions of the system provide availability of these objects.

It is a rather simple to be convinced that the datafiles created by means of the **Save** function contain definitions of objects in the Input *Mathematica* format irrespective of extension of a file name. It provides possibility of rather simple organization of processing of such files for various appendices. In particular, on the basis of structure of such files it is possible without their loading into the current session to obtain lists of names of the objects that are in them. For this purpose the **Nobj** procedure can be used, whose call **Nobj[x, y]** returns the list of names of the objects in string format that have been earlier saved in a *x* file by means of the **Save** function whereas through the second factual *y* argument the list of headings in string format of these objects is returned. Such decision is rather essential since in a datafile can be objects of the same name with various headings, exactly that identify uniqueness of object.

At that, can arise a need not to upload by means of the **Get** function into the current session completely a file that has been earlier created by means of the **Save** function with activation of all objects containing in it, but to upload the objects containing in the file selectively, i.e. to create a kind of libraries of the user tools. Concerning the packages created by means of a chain *"File → Save As → Mathematica Package (*.m)"* of the *GUI* commands, the problem can be solved by means of the **Aobj** whose call **Aobj[x, y]** makes *active* in the current session all objects with *y* names from *m*-file *x* that has been earlier created by the above chain of the *GUI* commands. The fragment below represents source codes of the above procedures **Aobj** and **Nobj** along with the most typical examples of their application.

In[2626]:= Art1 := #^2 &; Art2 = #^3 &; Art3 := #^4 &; Art4 = #^5 &; Art := 27; Kr = 20; Agn[y_] := 69; Avz[x_] := 90*x + 590; SetAttributes[Avz, {Listable, Protected}]
In[2627]:= Save["C:/Temp/Obj.m", {Adrive, SetDir, Art1, Art2, Art3, Art4, Art, Nobj, Kr, Agn, Avz}]
In[2628]:= Nobj[x_ /; FileExistsQ[x] && StringTake[x, -2] == ".m",
y_ /; ! HowAct[y]] := Module[{a, b, c, d, p, h, t, k = 1},
If[FileExistsQ[x] && MemberQ[{"Table", "Package"}, Quiet[FileFormat[x]]],
{a, b, d, h} = {OpenRead[x], {}, "90", {}};
While[! SameQ[d, "EndOfFile"], d = ToString[Read[a, String]];
If[! SuffPref[d, " ", 1], If[! StringFreeQ[d, "::usage = \""], AppendTo[b,
StringSplit[StringTake[d, {1, Flatten[StringPosition[d, "::usage"]][[1]] - 1}], " /: "][[1]]],
p = Quiet[Check[StringTake[d, {1, Flatten[StringPosition[d, {" := ", " = "}]][[1]] - 1}],
$Failed]];
If[! SameQ[p, $Failed], If[SymbolQ[p] && StringFreeQ[p, {" ", "{", "`"}] ||
StringFreeQ[p, {" ", "{", "`"}] && HeadingQ1[p] === True, AppendTo[b, p]]]]]; k++];
Close[a]; b = Sort[DeleteDuplicates[b]]; h = Select[b, ! SymbolQ[#] &];
t = Map[If[SymbolQ[#], #, HeadName[#]] &, h]; b = MinusList[b, h];
b = Sort[DeleteDuplicates[Join[b, t]]];
y = MinusList[Sort[DeleteDuplicates[Join[h, Select[Map[If[! UnevaluatedQ[HeadPF, #],
HeadPF[#]] &, b], ! SameQ[#, Null] &]]]], b]; b, $Failed]]

In[2629]:= Clear[ArtKr]; Nobj["C:\\Temp\\Obj.m", ArtKr]
Out[2629]= {"Adrive", "Agn", "Art", "Art1", "Art2", "Art3", "Art4", "Avz",
"BlockFuncModQ", "ClearAllAttributes", "Contexts1", "Definition2", "GenRules",
"HeadingQ", "HeadingQ1", "HeadName", "HeadPF", "HowAct", "Kr", "ListListQ",
"ListStrToStr", "Map13", "Map3", "Map9", "Mapp", "MinusList", "Nobj", "ProcQ",
"PureDefinition", "RedSymbStr", "Sequences", "SetDir", "StrDelEnds", "StringMultiple",

"StringSplit1", "SubsDel", "SuffPref", "SymbolQ", "SymbolQ1", "SysFuncQ", "SystemQ", "ToString1", "UnevaluatedQ"}
In[2630]:= **ArtKr**
Out[2630]= {"Adrive[]", "Agn[y_]", "Avz[x_]", "BlockFuncModQ[x_, y__]", "ClearAllAttributes[x__]", "Contexts1[]", "Definition2[x_ /; SymbolQ[x] === HowAct[x]]", "HeadingQ1[x_ /; StringQ[x]]", "HeadingQ[x_ /; StringQ[x]]", "HeadName[x_ /; HeadingQ[x] || HeadingQ1[x]]", "HowAct[x_]", ..., "ToString1[x_]", "UnevaluatedQ[F_ /; SymbolQ[F], x__]"}

In[2650]:= **Aobj[x_ /; FileExistsQ[x] && FileExtension[x] == "m", y_ /; SymbolQ[y] || ListQ[y] && AllTrue[Map[SymbolQ[#] &, y], TrueQ]] :=
Module[{a, b = "(*", c = "*)", d = $AobjNobj, p = {Read[x, String], Close[x]}[[1]], h = Mapp[StringJoin, Map[ToString, Flatten[{y}]], "["], k, j, g, s, t = {}, v = {}},
If[p != "(* ::Package:: *)", $Failed, a = ReadFullFile[x];
If[StringFreeQ[a, d], $Failed, a = StringSplit[a, d][[2 ;; -1]]];
a = Map[StringReplace[#, {b -> "", c -> ""}] &, a]; a = Select[a, SuffPref[#, h, 1] &];
For[k = 1, k <= Length[h], k++, g = h[[k]];
For[j = 1, j <= Length[a], j++, s = a[[j]];
c = StrSymbParity[s, g, "[", "]"]; c = If[c == {}, False,
HeadingQ1[Quiet[ToString[ToExpression[c[[1]]]]]] || HeadingQ[c[[1]]]];
If[SuffPref[s, g, 1] && c, AppendTo[t, s];
AppendTo[v, StringTake[g, {1, -2}]]]]]; Map[ToExpression, t];
If[v != {}, Print["Software for " <> ToString[v] <> " is downloaded"],
Print["Software for " <> ToString[Flatten[{y}]] <> " was not found"]]]]]**

In[2651]:= **Art1[] := #^2 &**
In[2652]:= **Art2[] = #^3 &;**
In[2653]:= **Art3[] := #^4 &**
In[2654]:= **Art4[] = #^5 &;**
In[2655]:= **Art[] := 27**
In[2656]:= **Kr[] = 20;**
In[2657]:= **Agn[y_] := 69**
In[2658]:= **Avz[x_] := 90*x + 590**
In[2659]:=**Aobj["c:\\tmp\\Obj.m", {Art1, Art2, Art3, Art4, Art, Kr, Agn, Avz}]**
"Software for {Nobj, Avz, Agn, ArtKr, Sv} is downloaded"
In[2659]:=**Aobj["C:\\Tmp\\Obj.m", {Nobj90, Avz590, Agn69, Vsv47}]**
"Software for {Nobj90, Avz590, Agn69, Vsv47} was not found"
In[2660]:= **Map[PureDefinition, {Art1, Art2, Art3, Art4, Art, Kr, Agn, Avz}]**
Out[2660]= {"Art1[] := #1^2 & ", "Art2[] = #1^3 & ", "Art3[] := #1^4 & ", "Art4[] = #1^5 & ", "Art[] := 27", "Kr[] = 20", "Agn[y_] := 69", "Avz[x_] := 90*x + 590"}

The top part of the previous fragment represents the saving in a *m*-file of the *Mathematica* objects from this fragment and the objects given a little above in the same section. Further the source code of the **Nobj** procedure and an example of its application is presented. Right there it should be noted that performance of the **Nobj** procedure will demand certain time costs. At that, if the main result of the procedure call **Nobj[x, y]** contains the list of names in string format of the means contained in a *x* file, through the *second y* argument the headings of the tools possessing them are returned.

Whereas the second part of the fragment represents source code of the **Aobj** procedure with an example of its usage for activization in the current session of the objects {*Art1, Art2, Art3, Art4, Art, Kr, Agn, Avz*} that are in a *m*-file that is earlier created by means of chain *"File → Save As → Mathematica Package (*.m)"* of *GUI* commands. Verification confirms *availability* of the specified objects in the current session. Moreover, as the second *y* argument at the call **Aobj** a separate symbol or their list can be. Besides that is supposed, that before saving in a *m*-datafile *x* all definitions of objects in the current document should have headings and be evaluated in separate the *Input* paragraphs. The successful call **Aobj[*x*, *y*]** returns *Null*, i.e. nothing with output of the message concerning those tools which were uploaded from a *m*-datafile *x* or that are absent in the datafile. The procedures **Nobj** and **Aobj** process the main erroneous situations with returning on them the value *$Failed*. At that, both procedures can be extended by the means of replenishment their by the new useful enough functions.

The following **Aobj1** procedure is an useful extension of the previous **Aobj** procedure. Like the **Aobj** procedure the **Aobj1** procedure also is used for activation in the current session of the objects which are in a *m*-file that is earlier created by means of chain *"File → Save As → Mathematica Package (*.m)"* of *GUI* commands. The successful call **Aobj1[*x,y*]** returns *Null*, i.e. nothing with output of the messages concerning those tools that were uploaded from a *m*-file *x* and which are absent in the datafile. Moreover, as the second *y* argument at the call **Aobj1** the separate symbol or their list can be. Besides that is supposed, before saving in a *m*-file *x* all definitions of objects in the saved document should be evaluated in the separate *Input* paragraphs on the basis of delayed assignments, though the existence of headings not required. Right there it should be noted, that for ability of correct processing of the *m*-files created in the specified manner the predetermined *$AobjNobj* variable is used that provides correct processing of the datafiles containing the procedures, in particular, **Aobj** and **Aobj1**. The following fragment represents source code of the **Aobj1** procedure along with the most typical examples of its application.

```
In[2672]:= Aobj1[x_ /; FileExistsQ[x] && FileExtension[x] == "m", y_ /; SymbolQ[y] ||
ListQ[y] && AllTrue[Map[SymbolQ[#] &, y], TrueQ]] :=
Module[{a, c="*)(*", d=$AobjNobj, k, t={}, g={}, h=Map[ToString, Flatten[{y}]], p, j=1, v},
a = StringSplit[ReadFullFile[x], d][[2 ;; -1]]; a = Map[StringTake[#, {3, -3}] &, a];
For[j, j <= Length[h], j++, p = h[[j]];
For[k = 1, k <= Length[a], k++, If[SuffPref[a[[k]], Map[StringJoin[p, #] &, {"[", "=", ":"}], 1],
AppendTo[t, StringReplace[a[[k]], c -> ""]]; AppendTo[g, p], Null]]];
v = {t, MinusList[h, g]}; If[v[[1]] != {}, ToExpression[v[[1]]];
Print["Software for " <> ToString[g] <> " is downloaded"], Null];
If[v[[2]] != {}, Print["Software for " <> ToString[v[[2]]] <> " was not found"], Null]]

In[2673]:= Aobj1["C:\\Temp/Obj42.m", {Nobj90, Avz590, Agn69, Vsv47}]
"Software for {Nobj90, Avz590, Agn69, Vsv47} was not found"
In[2674]:= Aobj1["C:\\Temp\Obj42.m", {Art1, Art2, Art3, Art4, Art, Agn, Avz, Rans, IAN,
Rae, Nobj}]
```

"Software for {Art1, Art2, Art3, Art4, Art, Agn, Avz, Nobj} is downloaded Software for {Rans, IAN, Rae, Nobj} was not found"

There is a number of other rather interesting procedures for ensuring work with files of the *Mathematica Input*-format whose names have extensions {".nb", ".m", ".txt"}, etc. All such tools are based on the basis of analysis of structure of the contents of files returned by access functions, in particular, **ReadFullFile**. Some of them gives a possibility to create the rather effective user libraries containing definitions of the *Mathematica* objects. These and certain other tools have been implemented as a part of the special package supporting the releases *8 ÷ 11* of *Mathematica* system [48]. The part of these means will be considered in the present book slightly below.

Certain remarks should be made concerning the **Save** function which saves the objects in a given file in the *Append* mode; in addition, undefinite symbols in the datafile are not saved without output of any messages, i.e. the **Save** call returns *Null*, i.e. nothing. Meanwhile, at saving of a procedure or function with a name *Avz* in a file by means of the **Save** in the file all active objects of the same *Avz* name in the current session with different headings – *the identifiers of their originality* – are saved too. For elimination of this situation a generalization of the **Save** function concerning possibility of saving of *Mathematica* objects with concrete headings is offered. Thus, the **Save1** procedure solves the problem whose source code with typical examples of its application are represented by means of the following fragment.

```
In[2742]:= A[x_] := x^2; A[x_, y_] := x+y; A[x_, y_, z_] := x+y+z; A[x__] := {x}; DefFunc3[A]
Out[2742]= {"A[x_] := x^2", "A[x_, y_] := x + y", "A[x_, y_, z_] := x + y + z", "A[x__] := {x}"}
In[2743]:= Save1[x_ /; StringQ[x], y_ /; DeleteDuplicates[Map[StringQ, Flatten[{y}]]][[1]]]:=
Module[{Rs, t = Flatten[{y}], k = 1},
Rs[n_, m_] := Module[{b, c = ToString[Unique[b]], a = If[SymbolQ[m], Save[n, m],
If[StringFreeQ[m, "["], $Failed, StringTake[m, {1, Flatten[StringPosition[m, "["]][[1]] – 1}]]]},
If[a === Null, Return[], If[a === $Failed, Return[$Failed],
If[SymbolQ[a], b = DefFunc3[a], Return[$Failed]]]];
If[Length[b] == 1, Save[n, a], b = Select[b, SuffPref[#, m, 1] &]];
If[b != {}, b = c <> b[[1]], Return[$Failed]]; ToExpression[b]; a = c <> a;
ToExpression["Save[" <> ToString1[n] <> "," <> ToString1[a] <> "]"];
BinaryWrite[n, StringReplace[ToString[StringJoin[Map[FromCharacterCode,
BinaryReadList[n]]]], c -> ""]]; Close[n]; ]; For[k, k <= Length[t], k++, Rs[x, t[[k]]]]]
In[2744]:= Save1["rans_ian.m", {"A[x_, y_, z_]", "A[x__]"}]
In[2745]:= Clear[A]; DefFunc3[A]
Out[2745]= DefFunc3[A]
In[2746]:= << "rans_ian.m"
In[2747]:= B[x_] := x^2; DefFunc3[A]
Out[2747]= {"A[x_, y_, z_] := x + y + z", "A[x__] := {x}"}
In[2748]:= Agn = 69; Save1["Avz.m", {"A[x_, y_, z_]", "B", "A[x__]", "Agn"}]
In[2749]:= Clear[A, B, Agn]; Map[DefFunc3, {A, B, Agn}]
Out[2749]= {DefFunc3[A], DefFunc3[B], DefFunc3[Agn]}
In[2750]:= << "Avz.m"
```

Out[2750]= 69
In[2751]:= **DefFunc3[A]**
Out[2751]= {"A[x_, y_, z_] := x + y + z", "A[x__] := {x}"}
In[2752]:= **{DefFunc3["B"], Agn}**
Out[2752]= {{"B[x_] := x^2"}, 69}

The procedure call **Save1**[*x, y*] saves in a datafile defined by the first factual *x* argument, the definitions of the objects determined by the second factual *y* argument – *the name of an active object in the current session or its heading in string format, or their combinations in the list format*. The **Save1** procedure can be used as standard **Save** function, and solving a saving problem of the chosen objects activated in the current session in the file differentially on the basis of their headings. Thus, a successful procedure call returns *Null*, carrying out the demanded savings; otherwise, $*Failed* or unevaluated call are returned. The previous fragment presents results of application of the **Save1** procedure for a selective saving in files of the objects that have been activated in the *Mathematica* current session. In a number of cases the procedure **Save1** represents undoubted interest.

In a number of cases there is an urgent need of saving in a file of state of the current session with possibility of its subsequent restoration by means of uploading of a file into the current session different from the previous session. In this context, **SaveCurrentSession** procedure and **RestoreCS** procedure are rather useful for saving and restoration of state of the current session respectively. Thus, the call **SaveCurrentSession[]** saves a state of the *Mathematica* current session in the *m*–file "SaveCS.m" with returning of the name of a *target* file. Whereas the call **SaveCurrentSession**[*x*] saves a state of the *Mathematica* current session in a *m*–file *x* with returning of the name of the target *x* file; at that, if a *x* file has not ".*m*" extension then this extension is added to the *x* string. The call **RectoreCS[]** restores *Mathematica* current session that has been previously stored by means of the **SaveCurrentSession** procedure in "SaveCS.m" file with returning the *Null*, i.e. nothing. Whereas the call **RectoreCS**[*x*] restores the current *Mathematica* session that has been previously stored by means of the procedure **SaveCurrentSession** in a *m*–file *x* with returning the *Null*. In absence of the above datafile the procedure call returns $*Failed*. The next fragment represents source codes of the above procedures along with typical examples of their application.

In[2742]:= SaveCurrentSession[x___String] := Module[{a = Names["*"],
b = If[{x} == {}, "SaveCS.m", If[SuffPref[x, ".m", 2], x, x <> ".m"]]}, Save1[b, a]; b]

In[2743]:= **SaveCurrentSession["Tallinn"]**
Out[2743]= "Tallinn.m"

In[2744]:= RestoreCS[x___String] := Module[{a = If[{x} == {}, "SaveCS.m",
If[FileExistsQ[x] && FileExtension[x] == "m", x, $Failed]]},
If[a === $Failed, $Failed, On[General]; Quiet[Get[a]]; Off[General]]]

In[2745]:= **RestoreCS["Tallinn.m"]**
In[2746]:= **RestoreCS["AvzAgnVsv.m"]**
Out[2746]= $Failed

So, the represented means are rather useful in a case when is required to create copies of the current sessions at certain moments of operating with the system.

The **DumpSave** function serves as other tool for saving of definitions of the objects in files, creating files of binary format which is optimized for input into the *Mathematica* system. Names of files of this format have "*mx*" extension, and analogously to the previous format they can be uploaded into the current session by the **Get** function. Unlike the **Save** function, the call of **DumpSave** returns the list of names, or definitions of the objects saved in a *mx*-file. Meanwhile, it must be kept in mind an essential circumstance that the files created by means of the **DumpSave** function not only are most optimum for input into *Mathematica*, but also can't be uploaded on a computing platform different from the platform on that they were created. Many interesting examples of application of the function **DumpSave** can be found in [30-33], some from them will be presented and a little below. Thus, it is necessary to work with datafiles of the binary format only in the case when their usage in rather broad aspect isn't planned, i.e. in the sense this format has obviously internal character, without providing of the portability of the created means.

In a lot of cases there is a necessity of uploading into the current session of files of types {*nb, m, mx, txt*} or datafiles of the *ASCII* format without name extension that are located in one of directories of file system of the computer; moreover, having a full name of datafile we can not have a certain information concerning its location in file system of the computer. In this context the **LoadFile** procedure solves the problem whose source code and typical examples of its application the following fragment represents.

In[2575]:= **LoadFile[F_ /; StringQ[F]] := Module[{a, b, c},**
If[! MemberQ[{"nb", "m", "mx", "txt", ""}, FileExtension[F]],
Return["File <" <> F <> "> has an inadmissible type"], a = Flatten[{FindFile[F]}];
a = If[a === {$Failed}, SearchFile[F], a]; $Load$Files$ = a];
If[a == {}, Return["File <" <> F <> "> has not been found"],
Quiet[Check[Get[$Load$Files$[[1]]], c = {$Failed}, {Syntax::sntxc, Syntax::sntxi}]];
If[c === {$Failed}, "File <" <> $Load$Files$[[1]] <> "> has inadmissible syntax",
"File <" <> $Load$Files$[[1]] <> "> has been loaded; \n$Load$Files$ defines the list
with full paths to the found files."], Return["File <" <> F <> "> has not been found"]]]
In[2576]:= **LoadFile["C:\\Temp\\Obj42.m"]**
Out[2576]= "File <C:\\Temp\\Obj42.m> has been loaded; $Load$Files$ defines the list with full paths to the found files."
In[2577]:= **$Load$Files$**
Out[2577]= {"C:\\Temp\\Obj42.m"}
In[2578]:= **LoadFile["AvzAgn.m"]**
Out[2578]= "File <C:\\Mathematica\\AvzAgn.m> has been loaded; $Load$Files$ defines the list with full paths to the found files."
In[2579]:= **$Load$Files$**
Out[2579]= {"C:\\Mathematica\\AvzAgn.m"}
In[2580]:= **LoadFile["Obj4769.m"]**
Out[2580]= "File <Obj4769.m> has not been found"

The procedure call **LoadFile[*w*]** uploads into the current session a datafile given by its *w* name and with an extension {*m, nb, mx, txt*} or at all without extension. At that, at finding of the list of datafiles with an identical name *w* uploading of the first of the list with return of the corresponding message is made, while through the global $Load$Files$ variable the procedure returns the list of all *w* files found in search process. The procedure processes the main erroneous situations, including syntax of the found datafile, unacceptable for the **Get** function. In the case of lack of *w* files through the $Load$Files$ variable the empty list, i.e. {} is returned.

A rather simple and in certain cases the useful **MathematicaDF** procedure completes this section, its call **MathematicaDF[]** returns the list of the *ListList* type, whose two–element members by the first elements contain type of the elements of the *Mathematica* file system whereas by the second elements contain quantity of elements of this type. At that, the value *"NoExtension"* defines files without extension, *"Dir"* defines directories whereas the others defines type of extension of a datafile. The following fragment represents source code of the **MathematicaDF** procedure along with a typical example of its application concerning the *Mathematica* system of the current version *11.2.0*.

In[2982]:= MathematicaDF[] := Module[{a = "Art27$Kr20$", b = {}, c = "", d},
Run["Dir " <> " /A/B/S " <> StrStr[$InstallationDirectory] <> " > " <> a];
While[! SameQ[c, EndOfFile], c = Read[a, String];
Quiet[If[DirectoryQ[c], AppendTo[b, "dir"],
If[FileExistsQ[c], d = ToLowerCase[FileExtension[c]];
AppendTo[b, If[d === "", "NoExtension", d]], AppendTo[b, "NoFile"]]]]];
DeleteFile[Close[a]];
Sort[Map[{#[[1]], Length[#]} &, Gather[b, #1 === #2 &]], Order[#1[[1]], #2[[1]]] == 1 &]]

In[2983]:= MathematicaDF[]
Out[2983]= {{"1", 1}, {"2", 1}, {"3", 1}, {"4", 1}, {"a", 104}, {"accdb", 1}, {"access", 2}, {"aco", 1}, {"adoc", 6}, {"aff", 41}, {"aif", 1}, {"alias", 1}, {"bak", 1}, {"bat", 2}, {"bfc", 2}, {"bin", 2}, {"bmp", 1}, {"byu", 1}, {"c", 65}, {"cache", 4}, ..., {"vtk", 1}, {"wav", 5}, {"webp", 1}, {"wl", 19}, {"woff", 6}, {"xbm", 1}, {"xhtml", 1}, {"xls", 2}, {"xlsx", 1}, {"xml", 167}, {"xsl", 4}, {"xyz", 1}, {"zip", 2}}
In[2984]:= Plus[Sequences[Map[#[[2]] &, %]]]
Out[2984]= 33975

At last, the procedure call **OpSys[]** returns the type of operational system. The procedure is an useful in certain appendices above all of system character. The next fragment represents source code of the procedure with an example of its application.

In[5334]:= OpSys[] := Module[{a = ToString[Unique["s"]], b}, Run["SystemInfo >" <> a];
b = StringTrim[StringTake[ReadList[a, String][[2]], {9, -1}]]; DeleteFile[a]; b]
In[5335]:= OpSys[]
Out[5335]= "Microsoft Windows 7 Professional"

On that the representation of access means to the system files is completed, and means of operating with external datafiles will be represented in the next section. Meanwhile, the represented means of processing of system datafiles in a number of cases represent a quite certain interest, first of all, for various applications of the system character. So, certain tools of the *MathToolBox* package use the above tools [48,50].

7.2. Tools of the *Mathematica* system for operating with external datafiles

According to such an quite important indicator as means of access to files, the *Mathematica* system, in our opinion, possesses a number of advantages in comparison with the *Maple* system. First of all, *Mathematica* carries out automatic processing of hundreds of formats of data and their subformats on the basis of the unified use of symbolical expressions. For each specific format the correspondence between internal and external representation of a format is defined, using the general mechanism of data elements of *Mathematica* system. For today *Mathematica* as a whole supports many various formats of files for various purposes, their list can be received by means of the predetermined variables *$ImportFormats* *(the imported files)* and *$ExportFormats* *(the exported files)* in quantities *178* and *148* respectively. Whereas the basic formats of files are considered rather in details in [33,50].

By the function call **FileFormat[x]** an attempt to define an input format for a file given by a *x* name in the string format is made. In a case of existence for a *x* file of name extension the **FileFormat** function is, almost, similar to the **FileExtension** function, returning the available extension, except for a case of packages *(m–datafiles)* when instead of extension the file type *"Package"* is returned. At that, in some cases the format identification is done incorrectly, in particular, the attempt to test a *doc*-file without an extension returns *"XLS"*, ascribing it to the datafiles created by *Excel 95/97/2000/XP/2003* that is generally incorrect.

In[2557]:= **Map[FileFormat, {"MathToolBox_1.nb", "MathToolBox_1.m"}]**
Out[2557]= {"NB", "Package"}
In[2558]:= **FileFormat["D:\\MathToolBox\\Art1"]**
Out[2558]= "Text"
In[2559]:= **FileExtension["D:\\MathToolBox\\Art1"]**
Out[2559]= ""
In[2560]:= **FileFormat["Art1"]**
FileFormat::nffil: File not found during FileFormat[Art1]... >>
Out[2560]= $Failed
In[2561]:= **FileFormat["D:\\MathToolBox\\MathToolBox_1"]**
FileFormat::nffil: File not found during FileFormat[D:\MathToolBox\MathToolBox_1]... >>
Out[2561]= $Failed
In[2562]:= **Map[FileFormat, {"C:/AVZ_P", "C:/AVZ_P1", "C:/Temp/Der"}]**
Out[2562]= {"NB", "Package", "XLS"}
In[2563]:= **FileFormat["C:\\Temp\\Der.doc"]**
Out[2563]= "DOC"

In[2564]:= **FileFormat1[x_ /; StringQ[x]] := Module[{a},**
If[FileExistsQ[x], {x, FileFormat[x]}, a = SearchFile[x];
If[a == {}, {}, a = Map[{#, FileFormat[#]} &, a]; If[Length[a] == 1, a[[1]], a]]]]

In[2565]:= **FileFormat1["MathToolBox.m"]**
Out[2565]= {{"C:\\Users\\Mathematica\\MathToolBox.m", "Package"},
{"C:\\Temp\\Mathematica\\MathToolBox.m", "Package"},
{"C:\\Mathematica\\MathToolBox.m", "Package"},
{"D:\\Temp\\Mathematica\\MathToolBox.m", "Package"}}
In[2566]:= **FileFormat1["Z0123456789"]**

Out[2566]= {}
In[2567]:= **FileFormat1["C:\\Users\\Mathematica\\MathToolBox.m"]**
Out[2567]= {"C:\\Users\\Mathematica\\MathToolBox.m", "Package"}
In[2610]:= **Map[FileFormat, {"C:/", "C:\\"}]**
General::cdir: Cannot set current directory to $RXE7FCO.>>
General::cdir: Cannot set current directory to $RRMBM4A.>>
=====
General::stop: Further output of General::dirdep will be suppressed during this calculation...>>
Out[2610]= {"KML", "KML"}

In[2611]:= **FileFormat2[x_ /; StringQ[x]] := Module[{a, b = {}, c, k = 1},
If[StringLength[x] == 3, If[MemberQ[{":/", ":\\"}, StringTake[x, -2]] &&
MemberQ[Adrive[], ToUpperCase[StringTake[x, 1]]], Return["Directory"], Null],
If[DirectoryQ[x], Return["Directory"], a = SearchFile[x]];
If[a == {}, Return[{}], For[k, k <= Length[a], k++, c = a[[k]];
AppendTo[b, {c, FileFormat[c]}]]]; If[Length[b] == 1, b[[1]], b]]**

In[2612]:= **Map[FileFormat2, {"C:/", "C:\\", "C:/Temp", "C:\\Temp"}]**
Out[2612]= {"Directory", "Directory", "Directory", "Directory"}
In[2613]:= **FileFormat2["Obj47.m"]**
Out[2613]= {{"C:\\Users\\Aladjev\\Mathematica\\Obj47.m", "Package"},
{"D:\\MathToolBox\\Obj47.m", "Package"}}

Moreover, by the function call **FileFormat[x]** an attempt to define the format of a *x* datafile is made, that is located only in the subdirectories determined by *$Path* variable, otherwise returning *$Failed* with print of the appropriate message as illustrates an example of previous fragment. For elimination of similar situation the simple enough **FileFormat1** procedure is offered which extends the possibilities of the **FileFormat** function, and uses the **SearchFile** procedure which will be presented a little below. The procedure call **FileFormat1[x]** returns the simple or nested list, first element of a simple list defines the full path to a *x* file whereas the second element – its format that is recognized by the **FileFormat** function; in addition, the required datafile can be located in any directory of file system of the computer; absence of a *x* datafile initiates the return of the empty list, i.e. {}. Moreover, at finding several files with an identical name the nested list whose sublists have the specified format is returned. The previous fragment represents source code of the **FileFormat1** procedure with typical examples of its application. In certain cases the **FileFormat1** procedure is more preferable than standard **FileFormat** function.

As it is noted above, the call **FileFormat[F]** tries to define an *Import*-format for import of a datafile or *URL* corresponding to *F* argument; meanwhile, on main directories of external memory (*disk, flash memory, etc.*) the call causes erroneous situation; in addition, the function recognizes only the datafiles which are in the directories determined by *$Path* variable; for elimination of the last situation the **FileFormat1** procedure above has been offered while the procedure can be quite simply extended for the purpose of elimination and the 1[st] situation. The **FileFormat2** procedure was programmed on the basis of **FileFormat1** procedure, this procedure quite correctly processes the main directories, *inaccessible* and *nonexistent* devices of the external memory, and also files from directories of file system of the computer. The previous fragment represents source code of the procedure with typical examples of its use. Thus, earlier represented **FileFormat1** procedure provides check of format of the files which are located in directories of file system of the computer irrespectively from their presence in the **$Path** variable. Whereas **FileFormat2** procedure in addition *correctly* processes the main directories of external memory, bearing in mind the *important* circumstance that they are the key elements of file system of the computer. Indeed, the examples of the previous fragment illustrate that the function call **FileFormat[x]** on main directory of *x* volume returns "KML" format that is the *GIS* standard format that serves for storage of cartographical information instead of the *Directory* format. The call **FileFormat2[x]** eliminates this defect with return on similar objects "Directory", while in other situations a call **FileFormat2[x]** is equivalent to the call **FileFormat1[x]**.

At last, a version of the standard **FileFormat** function attempts to identify file type without extension, being based on information of the creator of file that is contained in the contents of the file. The **FileFormat3** procedure rather accurately identifies datafiles of the following often used types {*DOC, PDF, ODT, TXT, HTML*}. In addition, concerning the *TXT* type the verification of a datafile is made in the latter case, believing that the datafile of this type has to consist only of symbols with the following decimal codes:

0 ÷ 127 – ASCII symbols
1 ÷ 31   – the control ASCII symbols
32 ÷ 126 – the printed ASCII symbols
97 ÷ 122 – letters of the Latin alphabet in the lower register
129 ÷ 255 – Latin–1 symbols of ISO
192 ÷ 255 – letters of the European languages

The procedure call **FileFormat3[x]** returns the type of a file given by a name or a classifier *x*; at that, if the datafile has an extension, it relies as the extension of the datafile. Whereas the call **FileFormat3[x, y]** with the second optional argument – an arbitrary *y* expression – in a case of file without extension returns its full name with extension defined for it, at the same time renaming the *x* datafile, taking into account the calculated format. The fragment below represents source code of the **FileFormat3** procedure along with the most typical examples of its application.

```
In[2554]:= FileFormat3[x_ /; FileExistsQ[x], t___] := Module[{b, c, a = FileExtension[x]},
If[a != "", ToUpperCase[a], c = If[Quiet[StringTake[Read[x, String], {1, 5}]] === "%PDF-",
{Close[x], "PDF"}[[-1]], Close[x]; b = ReadFullFile[x];
If[! StringFreeQ[b, {"MSWordDoc", "Microsoft Office Word"}], "DOC",
If[! StringFreeQ[b, ".opendocument.textPK"], "ODT",
If[! StringFreeQ[b, {"!DOCTYPE HTML", "text/html"}], "HTML",
If[MemberQ3[Range[0, 255], DeleteDuplicates[Flatten[Map[ToCharacterCode[#] &,
DeleteDuplicates[Characters[b]]]]]], "TXT", Undefined]]]]];
If[{t} != {}, Quiet[Close[x]]; RenameFile[x, x <> "." <> c], c]]]

In[2555]:= Map[FileFormat3, {"C:\\Temp.Burthday", "C:\\Temp.cinema",
"C:/Temp/ransian", "C:/Temp/Book_Grodno", "C:/Temp/Math_Trials"}]
Out[2555]= {"DOC", "TXT", "HTML", "PDF", "DOC"}
```

In[2556]:= **FileFormat3["C:/Temp/Math_Trials", 590]**
Out[2556]= "C:\\Temp\\Math_Trials.DOC"

Using the algorithm implemented by **FileFormat3** procedure it is rather simple to modify it for testing of other types of datafiles whose full names have no extension. That can be rather useful in the processing problems of datafiles. In a certain relation the **Format3** procedure complements the standard **Format** function along with procedures **Format1** and **Format2**.

The *Mathematica* provides effective enough system-independent access to all aspects of the files of any size. For ensuring operations of opening and closing of files the following basic functions of access are used: **Close, OpenRead, OpenWrite, OpenAppend**. Moreover, the name or full path to a file in the string format acts as the only formal argument of the first three functions; at that, the function call **OpenWrite[]** without factual arguments is allowed, opening a new datafile located in the subdirectory intended for temporary files for writting. While the **Close** function closes a datafile given by its name, full path or a *Stream*-object. In attempt to close a closed or nonexistent datafile the system causes the erroneous situation. For elimination of such situation, undesirable in many cases, it is possible to use the simple **Closes** function providing the closing of any datafile including a closed or nonexistent file, without output of any erroneous messages with returning *Null*, i.e. nothing, but, perhaps, the name or full path to the closed datafile:

In[2351]:= **Close["D:/Math_myLib/test74.txt"]**
General::openx: D:/Math_myLib/test74.txt is not open...>>
Out[2351]= Close["D:/Math_myLib/test74.txt"]

In[2352]:= **Closes[x_] := Quiet[Check[Close[x], Null]]**

In[2353]:= **Closes["D:/Math_myLib/test74.txt"]**

At that, an object of the following a rather simple format is understood as a *Stream* object of the functions of access such as **OpenRead, OpenWrite** and **OpenAppend**:

$$\{OutputStream \,|\, InputStream\}[<Datafile>, <Logical\ IO\ channel>]$$

By the function call **Streams[]** the list of *Stream*-objects of files opened in the current session including system files is returned. For obtaining the list of all *Stream* objects of files different from the system files it is possible to use the function call **StreamsU[]**.

In[2642]:= **Streams[]**
Out[2642]= {OutputStream["stdout", 1], OutputStream["stderr", 2]}
In[2643]:= **S1 = OpenRead["C:/Temp/Math_Trials.doc"]**
Out[2643]= InputStream["C:/Temp/Math_Trials.doc", 163]
In[2644]:= **S2 = OpenWrite["C:\\Temp/Book_Grodno.pdf"]**
Out[2644]= OutputStream["C:\\Temp/Book_Grodno.pdf", 164]
In[2645]:= **Streams[]**
Out[2645]= {OutputStream["stdout", 1], OutputStream["stderr", 2],
InputStream["C:/Temp/Math_Trials.doc", 163],
OutputStream["C:\\Temp/Book_Grodno.pdf", 164]}
In[2646]:= **OpenWrite[]**
Out[2646]= OutputStream["C:\\Users\\Aladjev\\AppData\\Local\\Temp\\m-17629ca3-d621-4844-bfa1-a604585066f2", 165]

In[2647]:= **StreamsU[] := Select[Streams[], ! MemberQ[{"[stdout]", "[stderr]"}, StringTake[ToString[#1], {13, 19}]] &]**

In[2648]:= **StreamsU[]**
Out[2648]= {InputStream["C:/Temp/Math_Trials.doc", 163], OutputStream["C:\\Temp/Book_Grodno.pdf", 164], OutputStream["C:\\Users\\Aladjev\\AppData\\Local\\Temp\\m-17629ca3-d621-4844-bfa1-a604585066f2", 165]}

In[2649]:= **Close["C:\\Temp/Book_Grodno.pdf"]**
Out[2649]= "C:\\Temp/Book_Grodno.pdf"

In[2650]:= **StreamsU[]**
Out[2650]= {InputStream["C:/Temp/Math_Trials.doc", 163], OutputStream["C:\\Users\\Aladjev\\AppData\\Local\\Temp\\m-17629ca3-d621-4844-bfa1-a604585066f2", 165]}

In[2658]:= **CloseAll[] := Map[Close, StreamsU[]]**

In[2659]:= **CloseAll[]**
Out[2659]= {"C:/Temp/Math_Trials.doc", "C:\\Users\\Aladjev\\AppData\\Local\\Temp\\m-17629ca3-d621-4844-bfa1-a604585066f2"}

In[2660]:= **Streams[]**
Out[2660]= {OutputStream["stdout", 1], OutputStream["stderr", 2]}

It must be kept in mind that after the termination of work with an opened file, it remains opened up to its explicit closing by the **Close** function. For closing of all channels and files opened in the current session of the system, excepting system files, it is possible to apply quite simple **CloseAll** function, whose call **CloseAll[]** closes all mentioned open both files and channels with return of the list of files.

Similar to the *Maple* the *Mathematica* system also has opportunity to open the same file on different streams and in various modes, using different coding of its name or path by using alternative registers for letters or/and replacement of "\\" separators of the subdirectories on "/", and vice versa at opening of datafiles. The fragment below illustrates application of similar approach for opening of the same file on two different channels on reading with the subsequent alternating reading of records from it.

In[2534]:= **F = "C:\\Mathematica\\AvzAgn.m"; {S, S1} = {OpenRead[F], OpenRead[If[UpperCaseQ[StringTake[F, 1]], ToLowerCase[F], ToUpperCase[F]]]}**
Out[2534]= InputStream["C:\\Mathematica\\AvzAgn.m", 118], InputStream["c:\\mathematica\\avzagn.m", 119]}

In[2535]:= **t = {}; For[k = 1, k <= 3, k++, AppendTo[t, {Read[S], Read[S1]}]]**
Out[2535]= {"RANS1", "RANS1", "RANS2", "RANS2", "RANS3", "RANS3"}

Meanwhile, it must be kept in mind that the special attention at opening of the same file on different channels is necessary and, above all, at various modes of access to the datafile in order to avoid of the possible especial and erroneous situations, including distortion of data in the datafile. Whereas in certain cases this approach at operating with large enough files can give quite notable temporal effect along with simplification of certain algorithms of data processing which are in datafiles. The interesting enough examples of use of such approach can be found in our books [30-33,50].

Similar to the *Maple* system the *Mathematica* system has very useful means for work with the pointer defining the current position of scanning of a datafile. The following functions provide such work, namely: **StreamPosition, Skip, SetStreamPosition, Find**. The functions **StreamPosition, SetStreamPosition** allow to make monitoring of the current position of the pointer of an open file and to establish for it a new position respectively. Moreover, on the closed or nonexistent datafiles the calls of these functions cause erroneous situations.

Reaction to the status of a datafile of the **Skip** function is similar, whereas the function call **Find** opens a stream on reading from a file. The sense of the represented functions is rather transparent and in more detail it is possible to familiarize with them, for instance, in books [30,33]. In connection with the means arises the question of definition of the status of a file – opened, closed or doesn't exist. In this regard **FileOpenQ** procedure can be an useful tool, whose source code with examples of application represents the next fragment together with an example of use of the standard **Skip** function.

In[2542]:= **FileOpenQ[F_ /; StringQ[F]] :=**
Module[{A, a = FileType[F], b, d, x = inputstream, y = outputstream, c = Map[ToString1, StreamsU[]], f = ToLowerCase[StringReplace[F, "\\" -> "/"]]},
A[x_] := Module[{a1 = ToString1[x], b1 = StringLength[ToString[Head[x]]]},
ToExpression["{" <> StrStr[Head[x]] <> "," <> StringTake[a1, {b1 + 2, -2}] <> "}"]];
If[MemberQ[{Directory, None}, a], $Failed, Clear[inputstream, outputstream];
d = ToExpression[ToLowerCase[StringReplace[ToString1[Map[A, StreamsU[]]], "\\\\" -> "/"]]]; a = Map[Flatten, Select[d, #[[2]] === f &]];
If[a == {}, {inputstream, outputstream} = {x, y}; False,
a = {ReplaceAll[a, {inputstream -> "read", outputstream -> "write"}],
{inputstream, outputstream} = {x, y}}[[1]]]; If[Length[a] == 1, a[[1]], a]]

In[2543]:= **OpenRead["C:\\Temp\\cinema_2017.txt"]; Write["rans.ian"];**
Write["C:\\Temp/Summ.doc"]; Write["C:\\Temp/Grin.pdf"]
In[2544]:= **Map[FileOpenQ, {"rans.ian", "C:\\Temp\\Grin.pdf", "C:\\Temp/Summ.doc", "C:\\Temp/cinema_2017.txt"}]**
Out[2544]= {{"write", "rans.ian", 85}, {"write", "c:/temp/grin.pdf", 87}, {"write", "c:/temp/summ.doc", 86}, {"read", "c:/temp/cinema_2017.txt", 84}}
In[2545]:= **Map[FileOpenQ, {"C:\\Temp\\Books.doc", "C:\\Books.doc"}]**
Out[2545]= {{}, $Failed}

The procedure call **FileOpenQ[F]** returns the nested list {{*R, F, Channel*},...} if a *F* datafile is open on reading/writing (*R* = {*"read"* | *"write"*}), *F* defines actually the *F* file in the stylized format (*LowerCase* + *all "\\" are replaced on "/"*) while *Channel* defines the logical channel on which the *F* datafile in the mode specified by the first element of the *R* list was open; if *F* file is closed, the empty list is returned, i.e. {}, if *F* file is absent, then $*Failed* is returned. At that, the nested list is used with the purpose, that *F* file can be opened according to syntactically various datafile specifiers, for example, *"Agn1947"* and *"19AGN47"*, allowing to carry out its processing in the different modes simultaneously.

The **FileOpenQ1** is an useful enough extension of the **FileOpenQ** considered above. The procedure call **FileOpenQ1[F]** returns the nested list of the format {{R, x, y, ..., z}, {{R, x1, y1, ..., z1}} if a F file is open for reading or writing (R = {"in" | "out"}), and F defines the file in any format (Register + "/" and/or "\\"); if the F file is closed or is absent, the empty list is returned, i.e. {}. Moreover, sublists {x, y, ..., z} and {x1, y1, ..., z1} define files or full paths to them that are open for reading and writing respectively. Moreover, if in the current session all user files are closed, except system files, the call **FileOPenQ1[x]** on an arbitrary x string returns $Failed. The files and paths to them are returned in formats which are determined in the list returned by the function call **Streams[]**, irrespective of format of F file. The fragment below represents source code of the **FileOpenQ1** procedure along with typical examples of its application.

In[3646]:= **FileOpenQ1[F_ /; StringQ[F]] := Module[{a = StreamFiles[], b, c, d, k = 1, j},**
If[a === "AllFilesClosed", Return[False], c = StringReplace[ToLowerCase[F], "/" –> "\\"];
b = Mapp[StringReplace, Map[ToLowerCase, a], "/" –> "\\"]];
For[k, k <= 2, k++, For[j = 2, j <= Length[b[[k]]], j++, If[Not[SuffPref[b[[k]][[j]], c, 2] ||
SuffPref[b[[k]][[j]], "\\" <> c, 2]], a[[k]][[j]] = Null; Continue[], Continue[]]]];
b = Mapp[Select, a, ! # === Null &]; b = Select[b, Length[#] > 1 &];
If[Length[b] == 1, b[[1]], b]]

In[3647]:= **CloseAll[]; FileOpenQ1["AvzAgnArtKrSv"]**
Out[3647]= False
In[3648]:= **OpenWrite["Kherson.doc"]; OpenWrite["C:/Temp/Books.doc"];**
OpenWrite["RANS"]; OpenRead["C:/Temp/Cinema_2017.txt"];
Read["C:/Temp\\Cinema_2017.txt", Byte];
In[3649]:= **Map[FileOpenQ1, {"Kherson.doc", "C:/Temp\\Books.doc", "RANS", "C:/Temp\\Cinema_2017.txt", "Agn"}]**
Out[3649]= {{"out", "Kherson.doc"}, {"out", "C:/Temp\\Books.doc"}, {"out", "RANS"}, {"in", "C:/Temp\\Cinema_2017.txt"}, {}}
In[3650]:= **Map[FileOpenQ, {"Kherson.doc", "C:/Temp\\Books.doc", "RANS", "C:/Temp\\Cinema_2017.txt", "Agn"}]**
Out[3650]= {{"write", "kherson.doc", 458}, {"write", "c:/temp/books.doc", 459}, {"write", "rans", 460}, {"read", "c:/temp/cinema_2017.txt", 461}, $Failed}

So, functions of access **Skip, Find, StreamPosition** and **SetStreamPosition** provide quite effective means for a rather thin manipulation with files and in combination with a number of other functions of access they provide the user with the standard set of functions for files processing, and give opportunity on their base to create own means allowing how to solve specific problems of work with datafiles, and in a certain degree to extend standard means of the system. A number of similar means is presented and in the present book, and in our *MathToolBox* package [48]. In addition to the represented standard operations of datafiles processing, a number of other means of the package rather significantly facilitates effective programming of higher level at the solution of many problems of datafiles processing and management of the *Mathematica* system. Naturally, the consideration rather in details of earlier presented tools of access to files and the subsequent tools doesn't enter purposes of the present book therefore we will present relatively them only short excursus in the form of a brief information with some comments on the represented means *(see also books on the Mathematica system in [50])*.

Among standard means of processing, the following functions can be noted: **FileNames** – depending on the coding format returns the list of full paths to the files and/or directories contained in the given directory onto arbitrary nesting depth in file system of the computer. Whereas the functions **CopyFile, RenameFile, DeleteFile** serve for copying, renaming and removal of the given files accordingly. Except the listed means for work with datafiles the *Mathematica* has a number of rather useful functions which here aren't considered but with that the interested reader can familiarize in reference base of *Mathematica* system or in the corresponding literature [52,58,66]. Along with the above functions **OpenRead, OpenWrite, Read, Write, Skip** and **Streams** of the lowest level of access to files, the functions **Get, Put, Export, Import, ReadList, BinaryReadList, BinaryWrite, BinaryRead** are not less important for support of access to files which support operations of reading and writing of data of the required format. With these means along with a whole series of rather interesting examples and features of their use, at last with certain critical remarks to their address the reader can familiarize in [30-33,50]. Meantime, these means of access together with already considered tools and tools remaining without our attention form a rather developed system of effective processing of datafiles of various formats.

On the other hand, along with actually processing of the internal contents of datafiles, the *Mathematica* system has a number of tools for search of files, their testing, work with their names, etc. We will list only some of them, namely: **FindFile, FileExistsQ, FileBaseName, FileNameDepth, FileNameSplit, ExpandFileName, FileNameJoin, FileNameTake.** With the given means along with a whole series of rather interesting examples and features of their use, at last with certain critical remarks to their address the reader can familiarize in [30-33,50]. In particular, as it was noted earlier, the **FileExistsQ** function like certain other functions of access in the course of search is limited only to the directories determined in the predetermined *$Path* variable. For the purpose of elimination of this shortcoming a simple enough **FileExistsQ1** procedure has been offered. The following fragment represents source code of the **FileExistsQ1** procedure along with typical examples of its application.

In[2534]:= **FileExistsQ1[x__ /; StringQ[{x}[[1]]]] := Module[{b = {x}, a = SearchFile[{x}[[1]]]},
If[a == {}, False, If[Length[b] == 2 && ! HowAct[b[[2]]], ToExpression[ToString[b[[2]]] <>
" = " <> ToString1[a]], Null]; True]]**

In[2535]:= {FileExistsQ1["Mathematica.doc", t47], t47}
Out[2535]= {True, {"C:\\Mathematica\\Mathematica.doc",
"E:\\Mathematica\\Mathematica.doc"}}
In[2536]:= **FileExistsQ["Books.doc"]**
Out[2536]= False
In[2537]:= **FileExistsQ1["Books.doc"]**
Out[2537]= True
In[2538]:= **FileExistsQ1["Book_avz.doc"]**
Out[2538]= False

The procedure call **FileExistsQ1[x]** with one actual argument returns *True* if x determines a datafile, really existing in the file system of the computer and *False* otherwise; whereas the call **FileExistsQ1[x, y]** in addition through the actual *y* argument – an undefinite variable – returns the list of full paths to the found *x* datafile if the main result of the call is *True*.

The previous procedure enough essentially uses the **SearchFile** procedure providing search of the given file in file system of the computer. In addition, the procedure call **SearchFile[f]** returns the list of paths to a *f* file found within file system of the computer; in the absence of the required file *f* the procedure call **SearchFile[f]** returns the empty list. We will note, the procedure **SearchFile** essentially uses the standard **Run** function of the *Mathematica* that is used by a number of means of our *MathToolBox* package [48]. The next fragment presents source code of the **SearchFile** procedure along with typical examples of its use.

In[2532]:= SearchFile[F_ /; StringQ[F]] :=
Module[{a, b, f, dir, h = StringReplace[ToUpperCase[F], "/" -> "\\"]},
{a, b, f} = {Map[ToUpperCase[#] <> ":\\" &, Adrive[]], {}, ToString[Unique["d"]] <> ".txt"};
dir[y_ /; StringQ[y]] := Module[{a, b, c, v}, Run["Dir " <> "/A/B/S " <> y <> " > " <> f];
c = {}; Label[b];
a = StringReplace[ToUpperCase[ToString[v = Read[f, String]]], "/" -> "\\"];
If[a == "ENDOFFILE", Close[f]; DeleteFile[f];
Return[c], If[SuffPref[a, h, 2], If[FileExistsQ[v], AppendTo[c, v]]; Goto[b], Goto[b]]]];
For[k = 1, k <= Length[a], k++, AppendTo[b, dir[a[[k]]]]]; Flatten[b]]

In[2533]:= **SearchFile["MathToolBox.nb"]**
Out[2533]= {"C:\\Users\\Aladjev\\Mathematica\\MathToolBox.nb", "E:\\MathToolBox\\MathToolBox.nb"}

In[2534]:= **SearchFile["init.m"]**
Out[2534]= {"C:\\Program Files\\Wolfram Research\\Mathematica\\11.0\\AddOns\\Applications\\ AuthorTools\\Kernel\\init.m", ..., "C:\\Users\\All Users\\Mathematica\\ Kernel\\init.m"}

In[2535]:= **Length[%]**
Out[2535]= 115

In[2536]:= **SearchFile["Mathematica.doc"]**
Out[2536]= {"C:\\Mathematica\\Mathematica.doc", "E:\\Mathematica\\Mathematica.doc"}

In[2537]:= **SearchFile["AVZ_AGN_VSV_ART_KR.590"]**
Out[2537]= {}

In[2538]:= **SearchFile["Cinema_2017.txt"]**
Out[2538]= {"C:\\Temp\\Cinema_2017.txt"}

In[2587]:= SearchFile1[x_ /; StringQ[x]] := Module[{a, b, c, d, f = {}, k = 1},
If[PathToFileQ[x], If[FileExistsQ[x], x, {}], a = $Path; f = Select[Map[If[FileExistsQ[# <> "\\" <> ToUpperCase[x]], #, "Null"] &, a], # != "Null" &];
If[f != {}, f, d = Map[# <> ":\\" &, Adrive[]];
For[k, k <= Length[d], k++, a = Quiet[FileNames["*", d[[k]], Infinity]];
f = Join[f, Select[Map[If[FileExistsQ[#] && SuffPref[ToUpperCase[#], "\\" <> ToUpperCase[x], 2], #, "Null"] &, a], # != "Null" &]]]; If[f == {}, {}, f]]]]

In[2588]:= **SearchFile1["BurthDay.doc"]**

Out[2588]= {"C:\\Temp\\Burthday.doc",
"E:\\ARCHIVE\\MISCELLANY\\Burthday.doc", "E:\\Temp\\Burthday.doc"}

In[2589]:= **SearchFile1["Cinema_2017.txt"]**

Out[2589]= {"C:\\Program Files\\Wolfram Research\\Mathematica\\11.0\\ SystemFiles\\Links\\Cinema_2017.txt"}

In[2590]:= **SearchFile1["C:\\Mathematica\\Tuples.doc"]**

Out[2590]= "C:\\Mathematica\\Tuples.doc"

The **SearchFile1** procedure that is a functional analog of **SearchFile** completes the previous fragment. The call **SearchFile[F]** returns the list of full paths to a *F* datafile found within file system of the computer; in the case of absence of the required *F* datafile the procedure call **SearchFile[F]** returns the empty list, i.e. {}. Unlike the previous procedure the **SearchFile1** seeks out a datafile in 3 stages: *(1)* if the required file is given by the full path only existence of the concrete file is checked, at detection the full path to it is returned, *(2)* search is done in the list of directories determined by the predetermined *$Path* variable, *(3)* a search is done within all file system of the computer. The procedure **SearchFile1** essentially uses procedure **Adrive** which is used by a number of our means of access [48]. It should be noted that speed of both procedures generally essentially depends on the sizes of file system of the computer, first of all, if a required file isn't defined by the full path and isn't in the directories defined by the *$Path* variable. In addition, in this case the search is done if possible even in directory *"C:/$Recycle.bin"* of the system *Windows 7 Professional*.

Along with tools of processing of external files the system has also the set of useful enough means for manipulation with directories of both the *Mathematica*, and file system of the personal computer in general. We will list only some of these important functions, namely:

DirectoryQ[j] – *the call returns True if a j string defines an existing directory, and False otherwise; unfortunately, the standard procedure at coding "/" at the end of j string returns False irrespective of existence of the tested directory; a quite simple DirQ procedure eliminates a defect of this standard tool.*

In[2602]:= **DirQ[d_ /; StringQ[d]] := DirectoryQ[StringReplace[d, "/" -> "\\"]]**

In[2603]:= **Map1[{DirectoryQ, DirQ}, {"C:/Mathematica\\"}]**
Out[2603]= {True, True}
In[2604]:= **Map1[{DirectoryQ, DirQ}, {"C:/Mathematica/"}]**
Out[2604]= {False, True}
In[2605]:= **Map1[{DirectoryQ, DirQ}, {"C:/Mathematica"}]**
Out[2605]= {True, True}

DirectoryName[d] – *the call returns a path to a directory containing d datafile; moreover, if d is a real subdirectory, a chain of subdirectories to it is returned; in addition, taking into account the file concept that identifies files and subdirectories, and the circumstance that the call **DirectoryName[d]** doesn't consider actual existence of d, the similar approach in a certain measure could be considered justified, but on condition of taking into account of reality of the tested d path such approach causes certain questions. Therefore from this standpoint a rather simple **DirName** procedure which returns "None" if d is a subdirectory, the path to a subdirectory containing d file, and $Failed otherwise is offered. At that, the search is done within all file system of the computer, but only not within system of subdirectories determined by means of the predetermined $Path variable.*

In[2605]:= DirName[F_ /; StringQ[F]] := If[DirQ[F], "None", If[! FileExistsQ1[F], $Failed, Quiet[Check[FileNameJoin[FileNameSplit[F][[1; -2]]], "None"]]]]

In[2606]:= Map[DirectoryName, {"C:/Temp/Cinema_2017.txt", "C:/Temp"}]
Out[2606]= {"C:\\Temp\\", "C:\\"}

In[2607]:= Map[DirName, {"C:/Temp/cinema_2017.txt", "C:/Temp", "G:\\"}]
Out[2607]= {"Temp", "None", $Failed}

CreateDirectory[d] – *the call creates the given d directory with return of the path to it; meanwhile this tool doesn't work in the case of designation of the nonexistent device of external memory (flash card, disk, etc.) therefore we created a rather simple CDir procedure that resolves this problem: the procedure call CDir[d] creates the given d directory with return of the full path to it; in the absence or inactivity of the device of external memory the directory is created on a device from the list of all active devices of external memory that has the maximal volume of available memory with returning of the full path to it:*

In[2612]:= CDir[d_ /; StringQ[d]] := Module[{a}, Quiet[If[StringTake[d, {2, 2}] == ":", If[MemberQ[a, StringTake[d, 1]], CreateDirectory[d], a = Adrive[]; CreateDirectory[Sort[a, FreeSpaceVol[#1] >= FreeSpaceVol[#2] &][[1]] <> StringTake[d, {2, -1}]]], CreateDirectory[d]]]]

In[2613]:= CreateDirectory["G:\\Temp\\GSV/ArtKr"]
CreateDirectory::fdnfnd: Directory or file G not found...>>
Out[2613]= $Failed

In[2614]:= CDir["A:/Temp\\AVZ\\Tallinn\\IAN\\Grodno/Kherson"]
Out[2614]= "C:\\Temp\\AVZ\\Tallinn\\IAN\\Grodno\\Kherson"

CopyDirectory[w1, w2] – *the function call completely copies a w1 directory into a w2 directory, however in the presence of the accepting w2 directory the function call CopyDirectory[w1, w2] causes an erroneous situation with return of $Failed that in a number of cases is undesirable. For the purpose of elimination of such situation a rather simple CopyDir procedure can be offered, which in general is similar to the standard CopyDirectory, but with the difference that in the presence of the accepting w2 directory the w1 directory is copied as a subdirectory of the w2 with returning of the full path to it, for example:*

In[2625]:= CopyDirectory["C:/Mathematica", "C:/Temp"]
CopyDirectory::filex: Cannot overwrite existing file C:/Temp...>>
Out[2626]= $Failed

In[2626]:= CopyDir[d_ /; StringQ[d], p_ /; StringQ[p]] := Module[{c = p}, If[PrefixQ[StandPath[d], StandPath[p]], $Failed, Do[If[Quiet[Check[CopyDirectory[d, c], $Failed]] === $Failed, c = c <> "\\" <> FileNameSplit[d][[-1]], Return[]], {j, 1, Infinity}]]; c]

In[2627]:= CopyDir["C:/Mathematica", "C:/Temp"]
Out[2627]= "C:\\Temp\\Mathematica"

DeleteDirectory[W] – *the call deletes from file system of the computer the given W directory with returning Null, i.e. nothing, regardless of attributes of the directory (Archive, Read–only, Hidden, and System). Meanwhile, such approach, in our opinion, is not quite justified, relying only on the circumstance that the user is precisely sure that he deletes. Whereas in the general case there has to be an insurance from removal, in particular, of datafiles and directories having such attributes as Read-only (R), Hidden (H) and System (S). To this end, in particular, it is possible before removing of an* *element of file system to previously check up its attributes what the useful enough* **Attrib** *procedure considered in the following section provides.*

The reader can familiarize with other useful means of processing of files and directories in reference base on the *Mathematica* system and, in particular, in books such as [28-33,51-55, 61,63,65,67].

7.3. Tools of the *Mathematica* system for processing of attributes of directories and datafiles

The *Mathematica* system has no means for work with attributes of datafiles and directories what, in our opinion, is a rather essential shortcoming, first of all, at creation on its basis of various data processing systems. By the way, the similar means are absent also in the *Maple* therefore we created for it a set of procedures {*Atr, F_atr, F_atr1, F_atr2*} which have solved this problem [47]. These means represented below solve the similar problem for the system *Mathematica* too. The following fragment represents the **Attrib** procedure which provides processing of attributes of datafiles and directories.

```
In[2670]:= Attrib[F_/; StringQ[F], x_/; ListQ[x] && AllTrue[Map3[MemberQ, {"-A", "-H",
"-S", "-R", "+A", "+H", "+S", "+R"}, x], TrueQ] || x == {} || x == "Attr"] :=
Module[{a, b = "attrib ", c, d = " > ", h = "attrib.exe", p, f, g, t, v},
a = ToString[v = Unique["ArtKr"]];
If[Set[t, LoadExtProg["attrib.exe"]] === $Failed, Return[$Failed], Null];
If[StringLength[F] == 3 && DirQ[F] && StringTake[F, {2, 2}] == ":",
Return["Drive " <> F], If[StringLength[F] == 3 && DirQ[F], f = StandPath[F],
If[FileExistsQ1[StrDelEnds[F, "\\", 2], v], g = v;
f = StandPath[g[[1]]]; Clear[v], Return["<" <> F <> "> is not a directory or a file"]]]];
If[x === "Attr", Run[b <> f <> d <> a],
If[x === {}, Run[b <> " -A -H -S -R " <> f <> d <> a],
Run[b <> StringReplace[StringJoin[x], {"+" -> " +", "-" -> " -"}] <> " " <> f <> d <> a]]];
If[FileByteCount[a] == 0, Return[DeleteFile[a]], d = Read[a, String]; DeleteFile[Close[a]]];
h = StringSplit[StringTrim[StringTake[d, {1, StringLength[d] - StringLength[f]}]]];
Quiet[DeleteFile[t]];
h = Flatten[h /. {"HR" -> {"H", "R"}, "SH" -> {"S", "H"}, "SHR" -> {"S", "H", "R"},
"SRH" -> {"S", "R", "H"}, "HSR" -> {"H", "S", "R"}, "HRS" -> {"H", "R", "S"},
"RSH" -> {"R", "S", "H"}, "RHS" -> {"R", "H", "S"}}];
If[h === {"File", "not", "found", "-"} || MemberQ[h, "C:\\Documents"],
"Drive " <> f, {h, g[[1]]}]]

In[2671]:= Attrib["C:\\Temp\\Cinema_2017.txt", {"+A", "+S", "+R"}]
In[2672]:= Attrib["Cinema_2017.txt", {"+A", "+S", "+R"}]
In[2673]:= Attrib["C:\\Temp\\Cinema_2017.txt", "Attr"]
Out[2673]= {{"A", "S", "R"}, "C:\\Temp\\Cinema_2017.txt"}
In[2674]:= Attrib["Cinema_2017.txt", "Attr"]
Out[2674]= {{"A", "S", "R"}, "C:\\Program Files\\Wolfram
Research\\Mathematica\\11.0\\Cinema_2017.txt"}
```

In[2675]:= **Attrib["C:\\Temp\\Cinema_2017.txt", {}]**
In[2676]:= **Attrib["C:\\Temp\\Cinema_2017.txt", "Attr"]**
Out[2676]= {{}, "C:\\Temp\\Cinema_2017.txt"}
In[2677]:= **Attrib["C:\\", "Attr"]**
Out[2677]= "Drive C:\\"
In[2678]:= **Attrib["G:\\", "Attr"]**
Out[2678]= "<G:\\> is not a directory or a datafile"
In[2679]:= **Attrib["re.jsx.jpg", "Attr"]**
Out[2679]= {{"A"}, "C:\\Users\\Aladjev\\Documents\\re.jsx.jpg"}
In[2680]:= **Attrib["re.jsx.jpg", {"+A", "+S", "+H", "+R"}]**
In[2681]:= **Attrib["re.jsx.jpg", "Attr"]**
Out[2681]= {{"A", "S", "H", "R"}, "C:\\Users\\Aladjev\\Documents\\re.jsx.jpg"}
In[2682]:= **Attrib["re.jsx.jpg", {"–S", "–R", "–H"}]**
In[2683]:= **Attrib["re.jsx.jpg", "Attr"]**
Out[2683]= {{"A"}, "C:\\Users\\Aladjev\\Documents\\re.jsx.jpg"}
In[2684]:= **Attrib["c:/temp\\", "Attr"]**
Out[2684]= {{}, {"C:\\Temp"}}
In[2685]:= **Attrib["c:/temp\\", {"+A"}]**
In[2686]:= **Attrib["c:\\Temp\\", "Attr"]**
Out[2686]= {{"A"}, "C:\\Temp"}

The successful procedure call **Attrib[*f*, "*Attr*"]** returns the list of attributes of a given file or directory *f* in the context *Archive ("A")*, *Read–only ("R")*, *Hidden ("H")* and *System ("S")*. At that, also other attributes inherent to the system datafiles and directories are possible; thus, in particular, on the main directories of devices of external memory *"Drive f"*, whereas on a nonexistent directory or file the message *"f isn't a directory or datafile"* is returned. At that, the call is returned in the form of list of the format {*x*, *y*, ..., *z*, *F*} where the last element determines a full path to a file or directory *f*; the files and subdirectories of the same name can be in various directories, however processing of attributes is made only concerning the first file/directory from the list of the objects of the same name. If the full path to a datafile or directory *f* is determined as the first argument of the **Attrib** procedure, specifically only this object is processed. The elements of the returned list that precede its last element define attributes of a processed directory or datafile. The procedure call **Attrib[*f*, {}]** returns *Null*, i.e. nothing, canceling all attributes for a processed file or directory *f* while the procedure call **Attrib[*f*, {"*x*","*y*",...,"*z*"}]** where *x*, *y*, *z*∈{"–A", "–H", "–S", "–R", "+A", "+H", "+S", "+R"}, also returns *Null*, i.e. nothing, setting/cancelling the attributes of the processed datafile or directory *f* determined by the second argument. At impossibility to execute processing of attributes the call **Attrib[*f*, *x*]** returns the corresponding messages. Procedure **Attrib** allows to carry out processing of attributes of both the file, and the directory located in any place of file system of the computer. This procedure is represented to us as a rather useful means for operating with file system of the computer.

In turn, the next **Attrib1** procedure in many respects is similar to the **Attrib** procedure both in the functional, and in the descriptive relation, but the **Attrib1** procedure has also certain differences. The successful procedure call **Attrib[*f*, "*A*"]** returns the list of attributes in the string format of a directory or a file *f* in the context *Archive ("A")*, *Read–only ("R")*, *Hidden*

("H"), *System* ("S"). The procedure call **Attrib1[*f*, {}]** returns *Null*, i.e. nothing, canceling all attributes for the processed datafile/directory *f* whereas the procedure call **Attrib1[*f*, {"*x*", "*y*",...,"*z*"}]** where *x*, *y*, *z* ∈ {"-A", "-H", "-S", "-R", "+A", "+H", "+S", "+R"}, also returns *Null*, i.e. nothing, setting/cancelling the attributes of the processed file or directory *f* determined by the second argument, whereas call **Attrib1[*f*, *x*, *y*]** with the 3rd optional *y* argument – an expression – in addition deletes the program file *"attrib.exe"* from the directory determined by the call **Directory[]**. The next fragment represents source code of the **Attrib1** procedure along with the most typical examples of its application.

In[2670]:= **Attrib1[F_/; StringQ[F], x_/; ListQ[x] && AllTrue[Map3[MemberQ, {"-A", "-H", "-S", "-R", "+A", "+H", "+S", "+R"}, x], TrueQ] || x == {} || x == "Attr", y___] :=**
Module[{a = "$ArtKr$", b = "attrib ", c, d = " > ", h = "attrib.exe", p, f, g = Unique["agn"]},
If[LoadExtProg["attrib.exe"] === $Failed, Return[$Failed], Null];
If[StringLength[F] == 3 && DirQ[F] && StringTake[F, {2, 2}] == ":",
Return["Drive " <> F], If[StringLength[F] == 3 && DirQ[F], f = StandPath[F],
If[FileExistsQ1[StrDelEnds[StringReplace[F, "/" -> "\\"], "\\", 2], g];
f = StandPath[g[[1]]]; Clear[g], Return["<" <> F <> "> is not a directory or a datafile"]]]];
If[x === "Attr", Run[b <> f <> d <> a], If[x === {}, Run[b <> " -A -H -S -R " <> f <> d <> a],
Run[b <> StringReplace[StringJoin[x], {"+" -> " +", "-" -> " -"}] <> " " <> f <> d <> a]]];
If[FileByteCount[a] == 0, Return[DeleteFile[a]], d = Read[a, String]; DeleteFile[Close[a]]];
h = StringSplit[StringTrim[StringTake[d, {1, StringLength[d] - StringLength[f]}]]];
Quiet[DeleteFile[f]];
If[{y} != {}, DeleteFile[Directory[] <> "\\" <> "attrib.exe"], Null];
h = Flatten[h /. {"HR" -> {"H", "R"}, "SH" -> {"S", "H"}, "SHR" -> {"S", "H", "R"},
"SRH" -> {"S", "R", "H"}, "HSR" -> {"H", "S", "R"}, "HRS" -> {"H", "R", "S"},
"RSH" -> {"R", "S", "H"}, "RHS" -> {"R", "H", "S"}}];
If[h === {"File", "not", "found", "-"} || MemberQ[h, "C:\\Documents"], "Drive " <> f, h]]

In[2671]:= **Mapp[Attrib1, {"C:/tmp/a b c", "C:/tmp/I a n.doc"}, {"+A", "+R"}]**
Out[2671]= {Null, Null}
In[2672]:= **Mapp[Attrib1, {"C:/tmp/a b c", "C:\\tmp\\I a n.doc"}, "Attr"]**
Out[2672]= {{"A", "R"}, {"A", "R"}}
In[2673]:= **Attrib1["G:\\Temp\\Cinema_2017.txt", "Attr"]**
Out[2673]= {"A", "S", "R"}
In[2674]:= **Attrib1["G:\\Temp\\Cinema_2017.txt", {}]**

At the same time, the possible messages *"cmd.exe – Corrupt File"* which arise at operating of the above procedures **Attrib** and **Attrib1** should be ignored. Both procedures essentially use our procedures **LoadExtProg, StrDelEnds, StandPath, FileExistsQ1** and **DirQ** along with usage of the standard **Run** function and the *Attrib* function of the *MS DOS* operating system. In addition, the possibility of removal of the *"attrib.exe"* program datafile from the directory that is defiined by the call **Directory[]** after a call of the **Attrib1** procedure leaves the *Mathematica* system unchanged. So, in implementation of both procedures the system **Run** function was enough essentially used, which has the following coding format:

Run[s1, ..., sn] – *in the basic operational system (for example, MS DOS) executes a command that is formed from expressions sj (j=1..n) that are parted by blank symbols with return of code of success of the command completion in the form of an integer. As a rule, the Run function doesn't demand of an interactive input, but on certain operational platforms it generates text messages. To some extent the Run function is similar to the {system, ssystem} functions of the Maple system. In [33] rather interesting examples of application of Run for performance in the environment of the Mathematica with the MS DOS commands are represented.*

We will note that use of **Run** function illustrates one of useful enough methods of providing the interface with the basic operational platform, but here two very essential moments take place. Above all, the function on some operational platforms (*e.g., Windows XP Professional*) demands certain external reaction of the user at an exit from the *Mathematica* software into an operational environment, and secondly, a call by means of the **Run** function of functions or the system *DOS* commands assumes their existence in the directories system determined by the *$Path* variable since otherwise the *Mathematica* doesn't recognize them.

For instance, similar situation takes place in the case of use of the external *DOS* commands, for this reason in realization of the procedures **Attrib** and **Attrib1** that through the **Run** use the external *attrib* command of *DOS* system, a connection to system of directories of *$Path* of the directories containing the *"attrib.exe"* utility has been provided whereas for internal commands of the *DOS* it isn't required. Once again, possible messages *"cmd.exe – Corrupt File"* that can arise at execution of the **Run** function should be ignored.

Thus, at using of the internal *Dir* command of *MS DOS* system of an extension of the list of directories defined by the *$Path* is not required. At the same time, on the basis of standard reception on the basis of extension of a list defined by the *$Path* variable the *Mathematica* doesn't recognize the external *DOS* commands. In this regard a rather simple procedure has been created whose call **LoadExtProg[x]** provides search in file system of the computer of a program *x* given by the full name with its subsequent copying into the subdirectory defined by the call **Directory[]**. The successful procedure call **LoadExtProg[x]** searches out *x* datafile in file system of the computer and copies it into the directory defined by the call **Directory[]**, returning **Directory[]** <> "\\" <> *x*, if the file already was in this subdirectory or has been copied into this directory. The first directory containing the found *x* file supplements the list of the directories defined by the predetermined *$Path* variable. Whereas the procedure call **LoadExtProg[x, y]** with the second optional *y* argument – *an undefinite variable* – in addition through *y* returns the list of all full paths to the found *x* datafile without a modification of the directories list determined by the predetermined *$Path* variable. In case of absence of a possibility to find the required *x* datafile *$Failed* is returned. The next fragment represents source code of the **LoadExtProg** procedure with examples of its application, in particular, for loading into the directory defined by the function call **Directory[]** of a copy of external *"attrib.exe"* command of *MS DOS* with check of the result.

In[2566]:= LoadExtProg[x_ /; StringQ[x], y___] :=
Module[{a = Directory[], b = Unique["agn"], c, d, h},
If[PathToFileQ[x] && FileExistsQ[x], CopyFileToDir[x, Directory[]],
If[PathToFileQ[x] && ! FileExistsQ[x], $Failed, d = a <> "\\" <> x;
If[FileExistsQ[d], d, h = FileExistsQ1[x, b]; If[h, CopyFileToDir[b[[1]], a];
If[{y} == {}, AppendTo[$Path, FileNameJoin[FileNameSplit[b[[1]]][[1 ;; –2]]]], y = b]; d,

$Failed]]]]]

In[2567]:= **LoadExtProg["C:\\\attrib.exe"]**
Out[2567]= $Failed
In[2568]:= **LoadExtProg["attrib.exe"]**
Out[2568]= "C:\\Users\\Aladjev\\Documents\\attrib.exe"
In[2569]:= **FileExistsQ[Directory[] <> "\\" <> "attrib.exe"]**
Out[2569]= True
In[2570]:= **LoadExtProg["tlist.exe"]**
Out[2570]= $Failed
In[2571]:= **LoadExtProg["tasklist.exe", t74]**
Out[2571]= "C:\\Users\\Aladjev\\Documents\\tasklist.exe"
In[2572]:= **t74**
Out[2572]= {"C:\\WINDOWS\\System32\\tasklist.exe",
"C:\\WINDOWS\\winsxs\\amd64_microsoft\\-windows-
tasklist_31bf3856ad364e35_6.1.7600.16385_none_843823d87402ab36\\tasklist.exe",
"C:\\WINDOWS\\winsxs\\x86_microsoft-windows-
tasklist_31bf3856ad364\\e35_6.1.7600.16385_none_28198854bba53a00\\tasklist.exe"}
In[2573]:= **Attrib1["C:\\Temp\\Cinema_2016.txt", "Attr"]**
Out[2573]= {"A", "S", "R"}

Therefore, in advance by means of the call **LoadExtProg[*x*]** it is possible to provide access to a necessary *x* file if of course it exists in file system of the computer. So, using the procedure **LoadExtProg** in combination the system **Run** function, it is possible to execute a number of very useful {*.exe* | *.com*}–programs in the *Mathematica* software – the programs of different purpose which are absent in file system of the *Mathematica* thereby significantly extending the *functionality* of *Mathematica* that can be demanded by wide range of various appendice.

The above **LoadExtProg** along with **FileExistsQ1** procedure also uses the **CopyFileToDir** procedure whose the call **CopyFileToDir[*x*, *y*]** provides copying of a file or directory *x* into a *y* directory with return of the full path to the copied file or directory. If the copied datafile already exists, it isn't updated if the target directory already exists, the *x* directory is copied into its subdirectory of the same name. The fragment below represents source code of the **CopyFileToDir** procedure with examples of its application.

In[2557]:= **CopyFileToDir[x_ /; PathToFileQ[x], y_ /; DirQ[y]] :=**
Module[{a, b}, If[DirQ[x], CopyDir[x, y], If[FileExistsQ[x], a = FileNameSplit[x][[–1]];
If[FileExistsQ[b = y <> "\\" <> a], b, CopyFile[x, b]], $Failed]]]

In[2558]:= **CopyFileToDir["C:\\Temp\\Cinema_2017.txt", Directory[]]**
Out[2558]= "C:\\Users\\Aladjev\\Documents\\Cinema_2017.txt"
In[2559]:= **CopyFileToDir["C:\\Temp", "C:\\MathToolBox\\Temp"]**
Out[2559]= "C:\\MathToolBox\\Temp\\Temp"
In[2560]:= **CopyFileToDir["C:/Temp\\R a n s.htm", "C:\\Mathematica"]**
Out[2560]= "C:\\Mathematica\\R a n s.htm"

The given procedure has a variety of appendices in problems of processing of file system of the computer.

In conclusion of the section a rather useful procedure is represented which provides only two functions – *(1)* obtaining the list of the attributes ascribed to a file or directory, and *(2)* removal of all ascribed attributes. The call **Attribs[*x*]** returns the list of attributes in string format which are ascribed to a datafile or directory *x*. On the main directories of volumes of direct access the procedure call **Attribs** returns *$Failed*. Whereas the call **Attribs[*x*, *y*]** with the second optional *y* argument – an expression – deletes all attributes which are ascribed to a file or a directory *x* with returning *0* at a successful call. The following fragment represents source code of the procedure along with the most typical examples of its application.

```
In[2660]:= Attribs[x_ /; FileExistsQ[x] || DirectoryQ[x], y___] :=
Module[{b, a = StandPath[x], c = "attrib.exe", d = ToString[Unique["g"]], g},
If[DirQ[x] && StringLength[x] == 3 && StringTake[x, {2, 2}] == ":", $Failed,
g[] := Quiet[DeleteFile[Directory[] <> "\\" <> c]]; If[! FileExistsQ[c], LoadExtProg[c]];
If[{y} == {}, Run[c <> " " <> a <> " > ", d]; g[];
b = Characters[StringReplace[StringTake[Read[d, String], {1, -StringLength[a] - 1}],
" " -> ""]]; DeleteFile[Close[d]]; b, a = Run[c <> " -A -H -R -S " <> a]; g[]; a]]]

In[2661]:= Attribs["C:\\Temp\\Avz"]
Out[2661]= {"A", "S", "H", "R"}
In[2662]:= Map[Attribs, {"C:/", "E:\\", "D:\\"}]
Out[2662]= {$Failed, Attribs["E:\\"], $Failed}
In[2663]:= Attribs["C:/Temp/Agn/aaa bbb ccc"]
Out[2663]= {"A", "R"}
In[2664]:= Attribs["C:/Temp/Agn/Elisa.pdf"]
Out[2664]= {"R"}
In[2665]:= Attribs["C:/Temp/Agn/Vsv\\G r s u.doc"]
Out[2665]= {"A", "R"}
In[2666]:= Attribs["C:/Temp/Agn/Vsv\\G r s u.doc", 90]
Out[2666]= 0
In[2667]:= Attribs["C:/Temp/Agn/Vsv\\G r s u.doc"]
Out[2667]= {}
```

It should be noted that as *x* argument the usage of an existing datafile, full path to a file, or a directory is supposed. At that, the file *"attrib.exe"* is removed from the directory defined by the call **Directory[]** after a call of the procedure. The **Attribs** procedure is rather fast-acting, supplementing the procedures **Attrib, Attrib1**. The **Attribs** procedure is effectively applied in programming of tools of access to elements of file system of the computer at processing their attributes. Thus, it should be noted once again that the *Mathematica* has no standard means for processing of attributes of files and directories therefore the offered procedures **Attrib, Attrib1** and **Attribs** in a certain measure fill this niche.

So, the declared possibility of extension of the system of directories which is defined by the *$Path* variable, generally doesn't operate already concerning the external *DOS* commands what well illustrates both consideration of the above procedures **Attrib, LoadExtProg** and **Attrib1**, and an example with the external *"tlist"* command which is provided display of all active processes of the current session with *Windows XP Professional* system, for example:

```
In[2565]:= Run["tlist", " > ", "C:\\Temp\\tlist.txt"]
```

Out[2565]= 1
In[2566]:= **LoadExtProg["tlist.exe"]; Run["tlist", " > ", "C:/Temp/tlist.txt"]**
Out[2566]= 0
0 System Process
4 System
488 smss.exe
520 avgchsvx.exe
=====
3936 Skype.exe
4056 AVGIDSMonitor.exe
3316 AmplusnetPrivacyTools.exe
2256 FreeCommander.exe
2248 WINWORD
4348 avgrsx.exe
4380 avgcsrvx.exe
5248 Mathematica.exe
4760 MathKernel.exe
4780 cmd
4808 tlist.exe

The first example of the previous fragment illustrates, the attempt by means of the **Run** to execute the external *tlist* command of *DOS* completes unsuccessfully *(return code 1)*, while a result of the procedure call **LoadExtProg["*tlist.exe*"]** with searching and download into the directory defined by the call **Directory[]** of the *"tlist.exe"* file, allows to successfully execute by means of the **Run** function the external *tlist* command with preservation of result of its performance in a *txt*-file whose contents is represented by the shaded area. The contents of the shaded area depend on the basic operating system, for example, *Windows 7 Professional* with *DOS "Tasklist.exe"* command.

Meanwhile, use of external software on the basis of the **Run** function along with possibility of extension of functionality of the *Mathematica* system causes a rather serious portability question. So, the means developed by means of this technique with use of the external *DOS* commands are subject to influence of variability of the *MS DOS* commands depending on version of basic operating system. In a number of cases it demands a certain adaptation of the software according to the basic operating system.

7.4. Additional tools for processing of datafiles and directories of file system of the computer

This section represents means of processing of datafiles and directories of file system of the computer which supplement and in certain cases and extend means of the previous section. Unlike the functions **DeleteDirectory** and **DeleteFile** the **DelDirFile** procedure removes a directory or file *x* from file system of the computer, returning *Null*, i.e. nothing. In addition, the procedure call **DelDirFile[*x*]** with one *x* argument is analogous to a call **DeleteFile[*x*]** or **DeleteDirectory[*x*]** depending on the type of the *x* argument – a file or a directory. Whereas the call **DelDirFile[*x, y*]** with the 2nd *y* optional argument – an arbitrary expression – deletes a file or a catalog even if *x* file or elements of *x* directory of file system of the computer have

Read-only attribute; in this case before its removal the attributes of *x* element are cancelled, providing correct removal of *x* element what unlike the system tools expands opportunities for removal of elements of file system of the computer. The procedure eccentially uses our procedures **Attribs, DirQ** and **StandPath**. The fragment below represents source code of the **DelDirFile** procedure along with examples of its application.

```
In[2560]:= DelDirFile[x_ /; StringQ[x] && DirQ[x] || FileExistsQ[x], y__]:=
Module[{c, f, a = {}, b = "", k = 1},
If[DirQ[x] && If[StringLength[x] == 3 && StringTake[x, {2, 2}] == ":", False, True],
If[{y} == {}, Quiet[DeleteDirectory[x, DeleteContents -> True]], a = {}; b = "";
c = StandPath[x]; f = "$Art2618Kr$";
Run["Dir " <> c <> " /A/B/OG/S > " <> f]; Attribs[c, 90];
For[k, k < Infinity, k++, b = Read[f, String];
If[SameQ[b, EndOfFile], DeleteFile[Close[f]]; Break[], Attribs[b, 90]]];
DeleteDirectory[x, DeleteContents -> True]], If[FileExistsQ[x], If[{y} != {}, Attribs[x, 90]];
Quiet[DeleteFile[x]], $Failed]]]

In[2561]:= Map[DelDirFile, {"F:\\", "D:/"}]
Out[2561]= {DelDirFile["F:\\"], $Failed}
In[2562]:= DeleteFile["C:\\Temp\\Excel75.pip"]
DeleteFile::privv: Privilege violation during DeleteFile... >>
Out[2562]= $Failed
In[2563]:= DelDirFile["C:\\Temp\\Excel75.pip", 590]
In[2564]:= FileExistsQ["C:\\Temp\\Excel75.pip"]
Out[2564]= False
In[2565]:= Map1[{DirectoryQ, Attribs}, {"C:\\Temp\\Agn"}]
Out[2565]= {True, {"A", "S", "H", "R"}}
In[2566]:= DelDirFile["C:\\Temp\\Agn"]
Out[2566]= $Failed
In[2567]:= DelDirFile["C:\\Temp\\Agn", 590]
In[2568]:= DirectoryQ["C:\\Temp\\Agn"]
Out[2568]= False
```

Meanwhile, before representation of the following means it is expedient to determine one rather useful procedure whose essence is as follows. As it was already noted above, a file qualifier depends both on a register of symbols, and the used dividers of directories. Thus, the same file with different qualifiers **"c:\\Temp\\cinema.txt"** and **"c:/temp/cinema.txt"** opens in two various streams. Therefore its closing by means of the standard **Close** function doesn't close the *"cinema.txt"* file, demanding closing of all streams on which it was earlier open. For solution of this problem the **Close1** procedure presented by the next fragment has been determined.

```
In[2580]:= Streams[]
Out[2580]= {OutputStream["stdout", 1], OutputStream["stderr", 2]}
In[2581]:= Read["C:/Temp\\cinema.txt"]; Read["C:/Temp/Cinema.txt"];
Read["C:/Temp\\cinema.txt"]; Read["c:/temp/burthday.doc"];
Read["C:/temp\\BurthDay.doc"];
```

In[2582]:= **Streams[]**
Out[2582]= {OutputStream["stdout", 1], OutputStream["stderr", 2],
InputStream["C:/Temp\\cinema.txt", 697], InputStream["C:/Temp/Cinema.txt", 700],
InputStream["c:/temp/burthday.doc", 705], InputStream["C:/temp\\BurthDay.doc", 706]}

In[2583]:= **Close["C:/Temp\\cinema.txt"]**
Out[2583]= "C:/Temp\\cinema.txt"

In[2584]:= **Streams[]**
Out[2584]= {OutputStream["stdout", 1], OutputStream["stderr", 2],
InputStream["C:/Temp/Cinema.txt", 700], InputStream["c:/temp/burthday.doc", 705],
InputStream["C:/temp\\BurthDay.doc", 706]}

In[2585]:= **Close1[x__String] := Module[{a = Streams[][[3 ;; -1]], b = {x}, c = {}, k = 1, j},
If[a == {} || b == {}, {}, b = Select[{x}, FileExistsQ[#] &];
While[k <= Length[a], j = 1; While[j <= Length[b],
If[ToUpperCase[StringReplace[a[[k]][[1]], {"\\" -> "", "/" -> ""}]] ==
ToUpperCase[StringReplace[b[[j]], {"\\" -> "", "/" -> ""}]], AppendTo[c, a[[k]]]]; j++]; k++];
Map[Close, c]; If[Length[b] == 1, b[[1]], b]]]**

In[2586]:= **Close1["C:/Temp\\cinema.txt", "C:/temp\\BirthDay.doc"]**
Out[2586]= {"C:/Temp\\cinema.txt", "C:/temp\\BurthDay.doc"}

In[2587]:= **Streams[]**
Out[2587]= {OutputStream["stdout", 1], OutputStream["stderr", 2]}

In[2588]:= **Close1[]**
Out[2588]= {}

In[2589]:= **Close1["C:/Temp\\cinema.txt", "C:/temp\\BurthDay.doc"]**
Out[2589]= {}

In[2590]:= **Close1["C:/Temp\\Agn/Cinema.txt", AvzAgnVsvArtKr]**
Out[2590]= Close1["C:/Temp\\Agn/Cinema.txt", AvzAgnVsvArtKr]

In[2591]:= **Closes[x_] := Quiet[Check[Close[x], Null]]**

In[2591]:= **Closes["C:\\Temp\\Svetlana\\Kherson\\Cinema.txt"]**

In[2667]:= **Close2[x__String] :=
Module[{a = Streams[][[3 ;; -1]], b = {}, c, d = Select[{x}, StringQ[#] &]},
If[d == {}, {}, c[y_] := ToLowerCase[StringReplace[y, "/" -> "\\"]];
Map[AppendTo[b, Part[#, 1]] &, a]; d = DeleteDuplicates[Map[c[#] &, d]];
Map[Close, Select[b, MemberQ[d, c[#]] &]]]]**

In[2668]:= **Close2[]**
Out[2668]= {}

In[2669]:= **Close2["C:/Temp\\cinema.txt", "C:/temp\\BurthDay.doc"]**
Out[2669]= {"C:/Temp\\cinema.txt", "C:/Temp/Cinema.txt", "c:/temp/burthday.doc",
"C:/temp\\BurthDay.doc"}

In[2670]:= **Streams[]**
Out[2670]= {OutputStream["stdout", 1], OutputStream["stderr", 2]}

The procedure call **Close1[x, y, z,...]** closes all off really–existing datafiles in a {x, y, z,...} list irrespective of quantity of streams on which they have been opened by the various datafiles qualifiers with returning their list. In other cases the call on admissible factual arguments returns the empty list, while on inadmissible actual arguments a call is returned *unevaluated*. The previous fragment represents source code of the **Close1** procedure with examples of its use. In end of the fragment the simple **Closes** function and **Close2** procedure are presented. The call **Closes[x]** returns nothing, closing a *x* file, including the closed and empty datafiles without output of any erroneous messages. In certain applications the function is an quite useful means.

The **Close2** is a functional analog of the above procedure **Close1**. The call **Close2[x, y, z, ...]** closes all off really–existing datafiles in a {x, y, z, ...} list irrespective of quantity of streams on which they have been opened by various datafiles qualifiers with returning their list. In other cases the call on any admissible factual arguments returns the empty list, whereas on *inadmissible* actual arguments a call is returned *unevaluated*. The previous fragment presents source code of the **Close2** procedure and examples of its use. In a number of appendices the **Close1** and **Close2** are quite useful means.

The following **DelDirFile1** procedure – an useful enough extension of the **DelDirFile** on a case of open files in addition to the *Read-only* attribute of both the separate files, and the files being in the deleted directory. The call **DelDirFile1[x]** is equivalent to the call **DelDirFile[x, y]**, providing removal of a file or directory *x* irrespective of openness of a separate *x* file and the *Read-only* attribute ascribed to it, or existence of similar files in *x* directory. The fragment represents source code of the **DelDirFile1** procedure along with typical examples of its use.

```
In[2725]:= DelDirFile1[x_ /; StringQ[x] && FileExistsQ[x] || DirQ[x] &&
If[StringLength[x] == 3 && StringTake[x, {2, 2}] == ":", False, True]] :=
Module[{a = {}, b = "", c = StandPath[x], d, f = "$Art590Kr$", k = 1},
If[DirQ[x], Run["Dir " <> c <> " /A/B/OG/S > " <> f]; Attribs[c, 90];
For[k, k < Infinity, k++, b = Read[f, String];
If[SameQ[b, EndOfFile], DeleteFile[Close[f]]; Break[], Attribs[b, 90]; Close2[b]]];
DeleteDirectory[x, DeleteContents -> True], Close2[x]; Attribs[x, 90]; DeleteFile[x]]]

In[2726]:= Map[Attribs, {"C:/Temp\\Agn/Cinema_2017.txt",
"C:/Temp\\Agn/BurthDay.doc", "C:/Temp\\Agn"}]
Out[2726]= {{"A", "S", "H", "R"}, {"A", "S", "H", "R"}, {"A", "S", "H", "R"}}
In[2727]:= Read["C:/Temp\\Agn/Cinema_2017.txt"];
Read["C:/Temp\\Agn/BurthDay.doc"];
In[2728]:= Streams[]
Out[2728]= {OutputStream["stdout", 1], OutputStream["stderr", 2],
InputStream["C:/Temp\\Agn/Cinema_2017.txt", 131],
InputStream["C:/Temp\\Agn/BurthDay.doc", 132]}
In[2729]:= DelDirFile1["C:/Temp\\Agn"]
In[2730]:= Streams[]
Out[2730]= {OutputStream["stdout", 1], OutputStream["stderr", 2]}
In[2731]:= DirQ["C:\\Temp\\Agn"]
Out[2731]= False
In[2732]:= Attribs["C:\\GrGu_Books\\Cinema_2017.TXT"]
Out[2732]= {"A", "S", "H", "R"}
```

In[2733]:= **Read["C:\\GrGu_Books\\cinema_2017.TXT"];**
In[2734]:= **Streams[]**
Out[2734]= {OutputStream["stdout", 1], OutputStream["stderr", 2], InputStream["C:\\GrGu_Books\\cinema_2017.TXT", 149]}
In[2735]:= **DelDirFile1["C:\\GrGu_Books\\cinema_2017.TXT"]**
In[2736]:= **FileExistsQ["C:\\GrGu_Books\\cinema_2017.TXT"]**
Out[2736]= False

The tools representing quite certain interest at working with file system of the computer as independently, and as a part of means of processing of datafiles and directories complete this section. They are used and by a series of means of our *MathToolBox* package [48]. In particular, at working with files the **OpenFiles** procedure can be rather useful, whose call **OpenFiles[]** returns the two-element nested list, whose the first sublist with the first *"read"* element contains full paths to the files opened on reading, whereas the second sublist with the first *"write"* element contains full paths to files opened on writing in the current session. In the absence of such datafiles the procedure call returns the empty list, i.e. {}. Whereas the call **OpenFiles[x]** with one actual x argument – *a datafile classifier* – returns result of the above format relative to an open x file irrespective of a format of coding of its qualifier. If x defines a closed or a nonexistent datafile then the procedure call returns the empty list, i.e. {}. The fragment below represents source code of the procedure along with rather typical examples of its application.

In[2628]:= **OpenFiles[x___String] := Module[{a = Streams[][[3 ;; -1]], b, c, d, h1 = {"read"},**
h2 = {"write"}}, If[a == {}, {}, d = Map[{Part[#, 0], Part[#, 1]} &, a];
b = Select[d, #[[1]] == InputStream &]; c = Select[d, #[[1]] == OutputStream &];
b = Map[DeleteDuplicates, Map[Flatten, Gather[Join[b, c], #1[[1]] == #2[[1]] &]]];
b = Map[Flatten, Map[If[SameQ[#[[1]], InputStream], AppendTo[h1, #[[2 ;; -1]]],
AppendTo[h2, #[[2 ;; -1]]]] &, b]];
If[{x} == {}, b, If[SameQ[FileExistsQ[x], True],
c = Map[Flatten, Map[{#[[1]], Select[#, StandPath[#] === StandPath[x] &]} &, b]];
If[c == {{"read"}, {"write"}}, {}, c = Select[c, Length[#] > 1 &];
If[Length[c] > 1, c, c[[1]]], {}]]]]

In[2629]:= **OpenFiles[]**
Out[2629]= {{"read", "C:/Temp\\cinema.txt", "C:/Temp/Cinema.txt", "c:/temp/burthday.doc", "C:/temp\\BurthDay.doc", "C:/GrGu_Books/Burthday1.doc"}, {"write", "C:\\GrGu_Books\\Burthday1.doc"}}
In[2630]:= **OpenFiles["AvzArnVsvArtKr"]**
Out[2630]= {}
In[2631]:= **OpenFiles["C:\\Temp\\Cinema.txt"]**
Out[2631]= {"read", "C:/Temp\\cinema.txt", "C:/Temp/Cinema.txt"}
In[2632]:= **OpenFiles["C:\\GrGu_Books/Burthday1.doc"]**
Out[2632]= {{"read", "C:/GrGu_Books/Burthday1.doc"}, {"write", "C:\\GrGu_Books\\Burthday1.doc"}}

At that, as the full path it is understood or really full path to a datafile in file system of the computer, or its *full name* if it is located in the current directory determined by the function call **Directory[]**.

As the procedure similar to the **OpenFiles**, the following procedure can be used, whose call **StreamFiles[]** returns a nested list from 2 sublists, the first sublist with the first *"in"* element contains full paths/names of the files opened on the reading while the second sublist with the first *"out"* element contains full paths/names of the files opened on the recording. While in the absence of the open files the procedure call **StreamFiles[]** returns *"AllFilesClosed"*. A fragment below represents source code of the **OpenFiles** procedure with typical examples of its application.

In[2555]:= StreamFiles[] :=
Module[{a = Map[ToString1, StreamsU[]], b = {}, w = {"out"}, r = {"in"}, c, k = 1},
If[a == {}, Return["AllFilesClosed"], For[k, k <= Length[a], k++, c = a[[k]];
If[SuffPref[c, "Out", 1], AppendTo[w, StrFromStr[c]], AppendTo[r, StrFromStr[c]]]]];
c = Select[Map[Flatten, {r, w}], Length[#] > 1 &]; If[Length[c] == 1, c[[1]], c]]

In[2556]:= StreamFiles[]
Out[2556]= {{"in", "C:/Temp\\cinema.txt", "C:/Temp/Cinema.txt",
"c:/temp/birthday.doc", "C:/temp\\BurthDay.doc"},
{"out", "C:\\GrGu_Books\\Burthday1.doc"}}
In[2557]:= Close["C:\\GrGu_Books\\Burthday1.doc"]
Out[2557]= "C:\\GrGu_Books\\Burthday1.doc"
In[2558]:= StreamFiles[]
Out[2558]= {"in", "C:/Temp\\cinema.txt", "C:/Temp/Cinema.txt",
"c:/temp/burthday.doc", "C:/temp\\BurthDay.doc"}
In[2559]:= CloseAll[]; StreamFiles[]
Out[2559]= "AllFilesClosed"
In[2560]:= Read["Book_3.doc"];
In[2561]:= StreamFiles[]
Out[2561]= {"in", "Book_3.doc"}

In a number of cases at work with files the following procedure can be very useful, whose call **IsFileOpen[*f*]** returns *True* if a *f* datafile determined by a name or full path is open, and *False* otherwise. If *f* argument does not define an existing file the procedure call is returned unevaluated. While the call **IsFileOpen[*f*, *h*]** with the 2nd optional *h* argument – *an undefinite variable* – through *h* returns the nested list whose elements are sublists of format {{*"read"* | *"write"*}, {*The list of streams on which the f file is open on reading|recording*}} if the main result is *True*. The fragment below represents source code of the **IsFileOpen** procedure along with examples of its application.

In[2550]:= IsFileOpen[F_ /; FileExistsQ[F], h___] := Module[{a = OpenFiles[F]},
If[a == {}, False, If[{h} != {} && ! HowAct[h], h = a, Null]; True]]

In[2551]:= OpenWrite["C:/temp/cinema_2017.doc"];
OpenRead["C:/temp\\cinema_2017.doc"];
In[2552]:= Streams[]

Out[2552]= {OutputStream["stdout", 1], OutputStream["stderr", 2], OutputStream["C:/temp/cinema_2017.doc", 24], InputStream["C:/temp\\cinema_2017.doc", 25]}

In[2553]:= **IsFileOpen["C:/Temp\\Cinema_2017.doc", t590]**

Out[2553]= True

In[2554]:= **t590**

Out[2554]= {{"read", {"C:/temp/cinema_2017.doc"}}, {"write", {"C:/temp\\cinema_2017.doc"}}}

In[2555]:= **Read["C:/temp/burthday.doc"];**

In[2556]:= **IsFileOpen["C:\\temp\\BurthDay.doc", h590]**

Out[2556]= True

In[2557]:= **h590**

Out[2557]= {"read", {"C:/temp/birthday.doc"}}

In[2558]:= **CloseAll[]; IsFileOpen["C:\\temp\\BurthDay.doc"]**

Out[2558]= False

The following an quite simple procedure is represented as a rather useful tool at operating with file system of the computer, whose the call **DirEmptyQ[w]** returns *True* if *w* directory is empty, otherwise *False* is returned. At that, the procedure call **DirEmptyQ[w]** is returned unevaluated if *w* isn't a real directory. The following fragment represents source code of the **DirEmptyQ** procedure with typical enough examples of its application.

In[2602]:= **DirEmptyQ[d_ /; DirQ[d]] :=**
Module[{a = "$DirFile$", b, c, p = StandPath[StringReplace[d, "/" -> "\\"]], h = " 0 File(s) "},
b = Run["Dir " <> p <> If[SuffPref[p, "\\", 2], "", "\\"] <> "*.* > " <> a];
If[b != 0, $Failed, Do[c = Read[a, String], {6}]]; DeleteFile[Close[a]]; ! StringFreeQ[c, h]]

In[2603]:= **Map[DirEmptyQ, {"C:\\Mathematica/Avz", "C:/temp", "C:\\", "C:/Mathematica", "Rans", "C:/Mathematica/Avz/Agn/Art/Kr"}]**

Out[2603]= {False, False, False, False, DirEmptyQ["Rans"], True}

In[2604]:= **DirEmptyQ["C:\\Mathematica/Avz/Agn/Art/Kr/"]**

Out[2604]= True

In[2605]:= **Map[DirEmptyQ, {"C:\\Mathematica/Avz", "C:/Temp/", "C:/"}]**

Out[2605]= {False, False, False}

In[2606]:= **DirEmptyQ["C:\\Program Files (x86)"]**

Out[2606]= False

In addition to the previous **DirEmptyQ** procedure the procedure call **DirFD[j]** returns the 2-element nested list whose the first element determines the list of subdirectories of the first nesting level of a *j* directory whereas the second element – the list of files of a *j* directory; if the *j* directory is empty, the procedure call returns the empty list, i.e. {}. The fragment below represents source code of the **DirFD** procedure with examples of its application.

In[2575]:= **DirFD[d_ /; DirQ[d]] :=**
Module[{a = "$DirFile$", b = {{}, {}}, c, h, t, p = StandPath[StringReplace[d, "/" -> "\\"]]},
If[DirEmptyQ[p], Return[{}], Null];
c = Run["Dir " <> p <> " /B " <> If[SuffPref[p, "\\", 2], "", "\\"] <> "*.* > " <> a];
t = Map[ToString, ReadList[a, String]]; DeleteFile[a];

Map[{h = d <> "\\" <> #; If[DirectoryQ[h], AppendTo[b[[1]], #], If[FileExistsQ[h], AppendTo[b[[2]], #], Null]]} &, t]; b]

In[2576]:= **DirFD["C:/Program Files/Wolfram Research/Mathematica/11.0\\Documentation\\English\\Packages"]**

Out[2576]= {{"ANOVA", "Audio", "AuthorTools", "BarCharts", "Benchmarking", "BlackBodyRadiation", "Calendar", "Combinatorica", "Compatibility", "ComputationalGeometry", "ComputerArithmetic", "Developer", "EquationTrekker", "ErrorBarPlots", "Experimental", "FiniteFields", "FourierSeries", "FunctionApproximations", "Geodesy", "GraphUtilities", ..., "WorldPlot", "XML"}, {}}

In[2577]:= **Length[%[[1]]]**
Out[2577]= 48

In[2578]:= **DirFD["C:\\Program Files"]**
Out[2578]= {{"Common Files", "Dell Inc", "DVD Maker", "Extras", "File Association Helper", "Intel", "Internet Explorer", "MSBuild", "PDFeditor", "Realtek", "Reference Assemblies", "Windows Defender", "Windows Journal", "Windows Mail", "Windows Media Player", "Windows NT", "Windows Photo Viewer", "Windows Portable Devices", "Windows Sidebar", "Wolfram Research"}, {}}

In[2579]:= **DirFD["C:\\Temp"]**
Out[2579]= {{"Dialog_files"}, {"Rans.txt", "Addresses_for_book.doc", "Books.doc", "Books.mht", "Burthday.doc", "cinema_2017.doc", "Cinema.txt", "Dialog.htm", "ISSN Application form.pdf", "Math_Trials.DOC", "potencial.txt", "regcleaner.exe"}}

In particular, in an example of the previous fragment the list of directories with records on the packages delivered with the *Mathematica 11.0.1.0* system is returned. So, with release *11.0.1.0* of the *Mathematica 48* packages of different purpose that is rather simply seen from the name of the subdirectories containing them are being delivered.

In addition to the **DirFD** procedure, the **DirFull** procedure presents a quite certain interest, whose call **DirFull[w]** returns list of all full paths to the subdirectories and files contained in a *w* directory and its subdirectories; the first element of this list – the *w* directory. While on an *empty w* directory the call **DirFull[w]** returns the *empty* list. The next fragment represents source code of the **DirFull** procedure along with examples of its application.

In[2595]:= **DirFull[x_ /; DirQ[x]] :=**
Module[{a = "$Art27Kr20$", c, b = StandPath[StringReplace[x, "/" -> "\\"]]},
If[DirEmptyQ[x], {}, Run["Dir /S/B/A ", b, " > ", a];
c = Map[ToString, ReadList[a, String]]; DeleteFile[a]; Prepend[c, b]]]

In[2596]:= **DirFull["C:\\Mathematica\\avz\\agn/Art/Kr"]**
Out[2596]= {}

In[2597]:= **DirFull["C:\\Users\\Aladjev\\DownLoads"]**
Out[2597]= {"c:\\users\\aladjev\\downloads",
"c:\\users\\aladjev\\downloads\\1415971737.pdf",
"c:\\users\\aladjev\\downloads\\Arve_23618448.pdf",
"c:\\users\\aladjev\\downloads\\desktop.ini",
"c:\\users\\aladjev\\downloads\\Mathematica_11.0_WIN.zip",
"c:\\users\\aladjev\\downloads\\Nokia_225.PDF"}

In addition to the **DirFull** procedure the call **TypeFilesD**[*d*] of the procedure **TypeFilesD** returns the sorted list of types of files located in a *d* directory with returning *"undefined"* on files without of a name extension. In addition, the files located in the *d* directory and in all its subdirectories of an arbitrary nesting level are considered too. Moreover, on the empty *d* directory the procedure call **TypeFilesD**[*d*] returns the empty list, i.e. {}. The next fragment represents source code of the **TypeFilesD** procedure along with typical enough examples of its application.

In[5180]:= **TypeFilesD[x_ /; DirQ[x]] :=**
Module[{a = "$Art27Kr20$", d = {}, c, p, b = StandPath[StringReplace[x, "/" -> "\\"]]},
If[DirEmptyQ[x], {}, Run["Dir /S/B/A ", b, " > ", a];
c = Map[ToString, ReadList[a, String]]; DeleteFile[a];
Sort[Select[DeleteDuplicates[Map[If[DirectoryQ[#], Null, If[FileExistsQ[#],
p = ToLowerCase[ToString[FileExtension[#]]];
If[! SameQ[p, ""], p, "undefined"]], Null] &, c]], ! SameQ[#, Null] &]]]]

In[5181]:= **TypeFilesD["C:\\Temp\\"]**
Out[5181]= {"txt", "doc", "mht", "htm", "pdf", "exe", "jpg", "js", "css", "png", "gif", "php", "json", "undefined", "query", "xml"}

In[5182]:= **TypeFilesD["C:/Tallinn\\Grodno/Kherson"]**
Out[5182]= {}

In[5183]:= **TypeFilesD["C:\\Mathematica"]**
Out[5183]= {"css", "doc", "gif", "htm", "jpg", "js", "json", "pdf", "png", "tmp"}

In[5184]:= **TypeFilesD["C:\\Program Files (x86)\\Maple 11"]**
Out[5184]= {"access", "afm", "bfc", "cfg", "cpl", "csv", "dat", "del", "dll",...}

The **FindFile1** procedure serves as an useful expansion of the standard **FindFile** function, providing search of a file within file system of the computer. The call **FindFile1**[*x*] returns a full path to the found file *x*, or the list of full paths *(if a x file is located in different directories of file system of the computer)*, otherwise the call returns the empty list, i.e. {}. Whereas the call **FindFile1**[*x*, *y*] with the 2nd optional *y* argument – *full path to a directory* – returns full path to the found *x* datafile, or the list of full paths located in the *y* directory and its subdirectories. Furthermore, the **FindFile2** function serves as other useful extension of standard **FindFile** function, providing search of an *y* file within a *x* directory. The function call **FindFile2**[*x*, *y*] returns the list of full paths to the found *y* file, otherwise the call returns the empty list, i.e. {}. Search is done in the *x* directory and all its subdirectories. The next fragment represents source codes of the **FindFile1** procedure and **FindFile2** function with typical examples of their application.

In[2550]:= **FindFile1[x_ /; StringQ[x], y___] := Module[{c, d = {}, k = 1, a = If[{y} != {} &&**
PathToFileQ[y], {y}, Map[# <> ":\\" &, Adrive[]]], b = "\\" <> ToLowerCase[x]},
For[k, k <= Length[a], k++, c = Map[ToLowerCase, Quiet[FileNames["*", a[[k]],
Infinity]]]; d = Join[d, Select[c, SuffPref[#, b, 2] && FileExistsQ[#] &]]];
If[Length[d] == 1, d[[1]], d]]

In[2551]:= **FindFile1["Rans_15_10_17.doc"]**
Out[2551]= {"C:\\Temp\\Rans_15_10_17.doc", "F:\\Rans_15_10_17.doc"}
In[2552]:= **FindFile1["Cinema_2017.txt", "C:\\Temp"]**

Out[2552]= "c:\\temp\\cinema_2017.txt"
In[2553]:= FindFile1["Cinema_2017.txt"]
Out[2553]= {"C:\\GrGU_Books\\Cinema_2017.txt", "C:\\Program Files\\Wolfram Research\\Mathematica\\11.0\\Cinema_2017.txt", "C:\\Program Files\\Wolfram Research\\Mathematica\\11.0\\SystemFiles\\Cinema_2017.txt", "C:\\Temp\\Cinema_2017.txt", "E:\\ Cinema_2017.txt"}
In[2554]:= FindFile1["AvzAgnVsvArtKr"]
Out[2554]= {}
In[2555]:= t3 = TimeUsed[]; FindFile1["unins000.msg"]; TimeUsed[] - t3
Out[2555]= 5.96
In[2556]:= t4 = TimeUsed[]; FileExistsQ1["unins000.msg"]; TimeUsed[] - t4
Out[2556]= 5.164
In[3941]:= FindFile2[x_ /; DirectoryQ[x], y_ /; StringQ[y]] :=
Select[FileNames["*.*", x, Infinity], StandPath[FileNameSplit[#][[-1]]] == StandPath[y] &]
In[3942]:= FindFile2[$InstallationDirectory, "PacletDB.m"]
Out[3942]= {"C:\\Program Files\\Wolfram Research\\Mathematica\\11.0\\Documentation\\English\\PacletDB.m"}

In particular, examples of the previous fragment indicate, the **FindFile1** in many respects is functionally similar to the **FileExistsQ1** procedure however in the time relation is somewhat less *fast-acting* in the same file system of the computer *(the interesting questions of datafiles and directories processing can be found in the collection* [50]).

It is possible to present the **SearchDir** procedure as one more *indicative* example, whose call **SearchDir[d]** returns the list of all paths in file system of the computer which are completed by a *d* subdirectory; in case of lack of such paths the procedure call **SearchDir[d]** returns the empty list. In combination with the procedures **FindFile1** and **FileExistsQ1** the **SearchDir** procedure is useful at working with file system of the computer, that confirms their use for the solution of problems of similar type. The following fragment represents source code of the **SearchDir** procedure with examples of its application.

In[2595]:= SearchDir[d_ /; StringQ[d]] := Module[{a = Adrive[], c, t = {}, p,
b = "\\" <> ToLowerCase[StringTrim[d, ("\\" | "/")...]] <> "\\", g = {}, k = 1, v},
For[k, k <= Length[a], k++, p = a[[k]];
c = Map[ToLowerCase, Quiet[FileNames["*", p <> ":\\", Infinity]]];
Map[If[! StringFreeQ[#, b] || SuffPref[#, b, 2] && DirQ[#], AppendTo[t, #], Null] &, c]];
For[k = 1, k <= Length[t], k++, p = t[[k]] <> "\\"; a = StringPosition[p, b];
If[a == {}, Continue[], a = Map[#[[2]] &, a];
Map[If[DirectoryQ[v = StringTake[p, {1, # - 1}]], AppendTo[g, v], Null] &, a]]];
DeleteDuplicates[g]]

In[2596]:= SearchDir["AvzAgnVsvArtKr"]
Out[2596]= {}
In[2597]:= SearchDir["\\Temp/"]
Out[2597]= {"c:\\temp", "c:\\users\\aladjev\\appdata\\local\\temp", ..., "c:\\windows\\winsxs\\temp"}
In[2598]:= SearchDir["Mathematica"]

Out[2598]= {"c:\\mathematica", "c:\\programdata\\mathematica", "c:\\program files\\wolfram research\\mathematica", ..., "e:\\mathematica"}

It is once again expedient to note that the mechanism of the objects typification which the *Mathematica* system has, is a significantly inferior to the similar mechanism of the *Maple* system, but only relatively to the builtin types of testing of objects. Meanwhile, and tools of the *Mathematica* system allow to test types of the most important objects. In particular, the system **FileType** function provides the checking be a directory or datafile as illustrate the following simple enough examples, namely:

In[3742]:= **FileType["D:\\Math_myLib"]**
Out[3742]= Directory
In[3743]:= **FileType["C:\\Temp\\Cinema_2017.txt"]**
Out[3743]= File
In[3744]:= **FileExistsQ["D:\\Math_myLib\\ArtKr.mx"]**
Out[3744]= True
In[3745]:= **FileExistsQ["D:\\Math_myLib"]**
Out[3745]= True

In the tool time, these means yield to our procedures *isFile* and *isDir* for the *Maple* system, providing testing of files and directories respectively [47]. So, the **isFile** procedure not only tests the existence of a file, but also the mode of its opening, what in certain cases is a rather important. There are other interesting enough tools for testing of the state of directories and files, including their types [25,47,50]. On the other hand, the *Mathematica* system posesses the **FileExistsQ** function which returns *True* if a tested object is a file or directory what from standpoint of file system of the computer is quite correctly while for the user working with files it is not the same what rather visually illustrates the following very simple example:

In[2645]:= **F := "C:\\Mathematica"; If[FileExistsQ[F], OpenRead[F]; Read[F], Message[F::file, "file is absent"]]**
OpenRead::noopen: Cannot open C:\\Mathematica... >>
Read::openx: C:\\Mathematica is not open... >>
Out[2645]= Read["D:\\Mathematica"]

Check by means of the **FileExistsQ** function defines existence of a *F* datafile *(though instead of it the directory is specified)*, then the attempt to open this *F* datafile on the reading with the subsequent reading its first logical record are done, but both these procedures of access are completed with return of erroneous diagnostics. Therefore for this purpose it is necessary to use the testing function **IsFile** combining the **FileExistsQ** and **DirectoryQ** or even somewhat more complex organized procedure whose call **FileQ[*f*]** returns *True* if a *f* string determines a real–existing datafile, and *False* otherwise. The **FileQ** procedure serves sooner for a certain illustration of development tools of the procedures oriented on working with file system of the computer. The following fragment represents source codes of both tools with examples of their application.

In[2622]:= **IsFile[x_] := If[FileExistsQ[x], If[! DirectoryQ[x], True, False], False];**
Map[FileType, {"c:\\mathem", "c:\\mathem\\ap.doc"}]
Out[2622]= {Directory, File}
In[2623]:= **FileQ[f_ /; StringQ[f]] := Module[{d = Adrive[], s = {}, k = 1,**

```
a = ToLowerCase[StringReplace[Flatten[OpenFiles[]], "\\\\" -> "/"]],
b = ToLowerCase[StringReplace[Directory[], "\\" -> "/"]],
c = ToLowerCase[StringReplace[f, "\\" -> "/"]]},
For[k, k <= Length[d], k++, AppendTo[s, d[[k]] <> ":"]];
If[StringLength[c] < 2 || ! MemberQ[ToLowerCase[s], StringTake[c, {1, 2}]],
c = b <> "/" <> c, Null];
If[DirQ[c], False, If[MemberQ[a, c], True,
If[Quiet[OpenRead[c]] === $Failed, False, Close[c]; True]]]]
In[2624]:= Map[FileQ, {"C:/Temp/Cinema.txt", "Book_3.doc", "E:/Art.Kr"}]
Out[2624]= {True, True, False}
```

For the differentiated testing of datafiles the **FileType** function is used too:

```
In[2552]:= Map[FileType, {"C:/Mathematica", "C:/Mathematica/ap.doc"}]
Out[2552]= {Directory, File}
```

The *Mathematica* system has also some other similar testing means oriented on processing of elements of file system of the computer. Certain similar functions have been considered slightly above along with our tools. So, the next fragment represents procedure, whose call **EmptyFileQ[f]** returns *True* if a *f* datafile is empty, and *False* otherwise.

```
In[2640]:= EmptyFileQ[f_ /; StringQ[f], y___] := Module[{a, b, c, d = {}, k = 1},
If[FileExistsQ[f], b = {f}, c = Art27Kr20; ClearAll[Art27Kr20];
a = FileExistsQ1[f, Art27Kr20]];
If[! a, Return[$Failed], b = Art27Kr20; Art27Kr20 = c];
While[k <= Length[b], AppendTo[d, Quiet[Close[b[[k]]]]];
If[Quiet[Read[b[[k]]]] === EndOfFile, Quiet[Close[b[[k]]]]; True], Quiet[Close[b[[k]]]];
False]]; k++]; d = If[Length[d] == 1, d[[1]], d];
If[{y} != {}, {d, If[Length[b] == 1, b[[1]], b]}, d]]
In[2641]:= Map[EmptyFileQ, {"c:/temp/cinema.txt", "c:/temp/cinema.doc"}]
Out[2641]= {False, True}
In[2642]:= EmptyFileQ["cinema.txt"]
Out[2642]= {False, True, False, False, False, True, False}
In[2643]:= EmptyFileQ["C:\\Cinema.txt", 590]
Out[2643]= {{False, True, False, False, False, True, False}, "C:\\GrGU_Books\\Cinema.txt",
"C:\\Mathematica\\Cinema.txt",
"C:\\Program Files\\Wolfram Research\\Mathematica\\11.0\\Cinema.txt",
"C:\\Program Files\\Wolfram Research\\Mathematica\\11.0\\SystemFiles\\Links\\
Cinema.txt", "C:\\Temp\\Cinema.txt", "E:\\Cinema.txt", "E:\\CD_Book\\Cinema.txt"}}
In[2644]:= EmptyFileQ["Appendix.doc", 590]
Out[2644]= $Failed
In[2645]:= EmptyFileQ["C:\\Temp\\Cinema_2017.txt", 590]
Out[2645]= {False, "C:\\Temp\\Cinema_2017.txt"}
```

If a *f* file is absent in file system of the computer, the call **EmptyFileQ[f]** returns the *$Failed*. Moreover, if in the course of search of the *f* file its multiplicity in file system of the computer is detected, all datafiles from list of the found files are tested, including also files which are located in the *Recycle Bin* directory. In addition, the procedure call **EmptyFileQ**[*f, y*] with two factual arguments where optional *y* argument – an expression, returns the nested two-element list whose first sublist determines *emptiness/nonemptiness (True | False)* of the *f* file in the list of files of the same name whereas the second sublist defines full paths to the *f* files of the same name. At that, between both sublists the one–to–one correspondence takes place. The previous fragment represents both source code, and the typical examples of application of the **EmptyFileQ** procedure.

The **FindSubDir** procedure provides search of the full paths which contain a *x* subdirectory given by a full name in file system of the computer or in file system of the given devices of direct access that are defined by names in string format. The procedure call **FindSubDir**[*x*] returns the list of full paths within all file system of the computer, while the procedure call **FindSubDir**[*x, y, z, ...*] – within only file system of the {*y, z, ...*} devices. The next fragment represents source code of the **FindSubDir** procedure with examples of its application.

In[2542]:= FindSubDir[x_ /; StringQ[x], y___] := Module[{b = {}, c = "", p, t, k = 1,
a = If[{y} == {}, Adrive[], {y}], f = "Art27Kr20.txt", h = ToLowerCase[x]},
While[k <= Length[a], Run["Dir ", a[[k]] <> ":\\", " /B/S/L > "<> f];
While[! SameQ[c, "EndOfFile"], c = ToString[Read[f, String]];
t = FileNameSplit[c]; p = Flatten[Position[t, h]];
If[p != {} && DirectoryQ[FileNameJoin[t[[1 ;; p[[1]]]]]], AppendTo[b, c]];
Continue[]]; Closes[f]; c = ""; k++]; {DeleteFile[f], b}[[2]]]

In[2543]:= FindSubDir["Dell Inc"]
Out[2543]= {"c:\\program files\\dell inc",
"c:\\program files\\dell inc\\dell edoc viewer",
"c:\\program files\\dell inc\\dell edoc viewer\\eddy.ini", ...,
"c:\\program files\\dell inc\\dell edoc viewer\\sweepdocs.exe"}
In[2544]:= FindSubDir["Dell Inc", "F"]
Out[2544]= {}
In[2545]:= FindSubDir["MathToolBox", "C", "E"]
Out[2545]= {"e:\\MathToolBox", "e:\\MathToolBox\\MathToolBox.cdf",
"e:\\MathToolBox\\MathToolBox.m", "e:\\MathToolBox\\MathToolBox.mx",
"e:\\MathToolBox\\MathToolBox.nb"}

The following **FilesDistrDirs** procedure in a certain degree bears structural character for a directory given by the actual argument of the procedure. The call **FilesDistrDirs**[*x*] returns the nested list whose elements are sublists of the following format {*dir_p, f1, f2, f3, ..., fn*}, where *dir_p* – a *x* directory and all its subdirectories of any nesting level, whereas *f1, f2, f3, ..., fn* – names of the datafiles located in this directory. The following fragment represents source code of the **FilesDistrDirs** procedure along with an example of its application.

In[2555]:= FilesDistrDirs[x_ /; DirQ[x]] :=
Module[{a = {}, b, d, g, h = {}, t, c = FromCharacterCode[17], f = "$Art27Kr20$", k = 1},
Run["Dir " <> StandPath[x] <> "/A/B/OG/S > " <> f];
For[k, k < Infinity, k++, b = Read[f, String];
If[SameQ[b, EndOfFile], DeleteFile[Close[f]]; Break[], AppendTo[a, b]]];

```
b = Gather[PrependTo[a, StringReplace[x, "/" -> "\\"]], DirQ[#1] === DirQ[#2] &];
d = {Sort[Map[StringJoin[#, "\\"] &, b[[1]]], StringCount[#1, "\\"] >=
StringCount[#2, "\\"] &], Quiet[Check[b[[2]], {}]]}; a = Map[ToLowerCase, Flatten[d]];
For[k = 1, k <= Length[d[[1]]], k++, t = ToLowerCase[d[[1]][[k]]];
AppendTo[h, g = Select[a, SuffPref[#, t, 1] && StringFreeQ[StrDelEnds[#, t, 1], "\\"] &]];
a = MinusList[a, g]]; a = {}; For[k = 1, k <= Length[h], k++, b = h[[k]];
AppendTo[a, {b[[1]], Map[StrDelEnds[#, b[[1]], 1] &, b[[2 ;; -1]]]}]]; Map[Flatten[#] &, a]]
In[2556]:= FilesDistrDirs["C:\\GrGU_Books"]
Out[2556]= {{"c:\\grgu_books\\MathToolBox\\", "MathToolBox.m", "MathToolBox.mx",
"MathToolBox.nb", "MathToolBox.txt"}, {"c:\\grgu_books\\", "burthday.doc", "cinema.txt",
"general_statistics.pdf", "general_statistics_cover.pdf", "iton16_5.pdf", "school.pdf"}}
```

A rather simple **PathToFileQ** function is a useful tool at operating with files and directories, whose call **PathToFileQ**[*x*] returns *True* if a *x* defines a potentially admissible full path to a directory or file, and *False* otherwise. The following fragment represents source code of the function with an example of its application.

```
In[2555]:= PathToFileQ[x_ /; StringQ[x]] := If[StringLength[x] >= 3,
If[MemberQ[Join[CharacterRange["a", "z"], CharacterRange["A", "Z"]],
StringTake[x, 1]] && StringTake[x, {2, 2}] == ":" &&
And[Map3[StringFreeQ, x, {"/", "\\"}]] != {True, True}, True, False], False]
In[2556]:= Map[PathToFileQ, {"C:", "C:/", "G:/MathToolBox", "H:\\agn", "C:/Temp",
"C:/Temp\\Mathematica", "C:/GrSU_Books"}]
Out[2556]= {False, True, True, True, True, True, True}
```

Considering the circumstance, that ideology of the file organization of the computer quite allows in a number of cases of work with means of access for identify files and directories, the function is represented as an useful enough tool for both types of elements of file system of the computer.

In a number of cases arises a necessity of reading out of a datafile entirely, excluding from its contents the symbols "\r\n" – *carriage return* and *line feed*. The following **ReadFullFile** procedure quite successfully solves the given problem. The procedure call **ReadFullFile**[*f*] returns contents of a *f* datafile with replacement of its "\r\n" symbols onto "" symbols; if the *f* datafile is absent in file system of the computer, the procedure call returns the $*Failed*. Whereas the call **ReadFullFile**[*f, y*] in addition through the second optional *y* argument – *an undefinite variable* – returns a full name or a full path to the *f* file; in addition, if *y* is a string, then *y* replaces in the returned contents of the *f* file all "\r\n" symbols onto the *y* string. The following fragment represents source code of the procedure with examples of its use.

```
In[2554]:= ReadFullFile[f_ /; StringQ[f], y___] := Module[{a, b = $Art6Kr$},
If[FileExistsQ[f], a = f, ClearAll[$Art6Kr$];
If[! FileExistsQ1[f, $Art6Kr$], Return[$Failed], a = $Art6Kr$[[1]]]]; $Art6Kr$ = b;
StringReplace[StringJoin[Map[FromCharacterCode, BinaryReadList[a]]], "\r\n" ->
If[{y} != {}, If[StringQ[y], y, If[! HowAct[y], y = a; "", ""]], ""]]]
In[2555]:= ReadFullFile["Cinema_2017.txt", w74]
```

Out[2555]= "http://www.sagemath.org/http://kino-goda.com/load/smotret_onlajn/
serialy/shef_novaja_zhizn/18-1-0-3462
http://cinemaxx.ru/legends-of-the-criminal-investigation/29998-legendy-ugolovnogo-
rozyska-iuda-iz-kremlya.html
http://kinokong.net/26962-chuma-devyanostye-16-11-2015.html
http://cinemaxx.ru/9/31367-vysokie-stavki-2015.html
In[2556]:= **w74**
Out[2556]= "C:\\Temp\\cinema_2017.txt"
In[2557]:= **ReadFullFile["AvZAgnVsvArtKr.doc"]**
Out[2557]= $Failed
In[2558]:= **ReadFullFile["DataFile.txt"]**
Out[2558]= "AvzAgnVsvArtKrRansIan2017"
In[2559]:= **ReadFullFile["DataFile.txt", " | "]**
Out[2559]= "Avz | Agn | Vsv | Art | Kr | Rans | Ian | 2017 | "

Once again it is necessary to remind, that all elements of file system of the computer should be coded with the separators determined by the predefined *$PathnameSeparator* variable, by default as a *separator* the double backslash "\\" is used. In addition, in the *Mathematica* system in general the double backslash "\\" and slash "/" are distinguished as separators, namely: if the double backslash plays a part of standard separator of elements of file system of the computer, then the slash can also carry out this function, excepting a case when the slash is coded at the end of a chain of directories or at its use in a call of the **Run** function as a whole. For elimination of the first situation we created the simple enough **DirQ** function considered above.

In[2567]:= **Map[DirectoryQ, {"C:\\Program Files (x86)/Maple 11/", "C:/Program Files (x86)/Maple 11\\", "C:/Program Files (x86)/Maple 11"}]**
Out[2567]= {False, True, True}
In[2568]:= **Map[DirQ, {"C:\\Program Files (x86)/Maple 11/", "C:/Program Files (x86)/Maple 11\\", "C:/Program Files (x86)/Maple 11"}]**
Out[2568]= {True, True, True}

At that, the call **SetPathSeparator[*x*]** of a simple procedure makes setting of the separator "\\" or "/" for paths to files/directories for a period of the current session with returning of a new separator in the string format as the next simple enough fragment rather visually illustrates, namely:

In[2642]:= **$PathnameSeparator**
Out[2642]= "\\"
In[2643]:= **SetPathSeparator[x_ /; MemberQ[{"/", "\\"}, x]] := Module[{},
Unprotect[$PathnameSeparator]; $PathnameSeparator = x;
SetAttributes[$PathnameSeparator, Protected]]**
In[2644]:= **{SetPathSeparator["/"]; $PathnameSeparator, SetPathSeparator["\\"];
$PathnameSeparator}**
Out[2644]= {"/", "\\"}
In[2645]:= **StandPath[x_ /; StringQ[x]] := Module[{a, b = "", c, k = 1},
If[MemberQ[Flatten[Outer[StringJoin, CharacterRange["a", "z"], {":/", ":\\"}]],**

```
c = ToLowerCase[x]], StringReplace[c, "/" -> "\\"], If[PathToFileQ[x],
a = FileNameSplit[StringReplace[ToLowerCase[ToLowerCase[x]], "/" -> "\\"]];
For[k, k <= Length[a], k++, c = a[[k]];
If[! StringFreeQ[c, " "], b = b <> StrStr[c] <> "\\", b = b <> c <> "\\"]];
StringTake[b, {1, -2}], ToLowerCase[x]]]]
```

In[2646]:= **StandPath["C:/Program Files\\Wolfram Research/Mathematica/11.0/"]**
Out[2646]= "c:\\\"program files\"\\\"wolfram research\"\\mathematica\\11.0"
In[2647]:= **Map[StandPath, {"C:/", "C:\\", "E:/"}]**
Out[2647]= {"c:\\", "c:\\", "e:\\"}
In[2648]:= **StandPath["AvzAgnVsvArtKt.TXT"]**
Out[2648]= "avzagnvsvartkt.txt"

So, for the *Mathematica* system in most cases similar to the *Maple* system is also possible to use both types of separators of elements of a file system, however the told concerns only to the *Windows* system, for other platforms the differences which in a number of cases are an essential enough for programming are possible. As it was noted above, using the different formats for names of the datafiles and full paths to them, we obtain a possibility to open the same physical file in the different streams, that in some cases provides at times *simplification* of processing of datafiles. Meanwhile, in certain cases similar opportunity complicates the algorithms linked with processing of datafiles, for example, a file created on the basis of one one format name, generally, won't be recognized by standard means on the basis of another format, for example:

In[2652]:= **Write["RANS_IAN.txt"]; Close["Rans_Ian.txt"]**
General::openx: Rans_Ian.txt is not open... >>
Out[2652]= Close["Rans_Ian.txt"]
In[2653]:= **Close["RANS_IAN.txt"]**
Out[2653]= "RANS_IAN.txt"

Thus, correct use of datafiles names and paths to them assumes, generally, work with the same format, as it illustrates the above example. Therefore as a quite simple reception that allows to unify names of datafiles/directories and paths to them it is possible to offer the following standard – *the symbols that compose names of files and paths to them are encoded in the lower case whereas as separators the double backslashes "\\" are used.*

The problem is solved successfully by 2 simple procedures **StandPath** and **FileDirStForm**, the source code of the first procedure with examples of application are represented in the previous fragment. So, the procedure call **StandPath[*x*]** in the above standardized format returns a datafile, directory or full paths to them. Moreover, the **StandPath** procedure for testing of an admissibility of an argument *x* as a real path uses the **PathToFileQ** function presenting independent interest and providing the correctness of processing of the paths containing gap symbols. So, the usage by the **DirFD** procedure of the **StandPath** procedure allows to obtain an quite correctly contents of any directory of file system of the computer which contains gap symbols and on which the *Dir* command of *DOS* system doesn't yield result as very visually the simple examples illustrate [30-33]. The **StandPath** procedure can be used rather effectively at development of different tools of access in file system of the computer; moreover, the procedure is used by a number of means of access to the files that are considered in the present book along with the means represented in the *MathToolBox* package [48,50].

The *Mathematica* system has two standard functions **RenameDirectory** and **RenameFile** for ensuring renaming of directories and files of file system of the computer respectively. Meanwhile, from the point of view of the datafile concept these functions would be very expedient to be executed by uniform tools because in this concept directories and datafiles are in many respects are identical and their processing can be executed by the same tools. At the same time the mentioned standard functions and on restrictions are quite identical: for renaming of x name of an element of file system onto a new y name the element with the y name has to be absent in the system, otherwise $*Failed* with a certain diagnostic message are returned. At that, if as y *only* a new name without full path to a new y element is coded, its copying into the current directory is made; in case of a x directory it with all contents is copied into the current directory under a new y name. Therefore, similar organization is a rather inconvenient in many respects, what stimulated us to determine for renaming of the directories and datafiles the uniform **RenDirFile** procedure which provides renaming of a x element *(directory or file)* in situ with preservation of its type and all its attributes; at that, as an y argument a new name of the x element is used. Therefore, the successful procedure call **RenDirFile[x, y]** returns the full path to the renamed x element. In the case of existence of y element the message *"Directory/ datafile <y> already exists"* is returned. In other unsuccessful cases the procedure call returns $*Failed* or is returned unevaluated. The following fragment represents source code of the **RenDirFile** procedure along with examples of its typical use.

In[2632]:= **RenDirFile[x_, y_ /; StringQ[y]] :=**
Module[{a, c = {"/", "\\"}, b = StringTrim[x, {"/", "\\"}]},
If[FileExistsQ[b] || DirectoryQ[b], c = StringTrim[y, c];
a = If[FileExistsQ[b], RenameFile, RenameDirectory];
If[PathToFileQ[b] && PathToFileQ[c] && FileNameSplit[b][[1 ;; -2]] ==
FileNameSplit[c][[1 ;; -2]], Quiet[Check[a[b, c], "Directory/datafile <" <> y <>
"> already exists"]], If[PathToFileQ[b] && ! PathToFileQ[c],
Quiet[Check[a[b, FileNameJoin[Append[FileNameSplit[b][[1 ;; -2]],
StringReplace[c, {"/" -> "", "\\" -> ""}]]]], "Directory/datafile <" <> y <>
"> already exists"]], If[! PathToFileQ[b] && ! PathToFileQ[c],
Quiet[Check[a[b, StringReplace[c, {"/" -> "", "\\" -> ""}]],
"Directory/datafile <" <> y <> "> already exists"]], $Failed]]], Defer[RenDirFile[x, y]]]]

In[2633]:= **RenDirFile["C:/Temp\\Books.doc", "Books_GrSU.doc"]**
Out[2633]= "c:\\temp\\books_grsu.doc"
In[2634]:= **RenDirFile["C:/Temp/Noosphere Academy", "Rans_Ian"]**
Out[2634]= "c:\\temp\\rans_ran"
In[2635]:= **RenDirFile["C:\\Temp/Kino Online.txt", "Cinema Online.txt"]**
Out[2635]= "c:\\temp\\cinema online.txt"
In[2636]:= **RenDirFile["RANS_IAN.txt", "ArtKr.txt"]**
Out[2636]= "C:\\Users\\Aladjev\\Documents\\artkr.txt"
In[2637]:= **RenDirFile["RANS_IAN.txt", "ArtKr.txt"]**
Out[2637]= RenDirFile["RANS_IAN.txt", "ArtKr.txt"]

In[2638]:= **RenDirFile["C:/Temp\\agn", "Agn"]**
Out[2638]= "Directory/datafile <Agn> already exists"
In[2639]:= **RenDirFile["C:/Temp\\Avz.doc", "Agn.doc"]**
Out[2639]= "c:\\temp\\agn.doc"

The special means of processing of datafiles and directories are considered below.

7.5. Certain special tools for processing of datafiles and directories

In this section some special means of processing of directories and files are represented; in certain cases they can be useful enough. So, removal of a file in the current session is made by means of the standard **DeleteFile** function whose the call **DeleteFile[{x, y, z, ...}]** returns *Null*, i.e. nothing in case of successful removal of the given datafile or their list, and *$Failed* otherwise. At that, in the list of files only those are deleted that have no *Protected*-attribute. Moreover, this operation doesn't save the deleted files in the system *$Recycle.Bin* directory that in certain cases is extremely undesirable, first of all, in the light of possibility of their subsequent restoration. The fact that the system function **DeleteFile** is based on the *MS DOS* command *Del* that according to specifics of this operating system immediately deletes a file from file system of the computer without its preservation, which significantly differs from similar operation of the *Windows* system that by default saves the deleted file in the special *$Recycle.Bin* directory.

For elimination of similar shortcoming the **DeleteFile1** procedure has been offered, whose source code with examples of its use are represented by the fragment below. The successful procedure call **DeleteFile1[x]** returns *0*, deleting files given by an argument *x* with saving them in the *$Recycle.Bin* directory of the *Windows* system. Meanwhile, the files removed by means of the procedure call **DeleteFile1[x]** are saved in *$Recycle.Bin* directory, however they are invisible to viewing by the system means, for example, by means of *Ms Explorer*, complicating cleaning of the given system directory. While the procedure call **DeleteFile1[x, t]** with the 2nd optional *t* argument – an undefinite variable – through it in addition returns the list of files which for one reason or another were not removed. In addition, in the system *$Recycle.Bin* directory a copy only of the last deleted file always turns out. This procedure is oriented on *Windows XP* and *Windows 7*, however it can be spread to other operational platforms. The fragment below represents source code of the **DeleteFile1** procedure along with some examples of its application.

For restoration from the system directory *$Recycler.Bin* of the packages that were removed by means of the **DeleteFile1** procedure in the *OS Windows XP Professional*, the procedure **RestoreDelPackage** providing restoration from the system directory *$Recycler.bin* of such packages has been offered [30,48]. The successful call **RestoreDelPackage[F, "Context'"]**, where the first argument *F* defines the name of a file of the format {*"cdf"*, *"m"*, *"mx"*, *"nb"*} that is subject to restoration whereas the second argument – the context associated with a package returns the list of full paths to the restored datafiles, at the same time by deleting from the directory *$Recycler.Bin* the restored datafiles with the necessary package. At that, this tools is supported on the *Windows XP* platform, whereas on the *Windows 7* platform the **RestoreDelFile** procedure is of a certain interest, restoring datafiles from the directory *$Recycler.Bin* that earlier were removed by means of the **DeleteFile1** procedure.

The successful call **RestoreDelFile[F, r]**, where the first argument *F* defines the name of a datafile or their list that are subject to restoration whereas the second argument defines the name of a target directory or full path to it for the restored datafiles returns the list of paths to the restored files; at the same time, the deleting of the restored files from the *$recycler.bin* directory isn't done. In the absence of the requested files in the *$Recycler.Bin* directory the procedure call returns the *empty* list. It should be noted that only *nonempty* files are restored. If the second *r* argument defines a directory name in string format, but not the full path to it, a target *r* directory is created in the active directory of the current session. The fragment below represents source code of the procedure along with examples of its application.

On the other hand, for removal from the *$Recycle.Bin* directory of the files saved by means of the **DeleteFile1** procedure on the *Windows XP* platform, the procedure is used whose call **ClearRecycler[]** returns *0*, deleting files of specified type from the system *$Recycle.bin* directory with saving in it of the files removed by means of *Windows XP* or its appendices. In addition, the *Dick Cleanup* command in *Windows XP* in some cases completely does not clear *Recycler* directory from files what successfully does the call **ClearRecycler["ALL"]**, returning *0* and providing removal of all files from the system *Recycler* directory. In [30,48] it is possible to familiarize with source code of the **ClearRecycler** procedure and examples of its usage. On the *Windows 7* platform the **ClearRecyclerBin** procedure provides removal from the *Recycler* directory of all directories and files or only of those that are caused by the **DeleteFile1** procedure. The successful procedure call **ClearRecyclerBin[]** returns *Null*, and provides removal from the system *$Recycle.Bin* directory of directories and files which are caused by the **DeleteFile1** procedure. While the procedure call **ClearRecyclerBin[x]**, where *x – an expression* – also returns *Null*, i.e. nothing, and provides removal from the *$recycle.bin* directory of all directories and datafiles whatever the cause of their appearance in the given directory. In addition, the procedure call on the empty *Recycler* directory returns *$Failed* or nothing, depending on the operating platform. The fragment below represents source code of the procedure with typical examples of its application.

```
In[2552]:= DeleteFile1[x_ /; StringQ[x] || ListQ[x], y___] :=
Module[{d, p, t, a = Map[ToString, Flatten[{x}]], b, c = $ArtKr$},
b = If[! StringFreeQ[Ver[]," XP "], FilesDistrDirs[BootDrive[]][[1]] <> ":\\Recycler"][[1]],
p = 90; ClearAll[$ArtKr$];
If[FileExistsQ1["$recycle.bin", $ArtKr$], d = $ArtKr$[[1]], Return[$Failed]];
b = SortBy[Select[Flatten[FilesDistrDirs[d]], DirectoryQ[#] &], Length[#] &][[2]]];
$ArtKr$ = c;
c = Map[StandPath, Map[If[StringFreeQ[#, ":"], Directory[] <> "\\" <> #, #] &, a]];
t = Map[Run["Copy /Y " <> # <> " " <> If[p == 90, b <> FileNameSplit[#][[-1]], b[[1]]]] &, c];
t = Position[t, 1]; c = If[t != {}, MinusList[c, b = Extract[c, t]], Null];
If[t != {} && {y} != {} && ! HowAct[y], Quiet[y = b], Quiet[y = {}]];
Map[{Attrib[#, {}], Quiet[DeleteFile[#]]} &, c]; 0]

In[2553]:= DeleteFile1[{"Buthday1.doc", "c:/Mathematica\\desktop1.ini",
"C:/Temp/Agn/cinema.txt", "Help.txt", "Cinema.txt", "copy.txt"}, t69]
Out[2553]= 0
In[2554]:= t69
```

Out[2554]= {"c:\\temp\\agn\\cinema.txt", "c:\\users\\aladjev\\documents\\help.txt", "c:\\users\\aladjev\\documents\\cinema.txt", "c:\\users\\aladjev\\documents\\z.txt"}
In[2555]:= **DeleteFile1[{"AvzKr.m", "AgnArt.nb"}]**
Out[2555]= 0
In[2556]:= **DeleteFile1["C:/Documents and Settings/Cinema Online.txt"]**
Out[2556]= 0
In[2642]:= **RestoreDelFile[f_ /; StringQ[f] || ListQ[f], r_ /; StringQ[r]] :=
Module[{b = ToString[Unique["ag"]], c, p = $ArtKr$, t = Map[StandPath, Flatten[{f}]], h},
ClearAll[$ArtKr$]; If[FileExistsQ1["$recycle.bin", $ArtKr$], d = $ArtKr$[[1]]; $ArtKr$ = p,
Return[$Failed]]; Run["Dir " <> d <> "/B/S/L > " <> b];
If[EmptyFileQ[b], $Failed, Quiet[CreateDirectory[r]]; c = ReadList[b, String]];
DeleteFile[b]; h[x_, y_] := If[FileExistsQ[x] && SuffPref[x, "\\" <> y, 2],
CopyFileToDir[x, StandPath[r]], "Null"];
c = Select[Flatten[Outer[h, c, t]], ! SameQ[#, "Null"] &]]**
In[2643]:= **RestoreDelFile[{"Books.txt", "History.doc"}, "restore"]**
Out[2643]= {}
In[2644]:= **RestoreDelFile[{"Cinema.txt", "Birthday.doc"}, "restore"]**
Out[2644]= {"restore\\birthday.doc", "restore\\cinema.txt"}
In[2645]:= **RestoreDelFile["Cinema.txt", "c:/Temp/restore"]**
Out[2645]= {"c:\\temp\\restore\\cinema.txt"}
In[2646]:= **RestoreDelFile[{"Cinema.txt", "Burthday.doc", "Grodno1.doc", "z.txt"}, "C:/restore"]**
Out[2646]= {"C:\\restore\\birthday.doc", "C:\\restore\\cinema.txt", "C:\\restore\\z.txt"}
In[2660]:= **ClearRecyclerBin[x___] :=
Module[{a, c = $ArtKr$, d, p, b = ToString[Unique["ag"]]}, ClearAll[$ArtKr$];
If[! FileExistsQ1["$recycle.bin", $ArtKr$], $Failed, d = StandPath[$ArtKr$[[1]]]; $ArtKr$=c;
Run["Dir " <> d <> "/B/S/L > " <> b]; p = ReadList[b, String];
DeleteFile[b]; If[p == {}, Return[$Failed], Map[If[{x} == {},
If[SuffPref[a = FileNameSplit[#][[-1]], "$", 1] || a === "desktop.ini", Null, Attrib[#, {}];
If[FileExistsQ[#], Quiet[Check[DeleteFile[#],
DeleteDirectory[#, DeleteContents -> True]]],
Quiet[Check[DeleteDirectory[#, DeleteContents -> True], DeleteFile[#]]]]],
If[FileNameSplit[#][[-1]] == "desktop.ini", Null, Attrib[#, {}];
If[DirQ[#], Run["RD /S/Q " <> #], Run["Del /F/Q " <> #]]]] &, p];]]**
In[2661]:= **ClearRecyclerBin[]**
In[2662]:= **ClearRecyclerBin[590]**
In[2663]:= **ClearRecyclerBin[]**

These means rather essentially expand the functions of the *Mathematica* of restoration of datafiles of any type and directories, removed by means of *Windows*, its applications, our **DeleteFile1** procedure along with effective enough cleansing of the *$Recycle.Bin* directory.

Meanwhile, a number of means of processing of datafiles and directories was based on the **BootDrive** procedure that is correct for *Windows 2000 | 2003 | NT | XP* while since *Windows 7*, it is necessary to use the **BootDrive1** function whose source code along with an example are presented below. The call **BootDrive1[]** returns the 3-element list, whose first element – homedrive, the second – the system catalog, and the third element – the type of the current operating system.

In[4842]:= **BootDrive1[]** := Mapp[Part, GetEnvironment[{"SystemDrive", "SystemRoot", "OS"}], 2]

In[4843]:= **BootDrive1[]**
Out[4843]= {"C: ", "C:\\Windows", "Windows_NT"}

Furthermore, this function can be used for an operation system, supported by the system *Mathematica*. In addition, the type of an operating system in some cases by means of the call **GetEnvironment[]** is returned incorrectly; the presented example concerns *Windows 7*, but *Windows_NT* has been received.

Values of the global variables **$System, $SystemID** and **$OperatingSystem** determine the strings describing the current operational platform. Meanwhile, in a number of cases the specification of the current operational platform represented by them can be insufficient, in that case it is possible to use the **PCOS** procedure, whose call **PCOS[]** returns the 2-element list, whose the first element determines the name of the computer owner, while the second element – the type of an operating platform. The fragment below represents source code of the **PCOS** procedure along with an example of its application.

In[2593]:= {$System, $SystemID, $OperatingSystem}
Out[2593]= {"Microsoft Windows (64-bit)", "Windows-x86-64", "Windows"}

In[2594]:= PCOS[] := Module[{a = ToString[Unique["agn"]], b},
Run["SYSTEMINFO > " <> a]; b = Map[StringSplit[#] &, ReadList[a, String][[1 ;; 2]]];
DeleteFile[a]; b = Map[#[[3 ;; -1]] &, b];
{b[[1]][[1]], StringReplace[ListToString[b[[2]], " "], "\"" -> ""]}]

In[2595]:= PCOS[]
Out[2595]= {"ALADJEV-PC", "Microsoft Windows 7 Professional"}

In[4857]:= OSplatform[] := Module[{a = "$Art27$Kr20$", b = {}}, Run["systeminfo > " <> a];
Do[AppendTo[b, Read[a, String]], 3]; DeleteFile[Close[a]];
b = Map[StringSplit[#, ":"] &, b[[2 ;; 3]]]; Map[StringTrim[#[[2]]] &, b]]

In[4858]:= OSplatform[]
Out[4858]= {"Microsoft Windows 7 Professional", "6.1.7601 Service Pack 1 Build 7601"}

While the call of **OSplatform[]** procedure represented at the end of the previous fragment, in string format returns the 2-element list, whose the first element – the type of the current operating system, and the second element – main characteristics of this system. An example illustrates aforesaid.

The **$SysInfo** is the list describing the main parameters of computer system on which the *Mathematica* is being run; elements of the list have the format *"Parameter: its value"* whose essence are represented below. This procedure uses two support functions having a certain independent interest too. So, the function call **ElemNoList[x]** returns a string, different from any element of a *x* list containing only the strings. Whereas the call **Part1[x, j]** returns the list of the parts of a *j* list that are determined by the *j* tuple containing the integers or spans. The following fragment presents source codes of the above means with typical examples of their application.

In[6890]:= $SysInfo := Module[{a = ElemNoList[FileNames[]]},
Run["Systeminfo /FO LIST > " <> a];
{Map[RedSymbStr[#, " ", " "] &, Part1[StringSplit[ReadString[a],"\r\n"],
1 ;; 3, 12 ;; 14, 18, 19]], DeleteFile[a]}[[1]]]

In[6891]:= $SysInfo
Out[6891]= {"Host Name: ALADJEV-PC", "OS Name: Microsoft Windows 7 Professional",
"OS Version: 6.1.7601 Service Pack 1 Build 7601",
"System Manufacturer: Dell Inc.", "System Model: OptiPlex 3020",
"System Type: x64-based PC", "Windows Directory: C:\\Windows",
"System Directory: C:\\Windows\\system32"}

In[6892]:= ElemNoList[x_ /; ListStrQ[x]] := Sort[Map[StringReplace[#, " " -> "a"] &, x],
StringLength[#1] <= StringLength[#2] &][[-1]] <> "a"

In[6893]:= ElemNoList[{"a b c", "c   hh   d", "mpt 79", "agn 69"}]
Out[6893]= "caaaahhaaada"

In[6894]:= Part1[x_ /; ListQ[x], j__ /; MemberQ3[{Integer, Span}, Map[Head, {j}]]] :=
Quiet[Check[Flatten[Map[Part[x, #] &, Flatten[{j}]]], x]]

In[6895]:= Part1[{a, b, c, d, g, f, h, n, p, s, 69, 74, v, j, k}, 1 ;; 3, 5, 7 ;; 10, 12, 14;;15]
Out[6895]= {a, b, c, g, h, n, p, s, 74, j, k}

The next useful procedure bears the general character at operating with the devices of direct access and are useful enough in a number of applications, above all, of the system character. The following procedure to a great extent is an analog of *Maple* procedure *Vol_Free_Space* that returns a volume of free memory on devices of direct access. The call **FreeSpaceVol[x]** depending on type of an actual *x* argument which should define the logical name in string format of a device, returns simple or a nested list; elements of its sublists determine a device name, a volume of free memory on a volume of direct access, and an unit of its *measurement* respectively. In the case of absence or inactivity of the *x* device the call returns the message *"Device is not ready"*. The following fragment represents source code of the **FreeSpaceVol** procedure along with typical examples of its application.

In[2590]:= FreeSpaceVol[x_ /; MemberQ3[Join[CharacterRange["a", "z"],
CharacterRange["A", "Z"]], Flatten[{x}]]] :=
Module[{a = ToString[Unique["ag"]], c, d = Flatten[{x}], f},
f[y_] := Module[{n, b}, n = Run["Dir " <> y <> ":\\ > " <> a];
If[n != 0, {y, "Device is not ready"},
b = StringSplit[ReduceAdjacentStr[ReadFullFile[a], " ", 1]][[-3 ;; -2]];
{y, ToExpression[StringReplace[b[[1]], "ÿ" -> ""]], b[[2]]}]];
c = Map[f, d]; DeleteFile[a]; If[Length[c] == 1, c[[1]], c]]

In[2591]:= **FreeSpaceVol["c"]**
Out[2591]= {"c", 437735911424, "bytes"}
In[2592]:= **FreeSpaceVol[{"c", "d", "e", "a"}]**
Out[2592]= {{"c", 437735911424, "bytes"}, {"d", 0, "bytes"}, {"e", 12257828864, "bytes"}, {"a", "Drive is not ready"}}

The procedure below facilitates the solution of the problem of use of external *Mathematica* programs or operational platform. The procedure call **ExtProgExe**[*x, y, h*] provides search in file system of the computer of a {*exe*|*com*} file with program with its subsequent execution on *y* parameters of the command string. Both arguments *x* and *y* should be coded in string format. Successful performance of this procedure returns the *full path* to "*$TempFile$*" file of *ASCII* format containing result of execution of a *x* program, and this file can be processed by means of standard means on the basis of its structure. At that, in case of absence of the file with the demanded *x* program the procedure call returns $*Failed* while at using of the third *h* optional argument – *an arbitrary expression* – the file with the *x* program uploaded into the current directory defined by the function call **Directory[]**, is removed from this directory; also the "*$TempFile$*" datafile is removed if it is empty or implementation of the *x* program was terminated abnormally. The fragment below represents source code of the **ExtProgExe** procedure along with typical examples of its application.

In[2558]:= **ExtProgExe[x_ /; StringQ[x], y_ /; StringQ[y], h___] :=**
Module[{a = "$TempFile$", b = Directory[] <> "\\" <> x, c},
Empty::datafile = "Datafile $TempFile$ is empty; the datafile had been deleted.";
If[FileExistsQ[b], c = Run[x, " ", y, " > ", a], c = LoadExtProg[x];
If[c === $Failed, Return[$Failed]]; c = Run[x, " ", y, " > ", a];
If[{h} != {}, DeleteFile[b]]]; If[c != 0, DeleteFile[a]; $Failed, If[EmptyFileQ[a], DeleteFile[a];
Message[Empty::datafile], Directory[] <> "\\" <> a]]]

In[2559]:= **ExtProgExe["HostName.exe", "", 1]**
Out[2559]= "C:\\Users\\Aladjev\\Documents\\$TempFile$"
In[2560]:= **ExtProgExe["Rans_Ian.exe", "", 1]**
Out[2560]= $Failed
In[2561]:= **ExtProgExe["tasklist.exe", "/svc ", 1]**
Out[2561]= "C:\\Users\\Aladjev\\Documents\\$TempFile$"
In[2562]:= **ExtProgExe["systeminfo.exe", "", 1]**
Out[2562]= "C:\\Users\\Aladjev\\Documents\\$TempFile$"
In[2563]:= **Select[Map[StringTake[#, {3, -1}] &, ReadList[Directory[] <> "\\" <> "$TempFile$", String]], # != "" &]**
Out[2563]= {"ALADJEV-PC", "Microsoft Windows 7 Professional", "Microsoft Corporation", "Multiprocessor Free", "Aladjev", "Microsoft", "00371-OEM-8992671-00524", "9.08.2014, 21:45:35", "12.02.2016, 14:00:53", "Dell Inc.", "OptiPlex 3020", "x64-based PC", "Dell Inc. A03, 14.04.2014", "C:\\Windows", "C:\\Windows\\system32", "en-us; English (US)", "\\Device\\HarddiskVolume2", "et; Estonian", "(UTC+02:00) Helsinki, Kyiv, Riga, Sofia, Tallinn, Vilnius", "C:\\pagefile.sys", "WORKGROUP", "\\\\ALADJEV-PC"}
In[2564]:= **ExtProgExe["qprocess.exe", "*"]**
Out[2564]= "C:\\Users\\Aladjev\\Documents\\$TempFile$"

In[2565]:= k = 1; h = ""; While[! SameQ[h, EndOfFile], h = Read["$TempFile$", String];
Print[h]; k++]; Close["$TempFile$"];
(unknown) services 0 0
(unknown) services 0 4 system
=====
> aladjev console 1 5168 cmd.exe
> aladjev console 1 5924 conhost.exe
> aladjev console 1 5436 qprocess.exe
EndOfFile

The following procedure is an useful enough generalization of standard **CopyFile** function whose call **CopyFile[w1, w2]** returns the full name of the datafile it copies to and $*Failed* if it cannot do the copy; in addition, file *w1* must already exist, whereas *w2* file must not. Thus, in the program mode the standard function is insufficiently convenient. The procedure call **CopyFile1[w1, w2]** returns the full path to the datafile that had been copied. In contrast to the standard function, the procedure call **CopyFile1[w1, w2]** returns the list of format {*w2*, *w2**}, where *w2* – the full path to the copied file and *w2** – the full path to the previously existing copy of a datafile *"xyz.abc"* in the format *"xyz.abc"*, if the target directory for *w2* already contained *w1* file. In the case *w1* ≡ *w2* *(where identity is considered up to standardized paths of both files)* the procedure call returns the standardized path to the *w1* datafile, doing nothing. In the other successful cases the call **CopyFile[w1, w2]** returns the full path to the copied datafile. Even, if the nonexistent path to the target directory for the copied datafile is defined, then such path taking into account *available* devices of direct access will be created. The fragment below represents source code of the **CopyFile1** procedure along with typical examples of its application which illustrate quite clearly the aforesaid.

In[3545]:= **CopyFile1[x_ /; FileExistsQ[x], y_ /; StringQ[y]] :=
Module[{a, b, c, d, p = StandPath[x], j = StandPath[y]},
b = StandPath[If[Set[a, DirectoryName[j]] === "", Directory[],
If[DirectoryQ[a], a, CDir[a]]]]; If[p == j, p, If[FileExistsQ[j], Quiet[Close[j]];
Quiet[RenameFile[j, c = StringReplace[j, Set[d, FileBaseName[j]] -> "$" <> d <> "$"]]];
CopyFileToDir[p, b];
{b <> "\\" <> FileNameTake[p], j = b <> "\\" <> c}, CopyFileToDir[p, b]]]]**

In[3546]:= **CopyFile1["c:/temp/cinema.txt", "G:\\Grodno\\cinema.txt"]**
Out[3546]= "c:\\grodno\\cinema.txt"
In[3547]:= **CopyFile1["C:/temp/CD.doc", "CD.DOC"]**
Out[3547]= {"c:\\users\\aladjev\\documents\\cd.doc",
"c:\\users\\aladjev\\documents\\cd.doc"}
In[3548]:= **CopyFile1["c:/temp/CD.doc", "c:\\temp\\CD.DOC"]**
Out[3548]= "c:\\temp\\cd.doc"

At last, the procedure below provides search in the given directory of chains of directories and files containing a *x* string as own components. The call **DirFilePaths[x, y]** returns the 2-element list whose first element is a list of full paths to subdirectories of a *y* directory which contain *x* components while the second element is the list of full paths to files whose names coincide with the *x* string.

In[3642]:= **DirFilePaths[x_ /; StringQ[x], y_: BootDrive1[][[1]] <> "*.*"] :=**
Module[{c = {}, h, d = {}, b = ToString[Unique["avz"]], a = StringTrim[StandStrForm[x],
"\\"]}, Run["DIR /A/B/S " <> StandPath[y] <> " > " <> b];
h = ReadList[b, String]; DeleteFile[b];
Map[If[! StringFreeQ[StandPath[#], {"\\" <> a <> "\\", "\\" <> a}],
If[DirectoryQ[#], AppendTo[c, #], AppendTo[d, #]], Null] &, h]; {c, d}]

In[3643]:= **DirFilePaths["cinema_2017.txt", "c:\\Temp/"]**
Out[3643]= {{}, {"c:\\temp\\Cinema_2017.txt"}}

In[3644]:= **DirFilePaths["CuteWriter.exe", "C:/Users/Aladjev/"]**
Out[3644]= {{}, {"c:\\users\\aladjev\\Downloads\\CuteWriter.exe"}}

In[3645]:= **DirFilePaths["Mathematica_11.0.1_Win.zip"]**
Out[3645]= {{}, {"c:\\Users\\Temp\\Mathematica_11.0.1_WIN.zip"}}

In the absence of the second optional *y* argument the procedure call instead of it supposes **BootDrive1[][[1]] <> "*.*"**. The previous fragment presents source code of the procedure with some examples of its use. In certain cases of access to file system the given procedure is an useful enough means.

In a number of problems of processing of file system of the computer along with work with files the following **VolDir** procedure can present a quite certain interest. The procedure call **VolDir[*x*]** returns the nested 2–element list, whose the first element determines the volume occupied by a *x* directory in bytes, whereas the second element determines the size of free space on a hard disk with the given directory. Whereas procedure call **DirsFiles[*x*]** returns the nested 2–element list, whose first element defines the list of directories contained in a *x* directory, including *x*, and the second element defines the list of all datafiles contained in the given directory. The following fragment presents source codes of the above procedures with examples of their application.

In[3625]:= **VolDir[x_ /; DirectoryQ[x] || MemberQ[Map[# <> ":" &, Adrive[]],**
ToUpperCase[x]]] := Module[{a = ToString[Unique["agn"]], b, c, d = StandPath[x]},
b = Run["DIR /S " <> d <> " > " <> a];
If[b != 0, $Failed, c = Map[StringTrim, ReadList[a, String][[-2 ;; -1]]]]; DeleteFile[a];
c = Map[StringTrim, Mapp[StringReplace, c, {"ÿ" -> "", "bytes" -> "", "free" -> ""}]];
ToExpression[Map[StringSplit[#][[-1]] &, c]]]

In[3628]:= **Map[VolDir, {"C:/users/aladjev/downloads", "e:/MathtoolBox"}]**
Out[3628]= {{2400652450, 437738401792}, {30028491, 12269903872}}

In[3655]:= **DirsFiles[x_ /; DirectoryQ[x] || MemberQ[Map[# <> ":" &, Adrive[]],**
ToUpperCase[x]]] :=
Module[{a = ToString[Unique["ag"]], b = {x}, c = {}, d = StandPath[x], f},
If[Run["DIR /A/B/S " <> d <> " > " <> a] != 0, $Failed, f=ReadList[a, String]; DeleteFile[a];
Map[If[DirectoryQ[#], AppendTo[b, #], If[FileExistsQ[#], AppendTo[c, #], Null]] &, f];
{b, c}]]

In[3656]:= **DirsFiles["C:\\Users\\Aladjev\\DownLoads"]**
Out[3656]= {{"c:\\Users\\Aladjev\\DownLoads"},
{"c:\\users\\aladjev\\downloads\\Mathematica_11.0.1_WIN.zip", ... }}

By the by, it should be noted that at processing of the list structures of a rather large size the unpredictable situations are quite possible [30-33,50].

So, the means represented in the given chapter sometimes a rather significantly simplify programming of the tasks dealing with file system of the computer. Along with that, these tools extend functional means of access, illustrating a number of useful enough methods of programming of problems of similar type. These means in a number of cases significantly supplement the standard access tools supported by system, facilitating programming of a number of very important appendices which deal with the datafiles of various format. Our experience of programming of the access tools that extend the similar means of the systems *Maple* and *Mathematica* allows to notice that *basic* access tools of the *Mathematica* system in combination with its global variables allow to program more simply and effectively the user original access means. Moreover, the created access means possess sometimes by the significantly bigger performance in relation to the similar means developed in the *Maple* software. So, in the environment of the *Mathematica* system it is possible to solve the tasks linked with rather complex algorithms of processing of files whereas in the software of the *Maple* system, first of all, in case of large enough datafiles the efficiency of such algorithms leaves much to be desired. In a number of appendices the means, represented in the present chapter along with other similar means from package [48] are represented as rather useful, by allowing at times to essentially simplify programming. At that, it must be kept in mind, a whole series of means that are based on the **Run** function and the *DOS* commands generally can be nonportable onto other versions of the system and operational platform, demanding the corresponding adaptation onto appropriate new conditions.

Chapter 8. The manipulations organization with the user packages in the *Mathematica* software

Similarly to the well-developed software the *Mathematica* is the extendable system, i.e. in addition to the builtin tools that quite cover requirements of quite wide range of the users, the system allows to program those tools that absent for the specific user in environment of the builtin language, and also to extend and correct standard software. Moreover, the user can find the missing tools that are not builtin, in numerous packages both in the packages delivered with *Mathematica*, and separately existing packages for various applied fields. The question consists only in finding of a package necessary for a concrete case containing definitions of the functions, modules and other objects demanded for an application that are programmed in the system. A *package* has standard organization and contains definitions of various objects, somehow the functions, procedures, variables, etc., that solve well-defined problems. In return the *Mathematica* provides a standard set of packages whose *composition* is defined by concrete version of the system. For receiving of composition of packages that are delivered with the current release of the *Mathematica* it is possible to use a procedure, whose call **MathPackages[]** returns list of names of packages, whose names with a certain confidence speak about their basic purpose. While the call **MathPackages[*x*]** with optional *x* argument – an undefinite variable – provides through it in addition return of the 3–element list whose first element defines the current release of the *Mathematica* system, the second element – the type of the license and the third element – the deadline of action of the license. The following fragment represents source code of the procedure along with examples of its typical application.

In[2590]:= **MathPackages[h___] :=**
Module[{c = $InstallationDirectory, b, a = "$Kr20Art27$", d},
d = Run["Dir " <> StandPath[c] <> "/A/B/O/S > $Kr20Art27$"];
If[d != 0, $Failed, d = ReadList[a, String]; DeleteFile[a];
b = Map[If[! DirectoryQ[#] && FileExtension[#] == "m", FileBaseName[#], "Null"] &, d];
b = Select[b, # != "Null" &];
b = MinusList[DeleteDuplicates[b], {"init", "PacletInfo"}];
If[{h} != {} && ! HowAct[h], h = {$Version, $LicenseType,
StringJoin[StringSplit[StringReplace[DateString[$LicenseExpirationDate],
" " -> "*"], "*"][[1 ;; -2]]]}]; Sort[b]]

In[2591]:= **MathPackages[]**
Out[2591]= {"AbelianGroup", "AbortProtect", "Abs", "AbsoluteDashing",
"AbsoluteOptions", "AbsolutePointSize", "AbsoluteThickness", "AbsoluteTime",
"accessodbc", "AccountData", ..., "ZTransform"}
In[2592]:= **Length[%]**
Out[2592]= 2835
In[2593]:= **MathPackages[Sv]; Sv**
Out[2593]= {"11.0.1 for Microsoft Windows (64–bit) (September 20, 2016)", "Professional",
"Tue7Nov"}

From the given fragment follows that the *Mathematica* system of version *11.0.1.0* contains *2835* packages oriented on different appendices, including the packages of strictly system purpose. Before use of tools which are contained in a certain applied package, this package should be previously loaded in the current *Mathematica* session by means of the function call **Get[*Package*]**.

8.1. Concept of the context, and its use in the software of the *Mathematica*

The *context* concept has been entered in *Mathematica* software for organization of *operation* with symbols that represent various objects *(modules, functions, variables, packages and so on)*, in particular, in order to avoid the possible conflicts with symbols of the same name. Main idea consists in that that the full name of an arbitrary symbol consists of two parts, namely: a context and a short name, i.e. the full name of a certain object has format: *"context'short name"* where the sign <`> *(backquote)* carries out the role of some marker, identifying context in the system. For example, *Avzag'Vs* represents a symbol with the *Avzag* context and with short *Vs* name. In addition, with such symbols it is possible to execute various operations as with usual names; at that, the system considers *aaa'xy* and *bbb'xy* as various symbols.

So, the most widespread use of context consists in its assignment to functionally identical or semantically connected symbols. For example,

AladjevProcedures`StandPath, AladjevProcedures`MathPackages

the procedures **StandPath** and **MathPackages** belong to the same group of the means which associate with *"AladjevProcedures'"* context which is ascribed to our *MathToolBox* package [48,50]. The current context is determined any moment of the system session, the context is in the global variable *$Context*:

In[2562]:= **$Context**
Out[2562]= "Global`"

In the current *Mathematica* session the current context by default is defined as *"Global'"*. Whereas the global variable *$ContextPath* determines the list of contexts after the *$Context* variable for search of a symbol entered into the current session. It is possible to reffer to the symbols from the current context simply by their short names; in addition, if this symbol is crossed with a symbol from the list defined by the *$ContextPath* variable, the *second* symbol will be used instead of the symbol from the current context, for example:

In[2563]:= **$ContextPath**
Out[2563]= {"AladjevProcedures`", "StreamingLoader`", "IconizeLoader`", "CloudObjectLoader`", "PacletManager`", "System`", "Global`"}

Whereas the calls **Context[*x*]** and **Contexts[]** return the context ascribed to a *x* symbol and the list of all contexts of the current session respectively:

In[2564]:= **Context[ActUcontexts]**
Out[2564]= "AladjevProcedures`"
In[2565]:= **Contexts[]**
Out[2565]= {"AladjevProcedures`", "AladjevProcedures`ActBFMuserQ`", "AladjevProcedures`ActCsProcFunc`", "AladjevProcedures`ActRemObj`, ..., "XML`Parser`", "XML`RSS`", "XML`SVG`", "$CellContext`"}

At that, by analogy with file system of the computer, contexts quite can be compared with directories. It is possible to determine the path to a file, specifying a directory containing it and a name of the file. At the same time, the current context can be quite associated with the current directory to the files of which can be referenced simply by their names. Furthermore, like file system the contexts can have hierarchical structure, in particular:

"Visualization`VectorFields`VectorFieldsDump`"

So, the path of search of a context of symbols in the *Mathematica* system is similar to a path of search of program datafiles. At the beginning of the session the current context by default is *"Global`"*, and all symbols entered into the session will be associated with this context, except for the builtin symbols, for example, **Do**, that are associated with *"System`"* context. The path of search of contexts by default includes the contexts for system–defined symbols. Whereas for the symbols removed by means of the **Remove** function, the context can not be determined, for example:

In[2565]:= **Avz := 590; Context["Avz"]**
Out[2565]= "Global`"
In[2566]:= **Remove["Avz"]; Context["Avz"]**
Context::notfound: Symbol Avz not found...>>
Out[2566]= Context["Avz"]

At using of the contexts there is no guarantee that 2 symbols of the same name are available in various contexts. Therefore the *Mathematica* defines as a maximum priority the priority of choice of that symbol with this name, whose context is the first in the list which is defined by the global variable *$ContextPath*. Thence, for placement of such context at the beginning of the specified list it is possible to use the next construction:

In[2568]:= **$ContextPath**
Out[2568]= {"AladjevProcedures`", "StreamingLoader`", "IconizeLoader`", "CloudObjectLoader`", "PacletManager`", "System`", "Global`"}
In[2569]:= **PrependTo[$ContextPath, "RansIanAvz`"]**
Out[2569]= {"RansIanAvz`", "AladjevProcedures`", "TemplatingLoader`", "PacletManager`", "System`", "Global`"}
In[2570]:= **$ContextPath**
Out[2570]= {"RansIanAvz`", "AladjevProcedures`", "TemplatingLoader`", "PacletManager`", "System`", "Global`"}

The next a rather useful procedure provides assignment of the given context to a *definite* or *undefinite* symbol. The procedure call **ContextToSymbol1**[*x, y, z*] returns *Null*, i.e. nothing, providing assignment of a certain *y* context to a *x* symbol; in addition, the third optional *z* argument – the string, defining for *x* an usage; at its absence for an undefinite *x* symbol the usage – empty string, i.e. "", whereas for a definite *x* symbol the usage has view *"Help on x"*. The next fragment represents source code of the **ContextToSymbol1** procedure along with the most typical examples of its application.

In[2725]:= **ContextToSymbol1[x_ /; AladjevProcedures`SymbolQ[x], y_ /; AladjevProcedures`ContextQ[y], z___] := Module[{a, b = ToString[x]}, Off[General::shdw];
a = StringReplace["BeginPackage[\"AvzAgnVsvArtKr`\"]\n90::usage=74\n**

Begin[\"`90`\"]\n500\nEnd[]\nEndPackage[]", {"AvzAgnVsvArtKr`" -> y, "74" -> If[AladjevProcedures`PureDefinition[x] === $Failed, "\"\"", If[{z} != {} && StringQ[z], AladjevProcedures`ToString1[z], AladjevProcedures`ToString1["Help on " <> b]]], "90" -> b, "500" -> If[AladjevProcedures`PureDefinition[x] === $Failed, b, AladjevProcedures`PureDefinition[x]]}];

Remove[x]; ToExpression[a]; On[General::shdw]]

In[2726]:= Sv[x_] := Module[{a = 90, b = 590}, (a + b)*x^2]
In[2727]:= Context[Sv]
Out[2727]= "Global`"
In[2728]:= ContextToSymbol1[Sv, "Agn`"]; Context[Sv]
Out[2728]= "Agn`"
In[2729]:= Sv[74]
Out[2729]= 3723680
In[2730]:= ?Sv
Help on Sv.
In[2731]:= Vsv[x_] := Module[{a = 590}, a*x]
In[2732]:= ContextToSymbol1[Vsv, "Tampere`", "Help on module Vsv."]
In[2733]:= Context[Vsv]
Out[2733]= "Tampere`"
In[2734]:= ArtKr[x_] := Module[{a = 90, b = 590}, (a + b)*x]
In[2734]:= ContextToSymbol1[ArtKr, "AladjevProcedures`", "Help on module ArtKr."]
In[2735]:= DumpSave["C:/Users/Aladjev\\Mathematica\\Tampere.mx", "AladjevProcedures`"]
Out[2735]= {"AladjevProcedures`"}
In[2736]:= ClearAll[ArtKr]; Clear["ArtKr::usage"]
In[3337]:= Get["C:\\Users\\Aladjev\\Mathematica\\Tampere.mx"]
In[3338]:= ?? ArtKr
"Help on module ArtKr."
"Art[x_] := Module[{a = 90, b = 590}, (a + b)*x]"
In[3339]:= PureDefinition[Rans]
Out[3339]= $Failed
In[3340]:= ContextToSymbol1[Rans, "AgnVsv`"]
In[3341]:= Context[Rans]
Out[3341]= "AgnVsv`"
In[3342]:= $Packages
Out[3342]= {"AgnVsv`", "HTTPClient`", "HTTPClient`OAuth`", ..., "AladjevProcedures`", "Tampere`", "Agn`",...}
In[3343]:= $ContextPath
Out[3343]= {"AgnVsv`", "AladjevProcedures`", "Tampere`", "Agn`",...}

At that, along with possibility of assignment of the given context to symbols the procedure **ContextToSymbol1** is an useful enough means for extension by the new means of the user package contained in a *mx*-file. The technology of similar updating is as follows. On the *first* step a *x* file of *mx*-format with the user's package having *y* context is loaded into the current session by the function call **Get[x]**. Then, in the same session the definition of a new *f* means with its *u* usage which describes the given tools is evaluated. In addition, by the procedure call **ContextToSymbol1**[*f*, *y*, *u*] the assignment of a *y* context to the *f* symbol along with its *u* usage is provided. Moreover, the *u* usage can be directly coded in the procedure call, or be determined by a certain *u* string. At last, by means of the function call **DumpSave**[*x*, *y*] the saving in the *mx*-file *x* of all objects having *y* context is provided. Such approach provides a rather effective mechanism of updating in the context of both definitions and usages of the tools entering the user's package which is located in a *mx*-file. Yet, the approach is limited by packages located in datafiles of the *mx*-format.

The rather useful procedure below in a certain relation expands the above procedure and provides assignment of the given context to a *definite* symbol. The successful procedure call **ContextToSymbol2**[*x*, *y*] returns two-element list of the format {*x*, *y*}, where *x* – the name of a processed definite *x* symbol and *y* – its new context, providing assignment of a certain *y* context to the definite *x* symbol; while the procedure call **ContextToSymbol2**[*x*, *y*, *z*] with the optional third *z* argument – an arbitrary expression – also returns two-element list of the above format {*x*, *y*}, providing assignment of certain *y* context to the definite *x* symbol with saving of symbol definition *x* and its attributes and usage in file "*x.mx*".

Thence, before a procedure call **ContextToSymbol2**[*x*, *y*] for change of the existing context of a *x* symbol on a new *y* symbol in the current session it is necessary to evaluate definition of a *x* symbol and its usage in the format *x::usage* = "*Help on a x object.*" *(if an usage exists of course)* with assignment to the *x* symbol of necessary attributes.

At that, along with possibility of assignment of the given context to symbols the procedure **ContextToSymbol2** is a rather useful means for extension by new tools of the user package contained in a *mx*-file. The technology of similar updating is as follows. On the *first* step the definition of a new *x* tool with its *u* usage that describes these tools is evaluated along with ascribing of the necessary attributes. Then, by means of the call **ContextToSymbol2**[*x*, *y*, *j*] the assignment of a *y* context to a *x* symbol along with its usage with saving of the updated *x* object in "*x.mx*" file is provided. At last, the call **Get**[*w*] loads into the current session the revised user package located in a *mx*-file *w* with an *y* context, whereas the subsequent call **DumpSave**[*p*, *y*] saves in the updated *mx*-file *w* all objects having *y* context, including the objects which earlier have been obtained by the procedure call **ContextToSymbol2**[*x*, *y*] or **Get**["*x.mx*"]. Such approach provides a rather effective mechanism of updating of the user packages located in *mx*-files.

In[3147]:= ContextToSymbol2[x_ /; SymbolQ[x], y_ /; ContextQ[y], z___] :=
Module[{a = Flatten[{PureDefinition[x]}], b = ToString[x], c = ToString[x] <> ".mx", d, h, t},
If[a === {$Failed}, $Failed, t = If[! StringQ[Set[t, ToExpression[b <> "::usage"]]],
Nothing, y <> b <> "::usage = " <> ToString1[t]]; a = Flatten[{a, t}];
Map[ToExpression, Map[StringReplace[#, b <> "[" -> y <> b <> "[", 1] &, a]];
d = Attributes[x]; AppendTo[$ContextPath, y]; DumpSave[c, y];
Unprotect[x, h]; ClearAll[x, h]; Get[c];
ToExpression["SetAttributes[" <> y <> b <> "," <> ToString[d] <> "]"];
If[{z} == {}, DeleteFile[c]; {x, y}, {x, y}]]]

In[3148]:= Rans[x_, y_] := Module[{a = 75, b = 70}, a*x + b*y]; SetAttributes[Rans, {Protected, Listable}]

```
In[3149]:= Context[Rans]
Out[3149]= "Global`"
In[3150]:= ContextToSymbol2[Rans, "Tallinn`"]
Out[3150]= {Rans, "Tallinn`"}
In[3151]:= Context[Rans]
Out[3151]= "Tallinn`"
In[3152]:= Definition[Rans]
Out[3152]= Attributes[Rans] = {Listable, Protected}
Rans[x_, y_] := Module[{a = 75, b = 70}, a*x + b*y]
In[3153]:= RemovePackage["Tallinn`"]; ClearAllAttributes[Rans, Art]; ClearAll[Rans]
In[3154]:= Art[x_, y_] := x*y; Art[x_, y_, z_] := x + y + z; Art::usage = "Help on object Art.";
SetAttributes[Art, {Protected, Listable}]
In[3155]:= Context[Art]
Out[3155]= "Global`"
In[3156]:= ContextToSymbol2[Art, "Tampere`", 590]
In[3157]:= Context[Art]
Out[3157]= {Art, "Tampere`"}
In[3158]:= FullDefinition[Art]
Out[3158]= Attributes[Art] = {Listable, Protected}
Art[x_, y_] := x*y
Art[x_, y_, z_] := x + y + z
Art /: Art::usage = "Help on object Art."
```

The above examples rather visually illustrate the offered approach.

The **ContextToSymbol3** procedure is a rather useful modification of the above procedure **ContextToSymbol2**. The successful procedure call **ContextToSymbol3[x, y]** returns two-element list of format {x, y}, where x – the name in string format of a definite x symbol, y – its new context, providing assignment of a certain y context to the definite x symbol; on the inadmissible arguments the procedure call is returned as unevaluated. The next fragment represents source code of the **ContextToSymbol3** procedure with typical examples its use.

```
In[3765]:= ContextToSymbol3[x_ /; StringQ[x] && SymbolQ[x] && ! NullQ[x] &&
! SameQ[x, "System`"], y_ /; ContextQ[y]] :=
Module[{a = Flatten[{PureDefinition[x]}], b, c, d, h},
b = StringSplit[a[[1]], {"[", " = ", " := "}][[1]]; h = Help[Symbol[b]];
c = Attributes[x]; ToExpression["Unprotect[" <> b <> "]"];
d = "BeginPackage[\"" <> y <> "\"]" <> "\n" <> If[NullQ[h], "", b <> "::usage=" <>
ToString1[h]] <> "\n" <> StringJoin[Map[# <> "\n" &, a]] <> "EndPackage[]";
Remove[x]; Quiet[ToExpression[d]];
ToExpression["SetAttributes[" <> b <> "," <> ToString[c] <> "]"]; {b, y}]
In[3766]:= V74[x_] := Module[{a = 42}, a*x]; V74[x_, y_] := Module[{}, x*y];
V74::usage = "Help on V74."; SetAttributes[V74, {Listable, Protected}]
In[3767]:= ContextToSymbol3[V74, "AvzAgnVsv`"]
Out[3767]= ContextToSymbol3[V74, "AvzAgnVsv`"]
In[3767]:= ContextToSymbol3["V74", "AvzAgnVsv`"]
```

Out[3767]= {"V74", "AvzAgnVsv`"}
In[3768]:= **Attributes[V74]**
Out[3768]= {Listable, Protected}
In[3769]:= **Definition[V74]**
Out[3769]= Attributes[V74] = {Listable, Protected}
V74[x_] := Module[{a = 42}, a*x]
V74[x_, y_] := Module[{}, x*y]
In[3770]:= **Context[V74]**
Out[3770]= "AvzAgnVsv`"
In[3771]:= **?V74**
Help on V74.
In[3779]:= **G69[x_, y_] := x + y**
In[3780]:= **ContextToSymbol3["G69", "AvzAgn`"]**
Out[3780]= {"G69", "AvzAgn`"}
In[3781]:= **Definition[G69]**
Out[3781]= G69[x_, y_] := x + y
In[3782]:= **?G69**
AvzAgn`G69
G69[x_, y_] := x + y
In[3783]:= **Attributes[G69]**
Out[3783]= {}
In[3784]:= **Context[G69]**
Out[3784]= "AvzAgn`"

At that, along with possibility of assignment of the given context to symbols the procedure **ContextToSymbol3** is an useful enough tool for *extension* by new means of the user package contained in a *mx*-file. The technology of similar updating is as follows. On the first step the definition of a new *x* tool with its *u* usage which describes the given tool is evaluated along with ascribing of the necessary attributes. Then, by means of the call **ContextToSymbol3[*x*, *y*]** the assignment of the *y* context to the *x* symbol is provided. At last, the call **Get[*p*]** *uploads* in the current session the revised user package located in a *mx*-file *p* with *y* context, while the subsequent call **DumpSave[*p*, *y*]** saves in updated *mx*-file *p* all objects having *y* context, including the objects which earlier have been obtained by the call **ContextToSymbol3[*x*, *y*]**. Such approach provides a rather effective mechanism of updating of the user packages that are located in the *mx*-files with contexts.

On the basis of the previous procedure, **RenameMxContext** procedure was programmed whose call **RenameMxContext[*x*, *y*]** returns the name of a *mx*-file *x* with replacement of its context by a new *y* context; at that, the package located in the existing *x* file can be uploaded into current session or not, while at use of the 3rd optional argument – *an arbitrary expression* – the call **RenameMxContext[*x*, *y*, *z*]** additionally removes the *x* package from the current session. The fragment below presents source code of the **RenameMxContext** procedure and examples of its application.

In[3772]:= **BeginPackage["RansIan`"]**
GSV::usage = "Help on GSV."
ArtKr::usage = "Help on ArtKr."

```
Begin["`ArtKr`"]
ArtKr[x_, y_, z_] := Module[{a = 74}, a*x*y*z]
End[]
Begin["`GSV`"]
GSV[x_, y_] := Module[{a = 69}, a*x*y]
End[]
EndPackage[];
In[3782]:= DumpSave["avzagn.mx", "RansIan`"]
Out[3782]= {"RansIan`"}
In[3783]:= CNames["RansIan`"]
Out[3783]= {"ArtKr", "GSV"}

In[3784]:= RenameMxContext[x_ /; FileExistsQ[x] && FileExtension[x] == "mx",
y_ /; ContextQ[y], z___] := Module[{a = ContextInMxFile[x], b = Get[x], c},
b = CNames[a]; c = Quiet[AppendTo[Map[a <> # <> "`" &, b], a]];
Map[Quiet[ContextToSymbol3[#, y]] &, b];
ToExpression["DumpSave[" <> ToString1[x] <> "," <> ToString1[y] <> "]"];
DeletePackage[a]; If[{z} != {}, x, DeletePackage[y]; x]]

In[3785]:= RenameMxContext["avzagn.mx", "Tampere`", 74]
Out[3785]= "avzagn.mx"
In[3786]:= CNames["Tampere`"]
Out[3786]= {"ArtKr", "GSV"}
In[3787]:= Map[Context, {"ArtKr", "GSV"}]
Out[3787]= {"Tampere`", "Tampere`"}
In[3788]:= Information[ArtKr]
"Help on ArtKr."
ArtKr[x_, y_, z_] := Module[{a = 74}, a*x*y*z]
```

Now, using the procedure **ContextToSymbol2** or **ContextToSymbol3**, the procedure which executes the adjunction of a *mx*-file with a package with new means can be presented. The procedure call **AdjunctionToMx[y, f]** returns full path to *mx*-file with a context updated by new *y* tools. In addition, a single *y* symbol or their list can be as the first argument and their *definitions* and *usage* should be previously evaluated in the current session. Moreover, if the *mx*-file had been already uploaded, it remains, otherwise it will be unloaded of the current session. The procedure call on a *f* datafile without context returns $Failed.

```
In[4769]:= AdjunctionToMx[y_ /; SymbolQ[y] || ListQ[y] &&
DeleteDuplicates[Map[SymbolQ[#] &, Flatten[{y}]]] == {True}, f_ /; FileExistsQ[f] &&
FileExtension[f] == "mx"] :=
Module[{a = ContextInMxFile[f], b},
If[a === $Failed, $Failed, If[MemberQ[$Packages, a], b = 74, Get[f]];
Map[Quiet[ContextToSymbol2[#, a]] &, Flatten[{y}]];
ToExpression["DumpSave[" <> ToString1[f] <> "," <> ToString1[a] <> "]"];
If[! SameQ[b, 74], RemovePackage[a], 69]; f]]

In[4770]:= G69[x_, y_] := x^2 + y^2; G69::usage = "Help on G69 function.";
V74[x_, y_] := x^3 + y^3; V74::usage = "Help on V74 function.";
```

In[4771]:= **AdjunctionToMx[{G69, V74}, "Rans.mx"]**
Out[4771]= "Rans.mx"
A new Mathematica session
In[1]:= **Get["Rans.mx"]**
In[2]:= **?G69**
"Help on G69 function."
In[3]:= **?V74**
"Help on V74 function."
In[4]:= **Definition[G69]**
Out[4]= G69[x_, y_] := x^2 + y^2
In[5]:= **Definition[V74]**
Out[5]= V74[x_, y_] := x^3 + y^3
In[6]:= **MemberQ4[CNames[ContextInMxFile["Rans.mx"]], {"G69", "V74"}]**
Out[6]= True

In addition to the above procedure the **CreationMx** procedure creates a new *mx*-file *f* with tools defined by the *y* argument *(a single symbol or their list)* and with a *x* context, returning full path to the *f* file. In addition, definitions and usage of the *y* symbols should be *previously* evaluated. Furthermore, if *mx*-file *f* already exists, it remains, but instead of it a new *mx*-file is created. The procedure call on a *x* context existing in **$Packages** returns *$Failed*.

In[3681]:= **CreationMx[x_ /; ContextQ[x], y_ /; SymbolQ[y] || ListQ[y] &&**
DeleteDuplicates[Map[SymbolQ[#] &, Flatten[{y}]]] == {True},
f_ /; FileExtension[f] == "mx"] := Module[{a, b, c},
If[MemberQ[$Packages, x], $Failed, a = If[FileExistsQ[f], Print["File " <>
ToString1[f] <> " exists."]; b = FileNameSplit[f]; c = b[[-1]];
FileNameJoin[ReplacePart[b, -1 -> "#$#" <> c]], f];
Map[Quiet[ContextToSymbol2[#, x]] &, Flatten[{y}]];
ToExpression["DumpSave[" <> ToString1[a] <> "," <> ToString1[x] <> "]"]; a]]
In[3682]:= **G69[x_, y_] := x^2 + y^2; G69::usage = "Help on G69 function.";**
V74[x_, y_] := x^3 + y^3; V74::usage = "Help on V74 function.";
In[3683]:= **CreationMx["Grodno2016`", {G69, V74}, "c:/temp/tallinn74.mx"]**
"File "C:\\Temp\\Tallinn74.mx" exists."
Out[3683]= "C:\\Temp\\#$#Tallinn74.mx"
A new Mathematica session
In[1]:= **Get["C:\\Temp\\#$#Tallinn74.mx"]**
In[2]:= **?G69**
"Help on G69 function."
In[3]:= **?V74**
"Help on V74 function."
In[4]:= **Definition[G69]**
Out[4]= G69[x_, y_] := x^2 + y^2
In[5]:= **Definition[V74]**
Out[5]= V74[x_, y_] := x^3 + y^3
In[6]:= **ContextInMxFile["C:\\Temp\\#$#Tallinn74.mx"]**

Out[6]= "Grodno2016`"

Sometimes, it is expedient to replace a context of tools of the user package uploaded into the current session. This problem is solved by means of the procedure **RemoveContext**, whose successful call **RemoveContext[*j*, *x*, *y*, *z*, ...]** returns nothing, replacing in the current session a *j* context ascribed to the means {*x*, *y*, *z*, ...} of the user package by the *"Global'"* context. In the absence of the {*x*, *y*, *z*, ...} tools with the *j* context the procedure call returns $Failed. The next fragment represents source code of the **RemoveContext** procedure with examples of its application.

In[3200]:= **Get["C:\\MathToolBox\\Grodno.mx"]**
In[3201]:= **CNames["Grodno`"]**
Out[3201]= {"Ga", "Gs", "GSV", "Vgs"}

In[3202]:= **RemoveContext[at_ /; ContextQ[at], x__] :=**
Module[{a = {}, b, c = {}, d = Map[ToString, {x}], f = "$Art27$Kr20$", Attr},
d = Intersection[CNames[at], d]; b = Flatten[Map[PureDefinition, d]];
If[b == {}, $Failed, Attr := Map[{#, Attributes[#]} &, d];
Do[AppendTo[a, StringReplace[b[[k]], at <> d[[k]] <> "`" -> ""]], {k, 1, Length[d]}];
Write[f, a]; Close[f]; Do[AppendTo[c, at <> d[[k]]], {k, 1, Length[d]}]; c = Flatten[c];
Map[{ClearAttributes[#, Protected], Remove[#]} &, d];
Map[ToExpression, Get[f]]; DeleteFile[f];
Map[ToExpression["SetAttributes[" <> #[[1]] <> "," <> ToString[#[[2]]] <> "]"] &, Attr];]]

In[3203]:= **Map[Context, {Ga, Gs}]**
Out[3203]= {"Grodno`", "Grodno`"}
In[3204]:= **RemoveContext["Grodno`", Ga, Gs]**
In[3205]:= **Map[Context, {Ga, Gs}]**
Out[3205]= {"Global`", "Global`"}
In[3206]:= **CNames["Grodno`"]**
Out[3306]= {"GSV", "Vgs"}
In[3207]:= **Definition[Ga]**
Out[3207]= Ga[x_Integer, y_Integer] := x*y + Gs[x, y]
In[3208]:= **Definition[Gs]**
Out[3208]= Gs[x_Integer, y_Integer] := x^2 + y^2
In[3209]:= **RemoveContext["Grodno`", Kr, Art]**
Out[3209]= $Failed

The function call **OptDef[*x*]** returns nothing, providing optimization in the above sense of definition of a *x* symbol, whereas the call **OptDef[*x*, *y*]**, where *y* – the context, also returns nothing, replacing in definition of the *x* symbol the designs <*a* <> *x* <> "`"> and <*a*> on <*y* <> *x* <> "`"> and <*y*> respectively {*a* = Context[*x*]}. While the call **ReplaceContextInMx[*x*, *f*]** returns the list of format {*a*, *b*, *f1*} where *a* and *b* – a new context and old context of a *mx*-file *f*, and *f1* – a new *mx*-file obtained from a *x* file by means of the substitution of its *a* context onto *b*. If *f* datafile is already loaded into the current session, it remains, otherwise package contained in it is unloaded. If *f* file no contain a context, $Failed is returned. The following fragment represents source codes of the both tools with examples of their applications.

In[3847]:= OptDef[x_ /; SymbolQ[x], y__] :=
Quiet[ToExpression[StringReplace[ToString1[Definition[x]], {Context[x] <>
ToString[x] <> "`" -> If[{y} != {} && ContextQ[y], y, ""], Context[x] -> If[{y} != {} &&
ContextQ[y], y, ""]}]]]

In[3849]:= ReplaceContextInMx[x_ /; ContextQ[x], f_ /; FileExistsQ[f] &&
FileExtension[f] == "mx"] := Module[{a = ContextInMxFile[f], b, c, d, t},
If[MemberQ[{$Failed, "AladjevProcedures`"}, a], $Failed, If[MemberQ[$Packages, a],
b = CNames[a]; Map[OptDef[#, x] &, b]; t = 6, Get[f]; b = CNames[a];
Map[OptDef[#, x] &, b]]; c = FileNameSplit[f]; d = c[[-1]];
c = FileNameJoin[ReplacePart[c, -1 -> "#$#" <> d]];
Map[Quiet[ContextToSymbol2[#, x]] &, b];
ToExpression["DumpSave[" <> ToString1[c] <> "," <> ToString1[x] <> "]"];
If[! SameQ[t, 6], RemovePackage[a], RemovePackage[x]; Get[f]]; {a, x, c}]]

In[3850]:= ReplaceContextInMx["Tallinn2017`", "Tallinn.mx"]
Out[3850]= {"RansIan`", "Tallinn2017`", "#$#Tallinn.mx"}

A new Mathematica session

In[9]:= Get["#$#Tallinn.mx"]
In[10]:= ?? GSV
"Help on GSV."
GSV[x_, y_, z_] := Module[{a = 6}, x*y*z + a]

Using the above approach, a procedure ensuring the expansion of a *mx*-file with a context with definitions of new tools can be programmed. So, the call **AddToMxFile[x, y]** returns a *mx*-file whither the expansion result of a *mx*-file with a context with definitions of new *y* tools that have been previously calculated in the current session is unloaded. As an *y* there can be a separate symbol or their list. While the procedure call **AddToMxFile[x, y, j]** where *j* – an arbitrary expression – removes the previously determined *y* symbols from the current session. If *x* file has been loaded, it remains in the current session, otherwise is unloaded. The **AddToMxFile** is an analog of the **AdjunctionToMx** [48].

In[1942]:= AddToMxFile[x_ /; FileExistsQ[x] && FileExtension[x] == "mx",
y_ /; SymbolQ[y] || ListQ[y] && DeleteDuplicates[Map[SymbolQ, y]] == {True}, z___]:=
Module[{a = ContextInMxFile[x], b, c, d = Flatten[{y}], f},
If[a === $Failed, $Failed, Map[Quiet[ContextToSymbol2[#, a]] &, d];
f = FileNameSplit[x]; c = f[[-1]]; f = FileNameJoin[ReplacePart[f, -1 -> "#$#" <> c]];
If[MemberQ[$Packages, a], b = 74, 69]; Get[x];
ToExpression["DumpSave[" <> ToString1[f] <> "," <> ToString1[a] <> "]"];
If[b === 74, 69, If[{z} = {}, 69, Map[Clear[ToExpression[#]] &, Map["Global`" <> # &,
Map[ToString, Map[Unprotect, d]]]]]];
ToExpression["RemovePackage[" <> ToString1[a] <> "]"]; f]]

In[1943]:= Gs::usage = "Help on Gs."; Gs[x_, y_] := Module[{a = 6}, x*y*a]
ArtKr::usage = "Help on ArtKr."; ArtKr[x_, y_, z_] := Module[{}, x/y/z]
In[1944]:= AddToMxFile["Tallinn.mx", {ArtKr, Gs}]

Out[1944]= "#$#Tallinn.mx"

A New Mathematica session

In[1945]:= **Get["#$#Tallinn.mx"]**

In[1946]:= **CNames[ContextInMxFile["#$#Tallinn.mx"]]**

Out[1946]= {"Art", "ArtKr", "GSV", "Gs"}

In[1947]:= **Information[ArtKr]**

"Help on ArtKr."

ArtKr[x_, y_, z_] := Module[{}, x/y/z]

As a result the *symbols* with the same short name whose contexts are located in a list defined by the *$ContextPath* variable further from the beginning, are inaccessible for access to them by means of their short names. Therefore for access to them it is necessary to use full names of the following format *"Context'Name"*; furthermore, at entering into the current session of the new symbols overlapping the symbols of the same name from the *$ContextPath* list the corresponding message is output.

The procedure call **AllContexts[]** returns list of contexts that contain in the system packages of the current *Mathematica* version, whereas the call **AllContexts[*x*]** returns *True*, if *x* is a context of the above type, and *False* otherwise. The fragment below represents source code of the procedure along with typical examples of its application.

In[3873]:= **AllContexts[y___] :=**
Module[{a = Directory[], c, h, b = SetDirectory[$InstallationDirectory]},
b = FileNames[{"*.m", "*.tr"}, {"*"}, Infinity];
h[x_] := StringReplace[StringJoin[Map[FromCharacterCode, BinaryReadList[x]]],
{"\n" -> "", "\r" -> "", "\t" -> "", " " -> "", "{" -> "", "}" -> ""}];
c = Flatten[Select[Map[StringCases[h[#], {"BeginPackage[\"" ~~ Shortest[W__] ~~ "`\"]",
"Needs[\"" ~~ Shortest[W__] ~~ "`\"]", "Begin[\"" ~~ Shortest[W__] ~~ "`\"]", "Get[\"" ~~
Shortest[W__] ~~ "`\"]", "Package[\"" ~~ Shortest[W__] ~~ "`\"]"}] &, b], # != {} &]];
c = DeleteDuplicates[Select[c, StringFreeQ[#, {"*", "="}] &]]; SetDirectory[a];
c = Flatten[Append[Select[Map[StringReplace[StringTake[#, {1, -2}],
{"Get[" -> "", "Begin[" -> "", "Needs[" -> "", "BeginPackage[" -> "",
"Package[" -> ""}, 1] &, c], # != "\"`Private`\"" &], {"\"Global`\"",
"\"CloudObjectLoader`\""}]];
c = Map[ToExpression, Sort[Select[DeleteDuplicates[Flatten[Map[If[StringFreeQ[#, ","],
#, StringSplit[#, ","]] &, c]]],
StringFreeQ[#, {"<>", "]", "["}] && StringTake[#, {1, 2}] != "\"`" &]]];
If[{y} != {}, MemberQ[c, y], c]]

In[3874]:= **AllContexts[]**

Out[3874]= {"ANOVA`", "ANOVA`ANOVA`", "App`", ..., "YelpLoad`"}

In[3875]:= **Length[%]**

Out[3875]= 725

In[3876]:= **AllContexts["URLUtilitiesLoader`"]**

Out[3876]= True

Whereas the call **ContextsCS[]** returns the list of active contexts of the current *Mathematica* session. The following fragment represents source code of the **ContextsCS** function with an example of its application.

In[3878]:= **ContextsCS[] := Sort[DeleteDuplicates[Flatten[Map[If[StringLength[#] == 1 || StringFreeQ[#, "`"], {"System`", "Global`"}, StringTake[#, {1, Flatten[StringPosition[#, "`"]][[-1]]}]] &, Names[]]]]**

In[3879]:= **ContextsCS[]**
Out[3879]= {"AladjevProcedures`ActBFMuserQ`", ..., "$CellContext`"}

The function call **SymbolsContext[*x*]** returns the list of all symbols that are associated with a *x* context which is activated in the current *Mathematica* session. In particular, the function is useful enough at receiving of names of all objects contained in the package with the given *x* context. The fragment below presents source code of the function with example of its use.

In[3883]:= **SymbolsContext[x_ /; ContextQ[x]] := Quiet[Select[Names[x <> "*"], ToString[Definition[#]] != "Null" && Attributes[#] != {Temporary} &]]**

In[3884]:= **SymbolsContext["AladjevProcedures`"]**
Out[3884]= {"AcNb", "ActBFM", "ActBFMuserQ", ..., "$Version2"}

At last, the procedure **ContextToFileName1** – a rather useful addition to standard function **ContextToFileName**. So, the call **ContextToFileName1[]** returns the list of contexts that are associated with system *m*-files, while the call **ContextToFileName1[*y*]** returns the full path to a *m*-file associated with an *y* context. The following fragment presents source code of the **ContextToFileName1** procedure with an example of its application.

In[3889]:= **ContextToFileName1[y___] := Module[{a = Directory[], c, d, b = SetDirectory[$InstallationDirectory]}, c = FileNames[{"*.m"}, {"*"}, Infinity]; d = Sort[DeleteDuplicates[Map[StringTake[#, {Flatten[StringPosition[#, "\\"]][[-1]] + 1, -3}] <> "`" &, c]]]; SetDirectory[a]; If[{y} != {} && ContextQ[{y}[[1]]], Map[b <> "\\" <> #1 &, Select[c, SuffPref[#, "\\" <> StringTake[y, {1, -2}] <> ".m", 2] &]], d]]**

In[3890]:= **ContextToFileName1["PacletManager`"]**
Out[3890]= {"C:\\Program Files\\Wolfram Research\\Mathematica\\11.0\\SystemFiles\\Autoload\\PacletManager\\PacletManager.m"}

At last, interesting enough questions in this context are considered enough in details in our books [30-33,50].

8.1.1. Interconnection of contexts and packages in the software of the *Mathematica* system

The *packages* are one of the main mechanisms of the *Mathematica* extension which contain definitions of the new symbols intended for use both outside of a package and in it. These symbols can correspond, in particular, to the new functions or objects defined in a package that extend the functional *Mathematica* possibilities. In addition, according to the adopted agreement all new symbols entered in a certain package are placed in a context whose name is connected with the name of the package. At *uploading* of a package in the current session, the given context is added into the beginning of the list defined by the global *$ContextPath* variable. As a rule, for ensuring of association of a package with a context the construction **BeginPackage["*x'*"]** coded at its beginning is used. At uploading of a package in the current session the *"x'"* context will update the current values of the global variables *$Context* and *$ContextPath*. Thus, *MathToolBox* package contains **BeginPackage["*AladjevProcedures'*"]** and at its uploading, the values of the specified variables accept the following view, namely:

In[2571]:= **$ContextPath**
Out[2571]= {"AladjevProcedures`", "StreamingLoader`", "IconizeLoader`", "CloudObjectLoader`", "PacletManager`", "System`", "Global`"}
In[2572]:= **MemberQ[Contexts["*"], "AladjevProcedures`"]**
Out[2572]= True
In[2573]:= **$Packages**
Out[2573]= {"HTTPClient`","HTTPClient`OAuth`", "StreamingLoader`", "HTTPClient`CURLInfo`", "HTTPClient`CURLLink`", "JLink`", "DocumentationSearch`", "AladjevProcedures`", "GetFEKernelInit`", "CloudObjectLoader`", "ResourceLocator`", "PacletManager`", "System`", "Global`"}

In[2574]:= **CNames[x_ /; ContextQ[x], y___] := Module[{a = Names[StringJoin[x, "*"]], b},**
b = Select[a, Quiet[ToString[Definition[ToString[#1]]]] != "Null" &];
If[{y} != {} && PureDefinition[y] === $Failed, y = Map[StringTrim[#, x] &,
Sort[DeleteDuplicates[Select[a, Quiet[Check[PureDefinition[#], $Failed]] ===
$Failed &]]]]];
Map[StringTrim[#, x] &, Select[b, Quiet[! SameQ[Attributes[#], {Temporary}] &&
ToString[Definition[#]]] != "Null" &]]]

In[2575]:= **CNames["AladjevProcedures`"]**
Out[2575]= {"AcNb", "ActBFM","ActBFMuserQ", "ActCsProcFunc", ..., "$TypeProc", "$UserContexts", "$Version1", "$Version2"}
In[2576]:= **Length[%]**
Out[2576]= 1142
In[2577]:= **CNames["AladjevProcedures`", h74]; h74**
Out[2577]= {"a", "A", "a1", "A$", "b", "b1", "c", "d", "f", "F", "f$", "inputstream", "Op$", "outputstream", "p", "s", "S1", "t", "t$", "x", "x$", "y", "y$", "z", "z$"}
In[2578]:= **CNames["System`"]**
Out[2578]= {"AASTriangle", "AbelianGroup", "AbortKernels", ..., "$UserName", "$Version", "$VersionNumber"}

At that, in the above fragment instead of return of the complete list determined by the call **Contexts["*"]** to save space only testing of existence in it of the specified context is done. From the full list defined by the call **Contexts["*"]** can be easily noticed that in it along with this context exist elements of a type *"AladjevProcedures'Name'"* that determine full names of all objects whose definitions are located in the *MathToolBox* package [48]. Whereas the **CNames** procedure represented in the previous fragment allows to differentially obtain the lists of all short names in a package with the given context – of the definitions that exist in it, and undefinite ones from the standpoint of the current session.

So, the procedure call **CNames[*x*]** returns the list of all short names in the package with a *x* context, which have definitions in it; whereas the procedure call **CNames[*x, y*]** in addition through *y* argument – *an undefinite variable* – returns the list of all undefinite short names in the package with a *x* context. In addition, the analysis of the list, returned through *optional y* argument provides additional possibility of check of contents of the package relative to the definiteness of all objects contained in it. The **CNames** procedure provides an easy way of the differentiated analysis of contents of packages formalized in form of the *Mathematica* documents of the formats {"*nb*", "*cdf*"}. The mechanism of contexts has a number of rather essential features which need to be taken into account during the work in the environment of the system, first of all, at use of the procedural paradigm. These features are considered rather in details in [33]. In particular, after uploading of a package into the current session all its objects will be associated with a context ascribed to the package whereas the objects of the same name, whose definitions are evaluated in the current session are associated with the *"Global`"* context. Whereas to the **CNames** procedure directly adjoins a rather simple function whose call **DefectiveVars**[c] returns the sorted list of the symbols which have a *c* context but don't have definition and, possibly, with the *Temporary* attribute, for example:

In[2580]:= **DefectiveVars**[c_ /; ContextQ[c]] :=
Sort[Complement[Names[c <> "*"], CNames[c]]]

In[2581]:= **DefectiveVars**["AladjevProcedures`"]
Out[2581]= {"a", "a$", "b", "b$", "c", "c$", "d", "d$", "f", "f$", "g", "g$", "n", "n$", "Op$", "p", "p$", "s", "s$", "t", "t$", "x", "x$", "y", "y$", "z", "z$"}

In[2582]:= **DefectiveVars**["Global`"]
Out[2582]= {"F", "G", "Global", "h", "h$", "j", "k", "k$", "m", "mp", "mp$", "m$", "pf", "Sf", "t1", "t1$", "t2", "t2$", "u", "u$", "v", "v$"}

For definition of the contexts of symbols the **ContextDef** procedure can be used, whose call **ContextDef**[*x*] returns the list of contexts associated with an arbitrary *x* symbol. If *x* symbol isn't associated with any context, the empty list is returned, i.e. {}. The following fragment represents source code of the **ContextDef** procedure along with typical examples of its use.

In[3326]:= **BeginPackage**["RansIan`"]
GSV::usage = "help on GSV."
Begin["`GSV`"]
GSV[x_, y_, z_] := Module[{a = 6}, x*y*z + a]
End[]
EndPackage[]
Out[3326]= "RansIan`"
Out[3327]= "help on GSV."
Out[3328]= "RansIan`GSV`"
Out[3330]= "RansIan`GSV`"
In[3332]:= GSV[x_Integer, z_Integer] := Module[{a = 590}, (x + z)*a]

In[3333]:= **ContextDef**[x_ /; SymbolQ[x]] :=
Module[{a = $ContextPath, b = ToString[x], c = {}},
Do[If[! SameQ[ToString[Quiet[Check[ToExpression["Definition1[" <>
ToString1[a[[k]] <> b] <> "]"], "Null"]]], "Null"], AppendTo[c, {a[[k]] <> b,
If[ToString[Definition[b]] != "Null", "Global`" <> b, Nothing]}]], {k, 1, Length[a]}];
Flatten[c]]

In[3334]:= **ContextDef[GSV]**
Out[3334]= {"RansIan`GSV", "Global`GSV"}
In[3335]:= **ProcQ[x_, y_] := x*y**
In[3336]:= **ContextDef[ProcQ]**
Out[3336]= {"AladjevProcedures`ProcQ", "Global`ProcQ"}
In[3337]:= **Definition["RansIan`GSV"]**
Out[3337]= GSV[RansIan`GSV`x_, RansIan`GSV`y_, RansIan`GSV`z_] :=
Module[{RansIan`GSV`a = 6}, RansIan`GSV`x*RansIan`GSV`y*RansIan`GSV`z + RansIan`GSV`a]
GSV[x_Integer, z_Integer] := Module[{a = 590}, (x + z)*a]
In[3338]:= **$ContextPath**
Out[3338]= {"RansIan`", "AladjevProcedures`", "StreamingLoader`", "CloudObjectLoader`", "PacletManager`", "System`", "Global`"}

Thus, at using of the objects of the same name, generally, to avoid misunderstandings it is necessary to associate them with the contexts which have been ascribed to them.

8.2. Definition of the user packages, and their usage in the *Mathematica*

The global **$Packages** variable defines the list of the contexts corresponding to all packages uploaded into the current session, for example:

In[2569]:= **$Packages**
Out[2569]= {"AladjevProcedures`", "GetFEKernelInit`", ..., "Global`"}
In[2570]:= **Get["C:\\MathToolBox\\Aladjev.m"]; $Packages**
Out[2570]= {"AladjevVZ`", "AladjevProcedures`", ..., "Global`"}

As it was already noted, each uploading of a new package into the current session adds the context corresponding to it to the beginning of list which is defined by the global **$Packages** variable. Generally speaking, in the presence of the loaded packages their means it is quite possible to consider as tools at the level of the builtin means of the *Mathematica* system. In effect, quite essential number of functions of the *Mathematica* system has been realized in the form of packages. Meanwhile, in the majority of the *Mathematica* versions preliminary loading of packages for receiving access to tools, contained in them is required. The *majority* of *Mathematica* versions is provided with a standard set of packages that contain *definitions* of very large number of functions. For their usage, as a rule, the appropriate packages it is necessary to upload professedly in the current session. The *Mathematica* has the *mechanism* of both preliminary loading, and automatic loading of packages as needed. Meanwhile here one very essential circumstance takes place, namely: the help on such package means aren't reflected in the help *Mathematica* system, and it can be received, for example, by means of the calls ?*Name* and ??*Name*. Similar organization is completely inconvenient, in particular, significantly conceding to the mechanism of organization of the help *Maple* system [27,50].

The main forms of preservation of definitions of the objects are a document *(notebook)* and a package *(package)* which are located in files of formats {*cdf*, *nb*} and {*m*, *mx*} respectively. At the same time between them there is a certain distinction. If uploading of the first into the current session allows to work with it as the document *(look over, execute, edit, save)*, then the package is intended only for uploading into the current session. In addition, documents partially or completely can be considered as the packages. In particular, for convenience of work with *MathToolBox* package, it is presented in *3* main platform-independent formats, namely {*cdf, nb, m*}. It should be noted that binary files of the *mx*-format optimized for fast uploading into the current session are nonportable both between versions of *Mathematica* system, and between operational platforms.

A package uploading into the current session. Generally, a typical package is provided with two types of symbols determining as the exported symbols, and symbols for internal use. For distinction these symbols are associated with different contexts. The standard reception consists in definition of the exported symbols in context with *Name`* name that corresponds to the package name. Then, at uploading of a package it supplements the list defined by the global **$ContextPath** variable for providing of the call of the symbols that are in this context by their *short names*. Whereas the definitions of all symbols intended for internal usage are located in a context with the name *Package`Private`* which isn't added to the **$ContextPath** list, without allowing to get access to the symbols of such context by their short names. As a rule for setting of contexts of a package and *global* variables such as **$ContextPath, $Context** the standard sequence of functions in the package is used:

**BeginPackage["*Package`*"]** – *the setting for a package of the current "Package`" context;*
F1::usage = "*Help*" – *the help on the exported F1 symbol; further allows to receive the help by means of calls* **?F1** *and* **Information[F1]**;
F2::usage = "*Help*" – *the help on the exported F2 symbol; further allows to receive the help by means of calls* **?F2** *and* **Information[F2]**;
=====
Begin["`Private`"] – *the setting of the "`Private`" context for local symbols;*
F1[*args*] := *Definition1*;... – *definitions of local and global symbols of a package;*
F2[*args*] := *Definition2*;... – *definitions of local and global symbols of a package;*
=====
End[]
EndPackage[] – *the closing bracket of the package; simultaneously adding the "Package`" context to the beginning of the **$ContextPath** list at package uploading into the current session.*

The previous fragment at the same time represents the typical scheme of a package. In our view, the given scheme is rather convenient for processing of packages of the various type, including their updatings. The package given below serves as an illustration of filling of this scheme, namely:

In[2565]:= **BeginPackage["Tallinn`"]**
G::usage = "Function G[x, y] := 74*x^2 + 69*y + 49 + S[x, y]."
Begin["`Private`"]
S[x_, y_] := x^3 + y^3
G[x_ /; IntegerQ[x], y_Integer] := 74*x^2 + 69*y + 49 + S[x, y]
End[]
EndPackage[]
Out[2565]= "Tallinn`"
Out[2566]= "Function G[x, y] := 74*x^2 + 69*y + 49 + S[x, y]."
Out[2567]= "Tallinn`Private`"
Out[2570]= "Tallinn`Private`"
In[2572]:= **{S[90, 590], G[90, 590]}**

Out[2572]= {S[90, 590], 206748159}
In[2573]:= **$ContextPath**
Out[2573]= {"Tallinn`", "AladjevProcedures`", "StreamingLoader`", "CloudObjectLoader`", "PacletManager`", "System`", "Global`"}
In[2574]:= **$Context**
Out[2574]= "Global`"
In[2575]:= **Information[S]**
Out[2575]= Global`S
In[2576]:= **Information[G]**
Out[2576]= Function G[x, y] := 74*x^2 + 69*y + 49 + S[x, y].
G[Tallinn`Private`x_/; IntegerQ[Tallinn`Private`x], Tallinn`Private`y_Integer] := 74*Tallinn`Private`x^2 + 69*Tallinn`Private`y + 49 + Tallinn`Private`S[Tallinn`Private`x, Tallinn`Private`y]
In[2577]:= **Tallinn`Private`S[90, 590]**
Out[2577]= 206108000
In[2578]:= **$Packages**
Out[2578]= {"URLUtilities`", "CloudObject`", "MailReceiver`", "JLink`", "Iconize`", "UUID`", "Security`", "Tallinn`", "AladjevProcedures`", "GetFEKernelInit`", "StreamingLoader`", "CloudObjectLoader`", "ResourceLocator`", "PacletManager`", "System`", "Global`"}

Indeed as shows experience of programming of the user software, its simply to program as packages of the specified format. Such package is activated in the current session by means of the *GUI* chain *"File → Save As…… → Package (*.m)"* is saved in a *m*-file. In subsequent taking into account an inner pattern of such *m*-file it can be exposed to processings of the various type. For example, the procedure call **ExtrSymbolsFromM[*x*]** returns list of names in the string format of all means whose definitions are contained in such *x m*-file. Whereas the procedure call **ExtrSymbolsFromM[*x*, *y*]**, where the second optional *y* argument – an indefinite symbol – through it additionally returns the list of names in the string format of all tools whose definitions are contained in such *x m*-file without any usage. The following fragment represents source code of the **ExtrSymbolsFromM** procedure with an example of its application.

In[3848]:= **ExtrSymbolsFromM[x_ /; FileExistsQ[x] && FileExtension[x] == "m", y___] := Module[{a = ReadFullFile[x], b = {}, c},**
c = Sort[DeleteDuplicates[Map[StringReplace[#, {"Begin[\"`" -> "", "`\"]" -> ""}] &, StringCases[a, Shortest["Begin[\"`" ~~ __ ~~ "`\"]"]]]]]; c = Select[c, # != "Finish" &];
If[{y} != {} && NullQ[y], DeleteDuplicates[Flatten[Map[If[StringFreeQ[a, # <> "::usage"], AppendTo[b, #], Nothing] &, c]]];
y = Select[b, StringFreeQ[#, {"Finish", "(*StyleBox["}] &]; c, c]]

In[3849]:= **ExtrSymbolsFromM["C:\\Mathem\\MathToolBox.m", gs]**
Out[3849]= {"AcNb", "ActBFM", "ActBFMuserQ", "ActCsProcFunc", …, "$UserContexts1", "$UserContexts2", "$Version1", "$Version2"}
In[3850]:= **Length[%]**
Out[3850]= 1142
In[3851]:= **gs**
Out[3851]= {}

We will note that the definition of help *(usage)* for the means exported by a package serves as a certain kind of indicator what exactly these means are exported by a package whereas definitions of means without usage define local symbols which outside of the package are invisible, however they can be used by both local, and global symbols of the package. Such organization is simpler and in some cases is a little more preferable. So, the organizational scheme of a package can be simplified, having assumed a rather simple view, presented by the following fragment. The fragment below visually illustrates a principle of formation of a package taking into account the made remarks.

**BeginPackage["*Package`*"]** – *the setting for a package of the current "Package`" context;*
F::usage = "*Help*" – *the help on the exported F symbols; further allows to receive the help by means of calls* **?F** *and* **Information[F]**;
Begin["`*F*`"] – *the setting of a "`F`" context for a global symbol;*
F[*Formal args*] = *Definition F;...* – *definitions of the global package symbols;*
V[*Formal args*] = *Definition V;...* – *definitions of the local package symbols;*
=====
End[]
EndPackage[] – *the closing bracket of the package; simultaneously adding the "Package`" context to the beginning of the* **$ContextPath** *list at package uploading into the current session.*

Thus, programming of a package can be simplified by means of definition of local variables without usage corresponding to them whereas all exports of the package are defined by the usage corresponding to them as illustrates the following simple enough fragment, namely:

In[2590]:= **BeginPackage["Tallinn74`"]**
G6::usage = "Function G6[x, y] := 74*x^2 + 69*y + 49 + S6[x, y]."
Begin["`G6`"]
S6[x_, y_] := x^4 + y^4
G6[x_ /; IntegerQ[x], y_Integer] := 74*x^2 + 69*y + 49 + S6[x, y]
End[]
EndPackage[]
Out[2590]= "Tallinn74`"
Out[2591]= "Function G6[x, y] := 74*x^2 + 69*y + 49 + S6[x, y]."
Out[2592]= "Tallinn74`G6`"
Out[2593]= "Tallinn74`G6`"
In[2595]:= **{S6[90, 590], G6[90, 590]}**
Out[2595]= {S6[90, 590], 121239860159}
In[2596]:= **$ContextPath**
Out[2596]= {"Tallinn74`", "AladjevProcedures`", "StreamingLoader`", "CloudObjectLoader`", "PacletManager`", "System`", "Global`"}
In[2597]:= **$Packages**
Out[2597]= {"Tallinn74`", "AladjevProcedures`", "HTTPClient`OAuth`", "HTTPClient`CURLInfo`", "HTTPClient`CURLLink`", "HTTPClient`", "GetFEKernelInit`", "TemplatingLoader`", "ResourceLocator`", "PacletManager`", "System`", "Global`"}
In[2598]:= **Information[S6]**
Global`S6
In[2598]:= **Information[G6]**
Function G6[x, y] := 74*x^2 + 69*y + 49 + S6[x, y].

G6[Tallinn74`G6`x_/; IntegerQ[Tallinn74`G6`x], Tallinn74`G6`y_Integer] :=
74*Tallinn74`G6`x^2 + 69*Tallinn74`G6`y + 49 + Tallinn74`G6`S6[Tallinn74`G6`x, Tallinn74`G6`y]

So, the call **Context[x]** of standard function returns a context associated with a *x* symbol. Meanwhile, a rather interesting question is determination of the *m*-file with a package containing the given context. The procedure call **FindFileContext[x]** returns the list of full paths to *m*-files with the packages containing the given *x* context; in the absence of such datafiles the procedure call returns the empty list. In addition, the call **FindFileContext[x, y, z, ...]** with optional {*y, z, ...*} arguments – the names in string format of devices of external memory of direct access – provides search of required files on the specified devices instead of search in all file system of the computer in a case of the procedure call with one factual argument. The search of the required *m*-files is done also in the *$Recycle.bin* directory of the *Windows 7* system as that very visually illustrates an example of the next fragment. It must be kept in mind, that the search within all file system of the computer can demand essential temporal expenditure. The fragment below represents source code of the **FindFileContext** procedure along with typical examples of its application.

In[2600]:= **FindFileContext[x_/; ContextQ[x], y___]** := Module[{b = {}, c = "", k = 1, j = 1,
d = StringJoin["BeginPackage[", StrStr[x], "]"], s = {}, a = If[{y} == {}, Adrive[], {y}],
f = "$Kr20_Art27$.txt"},
While[k <= Length[a], Run["Dir ", StringJoin[a[[k]], ":*.*"], StringJoin[" /A/B/O/S > ", f]];
While[! c === EndOfFile, c = Read[f, String];
If[! DirQ[c] && FileExtension[c] == "m", AppendTo[b, c]]; j++]; c = ""; j = 1; k++]; k = 1;
While[k <= Length[b], c = ToString[ReadFullFile[b[[k]]]];
If[! StringFreeQ[c, d], AppendTo[s, b[[k]]]]; k++]; DeleteFile[Close[f]]; s]

In[2601]:= **FindFileContext["Tallinn`"]**
Out[2601]= {"C:\\MathToolBox\\Tallinn.m"}

In[2602]:= **FindFileContext["AladjevProcedures`"]**
Out[2602]= {"C:\\GrGU_Books\\MathToolBox\\MathToolBox.m",
"C:\\Users\\Aladjev\\Mathematica\\MathToolBox.m"}

In[2603]:= **FindFileContext["AvzAgnSvetArtKr`", "F"]**
Out[2603]= {}

In[2604]:= **FindFileContext["AladjevProcedures`"]**
Out[2604]= {"C:\\$RECYCLE.BIN\\S-1-5-21-2596736632-989557747-1273926778-1000\\MathToolBox.m", "C:\\GrGU_Books\\MathToolBox\\MathToolBox.m",
"C:\\Users\\Aladjev\\Mathematica\\MathToolBox.m"}

For definition of the status of existence of a context *(absent context, the current context without file, the current context with a m–file, inactive context with a m–file)* the next **FindFileContext1** procedure can be used, whose source code with typical examples of use represents the next fragment, namely:

In[2608]:= **FindFileContext1[x_/; ContextQ[x]]** := Module[{a = FindFileContext[x],
b = If[MemberQ[$Packages, x], "Current", {}]}, If[a != {} && ! SameQ[b, {}], {b, a},
If[a != {} && SameQ[b, {}], a, If[a == {} && ! SameQ[b, {}], b, {}]]]]

In[2609]:= **FindFileContext1["Tallinn`"]**
Out[2609]= "Current"
In[2610]:= **FindFileContext1["AladjevProcedures`"]**
Out[2610]= {"Current", {"C:\\\$RECYCLE.BIN\\S-1-5-21-2596736632-989557747-1273926778-1000\\MathToolBox.m", "C:\\GrGU_Books\\MathToolBox\\MathToolBox.m", "C:\\Users\\Aladjev\\Mathematica\\MathToolBox.m"}}
In[2611]:= **FindFileContext1["Aladjev`"]**
Out[2611]= {"f:\\MathToolBox\\aladjev.m"}
In[2612]:= **FindFileContext1["RansIanRacRea`"]**
Out[2612]= {}
In[2613]:= **FindFileContext1["PacletManager`"]**
Out[2613]= {"Current", {"C:\\Program Files\\Wolfram Research\\Mathematica\\11.0\\SystemFiles\\Autoload\\PacletManager\\PacletManager.m"}}

Depending on the status of a x context the procedure call **FindFileContext1[x]** returns the following result, namely:

- {"Current", {*m–files*}} – *the current x context located in the indicated m–files;*
- "Current" – *the current x context, not associated with m–files;*
- {*m–files*} – *a x context is located in m–files, but not in the $Packages list;*
- {} – *a x context is formally correct, but not factual.*

As an essential addition to the above procedures **FindFileContext** and **FindFileContext1** is the **ContextInFile** procedure providing search of files of the types {*cdf, m, mx, nb, tr*} which contain the definitions of packages with the given context. Thus, the call **ContextInFile[x, y]** returns the list of full paths to files of the indicated types containing definitions of packages with a x context. At that, search is executed in a directory, defined by the second optional y argument; in its absence the search of files is executed in the "C:\\" directory. Return of the empty list, i.e. {}, determines absence of the sought-for datafiles in the given path of search. The next fragment represents source code of the **ContextInFile** procedure with examples of its application.

In[2578]:= **ContextInFile[x_ /; ContextQ[x], y___] :=**
Module[{b, d, h, Tav, c = "\$Art27Kr20\$"},
If[{y} != {} && DirQ[y], Run["DIR " <> StandPath[y] <> "/A/B/O/S > \$Art27Kr20\$"],
Run["DIR C:\\ /A/B/O/S > \$Art27Kr20\$"]]; d = ReadList[c, String]; DeleteFile[c];
Tav[t_ /; ListQ[t]] := Module[{m, v = {}, k, z, a = "BeginPackage[" <> ToString1[x] <> "]"},
Map[If[FileExistsQ[#] && MemberQ[{"cdf", "nb", "m", "mx", "tr"},
FileExtension[#]], If[MemberQ[{"tr", "m"}, FileExtension[#]] &&
! StringFreeQ[ReadFullFile[#], a], AppendTo[v, #], If[MemberQ[{"cdf", "nb"},
FileExtension[#]], {m, h, k} = {0, "", 1};
For[k, k < Infinity, k++, h = Read[#, String];
If[h === EndOfFile, Close[#]; Break[], If[! StringFreeQ[h, "BeginPackage"] &&
! StringFreeQ[h, x], m = 90; Close[#]; Break[], Continue[]]]];
If[m == 90, AppendTo[v, #], Null], If[FileExtension[#] == "mx",
z = StringPosition[ReadFullFile[#], {"CONT", "ENDCONT"}];

```
If[! StringFreeQ[StringTake[ReadFullFile[#], {z[[1]][[1]], z[[2]][[1]]}], " " <> x <> " "];
AppendTo[v, #], Null]]]], Null] &, t]; v]; Tav[d]]
```

In[2579]:= **ContextInFile["AladjevProcedures`", "C:\\Users\\Aladjev\\Mathematica"]**
Out[2579]= {"c:\\users\\aladjev\\mathematica\\MathToolBox.cdf",
"c:\\users\\aladjev\\mathematica\\MathToolBox.nb"}
In[2580]:= **ContextInFile["ArtKrSvetGal`"]**
Out[2580]= {}
In[2581]:= **ContextInFile["AladjevProcedures`", "E:\\"]**
Out[2581]= {"e:\\users\\aladjev\\mathematica\\MathToolBox.cdf",
"e:\\users\\aladjev\\mathematica\\MathToolBox.nb"}
In[2582]:= **ContextInFile["PacletManager`", "C:\\Program Files\\Wolfram Research\\Mathematica\\11.0\\SystemFiles\\Autoload"]**
Out[2582]= {"c:\\program files\\wolfram research\\mathematica\\11.0\\systemfiles\\autoload\\PacletManager\\PacletManager.m"}

The procedures **FindFileContext**, **FindFileContext1** and **ContextInFile** are useful enough during the operating with packages. Meanwhile, realization of search of datafiles with the given context within all file system of the computer, as a rule, can demand rather essential time costs. Below, some other useful procedures for work with packages and their contexts will be represented.

In a sense the procedures **ContextMfile** and **ContextNBfile** are inverse to the procedures **FindFileContext, FindFileContext1, ContextInFile,** their successful calls **ContextMfile[w]** and **ContextNBfile[w]** return the context associated with the package that is located in a w file of formats ".m" and {".nb", ".cdf"} accordingly; the file is given by means of name or full path to it. The fragment below represents source codes of the procedures **ContextMfile** and **ContextNBfile** along with the most typical examples of their application.

```
In[2570]:= ContextMfile[x_ /; FileExistsQ[x] && FileExtension[x] == "m"] :=
Module[{b, a = ReadFullFile[x], c}, b = SubString[a, {"BeginPackage[\"", "\"]"}];
c = If[b != {}, StringTake[b, {14, -2}]]; If[b === {}, $Failed, c = Flatten[StringSplit[c, ","]];
c = Select[Quiet[ToExpression[c]], ContextQ[#] &];
If[c == {}, {}, If[Length[c] > 1, c, c[[1]]]]]]
```

In[2571]:= **ContextMfile["c:\\users\\aladjev\\mathematica\\MathToolBox.m"]**
Out[2571]= "AladjevProcedures`"
In[2572]:= **ContextMfile["D:\\MathToolBox\\RansIan.m"]**
Out[2572]= $Failed
In[2573]:= **ContextMfile["C:/MathToolBox/MathToolBox_1.m"]**
Out[2573]= "AladjevProcedures`"
In[2574]:= **ContextMfile["C:/temp\\A A A\\Aladjev.m"]**
Out[2574]= "Aladjev`"
In[2575]:= **ContextMfile[$InstallationDirectory <> "\\SystemFiles\\Kernel\\Packages\\Experimental.m"]**
Out[2575]= "Experimental`"

In[2580]:= **ContextNBfile[x_ /; FileExistsQ[x] && MemberQ[{"cdf", "nb"}, FileExtension[x]]] := Module[{a = ""},**

Software Etudes in the Mathematica

```
While[! SameQ[a, EndOfFile], a = Read[x, String];
If[! StringFreeQ[ToString[a], "BeginPackage"],
a = Quiet[ToExpression[ToExpression[StringSplit[a, ","]][[3]]]]];
Break[]]; Continue[]]; Close[x]; If[! ContextQ[a] || SameQ[a, EndOfFile], $Failed, a]]
```

In[2581]:= **ContextNBfile["D:\\MATHTOOLBOX\\MathToolBox.nb"]**
Out[2581]= "AladjevProcedures`"
In[2582]:= **ContextNBfile["D:\\MATHTOOLBOX\\Book_3.nb"]**
Out[2582]= $Failed
In[2583]:= **ContextNBfile["D:\\MATHTOOLBOX\\MathToolBox.cdf"]**
Out[2583]= "AladjevProcedures`"
In[2584]:= **ContextNBfile["C:/MathToolBox/MathToolBox_1.nb"]**
Out[2584]= "AladjevProcedures`"
In[2585]:= **ContextNBfile["C:/Temp/A A A\\MathToolBox.nb"]**
Out[2585]= "AladjevProcedures`"

Thus, the **ContextNBfile** procedure similar to the **ContextMfile** procedure completes the previous fragment, but it is oriented onto the user packages located in files of {*".cdf"*, *".nb"*} format whose internal organization differs from the organization of *m*–files with packages. The procedure call **ContextNBfile[*x*]** returns the context associated with the package which is located in a *x* file of format {*".cdf"*, *".nb"*} that is given by means of a name or full path to it. If *x* datafile doesn't contain a context, the procedure call **ContextNBfile[*x*]** returns $*Failed*. Both procedures have a number of important enough appendices at operating with datafiles containing packages.

On the basis of the **ContextMfile** procedure for testing of system packages (*m–files*) which are located in a directory defined by $*InstallationDirectory* variable the **SystemPackages** procedure has been created whose procedure call **SystemPackages[]** returns the list whose two–element sublists have the format {*Package, its context*} while the call **SystemPackages[*x*]** thru optional *x* argument – an indefinite variable – in addition returns the list of the system packages that aren't possessing contexts, i.e. are used for internal needs of the system. The next fragment represents source code of the **SystemPackages** procedure along with typical examples of its application.

In[2678]:= **SystemPackages[y___] := Module[{a, b},**
a = FileNames["*.m", $InstallationDirectory, Infinity];
b = Quiet[DeleteDuplicates[Map[{FileBaseName[#], ContextMfile[#]} &, a]]];
b = Select[b, # != {} &];
If[{y} != {} && ! HowAct[y], y = Select[Map[If[SameQ[#[[2]], $Failed], #[[1]]] &, b],
! SameQ[#, Null] &]]; Select[b, ! SameQ[#[[2]], $Failed] &]]
In[2679]:= **SystemPackages[]**
Out[2679]= {{"Common", {"AuthorTools`Common`", "AuthorTools`MakeProject`"}}, ...,
{"YelpFunctions", "YelpFunctions`"}, {"YelpLoad", "YelpLoad`"}}
In[2680]:= **Length[%]**
Out[2680]= 387
In[2681]:= **SystemPackages[Sv]; Sv**

Out[2681]= {"AstronomyConvenienceFunctionsLoader", "AstronomyConvenienceFunctions", "PacletInfo", "Default", "init", "DataDropClientLoader", "DataDropClient", ..., "Implementation", "WSDL", "Yelp"}
In[2682]:= **Length[%]**
Out[2682]= 2510
In[2683]:= **t74 = TimeUsed[]; SystemPackages[Kr]; Kr; TimeUsed[] – t74**
Out[2683]= 38.204
In[2684]:= **Length[FileNames["*.*", $InstallationDirectory, Infinity]]**
Out[2684]= 31333
In[2768]:= **t70 = TimeUsed[]; a = FileNames["*.*", "C:\\", Infinity]; TimeUsed[] – t70**
General::dirdep: Cannot get deeper in directory tree: C:\\Documents...>>
General::cdir: Cannot set current directory to PerfLogs...>>
General::cdir: Cannot set current directory to cache...>>
General::dirdep: Cannot get deeper in directory tree: C:\\ProgramData...>>
General::stop: Further output of General::dirdep will be suppressed during this calculation...>>
General::cdir: Cannot set current directory to Favorites...>>
General::stop: Further output of General::cdir will be suppressed during this calculation...>>
Out[2768]= 2.777
In[2769]:= **t50 = TimeUsed[]; Run["DIR C:\\ /A/B/O/S > $Art27Kr20$"]; TimeUsed[] – t50**
Out[2769]= 0.005
In[2770]:= **Length[a]**
Out[2770]= 182485
In[2771]:= **t6 = ""; For[k = 1, k < Infinity, k++, If[t6 === EndOfFile, Break[], t6 = Read["$Art27Kr20$", String]; Continue[]]]; k**
Out[2771]= 200018

Inasmuch as, in particular, the directory containing the system *Mathematica 11.1* contains *31333* datafiles of different types, their testing demands certain time needs as illustrates an example of the previous fragment. At the same time it must be kept in mind that in a view of the told, the access to internal packages of the *Mathematica* by means of the mechanism of contexts is impossible. Here quite appropriate to make one rather essential remark.

Meanwhile, the **ContextMfile** procedure provides search only of the first context in a *m*-file with a package whereas generally multiple contexts can be associated with a package. The following **ContextMfile1** procedure provides the solution of this question in case of *multiple* contexts. The procedure call **ContextMfile1[*x*]** returns the list of contexts or a single context associated with a *x* datafile of {"*m*", "*tr*"} formats, in case of lack of contexts the empty list is returned. Furthermore, the additional *tr*-format allows to carry out search of contexts in the system files containing contexts. Moreover, in case **FileExistsQ[*w*]** = *False* the search of a file *w* is done in file system of the computer as a whole. Whereas the **ActUcontexts** procedure provides obtaining of the list of contexts of the current session which are associated with the user packages.

The procedure call **ActUcontexts[]** for obtaining of the list uses an algorithm which is based on the analysis of system datafiles of the {"*m*", "*tr*"} formats, while the call **ActUcontexts[*x*]** where optional *x* argument is arbitrary expression, is based on the search of system files of the next view "**StringTake[Context, {1, -2}] <> {".m" | ".tr"}**". If the first algorithm is more universal, whereas the second significantly more high-speed. The **ReadFullFile1** function used by the **ContextMfile1** procedure, is a modification of **ReadFullFile** procedure. While the procedure call **SysContexts[]** returns list of all system contexts activated in the current session, and the function call **SystemSymbols[]** returns all system symbols of the current session. The following fragment represents source codes of the above means with examples of their typical application.

In[2600]:= ContextMfile1[x_ /; MemberQ[{"m", "tr"}, FileExtension[x]]] :=
Module[{b = "BeginPackage[", c, d, a = Quiet[Check[ReadFullFile1[If[FileExistsQ[x],
x, Flatten[{FindFile1[x]}][[1]]]], {}]]}, If[a === {}, {}, c = StringPosition[a, b];
If[c == {}, {}, d = SubStrToSymb[StringTake[a, {Flatten[c][[2]], -1}], 1, "]", 1];
d = StringReplace[StringTake[d, {2, -2}], {"{" -> "", "}" -> ""}];
d = Map[ToExpression, StrToList[d]]; If[Length[d] == 1, d[[1]], d]]]]

In[2601]:= ContextMfile1["DocumentationSearch.m"]
Out[2601]= {"DocumentationSearch`", "ResourceLocator`"}
In[2602]:= ContextMfile1["IanRans.m"]
Out[2602]= {}
In[2603]:= ContextMfile1["MathToolBox.m"]
Out[2603]= "AladjevProcedures`"

In[2620]:= SubStrToSymb[x_ /; StringQ[x], n_ /; IntegerQ[n], y_ /; StringQ[y] &&
y != "", p_ /; MemberQ[{0, 1}, p]] := Module[{a, b = StringLength[x], c, d, k},
If[n <= 0 || n >= b || StringFreeQ[x, y], $Failed, c = StringTake[x, {n}];
For[If[p == 0, k = n - 1, k = n + 1], If[p == 0, k >= 1, k <= b], If[p == 0, k--, k++],
If[Set[d, StringTake[x, {k}]] != y, If[p == 0, c = d <> c, c = c <> d], Break[]]];
If[k < 1 || k > b, $Failed, If[p == 0, c = y <> c, c = c <> y]]]]

In[2620]:= SubStrToSymb["85123456786", 7, "8", 0]
Out[2620]= "8512345"

In[2740]:= SubStrToSymb["85123456786", 7, "2", 1]
Out[2740]= $Failed

In[2620]:= SubStrToSymb["85123456786", 1, "6", 1]
Out[2620]= "85123456"

In[2649]:= ActUcontexts[x___] := Module[{c, d = {}, k, j, a = MinusList[$Packages,
{"System`", "Global`"}], b = FileNames[{"*.m", "*.tr"}, $InstallationDirectory, Infinity]},
c = DeleteDuplicates[Map[StringTake[#, {1, Flatten[StringPosition[#, "`"]][[1]]}] &, a]];
If[{x} == {}, For[k = 1, k <= Length[c], k++, For[j = 1, j <= Length[b], j++,
If[FileBaseName[b[[j]]] <> "`" == c[[k]] ||
MemberQ[MemberQ[Quiet[ContextMfile1[b[[j]]]], c[[k]]], AppendTo[d, c[[k]]];
Break[]]]]; MinusList[c, d], c = Map[StringTake[#, {1, -2}] &, c];
For[k = 1, k <= Length[c], k++, For[j = 1, j <= Length[b], j++,
If[FileBaseName[b[[j]]] == c[[k]], AppendTo[d, c[[k]]]; Break[]]]; MinusList[c, d]]]

In[2650]:= ActUcontexts[590]
Out[2650]= {"Tallinn74`", "Tallinn`", "Grodno`", "AladjevProcedures`"}

In[2656]:= ReadFullFile1[x_/; FileExistsQ[x]] :=
StringReplace[Quiet[Check[ReadString[x], ""]], "\r\n" -> ""]

In[2657]:= ReadFullFile1["C:\\Temp\\Cinema_2017.txt"]
Out[2657]= http://cinemaxx.ru/9/31367-vysokie-stavki-2015.html

In[2670]:= SysContexts[]:= Module[{a = Contexts[], b = ActUcontexts[590]},
Select[a, ! SuffPref[#, b, 1] &]]

In[2671]:= SysContexts[]
Out[2671]= {"Algebra`", "Algebraics`Private`", "Algebra`Polynomial`", ...,
"XML`NotebookML`", "XML`Parser`", "XML`RSS`", "XML`SVG`", "$CellContext`"}

In[2672]:= Length[%]
Out[2672]= 1518

In[2694]:= SystemSymbols[] := Module[{a = Names["*"], c = ActUcontexts[590],
b = Join[Map[FromCharacterCode, Range[63488; 63596]], CNames["Global`"]]},
MinusList[a, Join[b, Flatten[Map[CNames[#] &, c]]]]]

In[2695]:= h = SystemSymbols[]; Length[h]
Out[2695]= 6493

It should be noted, that the above **ContextMfile1** procedure for the purpose of increase of performance significantly uses the **SubStrToSymb** procedure which belongs to means of processing of the string expressions. The procedure call **SubStrToSymb**[*x, n, y, p*] returns a substring of a *x* string bounded on the left *(p = 1)* by a *n* position and the first occurrence of *y* symbol, and on the right *(p = 0)* by *n* position and the first occurrence of *y* symbol, i.e., at *p = 0* and *p = 1* the search of *y* symbol is done right to left and left to right accordingly.

Moreover, in a case of absence at search of a required *y* symbol the call **SubStrToSymb**[*x, n, y, p*] returns $Failed whereas in other especial cases the call is returned unevaluated. At that, the given procedure along with the above-mentioned application has enough much of other interesting appendices at processing of various string expressions. The following fragment represents source code of the procedure with typical example of its application.

In[7647]:= SubStrToSymb[x_/; StringQ[x], n_/; IntegerQ[n], y_/; StringQ[y] &&
y != "", p_/; MemberQ[{0, 1}, p]] := Module[{a, b = StringLength[x], c, d, k},
If[n <= 0 || n >= b || StringFreeQ[x, y], $Failed, c = StringTake[x, {n}];
For[If[p == 0, k = n - 1, k = n + 1], If[p == 0, k >= 1, k <= b],
If[p == 0, k--, k++], If[Set[d, StringTake[x, {k}]] != y,
If[p == 0, c = d <> c, c = c <> d], Break[]]];
If[k < 1 || k > b, $Failed, If[p == 0, c = y <> c, c = c <> y]]]]

In[7648]:= SubStrToSymb["12a3b4c5d6e7f8g9", 14, "a", 0]
Out[7648]= "a3b4c5d6e7f8"

The *Mathematica* system posesses the **FileNames** function which allows to obtain the list of files of the given type in the specified directories of file system of the computer. For instance, our **SystemPackages** procedure uses this function for obtaining of *m*-files with the system packages. Meanwhile, in the tools considered earlier for operating with files and directories the constructions of type **"Run[DIR... ...]"** were generally used and that is why. First, in the case of large number of the tested files the considerable volume of *RAM* is required whereas on the basis of the specified construction the list of files is output into a *HD* file. Secondly – the specified construction demands smaller time expenses concerning **FileNames** function; in application, the function call on the main system directory causes erroneous situations, not allowing to receive the complete list of the datafiles contained in it. The last examples of the previous fragment illustrate the given reasons.

For receiving access to the package tools it is necessary that package containing them was uploaded into the current session, and the list determined by the *$ContextPath* variable has to include the context corresponding to the given package. A package can be loaded in any place of the current document by the call **Get["***context'***"]** or by the call **Needs["***context'***"]** to define uploading of a package if the context associated with the package is absent in the list defined by *$Packages* variable. In a case if package begins with **BeginPackage["***Package'***"]**, at its uploading into the lists determined by the variables *$ContextPath* and *$Packages* only context *"Package'"* is placed, providing access to exports of the package and system means.

If a package uses means of other packages, this package should begin with the construction **BeginPackage["***Package'***", {"***Package1'***", ..., "***Package2'***"}]** with indication of the list of the contexts associated with such packages. It allows to include, in addition, in the system lists *$ContextPath* and *$Packages* the demanded contexts. With features of loading of packages the reader can familiarize in [33,50].

A package like procedures allows nesting; at that, in the system all subpackages composing it are distinguished and registered. Moreover, the objects defined both in the main package, and in its subpackages are fully accessible in the current session after loading of the nested package as quite visually illustrates the following a rather simple fragment. Meanwhile, for performance of the aforesaid it is necessary to redefine system *$ContextPath* variable after loading of the nested package, having added all contexts of *subpackages* of the main package to the list determined by the variable:

```
In[2567]:= BeginPackage["Kiev`"]
W::usage = "Help on W."
Begin["`W`"]
W[x_Integer, y_Integer] := x^2 + y^2
End[]
BeginPackage["Kiev1`", {"Kiev`"}]
W1::usage = "Help on W1."
Begin["`W1`"]
W1[x_Integer, y_Integer] := x*y + W[x, y]
End[]
EndPackage[]
Out[2567]= "Kiev`"
Out[2568]= "Help on W."
Out[2569]= "Kiev`W`"
Out[2571]= "Kiev`W`"
Out[2572]= "Kiev1`"
```

Out[2573]= "Help on W1."
Out[2574]= "Kiev1`W1`"
Out[2576]= "Kiev1`W1`"
In[2578]:= **$ContextPath**
Out[2578]= {"Kiev1`", "Kiev`", "System`"}
In[2579]:= **$Packages**
Out[2579]= {"Kiev1`", "Kiev`", "AladjevProcedures`", "GetFEKernelInit`", "StreamingLoader`", "IconizeLoader`", "CloudObjectLoader`", "ResourceLocator`", "PacletManager`", "System`", "Global`"}
In[2580]:= **AladjevProcedures`CNames["Kiev`"]**
Out[2580]= {"W"}
In[2581]:= **AladjevProcedures`CNames["Kiev1`"]**
Out[2581]= {"W1"}
In[2582]:= **{W[42, 74], W1[42, 74]}**
Out[2582]= {7240, 10348}
In[2583]:= **Definition[W]**
Out[2583]= W[Kiev`W`x_Integer, Kiev`W`y_Integer] := Kiev`W`x^2 + Kiev`W`y^2
In[2584]:= **Definition[W1]**
Out[2584]= W1[Kiev`W1`x_Integer, Kiev`W1`y_Integer] := Kiev`W1`x*Kiev`W1`y + W[Kiev`W1`x, Kiev`W1`y]

After evaluation of definition of the user package of any nesting level it can be saved in files of the following three system formats, namely:

F.nb – a file with the standard document *(notebook)* of the *Mathematica* system; moreover, there is a possibility of converting of such files into datafiles of 9 formats, including formats {".cdf", ".m"};

F.m – a datafile with a package of source format of the *Mathematica* system;

F.mx – a file with a package in *DumpSave* format of the *Mathematica* system; this datafile is optimized under the used operational platform *(as a rule,* **Windows, MacOSX, Linux**).

However, because of certain features the use of the nested packages doesn't make a special sense.

As it was already noted, the objects defined in the main package and in its subpackages are accessible in the current session after loading of the main package into it, and redefinition of *$ContextPath* variable by means of addition into the list defined by it, of all contexts which are associated with subpackages of the main package. In this context the **ToContextPath** procedure automatizes the given problem, whose call **ToContextPath[*x*]** provides updating of contents of the current list determined by *$ContextPath* variable by means of adding to its end of all contexts of a *x m*-file containing simple or nested package. Thus, the following fragment represents source code of the **ToContextPath** procedure with a typical example of its application.

In[5127]:= **ToContextPath[x_ /; FileExistsQ[x] && FileExtension[x] == "m"] :=
Module[{c, a = ReadFullFile[x], b = "BeginPackage["}, c = StrSymbParity[a, b, "[", "]"];
Map[If[! StringFreeQ[#, {"`\"]", "`\"}]"}], StringTake[#, {14, -2}]] &, c];
c = ToExpression[Flatten[Map[StringSplit[#, ","] &, c]]];**

c = DeleteDuplicates[Map[If[ListQ[#], #[[1]], #] &, c]];
$ContextPath = DeleteDuplicates[Join[$ContextPath, c]]; $ContextPath

In[5128]:= ToContextPath["C:\\MathToolBox\\Kiev.m"]
Out[5128]= {"AladjevProcedures`", "TemplatingLoader`", "PacletManager`", "System`", "Global`", "Kiev`", "Kiev1`"}

The successful procedure call **ToContextPath[*x*]** returns the updated value for the system *$ContextPath* variable. Taking into account the told, it is recommended, inter alia, to make uploading of a nested *x* package *(m–file)* into the current session by means of the next pair of calls, namely **Get[*x*]; ToContextPath[*x*]**, providing access to all tools of the *x* package.

By the function call **Get["*Name'*"]** the *Mathematica,* first of all, does attempt automatically to upload the version of the *"Name.mx"* file which is optimized for the current platform if such file isn't found, the attempt is done to upload the *"Name.m"* file which contains code portable to other platforms. At that, it is supposed that a *m*–file with some package should be in one of the directories defined by the *Path* option for **Get**. If a directory name is used, attempt to read the *"init.m"* file intended for setting of packages of the directory is done. For providing the mode of automatic uploading of packages the **DeclarePackage** function is used. At the same time for removal of symbols of some context, more precisely, exports of a package with this context, the procedure call **RemovePackage["*Name'*"]** of is used [48,50].

As it was noted earlier, for each exported object of a certain package for it it is necessary to determine an *usage*. As a result of uploading of such package into the current session all its *exports* will be available whereas the local objects, located in a section, in particular *Private*, will be inaccessible in the current session. For testing of a package uploaded into the current session or unloaded package which is located in a *m*–file regarding existence in it of global and local objects the procedure **DefInPackage** can be used, whose the call **DefInPackage[*x*]**, where *x* defines a file or full path to it, or context associated with the package returns the nested list, whose the first element defines the package context, the second element – the list of local variables whereas the third element – the list of global variables of the *x* package. If the *x* argument doesn't define a package or a context, the call **DefInPackage[*x*]** is returned unevaluated. In a case of an unusable *x* context the procedure call returns *$Failed*. The next fragment represents source code of the **DefInPackage** procedure along with the most typical examples of its application.

In[2582]:= BeginPackage["Kherson`"]
Gs::usage = "Help on Gs."
Ga::usage = "Help on Ga."
Vgs::usage = "Help on Vgs."
Begin["`Private`"]
W[x_, y_] := x + y
Vt[y_] := y + Sin[y]
Sv[x_] := x^2 + 27*x + 20
End[]
Begin["`Gs`"]
Gs[x_Integer, y_Integer] := x^2 + y^2
End[]
Begin["`Ga`"]

```
Ga[x_Integer, y_Integer] := x*y + Gs[x, y]
End[]
Begin["`Vgs`"]
Vgs[x_Integer, y_Integer] := x*y
End[]
EndPackage[]
Out[2582]= "Kherson`"
Out[2583]= "Help on Gs."
Out[2584]= "Help on Ga."
Out[2585]= "Help on Vgs."
Out[2586]= "Kherson`Private`"
Out[2590]= "Kherson`Private`"
Out[2591]= "Kherson`Gs`"
Out[2593]= "Kherson`Gs`"
Out[2594]= "Kherson`Ga`"
Out[2595]= "Kherson`Ga`"
Out[2596]= "Kherson`Vgs`"
Out[2598]= "Kherson`Vgs`"
In[2599]:= Map[FunctionQ, {Ga, Gs, Vgs, W, Vt, Sv}]
Out[2599]= {True, True, True, False, False, False}
In[2600]:= BeginPackage["Kherson1`"]
Gs1::usage = "Help on Gs1."
Ga1::usage = "Help on Ga1."
Begin["`Gs1`"]
Gs1[x_Integer, y_Integer] := x^2 + y^2
End[]
Begin["`Ga1`"]
Ga1[x_Integer, y_Integer] := x*y + Gs1[x, y]
End[]
EndPackage[]
In[2640]:= StringDependAllQ[s_String, a_ /; StringQ[a] || ListQ[a] &&
! MemberQ[Map[StringQ, a], False]] :=
DeleteDuplicates[Map[StringFreeQ[s, #] &, If[StringQ[a], {a}, a]]] == {False}
In[2641]:= Map3[StringDependAllQ, "abcnq", {{"a", "n", "q"}, {"a", "x", "y"}}]
Out[2641]= {True, False}
In[2642]:= Map[! StringFreeQ["abcnq", #] &, {{"a", "b", "n", "q"}, {"a", "x", "y"}}]
Out[2642]= {True, True}
In[2778]:= StringDependQ1[x_ /; StringQ[x], y_ /; ListStringQ[y]] :=
Module[{a = x, b, k = 1}, For[k, k <= Length[y], k++, b = Flatten[StringPosition[a, y[[k]]]];
If[b != {}, a = StringTake[a, {b[[2]] + 1, -1}], Return[False]]]; True]
In[2779]:= Map3[StringDependQ1, "11abc222dcd3333xy44z6", {{"11", "222", "333"},
{"11", "22222", "333"}, {"333", "44", "6"}}]
Out[2779]= {True, False, True}
In[2858]:= MfilePackageQ[x_] := If[FileExistsQ[x] && FileExtension[x] == "m",
```

StringDependAllQ[ReadFullFile[x], {"(* ::Package:: *)", "(* ::Input:: *)", "::usage", "BeginPackage[\"", "EndPackage[]"}], False]

In[2859]:= MfilePackageQ["C:\\MathToolBox\\MathToolBox_1.m"]
Out[2859]= True

In[2860]:= Map[MfilePackageQ, {"C:\\MathToolBox\\69.nb", "Av.agn"}]
Out[2860]= {False, False}

In[2915]:= DefInPackage[x_ /; MfilePackageQ[x] || ContextQ[x]] :=
Module[{a, b = {"Begin[\"`", "`\"]"}, c = "BeginPackage[\"", d, p, g, t, k = 1, f, n = x},
Label[Avz];
If[ContextQ[n] && Contexts[n] != {}, f = "$Kr20Art27$";
Save[f, x]; g = FromCharacterCode[17]; t = n <> "Private`";
a = ReadFullFile[f, g]; DeleteFile[f]; d = CNames[n]; p = SubsString[a, {t, g}];
p = DeleteDuplicates[Map[StringCases[#, t ~~ Shortest[__] ~~ "[" <>
t ~~ Shortest[__] ~~ " := "] &, p]];
p = Map[StringTake[#, {StringLength[t] + 1, Flatten[StringPosition[#, "["]][[1]] - 1}] &,
Flatten[p]];
{n, DeleteDuplicates[p], d}, If[FileExistsQ[n], a = ReadFullFile[n];
f = StringTake[SubsString[a, {c, "`\"]"}], {15, -3}][[1]]];
If[MemberQ[$Packages, f], n = f; Goto[Avz]]; b = StringSplit[a, "*)(*"];
d = Select[b, ! StringFreeQ[StringReplace[#, " " -> ""], "::usage="] &];
d = Map[StringTake[#, {1, Flatten[StringPosition[#, "::"]][[1]] - 1}] &, d];
p = DeleteDuplicates[Select[b, StringDependAllQ[#, {"Begin[\"`", "`\"]"}] &]];
p = MinusList[Map[StringTake[#, {9, -4}] &, p], {"Private"}];
t = Flatten[StringSplit[SubsString[a, {"Begin[\"`Private`\"]", "End[]"}], "*)(*"]];
If[t == {}, {f, MinusList[d, p], p}, g = Map[StringReplace[#, " " -> ""] &, t[[2 ;; -1]]];
g = Select[g, ! StringFreeQ[#, ":="] &];
g = Map[StringTake[#, {1, Flatten[StringPosition[#, ":"]][[1]] - 1}] &, g];
g = Map[Quiet[Check[StringTake[#, {1, Flatten[StringPosition[#, "["]][[1]] - 1}], #]] &, g];
{f, g, d}], $Failed]]]

In[2916]:= DefInPackage["Kherson1`"]
Out[2916]= {"Kherson1`", {}, {"Ga1", "Gs1"}}}

In[2917]:= DefInPackage["C:\\MathToolBox\\Kiev.m"]
Out[2917]= {"Kiev`", {}, {"W", "W1"}}

In[2918]:= DefInPackage["C:\\MathToolBox\\Kherson1.m"]
Out[2918]= {"Kherson1`", {"W1", "Vt1", "Sv1"}, {"Gs1", "Ga1", "Vgs1"}}

In[2919]:= DefInPackage["C:\\MathToolBox\\Kherson.m"]
Out[2919]= {"Kherson`", {"Vt", "Sv", "W"}, {"Ga", "Gs", "Vgs"}}

In[2920]:= DefInPackage["Kherson`"]
Out[2920]= {"Kherson`", {"Vt", "Sv", "W"}, {"Ga", "Gs", "Vgs"}}

For simplification of the **DefInPackage** procedure algorithm the expediency of additional definition of two simple enough functions came to light, namely. The **StringDependAllQ** expands the **! StringFreeQ** construction if is required a testing of belonging to a string of all substrings from the given list. The call **StringDependAllQ[s, x]** returns *True* only in the case if a *x* string is substring of a *s* string, or each string from a *x* list belongs to a *s* string.

Whereas the call **StringDependQ1[x, y]** returns *True* if a *x* string contains an occurrence of a chain of the substrings determined by an *y* list of strings and in the order defined by their order in the *y* list, otherwise the *False* is returned. This procedure has a number of important enough appendices.

At last, the function call **MfilePackageQ[x]** returns *True* only in case if a *x* string defines a real file of *m*-format that is the standard package. The previous fragment represents source codes of both functions along with examples of their use. It is supposed, that local symbols of a package are in its *Private* section, that is quite settled agreement. Meanwhile, qua of the local objects of a package act as well those for which usage aren't defined. So, the procedure **DefInPackage** successfully processes the packages with other names of the local sections or without such sections at all, i.e. definitions of *local* symbols are located in package *arbitrarily*. We leave the *analysis* of algorithm of the procedure as a rather useful exercise for the reader.

In a number of cases there is a need of full removal from the current session of the package uploaded into it. Partially the given problem is solved by the standard functions **Clear** and **Remove**, however they don't clear the lists that are determined by variables *$ContextPath*, *$Packages* and by the call **Contexts[]** off the package information. This problem is solved by means of the **RemovePackage** procedure whose the call **RemovePackage[x]** returns *Null*, in addition, completely removing from the current session a package determined by *x* context, including all exports of the *x* package and respectively updating the above system lists. The following fragment represents source code of the **RemovePackage** procedure with the most typical examples of its application.

In[2820]:= RemovePackage[x_ /; ContextQ[x]] := Module[{a = CNames[x],
b = ClearAttributes[{$Packages, Contexts}, Protected]}, Quiet[Map[Remove, a]];
$Packages = Select[$Packages, StringFreeQ[#, x] &];
Contexts[] = Select[Contexts[], StringFreeQ[#, x] &];
SetAttributes[{$Packages, Contexts}, Protected];
$ContextPath = Select[$ContextPath, StringFreeQ[#, x] &];]

In[2821]:= $ContextPath
Out[2821]= {"Kherson1`", "Kherson`", "AladjevProcedures`", "TemplatingLoader`", "PacletManager`", "System`", "Global`"}
In[2822]:= $Packages
Out[2822]= {"Kherson1`", "Kherson`", "AladjevProcedures`", "GetFEKernelInit`", "StreamingLoader`", "CloudObjectLoader`", "ResourceLocator`", "PacletManager`", "System`", "Global`"}
In[2823]:= Contexts[]
Out[2823]= {"AladjevProcedures`", ..., "Kherson`", "Kherson1`", "Kherson1`Ga1`", "Kherson1`Gs1`", "Kherson`Ga`", "Kherson`Gs`", "Kherson`Private`", "Kherson`Vgs`", ...}
In[2824]:= RemovePackage["Kherson1`"]
In[2825]:= $Packages

Out[2825]= {"Kherson`", "AladjevProcedures`", "GetFEKernelInit`", "StreamingLoader`", "IconizeLoader`", "CloudObjectLoader`", "PacletManager`", "System`", "Global`"}
In[2826]:= **Map[PureDefinition, {"Ga1", "Gs1"}]**
Out[2826]= {$Failed, $Failed}

Meanwhile, it should be noted that the packages uploaded into the current session can have the objects of the same name; about that the corresponding messages are output. Qua of an active object acts the object whose context is in the list *$Packages* earlier, that quite visually illustrates the next fragment with the **RemovePackage** procedure usage. In this regard the procedure call **RemovePackage**[*x*] deletes a package with the given *x* context.

In[2587]:= **BeginPackage["Pac1`"]**
W::usage = "Help on W."
Begin["`W`"]
W[x_Integer, y_Integer] := x^2 + y^2
End[]
EndPackage[]
Out[2587]= "Pac1`"
Out[2588]= "Help on W."
Out[2589]= "Pac1`W`"
Out[2591]= "Pac1`W`"
In[2593]:= **BeginPackage["Pac2`"]**
W::usage = "Help on W."
Begin["`W`"]
W[x_Integer, y_Integer] := x^3 + y^3
End[]
EndPackage[]
Out[2593]= "Pac2`"
W::shdw: Symbol W appears in multiple contexts {Pac2`, Pac1`}; definitions...>>
Out[2594]= "Help on W."
Out[2595]= "Pac2`W`"
Out[2597]= "Pac2`W`"
In[2598]:= **$Packages**
Out[2598]= {"Pac2`", "Pac1`", "HTTPClient`", "HTTPClient`OAuth`", ..., "Global`"}
In[2599]:= **W[90, 590]**
Out[2599]= 206108000
In[2600]:= **Map[CNames, {"Pac1`", "Pac2`"}]**
Out[2600]= {{"W"}, {"W"}}
In[2601]:= **RemovePackage["Pac1`"]**
In[2602]:= **Map[CNames, {"Pac1`", "Pac2`"}]**
Out[2602]= {{"W"}, {}}
In[2603]:= **MemberQ[Contexts[], "Pac1`"]**
Out[2603]= False
In[2604]:= **Definition[W]**
Out[2604]= Null
In[2605]:= **Definition[Pac1`W]**
Out[2605]= Pac1`W[Pac1`W`x_Integer, Pac1`W`y_Integer] := Pac1`W`x^2 + Pac1`W`y^2

In[2606]:= **$Packages**
Out[2606]= {"Pac2`", "HTTPClient`", "HTTPClient`OAuth`", "HTTPClient`CURLInfo`", ..., "TemplatingLoader`", "ResourceLocator`", "PacletManager`", "System`", "Global`"}

The procedure **DeletePackage** is a version of the above **RemovePackage** procedure. The procedure call **DeletePackage[*x*]** returns *Null*, i.e. nothing, providing removing from the current session of the package, defined by a *x* context, including all its exported symbols and accordingly updating the system variables *$Packages*, *$ContextPath* and *Contexts*[]. The difference of the procedure **DeletePackage** from the **RemovePackage** procedure is that the symbols defined by the package, removes completely, so that their names are no longer recognized in the current session. The next fragment presents source code of the procedure **DeletePackage** along with accompanying examples.

In[3942]:= **Definition[StrStr]**
Out[3942]= StrStr[x_] := If[StringQ[x], "\"" <> x <> "\"", ToString[x]]
In[3943]:= **$Packages**
Out[3943]= {"AladjevProcedures`", "GetFEKernelInit`", "StreamingLoader`",...}
In[3944]:= **$ContextPath**
Out[3944]= {"AladjevProcedures`", "StreamingLoader`","IconizeLoader`",...}

In[3945]:= **DeletePackage[x_] := Module[{a},**
If[! MemberQ[$Packages, x], $Failed, a = Names[x <> "*"];
Map[ClearAttributes[#, Protected] &, Flatten[{"$Packages", "Contexts", a}]];
Quiet[Map[Remove, a]]; $Packages = Select[$Packages, # != x &];
$ContextPath = Select[$ContextPath, # != x &];
Contexts[] = Select[Contexts[], StringCount[#, x] == 0 &];
Quiet[Map[Remove, Names[x <> "*"]]];
Map[SetAttributes[#, Protected] &, {"$Packages", "Contexts"}];]]

In[3946]:= **DeletePackage["AladjevProcedures`"]**
In[3947]:= **?StrStr**
Information::notfound: Symbol StrStr not found...>>
In[3948]:= **Definition[StrStr]**
Out[3948]= Null
In[3949]:= **MemberQ[$Packages, "AladjevProcedures`"]**
Out[3949]= False
In[3950]:= **MemberQ[$ContextPath, "AladjevProcedures`"]**
Out[3950]= False

Natural addition to the **DeletePackage** and **RemovePackage** procedures is the procedure **DelOfPackage** providing removal from the current session of the given tools of a loaded package. Its call **DelOfPackage[*x*, *y*]** returns the *y* list of tools names of a package given by its *x* context which have been removed from the current session. While the procedure call **DelOfPackage[*x*, *y*, *z*]** with the third optional *z* argument – a *mx*–file – returns 2–element list whose the first element defines *mx*–file *z*, while the second element defines the *y* list of tools of a *x* package that have been removed from the current session and have been saved in *mx*–file *z*. At that, only tools of *y* which are contained in *x* package will be removed. The fragment below represents source code of the **DelOfPackage** procedure along with typical examples of its application.

In[4011]:= **DelOfPackage[x_ /; ContextQ[x], y_ /; SymbolQ[y] || (ListQ[y] &&**
AllTrue[Map[SymbolQ, y], TrueQ]), z___] :=
Module[{a, b, c}, If[! MemberQ[$Packages, x], $Failed,
If[Set[b, Intersection[Names[x <> "*"], a = Map[ToString, Flatten[{y}]]]] == {}, $Failed,
If[{z} != {} && StringQ[z] && SuffPref[z, ".mx", 2], ToExpression["DumpSave[" <>
ToString1[z] <> "," <> ToString[b] <> "]"]; c = {z, b}, c = b];
ClearAttributes[b, Protected]; Map[Remove, b]; c]]]

In[4012]:= **DelOfPackage["AladjevProcedures`", {Mapp, Map1}, "Map.mx"]**
Out[4012]= {"Map.mx", {"Map1", "Mapp"}}
In[4013]:= **Definition[Mapp]**
Out[4013]= Null
In[4014]:= **Context[Mapp]**
Out[4014]= "Global`"
In[4015]:= **Get["Map.mx"]**
Mapp::shdw: Symbol Mapp appears in multiple contexts... >>
In[4016]:= **Definition[Mapp]**
Out[4016]= Definition[AladjevProcedures`Mapp]
In[4017]:= **Context[Mapp]**
Out[4017]= "AladjevProcedures`"
In[4018]:= **DelOfPackage["AladjevProcedures`", {Map18, Map19, Map20}]**
Out[4018]= {"Map18", "Map19", "Map20"}

A convenient enough way of packages saving is represented by the **DumpSave** function, whose call **DumpSave[F, x]** returns the *x* context of a package saved in a binary *F* datafile in the format optimized for its subsequent uploading into the *Mathematica* system. A package saved in the described way is uploaded into the current session by means of the call **Get[F]** with automatical activation of all definitions contained in it; at that, only those datafiles are correctly uploaded which were saved on the same computing platform by the **DumpSave** function of the *Mathematica* system.

Concerning the files of *mx*-format with the user packages an interesting and useful problem of definition of the context and objects, whose definitions are in a datafile of the given type, without its uploading into the current session arises. The fragment below represents source code of the **ContMxFile** procedure with typical examples of its use, solving this problem.

In[2664]:= **DumpSave["MathToolBox.mx", "AladjevProcedures`"]**
Out[2664]= {"AladjevProcedures`"}
In[2665]:= **DumpSave["Kherson1.mx", "Kherson1`"]**
Out[2665]= {"Kherson1`"}
In[2666]:= **DumpSave["Kiev1.mx", "Kiev1`"]**
Out[2666]= {"Kiev1`"}
In[2667]:= **ContMxFile[x_ /; FileExistsQ[x] && FileExtension[x] == "mx", y___] :=**
Module[{a = ReadFullFile[x], b = "CONT", c = "ENDCONT", d = "`", h, t},
h = Flatten[StringPosition[a, {b, c}]][[1 ;; 4]];

```
h = Quiet[Check[StringReplace[StringTake[a, {h[[2]] + 1, h[[3]] - 2}], "\.10" -> ""],
Return[{}]]];
h = StringJoin[Select[Characters[h], SymbolQ[#] &]] <> d;
If[h == "", {}, If[MemberQ[$Packages, h] && {y} != {}, {h, CNames[h]},
If[! MemberQ[$Packages, h] && {y} != {}, Quiet[Get[x]];
{{h, CNames[h]}, RemovePackage[h]}[[1]], t = SubsString[a, {h, "`"}];
t = Select[t, ! MemberQ[ToCharacterCode[#], 0] &];
{h, Sort[DeleteDuplicates[Map[StringReplace[#, {h -> "", "`" -> ""}] &, t]]]}]]]]
In[2668]:= ContMxFile["Kiev1.mx"]
Out[2668]= {"Kiev1`", {"W", "W1", "W2", "W3"}}
In[2669]:= ContMxFile["Kiev1.mx", 90]
Out[2669]= {"Kiev1`", {"W", "W1"}}
In[2670]:= ContMxFile["E:\\MathToolBox\\MathToolBox.mx"]
Out[2670]= {"AladjevProcedures`", {"ActBFMuserQ", "ActRemObj", "Args1", ...}}
In[2671]:= Length[%[[2]]]
Out[2671]= 68
In[2672]:= ContMxFile["Tallinn.mx"]
Out[2672]= {"Grodno`", {"Gs", "Gs1", "Vgs", "Vgs1"}}
```

The procedure call **ContMxFile[x]** returns the nested list whose first element determines the context associated with the package contained in a *x* *mx*-datafile while the second element determines the list of names in the string format of all objects of this package irrespectively from existence for them of usage, i.e. of both local, and global objects. While the procedure call **ContMxFile[x, y]**, where *y* argument – *an arbitrary expression* – returns the nested list of similar structure, but with that difference that its second element defines the list of names of the objects of this package which are supplied with usage, i.e. only of global objects. Withal, it should be noted the **ContMxFile** procedure presented in the *previous* fragment is intended for use with the *mx*-files created on platform *Windows XP/7 Professional*, its use for other *OS* platforms can demand the appropriate adaptation. The reason of it consists in that the algorithm of the **ContMxFile** procedure is based on an analysis of structure of *mx*-files that depends on platform used at creation of such files. The following procedure **ContMxFile1** is a rather useful modification of the **ContMxFile** procedure which also uses an analysis of the structure of *mx*-files that depends on platform used at creation of such files. The procedure call **ContMxFile1[x]** returns the nested list whose the first element determines the context associated with the package contained in a *x* *mx*-file whereas the second element defines the list of names in string format of all objects of the package irrespectively from existence for them usage, i.e. local and global objects. Furthermore, similarly to the previous **ContMxFile** procedure the returned names determine objects whose definition returned by the function call **Definition** contains the context. In addition, is supposed that a *x* file is recognized by the **FileExistsQ** function. At that, the procedure algorithm essentially uses a function whose call **StrAllSymbNumQ[x]** returns *True* if a *x* string contains only symbols and/or integers, and *False* otherwise. The fragment below represents source codes of both means along with examples of their typical application.

```
In[2769]:= ContMxFile1[x_ /; FileExistsQ[x] && FileExtension[x] == "mx"] :=
```

Module[{a = ReadFullFile[x], b = "CONT", c = "ENDCONT", d, h, t},
h = Flatten[StringPosition[a, {b, c}]][[1 ;; 4]];
h = Quiet[Check[StringReplace[StringTake[a, {h[[2]] + 1, h[[3]] - 2}], "\.10" -> ""],
Return[{}]]];
h = StringJoin[Select[Characters[h], SymbolQ[#] &]] <> "`";
If[h == "", {}, d = StringPosition[a, h][[2 ;; -1]]; d = Map[StringTrim[#, "`"] &,
Map[SubStrToSymb[a, #[[2]] + 1, "`", 1] &, d]];
{h, Sort[Select[d, StrAllSymbNumQ[#] &]]}]]

In[2770]:= **ContMxFile1["C:\\Users\\Mathematica\\MathToolBox.mx"]**
Out[2770]= {"AladjevProcedures`", {"ActBFMuserQ", "ActCsProcFunc", "ActRemObj",
"ActUcontexts", "AllCurrentNb", ..., "WhichN", "XOR1", "$ProcName", "$TypeProc"}}
In[2771]:= **Length[%[[2]]]**
Out[2771]= 68

In[2772]:= **StrAllSymbNumQ[x_ /; StringQ[x]] := ! MemberQ[Map[SymbolQ[#] | |
Quiet[IntegerQ[ToExpression[#]]] &, Characters[x]], False]**
In[2773]:= **Map[StrAllSymbNumQ, {"PosListTest1", "BitGet`"}]**
Out[2773]= {True, False}

The procedures **ContMxFile** and **ContMxFile1** adjoin the following procedure, whose call **PackageMxCont[*x*]** returns the context of a *x mx*-file; the call **PackageMxCont[*x, y*]** thru the second optional *y* argument – an undefinite variable – returns the nested list whose the first element defines the context of *x*, whereas the second element determines the list of global symbols of the package which are contained in the *x mx*-file [28,33,48]. On *mx*-files without context or local/global symbols the procedure call **PackageMxCont[*x*]** returns $*Failed* or the empty list, i.e. {}, accordingly, for example:

In[2727]:= **PackageMxCont[x_ /; FileExistsQ[x] && FileExtension[x] == "mx", y___] :=
Module[{a, b, c, d}, If[IsPackageQ[x] === $Failed, $Failed, a = ContextsInFiles[x];
If[a === $Failed, $Failed, If[MemberQ[$Packages, a], d = 75, d = 70];
c = If[StringFreeQ[AladjevProcedures`OSplatform[][[1]], " 7 "],
AladjevProcedures`ContMxFile[x, 90], AladjevProcedures`ContMxW7[x]];
If[c == {} | | c[[2]] == {}, b = {}, b = a];
If[{y} != {} && ! AladjevProcedures`HowAct[y] && ! SameQ[a, {}], y = c, Null];
If[d == 70, AladjevProcedures`RemovePackage[a], Null]; b]]]**
In[2728]:= **{PackageMxCont["e:\\MathToolBox\\MathToolBox.mx", s], s}**
Out[2728]= {"AladjevProcedures`", {"AcNb", "ActBFM", "ActBFMuserQ", "ActCsProcFunc",
"ActRemObj", "ActUcontexts", "AddMxFile", "Aobj1", "Args",...}}
In[2729]:= **Length[%[[2]][[2]]]**
Out[2729]= 68
In[2730]:= **{PackageMxCont["PureDefinition.mx", s6], s6}**
Out[2730]= {$Failed, s6}

This procedure also is oriented onto the platform *Windows XP Professional*, in general, but on the platform *Windows 7 Professional* correctly returns the list of global symbols. So, for platform *Windows 7 Professional* the algorithm of the previous **ContMxFile** procedure is modified in the corresponding manner, taking into account the internal structure of the *mx*-files created on the specified platform. The algorithm is realized by procedure **ContMxW7**, whose call **ContMxW7[*x*]** returns the nested list whose the first element defines the context connected with the package contained in a *x mx*-file while the second element determines the list of names in the string format of all global objects of the package whose definitions contains a context ascribed to the package. Whereas on a *mx*-file without context the call returns $*Failed*. At that, is supposed that a *x* file is recognized by the **FileExistsQ** function. The next fragment represents source code of the **ContMxW7** procedure along with typical examples of its application.

In[2633]:= **ContMxW7[x_ /; FileExistsQ[x] && FileExtension[x] == "mx"] :=**
Module[{a = FromCharacterCode[Select[BinaryReadList[x], # != 0 &]], b = "CONT",
c = "ENDCONT", d = "`", h, t, g = {}, k, f, n},
h = StringPosition[a, {b, c}][[1 ;; 2]]; If[h[[1]] - h[[2]] == {-3, 0}, $Failed,
t = StringTrim[StringTake[a, {h[[1]][[2]] + 2, h[[2]][[1]] - 2}]];
a = StringTake[a, {h[[2]][[2]] + 1, -1}]; f = StringPosition[a, t];
Map[{c = "", For[k = #[[2]] + 1, k <= StringLength[a], k++, n = StringTake[a, {k, k}];
If[n == d, Break[], c = c <> n]];
If[StringFreeQ[c, StringTake[t, {1, -2}]], AppendTo[g, c], Null]} &, f];
{t, Select[Sort[g], StrAllSymbNumQ[#] &]}]]

In[2634]:= **ContMxW7["C:/users/aladjev/mathem/MathToolBox.mx"]**
Out[2634]= {"AladjevProcedures`", {"ActBFMuserQ", "ActRemObj", ..., "$TypeProc"}}
In[2635]:= **Length[%[[2]]]**
Out[2635]= 68
In[2636]:= **ContMxW7["C:\\users\\mathematica\\PureDefinition.mx"]**
Out[2636]= $Failed

Unlike the above procedures **ContMxFile** and **ContMxFile1**, the **ContMxFile2** procedure is based on another algorithm whose essence is as follows. First of all, the existence in a *x mx*-file of a package is checked; at its absence $*Failed* is returned. Then uploading in the current session of a package containing in the *x mx*-file is checked. At positive result the required result without loading of a *x* package is returned, otherwise the required result with loading of a package is returned. In both cases the call **ContMxFile2[*x*]** returns the two–element list, whose first element determines a package context whereas the second – the list of names in the string format of tools, contained in the package. At that, this procedure essentially uses the **IsPackageQ** procedure.

In[2878]:= **ContMxFile2[x_ /; FileExistsQ[x] && FileExtension[x] == "mx"]:=**
Module[{a = $Packages, b = "AvzAgnVsvArtKr`", c, h, g, d = Unique["ag"]},
h = ToString[d]; g = IsPackageQ[x, d];
If[g === $Failed, $Failed, If[g === True, {d, AladjevProcedures`CNames[d],
ToExpression["Remove[" <> h <> "]"]},
ToExpression["InputForm[BeginPackage[\"AvzAgnVsvArtKr`\"];
EndPackage[]]"]; Off[General::shdw]; Get[x]; c = $Packages[[1]];
b = {c, AladjevProcedures`CNames[c]};

AladjevProcedures`RemovePackage[c]; On[General::shdw]; b]]]

In[2879]:= ContMxFile2["c:\\users\\mathematica\\MathToolBox.mx"]
Out[2879]= {"AladjevProcedures`", {"AcNb", "ActBFM", ..., "$UserContexts"}, Null}
In[2880]:= Length[%[[2]]]
Out[2880]= 1142

In[2918]:= IsPackageQ[x_ /; FileExistsQ[x] && FileExtension[x] == "mx", y___] :=
Module[{a = ReadFullFile[x], b = "CONT", c = "ENDCONT", d, g = $Packages},
If[! StringContainsQ[a, "CONT" ~~ __ ~~ "ENDCONT"], $Failed,
d = StringPosition[a, {b, c}][[1 ;; 2]]; d = StringTake[a, {d[[1]][[2]] + 1, d[[2]][[1]] - 1}];
d = Select[Map[If[! StringFreeQ[d, #], #, Null] &, g], ! SameQ[#, Null] &];
If[{y} != {} && ! HowAct[y], y = If[d == {}, {}, d[[1]]], Null]; If[d != {}, True, False]]]

In[2919]:= {IsPackageQ["c:\\users/mathematica/MathToolBox.mx", y], y}
Out[2919]= {True, "AladjevProcedures`"}
In[2920]:= IsPackageQ["PureDefinition.mx"]
Out[2920]= $Failed
In[2921]:= IsPackageQ["c:\\users/aladjev\\mathematica\\Tallinn.mx"]
Out[2921]= False

The **IsPackageQ** procedure is intended for testing of any *mx*-file regarding existence of the user's package in it along with upload of such package into the current session. The call of the **IsPackageQ**[*x*] procedure returns *$Failed* if the *mx*-file doesn't contain a package, *True* if a package that is in the *x mx*-file is uploaded into the current session, and *False* otherwise. Moreover, the procedure call **IsPackageQ**[*x*, *y*] through the second optional *y* argument – an undefinite variable – returns the context associated with the package uploaded into the current session. In addition, is supposed that a *x* file is recognized by the testing function **FileExistsQ**, otherwise the procedure call is returned unevaluated. The previous fragment represents source codes of both procedures **ContMxFile2** and **IsPackageQ** with the typical examples of their application.

Meanwhile, the **DumpSave** function has one rather essential shortcoming, namely: it saves contexts that are only formally contexts, i.e. correspond to them only by the format. In this regard the **DumpSaveP** function is more preferable, whose call **DumpSaveP**[*f*, *x*] provides saving in a *f* file of the package with a *x* context on condition that this package contains the global symbols; otherwise the **DumpSaveP** function call returns *$Failed*. The next fragment represents source code of the function and examples of its application.

In[3342]:= PackageQ[x_ /; ContextQ[x]] := If[CNames[x] != {}, True, False]

In[3343]:= DumpSaveP[f_ /; StringQ[f], x_ /; ContextQ[x]] :=
If[PackageQ[x], DumpSave[f, x], $Failed]

In[3344]:= DumpSave["MathToolBox.mx", "AladjevProcedures`"]
Out[3344]= {"AladjevProcedures`"}
In[3345]:= RemovePackage["AladjevProcedures`"]
In[3346]:= Map[Definition, {ProcQ, RemovePackage, Mapp, Map14, Map6, Definition2, StrStr, ContextQ, CNames, ToString1}]
Out[3346]= {Null, Null, Null, Null, Null, Null, Null, Null, Null, Null}

```
In[3347]:= Quiet[Get["MathToolBox.mx"]]
In[3348]:= Definition[StrStr]
Out[3348]= StrStr[x_] := If[StringQ[x], "\"" <> x <> "\"", ToString[x]]
In[3349]:= PackageQ["AvzAgnVsvArtKr`"]
Out[3349]= False
In[3350]:= DumpSave["AvzAgnVsvArtKr.mx", "AvzAgnVsvArtKr`"]
Out[3350]= {"AvzAgnVsvArtKr`"}
In[3351]:= DumpSaveP["AvzAgnVsvArtKr.mx", "AvzAgnVsvArtKr`"]
Out[3351]= $Failed
```

The **DumpSaveP** function qua of the test for an admissibility of the second argument uses a logical function whose call **PackageQ[x]** returns *True* if *x* – a package containing the global symbols, and *False* otherwise. Naturally, a package without global symbols of any interest doesn't represent. Really, according to the system agreements the package has to determine global symbols without which that package can't be considered as such. In this regard the function call **DumpSaveP[f, x]** where *x* isn't a package, returns *$Failed*, allowing to process situations of this type very simply programmatically.

So, despite a formal correctness of definition of packages without the global symbols or *mx*-files without context, a testing of actual packages which are loaded into the current session is necessary what a simple function does, whose call **Packages[]** returns the list of contexts of the actual packages that are loaded into the current session [33,48,50]. The section below considers some additional means for manipulating with the user packages.

8.3. Additional tools for manipulating with the user packages in the *Mathematica* software

Tools of the *Mathematica* for operating with datafiles can be subdivided into two groups conditionally: the tools supporting the work with files which are automatically recognized at the address to them, and the tools supporting the work with files as a whole. This theme is quite extensive and is in more detail considered in [30-33,50,52,66], here some additional tools of work with the files containing the user's packages will be considered.

Since tools of access to datafiles of formats, even automatically recognized by *Mathematica*, don't solve a number of important enough problems, the user is compelled to program own means on the basis of standard tools and perhaps with use of own means. Qua of an useful enough example we will represent the procedure whose call **DefFromPackage[x]** returns 3-element list, whose first element is definition in string format of a *x* symbol whose context is different from *{"Global`", "System`"}*, the second element defines its usage while the third element defines attributes of the symbol. At that, on the symbols associated with 2 specified contexts, the procedure call returns only list of their attributes. The next fragment represents source code of the **DefFromPackage** procedure with examples of its application.

```
In[2742]:= DefFromPackage[x_ /; SymbolQ[x]] :=
Module[{a = Context[x], b = "", c = "", p, d = ToString[x], k = 1, h},
If[MemberQ[{"Global`", "System`"}, a], Return[Attributes[x]], h = a <> d;
ToExpression["Save[" <> ToString1[d] <> "," <> ToString1[h] <> "]"]];
For[k, k < Infinity, k++, c = Read[d, String]; If[c === " ", Break[], b = b <> c]];
```

```
p = StringReplace[RedSymbStr[b, " ", " "], h <> "`" -> ""];
{c, k, b} = {"", 1, ""}; For[k, k < Infinity, k++, c = Read[d, String];
If[c === " " || c === EndOfFile, Break[],
b = b <> If[StringTake[c, {-1, -1}] == "\\", StringTake[c, {1, -2}], c]]];
DeleteFile[Close[d]]; {p, StringReplace[b, " /: " <> d -> ""], Attributes[x]}]
In[2743]:= DefFromPackage[StrStr]
Out[2743]= {StrStr[x_] := If[StringQ[x], StringJoin["\"", x, "\""], ToString[x]], StrStr::usage =
"The call StrStr[x] returns an expression x in string format if x is different from string;
otherwise, the double string obtained from an expression x is returned.", {}}
In[2744]:= DefFromPackage[AvzAgn]
Out[2744]= {}
In[2745]:= SetAttributes[Ian, {Listable, Protected}]; DefFromPackage[Ian]
Out[2745]= {Listable, Protected}
In[2746]:= DefFromPackage[Cos]
Out[2746]= {Listable, NumericFunction, Protected}
```

The **DefFromPackage** procedure serves for obtaining of full information on *x* symbol whose definition is located in the user package loaded into the current session. Unlike the standard functions **FilePrint** and **Definition** this procedure, first, doesn't print, but returns specified information completely available for subsequent processing, and, secondly, this information is returned in an optimum format. At that, in a number of cases the output of definition of a symbol which is located in an active package by the standard means is accompanied with a context associated with the package which not only complicates its viewing, but also its the subsequent processing. The result of the **DefFromPackage** call also obviates this problem. The algorithm realized by the procedure is based on analysis of structure of a file received in result of saving of a "*y'x*" context, where *x* – a symbol at the call **DefFromPackage[x]** and "*y'*" – a context, associated with the loaded package containing the definition of *x* symbol. In more detail this algorithm realized by the **DefFromPackage** procedure is visible from its source code.

As the second example developing the algorithm of the previous procedure in the light of application of functions of access it is possible to represent an useful **FullCalls** procedure whose the call **FullCalls[x]** returns the list whose 1st element is the context associated with a package uploaded into the current session whereas its other elements – the symbols of this package which are used by the user procedure or function *x*, or nested list of sublists of this type at using by the *x* of symbols *(names of procedures or functions)* from several packages. The source code of the **FullCalls** procedure along with typical examples of its use are presented in the following fragment.

```
In[3435]:= FullCalls[x_ /; ProcQ[x] || FunctionQ[x]] :=
Module[{a = {}, b, d, c = "::usage = ", k = 1}, Save[b = ToString[x], x];
For[k, k < Infinity, k++, d = Read[b, String];
If[d === EndOfFile, Break[], If[StringFreeQ[d, c], Continue[], AppendTo[a,
StringSplit[StringTake[d, {1, Flatten[StringPosition[d, c]][[1]] - 1}], " /: "][[1]]]]]];
a = Select[a, SymbolQ[#] &]; DeleteFile[Close[b]];
a = Map[{#, Context[#]} &, DeleteDuplicates[a]];
```

a = If[Length[a] == 1, a, Map[DeleteDuplicates, Map[Flatten, Gather[a, #1[[2]] === #2[[2]] &]]]]; {d, k} = {{}, 1};
While[k <= Length[a], b = Select[a[[k]], ContextQ[#] &];
c = Select[a[[k]], ! ContextQ[#] &]; AppendTo[d, Flatten[{b, Sort[c]}]]; k++];
d = MinusList[If[Length[d] == 1, Flatten[d], d], {ToString[x]}]; If[d == {Context[x]}, {}, d]]

In[3436]:= FullCalls[StrStr]

Out[3436]= {}

In[3437]:= G[x_] := StrStr[x] <> "RansIan59090"; FullCalls[G]

Out[3437]= {"AladjevProcedures`", "StrStr"}

In[3438]:= F[x_ /; IntegerQ[x], y_ /; IntegerQ[y]] := x^2 + y^2; FullCalls[F]

Out[3438]= {}

In[3439]:= FullCalls[ProcQ]

Out[3439]= {"AladjevProcedures`", "Attributes1", "BlockFuncModQ", "ClearAllAttributes", "Contexts1", "Definition2", "HeadPF", "HowAct", "ListStrToStr", "Map3", "Mapp", "MinusList", "ProtectedQ", "PureDefinition", "StrDelEnds", "SuffPref", "SymbolQ", "SysFuncQ", "SystemQ", "ToString1", "UnevaluatedQ"}

In[3440]:= FullCalls[Attribs]

Out[3440]= {"AladjevProcedures`", "Adrive", "Attributes1", "CopyDir", "CopyFileToDir", "DirQ", "FileExistsQ1", "HowAct", "LoadExtProg", "Map3", "PathToFileQ", "ProtectedQ", "SearchFile", "StandPath", "StrDelEnds", "StrStr", "SuffPref", "SymbolQ", "ToString1"}

In[3441]:= GS[x_ /; RuleQ[x], y_ /; StringQ[y]] := ArtKr[StringLength[StringReplace[y, x]], 590] + Vgs[StringLength[y], 90]; FullCalls[GS]

Out[3441]= {{"AladjevProcedures`", "RuleQ"}, {"Kherson`", "ArtKr", "Vgs"}}

In[3442]:= GS["Avz" -> "2016", "AgnAvzVsvArtKr"]

Out[3442]= 7604

Thus, the procedure call **FullCalls[x]** provides possibility of testing of the user procedure or function, different from standard means, regarding use by it of means whose definitions are in packages loaded into the current session. In development of the procedure the **FullCalls1** can be offered whose source code with rather typical examples of its use are represented by the following fragment.

In[2661]:= FullCalls1[x_ /; ProcQ[x] || FunctionQ[x]] :=
Module[{a = {}, b, c = "", d, k = 1, n, p}, Save[b = ToString[x], {x, c}];
For[k, k < Infinity, k++, d = Read[b, String];
If[d === EndOfFile, Break[], If[d != " ", c = c <> d,
If[n = Flatten[StringPosition[c, " := "]]; n != {},
If[Quiet[HeadingQ[p = StringTake[c, {1, n[[1]] - 1}]]],
AppendTo[a, Quiet[HeadName[StringTake[c, {1, n[[1]] - 1}]]]]]; c = ""]]];
DeleteFile[Close[b]]; {b = FullCalls[x], Select[MinusList[a, {ToString[x]}],
! MemberQ[Flatten[b], #] &]}]

In[2662]:= ArtKr[x_Integer, y_Integer] := Module[{}, N[Sqrt[x^2 + y^2]]];
Vgs[x_Integer, y_Integer] := N[Sin[x] + Cos[y]]; GS[x_ /; RuleQ[x], y_ /; StringQ[y]] :=
ArtKr[StringLength[StringReplace[y, x]], 90] + Vgs[StringLength[y], 590];

In[2663]:= FullCalls1[GS]

Out[2663]= {{"AladjevProcedures`", "RuleQ"}, {"ArtKr", "ArtKr", "Vgs"}}
In[2664]:= **FullCalls1[StrStr]**
Out[2664]= {{}, {}}
In[2665]:= **FullCalls1[ProcQ]**
Out[2665]= {{"AladjevProcedures`", "Attributes1", "BlockFuncModQ", "ClearAllAttributes", "Contexts1", "Definition2", "HeadPF", "HowAct", "ListStrToStr", "Map3", "Mapp", "MinusList", "ProtectedQ", "PureDefinition", "Sequences", "StrDelEnds", "SuffPref", "SymbolQ", "SysFuncQ", "SystemQ", "ToString1", "UnevaluatedQ"}, {}}

The **FullCalls1** procedure tests a procedure/function x regarding use by it of both package tools, and the other tools, other than the standard tools. In particular, the call **FullCalls1[x]** returns the nested list whose the first element corresponds to result of the call **FullCalls[x]** whereas the second element defines the list of names of the means used by x, excluding the means belonging to the loaded user packages. Meanwhile, it must be kept in mind that both procedures process only the means used by x that are determined by the mechanism of the delayed calculations. Spreading of these procedures on mechanism of *immediate* calculations of any special difficulties doesn't cause, and such extension can represent an useful enough exercitation to the interested reader. We proceeded from the fact that the definition of both the procedures, and the functions on a number of fairly significant reasons it is advisable to determine by the mechanism of *delayed* calculations. In addition, both procedures **FullCalls** and **FullCalls1** are quite useful at programming a number of appendices. Right there quite pertinently to note, that the **Save** function used in realization of the procedures **FullCalls** and **FullCalls1** can be quite useful for organization of libraries of the user tools. Indeed, the call **Save[f, {a, b, ...}]** saves in a f datafile of the text format all definitions not only of objects with {a, b, c, ...} names, but also all definitions of means with which the specified objects are connected at all levels of their structural tree. At the same time, the function call writes into datafile in the *Append* mode, leaving the datafile closed. Moreover, the created file is easily edited by simple *text editors*, allowing rather simply to create software for its editing *(addition of objects, deleting of objects, replacement of objects, etc.)*. For loading of similar library into the current session the call **Get[f]** is a quite sufficient, having provided access to all tools whose definitions were earlier saved in the f file. The given question is considered rather in details in [30-33,50].

In a number of cases there is a necessity for uploading into the current session of the system *Mathematica* not entirely of a package, but only separate tools contained in it, for example, of a procedure or function, or their list. In the fragment below the procedure is represented, whose call **ExtrOfMfile[x, y]** returns *Null*, i.e. nothing, uploading in the current session the definitions only of those tools which are determined by an y argument and are located in a x datafile of *m*-format. In addition, in case of existence in the *m*-file of several means of the same name, the last is uploaded into the current session. While the call **ExtrOfMfile[x, y, z]** with the 3rd optional z argument – *an undefinite variable* – in addition through z returns the list of definitions of y means which are located in the x *m*-file. In case of absence in the x *m*-file of y tools the procedure call returns *$Failed*. The fragment below represents source code of the **ExtrOfMfile** procedure with examples of its application.

In[2572]:= **ExtrOfMfile[f_ /; FileExistsQ[f] && FileExtension[f] == "m",**
 s_ /; StringQ[s] || ListQ[s], z___] :=

```
Module[{Vsv, p = {}, v, m}, m = ReadFullFile[f];
If[StringFreeQ[m, Map["(*Begin[\"`" <> # <> "`\"]*)" &, Map[ToString, s]]], $Failed,
Vsv[x_, y_] := Module[{a = m, b = FromCharacterCode[17], c = FromCharacterCode[24],
d = "(*Begin[\"`" <> y <> "`\"]*)", h = "(*End[]*)", g = {}, t}, a = StringReplace[a, h -> c];
If[StringFreeQ[a, d], $Failed, While[! StringFreeQ[a, d], a = StringReplace[a, d -> b, 1];
t = StringTake[SubStrSymbolParity1[a, b, c][[1]], {4, -4}];
t = StringReplace[t, {"(*" -> "", "*)" -> ""}];
AppendTo[g, t]; a = StringReplace[a, b -> "", 1]; Continue[]];
{g, ToExpression[g[[-1]]]}]];
If[StringQ[s], v = Quiet[Check[Vsv[f, s][[1]], $Failed]],
Map[{v = Quiet[Check[Vsv[f, #][[1]], $Failed]], AppendTo[p, v]} &, Map[ToString, s]]];
If[{z} != {} && ! HowAct[z], z = If[StringQ[s], v, p]];]]
```

In[2573]:= **ExtrOfMfile["C:\\MathToolBox\\Kiev.m", "W"]**
In[2574]:= **ExtrOfMfile["C:\\MathToolBox\\Kiev.m", "W", w]**
In[2575]:= **{W[74, 69, 2016], w}**
Out[2575]= {8194273829, {"W[x_Integer, y_Integer] := x^2 + y^2", "W[x_Integer, y_Integer, z_Integer] := x^2 + y^2 + z^2", "W[x_Integer, y_Integer, z_Integer] := x^3 + y^3 + z^3"}}
In[2576]:= **ExtrOfMfile["C:/MathToolBox/Kiev.m", {"W", "W1", "GS"}, w2]**
In[2576]:= **w2**
Out[2576]= {{"W[x_Integer, y_Integer] := x^2 + y^2", "W[x_Integer, y_Integer, z_Integer] := x^2 + y^2 + z^2", "W[x_Integer, y_Integer, z_Integer] := x^3 + y^3 + z^3"}, {"W1[x_Integer, y_Integer] := x*y + W[x, y]"}, $Failed}
In[2577]:= **ExtrOfMfile["C:/Temp/Kiev.m", {"AgnVsvArtKr", "Avz"}]**
Out[2577]= $Failed
In[2578]:= **Remove[StrStr]**
In[2578]:= **Definition[StrStr]**
Out[2578]= Null
In[2579]:= **{ExtrOfMfile["c:/avz/mathematica/MathToolBox.m", "StrStr", g70], g70}**
Out[2579]= {Null, {"StrStr[x_] := If[StringQ[x], \"\\\"\"<>x<>\"\\\"\", ToString[x]]"}}
In[2580]:= **Definition[StrStr]**
Out[2580]= StrStr[x_] := If[StringQ[x], "\"" <> x <> "\"", ToString[x]]

It should be noted that this procedure can be quite useful in case of need of recovery in the current session of the damaged means without uploading of the user packages containing their definitions.

To certain extent, to the previous procedure the following procedure adjoins whose the call **ExtrDefFromM[x, y]** in tabular form returns an usage and definition of a *y* means contained in a *x m*-file with the user package. In case of absence of one of these components of a *y* tool a message *"Usage for y is absent"* or *"Definition for y is absent"* is returned accordingly; while in the absence of the both components $*Failed* is returned. At last, the call **ExtrDefFromM[x, y, z]** with the third optional *z* argument – *an arbitrary expression* – additionally in the current session the usage and definition of *y* tool are evaluated. We will note that procedure doesn't demand loading of a *x* package into the current session, allowing in it selectively to activate the means of the user package. The following fragment represents source code of procedure **ExtrDefFromM** along with examples of its application.

In[4290]:= **ExtrDefFromM**[x_ /; SymbolQ[x], y_ /; FileExistsQ[y] &&
FileExtension[y] == "m", z___] :=
Module[{a = ReadString[y], b = "(*Begin[\"`$`\"]*)", c = "(*End[]*)", d = ToString[x],
h = "(*$::usage=", c1, h1},
c = StringCases[a, Shortest[StringReplace[b, "$" -> d] ~~ __ ~~ c]];
h = StringCases[a, Shortest[StringReplace[h, "$" -> d] ~~ __ ~~ "*)"]];
h1 = If[h == {}, "Usage for " <> d <> " is absent", StringReplace[h[[1]],
{"(*" -> "", "*)" -> "", d <> "::usage=" -> ""}]];
c1 = If[c == {}, "Definition for " <> d <> " is absent", c = StringReplace[c[[1]],
{"\r\n" -> "", "(*" -> "", "*)" -> ""}]];
c = StringTake[c, {StringLength[d] + 12, -6}]];
If[h == {} && c == {}, $Failed, If[{z} != {}, Map[ToExpression,
d <> "::usage=" <> h1, c}], Null]; Table[{ToExpression[h1], c1}, 1]]]

In[4291]:= **ExtrDefFromM**[Ga, "C:\\MathToolBox\\Grodno.m", g70]
Out[3291]= {{"Help on Ga.", "Ga[x_Integer, y_Integer] := x*y + Gs[x, y]"}}
In[4292]:= **Information**[Ga]
"Help on Ga."
Ga[x_Integer, y_Integer] := x*y + Gs[x, y]
In[4293]:= **ExtrDefFromM**[ransian, "C:/MathtoolBox/MathtoolBox.m", g9]
Out[4293]= $Failed

The **DefFromM** procedure directly adjoines to the **ExtrOfMfile** procedure, whose the call **DefFromM**[x, y] returns definition of an object with an y name that is located in a x file of m-format with package while the procedure call **DefFromM**[x, y, z], where z – *an arbitrary expression*, in addition evaluates that definition in the current session, making the y object available. In order to simplify of algorithm of the **DefFromM** procedure the **SubListsMin** procedure is used, in general useful at operating with lists. The call **SubListsMin**[L, x, y, t] returns the sublists of a L list which are limited by {x, y} elements and have the minimum length; at t = "r" selection is executed from left to right, and at t = "l" from right to left. While the procedure call **SubListsMin**[L, x, y, t, z] with the optional fifth z argument – *an arbitrary expression* – returns sublists without the limiting {x, y} elements. The next fragment presents source codes of both procedures with examples of their application.

In[2742]:= **SubListsMin**[L_ /; ListQ[L], x_, y_, t_ /; MemberQ[{"r", "l"}, t], z___] :=
Module[{a, b, c, d = {}, k = 1, j}, {a, b} = Map[Flatten, Map3[Position, L, {x, y}]];
If[a == {} || b == {} || a == {} && b == {} || L == {}, {}, b = Select[Map[If[If[t == "r",
Greater, Less][#, a[[1]]], #] &, b], ! SameQ[#, Null] &];
For[k, k <= Length[a], k++, j = 1; While[j <= Length[b],
If[If[t == "r", Greater, Less][b[[j]], a[[k]]], AppendTo[d,
If[t == "r", a[[k]] ;; b[[j]], b[[j]] ;; a[[k]]]]; Break[]]; j++]];
d = Sort[d, Part[#1, 2] – Part[#1, 1] <= Part[#2, 2] – Part[#2, 1] &];
d = Select[d, Part[#, 2] – Part[#, 1] == Part[d[[1]], 2] – Part[d[[1]], 1] &];

```
d = Map[L[[#]] &, d]; d = If[{z} != {}, Map[#[[2 ;; -2]] &, d], d];
If[Length[d] == 1, Flatten[d], d]]]

In[2743]:= SubListsMin[{a, b, a, c, d, q, v, d, w, j, k, d, h, f, d, h}, a, h, "r", 90]
Out[2743]= {c, d, q, v, d, w, j, k, d}
In[2744]:= SubListsMin[{h, g, a, b, h, a, c, d, a, q, h, v, w, a, j, k, d, h, f, d, h}, a, h, "r"]
Out[2744]= {{a, b, h}, {a, q, h}}
In[2745]:= SubListsMin[{h, g, a, b, h, a, c, d, a, q, h, v, w, j, k, d, h, f, d, h}, a, h, "r", 590]
Out[2745]= {{b}, {q}}
In[2746]:= SubListsMin[{h, g, a, b, h, a, c, d, a, q, h, v, w, j, k, d, h, f, d, h}, a, h, "l"]
Out[2746]= {h, g, a}
In[2747]:= SubListsMin[{h, g, a, b, h, a, c, d, a, q, h, v, w, j, k, d, h, f, d, h}, a, h, "l", 590]
Out[2747]= {g}

In[2749]:= DefFromM[x_ /; FileExistsQ[x] && FileExtension[x] == "m", y_ /; SymbolQ[y],
z___] := Module[{a = ReadList[x, String], b, c, d},
{b, c} = {"(*Begin[\"`" <> ToString[y] <> "`\"]*)", "(*End[]*)"};
d = StringJoin[Map[StringTake[#, {3, -3}] &, Flatten[SubListsMin[a, b, c, "r", 90]]]];
If[{z} != {}, ToExpression[d]; d, d]]

In[2750]:= DefFromM["MathToolBox.m", StrStr]; Definition[StrStr]
Out[2750]= StrStr[x_] := If[StringQ[x], "\"" <> x <> "\"", ToString[x]]
```

Being based on the approach, used in the previous **ExtrOfMfile** procedure, and also on the mechanism of string patterns, we receive useful procedure which provides receiving of the list of means, whose definitions are located in the user package (*m–file*). The procedure call **ContentOfMfile[***f***]** returns the list of names in string format of all means, whose definitions are located in a package (*m–file*) defined by *f* argument. In absence in the *m*–file of *definitions* of tools in the standard package format the procedure call returns the empty list, i.e. {}. The next fragment represents source code of the **ContentOfMfile** procedure along with typical examples of its application.

```
In[2830]:= ContentOfMfile[f_ /; FileExistsQ[f] && FileExtension[f] == "m"] :=
Module[{b, a = ReadFullFile[f]}, b = StringSplit[a, {"(*", "*)"}];
b = Select[b, ! StringFreeQ[#, {"Begin[\"`", "`\"]"}] && StringFreeQ[#, "BeginPackage["] &];
b = Flatten[Map[StringCases[#, "\"`" ~~ __ ~~ "`\""] &, b]];
b = DeleteDuplicates[Map[StringTake[#, {3, -3}] &, b]]; Sort[Select[b, SymbolQ[#] &]]]

In[2841]:= ContentOfMfile["C:\\MathToolBox\\Kiev.m"]
Out[2841]= {"W", "W1"}
In[2842]:= ContentOfMfile["C:\\AAA\\MathToolBox.m"]
Out[2842]= {"AcNb", "ActBFM", "ActBFMuserQ", "ActCsProcFunc",...}
In[2843]:= Length[%]
Out[2843]= 1134
```

The previous **ContentOfMfile** procedure can be simplified and reduced to a function, using **SubsString** providing allocation of substrings from a string on condition of satisfaction of the allocated substrings to the set conditions. Using the **SubsString** procedure, it is a rather simple to modify the procedure **ContentOfMfile** in the form of **ContentOfMfile1** function, whose source code with certain examples of its use the following fragment represents.

In[3227]:= **ContentOfMfile1**[f_ /; FileExistsQ[f] && FileExtension[f] == "m"] :=
Sort[DeleteDuplicates[Select[Map[StringTake[#, {9, -4}] &, SubsString[ReadFullFile[f], {"Begin[\"`", "`\"]"}]], StringFreeQ[#, {"=",",","`", "[","]", "(",")", "^",";","{", "}","\\","/"}] &]]]

In[3228]:= **ContentOfMfile1**["C:\\Temp\\MathToolBox\\Kherson.m"]
Out[3228]= {"W", "W1"}

In[3229]:= **ContentOfMfile1**["C:/MathToolBox/MathToolBox.m"]
Out[3229]= {"AcNb", "ActBFM", "ActBFMuserQ", "ActCsProcFunc", ...}

In[3230]:= **Length**[%]
Out[3230]= 1134

In[3944]:= **ContentOfMfile2**[x_ /; FileExistsQ[x] && FileExtension[x] == "m"] :=
Sort[DeleteDuplicates[Map[StringReplace[#, {"Begin[\"`" -> "", "`\"]" -> ""}] &, SubsString[StringReplace[ReadFullFile[x], {" " -> "", "\n" -> "", "\t" -> "", "\r" -> ""}], {"Begin[\"`", "`\"]"}]]]]

In[3945]:= **ContentOfMfile2**["C:\\MathToolBox\\MathToolBox.m"]
Out[3945]= {"AcNb", "ActBFM", "ActBFMuserQ", "ActCsProcFunc", ...}

In[3946]:= **Length**[%]
Out[3946]= 1143

In[4258]:= **ContentsMx**[x_ /; FileExistsQ[x] && FileExtension[x] == "mx"] :=
Module[{a = ContextInMxFile[x], b},
If[a === $Failed, $Failed, If[MemberQ[$Packages, a], CNames[a], Get[x];
b = CNames[a]; RemovePackage[a]; b]]]

In[4259]:= **ContentsMx**["C:\\MathToolBox\\Grodno.mx"]
Out[4259]= {"Ga", "Gs", "GSV", "Vgs"}

While the **ContentOfMfile2** function is a functional analog of the above **ContentOfMfile1** function. In general it should be noted, that the *Mathematica* posesses a rather developed mechanism of the string patterns that allows to program developed means of processing of different string structures. The procedure call **ContentsMx**[*x*] returns the list of tools names contained in a *x mx*-file with a context; such file is not necessarily uploaded into the current session; if the *x* file has been already uploaded into the current session, then file remains in it, otherwise the file is unloaded from it. As other examples, procedures **ContentMusage** and **ContentMdefinitions** can serve. The call **ContentMusage**[*x*] returns the list of means names contained in a *x m*-file and which are provided with usage; the file is not necessarily uploaded in the current session. While the procedure call **ContentMdefinitions**[*x*] returns the list of tools names contained in a *x m*-file regardless of the presence for them of usage; in addition, the file is not necessarily uploaded in the current session. The fragment below represents source codes of the both procedures with examples of their application.

In[3011]:= **ContentMusage**[x_ /; FileExistsQ[x] && FileExtension[x] == "m"] :=
Module[{a = ReadString[x], b, c, d = "", g = {}},
b = Map[#[[1]] &, StringPosition[a, "::usage="]];
Do[Do[If[Set[c, StringTake[a, {j}]] === "*", AppendTo[g, d]; d = "";

Break[], d = c <> d], {j, b[[k]] - 1, 1, -1}], {k, 1, Length[b]}];
Sort[DeleteDuplicates[Select[g, SymbolQ[#] && StringFreeQ[#, "."] &]]]]

In[3012]:= a = ContentMusages["C:\\aaa\\MathToolBox.m"]; Length[a]
Out[3012]= 1140

In[3013]:= ContentM["pacletmanager.m"]
Out[3013]= {}

In[3014]:= ContentMdefinitions[x_ /; FileExistsQ[x] && FileExtension[x] == "m"] :=
Module[{a = ReadString[x], b = "(*Begin[`", c = "`]*)"},
a = StringCases[UniformString[a], Shortest[b ~~ __ ~~ c]];
a = Map[StringReplace[#, {b -> "", c -> ""}] &, a]; Sort[DeleteDuplicates[a]]]

In[3015]:= b = ContentMdefinitions["MathToolBox.m"]; Length[b]
Out[3015]= 1143

Note, the above and certain other tools presented in the book and in [33,48,50] are oriented, first of all, on the means conforming to the technique of organization of the user software offered by us.

Three procedures below are quite useful at manipulations with a package that is located in a *mx*-file. Thus, the procedure call **ContextMXfile[x]** returns the context which is associated with the package that is located in a *x mx*-file. Whereas the call **ContextInMxFile[x]** returns the context that is associated with a *x mx*-file. In the absence of a context the procedure call returns $*Failed*. In addition, loading of a *mx*-file into the current session isn't made in both cases. The **MxToTxt** procedure allows 2÷4 actual arguments. The call **MxToTxt[x, y]** returns *Null*, i.e. *nothing*, saving in a *y* file of *txt*-format and in the current session all definitions of a package which is located in a *mx*-file. In addition, all definitions of the *x* file are saved in an optimum format *(without the context associated with package)*. If the call **MxToTxt[x, y, z]** since the third argument, contains optional argument *"Del"*, the *x* package isn't uploaded into the current session, otherwise all its definitions are saved in the current session in the optimum format. If at the procedure call the arguments, starting with the third, contain an undefinite variable, thru it the list of all objects whose definitions are located in a *x* file with the user package is returned. The following fragment represents the source codes of the mentioned procedures together with the associated with them tools along with certain typical examples of their applications.

In[2825]:= ContextMXfile[x_ /; FileExistsQ[x] && FileExtension[x] == "mx"] :=
Module[{a, c, b = Flatten[Map7[Range, Sequences, {{48, 57}, {65, 90}, {96, 122}}]]},
a = BinaryReadList[x]; a = a[[1 ;; If[Length[a] >= 500, 500, Length[a]]]];
c = Flatten[Map3[PosSubList, a, {{67, 79, 78, 84}, {69, 78, 68, 67, 79, 78, 84}}]];
If[Length[c] < 5, $Failed, FromCharacterCode[Select[a[[c[[2]] + 1 ;; c[[5]] - 1]],
MemberQ[b, #1] &]]]]

In[2826]:= ContextMXfile["F:\\MathToolBox\\MathToolBox.mx"]
Out[2826]= "AladjevProcedures`"

In[3947]:= ContextInMxFile[x_ /; FileExistsQ[x] && FileExtension[x] == "mx"] :=
Module[{a = StringReplace[ReadFullFile[x], {" " -> "", "\n" -> "", "\t" -> "", "\r" -> ""}],
b = Range5[48 ;; 57, 65 ;; 90, 96 ;; 122]},

If[StringCount[SubString[a, {"Mathematica", "ENDCONT"}][[1]], "CONT"] == 1, $Failed,
FromCharacterCode[Select[ToCharacterCode[Sort[DeleteDuplicates[Map[StringReplace[
#, {"ENDCONT" -> "", "CONT" -> ""}] &, SubsString[a, {"CONT", "ENDCONT"}]]]][[1]]],
MemberQ[b, #] &]]]]

In[3948]:= ContextInMxFile["C:\\MathToolBox\\MathToolBox.mx"]
Out[3948]= "AladjevProcedures`"
In[3949]:= ContextInMxFile[$InstallationDirectory <>
"\\SystemFiles\\components\\urlutilities\\Kernel\\64bit\\urlutilities.mx"]
Out[3949]= "URLUtilities`"
In[3950]:= ContextInMxFile["C:\\MathToolBox\\Tallinn.mx"]
Out[3950]= $Failed
In[3951]:= ContextInMxFile[$InstallationDirectory <>
"\\SystemFiles\\components\\urlutilities\\Kernel\\32bit\\urlutilities.mx"]
Out[3951]= "URLUtilities`"

In[2827]:= ContextFromFile[x_ /; StringQ[x]] :=
If[Quiet[FileExistsQ[x]] && MemberQ[{"m", "nb", "mx", "cdf"}, FileExtension[x]],
Quiet[ToExpression[StringJoin["Context", ToUpperCase[If[FileExtension[x] == "cdf",
"nb", FileExtension[x]]], "file[", ToString1[x], "]"]]], $Failed]

In[2828]:= Map[ContextFromFile, {"E:\\Temp/Kherson.m", "Package.nb",
"C:\\Users\\Aladjev\\Mathematica\\MathToolBox.mx"}]
Out[2828]= {"Kherson`", "AladjevProcedures`", "AladjevProcedures`"}

In[2829]:= MxToTxt[x_ /; FileExistsQ[x] && FileExtension[x] == "mx", y_ /; StringQ[y],
z___] := Module[{b, c, a = ContextMXfile[x]}, LoadMyPackage[x, a];
b = CNames[a]; Map[{Write[y, Definition[#]], Write[y]} &, b];
Close[y]; If[MemberQ[{z}, "Del"], RemovePackage[a]];
c = Select[{z}, ! HowAct[#] && ! SameQ[#, "Del"] &];
If[c != {}, ToExpression[ToString[c[[1]]] <> "=" <> ToString[b]]];]

BeginPackage["Kherson`"]
Gs::usage = "Function Gs[x, y] := 74*x^2 + 69*y + 49 + S[x, y]."
G::usage = "Function G[x, y] := N[Sin[x] + Cos[y]] + S[x, y]."
V::usage = "Function S[x_, y_] := x^2 + y^2."
Begin["`Private`"]
V[x_, y_] := x^2 + y^2
Gs[x_ /; IntegerQ[x], y_ /; IntegerQ[y]] := 74*x^2 + 69*y + 49 + V[x, y]
G[x_ /; IntegerQ[x], y_ /; IntegerQ[y]] := N[Sin[x] + Cos[y]] + V[x, y]
End[]
EndPackage[]

In[2830]:= $Packages
Out[2830]= {"Kherson`", "AladjevProcedures`", "ResourceLocator`", "PacletManager`",
"StreamingLoader`", "System`", "Global`"}
In[2831]:= ContextMXfile["Kherson.mx"]
Out[2831]= "Kherson`"
In[2832]:= MxToTxt["Kherson.mx", "Kherson.txt"]

In[2833]:= **$Packages**
Out[2833]= {"Kherson`", "AladjevProcedures`", "GetFEKernelInit`", "StreamingLoader`", "ResourceLocator`", "PacletManager`", "StreamingLoader`", "CloudObjectLoader`", "System`", "Global`"}
In[2834]:= **MxToTxt["Kherson.mx", "Kherson.txt", g70]; g70**
Out[2834]= {G, Gs, V}
In[2835]:= **$Packages**
Out[2835]= {"Kherson`", "AladjevProcedures`", "GetFEKernelInit`", "StreamingLoader`", "ResourceLocator`", "PacletManager`", "StreamingLoader`", "CloudObjectLoader`", "System`", "Global`"}
In[2836]:= **MxToTxt["Kherson.mx", "Kherson.txt", "Del"]**
In[2837]:= **$Packages**
Out[2837]= {"AladjevProcedures`", "GetFEKernelInit`", "StreamingLoader`", "ResourceLocator`", "PacletManager`", "StreamingLoader`", "CloudObjectLoader`", "System`", "Global`"}
In[2838]:= **MxToTxt["Kherson.mx", "Kherson.txt", v74, "Del"]; v74**
Out[2838]= {G, Gs, V}
In[2839]:= **$Packages**
Out[2839]= {"AladjevProcedures`", "GetFEKernelInit`", "StreamingLoader`", "ResourceLocator`", "PacletManager`", "StreamingLoader`", "CloudObjectLoader`", "System`", "Global`"}

The **MxToTxt** procedure has 2 rather useful modifications **MxToTxt1** and **MxToTxt2** with which it is possible to familiarize in [30-33,48]. In particular, on the basis of the procedures **MxToTxt ÷ MxToTxt2** it is possible to create quite effective and simple libraries of the user means with system of their maintaining. The similar organization is rather habitual for the users having experience in traditional programming systems.

In turn, the **MxToMpackage** procedure provides converting of the package that is in a *mx*-file into the package of the format represented here and in books [31-33,50] which is a rather convenient at creation of the user packages.

The call **MxToMpackage[x]** returns the path to the file **FileBaseName[x] <> ".m"** which will contain the package of the above format contained in a *x mx*-file, whereas the procedure call **MxToMpackage[x, y]** returns the path to the file **FileBaseName[y] <> ".m"**; in addition, if a package from the *x mx*-file yet has been loaded into the current session, then it remains in it, otherwise it is unloaded from the current session. At impossibility of such converting, the procedure call is returned *unevaluated* or returns $Failed. The following fragment represents source code of the **MxToMpackage** procedure with examples of its application.

In[4968]:= **MxToMpackage[x_ /; FileExistsQ[x] && FileExtension[x] == "mx", y___] :=
Module[{a = ContextInMxFile[x], b, c = {}, d, f, u, s, h},
If[a === $Failed, $Failed, If[MemberQ[$Packages, a], h = 75, Quiet[Get[x]]];
If[{y} == {}, f = FileBaseName[x] <> ".m", f = FileBaseName[If[StringQ[y], y, x]] <> ".m"];
b = CNames[a];
Map[If[SameQ[Set[u, ToString[ToExpression[# <> "::usage"]]], # <> "::usage"], Null,
AppendTo[c, # <> "::usage = " <> u]] &, b];**

If[c == {}, $Failed, c = Flatten[Map[{"(*" <> # <> "*)", "(**)"} &, c]];
d = Flatten[Map[{"(*Begin[\"`" <> # <> "`\"]*)", Map["(*" <> #1 <> ";*)" &,
Flatten[{PureDefinition[#]}]], "(*" <> "SetAttributes[" <> # <> ",
Attributes[" <> # <> "]]" <> "*)", "(*End[]*)", "(**)"} &, b]]; s = OpenWrite[f];
Map[WriteLine[s, #] &, Join[{"(* ::Package:: *)", "(**)", "(* ::Input:: *)", "(**)",
"(*BeginPackage[\"" <> a <> "\"]*)", "(**)"}, c, d, {"(*EndPackage[]*)"}]];
If[! SameQ[h, 75], RemovePackage[a], Null]; Close[s]]]]

In[4969]:= MxToMpackage["C:\\Temp\\MathToolBox.mx", "Apackage"]
Out[4969]= "Apackage.m"
In[4970]:= MxToMpackage["C:\\MathToolBox\\MathToolBox.mx"]
Out[4970]= "MathToolBox.m"

The following equivalent procedures **ContextFromMx** and **ContextFromMx1** use different algorithms; their calls on a *mx*-file return a context ascribed to the user package, at context absence $*Failed* is returned. The fragment below presents source codes of these procedures and an auxiliary function along with typical examples of their application. The function call **StringFreeQ2**[*x*, {*a1, a2, a3, ...*}] returns *True* if all {*a1, a2, a3, ...*} substrings are absent in a *x* string, and *False* otherwise.

In[2770]:= ContextFromMx[x_ /; FileExistsQ[x] && FileExtension[x] == "mx"] :=
Module[{d = Map[FromCharacterCode, Range[2, 27]],
a = StringJoin[Select[Characters[ReadString[x]], SymbolQ[#] || IntegerQ[#] ||
# == "`" &]], b},
If[StringFreeQ2[a, {"CONT", "ENDCONT"}], $Failed,
b = StringCases[a, Shortest["CONT" ~~ __ ~~ "\.10ENDCONT"]];
If[b == {}, $Failed, StringReplace[b, Flatten[{GenRules[d, ""], "ENDCONT" -> "",
"CONT" -> ""}]][[1]]]]]

In[2771]:= ContextFromMx["c:\\users/aladjev/mathematica/Tallinn.mx"]
Out[2771]= "Grodno`"

In[2772]:= ContextFromMx1[x_ /; FileExistsQ[x] && FileExtension[x] == "mx"] :=
Module[{d = Map[FromCharacterCode, Range[2, 27]],
a = StringJoin[Select[Characters[ReadString[x]], SymbolQ[#] || IntegerQ[#] ||
# == "`" &]], b},
If[StringFreeQ2[a, {"CONT", "ENDCONT"}] || StringCases1[a, {"CONT", "ENDCONT"},
"___"] == {}, $Failed, b = StringPosition[a, {"CONT", "ENDCONT"}];
If[b == {}, $Failed, StringReplace[StringTake[a, {b[[1]][[1]], b[[2]][[2]]}],
Flatten[{GenRules[d, ""], "ENDCONT" -> "", "CONT" -> ""}]]]]]

In[2773]:= ContextFromMx1["C:/users/aladjev/mathematica/Tallinn.mx"]
Out[2773]= "Grodno`"

In[2774]:= StringFreeQ2[x_ /; StringQ[x], y_ /; StringQ[y] || ListQ[y] &&
AllTrue[Map[StringQ[#] &, y], TrueQ]] :=
! MemberQ[Map[StringFreeQ[x, #] &, Flatten[{y}]], False]

In[2775]:= **StringFreeQ2["12tvArt27nm3p42k6r74hKr20", {"a", "b", "c", "d"}]**
Out[2775]= True

At last, the procedure **ContextsInFiles** provides evaluation of the context ascribed to a file of the format {"*m*", "*mx*", "*cdf*", "*nb*"}. The procedure call **ContextsInFiles[*w*]** returns the single context ascribed to a *w* datafile of the above formats. In the absence of a context the call returns $*Failed*. At that, it must be kept in mind that the context in files of the specified format is sought relative to the key word *"BeginPackage"* that is typically used at beginning of a package. A return of list of format {*"Context1'"*, ..., *"Contextp'"*} is equivalent to existence in a *m*-file of construction of format **BeginPackage[**"*context1'*", {"*context2'*", ..., "*contextp'*"}**]** where {"*context2'*", ..., "*contextp'*"} define uploadings of the appropriate files if their contexts aren't in the $*Packages* variable. The next fragment represents source code of the procedure with the most typical examples of its application.

In[3051]:= **ContextsInFiles[x_ /; FileExistsQ[x] && MemberQ[{"m", "mx", "cdf", "nb"},**
FileExtension[x]]] := Module[{a = StringReplace[ReadFullFile[x], {" " -> "", "\n" -> "",
"\t" -> ""}], b, b1, d = Flatten[{Range[65, 90], Range[96, 122]}]},
If[FileExtension[x] == "m", b=StringCases[a, Shortest["BeginPackage[\"" ~~ __ ~~ "`\"]"]];
If[b === {}, b = $Failed, b = Map[StringTake[#, {15, -3}] &, b][[1]]];
b1 = StringCases[a, Shortest["BeginPackage[\"" ~~ __ ~~ "`\"}]"]];
If[b1 === {}, b1 = $Failed, If[! StringFreeQ[b1[[1]], {"{", "}"}],
b1 = StringReplace[b1[[1]], {"{" -> "", "}" -> "", "\"" -> ""}];
b1 = StringSplit[StringTake[b1, {14, -2}], ","], b1 = $Failed]]];
b = DeleteDuplicates[Flatten[{b, b1}]]; SetAttributes[ContextQ, Listable];
b = Select[b, AllTrue[Flatten[ContextQ[{#}]], TrueQ] &];
If[ListQ[b] && Length[DeleteDuplicates[b]] == 1, b[[1]], b], If[FileExtension[x] == "mx",
Quiet[Check[b = StringCases[a, Shortest["CONT" ~~ __ ~~ "ENDCONT"]][[1]];
b = Flatten[Map[ToCharacterCode, Characters[StringReplace[b,
{"CONT" -> "", "ENDCONT" -> ""}]]]];
StringJoin[Map[FromCharacterCode[#] &, Select[b, MemberQ[d, #] &]]], $Failed]],
Quiet[Check[a = StringCases[a,
Shortest["BeginPackage\",\"[\",\"\\\"\\<" ~~ __ ~~ "`\\>\\\"\",\"]\"}]"]][[1]];
a = StringReplace[a, "BeginPackage" -> ""];
b = Flatten[Map[ToCharacterCode, Characters[a]]];
StringJoin[Map[FromCharacterCode[#] &, Select[b, MemberQ[d, #] &]]], $Failed]]]]]

In[3052]:= **ContextsInFiles[$InstallationDirectory <>**
"\\SystemFiles\\components\\ccodegenerator\\systemsmodel.m"]
Out[3052]= {"CCodeGenerator`SystemsModel`", "CCodeGenerator`"}
In[3053]:= **ContextsInFiles[$InstallationDirectory <>**
"\\SystemFiles\\components\\ccodegenerator\\CCodeGenerator.m"]
Out[3053]= {"CCodeGenerator`", "CompiledFunctionTools`",
"CompiledFunctionTools`Opcodes`", "SymbolicC`", "CCompilerDriver`"}
In[3054]:= **ContextsInFiles["C:\\MathToolBox\\MathToolBox.m"]**
Out[3054]= "AladjevProcedures`"

In[3055]:= ContextsInFiles["C:\\MathToolBox\\Book_50.nb"]
Out[3055]= $Failed
In[3056]:= ContextsInFiles["C:\\MathToolBox\\Tallinn_75.txt"]
Out[3056]= ContextsInFiles["C:\\MathToolBox\\Tallinn_75.txt"]
In[3057]:= ContextsInFiles["C:\\MathToolBox\\MathToolBox.mx"]
Out[3057]= "AladjevProcedures`"
In[3058]:= ContextsInFiles[$InstallationDirectory <> "\\SystemFiles\\components\\Interpreter\\Kernel\\64Bit\\Interpreter.mx"]
Out[3058]= "Interpreter`"
In[3059]:= ContextsInFiles["C:\\MathToolBox\\MathToolBox.cdf"]
Out[3059]= "AladjevProcedures`"
In[3060]:= ContextsInFiles["C:\\MathToolBox\\MathToolBox.nb"]
Out[3060]= "AladjevProcedures`"

In addition to the previous **ContextsInFiles** procedure the **ContextsFromFiles** procedure allows to extract contexts from files of any format which are located in the given directories or are given by own full or short names. The call **ContextsFromFiles[]** without arguments returns the sorted list of contexts from all files located in the catalog *$InstallationDirectory* and in all its subdirectories whereas the call **ContextsFromFiles[*x*]** returns the sorted list of contexts from all datafiles located in a *x* directory and in all its subdirectories, at last the call **ContextsFromFiles[*x*]** on an existing *x* file returns the sorted list of contexts from the *x* file. The unsuccessful call returns *$Failed* or is returned unevaluated. The next fragment presents source code of the procedure with the most typical examples of its application.

In[4332]:= **ContextsFromFiles[x___String] := Module[{a = If[{x} == {}, FileNames["*", $InstallationDirectory, Infinity], If[DirQ[x], FileNames["*", x, Infinity], If[FileExistsQ[x], {x}, $Failed]]], b},
If[a === $Failed, $Failed,
b = Select[Map[Quiet[StringReplace[#, {": " -> "", " " -> "", "\"" -> ""}]] &,
Flatten[Map[StringCases[Quiet[Check[ReadFullFile[#], ""]],
(Shortest[": " ~~ __ ~~ "`"] | Shortest["\"" ~~ __ ~~ "`\""]) ..] &, a]]], ContextQ[#] &];
Sort[DeleteDuplicates[b]]]]**

In[4333]:= **ContextsFromFiles[$InstallationDirectory <> "\\AddOns\\Applications\\AuthorTools\\Kernel"]**
Out[4333]= {"AuthorTools`", "AuthorTools`MakeBilateralCells`"}
In[4334]:= **ContextsFromFiles[$InstallationDirectory <>
"\\AddOns\\Applications\\ClusterIntegration"]**
Out[4334]= {"ClusterIntegration`", "ClusterIntegration`CCS`",
"ClusterIntegration`CCSWin`", "ClusterIntegration`HPC`", "ClusterIntegration`HPCWin`",
"ClusterIntegration`Library`", "ClusterIntegration`LSF`", "ClusterIntegration`Palette`",
"ClusterIntegration`Parallel`", "ClusterIntegration`PBS`", "ClusterIntegration`SGE`",
"ClusterIntegration`SubKernels`", "ClusterIntegration`XGRID`", "CURLLink`", "JLink`",
"NETLink`", "Parallel`", "Parallel`Developer`", "ResourceLocator`", "SubKernels`"}
In[4335]:= **ContextsFromFiles["DiffReport.m"]**
Out[4335]= {"AuthorTools`Common`", "AuthorTools`DiffReport`"}
In[4336]:= **ContextsFromFiles["AvzRansIan.txt"]**

Out[4336]= $Failed

The procedure **ContextInMfile** provides evaluation of all *contexts* contained in a file of the *m*-format. The procedure call **ContextInMfile**[*x*] returns the list of contexts contained in a *x* *m*-file. In the absence of context the call returns the empty list, i.e. {}. At that, it must be kept in mind that contexts in *m*-files are sought relative to the key words {"*BeginPackage*","*Needs*", "Get", "Package"} which are used in *m*-files. The fragment below represents source code of the **ContextInMfile** procedure with typical examples of its application.

In[2947]:= **ContextInMfile**[x_ /; FileExistsQ[x] && FileExtension[x] == "m"] :=
Module[{d = Flatten[{Range[65, 90], Range[96, 123], {44, 125}}], b, c,
a = StringReplace[ReadFullFile[x], {" " -> "", "\n" -> "", "\t" -> "", "\r" -> ""}]},
b = Flatten[Map[SubsString[a, {#, "\"]"}] &,
{"Begin[\"", "Package[\"", "Get[\"", "Needs[\""}]];
c = Flatten[Map[SubsString[a, {#, "\"}]"}] &,
{"Begin[\"", "Package[\"", "Get[\"", "Needs[\""}]];
b = Map[StringReplace[#, {"\"" -> "", "{" -> "", "}" -> ""}] &,
Map[StringReplace[StringTake[#, {1, -2}],
{"Begin[\"" -> "", "Get[\"" -> "", "Needs[\"" -> "", "Package[\"" -> ""}, 1] &, Join[b, c]]];
DeleteDuplicates[Flatten[Map[StringSplit[#, ","] &,
Select[b, Complement[DeleteDuplicates[ToCharacterCode[#]], d] == {} &&
! SuffPref[#, "`", 1] &]]]]

In[2948]:= **ContextInMfile**[$InstallationDirectory <> "\\SystemFiles\\components\\ccompilerdriver\\ccompilerdriver.m"]
Out[2948]= {"ResourceLocator`", "CCompilerDriver`System`",
"CCompilerDriver`CCompilerDriverRegistry`", "CCompilerDriver`"}
In[2949]:= **ContextInMfile**["C:\\MathToolBox\\MathToolBox.m"]
Out[2949]= {"AladjevProcedures`"}
In[2950]:= **ContextInMfile**[$InstallationDirectory <> "\\SystemFiles\\components\\ccodegenerator\\systemsmodel.m"]
Out[2950]= {"CCodeGenerator`SystemsModel`", "CCodeGenerator`"}
In[2951]:= **ContextInMfile**[$InstallationDirectory <> "\\SystemFiles\\autoload\\pacletmanager\\kernel\\utils.m"]
Out[2951]= {"JLink`"}

It should be noted the above procedures operates on platforms *Windows XP Professional* and *Windows 7 Professional*. At that, the performance of procedures is higher if they are applied to a *mx*-file created on the current platform.

The binary *mx*-files are optimized for fast uploading. Wherein, they cannot be exchanged between different operating systems or versions of the *Mathematica*. Any *mx*-file contains version of *Mathematica*, the type of operating system in which it has been created and the context if it exists. The procedure call **ContextMathOsMx**[*x*] returns the three-element list whose the first element determines the context if it exists (*otherwise, $Failed is returned*), the second element defines list whose elements define version, releases of the *Mathematica* and the third element determines operating system in which the *x mx*-file has been created. The following fragment represents source code and examples of its application.

In[4122]:= **ContextMathOsMx[x_ /; FileExistsQ[x] && FileExtension[x] == "mx"] :=**
Module[{a = ReplaceAll[BinaryReadList[x], 0 -> 32], b, c, d, g, p},
a = StringJoin[Map[FromCharacterCode, a]];
c = Quiet[Check[StringTake[StringCases[a,
Shortest["CONT" ~~ __ ~~ "ENDCONT"]][[1]], {7, -10}], $Failed]];
b = StringCases[a, Shortest["Get.*)" ~~ __ ~~ If[c === $Failed,
"ENDCONT", "CONT"]]][[1]];
b = StringReplace[b, {"Get.*)" -> "", "ENDCONT" -> "", "CONT" -> ""}];
p = StringTrim[StringReplace[b, GenRules[Map[FromCharacterCode[#] &,
Range5[0 ;; 30]], " "]]];
d = StringReplace[StringCases[a, Shortest["\.03" ~~ __ ~~ "\.0f" | "\.06" | p]][[1]], p -> ""];
d = ReplaceAll[ToCharacterCode[d][[2 ;; -2]], {13 -> Nothing, 32 -> Nothing}]; {c, d, p}]

In[4123]:= **ContextMathOsMx ["C:\\users/aladjev/math/mathtoolBox.mx"]**
Out[4123]= {"AladjevProcedures`", {11}, "Windows-x86-64"}
In[4124]:= **ContextMathOsMx["avzagnvsvArtKr.mx"]**
Out[4124]= {$Failed, {11}, "Windows-x86-64"}
In[4125]:= **ContextMathOsMx[$InstallationDirectory <> "/SystemFiles/ ...**
/32Bit/GeneralUtilities.mx"]
Out[4125]= {$Failed, {11}, "Linux"}
In[4126]:= **ContextMathOsMx["C:/users/Aladjev/math/Avz_package.mx"]**
Out[4126]= {"AladjevProcedures`", {10, 4}, "Windows-x86-64"}

In view of distinctions of the *mx*-datafiles created on different platforms there is a natural expediency of creation of the tools testing any *mx*-file regarding a platform in which it was created in virtue of the **DumpSave** function. The following **TypeWinMx** procedure is one of such tools. The procedure call **TypeWinMx[*x*]** in string format returns type of operating platform on which a *x mx*-file was created; correct result is returned for case of the *Windows* platform, whereas on other platforms $*Failed* is returned. This is conditioned by absence of a possibility to carry out debugging on other platforms. The next fragment represents source code of the **TypeWinMx** procedure with examples of its application.

In[2785]:= **TypeWinMx[x_ /; FileExistsQ[x] && FileExtension[x] == "mx"] :=**
Module[{a, b, c, d}, If[StringFreeQ[$OperatingSystem, "Windows"], $Failed,
a = StringJoin[Select[Characters[ReadString[x]], SymbolQ[#] ||
Quiet[IntegerQ[ToExpression[#]]] || # == "-" &]];
d = Map[FromCharacterCode, Range[2, 27]];
b = StringPosition[a, {"CONT", "ENDCONT"}];
If[b[[1]][[2]] == b[[2]][[2]], c = StringCases1[a, {"Windows", "ENDCONT"}, "___"],
b = StringPosition[a, {"Windows", "CONT"}]; c = StringTake[a, {b[[1]][[1]], b[[2]][[2]]}]];
c = StringReplace[c, Flatten[{GenRules[d, ""], "ENDCONT" -> "", "CONT" -> ""}]];
If[ListQ[c], c[[1]], c]]]

In[2786]:= **TypeWinMx["ProcQ.mx"]**

Out[2786]= "Windows-x86-64"
In[2787]:= **TypeWinMx["MathToolBox_1.mx"]**
Out[2787]= "Windows"
In[2788]:= **TypeWinMx["MathToolBox.mx"]**
Out[2788]= "Windows-x86-64"

The call **DumpSave[x, y]** returns the list of *y* contexts of objects or objects with definitions which were ostensibly unloaded into a *x mx*-file irrespective of existence of definitions for these objects or their contexts in the list defined by system *$ContextPath* variable, without allowing to make program processing of results of the **DumpSave** calls. At that, the result of the **DumpSave** call can't be tested programmatically and elimination of this situation is promoted by a procedure, whose successful call **DumpSave1[x, y]** returns the nested list whose first element defines the path to a *x* file of *mx*-format *(if necessary, the ".mx" extension is ascribed to the datafile)* while the second element defines the list of objects and/or contexts from the list defined by *y* whose definitions are unloaded into the *x* datafile. In the absence of objects *(the certain symbols and/or contexts existing in the list determined by the $ContextPath variable)* which were defined by *y* argument, the **DumpSave1** call returns *$Failed*. The next fragment represents source codes of the procedure with other tools, useful at processing of files of *mx*-format, and contexts of symbols.

In[3120]:= **DumpSave1[x_, y_] := Module[{a, b, c},**
If[StringQ[x], If[FileExtension[x] == "mx", c = x, c = x <> ".mx"]; a = Flatten[{y}];
b = Select[a, (ContextQ[#] && MemberQ[$ContextPath, #]) || ! MemberQ[{"", "Null"},
Quiet[ToString[Definition[#]]]] &];
If[b != {}, {c, Flatten[DumpSave[c, b]]}, $Failed], $Failed]]

In[3121]:= **DumpSave1["MathToolBox42.mx", {"Art`", "Kr`", GS}]**
Out[3121]= $Failed

In[3124]:= **ReplaceSubLists[x_ /; ListQ[x], y_ /; RuleQ[y] || ListRulesQ[y]] :=**
Module[{a, f, d = FromCharacterCode[2016]}, f[z_ /; ListQ[z]] :=
StringJoin[Map[ToString1[#] <> d &, z]];
a = Map[f[Flatten[{#[[1]]}]] -> f[Flatten[{#[[2]]}]] &, Flatten[{y}]];
ToExpression[StringSplit[StringReplace[f[x], a], d]]]

In[3125]:= **ReplaceSubLists[{a, b, c, "d", m, x, b, c}, {{b, c} -> {x, y}, a -> {m, n}, "d" -> "590"}]**
Out[3125]= {m, n, x, y, "590", m, x, x, y}

In[3128]:= **SubsList[x_ /; ListQ[x], y_, z_] := Module[{b, c, a = FromCharacterCode[2017]},**
b = StringJoin[Map[ToString1[#] <> a &, x]];
c = Map[StringJoin[Map[ToString1[#] <> a &, Flatten[{#1}]]] &, {y, z}];
c = ToExpression[StringSplit[SubsString[b, {c[[1]], c[[2]]}], a]]; If[Length[c] == 1, c[[1]], c]]

In[3129]:= **SubsList[{a, b, c, d, x, y, x, b, c, n, a + b, x, y, z}, {b, c}, {x, y}]**
Out[3129]= {{b, c, d, x, y}, {b, c, n, a + b, x, y}}

In[3146]:= **ContextToSymbol[x_ /; SymbolQ[x], y_ /; ContextQ[y]] :=**
Module[{a = ToString[x], b = Flatten[{PureDefinition[x]}], c, d, f, h = Attributes[x]},
If[b === {$Failed}, $Failed, AppendTo[$ContextPath, y];

```
f = a <> ".mx"; Attributes[x] = {}; Quiet[ToExpression[Map[y <> # &, b]]];
c = ToExpression[y <> a]; ToExpression[y <> a <> "::usage = " <>
ToString1[d = ToExpression[a <> "::usage"]]]; DumpSave[f, {c, d}];
Remove[x]; Get[f]; ToExpression["SetAttributes[" <> a <> "," <> ToString[h] <> "]"];
DeleteFile[f]; {c, y}]]
In[3147]:= Agn[x_, y_] := x*y; Agn::usage = "Help on function Agn.";
In[3148]:= Context[Agn]
Out[3148]= "Global`"
In[3149]:= ContextToSymbol[Agn, "Tallinn`"]
Out[3149]= {Agn, "Tallinn`"}
In[3150]:= Context[Agn]
Out[3150]= "Tallinn`"
In[3151]:= Definition[Agn]
Out[3151]= Agn[x_, y_] := x*y
In[3152]:= ??Agn
"Help on function Agn."
Agn[x_, y_] := x*y
In[3158]:= Avz[x_, y_] := x + y; Avz::usage = "Help on function Avz.";
SetAttributes[Avz, {Listable, Protected}]; Context[Avz]
In[3159]:= "Global`"
In[3160]:= ContextToSymbol[Avz, "Grodno`"]
Out[3160]= {Avz, "Grodno`"}
In[3161]:= Context[Avz]
Out[3161]= "Grodno`"
In[3162]:= ??Avz
Out[3162]= "Help on function Avz."
Attributes[Avz] = {Listable, Protected}
Avz[x_, y_] := x + y
In[3166]:= ?? Agn
Grodno`Agn
Agn[x_, y_] := x*y
In[3250]:= ContextRepMx[x_ /; FileExistsQ[x] && FileExtension[x] == "mx",
y_ /; ContextQ[y], z___] := Module[{a = ContextMXfile[x], b, c, t},
If[SameQ[a, $Failed], $Failed, If[{z} != {} && FileExtension[z] == "mx", c = z, c = x];
If[MemberQ[$Packages, a], t = 75, Get[x]]; b = CNames[a];
Map[Quiet[ContextToSymbol[#, y]] &, b];
ToExpression["RemovePackage[" <> ToString1[a] <> "]"];
DumpSave[c, y]; If[t == 75, Get[c], RemovePackage[y]]; {c, a, y}]]
In[3252]:= ContextRepMx["Grodno.mx", "Tallinn`", "Grodno75.mx"]
Out[3252]= {"Grodno`", "Tallinn`", "Grodno75`"}
In[3253]:= MemberQ4[$Packages, {"Grodno`", "Tallinn`", "Grodno75`"}]
Out[3253]= False
In[3254]:= Get["Grodno75.mx"]
```

In[3255]:= **CNames["Tallinn`"]**
Out[3255]= {"Ga", "Gs", "GSV", "Vgs"}
In[3259]:= **Vgs[1942, 2016]**
Out[3259]= 3915072

In[3154]:= **ContextSymbol[x_ /; SymbolQ[x]] := Select[Map[If[MemberQ[CNames[#], ToString[x]] || MemberQ[CNames[#], # <> ToString[x]], #] &, DeleteDuplicates[$ContextPath]], ! SameQ[#1, Null] &]**

In[3155]:= **Map[ContextSymbol, {G, Gs, ProcQ, Sin}]**
Out[3155]= {{"Kherson`"}, {"Grodno`"}, {"AladjevProcedures`"}, {"System`"}}

Thus, the previous fragment represents as the main, and supportive means of processing of *mx*-files and contexts. The call **ReplaceSubLists[x, y]** returns the result of replacement of elements *(including adjacent)* of a *x* list on the basis of a rule or list of rules *y*; moreover, the lists can be as parts of rules. Whereas the procedure call **SubsList[x, y, z]** returns the list of sublists of the elements of a *x* list that are limited by {*y, z*} elements; qua of {*y, z*} elements can be lists too. If any of {*y, z*} elements doesn't belong *x*, the procedure call returns empty list. The presented procedures **ReplaceSubLists** and **SubsList** along with processing of lists are of interest for assignment to *mx*-files of a context in its absence.

While the procedure call **ContextToSymbol[x, y]** returns list of the format {*x*, {*y*}}, ascribing in the current session an *y* context to a *x* definite symbol. In particular, these tools is an quite useful in the case of necessity of saving of objects in *mx*-datafiles with a context as the above example illustrates. On the basis of 4 procedures **CNames, ContextMXfile, RemovePackage** and **ContextToSymbol** the procedure that provides replacement of contexts in *mx*-datafiles without their uploading into the current session has been created.

The procedure call **ContextRepMx[x, y]** provides replacement of a *j* context of a *x mx*-file by a new *y* context, returning the list of format {*x, w, y*} where *x* defines file with result of such replacement, *w* – an old context and *y* – a new context. At that, if context in *x* file is absent, the call returns $*Failed*. The call **ContextRepMx[x, y, z]** where *z* defines a *mx*-file with result of replacement returns {*z, j, y*}. Whereas the function call **ContextSymbol[x]** returns context associated with a *x* symbol.

Whereas unlike the above **ContextToSymbol** procedure the procedure call **ToContext[x, y]** returns *nothing*, providing the assignment of an *y* context to a symbol or their list *x*. The next fragment presents source code of the **ToContext** procedure with typical examples of its use.

In[3322]:= **ToContext[x_ /; SymbolQ[x] || ListQ[x] && AllTrue[Map[SymbolQ, x], TrueQ], y_ /; ContextQ[y]] := Module[{h = Flatten[{x}], a, attr}, a = Map[PureDefinition, h]; attr = Map[Attributes, h]; Map[ClearAttributes[#, Protected] &, h]; Map[Remove, h]; Quiet[ToExpression[{"BeginPackage[\"" <> y <> "\"]", ToString[Flatten[a]], "Map[Attributes[#[[1]]] = #[[2]]&," <> "Partition[Riffle[" <> ToString[h] <> "," <> ToString[attr] <> "], 2]]", "EndPackage[]"}];]**

In[3323]:= **Fs[x_] := x; Vs[x_, y_] := x*y; Fs[x_, y_] := x + y; Vs[x_List] := x; Vgs[x_, y_, z_] := Module[{}, x*y*z]; SetAttributes[Vgs, {Protected}]; SetAttributes[Vs, {Listable, Protected}]; Map[Attributes, {Fs, Vs, Vgs}]**

Out[3323]= {{Listable, Protected}, {}, {Protected}}
In[3324]:= **Map[Context, {Fs, Vs, Vgs}]**
Out[3324]= {"Global`", "Global`", "Global`"}
In[3325]:= **ToContext[{Fs, Vs, Vgs}, "Grodno`"]**
In[3326]:= **Map[Context, {Fs, Vs, Vgs}]**
Out[3326]= {"Grodno`", "Grodno`", "Grodno`"}
In[3327]:= **Definition[Vgs]**
Out[3327]= Vgs[x_, y_, z_] := Module[{}, x*y*z]
In[3328]:= **Definition[Vs]**
Out[3328]= Vs[x_, y_] := x*y
Vs[x_List] := x
In[3329]:= **Map[Attributes, {Fs, Vs, Vgs}]**
Out[3329]= {{}, {}, {}}
In[3330]:= **SetAttributes[Vs, {Listable}]; {Context[Vs], Attributes[Vs]}**
Out[3330]= {"Grodno`", {Listable, Protected}}

It must be kept in mind that a call **ToContext**[*x, y*], providing assignment of a new *y* context to the *x* symbols, at the same time doesn't keep attributes and options attributed to them. It is necessary to do it outside of the procedure.

At calculation of definition of a *x* symbol in the *current* session the symbol will be associated with the *"Global`"* context that remains at its loading in *mx*-file by means of the **DumpSave** function. Whereas in some cases there is a need of saving of symbols in *mx*-files with other contexts. The procedure **DumpSave2** solves the given problem whose call **DumpSave2**[*f, x, y*] returns nothing, loading into a *f mx*-file the definition of a symbol or their list *x* that have *"Global`"* context with *y* context. So, in the current session *x* symbols receive the *y* context. The fragment presents source code of the **DumpSave2** procedure with typical examples of its application.

In[3203]:= **DumpSave2[x_ /; FileExtension[x] == "mx", y_ /; SymbolQ[y] || ListQ[y] && AllTrue[Map[SymbolQ[#] &, y], TrueQ], z_ /; ContextQ[z]] :=
Module[{b, a = Select[Flatten[{y}], ! SameQ[PureDefinition[#], $Failed] &]},
If[a == {}, $Failed, a = Map[ToString, a];
Map[ToExpression["ContextToSymbol[" <> ToString[#] <> "," <> ToString1[z]<>"]"] &, a];
DumpSave[x, z];]]**
In[3204]:= **Agn[x_] := x; Agn[x_, y_] := x + y; Agn[x_Integer] := x + 590**
In[3205]:= **Avz[x_] := x^2; Avz[x_, y_] := 90*(x + y); Avz[x_Integer] := x + 590**
In[3206]:= **Ian[x_] := x^2; Ian[x_, y_] := x + y; Ian[x_, y_, z_] := x*y*z**
In[3207]:= **Map[Context, {Agn, Avz, Ian, xyz}]**
Out[3207]= {"Global`", "Global`", "Global`", "Global`"}
In[3208]:= **DumpSave2["Tallinn.mx", {Avz, Agn, Ian}, "Tallinn`"]**
In[3209]:= **Map[Context, {Agn, Avz, Ian, xyz}]**
Out[3209]= {"Tallinn`", "Tallinn`", "Tallinn`", "Global`"}
In[3210]:= **$Packages**

Out[3210]= {"AladjevProcedures`", "HTTPClient`OAuth`", "HTTPClient`CURLInfo`", "HTTPClient`CURLLink`", "HTTPClient`", "GetFEKernelInit`", "IconizeLoader`", "CloudObjectLoader`", "ResourceLocator`", "PacletManager`", "System`", "Global`"}
In[3211]:= **Clear[Agn, Avz, Ian]**
In[3212]:= **Map[PureDefinition, {Agn, Avz, Ian}]**
Out[3212]= {$Failed, $Failed, $Failed}
In[3213]:= **Get["Tallinn.mx"]**
In[3214]:= **PureDefinition[Agn]**
Out[3214]= {"Agn[x_Integer] := x + 590", "Agn[x_] := x", "Agn[x_, y_] := x + y"}
In[3215]:= **PureDefinition[Ian]**
Out[3215]= {"Ian[x_] := x^2", "Ian[x_, y_] := x + y", "Ian[x_, y_, z_] := x*y*z"}
In[3216]:= **ContextInMxFile["Tallinn.mx"]**
Out[3216]= "Tallinn`"

The previous fragment is completed by examples illustrating the principle of saving of the objects, whose definitions are evaluated in the current session, in *mx*-files with the given context. This principle was used at programming of the procedures endowing a symbol by a context.

As it was noted earlier, the objects of the same name have different headings, therefore in certain cases arises the question of their more exact identification. The following procedure provides one of such *approaches*, trying to associate the components composing such objects with the contexts ascribed to them. At the heart of the procedure algorithm lies a principle of creation for separate components of an object of the same name of packages in the *m*-files with the unique contexts ascribed to them. Further, having removed a *x* object of the same name from the current session, by means of loading of these *m*-files into the current session we have opportunity of access to components of the *x* object of the same name through the construction of *"Context`x"* format. The following fragment below represents source code of the **DiffContexts** procedure along with typical examples of its application.

In[2630]:= **DiffContexts[x_ /; SymbolQ[x] && ! UnevaluatedQ[HeadPF, x], y___] :=**
Module[{a = {"(*BeginPackage[\"\.12`\"]*)", "(*\.0f::usage=\"\" <> "*)",
"(*Begin[\"`\.06`\"]*)", "(*\.04*)", "(*End[]*)", "(*EndPackage[]*)"},
b = Map[FromCharacterCode, {18, 15, 6, 4}], c = Definition2[x][[1 ;; -2]], d,
h = ToString[x], k = 1, j, t = {}, p, f = {}, z},
If[Length[c] < 2, Context[x], z = HeadPF[x]; Clear[x];
For[k, k <= Length[c], k++, d = {}; For[j = 1, j <= Length[a], j++, AppendTo[d,
StringReplace[a[[j]], {b[[1]] -> h <> ToString[k], b[[2]] -> h, b[[3]] -> h, b[[4]] -> c[[k]]}]]];
AppendTo[t, p = h <> ToString[k] <> ".m"]; AppendTo[f, {h <> ToString[k] <> "`", z[[k]]}];
Map[{BinaryWrite[p, ToCharacterCode[#][[3 ;; -3]]], BinaryWrite[p, {32, 10}]} &, d];
Close[p]; Quiet[Get[p]]]; If[{y} != {}, Map[DeleteFile, t], Null]; Reverse[f]]]
In[2631]:= **T[x_] := x; T[x_, y_] := x*y; T[x_, y_, z_] := x*y*z**
In[2632]:= **DiffContexts[T]**
Out[2632]= {{"T3`", "T[x_, y_, z_]"}, {"T2`", "T[x_, y_]"}, {"T1`", "T[x_]"}}
In[2633]:= **Definition["T1`T"]**
Out[2633]= T1`T[T1`T`x_] := T1`T`x

In[2634]:= **Definition["T2`T"]**
Out[2634]= T2`T[T2`T`x_, T2`T`y_] := T2`T`x*T2`T`y
In[2635]:= **Definition["T3`T"]**
Out[2635]= T[T3`T`x_, T3`T`y_, T3`T`z_] := T3`T`x*T3`T`y*T3`T`z
In[2636]:= **Definition[T]**
Out[2636]= T[T3`T`x_, T3`T`y_, T3`T`z_] := T3`T`x*T3`T`y*T3`T`z
In[2637]:= **$Packages**
Out[2637]= {"T3`", "T2`", "T1`", "AladjevProcedures`", "GetFEKernelInit`", "StreamingLoader`", "ResourceLocator`", "PacletManager`", "IconizeLoader`", "CloudObjectLoader`", "System`", "Global`"}
In[2638]:= **DiffContexts[T, 590]**
Out[2639]= "T3`"
In[2639]:= **Definition["T1`T"]**
Out[2639]= T1`T[T1`T`x_] := T1`T`x
In[2640]:= **FileExistsQ["T1.m"]**
Out[2640]= True
In[2641]:= **T3`T[74, 69, 49]**
Out[2641]= 250194

The procedure call **DiffContexts[x]** returns the nested list of *ListList* type whose sublists by the first element define *context* whereas the second element determine *heading* of a certain component of a *x* object of the same name in format {{"xn'", "cn'"}, ..., {"x2'", "c2'"}, {"x1'", "c1'"}} whose order is defined by order of the contexts in the list defined by the *$Packages* variable, where *n* – number of components of the *x* object of the same name. Moreover, the "*xj.m*" datafiles with the packages with components definitions composing the *x* object of the same name remain in the current directory of the session (*j = 1..n*). At the same time the procedure call **DiffContexts[x, y]** with the 2nd *y* argument – *an arbitrary expression* – returns the above result, removing the *intermediate m*–files. While on *x* objects different from objects of the same name the call **DiffContexts[x]** returns the context of the *x* object.

A certain interest is represented by the **NamesCS** procedure whose the call **NamesCS[P, Pr, Pobj]** returns *Null*, i.e. nothing while through three arguments *P*, *Pr*, *Pobj* – the undefinite variables – are respectively returned the list of contexts corresponding to packages loaded into the current session, the list of the user procedures whose definitions are activated in the *Input* paragraph of the current session, and the nested list, whose sublists in the main have various length and are structurally formatted as follows:

– the first element of a sublist defines the context corresponding to a package which was uploaded in the current session of the **Mathematica** system at the time of the **NamesCS** procedure call;
– all subsequent elements of this sublist define objects of this package which in the current session of the **Mathematica** system were made active.

The next fragment represent source code of the **NamesCS** procedure with a typical example of its application.

In[2593]:= **NamesCS[P_/;! HowAct[P], Pr_/;! HowAct[Pr], Pobj_/;! HowAct[Pobj]] :=
Module[{b = Contexts[], c = $Packages, d, k = 1, p, n, m, h,
a = Quiet[Select[Map[ToExpression, Names["`*"]], ProcQ[#] &]]},**

{P, Pr} = {c, a}; c = Map[List, c];
For[k, k <= Length[b], k++, For[p = 1, p <= Length[c], p++, n = b[[k]]; m = c[[p]][[1]];
If[n === m, Null, If[SuffPref[n, m, 1], d = StringReplace[n, b -> ""];
If[d == "", Null, c[[p]] = Append[c[[p]],
ToExpression[StringTake[StringReplace[n, b -> ""], {1, -2}]]]]], Continue[]]]];
c = Map[DeleteDuplicates, c];
For[k = 1, k <= Length[c], k++, h = c[[k]];
If[Length[h == 1], h = Null, h = Select[h, StringQ[#] ||
ToString[Quiet[DefFunc[#]]] != "Null" &]]];
Pobj := Select[c, Length[#] > 1 && ! # === Null &];
Pobj = Mapp[Select, Pobj, If[! StringQ[#], True,
If[StringTake[#, -1] == "`", True, False]] &];]

In[2594]:= NamesCS[P, Pr, Pobj]
In[2595]:= {P, Pr}
Out[2595]= {{"T3`", "T2`", "T1`", "AladjevProcedures`", "GetFEKernelInit`", "HTTPClient`", "StreamingLoader`", "ResourceLocator`", "IconizeLoader`", "CloudObjectLoader`","PacletManager`", "System`", "Global`"}, {}}
In[2596]:= Pobj
Out[2596]= {{"T3`", T}, {"T2`", T}, {"T1`", T},
{"AladjevProcedures`", ActBFMuserQ, ActCsProcFunc,... ,
{"ResourceLocator`", Private},
{"PacletManager`", Collection`Private, Private,... },
{"QuantityUnits`", Private},
{"WebServices`", Information},
{"System`", BesselParamDerivativesDump, BinaryReadDump}}

Moreover, the list returned through *Pobj* argument – an undefinite symbol – contains only sublists, whose corresponding packages have objects that have been activated in the current *Mathematica* session.

Whereas the call **Npackage[x]** of very simple function returns the list of names in the string format of all objects whose definitions are located in a *x* package uploaded into the current session. In case of inactivity in the current session of the *x* package or in case of its absence the function call **Npackage[x]** returns $Failed. So, the following fragment represents source code of the **Npackage** function along with typical examples of its application.

In[2684]:= Npackage[x_ /; StringQ[x]] := If[MemberQ[Contexts1[], x],
Sort[Select[Names[x <> "*"], StringTake[#, -1] != "$" &&
ToString[Definition[#]] != "Null" &]], $Failed]
In[2685]:= Npackage["AladjevProcedures`"]
Out[2685]= "AcNb", "ActBFM", "ActBFMuserQ", ..., "$Version1", "$Version2"}
In[2686]:= Npackage["Tallinn`"]
Out[2686]= $Failed

The **ContOfContex** procedure also is represented as a rather interesting means whose call **ContOfContex[x]** returns the nested 2–element list whose first element defines the sublist of all names in string format of tools of the user package with a x context whose definitions in the current session are returned by the **Definition** function with the x context included in them while the second element defines the sublist of all names in string format of all means of the package with the x context whose definitions in the current session are returned by means of the **Definition** function without x context.

The fragment presents source code of the **ContOfContex** procedure with an example of its application concerning the context *"AladjevProcedures'"* associated with the *MathToolBox* package [48]. At the end of the fragment the *length* of both sublists of the returned result is calculated along with random inspection by means of the **Definition** function of definitions of tools from both sublists. From the received estimation follows, that the length of the first sublist of means of the above package whose definitions in the current session are returned by means of the **Definition** function call along with the context is significantly longer.

In[2705]:= **ContOfContext[x_ /; ContextQ[x]] :=**
Module[{b = {}, c = {}, h, k = 1, a = Select[CNames[x], # != "a" &]},
If[a == {}, $Failed, While[k <= Length[a], h = a[[k]];
If[StringFreeQ[StringReplace[ToString[Definition4[h]], "\\n \\n" -> ""], x <> h <> "`"],
AppendTo[c, h], AppendTo[b, h]]; k++]; {b, c}]]

In[2706]:= **ContOfContext["AladjevProcedures`"]**
Out[2706]= {{"ActBFMuserQ", "ActCsProcFunc", "ActRemObj", "ActUcontexts", ...},
{"AcNb", "ActBFM", "Adrive", "Adrive1", "Attributes1", ..., "$Version1", "$Version2"}}
In[2707]:= **Map[Length, %]**
Out[2707]= {66, 1058}
In[2708]:= **Definition["DirName"]**
Out[2708]= DirName[AladjevProcedures`DirName`F_ /;
StringQ[AladjevProcedures`DirName`F]] := If[DirQ[AladjevProcedures`DirName`F],
"None", If[! FileExistsQ1[AladjevProcedures`DirName`F], $Failed,
Quiet[Check[FileNameJoin[FileNameSplit[AladjevProcedures`DirName`F][[1; -2]]],
"None"]]]]
In[2709]:= **Definition["StrStr"]**
Out[2709]= StrStr[x_] := If[StringQ[x], StringJoin["\"", x, "\""], ToString[x]]
In[2710]:= **ContOfContext["AladjevProceduresAndFunctions`"]**
Out[2710]= $Failed

In[2716]:= **LoadPackage[x_ /; FileExistsQ[x] && FileExtension[x] == "mx"] := Module[{a},**
Quiet[ToExpression["Off[shdw::Symbol]"]; Get[x]; a = ToExpression["Packages[][[1]]"];
ToExpression["LoadMyPackage[" <> "\"" <> x <> "\"" <> "," <> "\"" <> a <> "\"" <> "]"];
ToExpression["On[shdw::Symbol]"]]]

In[2717]:= **LoadPackage["C:\\Users\\Mathematica\\MathToolBox.mx"]**
In[2718]:= **Definition["DirName"]**
Out[2718]= DirName[F_ /; StringQ[F]] := If[DirQ[F], "None", If[! FileExistsQ1[F], $Failed,
Quiet[Check[FileNameJoin[FileNameSplit[F][[1; -2]]], "None"]]]]

On inactive contexts x the procedure calls **ContOfContext[x]** return *$Failed* while in other cases the procedure call is returned unevaluated. Qua of one of possible appendices of the given procedure it is possible to note problems which deal with source codes of software of the user packages. With the aim of full elimination of similar distinction the **LoadPackage** procedure completing the previous fragment can be used. The call **LoadPackage[*x*]** returns *Null*, i.e. nothing, uploading the user package contained in a *x* datafile of *mx*-format into the current session of the *Mathematica* with activation of all definitions which contain in it in a mode similar to the mode of the *Input* paragraph of the *Mathematica* system.

Qua of useful addition to the **ContOfContex** procedure, the **NamesContext** procedure can be quite considered, whose call **NamesContext[*x*]** returns the list of names in string format of program objects of the current session which are associated with a *x* context. In a case of absence of this context the empty list is returned. If the *x* value is different from the context the procedure call is returned unevaluated. The following fragment represents source code of the **NamesContext** procedure along with typical examples of its application.

In[2840]:= **NamesContext[x_ /; ContextQ[x]] :=**
Module[{b, c = {}, k = 1, h, a = Names[x <> "*"]},
While[k <= Length[a], b = a[[k]];
h = Quiet[ToString[ToExpression["Definition[" <> b <> "]"]]];
If[h != "Null" && h != "Attributes[" <> b <> "] = {Temporary}" && ! SuffPref[b, "a$", 1],
AppendTo[c, a[[k]]]]; k++]; c]

In[2841]:= **NamesContext["AladjevProcedures`"]**
Out[2841]= "AcNb", "ActBFM", "ActBFMuserQ", ..., "$Version1", "$Version2"}
In[2842]:= **Length[%]**
Out[2842]= 1146
In[2843]:= **NamesContext["Global`"]**
Out[2843]= {"Agn", "Avz", "P", "Pobj", "ArtKr", "Pr", "RemoveContext"}
In[2844]:= **Length[%]**
Out[2844]= 6
In[2845]:= **NamesContext["System`"]**
Out[2845]= {"\[FormalA]", "\[FormalB]", ..., "\[SystemsModelDelay]", λ}
In[2846]:= **Length[%]**
Out[2846]= 5608
In[2847]:= **NamesContext["Tallinn`"]**
Out[2847]= {}

The procedure call **Contexts1[]** which is a simple modification of the **Contexts** function that provides testing of an arbitrary string for admissibility qua of a syntactically correct context returns the list of contexts corresponding to packages whose components have been loaded into the current *Mathematica* session. The following fragment represents source code of the procedure **Contexts1** with a typical example of its application.

In[2920]:= **Contexts1[] := Module[{a = {}, b = Contexts[], c, k = 1},**
For[k, k <= Length[b], k++, c = b[[k]];
If[Length[DeleteDuplicates[Flatten[StringPosition[c, "`"]]]] == 1 &&
StringTake[c, {-1, -1}] == "`", AppendTo[a, c], Next[]]]; a]

In[2921]:= **Contexts1[]**
Out[2921]= {"AladjevProcedures`", "Algebra`", "AlphaIntegration`",...}
In[2922]:= **Length[%]**

Out[2922]= 240

The following fragment represents source code of the **Contexts2** function being the simplest functional analog of the above procedure with a typical example of its application.

In[4557]:= **Contexts2[] := Sort[DeleteDuplicates[Map[StringTake[#,**
{1, Flatten[StringPosition[#, "`"]][[1]]}] &, Contexts[]]]]

In[4558]:= **Contexts2[]**
Out[4558]= {"AladjevProcedures`", "Algebra`", "Algebraics`", "AlphaIntegration`", ...}
In[4559]:= **Length[%]**
Out[4559]= 214

In some cases exists the problem of definition of *m*–files containing the definition of some object active in the current session. This problem is successfully solved by the procedure whose call **FindFileObject[x]** returns the list of datafiles containing definition of a *x* object, including the usage; in the absence of such *m*–files the procedure call returns the empty list, i.e. {}. The procedure call **FindFileObject[x, y, z,...]** with optional {*y, z,...*} arguments qua of which the names in the string format of devices of direct access are defined, provides search of *m*–files on the specified devices instead of search in all file system of the computer by the procedure call with one argument. The following fragment represents the source code of the **FindFileObject** procedure along with some typical examples of its application.

In[4363]:= **FindFileObject[x_ /; ! SameQ[ToString[DefOpt[ToString[x]]], "Null"], y___] :=**
Module[{b = {}, c = "", s = {}, d, k = 1, a = If[{y} == {}, Adrive[], {y}], f = "ArtKr",
h = "(*Begin[\"`" <> ToString[x] <> "`\"]*)", p = "(*" <> ToString[x] <> "::usage=", t},
While[k <= Length[a], Run["Dir ", a[[k]] <> ":\\", " /B/S/L > " <> f];
While[! SameQ[c, "EndOfFile"], c = ToString[Read[f, String]];
If[StringTake[c, {-2, -1}] == ".m", AppendTo[b, c]];
Continue[]]; Quiet[Close[f]]; c = ""; k++]; k = 1;
While[k <= Length[b], If[Select[ReadList[b[[k]], String], ! StringFreeQ[#, h] &&
StringFreeQ[#, p] &] != {}, AppendTo[s, b[[k]]]]; k++]; {DeleteFile[f], s}[[2]]]

In[4364]:= **FindFileObject[ProcQ, "C"]**
Out[4364]= {"c:\\$recycle.bin\\s-1-5-2596736632-989557747-1273926778-1000\\$r8tc3vj.m",
"c:\\aaa\\MathToolBox.m", "c:\\MathToolBox\\MathToolBox.m"}
In[4365]:= **Mapp[FindFileObject, {Mapp, AvzAgn}]**
Out[4365]= {{"c:\\grgu_books\\MathToolBox\\MathToolBox.m",
"e:\\MathToolBox\\MathToolBox.m"}, FindFileObject[AvzAgn]}

So, for identification of means of the user package whose definitions in the current session contain contextual references, the procedure can be used, whose the call **DefWithContext[x]** returns the 2-element nested list: it's the first element defines the list of names of tools of the package loaded from a *x m*–file whose definitions don't contain contextual references while the second element – the list of names of tools of the package whose definitions contain the contextual references. The following fragment represents source code of the procedure and examples of its application prior to the procedure call **ReloadPackage1** and after it, that is a rather evidently.

In[2982]:= **DefWithContext[x_ /; FileExistsQ[x] && FileExtension[x] == "m"] :=**

```
Module[{a = ContextMfile[x], b, c = {}, d = {}}, b = CNames[a];
Map[If[StringFreeQ[Definition4[#], a <> # <> "`"], AppendTo[c, #],
AppendTo[d, #]] &, b]; {c, d}]]
In[2983]:= DefWithContext["C:\\Mathematica\\MathToolBox.m"]
Out[2983]= {{"AcNb", "ActBFM", "Adrive", "Adrive1", ..., "$Version1", "$Version2"},
{"ActBFMuserQ", "ActCsProcFunc", "ActRemObj", ..., "$ProcName", "$TypeProc"}}
In[2984]:= Map[Length, %]
Out[2984]= {1058, 66}
In[2985]:= ReloadPackage1["C:\\Mathematica\\MathToolBox.m"]
In[2986]:= d = DefWithContext["C:\\Mathematica\\MathToolBox.m"];
In[2987]:= Map[Length, d]
Out[2987]= {1123, 0}
```

From the given fragment follows that practically *94.2%* of definitions of the means of our *MathToolBox* package loaded into the current session, which are received by means of the function call **Definition**[*x*] will contain context references of *"AladjevProcedures`x`"* format.

The next procedure is a rather useful version of the above **DefWithContext** procedure. The call **DefWithContext1**[*x*] returns the nested list whose elements represents lists of tools with a *x* context that is contained in the predefined *$Packages* variable of the *Mathematica*; the 1st list contains tools names *hj* in string format whose definitions no contain the expressions *x`hj`p*, while the second list contains tools names in string format whose definitions contain the expressions *x`hj`p* (i.e. their definitions obtained by means of the standard **Definition** *function are not optimized in the above sense*). Whereas the procedure call **ContentMx**[*x*] returns the list of means names in string format of a *x mx*-file whose definitions obtained by means of the standard **Definition** function are not optimized. The next fragment represents source codes of procedures **DefWithContext1** and **ContentMx** with examples of their application.

```
In[3674]:= DefWithContext1[x_ /; ContextQ[x] && MemberQ[$Packages, x]] :=
Module[{b = {}, c = {}},
Map[If[StringFreeQ[ToString1[Definition[#]], x <> # <> "`"], AppendTo[b, #],
AppendTo[c, #]] &, CNames[x]]; Map[Sort, {b, c}]]
In[3675]:= DefWithContext1["AladjevProcedures`"]
Out[3675]= {{"AcNb", "ActBFM", ..., "$Version2"}, {"ActBFMuserQ", ..., "$TypeProc"}}
In[3676]:= Map[Length, %]
Out[3676]= {1057, 66}
In[3687]:= ContentMx[x_ /; FileExistsQ[x] && FileExtension[x] == "mx"] :=
Module[{a = ReadString[x], b, c = ContextFromMx[x]},
If[c === $Failed, {}, b = StringCases[a, Shortest[c ~~ __ ~~ "`"]][[2 ;; -1]];
Sort[Select[Map[StringTake[#, {1, -2}] &, Map[StringReplace[#, c -> ""] &, b]],
SymbolQ[#] &]]]]
In[3688]:= Length[ContentMx["C:/aladjev/mathtoolbox/mathtoolbox.mx"]]
Out[3688]= 68
```

The **ContentMx1** procedure that also is based on internal structure of a *mx*-file in *Windows 7 Professional* is an useful version of the **ContentMx** procedure [48,50]. The next procedure is another tool of extraction from a *mx*-file of means names in string format whose definitions obtained by means of the standard **Definition** function aren`t optimized in the above sense.

In[3384]:= ContentMxFile[x_ /; FileExistsQ[x] && FileExtension[x] == "mx"] :=
Module[{a = ReplaceAll[BinaryReadList[x], 0 -> 32], b, c, d},
a = StringJoin[Map[FromCharacterCode, a]];
c = Quiet[Check[StringTake[StringCases[a, Shortest["CONT" ~~ __ ~~ "ENDCONT"]][[1]], {7, -10}], $Failed]];
If[c === $Failed, d = DeleteDuplicates[Flatten[StringPosition[a, "\.0b"]]];
d = Map[ExtrSubString[a, # - 2, -1, LetterQ[#] || DigitQ[#] &] &, d];
Sort[Select[d, Quiet[Check[SystemQ[#], False]] &]],
b = StringCases[a, Shortest[c ~~ __ ~~ "`"]][[2 ;; -1]];
b = Sort[DeleteDuplicates[Map[StringReplace[StringTake[#, {1, -2}], c -> ""] &, b]]];
Select[b, StringFreeQ[#, StringTake[c, {1, -2}]] &]]]

In[3385]:= Length[ContentMxFile["GeneralUtilities.mx"]]
Out[3385]= 843

The procedure call **ContentMxFile[x]** returns the list of names of tools of a *x mx*-file with non-optimized definitions in the above sense if the file contains a context, or the list of the names of system tools otherwise. The fragment above represents source codes of the both procedures with examples of their application.

At loading of the user package into the current session its context will be located in the list determined by the **$Packages** variable while at attempting to receive definitions of its tools by means of the **Definition** function some such definitions will contain context associated with this package. First of all, such definitions are much less readable however not this most important. For software which is based on optimum format and using similar definitions, in the process of work with them the erroneous situations are possible as it was already noted above. For the purpose of receiving definitions of means of the user package in the optimal format the **LoadMyPackage** procedure can be used. The procedure call **LoadMyPackage[x, y]** at the very beginning of the current session of the *Mathematica* returns *Null*, i.e. nothing, loading the user package *x* with an *y* context ascribed to it, with the subsequent *reevaluation* of definitions of its means, providing the optimal format of these definitions.

In[2593]:= LoadMyPackage[x_ /; FileExistsQ[x] && FileExtension[x] == "mx", y_] :=
Module[{a, Cn, Ts, k = 1},
Ts[g_] := Module[{p = "$Art27Kr20$.txt", b = "", c, d, v = 1}, Write[p, g]; Close[p];
While[v < Infinity, c = Read[p, String];
If[SameQ[c, EndOfFile], Close[p]; DeleteFile[p]; Return[b], b = b <> c]; Continue[]]];
Cn[t_] := Module[{s = Names[StringJoin[t, "*"]], b},
b = Select[s, Quiet[ToString[Definition[ToString[#1]]]] != "Null" &]];
Quiet[Get[x]]; a = Cn[y]; While[k <= Length[a],
Quiet[ToExpression[StringReplace[StringReplace[Ts[ToExpression["Definition[" <> a[[k]] <> "]"]], y -> ""], a[[k]] <> "`" -> ""]]]; k++]]

In[2594]:= LoadMyPackage["MathToolBox.mx", "AladjevProcedures`"]
In[2595]:= Definition["ContextQ"]

Out[2595]= ContextQ[x_] := StringQ[x] && StringLength[x] > 1 &&
Quiet[SymbolQ[Symbol[StringTake[x, {1, -2}]]]] && StringTake[x, {-1, -1}] == "`" &&
! StringTake[x, {1, 1}] === "`"

The previous fragment adduces source code of **LoadMyPackage** procedure with example of its application. Similar approach is recommended to be used at loading of the user package, saved in a file of *mx*-format, for elimination of the specified undesirable moments and for simplification of programming with use of its means, and for extension of the system on the basis of its means. Furthermore, the call **LoadMyPackage[x, y]** with the noted purposes can be executed and in the presence of the loaded user package *x* with *y* context. So, saving of a package in a *mx*-file with its subsequent uploading in each new session by the **Get** function, providing access to all package tools with receiving their definitions in the *optimized* format *(in the above-mentioned sense)* is the most effective.

In the course of operating in the current session with tools of an uploaded package *(from a m-file)* situations when certain of its activated means for one reason or another are removed of the current session or are distorted are quite real. For their restoration the **ReloadPackage** procedure can be used.

In[2992]:= ReloadPackage[x_ /; FileExistsQ[x] && FileExtension[x] == "m", y___List, t___]:=
Module[{a = NamesMPackage[x], b = ContextMfile[x], c = "$Art27Kr20$.txt", p, k = 1,
d = If[{y} != {}, ToExpression[Map14[StringJoin, Map[ToString, y], "[", 90]], {}]}, Put[c];
While[k <= Length[a], p = a[[k]];
PutAppend[StringReplace[ToString1[ToExpression["Definition[" <> p <> "]"]],
b <> p <> "`" -> ""], c]; k++];
If[d == {}, ToExpression["Clear[" <> StringTake[ToString[a], {2, -2}] <> "]"], Null];
While[b != "EndOfFile", b = ToString[Read[c]];
If[b === "EndOfFile", Break[]];
If[d == {}, Quiet[ToExpression[b]]; Continue[],
If[If[{t} == {}, MemberQ, ! MemberQ][d, StringTake[b, {1, Quiet[StringPosition[b,
"[", 1]][[1]][[1]]}]], Quiet[ToExpression[b]]; Break[], Continue[]]]]; DeleteFile[Close[c]]]
In[2993]:= ReloadPackage["C:\\Mathematica\\MathToolBox.m"]
In[2994]:= **Definition[StrStr]**
Out[2994]= StrStr[x_] := If[StringQ[x], "\"" <> x <> "\"", ToString[x]]
In[2995]:= **Clear[StrStr]; Definition[StrStr]**
Out[2995]= Null
In[2996]:= **ReloadPackage["C:\\Mathematica\\MathToolBox.m"]**
In[2997]:= **Definition[StrStr]**
Out[2997]= StrStr[x_] := If[StringQ[x], "\"" <> x <> "\"", ToString[x]]

The successful procedure call **ReloadPackage[x]** returns nothing, providing in the current session the activation of all tools of a package which is located in a *x m*-file as though their definitions were calculated in an input stream. If the call **ReloadPackage[x, y]** contains the second optional *y* argument qua of which the list of names is used, the reboot is made only for the package tools with the given names. At the same time the call **ReloadPackage[x, y, t]** in addition with the third optional argument where *t* – an arbitrary expression, also returns

Software Etudes in the Mathematica

nothing, providing reboot in the current session of all tools of the *x* package, excluding only means with the names given in the *y* list. The previous fragment presents source code of the **ReloadPackage** procedure with typical examples of its use. For instance, it is illustrated that reboot of a package provides more compact output of definitions of tools that are contained in it, i.e. the output of definitions is made in the so-called optimal format *(without contexts)*. The fragment below represents source code of the **ReloadPackage1** procedure, functionally equivalent to **ReloadPackage** procedure, with typical examples of its use.

In[4436]:= ReloadPackage1[x_ /; FileExistsQ[x] && FileExtension[x] == "m", y_: 0, t_: 0] :=
Module[{a = NamesMPackage[x], b = ReadFullFile[x], c, d = Map[ToString, Flatten[{y}]]},
c = Flatten[Map[SubsString[b, {"*)(*Begin[\"`" <> # <> "`\"]*)(*", "*)(*End[]*)"}, 90] &, a]];
c = Map[StringReplace[#, "*)(*" -> ""] &, c];
Map[If[d == {"0"}, Quiet[ToExpression[#]], If[ListQ[y], If[{t} == {0},
If[MemberQ[d, StringTake[#, Flatten[StringPosition[#, {"[", " :=", "="}]][[1]] - 1]],
ToExpression[#], If[! MemberQ[d, StringTake[#, Flatten[StringPosition[#,
{"[", " :=", "="}]][[1]] - 1]], ToExpression[#]]]]] &, c];]

In[4437]:= Map[Clear, {StrStr, Map2}]
Out[4437]= {Null, Null}
In[4438]:= Definition[StrStr]
Out[4438]= Null
In[4439]:= Definition[Map2]
Out[4439]= Null
In[4440]:= ReloadPackage1["C:\\Mathematica\\MathToolBox.m", {StrStr, Map2}]
In[4441]:= Definition[StrStr]
Out[4441]= StrStr[x_] := If[StringQ[x], "\"" <> x <> "\"", ToString[x]]
In[4442]:= Definition[Map2]
Out[4442]= Map2[F_ /; SymbolQ[F], c_ /; ListQ[c], d_ /; ListQ[d]] :=
(Symbol[ToString[F]][#1, Sequences[d]] &) /@ c

The successful procedure call **ReloadPackage1**[*x*] returns *nothing*, providing in the current session the activation of all tools of a package which is located in a *x m*-file as though their definitions were calculated in an input stream. If the call **ReloadPackage1**[*x, y*] contains the second optional *y* argument qua of which the list of names is used, the reboot is made only for the package means with the given names. Furthermore, the call **ReloadPackage1**[*x, y, t*] in addition with the third optional argument where *t* – an arbitrary expression, also returns nothing, providing reboot in the current session of all means from the *x* package, excluding only means with the names given in the *y* list. At that, similar to **ReloadPackage** procedure the **ReloadPackage1** procedure, in particular, provides output of definitions in the optimal format in the above sense too. The given modification is of interest from the standpoint of the approaches used in it. Such approach allows to get rid of contextual links in definitions of the functions or procedures uploaded into the current session from the user package. At that, with methods of uploading of the user packages into the current session it is possible to familiarize enough in details in our collection [50].

As it was noted earlier, in the result of loading into the current session of the user package from a file of format {*m, nb*} with its subsequent activation an essential part of definitions of its tools received by the call of standard **Definition** function will include contextual links of the *"Context'x'"* format, where *x* – a name of tools and *"Context"* – a context ascribed to the given package. Tools of identification of those objects of the user package whose definitions have contextual references are represented above. However, these means suppose that the analyzed package is activated in the current session. While the next procedure provides the similar analysis of an unuploaded package located in a datafile of *mx*-format. The fragment below represents source code of the **MxPackNames** procedure with an example of its usage. The procedure call **MxPackNames[*x*]** returns the list of names of objects in string format of *y nb*-file which is an analog of a *x mx*-file, whose definitions in case of loading of the *y* file into the current *Mathematica* session with *subsequent* activation system **Definition** function will return with contextual links of the above format.

In[3235]:= **MxPackNames[x_ /; FileExistsQ[x] && FileExtension[x] == "mx"]** :=
Module[{b, c, d, g = {}, k, j,
a = FromCharacterCode[Select[ToCharacterCode[ReadFullFile[x]], # > 31 &]]},
b = StringPosition[a, {"CONT", "ENDCONT"}][[1 ;; 2]];
If[b[[1]][[2]] == b[[2]][[2]], {}, b = StringTake[a, {b[[1]][[2]] + 2, b[[2]][[1]] – 1}];
b = Map[#[[2]] + 1 &, StringPosition[a, b][[2 ;; –1]]];
For[k = 1, k <= Length[b], k++, c = "";
For[j = b[[k]], j < Infinity, j++, d = StringTake[a, {j, j}];
If[d == "`", Break[], c = c <> d]]; AppendTo[g, c]];
Sort[Select[g, StringFreeQ[#, {"[", "("}] &]][[2 ;; –1]]]]

In[3236]:= **MxPackNames["C:\\Mathematica\\MathToolBox.mx"]**
Out[3236]= {"ActCsProcFunc", "ActRemObj", ..., "$Line1", "$ProcName", "$TypeProc"}
In[3237]:= **Length[%]**
Out[3237]= 67
In[3238]:= **N[67*100/Length[CNames["AladjevProcedures`"]], 5]**
Out[3238]= 5.99

Examples of the previous fragment once again confirm that quantity of tools of our package *MathToolBox*, uploaded into the current session from a *nb*-file, whose definitions received by the **Definition** function contain contextual references in the amount 6%.

The question of obtaining the list of *names* of objects whose definitions with their usage are located in a package being in a datafile of format {*m*, *nb*} is represented interesting enough. At that, it is supposed that uploading of a package into the current session isn't obligatory. Such problem is solved by quite useful procedure, whose call **PackNames[*x*]** returns the list of names of the above objects in a package, being in a *x* datafile of format {*m*, *nb*}. The next fragment represents source code of the **PackNames** procedure with an example of its usage with the *MathToolBox* package that is located in the *ASCII* datafiles *"MathToolBox.m"* and *"MathToolBox.nb"* [48,50].

In[2872]:= **PackNames[x_ /; FileExistsQ[x] && MemberQ[{"m", "nb"}, FileExtension[x]]] :=**
Module[{b, c = {}, d = "", k = 1, j, h, a = StringReplace[ReadFullFile[x], {" " -> "", "\n" -> ""}]},
If[FileExtension[x] == "m", Sort[Map[StringTake[#, {9, –4}] &,
StringCases[a, Shortest["Begin[\"`" ~~ __ ~~ "`\"]"]]]],

```
b = Quiet[SubsString1[a, {"RowBox[{RowBox[{RowBox[{", "\"::\"", "\"usage\"}]"},
StringQ[#] &, 0]]; b = Map[StringTake[#, {2, -6}] &, b];
Select[Sort[(If[SymbolQ[#1], #1] &) /@ b], ! SameQ[#, Null] &]]]
```

In[2873]:= **PackNames["C:\\MathToolBox\\MathToolBox.m"]**
Out[2873]= {"AcNb", "ActBFM", "ActBFMuserQ", "ActCsProcFunc",...}
In[2874]:= **Length[%]**
Out[2874]= 1150
In[2875]:= **PackNames["C:\\MathToolBox\\MathToolBox.nb"]**
Out[2875]= {"AcNb", "ActBFM", "ActBFMuserQ", "ActCsProcFunc",...}
In[2876]:= **Length[%]**
Out[2876]= 1132

It should be noted that algorithm of **PackNames** procedure significantly uses **SubsString1** procedure which is the **SubsString** procedure extension, being of interest in programming of the problems connected with processing of strings. Here, in connection with the aforesaid it is quite appropriate to raise an important enough concerning the global variables defined by a procedure.

The following **PackNames1** procedure solves the problem of obtaining of the names list of the objects whose definitions with usage are in a package, being in a file of the *mx*-format. Furthermore, it is supposed that package loading into the current session isn't obligatory. The problem is solved by a quite useful procedure, whose call **PackNames1[*x*]** returns the names list of the above objects in a package, being in a *x* datafile of the *mx*-format whose definitions are associated with a context of *x mx*-file, for example, by means of the function **Definition**. The fragment below represents source code of the procedure with an example of its typical application.

In[3917]:= **PackNames1[x_ /; FileExistsQ[x] && FileExtension[x] == "mx"] :=**
Module[{a = ReadFullFile[x], b = ContextFromMx[x]},
If[b === $Failed, {}, a = StringCases[a, Shortest[b ~~ __ ~~ "`"]];
a = Select[a, StringFreeQ[#, {"\.0b", "[", "{"}] &];
Sort[Map[StringReplace[#, {b -> "", "`" -> ""}] &, a]]]]

In[3918]:= **PackNames1["C:\\MathToolBox\\MathToolBox.mx"]**
Out[3918]= {"ActBFMuserQ", "ActCsProcFunc", "ActRemObj",...}
In[3919]:= **Length[%]**
Out[3919]= 68
In[3920]:= **N[68*100/Length[CNames["AladjevProcedures`"]], 5]**
Out[3920]= 6.0552

Thus, the *MathToolBox* package contained in a *mx*-file at its uploading into the current session by means of the **Get** function activates all definitions that contained in the *mx*-file. Furthermore, among these definitions returned by the standard **Definition** function nearly *6.1%* of definitions not include a context associated with a package from *mx*-file. The above procedure essentially uses our procedures **ContextFromMx** and **ReadFullFile** described in the present book along with **Shortest** function whose call **Shortest[*h*]** is a pattern object that matches the shortest sequence consistent with a *h* pattern.

The following **PackNames2** procedure using **Shortest** function, whose call **Shortest[h]** is a pattern object which matches the shortest sequence consistent with a *h* pattern, solves the problem of obtaining of the names list of objects whose definitions are in a package, being in a file of the *nb*-format. In addition, it is supposed that package loading into the current session isn't obligatory. The given problem is solved by means of a quite useful procedure, whose call **PackNames2[x]** returns the names list of the above objects in a package, being in a *x* datafile of the *nb*-format. The fragment below represents source code of the procedure along with a typical example of its application.

```
In[2964]:= PackNames2[x_ /; FileExistsQ[x] && FileExtension[x] == "nb"] :=
Module[{a = StringReplace[ReadFullFile[x], {" " -> "", "\n" -> ""}], c},
a = StringCases[a, Shortest["RowBox[{\"Begin\",\"[\",\"\\\"\\<`" ~~ __ ~~
"`\\>\\\"\",\"]\"}]"]];
a = Select[a, StringCount[#, "RowBox"] == 1 &];
Sort[DeleteDuplicates[Map[{c = DeleteDuplicates[Flatten[StringPosition[#, "`"]]],
StringTake[#, {c[[1]] + 1, c[[2]] - 1}]}[[2]] &, a]]]

In[2965]:= PackNames2["C:\\MathToolBox\\MathToolBox.nb"]
Out[2965]= {"AcNb", "ActBFM", "ActBFMuserQ", "ActCsProcFunc", ...}
In[2966]:= Length[%]
Out[2966]= 1143
```

The method based on use of construction of the type **Simplest[a ~~ __ ~~ b]** and used, for example, by the procedures **PackNames ÷ PackNames2** is very effective at organization of choice of substrings from a string provided that choice of substrings *a* and *b* is correct.

According to agreements of procedural programming, a variable defined in the procedure qua of *global* variable is visible outside of the procedure, i.e. can change own value both in the procedure, and outside of it, more precisely, field of its definition is the current session as a whole. In principle, this agreement is fair and for the current session of *Mathematica* system, but with very essential stipulations which are discussed in [30,33] with interesting enough examples. If a certain procedure defining global variables has been activated in the *Input* stream, the above agreement is valid. Meanwhile, if such procedure is located in a file of format {*m*|*nb*}, then the subsequent uploading of such file into the current session makes active all tools contained in the file, making them available, however the mechanism of the global variables as a whole doesn't work. In our work [33] an approach eliminating defects of the mechanism of global variables is represented.

For providing the mechanism of global variables *(including)*, an useful **LoadNameFromM** procedure was created whose call **LoadNameFromM[f, n]** provides loading and activation in the current session of a *n* procedure or their list saved in a *f* file of the *m*-format with a package. The following fragment represents source code of the procedure with an example.

```
In[2588]:= LoadNameFromM[F_ /; FileExistsQ[F] && FileExtension[F] == "m" &&
StringTake[ToString[ContextFromFile[F]], -1] == "`", p_ /; StringQ[p] || ListStringQ[p]]:=
Module[{a = ReadFullFile[F], b = {}, c = "*)(*End[]*)", d, h = Flatten[{p}]},
h = Select[h, ! StringFreeQ[a, "`" <> # <> "`"] &]; If[h == {}, $Failed,
b = Map[SubString[a, {"(*Begin[\"`" <> # <> "`\"]*)(*", c}, 90] &, h];
```

b = If[Length[b] == 1, Flatten[b], Map[#[[1]] &, b]];
Map[ToExpression, Map[StringReplace[#, "*)(*" -> " "] &, b]];]]

In[2589]:= LoadNameFromM["C:\\Temp\\MathToolBox.m", "StrStr"]
In[2590]:= Definition[StrStr]
Out[2590]= StrStr[x_] := If[StringQ[x], "\"" <> x <> "\"", ToString[x]]

The previous fragment represents source code of the given procedure with an example of its usage. The procedure in a certain relation is adjoined the **ExtrPackName** procedure too. The algorithm of the procedure is based on analysis of *internal* structure of a file of the *m*-format with the user package. The successful procedure call **ExtrPackName[f, w]** returns *Null*, i.e. nothing, with simultaneous return of the evaluated definition of a *w* object which is located in a *f m*-file with the user package, making the definition available in the current session. If format of a *f* file is other than *m*-format, the procedure call returns *$Failed*, while in absence in the *f* file of the requested *w* object the call **ExtrPackName[f, w]** returns the corresponding message. The fragment below represents source code of the **ExtrPackName** procedure along with some typical examples of its application.

In[2883]:= ExtrPackName[F_ /; StringQ[F], N_ /; StringQ[N]] := Module[{a, b, c, d, Art, Kr},
If[FileExistsQ[F] && FileExtension[F] == "m" &&
StringTake[ToString[ContextFromFile[F]], -1] == "`", a = OpenRead[F], Return[$Failed]];
If[Read[a, String] != "(* ::Package:: *)", Close[a]; $Failed,
{c, d} = {"", StringReplace["(*Begin[\"`Z`\"]*)", "Z" -> N]}];
Label[Art]; b = Read[a, String]; If[b === EndOfFile, Close[a];
Return["Definition of " <> N <> " is absent in file <" <> F <> ">"], Null];
If[b != d, Goto[Art], Label[Kr]; b = StringTake[Read[a, String], {3, -3}];
c = c <> b <> " "; If[b == "End[]", Close[a];
Return[ToExpression[StringTake[c, {1, -8}]]], Goto[Kr]]]]

In[2884]:= ExtrPackName["F:\\Mathematica\\MathToolBox.m", "Df"]
In[2885]:= ExtrPackName["F:\\Mathematica\\MathToolBox.m", "Subs"]
In[2886]:= ExtrPackName["F:\\Mathematica\\MathToolBox.m", "ArtKr"]
Out[2886]= "Definition of ArtKr is absent in file <F:\\Mathematica\\MathToolBox.m>"
In[2887]:= ExtrPackName["C:\\Temp\\MathToolBox_6.m", "ProcQ"]
Out[2887]= $Failed
In[2888]:= Df[(Sin[1/x^2] + Cos[1/x^2])/x^2, 1/x^2]
Out[2888]= x^2*(-(-1 + x^2)*Cos[1/x^2] - (1 + x^2)*Sin[1/x^2])
In[2889]:= Subs[(Sin[1/x^2] + Cos[1/x^2])/x^2, 1/x^2, h]
Out[2889]= (Cos[h] + Sin[h])/h
In[2890]:= ExtrPackName["C:\\Temp\\Tallinn.m", "Gs"]; Definition[Gs]
Out[2890]= Gs[x_ /; IntegerQ[x], y_ /; IntegerQ[y]] := x^2 + y^2

The procedure provides activation in the current session of concrete function or procedure that is located in a *m*-file without loading of the file completely. By functionality the given procedure is crossed with the **LoadNameFromM** procedure considered above, however it possesses certain additional useful opportunities.

As a rule, enough many of the user packages contain in own structure the variables of some types which appear at their uploading into the current session of the system. For definition of such variables the procedure can be used, whose call **UserPackTempVars**[*x*] returns the 3-element nested list where the first sublist determines the undefinite variables associated with the package defined by a *x* context, the second sublist defines the temporary variables associated with the package and having names of format "**Name$**" whereas the third sublist defines symbols of "**Name$Integer**" format that in the current session aren't distinguished as symbols. The **TempInPack** function, based on the **TemporaryQ** function is a version of the above procedure [48,50].

In[2684]:= UserPackTempVars[x_ /; ContextQ[x]] :=
Module[{a = {}, p, b = {}, d = {}, c = Names[x <> "*"], h = {}},
Quiet[Map[{p = Definition2[#], If[UnevaluatedQ[Definition2, #], AppendTo[d, #],
If[p[[2]] == {} && p[[1]] == "Undefined", AppendTo[a, #], If[p[[2]] == {Temporary},
AppendTo[b, #], 6]]]} &, c]];
Map[{p = Flatten[StringPosition[#, "$"]], If[p[[-1]] == StringLength[#], AppendTo[a, #],
If[IntegerQ[ToExpression[StringTake[#, {p[[-1]] + 1, StringLength[#]}]]],
AppendTo[h, #]]]} &, b]; {d, a, h}]

In[2685]:= UserPackTempVars["AladjevProcedures`"]
Out[2685]= {{"a", "A", "a1", ..., "z"}, {"a1$", ..., "z$"}, {"a$1868", "b$1868"}}

In[2695]:= $UserContexts:= Select[Map[If[Flatten[UserPackTempVars[#][[2 ;; 3]]] != {}, #] &,
Select[$Packages, ! MemberQ[{"Global`", "System`"}, #] &]], ! SameQ[#, Null] &]

In[2696]:= $UserContexts
Out[2696]= {"AladjevProcedures`", "RansIan`"}

Definition of the global *$UserContexts* variable defining list of contexts of the user packages uploaded into the current session completes the previous fragment. In addition, the variable determines only contexts of the packages which generate in the current session the variables of 2 types presented above according to **UserPackTempVars** procedure. The example below presents one more realization of the above *$UserContexts* function. Global *$UserContexts1* variable returns list of the user contexts which have been made active in the current session.

In[3858]:= $UserContexts1 := Module[{a = Map[{#, ToString[FindFile[#]]} &,
DeleteDuplicates[Map[StringSplit[#, "`"][[1]] <> "`" &, Complement[Contexts[],
{"Global`", "System`"}]]]], b},
b = Select[a, StringFreeQ[#[[2]], "\\Mathematica\\"] &];
b = Select[b, CNames[#[[1]]] != {} &];
b = Select[b, Complement[DeleteDuplicates[Map[PureDefinition, CNames[#[[1]]]]],
{$Failed, "System"}] != {} &]; Map[#[[1]] &, b]]

In[3859]:= $UserContexts1
Out[3859]= {"AladjevProcedures`", "RansIan`"}

Depending on a state of the current session the execution of the above 3 tools can demand certain time expenses. Whereas the global variable, whose call *$UserContexts2* returns the list of all user contexts that have been made active in the current session is essentially more quick, basing on the other algorithm. The following fragment represents source code of the global variable with an example of its application.

In[3884]:= **$UserContexts2 := Module[{a = ToString[FileNames["*", $InstallationDirectory, Infinity]], b = Complement[$Packages, {"System`", "Global`"}]}, Select[b, StringFreeQ[a, "\\" <> StringSplit[#, "`"][[1]] <> "."] &]]**

In[3885]:= **$UserContexts2**
Out[3885]= {"AladjevProcedures`", "RansIan`"}

Along with the user contexts the processing of system contexts is of quite certain interest in connection with their close association with the system packages. In particular, he call of the global **$SysPackagesContexts** variable returns the sorted list of the contexts associated with *m*-files from the system catalog **$InstallationDirectory**. Whereas the call of global variable **$CurrentUserPackages** returns the sorted list of the user contexts with packages activated in the current session. In its turn, the call of the *global* **$SysContextsInM** variable returns the list of the contexts restricted by the package brackets **BeginPackage[.....]** and **EndPackage[]** which are contained in *m*-files from system catalog **$InstallationDirectory**. The following procedure has of quite certain interest at processing files, first of all types {*"m"*, *"nb"*, *"cdf"*} regarding detection in them of formally correct contexts. The procedure call **ExtrContexts[x]** returns the sorted list of formally correct contexts contained in a really existing *x* datafile. Furthermore, at absence of the *x* file the unevaluated procedure call is returned, whereas at absence of any contexts *$Failed* is returned. At last, using the above **ExtrContexts** procedure an useful global variable extending the *$SysContextsInM* variable can be programmed; its call *$SysContextsInM1[x, y]* returns the sorted list of contexts contained in datafiles from a *x* directory; at that, if the second optional *y* argument is absent then all files of the *x* directory in all subdirectories of the *x* are analyzed, in opposite case only all files with *y* extension are analyzed. The fragment below represents source codes of the above 5 means with examples of their application.

In[4885]:= **$SysPackagesContexts := Map[# <> "`" &, Sort[DeleteDuplicates[Map[FileBaseName, FileNames["*.m", $InstallationDirectory, Infinity]]]]]**

In[4886]:= **$SysPackagesContexts**
Out[4886]= {"AbelianGroup`", "AbortProtect`", "Abs`", ..., "ZTest`", "ZTransform`"}
In[4837]:= **Length[%]**
Out[4837]= 2838

In[4847]:= **$CurrentUserPackages := Select[Complement[$ContextPath, {"Global`", "System`"}], ! MemberQ[$SysPackagesContexts, StringSplit[#, "`"][[1]] <> "`"] &]**

In[4848]= **$CurrentUserPackages**
Out[4848]= {"AladjevProcedures`", "RansIan`"}

In[5812]:= **$SysContextsInM :=**
Module[{a = FileNames["*.m", $InstallationDirectory, Infinity], b},
b = Map[Quiet[Check[StringCases[ReadFullFile[#],
Shortest["BeginPackage[" ~~ __ ~~ "]"]][[1]], Nothing]] &, a];
b = Map[StringCases[#, "\"" ~~ __ ~~ "`\""] &, b];

```
b = Flatten[Map[StringSplit[StringReplace[#, {"\"" -> "", "`\"" -> "`"}],
{" ", ",", "{", "}"}] &, b]];
Sort[DeleteDuplicates[Select[b, ContextQ[#] &]],
StringCount[#1, "`"] <= StringCount[#2, "`"] &]]
```

In[5813]:= **$SysContextsInM**
Out[5813]= {"AuthorTools`", ..., "DeviceAPI`Drivers`Demos`WriteDemo`Dump`"}
In[5814]:= **Length[%]**
Out[5814]= 305

```
In[5817]:= ExtrContexts[x_ /; FileExistsQ[x]] :=
Module[{a = ReadFullFile[x], b, c = {}, d = Flatten[{CharacterRange["A", "Z"],
CharacterRange["a", "z"], "`"}], g, h = ""},
b = DeleteDuplicates[Flatten[StringPosition[a, "`"]]];
If[b == {}, $Failed, Do[h = "`"; Do[If[MemberQ[d, Set[g, StringTake[a, {j, j}]]], h = g <> h,
AppendTo[c, h]; Break[]], {j, b[[k]] - 1, 1, -1}], {k, 1, Length[b]}];
Sort[Select[DeleteDuplicates[c], ContextQ[#] &]]]]
```

In[5818]:= **ExtrContexts["C:\\temp\\generalutilities.m"]**
Out[5818]= {"GeneralUtilities`", "GeneralUtilitiesLoader`"}
In[5819]:= **ExtrContexts["C:\\temp\\PacletInfo.m"]**
Out[5819]= {"Factual`", "FactualFunctions`", "FactualLoad`"}
In[5820]:= **ExtrContexts["C:\\temp\\GCCCompiler.m"]**
Out[5820]= {"CCompilerDriver`", "CCompilerDriver`GCCCompiler`", "`Private`",
"CCompilerDriver`CCompilerDriverBase`", "CCompilerDriver`CCompilerDriverRegistry`"}
In[5821]:= **ExtrContexts["C:\\temp\\Cinema_2017.txt"]**
Out[5821]= $Failed

```
In[5823]:= $SysContextsInM1[x_ /; DirQ[x], y___String] :=
Module[{a = FileNames["*." <> If[{y} == {}, "*", y], x, Infinity], b},
b = Sort[ReplaceAll[DeleteDuplicates[Flatten[Map[ExtrContexts, a]]],
$Failed -> Nothing]];
Sort[DeleteDuplicates[Select[b, ContextQ[#] &]],
StringCount[#1, "`"] <= StringCount[#2, "`"] &]]
```

In[5824]:= **$SysContextsInM1[$InstallationDirectory <> "\\SystemFiles\\Devices", "m"]**
Out[5824]= {"DeviceAPI`", ...,"DeviceAPI`Drivers`Demos`WriteDemo`Dump`"}
In[5825]:= **Length[%]**
Out[5825]= 33

Qua of an addition to the above means the **NamesNbPackage** procedure can represent a certain interest, whose call **NamesNbPackage[W]** returns the list of names in string format of all tools which are located in a *W* file of *nb-*format with a package and that are supplied with *"usage"*. The fragment below represents source code of **NamesNbPackage** procedure with an example of its application to *nb-*file with *MathToolBox* package. Whereas the call **NamesNbPackage1[W]** *(procedure is an effective enough modification of the previous procedure)* returns the similar list of names in string format of all tools which are located in a *W* file of *nb*-format with a package; it is supposed that all means are provided with *"usage"*; in the absence of such means the empty list, i.e. {} is returned.

In[2628]:= **NamesNbPackage[f_ /; IsFile[f] && FileExtension[f] == "nb" &&**
! SameQ[ContextFromFile[f], $Failed]] := Module[{Res = {}, Tr},
Tr[x_ /; StringQ[x]] := Module[{c, d, h, g = "\"::\"", v = "\"=\"", p = "\"usage\"",
a = OpenRead[x], s = "   RowBox[{"}, Label[c]; d = Read[a, String];
If[d === EndOfFile, Close[a]; Return[Res], Null];
If[DeleteDuplicates[Map3[StringFreeQ, d, {s, g, p, v}]] == {False} && SuffPref[d, s, 1],
h = Flatten[StringPosition[d, g]];
AppendTo[Res, StringTake[d, {12, h[[1]] - 3}]]; Goto[c], Goto[c]]];
Map[ToExpression, Sort[Tr[f]]]]

In[2629]:= **NamesNbPackage["C:\\Mathematica\\MathToolBox.nb"]**
Out[2629]= {"AcNb", "ActBFM", "ActBFMuserQ", "ActCsProcFunc", ... }

In[2630]:= **NamesNbPackage1[f_ /; IsFile[f] && FileExtension[f] == "nb" &&**
! SameQ[ContextFromFile[f], $Failed]] :=
Module[{c, d, g = "::", a = OpenRead[f], p = "usage", v = "=", Res = {}, s = "   RowBox[{"},
Label[c]; d = Read[a, String]; If[d === EndOfFile, Close[a];
Return[Sort[Map[ToExpression, Res]]],
If[DeleteDuplicates[Map3[StringFreeQ, d, {s, g, p, v}]] == {False} && SuffPref[d, s, 1],
AppendTo[Res, StringReplace[StringSplit[d, ","][[1]], s -> ""]]; Goto[c]]; Goto[c]]]

In[2631]= **NamesNbPackage1["C:\\MathToolBox\\MathToolBox.nb"]**
Out[2631]= {"AcNb", "ActBFM", "ActBFMuserQ", "ActCsProcFunc", ... }
In[2632]:= **Length[%]**
Out[2632]= 1135

The following **NamesMPackage** procedure represents an analog of 2 previous procedures **NamesNbPackage** and **NamesNbPackage1**, oriented on a case of the user packages that are located in files of *m*-format. Successful procedure call **NamesMPackage1[*x*]** returns the list of names in string format of tools which are located in a *x* file of *m*-format with a package; it is supposed that all tools are provided with *"usage"*; in the absence of such tools the empty list is returned. The fragment below represents source code of **NamesMPackage** procedure with an example. This procedure well supplements the procedures **NamesNbPackage** and **NamesNbPackage1**.

In[3342]:= **NamesMPackage[f_ /; IsFile[f] && FileExtension[f] == "m" &&**
! SameQ[ContextFromFile[f], $Failed]] :=
Module[{c, d, Res = {}, s = "::usage=\"", a = OpenRead[f]},
Label[c];
d = Read[a, String]; If[SuffPref[d, "(*Begin[\"`", 1] || d === EndOfFile, Close[a];
Return[Sort[DeleteDuplicates[Res]]], If[SuffPref[d, "(*", 1] && ! StringFreeQ[d, s],
AppendTo[Res, StringTake[d, {3, Flatten[StringPosition[d, s]][[1]] - 1}]]; Goto[c], Goto[c]]]]

In[3343]:= **NamesMPackage["C:\\MathToolBox\\MathToolBox.m"]**
Out[3343]= {"AcNb", "ActBFM", "ActBFMuserQ", "ActCsProcFunc", ... }

In[3344]:= **Length[%]**
Out[3344]= 1137

The **ContextFromFile** function represented in the above fragment generalizes 3 procedures **ContextMfile, ContextMXfile** and **ContextNBfile**, returning the context associated with the packages saved in datafiles of the format {".cdf", ".m", ".mx", ".nb"}, and $Failed otherwise.

The question of extraction of definitions of functions and procedures from an unuploaded package which is located in a file of *m*–format is rather actual. In this regard we will present a procedure that solves this problem for the package located in a file of format {"cdf", "nb"}. The principal organization of a datafile of these formats with a package is represented at the beginning of the following fragment which is used and as one of examples. This package is previously saved in a file of format {".cdf", ".nb"} by means of chain of the *GUI* commands "*File → Save As*" (*GUI is abbreviation of the Graphic User Interface*).

BeginPackage["Grodno`"]
Gs::usage = "Help on Gs."
Ga::usage = "Help on Ga."
Vgs::usage = "Help on Vgs."
GSV::usage = "Help on GSV."
Begin["`Private`"]
Sv[x_] := 20*x^2 + 27*x + 590
End[]
Begin["`Gs`"]
Gs[x_Integer, y_Integer] := x^2 + y^2
End[]
Begin["`Ga`"]
Ga[x_Integer, y_Integer] := x*y + Gs[x, y]
End[]
Begin["`Vgs`"]
Vgs[x_Integer, y_Integer] := x*y
End[]
Begin["`GSV`"]
GSV[x_Integer, y_Integer] := Module[{a = 90, b = 590, c = 2016}, x*y + Gs[x, y]*(a + b + c)] + a*Sin[x]/(b + c)*Cos[y]
End[]
EndPackage[]

In[2669]:= **ExtrFromNBfile[x_ /; FileExistsQ[x] && MemberQ[{"cdf", "nb"}, FileExtension[x]], n_ /; StringQ[n]] :=**
Module[{a = ToString1[Get[x]], b = "`" <> n <> "`", c, d, p},
If[StringFreeQ[a, "\\\"`" <> n <> "`\\\"\""], $Failed,
a = StringTake[a, {Flatten[StringPosition[a, "Notebook["]][[1]], -1}];
c = StringCases[a, Shortest["RowBox[{\"Begin\", \"[\", \"\\\"" <> b <> "\\\"\", \"]\"}]" ~~ __ ~~ "RowBox[{\"End\", \"[\", \"]\"}]"]][[1]];
p = If[StringFreeQ[c, "[IndentingNewLine]"], 75, 70];
c = StringReplace[c, ", \"\\[IndentingNewLine]" -> ""];
d = Map[#[[1]] &, StringPosition[c, "RowBox"]];

```
c = StringTake[c, {d[[2]], If[p == 75, d[[-1]] - 9, d[[-2]] - 4]}];
d = DisplayForm[ToExpression[c]];
CDFDeploy[n, d, "Target" -> "CDFPlayer"];
d = StringTake[ToString[Import[n <> ".cdf", "Plaintext"]], {1, -5}];
DeleteFile[{n <> ".cdf", n <> ".png"}]; d]]
```

In[2670]:= **ExtrFromNBfile["C:/MathToolBox/MathToolBox.nb", "StrStr"]**
Out[2670]= "StrStr[x_] := If[StringQ[x], \"\\\"\" <> x <> \"\\\"\", ToString[x]]"
In[2671]:= **ExtrFromNBfile["C:/MathToolBox/MathToolBox.cdf", "StrStr"]**
Out[2671]= "StrStr[x_] := If[StringQ[x], \"\\\"\" <> x <> \"\\\"\", ToString[x]]
In[2672]:= **ExtrFromNBfile["C:\\Mathematica\\Grodno.nb", "GSV"]**
Out[2672]= "GSV[x_Integer, y_Integer] := Module[{a = 90, b = 590, c = 2016}, x*y + Gs[x, y]* (a + b + c)] + a*Sin[x]/(b + c)*Cos[y]"

The successful procedure call **ExtrFromNBfile[*x*, *y*]** returns the definition of an object in the string format with a name *y* given in string format from an unuploaded *x* datafile of format {"*cdf*", "*nb*"}, at the same time activating the definition in the current session; otherwise, the call returns $*Failed*. Qua of an useful property of this procedure is the circumstance that the *x* file not require of uploading into the current session.

All tools represented above for processing of datafiles of formats {"*cdf*", "*nb*"} with the user packages were debugged in the software of *Mathematica* of versions *10.0.0 ÷ 11.2.0*; at that, their structural organization is the cornerstone of algorithms realized by these means. The **ExtrFromNBfile1** procedure represented below is a certain analog of the above procedure **ExtrFromNBfile**. The following fragment presents source code of the procedure along with examples of its application.

In[3063]:= **ExtrFromNBfile1[x_ /; FileExistsQ[x] && MemberQ[{"cdf", "nb"}, FileExtension[x]], n_ /; StringQ[n], m___] :=**
Module[{a = ToString[InputForm[Get[x]]], c = "`" <> n <> "`", b = "RowBox[{\"End\", \"[\", \"]\"}]", d, h, t}, d = StringCases[a, c ~~ Shortest[X__] ~~ b];
If[d == {}, {}, d = StringTake[d, {Flatten[StringPosition[d, "RowBox[{"]][[1]], -1}];
d = StringReplace[d[[1]], b -> ""]; h = d;
While[! SyntaxQ[h], h = StringTake[h, {1, -2}]]; h = DisplayForm[ToExpression[t = h]];
NotebookEvaluate[NotebookOpen[x, Visible -> False], EvaluationElements -> All];
CDFDeploy[n, h, "Target" -> "CDFPlayer"];
DeleteFile[n <> ".png"]; If[{m} != {} && ! HowAct[m],
m = Directory[] <> "\\" <> n <> ".cdf", Null]; h]]

In[3064]:= **ExtrFromNBfile1["C:/mathtoolbox/mathtoolbox.nb", "StrStr", t6]**
Out[3064]//DisplayForm=
StrStr[x_] := If[StringQ[x], "\"" <> x <> "\"", ToString[x]]
In[3065]:= **t6**
Out[3065]= "C:\\Users\\Aladjev\\Documents\\StrStr.cdf"

The successful procedure call **ExtrFromNBfile1[*x*, *y*]** returns the definition of an object in the *DisplayForm* format with an *y* name given in string format from an unuploaded *x* file of format {"*cdf*", "*nb*"}, activating an *y* object in the current session; otherwise, the call returns the empty list, whereas the call **ExtrFromNBfile1[*x*, *y*, *t*]**, where *t* – an undefinite variable – through *t* additionally returns full path to *cdf*-file with definition of the *y* object. Qua of an useful property of this procedure is the circumstance that the *x* file not require of uploading into the current session.

The procedure call **ExtrFromNBfile2[*x*, *y*]** returns the definition of an object with an *y* name given in string format from the unuploaded or the uploaded user package located in a *x* file of the format {".cdf", ".nb"}. At that, the *x* file not require of loading into the current session. The next fragment represents source code of the **ExtrFromNBfile2** procedure with examples of its application.

In[4202]:= **ExtrFromNBfile2[x_ /; FileExistsQ[x] && MemberQ[{"cdf", "nb"}, FileExtension[x]], n_ /; StringQ[n]] := Module[{a = ContextFromFile[x], b, c, d},**
If[a === $Failed, $Failed, d = If[PathToFileQ[x], x, Directory[] <> "\\" <> x];
If[MemberQ[$Packages, a], c = Map[StringReplace[#, a <> n <> "`" -> ""] &,
Flatten[{PureDefinition[n]}]];
If[ListQ[c] && Length[c] == 1, c[[1]], c], Quiet[Activate[ExtrFromNBfile1[x, n]]]];
If[! MemberQ[CNames[a], n], $Failed, b = Flatten[{PureDefinition[n]}];
c = Map[StringReplace[#, a <> n <> "`" -> ""] &, b];
RemovePackage[a]; Unprotect[n]; Quiet[Remove[n]];
If[ListQ[c] && Length[c] == 1, c[[1]], c]]]]]

In[4203]:= **ExtrFromNBfile2["Grodno.nb", "GSV"]**
Out[4203]= "GSV[x_, y_] := Module[{a, b, c}, x*y + Gs[x, y]*(a + b + c)]"
In[4204]:= **ExtrFromNBfile2["Grodno.nb", "Vgs"]**
Out[4204]= "Vgs[x_Integer, y_Integer] := x*y + StringLength[\"ArkKr\"]"
In[4205]:= **MemberQ[$Packages, "Grodno`"]**
Out[4205]= False
In[4206]:= **Definition[Vgs]**
Out[4206]= Null
In[4207]:= **Get["Grodno.mx"]**
In[4208]:= **ExtrFromNBfile2["Grodno.nb", "Vgs"]**
Out[4208]= "Vgs[x_Integer, y_Integer] := x*y + StringLength[\"ArkKr\"]"
In[4209]:= **Context[Vgs]**
Out[4209]= "Grodno`"

At last, algorithm of the following procedure similar to previous ones is based on internal format of a {*cdf*, *nb*} file too, however uses other approach. The call **ExtrFromNBfile3[*x*, *n*]** returns in string format the definition of an object located in a *x* file of format {*cdf*, *nb*} that is defined by a *n* name in string format or by their list; if the names list is as a *n* argument, the list of their definitions is returned generally speaking. Whereas the call **ExtrFromNBfile3[*x*, *n*, *y*]** with third optional *y* argument – an undefined variable – through it returns the list of elements of the kind {*mnw*, *$Failed*} that defines *mnw* names whose definitions are absent in the *x* file with the user package. It is assumed that the user package located in the *x* file is arranged in the above format, and tools definitions of the same name which are in it, are in different blocks of format "**Begin[...] ... End[]**". The fragment below represents source code of the procedure with typical examples of its application.

In[4769]:= ExtrFromNBfile3[x_ /; FileExistsQ[x] && MemberQ[{"cdf", "nb"},
FileExtension[x]], n_ /; StringQ[n] || ListQ[n] && n != {} && AllTrue[Map[StringQ[#] &,
Flatten[{n}]], TrueQ], y___] := Module[{a = Get[x], b, c, d = {}, g = {}, h = Flatten[{n}], k = 1},
b = DisplayForm[a]; CDFDeploy[c = "$Art27$Kr20$.cdf", b, "Target" -> "CDFPlayer"];
b = ToString1[Import[c, "Plaintext"]]; DeleteFile[c];
For[k, k <= Length[h], k++, If[StringFreeQ[b, "Begin[\\\"`" <> h[[k]] <> "`\\\"]"],
AppendTo[g, {h[[k]], $Failed}],
c = DeleteDuplicates[StringCases[b, Shortest["Begin[\\\"`" <> h[[k]] <>
"`\\\"]" ~~ __ ~~ "End[]"]]];
c = Map[StringTake[#, {Flatten[StringPosition[#, h[[k]] <> "["]][[1]], -6}] &, c];
c = Map[StringReplace[#, {"\\r" -> "", "\\n" -> "", "\\" -> ""}] &, c];
AppendTo[d, c]]]; d = Flatten[d];
If[{y} != {} && ! HowAct[y], y = If[Length[g] == 1, g[[1]], g], Null];
If[Length[d] == 1, d[[1]], d]]

In[4770]:= ExtrFromNBfile3["C:/MathToolBox/MathToolBox.nb", "StrStr"]
Out[4770]= "StrStr[x_] := If[StringQ[x], \"\"\"<>x<>\"\"\", ToString[x]]"
In[4771]:= ExtrFromNBfile3["h:/grodno.nb", {"Vgs", "Ga", "Art", "Kr"}, g70]
Out[4771]= {"Vgs[x_Integer, y_Integer] := x*y", "Ga[x_Integer, y_Integer] := x*y + Gs[x, y]"}
In[4772]:= g70
Out[4772]= {{"Art", $Failed}, {"Kr", $Failed}}

In some cases the approach used in the previous procedure seems to us as an useful enough at programming of means based on the internal {"cdf", "nb"} format. In particular, for these purposes, the following procedure may be a rather useful means. The call **CdfNbToText[x]** returns the full path to a *txt*-file that contains in text format the content of *x* file of the type {"cdf", "nb"}. Whereas the call **CdfNbToText[x, y]** with 2nd optional argument – *an arbitrary expression* – returns the 2–element list whose 1st element is the above path to the *txt*-file, and the second element – the content of the *txt*-file. The fragment below represents source code of the **CdfNbToText** procedure along with examples of its application.

In[3215]:= CdfNbToText[x_ /; FileExistsQ[x] && MemberQ[{"cdf", "nb"},
FileExtension[x]], y___] := Module[{a = Get[x], b, c}, b = DisplayForm[a];
CDFDeploy[c = "$Art27$Kr20$.cdf", b, "Target" -> "CDFPlayer"];
b = ToString1[Import[c, "Plaintext"]]; Quiet[DeleteFile[{c, FileBaseName[c] <> ".png"}]];
c = DirectoryName[x] <> FileBaseName[x] <> ".txt";
StringReplace[b, {"\\r" -> "", "\\t" -> "", "\\n" -> "\n", "\\" -> ""}];
WriteString[c, b]; Close[c]; If[{y} != {}, {c, b}, c]]

In[3216]:= CdfNbToText["c:\\MathToolBox\\Grodno75.nb", 590]
Out[3216]= {"c:\\MathToolBox\\Grodno75.txt",
"\"Notebook[{BeginPackage[\"Grodno75`\"]
Gs::usage = \"Help on Gs.\"
Vgs::usage = \"Help on Vgs.\"
Begin[\"`Gs`\"]
Gs[x_Integer, y_Integer] := x^2 + y^2

```
End[]
Begin[\"`Vgs`\"]
Vgs[x_Integer, y_Integer] := x*y
End[]
EndPackage[]},
WindowSize -> {1904, 998}, WindowMargins -> {{0, Automatic}, {Automatic, 0}},
FrontEndVersion -> \"10.4 for Microsoft Windows (64-bit) (February 25, 2016)\",
StyleDefinitions -> \"Default.nb\"]\""}
In[3228]:= CdfNbToText["C:\\MathToolBox\\MathToolBox.nb"]
Out[3228]= "C:\\MathToolBox\\MathToolBox.txt"
```

The function call **EvaluateCdfNbFile[*w*]** returns nothing, calculating in the current session a *w* file of format *{"cdf", "nb"}* without its visualization and loading in the current session. Whereas the call **EvaluateCdfNbFile[*w*, *y*]** with the 2nd optional *y* argument – an arbitrary expression – does the above actions, visualizing additionally the *w* file. The procedure call **ContentsCdfNb[*x*]** returns the sorted list of objects names whose definitions are in a *x* file of the format *{"cdf", "nb"}*. The fragment below represent source codes of the function and procedure with examples of their typical applications.

```
In[3066]:= EvaluateCdfNbFile[x_ /; FileExistsQ[x] && MemberQ[{"cdf", "nb"},
FileExtension[x]], y___] :=
NotebookEvaluate[NotebookOpen[x, If[{y} != {}, Visible -> True, Visible -> False]],
EvaluationElements -> All]

In[3067]:= EvaluateCdfNbFile["C:\\MathToolBox\\Grodno.nb"];
In[3068]:= Definition[GSV]
Out[3068]= GSV[x_Integer, y_Integer] := Module[{a = 90, b = 590, c = 2016}, x*y + Gs[x, y]*
(a + b + c)] + (a*Sin[x]*Cos[y])/(b + c)
In[3069]:= CNames["Grodno`"]
Out[3069]= {"Ga", "Gs", "GSV", "Vgs"}

In[3111]:= ContentsCdfNb[x_ /; FileExistsQ[x] && MemberQ[{"cdf", "nb"},
FileExtension[x]]] :=
Module[{a = ToString1[Get[x]],
b = "RowBox[{\"Begin\", \"[\", \"\\\"`", c = "`\\\"\", \"]\"}]", d},
d = StringCases[a, b ~~ Shortest[X__] ~~ c];
DeleteDuplicates[Sort[Map[StringReplace[#, {b -> "", c -> ""}] &, d]]]]

In[3112]:= Length[ContentsCdfNb["C:/MathToolBox/MathToolBox.cdf"]]
Out[3112]= 1143
```

In particular, this function is a rather useful tool, allowing to receive in the current session the evaluated definitions contained in datafiles of the format *{"cdf", "nb"}* without loading of files into the current session. Whereas the procedure allows to obtain the contents of the *{"cdf", "nb"}*-files without uploading their into the current *Mathematica* session. In a lot of applications, the given means are quite useful in the program mode.

The following fragment represents one more means in two versions basing on an analysis of internal structure of the *cdf/nb*-files which allow to receive in the current session the means names of a *cdf/nb*-file that are provided by an usage. The procedure call **ContentCdfNb[*x*]** returns the list of the names in string format of means of a *cdf/nb*-file *x* which are provided by the usage. At that, performance of the procedure significantly depends on quantity of the means with usage located in the analyzed *cdf/nb*-file *x*. The **ContentCdfNb1** procedure is a more quick analog of the previous procedure. The fragment represents source codes of the both procedures with examples of their application.

In[1942]:= **ContentCdfNb[x_ /; FileExistsQ[x] && MemberQ[{"cdf", "nb"},**
FileExtension[x]]] := Module[{a = ReadString[x], b, c, d = "", g = {}},
b = Map[#[[1]] &, StringPosition[a, ", \":::\", \"usage\"}"]];
Do[Do[If[Set[c, StringTake[a, {j}]] === "{", AppendTo[g, d]; d = "";
Break[], d = c <> d], {j, b[[k]] - 1, 1, -1}], {k, 1, Length[b]}];
c = Sort[DeleteDuplicates[ToExpression[g]]];
Select[c, NameQ[#] && UpperCaseQ[StringTake[#, {1}]] || StringTake[#, {1}] == "$" &]]

In[1943]:= **Length[ContentCdfNb["C:\\Math\\MathToolBox.nb"]]**
Out[1943]= 1142

In[1942]:= **ContentCdfNb1[x_ /; FileExistsQ[x] && MemberQ[{"cdf", "nb"},**
FileExtension[x]]] :=
Module[{b = Range5[36, 48 ;; 58, 65 ;; 90, 97 ;; 123, 125], a = BinaryReadList[x], c},
a = Map[If[MemberQ[b, #], #, Nothing] &, a];
a = StringReplace[StringJoin[Map[FromCharacterCode, a]], "RowBox" -> ""];
b = StringCases[a, Shortest["{{{" ~~ __ ~~ "::usage"]];
c = StringCases[a, Shortest["{{" ~~ __ ~~ "::usage"]];
b = DeleteDuplicates[Join[b, c]]; b = Select[b, ! StringFreeQ[#, "::usage"] &];
b = Map[StringReplace[#, {"{" -> "", "::usage" -> ""}] &, b];
Sort[DeleteDuplicates[Select[b, SymbolQ[#] &]]]]

Note, to extract the tools names whose definitions are in a *txt*-file that is the result of a *nb*-document saving, the **ContentsTxt** procedure can be useful.

It is known that definitions of tools of the user packages kept in files of format {"*cdf*", "*nb*"}, have to be supplied with usage of the corresponding format. That requirement is obligatory for ensuring availability of these tools at evaluation of such datafiles in the current session. In this connexion it is expedient to have the means for testing of supply of means of such {"*cdf*", "*nb*"}-files with corresponding usage. The call **TestCdfNbFile[x]** returns the sorted list of tools of a *x* file of the format {"*cdf*", "*nb*"} which have not usage; otherwise the empty list is returned. While the call **TestCdfNbFile[x, y]** where *y – an undefinite variable –* through *y* additionally returns the list of tools names, whose definition are in the *x* file with the user package. The fragment below represents source code of the procedure with examples of its application.

In[3375]:= **TestCdfNbFile[x_ /; FileExistsQ[x] && MemberQ[{"cdf", "nb"},**
FileExtension[x]], y__] :=
Module[{a = ToString[InputForm[Get[x]]], b = "RowBox[{\"Begin\", \"[\", \"\\\"`",
c = "`\\\"\", \"]\"}]", d = "RowBox[{\"590\", \"::\", \"usage\"}]", h = {}, p},
p = StringCases[a, b ~~ Shortest[X__] ~~ c];

```
p = Map[StringReplace[#, {b -> "", c -> ""}] &, p];
Map[If[StringFreeQ[a, StringReplace[d, "590" -> #]], AppendTo[h, #], Null] &, p];
If[{y} != {} && ! HowAct[y], y = Sort[DeleteDuplicates[p]], Null];
Select[h, StringFreeQ[#, {"StyleBox[", "Finish"}] &]]

In[3377]:= TestCdfNbFile["C:\\MathToolBox\\MathToolBox.nb"]
Out[3377]= {}
In[3378]:= TestCdfNbFile["C:\\MathToolBox\\MathToolBox.nb", gs]
Out[3378]= {}
In[3379]:= Length[gs]
Out[3379]= 1143
```

As it was already noted, definitions of the user package without the usage corresponding to them, are ignored at loading of the package into the current session. Thus, the means testing such situations are represented to us as rather important. So, the call **ContentOfNbCdf[*w*]** returns the sorted list of objects names whose definitions are located in a *w* file of the {"*cdf*", "*nb*"} format without uploading of *w* datafile into the current session. While the procedure call **ContentOfNbCdf[*w*, *y*]** where *y* – *an undefinite symbol* – additionally through *y* returns three–element list whose the first element represents the sorted list of objects names whose definitions are located in the *w* file and have usage, the *second* element represents the sorted list of objects names whose definitions are located in the *w* file and have not usage, the third element presents the sorted list of objects names that have not the corresponding *definitions*. The given procedure allows to verify the contents of the {"*cdf*", "*nb*"}–files without loading their into the current session.

```
In[3327]:= ContentOfNbCdf[x_ /; FileExistsQ[x] && MemberQ[{"cdf", "nb"},
FileExtension[x]], y___ ] := Module[{a = ToString[Get[x]], b, c = {}, d = {}},
b = Sort[DeleteDuplicates[Select[Map[StringTrim[#, {" \"`", "`\""}] &,
StringCases[a, {Shortest[" \"`" ~~ __ ~~ "`\""], Shortest["`" ~~ __ ~~ "`"]},
Overlaps -> True]], SymbolQ[#] && # != "Private" &]]];
If[{y} != {} && ! HowAct[y], Map[If[! StringFreeQ[a, "{" <> # <> ", ::, usage}"],
AppendTo[c, #], AppendTo[d, #]] &, b];
y = {c, d, Select[Select[Map[SubsPosSymb[a, # - 1, {"{"}, 0] &,
Map[First, StringPosition[a, ", ::, usage}"]]], ! MemberQ[b, #] &], SymbolQ[#] &&
# != "p" &]}; b, b]]

In[3328]:= Length[ContentOfNbCdf["C:/mathtoolbox\\mathtoolbox.cdf"]]
Out[3328]= 1143
In[3329]:= ContentOfNbCdf["C:\\MathToolBox\\Grodno.nb"]
Out[3329]= {"Ga", "Gs", "GSV", "Vgs"}
In[3330]:= {ContentOfNbCdf["C:\\MathToolBox/Grodno.cdf", g70], g70}
Out[3330]= {{"Ga", "Gs", "GSV", "Vgs"}, {{"Ga", "Gs", "GSV", "Vgs"}, {}, {}}}
In[3332]:= {ContentOfNbCdf["C:\\MathToolBox/Grodno6.nb", v75], v75}
Out[3332]= {{"Ga", "Gs", "GSV", "Vgs"}, {{"Gs", "GSV", "Vgs"}, {"Ga"}, {}}}
```

Lastly, the procedure call **UsagesCdfNb[*x,y*]** provides usage output relative to the means defined by a separate symbol or their list *y* which are in a *x* file of the {"*cdf*", "*nb*"} format without its loading into the current session. For a single means the result is returned in the format *"y::usage"* or *"y::No"* if the usage for a means with N name is absent in the *x* file.

In[3154]:= UsagesCdfNb[x_ /; FileExistsQ[x] &&
MemberQ[{"cdf", "nb"}, FileExtension[x]], y_ /; SymbolQ[y] || ListQ[y] &&
AllTrue[Map[SymbolQ[#] &, y], TrueQ]] :=
Module[{a = ToString[InputForm[Get[x]]],
b = "RowBox[{RowBox[{\"590\", \"::\", \"usage\"}], \"=\", ", c = "}],
\"\[IndentingNewLine]\"}]",
b1 = "RowBox[{RowBox[{\"590\", \"::\", \"usage\"}], \"=\", ", c1 = "}]", f, p, g},
f[t_] := Module[{z = StringReplace[b, "590" -> t],
z1 = StringReplace[b1, "590" -> t], h, d}, d = Join[StringCases[a, z ~~ Shortest[X__] ~~ c],
StringCases[a, z1 ~~ Shortest[X__] ~~ c1]];
If[d == {}, {}, ToExpression[ToExpression[StringReplace[d[[1]],
{z -> "", c -> "", z1 -> "", c1 -> ""}]]]]];
g = Map[{p = f[#], If[p === {}, # <> "::" <> "No" <> "\n", # <> "::" <> p <> "\n"]}[[2]] &,
Map[ToString, Flatten[{y}]]]; If[Length[g] == 1, g[[1]], StringJoin[g]]]

In[3155]:= Help[x_] := Module[{a}, If[! SymbolQ[x], Null, a = x::usage;
If[SameQ[ToString[x] <> "::usage", ToString[a]], Null, a]]]

In[3156]:= Help[Sin]
Out[3156]= "Sin[z] gives the sine of z."

In[3157]:= UsagesCdfNb["C:/h/MathToolBox.nb", {"Attribs", GSV, StrStr}]
Out[3157]= Attribs::This procedure provides only two functions – (1) obtaining the list of the attributes ascribed to a datafile or directory, and (2) removal of all ascribed attributes. The call Attribs[x] returns the list of attributes in the string format which are ascribed to a datafile or directory x. On the main directories of volumes of direct access the procedure call Attribs returns $Failed. While the call Attribs[x, y] with the second optional argument y – an expression – deletes all attributes which are ascribed to a datafile or directory x with returning at a successful call 0. At that, the file "attrib.exe" is removed from the directory defined by the call Directory[] after a call of the procedure.
GSV::No
StrStr::The call StrStr[x] returns an expression x in string format if x is different from string; otherwise, the double string obtained from an expression x is returned."

While the call **Help**[*x*] of a rather simple **Help** procedure in string format returns the usage on a *x* symbol that is suitable for program processing.

On the basis of the above 2 procedures **UsageCdfNb** and **ExtrFromNBfile1**, the procedure **ActivateMeansFromCdfNb** can be programmed. The call **ActivateMeansFromCdfNb**[*x*, *y*] returns nothing, evaluating in the current session a separate tools or their list whose names are determined by *y* argument along with their usage whose definitions are in a *x* file of the {*"cdf"*, *"nb"*} format. At that, loading of the *x* file into the current session isn't required. The following fragment represents source code of the procedure with examples of its use.

In[4082]:= **ActivateMeansFromCdfNb**[x_ /; FileExistsQ[x] &&
MemberQ[{"cdf", "nb"}, FileExtension[x]], y_ /; SymbolQ[y] || ListQ[y] &&

AllTrue[Map[SymbolQ[#] &, y], TrueQ]] :=
Module[{a = Map[ToString, Flatten[{y}]], b, c}, b = UsageCdfNb[x, a];
b = StringSplit["\n" <> b, Map["\n" <> # <> "::" -> # <> "::" &, a]];
Do[ToExpression[b[[2*k - 1]] <> "usage=" <> ToString1[b[[2*k]]]], {k, 1, Length[b]/2}];
Map[Quiet[{ClearAll[c], ExtrFromNBfile1[x, #, c], DeleteFile[c]}] &, a];]

In[4083]:= ActivateMeansFromCdfNb["C:\\MathToolBox\\Grodno.nb", {Ga, Gs, GSV, Vgs, AvzAgn}]
In[4084]:= ?Ga
"Help on Ga."
In[4085]:= Definition[Ga]
Out[4085]= Ga[Grodno`Ga`x_Integer, Grodno`Ga`y_Integer] := Grodno`Ga`x*Grodno`Ga`y+ Gs[Grodno`Ga`x, Grodno`Ga`y]
In[4086]:= Definition[AvzAgn]
Out[4086]= Null
In[4087]:= ?AvzAgn
No

The **ExtrFromMfile** procedure is a specifical complement of the previous **ExtrFromNBfile** procedure, providing extraction of definitions of functions and procedures along with their usage from an unuploaded package that is in a file of *m*-format. The call **ExtrFromMfile**[*x*, *y*] returns the definition of an object in the string format with a name or list of their names *y* given in string format from an unuploaded *x* file of *m*-format, at the same time activating these definitions and usage corresponding to them in the current session; otherwise, the call returns empty list, i.e. {}. The following fragment represents source code of **ExtrFromMfile** procedure along with typical examples of its application.

In[2608]:= ExtrFromMfile[x_ /; FileExistsQ[x] && FileExtension[x] == "m",
y_ /; SymbolQ[y] || ListQ[y] && AllTrue[Map[SymbolQ, y], TrueQ]] :=
Module[{a = ReadString[x], b, c, d, d1, n}, b = StringSplit[a, {"(**)", "(* ::Input:: *)"}];
b = Map[If[! StringFreeQ[#, {"::usage=", "BeginPackage[\"", "End[]"}], #, Null] &, b];
b = Select[b, ! SameQ[#, Null] &]; c = Map[ToString, Flatten[{y}]];
d = Map["Begin[\"`" <> # <> "`\"]" &, c]; d1 = Map["(*" <> # <> "::usage=" &, c];
b = Select[b, ! StringFreeQ[#, Join[d, d1]] &]; b = Map[StringTake[#, {3, -5}] &, b];
c = Map[If[SuffPref[#, d1, 1], StringTake[#, {3, -1}], n = StringReplace[#, GenRules[d, ""]];
n = StringReplace[n, "*)\r\n(*" -> ""]; StringTake[n, {3, -6}]] &, b]; ToExpression[c]; c]
In[2609]:= ExtrFromMfile["C:/Temp/MathToolBox.m", {StrStr, HowAct}]
Out[2609]= {"HowAct::usage=\"The call HowAct[Q] returns the value True if Q is an object active in the current session, and the False otherwise. In many cases the procedure HowAct is more suitable than standard function ValueQ, including local variables in procedures.",
"StrStr::usage=\"The call StrStr[x] returns an expression x in string format if x is different from string; otherwise, the double string obtained from an expression x is returned.",
"StrStr[x_]:=If[StringQ[x],\"\\\"\"<>x<>\"\\\"\",ToString[x]]",
"HowAct[x_]:=If[Quiet[Check[ToString[Definition[x]],True]]===\"Null\", False,

If[Quiet[ToString[Definition[P]]]===\"Attributes[\"<>ToString[x] <>\"] = {Temporary}\", False, True]]"}

In[2610]:= ExtrFromMfile["C:\\Mathematica\\MathToolBox.m", StrStr]
Out[2610]= {"StrStr::usage = \"The call StrStr[x] returns an expression x in string format if x is different from the string; otherwise, the double string obtained from an expression x is returned.", "StrStr[x_] := If[StringQ[x], \"\\\"\" <> x <> \"\\\"\", ToString[x]]"}

The call **ExtrFromM**[*x*, *y*] returns nothing, evaluating in the current session a separate tools or their list whose names are defined by an *y* argument which are supplied with usage and whose definitions are in a *x* file of the *"m"* format. While the call **ExtrFromM**[*x*, *y*, *z*] where *z* – *an undefinite symbol* – via *z* returns the four-element list whose elements are names lists of the *y*, which have: *(1)* definitions and usage, *(2)* usage without definitions, *(3)* definitions without usage, *(4)* neither definitions or usage. At that, loading of the *x* file into the current session isn't required. The following fragment represents source code of the procedure with examples of its application.

In[3615]:= **ExtrFromM[x_ /; FileExistsQ[x] && FileExtension[x] == "m",**
y_ /; SymbolQ[y] || ListQ[y] && AllTrue[Map[SymbolQ[#] &, y], TrueQ], z___] :=
Module[{a = ReadString[x], c, d = {}, h = {}, g = {}, s = {}, t = {},
b = DeleteDuplicates[Map[ToString, Flatten[{y}]]], k = 1},
c = Map[Flatten[{StringCases[a, "(*" <> # <> "[" ~~ Shortest[X__] ~~ "*)"],
StringCases[a, "(*" <> # <> "::usage" ~~ Shortest[X__] ~~ "*)"]}] &, b];
For[k, k <= Length[c], k++, If[c[[k]] == {}, AppendTo[t, b[[k]]], If[Length[c[[k]]] == 1,
If[SuffPref[c[[k]][[1]], "(*" <> b[[k]] <> "::usage", 1], AppendTo[d, b[[k]]],
AppendTo[h, b[[k]]]], AppendTo[s, b[[k]]]; AppendTo[g, {StringTake[c[[k]][[1]], {3, -3}],
StringTake[c[[k]][[2]], {3, -3}]}]]]]; Quiet[Map[ToExpression, g]];
If[{z} != {} && ! HowAct[z], z = {s, d, h, t}, Null];]

In[3616]:= **ExtrFromM["C:\\MathToolBox\\Grodno.m", {Gs, Ga, GSV}, t]**
In[3617]:= **t**
Out[3617]= {{"Gs", "Ga", "GSV"}, {}, {}, {}}
In[3618]:= **Definition[Ga]**
Out[3618]= Ga[x_Integer, y_Integer] := x*y + Gs[x, y]
In[3619]:= **ExtrFromM["C:\\MathToolBox\\Grodno.m", {Sg, Ga, Gh}, t6]**
In[3620]:= **t6**
Out[3620]= {{"Ga"}, {}, {}, {"Sg", "Gh"}}
In[3621]:= **ExtrFromM["C:/Package/Grsu.m", {Sg, Vt, Ga, Vgs, GSV, Gs}, j]**
In[3622]:= **j**
Out[3622]= {{"GSV", "Gs"}, {"Vgs"}, {"Ga"}, {"Sg", "Vt"}}

The problem of editing of a package which is located in a *m*–file is interesting enough; the following **RedMfile** procedure solves this problem whose source code with examples of its application represents the following fragment.

In[2864]:= **PosListTest[l_List, p_ /; PureFuncQ[p]] := Module[{a = {}, k = 1},**
While[k <= Length[l], If[Select[{l[[k]]}, p] != {}, AppendTo[a, k]]; k++]; a]

In[2865]:= **PosListTest[{1, 2, 3, 4, 5, 6, 7, 8, 9, 10, 18, 26}, EvenQ[#] &]**

Out[2865]= {2, 4, 6, 8, 10, 11, 12}
In[2866]:= RedMfile[x_ /; FileExistsQ[x] && FileExtension[x] == "m", p_ /; SymbolQ[p],
r_ /; MemberQ[{"add", "delete", "replace"}, r]] :=
Module[{a = ReadList[x, String], d = ToString[p], h, save,
b = "(*Begin[\"`" <> ToString[p] <> "`\"]*)", c = "(*End[]*)"},
If[MemberQ[! ContentOfMfile[x], ToString[p]] && r == "delete" || MemberQ[{"add",
"replace"}, r] && ! (ProcQ[p] || QFunction[p]), $Failed, save[q_] := Module[{f, k = 1},
f = DirectoryName[x] <> FileBaseName[x] <> "$.m";
While[k <= Length[q], WriteString[f, q[[k]], "\n"]; k++]; Close[f]];
If[! MemberQ[a, "(* ::Package:: *)"], $Failed, If[r === "delete",
h = Select[a, SuffPref[#, "(*" <> d <> "::usage", 1] &];
If[h == {}, x, a = Select[a, ! SuffPref[#, "(*" <> d <> "::usage", 1] &];
d = SubListsMin[a, b, c, "r"]; d = MinusList[a, d];
save[d]], If[r === "add" && Select[a, SuffPref[#, "(*" <> d <> "::usage=", 1] &] == {} &&
Head[p::usage] == String && (ProcQ[p] || FunctionQ[p]),
h = PosListTest[a, SuffPref[#, {"(*BeginPackage[", "(*EndPackage[]"}, 1] &];
a = Insert[a, "(*" <> d <> "::usage= " <> ToString1[p::usage] <> "*)", h[[1]] + 1];
a = Flatten[Insert[a, {"(*Begin[\"`" <> d <> "`\"]*)", "(*" <> PureDefinition[p] <> "*)",
"(*End[]*)"}, h[[2]] + 1]]; save[a],
If[r === "replace" && Head[p::usage] == String && (ProcQ[p] || FunctionQ[p]),
h = PosListTest[a, SuffPref[#, "(*Begin[\"`".<> d <> "`\"]*)", 1] &];
If[h == {}, $Failed, a[[h[[1]] ;; h[[1]] + 2]] = {"(*Begin[\"`" <> d <> "`\"]*)",
"(*" <> PureDefinition[p] <> "*)", "(*End[]*)"};
h = PosListTest[a, SuffPref[#, "(*" <> d <> "::usage=", 1] &];
a[[h[[1]]]] = "(*" <> d <> "::usage= " <> ToString1[p::usage] <> "*)"; save[Flatten[a]]]], x]]]]
=====
(* ::Package:: *) *Contents of an initial m-file*
(* ::Input:: *)
(*BeginPackage["Grodno`"]*)
(*Gs::usage = "Help on Gs."*)
(*Vgs::usage = "Help on Vgs."*)
(*Begin["`Gs`"]*)
(*Gs[x_Integer, y_Integer] := x^2 + y^2*)
(*End[]*)
(*Begin["`Vgs`"]*)
(*Vgs[x_Integer, y_Integer] := x*y*)
(*End[]*)
(*EndPackage[]*)
=====
In[2867]:= Avz[x_] := Module[{}, x^2 + 590]; Vgs[x_, y_] := x^2 + y^2
In[2868]:= Avz::usage = "Help on Avz."; Vgs::usage = "Help on Vgs_1.";
In[2869]:= RedMfile["C:\\Mathematica\\Grodno.m", Vgs, "delete"]

Out[2869]= "C:\\Mathematica\\Grodno$.m"
(* ::Package:: *) *Contents of m-file after the "delete" operation*
(* ::Input:: *)
(*BeginPackage["Grodno`"]*)
(*Gs::usage = "Help on Gs."*)
(*Begin["`Gs`"]*)
(*Gs[x_Integer, y_Integer] := x^2 + y^2*)
(*EndPackage[]*)
In[2870]:= **RedMfile["C:\\Mathematica\\Grodno.m", Avz, "add"]**
Out[2870]= "C:\\Mathematica\\Grodno$.m"
(* ::Package:: *) *Contents of m-file after the "add" operation*
(* ::Input:: *)
(*BeginPackage["Grodno`"]*)
(*Avz::usage = "Help on Avz."*)
(*Gs::usage = "Help on Gs."*)
(*Vgs::usage = "Help on Vgs."*)
(*Begin["`Gs`"]*)
(*Gs[x_Integer, y_Integer] := x^2 + y^2*)
(*End[]*)
(*Begin["`Vgs`"]*)
(*Vgs[x_Integer, y_Integer] := x*y*)
(*End[]*)
(*Begin["`Avz`"]*)
(*Avz[x_] := Module[{}, x^2 + 590]*)
(*End[]*)
(*EndPackage[]*)
In[2871]:= **RedMfile["C:\\Mathematica\\Grodno.m", Vgs, "replace"]**
Out[2871]= "C:\\Mathematica\\Grodno$.m"
(* ::Package:: *) *Contents of m-file after the "replace" operation*
(* ::Input:: *)
(*BeginPackage["Grodno`"]*)
(*Gs::usage = "Help on Gs."*)
(*Vgs::usage = "Help on Vgs_1."*)
(*Begin["`Gs`"]*)
(*Gs[x_Integer, y_Integer] := x^2 + y^2*)
(*End[]*)
(*Begin["`Vgs`"]*)
(*Vgs[x_, y_] := x^2 + y^2*)
(*End[]*)
(*EndPackage[]*)
In[2872]:= **RedMfile["C:\\Mathematica\\Grodno.m", Gs, "add"]**
Out[2872]= Null
In[2873]:= **RedMfile["C:\\Mathematica\\Grodno.m", GsArtKr, "add"]**
Out[2873]= $Failed

First of all, the previous fragment is preceded by a rather simple procedure, whose the call **PosListTest[*l*, *p*]** returns the list of positions of a *l* list that satisfy the test defined by a pure *p* function. Further it is supposed that a *x* datafile of *m*-format structurally corresponds to the standard file with a package; an example of such file of *m*-format is given in the first shaded area of the previous fragment. The procedure call **RedMfile[*x*, *n*, *y*]** returns the full path to a *m*-file, whose **FileBaseName** has view **FileBaseName[*x*]** <> "$" which is a result of application to the initial *m*-file of an *y* operation concerning its object determined by a *n* name, namely:

"delete" – from a *x* datafile the usage and definition of object with a *n* name are removed, the initial datafile doesn't change; if such object in the datafile is absent, the full path to the initial datafile is returned;

"add" – usage and definition of an object with a *n* name are added into a *x* file whereas the initial file doesn't change; if the object of the same name in the file already exists, the *Null* is returned, i.e. nothing;

"replace" – usage and definition of object with a *n* name are replaced in a *x* file whereas the initial datafile doesn't change; if such object in a file is absent, the $*Failed* is returned.

If an initial *x* file has structure, different from specified, the procedure call returns $*Failed*; in addition, successful performance of operations *"add"* and *"replace"* requires preliminary evaluation in the current session of the construction *n::usage* with definition for *n* object as illustrate example of the previous fragment. At that, if a *n* object is undefined the procedure call returns $*Failed*. In general, the procedure allows a number of interesting extensions and modifications which we leave to the interested reader.

Absolutely other situation if necessary to update an object from a package which is located in a datafile of *mx*-format. In this case the next scheme can be used, namely: on the *first* step the function call **Get[*x*]** loads into the current session a *x* file of *mx*-format with a package what provides the availability of all means contained in it. Whereas on the second step the usage and definition of an object *(function or procedure)* that should be subjected to updating along with result of a concrete call of the object are checked. Then, on the *next* step from the current session by means of the **Clear** function the demanded object is removed and for it a new usage is defined. Then, a new definition for the object whose all parameters, including local variables and formal arguments, will be linked with a package context is calculated, accepting the following format, namely:

Context_from_File`Object_Name`Variable_of_New_Definition

Then by means of the function call **DumpSave[*y*, "*Context*'"]** definitions of all objects of the current session which are supplied with a "*Context*'" context, together with their usage are saved in a new *y* file of *mx*-format. At last, the final stage in a new current session tests the correctness of the received *y* file of *mx*-format with package – of the result of modification of the initial *x* file of the *mx*-format with a package. With rather obvious changes the above algorithm quite successfully works and in case of modification of files of *mx*-format with a package on the basis of operations of addition and removal. The represented algorithm is a a rather simple, however has a shortcoming if necessary to modify a datafile of *mx*-format with a package by means of quite large source codes of objects; for similar case a reception described in [30-33] can be used. Meanwhile, it must be kept in mind, that the represented algorithm of modification of *mx*-files with packages belongs to a case when files of the *mx*-format belong to the same operational platform, as their planned modification.

Software Etudes in the Mathematica

The following **RedMxFile** procedure provides automation of a modification of datafiles of *mx*-format that is considered above. The call **RedMxFile**[*x, y, r, f*] returns the full path to a *mx*-datafile, whose **FileBaseName** has view **FileBaseName**[*x*] <> "$" which is the result of application to the initial *mx*-file of an operation *r* concerning its object determined by an *y* name, namely:

"delete" – from a *x* datafile the usage and definition of object with an *y* name are removed, the initial datafile doesn't change; if such object in the datafile is absent, the procedure call returns $*Failed*;

"add" – usage and definition of an object with a name *y* are added into a *x* file whereas the initial file doesn't change; if such object in the file already exists, the procedure call returns $*Failed*; the fourth *f* argument defines a *mx*-file containing the usage and definition of the supplemented *y* object;

"replace" – usage and definition of object with a name *y* are replaced in a *x* file whereas the initial datafile doesn't change; if such object in a datafile is absent, the procedure call returns $*Failed*; the fourth *f* argument determines a *mx*-file containing a package with context of the initial *x mx*-file along with usage and definition of the added *y* object. At that, if *y* object is undefined the procedure call returns $*Failed*.

So, return of the path to an updated datafile "*x*$.*mx*" serves as an indicator of success of the **RedMxFile** procedure call. In addition, successful performance of operations *"replace"* and *"add"* requires preliminary evaluation in the current session of the expressions of the next formats, namely:

Cont`Name[...] := *Definition of a Name object*
Cont`Name::usage = "*Help on the Name object.*"

where *Name* – the name of an object and "*Cont`*" is a context ascribed to the updated initial *x mx*-file, with the subsequent saving of the forenamed evaluated object **Cont`Name** in a *f mx*-file. The unsuccessful call returns $*Failed* or is returned unevaluated. The next fragment represents source code of the **RedMxFile** procedure with examples of its application.

In[2632]:= RedMxFile[x_ /; FileExistsQ[x] && FileExtension[x] == "mx",
y_ /; StringQ[y] && SymbolQ[y], r_ /; MemberQ[{"add", "delete", "replace"}, r], f___] :=
Module[{a, c, c1 = ContextFromFile[x], c2, save, t},
If[MemberQ[$Packages, c1] && CNames[c1] != {}, t = 75, Get[x]];
save[z_] := Module[{p = DirectoryName[z] <> FileBaseName[z] <> "$.mx"},
ToExpression["DumpSave[" <> ToString1[p] <> "," <> ToString1[c1] <> "]"]; p];
If[r == "delete" && MemberQ[CNames[c1], y], Unprotect[y];
Remove[y]; c = save[x], If[r == "replace" && MemberQ[a, y] && {f} != {} &&
FileExistsQ[f] && FileExtension[f] == "mx", Unprotect[y]; Remove[y]; Get[f];
c = save[x], If[r == "add" && {f} != {} && FileExistsQ[f] &&
FileExtension[f] == "mx", Unprotect[y]; Remove[y]; Get[f];
c = save[x], c = $Failed]]]; If[t == 75, Null, RemovePackage[c1]]; c]

In[3186]:= ContextFromFile["Grodno.mx"]
Out[3186]= "Grodno`"
In[3148]:= Get["Grodno.mx"]; CNames["Grodno`"]

Out[3148]= {"Ga", "Gs", "GSV", "Vgs"}
In[3149]:= RemovePackage["Grodno`"]
In[3150]:= CNames["Grodno`"]
Out[3150]= {}
In[3151]:= Grodno`ArtKr[x_, y_, z_] := Module[{a = 75}, a*(x + y + z)];
Grodno`ArtKr::usage = "Help on module ArtKr.";
In[3152]:= Context[ArtKr]
Out[3152]= "Global`"
In[3153]:= DumpSave["ArtKr.mx", Grodno`ArtKr]
Out[3153]= {Grodno`ArtKr}
In[3156]:= Remove[Grodno`ArtKr, ArtKr]
In[3157]:= RedMxFile["Grodno.mx", "ArtKr", "add", "ArtKr.mx"]
Out[3157]= "Grodno$.mx"
In[3158]:= RemovePackage["Grodno`"]
In[3159]:= Get["Grodno$.mx"]
In[3160]:= CNames["Grodno`"]
Out[3160]= {"ArtKr", "Ga", "Gs", "GSV", "Vgs"}
In[3161]:= Definition[ArtKr]
Out[3161]= ArtKr[x_, y_, z_] := Module[{a = 75}, a*(x + y + z)]
In[3162]:= Context[ArtKr]
Out[3162]= "Grodno`"
In[3163]:= ?ArtKr
"Help on module ArtKr."
In[3192]:= RedMxFile["Grodno.mx", "GSV", "delete"]; RemovePackage["Grodno`"];
Clear[Grodno`GSV]
In[3194]:= Get["Grodno$.mx"]; CNames["Grodno`"]
Out[3194]= {"Ga", "Gs", "Vgs"}

Thus, for providing of the operation *"add"* or *"replace"* a file of *mx*-format with a package should be previously created that contains definition of an object used for *updating (addition, replacement)* of a main *mx*-file with the package. It must be kept in mind that both updating and updated *mx*-files have to be created on the same operational platform. At that, qua of result of the procedure call both packages are removed from the current session. In general, the **RedMxFile** procedure allows a number of extensions which we leave to the interested reader. Meanwhile, it should be noted, this procedure in a number of the relations is based on receptions, artificial for the standard procedural paradigm providing correct procedure calls in the software system of the dependent on its version. We will note, that in addition to the offered means of updating of *mx*-files there are other rather simple methods of support of the operation with updating of the *mx*-files both in situ, and in the form of new files.

An quite useful procedure provides converting of a package located in a file of *mx*-format into a file of *m*-format. The call **MxFileToMfile[x, y]** returns the path to an *y* file that is the result of converting of a *x mx*-file with a package into *y* file of *m*-format. In addition, the procedure call deletes the above packages *x* and *y* from the current session. The following fragment represents source code of the procedure with an example of application, whereas with the examples of the contents of the initial and converted files *x* and *y* with the package the interested reader can familiarize in our books [30–33,50].

In[2672]:= MxFileToMfile[x_ /; FileExistsQ[x] && FileExtension[x] == "mx",
y_ /; StringQ[y] && FileExtension[y] == "m"] := Module[{b, c, a = ContextFromFile[x], k=1},
Quiet[Check[Get[x]; b = CNames[a];
WriteString[y, "(* ::Package:: *)", "\n", "(* ::Input:: *)", "\n",
"(*BeginPackage[\"" <> a <> "\"]*)", "\n"];
While[k <= Length[b], c = b[[k]] <> "::usage";
WriteString[y, "(*" <> c <> " = " <> ToString1[ToExpression[a <> c]], "*)", "\n"]; k++];
k = 1; While[k <= Length[b], c = b[[k]];
WriteString[y, "(*Begin[\"`" <> c <> "`\"]*)", "\n",
"(*" <> PureDefinition[a <> c] <> "*)", "\n", "(*End[]*)", "\n"]; k++];
WriteString[y, "(*EndPackage[]*)", "\n"];
Map[{Clear1[2, a <> # <> "::usage"], Clear1[2, a <> #]} &, b];
$ContextPath = MinusList[$ContextPath, {a}]; Close[y]], Return[$Failed]]]]

In[2673]:= MxFileToMfile["C:\\Mathematica\\Grodno.mx", "Tallinn.m"]
Out[2673]= "Tallinn.m"

Whereas the **MfileToMx** procedure provides converting of a package located in a file of *m*-format into a file of *mx*-format. The procedure call **MfileToMx[x]** returns the path to a file which is the result of converting of a *x* *m*-file with a package into a file of *mx*-format, whose name coincides with the name of the initial *x* file with replacement of the "*m*" extension on "*mx*". Moreover, the procedure call deletes a *x* package from the current session if upto the **MfileToMx** procedure call the file wasn't uploaded, and otherwise no. The fragment below represents source code of the **MfileToMx** procedure with a typical example of its use.

In[2721]:= MfileToMx[x_ /; FileExistsQ[x] && FileExtension[x] == "m"] :=
Module[{a = ContextFromFile[x], b, d, c = ToString1[x <> "x"]},
If[a === $Failed, $Failed, If[MemberQ[$ContextPath, a], ToExpression["DumpSave[" <>
c <> "," <> ToString1[a] <> "]"]; x <> "x", b = ReadList[x, String];
d = Select[Map[StringReplace[#, {"(*" -> "", "*)" -> ""}] &, b[[3 ;; -1]]], # != "" &];
Quiet[ToExpression[d]];
ToExpression["DumpSave[" <> c <> "," <> ToString1[a] <> "]"];
Map[Clear1[2, a <> #] &, CNames[a]];
$ContextPath = MinusList[$ContextPath, {a}]; x <> "x"]]]

In[2722]:= MfileToMx["C:\\Mathematica\\Rans_Ian.m"]
Out[2722]= "C:\\Mathematica\\Rans_Ian.mx"

This procedure represents a certain interest in a number of appendices.

The question of documenting of the user package is an important enough its component; in addition, absence in a package of an usage for an object contained in it does such object as inaccessible at loading the package into the current session. Thus, description of each object of the user package has to be supplied with the corresponding usage. At the same time, it must be kept in mind, that mechanism of documenting of the user libraries in *Maple* system is much more developed than similar mechanism of documenting of the user package in the *Mathematica* system. Thus, if the mechanism of formation of the user libraries in the *Maple* is simple enough, providing a simple documenting of library means and providing access both to means of library, and to their references at the level of the system tools in the system *Mathematica* the similar mechanism is absent. Receiving of usage concerning a *x* package means is possible only by means of calls **?x** or **Information[x]** provided that the package has been loaded into the current session. Meanwhile, in case the package contains many means, for obtaining the usage concerning the demanded means it is necessary to be sure in their existence, first of all. The **PackageUsage** procedure can be rather useful to these purposes, whose source code along with examples of its use are represented below.

In[5313]:= **PackageUsage[x_ /; FileExistsQ[x] && FileExtension[x] == "m"] :=**
Module[{a = StringSplit[ReadString[x], {"(**)", "*)\r\n(*"}], b, c, d, f},
b = Select[a, ! StringFreeQ[#, {"::usage=", "::usage = "}] &];
If[b == {}, {}, FileNameSplit[x]; d = FileBaseName[c[[-1]]] <> "_Usage.txt";
f = FileNameJoin[Join[c[[1 ;; -2]], {d}]];
Map[{WriteString[f, StringReplace[#, "::usage" -> ""]], WriteString[f, "\n\n"]} &, b];
Close[f]]]

In[5314]:= **PackageUsage["MathToolBox.m"]**
Out[5314]= "MathToolBox_Usage.txt"
In[5315]:= **PackageUsage["C:\\users\\aladjev\\mathem\\Tampere.m"]**
Out[5315]= "C:\\users\\aladjev\\mathem\\Tampere_Usage.txt"
Gs = "Help on Gs."
Rans = "Help on Ga."
Vgs = "Help on Vgs."
GSV = "Help on GSV."

The procedure call **PackageUsage[x]** returns the path to a file in which the *"m"* extension of a *x* file is replaced on *"_Usage.txt"*; the received datafile contains usage of the user package formed standardly in the form of a *nb*-document *(see above)* with the subsequent its saving in a *x m*-file by means of chain of the commands *"File -> Save As"* of the *GUI*. The usage on the specific package *y* means has the format *y* = *"Help on y"*. The received *txt*-file allows to look through easily its contents regarding search of necessary means of the user package.

For testing of contents of a file of *mx*-format with the user package in the context of names of means whose definitions are located in this file, the **NamesFromMx** procedure is a rather useful means. The procedure call **NamesFromMx[x]** returns list of names in string format of means whose definitions are in *x* file of *mx*-format with the user package. If this package wasn't loaded into the current session, the procedure call leaves it loaded. Fragment below represents source code of the procedure **NamesFromMx** along with typical examples of its application.

In[5190]:= **NamesFromMx[x_ /; FileExistsQ[x] && FileExtension[x] == "mx"] :=**
Module[{a = ContextFromFile[x], b},
If[a === $Failed, {}, If[MemberQ[$ContextPath, a], CNames[a], Get[x];
b = CNames[a]; Map[Close1[2, a <> #] &, b];
$ContextPath = MinusList[$ContextPath, {a}]; b]]]

In[5191]:= **NamesFromMx["C:\\MathToolBox\\MathToolBox.mx"]**

Out[5191]= {"AcNb", "ActBFM", "ActBFMuserQ", "ActCsProcFunc",...}
In[5192]:= **Length[%]**
Out[5192]= 1144
In[5193]:= **NamesFromMx["C:\\Temp\\Mathematica\\Grodno.mx"]**
Out[5193]= {"Ga", "Gs", "GSV", "Sv", "Vgs"}
In[5194]:= **$ContextPath**
Out[5194]= {"AladjevProcedures`", "StreamingLoader`", "IconizeLoader`", "CloudObjectLoader`", "PacletManager`", "System`", "Global`"}
In[5195]:= **Definition[GSV]**
Out[5195]= Null

While the **NamesFromMx1** procedure unlike **NamesFromMx** procedure does not demand for obtaining the list of names, whose definitions are located in a *mx*-file with user package, real loading into the current session of this datafile. The procedure call **NamesFromMx1[x]** returns the list of names of tools whose definitions are located in a *x* datafile of *mx*-format with the user package. The fragment below represents source code of the **NamesFromMx1** procedure along with some typical examples of its application.

In[3570]:= **NamesFromMx1[x_ /; FileExistsQ[x] && FileExtension[x] == "mx"] :=**
Module[{c, d = {}, p, h = "", k = 1, j, m, n, a = ContextFromFile[x],
b = ToString[ReadFullFile[x]]},
If[a === $Failed, {}, b = StringJoin[Map[FromCharacterCode, Select[ToCharacterCode[b],
 # > 32 && # < 128 &]]];
{n, m} = Map[StringLength, {a, b}]; c = Map[#[[1]] + n &, StringPosition[b, a]][[2 ;; -1]];
While[k <= Length[c], For[j = c[[k]], j <= m, j++, p = StringTake[b, {j, j}];
If[p == "`", AppendTo[d, h]; h = ""; Break[], h = h <> p]]; k++];
Sort[MinusList[Select[d, SymbolQ[#] &], {"Private"}]]]]

In[3571]:= **NamesFromMx1["C:\\Temp\\Mathematica\\Kiev.mx"]**
Out[3571]= {"Art", "Avz", "GSV"}
In[3572]:= **Length[NamesFromMx1["C:/MathToolBox/MathToolBox.mx"]]**
Out[3572]= 68

At that, the procedure call **NamesFromMx1[x]** returns only those names of means whose definitions received by means of the **Definition** contain the context associated with package contained in a *x mx*-file. While on the other side certain modifications of **NamesFromMx1** procedure allow to obtain more complete list of names of means whose definitions with context are located in a *x* file of *mx*-format with a package. The next fragment presents one of such modifications qua of which the procedure acts, whose the call **NamesFromMx2[x]** returns the list of names in string format of means, whose definitions are in a *mx*-file with package. Along with sourse code of the procedure the examples of its usage are presented. At that, the both procedures demand enough considerable time costs on files of *mx*-format with package of a rather large size.

In[3584]:= **NamesFromMx2[x_ /; FileExistsQ[x] && FileExtension[x] == "mx"] :=**
Module[{a = ToString[ReadFullFile[x]], b},
b = Select[ToCharacterCode[a], # == 255 || (# > 31 && # < 123 &&
! MemberQ[Flatten[{Range[37, 47], Range[91, 95]}], #]) &];

```
b = ReduceList[b, 255, 1, 1]; b = Select[Quiet[SplitList[b, 96]], # != {} &];
b = Quiet[Map[FromCharacterCode, b]]; b = DeleteDuplicates[Select[b, SymbolQ[#] &]];
Sort[Select[b, ! MemberQ[{"Private", "System"}, #] &&
StringFreeQ[#, {StringTake[ContextFromFile[x], {1, -2}], "ÿ"}] &]]]
In[3585]:= NamesFromMx2["C:\\Temp\\Mathematica\\Kiev.mx"]
Out[3585]= {"Art", "Avz", "GSV"}
In[3586]:= Length[NamesFromMx2["C:\\Temp\\MathToolBox.mx"]]
Out[3586]= 690
```

For the purpose of a certain reduction of time costs, the above algorithm of the procedure **NamesFromMx2** can be modified, using the following means extending the *Mathematica* system. The *Map11* function considered above, and the procedure **SplitList1**, given by the fragment below, act as such means.

```
In[5173]:= SplitList1[x_ /; ListQ[x], y_ /; ListQ[y], z_ /; ListQ[z]] :=
Module[{c, a = Map12[ToString, {x, y, z}], b = ToString[Unique["$"]]},
c = Map11[StringJoin, a, b]; c = Map[StringJoin, c];
c = SubsString1[c[[1]], {c[[2]], c[[3]]}, StringQ[#] &, 0];
ToExpression[Map11[StringSplit, c, b]]]
In[5174]:= SplitList1[{x, y, z, a, b, c, d, p, m, n, p, x, y, z, 42, 47, 67, 90, m, n, p}, {x, y, z}, {m, n, p}]
Out[5174]= {{a, b, c, d, p}, {42, 47, 67, 90}}
In[5174]:= SplitList1[{x, y, z, a, b, c, d, p, x, y, z, 42, 47, 67}, {x, y, z}, {m, n, p}]
Out[5174]= {}
```

The procedure call **SplitList1**[*x*, *y*, *z*] returns the sublists of a *x* list which are limited by its sublists *y* and *z* excepting the limiting sublists *y* and *z*. In lack of of such sublists the empty list, i.e. {}, is returned. Along with that, this procedure extends the above **SplitList** tool.

When uploading the package along with the main exports can be generated so-called *excess* symbols whose analysis represents an quite certain interest. So, the call **ExcessVarsPack**[*x*] returns the nested four-element list of the names of the excess symbols that are generated by the loading of the package with a context *x* into the current session. The procedure call with *x* context that is absent in the list defined by the $*Packages* variable is returned *unevaluated*. The elements of the above nested list are defined as follows: *(1)* list of names of the excess temporary definite symbols with a *x* context of the package, *(2)* list of names of the excess temporary undefinite symbols with *x* context of the package, *(3)* list of names of the excess definite symbols with a *x* context of the package, *(4)* list of names of the excess undefinite symbols with *x* context of the package, finally *(5)* list of other excess symbols of the package with *x* context. The next fragment represents source code of the **ExcessVarsPack** procedure with examples of its application.

```
In[3594]:= ExcessVarsPack[x_ /; ContextQ[x] && MemberQ[$Packages, x]] :=
Module[{a = {{}, {}, {}, {}, {}},
b = Sort[DeleteDuplicates[MinusList[Names[x <> "*"], CNames[x]]]]},
Map[If[TemporaryQ[#] && PureDefinition[#] != $Failed, AppendTo[a[[1]], #],
If[TemporaryQ[#] && PureDefinition[#] === $Failed, AppendTo[a[[2]], #],
If[! SameQ[PureDefinition[#], $Failed] && Context[#] == x, AppendTo[a[[3]], #],
```

If[SameQ[PureDefinition[#], $Failed] && Context[#] == x, AppendTo[a[[4]], #], AppendTo[a[[5]], #]]]] &, b]; a]

In[3595]:= ExcessVarsPack["AladjevProcedures`"]
Out[3595]= {{}, {"a", "A", "a1", "b", "b1", "c", "d", "f", "F", "inputstream", "outputstream", "t", "x", "y", "z"}, {"a$6428", "b$6428"}, {}, {}}

In[3596]:= ExcessVarsPack["PacletManager`"]
Out[3596]= {{}, {"PacletManager", "PacletSite"}, {"Paclet", "PacletSiteUpdate", "$AllowDataUpdates", "$AllowDocumentationUpdates", "$AllowInternet", "$BasePacletsDirectory", "$InternetProxyRules", "$UserBasePacletsDirectory"}, {}, {}}

As it was noted, the *Mathematica* has a large enough number of the global variables which describe, for example, characteristics of the system, an operating platform, the full paths to its main directories along with a number of other indicators of current state of the system. Thus, the user has a quite real possibility quite effectively to develop own means, including the means which extend possibilities of the system itself. In reality, on the basis of a number of such global variables and a number of enough developed means it is possible to develop the original tools; at that, the development of their analogs in the *Maple* often demands the more essential efforts and non-standard approaches. Our experience in the given direction confirms the told. Some quite simple examples were given in [25-27] and, most often, they concerned the tools of access. Considerable interest for the advanced programming in the system the problem of determination of name of the current document {*mws–file, nb–file*} represents too. In the *Maple* for this purpose the *mwsname* procedure whose development demanded a certain non-standard approach was created. While the development of similar means for *Mathematica* system appeared much simpler, what the following a rather simple **NbName** function illustrates, whose source code with examples of its use are presented by the following fragment.

In[3744]:= NbName[] := Map[StringReplace[#, {"]" -> "", ">>" -> "", "NotebookObject[<<" -> ""}] &, Map[ToString, Notebooks[]]]

In[3745]:= NbName[]
Out[3745]= {"0-142.nb", "MathToolBox.nb", "Messages"}

In[3746]:= AcNb[] := StringSplit[NotebookFileName[], {"\\", "/"}][[-1]]

In[3747]:= CurrentNb[] := StringTake[StringCases[ToString[NotebookSelection[]], "<<" ~~ __ ~~ ">>"][[1]], {3, -3}]

In[3748]:= {AcNb[], CurrentNb[]}
Out[3748]= {"0-100.nb", "0-142.nb"}

The procedure call **NbName[]** returns the list of *nb*–documents which have been uploaded into the current session; at that, their order in the list is defined by order of their uploading into the current session so, that the first element defines the current document of the {*"cdf"*, *"nb"*} format. While, the function calls **AcNb[]** and **CurrentNb[]** return name of the current document or package that has been earlier saved in a file of the {*".cdf"*, *".nb"*} format.

While the call of the **$FileCurrentNb** variable retuns full path to the current *nb*–document loaded in the session what the following examples enough visually illustrate. At that, if the call of the **$FileCurrentNb** returns only file name then the document corresponded it earlier hasn't been saved in *nb*-file.

In[4503]:= $FileCurrentNb := Module[{a, b, c, d}, d = NotebookInformation[];
If[Select[d, #[[1]] === "FileName" &] == {},
Select[FileNameJoin[d][[1]], #[[1]] === "WindowTitle" &][[1]][[2]] <> ".nb",
a = FileNameJoin[d[[1]][[2]][[1]][[2 ;; -1]]];
b = Quiet[Check[Flatten[StringPosition[c = CurrentNb[], " - W"]][[1]], 75]];
a <> "\\" <> If[b == 75, c, AddDelPosString[c, b - 1, ".nb", g]]]]

In[4504]:= $FileCurrentNb
Out[4504]= "C:\\AVZ\\14.nb"
In[4505]:= $FileCurrentNb
Out[4505]= "C:\\Program Files\\Wolfram Research\\Mathematica\\11.0\\Documentation\\English\\System\\ReferencePages\\Symbols\\NotebookGet.nb"
In[4506]:= $FileCurrentNb
Out[4506]= "Untitled-6.nb"

In turn, the call of **$FileCurrentNb1** variable realized by a module returns the list of *ListList* type whose 2-element sublists define names of *nb*-documents and full paths to directories from that they have been loaded into the current session. At the same time, a *nb*-documents created in the current session and earlier not saved in *nb*-files instead of the directories are marked with *"CS"* – the current session. The source code of the variable **$FileCurrentNb1** with its application are represented by the following fragment.

In[4529]:= $FileCurrentNb1 := Module[{a, b, c, h = {}, g = {}, s = {}}, a = Notebooks[];
Do[b = NotebookInformation[a[[j]]];
AppendTo[g, Select[b, #[[1]] === "WindowTitle" &][[1]][[2]]], {j, 1, Length[a] - 1}];
Map[{c = Flatten[StringPosition[#, " - W"]];
AppendTo[h, If[c == {}, #, AddDelPosString[#, c[[1]] - 1, ".nb", gs]]]} &, g];
Do[b = NotebookInformation[a[[j]]];
c = Flatten[Select[b, #[[1]] === "FileName" &]]; If[c == {}, AppendTo[s, "CS"],
AppendTo[s, (c)[[1]][[2]][[1]]]], {j, 1, Length[a] - 1}];
s = Map[Quiet[Check[FileNameJoin[#[[2 ;; -1]]], #]] &, s]; Partition[Riffle[h, s], 2]]

In[4530]:= $FileCurrentNb1
Out[4530]= {{"14.nb", "C:\\AVZ"}, {"MathToolBox.nb", "C:\\AVZ"}, {"Untitled-6", "CS"}, {"Rearranging & Restructuring Lists.nb", "C:\\Program Files\\Wolfram Research\\Mathematica\\11.0\\Documentation\\English\\System\\Guides"}}

Whereas the call of the **$DefInCS** variable returns the list of the *nb*-documents loaded into the current session and whose elements have formats *"xyzg.nb"*, {*"Sys.nb"*, *"Sys"*} and/or {*"Search Results: hhh.nb"*, *"No"*} which define the user document, the system document, as a rule with system documentation and a request for search of the reference on a *"hhhhh.nb"* document that is absent in the *Mathematica*. The source code of the **$DefInCS** variable and its application are represented by the following fragment.

In[4494]:= $DefInCS := Module[{a = Map[ToString, Notebooks[]]},

a = Map[StringReplace[#, {"NotebookObject[<<"-> "", ">>]" -> ""}] &, a];
Map[If[SuffPref[#, ".nb", 2], #, If[StringFreeQ[#, " - W"], Nothing,
{StringTrim[AddDelPosString[#, Flatten[StringPosition[#, " - W"]]][[1]] - 1, ".nb", g]],
If[StringFreeQ[#, "Results: "], "Sys", "No"]}]] &, a]]

In[4495]:= **$DefInCS**
Out[4495]= {"14.nb", {"StringTrim.nb", "Sys"}, "MathToolBox.nb"}
In[4496]:= **$DefInCS**
Out[4496]= {"14.nb", "MathToolBox.nb", {"None.nb", "Sys"}}
In[4497]:= **$DefInCS**
Out[4497]= {"14.nb", "MathToolBox.nb", {"Search Results: Save2.nb", "No"}}

The procedure call **ObjInCurrentNb[]** returns the nested list of the objects activated in a *nb*-document of the current session. In addition, the objects are grouped according to the contexts attributed to them. In each sublist of the returned list the first element defines the context while the others define names of objects in string format that have this context. The following fragment represents source code of the **ObjInCurrentNb** procedure along with an example of its application in the current *MathToolBox.nb* document [48,50].

In[2920]:= **ObjInCurrentNb[]** := Module[{b, c = {}, d, k, h = {},
a = StringReplace[ToString[NotebookGet[]], {" " -> "", "\n" -> "", "\r" -> "", "\t" -> ""}]},
b = StringCases[a, Shortest["RowBox[{RowBox[{" ~~ __ ~~ ",["]];
b = DeleteDuplicates[Select[b, StringFreeQ[#, {"Cell", "BoxData"}] &&
StringCount[#, "RowBox"] == 2 &]];
b = Map[StringReplace[#, {"RowBox[{" -> "", ",[" -> ""}] &, b];
Map[If[Set[d, Quiet[Check[Context[#], $Failed]]] === $Failed, Null,
AppendTo[c, {#, d}]] &, b];
c = Map[DeleteDuplicates, Map[Flatten, Gather[c, #1[[2]] == #2[[2]] &]]];
If[c == {}, {}, c = If[NestListQ[c], c, {c}]];
Do[AppendTo[h, Sort[c[[k]], ContextQ[#] &]], {k, 1, Length[c]}]; c = {};
Do[AppendTo[c, Flatten[{h[[k]][[1]], Select[h[[k]][[2 ;; -1]],
! SameQ[PureDefinition[#], $Failed] &]}]], {k, 1, Length[h]}];
h = Map[Flatten[{#[[1]], Sort[#[[2 ;; -1]]]}] &, c]; If[Length[h] == 1, Flatten[h], h]]]

In[3529]:= **ObjInCurrentNb[]**
Out[3529]= {{"AladjevProcedures`", ..., "XOR1"}, {"System`", ..., "$Packages"}, {"Global`", g}}
In[3530]:= **Map[Length, %]**
Out[3520]= {938, 156, 1}

The **ObjInCurrentNb1** procedure is an useful extension of the previous **ObjInCurrentNb** procedure. Similarly, procedure call **ObjInCurrentNb1[*x*]** returns the nested list of objects located in a *x nb*-document opened in the current session or in a *x nb*-file. These objects are grouped according to the contexts attributed to them. At that, in each sublist of the returned list the first element defines the context whereas the others define names of objects in string format that have this context. Furthermore, an attempt to analyze *x nb*-document opened in the current session without its saving in a *nb*-file returns the result of analysis in the current *nb*-file (*i.e. nb-document in which the call* **ObjInCurrentNb1[*x*]** *was done*). The fragment below represents source code of the **ObjInCurrentNb1** procedure with examples of its use in the current document. At that, the **ObjInCurrentNb1** procedure essentially uses the procedures **AllCurrentNb**, **OpenCurrentNb** and **NotebookSave1**, that are considered below and which have a rather independent meaning.

```
In[4926]:= ObjInCurrentNb1[x_ /; MemberQ[Map[#[[1]] &, AllCurrentNb[]],
FileNameTake[x]] || FileExistsQ[x] && FileExtension[x] == "nb"] :=
Module[{a, b, c = {}, d, k, h = {}, f, cnb = NbName[][[1]]},
a = If[x === NbName[][[1]], ToString[NotebookGet[]], If[MemberQ[Map[#[[1]] &,
AllCurrentNb[]], FileNameTake[x]], k = Flatten[Select[AllCurrentNb[], #[[1]] ===
FileNameTake[x] && #[[2]] != "nb has been not saved" &]];
If[k == {}, f = If[SuffPref[x, ".nb", 2], x, x <> ".nb"];
f = Directory[] <> "\\" <> f; NotebookSave1[FileNameTake[x], f];
b = ReadFullFile[f]; {OpenCurrentNb[cnb], b}[[2]], ReadFullFile[k[[2]]]],
ReadFullFile[x]]];
If[a === $Failed, $Failed, a = StringReplace[a, {" " -> "", "\n" -> "", "\r" -> "", "\t" -> "",
"\\\\" -> "", "\"" -> ""}]];
b = Join[SubsString[a, {"RowBox[{", ",[,"}], SubsString[a, {"<`", "`>"}]];
b = DeleteDuplicates[Select[b, StringFreeQ[#, {"Cell", "BoxData"}] &&
StringCount[#, "RowBox"] == 1 || StringFreeQ[#, "`"] &]];
b = Map[StringReplace[#, {"RowBox[{" -> "", ",[," -> ""}] &, b];
b = Select[b, SymbolQ[#] &];
If[b == {}, {}, Map[If[Set[d, Quiet[Check[Context[#], $Failed]]] === $Failed, Null,
AppendTo[c, {#, d}]] &, b];
c = Map[DeleteDuplicates, Map[Flatten, Gather[c, #1[[2]] == #2[[2]] &]]];
c = If[NestListQ[c], c, {c}];
Do[AppendTo[h, Sort[c[[k]], ContextQ[#] &]], {k, 1, Length[c]}]; c = {};
Do[AppendTo[c, Flatten[{h[[k]][[1]], Select[h[[k]][[2 ;; -1]],
! SameQ[PureDefinition[#], $Failed] &]}]], {k, 1, Length[h]}];
h = Map[Flatten[{#[[1]], Sort[#[[2 ;; -1]]]}] &, c]; c = {};
Map[If[Length[#] > 1, AppendTo[c, #], Null] &, h]; If[Length[c] == 1, Flatten[c], c]]]
In[4927]:= ObjInCurrentNb1["Untitled-6"]
Out[4927]= {"Global`", "G"}
In[4928]:= ObjInCurrentNb1[CurrentNb[]]
Out[4928]= {{"System`", "AppendTo", ... }, {"AladjevProcedures`", "NestListQ", ... },
{"Global`", "ObjInCurrentNb1"}}
```

The next procedure is a rather useful tools at operating with *nb*-documents in the current session. The procedure call **AllCurrentNb[]** returns the nested list of *ListList* type, the first element of each sublist determines a name in string format of *nb*-document activated in the current session whereas the *second* element defines the *nb*-file from which it was uploaded into the current session. If *nb*-document was created in the current session without saving, the *second* element of the sublist is the message *"nb has been not saved"*. In addition, the first sublist of the returned list defines the current *nb*-document. If the returned list contains one sublist, it is converted in simple 2-element list of the above format. The following fragment represents source code of the **AllCurrentNb** procedure with an example of its application.

In[2964]:= AllCurrentNb[] := Module[{a = Notebooks[], b, c = {}, d, k},
b = Flatten[Map[SubsString[#, {"<<", ">>"}, 0] &, Map[ToString, a]]];
d = Map[Quiet[Check[NotebookFileName[#], "nb has been not saved"]] &, a];
Do[AppendTo[c, {b[[k]], d[[k]]}], {k, 1, Length[b]}];
c = Select[c, #[[1]] != "Messages" &]; If[Length[c] == 1, Flatten[c], c]]

In[2965]:= AllCurrentNb[]
Out[2965]= {{"27_20.nb", "C:\\MathToolBox\\27_20.nb"}, {"Untitled-6", "nb has been not saved"}, {"MathToolBox.nb", "C:\\MathToolBox\\MathToolBox.nb"}}

The next **NotebookSave1** procedure adjoins directly the previous **AllCurrentNb** procedure, significantly extending standard **NotebookSave** function. At that, that procedure provides saving in a *nb*-file of an arbitrary *nb*-document opened in the current session. Moreover, the procedure provides saving of *nb*-documents earlier saved in *nb*-files, along with the *nb*-documents opened only in the current session without their preliminary saving in *nb*-files, including documents "*Untitled-n*" and "*Messages*". The procedure call **NotebookSave1[x, y]** returns the path to a *nb*-file determined by the *second* y argument into that has been loaded a *x nb*-document opened in the current session. The saving of *nb*-documents opened in the current session is done by the following manner, namely:

*(1) if a **nb**-document has been opened in the current session from a **nb**-file then it will be saved in the same **nb**-file, but not in an y datafile;*

*(2) if a **nb**-document has been opened only in the current session without its preliminary saving in a **nb**-file then it will be saved in an y file; at that **nb**-document x receives y name in the current session;*

*(3) if a x **nb**-document is not contained among **nb**-documents opened in the current session then the procedure call returns Null, i.e. nothing.*

The fragment below represents source code of the **NotebookSave1** procedure with typical examples of its application.

In[2971]:= NotebookSave1[x_ /; StringQ[x], y_ /; StringQ[y]] :=
Module[{a = Notebooks[], b, c = {}, d, k},
b = Flatten[Map[SubsString[#, {"<<", ">>"}, 0] &, Map[ToString, a]]];
d = Map[Quiet[Check[NotebookFileName[#], $Failed]] &, a];
Do[AppendTo[c, {b[[k]], d[[k]]}], {k, 1, Length[b]}]; c = If[Length[c] == 1, Flatten[c], c];
Do[If[c[[k]][[1]] == FileNameTake[x] && c[[k]][[2]] === $Failed, NotebookSave[a[[k]], y];
Return[y], If[c[[k]][[1]] == FileNameTake[x], NotebookSave[a[[k]], c[[k]][[2]]];
Return[c[[k]][[2]]], Null]], {k, 1, Length[c]}]]

In[2972]:= NotebookSave1["35-12.nb", "C:\\temp\\hhh.nb"]
Out[2972]= "C:\\MathToolBox\\35-12.nb"
In[2973]:= NotebookSave1["Untitled-6", "C:\\Temp\\Untitled6.nb"]
Out[2973]= "C:\\Temp\\Untitled6.nb"
In[2974]:= NotebookSave1["Messages", "C:\\Temp\\Messages.nb"]
Out[2974]= "C:\\Temp\\Messages.nb"

It should be noted that procedures **AllCurrentNb, ObjInCurrentNb1, OpenCurrentNb** and **NotebookSave1** in the program mode allow both to receive list of *nb*-documents opened in the current session and to save them in the given files, and to analyze them regarding the main objects which are contained in them.

The procedure call **OpenCurrentNb[*x*]** in the program mode allows to open window with a *nb*-document *x* opened in the current session or located in file of {*"cdf"*, *"nb"*} formats with returning *Null*, i.e. nothing. The fragment represents source code of the procedure with an example of its application.

In[3934]:= **OpenCurrentNb[x_ /; StringQ[x] && (SuffPref[x, {".cdf", ".nb"}, 2] || SuffPref[x, "Untitled-", 1]) || x == "Messages"] :=**
Module[{a = Notebooks[], b, c = {}, d, k, h},
If[FileExistsQ[x] && Select[AllCurrentNb[], #[[1]] == FileNameTake[x] &] == {},
NotebookOpen[x], h = FileNameTake[x];
b = Flatten[Map[SubsString[#, {"<<", ">>"}, 0] &, Map[ToString, a]]];
d = Map[Quiet[Check[NotebookFileName[#], "nb has been not saved"]] &, a];
Do[AppendTo[c, {b[[k]], d[[k]]}], {k, 1, Length[b]}];
b = If[Length[c] == 1, Flatten[c], c]; If[NbName[][[1]] == h, Null,
If[Select[b, #[[1]] == h &] == {}, $Failed, c = Partition[Riffle[Map[#[[1]] &, b], a], 2];
SetSelectedNotebook[Select[c, #[[1]] == h &][[1]][[2]]]]];]]

In[3935]:= **OpenCurrentNb["0-142.nb"]**

At last, the procedure call **NbDocumentQ[*x*]** returns *True* if *x* is a real *nb*-document opened in the current session or located in a *x nb*-file, otherwise *False* is returned. Whereas the call **NbDocumentQ[*x*, *y*]** with the second optional *y* argument – *an indefinite variable* – through *y* returns the *nb*-document type: *"current"* (current *nb*-document), *"opened"* (*nb*-document, opened in the current session), or *"file"* (a *nb*-document located in a *nb*-file *x*) if the main return is *True*, otherwise *y* is returned indefinite. The fragment presents source code of the **NbDocumentQ** procedure along with typical examples of its application.

In[3947]:= **NbDocumentQ[x_, t___] := Module[{a, b = FileNameTake[x], c},**
If[StringQ[x] && (SuffPref[x, {".cdf", ".nb"}, 2] || SuffPref[x, "Untitled-", 1]),
If[Select[AllCurrentNb[], #[[1]] == b &] != {},
If[{t} != {} && ! HowAct[t],
If[NbName[][[1]] == b, t = "current", t = "opened"], Null]; True, a = AllCurrentNb[];
On[Definition::notfound]; c = Quiet[Check[Get[x], False]]; Off[Definition::notfound];
If[c[[0]] === Notebook, If[{t} != {} && ! HowAct[t], t = "file", Null]; True, False]], False]]

In[3948]:= **{NbDocumentQ["Untitled-3", h74], h74}**
Out[3948]= {True, "opened"}
In[3949]:= **{NbDocumentQ["0-142.nb", h69], h69}**
Out[3949]= {True, "current"}
In[3950]:= **{NbDocumentQ["C:\\MathToolBox\\0-74.nb", h49], h49}**
Out[3950]= {True, "file"}

Whereas the function is a simplistic version of the **NbDocumentQ** procedure represented above. The function call **NbCurrentQ[x]** returns *True*, if a *x nb*-document is opened in the current session, and *False* otherwise. The following fragment represents source code of the **NbCurrentQ** function with examples of its application.

In[4135]:= **NbCurrentQ[x_] := If[StringQ[x] && (SuffPref[x, {".cdf",".nb"}, 2] || SuffPref[x, "Untitled-", 1]) || x == "Messages", If[Select[Map[ToString, Notebooks[]], ! StringFreeQ[#, "<<" <> x <> ">>"] &] != {}, True, False], False]**

In[4136]:= **NbCurrentQ["MathToolBox.nb"]**
Out[4136]= True
In[4137]:= **NbCurrentQ["2016-6.nb"]**
Out[4137]= False
In[4138]:= **NbCurrentQ["Messages"]**
Out[4138]= True

In turn, the procedure call **FileCurrentNb[x]** returns the file containing a *nb*-document *x* uploaded in the current session; if the *nb*-document wasn't open in the current session the *$Failed* is returned, whereas on a *x* document with the name "*Untitled-n*" or "*Messages*" the message "*x wasn't saved*" is returned. The following fragment represents source code of the **FileCurrentNb** procedure with typical examples of its application.

In[3708]:= **FileCurrentNb[x_ /; StringQ[x] && (SuffPref[x, {".cdf", ".nb"}, 2] || SuffPref[x, "Untitled-", 1]) || x == "Messages"] := Module[{a = Notebooks[], b, c, k}, b = Map[ToString, a]; Do[If[! StringFreeQ[b[[k]], "<<" <> x <> ">>"], c = Return[Quiet[Check[NotebookDirectory[a[[k]]], "500"]]], c = "90"], {k, 1, Length[a]}]; If[DirectoryQ[c], c <> x, If[c == "90", $Failed, x <> " was not saved"]]]**

In[3709]:= **FileCurrentNb["MathToolBox.nb"]**
Out[3709]= "C:\\MathToolBox\\MathToolBox.nb"
In[3710]:= **FileCurrentNb["2016-6.nb"]**
Out[3710]= $Failed
In[3711]:= **FileCurrentNb["Messages"]**
Out[3711]= "Messages was not saved"

The function call **NbFileEvaluate[x]** evaluates all calculated cells in the notebook located in a *x* file of {"*cdf*", "*nb*"} format with its opening in a new window. At that, the call evaluates the notebook as if all cells had been evaluated with hot keys *Shift+Enter*. Messages, print output and other side effects are placed in the notebook along with outputs. If the call is used on a *x* file which is not open, the *Mathematica* will invisibly open the file, evaluate it entirely, saves, and closes the file. Whereas the call **NbFileEvaluate[x, y]** with the second *y* argument – an arbitrary expression – opens a *x* file, evaluates it entirely and will leave the notebook completely unmodified. The next fragment represents source code of the function **NbFileEvaluate** with an example of its application.

In[5]:= **NbFileEvaluate[x_ /; FileExistsQ[x] && MemberQ[{"cdf", "nb"}, FileExtension[x]], y___] := Quiet[Quiet[NotebookEvaluate[NotebookOpen[x], InsertResults -> If[{y} != {}, False, True]]]]**

In[6]:= **NbFileEvaluate["C:\\MathToolBox\\MathToolBox.nb"]**

This function is an useful means, in particular, at need in the program mode of activation in the current session of a package, located in a file of the {"*cdf*", "*nb*"} format. The example of the previous fragment illustrates use of this function for uploading in the current session of *MathToolBox*, located in the *nb*-file. The **NbFileEvaluate** procedure is adjoined directly by the **MfileEvaluate** procedure whose description should be preceded by the **DefToString** procedure, and that is essentially used by the **MfileEvaluate** procedure. The procedure call **DefToString[*x*]** in string format returns the definition of an object whose *x* name is coded in the string format. The following fragment represents source codes of the **DefToString** and **MfileEvaluate** procedures with examples of their application.

In[4242]:= DefToString[x_ /; StringQ[x]] :=
Module[{a = Definition[x], c, b = ToString[Unique["agn"]]},
Write[b, a]; Close[b]; a = ReadString[b]; DeleteFile[b];
If[Set[c, Attributes[x]] == {}, a, b = StringPosition[a, "\r\n \r\n"][[1]];
a = StringTake[a, {b[[2]] + 1, -1}] <> StringTake[a, b] <> "Attributes[" <>
ToString[x] <> "] = " <> ToString[c] <> ";"];
StringReplace[a, {"\r\n \r\n" -> "\r\n", "\r\n\r\n" -> ""}]]

In[4243]:= M[x_] := Module[{a = "12", b = "56"}, x^2];
M[x_, y_] := Module[{a = "12", b = "56"}, x + y]; SetAttributes[M, {Protected, Listable}]
In[4244]:= Definition[M]
Out[4244]= Attributes[M] = {Listable, Protected}
M[x_] := Module[{a = "12", b = "56"}, x^2]
M[x_, y_] := Module[{a = "12", b = "56"}, x + y]
In[4245]:= S = DefToString["M"]
Out[4245]= "M[x_] := Module[{a = \"123\", b = \"567\"}, x^2]
M[x_, y_] := Module[{a = \"123\", b = \"567\"}, x + y]
Attributes[M] = {Listable, Protected};"
In[4246]:= ClearAttributes[M, Protected]; ClearAll[M]
In[4247]:= ToExpression[S]
In[4248]:= Definition[M]
Out[4248]= Attributes[M] = {Listable, Protected}
M[x_] := Module[{a = "12", b = "56"}, x^2]
M[x_, y_] := Module[{a = "12", b = "56"}, x + y]
In[4250]:= MfileEvaluate[x_ /; FileExistsQ[x] && FileExtension[x] == "m",
y_ /; MemberQ[{1, 2, 3, 4}, y]] := Module[{a, b, c, d, h, f},
f[z_]:= Select[z, "Attributes["<>#<>"] = {*Temporary*}" != Quiet[ToString[Definition[#]]] &];
a = StringCases[ReadString[x], "BeginPackage[\"" ~~ Shortest[__] ~~ "`\"]"];
a = Map[Quiet[Check[StringTake[#, {15, -3}], Null]] &, a];
a = Select[a, Complement[Characters[#], Join[CharacterRange["A", "Z"],
CharacterRange["a", "z"], {"`"}]] == {} &];
If[MemberQ[{{}, {"AladjevProcedures`"}}, a], $Failed,
Quiet[NotebookEvaluate[NotebookOpen[x, Visible -> False]]]; b = a[[1]];

```
h = Names[b <> "*"]; c = Sort[DeleteDuplicates[Map[StringReplace[#, b -> ""] &, h]]];
If[y == 1, f[c], If[y == 2, d = {{}, {}};
Map[If[Quiet[ToString[Definition[#]]] != "Null", AppendTo[d[[1]], #],
AppendTo[d[[2]], #]] &, c];
If[d[[1]] == {}, Null, c = Map[Quiet[ToExpression[StringReplace[DefToString[#],
{b -> "", # <> "`" -> ""}]]] &, d[[1]]]];
d = Map[StringReplace[#, b -> ""] &, d];
Map[Sort, Map[f, d]], If[y == 3, b, Map[{Print[StringReplace[#, b -> ""]],
ToExpression["?" <> ToString[#]]} &, h];]]]]]
In[4251]:= MfileEvaluate["C:\\MathToolBox\\MathToolBox.m", 1]
Out[4251]= $Failed
In[4252]:= MfileEvaluate["C:\\Temp\\Combinatorica.m", 3]
Out[4252]= "Combinatorica`"
In[4252]:= MfileEvaluate["C:\\Temp\\Combinatorica.m", 4]
AcyclicQ
AcyclicQ[g] yields True if graph g is acyclic... >>
=====
In[4252]:= MfileEvaluate["C:\\Temp\\Combinatorica.m", 1]
Out[4252]= {"AcyclicQ", "AddEdge", "AddEdges", "AddVertex",...}
In[4252]:= Length[%]
Out[4252]= 462
In[4252]:= MfileEvaluate["C:\\Temp\\Combinatorica.m", 2]
Out[4252]= {{"AcyclicQ",...,"Zoom"}, {"PathConditionGraph",...,"VertexNumberPosition"}}
```

The call **MfileEvaluate[x, y]** evaluates a package located in a *x m*-file and depending on a value of the second *y* argument performs the following actions concerning the *x m*-file with a package, namely:

y=1 – returns the list of all objects names whose definitions are in the x m-file;

y=2 – returns the 2-element list whose the first element determines the list of objects names of m-file that are available in the current session while the second element – the list of names of the m-file that are not available in the current session;

y=3 – returns the context ascribed to a package located in the x m-file;

y=4 – prints the usage concerning all objects located in the x m-file in the format:

Name

The usage concerning **Name**.

The call **MfileEvaluate[x, y]** – *x* determines a *m*-file not contained a package or *m*-file with a package containing the procedure definition – returns *$Failed*.

The previous procedure is adjoined directly by the procedure programmed on an other idea and whose call **MfileLoad[x]** evaluates the package located in a *x m*-file, returning *Null*, i.e. nothing. While the call **MfileLoad[x, y]** with the second optional *y* argument – an indefinite variable – thru *y* additionally returns the 3-element list whose elements define the context ascribed to the *x* package, list of main objects names whose definitions are in the package, and the list of names with the given context accordingly. In particular, the third element can define objects of the system packages built in the system as it takes place for *Combinatorica* package, options, etc. The call on a *m*-file not contained any package returns $Failed.

In[4242]:= MfileLoad[x_ /; FileExistsQ[x] && FileExtension[x] == "m", y___] :=
Module[{a = ReadString[x], b, c, d, h, p}, b = Flatten[StringPosition[a, "BeginPackage[\""]];
If[b == {}, $Failed, c[z_] := Select[z, ! MemberQ[{"Attributes[" <> # <> "] = {Temporary}", "Null", False}, Quiet[Check[ToString[Definition[#]], False]]] &];
d = StringCases[a, "BeginPackage[\"" ~~ Shortest[__] ~~ "`\"]"];
d = Map[Quiet[Check[StringTake[#, {15, -3}], Null]] &, d];
d = Select[d, Complement[Characters[#], Join[CharacterRange["A", "Z"], CharacterRange["a", "z"], {"`"}]] == {} &][[1]];
Quiet[ToExpression[StringReplace[StringTake[a, {b[[1]], -1}], {"(*" -> "", "*)" -> ""}]]];
b = Map[StringReplace[#, d -> ""] &, Names[d <> "*"]];
Map[Quiet[ClearAttributes[#, {Protected, ReadProtected}]] &, b];
If[{y} != {} && SameQ[ToString[Definition[y]], "Null"], y = {d, Set[p, c[b]],
Select[Complement[b, p], "Attributes[" <> # <> "] = {Temporary}" !=
Quiet[ToString[Definition[#]]] &]};, Null]]]

In[4243]:= {MfileLoad["C:\\MathToolBox\\MathToolBox.m", g70], g70}
Out[4243]= {Null, {"AladjevProcedures`", {"AcNb", ..., "$Version2"}, {"a", "a1", "b", ...}}
In[4244]:= Map[Length, {g70[[2]], g70[[3]]}]
Out[4244]= {1127, 14}

For convenience of uploading of a package into the current session the **Need** procedure generalizing in a certain degree the standard **Needs** function can be used. The source code of the **Need** procedure with examples of its application are represented by the following fragment.

In[2672]:= Need[x__] := Module[{a = Directory[], c, p, d = {x}[[1]], f, b = If[Length[{x}] > 1 && StringQ[{x}[[2]]], {x}[[2]], "Null"]},
If[! ContextQ[d], $Failed, If[b == "Null", Quiet[Check[Get[d], $Failed]],
If[b != "Null" && ! MemberQ[{"m", "mx"}, FileExtension[b]] || ! FileExistsQ[b], $Failed,
If[MemberQ[$Packages, d], True, CopyFile[b, f = a <> "\\" <> FileNameSplit[b][[-1]]];
Get[f]; DeleteFile[f]; True]]]]]

In[2673]:= Need["Grodno`", "C:\\mathematica\\Grodno.mx"]
Out[2673]= True
In[2674]:= **$Packages**
Out[2674]= {"Grodno`", "AladjevProcedures`", "GetFEKernelInit`", ... }
In[2675]:= **CNames["Grodno`"]**
Out[2675]= {"Ga", "Gs", "GSV", "Vgs"}

The procedure call **Need**[*x*] loads a package that corresponds to a *x* context into the current session provided that the corresponding datafile of format {"*m*" | "*mx*"} is located in one of the directories determined by the system variable $*Path* with returning *True*; otherwise, the call returns $*Failed*. Whereas the procedure call **Need**[*x*] loads a package that corresponds to a *x* context into the current session provided that the corresponding file of the format {"*m*" |

"*mx*" } is located or in one of the directories determined by the system variable $Path$, or is determined by *y* argument with return *True*; otherwise, the call returns *$Failed*. So, having created a *nb*-document with definitions of objects, having supplied them with usage with its subsequent evaluation and preservation by means of function {**Save**|**DumpSave**} in a file of format {"*m*"|"*mx*"} respectively, we have a possibility in the subsequent sessions to upload it into the current session by means of the **Needs** function or the **Need** procedure with receiving access to the program objects that contain in it. Moreover, for the purpose of increase of efficiency of uploading of a package it is recommended to use a file of *mx*-format in which it was earlier saved by means of call **DumpSave[x]** where the *x* argument defines a context associated with the saved package. With questions of loading of the user packages into the current session along with rather useful recommendations the interested reader can familiarize in [28,30-33,50]. In particular, it should be noted the undesirability of use of the identical contexts for the user packages, leading in some cases to unpredictable results, but not all so negatively.

When processing of *mx*-files with user packages in some cases there is need to change the contexts assigned to these datafiles. This problem is successfully solved by the procedure whose call **ContextForPackage[x, y]** returns two–element list whose first element defines a new *y* context, assigned to the user package from *x mx*-file, whereas the second element defines path to the file which contains the updated *x* file. The updated file is saved in the same directory as the *x* file, but with the name **FileBaseName[x]** <> "*$.mx*". At the same time, irrespective of whether the initial file *x* has been loaded into the current session, as a result of the procedure call the file is removed from the current session, remaining in the external memory without change. At the same time, if the initial package from a *x* file has been already uploaded up the procedure call, then the package with the updated *y* context remains in the current session, otherwise it is removed from the current session. The next fragment represents source code of the procedure with examples of its application.

```
In[4769]:= ContextForPackage[x_ /; FileExistsQ[x] && FileExtension[x] == "mx",
y_ /; ContextQ[y] && ! MemberQ[$Packages, y]] := Module[{a = ContextInMxFile[x], b, c},
If[a === $Failed, $Failed, If[a == y, {y, x}, If[MemberQ[$Packages, a], b = 75, Get[x]];
Map[ContextToSymbol[#, y] &, CNames[a]];
DumpSave[c = FileNameJoin[Reverse[ReplacePart[Reverse[FileNameSplit[x]],
1 -> FileBaseName[x] <> "$.mx"]]], y]; RemovePackage[a];
If[b == 75, Null, RemovePackage[y]]; {y, c}]]]

In[4770]:= ContextInMxFile["Grodno.mx"]
Out[4770]= "Grodno`"
In[4771]:= ContextForPackage["Grodno.mx", "Tallinn`"]
Out[4771]= {"Tallinn`", "Grodno$.mx"}
In[4772]:= {CNames["Grodno`"], MemberQ[$Packages, "Grodno`"]}
Out[4772]= {{}, False}
In[4773]:= CNames["Tallinn`"]
Out[4773]= {"Ga", "Gs", "GSV", "Vgs"}
In[4774]:= Definition[Vgs]
Out[4774]= Vgs[x_Integer, y_Integer] := x*y
```

In[7475]:= **Map[Context[#] &, CNames["Tallinn`"]]**
Out[4775]= {"Tallinn`", "Tallinn`", "Tallinn`", "Tallinn`"}
In[4776]:= **$Packages**
Out[4776]= {"AladjevProcedures`", "GetFEKernelInit`", "PacletManager`",...}
In[4777]:= **Get["Grodno$.mx"]**
In[4778]:= **$Packages**
Out[4778]= {"Tallinn`", "AladjevProcedures`", "GetFEKernelInit`",...}
In[4779]:= **??Vgs**
Tampere`Vgs
Vgs[x_Integer, y_Integer] := x*y

This procedure can be a rather useful tools in case of certain types of processing of *mx*-files with the user packages. For example, such approach can be used for replenishment of a *mx*-file with the user package with new means as the above-considered **RedMxFile** procedure illustrates. While the next **AddMxFile** procedure illustrates the use of **ContextForPackage** procedure for merging of *mx*-files with the user packages with saving of the result in a *mx*-file with an ascribed *y* context. It is supposed that the merged *mx*-files haven't been loaded in the current session and have been supplied with appropriate contexts. The procedure call **AddMxFile[x, y]** returns the two-element list whose the first element determines *y* context, whereas the second element determines *mx*-file with the result of merging of *mx*-files that are defined by the *x* list. At last, the call **AddMxFile[x, y, z]** with the 3rd optional *z* argument – an arbitrary expression – additionally allows to save in the current session the means with the *y* context, otherwise the package with an *y* context is unloaded from the current session. The following fragment represents source code of the procedure with examples of its use.

In[4174]:= **AddMxFile[x_ /; ListQ[x] && Length[x] >= 1 &&**
AllTrue[Map[FileExistsQ[#] && FileExtension[#] == "mx" &, x], TrueQ] &&
AllTrue[Map[! MemberQ[$Packages, ContextInMxFile[#]] &, x], TrueQ],
y_ /; ContextQ[y], z___] := Module[{a = {}, b, k},
Do[AppendTo[a, ContextForPackage[x[[k]], y]], {k, 1, Length[x]}];
DumpSave[b = StringTake[y, {1, -2}] <> ".mx", y];
If[{z} == {}, RemovePackage[y], Null]; {y, b}]

In[4174]:= **AddMxFile[{"Grodno.mx", "Tallinn.mx"}, "RansIan`"]**
Out[4174]= {"RansIan`", "RansIan.mx"}
In[4174]:= **{CNames["RansIan`"], MemberQ[$Packages, "RansIan`"]}**
Out[4174]= {{}, False}
In[4174]:= **Get["RansIan.mx"]**
In[4174]:= **CNames["RansIan`"]**
Out[4174]= {"Agn1", "Avz1", "Ga", "Gs", "GSV", "Ian1", "Vgs"}
In[4174]:= **$Packages**
Out[4174]= {"RansIan`", "JLink`", "DocumentationSearch`", "AladjevProcedures`", "CURLInfo`", "OAuthSigning`", "CURLLink`HTTP`", "CURLLink`", "GetFEKernelInit`", "StreamingLoader`", "IconizeLoader`", "CloudObjectLoader`", "ResourceLocator`", "PacletManager`", "System`", "Global`"}
In[4174]:= **Definition[Vgs]**

Out[4174]= Vgs[x_Integer, y_Integer] := x*y
In[4174]:= **Definition[Agn1]**
Out[4174]= Agn1[x_Integer] := x + 590
Agn1[x_] := x
Agn1[x_, y_] := x + y
In[4174]:= **?? Vgs**
RanslanʼVgs
Vgs[x_Integer, y_Integer] := x*y

In[4230]:= SaveInMx[x_/; FileExtension[x] == "mx", y_/; SymbolQ[y] || ListQ[y] &&
AllTrue[Map[SymbolQ[#] &, y], TrueQ], z_/; ContextQ[z]] :=
Module[{b, a = Flatten[Select[Map[PureDefinition[#] &, Flatten[{y}]],
! SameQ[#, $Failed] &]]},
Map[ToExpression[z <> #] &, a]; AppendTo[$ContextPath, z]; DumpSave[x, z];]

In[4231]:= Agn[x_, y_] := Module[{a = 90}, a*(x + y)]; Agn[x_] := x + 590
In[4232]:= SaveInMx["Grodno.mx", {Avz, Agn}, "Grodno`"];
In[4233]:= $ContextPath = MinusList[$ContextPath, {"Grodno`"}]; Clear[Avz, Agn];
Get["Grodno.mx"]
In[4234]:= **PureDefinition[Agn]**
Out[4234]= {"Agn[x_, y_] := Module[{a = 90}, a*(x + y)]", "Agn[x_] := x + 590"}

The previous fragment represents source code of **SaveInMx** procedure along with examples of it use. The procedure call **SaveInMx**[*x, y, z*] returns nothing, saving in a *x mx*-file with *z* context the definition of a symbol or a list of symbols *y* that have the *"Global'"* context. The **SaveInMx** procedure to a certain extent supplements earlier represented tools of the same plan.

In a number of cases exists a necessity of testing of a file regarding that whether it contains a package. This problem is solved by an quite simple function, whose call **PackageFileQ**[*x*] returns *True* if *x* argument defines a file of formats {*"cdf", "mx", "m", "nb"*} with a package, otherwise *False* is returned. The following fragment represents source code of the function with an example of its application.

In[2542]:= **PackageFileQ[x_] := If[StringQ[x] && FileExistsQ[x] &&**
MemberQ[{"cdf", "m", "mx", "nb"}, FileExtension[x]],
If[SameQ[ContextFromFile[x], $Failed], False, True], False]

In[2543]:= **Map[PackageFileQ, {"gru.mx", "pack.m", "pack.nb", "pack.cdf"}]**
Out[2543]= {True, True, True, True}

The previous fragment represents source code of the **PackageFileQ** function with examples of its use. The given function turned out as a rather useful tool for a number of means of our *MathToolBox* package [48,50].

At last, for convenience of loading of the user package located in a *x mx*-file into the current session the **LoadPackage** procedure can be used, whose call **LoadPackage**[*x*] returns *Null*, i.e. nothing, uploading the package into the current session with activation of all definitions that are contained in it in the mode similar to the mode of *Input* paragraph, i.e. in an *optimal* format in the above sense *(without package context)*. The next fragment represents source code of the **LoadPackage** procedure with examples of its application.

In[3422]:= **LoadPackage[x_ /; FileExistsQ[x] && FileExtension[x] == "mx"] :=**
Module[{a}, Quiet[ToExpression["Off[shdw::Symbol]"];
Get[x]; a = ToExpression["Packages[][[1]]"];
ToExpression["LoadMyPackage[" <> "\"" <> x <> "\"" <> "," <> "\"" <> a <> "\"" <> "]"];
ToExpression["On[shdw::Symbol]"]]]

In[3423]:= **LoadPackage["C:\\Temp\\Mathematica\\MathToolBox.mx"]**
In[3424]:= **Definition[StrStr]**
Out[3424]= StrStr[x_] := If[StringQ[x], "\"" <> x <> "\"", ToString[x]]

Meantime it must be kept in mind, in case of loading in the described way into the current session of other user package the availability of package the *MathToolBox* or the activated **LoadPackage** procedure is required. These tools is convenient at processing of definitions of the package tools in the above optimized format, i.e. without a package context.

In books [30-33] and here the organization of the user package, simple and convenient for modifications and saved in *m*–file by means of chain of *GUI* commands *"File -> Save As -> Mathematica Package (*.m)"* is presented. The procedure call **ContCodeUsageM[*x*]** returns the sorted list of names in string format of objects which are contained in the *x m*–file with a package. Whereas the call **ContCodeUsageM[*x, y*]** returns the usage in string format of an object which is contained in a *x m*–file with package and has *y* name. Furthermore, the call **ContCodeUsageM[*x, y, z*]** with the 3rd optional *z* argument – *an arbitrary expression* – returns the source code in string format of an object which is in a *x m*–file with a package and has *y* name. The next fragment represents source code of the procedure **ContCodeUsageM** along with typical examples of its application.

In[5741]:= **ContCodeUsageM[x_ /; FileExistsQ[x] && FileExtension[x] == "m", y__] :=**
Module[{b = {y}, a = StringJoin[Map[FromCharacterCode, BinaryReadList[x]]]},
If[Length[b] > 1 && Head[b[[1]]] == Symbol, StringTake[StringReplace[StringCases[a,
"Begin[\"`" <> ToString[b[[1]]] <> "`\"]" ~~ Shortest[J__] ~~ "End[]"][[1]], "*)\r\n(*" ->
"\r"], {13 + StringLength[ToString[b[[1]]]], -7}],
If[b != {} && Head[b[[1]]] == Symbol, StringReplace[StringTake[StringCases[a,
ToString[b[[1]]] <> "::usage=" ~~ Shortest[J__] ~~ "(**)"][[1]], {1, -9}], "::usage=" -> "::", 1],
Sort[DeleteDuplicates[Map[StringTake[#, {9, -4}] &, StringCases[a, "Begin[\"`" ~~
Shortest[J__] ~~ "`\"]"]]]], $Failed]]

In[5742]:= **Length[ContCodeUsageM["C:/MathToolBox/MathToolBox.m"]]**
Out[5742]= 1143

In[5743]:= **ContCodeUsageM["C:/MathToolBox/MathToolBox.m", StrStr]**
Out[5743]= "StrStr::\"The call StrStr[x] returns an expression x in string ... obtained from an expression x is returned.\""

In[5744]:= **ContCodeUsageM["c:/Mathtoolbox/Mathtoolbox.m", StrStr, 90]**
Out[5744]= "StrStr[x_] := If[StringQ[x], \"\\\"\" <> x <> \"\\\"\", ToString[x]]"

The following procedure concerns the case of organization of the user packages, mentioned above and saved in *m*–files by means of the above chain of *GUI* commands. The package

Software Etudes in the Mathematica

MathToolBox was organized and modified exactly in such way [48,50]. The procedure call **ConvertMtoMx[x, y]** returns *Null*, i.e. nothing, providing converting of a x m–file created by the above method into file with the same main name, but with *"mx"* extension; through the 2nd y argument – a symbol – the list of names in string format of objects that are in the x m–file with a package is returned. Whereas the procedure call **ConvertMtoMx[x, y, z]** with the third optional z argument – *an arbitrary expression* – in addition load a package contained in a x file from the current session. The next fragment represents source code of the procedure along with typical examples of its application.

```
In[5755]:= ConvertMtoMx[x_ /; FileExistsQ[x] && FileExtension[x] == "m",
y_ /; Head[y] == Symbol, z___] :=
Module[{a, b, c, d, h = {}, f = StringTake[x, {1, -2}] <> "mx", p = "\""},
a = StringReplace[StringJoin[Map[FromCharacterCode, BinaryReadList[x]]], {"(**)" -> "",
"*)\r\n(*" -> "\r", "*)\r\n\r\n(*" -> "\r", "*)\r\n\r\n(\r\n*" -> "\r",
"(* :: " -> "::", "End[]" -> ""}];
a = StringTake[a, {Flatten[StringPosition[a, "BeginPackage["]][[1]] - 1, -4}];
b = StringCases[a, "Begin[\"`" ~~ Shortest[X__] ~~ "`\"]"];
c = StringTake[StringCases[a, "BeginPackage[\"" ~~ Shortest[J__] ~~ "\"]"][[1]], {14, -2}];
Quiet[ToExpression[StringTake[StringReplace[a, Map[Rule[#,""] &, b]], {1, -2}]]];
ToExpression["DumpSave[" <> p <> f <> p <> "," <> c <> "]"];
y = Sort[Map[StringTake[#, {9, -4}] &, b]]; If[{z} != {}, Map[ClearAll, y]];
d = "ClearAttributes[{$Packages, Contexts}, Protected];
$Packages = Select[$Packages, StringFreeQ[#, g] &];
Contexts[] = Select[Contexts[], StringFreeQ[#, g] &];
SetAttributes[{$Packages, Contexts}, Protected];
$ContextPath = Select[$ContextPath, StringFreeQ[#, g] &]";
ToExpression[StringReplace[d, ",g" -> "," <> c]];, Null]]

In[5756]:= Clear[StrStr]; ConvertMtoMx["C:/MathToolBox.m", StrStr, 90]
In[5757]:= Get["C:\\MathToolBox.m"]
In[5758]:= Definition[StrStr]
Out[5758]= StrStr[x_] := If[StringQ[x], "\"" <> x <> "\"", ToString[x]]
```

The procedure call **PackReplaceQ[x]** returns *True* if definitions contained in a x m–file with the user package replace definitions activated in the current session, and *False* otherwise at uploading of the x file into current session. Furthermore, the procedure call leaves the x file unloaded. While the call **PackReplaceQ[x, y]** thru optional y argument – *an indefinite symbol* – returns list of all objects of the current session whose definitions will be *replaced* at loading of the x file into current session. The next fragment represents source code of the procedure with typical examples of its application.

```
In[5949]:= PackReplaceQ[x_ /; FileExistsQ[x] && FileExtension[x] == "m", y___] :=
Module[{a = $Packages, b = ContentOfMfile[x], c},
c = Select[Select[Flatten[Map[Quiet[Cnames[#]] &, a]], StringFreeQ[#,"`"] &],
MemberQ[b, #] &];
```

593

```
If[{y} != {} && ! HowAct[y], y = c, Null]; If[c == {}, False, True]]
In[5950]:= StrStr[x_] := x; PackReplaceQ["C:/mathtoolbox/mathtoolbox.m"]
Out[5950]= True
```

The tools, presented in this chapter along with other tools of our *MathToolBox* [48] allow to solve a number of important problems of processing of the user packages which are in files of {"*cdf*", "*mx*", "*m*", "*nb*"} formats. The *MathToolBox* package represents toolbox oriented on the wide enough circle of appendices including the system ones. The package represents also a certain interest from standpoint of useful enough approaches and receptions used at programming a number of the tools entering it, including tools for non-standard processing of the user packages. Such acquaintance with source codes of tools which are in the package *MathToolBox* and with the organization of the package as a whole will allow to acquaint of the reader more deeply with built-in language of the *Mathematica* system and to examine a rather simple and effective organization of the user packages.

Once again pertinently to pay attention to the next moment. A number of tools represented in the package are focused on the solution of identical problems, however they use various algorithms programmed with usage of various approaches. They not only illustrate variety of useful enough receptions but also reveal their shortcomings and advantages useful both in practical and system programming. In our opinion, such approach opens a wide enough field for awakening of creative activity of the reader in respect of improvement of his skills in the programming in the *Mathematica* system.

At that, one rather essential moment should be noted, namely. In the course of editing and debugging of source codes of objects for the *Mathematica* of version **10.0** rather often arises the situation with diagnostics *"Wolfram Mathematica 10.0 isn't responding"*, supposing, as a rule, closing of the *Mathematica* system. Moreover, the *second* possible reaction *"Wait for the program to respond"* to the situation is useless in most cases. As a whole, the dependability of functioning of the *Mathematica* causes certain *questions*. Unfortunately, the similar situation hasn't improved also in the latest version *Mathematica* **11.2.0**. This situation which does not have accurate diagnostics is a rather serious omission of the developers of the *Mathematica*. Thus, once again it should be noted that during of active operation with *Mathematica* on a number enough difficult applications with all definiteness have become clear that the very unpleasant above described situation arises rather often that is very unpleasant due to an impossibility of saving of the current *nb*-document at arising moment of the above especial situation. In general, the *Mathematica* system is a rather sensitive to the versions.

For example, the **UsagesMNb** procedure correctly operates only on files of *nb*-type which have been created in the *Mathematica* of versions **10.3.0.0** and below because of change of *internal* formats of these files, beginning with the system *Mathematica* of version **10.4.0.0**. In particular, in a whole, the optimized binary format of the *mx*-files is determined by both the operating platform and the *Mathematica* version. Therefore, certain means of our package [48,50], whose algorithms are based on the internal format of files, can demand appropriate adapting to new versions of *Mathematica*. It is also necessary to note, that for certain cyclic calculations the infinite calculations can arise that are irremovable by means of the system means, demanding the termination of the *Mathematica* system through *Task Manager* and not allowing to save the current *nb*-document. At last, at operation with the *Mathematica* also more complex especial situations, sometimes, not processed by both the *Mathematica* system, and the *Windows* system are possible, requiring reboot of the computer.

The following section represents certain reasons on the organization of the user software. Meanwhile, earlier we already provided the organization of the user packages which is a rather convenient at various processings (*e.g. editing, programming of various means for their processing, etc.*). At the same time, many means presented in the present book are oriented to this organization, first of all. Our *MathToolBox* package attached to the present book can be a bright example of such organization [48,50].

8.4. The organization of the user software in the *Mathematica* system

The *Mathematica* no possess comfortable enough means of the organization of the user libraries as in the case of the *Maple*, creating certain difficulties at the organization of the user software developed in its environment. For saving of definitions of objects and results of calculations the *Mathematica* uses datafiles of various organization. At that, files of text format which not only are easily loaded into the current session, in general are most often used, but also are convenient enough for processing by other known means, for example, the word processors. Moreover, the text format provides a portability on other computing platforms. One of the main prerequisites of saving in files is possibility of use of definitions and their *usage* of the *Mathematica* objects in the subsequent sessions of the system. At that, with questions of standard saving of the objects (*blocks, modules, functions, etc.*) the interested reader can familiarize in details in [28-33,51-53,61,63,66,68], some of them were considered in the present book in the context of organization of packages while here we present simple tools of organization of the user libraries in the *Mathematica* system.

Meanwhile, here it is expedient to make a number of very essential remarks on usage of the above system means. First, the mechanism of processing of erroneous and especial *situations* represents a rather powerful instrument of programming practically of each quite complex algorithm. However, in the *Mathematica* such mechanism is characterized by a number of essential shortcomings, for example, successfully using in the *Input* mode the mechanism of output of messages concerning erroneous {Off, On} situations, in body of procedures such mechanism generally doesn't work as illustrates the following a rather simple fragment:

In[2602]:= **Import["D:\\Math_myLib\\ArtKr_2017.m"]**
Import::nffil: File not found during Import... >>
Out[2602]= $Failed
In[2603]:= **Off[Import::nffil]**
In[2604]:= **Import["D:\\Math_myLib\\ArtKr_2017.m"]**
Out[2604]= $Failed
In[2605]:= **On[Import::nffil]**
In[2606]:= **F[x_] := Module[{a}, Off[Import::nffil]; a := Import[x]; On[Import::nffil]; a]**
In[2607]:= **F["D:\\Math_myLib\\ArtKr_2017.m"]**
Import::nffil: File not found during Import... >>
Out[2607]= $Failed

So, at creation of complex enough procedures in which is required to solve questions of the blocking of output of a number of erroneous messages, tools of the *Mathematica* system are presented to us as insufficiently developed tools. The interested reader can familiarize with other peculiarities of the specified system means in [28-33,50]. Now, we will present certain approaches concerning the organization of the user libraries in the *Mathematica*. Some of them can be useful in practical work with the *Mathematica* system.

In view of the scheme of the organization of library considered in [22,25-27] concerning the *Maple* with organization different from the main library, we will present realization of the similar user library for a case of the *Mathematica* system. On the first step in file system of the computer a directory, let us say, "C:\\Math_myLib" is created which will contain *txt*-files with definitions of the user procedures/functions along with their usage. In principle, it is possible to place any number of definitions into such *txt*-files, however in this case it is previously necessary to call a procedure whose name coincides with name of the *txt*-file, whereupon in the current session all procedures/ functions whose definitions are located in the file along with usage are available. That is really convenient in a case when in a single file are located the main procedure and all means accompanying it, excluding the standard system means.

On the second step the procedures and/or functions together with their usage are created and debugged with their subsequent saving in the required file of a library subdirectory:

In[2601]:= NF[x_] := Sin[x]*Cos[x]; ArtKr[x_, y_] := Sqrt[Sin[x] + 90*NF[y]]
In[2602]:= NF::usage = "Help on NF."; Rans::usage = "Help on Rans.";
Rans[x_] := Module[{}, x^2]; ArtKr::usage = "Help on function ArtKr.";
In[2603]:= **CreateDirectory["C:\\Math_myLib"];**
In[2604]:= **Save["C:\\Math_myLib\\Userlib.txt", {NF, ArtKr, "NF::usage", "ArtKr::usage",**
"Rans::usage", Rans}]
In[2605]:= **Clear[NF, ArtKr, Rans]; ArtKr::usage = ""; NF::usage = "";**
In[2606]:= **?ArtKr**
In[2607]:= **Definition[ArtKr]**
Out[2607]= Null
In[2608]:= **Get["C:\\Math_myLib\\Userlib.txt"];**
In[2609]:= **Definition[ArtKr]**
Out[2609]= ArtKr[x_, y_] := Sqrt[Sin[x] + 90*NF[y]]
In[2610]:= **?ArtKr**
"Help on function ArtKr."

To save the definitions and usage in datafiles of *txt*-format perhaps in two ways, namely: *(1)* by the function call **Save**, saving the previously evaluated definitions and usage in a file given by its first argument as illustrates the previous fragment; at that, saving is made in the *append-mode*, or *(2)* by creating *txt*-files with *names* of objects and their *usage* whose contents are formed by means of a simple word processor, for example, *Notepad*. At that, by means of the **Save** function we have possibility to create libraries of the user means, located in an arbitrary directory of file system of the computer.

The following fragment represents the **CallSave** procedure whose the call **CallSave[*x, y, z*]** returns the result of a call *y*[*z*] of a procedure or function *y* on a *z* list of factual arguments passed the *y* provided that object definition *y* with usage are located in a *x* *txt*-file that has been earlier created by means of **Save** function. If an object with the given *y* name is absent in the *x* file, the procedure call returns $Failed. If a *x* datafile contains definitions of several procedures or functions of the same name *y*, the procedure call is executed relative to their definition whose *formal* arguments correspond to a z list of *actual* arguments. If the y defines the list, the call returns the names list of all means located in the x file. The fragment below represents source code of the **CallSave** procedure along with examples of its use relative to the concrete file created by means of the standard **Save** function.

In[3582]:= NF[x_] := Sin[x]*Cos[x]; ArtKr[x_, y_] := Sqrt[Sin[x] + 90*NF[y]]
NF::usage = "Help on NF."; Rans::usage = "Help on Rans."; Rans[x_] := Module[{}, x^2];
Rans[x_, y_] := Module[{}, x + y]; ArtKr::usage = "Help on ArtKr.";
In[3583]:= Save2["C:/Math_myLib\\Userlib.txt", {NF, ArtKr, "NF::usage", "ArtKr::usage", "Rans::usage", Rans}]
In[3584]:= Clear[ArtKr, NF, Rans]; NF::usage = ""; ArtKr::usage = ""; Rans::usage = "";
In[3585]:= CallSave[x_ /; FileExistsQ[x], y_ /; SymbolQ[y] || ListQ[y], z_ /; ListQ[z]] :=
Module[{b, c, d, nf, u, p, t, v, n,
a = StringReplace[StringTake[ToString[InputForm[ReadString[x]]], {2, -2}],
"\\r\\n\\r\\n" -> "\\r\\n \\r\\n"], s = Map[ToString, Flatten[{y}]]},
b = StringSplit[a, "\\r\\n \\r\\n"]; n = Select[b, StringFreeQ[#, " /: "] &];
nf[g_] := StringTake[g, {1, Flatten[StringPosition[g, "[", 1]][[1]] - 1}];
c = Select[b, SuffPref[#, p = Flatten[{Map4[StringJoin, s, "["],
Map4[StringJoin, s, " /: "]}], 1] &]; {d, u, t, v} = {{}, {}, Map[# <> " /: " &, s], {}};
Map[If[SuffPref[#, t, 1], AppendTo[u, DelSuffPref[StringReplace[StringTrim[#, t],
"\\" -> ""], "rn", 2]], AppendTo[d, #]] &, c]; Map[ToExpression, {d, u}];
If[d == {}, $Failed, If[Length[d] == 1, Symbol[nf[d[[1]]]][Sequences[z]],
If[Length[DeleteDuplicates[Map[nf[#] &, d]]] == 1,
Map[Symbol[nf[#]][Sequences[z]] &, d][[1]], Map[nf[#] &, n]]]]]
In[3586]:= **CallSave["C:\\Math_myLib\\Userlib.txt", {NF, ArtKr, Rans}, {90, 500}]**
Out[3586]= {"NF", "ArtKr", "Rans", "NF", "ArtKr", "Rans", "Rans"}
In[3587]:= **CallSave["C:\\Math_myLib\\Userlib.txt", ArtKr, {90, 500}]**
Out[3587]= Sqrt[Sin[90] + 90*Cos[500]*Sin[500]]
In[3588]:= **CallSave["C:\\Math_myLib\\Userlib.txt", NF, {90, 500}]**
Out[3588]= NF[90, 500]
In[3589]:= **CallSave["C:\\Math_myLib\\Userlib.txt", ArtKr, {500}]**
Out[3589]= ArtKr[500]
In[3590]:= **CallSave["C:\\Math_myLib\\Userlib.txt", NF, {500}]**
Out[3590]= Cos[500]*Sin[500]
In[3591]:= **CallSave["C:\\Math_myLib\\Userlib.txt", Rans, {590}]**
Out[3591]= 348100
In[3592]:= **CallSave["C:\\Math_myLib\\Userlib.txt", Rans, {90, 590}]**
Out[3592]= 680
In[3593]:= **?ArtKr**
"Help on ArtKr."
In[3594]:= **CallSave["C:\\Math_myLib\\Userlib.txt", Art, {90, 590}]**
Out[3594]= $Failed
In[3600]:= **Save2[x_ /; StringQ[x], y_ /; SymbolQ[y] || ListQ[y]] :=**

If[FileExistsQ[x], Save[x, "\\r\\n \\r\\n"]; Save[x, y], Save[x, y]]
In[3601]:= Avz[x_, y_, z_] := Module[{a = 590, b = 90}, a*b*x*y*z];
Avz::usage = "Help on Avz." ;
In[3602]:= Save2["C:\\Math_myLib\\Userlib.txt", {Avz, "Avz::usage"}]
In[3603]:= Clear[Avz]; Avz::usage = "";
In[3604]:= CallSave["C:\\Math_myLib\\Userlib.txt", Avz, {74, 90, 590}]
Out[3604]= 208651140000
In[3605]:= ?Avz
"Help on Avz."

Meantime, the **CallSave** procedure provides the call of a necessary function or procedure which is located in a *txt*-file created by means of the standard **Save** function; at that, such user library rather reminds an archive because doesn't allow the updating. Whereas for extension of such libraries by new means it is necessary to use the simple **Save2** function, whose call **Save2[x, y]** append to a *x* datafile the definitions of the tools given by a name or their list *y* in the format convenient for the subsequent processing by a number of tools, in particular, by the **CallSave** procedure. In the previous fragment a source code of the **Save2** function with examples of its usage are represented. Thus, the similar organization of the user library provides a simple mode of its maintaining, whereas the **CallSave** procedure allows extensions on rather broad circle of functions of operating with the user library. In particular, the principle of modification of text files with definitions and usage of functions and procedures not only is very simple, but allows to keep history of their modifications that in a number of cases is a rather actual. In our opinion, the represented approach quite can be used for the organization of simple and effective user libraries of traditional type.

The mentioned simple approach to the organization of the user means in the *Mathematica* system is only one of possible methods, giving opportunity of creation of own libraries of procedures/functions with access to them at the level of the system means. The interested reader can familiarize with these questions more in details, for example, in books [30-33,50].

Qua of other a rather useful approach we will represent the **CALLmx** procedure whose call provides saving in library directory of definitions of objects and their usage in the format of *mx*-files with possibility of their subsequent loading into the current session. The fragment below represents source code of the **CALLmx** procedure with some examples of its use.

In[4650]:= NF[x_] := Sin[x]*Cos[x] + x^3
In[4651]:= ArtKr[x_, y_] := Sqrt[42*Sin[x] + 47*Cos[y]] + x*y
In[4652]:= CALLmx[y_, z_ /; MemberQ[{1, 2}, z], d___] :=
Module[{c = {}, h, k = 1, s, a = If[{d} == {}, Directory[], If[StringQ[d] && DirectoryQ[d],
d, Directory[]]], b = Map[ToString, If[ListQ[y], y, {y}]]},
If[z == 1, While[k <= Length[b], s = b[[k]]; h = a <> "\\" <> s <> ".mx";
If[! MemberQ[{"Null", $Failed}, Definition4[s]], ToExpression["DumpSave[" <>
ToString1[h] <> "," <> ToString[s] <> "]"];
AppendTo[c, s]]; k++]; Prepend[c, a], While[k <= Length[b], s = b[[k]];
h = a <> "\\" <> s <> ".mx"; If[FileExistsQ[h], Get[h]; AppendTo[c, s]]; k++]; c]]
In[4653]:= NF::usage = "Help on NF"; ArtKr::usage = "Help on ArtKr";

In[4654]:= CALLmx[{NF, ArtKr, "NF::usage", "ArtKr::usage"}, 1]
Out[4654]= {"C:\\Users\\Aladjev\\Documents", "NF", "ArtKr"}
In[4655]:= Clear[NF, ArtKr]
In[4656]:= CALLmx[{NF, ArtKr}, 2]
Out[4656]= {"NF", "ArtKr"}
In[4657]:= AGN = Sqrt[NF[42.47]^2 + ArtKr[19.89, 19.96]^4]
Out[4657]= 180710.0
In[4658]:= ?ArtKr
"Help on ArtKr."

The procedure call **CALLmx[y, 1, d]** returns the list whose the first element defines library directory while the others – the names of objects from *y* argument (*a separate name or their list*) whose definitions are evaluated in the current session; in the presence of the evaluated usage for objects they are saved in a file too; the optional *d* argument defines a directory in which the evaluated definitions of objects and their *y* usage in the form of *mx*-files with the names "*Name.mx*" where *Name* is the names of the objects defined by the *y* argument will be located; in a case of absence of the *d* argument as a library directory a directory which is defined by the call **Directory[]** is choosen. While the call **CALLmx[y, 2, d]** provides loading into the current session of objects whose names are determined by an *y* argument from a library directory defined by the third *d* argument; in its absence the **Directory[]** directory is supposed. At that, it should be noted that in one datafile is most expedient to place only the main procedure and functions associated with it, excepting *references* on standard functions. It allows to form procedural files enough simply.

It is possible to represent the **UserLib** procedure that supports a number of useful functions as one more rather simple example of maintaining the user libraries. The call **UserLib[W, f]** provides a number of important functions on maintaining of a simple user library located in a *W* datafile of *txt*-format. Qua of the second actual *f* argument the two-element list acts for which admissible pairs of values of elements can be, namely:

{"*names*", "*list*"} – return of the list of objects names, whose definitions are located in a library file; in case of the empty file the call is returned unevaluated;

{"*print*", "*all*"} – output to the screen of full contents of a library *W* file; in the case of the empty file the procedure call is returned unevaluated;

{"*print*", "*Name*"} – output to the screen of definition of object with name **Name** whose definition is in the library *W* file; in a case of empty file the call is returned unevaluated; in the absence in library *W* file of the demanded tools the procedure call returns Null, i.e. nothing, in such case the procedure call prints the message of the following kind "**Name** is absent in the **W** Library";

{"*add*", "*Name*"} – saving in the library *W* file in the append-mode of an object with a **Name** name; the definition of a saved tools has to be previously evaluated in the current session in the Input mode;

{"*load*", "*all*"} – loading into the current session of all means whose definitions are in the *W* library file; in case of the empty file the call is returned unevaluated;

{"*load*", "*N*"} – uploading into the current session of an object with N name whose definition is in the *W* library file; in case of the empty file the procedure call is returned unevaluated; in the absence in the *W* library file of a demanded tool the procedure call returns Null, i.e. nothing, in such case the procedure call prints the message of the following kind "N" is absent in the *W* library.

In other cases the **UserLib** procedure call is returned unevaluated. There is a good enough opportunity to extend the procedure with a lot of useful enough functions such as: deletion from a library of definitions with usage of the specified tools or their obsolete versions, etc. With this procedure is possible to familiarize more in details, for example, in [30-33,48,50].

The *list* structure of the *Mathematica* system allows to rather easily simulate the operating with structures of other systems of computer mathematics, for example, the *Maple* system. So, in the *Maple* system the tabular structure as one of the most important structures is used that is rather widely used both for the organization of data structures, and for organization of the libraries of software. The similar tabular organization is widely used for organization of package modules of the *Maple* along with a number of means of our **UserLib** library [47]. For simulation of the main operations with the tabular organization similar to the *Maple*, in the *Mathematica* system the **Table1** procedure can be used. The procedure call **Table1[L, x]** considers a *L* list of the *ListList* type, whose 2-element sublists {*x, y*} correspond to a {*index, entry*} of the *Maple* tables respectively as the table. As the second *x* argument can be: *(1)* list {*a, b*}, *(2)* word {"*index*" | "*entry*"} along with an expression of other type *(3)*. The procedure call **Table1[L, x]** returns the list of *ListList* type received from an initial *L* list as follows.

In the case *(1)* in the presence in *L* of a sublist with the first element *a* it is replaced onto list {*a, b*}, otherwise it supplements *L*; if the *x* argument has view {*a, Null*}, in the presence in *L* of a sublist with the 1st element *a* the sublist is removed. At that, for case *(2)* the list {*indices | entries*} accordingly of a *L* list is returned, whereas in the case *(3)* the procedure call returns an entry for a *x* index if such in this table really exists. Whereas, on other tuples of the actual arguments the procedure call **Table1[x, y]** returns $Failed. The following fragment presents source code of the **Table1** procedure together with the most typical examples of its use. The represented examples of the **Table1** procedure use rather visually illustrate its functionality.

```
In[4412]:= Table1[L_ /; ListListQ[L], x_] := Module[{a = {}, c = L, d = {}, k = 1, b = Length[L]},
If[ListListQ[L] && Length[L[[1]]] == 2,
For[k, k <= b, k++, AppendTo[a, L[[k]][[1]]]; AppendTo[d, L[[k]][[2]]]];
{a, d} = Map[DeleteDuplicates, {a, d}];
If[x === "index", a, If[x === "entry", d, If[ListQ[x] && Length[x] == 2,
If[! MemberQ[a, x[[1]]], AppendTo[c, x],
Select[Map[If[#1[[1]] === x[[1]] && ! SameQ[x[[2]], Null], x,
If[#[[1]] === x[[1]] && x[[2]] === Null, Null, #]] &, L],
! SameQ[#, Null] &]], Quiet[Check[Select[Map[If[#[[1]] === x, #[[2]]] &, L],
! SameQ[#, Null] &][[1]], $Failed]]]], $Failed]]

In[4413]:= Tab1 := {{a, a74}, {b, b42}, {c, c47}, {Kr, d20}, {Art, h27}}
In[4414]:= Table1[Tab1, "entry"]
Out[4414]= {a74, b42, c47, d20, h27}
In[4415]:= Table1[Tab1, "index"]
Out[4415]= {a, b, c, Kr, Art}
In[4416]:= Table1[Tab1, {ArtKr, 2017}]
Out[4416]= {{a, a74}, {b, b42}, {c, c47}, {Kr, d20}, {Art, h27}, {ArtKr, 2017}}
In[4417]:= Table1[Tab1, {Kr, 2017}]
Out[4417]= {{a, a74}, {b, b42}, {c, c47}, {Kr, 2017}, {Art, h27}}
```

In[4418]:= **Table1[Tab1, Art]**
Out[4418]= h27
In[4419]:= **Table1[Vsv, ArtKr]**
Out[4419]= Table1[Vsv, ArtKr]
In[4420]:= **Table1[Tab1, {Vsv, Agn}]**
Out[4420]= {{a, a74}, {b, b42}, {c, c47}, {Kr, d20}, {Art, h27}, {Vsv, Agn}}

On the basis of tabular organization supported by the **Table1** procedure it is rather simply possible to determine the user libraries. Qua of one of such approaches we will present an example of *LibBase* library whose structural organization has format of the *ListList* list and whose elements have length two. The principled kind of such library is given below:

LibBase := {{Help, {"O1::usage = \"Help on O1\"", ..., "Ok::usage = \"Help on Ok\"}}, {O1, PureDefinition[O1]}, {O2, PureDefinition[O2]}, ..., {Ok, PureDefinition[Ok]}}

The first element of the 2-element first sublist of the *LibBase* list is *Help* whereas the second represents the usage list in string format for all objects, whose definitions are in the *LibBase* library; at that, their actual presence in the library isn't required. Other elements of *LibBase* library - 2-element sublists of format {Oj, **PureDefinition**[Oj]}, where Oj - an j-object name, and **PureDefinition**[Oj] - its definition, represented in string optimal format. The following fragment represents the **TabLib** procedure supporting work with the above *LibBase* library along with concrete examples which rather visually clarify the essence of such maintenance.

In[5248]:= **LibBase := {{Help, {"NF::usage = \"Help on function NF.\"", "ArtKr::usage = \"Help on function ArtKr.\""}}, {NF, "NF[x_, y_] := x + y"}, {ArtKr, "ArtKr[x_, y_] := Sqrt[27*x + 20*y]"}}**

In[5249]:= **DumpSave["LibBase.mx", LibBase]**
Out[5249]= {{{Help, {"NF::usage = \"Help on function NF.\"", "ArtKr::usage = \"Help on function ArtKr.\""}}, {NF, "NF[x_, y_] := x+y"}, {ArtKr, "ArtKr[x_, y_] := Sqrt[27*x+20*y]"}}}

In[5250]:= **TabLib[Lib_ /; FileExistsQ[Lib] && FileExtension[Lib] == "mx", x_, y___] := Module[{a = Get[Lib], b, c},**
If[MemberQ[{"index", "entry"}, x], Table1[LibBase, x],
Map[ToExpression, LibBase[[1]][[2]]];
If[ListQ[x] && Length[x] == 2, c = If[SameQ[x[[2]], Null], x, {x[[1]], PureDefinition[x[[1]]]}]; b = Table1[LibBase, c];
If[! SameQ[b, $Failed], LibBase = b;
ToExpression["DumpSave[" <> ToString1[Lib] <> "," <> "LibBase]"]], If[StringQ[x] && ! StringFreeQ[x, "::usage = "], c = Quiet[LibBase[[1]][[2]] = AppendTo[LibBase[[1]][[2]], x]];
LibBase = ReplacePart[LibBase, {1, 2} -> c];
ToExpression["DumpSave[" <> ToString1[Lib] <> "," <> "LibBase]"],
If[Table1[LibBase, x] === $Failed, $Failed, b = Table1[LibBase, x];
If[! SameQ[b, $Failed], ToExpression[b]; x[y]], $Failed]]]]]

In[5251]:= **Clear[LibBase]; TabLib["LibBase.mx", "index"]**
Out[5251]= {Help, NF, ArtKr}
In[5252]:= **TabLib["LibBase.mx", "entry"]**

Out[5252]= {{"NF::usage = \"Help on function NF.\"", "ArtKr::usage = \"Help on function ArtKr.\""}, "NF[x_, y_] := x + y", "ArtKr[x_, y_] := Sqrt[27*x + 20*y]"}
In[5253]:= **NF[x_] := Sin[x]*Cos[x] + x^3**
In[5254]:= **ArtKr[x_, y_] := 42*Sin[x] + 47*Cos[y] + x*y**
In[5255]:= **TabLib["LibBase.mx", {ArtKr, PureDefinition[ArtKr]}]**
Out[5255]= {{{Help, {"NF::usage = \"Help on function NF.\"", "ArtKr::usage = \"Help on function ArtKr.\""}}, {ArtKr, "ArtKr[x_, y_] := 42*Sin[x] + 47*Cos[y] + x*y"}}}
In[5256]:= **TabLib["LibBase.mx", {NF, PureDefinition[NF]}]**
Out[5256]= {{{Help, {"NF::usage = \"Help on function NF.\"", "ArtKr::usage = \"Help on function ArtKr.\""}}, {NF, "NF[x_] := Sin[x]*Cos[x] + x^3"}, {ArtKr, "ArtKr[x_, y_] := 42*Sin[x] + 47*Cos[y] + x*y"}}}
In[5257]:= **TabLib["LibBase.mx", "index"]**
Out[5257]= {Help, ArtKr, NF}
In[5258]:= **Clear[ArtKr, LibBase, NF]**
In[5259]:= **TabLib["LibBase.mx", ArtKr, 90.42, 590.2016]**
Out[5259]= 53435.6
In[5260]:= **TabLib["LibBase.mx", NF, 500.2016]**
Out[5260]= 1.25151*10^8
In[5261]:= **TabLib["LibBase.mx", ArtKr]**
Out[5261]= ArtKr[]
In[5262]:= **TabLib["LibBase.mx", {NF, Null}]**
Out[5262]= {{{Help, {"NF::usage = \"Help on function NF.\"", "ArtKr::usage = \"Help on function ArtKr.\""}}, {ArtKr, "ArtKr[x_, y_] := 42*Sin[x] + 47*Cos[y] + x*y"}}}
In[5263]:= **TabLib["LibBase.mx", Avz42]**
Out[5263]= $Failed
In[5264]:= **TabLib["LibBase.mx", "Avz::usage = \"Help on object Avz.\""]**
Out[5264]= {{{Help, {"NF::usage = \"Help on function NF.\"", "ArtKr::usage = \"Help on function ArtKr.\"", "Avz::usage = \"Help on object Avz.\""}}, {ArtKr, "ArtKr[x_, y_] := 42*Sin[x] + 47*Cos[y] + x*y"}}}
In[5265]:= **LibBase**
Out[5265]= {{Help, {"NF::usage = \"Help on function NF.\"", "ArtKr::usage = \"Help on function ArtKr.\"", "Avz::usage = \"Help on function Avz.\""}}, {ArtKr, "ArtKr[x_, y_] := 42*Sin[x] + 47*Cos[y] + x*y"}}
In[5266]:= **??NF**
"Help on function NF."
NF[x_] := Sin[x]*Cos[x] + x^3
In[5267]:= **?ArtKr**
"Help on function ArtKr."

The main operations with the library organized thus are supported by the procedure **TabLib** whose source code with some examples of its use are represented by the previous fragment. The procedure call **TabLib[x, y]** depending on the second argument *y* returns or the current contents of the library that is in a *x mx*–file, or names of the objects that are in the library, or their definitions, namely:

TabLib[*x*, "*index*"] – returns the list of objects names whose definitions are located in the *x* library, including the *Help* name of help base of the library;

TabLib[*x*, "*entry*"] – returns the list of objects definitions which are contained in a *x* library, including also the help base *Help* of the library;

TabLib[*x*, {*N*, *Df*}] – returns the contents of a *x* library after its extension by means of a new *Df* definition of object with *N* name if *Df* is different from *Null*; at that, obsolete definition of the *N* object is updated;

TabLib[*x*, {*N*, *Null*}] – returns the contents of *x* library as a result of removing from it of the definition of an object with a *N* name; at that, its usage remains;

TabLib[*x*, *N*, *y*, *z*, ...] – returns the result of call *N*[*y*, *z*, ...] of a *N* object from a *x* library; if the *N* object is absent in the library, $Failed is returned;

TabLib[*x*, *n*] – if *n* is usage for *n* object, it supplements the help base of *x* library with return of the updated contents of the library.

In other cases the procedure call returns *$Failed* or is returned unevaluated. Qua of a certain initial library **LibBase** intended for filling its by necessary contents a *ListList* list of the above format is used. An initial library **LibBase** should be determined before the first procedure call **TabLib**. Naturally, for real application of the **TabLib** procedure qua of a ready software for organization of the user libraries it demands an extension of functionality, meantime, it is presented as a certain illustrative example of one of possible approaches to the solution of task of organization of the user software. We leave the problem for the interested user as a rather useful practice. In principle, the presented library organization provided by **TabLib** procedure and that is based on the tabular organization which is supported by the **Table1** procedure represents a certain analog of a *Maple*-package of tabular type. The represented library has only a basic set of functions which, meanwhile, provides its an quite satisfactory functioning. Meanwhile, on the basis of the offered approach quite really to create the fast rather small libraries of the user procedures and functions which will be very convenient in operation. At that, the similar quite simple means can serve as good means for maintenance of the libraries of the user procedures or functions which have a text format, and which are simply edited by routine word processors, for example, *Notepad*. The interested reader can develop own means of library organization in the *Mathematica*, using approaches offered by us along with others. However, exists a problem of the organization of convenient help bases for the user libraries. A number of approaches in this direction can be found in [50]. In particular, on the basis of the list structure supported by *Mathematica*, it is a rather simply possible to determine help bases for the user libraries. On this basis as one of approaches an example of the **BaseHelp** procedure has been presented, whose structural organization has the list format [30-33,50].

Meanwhile, it is possible to create the help bases on the basis of packages containing usage on tools of the user library which are saved in datafiles of *mx*-format. At that, for complete library it is possible to create only one help *mx*-file, uploading it as required into the current session by means of the **Get** function with receiving in the subsequent of access to all usage that are in the datafile. The next **Usage** procedure can represent an quite certain interest for organization of a *help database* for the user libraries. The procedure provides maintaining a help base *irrespective* of library that is rather convenient in a number of cases of organization of the user software. The next fragment presents source code of the **Usage** procedure along with the most typical examples of its application.

In[3600]:= G::usage = "Help on function G."; V::usage = "Help on function V.";
S::usage = "Help on function S."; Art::usage = "Help on procedure Art.";
Kr::usage = "Help on procedure Kr.";

In[3601]:= Usage[x_ /; StringQ[x], y___] := Module[{a, b, h = ""},
If[! FileExistsQ[x], Put[x], Null];
If[{y} == {} && ! EmptyFileQ[x], While[! SameQ[h, EndOfFile],
Quiet[ToExpression[h = Read[x, Expression]]]]; Close[x];,
If[{y} == {} && EmptyFileQ[x], $Failed, If[Quiet[Check[ListQ[y], False]] && {y} != {} &&
ListSymbolQ[y], a = DeleteDuplicates[Select[y, Head[#::usage] === String &]];
If[a != {}, PutAppend[Sequences[Map[ToString[#] <> "::usage = " <>
"\"" <> #::usage <> "\"" &, a]], x], $Failed],
If[! Quiet[Check[ListQ[y], False]], b = DeleteDuplicates[Reverse[ReadList[x, Expression]]];
Put[Sequences[Select[b, ! SuffPref[#1, Map[ToString[#] <> "::usage" &,
Flatten[{y}]], 1] &]], x], $Failed]]]]]

In[3602]:= Usage["C:/MathLib/HelpBase.m", {Art, Kr, G, V, Art, Kr, Vsv}]

A new session with the Mathematica system
In[2216]:= Usage["C:\\MathLib\\HelpBase.m"]
In[2217]:= **?G**
Help on function G.
In[2218]:= **Information[V]**
Help on function V.
In[2219]:= **?Kr**
Help on function Kr.
In[2220]:= **?Art**
Help on procedure Art.

For initial filling of a help database in the current session all known usage on tools that are planned on inclusion into the user library are evaluated as visually illustrates the *1st Input* paragraph of the previous fragment. Then by the procedure call **Usage**[*x, y*] the saving in a *x*–file of the *ASCII* format of all usage relating to software tools that are defined by a *y* list is provided. In addition, saving is executed in the *append*–mode into the end of the *x*–file; if the specified *x* file is absent, the *empty x*–file is created. Whereas the call **Usage**[*x, y, z,...*] where arguments, since the 2nd, represent names {*y, z,...*} of software means, deletes from the help base the usage on these tools. In addition, the call **Usage**[*x*] activates all usage containing in *x* base in the current session, doing them available irrespectively from existence of the tools described by these usage. The successful call of the **Usage** procedure returns *Null*, otherwise, the value *$Failed* is returned, in particular, in case of the call **Usage**[*x*] at the absent or empty file *x*. The represented approach is seems as a rather convenient. In addition, the history of modifications of a datafile *x* is saved while qua of active usage the last usage supplementing the datafile acts.

For receiving usage on tools that are located in packages, it is possible to use the **UsageMNb** procedure, whose source code along with typical examples of application, are presented by the following fragment.

In[4242]:= **UsagesMNb**[x_ /; FileExistsQ[x] && MemberQ[{"m", "nb"}, FileExtension[x]]]:= Module[{a, b, c},
If[FileExtension[x] == "m", a = Select[ReadList[x, String], ! StringFreeQ[#, "::usage="] &];
a = Map[StringTake[#, {3, -3}] &, a];
a = Map[If[SymbolQ[StringTake[#, {1, Flatten[StringPosition[#, "::usage="]][[1]] – 1}]], #] &, a]; Select[a, ! SameQ[#, Null] &], c = "$.m"; b = ContextFromFile[x];
ToExpression["Save[" <> StrStr[c] <> ", " <> StrStr[b] <> "]"];
b = Select[Quiet[ReadList["$.m", Expression]], ! MemberQ[{Null, {Temporary}}, #] &];
DeleteFile["$.m"]; b]]

In[4243]:= **UsagesMNb**["C:/users/aladjev/mathematica/MathToolBox.mx"]
Out[4243]= UsageMNb["C:/users/aladjev/mathematica/MathToolBox.mx"]
In[4244]:= **UsagesMNb**["c:\\users/aladjev/mathematica/MathToolBox.m"]
Out[4244]= {"UprocQ::usage=\"The call UprocQ[x] returns False if x is not a procedure; otherwise, two-element list of the format {True, {\"Module\"| \"Block\"| \"DynamicModule\"}} is returned.\",...}
In[4245]:= **UsagesMNb**["C:/users/aladjev/mathematica/MathToolBox.nb"]
Out[4245]= {"The call Names1[] returns the nested 4-element list, whose the first element determines the list of names of the procedures, the second – the list of names of functions/modules, the third element – the list of names whose definitions have been evaluated in the current session of the system, while the fourth element determines the list of other names associated with the current session.",...}

The procedure call **UsagesMNb**[*x*] returns the usage list on a software of the user package which is in a *x* file of {"*m*", "*nb*"} format; these usage are returned in string format. At that, for a *x* file of *m*-format the usage list containing a prefix *"Name::usage="* is returned while for a *x* file of *nb*-format the usage list without such prefix is returned. Furthermore, if for a package from a *x* file of *m*-format its uploading into the current session isn't required, for a package from the *x* file of *nb*-format its real uploading is required. Unlike the procedures **HelpPrint**, **HelpBasePac** the procedure **UsagesMNb** provides possibility of both perusal of help databases of the user packages, and their processing. This procedure is correct for the *Mathematica* system of versions *10.3.0* and below.

At last, the call of simple function **Usages1**[*x*] provides the output of all usage that describe the tools contained in the user package associated with a *x* context. The following fragment presents source code of the **Usages1** function with a typical example of its application.

In[2699]:= Usages1[x_ /; ContextQ[x]] := Map[{Print[#], ToExpression["?" <> #]} &, CNames[x]]

In[2700]:= Usages1["AladjevProcedures`"]
"AcNb"
The call AcNb[] returns full name of the current document earlier saved as a nb–file.
=====

The above example illustrates the format returned by the function call.

605

In conclusion we will give one more a rather useful approach to formation of the user help base on an example of the following procedure. The procedure call **SystemUsages[x]** shows the window containing the usage for system tool with a name x whereas the procedure call with the second optional *y* argument – *an uncertain symbol* – through it returns the list of the names in string format of all system tools which have reference information. At absence in the directory with references of the file *"x.nb"*, the procedure call returns $Failed. The next fragment represents source code of the **SystemUsages** procedure with examples of its use.

In[4570]:= **SystemUsages[x_ /; SymbolQ[x], j___]** := Module[{a = $InstallationDirectory <>
"\\Documentation/English/System/ReferencePages/Symbols", b, c},
c = ToString[x] <> ".nb"; If[! FileExistsQ[a <> "/" <> c], $Failed,
$Path = PrependTo[$Path, a]; If[{y} != {} && NullQ[y], b = SetDirectory[]; SetDirectory[a];
y = Map[StringReplace[#, ".nb" -> ""] &, FileNames[]]; SetDirectory[b], 6];
NotebookGet[NotebookOpen[FindFile[c]]];]]

In[4571]:= **SystemUsages[Name42]**
Out[4571]= $Failed
In[4572]:= **SystemUsages[Sin, gs]**
The window with the reference on **Sin** function is shown
In[4573]:= **Length[gs]**
Out[4573]= 5058

For use of this procedure for the organization of help base for the user means it is enough: *(1)* to create in a certain directory a set of *nb*–documents with reference information, *(2)* to replace in the **SystemUsages** procedure the value of local *a* variable onto the full path to the directory with reference information, *(3)* to use the call **SystemUsages[x]** for the operational obtaining the reference information concerning the user *x* tool. This mechanism is a rather transparent and doesn't demand additional explanations.

8.5. A *MathToolBox* package for the *Mathematica* system

The computer mathematics has found application in many fields of science such as physics, mathematics, education, computer sciences, engineering, computational biology, chemistry, technology, etc. *Computer mathematics systems (CMS)* such as the *Mathematica* are becoming more and more popular in teaching, research and industry. Researchers use the well-known *Mathematica* system as an essential enough means for solving problems related to various investigations. The system is ideal tool for formulating, solving and exploring very different mathematical models.

Its symbolic manipulation facilities extend greatly over a range of the problems that can be solved with its help. The educators in universities have revitalized traditional curricula by introducing problems and exercises that enough widely use the *Mathematica's* interactive mathematics and physics. Whereas the students can concentrate on the more fundamental concepts rather than on various plural tedious algebraic manipulations. Finally, engineers and experts in industries use the system *Mathematica* as an efficient means replacing many traditional resources such as reference books, spreadsheets, calculators, and programming languages. These users easily solve mathematical problems, creating various projects and consolidating their computations into professional report. Meanwhile, our experience with the system *Mathematica* of releases *8 ÷ 11* enabled us not only to estimate its advantages in regard to other similar *CMS*, above all the *Maple*, but has also revealed a number of faults and shortcomings that were eliminated by us. In particular, *Mathematica* does not support a number of functions important for procedural programming and datafiles processing. As a result, the *MathToolBox* package oriented on solution of the above problems was created [33,48,50]. The given package contains more than *1140* tools which eliminate restrictions of a number of standard means of the *Mathematica*, and expand its software environment with new means. In this context, the package can serve as a certain additional means of modular programming, especially useful in the numerous applications where certain non-standard evaluations have to accompany programming. At that, tools presented in the given package have a direct relationship to certain principal questions of *procedure–functional* programming in *Mathematica*, not only for the decision of applied problems, but, above all, for creation of software extending frequently used facilities of the system and/or eliminating their defects or extending the system with new facilities. The software presented in this package contains a series of rather useful and effective receptions of programming in the *Mathematica*, and extends its software which allows in the system to programme the tasks of various purpose more simply and effectively. The additional means composing the above package embrace the next sections of the *Mathematica* system, namely:

– *additional means in interactive mode of the **Mathematica** system*
– *additional means of processing of expressions in the **Mathematica** system*
– *additional means of processing of symbols and strings in the **Mathematica***
– *additional means of processing of sequences and lists in the **Mathematica***
– *additional means expanding standard **Mathematica** functions or its software as a whole (control structures branching and loop, etc.)*
– *definition of procedures in the **Mathematica** software*
– *definition of the user functions and pure functions in the **Mathematica** software*
– *means of testing of procedures and functions in the **Mathematica** software*
– *headings of procedures and functions in the **Mathematica** software*
– *formal arguments of procedures and functions*
– *local variables of modules and blocks; means of their processing*
– *global variables of modules and blocks; means of their processing*
– *attributes, options and values by default for arguments of the user blocks, functions and modules; additional means of their processing*
– *some useful additional means for processing of blocks, functions and modules*
– *additional means of the processing of internal **Mathematica** datafiles*
– *additional means of the processing of external **Mathematica** datafiles*
– *additional means of the processing of attributes of directories and datafiles*
– *additional and some special means of processing of datafiles and directories*
– *additional means of operating with packages and contexts ascribed to them*
– *organization of the user software in the **Mathematica** system.*

This package, is mostly for people who want the more deep understanding in *Mathematica* programming, and particularly those the users who would like to make a transition from the beginning user to the programmer, or perhaps those who already have certain limited experience in the *Mathematica* programming but want to improve their possibilities in the system. The expert programmers will probably find an useful information too. The archive

Archive75.zip with the package which owns the *FreeWare* license can be freely downloaded from the website represented in [48]. The archive contains five datafiles: ***MathToolBox.cdf, MathToolBox.mx, MathToolBox.m, MathToolBox.nb, MathToolBox.txt.*** So, with the aim of perlustration of the package it is possible to use file ***MathToolBox.cdf*** with *CDF Player* while file ***MathToolBox.m,*** or ***MathToolBox.txt*** with an arbitrary word processor. This approach allows to satisfy the user on different operating platforms. The package contains more than ***1140*** means which eliminate restrictions of a number of standard means of the system, and extend its software with new means. In this context, the package can serve as a rather useful means of programming, first of all, useful in numerous applications where the certain non-standard *evaluations* have to accompany programming. At that, the memory size demanded for the ***MathToolBox*** package in the ***Mathematica 11.0.1*** *(on platform Windows 7 Professional version 6.1.7601)* yields the next result, namely:

In[1]:= **MemoryInUse[]**
Out[1]= 32154496
In[2]:= **Get["C:\\Avz\\MathToolBox.mx"]**
In[3]:= **MemoryInUse[]**
Out[3]= 45550472
In[4]:= **N[(% - %%%)/1024^2]**
Out[4]= 12.7754

i.e. in the ***Mathematica*** the ***MathToolBox*** package demands more ***12.7 MB***, while amount of software whose definitions are located in the package, at the moment of its loading into the current session of the ***Mathematica*** system is available on the basis of the following simple calculations:

In[1]:= **Get["C:\\Avz\\MathToolBox.mx"]**
In[2]:= **Length[CNames["AladjevProcedures`"]]**
Out[2]= 1142

It should be borne in mind that debugging of the package tools was done in software of the ***Mathematica*** of versions ***9–10***, and significantly in software of the version ***11.0.1.*** Hence, in some cases there can be certain slips at their performance that are rather simply eliminated. Unfortunately, regardless of sufficient stability of the built-in ***Mathematica*** language, upon transition from the younger version of the ***Mathematica*** to more senior a certain adjustment can be needed. As a rule, similar adjustment for the used version of the ***Mathematica*** is not very complex.

In conclusion of the given book we once again emphasize the following point of view: along with illustrative purposes the tools, presented in it quite can be used as enough useful tools extending the ***Mathematica*** software which rather significantly facilitate programming of a wide range of the problems, first of all, having the system character. At that, in our opinion, the detailed analysis of their source code can be a rather effective remedy on the path of the deeper mastering of programming in the ***Mathematica.*** Experience of holding of the master classes of various levels on the systems ***Mathematica*** and ***Maple*** with all evidence confirms expediency of joint use of both standard tools of the systems of computer mathematics, and the user means that have been created in the course of programming of various appendices.

References

1. *Aladjev V.Z., Hunt Ü., Shishakov M.L.* Mathematics on Personal Computer.– Gomel: BELGUT Press, 1996, 498 p., ISBN 34206140233.

2. *Aladjev V.Z., Shishakov M.L.* An Introduction into Mathematical Package **Mathematica 2.2**.– Moscow: Filin Press, 1997, 363 p.

3. *Aladjev V.Z., Hunt Ü.J., Shishakov M.L.* Basics of Computer Informatics: Textbook.– Tallinn: Russian Academy of Noosphere & TRG, 1997, 396 p.

4. *Aladjev V.Z., Hunt Ü.J., Shishakov M.L.* Basics of Computer Informatics: Textbook.– Moscow, Filin Press, 1998, 496 p., ISBN 5895680682.

5. *Aladjev V.Z., Hunt Ü.J., Shishakov M.L.* Basics of Computer Informatics: Textbook, Second edition.– Moscow, Filin Press, 1999, 545 p.

6. *Aladjev V.Z., Vaganov V.A., Hunt Ü.J., Shishakov M.L.* Introduction into Environment of the Mathematical Package **Maple V**.– Minsk: International Academy of Noosphere, 1998, 452 p., ISBN 1406425698.

7. *Aladjev V.Z., Vaganov V.A., Hunt Ü.J., Shishakov M.L.* Programming in Environment of the Mathematical Package **Maple V**.– Minsk–Moscow: Russian Ecology Academy, 1999, 470 p., ISBN 4101212982.

8. *Aladjev V.Z., Bogdevicius M.A.* Solution of Physical, Technical and Mathematical Problems with **Maple V**.– Tallinn–Vilnius, TRG, 1999, 686 p.

9. *Aladjev V.Z., Vaganov V.A., Hunt Ü.J., Shishakov M.L.* Workstation for the Mathematician.– Tallinn–Gomel–Moscow: Russian Academy of Natural Sciences, 1999, 608 p., ISBN 3420614023.

10. *Aladjev V.Z., Shishakov M.L.* Workstation of the Mathematician.– Moscow: Laboratory of Basic Knowledge, 2000, 752 p., ISBN 5932080523.

11. *Aladjev V.Z., Bogdevicius M.A.* **Maple 6**: Solution of Mathematical, Statistical, Physical and Engineering Problems.– Moscow: Laboratory of Basic Knowledge, 2001, 850 p., ISBN 593308085X.

12. *Aladjev V.Z., Bogdevicius M.A.* Special Questions of Operation in Software Environment of the Mathematical Package **Maple**.– Vilnius: International Academy of Noosphere & Vilnius Gediminas Technical Univ., 2001, 208 p.

13. *Aladjev V.Z., Bogdevicius M.A.* Interactive **Maple**: Solution of Statistical, Mathematical, Engineering and Physical Problems.– Tallinn: International Academy of Noosphere, 2001–2002, CD with Booklet, ISBN 9985927710.

14. *Aladjev V.Z., Vaganov V.A., Grishin E.P.* Additional Software Tools of the Mathematical Package **Maple** of releases 6 and 7.– Tallinn: International Academy of Noosphere, 2002, 314 p. + CD, ISBN 9985927737.

15. *Aladjev V.Z.* Effective Operation in the Mathematical Package **Maple**.– Moscow: Laboratory of Basic Knowledge, 2002, 334 p., ISBN 593208118X.

16. *Aladjev V.Z., Liopo V.A., Nikitin A.V.* Mathematical Package **Maple** in Physical Modeling.– Grodno: Grodno State University, 2002, 416 p.

17. *Aladjev V.Z., Vaganov V.A.* Computer Algebra System **Maple**: *A New Software Library.*– Tallinn: International Academy of Noosphere, the Baltic Branch, 2002, CD with Booklet, ISBN 9985927753.

18. *Aladjev V.Z., Bogdevicius M.A., Prentkovskis O.V.* *A New Software for Mathematical Package* **Maple** *of Releases 6, 7 and 8.*– Vilnius: Vilnius Gediminas Technical University & International Academy of Noosphere, 2002, 404 p., ISBN 9985927745, 9986055652.

19. *Aladjev V.Z., Vaganov V.A.* *Systems of Computer Algebra: A New Software Toolbox for* **Maple**.– Tallinn: International Academy of Noosphere, the Baltic Branch, 2003, 270 p., ISBN 9985927761.

20. *Aladjev V.Z., Bogdevicius M., Vaganov V.A.* *Systems of Computer Algebra: A New Software Toolbox for* **Maple**. *Second edition.*– Tallinn: Intern. Academy of Noosphere, 2004, 462 p., ISBN 9985927788.

21. *Aladjev V.Z.* *Computer Algebra Systems: A New Software Toolbox for the* **Maple**.– CA: Palo Alto: Fultus Corporation, 2004, 575 p., ISBN 1596820004.

22. *Aladjev V.Z.* *Computer Algebra Systems: A New Software Toolbox for* **Maple**.– CA: Palo Alto: Fultus Corporation, 2004, Acrobat eBook, ISBN 1596820152.

23. *Aladjev V.Z. et al.* *Electronic Library of Books and Software for Scientists, Experts, Teachers and Students in Natural and Social Sciences.*– CA: Palo Alto: Fultus Corporation, 2005, CD, ISBN 1596820136.

24. *Aladjev V.Z., Bogdevicius M.A.* **Maple**: *Programming, Physical and Engineering Problems.*– Palo Alto: Fultus Corp., 2006, 404 p., ISBN 1596820802, eBook, ISBN 1596820810, http://writers.fultus.com/aladjev/index.html

25. *Aladjev V.Z.* *Computer Algebra Systems.* **Maple**: *the Art of Programming.*– Moscow: BINOM Press, 2006, 792 p., ISBN 5932081899.

26. *Aladjev V.Z.* *Foundations of programming in* **Maple**: *Textbook.*– Tallinn: International Academy of Noosphere, 2006, 300 p., *(pdf)*, ISBN 998595081X. *(can be freely uploaded from website http://www.aladjev-maple.narod.ru)*

27. *Aladjev V.Z., Boiko V.K., Rovba E.A.* *Programming and Applications Elaboration in* **Maple**.– Grodno: GRSU, Tallinn: International Academy of Noosphere, 2007, 456 p., ISBN 9789854178912, ISBN 9789985950821.

28. *Aladjev V.Z., Vaganov V.A.* *Modular Programming:* **Mathematica** *vs* **Maple**, *and vice versa.*– CA: Palo Alto, Fultus Corporation, 2011, 418 p.

29. *Aladjev V.Z., Bezrukavyi A.S., Haritonov V.N., Hodakov V.E.* *Programming:* **Maple** *or* **Mathematica**?– Ukraine: Herson, Oldi–Plus Press, 2011, 474 p., ISBN 9789662393460.

30. *Aladjev V.Z., Boiko V.K., Rovba E.A.* *Programming in the Packages* **Mathematica** *and* **Maple**: *Comparative Aspect.*– Belarus: Grodno, Grodno State University, 2011, 517 p., ISBN 9789855154816.

31. *Aladjev V.Z., Grinn D.S., Vaganov V.A.* *The extended functional tools for the package* **Mathematica**.– Ukraine: Kherson: Oldi–Plus Press, 2012, 404 p., ISBN 9789662393590.

32. *Aladjev V.Z., Grinn D.S.* *Extension of functional environment of the system* **Mathematica**.– Ukraine: Kherson: Oldi–Plus Press, 2012, 552 p., ISBN 9789662393729.

33. *Aladjev V.Z., Grinn D.S., Vaganov V.A.* *The selected system problems in* **Mathematica** *software.*– Ukraine: Kherson: Oldi–Plus Press, 2013, 556 p., ISBN 9789662890129.

34. *Aladjev V.Z., Bogdevicius M.* Use of package **Maple** for solution of physical and engineering problems // Int. Conf. *Transbaltica-99.*– Vilnius: Technics Press.

35. *Aladjev V.Z., Hunt U.* Workstation for mathematicians // Conference *Transbaltica–99.*– Vilnius: Technics Press, April 1999.

36. *Aladjev V.Z., Hunt U.* Workstation for mathematicians // Conf. «Perfection of Mechanisms of Management», Institute of Modern Knowledge, Grodno, 1999.

37. *Aladjev V.Z., Shishakov M.* Programming in package **Maple** // 2nd Int. Conf. «Computer Algebra in Fundamental and Applied Researches and Education».– Byelorussia: Minsk, 1999.

38. *Aladjev V.Z., Shishakov M.L.* A Workstation for mathematicians // 2nd Conf. «Computer Algebra in Fundamental and Applied Researches and Education».– Byelorussia: Minsk, 1999.

39. *Aladjev V.Z., Shishakov M.L., Trokhova T.A.* Educational computer laboratory of the engineer // Proc. 8th Byelorussian Mathem. Conf., Minsk, 2000.

40. *Aladjev V.Z. et al.* Modelling in software environment of the mathematical package **Maple** // Int. Conf. on Math. Mod. *MKMM–2000.*– Herson, 2000.

41. *Aladjev V.Z., Shishakov M.L., Trokhova T.A.* A workstation for solution of systems of differential equations // 3rd International Conf. «Differential Equations and Applications».– Saint–Petersburg, Russia, 2000.

42. *Aladjev V.Z., Shishakov M.L., Trokhova T.A.* Computer laboratory for engineering researches // Int. Conf. *ACA-2000.*– Saint–Petersburg, Russia, 2000

43. *Aladjev V.Z., Bogdevicius M., Hunt U.J.* A Workstation for mathematicians / Lithuanian Conf. *TRANSPORT–2000.*– Vilnius: Technics Press, April 2000.

44. *Aladjev V.Z.* Computer Algebra // Alpha, no. *1.*– Grodno: GRSU, 2001.

45. *Aladjev V.Z.* Modern computer algebra for modeling of the transport systems // Intern. Conf. *TRANSBALTICA–2001.*– Vilnius: Technics Press, April 2001.

46. *Aladjev V.Z.* Computer Algebra System **Maple**: A New Software Library // International Conference «Computer Algebra Systems and Their Applications», Saint–Petersburg, Russia, 2003.

47. *Aladjev V.Z.* A Library **UserLib6789** for system **Maple.**– The library can be freely downloaded from website **https://yadi.sk/d/hw1rnmsbyfVKz**.

48. *Aladjev V.Z.* The **MathToolBox** package with Freeware license can be downloaded from website **https://yadi.sk/d/oC5lXLWa3PVEhi**.

49. *Aladjev V.Z.* Modular programming: **Maple** or **Mathematica** – A subjective standpoint / Intern. school «Mathematical and computer modeling of fundamental objects and phenomena in systems of computer mathematics», ed. **Y.G. Ignat'ev.**– Kazan: Kazan Univ. Press, 2014.

50. *Aladjev V.Z., Boiko V.K. et al.* Books miscellany on Cellular Automata, General Statistics Theory, **Maple** and **Mathematica.**– Tallin: International Academy of Noosphere, CD–edition, 2016, ISBN 9789949987603.

51. *Arantes R.D.* A computational reference guide on experimental mathematics, algorithmic number theory and symbolic computing.– Rio de Janeiro: Federal University, Caixa Postal 11502, 220022–970, 2004.

52. *Mangano S.* Mathematica Cookbook.– CA: Sebastopol: O'Reilly Media, Inc., 2010, 828 p., ISBN 9780596520991.

53. **Wellin P. et al.** *An introduction to programming with* **Mathematica**, 3rd *ed.–* Cambridge University Press, 2005, 550 p., ISBN 0521846781.

54. **Sisson P.** *College Algebra*, 2nd *ed.–* Hawkes Learning Systems, 2008.

55. **Gregor J., Tier J.** *Discovering Mathematics: A Problem–Solving Approach to Mathematical Analysis with* **Mathematica** *and* **Maple.–** Springer, 2010, 254 p.

56. **Alberty R.** *Applications of* **Mathematica.–** Wiley Press, 2011, 456 p.

57. **Shiskowski K., Frinkle K.** *Principles of Linear Algebra with* **Mathematica.–** Wiley, 2011, 616 p., ISBN 9780470637951.

58. **Kilian A.** *Programmieren mit Wolfram* **Mathematica.–** Springer, 2010.

59. **Hollis S.** *CalcLabs with* **Mathematica** *for Multivariable Calculus.–* Brooks/ Cole, 2012, 274 p., ISBN 9780840058133.

60. **Annong Xu.** *Introduction to Scientific Computing: Numerical Analysis With* **Mathematica.–** China Machine Press, 2010, ISBN 9787111310914.

61. **Core Language:** *Tutorial Collection.–* Wolfram Research Inc., 2008, 358 p.

62. **Hastings K.J.** *Introduction to Probability with* **Mathematica.–** CRC Press, 2009, 465 p., ISBN 9781420079388.

63. **Wellin P.R.** *Programming with* **Mathematica:** *An Introduction*, 2013.

64. **Koberlein B., Meisel D.** *Astrophysics through Computation: With* **Mathematica** *Support*, 2013, ISBN 9781107010741.

65. **Boccara N.** *Essentials of* **Mathematica:** *With Applications to Mathematics and Physics.–* Springer, 2007, ISBN 9780387495132.

66. **Shifrin L.** **Mathematica** *Programming: An Advanced Introduction.–* Brunel University, 2008, *http://www.mathprogramming-intro.org/2008*.

67. **Wagon S.** **Mathematica**® *in Action: Problem Solving Through Visualization and Computation*, 3rd ed., 2010, 574 p., ISBN 9780387754772.

68. **Mathematica 9** *documentation center: complete reference for* **Mathematica 9**, *http://reference.wolfram.com/mathematica/guide/Mathematica.html*.

69. *The fourth international seminar and international school «Mathematical and computer modeling of fundamental objects and phenomena in systems of computer mathematics» / Ed. Prof.* **Yu. G. Ignat'ev.–** Kazan: Kazan Univ. Press, 2014.

70. *The Intern. scientifically–practical conference and seminar–school of mathemat. modelling in CAS / Ed. Prof.* **Yu. G. Ignat'ev.–** Kazan: AN RT Press, 2016.

71. **Aladjev V.Z., Vaganov V.A.** *Extension of the* **Mathematica** *system functionality.–* USA: Seattle, CreateSpace, An Amazon.com Company, 2015, 590 p., ISBN 9781514237823.

72. **Aladjev V.Z.** *Classical Cellular Automata.–* Saarbrucken: Scholar`s Press, 2014, 517 p., ISBN 9783639713459.

73. **V.Z. Aladjev, V.K. Boiko.** Tools for computer research of cellular automata dynamics // Intern. school "Mathematical Modelling of Fundamental Objects and Phenomena in the Systems of Computer Mathematics"; Intern. scientific and practical conference "Information Technologies in Science and Education" (**ITON-2017**), November 4 – 6, 2017, Kazan, pp. 7 – 16.

About the Authors

Professor *Aladjev V.Z.* was born on *June 14, 1942* in the town *Grodno (West Byelorusia)*. Now, he is the First vice–president of *International Academy of Noosphere (IAN)*, and academician–secretary of Baltic branch of the *IAN* whose scientific results have received international recognition, first, in the field of Cellular Automata theory. Many applied researches of *Aladjev V.* refers to computer science, notably well–known books on computer mathematics systems *(MathCad, Mathematica, Maple, etc.)*. Along with these original editions he developed a rather large library of a new software *(more 850)* for *Maple* which is now widely used in the *CIS* and beyond. The packages *AVZ_Package (more 800 tools)* and *MathToolBox (more 1140 tools)* represent a considerable interest too, whose means quite significantly expand the *Mathematica* and to some extent eliminate limitations of its standard means. Many of his works in the given direction are presented on the Internet and included in the mandatory or supplementary literature in university programs. He is full member of a number of the Russian and the International Academies. Prof. Dr. *Aladjev V.Z.* is the author of more *500* scientific publications, including *90* books and monographs, published in the *USSR, Russia, Germany, Belarus, Germany, Estonia, Ukraine, Lithuania, Czechoslovakia, Hungary, Japan, USA, Netherlands, Great Britain* and *Bulgaria*. Since *1972 Aladjev V.Z.* is a reviewer and a member of the editorial board of international mathematical journal *"Zentralblatt für Mathematik"* and since *1980 Aladjev V.Z.* is a full member of the *IAMM (International Accociation on the Mathematical Modelling, USA)*. Prof. *Aladjev V.* created the Estonian School on the mathematical theory of the Homogeneous structures *(Cellular automata)*, whose fundamental results have received international recognition and became as a basis for the new branch of modern mathematical cybernetics. He participates as a member of organizing committee and/or a guest lecturer in many international scientific forums in mathematics and cybernetics. In *May, 2015* Dr. Prof. *Aladjev V.Z.* was awarded by Gold medal *"European Quality"* of the *ESIC*.

Dr. *Shishakov M.L.* was born on *October 21, 1957* in the Gomel area *(Belarus)*. In *1974* after leaving school he has entered the Leningrad Polytechnic institute on electro–mechanical faculty, that he has successfully finished in *1980*, having defended the diploma *"Automatics and telemechanics"*. In the term of study in institute *Shishakov M.L.* awakely was engaged in research work in field of analysis and synthesis of the discrete logical devices and functions, having received in *1979* on the All-Union conference of student research works *(Tbilisi)* the Diploma of the 2nd degree. The labor activity he of the beginnings at Gomel state university at physical faculty on stand Radio physics, then in Computer center of Gomel Polytechnic institute *(CC GPI)*. From *1985* to *1994* he is chief of *CC GPI*. In *1993 Shishakov M.* has defended candidate thesis on speciality *"Systems of design automation"*. For the season of activity in the *GPI* he has published more than *60* research works, including text–books on the *CAD* problems. In a cycle of activities *Shishakov M.* has offered and significantly researched a fuzzy hypergraph structure model of technical object for the *CAD* of functional diagrams of devices, formalism of presentation of space of engineering solutions is designed, etc. Many of technological activities of Dr. *Shishakov M.L.* are dedicated to operational use of heuristic methods to synthesis of kinematic scheme of the gears. A number of his research activities was dedicated to operational use of the heuristic methods to synthesis kinematic schemes of the gears. Dr. *Shishakov M.* has a number of the publications on information technology in different application fields, including *25* books and monographies. In *June 1998* Dr. *Shishakov M.* was elected as a member of the *IAN* on section of the information science and information technologies. Fields of the basic *Shishakov M.L.* interests are: cybernetics, problems of *CAD* and designing of the mobile software, theory of statistics, the artificial intelligence, computer telecommunication, information science, and applied software for solution of different problems of technical and manufacturing nature. At present, *Shishakov M.L.* is the director of Belarusian–Swiss company *TDF Ecotech*, that works in the field of *"green"* energy - it builds and operates mini-power plants running on wind, biogas, solar and gas produced from municipal landfills.

REAG is an international group of companies specializing in renewable energy sources

The **REAG** builds and operates the appropriate facilities for the production of renewable energy through its subsidiary companies *(with a focus on the Eastern European region)*. This group of companies is controlled by the parent company, based in Switzerland.

Main investment objectives include the directions such as:

> the degassing of SDW landfills,
> photovoltaic outdoor units,
> wind power plants and
> hydraulic power plants,

to produce green electricity with these units and apply power from the public networks.

As a technology company, **REAG** is interested in not only the latest technologies, which are used in its own plants, but also in technological researches and further developments.

For this reason, **REAG** is glad to support scientific work in the widest range of forms and also draws attention to its technology projects as a part of the *sponsorship* of scientific work.

Particularly, we have supported the present work of Prof. Dr. **Victor Aladjev** and *Akadeemia Balti Ühing* as a sponsor. Mathematics is one of the essential foundations of any scientific work, so research and teaching in this field are essential to the technological progress of our society.

REAG *RenewableEnergy AG*
Headquarter: Switzerland

May 2017

Made in United States
Orlando, FL
26 January 2023